GET YOUR CAPTAIN'S LICENSE

Charlie Wing

International Marine
Camden, Maine

International Marine/
Ragged Mountain Press

A Division of The McGraw·Hill Companies

Published by International Marine, a division of The McGraw-Hill Companies

10 9 8 7 6 5 4 3 2

Copyright © 1998 by Charlie Wing

P/N 071093-7
Part of 0-07-913677-X
Cataloging-in-Publication data is available from the Library of Congress

All rights reserved. The publisher takes no responsibility for the use of any of the materials or methods described in this book, nor for the products thereof. The name "International Marine" and the International Marine logo are trademarks of the McGraw-Hill Companies

Printed in the United States of America.

Questions regarding the content of this book should be addressed to:
    International Marine,
    P.O. Box 220, Camden, ME 04843

Questions regarding the ordering of this book should be addressed to:
    The McGraw-Hill Companies
    Customer Service Department
    P.O. Box 547, Blacklick, OH 43004
    Retail customers: 1-800-262-4729
    Bookstores: 1-800-233-4726

Printed by Quebecor, Dubuque, Iowa

CONTENTS

WHAT THIS BOOK IS ABOUT

Captain. What boater hasn't coveted the title—because of the knowledge and experience it implies and because of the opportunities it offers. The reality is that most small-boat captain jobs pay mediocre wages. On the other hand, operating a boat is more fun than almost any other thing I can think of. To actually be paid to run someone else's vessel, instead of endlessly pouring money into your own, is a proposition that is hard to beat. In addition, boating regulations get tougher every year. It is, in fact, illegal to accept as much as a beer from a guest on your boat unless you hold the proper Coast Guard–issued operator's license.

In the process of obtaining my own "ticket," I became aware of just how little I had previously known. Even with a Ph.D. in oceanography and 25,000 miles under the keel of my own boat, I could not have passed the Coast Guard license exam in 100 tries without further study.

Nothing is more fun and idyllic than a blue-sky day on the water, but the ocean—even a lake or river—can be a hostile environment. Losing crew overboard, going aground on a lee shore, witnessing a heart attack 10 miles offshore, and having fire in the engine compartment are all possibilities, too. The knowledge and judgment demanded by the Coast Guard of its licensees are really no more than the prudent boater should expect of himself or herself.

This book and its accompanying CD are designed to make the assimilation of this knowledge as simple as possible. Some study guides and classroom courses drill the student with just the answers required to pass the exam. The educational philosophy is that passing the exam is all that counts; whether the student comprehends and retains the material is irrelevant. Our approach is to explain the principles so the student can not only answer the questions at the examination, but also come up with the answers in real-life situations years down the waterway.

Coast Guard examinations are divided into six subject areas: Rules of the Road, Deck General, Navigation General, Safety, Navigation Problems, and Sail. Each subject area covers numerous specific topics. As you will see in the Contents, this book is organized in the same way. Each subject area is a chapter unto itself. Each chapter contains lean, information-packed summaries of the topics, followed by the entire set of questions in that subject area from the Coast Guard database. Answers to the questions appear at the end of each chapter.

The instructional text and illustrations provide the answers to an estimated 95% of the questions. No reasonable amount of text—not even all 31 of the books the Coast Guard recommends (page 8)—could answer the more esoteric questions in the database, however. For example:

00618. What is the mark on a lead line indicating 13 fathoms?

A. white linen rag
B. red woolen rag
C. 3 knots
D. 3 strips of leather

Some information can thus be gotten only from reading the questions and answers. If you plan to use the *AutoExam* CD to practice taking exams, consider marking the correct answer to all of the printed questions. For example:

00618. What is the mark on a lead line indicating 13 fathoms?

A. white linen rag
B. red woolen rag
C. 3 knots
D. 3 strips of leather

Now question 00618 can be read as, "The mark on a lead line indicating 13 fathoms is 3 strips of leather."

Once you have read an entire chapter, including questions and answers, start taking practice exams, either by selecting random questions from the back of the chapter or letting *AutoExam* do it for you. If you consistently pass the practice exams, move on to the next chapter. If not, read the chapter and—yes—all of the questions again. And again. Find a boating friend—or better, three—who also want tickets. Make up a game of "Trivial Pursuit" using the questions and answers. Learning the material can be fun!

The only thing we didn't include (it would have increased the cost of the book by $20 or more) is the set of charts the Coast Guard uses in the navigation section of the exam. If you have the money, buy them. Otherwise, borrow them from cruising friends or become intimate with them at a chandlery. They are

11462 *Fowey Rocks to Alligator Reef*
12221 *Chesapeake Bay Entrance*
12354 *Long Island Sound—Eastern Part*
13205 *Block Island Sound and Approaches*
18531 *Columbia River—Vancouver to Bonneville*

Happy *AutoExam*ining, and good luck, Cappy!

USING THE *AUTOEXAM* SOFTWARE

Drawing upon the complete database of more than 6,000 applicable Coast Guard questions, *AutoExam* automatically generates and grades examinations for four types of Coast Guard license:

1. OUPV (Six-Pack) License
2. Master and Mate Inland License
3. Master and Mate Near Coastal License
   Part 1: General Deck and Safety (70% pass)
       60 questions (combined) for Licenses 1 and 2
       70 questions (combined) for License 3
   Part 2: General Navigation (70% pass)
       20 questions
   Part 3: Navigation Problems (70% pass)
       10 questions
   Part 4: Rules of the Road (90% pass)
       30 questions
4. Sail/Auxiliary Sail Endorsement (70% pass)
       10 questions

The software consists of three main sections: Take Exams, Review Exams, and Print Exams.

Let's walk through a typical session:

1. From the Main Menu, select the **Exams** button.

2. You will be asked to enter your initials (Screen 1). Entering your initials enables a tracking mechanism which logs your performance for later review.

3. When you click **OK**, the Take Exams section appears (Screen 2). At this point you may be interested in configuring an exam just to see how you would do. Click on **Exam Options**.

4. Let's try a Six-Pack License, Part 1, the General Deck and Safety portion of the exam. As shown in Screen 3, *AutoExam* automatically selects it for you and sets the question count to sixty. If you wish a different exam, simply click on **Custom** and enter the Part and Questions count.

The Review Options allow you either to get your final score at the completion of a Part or to receive continuous feedback as you progress.

Would you like a second chance on questions you answer incorrectly? If so, select **Retry incorrect responses**. *AutoExam* will record the incorrectly answered questions, allowing you to try again.

Screen 1

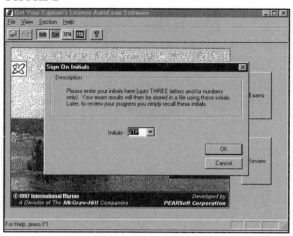

Screen 2

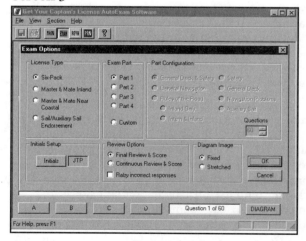

Screen 3

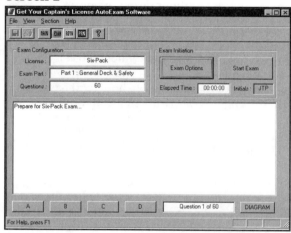

Note the Diagram Image options of **Fixed** or **Stretched**. When an exam question references a diagram, AutoExam enables the **DIAGRAM** button in the lower right corner of the screen. Clicking the **DIAGRAM** button brings up the image, which can then be adjusted to any size, as in Screen 4.

Now that we have set all exam options, let's take the exam. Click on **Start Exam** and the first question appears (Screen 4). Answer the question by clicking the correct button: **A**, **B**, **C**, or **D**. Your answer will be recorded and the next question will appear.

If you would rather print an exam to take with you, click on the **PRIN** toolbar button and you'll get a full randomly generated exam ready to go (Screen 5).

The Review Section (Screen 6) allows you to review all aspects of previous exams. As you move through the list of questions, the correct answers appear side-by-side with your responses. Using the **Newer/Older** buttons allows you to review all past exams, including the date and time the exam started, as well as elapsed time.

If at any point you need further guidance, press the Help key, **F1**.

Now get comfortable and start practicing. *AutoExam* never runs out of questions and never tires of randomly generating fresh exams. When you reach the point of consistently passing all parts, call your local Regional Exam Center and tell them you are ready for the real thing. Good luck!

Screen 4

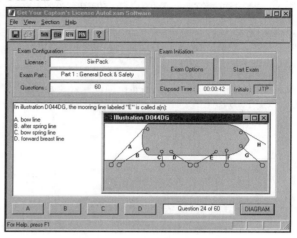

Screen 5

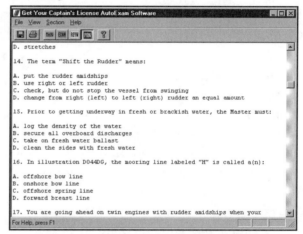

Screen 6

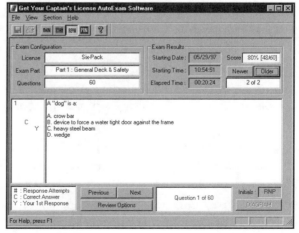

RECOMMENDED REFERENCES

The references listed below are those recommended by the Coast Guard for exam preparation. The books in bold type are available during the exam. Supposedly, answers to all of the more than 6,000 questions can be found in the books listed.

Whether it is worth your time to read all of the books is doubtful. Better to read "Chapman" (reference 19) two or three times than all books once.

Our recommendations are:
1. Become familiar with the books in bold so that you can quickly find answers during the exam.
2. Read Chapman (19) entirely at least twice.
3. Read the chapters in this book at least twice.
4. Read all of the questions and answers.
5. Use *AutoExam* until you consistently make grades well above passing.

REFERENCES
(Bold items are provided at exam)

1. *American Merchant Seaman's Manual*, by W. B. Hayler
2. **American Practical Navigator** (Bowditch), Defense Mapping Agency Pub. #9
3. **Code of Federal Regulations (CFR),** Titles 33 and 46, Government Printing Office
4. *Encyclopedia of Nautical Knowledge*, by William A. MacEwen and A.H. Lewis
5. **International Code of Signals,** H.O. PUB. No. 102, Defense Mapping Agency
6. *Introduction to Steel Shipbuilding*, by Elijah Baker III
7. *Knight's Modern Seamanship*, by John V. Noel, Jr.
8. **Light Lists,** U.S. Coast Guard
9. *Manual for Lifeboatmen*, U.S. Coast Guard
10. *Marine Fire Prevention, Firefighting and Fire Safety*, Maritime Administration, U.S. Dept. of Commerce
11. *Marine Radiotelephone User's Handbook*, Radio Technical Commission for Maritime Services
12. *Merchant Marine Officer's Handbook*, by Edward A. Turpin and William A. MacEwen
13. *Meteorology with Marine Applications*, by William L. Donn
14. *Modern Ships*, by Reginald Carpenter
15. **Nautical Almanac,** U.S. Naval Observatory
16. *Navigation and Piloting* (Duttons), by Elbert S. Maloney
17. *Navigation Rules: International—Inland*, U.S. Coast Guard
18. *Oil Pollution Control for Tankermen*, U.S. Coast Guard
19. *Piloting, Seamanship and Small Boat Handling* (Chapman), by Elbert S. Maloney
20. *Radar Navigation Manual*, Defense Mapping Agency, NAVPUB 1310
21. **Radio Navigation Aids,** Pub. 117, Defense Mapping Agency
22. **Sight Reduction Tables for Marine Navigation,** Pub. 229, Defense Mapping Agency
23. *Ship's Medicine Chest & Medical Aid at Sea*, U.S. Dept. of Health, Education and Welfare
24. *Stability & Trim for the Ship's Officer*, by William E. George
25. *This Is Sailing*, by Richard Creagh-Osborne
26. **Tidal Current Tables,** U.S. Dept. of Commerce, N.O.A.A., N.O.S.
27. **Tide Tables,** U.S. Dept. of Commerce, N.O.A.A., N.O.S.
28. *Tugs, Towboats and Towing*, by Edward M. Brady
29. **U. S. Coast Pilots,** U.S. Dept. of Commerce, National Ocean Survey
30. *Weather for the Mariner*, by William J. Kotsch

QUALIFYING FOR A LICENSE

The Licensing Process

To obtain a license for either Operator of Uninspected Passenger Vessels or Master of Inspected Vessels to 100 gross tons, you must clear two hurdles:

• Prove to the Coast Guard that you *qualify* (meet all of the regulatory requirements for the license).

• Pass a written *exam* which includes multiple-choice questions on rules of the road, general navigation, safety and seamanship, and 10 hands-on multiple-part chart navigation problems.

You can not schedule an examination (hurdle 2) until the Coast Guard has evaluated your application and its supporting documentation.

A Changing Process

In line with the streamlining of all government activities, the Coast Guard is studying privatization of the examination process. The goal is to have the Coast Guard get out of the examination business entirely.

Instead, private schools would be accredited by the Coast Guard to conduct courses, administer exams, and grant certificates qualifying an applicant for the knowledge portion of the license. Instuctors at the schools would be Coast Guard licensed, and the quality of the courses would be periodically monitored. The list of schools offering the courses would be available from the Coast Guard Regional Examination Centers (RECs). Such schools presently exist. The courses are excellent, but considerably more expensive ($500–$1,000) than the price of a book. In order not to price applicants out of the process, applicants will still be able to study at home then take the exam at a school for a lesser fee.

Further down the road the Coast Guard anticipates the use of computer simulation to examine the applicant's vessel-handling abilities and knowledge of the rules of the road.

Where to Apply

All phases of the licensing process are handled presently by RECs at each of the 17 Coast Guard Districts (addresses and telephone numbers listed on the facing page). This chapter supplies all of the information and forms you will require, but we suggest that you call the REC in your district for their *Small Vessel Licensing Information Package* to ensure that requirements haven't changed.

You will find that REC personnel are professional, courteous, and eager to assist, but will interpret the regulatory requirements strictly.

A Coast Guard document is a professional license—difficult to acquire and worthy of respect. We suggest you grant REC personnel and the licensing process the same respect. Lest you need further motivation, be aware that falsification of any information—such as sea service experience—is punishable by up to a $10,000 fine, five years in jail, or both!

Which License to Apply For

Operating licenses for up to 100 gross ton vessels fall into six categories, as shown on the page at right. As you go through the requirements and the content of the exams for each, you should be struck by the fact that—except for the limited licenses (numbers 1 and 4)—the only significant differences are in experience (what the Coast Guard terms *sea service*). Our recommendation is to compute the sea service you can document and apply for the highest level license for which you are qualified. There is little sense settling for a Six-Pack (a term the Coast Guard detests), if the exam is the same as that for a 100-ton Master!

Tonnage Limits

Licenses are issued in increments of 50 GT, except when the service was gained on vessels of less than 5 GT, in which case the limit will be 25 GT. Otherwise, the tonnage limit is calculated as the greater of:

1. the tonnage on which at least 25% of the required service was gained, or

2. 150% of the tonnage on which at least 50% of the required service was gained

Route (Waters):

The waters in which the license is valid depends on where the required sea service was gained:

Inland—inland of the Boundary Line, as specified in 46 CFR part 7. The Boundary Line is NOT THE SAME as the COLREGS Demarcation Line which separates International and Inland Rules of the Road waters. Contact the Coast Guard office in your area of operation for a definition.

Near Coastal—waters to seaward of the Boundary Line to 200 miles offshore. A Near Coastal license may be restricted to a smaller distance offshore, such as 100 miles. A Near Coastal license is also valid in Inland and Great Lakes waters.

Great Lakes—obviously valid in the Great Lakes. An Inland license is not valid in the Great Lakes unless it specifies Inland and Great Lakes.

Coast Guard Regional Examination Centers

ANCHORAGE, AK
USCG Regional Exam Center
510 L Street, Suite 100
Anchorage, AK 99501
(907) 271-6732/36

BALTIMORE, MD
USCG Regional Exam Center
Customhouse, 40 South Gay Street
Baltimore, MD 21202
(410) 962-5132

BOSTON, MA
USCG Regional Exam Center
455 Commercial Street
Boston, MA 02109-1045
(617) 223-3040/41/42

CHARLESTON, SC
USCG Regional Exam Center
196 Tradd Street
Charleston, SC 29401
(803) 724-7692/93/94

HONOLULU, HI
USCG Regional Exam Center
433 Ala Moana Boulevard (Pier 4)
Honolulu, HI 96813-4909
(808) 522-8259

HOUSTON, TX
USCG Regional Exam Center
8876 Gulf Freeway, Suite 200
Houston, TX 77017
(713) 947-0044

JUNEAU, AK
USCG Regional Exam Center
2760 Sherwood Lane, Suite 2A
Juneau, AK 99801
(907) 463-2450

LONG BEACH, CA
USCG Regional Exam Center
165 North Pico Avenue
Long Beach, CA 90802-1096
(310) 980-4485

MEMPHIS, TN
USCG Regional Exam Center
200 Jefferson Avenue, Suite 1302
Memphis, TN 38103
(901) 544-3297/98

MIAMI, FL
USCG Regional Exam Center
Claude Pepper Fed. Bldg., 6th Floor
51 S.W. First Avenue
Miami, FL 33130
(305) 536-6548/49

NEW ORLEANS, LA
USCG Regional Exam Center
1440 Canal Street
New Orleans, LA 70112-2711
(504) 589-6183/84/85

NEW YORK, NY
USCG Regional Exam Center
Battery Park Building
New York, NY 10004
(212) 668-6395

PORTLAND, OR
USCG Regional Exam Center
6767 North Basin Avenue
Portland, OR 97217
(503) 240-9347

SAN FRANCISCO, CA
USCG Regional Exam Center
Government Island
Building 14, Room 109
Alameda, CA 94501-5100
(510) 437-3096

SEATTLE, WA
USCG Regional Exam Center
1519 Alaskan Way S., Bldg. 1
Seattle, WA 98134
(206) 286-5510

ST. LOUIS, MO
USCG Regional Exam Center
1222 Spruce Street, Suite 8.104E
St. Louis, MO 63103-2835
(314) 539-2657

TOLEDO, OH
USCG Regional Exam Center
501 Federal Building
234 Summit Street
Toledo, OH 43604
(419) 259-6395

EXPERIENCE REQUIREMENTS

UNINSPECTED VESSELS

1. **License for Operating Uninspected Passenger Vessels at Yacht Clubs, Marinas, Formal Camps or Educational Institutions**—*AKA "Launchtender"*

   a. Minimum age: 17

   b. Satisfactory completion within the past five years of a safe boating course approved by the National Association of State Boating Law Administrators or conducted by the USPS, Red Cross, or CG Auxiliary

   c. 90 days operating same type of vessel within the preceding three years

   d. Letter from prospective employer stating type of vessel and area of operation

2. **License for Operating Uninspected Passenger Vessel Upon Inland Waters**—*AKA "Six-Pack"*

   a. Minimum age: 18

   b. 360 days operating a small vessel

   c. 90 of the 360 days must have been within the past three years

3. **License for Operating Uninspected Passenger Vessel Upon Near Coastal Waters**—*AKA "Six-Pack"*

   a. Minimum age: 18

   b. 360 days operating a small vessel, of which 90 days must have been on ocean or near coastal waters

   c. 90 of the 360 days must have been within the past three years

INSPECTED VESSELS

4. **License for Operating Inspected Inland Passenger Vessels at Yacht Clubs, Marinas, Formal Camps or Educational Institutions**

   a. Minimum age: 18

   b. Satisfactory completion within the past 5 years of a safe boating course approved by the National Association of State Boating Law Administrators or conducted by the USPS, Red Cross, or CG Auxiliary

   c. 120 days operating same type of vessel, of which 90 days must be within the preceding three years

   d. Letter from prospective employer stating type of vessel and area of operation

5. **Master of Inland Steam or Motor Vessels of Not More Than 100 Gross Tons**

   a. Minimum age: 19

   b. 360 days operating a small vessel, of which 90 days must have been within the preceding three years

   c. For Auxiliary Sail Endorsement, 180 days service on a sail or auxiliary sail vessel

6. **Master of Near Coastal Steam or Motor Vessels of Not More Than 100 Gross Tons**

   a. Minimum age: 19

   b. 720 days operating a small vessel, of which 90 days must have been within the preceding three years

   c. Of the 720 total days, 360 must have been on ocean or near coastal waters

   d. For Auxiliary Sail Endorsement, 360 days service on a sail or auxiliary sail vessel

ENDORSEMENTS

Auxiliary Sail Endorsement

   a. On an Inland Master License, a minimum of 180 days of service on a sail or auxiliary sail vessel

   b. On a Near Coastal Master License, a minimum of 360 days of service on a sail or auxiliary sail vessel

COMPLETING THE FORMS

1. Application Form (Page 18)

Applicants for an original license, complete Sections I, II, III, IV, VI, VII and IX. Applicants for a duplicate license, complete Sections I, II, V, VI, VII and IX. Applicants for a license renewal, endorsement, or replacement, complete Sections I, II, III, VI, VII and IX.

Applicants for an original license submit two sets of fingerprints. You can have fingerprints made at your police station or at the Coast Guard REC. The prints will be forwarded to the FBI for verification of the arrest and conviction information on your application.

All applicants for an original license are required to supply three recommendations attesting to the applicant's suitability for a Coast Guard License.

Applications are valid for one year from receipt. After one year you must submit a new application. Original supporting documentation submitted with the application will be returned to the applicant.

2. Physical Exam Form (Page 21)

The Coast Guard Physical Examination Form (CG-719K) must be completed in full by a licensed physician, a licensed physician's assistant, or a licensed nurse practitioner. The examination must be completed before submission of the application and no more than 12 months before issuance of the license.

An incomplete examination form will delay your application. Make sure the physician completes Block 15. If medication side effects are experienced, they must be listed. If no side effects are experienced, a statement to that effect must be entered.

Blood pressure may not be higher than 150/90, regardless of treatment or medication. Uncorrected vision should be at least 20/200, correctable to 20/40, in each eye. A waiver for simple myopia over 20/200 may be granted.

Not meeting a vision, hearing, or general physical condition requirement does not automatically disqualify the applicant. The examining physician may attach a request for waiver based on the opinion that the condition does not endanger the vessel or her passengers. Conditions the Coast Guard probably would not accept include major psychological disorder, unstable diabetes, heart condition and epilepsy.

The Coast Guard has access to your records through the FBI, so be sure to list all convictions for drugs and OUI. Prior conviction does not automatically disqualify you. Severity and age at convictions are considered. If the state won't give you a license, however, you can be sure the Coast Guard won't either.

3. Drug Test (Page 23)

All applicants must be certified "Drug Free." An individual can be documented "Drug Free" by:

- The examining physician or program vendor collects a urine sample and sends it (in accordance with *49 CFR 40*) to a Substance Abuse and Mental Health Services Administration (SAMHSA) approved lab. Upon receipt of the laboratory results, the physician or vendor completes the form on page 23 and returns it to the REC. *Do not submit copies of the custody control forms or laboratory forms to the REC.* Tests performed by non-approved labs will not be accepted The lab test must be performed within six months of the application. See pages 15–17 for a list of approved labs to show your doctor. If your doctor is not affiliated with one of these labs, you may contact a drug program vendor.

- A letter on company letterhead from a marine employer signed by a company official indicating that the applicant has a) passed a test for dangerous drugs required by the Coast Guard within the previous six months with no subsequent positive chemical tests during the remainder of the six month period; or b) during the previous 185 days, has been subject to a Coast Guard-required random testing program for at least 60 days and did not fail or refuse to participate in a Coast Guard-required chemical test for dangerous drugs.

- A letter from an active-duty military command or a federal employee supervisor indicating that the applicant has a) passed a test for dangerous drugs within the previous six months with no subsequent positive chemical tests during the remainder of the six month period; or b) during the previous 185 days been subject to a random testing program for at least 60 days and did not fail or refuse to participate in a chemical test for dangerous drugs.

4. Sea Service Form (Page 24)

You must tabulate your experience in operating vessels on the Sea Service Form. If necessary use additional copies to account for service on more than four vessels.

One day of service consists of a minimum of four hours underway—not at the dock. Do not claim additional days on any one day even if you served more than eight hours.

Service before the age of 13 does not count. The value of service attained before the age of 16 will be judged by the evaluator.

5. Documentation of Sea Service

Service listed on the Sea Service Form must be supported by proof of vessel ownership. State registration, documentation certificate, bill of sale, and insurance policy may be acceptable proofs. Service on other vessels must be supported by letters in the form of the Supplemental Small Boat Experience Letter.

6. Proof of Age and Citizenship

Age and citizenship must be verified by one of:

- Birth Certificate (original or certified copy)

- Passport (original or certified copy)

- Baptismal Certificate (issued within a year of birth)

- Certificate of Naturalization (original only)

- If your current name is different from what appears on your proof of citizenship, supply documentation of the name change. A married woman must present marriage licenses and divorce decrees.

7. Proof of Social Security Number

A photocopy of your Social Security Card may be submitted for evaluation, but you must supply an original or duplicate card before the license will be issued. If you do not have your original card, apply for a duplicate from the Social Security Administration.

8. First Aid Card

Applicants for all licenses, except Launchtender, must present a certificate for a first aid course, dated within 12 months of the application date. Acceptable courses include:

- American Red Cross Standard First Aid and Emergency Care

- American Red Cross Multi-Media Standard First Aid

- Any other Coast Guard approved first aid course

9. CPR Certificate

Applicants for all licenses, except Launchtender, must present a certificate for a cardiopulmonary resuscitation (CPR) course. The certificate must be valid at the time of the application. Acceptable courses include:

- American Red Cross CPR

- American Heart Association CPR

- Any other Coast Guard approved CPR course

10. Boating Course Certificate

Applicants for limited licences (Launchtender, etc.) must present evidence of satisfactory completion within the past five years of a safe boating course approved by the National Association of State Boating Law Administrators or one of the public education courses conducted by the U.S. Power Squadrons, the Coast Guard Auxiliary, or the American Red Cross.

11. Fees

The fees depend on the category of license. In order to assess fees fairly and to ensure that applicants pay only for services received, the Coast Guard divides the fee assessment into three phases:

Evaluation—processing the application, including review of documents and records submitted with the application.

Examination—scheduling, proctoring, and grading examination sections, as well as notifying applicants of results.

Issuance—preparing, reviewing, and signing documents by appropriate REC personnel.

You pay only for the phases you use. Fees may be paid in person or mailed to the REC. Check, money order, or cash in the exact amount are accepted in person. For mail-ins, fees must be paid by check or money order. Checks and money orders are to be made out to the U.S. Coast Guard and must include the applicant's social security number so that the payment is credited to the correct applicant.

Employees of youth-oriented, non-profit organizations teaching youths maritime skills may qualify for *no-fee licenses*. Contact the REC for details.

Fee Schedule

	Evaluation	Exam	Issuance
Original License (includes endorsements)	$65	$80 [1]	$35
Renewal License	$45	$45	$35
Duplicate/Replacement	0	0	$35
Endorsement Only	$45	$45	$35
Continuity Endorsement [2]	0	0	$35

[1] *For certain licenses (Launchtender and upgrades) requiring only a partial exam, the exam fee is $45.*

[2] *A Continuity Endorsement is an endorsement on an expired license which preserves the license in an inactive state until a requirement such as sea service is fulfilled.*

SAMHSA-APPROVED DRUG TEST LABS

The following is a list of laboratories which meet minimum SAMHSA standards to analyze urine drug samples as of 13 January, 1997. Your doctor should send your urine sample to one of these labs. It is equally important to ensure that the individual accepting the sample is authorized by the laboratory to act as a "collection site."

AEGIS ANALYTICAL LABORATORIES, INC.
824 GRASSMERE PARK ROAD, SUITE 21
NASHVILLE, TN 37211
(615) 331-5300

ALABAMA REFERENCE LABORATORIES, INC.
543 SOUTH HULL STREET
MONTGOMERY, AL 36103
(800) 541-4931 / (205) 263-5745

AMERICAN MEDICAL LABORATORIES, INC.
14225 NEWBROOK DRIVE
CHANTILLY, VA 22021
(703) 802-6900

ASSOCIATED PATHOLOGISTS LABORATORIES, INC.
4230 SOUTH BURNHAM AVENUE, SUITE 250
LAS VEGAS, NV 89119-5412
(702) 733-7866 / (800) 433-2750

ASS. REG. AND UNIVERSITY PATHOLOGISTS, INC.
500 CHIPETA WAY
SALT LAKE CITY, UT 84108
(801) 583-2787 / (800) 242-2787

BAPTIST MEDICAL CENTER TOXICOLOGY LAB
9601 I-630, EXIT 7
LITTLE ROCK, AR 72205-7299
(501) 227-2783

BAYSHORE CLINICAL LABORATORY
4555 WEST SCHROEDER DRIVE
BROWN DEER, WI 53223
(414) 355-4444 / (800) 877-7016

CEDARS MEDICAL CTR., DEPT. OF PATHOLOGY
1400 NORTHWEST 12TH AVENUE
MIAMI, FL 33136
(305) 325-5810

CENTINELA HOSPITAL AIRPORT TOXICOLOGY LAB
9601 S. SEPULVEDA BOULEVARD
LOS ANGELES, CA 90045
(310) 215-6020

CLINICAL REFERENCE LAB
11850 WEST 85TH STREET
LENEXA, KS 66214
(800) 445-6917

COMPUCHEM LABS, INC.
1904 ALEXANDER DRIVE
RESEARCH TRIANGLE PARK, NC 27709
(919) 549-8263 / (800) 833-3984

CORNING CLINICAL LABORATORIES
2320 SCHUETZ ROAD
ST. LOUIS, MO 63146
(800) 288-7293

CORNING CLINICAL LABORATORIES
4771 REGENT BOULEVARD
IRVING, TX 75063
(800) 526-0947

CORNING CLINICAL LABORATORIES
4444 GIDDINGS ROAD
AUBURN HILLS, MI 48326
(800) 444-0106 / (810) 373-9120

CORNING METPATH CLINICAL LABORATORIES
1355 MITTEL BOULEVARD
WOOD DALE, IL 60191
(708) 595-3888

CORNING METPATH CLINICAL LABS
ONE MALCOLM AVENUE
TETERBORO, NJ 07608
(201) 393-5000

CORNING CLINICAL LABS
875 GREENTREE RD., 4 PARKWAY CENTER
PITTSBURGH, PA 15220
(800) 284-7515

CORNING NAT. CENTER FOR FORENSIC SCIENCE
1901 SULPHUR SPRING ROAD
BALTIMORE, MD 21227
(410) 536-1485 / (800) 522-9235

CORNING METPATH CLINICAL LABORATORIES
7470-A MISSION VALLEY ROAD
SAN DIEGO, CA 92108-4406
(708) 446-4728 / (619) 686-3200

COX MEDICAL CENTERS, DEPT. OF TOXICOLOGY
1423 NORTH JEFFERSON AVENUE
SPRINGFIELD, MO 65802
(800) 876-3652 / (417) 836-3093

DEPT. OF THE NAVY DRUG SCREENING LAB
BUILDING 38-H
GREAT LAKES, IL 60088-5223
(708) 688-2045 / (708) 688-4171

DIAGNOSTIC SERVICES INC., dba DSI
4048 EVANS AVENUE, SUITE 301
FORT MYERS, FL 33901
(813) 936-5446 / (800) 735-5416

DOCTORS LABORATORY, INC.
P. O. BOX 2658, 2906 JULIA DRIVE
VALDOSTA, GA 31604
(912) 244-4468

DRUGPROOF, DIV. OF
LABORATORY OF PATHOLOGY, OF SEATTLE, INC.
1229 MADISON STREET, SUITE 500
NORDSTROM MEDICAL TOWER
SEATTLE, WA 98104
(800) 898-0180 / (206) 386-2672

DRUGSCAN, INC.
P.O. BOX 2969, 1119 MEARNS ROAD
WARMINSTER, PA 18974
(215) 674-9310

ELSOHLY LABORATORIES,INC.
5 INDUSTRIAL PARK DRIVE
OXFORD, MS 38655
(601) 236-2609

GENERAL MEDICAL LABORATORIES
36 SOUTH BROOKS STREET
MADISON, WI 53715
(608) 267-6267

HARRISON LABORATORIES, INC.
9930 W. HIGHWAY 80
MIDLAND, TX 79706
(800) 725-3784 / (915) 563-3300

JEWISH HOSPITAL OF CINCINNATI, INC.
3200 BURNET AVENUE
CINCINNATI, OH 45229
(513) 569-2051

LAB ONE, INC.
8915 LENEXA DRIVE
OVERLAND PARK, KS 66214
(913) 888-3927 / (800) 728-4064

LABORATORY CORP. OF AMERICA HOLDINGS
69 FIRST AVENUE
RARITAN, NJ 08869
(800) 437-4986

LABORATORY SPECIALISTS, INC.
113 JARRELL DRIVE
BELLE CHASSE, LA 70037
(504) 392-7961

MARSHFIELD LABORATORIES
1000 NORTH OAK AVENUE
MARSHFIELD, WI 54449
(715) 389-3734 / (800) 222-5835

MEDEXPRESS/NATIONAL LABORATORY CTR.
4022 WILLOW LAKE BOULEVARD
MEMPHIS,TN 38175
(901) 795-1515 / (800) 526-6339

MEDICAL COLLEGE HOSPITALS
TOXICOLOGY LAB, DEPT. OF PATHOLOGY
3000 ARLINGTON AVENUE
TOLEDO, OH 43699-0008
(419) 381-5213

MEDLAB CLINICAL TESTING, INC.
212 CHERRY LANE
NEW CASTLE, DE 19720
(302) 655-5227

MEDTOX LABORATORIES, INC.
402 WEST COUNTY ROAD
ST.PAUL, MN 55112
(612) 636-7466 / (800) 832-3244

METHODIST HOSPITAL OF INDIANA, INC.
DEPT. OF PATHOLOGY AND LAB MEDICINE
1701 N. SENATE BOULEVARD
INDIANAPOLIS, IN 46202
(317) 929-3587

METHODIST MEDICAL CENTER
TOXICOLOGY LABORATORY
221 N.E. GLEN OAK AVENUE
PEORIA, IL 61636
(309) 671-5199 / (800) 752-1835

METROLAB-LEGACY LAB SERVICES
235 N. GRAHAM STREET
PORTLAND, OR 97227
(503) 413-4512 / (800) 237-7808

MINNEAPOLIS V.A. MEDICAL CENTER
FORENSIC TOXICOLOGY LABORATORY
1 VETERANS DRIVE
MINNEAPOLIS, MN 55417
(612) 725-2088

NATIONAL TOXICOLOGY LABORATORIES, INC.
1100 CALIFORNIA AVENUE
BAKERSFIELD, CA 93304
(805) 322-4250

NORTHWEST TOXICOLOGY, INC.
1141 EAST 3900 SOUTH
SALT LAKE CITY, UT 84124
(800) 322-3361

OREGON MEDICAL LABORATORIES
P.O. BOX 972
722 EAST 11TH AVENUE
EUGENE, OR 97440-0972
(541) 687-2134

PATHOLOGY ASSOCIATES MEDICAL LABS
EAST 11604 INDIANA
SPOKANE, WA 99206
(509) 926-2400 / (800) 541-7891

PREMIER ANALYTICAL LABORATORIES
15201 I-10 EAST, SUITE 125
CHANNELVIEW, TX 77530
(713) 457-3784 / (800) 888-4063

PHARMCHEM LABORATORIES, INC.
1505-A O'BRIEN DRIVE
MENLO PARK,CA 94025
(415) 328-6200 / (800) 446-5177

PHARMCHEM LABORATORIES, INC.
TEXAS DIVISION
7606 PEBBLE DRIVE
FORT WORTH, TX 76118
(817) 595-0294

PHYSICIANS REFERENCE LABORATORY
7800 WEST 110TH STREET
OVERLAND PARK, KS 66210
(913) 338-4070 / (800) 821-3627

POISONLAB, INC.
7272 CLAIREMONT MESA ROAD
SAN DIEGO, CA 92111
(619) 279-2600 / (800) 882-7272

PRESBYTERIAN LAB SERVICES
1851 EAST THIRD STREET
CHARLOTTE, NC 28204
(800) 473-6640

PUCKETT LABORATORY
4200 MAMIE STREET
HATTIESBURG, MS 39402
(601) 264-3856 / (800) 844-8378

SCIENTIFIC TESTING LABS, INC.
463 SOUTHLAKE BOULEVARD
RICHMOND, VA 23236
(804) 378-9130

SCOTT & WHITE DRUG TESTING LABORATORY
600 SOUTH 25TH STREET
TEMPLE, TX 76504
(800) 749-3788

S.E.D. MEDICAL LABORATORIES
500 WALTER NE, SUITE 500
ALBUQUERQUE, NM 87102
(505) 848-8800 / (800) 999-LABS

SIERRA NEVADA LABORATORIES, INC.
888 WILLOW STREET
RENO, NV 89502
(800) 648-5472

SMITHKLINE BEECHAM CLINICAL LABS
7600 TYRONE AVENUE
VAN NUYS, CA 91045
(818) 877-2520 / (800) 877-2520

SMITHKLINE BEECHAM CLINICAL LAB
801 EAST DIXIE AVENUE
LEESBURG, FL 34748
(904) 787-9006

SMITHKLINE BEECHAM CLINICAL LAB
3175 PRESIDENTIAL DRIVE
ATLANTA, GA 30340
(770) 452-1590

SMITHKLINE BEECHAM CLINICAL LABORATORIES
506 EAST STATE PARKWAY
SCHAUMBURG, IL 60173
(708) 885-2010 / (800) 447-4379

SMITHKLINE BEECHAM CLINICAL LABORATORIES
400 EGYPT ROAD
NORRISTOWN, PA 19403
(800) 523-5447 / (610) 631-4600

SMITHKLINE BEECHAM CLINICAL LABORATORIES
8000 SOVEREIGN ROW
DALLAS, TX 75247
(214) 638-1301

SOUTH BEND MEDICAL FOUNDATION, INC.
530 NORTH LAYFAYETTE BOULEVARD
SOUTH BEND, IN 46601
(219) 234-4176

SOUTHWEST LABORATORIES
2727 W. BASELINE ROAD, SUITE 6
TEMPE, AZ 85283
(602) 438-8507

ST. ANTHONY HOSPITAL (TOXICOLOGY LABORATORY)
P. O. BOX 205
1000 NORTH LEE STREET
OKLAHOMA CITY, OK 73102
(405) 272-7052

TOXICOLOGY & DRUG MONITORING LABORATORY
UNIVERSITY OF MISSOURI HOSPITAL & CLINICS
2703 CLARK LANE, SUITE B, LOWER LEVEL
COLUMBIA, MO 65202
(314) 882-1273

TOXICOLOGY TESTING SERVICE, INC.
5426 N.W. 79TH AVENUE
MIAMI, FL 33166
(305) 593-2260

TOXWORX LABS INC.
6160 VARIEL AVENUE
WOODLAND HILLS, CA 91367
(818) 226-4373 / (800) 966-2211

UNILAB
18408 OXNARD STREET
TARZANA, CA 91356
(800) 492-0800 / (818) 343-8191

UTMB PATHOLOGY-TOXICOLOGY LAB,
UNIVERSITY OF TEXAS, MEDICAL BRANCH,
CLINICAL CHEMISTRY DIVISION
301 UNIVERSITY BOULEVARD
ROOM 5.158, OLD JOHN SEALY
GALVESTON, TX 77555
(409) 772-3197

DEPARTMENT OF TRANSPORTATION U.S.COAST GUARD	APPLICATION FOR LICENSE AS OFFICER, STAFF OFFICER, OPERATOR, AND MERCHANT MARINER'S DOCUMENT	1. PORT *(REC)*

SECTION I. MARINER'S CREDENTIALS APPLICATION

2. NAME   *(LAST)*   *(FIRST)*   *(MIDDLE)*

3. ADDRESS	4. DATE	5. SSN	6. DATE OF BIRTH
	7. PLACE OF BIRTH		
	8. CITIZENSHIP		9. TELEPHONE NUMBER

10. TYPE OF TRANSACTION (CHECK APPROPRIATE BOXES

	ORIGINAL	RENEWAL	DUPLICATE	EMDORSEMENT	SUPPLEMENTAL	REPLACEMENT	EXCHANGE	10a. MMD NUMBER
☐ LICENSE	☐	☐	☐	☐	☐			(CG USE ONLY)
☐ MERCHANT MARINER DOCUMENT	☐		☐					10b. BK. NUMBER
☐ CONTINUOUS DISCHARGE BOOK	☐		☐			☐	☐	
☐ DISCHARGES			☐					(CG USE ONLY)

11. APPLYING FOR

12. HAIR	13. EYES	14. WEIGHT	15. HEIGHT	16. COMPLEXION

17. NAME AND ADDRESS OF NEXT OF KIN	18. RELATIONSHIP
	19. PARENTAL CONSENT FOR MMO *(UNDER 18)* ☐ YES *(ATTACHED)* ☐ NO

SECTION II. PRESENT OR PREVIOUS MMD/LICENSE HISTORY

20. DESCRIPTION OF LICENSE OR MMD	21. PLACE OF ISSUE	22. DATE OF ISSUE	23. LICENSE SERIAL N0/MMD NO

24.	YES	NO	INDICATE ANSWER BY PLACING YOUR INITIALS IN PROPER COLUMN
			HAS ANY COAST GUARD DOCUMENT OR LICENSE HELD BY YOU EVER BEEN REVOKED, SUSPENDED, OR VOLUNTARILY SURRENDERED? *(If yes, attach statement)*

25. RECORD OF QUALIFYING SERVICE/TRAINING *(IF APPLICABLE, CHECK APPROPRIATE BOXES)*

☐ MERCHANT MARINE SEA SERVICE DISCHARGE(S) ATTACHED   ☐ MILITARY SEA SERVICE–TRANSCRIPT OR HISTORY OF ASSIGNMENTS ATTACHED

☐ LETTER(S) OF SEA SERVICE ATTACHED   ☐ COMPLETION OF CG APPROVED SCHOOL/COURSE CERTIFICATE(S) ATTACHED

SECTION III. U.S. CITIZENSHIP AND MILITARY RECORD *(FOR ORIGINAL LICENSES, AND, U.S. MMD ONLY)*

26. PROOF OF U.S. CITIZENSHIP SUBMITTED (CG USE ONLY)

27. INDICATE STATE IF NATURALIZED BY COURT	28. DATE NATURALIZED

29. HAVE YOU EVER SERVED IN THE U.S. ARMED FORCES? ☐ YES ☐ NO	30. DATE ENTERED	31. DATE SEPARATED

32. SERVICE NUMBER	33. FULL NAME *(IF DIFFERENT FROM BLOCK 2)*	34. BRANCH OF SERVICE	35. TYPE OF DISCHARGE

SECTION IV. CHARACTER REFERENCES *(FOR ORIGINAL LICENSES ONLY)*

36. THREE NOTARIZED LETTERS OF REFERENCE/RECOMMENDATION THAT INCLUDE THE ORIGINATOR'S NAME, ADDRESS, TELEPHONE NUMBER, AND OCCUPATION ARE ATTACHED	☐ YES (ATTACHED)	☐ NO

SECTION V. REQUEST FOR DUPLICATE LICENSE, MMD, OR CD *(LIST INFORMATION ON LOST LICENSE/MMD)*

37. LICENSE SERIAL NUMBER	38. DATE AND PLACE LICENSE ISSUED
39. MMD NUMBER	40. DATE AND PLACE MMD ISSUED

41. ☐ CERTIFICATES OF DISCHARGE *(IF REQUEST IS FOR ALL DISCHARGES, SPECIFY OR ATTACH LIST OF VESSELS AND DATES OF SERVICE)*

42. SIGNED STATEMENT ATTACHED EXPLAINING THE PARTICULARS OF HOW, WHEN, AND WHERE THE CREDENTIALS WERE LOST/STOLEN AND APPLICANT'S EFFORT TO RECOVER THEM

☐ YES (ATTACHED)   ☐ NO

DEPARTMENT OF TRANSPORTATION U.S.COAST GUARD	**APPLICATION FOR LICENSE AS OFFICER, STAFF OFFICER, OPERATOR, AND MERCHANT MARINER'S DOCUMENT**

SECTION VI. NARCOTICS, DWI/DUI, AND CONVICTIONS RECORD

YES (INITIALS)	NO (INITIALS)	INDICATE ANSWER BY PLACING YOUR INITIALS IN PROPER COLUMN.
		Have you ever been convicted of violating a dangerous drug law of the United States, District of Columbia, or any state or territory of the United States, including marijuana? *(If yes, attach statement.)*
		Have you ever been a user of/or addicted to a dangerous drug? (including marijuana) *(If yes, attach statement.)*
		Have you ever been convicted by any court – including military court – for an offense other than a minor traffic violation? (Conviction means found guilty by judgement or by plea and includes cases of deferred adjudication (*nolo contendere*, adjudication withheld, etc.) or where the court required you to attend classes, make contributions of time or money, receive treatment, submit to any manner of probation or supervision, or forgo appeal of a trial court finding. Expunged convictions must be reported unless the expungement was based upon a showing that the court's earlier conviction was in error.) *(If yes, attach statement.)*
		Have you ever been convicted of a traffic violation arising in connection with a fatal traffic accident, reckless driving or racing on the highway or operating a motor vehicle while under the influence of, or impaired by, alcohol or a controlled substance. *(If yes, attach statement.)*
		Have you ever had a driver's license revoked or suspended for refusing to submit to an alcohol or drug test? *(If yes, attach statement.)*
		Have you ever been given a Coast Guard letter of warning or been assessed a civil penalty for violation of maritime or environmental regulations? *(If yes, attach statement.)*

SECTION VII. CERTIFICATION AND OATH – IMPORTANT – READ BEFORE SIGNING

Whoever, in any manner within the jurisdiction of any department or agency of the U.S. knowingly and willfully falsifies, conceals or covers up by any trick, scheme, or device a material fact, or makes any false, fictitious or fraudulent statements or representations, or makes or uses any false writing or document knowing the same to contain any false, fictitious, or fraudulent statement or entry, shall be fined under this title or imprisoned not more than 5 years, or both (18 USC 1001).

I CERTIFY that the information on this application is true and correct and that I have not submitted an application of any type to the Officer in Charge, Marine Inspection in any port and been rejected or denied within 12 months of this application.	43. SIGNATURE OF APPLICANT

44. DATE	45. SIGNATURE OF VERIFYING OFFICIAL (CG USE ONLY)	46. PORT OF (CG USE ONLY)

OATH FOR LICENSE *(To be completed when original license is received)*

I do solemnly swear or affirm that I am a citizen of the United States and that I will faithfully and honestly, according to my best skill and judgement, and without concealment or reservation, perform all the duties required of me by the laws of the United States. I agree to have a thorough physical examination each year if I act as a pilot under authority of the License being issued.	47. DATE

48. SIGNATURE OF LICENSEE	49. SIGNATURE AND TITLE OF WITNESSING OFFICIAL

OATH FOR MERCHANT MARINER'S DOCUMENT ONLY *(To be administered when original MMD is received)*

I HEREBY SWEAR (or affirm) that I will faithfully and honestly perform all duties required of me by law and carry out the lawful orders of my superior officers on shipboard.	50. DATE

51. SIGNATURE OF MARINER	52. SIGNATURE AND TITLE OF WITNESSING OFFICIAL

SECTION VIII. LICENSE/MMD ISSUED (FOR REC USE ONLY)

LICENSE/ENDORSEMENTS AND DOCUMENTS RATINGS ISSUED

☐ DUPLICATE DISCHARGES ISSUED TO APPLICANT

DATE	SIGNATURE OF ISSUING OFFICIAL	PORT OF

FOR NATIONAL MARITIME CENTER USE ONLY *(DUPLICATE TRANSACTIONS)*

NAME ON RECORD (LAST, FIRST, M)		DUPLICATE NO.	SOCIAL SECURITY NUMBER	DATE NATURALIZED
CITIZENSHIP	DATE OF BIRTH	PLACE OF BIRTH		COLLECT ADDITIONAL FEE OF:

RATINGS/ENDORSEMENTS AUTHORIZED

<table>
<tr><td>DEPARTMENT OF
TRANSPORTATION
U.S.COAST GUARD</td><td>**APPLICATION FOR LICENSE AS OFFICER OPERATOR, OR
STAFF OFFICER AND MERCHANT MARINER'S DOCUMENT**</td></tr>
</table>

SECTION IX. MARINER CONSENTS

NATIONAL DRIVER'S REGISTRY – I authorize the National Driver's Registry (NDR) through a designated State Department of Motor Vehicles, to furnish to the U.S. Coast Guard (USCG) information pertaining to my driving record. This consent constitutes authorization for a single access to the information contained in the NDR to verify information provided in this application. I understand the Coast Guard will make the information received from the NDR available to me for review and written comment prior to taking any action against my license, or U. S. Merchant Mariner's Document. Authority: 46 USC 7101(g) and 46 USC 7302(c).

SIGNATURE OF APPLICANT _____   DATE _____

MARINER'S TRACKING SYSTEM

I consent to voluntary participation in the Mariner's Tracking System to be used by the Maritime Administration (MARAD) in the event of a national emergency or sealift crisis. In such an emergency situation, MARAD would disseminate your contact information to an appropriate maritime employment office to determine your availability for possible employment on a sealift vessel. This is not a reserve program nor does it guarantee call-up for employment. This authorization may be revoked at any time by contacting a U.S. Coast Guard Regional Examination Center.

SIGNATURE OF APPLICANT _____   DATE _____

MERCHANT MARINE PERSONNEL PHYSICAL EXAMINATION REPORT

PRIVACY ACT STATEMENT

As required by 5 USC 552a(e)(3), the following information is provided when supplying personal information to the U. S. Coast Guard.

1. Authority for solicitation of the information: 46 USC 2104(a), 7101(c)–(e), 7306(a)(4), 7313(c)(3), 7317(a), 8703(b), 9102(a)(5).
   (See 46 CFR subparts and paragraphs 10.205(d), 10.207(e), 10.209(d), 12.05–5, 12.20–3)

2. Principal purposes for which the information is used:
   (1) To determine if an applicant is physically capable of performing shipboard duties.
   (2) To ensure that the applicant's physical is conducted by a duly licensed physician/physician's assistant and to verify the information as needed.

3. The routine uses which may be made of this information:
   (1) This form becomes part of the applicant's file as documentary evidence that the regulatory physical requirement has been satisfied and the applicant is physically competent to hold a merchant marine license or document.
   (2) This information becomes part of the total license or document file and is subject to review by federal agency casualty investigators.

4. Disclosure of this information is voluntary, but failure to provide this information will result in nonissuance of a license or merchant mariner's document.

INSTRUCTIONS FOR THE PHYSICIAN

The United States Code requires a physical examination to determine that all holders of Coast Guard issued Licenses and Merchant Mariner's Documents are of sound health with no physical limitations that would hinder or prevent performance of duties. In general, all mariners must be capable of working in cramped spaces on rolling vessels. They must be able to climb steep stairs or vertical ladders. In an emergency such as a vessel fire or flooding, the mariner must be able to fully participate in the firefighting and lifesaving of passengers and crewmembers. In addition, mariners must be physically able to stand an alert, 4 to 6 hour watch. To do this, they must be free from any sudden onset of a medical condition which would affect their watchkeeping abilities.

Detailed guidelines on potentially disqualifying medical conditions may be obtained from any U.S. Coast Guard Regional Examination Center (NVIC 6–89) or by calling Coast Guard Headquarters (G–MVP–2), at 202-267-6828. Examples of impairment that could lead to disqualification include: impaired vision, color vision or hearing; poorly controlled diabetes; multiple or recent myocardial infarctions; psychiatric disorders; and convulsive disorders. In short, any condition that poses an inordinate risk of sudden incapacitation or debilitating complication, and any condition requiring medication that impairs judgement or reaction time are potentially disqualifying and will require a detailed evaluation.

The Coast Guard will use this physical examination to determine the applicant's eligibility to hold a license or document.

1. Name (Last, First, MI)	2. Social Security Number

3. Height	4. Weight (pounds)	5. Eye Color	6. Hair Color	7. Distinguishing Marks

8. Blood Pressure	9. Pulse (resting)
Systolic Diastolic	☐ Regular ☐ Irregular

10a. Vision	10b. Field of Vision
Uncorr. Right 20/ Corr. to 20/ Uncorr. Left 20/ Corr. to 20/	_____ Degrees ☐ Normal ☐ Abnormal

11. Color Vision

☐ Normal   ☐ Abnormal   * Color sense must be tested by one of the following.   * Color sensing lenses are prohibited.

Pseudoisochromatic plates		Eldridge – Green Perception Lantern	SAMCTT – School of Aviation Medicine
Divorine 2nd Edition		Farnsworth Lantern	Titmus Optical Vision Test
AOC Revised Edition		Keystone Orthoscope	Williams Lantern
Ishihara 16–, 24–, 38– Plate Ed		Keystone Telebinocular	

12. Hearing

☐ Normal   ☐ Impaired

An audiometer and speech discrimination tests are only required if the applicant has, or is suspected to have impaired hearing.

Audiometer (Threshold Values)	500 (Hz)	1000 (Hz)	2000 (Hz)	3000 (Hz)	Functional Speech Discrimination Test at 55 db
Right Ear					Left Ear _____ % Right Ear _____ %
Left Ear					**External Auditory Canal**
Right Ear – aided					☐ Normal ☐ Abnormal
Left Ear – aided					

13. Indications of current or past Drug/Alcohol Abuse
☐ Yes   ☐ No   of yes, explain inBlock16.

14. Doctor's assessment – Does the applicant have or has he/she ever suffered from any of the following?   * If yes, explain in Block 16.

Yes	No		Yes	No		Yes	No	
		Deteriorating eye disease			Severe digestive disorder			Periods of unconsciousness
		Severe speech impediment			Chronic renal failure			Sleepwalking
		Diabetes			Communicable disease			Recent or repetitive surgery
		Thyroid disfunction			Asthma or lung disease			Amputations
		Epilepsy, seizures, paralysis			Psychiatric disorder			Impaired range of motion
		Heart or vascular disease			Depression			Impaired balance or coordination
		Heart surgery			Attempted suicide			Other illness or disability
		Blood disorder			Loss of memory			
		High blood pressure			Dizziness or fainting			

15. Medications taken: include dosage, purpose, and side effects.

No prescription medications ☐

16. Comments on findings

No significant medical history ☐

Considering the findings in this examination, and noting the duties to be performed by the applicant aboard a merchant vessel of the United States of America, I consider the applicant

☐ competent   ☐ needs further evaluation   ☐ not competent

Printed/Typed Name of Physician/Physician's Assistant/Nurse Practioner

OFFICE ADDRESS (ZIP CODE)

State License Number

Telephone

Physician/Physician's Assistant/Nurse Practioner Signature   Date

I certify that all information provided by me is complete and true to the best of my knowledge.

Signature of Applicant   Date

Regional Examination Center
U.S. Coast Guard
Marine Safety Office

Date: _____

Applicant's name _____

Applicant's Social Security number: _____

Dear Commanding Officer:

I have reviewed the above named individual's urinalysis lab report in accordance with Department of Transportation procedures at 49 CFR Part 40 and have determined that he/she

_____ is "Drug Free"

_____ is not "Drug Free"

The sample was tested by the following SAMHSA-approved laboratory:

Lab name: _____

Address: _____

_____

Date sample was collected: _____

Examining Physician's Signature: _____

Examining Physician's Name: _____

Examining Physician's License Number: _____

Examining Physician's Address and Phone Number: _____

_____

_____

_____

PLEASE DO NOT SUBMIT LAB REPORTS

DEPARTMENT OF TRANSPORTATION U.S. COAST GUARD CG–865 (Rev. 6-82)	SEA SERVICE FORM (SMALL BOAT EXPERIENCE) *See Privacy Act Statement on Instruction Sheet*	

NAME		SOCIAL SECURITY NO.	FILING DATA *(C.G. USE ONLY)*
(Last)	*(First)*	Middle Init. *(Suffix)*		

VESSEL NAME: _____ OFFICIAL NO. OR STATE REGISTRATION NO. _____ LENGTH OF VESSEL: _____

GROSS TONS: _____ PROPULSION: _____ SERVED AS: _____

VESSEL WAS OERATED BY THE APPLICANT UPON THE WATERS OF: _____

_____ BETWEEN _____ TO _____
(Name body or bodies of water)   *(Geographical Point)*   *(Geographical Point)*

NAME OF OWNER OR OWNERS OF BOAT IF OTHER THAN APPLICANT: _____

WRITE IN THE BLOCK UNDER THE APPROPRIATE MONTH THE NUMBER OF DAYS THAT YOU OPERATED OR SERVED ON THE ABOVE NAMED BOAT.

JANUARY *(Year)*	FEBRUARY *(Year)*	MARCH *(Year)*	APRIL *(Year)*	MAY *(Year)*	JUNE *(Year)*
JULY *(Year)*	AUGUST *(Year)*	SEPTEMBER *(Year)*	OCTOBER *(Year)*	NOVEMBER *(Year)*	DECEMBER *(Year)*

VESSEL NAME: _____ OFFICIAL NO. OR STATE REGISTRATION NO. _____ LENGTH OF VESSEL: _____

GROSS TONS: _____ PROPULSION: _____ SERVED AS: _____

VESSEL WAS OERATED BY THE APPLICANT UPON THE WATERS OF: _____

_____ BETWEEN _____ TO _____
(Name body or bodies of water)   *(Geographical Point)*   *(Geographical Point)*

NAME OF OWNER OR OWNERS OF BOAT IF OTHER THAN APPLICANT:

WRITE IN THE BLOCK UNDER THE APPROPRIATE MONTH THE NUMBER OF DAYS THAT YOU OPERATED OR SERVED ON THE ABOVE NAMED BOAT.

JANUARY *(Year)*	FEBRUARY *(Year)*	MARCH *(Year)*	APRIL *(Year)*	MAY *(Year)*	JUNE *(Year)*
JULY *(Year)*	AUGUST *(Year)*	SEPTEMBER *(Year)*	OCTOBER *(Year)*	NOVEMBER *(Year)*	DECEMBER *(Year)*

VESSEL NAME _____ OFFICIAL NO. OR STATE REGISTRATION NO. _____ LENGTH OF VESSEL: _____

GROSS TONS: _____ PROPULSION _____ SERVED AS: _____

VESSEL WAS OPERATED BY THE APPLICANT UPON THE WATERS OF: _____

_____ BETWEEN _____ TO _____
(Name body or bodies of water)   (Geographical Point)   (Geographical Point)

NAME OF OWNER OR OWNERS OF BOAT IF OTHER THAN APPLICANT: _____

WRITE IN THE BLOCK UNDER THE APPROPRIATE MONTH THE NUMBER OF DAYS THAT YOU OPERATED OR SERVED ON THE ABOVE NAMED BOAT.

JANUARY (Year)	FEBRUARY (Year)	MARCH (Year)	APRIL (Year)	MAY (Year)	JUNE (Year)
JULY (Year)	AUGUST (Year)	SEPTEMBER (Year)	OCTOBER (Year)	NOVEMBER (Year)	DECEMBER (Year)

VESSEL NAME _____ OFFICIAL NO. OR STATE REGISTRATION NO. _____ LENGTH OF VESSEL: _____

GROSS TONS: _____ PROPULSION _____ SERVED AS: _____

VESSEL WAS OPERATED BY THE APPLICANT UPON THE WATERS OF: _____

_____ BETWEEN _____ TO _____
(Name body or bodies of water)   (Geographical Point)   (Geographical Point)

NAME OF OWNER OR OWNERS OF BOAT IF OTHER THAN APPLICANT: _____

WRITE IN THE BLOCK UNDER THE APPROPRIATE MONTH THE NUMBER OF DAYS THAT YOU OPERATED OR SERVED ON THE ABOVE NAMED BOAT.

JANUARY (Year)	FEBRUARY (Year)	MARCH (Year)	APRIL (Year)	MAY (Year)	JUNE (Year)
JULY (Year)	AUGUST (Year)	SEPTEMBER (Year)	OCTOBER (Year)	NOVEMBER (Year)	DECEMBER (Year)

DATE SUBMITTED	SIGNATURE OF APPLICANT	PAGE _____ of _____

Regional Examination Center
U.S. Coast Guard
Marine Safety Office

SUPPLEMENTAL SMALL BOAT EXPERIENCE SHEET

To validate underway time on the Small Vessel SEA SERVICE form (CG–865) aboard a vessel which you do not own, you must submit a letter from the owner using the basic format below. The letter should be submitted on company letterhead stationery whenever possible. The owner may expect licensing evaluators to verify this information by phone or letter. DO NOT ask an owner or captain to stretch the truth for you. Submitting a fraudulent application is a criminal offense, punishable by a $10,000 fine, 5 years in jail, or both. A captain giving a false letter of sea service can lose his license.

USCG Regional Exam Center
Street Address
City, ST ZIP

Dear License Evaluator:

Mr./Ms. _____ worked in the capacity of _____ , aboard the vessel (name) _____ , Official No. _____ , gross tonnage _____ , propelled by _____ , length _____ , from (dates) _____ , to _____ , for a total of _____ underway days of approximately _____ hours each. The vessel operated between the geographical points of _____ and _____ at a distance of _____ miles offshore.

Sincerely,

_____
Owner's Signature

_____
Printed Name

_____

_____
Address

_____
Telephone Number

_____
USCG License Number if applicable

RULES OF THE ROAD

PART A—GENERAL

RULE 1. Application

(a) The International Rules ("Colregs") apply on all oceans and connected navigable waters, except inside the dashed magenta Colregs Demarcation lines shown on charts, where Inland Rules apply.

(b) In spite of (a), special rules may apply to harbors, rivers, and canals.

(c) Vessels fishing in a fleet and warships may use special lights, shapes, and sound signals, as long as they cannot be confused with those in the Rules.

(d) Vessels of unusual construction or use may deviate in the characteristics of light and sound-signalling devices, as long as they comply as closely as possible.

RULE 2. Responsibility

(a) The owner, master, and crew are all charged with obeying the Rules.

(b) Special circumstances allow you to deviate from the Rules, if necessary, to avoid immediate danger.

RULE 3. General Definitions

Vessel: craft which can be used for transportation on the water, including hovercraft and seaplanes.

Power-driven vessel: vessel propelled in whole or in part by machinery.

Sailing vessel: vessel being propelled by sail alone.

Vessel engaged in fishing: vessel fishing with equipment that restricts maneuverability (nets, trawls, etc.). Does not include fishing boats when not fishing, nor angling or trolling recreational boats.

Seaplane: aircraft which can maneuver on water.

Vessel not under command: vessel unable to maneuver due to circumstances such as equipment failure.

Vessel restricted in her ability to maneuver: vessel which, due to her work, can not maneuver easily (*examples*—buoy tending, laying cable, dredging, surveying, diving, transferring materials, launching or recovering aircraft, minesweeping, towing).

Vessel constrained by her draft: vessel which will go aground if it deviates much from its course.

Underway: vessel not anchored, grounded, or otherwise attached to shore. Includes vessel dead in water and not making way.

Length and breadth: length overall (LOA) and beam.

In sight: seen with the eyes.

Restricted visibility: any atmospheric condition which reduces visibility.

PART B—STEERING AND SAILING
Section I—Conduct of Vessels in Any Condition of Visibility

RULE 4. Application

The rules in this section apply generally, regardless of whether the vessels can see each other.

RULE 5. Look-out

Every vessel is required to use all available means, including a proper lookout, at all times to be aware of other vessels and the possibility of collision.

RULE 6. Safe Speed

Vessels are required to limit speed, considering all factors, in order to be able to avoid collision. Factors include visibility, traffic, maneuverability, background lights, wind and sea, currents, navigational hazards, depth, draft, and the limitations of radar.

RULE 7. Risk of Collision

A vessel must use all available means to determine if collision with another boat is possible. Collision is possible if the compass bearing (or relative bearing, if on a steady course) to another vessel remains constant while the distance is decreasing. In case of doubt, assume collision is possible.

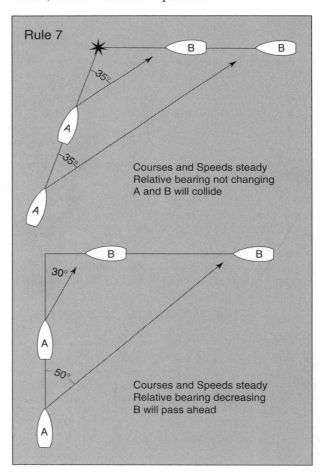

Rule 7

Courses and Speeds steady
Relative bearing not changing
A and B will collide

Courses and Speeds steady
Relative bearing decreasing
B will pass ahead

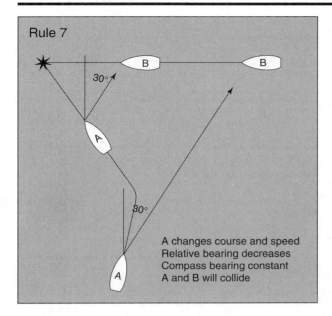

Rule 7

30°

30°

A changes course and speed
Relative bearing decreases
Compass bearing constant
A and B will collide

RULE 8. Action to Avoid Collision

(a) If you must take action to avoid collision, the action must be substantial and early enough to indicate clearly to the other vessel you are taking action.

(b) Changes of course and/or speed should be large enough to be obvious to the other vessel. At night, for example, the change of course should be large enough to show a different sidelight.

(c) Change of course is preferable to change of speed (because it is more obvious), unless it will result in another bad situation.

(d) The action must result in passing at safe distance.

(e) If necessary, a vessel shall (must) slow or stop in order to avoid collision.

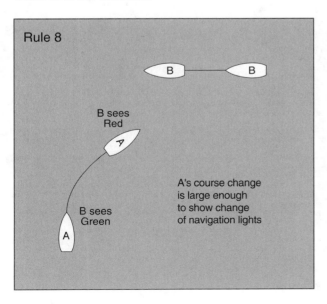

Rule 8

B sees
Red

B sees
Green

A's course change
is large enough
to show change
of navigation lights

RULE 9. Narrow Channels

(a) Stay on the starboard side of a narrow channel.

(b,c) Sailboats, fishing boats, and boats under 20 meters (65 feet) should not impede the progress of vessels confined to the channel.

(d) Do not cross a channel if it will impede the progress of a vessel confined to the channel.

(e) If an overtaken vessel must take action to be safely passed, the vessels must use the signals in Rule 34. The overtaking vessel is also subject to Rule 13.

(f) Vessels approaching a bend obscuring visibility must sound one long (4–6 second) blast. Vessels approaching in opposite direction should respond in like manner.

(g) Do not anchor in a narrow channel.

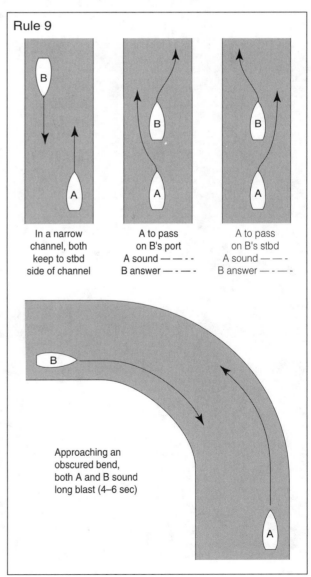

Rule 9

In a narrow channel, both keep to stbd side of channel

A to pass on B's port
A sound — — - -
B answer — - — -

A to pass on B's stbd
A sound — — -
B answer — - — -

Approaching an obscured bend, both A and B sound long blast (4–6 sec)

RULE 10. Traffic Separation Schemes (TSS)

(a) This applies to official Traffic Separation Schemes.

(b)When using a TSS, use the correct lane, keep clear of separation lines and zones, and try to enter and leave at the termination points. If you must enter or exit elsewhere, do so at a small angle.

(c) Try not·to cross a TSS, but if you must, do so at a right angle.

(d) In general, use the TSS, but sailboats and vessels under 20 meters (65 feet) may use the inshore zones.

(e) Other than when entering, leaving, or crossing a TSS, do not cross a separation line or enter a separa-tion zone except to avoid immediate danger or to engage in fishing in the separation zone.

(f) Be especially careful near terminations because vessels will be heading in all directions.

(g) Do not anchor in a TSS or near terminations.

(h) Unless using a TSS, stay as far as possible from it.

(i, j) Sailboats, fishing boats, and all boats under 20 meters (65 feet) should not impede the progress of vessels in traffic lanes.

(k,l) Vessels involved in maintenance of navigation aids and vessels working on underwater cables are exempt from Rule 10.

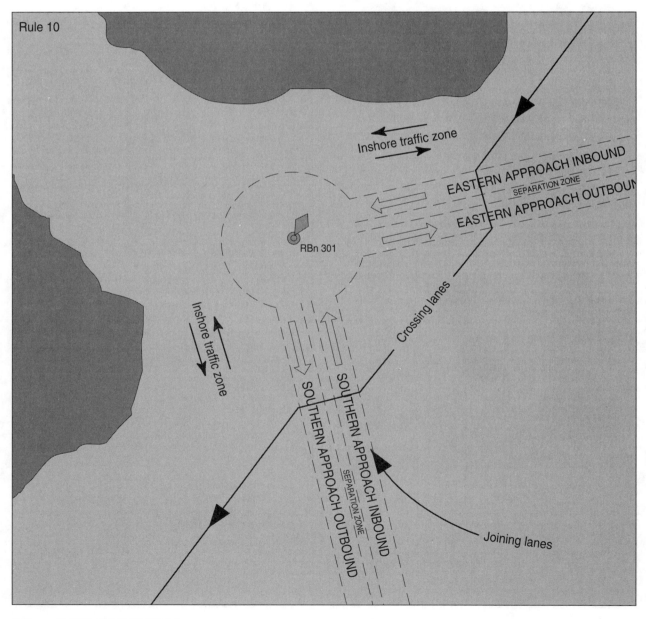

Section II—Conduct of Vessels in Sight

RULE 11. Application
Section II applies to vessels that can see each other.

RULE 12. Sailing Vessels
(1) If two sailboats are on different tacks (any point of sail), the boat on port tack stay clear.

(2) If two sailboats are on the same tack (any point of sail), windward boat stay clear.

(3) If in doubt as to the other boat's tack, keep clear. Windward side is the side opposite that on which the mainsail (or largest fore-and-aft sail) is carried.

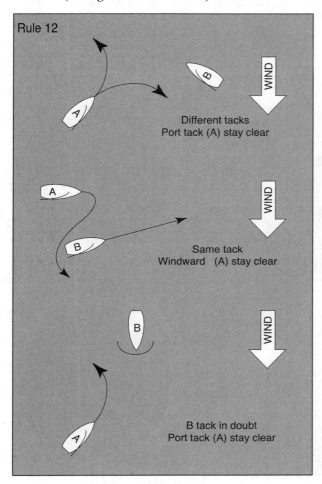

RULE 13. Overtaking
(a) Regardless of any other rule, an overtaking vessel must keep out of the way.

(b) A vessel is overtaking when approaching another vessel from within the arc of its sternlight (more than 22.5 degrees abaft her beam).

(c) If in doubt, assume you are overtaking.

(d) After passing forward of the arc of the sternlight, you are considered overtaking until past and clear.

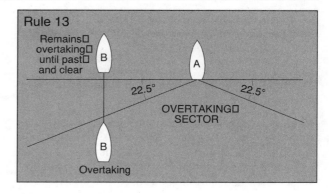

RULE 14. Head-on Situation
Power-driven vessels meeting head-on should both alter course to starboard and pass port-to-port. If there is any doubt as to whether the meeting is head-on or crossing, assume head-on.

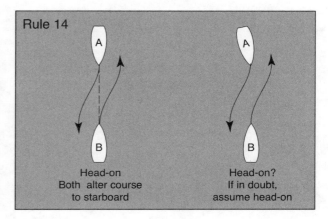

RULE 15. Crossing Situation
When two power-driven vessels cross paths, one on your starboard should stand on, i.e. not change course or speed; one on your port must give way. The give-way vessel should not pass ahead of the stand-on vessel. Remember, the vessel on your starboard sees your green (go) light, while the vessel on your port sees your red (stop) light.

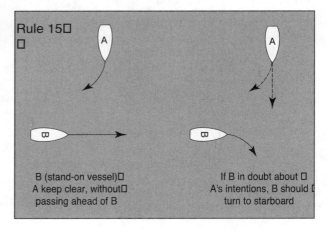

RULE 16. Action by Give-way Vessel

The give-way vessel should make her give-way action early and obvious.

RULE 17. Action by Stand-on Vessel

The stand-on vessel is required to maintain constant course and speed.

If the give-way vessel does not make early and obvious action, then the stand-on vessel *may* take action to avoid collision. If collision is likely in spite of tardy action by the give-way vessel, the stand-on vessel *must* take action, as well.

In taking action, the stand-on vessel must not alter course to port for a give-way vessel on her port. Turn away from the give-way vessel, not into its path.

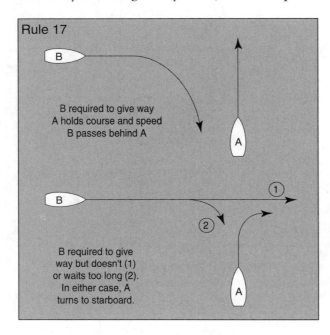

RULE 18. Responsibilities Between Vessels

Rule 18 establishes a "pecking order" between vessel types. Vessels above you have the right-of-way; you have right-of-way over vessels below you. The list:

> Vessel not under command
> Vessel restricted in ability to maneuver
> Vessel constrained by draft
> Vessel engaged in fishing
> Sailing vessel
> Power-driven vessel
> Seaplane

The status a vessel claims is indicated by the lights or shapes she displays. Note that a fishing vessel not displaying either fishing or trawling lights or shapes, a sailing vessel using its engine, and a tug not displaying the lights or shapes for a vessel restricted in ability to maneuver—are all simply power-driven vessels.

Section III—Conduct of Vessels in Restricted Visibility

RULE 19. Conduct of Vessels in Restricted Visibility

Vessels must proceed at safe speed (allowing avoidance upon sighting), determined by conditions.

If you see another vessel only on radar, you must evaluate risk of collision. If risk exists (constant bearing, decreasing range), you must take avoiding action without: 1) altering course to port for vessels forward of your beam (unless overtaking); 2) altering course toward vessels abeam or abaft your beam.

Unless you know there is no risk of collision, when you hear the fog signal of another vessel forward of your beam, you must reduce your speed to bare steerageway or, if necessary, stop.

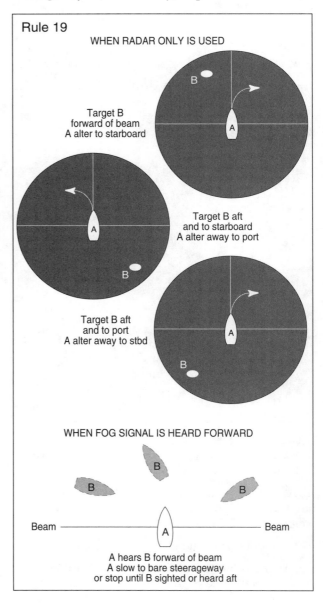

RULE 20. Application

Lights must be displayed at night (sunset to sunrise) and during the day in restricted visibility. Shapes must be displayed from sunrise to sunset, regardless of visibility. Lights that could be confused with the official required lights or impair your lookout are prohibited.

RULE 21. Definitions

Masthead light (also known as *steaming light*): white light on centerline showing forward from 22.5° abaft the beam on either side (225° arc).

Sidelights: green on starboard and red on port, each visible from dead ahead to 22.5° abaft the beam. On vessels less than 20 meters (65 feet), the sidelights may be combined in one unit on the centerline.

Sternlight: white light at the stern showing aft from 22.5° abaft the beam on either side (135° arc).

Towing light: same as a sternlight, except yellow.

All-around light: light of any color that shows 360°.

Flashing light: light flashing 120 per min. minimum.

RULE 22. Visibility of Lights

Type of Light	Vessel Length in meters	Visibility, in miles
Masthead	under 12	2
	12 up to 20	3
	20 up to 50	5
	50 or more	6
Side	under 12	1
	12 up to 50	2
	50 or more	3
Stern, Towing, and All-around	under 50	2
	50 or more	3

RULES 23–31. Lights for Vessel Types

To simplify the presentation of Rules 23 through 31, which describe the required lights for different vessels, we will first group the lights and shapes by activity. By considering what the vessel is doing, we can then specify the lights or shapes she must display.

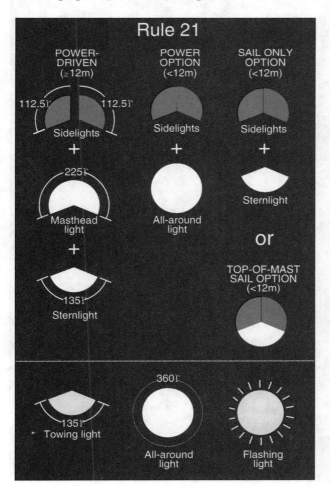

POWER-DRIVEN VESSELS UNDERWAY (Rule 23)

VESSEL	GROUPS	SHAPES	VIEW FROM SIDE	BOW	STERN
Power-driven Vessel ≥50 m (164 ft)	Masthead (2) Side Stern *Substitute All-round for 2nd Masthead + Stern on W. Rivers and Waterways*	None			
Power-driven Vessel <50 m (164 ft)	Masthead Side Stern	None			
Power-driven Vessel <20 m (65 ft)	Masthead Side Stern	None			
Power-driven Vessel <12 m (39.4 ft)	Masthead Side Stern (All-around + Bow option)	None			
Power-driven Vessel <7 m (23 ft)	Masthead Side Stern All-around + Bow option *All-around option (Int'l only)*	None			
Submarine	Masthead (2) Side Stern Flashing Y, 1/sec for 3 sec, followed by 3 sec. off	None			
Hovercraft, non-displacement mode	Masthead (2) Side Stern Flashing Y	None			
Police Customs Lifeboat	Masthead Side Stern Flashing Blue	None			

TOWING & PUSHING (Rule 24)

VESSEL	GROUPS	SHAPES	VIEW FROM SIDE	BOW	STERN
Towing <50 m (Tow ≤ 200 m)	Masthead (2) Side Stern Tow	None			
Towing ≥50m (Tow ≤ 200 m)	Masthead (3) Side Stern Tow				
Towing (Tow > 200 m)	Masthead (3) Side Stern Tow	◆			
Alongside or pushing <50 m	Masthead (2) Side Stern *Subst. 2 Tow for Stern (Inland only)*	None			
Being towed	Side Stern	◆ If tow >200m			
Pushed ahead	Masthead (2) Side Stern Flashing (inland)	None			
Pushed alongside	Masthead (2) Side Stern	None			
Composite <50 m (treat as single power vessel)	Masthead Side Stern	None			
Composite ≥50 m (treat as single power vessel)	Masthead Side Stern	None			
Partly submerged ≤100 m long (<25 m wide) (≥25 m wide)	All-round fore & aft All-round fore & aft +All-round on beam	◆ ◆			
Partly submerged >100 m long (<25 m wide) (≥25 m wide)	All-round fore & aft and every 100 m All-round fore & aft +beam every 100 m	◆ ◆ aft fwd If tow >200 m			

SAILING VESSELS UNDERWAY & VESSELS UNDER OARS (Rule 25)

VESSEL	GROUPS	SHAPES	VIEW FROM SIDE	BOW	STERN
Sailing only (any length)	Side Stern	None			
Sailing only (<20 m option)	Tri-color	None			
Sailing only (any length option)	Side Stern R/G	None			
Motorsailing ≥50 m (164 ft)	Masthead Side Stern	▼			
Motorsailing <50 m (164 ft)	Masthead Side Stern	▼			
Motorsailing <12 m (39.4 ft)	Masthead Side Stern (All-around + Bow option)	None under Inland			
Rowing and sailing <7 m	Side Stern	None			
Rowing and sailing <7 m options/	All-round or show only to prevent collision	None			

FISHING VESSELS (Rule 26)

VESSEL	GROUPS	SHAPES	VIEW FROM SIDE	BOW	STERN
Trawling Underway ≥50 m	Masthead (2) Side Stern G/W				
Trawling Underway <50 m	Side Stern G/W				
Trawling Stopped	G/W				
Other fishing Underway ≥50 m	Masthead Side Stern R/W				
Other fishing Underway <50 m	Side Stern R/W				
Other fishing Stopped	R/W				
Other fishing Gear out >150 m Underway	Side Stern R/W All-round	gear side			
Other fishing Gear out >150 m Stopped	R/W All-round	gear side			

NOT UNDER COMMAND or RESTRICTED IN ABILITY TO MANEUVER (Rule 27)

VESSEL	GROUPS	SHAPES	VIEW FROM SIDE	BOW	STERN
Not Under Command —Making Way	Side Stern R/R				
Not Under Command —Not Making Way	R/R				
Restricted in Ability to Maneuver <50 m —Making Way	Masthead Side Stern R/W/R				
Restricted in Ability to Maneuver ≥50 m —Making Way	Masthead Side Stern R/W/R				
Restricted in Ability to Maneuver —Not Making Way	R/W/R				
Restricted in Ability to Maneuver <50 m —Anchored	R/W/R All-round				
Restricted in Ability to Maneuver ≥50 m —Anchored	R/W/R 2 All-round				
Dredging or Underwater Operations	R/W/R R/R G/G	obstr. side / clear side			
Diving, but unable to display all Underwater Operations lights	R/W/R	Int'l Code Flag "A"			
Mine-clearing ≥50 m Underway	Masthead Side Stern G △				
Mine-clearing <50 m Underway	Masthead Side Stern G △	None			

VESSELS CONSTRAINED BY THEIR DRAFT (Rule 28)

VESSEL	GROUPS	SHAPES	VIEW FROM SIDE	BOW	STERN
Constrained by Draft ≥50 m	Masthead (2) Side Stern R/R/R	cyl.			
Constrained by Draft <50 m	Masthead Side Stern R/R/R	cyl.			

PILOT VESSELS (Rule 29)

VESSEL	GROUPS	SHAPES	VIEW FROM SIDE	BOW	STERN
Pilot on Duty Underway	Masthead Side Stern W/R	Int'l Code Flag "H"			
Pilot on Duty Stopped	W/R	Int'l Code Flag "H"			
Pilot on Duty Anchored	All-round W/R	Int'l Code Flag "H"			

ANCHORED VESSELS & VESSELS AGROUND (Rule 30)

VESSEL	GROUPS	SHAPES	VIEW FROM SIDE	BOW	STERN
Anchored ≥7 m <50 m	All-round (1)	●			
Anchored 50—100 m	All-round (2)	●			
Anchored ≥100 m	All-round (2) All deck lights	●			
Aground <50 m	All-round (1) R/R	● ● ●			
Aground ≥50 m	All-round (2) R/R	● ● ●			

SEAPLANE (Rule 31)

VESSEL	GROUPS	SHAPES	VIEW FROM SIDE	BOW	STERN
Seaplane Underway	Masthead Side Stern	None			

PART D—SOUNDS AND SIGNALS

RULE 32. Definitions

Short blast: 1 second (●)

Long blast: 4–6 seconds (—)

Whistle: any sound device meeting the specifications:

Length	Hertz	Decibels	Range
12≤20 m	280–700 (*250–525*)	120	0.5 nm
20≤75 m	280–700 (*250–525*)	130	1.0 nm

RULE 33. Equipment for Sound Signals

The type of required sound-making apparatus depends on the length of the vessel.

Length	Any Means	Whistle	Bell	Gong
<12 m	✔			
12 to <100 m		✔	✔	
≥100 m		✔	✔	✔

RULE 34. Maneuvering and Warning Signals

Under the International Rules, the signals below announce action to be taken. No delay for agreement is required before action.	*Under the Inland Rules, the signals below announce proposed action. Proposed maneuver should be delayed until the other boat agrees.*
When a maneuver is required in open water and within sight of each other:	*When meeting or crossing within ¹/₂ mile of each other and within sight:*
I am altering course to starboard ●	*I will leave you on my port* ●
I am altering course to port ● ●	*I will leave you on my starboard* ● ●
I am operating astern propulsion ● ● ●	*I am operating astern propulsion* ● ● ●
In sight in a narrow channel or fairway:	*In sight in a narrow channel or fairway:*
I intend to overtake on your starboard — — ●	*I intend to overtake on your starboard* ●
I intend to overtake on your port — — ● ●	*I intend to overtake on your port* ● ●
I agree to be overtaken — ● — ●	*I agree to be overtaken — answer* ● or ● ●
I don't understand your intentions ● ● ● ● ●	*I don't understand your intentions* ● ● ● ● ●
Approaching a bend in a channel —	*Approaching a bend in a channel* —
	Leaving berth or dock —

RULE 35. Sound Signals in Restricted Visibility

Power making way	— @ 2 min.	Being towed, if manned	— ● ● ● @ 2 min.
Power stopped	— — @ 2 min.	At anchor <100 m	rapid 5-sec. bell @ 1 min.
Not under command	— ● ● @ 2 min.	≥100 m	5 sec. fore, then 5 sec. aft
Restricted	— ● ● @ 2 min.	added option	● — ●
Constrained by draft	— ● ● @ 2 min.	Aground	3 distinct claps of bell
Sailing	— ● ● @ 2 min.		+ rapid 5-sec. bell
Fishing	— ● ● @ 2 min.		+ 3 claps, all @ 1 min.
Towing or pushing	— ● ● @ 2 min.	Vessel <12 m option	any sound @ 2 min.
Fishing, at anchor	— ● ● @ 2 min.	Pilot vessel	added option ● ● ● ●
Restricted, at anchor	— ● ● @ 2 min.		

@ means that the signal must be sounded at an interval less than or equal to the value indicated.

RULE 36. Signals to Attract Attention

In attracting the attention of another vessel, you may use any light or sound signal that cannot be mistaken for any of the signals given in the Rules. The only exception is a prohibition of high intensity flashing or revolving lights—such as strobes—in the International Rules.

RULE 37. Distress Signals

Vessels in distress and requiring assistance shall use one or more of the distress signals listed in Annex IV of the Rules (see below). The only exception is permission to use strobes in Inland waters.

ANNEX IV. Distress Signals

- A gun fired once per minute

- Continuous sounding of fog horn

- Red star rockets or shells

- Morse Code SOS (● ● ● ▬ ▬ ▬ ● ● ●) by radio, light, sound, or any other method

- Spoken word "Mayday" on radio

- International Flags "N" + "C"

- Square flag and a ball

- Flames on deck, such as burning oil in a barrel

- Rocket parachute flare

- Red hand flare

- Orange colored smoke

- Slow, repeated raising and lowering of arms at sides

- Radiotelegraph alarm signal

- Radiotelephone alarm signal

- EPIRB

- Dye marker

- Orange canvas with black square and circle

- *High intensity flashing white light (strobe), at 50-70/minute*

INLAND—ONLY QUESTIONS

00001. You are navigating in a narrow channel and must remain in the channel for safe operation. Another vessel is crossing the channel ahead of you from your starboard and you doubt whether your vessel will pass safely. Which statement is true?

A. You must stop your vessel, since the other vessel has the right of way.
B. You must sound 1 short blast of the whistle, and turn to starboard.
C. You must sound the danger signal.
D. You must stop your engines, and the sounding of the danger signal is optional.

00002. What is the required whistle signal for a power-driven vessel leaving a dock or berth?

A. 1 short blast
B. 1 prolonged blast
C. 2 short blasts
D. 1 long blast

00003. In a narrow channel, you are underway on vessel "A" and desire to overtake vessel "B". After you sound 2 short blasts on your whistle, vessel "B" sounds 5 short rapid blasts on the whistle. You should:

A. pass with caution on the port side of vessel "B"
B. hold your relative position, and then sound another signal after the situation has stabilized
C. answer the 5 short blast signal then stop your vessel until the other vessel initiates a signal
D. slow or stop and expect radical maneuvers from "B"

00004. A vessel is proceeding downstream in a narrow channel on the Western Rivers when another vessel is sighted moving upstream. Which vessel has the right of way?

A. The vessel moving upstream against the current.
B. The vessel moving downstream with a following current.
C. The vessel located more towards the channel centerline.
D. The vessel sounding the first whistle signal.

00005. You are overtaking a vessel in a narrow channel and wish to leave her on your starboard side. You may:

A. attempt to contact her on the radiotelephone to arrange for the passage
B. proceed to overtake her without sounding whistle signals
C. sound 5 short blasts
D. any of the above

00006. A vessel displaying a flashing blue light is:

A. transferring dangerous cargo
B. a law enforcement vessel
C. a work boat
D. engaged in a race

00007. When power-driven vessels are crossing, a signal of 1 short blast by either vessel means:

A. "I intend to leave you on my port side"
B. "I intend to hold course and speed"
C. "I intend to change course to starboard"
D. "I request a departure from the Rules"

00008. If you were coming up on another vessel from dead astern and desired to overtake on the other vessel's starboard side, what whistle signal would you sound?

A. 1 short blast
B. 1 prolonged blast
C. 2 short blasts
D. 2 prolonged blasts

00009. Which statement is true concerning narrow channels?

A. You should keep to that side of the channel which is on your port side.
B. You should avoid anchoring in a narrow channel.
C. A vessel having a following current will propose the manner of passage in any case where 2 vessels are meeting.
D. all of the above

00010. Which term is NOT defined in the Inland Navigation Rules?

A. seaplane
B. restricted visibility
C. underway
D. vessel constrained by her draft

00011. When you are overtaking another vessel and desire to pass on her left or port hand side, you should sound:

A. 1 short blast
B. 1 long blast
C. 2 short blasts
D. 2 prolonged blasts

00012. Your vessel is meeting another vessel head to head. To comply with the steering and sailing rules, you should:

A. sound the danger signal
B. sound 1 prolonged and 2 short blasts
C. exchange 2 short blasts
D. exchange 1 short blast

00013. Yellow lights are NOT used to identify:

A. U.S. submarines
B. vessels towing by pushing ahead
C. law enforcement vessels
D. dredge pipelines on trestles

00014. You have made your vessel up to a tow and are moving from a pier out into the main channel. Your engines are turning ahead. What whistle signal should you sound?

A. 1 prolonged and 2 short blasts
B. 3 long blasts
C. 1 prolonged blast
D. 5 or more short rapid blasts

00015. Under the Inland Navigational Rules, what is the meaning of the 2 short blast signal used when meeting another vessel?

A. "I am turning to starboard."
B. "I am turning to port."
C. "I intend to leave you on my starboard side."
D. "I intend to leave you on my port side."

00016. For the purpose of the Inland Rules, the term "Inland Waters" includes:

A. the Western Rivers
B. the Great Lakes on the United States side of the International Boundary
C. harbors and rivers shoreward of the COL-REGS demarcation lines
D. all of the above

00017. A vessel crossing a river on the Western Rivers has the right of way over:

A. vessels ascending the river
B. vessels descending the river
C. all vessels ascending and descending the river
D. none of the above

00018. What lights are required for a barge, not part of a composite unit, being pushed ahead?

A. sidelights and a stern light
B. sidelights, a special flashing light, and a stern light
C. sidelights and a special flashing light
D. sidelights, a towing light, and a stern light

00019. A power-driven vessel operating in a narrow channel with a following current on the Great Lakes or Western Rivers is meeting an upbound vessel. Which statement is true?

A. The downbound vessel has the right-of-way.
B. The downbound vessel must initiate the required maneuvering signals.

C. The downbound vessel must propose the manner and place of passage.
D. all of the above

00020. Your vessel is proceeding down a channel, and can safely navigate only within the channel. Another vessel is crossing your bow from port to starboard, and you are in doubt as to her intentions. Which statement is true?

A. The sounding of the danger signal is optional.
B. The sounding of the danger signal is mandatory.
C. You should sound 2 short blasts.
D. You should sound 1 prolonged and 2 short blasts.

00021. The stand-on vessel in a crossing situation sounds 1 short blast of the whistle. This means that the vessel:

A. intends to hold course and speed
B. is changing course to starboard
C. is changing course to port
D. intends to leave the other on her port side

00022. You are crossing the course of another vessel which is to your starboard. You have reached an agreement by radiotelephone to pass astern of the other vessel. You must:

A. sound 1 short blast
B. sound 2 short blasts
C. change course to starboard
D. none of the above

00023. Passing signals shall be sounded on inland waters by:

A. all vessels upon sighting another vessel rounding a bend in the channel
B. towing vessels when meeting another towing vessel on a clear day
C. power-driven vessels when crossing less than half a mile ahead of another power-driven vessel
D. all of the above

00024. You are proceeding up a channel in Chesapeake Bay and are meeting an outbound vessel. Responsibilities include:

A. keeping to that side of the channel which is on your vessel's port side
B. stopping your vessel and letting the outbound vessel initiate the signals for meeting and passing
C. appropriately answering any whistle signals given by the other vessel
D. giving the outbound vessel the right of way

00025. When overtaking another power-driven vessel in a narrow channel, a vessel desiring to overtake on the other vessel's starboard side would sound a whistle signal of:

A. 1 short blast
B. 2 short blasts
C. 2 prolonged blasts followed by 1 short blast
D. 2 prolonged blasts followed by 2 short blasts

00026. A law enforcement boat may display a:

A. blue flag
B. flashing blue light
C. flashing red light
D. flashing amber light

00027. Your vessel is meeting another vessel head to head. To comply with the steering and sailing rules you should exchange:

A. 1 short blast, alter course to the left and pass starboard to starboard
B. 1 short blast, alter course to the right and pass port to port
C. 2 short blasts, alter course to the left and pass starboard to starboard
D. 2 short blasts, alter course to the right and pass port to port

00028. A vessel overtaking another in a narrow channel, and wishing to pass on the other vessel's port side, would sound a whistle signal of:

A. 1 short blast
B. 2 short blasts
C. 2 prolonged blasts followed by 1 short blast
D. 2 prolonged blasts followed by 2 short blasts

00029. A fleet of moored barges extends into a navigable channel. What is the color of the lights on the barges?

A. red
B. amber
C. white
D. none of the above

00030. What signal must a power-driven vessel give, in addition to 1 prolonged blast, when backing out of a berth with another vessel in sight?

A. 2 short blasts
B. 1 blast
C. 3 short blasts
D. 4 blasts

00031. At night, a light signal consisting of 2 flashes by a vessel indicates:

A. an intention to communicate over radiotelephone
B. that the vessel is in distress
C. an intention to leave another vessel to port
D. an intention to leave another vessel to stbd

00032. You are overtaking a vessel in a narrow channel and wish to leave her on your starboard side. You may:

A. proceed to overtake her without sounding whistle signals
B. attempt to contact her on the radiotelephone to arrange for the passage
C. sound 4 short blasts
D. any of the above

00033. For the purpose of the Inland Rules, the term "inland waters" includes:

A. the Great Lakes on the United States side of the International boundary
B. the water surrounding any islands of the United States
C. the coastline of the United States, out to 1 mile offshore
D. any lakes within state boundaries

00034. A barge more than 50 meters long is required to show how many white anchor lights when anchored in a Secretary of Transportation approved "special anchorage area"?

A. 2
B. 1
C. 3
D. 4

00035. You are on vessel "B" and vessel "A" desires to overtake you on the starboard side as shown in DIAGRAM 9. After the vessels have exchanged 1 blast signals, you should:

A. alter course to the left
B. slow your vessel until vessel "A" has passed
C. hold course and speed
D. alter course to the left or right to give vessel "A" more sea room

00036. Which of the following is not contained in the Inland Navigational Rules?

A. an inconspicuous, partly submerged vessel
B. a seaplane
C. an air-cushion vessel
D. a vessel constrained by her draft

00037. You are operating a vessel through a narrow channel and your vessel must stay within the channel to be navigated safely. Another vessel is crossing your course from starboard to port, and you are in doubt as to her intentions. You:

A. may sound the danger signal
B. must sound the danger signal
C. should sound 1 short blast to show that you are holding course and speed
D. are required to back down

00038. Your vessel is meeting another vessel head to head. To comply with the rules, you should exchange:

A. 1 short blast, alter course to the left and pass starboard to starboard
B. 2 short blasts, alter course to the left and pass starboard to starboard
C. 1 short blast, alter course to the right and pass port to port
D. 2 short blasts, alter course to the right and pass port to port

00039. Which of the following is used to indicate the presence of a partly submerged object being towed?

A. a diamond shape on the towed object
B. an all-round light at each end of the towed object
C. a searchlight from the towing vessel in the direction of the tow
D. all of the above

00040. What type of light is required on a vessel to signal passing intentions?

A. an all-round white light only
B. an all-round yellow light only
C. an all-round white or yellow light
D. any colored light is acceptable

00041. 2 vessels in a crossing situation have reached agreement by radiotelephone as to the intentions of the other. In this situation, whistle signals are:

A. required
B. not required, but may be sounded
C. required if crossing within half a mile
D. required when crossing within 1 mile

00042. You are underway in a narrow channel, and you are being overtaken by a vessel astern. After the overtaking vessel sounds the proper signal indicating his intention to pass your vessel on your starboard side, you signal your agreement by sounding:

A. 1 short blast
B. 2 prolonged blasts
C. 2 prolonged followed by 2 short blasts
D. 1 prolonged, 1 short, 1 prolonged and 1 short blast in that order

00043. You are meeting another vessel and sound a 1 short blast passing signal. The

other vessel answers with 2 blasts. What should be your action?

A. pass on the other vessel's starboard side.
B. sound the danger signal.
C. pass astern of the other vessel.
D. hold your course and speed.

00044. What lights are required for a barge being pushed ahead, not being part of a composite unit?

A. sidelights and a stern light
B. sidelights and a special flashing light
C. sidelights, a towing light, and a stern light
D. sidelights, a special flashing light, and stern light

00045. When overtaking another power-driven vessel in a narrow channel, a vessel desiring to overtake on the other vessel's port side, would sound a whistle signal of:

A. 1 short blast
B. 2 short blasts
C. 2 prolonged blasts followed by 1 short blast
D. 2 prolonged blasts followed by 2 short blasts

00046. At night, a barge moored in a slip used primarily for mooring purposes shall:

A. not be required to be lighted
B. show a white light at each corner
C. show a red light at the bow and stern
D. show a flashing yellow light at each corner

00047. A flashing blue light is used to identify:

A. law enforcement vessels
B. U.S. submarines
C. air-cushion vessels in the nondisplacement mode
D. dredge pipelines on trestles

00048. Which statement is true concerning the fog signal of a vessel 15 meters in length anchored in a "special anchorage area" approved by the Secretary of Transportation?

A. The vessel is not required to sound a fog signal.
B. The vessel shall ring a bell for 5 seconds every minute.
C. The vessel shall sound 1 blast of the foghorn every 2 minutes.
D. The vessel shall sound 3 blasts on the whistle every 2 minutes.

00049. A power-driven vessel, when leaving a dock or berth, is required to sound:

A. 4 short blasts
B. 1 long blast

C. 1 prolonged blast
D. No signal is required.

00050. Vessels "A" and "B" are meeting on a river as shown in DIAGRAM 29, and will pass about 1/4 mile apart. Which statement is true?

A. Both vessels should continue on course and pass without sounding any whistle signals.
B. The vessels should exchange 2 blast whistle signals and pass port to port.
C. The vessels should exchange 2 blast whistle signals and pass starboard to starboard.
D. The vessels should pass port to port and must sound whistle signals only if either vessel changes course.

00051. Which is true of a downbound power-driven vessel, when meeting an upbound vessel on the Western Rivers?

A. She has the right of way.
B. She shall propose the manner of passage.
C. She shall propose the place of passage.
D. all of the above

00052. Whistle signals shall be exchanged by vessels in sight of one another when:

A. they are passing within half a mile of each other.
B. passing agreements have been made by radio.
C. course changes are necessary to pass.
D. doubt exists as to which side the vessels will pass on.

00053. You are on vessel "A" and vessel "B" desires to overtake you on the starboard side as shown in DIAGRAM 38. After the vessels have exchanged 1 blast signals you should:

A. alter course to the left
B. slow your vessel until vessel "B" has passed
C. hold course and speed
D. alter course to the left or right to give vessel "B" more sea room

00054. A barge more than 50 meters long is required to show how many white anchor lights when anchored in a Secretary of Transportation approved "special anchorage area"?

A. 1
B. 2
C. 3
D. 4

00055. The lights illustrated in DIAGRAM 75 are those of a:

A. pipeline
B. vessel towing by pushing ahead

C. vessel being towed astern
D. vessel underway and dredging

00056. You are navigating in a narrow channel and must remain in the channel for safe operation. Another vessel is crossing the channel ahead of you from your starboard and you are doubtful as to the intention of the crossing vessel. You must:

A. stop your vessel, since the other vessel has the right of way
B. sound 1 short blast of the whistle, and turn to starboard
C. sound the danger signal
D. stop your engines, and the sounding of the danger signal is optional

00057. While underway during the day you sight a small motorboat showing a flashing blue light. The blue light indicates a:

A. law enforcement boat
B. boat involved in a race
C. workboat
D. rescue boat

00058. While underway, you sight the lights illustrated in DIAGRAM 81, with the yellow lights flashing. You should:

A. wait until the vessel ahead crosses your bow
B. stop until the red lights turn green
C. proceed leaving all the lights on your starboard side
D. pass between the 2 sets of vertical red lights

00059. When power-driven vessels are in a crossing situation, 1 short blast by either vessel would mean:

A. "I intend to leave you on my port side"
B. "I intend to hold course and speed"
C. "I intend to change course to starboard"
D. "I request a departure from the rules"

00060. 2 vessels are meeting on a clear day and will pass less than half a mile apart. In this situation whistle signals:

A. must be exchanged
B. may be exchanged
C. must be exchanged if passing agreements have not been made by radio
D. must be exchanged only if course changes are necessary by either vessel

00061. You are overtaking another vessel in a narrow channel. You wish to overtake her on her starboard side. You should sound a whistle signal of:

A. 1 short blast
B. 2 prolonged blasts followed by 1 short blast
C. 1 prolonged and 1 short blast
D. at least 5 short blasts

00062. Which is true of a downbound vessel, when meeting an upbound vessel on the Western Rivers?

A. She has the right of way only if she is a power-driven vessel.
B. She has the right of way only if she has a tow.
C. She does not have the right of way, since the other vessel is not crossing the river.
D. She must wait for a whistle signal from the upbound vessel.

00063. A vessel of less than 20 meters at anchor at night in a "special anchorage area designated by the secretary":

A. must show 1 white light
B. need not show any lights
C. must show 2 white lights
D. must show a light only on the approach of another vessel

00064. At night, what lights are required on barges moored in group formation at a bank of a river?

A. a white light placed at the corners farthest from the bank on each of the upstream and downstream ends of the group.
B. a white light placed at the corners farthest from the bank of each barge in the group.
C. a flashing yellow light placed at each of the upstream and downstream ends of the group.
D. 2 red lights in a vertical line placed at the corners farthest from the bank on each of the upstream and downstream ends of the group.

00065. A vessel intends to overtake another vessel on the overtaken vessel's port side. What whistle signal should be sounded in order to state this intention?

A. 1 short blast
B. 2 short blasts
C. 2 prolonged and 1 short blast
D. 2 prolonged and 2 short blasts

00066. A towing vessel pushing ahead on the Western Rivers above the Huey P. Long bridge must show:

A. sidelights only
B. sidelights and towing lights
C. sidelights, towing lights, and 2 masthead lights
D. sidelights, towing lights, and 3 masthead lights

00067. A power-driven vessel, when leaving a dock or berth, is required to sound:

A. 2 short blasts
B. 1 long blast
C. 1 prolonged blast
D. the danger signal

00068. Which is a characteristic of a "special flashing light"?

A. It must be yellow in color.
B. It must be placed as far forward as possible.
C. It must not show through an arc of more than 225°.
D. all of the above

00069. For the purpose of the Inland Navigation Rules, the term "Inland Waters" includes:

A. the Western Rivers, extending to the COLREGS demarcation line
B. harbors and rivers to the outermost aids to navigation
C. waters along the coast of the United States to a distance of 2 miles offshore
D. none of the above

00070. Vessels "A" and "B" are meeting in a narrow channel as shown in DIAGRAM 29. Which of the following is true concerning whistle signals between vessels?

A. Both vessels should sound 2 short blasts.
B. Both vessels should sound 1 short blast.
C. Vessel "A" should sound 1 short blast and vessel "B" should sound 2 short blasts.
D. Neither vessel should sound any signal as no course change is necessary.

00071. Which is true of a downbound power-driven vessel, when meeting an upbound vessel on the Western Rivers?

A. She has the right of way.
B. She shall propose the manner of passage.
C. She shall initiate maneuvering signals.
D. all of the above

00072. You are approaching a vessel showing the lights shown in DIAGRAM 75. This is a(n):

A. meeting situation
B. crossing situation
C. overtaking situation
D. special circumstance situation

00073. You are overtaking a vessel in a narrow channel and wish to leave her on your starboard side. You may:

A. sound 1 short blast
B. sound 4 short blasts
C. overtake without sounding whistle signals
D. attempt to contact her on the radiotelephone to arrange for the passage

00074. Which term is NOT used in the Inland Navigational Rules?

A. a vessel engaged in mineclearing operations
B. a vessel constrained by her draft
C. a vessel towing
D. a vessel engaged in fishing

00075. You are on vessel "A", and vessel "B" desires to overtake you on the starboard side as shown in DIAGRAM 31. After the vessels have exchanged 1 blast signals, you should:

A. alter course to the left
B. slow your vessel until vessel "B" has passed
C. hold course and speed
D. alter course to the left to give vessel "B" more sea room

00076. A special flashing light is used on a vessel:

A. being pushed ahead
B. towed alongside
C. towed astern
D. any of the above

00077. Vessels "A" and "B" are meeting on a river as shown in DIAGRAM 41, and will pass about 1/4 mile apart. What action should the vessels take?

A. Both vessels should continue on course and pass without sounding any whistle signals.
B. The vessels should exchange 2 blast whistle signals and pass starboard to starboard.
C. The vessels should exchange 1 blast whistle signals and pass starboard to starboard.
D. The vessels should pass starboard to starboard and must sound whistle signals only if either vessel changes course.

00078. Under the Inland Navigational Rules, what is the meaning of a 1 short blast signal used in a meeting situation with another vessel?

A. "I am turning to starboard."
B. "I am turning to port."
C. "I intend to leave you on my starboard side."
D. "I intend to leave you on my port side."

00079. On the Western Rivers, a vessel crossing a river must:

A. only keep out of the way of a power-driven vessel descending the river
B. keep out of the way of any vessel descending the river

C. keep out of the way of a power-driven vessel ascending or descending the river
D. keep out of the way of any vessel ascending or descending the river

00080. While underway at night, you see 2 yellow lights displayed in a vertical line. This should indicate to you a(n):

A. opening in a pipeline
B. vessel broken down
C. vessel towing by pushing ahead
D. vessel fishing

00081. When 2 vessels are meeting on a narrow inland waterway, specified by the secretary, which vessel shall sound the first passing signal?

A. the vessel going upstream
B. the vessel coming downstream
C. the vessel that is towing
D. either vessel

00082. A vessel leaving a dock or berth must sound a prolonged blast of the whistle only if:

A. other vessels can be seen approaching
B. she is a power-driven vessel
C. visibility is restricted
D. her engines are going astern

00083. If your tug is pushing a barge ahead at night, what light(s) should show aft on your vessel?

A. a white stern light
B. 2 red lights
C. 2 towing lights
D. 3 white lights

00084. You are in charge of a power-driven vessel crossing a river on the Western Rivers. You must keep out of the way of a:

A. sail vessel descending the river
B. power-driven vessel ascending the river
C. vessel restricted in its ability to maneuver crossing the river
D. any of the above

00085. A vessel crossing a river on the Great Lakes or Western Rivers, must keep out of the way of a power-driven vessel:

A. descending the river with a tow
B. ascending the river with a tow
C. ascending the river without a tow
D. all of the above

00086. What is the whistle signal used to indicate a power-driven vessel leaving a dock?

A. 1 short blast
B. 3 short blasts
C. 1 prolonged blast
D. 3 prolonged blasts

00087. Which statement is true concerning the light used for maneuvering signals?

A. It must be synchronized with the whistle.
B. It may be white or yellow.
C. It must be an all-round light.
D. all of the above

00088. 2 power-driven vessels are meeting in the situation shown in DIAGRAM 37. 1 short blast by vessel "A" means:

A. "I am altering my course to starboard."
B. "I intend to leave you on my port side."
C. "My intention is to hold course and speed."
D. "I intend to pass on your starboard side."

00089. You are operating a vessel through a narrow channel and your vessel must stay within the channel to be navigated safely. Another vessel is crossing your course from starboard to port, and you are in doubt as to her intentions. You:

A. may sound the danger signal
B. must sound the danger signal
C. should sound 1 short blast to indicate that you are holding course and speed
D. are required to back down

00090. 2 vessels are in a starboard to starboard passing situation and will pass well clear approximately 1/4 mile apart. Which action should each vessel take?

A. Blow a 1 blast whistle signal and turn to starboard.
B. Maintain course and sound no signal.
C. Blow a 2 blast whistle and maintain course.
D. Blow a 3 blast whistle signal and turn to port.

00091. Which statement is true concerning the Inland Navigation Rules?

A. They require compliance with VTS Regulations.
B. They define moderate speed.
C. They require communication by radiotelephone to reach a passing agreement.
D. all of the above

00092. A power-driven vessel pushing ahead or towing alongside on the Mississippi River, below the Huey P. Long Bridge, shall carry:

A. 2 masthead lights, sidelights and stern light
B. 2 masthead lights, sidelights and 2 towing lights

C. sidelights and 2 towing lights
D. 1 masthead light, sidelights and stern light

00093. While underway in a harbor you hear a vessel sound a prolonged blast. This signal indicates that this vessel:

A. desires to overtake your vessel
B. is at anchor
C. is backing her engines
D. is moving from a dock

00094. You are overtaking another vessel and sound a whistle signal indicating that you intend to pass the vessel along its starboard side. If the other vessel answers your signal with 5 short and rapid blasts, you should:

A. not overtake the other vessel until both vessels exchange the same passing signal
B. not overtake the other vessel until she sounds another 5 short and rapid blast signal
C. pass the other vessel along her starboard side
D. sound 5 short and rapid blasts and pass along her starboard side

00095. You are meeting another vessel in inland waters, and she sounds 1 short blast on the whistle. This means that she:

A. is changing course to starboard
B. is changing course to port
C. intends to leave you on her port side
D. desires to depart from the Rules

00096. You are approaching a sharp bend in a river. You have sounded a prolonged blast and it has been answered by a vessel on the other side of the bend. In this situation, which statement is true?

A. Both vessels must exchange passing signals when they sight each other.
B. No further whistle signals are necessary.
C. The vessel down river must stop her engines and navigate with caution.
D. Both vessels must immediately sound passing signals whether or not they are in sight of one another.

00097. Which statement is true concerning a passing agreement made by radiotelephone?

A. Such an agreement is prohibited by the Rules.
B. A vessel which has made such an agreement must also sound whistle signals.
C. Whistle signals must still be exchanged when passing within half a mile of each other.
D. If agreement is reached by radiotelephone, whistle signals are optional.

00098. You are onboard the stand-on vessel in a crossing situation. Upon sounding a 1 blast whistle signal the give-way vessel answers with a 2 blast whistle signal. You should then sound the danger signal and:

A. maintain course and speed as you are the stand-on vessel
B. come around sharply to port
C. stop and back your vessel if necessary until signals are agreed on
D. maneuver around the stern of other vessel

00099. A power-driven vessel when pushing ahead or towing alongside on the Western Rivers shall carry:

A. 2 masthead lights, sidelights, and stern light
B. 2 masthead lights, sidelights, and 2 towing lights
C. sidelights and 2 towing lights
D. 1 masthead light, sidelights, and stern light

00100. Law enforcement vessels are permitted to show:

A. 2 red lights in a vertical line
B. a flashing yellow light
C. a green light at the masthead
D. a flashing blue light

00101. You are overtaking another vessel in a narrow channel. The other vessel will have to move to allow you to pass. You wish to overtake the other vessel on her starboard side. Your first whistle signal should be:

A. 1 short blast
B. 2 short blasts
C. 2 prolonged blasts followed by 1 short blast
D. 2 prolonged blasts followed by 2 short blasts

00102. Which statement is true concerning the Inland Navigational Rules?

A. The Rules require vessels to comply with VTS (vessel traffic service) regulations.
B. The Rules use the term "safe speed".
C. The Rules provide for action to be taken by a stand-on vessel in a crossing situation prior to being in extremis.
D. all of the above

00103. Which of the following light displays would mark the opening in a pipeline where vessels could pass through?

A. 3 red lights in a vertical line on each side of the opening
B. 2 red lights in a vertical line on each side of the opening
C. 3 white lights in a vertical line on each side of the opening

D. 2 white lights in a vertical line on each side of the opening

00104. What light(s) shall be shown at night on a moored barge which reduces the navigable width of any channel to less than 80 meters?

A. a white light placed on the 2 corners farthest from the bank
B. 2 yellow lights in a vertical line at the stern
C. a red light placed on all 4 corners
D. a red light placed on the 2 corners farthest from the bank

00105. You are overtaking another vessel in a narrow channel. The other vessel will have to move to allow you to pass. You wish to overtake the other vessel and leave her on your starboard side. Your first whistle signal should be:

A. 1 short blast
B. 2 short blasts
C. 2 prolonged blasts followed by 1 short blast
D. 2 prolonged blasts followed by 2 short blasts

00106. You are overtaking another vessel and sound a whistle signal indicating that you intend to pass the vessel along its starboard side. If the other vessel answers your signal with 5 short and rapid blasts, you should:

A. pass the other vessel along her starboard side
B. sound 5 short and rapid blasts and pass along her starboard side
C. not overtake the other vessel until both vessels exchange the same passing signal
D. not overtake the other vessel until she sounds another 5 short and rapid blast signal

00107. A vessel intends to overtake another vessel on the overtaken vessel's port side. What whistle signal should be sounded in order to state this intention?

A. 1 prolonged and 1 short blast
B. 1 short blast
C. 2 prolonged and 2 short blasts
D. 2 short blasts

00108. You are overtaking another vessel in a narrow channel. The other vessel will have to move to allow you to pass. You wish to overtake the other vessel and leave her on your starboard side. Your first whistle signal should be:

A. 2 prolonged blasts followed by 1 short blast
B. 2 prolonged blasts followed by 2 short blasts
C. 1 short blast
D. 2 short blasts

00109. You are underway on vessel "A" and desire to overtake vessel "B" as shown in DIA-

GRAM 17. After you sound 2 short blasts on your whistle, vessel "B" sounds 5 short rapid blasts on the whistle. You should:

A. alter course to starboard and pass on the starboard side of "B"
B. keep sounding passing signals until the same signal is received from vessel "B"
C. answer the 5 short blast signal then pass on the port side
D. pass with caution on the port side of vessel "B"

00110. Which statement is true concerning the fog signal of a vessel 25 meters in length anchored in a "special anchorage area" approved by the Secretary of Transportation?

A. The vessel is not required to sound a fog signal.
B. The vessel shall ring a bell for 5 seconds every minute.
C. The vessel shall sound 1 blast of the foghorn every 2 minutes.
D. The vessel shall sound 3 blasts on the whistle every 2 minutes.

00111. Which of the following light displays would mark the opening in a pipeline where vessels could pass through?

A. 2 red lights in a vertical line on each side of the opening.
B. 3 red lights in a vertical line on each side of the opening.
C. 2 yellow lights in a vertical line on each side of the opening.
D. 3 white lights in a vertical line on each side of the opening.

00112. While underway, you sight the lights illustrated in DIAGRAM 81 with the yellow lights flashing. You should:

A. wait until the vessel ahead crosses your bow
B. stop until the red lights turn green
C. pass between the 2 sets of vertical red lights
D. proceed, leaving all the lights on your starboard side

00113. At night a barge moored in a slip used primarily for mooring purposes shall:

A. show a flashing yellow light at each corner
B. show a white light at each corner
C. show a red light at the bow and stern
D. not be required to be lighted

00114. At night, what lights are required on barges moored in a group formation at a river bank?

A. a flashing yellow light placed at each of the upstream and downstream ends of the group
B. a white light placed at the corners farthest from the bank of each barge in the group
C. a white light placed at the corners farthest from the bank on each of the upstream and downstream ends of the group
D. 2 red lights in a vertical line placed at the corners farthest from the bank on each of the upstream and downstream ends of the group

00115. Which is a characteristic of a "special flashing light"?

A. It may show through an arc of 180.
B. It flashes at the rate of 120 flashes per minute.
C. It is optional below the Baton Rouge Highway Bridge.
D. all of the above

00116. Which is a characteristic of a "special flashing light"?

A. It must be white in color.
B. It must show through an arc of not less than 225°.
C. It must be placed as nearly as practicable on the fore and aft center line of a tow.
D. all of the above

00117. Which is a characteristic of a "special flashing light"?

A. It is required for all vessels being pushed ahead as part of a composite unit.
B. It must show through an arc of not less than 180 nor more than 225°.
C. It must be of the same character and construction as the masthead light.
D. all of the above

00118. If your tug is pushing a barge ahead at night, what light(s) should show aft on your vessel?

A. A towing light above the stern light
B. 2 towing lights
C. A stern light
D. A towing light below the stern light

00119. Which of the following may be used to indicate the presence of a partly submerged object being towed?

A. A black cone, apex upward
B. 2 all-round white lights at each end of tow
C. The beam of a search light from the towing vessel in the direction of the tow
D. all of the above

00120. Which of the following may be used to indicate the presence of a partly submerged object being towed?

A. a black cone, apex downward
B. an all-round white light at each end of tow
C. a flare-up light
D. all of the above

00121. A special flashing light is used on a vessel which is:

A. operating in the nondisplacement mode
B. towed astern
C. dredging
D. being pushed ahead

00122. A barge more than 50 meters long is required to show how many white anchor lights when anchored in a Secretary of Transportation approved "special anchorage area"?

A. none
B. 1
C. 2
D. 1, on the near approach of another vessel

00123. Which of the following is not contained in the Inland Navigation Rules?

A. an inconspicuous, partly submerged object
B. lights on pipelines
C. a vessel constrained by her draft
D. an air-cushion vessel

00124. Which term is NOT defined in the Inland Navigation Rules?

A. towing light
B. vessel constrained by her draft
C. in sight
D. restricted visibility

00125. For the purpose of the Inland Navigation Rules, the term "Inland Waters" includes:

A. any waters marked by U.S. aids to navigation
B. harbors and rivers to the outermost aids to navigation
C. waters along the coast of the United States to a distance of 2 miles offshore
D. the Western Rivers, extending to the COLREGS demarcation line

00126. For the purpose of the Inland Navigation Rules, the term "Inland Waters" includes:

A. the waters surrounding any islands of the U.S.
B. the Great Lakes on the United States side of the boundary
C. the coastline of the United States, out to 1 mile offshore
D. any lakes within state boundaries

00127. You are on board the stand-on vessel in a crossing situation. You sound a 1 blast whistle signal, and the give-way vessel answers with a 2-blast signal. You should then sound the danger signal and:

A. maintain course and speed
B. come around sharply to port
C. maneuver around the stern of the other vessel
D. stop and back your vessel if necessary until signals are agreed upon

00128. In a narrow channel, you are underway on vessel "A" and desire to overtake vessel "B". After you sound 2 short blasts on your whistle, vessel "B" sounds 5 short rapid blasts on the whistle. You should:

A. pass with caution on the port side of vessel "B"
B. wait for the other vessel to initiate a signal
C. initiate another signal after the situation has stabilized
D. immediately answer with the danger signal, and then sound 1 short blast

00129. You are proceeding up a channel in inland waters and are meeting an outbound vessel. Your responsibilities include:

A. keeping to that side of the channel which is on your vessel's port side
B. exchanging whistle signals if passing within half a mile
C. stopping your vessel and letting the outbound vessel initiate signals for passing
D. giving the outbound vessel the right of way

00130. You are operating a vessel through a narrow channel and your vessel must stay within the channel to be navigated safely. Another vessel is crossing your course from starboard to port, and you are in doubt as to her intentions. You:

A. may sound the danger signal
B. are required to back down
C. should sound 1 short blast to indicate that you are holding course and speed
D. must sound the danger signal

00131. You are navigating in a narrow channel and must remain in the channel for safe operation. Another vessel is crossing the channel ahead of you from your starboard and you are doubtful as to the intention of the crossing vessel. You must:

A. stop your vessel, since the other vessel has the right of way
B. sound the danger signal
C. contact him on the radiotelephone to make a passing agreement
D. stop your engines until you have slowed to bare steerageway

00132. Which is true of a downbound power-driven vessel, when meeting an upbound vessel on the Western Rivers?

A. She shall not impede the upbound vessel
B. She shall pass on the port side of the other
C. She shall propose the place of passage
D. all of the above

00133. A power-driven vessel operating in a narrow channel with a following current on the Great Lakes or Western Rivers is meeting an upbound vessel. Which statement is true?

A. The downbound vessel has the right of way.
B. The upbound vessel must initiate the required maneuvering signals.
C. The upbound vessel must propose the manner of passing.
D. all of the above

00134. Which is true of a downbound vessel, when meeting an upbound vessel on the Western Rivers?

A. Neither vessel has the right of way.
B. The downbound vessel has the right of way only if she is power-driven.
C. She does not have the right of way, since the other vessel is not crossing the river.
D. She must wait for a whistle signal from the upbound vessel.

00135. Which statement is true concerning the Inland Navigation Rules?

A. They require communication by radiotelephone to reach a passing agreement.
B. They have rules for traffic separation schemes.
C. They require compliance with VTS regulations.
D. all of the above

00136. Yellow lights are NOT used to identify:

A. a dredge pipeline on a trestle
B. the heads of tows being pushed ahead by towboats
C. purse seiners
D. a seaplane on the water

00137. A vessel is displaying an alternating red and yellow light. This indicates that the vessel is:

A. in distress
B. fishing with lines extending out over 500 ft
C. engaged in public safety activities
D. restricted in its ability to maneuver

00138. A law enforcement vessel patrolling a marine regatta may show either a flashing blue light or:

A. 2 amber lights in a horizontal line
B. an alternately flashing red and yellow light
C. a high intensity flashing light (strobe)
D. a fixed green light over a red flashing light

00139. A vessel engaged in public safety activities may display a special light. Which of the following is NOT considered a public safety activity?

A. search and rescue
B. patrolling a regatta
C. firefighting
D. setting a buoy

00140. You are the stand-on vessel in a crossing situation. The other vessel is showing an alternating red and yellow light. What action should you take?

A. Stand on
B. Heave to
C. Alter course to assist
D. Yield the right of way

00141. You are the stand-on vessel in an overtaking situation. The other vessel is showing an alternately flashing red and yellow light. What action should you take?

A. Alter course to assist
B. Yield right of way
C. Stand on
D. Heave to

00142. The special light assigned for a vessel engaged in public safety activities must be located:

A. on top of the mast or highest structure on the vessel
B. so as not to interfere with the visibility of the navigation lights
C. as far forward as possible
D. so that it is not visible more than 22 1/2° abaft the beam

00143. A light used to signal passing intentions must be an:

A. alternating red and yellow light
B. alternating white and yellow light
C. all-round white or yellow light
D. all-round white light only

00144. A light used to signal passing intentions must be an:

A. all-round yellow light only
B. all-round white light only
C. alternating red and yellow light
D. all-round white or yellow light

00145. A light used to signal passing intentions must be a(n):

A. all-round white or yellow light
B. all-round yellow light only
C. all-round white light only
D. 225° white light only

00146. What characteristic must a light have if used to signal passing intentions?

A. an all-round white light.
B. an alternating blue and white light.
C. either an all-round white or an all-round yellow light.
D. an alternating red and yellow light.

00147. What characteristic must a light used to indicate passing intentions have?

A. an alternating red and yellow light.
B. an all-round white light.
C. an all-round yellow light.
D. either an all-round white or an all-round yellow light.

00148. In a narrow channel, you are underway on vessel "A" and desire to overtake vessel "B". After you sound 2 short blasts on your whistle, vessel "B" sounds 5 short rapid blasts on the whistle. You should:

A. pass with caution on the port side of vessel "B"
B. wait for the other vessel to initiate a signal
C. initiate another signal after the situation has stabilized
D. immediately answer with the danger signal, and then sound 1 short blast

00149. A power-driven vessel pushing ahead or towing alongside on the Mississippi River, above the Huey P. Long Bridge, shall carry:

A. 2 masthead lights, sidelights and stern light
B. 2 masthead lights, sidelights and 2 towing lights
C. sidelights and 2 towing lights
D. 1 masthead light, sidelights and stern light

00150. A power-driven vessel, when leaving a dock or berth, must sound what signal?

A. 3 short blasts
B. a long blast
C. a prolonged blast
D. no signal is required.

00163. A commercial vessel engaged in public safety activities may display a(n):

A. flashing yellow light
B. flashing blue light
C. alternately flashing blue and red light
D. alternately flashing red and yellow light

00216. Passing signals shall be sounded by a power-driven vessel intending to overtake:

A. any vessel when within half a mile of that vessel
B. another power-driven vessel when both power-driven vessels are in sight of one another
C. any vessel when both are in sight of one another
D. another power-driven vessel only when within half a mile of that power-driven vessel

00220. Your vessel is meeting another vessel head to head. To comply with the rules, you should exchange:

A. 1 short blast, alter course to the left and pass starboard to starboard
B. 2 short blasts, alter course to the left, and pass starboard to starboard
C. 1 short blast, alter course to the right, and pass port to port
D. 2 short blasts, alter course to the right, and pass port to port

00221. A barge more than 50 m long would be required to show how many white anchor lights when anchored in a Secretary of Transportation approved "special anchorage area"?

A. 4
B. 3
C. 2
D. 1

00222. A barge more than 50 m long would be required to show how many white anchor lights when anchored in a Secretary of Transportation approved "special anchorage area"?

A. 1
B. 3
C. 4
D. 2

00223. A barge more than 50 m long would be required to show how many white anchor lights when anchored in a Secretary of Transportation approved "special anchorage area"?

A. 2
B. 1
C. 1, on the near approach of another vessel
D. None

00224. A barge more than 50 m long would be required to show how many white anchor lights when anchored in a Secretary of Transportation approved "special anchorage area"?

A. none
B. 2
C. 1
D. 1, on the near approach of another vessel

00225. A barge more than 50 m long would be required to show how many white anchor lights when anchored in a Secretary of Transportation approved "special anchorage area"?

A. 1
B. none
C. 1, on the near approach of another vessel
D. 2

00227. A commercial vessel engaged in public safety activities may display a(n):

A. alternately flashing red and yellow light
B. flashing blue light
C. flashing yellow light
D. alternately flashing blue and red light

00262. When power-driven vessels are in sight of one another, passing signals shall be sounded when:

A. meeting or crossing within half a mile of each other
B. meeting within 1 mile of each other
C. meeting or crossing at any distance
D. crossing within 1 mile of each other

00352. A commercial vessel engaged in public safety activities may display a(n):

A. flashing blue light
B. alternately flashing red and yellow light
C. flashing yellow light
D. alternately flashing blue and red light

00727. Passing signals shall be sounded on inland waters by:

A. all vessels when meeting, crossing or overtaking and in sight of one another
B. all vessels meeting or crossing at a distance within half a mile of each other and in sight of one another
C. power-driven vessels overtaking and in sight of one another
D. power-driven vessels meeting or crossing at a distance within half a mile of each other and NOT in sight of one another due to heavy fog

BOTH INTERNATIONAL & INLAND QUESTIONS

04000. A vessel 75 meters in length and restricted in her ability to maneuver is carrying out her work at anchor. What signal will she sound in restricted visibility?

A. 5 second ringing of a bell at intervals of not more than 1 minute
B. 1 prolonged blast followed by 2 short blasts at intervals of not more than 2 minutes
C. 5 second ringing of a bell and 5 second sounding of a gong at intervals of not more than 1 minute
D. 4 short blasts at intervals of not more than 2 minutes

04002. While underway in fog, you hear a prolonged blast from another vessel. This signal indicates a:

A. sailboat underway
B. vessel underway, towing
C. vessel underway, making way
D. vessel being towed

04003. Which of the following is used to show the presence of a partly submerged object being towed?

A. a diamond shape on the towed object
B. an all-round light at each end of the towed object
C. a searchlight from the towing vessel in the direction of the tow
D. all of the above

04004. At night, a barge being towed astern must display:

A. red and green sidelights only
B. a white stern light only
C. sidelights and a stern light
D. 1 all-round white light

04005. Which of the following may be used as a distress signal?

A. directing the beam of a searchlight at another vessel
B. a smoke signal giving off orange colored smoke
C. a whistle signal of 1 prolonged and 3 short blasts
D. International Code Signal "PAN" spoken over radiotelephone

04006. If your vessel is approaching a bend and you hear a prolonged blast from around the bend, you should:

A. back your engines
B. stop your engines and drift
C. answer with 1 prolonged blast
D. sound the danger signal

04007. Failure to understand the course or intention of an approaching vessel should be indicated by.

A. 1 short blast
B. 1 prolonged blast
C. not less than 5 short blasts
D. not less than 5 prolonged blasts

04008. If you are the stand-on vessel in a crossing situation, you may take action to avoid collision by your maneuver alone. When may this action be taken?

A. at any time you feel it is appropriate
B. only when you have reached extremis
C. when you determine that your present course will cross ahead of the other vessel
D. when it becomes apparent to you that the give-way vessel is not taking appropriate action

04009. Your 15-meter tug is underway and crossing a deep and narrow channel. A large container vessel is off your port bow on a steady bearing. Which statement is true concerning this situation?

A. You should maintain course and speed.
B. The container vessel has the right of way as it is the larger vessel.
C. You are not to impede the safe passage of the container vessel in the channel.
D. none of the above

04010. If your vessel is underway in fog and you hear 1 prolonged and 3 short blasts, this is a:

A. vessel not under command
B. sailing vessel
C. vessel being towed (manned)
D. vessel being towed (unmanned)

04011. A pilot vessel on pilotage duty at night will show sidelights and a stern light:

A. when at anchor
B. only when making way
C. at any time when underway
D. only when identifying lights are not shown

04012. A vessel which displays the day signal as shown in DIAGRAM 6 is engaged in:

A. submarine cable laying
B. pilotage duty
C. fishing
D. mineclearance

04013. A vessel displaying the dayshapes illustrated in DIAGRAM 11, is:
A. towing
B. conducting underwater operations

C. drifting
D. aground

04014. A power-driven vessel underway in fog making NO way must sound what signal?

A. 1 long blast
B. 2 prolonged blasts
C. 1 prolonged blast
D. 1 prolonged and 2 short blasts

04015. A 95-meter vessel aground shall sound which fog signal?

A. a rapid ringing of a bell for 5 seconds every 2 minutes
B. a whistle signal of 1 short, 1 prolonged, and 1 short blast
C. a long blast of the whistle at intervals not to exceed 1 minute
D. a rapid ringing of a bell for 5 seconds, preceded and followed by 3 separate and distinct strokes on the bell

04016. Which statement is true concerning a vessel equipped with operational radar?

A. She must use this equipment to obtain early warning of risk of collision.
B. The radar equipment is only required to be used in restricted visibility.
C. The use of a radar excuses a vessel from the need of a look-out.
D. The safe speed of such a vessel will likely be greater than that of vessels without radar.

04017. A 200-meter vessel is aground in fog. Which signal is optional?

A. A bell signal
B. A gong signal
C. A whistle signal
D. all of the above

04018. Which of the following is a distress signal?

A. a triangular flag above or below a ball
B. the International Code Signal of distress indicated by "JV"
C. a green smoke signal
D. flames on vessel as from a burning tar barrel

04019. Which vessel must show forward and after masthead lights when making way?

A. a 75-meter vessel restricted in her ability to maneuver
B. a 100-meter sailing vessel
C. a 150-meter vessel engaged in fishing
D. a 45-meter vessel engaged in towing

04020. A vessel must proceed at a safe speed:

A. in restricted visibility
B. in congested waters
C. during darkness
D. at all times

04021. A light signal of 3 flashes means:

A. "I am in doubt as to your actions"
B. "My engines are full speed astern"
C. "I desire to overtake you"
D. "I am operating astern propulsion"

04022. A sailing vessel underway may exhibit:

A. red light over a green light at the masthead
B. green light over a red light at the masthead
C. 2 white lights in a vertical line at the stern
D. all-round white light at the bow

04023. A sailing vessel is overtaking a tug and tow as shown in DIAGRAM 43. Which statement is correct?

A. The sailing vessel is the stand-on vessel because it is overtaking.
B. The sailing vessel is the stand-on vessel because it is under sail.
C. The tug is the stand-on vessel because it is being overtaken.
D. The tug is the stand-on vessel because it is towing.

04024. The word "vessel", in the Rules, includes:

A. sailing ships
B. nondisplacement craft
C. seaplanes
D. all of the above

04025. A sailing vessel with the wind abaft the beam is navigating in fog. She should sound:

A. 3 short blasts
B. 1 prolonged blast
C. 1 prolonged and 2 short blasts
D. 2 prolonged blasts

04026. Which of the following actions would indicate a distress signal?

A. firing of green star shells
B. sounding 5 short blasts on the whistle
C. answering a 1 blast whistle signal with 2 blasts
D. having a flaming barrel of oil on deck

04027. If a towing vessel and her tow are severely restricted in their ability to change course, they may show lights in addition to their towing identification lights. These additional lights may be shown if the tow is:

A. pushed ahead
B. towed alongside
C. towed astern
D. any of the above

04028. If 2 sailing vessels are running free with the wind on the same side, which 1 must keep clear of the other?

A. the one with the wind closest abeam
B. the one with the wind closest astern
C. the one to leeward
D. the one to windward

04029. The masthead light may be located at other than the fore and aft centerline of a vessel:

A. less than 20 meters in length
B. less than 12 meters in length
C. which has separate sidelights carried on the outboard extremes of the vessel's breadth
D. engaged in fishing

04030. The NAVIGATION RULES define a "vessel not under command" as a vessel which:

A. from the nature of her work is unable to keep out of the way of another vessel
B. through some exceptional circumstance is unable to maneuver as required by the rules
C. by taking action contrary to the rules has created a special circumstance situation
D. is moored, aground or anchored in a fairway

04031. Additional light signals are provided in the Annexes to the Rules for vessels:

A. engaged in fishing
B. not under command
C. engaged in towing
D. under sail

04032. Which vessel may combine her sidelights in 1 lantern on the fore and aft centerline of the vessel?

A. a 16-meter sailing vessel
B. a 25-meter power-driven vessel
C. a 28-meter sailing vessel
D. any non-self-propelled vessel

04033. The duration of a prolonged blast of the whistle is:

A. 2 to 4 seconds
B. 4 to 6 seconds
C. 6 to 8 seconds
D. 8 to 10 seconds

04034. A vessel "restricted in her ability to maneuver" is 1 which:

A. from the nature of her work is unable to maneuver as required by the rules
B. through some exceptional circumstance is unable to maneuver as required by the rules
C. due to adverse weather conditions is unable to maneuver as required by the rules
D. has lost steering and is unable to maneuver

04035. When underway in restricted visibility, you might hear, at intervals of 2 minutes, any of the following fog signals EXCEPT:

A. 1 prolonged blast
B. 2 prolonged blasts
C. 1 prolonged and 2 short blasts
D. ringing of a bell for 5 seconds

04036. You are approaching a narrow channel. You see a vessel that can only be navigated safely within the channel. You should:

A. not cross the channel if you might impede the other vessel
B. initiate an exchange of passing signals
C. sound the danger signal
D. hold your course and speed

04037. A vessel of less than 20 meters in length may display a basket as a dayshape when she is engaged in:

A. trawling
B. diving operations
C. trolling
D. all of the above

04038. A bell is used to sound a fog signal for a:

A. power-driven vessel underway
B. sailing vessel at anchor
C. vessel engaged in fishing
D. vessel not under command

04039. You are seeing another vessel approaching, and its compass bearing does not significantly change. This would indicate that:

A. you are the stand-on vessel
B. risk of collision exists
C. a special circumstances situation exists
D. the other vessel is dead in the water

04040. Which of the dayshapes in DIAGRAM 16 indicates a vessel with a tow exceeding 200 meters in length?

A. A
B. B
C. C
D. D

04041. What lights are required for a barge being towed alongside?

A. sidelights and a stern light
B. sidelights, a special flashing light, and a stern light
C. sidelights and a special flashing light
D. sidelights, a towing light, and a stern light

04042. A towing vessel pushing a barge ahead and rigidly connected in a composite unit shall show the lights of:

A. a vessel towing by pushing ahead
B. a power-driven vessel, not towing
C. a barge being pushed ahead
D. either answer A or answer B

04043. You are the watch officer on a power-driven vessel and notice a large sailing vessel approaching from astern. You should:

A. slow down
B. sound 1 short blast and change course to starboard
C. sound 2 short blasts and change course to port
D. hold your course and speed

04044. You see a vessel's green sidelight bearing due east from you. It might be heading:

A. east
B. northeast
C. northwest
D. southwest

04045. A vessel shall be deemed to be overtaking when she is in such a position, with reference to the vessel she is approaching, that she can see at night:

A. only the stern light of the vessel
B. the stern light and 1 sidelight of the vessel
C. only a sidelight of the vessel
D. any lights except the masthead lights of the vessel

04046. You are underway on vessel "A" and sight vessel "B" which is a vessel underway and fishing. Which statement is true? (see DIAGRAM 14)

A. Vessel "A" must keep out of the way of vessel "B" because "B" is to port.
B. Vessel "A" must keep out of the way of vessel "B" because "B" is fishing.
C. Vessel "B" must keep out of the way of vessel "A" because "A" is to starboard.
D. In this case, both vessels are required by the Rules to keep clear of each other.

04047. A vessel trawling will display a:

A. red light over a white light
B. green light over a white light

C. white light over a red light
D. white light over a green light

04048. If it becomes necessary for a stand-on vessel to take action to avoid collision, she shall NOT, if possible:

A. decrease speed
B. increase speed
C. turn to port for a vessel on her own port side
D. turn to starboard for a vessel on her own port side

04049. Your vessel is NOT making way, but is not in any way disabled. Another vessel is approaching you on your starboard beam. Which statement is true?

A. The other vessel must give way since your vessel is stopped.
B. Your vessel is the give-way vessel in a crossing situation.
C. You should be showing the lights or shapes for a vessel not under command.
D. You should be showing the lights or shapes for a vessel restricted in her ability to maneuver.

04050. A sailing vessel which is also propelled by machinery shall show during daylight hours a:

A. black diamond
B. black cone
C. black ball
D. basket

04051. The rules concerning lights shall be complied with in all weathers from sunset to sunrise. The lights:

A. shall be displayed in restricted visibility during daylight hours
B. need not be displayed when no other vessels are in the area
C. shall be set at low power when used during daylight hours
D. need not be displayed by unmanned vessels

04052. The lights shown in DIAGRAM 44, would be displayed by a vessel when it is:

A. aground
B. not under command and dead in the water
C. not under command and is making way
D. laying or picking up navigation marks

04053. 2 vessels meeting in a "head on" situation are directed by the Rules to:

A. alter course to starboard and pass port to port
B. alter course to port and pass starboard to starboard

C. decide on which side the passage will occur by matching whistle signals
D. slow to bare steerageway

04054. A vessel is "engaged in fishing" when:

A. her gear extends more than 100 meters from the vessel
B. she is using any type of gear, other than lines
C. she is using fishing apparatus which restricts her maneuverability
D. she has any fishing gear on board

04055. When shall the stand-on vessel change course and speed?

A. The stand-on vessel may change course and speed at any time as it has the right-of-way
B. After the give-way vessel sounds 1 blast in a crossing situation
C. When action by the give-way vessel alone cannot prevent collision
D. When the 2 vessels become less than half a mile apart

04056. A sailing vessel with the wind abaft the beam is navigating in restricted visibility. She should sound:

A. 3 short blasts
B. 1 prolonged blast
C. 1 prolonged and 2 short blasts
D. 2 prolonged blasts

04057. You are on watch, when you sight a vessel displaying the code flag "LIMA" below which is a red ball. This indicates a vessel:

A. with trolling lines out
B. getting ready to receive aircraft
C. aground
D. in distress

04058. Which factor is listed in the Rules as 1 which must be taken into account when determining safe speed?

A. the construction of the vessel
B. the maneuverability of the vessel
C. the experience of vessel personnel
D. all of the above

04059. Which statement is true concerning seaplanes on the water?

A. A seaplane must show appropriate lights but need not exhibit shapes.
B. A seaplane should exhibit the lights for a vessel constrained by her draft.
C. In situations where a risk of collision exists, a seaplane should always give way.
D. A seaplane on the water shall, in general, keep well clear of all vessels.

04060. A vessel approaching your vessel from 235° relative is in what type of situation?

A. meeting
B. overtaking
C. crossing
D. passing

04061. Vessels "A" and "B" are crossing as shown in DIAGRAM 26. Which statement is true?

A. The vessels should pass starboard to starboard.
B. Vessel "B" should pass under the stern of vessel "A".
C. Vessel "B" should alter course to the right.
D. Vessel "A" must keep clear of vessel "B".

04062. You are in charge of a power-driven vessel navigating at night. You sight the red sidelight of another vessel on your port bow. Its after masthead light is to the right of the forward masthead light. You should:

A. hold course and speed
B. alter course to port
C. stop engines
D. sound the danger signal

04064. Which statement is TRUE, according to the Rules?

A. A vessel engaged in fishing shall, so far as possible, keep out of the way of a vessel restricted in her ability to maneuver.
B. A vessel not under command shall keep out of the way of a vessel engaged in fishing.
C. A sailing vessel has the right of way over a vessel engaged in fishing.
D. A vessel restricted in her ability to maneuver shall keep out of the way of a vessel not under command.

04065. You are underway in fog when you hear the rapid ringing of a bell for 5 seconds followed by the sounding of a gong for 5 seconds. This signal indicates a vessel:

A. aground
B. more than 100 meters in length, at anchor
C. fishing while making no way
D. fishing in company with another vessel

04066. The wind is ESE, and a sailing vessel is steering NW. What fog signal should she sound?

A. 1 blast at 1-minute intervals
B. 1 blast at 2-minute intervals
C. 2 blasts at 1-minute intervals
D. 1 prolonged and 2 short blasts at 2-minute intervals

04067. At night, what lights are required to be shown by a dredge on the side of the dredge which another vessel may pass?

A. 1 red light
B. 2 red lights
C. 1 white light
D. 2 green lights

04068. In the situation illustrated in DIAGRAM 2, Vessel I is a power-driven vessel. Vessel II is a sailing vessel with the wind dead aft. Which of the following statements about this situation is correct?

A. Vessel I should keep out of the way of Vessel II.
B. Vessel II should keep out of the way of Vessel I.
C. Vessel II would normally be the stand-on vessel, but should stay out of the way in this particular situation.
D. The Rules of Special Circumstances applies, and neither vessel is the stand-on vessel.

04069. What lights are shown by a vessel restricted in her ability to maneuver to indicate that the vessel is making way?

A. masthead lights, sidelights and stern light
B. masthead lights and sidelights only
C. sidelights and stern light only
D. sidelights only

04070. You are underway and hear a vessel continuously sounding her fog whistle. This indicates the other vessel:

A. desires to communicate by radio
B. desires a pilot
C. is in distress
D. is aground

04071. While operating a power-driven vessel in fog, you see another vessel on radar who is half a mile distant on your port bow. You should:

A. sound the danger signal
B. exchange passing signals
C. sound 1 long blast
D. make no change in your fog signal

04072. A 30-meter tug is underway and not towing. At night, it must show sidelights and:

A. 1 masthead light and a stern light
B. 2 masthead lights and a stern light
C. 3 masthead lights and a stern light
D. a stern light

04073. While underway in fog, you hear a signal of 1 prolonged blast followed by 3 short blasts. This is the fog signal for a vessel:

A. towing
B. manned being towed
C. unmanned being towed
D. at anchor

04074. Which statement is true concerning a vessel of 75 meters in length, at anchor?

A. She must show an all-round white light fwd.
B. She must show a second all-round white light aft.
C. She may use her working lights to illuminate her decks.
D. all of the above

04075. You are approaching another vessel. She is about 1 mile distant and is on your starboard bow. You believe she will cross ahead of you. She then sounds a whistle signal of 5 short blasts. You should:

A. answer the signal and hold course and speed
B. reduce speed slightly to make sure she will have room to pass
C. make a large course change, and slow down if necessary
D. wait for another whistle signal from the other vessel

04076. If a rowboat underway does not show the lights specified for a sailing vessel underway, it shall show a:

A. white light from sunset to sunrise
B. combined lantern showing green to starboard and red to port and shown from sunset to sunrise
C. combined lantern showing green to starboard and red to port and shown in sufficient time to prevent collision
D. white light shown in sufficient time to prevent collision

04077. A vessel at anchor shall display between sunrise and sunset on the forward part of the vessel where it can best be seen:

A. 1 black ball
B. 2 black balls
C. 1 red ball
D. 2 orange and white balls

04078. You are underway in fog and hear a fog signal of 2 prolonged blasts on your starboard quarter. You should:

A. stop your vessel
B. change your course to the left
C. change course to the right
D. hold your course and speed

04079. You see a vessel displaying a basket in the rigging. It could be a:

A. 100-meter vessel engaged in fishing
B. 30-meter vessel trawling
C. 15-meter vessel trolling
D. 15-meter vessel engaged in fishing while at anchor

04080. You are underway, in fog, when you hear a whistle signal of 1 prolonged blast followed by 2 short blasts. This signal could indicate a vessel:

A. not under command
B. being towed
C. aground
D. all of the above

04081. You are aboard vessel "A" , a power-driven vessel, on open waters and vessel "B", a sailing vessel, is sighted off your port bow as shown in DIAGRAM 27. Which vessel is the stand on vessel?

A. Vessel "A" because it is towing
B. Vessel "A" because it is to starboard of vessel "B"
C. Vessel "B" because it is sailing
D. Vessel "B" because it is to port of vessel "A"

04082. Which vessel must exhibit 3 white masthead lights in a vertical line?

A. any vessel towing astern
B. a vessel whose tow exceeds 200 m astern
C. a vessel not under command, at anchor
D. a vessel being towed

04083. All of the following are distress signals EXCEPT:

A. the continuous sounding of any fog signal apparatus
B. giving 5 or more short and rapid blasts of the whistle
C. firing a gun at intervals of about a minute
D. a barrel with burning oil in it, on deck

04084. If you are approaching a bend, and hear a whistle signal of 1 prolonged blast from around the bend, you should answer with a signal of:

A. a short blast
B. a prolonged blast
C. 1 short, 1 prolonged, and 1 short blast
D. a long blast

04085. Which vessel must show an after masthead light, if over 50 meters in length?

A. a vessel engaged in fishing
B. a vessel at anchor
C. a vessel not under command
D. a vessel trawling

04086. You are on vessel "A" and approaching vessel "B" as shown in DIAGRAM 15. You are not sure whether your vessel is crossing or overtaking vessel "B". You should:

A. change course to make the situation definitely either crossing or overtaking
B. consider it to be a crossing situation
C. consider it to be an overtaking situation
D. consider it a crossing situation if you can cross ahead safely

04087. A "flashing light", according to the definition given in the rules, is a light that:

A. is red in color
B. is visible over an arc of the horizon of 360°
C. flashes at regular intervals at a frequency of 120 flashes or more per minute
D. all of the above

04088. The term "restricted visibility" as used in the Rules refers:

A. only to fog
B. only to visibility of less than 1/2 mile
C. to visibility where you cannot see shore
D. to any condition where visibility is restricted

04089. A vessel engaged in mineclearing shows special identity lights:

A. in addition to the lights required for a power-driven vessel
B. which mean that other vessels should not approach within 1000 meters of the mineclearing vessel
C. which are green and show all-round
D. all of the above

04090. According to the Navigation Rules, you may depart from the Rules when:

A. no vessels are in sight visually
B. no vessels are visible on radar
C. you are in immediate danger
D. out of sight of land

04091. An authorized light to assist in the identification of submarines operating on the surface is a(n):

A. blue rotating light
B. intermittent flashing amber/yellow light
C. flashing white light
D. flashing sidelight

04092. You sight a vessel displaying a basket in the rigging. It could be a:

A. 100-meter vessel fishing
B. 30-meter vessel trawling

C. 15-meter vessel trolling
D. 15-meter vessel fishing while at anchor

04093. Which statement is true concerning 2 sailing vessels?

A. A sailing vessel with the wind forward of the beam on her port side shall keep out of the way of a sailing vessel with the wind forward of the beam on the starboard side.
B. When both vessels have the wind on the same side, the vessel to leeward shall keep out of the way.
C. A sail vessel with the wind aft of the beam must keep out of the way of a vessel sailing into the wind.
D. none of the above

04094. You are aboard vessel "A" which is towing on open waters when vessel "B", a sailing vessel, is sighted off your port bow, as shown in DIAGRAM 20. Which vessel has the right of way?

A. Vessel "A" is the stand-on vessel because it is towing.
B. Vessel "A" is the stand-on vessel because it is to starboard of vessel "B".
C. Vessel "B" is the stand-on vessel because it is sailing.
D. Vessel "B" is the stand-on vessel because it is to port of vessel "A".

04095. When underway in a channel, you should keep:

A. in the middle of the channel
B. to the starboard side of the channel
C. to the port side of the channel
D. to the side of the channel that has the widest turns

04096. While underway, in fog, you hear a whistle signal of 1 prolonged blast followed by 2 short blasts. This signal is sounded by a vessel:

A. not under command
B. being towed
C. at anchor
D. aground

04097. When navigating in restricted visibility, a power-driven vessel shall:

A. stop her engines when hearing a fog signal forward of her beam, even if risk of collision does not exist
B. have her engines ready for immediate maneuver
C. when making way, sound 1 prolonged blast at intervals of not more than 1 minute
D. operate at a speed to be able to stop in the distance of her visibility

04098. You can indicate that your vessel is in distress by:

A. displaying a large red flag
B. displaying 3 black balls in a vertical line
C. sounding 4 or more short rapid blasts on the whistle
D. continuously sounding the fog whistle

04099. During the day, a dredge will indicate the side on which it is safe to pass by displaying:

A. 2 balls in a vertical line
B. 2 diamonds in a vertical line
C. a single black ball
D. no shape is shown during the day

04100. A 45-meter vessel is pulling a 210-meter tow. She may exhibit:

A. a masthead light forward, and 2 masthead lights in a vertical line aft
B. 3 masthead lights forward and 1 aft
C. 2 masthead lights forward and no after masthead light
D. none of the above

04101. Which of the following statements is true concerning the danger signal?

A. Vessels must be in sight of each other in order to use the danger signal.
B. Only the stand-on vessel can sound the danger signal.
C. Distress signals may be used in place of the danger signal.
D. The danger signal consists of 4 or more short blasts of the whistle.

04102. A distress signal:

A. consists of 5 or more short blasts of the fog signal apparatus
B. may be used separately or with other distress signals
C. consists of the raising and lowering of a large white flag
D. is used to indicate doubt about another vessel's intentions

04103. What is the danger signal?

A. a continuous sounding of the fog signal
B. firing a gun every minute
C. 5 or more short rapid blasts on the whistle
D. 1 long blast on the whistle

04104. A vessel is "in sight" of another vessel when:

A. she can be observed visually or by radar
B. she can be observed visually from the other vessel

C. she can be seen well enough to determine her heading
D. her fog signal can be heard

04105. Which statement is true concerning 2 sailing vessels approaching each other?

A. A sailing vessel overtaking another is the give-way vessel.
B. When each is on a different tack, the vessel on the starboard tack shall keep out of the way.
C. A sailing vessel seeing another to leeward on an undetermined tack shall hold her course.
D. all of the above

04106. What type of vessel or operation is indicated by a vessel showing 2 cones with the apexes together?

A. sailing vessel
B. vessel trawling
C. mineclearing
D. dredge

04107. A power-driven vessel has on her port side a sailing vessel which is on a collision course. The power-driven vessel is to:

A. maintain course and speed
B. keep clear
C. sound 1 blast and turn to starboard
D. stop her engines

04108. At specified intervals, a vessel towing in fog shall sound:

A. 1 prolonged blast
B. 2 prolonged blasts
C. 1 prolonged and 2 short blasts in succession
D. 1 prolonged and 3 short blasts in succession

04109. A vessel towing in fog shall sound a fog signal of:

A. 1 prolonged blast every 2 minutes
B. 2 prolonged blasts every 2 minutes
C. 1 prolonged and 2 short blasts every 2 minutes
D. 1 prolonged blast every 2 minutes

04110. Continuous sounding of a fog whistle by a vessel is a signal:

A. that the vessel is anchored
B. for a request that the draw span of a bridge be opened
C. of distress
D. that the vessel is broken down and drifting

04111. A 50-meter vessel is towing astern and the length of the tow is 100 meters. In addition to sidelights, she may show:

A. 2 masthead lights forward, a stern light, and towing light above the stern light
B. a masthead light forward, 2 masthead lights aft, a stern light, and a towing light above the stern light
C. no masthead light forward, 2 masthead lights aft, a stern light, and a towing light above the stern light
D. 3 masthead lights forward, 1 masthead light aft, and 2 towing lights in a vertical line at the stern

04112. A vessel, which is unable to maneuver due to some exceptional circumstance, shall exhibit:

A. during the day, 3 balls in a vertical line
B. during the day, 3 shapes, the highest and lowest being balls and the middle being a diamond
C. when making way at night, 2 all-round red lights, sidelights, and a stern light
D. when making way at night, masthead lights, sidelights, and a stern light

04113. Which signal, other than a distress signal, can be used by a vessel to attract attention?

A. searchlight
B. continuous sounding of a fog-signal apparatus
C. burning barrel
D. orange smoke signal

04114. Which statement is true concerning the light used with whistle signals?

A. Use of such a light is required.
B. The light shall have the same characteristics as a masthead light.
C. It is only used to supplement short blasts of the whistle.
D. all of the above

04115. What is the minimum sound signaling equipment required aboard a vessel 14 meters in length?

A. a bell only
B. a whistle only
C. a bell and a whistle
D. any means of making an efficient sound signal

04116. The towing light is defined as a(n):

A. flashing amber light
B. yellow light having the same characteristics as the stern light
C. all-round yellow light
D. yellow light having the same characteristics as the masthead light

04117. An all-round flashing yellow light may be exhibited by a(n):

A. vessel not under command
B. air cushion vessel in the nondisplacement mode
C. vessel towing a submerged object
D. vessel engaged in diving operations

04118. When should the fog signal of a manned vessel being towed be sounded?

A. after the towing vessel's fog signal
B. before the towing vessel's fog signal
C. approximately 1 minute after the towing vessel's fog signal
D. if the towing vessel is sounding a fog signal, the manned vessel being towed is not required to sound any fog signal.

04119. A lantern combining the 2 sidelights of a vessel's running lights may be shown on a:

A. 15-meter sailing vessel
B. 20-meter vessel engaged in fishing and making way
C. 25-meter power-driven vessel trolling
D. 25-meter pilot vessel

04120. A vessel engaged in fishing during the day would show:

A. 1 black ball
B. 2 cones with bases together
C. a cone, apex downward
D. 2 cones, apexes together

04121. A sailing vessel is NOT required to keep out of the way of a:

A. power-driven vessel
B. vessel not under command
C. vessel restricted in her ability to maneuver
D. vessel engaged in fishing

04122. Which vessel may sound the danger signal?

A. the stand-on vessel in a crossing situation.
B. the give-way vessel in a crossing situation.
C. a vessel at anchor.
D. all of the above

04123. While underway in fog, you hear a vessel sound 1 prolonged blast followed by 2 short blasts on the whistle. What does this signal indicate?

A. a vessel towing
B. a vessel engaged in pilotage duty
C. a vessel being towed
D. a vessel aground

04124. In DIAGRAM 28, vessel "A" is underway and towing, when vessel "B" is sighted off the starboard bow. Which vessel is the stand-on vessel?

A. Vessel "A" is the stand-on vessel because it is to port.
B. Vessel "A" is the stand-on vessel because it is towing.
C. Vessel "B" is the stand-on vessel because it is to starboard of vessel "A".
D. Neither vessel is the stand-on vessel.

04125. If you saw flames aboard a vessel but could see the vessel was not on fire, you would know that the:

A. crew was trying to get warm
B. vessel required immediate assistance
C. vessel was attempting to attract the attention of a pilot boat
D. vessel was being illuminated for identification by aircraft

04126. By day, when it is impracticable for a small vessel engaged in diving operations to display the shapes for a vessel engaged in underwater operations, it shall display.

A. 3 black balls in a vertical line
B. 2 red balls in a vertical line
C. a black cylinder
D. a rigid replica of the International Code flag "A"

04127. A vessel will NOT show sidelights when:

A. underway but not making way
B. making way, not under command
C. not under command, not making way
D. trolling underway

04128. Which display indicates a vessel conducting mineclearance operations?

A. 3 balls in a vertical line
B. 2 balls in a vertical line
C. 1 ball near the foremast and 1 ball at each yardarm
D. 1 diamond near the foremast and 1 ball at each yardarm

04129. Which vessel may show 2 masthead lights in a vertical line?

A. a vessel less than 50 meters in length with a 20-meter tow
B. a sailing vessel towing a small vessel astern
C. a vessel restricted in her ability to maneuver
D. a vessel engaged in dredging

04130. The duration of each blast of whistle signals used in meeting and crossing situations is:

A. about 1 second
B. 2 or 4 seconds
C. 4 to 6 seconds
D. 8 to 10 seconds

04131. What dayshape should a vessel being towed exhibit if the tow EXCEEDS 200 meters?

A. 2 balls
B. 2 diamonds
C. 1 ball
D. 1 diamond

04132. A sailing vessel is meeting a vessel engaged in fishing in a narrow channel. Which statement is true?

A. The fishing vessel shall not hinder the passage of the sailing vessel.
B. The fishing vessel has the right of way.
C. Each vessel should move to the edge of the channel on her port side.
D. Each vessel should be displaying signals for a vessel constrained by her draft.

04133. Which statement is true when you are towing more than 1 barge astern at night?

A. Only the last barge in the tow must be lighted.
B. Only the first and last barges in the tow must be lighted.
C. Each barge in the tow must be lighted.
D. Only manned barges must be lighted.

04134. Vessel "A" is overtaking vessel "B" as shown in DIAGRAM 9. Which vessel is the stand-on vessel?

A. Vessel "A"
B. Vessel "B"
C. neither vessel
D. both vessels must keep clear of the other

04135. A vessel is being propelled both by sail and by engines. Under the Rules, the vessel is:

A. considered a "special circumstance" vessel
B. not covered under any category
C. considered a sail vessel
D. considered a power-driven vessel

04136. The white masthead light required for a power-driven vessel under the Rules is visible over how many degrees of the horizon?

A. 022.5
B. 112.5
C. 225.0
D. 360.0

04137. Which statement is true concerning lights and shapes for towing vessels?

A. If a tow exceeds 200 meters in length, the towing vessel will display a black ball during daylight.
B. When towing astern, a vessel will carry her identification lights at the masthead in addition to her regular masthead light.
C. When towing astern, the towing vessel may show either a stern light or a towing light, but not both.
D. If the towing vessel is over 50 meters in length, she must carry forward and after masthead lights.

04138. A vessel may use any sound or light signals to attract the attention of another vessel as long as:

A. white lights are not used
B. red and green lights are not used
C. the vessel signals such intentions over the radiotelephone
D. the signal cannot be mistaken for a signal authorized by the Rules

04139. What type of vessel or operation is indicated by a vessel displaying 2 cones with the apexes together?

A. sailing
B. trawling
C. minesweeping
D. dredging

04140. The rule regarding look-outs applies:

A. in restricted visibility
B. between dusk and dawn
C. in heavy traffic
D. all of the above

04141. While underway and towing, your vessel enters fog. What fog signal should you sound?

A. 1 prolonged blast
B. 2 prolonged blasts
C. 1 prolonged blast and 2 short blasts
D. 3 distinct blasts

04142. A vessel engaged in fishing must display a light in the direction of any gear that extends outward more than 150 meters. The color of this light is:

A. white
B. green
C. red
D. yellow

04143. Which statement is true concerning a towing light when a towing vessel is towing astern?

A. When a towing light is shown, no stern light is necessary.
B. When a stern light is shown, no towing light is necessary.
C. The towing light is shown below the stern light.
D. The towing light is shown above the stern light.

04144. At night, a vessel which is less than 7 meters in length and anchored in an area where other vessels do not normally navigate is:

A. not required to show any anchor lights
B. required to show a flare-up light
C. required to show 1 white light
D. required to show sidelights and a stern light

04145. You are in charge of a 120-meter power-driven vessel at anchor in fog, sounding the required anchor signals. You hear the fog signal of a vessel underway off your port bow. You may sound:

A. at least 5 short and rapid blasts
B. 2 short blasts
C. 1 short, 1 prolonged, 1 short blast
D. 3 short blasts

04146. When taking action to avoid collision, you should:

A. make sure the action is taken in enough time
B. not make any large course changes
C. not make any large speed changes
D. all of the above

04147. Which vessel would have no white lights visible when meeting her head-on?

A. a vessel trawling
B. a vessel restricted in her ability to maneuver
C. a vessel mineclearing
D. a vessel not under command

04148. You are in restricted visibility and hear a fog signal forward of the beam. Nothing appears on your radar screen. The Rules require you to:

A. stop your engines
B. sound 2 prolonged blasts of the whistle
C. sound the danger signal
D. slow to bare steerageway

04149. A vessel displaying the lights illustrated in DIAGRAM 84 is:

A. not under command
B. showing improper lights
C. towing
D. dredging

04150. A towing vessel 30 meters in length is pushing barges ahead. How many white masthead lights is the vessel required to show at night?

A. 1
B. 2
C. 3
D. 4

04151. While underway in fog you hear a vessel sound 1 prolonged blast followed by 2 short blasts. What does this signal indicate?

A. a vessel towing
B. a vessel being towed
C. a pilot vessel engaged on pilotage duty
D. a vessel aground

04152. A power-driven vessel with a 150-meter stern tow shall display:

A. 3 masthead lights in a vertical line
B. a towing light above the stern light
C. 2 towing lights in a vertical line
D. a red light over a white light at the masthead

04153. A vessel transferring cargo while underway is classified by the Rules as a vessel:

A. not under command
B. in special circumstances
C. restricted in her ability to maneuver
D. constrained by her draft

04154. Which of the following vessels, when anchored at night, would not be required to show anchor lights?

A. a power-driven vessel
B. a vessel engaged on pilotage duty
C. a vessel dredging
D. a vessel restricted in her ability to maneuver

04155. A vessel which is towing and showing 3 forward white masthead lights in a vertical line is indicating that the length of the:

A. towing vessel is less than 50 meters
B. towing vessel is greater than 50 meters
C. tow is less than 200 meters
D. tow is greater than 200 meters

04156. Which vessel is "underway" under the Rules of the Road?

A. a vessel at anchor with the engine running
B. a vessel with a line led to a tree onshore
C. a vessel drifting with the engine off
D. a vessel aground

04157. Which vessel may exhibit identifying lights when not engaged in her occupation?

A. a trawler
B. a fishing vessel
C. a tug
D. none of the above

04158. A 25-meter vessel trawling will show the dayshape(s) consisting of:

A. a basket
B. 2 balls
C. 2 cones, apexes together
D. a cone, apex downward

04159. A power-driven vessel underway shall keep out of the way of a:

A. vessel not under command
B. vessel engaged in fishing
C. sailing vessel
D. all of the above

04160. A fog signal of 1 short, 1 prolonged, and 1 short blast can be sounded by a:

A. vessel at anchor
B. vessel aground
C. trawler shooting its nets
D. all of the above

04161. A continuous sounding of a fog-signal apparatus indicates:

A. the vessel is in distress
B. the vessel has completed loading dangerous cargo
C. it is safe to pass
D. the vessel is anchored

04162. A vessel at night, displaying the lights illustrated in DIAGRAM 83 is:

A. fishing
B. not under command
C. towing
D. being towed

04163. Your vessel is underway in reduced visibility. You hear, about 22 degrees on the starboard bow, a fog signal of another vessel. Which of the following actions should you take?

A. Alter the course to starboard to pass around the other vessel's stern.
B. Slow your engines and let him pass ahead.
C. Reduce your speed to bare steerageway.
D. Alter course to port to pass him on his port side.

04164. While underway in fog you hear a whistle signal consisting of 1 prolonged blast followed immediately by 2 short blasts. Such a signal is sounded in fog by:

A. vessels at anchor, not engaged in fishing
B. vessels underway and towing
C. vessels in danger
D. pilot vessels

04165. Which statement is true of a 30 meter sailing vessel underway?

A. She must show sidelights and a stern light in restricted visibility.
B. She may show an all-round white light at the top of the mast.
C. She need not show a stern light if she is showing all-round lights on the mast.
D. If she is using propelling machinery, she shall show forward a shape consisting of 2 cones, apexes together.

04166. A power-driven vessel when towing another vessel astern (tow less than 200 meters) shall show:

A. 2 masthead lights in a vertical line instead of the forward masthead light
B. 2 masthead lights in a vertical line instead of either the forward or after masthead lights
C. 2 towing lights in a vertical line at the stern
D. a small white light aft of the funnel

04167. A vessel which is "restricted in her ability to maneuver" under the Rules, is a vessel which is:

A. mineclearing
B. engaged in fishing
C. at anchor
D. not under command

04168. When a vessel signals her distress by means of a gun or other explosive signal, the firing should be at intervals of approximately:

A. 10 minutes
B. 1 minute
C. 1 hour
D. 3 minutes

04169. A "head on" or "end on" situation shall be deemed to exist at night when a vessel sees the other vessel ahead and:

A. 1 sidelight and the masthead light are visible
B. the vessels will pass closer than half a mile
C. both vessels sound 1 prolonged blast
D. both sidelights are visible

04170. A 20-meter vessel is towing another vessel astern. The length of the tow from the stern of the towing vessel to the stern of the tow is 75 meters. How many white towing identification lights shall the towing vessel show at night?

A. 1
B. 2
C. 3
D. 4

04171. A vessel fishing, and at anchor, should show:

A. an anchor light
B. sidelights and a stern light
C. 3 lights in a vertical line, the highest and lowest being red, and the middle being white
D. none of the above

04172. A vessel showing the day signal shown in DIAGRAM 19 is a:

A. work boat at anchor
B. vessel fishing
C. dredge at anchor
D. vessel being towed

04173. A power-driven vessel underway shall keep out of the way of a vessel:

A. not under command
B. restricted in her ability to maneuver
C. engaged in fishing
D. all of the above

04174. A vessel sounding a fog signal of 1 short, 1 prolonged and 1 short blast is indicating that the vessel is:

A. fishing
B. in distress
C. at anchor
D. not under command

04175. A vessel displaying the lights illustrated in DIAGRAM 57 is:

A. restricted in her ability to maneuver and not making way
B. engaged in fishing and not making way
C. a pilot vessel underway and making way on pilotage duty
D. towing and making way

04176. 2 all-round red lights displayed in a vertical line are shown by a:

A. vessel being towed
B. tug or towboat pushing a barge ahead
C. vessel at anchor
D. vessel not under command

04177. Your vessel is underway in reduced visibility. You hear, about 30 degrees on the starboard bow, a fog signal of another vessel. Which of the following actions should you take?

A. Alter course to starboard to pass around the other vessel's stern.
B. Slow your engines and let him pass ahead.
C. Reduce your speed to bare steerageway.
D. Alter course to port and pass him on his port side.

04178. You are underway in fog and you hear 1 prolonged blast followed by 2 short blasts. This is a ____vessel:

A. towing
B. engaged on pilotage duty
C. aground in a fairway
D. stopped and making no way

04179. A sailing vessel is NOT allowed to show the all-round red over green lights on the mast if:

A. she is showing sidelights
B. her sidelights are combined and shown on the fore and aft centerline of the vessel
C. she is showing a stern light
D. her sidelights and stern light are combined in 1 lantern and shown on the mast

04180. A power-driven vessel, when towing astern, shall show:

A. 2 towing lights in a vertical line
B. a towing light in a vertical line above the stern light
C. 2 towing lights in addition to stern light
D. a small white light in lieu of the stern light

04181. According to the Rules, which vessel is NOT "restricted in her ability to maneuver"?

A. a vessel servicing a navigation marker
B. a sailing vessel
C. a vessel mineclearing
D. a vessel dredging

04182. Distress signals may be:

A. red flares
B. smoke signals
C. sound signals
D. any of the above

04183. When anchoring a 25-meter vessel at night, you must show:

A. 1 all-round white light
B. 2 all-round white lights
C. 1 all-round white light and the sidelights
D. the sidelights and a stern light

04184. You are approaching another vessel at night. You can see both red and green sidelights and, above the level of the sidelights, 3 white lights in a vertical line. The vessel may be:

A. not under command
B. towing a tow more than 200 meters astern
C. trawling
D. underway and dredging

04185. A vessel engaged in fishing, and at anchor, should exhibit:

A. an anchor light
B. sidelights and stern light
C. 3 lights in a vertical line, the highest and lowest being red, and the middle being white
D. none of the above

04186. A vessel fishing should display which of the following day signals shown in DIAGRAM 1?

A. A
B. B
C. C
D. D

04187. In a crossing situation on open waters, a sailing vessel shall keep out of the way of all the following vessels EXCEPT:

A. a vessel not under command
B. a vessel restricted in her ability to maneuver
C. a power-driven vessel approaching on her starboard side
D. a vessel fishing

04188. You are on a 120-meter power-driven vessel at anchor in fog. You hear the fog signal of a vessel approaching off your port bow. You may sound:

A. at least 5 short and rapid blasts
B. 2 short blasts
C. 1 short, 1 prolonged, and 1 short blast
D. 1 prolonged blast

04189. You see a vessel displaying the day signal shown in DIAGRAM 6. The vessel is:

A. not under command
B. fishing with trawls
C. laying cable
D. aground

04190. A power-driven vessel making way through the water sounds a fog signal of:

A. 1 prolonged blast at intervals of not more than 2 minutes
B. 2 prolonged blasts at intervals of not more than 2 minutes
C. 1 prolonged blast at intervals of not more than 1 minute
D. 2 prolonged blasts at intervals of not more than 1 minute

04191. You are on watch in the fog. Your vessel is proceeding at a safe speed when you hear a fog signal ahead of you. The Rules require you to navigate with caution until the danger of collision is over and to:

A. slow to less than 2 knots
B. reduce to bare steerageway
C. stop your engines
D. begin a radar plot

04192. In restricted visibility, a vessel fishing with nets shall sound at intervals of 2 minutes:

A. 1 prolonged blast
B. 1 prolonged followed by 2 short blasts
C. 1 prolonged followed by 3 short blasts
D. 2 prolonged blasts in succession

04193. A 20-meter sailing vessel underway must exhibit a:

A. stern light
B. combined lantern
C. red light over a green light at the masthead
D. all of the above

04194. At night, you are towing a partly submerged vessel, 20 meters in length and 4 meters in breadth. What lights must you display on the towed vessel?

A. A white light at the stern
B. 2 white lights side by side at the stern
C. A white light at the forward end and a white light at the after end
D. 2 red lights in a vertical line at the aft end

04195. All of the following vessels shall be regarded as "restricted in their ability to maneuver" EXCEPT a vessel:

A. laying a pipeline
B. dredging
C. mineclearing
D. not under command

04196. What lights must be shown on a barge being towed astern at night?

A. a white light at each corner
B. a white light fore and aft
C. sidelights and a stern light
D. a stern light only

04197. A vessel which is unable to maneuver due to some exceptional circumstance, shall show 2 red lights in a vertical line and:

A. during the day, 3 balls in a vertical line
B. during the day, 3 shapes, the highest and lowest being balls and the middle being a diamond

C. when making way at night, sidelights and a stern light
D. when making way at night, masthead lights, sidelights, and a stern light

04198. You are underway and approaching a bend in the channel where vessels approaching from the opposite direction cannot be seen. You should sound:

A. 1 blast, 4 to 6 seconds in duration
B. 3 blasts, 4 to 6 seconds in duration
C. 1 continuous blast until you are able to see around the bend
D. 1 blast, 8 to 10 seconds in duration

04199. A vessel which is fishing must show sidelights and a stern light only when:

A. anchored
B. underway
C. dead in the water
D. underway and making way

04200. You encounter a vessel displaying the dayshapes shown in DIAGRAM 4. Which of the following is it?

A. vessel under sail also being propelled by machinery
B. small tug with tow greater than 200 meters astern
C. a vessel trawling
D. small fisherman with nets out more than 150 meters

04201. A power-driven vessel towing astern shall show:

A. 2 towing lights in a vertical line
B. a towing light in a vertical line above the stern light
C. 2 towing lights in addition to the stern light
D. a small white light in lieu of the stern light

04202. You are underway in fog when you hear the following signal: 1 short blast, 1 prolonged blast and 1 short blast in succession. Which of the following would it be?

A. a sailing vessel underway with the wind abaft the beam
B. a power-driven vessel underway and making way through the water
C. a vessel at anchor
D. a vessel towing

04203. If you hear the firing of a gun at 1 minute intervals from another vessel, this indicates that:

A. the gun is being used to sound passing signals

B. the vessel is in distress
C. all vessels are to clear the area
D. all is clear and it is safe to pass

04204. Fog signals, required under the Rules for vessels underway, shall be sounded:

A. only on the approach of another vessel
B. only when vessels are in sight of each other
C. at intervals of not more than 1 minute
D. at intervals of not more than 2 minutes

04205. A towing vessel is towing 2 barges astern. The length of the tow from the stern of the tug to the stern of the last barge is 250 meters. How many forward white masthead lights should be displayed on the towboat at night?

A. 1
B. 2
C. 3
D. 4

04206. At night, a vessel shall indicate that she is restricted in her ability to maneuver by showing in a vertical line 2:

A. red lights
B. red lights and 2 white lights
C. red lights with a white light in between
D. white lights with a red light in between

04207. Your power-driven vessel is underway when you sight a sailing vessel on your port bow. Which vessel is the "stand-on" vessel?

A. the sailboat, because it is to port of you
B. the sailboat, because it is under sail
C. your vessel, because it is power-driven
D. your vessel, because it is to starboard of the sailboat

04208. 5 or more short blasts on a vessel's whistle indicates that she is:

A. in doubt that another vessel is taking sufficient action to avoid a collision
B. altering course to starboard
C. altering course to port
D. the stand-on vessel and will maintain course and speed

04209. Which statement concerning maneuvering in restricted visibility is FALSE?

A. A vessel which cannot avoid a close-quarters situation with a vessel forward of her beam shall reduce her speed to bare steerageway.
B. A vessel which hears a fog signal forward of her beam shall stop her engines.
C. A vessel which hears a fog signal forward of the beam shall navigate with caution.

D. If a vessel determines by radar that a close-quarters situation is developing, she shall take avoiding action in ample time.

04210. A vessel being towed astern shall show at night:

A. the lights required for a power-driven vessel underway
B. only the required masthead lights
C. a stern light only
D. sidelights and a stern light

04211. In order for a stand-on vessel to take action in a situation, she must determine that the other vessel:

A. is restricted in her ability to maneuver
B. has sounded the danger signal
C. is not taking appropriate action
D. has not changed course since risk of collision was determined

04212. While underway your vessel approaches a bend in a river where, due to the bank, you cannot see around the bend. You should:

A. keep to the starboard side of the channel and sound 1 short blast
B. sound the danger signal
C. sound 1 prolonged blast
D. slow your vessel to bare steerageway

04213. Which statement concerning whistle signals is FALSE?

A. When a pushing vessel and a vessel pushed are connected in a composite unit, the unit sounds the fog signal of a power-driven vessel.
B. A vessel at anchor may sound 1 short, 1 prolonged, and 1 short blast.
C. A pilot vessel may sound an identity signal on the whistle.
D. A vessel engaged in towing in fog shall sound a fog signal at intervals of 1 minute.

04214. A sailing vessel of over 20 meters in length underway must show a:

A. red light over a green light at the masthead
B. white masthead light
C. combined lantern
D. stern light

04215. An inconspicuous, partly submerged vessel or object being towed, where the length of tow is 100 meters, shall show:

A. yellow lights at each end
B. 2 red lights in a vertical line
C. a black ball
D. a diamond shape

04216. You are approaching a narrow channel. You see a vessel that can only be navigated safely within the channel. You should:

A. initiate an exchange of passing signals
B. not cross the channel if you might impede the other vessel
C. sound the danger signal
D. hold your course and speed

04217. A man aboard a vessel, signaling by raising and lowering his outstretched arms to each side, is indicating:

A. danger, stay away
B. all is clear, it is safe to pass
C. the vessel is anchored
D. a distress signal

04218. A vessel showing the day signal shown in DIAGRAM 7 is:

A. not under command
B. a dredge underway and dredging
C. fishing
D. a hydrographic survey vessel underway

04219. Your 15-meter vessel is crossing a narrow channel and a large cargo vessel to port is within the channel and crossing your course. What is your responsibility?

A. Hold course and speed
B. Sound the danger signal
C. Initiate an exchange of passing signals
D. Do not cross the channel if you might impede the other vessel

04220. A vessel being towed shall show:

A. masthead lights
B. sidelights
C. a special flashing light
D. all of the above

04221. A power-driven vessel making way through the water would sound which of the following fog signals?

A. 2 short blasts every 1 minute
B. 1 short blast every 1 minute
C. 2 prolonged blasts every 2 minutes
D. 1 prolonged blast every 2 minutes

04222. You are towing 2 barges astern. The length of the tow from the stern of the tug to the stern of the last barge is 150 meters. How many forward white towing identification lights should be displayed on the towboat at night?

A. 1
B. 2

C. 3
D. 4

04223. Which vessel may show 3 lights in a vertical line, the top and bottom being red and the middle being white?

A. a vessel engaged in diving operations
B. a pilot vessel
C. a vessel trawling
D. all of the above

04224. A power-driven vessel has on her port side a sailing vessel which is on a collision course. The power-driven vessel is required to:

A. maintain course and speed
B. keep clear
C. sound 1 blast and turn to starboard
D. stop her engines

04225. A towing light will be carried above a vessel's stern light:

A. only if she is towing astern
B. only if the tow exceeds 200 meters
C. at any time when towing
D. if the towing vessel is restricted in her maneuverability

04226. What dayshape must be shown by a vessel 25 meters in length aground during daylight hours?

A. 1 black ball
B. 2 black balls
C. 3 black balls
D. 4 black balls

04227. An orange flag showing a black circle and square is recognized as being a:

A. signal indicating a course change
B. distress signal
C. signal of asking to communicate with another vessel
D. signal indicating danger

04228. When is a stand-on vessel first allowed to take action in order to avoid collision?

A. when the 2 vessels are less than half a mile from each other
B. when the give-way vessel is not taking appropriate action to avoid collision
C. when collision is imminent
D. The stand-on vessel is not allowed to take action at anytime.

04229. You are crossing a narrow channel in a 15-meter vessel when you sight a tankship off your port bow coming up the channel. Which statement is correct?

A. Yours is the give-way vessel because it is less than 30 meters long.
B. You may not impede the safe passage of the tankship.
C. The tankship has the right of way because it is to port of your vessel.
D. The tankship has the right of way because it is the larger of the 2 vessels.

04230. In restricted visibility, a vessel restricted in her ability to maneuver, at anchor, would sound a fog signal of:

A. the rapid ringing of a bell for 5 seconds every minute
B. 2 long and 2 short blasts every 2 minutes
C. 1 long and 2 short blasts every 2 minutes
D. 2 long and 1 short blast every 2 minutes

04231. A 15-meter sailing vessel would be required to show:

A. sidelights, stern light, and a red light over a green light on the mast
B. sidelights, and stern light, but they may be in a combined lantern on the mast
C. separate sidelights and stern light
D. sidelights only

04232. The use of the danger signal:

A. replaces directional signals
B. makes the other vessel the give-way vessel
C. indicates doubt as to the other vessel's action
D. makes it necessary to slow or stop

04233. While underway in fog, you hear the fog signal of another vessel ahead. If a risk of collision exists, you must:

A. slow to bare steerageway and navigate with caution
B. sound 3 short blasts and back engines
C. stop engines and navigate with caution
D. continue on your course and speed until the other vessel is sighted

04234. What lights, if any, would you exhibit at night if your vessel were broken down and being towed by another vessel?

A. none
B. same as a power-driven vessel underway
C. a white light forward and a white light aft
D. the colored sidelights and white stern light

04235. A vessel displaying the dayshapes illustrated in DIAGRAM 7 is:

A. broken down
B. fishing
C. a dredge
D. transferring dangerous cargo

04236. If your vessel is underway in fog and you hear 1 prolonged and 3 short blasts, this indicates a:

A. vessel not under command
B. sailing vessel
C. vessel in distress
D. vessel being towed

04237. At night, what lights would you see on a vessel engaged in fishing?

A. 2 red lights, 1 over the other
B. a green light over a red light
C. a red light over a white light
D. a white light over a red light

04238. During daylight hours, what should a vessel display to indicate that it is fishing?

A. a black ball
B. a green ball
C. a basket
D. a white flag

04239. You are on a vessel nearing a bend in the channel where, because of the height of the bank, you cannot see a vessel approaching from the opposite direction. You should sound:

A. 1 short blast
B. 1 prolonged blast
C. 1 long blast
D. 5 or more short blasts

04240. Which vessel is considered to be a "vessel restricted in her ability to maneuver" under the Navigational Rules?

A. a vessel at anchor
B. a vessel dredging
C. a vessel fishing
D. a vessel towing

04241. A tug is towing 3 manned barges in line in fog. The first vessel of the tow should sound:

A. no fog signal
B. 1 short blast
C. 1 prolonged and 3 short blasts
D. 1 prolonged, 1 short and 1 prolonged blast

04242. All fog signals shall be sounded every 2 minutes with the exception of a vessel:

A. underway or making way
B. under sail or under tow
C. anchored or aground
D. not under command or restricted in her ability to maneuver

04243. In reduced visibility, you hear 2 prolonged blasts of a whistle. This signal is sounded by a:

A. power-driven vessel dead in the water
B. sailing vessel on the port tack
C. vessel not under command
D. vessel fishing with nets

04244. A 200-meter vessel restricted in its ability to maneuver, at anchor, will sound a fog signal of:

A. a 5 second ringing of a bell forward and a 5 second sounding of a gong aft at intervals of 1 minute
B. 1 long and 2 short blasts every 2 minutes
C. 1 long and 3 short blasts every minute
D. 1 long and 3 short blasts every 2 minutes

04245. Underway at night, a vessel displaying the lights illustrated in DIAGRAM 62 is:

A. engaged in fishing
B. mine sweeping
C. a pilot boat
D. under sail

04246. A partially submerged object towed by a vessel must show during the day:

A. a diamond shape when the length of the tow is 200 meters or less
B. a diamond shape only when the length of the tow exceeds 200 meters in length
C. 1 black ball
D. 1 black ball only when the length of the tow exceeds 200 meters in length

04247. What dayshape is to be shown by a vessel aground?

A. a cylinder
B. 2 cones with their apexes together
C. 2 black balls in a vertical line
D. 3 black balls in a vertical line

04248. Which of the following is NOT a distress signal?

A. red flares or red rockets
B. continuous sounding of fog signal
C. Int'l Code Flags "November" and "Charlie"
D. basket hanging in the rigging

04249. Which statement is true concerning a vessel equipped with operational radar?

A. She must use this equipment to obtain early warning of risk of collision.
B. The use of a radar excuses a vessel from the need of a look-out.

C. The radar equipment is only required to be used in restricted visibility.
D. The safe speed of such a vessel will likely be greater than that of vessels without radar.

04250. A vessel displaying the lights illustrated in DIAGRAM 60 is:

A. towing
B. being towed
C. broken down
D. fishing

04251. At night, if you see a vessel ahead displaying the lights in DIAGRAM 70, you should:

A. provide assistance as the vessel is in distress
B. stay clear as the vessel is transferring dangerous cargo
C. stay clear as the vessel is fishing
D. change course to the right as the vessel is crossing your bow

04252. In daytime, a 19-meter vessel underway and fishing with nets or lines may indicate her occupation by displaying a:

A. black cone
B. black or white vertically striped ball
C. black ball
D. basket

04253. A pilot vessel on pilotage duty shall show identity lights:

A. at any time while underway
B. while at anchor
C. while alongside a vessel
D. all of the above

04254. You are operating in restricted visibility and hear a fog signal forward of the beam. Nothing appears on your radar screen. The Rules require you to:

A. stop your engines
B. sound 2 prolonged blasts of the whistle
C. sound the danger signal
D. slow to bare steerageway

04255. A stand-on vessel in a crossing situation is allowed to take action when:

A. collision is imminent
B. the distance between the vessels is less than 1 mile
C. it becomes apparent to her that the giveway vessel is not taking appropriate action
D. the relative speed of the vessels indicates that they will meet in less than 3 minutes

04256. If you approach a vessel in a narrow channel, and that vessel can only be navigated safely within the channel, you should:

A. hold your course and speed
B. sound the danger signal
C. initiate an exchange of passing signals
D. not cross the channel if you might impede the other vessel

04257. Which vessel is required to sound a fog signal of 1 prolonged followed by 2 short blasts?

A. a vessel not under command
B. a sailing vessel, underway
C. a vessel restricted in its ability to maneuver, at anchor
D. all of the above

04258. At night, a broken down vessel being towed would show the same lights as:

A. a power-driven vessel underway
B. the towing vessel
C. a barge
D. a vessel at anchor

04259. What is the optional whistle signal which may be sounded by a vessel at anchor?

A. 2 prolonged followed by 1 short blast
B. 1 short followed by 2 prolonged blasts
C. 1 short, 1 prolonged, followed by 1 short blast
D. 4 short blasts

04260. The minimum length of a power-driven vessel that must show forward and after masthead lights is:

A. 30 meters
B. 50 meters
C. 75 meters
D. 100 meters

04261. What light(s), if any, would you show at night if your vessel was broken down and being towed by another vessel?

A. none
B. same as for a power-driven vessel underway
C. a white light forward and a white light aft
D. colored sidelights and a white stern light

04262. A vessel not under command making way at night would show:

A. 2 all-round red lights in a vertical line
B. anchor lights and running lights
C. 2 all-round white lights in a vertical line, sidelights and a stern light
D. 2 all-round red lights in a vertical line, sidelights, and a stern light

04263. In a dense fog, you hear a whistle signal of 1 prolonged blast followed by 3 short blasts. This signal is blown by a:

A. manned vessel being towed
B. fishing vessel underway trawling
C. pilot vessel underway making a special signal
D. vessel not under command

04264. Because of her occupation, a vessel shows a dayshape of 2 cones with apexes together. If under 20 meters length, she may instead show:

A. a diamond shape
B. 2 balls in a vertical line
C. a basket
D. none of the above

04265. While underway and pushing a barge ahead, your vessel enters a heavy rain storm. You should sound:

A. a long blast every 2 minutes
B. 2 long blasts every 2 minutes
C. 1 long and 2 short blasts every 2 minutes
D. 1 long blast every 2 minutes

04266. On open waters, a power-driven vessel shall keep out of the way of a:

A. vessel on her port side crossing her course
B. vessel that is overtaking her
C. seaplane on the water
D. sailing vessel

04267. You are overtaking a vessel at night and you see a yellow light showing above the stern light of the overtaken vessel. The overtaken vessel is:

A. underway and dredging
B. pushing ahead or towing alongside
C. towing astern
D. a pilot vessel

04268. Your vessel is at anchor in fog. The fog signal of another vessel, apparently underway, has been growing louder and the danger of collision appears to exist. In addition to the required fog signal, what signal may be used to indicate your presence?

A. 5 or more short rapid whistle blasts
B. 1 short, 1 long, and 1 short whistle blast
C. 1 long followed by 2 short whistle blasts
D. No other signal may be used

04269. All of the following are distress signals under the Rules EXCEPT:

A. International Code Signal "AA"
B. orange-colored smoke

C. red flares
D. the repeated raising and lowering of out-stretched arms

04270. A vessel displaying the lights illustrated in DIAGRAM 70 is a:

A. pilot boat
B. sailboat
C. fishing vessel
D. motorboat

04271. A tug is towing 3 manned barges in line in fog. The third vessel of the tow should sound:

A. no fog signal
B. 1 short blast
C. 1 prolonged and 3 short blasts
D. 1 prolonged, 1 short and 1 prolonged blast

04272. A power-driven vessel, when towing another vessel astern shall show:

A. 2 towing lights in a vertical line
B. a towing light above the stern light
C. a towing light below the stern light
D. only a stern light at the stern

04273. Which vessel is NOT classified as "restricted in her ability to maneuver"?

A. a vessel picking up a navigation mark
B. a vessel transferring cargo while underway
C. a vessel whose anchor is fouled
D. a vessel in a towing operation that restricts the ability of the vessel and her tow to change their course

04274. During the day, a vessel picking up a submarine cable shall carry:

A. 3 shapes, the highest and lowest shall be red balls, and the middle a white diamond
B. 2 black balls
C. 3 shapes; the highest and lowest shall be black balls, and the middle a red diamond
D. 3 shapes; the highest and lowest shall be black balls and the middle a black diamond

04275. While underway in fog, you hear a prolonged blast from another vessel. This signal indicates a:

A. sailboat underway
B. power-driven vessel underway, towing
C. power-driven vessel underway
D. vessel being towed

04276. While underway your vessel enters fog. You stop your engines and the vessel is dead in the water. What fog signal should you sound?

A. 1 prolonged blast every 2 minutes
B. 2 prolonged blasts every 2 minutes
C. 3 short blasts every 2 minutes
D. 1 long and 2 short blasts every 2 minutes

04277. You are underway in a fog when you hear a whistle signal of 1 prolonged blast followed by 2 short blasts. This signal could indicate all of the following EXCEPT a vessel:

A. being towed
B. not under command
C. fishing with trawls
D. towing astern

04278. A light signal consisting of 3 flashes means:

A. "I am in doubt as to your actions"
B. "My engines are full speed astern"
C. "I desire to overtake you"
D. "I am operating astern propulsion"

04279. You are watching another vessel approach and her compass bearing is not changing. This indicates that:

A. you are the stand-on vessel
B. a risk of collision exists
C. a special circumstances situation exists
D. the other vessel is dead in the water

04280. Vessels I and II are underway as shown in DIAGRAM 33. Vessel I is a sailing vessel with the wind dead aft. Vessel II is a power-driven vessel trawling. Which statement is true?

A. Vessel I is to keep clear because the other vessel is fishing.
B. Vessel II is to keep clear because it is a power-driven vessel.
C. Vessel II is to keep clear because the other vessel is to its starboard.
D. Both vessels are to take action to stay clear of each other.

04281. A vessel 30 meters in length and aground would display a dayshape consisting of:

A. a cylinder
B. 1 black ball
C. 2 black balls in a vertical line
D. 3 black balls in a vertical line

04282. A vessel displaying the lights illustrated in DIAGRAM 63 is:

A. towing astern
B. underway and more than 50 m in length
C. broken down
D. fishing

04283. Which of the following is NOT a distress signal?

A. a continuous sounding of the fog horn
B. firing a gun every minute
C. 5 or more short rapid blasts on the whistle
D. a square flag and ball flown from the mast

04284. Which statement is true concerning a vessel equipped with operational radar?

A. The Master of the vessel must be on the bridge when the radar is in use.
B. The radar equipment is only required to be used in restricted visibility.
C. The use of a radar excuses a vessel from the need of a look-out.
D. This equipment must be used to obtain early warning of risk of collision.

04285. While underway in fog you hear another vessel sounding 2 prolonged blasts every 2 minutes. This signal indicates a vessel:

A. making way through the water
B. towing
C. drifting
D. anchored

04286. A vessel which is underway at night and displaying the lights illustrated in DIAGRAM 69 is:

A. engaged in trawling
B. minesweeping
C. under sail
D. a pilot boat

04287. Fog signals for vessels not underway, other than fishing vessels or those restricted in their ability to maneuver, shall be sounded at intervals of not more than:

A. 15 minutes
B. 5 minutes
C. 2 minutes
D. 1 minute

04288. A vessel is carrying 3 lights in a vertical line. The highest and lowest of these are red and the middle light is white. Which statement is always true?

A. During the day, she would display 3 balls in a vertical line.
B. If making way, she would show masthead lights at night.
C. If at anchor, she need not show anchor lights while displaying identifying lights.
D. Her fog signal would consist of a rapid ringing of a bell for 5 seconds every minute.

04289. You are on a power-driven vessel in fog. Your vessel is proceeding at a safe speed when you hear a fog signal ahead of you. In this situation, the Rules require you to navigate with caution until the danger of collision is over and to:

A. slow to less than 2 knots
B. reduce to bare steerageway
C. stop your engines
D. initiate a radar plot

04290. While underway in a fog you hear a signal of 3 strokes of a bell, a rapid ringing of the bell and 3 more strokes of the bell. This signal is made by a vessel:

A. at anchor and giving warning
B. aground
C. at anchor and greater than 100 m in length
D. not under command and at anchor

04291. The maximum length of a power-driven vessel which may show an all-round white light and sidelights instead of a masthead light, sidelights and a stern light is:

A. 7 meters
B. 10 meters
C. 11 meters
D. 20 meters

04292. While underway in fog, you hear a signal of 1 prolonged blast followed by 3 short blasts. This is the fog signal for a vessel:

A. towing
B. being towed (manned)
C. under sail
D. at anchor

04293. Which vessel is to sound a fog signal of 1 prolonged followed by 2 short blasts?

A. a vessel not under command
B. a sailing vessel underway
C. a vessel restricted in ability to maneuver, at anchor
D. all of the above

04294. At night you observe a vessel ahead to show 3 flashes of a white light. This signal indicates that the vessel ahead is:

A. in distress
B. approaching a bend in the channel
C. operating astern propulsion
D. intending to overtake another vessel

04295. The use of the danger signal:

A. replaces directional signals
B. makes the other the stand-on vessel

C. indicates doubt as to another vessel's actions
D. is used as a "MAYDAY" signal

04296. Which power-driven vessel is NOT required to carry a light in the position of the after masthead light?

A. a pushing vessel and a vessel being pushed, in a composite unit and 100 m in length
B. a vessel of 60 m in length towing astern
C. a vessel of 45 m in length trolling
D. any vessel constrained by her draft

04297. Which requirement must be met in order for a stand-on vessel to take action to avoid collision in accordance with Rule 17?

A. Risk of collision must have been deemed to exist.
B. The give-way vessel must have taken no action.
C. The vessels must be within half a mile of each other.
D. There are no requirements to be met. The stand-on vessel may take action anytime.

04298. A vessel being towed alongside shall exhibit:

A. 1 all-round white light
B. sidelights and a stern light
C. only the outboard sidelight and a stern light
D. a masthead light, sidelights, and a stern light

04299. You are crossing a narrow channel on your 15-meter vessel with a deeply loaded cargo vessel proceeding down the channel as shown in DIAGRAM 40. In this situation, which statement is correct?

A. You have the right of way because you are less than 65 feet in length.
B. You cannot impede the passage of the cargo vessel.
C. The cargo vessel has the right of way because it is running with the current.
D. The Rule of Special Circumstances applies in this case.

04300. At night, a vessel displaying the lights illustrated in DIAGRAM 46 is:

A. sailing
B. fishing and making way
C. a pilot boat making way
D. fishing and anchored

04301. In which situation would risk of collision exist?

A. A vessel is 22 degrees on your port bow, range increasing, bearing changing slightly to the right.

B. A vessel is broad on your starboard beam, range decreasing, bearing changing rapidly to the right.
C. A vessel is 22 degrees abaft your port beam, range increasing, bearing is constant.
D. A vessel is on your starboard quarter, range decreasing, bearing is constant.

04302. A vessel nearing a bend or an area of a channel or fairway where other vessels may be obscured by an intervening obstruction shall sound:

A. 1 long blast
B. 1 prolonged blast
C. the danger signal
D. 2 short blasts

04303. In fog, you hear apparently forward of your beam a fog signal of 2 prolonged blasts in succession every 2 minutes. This signal indicates a:

A. power-driven vessel making way through the water
B. vessel being pushed ahead
C. vessel restricted in her ability to maneuver
D. power-driven vessel underway but stopped and making no way through the water

04304. A vessel being towed will show:

A. a forward masthead light
B. sidelights
C. a towing light
D. all of the above

04305. In fog, a vessel being towed, if manned, shall sound a fog signal of:

A. 2 short blasts
B. 3 short blasts
C. 1 prolonged and 2 short blasts
D. 1 prolonged and 3 short blasts

04306. Which vessel is directed not to impede the passage of a vessel which can only navigate inside a narrow channel?

A. a vessel of less than 20 meters in length
B. a vessel not under command
C. a vessel engaged in surveying
D. all of the above

04307. While you are underway, navigation lights must be displayed on your vessel:

A. during all periods of reduced visibility
B. at all times
C. at night only when other vessels may be in area
D. at night only when vessels are detected on radar

04308. When underway in fog, you might hear any of the following fog signals EXCEPT:

A. 1 prolonged blast at intervals of 1 minute
B. 2 prolonged blasts at intervals of 1 minute
C. 1 prolonged and 2 short blasts at intervals of 2 minutes
D. ringing of a bell for 5 seconds at intervals of 2 minutes

04309. What dayshape must be shown on a partially submerged vessel which is being towed?

A. a diamond
B. a cone
C. 1 black ball
D. 2 black balls in a vertical line

04310. Which vessel is to be regarded as a vessel "restricted in her ability to maneuver"?

A. a vessel fishing with trawls
B. a vessel which has lost the use of her steering gear
C. a vessel with a draft of such depth that she cannot change her course
D. a vessel engaged in mineclearing

04311. Which of the following vessels would show 3 dayshapes in a vertical line, the highest and lowest being balls and the middle shape being a diamond?

A. vessel not under command
B. vessel constrained by her draft
C. vessel minesweeping
D. vessel restricted in her ability to maneuver

04312. A power-driven vessel "not under command" at night must show how many lights in a vertical line?

A. 3 red
B. 2 red
C. 2 white
D. 3 white

04313. While underway at night, you sight a vessel ahead displaying the lights shown in DIAGRAM 71. How should the vessels pass?

A. Both vessels should alter course to starboard and pass port to port.
B. Both vessels should alter course to port and pass starboard to starboard.
C. Your vessel should hold course and speed and the other vessel should keep clear.
D. You should sound an appropriate overtaking signal.

04314. In order for a vessel to be "engaged in fishing" she must be:

A. underway
B. using gear which extends more than 50 meters outboard
C. using a seine of some type
D. using gear restricting her maneuverability

04315. While underway and in sight of another vessel you put your engines on astern propulsion. Which statement concerning whistle signals is true?

A. You must sound 3 short blasts on the whistle.
B. You must sound 1 blast if backing to starboard.
C. You must sound whistle signals only if the vessels are meeting.
D. You need not sound any whistle signals.

04316. When shall the stand-on vessel in a crossing situation take action to avoid the other vessel?

A. when a risk of collision exists.
B. when action by the give-way vessel alone will not prevent a collision.
C. when the bearing to give-way vessel becomes steady.
D. when the vessels become less than 1/2 mile apart.

04317. What signal would a vessel aground show during daylight?

A. 1 black ball
B. 2 black balls
C. 3 black balls
D. 4 black balls

04318. Which of the following would NOT be a distress signal?

A. flames on a vessel
B. vertical motion of a white lantern at night
C. code flags "November" and "Charlie"
D. dye marker on the water

04319. Which statement about a 25-meter auxiliary sailboat is true?

A. The sidelights and stern light may be combined in 1 lantern.
B. When operating under sail, her fog signal would consist of 1 prolonged blast.
C. She may show a green light over a red light at the masthead.
D. She must show fixed sidelights, and may not use a portable lantern.

04320. Which of the following vessels shall not impede the passage of a vessel which can safely navigate only within a narrow channel or fairway?

A. a vessel of less than 20 meters in length
B. a vessel sailing
C. a vessel fishing
D. all of the above

04321. While underway in a fog, you hear a whistle signal of 1 prolonged blast followed by 2 short blasts. This signal could mean all of the following EXCEPT a vessel:

A. not under command
B. towing astern
C. fishing with trawls
D. being towed

04322. In which situation would you consider a risk of collision to exist?

A. A vessel is 22° on your port bow, range increasing, bearing changing slightly to right.
B. A vessel is broad on your starboard beam, range decreasing, bearing changing rapidly to the right.
C. A vessel is 22° abaft your port beam, range increasing, bearing is constant.
D. A vessel is on your starboard quarter, range decreasing, bearing is constant.

04323. A vessel displaying the lights illustrated in DIAGRAM 53 is a:

A. vessel engaged on pilotage duty
B. vessel engaged in fishing
C. vessel under sail
D. power-driven vessel underway

04324. Vessel "A" is overtaking vessel "B". Vessel "B":

A. should change course to the right
B. should slow until vessel "A" has passed
C. should hold her course and speed
D. may steer various courses and vessel "A" must keep clear

04325. A vessel aground in fog shall sound, in addition to the proper anchor signal, which of the following?

A. 3 strokes before and after sounding on the gong
B. 3 strokes before and after the ringing of the bell
C. 4 short blasts on the whistle
D. 1 prolonged and 1 short blast on the whistle

04326. A vessel which, because of her occupation, shows a dayshape of 2 cones with their apexes together may, if under 20 meters in length, show:

A. a diamond shape
B. 2 balls in a vertical line

C. a basket
D. none of the above

04327. 2 vessels are approaching each other near head on. What action should be taken to avoid collision?

A. The first vessel to sight the other should give way.
B. The vessel making the slower speed should give way.
C. Both vessels should alter course to starboard.
D. Both vessels should alter course to port.

04329. Your vessel is 25 meters long and anchored in restricted visibility. You are required to sound the proper fog signal at intervals of not more than:

A. 30 seconds
B. 1 minute
C. 2 minutes
D. 3 minutes

04330. While underway in fog, you hear a short blast, a prolonged blast and a short blast of a whistle. This signal indicates a:

A. vessel towing in fog
B. sailboat underway in fog
C. vessel being towed in fog
D. vessel anchored in fog

04331. You see the lights illustrated in DIAGRAM 77. Which of the following would it be?

A. a vessel pushing barges ahead
B. a vessel towing barges astern
C. a pipeline
D. a stationary dredge

04332. In a crossing situation in which you are the stand-on vessel, you may hold your course and speed until:

A. the other vessel takes necessary action
B. the other vessel gets to within half a mile of your vessel
C. action by the give-way vessel alone will not prevent collision
D. the other vessel gets to within a quarter mile of your vessel

04333. The arc of visibility for sidelights is from right ahead to:

A. 22.5 degrees abaft the beam
B. abeam
C. 22.5 degrees forward of the beam
D. 135 degrees abaft the beam

04334. In narrow channels, vessels of less than what length shall not impede the safe passage of vessels which can navigate only inside that channel?

A. 20 meters
B. 50 meters
C. 65 meters
D. 100 meters

04335. At night a vessel displaying the lights illustrated in DIAGRAM 82 is:

A. sailing
B. fishing
C. a pilot boat
D. anchored

04336. While underway and in sight of another vessel, you put your engines full astern. Which statement concerning whistle signals is true?

A. You must sound 3 short blasts on the whistle.
B. You must sound 1 blast if backing to starboard.
C. You must sound whistle signals only if the vessels are meeting.
D. You need not sound any whistle signals.

04337. A vessel showing a yellow light over a white light at night is a vessel:

A. engaged in piloting
B. towing astern
C. engaged in fishing
D. in distress

04338. A vessel hearing a fog signal forward of her beam shall reduce speed to:

A. moderate speed
B. safe speed
C. half speed
D. the minimum where the vessel can be kept on course

04339. 2 vessels are in an overtaking situation. Which of the following lights on the overtaken vessel shall be visible to the vessel overtaking?

A. 2 masthead lights and a stern light
B. 1 masthead light, sidelights and stern light
C. Sidelights only
D. Stern light only

04340. While underway and making way your vessel enters fog. What fog signal should you sound every 2 minutes?

A. 1 prolonged blast
B. 2 prolonged blasts
C. 3 short blasts
D. A prolonged blast and 3 short blasts

04341. On open water, a vessel fishing is in a crossing situation with a vessel sailing located on the fishing vessel's starboard side. Which vessel is the stand-on vessel?

A. the fishing vessel because it is to port of the sailing vessel.
B. the fishing vessel because it is fishing.
C. the sailing vessel because it is to starboard of the fishing vessel.
D. the sailing vessel because it is sailing.

04342. The lights prescribed by the Rules shall be exhibited:

A. from sunrise to sunset in restricted visibility
B. at all times
C. only from sunset to sunrise
D. whenever a look-out is posted

04343. Risk of collision may exist:

A. if the compass bearing of an approaching vessel does NOT appreciably change
B. even when an appreciable bearing change is evident, particularly when approaching a vessel at close range
C. if you observe both sidelights of a vessel ahead for an extended period of time
D. all of the above

04344. "Safe speed" is defined as speed where:

A. you can stop within your visibility range
B. you can take proper and effective action to avoid collision
C. you are traveling slower than surrounding vessels
D. no wake comes from your vessel

04345. A vessel showing a green light over a white light in a vertical line above the level of the sidelights is:

A. engaged in underwater construction
B. under sail and power
C. a pilot vessel
D. trawling

04346. A vessel or object being towed at night must show:

A. a white all-round light
B. sidelights and a stern light
C. a flashing yellow light
D. forward and after masthead lights

04347. To determine if risk of collision exists, a vessel must use:

A. radar scanning
B. radar plotting

C. compass bearings
D. all of the above

04348. You are on vessel "A" pushing a barge ahead and meeting vessel "B" as shown in DIAGRAM 12. How should the vessels pass?

A. Both vessels must alter course to starboard and pass port to port.
B. Both vessels must alter course to port and pass starboard to starboard.
C. Vessel "A" should maintain course and vessel "B" alter course.
D. The vessels should determine which will alter course by sounding whistle signals.

04349. If a vessel is engaged in fishing, according to the definitions in the Rules, it will have:

A. gear extending from the side or stern
B. gear that restricts maneuverability
C. less than 50 percent trolling lines
D. none of the above

04350. While underway in fog you hear rapid ringing of a bell. What does this signal indicate?

A. a vessel backing down
B. a sailboat underway
C. a vessel at anchor
D. a vessel drifting

04351. 2 power-driven vessels are crossing so as to involve risk of collision. Which statement is true, according to the Rules?

A. The vessel which has the other on her own port side shall keep out of the way.
B. If the stand-on vessel takes action, she shall avoid changing course to port.
C. If the give-way vessel takes action, she shall avoid changing course to starboard.
D. The give-way vessel should keep the other vessel to her starboard.

04352. What is the minimum vessel length which must show 2 white masthead lights when underway at night?

A. 7 meters
B. 20 meters
C. 50 meters
D. 100 meters

04353. Every vessel that is to keep out of the way of another vessel must take positive action early to comply with this obligation and must:

A. avoid crossing ahead of the other vessel
B. avoid passing astern of the other vessel
C. sound 1 prolonged blast to indicate compliance
D. alter course to port for a vessel on port side

04354. At night, a power-driven vessel less than 12 meters in length may, instead of the normal running lights, show sidelights and 1:

A. white light
B. yellow light
C. flashing white light
D. flashing yellow light

04355. You are crossing a narrow channel in an 18-meter tug when you sight a loaded tankship off your port bow coming up the channel. Which statement is correct?

A. Neither vessel has the right of way because the tankship is crossing.
B. You cannot impede the safe passage of the tankship.
C. The tankship has the right of way because it is in the channel.
D. The tankship has the right of way because it is the larger of the 2 vessels.

04356. A vessel engaged in fishing underway sounds the same fog signal as a:

A. power-driven vessel stopped and making no way through the water
B. vessel being towed
C. vessel restricted in her ability to maneuver at anchor
D. sailing vessel at anchor

04357. A vessel 15 meters in length which is proceeding under sail as well as being propelled by machinery shall exhibit during daytime:

A. 1 black ball
B. a basket
C. a cone with its apex downward
D. 2 cones with their apexes together

04358. Which of the following should not impede the navigation of a power-driven vessel?

A. a vessel not under command
B. a vessel engaged in fishing
C. a sailing vessel
D. a seaplane

04359. Your vessel is underway but stopped and making no way through the water when fog sets in. What fog signal would you sound?

A. 1 prolonged blast on the whistle
B. 1 prolonged blast and 2 short blasts on the whistle
C. 2 prolonged blasts on the whistle
D. 1 short, 1 prolonged, and 1 short blast on the whistle

04360. While underway, you see a vessel displaying the dayshapes shown in DIAGRAM 6. What action should you take?

A. Maintain course and speed.
B. Provide assistance, the other vessel is in distress.
C. Stay clear, the other vessel cannot get out of the way.
D. Stop your vessel and sound passing signals.

04361. A vessel towed alongside shall show:

A. 1 all-round white light
B. sidelights and a stern light
C. only the outboard sidelight and a stern light
D. a masthead light, sidelights, and a stern light

04362. A vessel underway and fishing shall keep out of the way of a:

A. power-driven vessel underway
B. vessel not under command
C. vessel sailing
D. vessel engaged on pilotage duty

04363. A vessel displaying the day shape illustrated in DIAGRAM 10 is:

A. broken down
B. anchored
C. towing
D. fishing

04364. The whistle signal for a vessel operating astern propulsion is:

A. 1 long blast
B. 1 prolonged blast
C. 3 short blasts
D. 4 or more short blasts

04365. A vessel restricted in her ability to maneuver which is at anchor must show at night which of the following lights?

A. 3 all-round red-white-red lights in a vertical line and anchor lights
B. 3 all-round red-white-red lights in a vertical line only
C. anchor lights only
D. anchor lights and sidelights only

04366. Which vessel is a "vessel restricted in her ability to maneuver" under the Rules?

A. a vessel mineclearing
B. a vessel engaged in fishing
C. a vessel at anchor
D. a vessel not under command

04367. Which of the following would NOT be a distress signal?

A. "MAYDAY" sent by radiotelephone
B. continuous sounding of fog horn
C. green star shells fired from a launcher
D. square flag and ball in a vertical line

04368. In a dense fog you hear a whistle signal ahead of 1 prolonged blast followed by 3 short blasts. This signal indicates a:

A. fishing vessel underway trawling
B. manned vessel being towed
C. pilot vessel underway making a special signal
D. vessel not under command

04369. If a towing vessel and her tow are severely restricted in their ability to deviate from their course, they may show lights in addition to their towing identification lights. These additional lights may be shown if the tow is:

A. pushed ahead
B. towed alongside
C. towed astern
D. any of the above

04370. At night, which lights would indicate to you that a vessel is fishing?

A. 2 red lights, 1 over the other
B. a green light over a red light
C. a red light over a white light
D. a white light over a red light

04371. A head-on situation at night would be 1 in which you see:

A. 1 sidelight of a vessel ahead of you
B. 1 sidelight and a masthead light of a vessel ahead of you
C. 1 sidelight, a masthead light and a range light of a vessel ahead of you
D. both sidelights of a vessel ahead of you

04372. You are the stand-on vessel in a crossing situation. If the give-way vessel is not taking sufficient action to avoid collision, and you are in doubt, you should sound:

A. 1 short blast and maintain course
B. 1 short blast and back down
C. no signal and maneuver at will
D. the danger signal

04373. A lantern combining the 2 sidelights of a vessel's running lights may be shown on a:

A. 10-meter sailing vessel
B. 20-meter vessel fishing and making way
C. 25-meter power-driven vessel trolling
D. 25-meter pilot vessel

04374. A vessel aground would show the same dayshape as a:

A. vessel towing a submerged object
B. dredge underway and dredging
C. hydrographic survey vessel at anchor and surveying
D. none of the above

04375. You are underway in a fog when you hear a signal of 3 strokes of a bell, a rapid ringing of the bell, and 3 more strokes of the bell. This signal indicates a vessel:

A. at anchor, giving warning
B. aground
C. at anchor, greater than 100 meters
D. not under command at anchor

04376. A power driven vessel "not under command" at night must show her sidelights when:

A. making headway
B. making no headway
C. moored to a buoy
D. at anchor

04377. The term "prolonged blast" means a blast of from:

A. 2 to 4 seconds duration
B. 4 to six seconds duration
C. six to eight seconds duration
D. eight to ten seconds duration

04378. While you are underway, navigation lights must be displayed on your vessel:

A. during all periods of reduced visibility
B. at all times
C. at night only when other vessels may be in the area
D. at night only when vessels are detected on radar

04379. Which statement is true concerning risk of collision?

A. The stand-on vessel must keep out of the way of the other vessel when risk of collision exists.
B. Risk of collision always exists when 2 vessels pass within 1 mile of each other.
C. Risk of collision always exists when the compass bearing of an approaching vessel changes appreciably.
D. Risk of collision may exist when the compass bearing of an approaching vessel is changing appreciably.

04380. A vessel nearing a bend where other vessels may be obscured shall sound:

A. 1 short blast
B. 1 long blast
C. 2 short blasts
D. 1 prolonged blast

04381. A vessel that is defined as "restricted in her ability to maneuver" is unable to keep out of the way of another vessel due to:

A. her draft
B. the nature of her work
C. some exceptional circumstances
D. a danger of navigation

04382. While underway in fog, you hear a vessel sound 4 short blasts in succession. What does this signal indicate?

A. a pilot vessel
B. a vessel being towed
C. a vessel fishing
D. a sailboat

04383. You are in charge of a stand-on vessel in a crossing situation. The other vessel is 1.5 miles to port. You have determined that risk of collision exists. You should:

A. take avoiding action immediately upon determining that risk of collision exists
B. immediately sound the danger signal
C. take avoiding action only after providing the give-way vessel time to take action, and determining that her action is not appropriate
D. hold your course and speed until the point of extremis, and then sound the danger signal, taking whatever action will best avert collision

04384. Vessel "A" and vessel "B", which is towing, are meeting head and head as shown in DIAGRAM 8. How must the vessel pass?

A. Vessel "A" must alter course while vessel "B" continues on its present course.
B. The vessels should determine which will alter course by exchanging whistle signals.
C. Both vessels should alter course to port and pass starboard to starboard.
D. Both vessels should alter course to starboard and pass port to port.

04385. To be considered "engaged in fishing" according to the Rules of the Road, a vessel must be:

A. using fishing apparatus which restricts maneuverability
B. using trolling lines
C. power-driven
D. showing lights or shapes for a vessel restricted in her ability to maneuver

04386. While underway in fog you hear a rapid ringing of a bell ahead. This bell indicates a:

A. vessel at anchor
B. vessel in distress

C. sailboat underway
D. vessel backing out of a berth

04387. An overtaking situation would be 1 in which 1 vessel is approaching another from more than how many degrees abaft the beam?

A. 0 degrees
B. 10 degrees
C. 22.5 degrees
D. none of the above

04389. An overtaking situation at night would be 1 in which 1 vessel sees which of the following lights of a vessel ahead?

A. masthead lights and sidelights
B. sidelights and stern light
C. sidelights only
D. stern light only

04390. What lights must sailboats show when underway at night?

A. 1 all-round white light
B. a stern light
C. red and green side lights
D. red and green side lights and a stern light

04391. You are crossing a narrow channel in a small motorboat when you sight a tankship off your port bow coming up the channel. Which statement is correct?

A. Yours is the give-way vessel because you are crossing the channel.
B. You cannot impede the safe passage of the tankship.
C. The tankship has the right of way because it is to port of your vessel.
D. The tankship has the right of way because it is the larger of the 2 vessels.

04392. Which vessel does NOT sound a fog signal of 1 prolonged followed by 2 short blasts?

A. a vessel dredging
B. a vessel being towed
C. a vessel engaged in fishing
D. a sailing vessel

04393. Which light(s) is(are) among those shown by a 200-meter vessel at anchor?

A. in the forepart of the vessel, a 225° white light
B. in the aft part of the vessel, a 135° white light
C. any available working lights to illuminate the decks
D. in the fore part of the vessel, a 135° white light

04394. A partly submerged vessel or object being towed, which is not readily noticeable, shall show:

A. yellow lights at each end
B. 2 red lights in a vertical line
C. a black ball
D. a diamond shape

04395. At night, if you saw the lights illustrated in DIAGRAM 73, what would they indicate?

A. a fishing vessel trolling
B. a vessel laying submarine cable
C. a vessel towing astern
D. a vessel dredging

04396. Concerning the identification signal for a pilot vessel, in fog, which statement is true?

A. When at anchor, the pilot vessel is only required to sound anchor signals.
B. The identification signal must be sounded any time the pilot vessel is underway.
C. The pilot vessel may only sound the identity signal when making way.
D. all of the above

04397. In a crossing situation, a vessel fishing must keep out of the way of a vessel which is:

A. under sail
B. towing
C. restricted in her ability to maneuver
D. engaged in pilot duty

04398. A towboat displaying the dayshape illustrated in DIAGRAM 10 .

A. is at anchor
B. is not under command
C. has a tow that exceeds 200 meters in length
D. has a tow that is carrying dangerous cargo

04399. Which vessel would display a cone, apex downward?

A. a fishing vessel with outlying gear
B. a vessel proceeding under sail and power
C. a vessel engaged in diving operations
D. a vessel being towed

04400. When action to avoid a close quarters situation is taken, a course change alone may be the most effective action provided that:

A. it is done in a succession of small course changes
B. it is not done too early
C. it is a large course change
D. the course change is to starboard

04401. You are underway in heavy fog and hear the fog signal of a vessel which is in an undetermined position ahead of your vessel. As far as circumstances permit, you must:

A. slow to moderate speed and then navigate with caution
B. maintain speed and sound the danger signal
C. stop engines and then navigate with caution
D. slow to bare steerageway and then navigate with caution

04402. A vessel at anchor will show a:

A. ball
B. cone
C. cylinder
D. double cone, apexes together

04403. What dayshape must be shown by a vessel fishing which has gear extending more than 150 meters horizontally outward from it?

A. 1 black ball
B. 1 diamond shape
C. 1 cone with its apex upwards
D. 1 basket

04404. A vessel in a towing operation which severely restricts the towing vessel and her tow in their ability to change course shall, when making way, exhibit:

A. the lights for a towing vessel
B. the lights for a vessel restricted in its ability to maneuver
C. sidelights and sternlights
D. all of the above

04405. A vessel underway but not making way and fishing other than trawling would show which of the following lights?

A. a white light over a red light
B. a red light over a white light
C. a white light over a red light, sidelights and a stern light
D. a red light over a white light, sidelights and a stern light

04406. 2 power-driven vessels are crossing as shown in DIAGRAM 42 . Vessel "A" sounds 3 short blasts on the whistle. This signal means that vessel "A":

A. intends to hold course and speed
B. is sounding the danger signal
C. is backing engines
D. proposes to cross ahead of the other vessel

04407. A 200-meter vessel is aground in restricted visibility. Which signal is optional?

A. a bell signal
B. a gong signal
C. a whistle signal
D. all of the above

04408. A fishing vessel displaying the lights illustrated in DIAGRAM 67 is:

A. anchored
B. underway but not fishing
C. tending a small fishing boat
D. fishing by trawling

04409. A vessel or object being towed shall display a(n):

A. forward masthead light
B. after masthead light
C. stern light
D. all of the above

04410. The rules state that vessels may depart from the requirements of the Rules when:

A. there are no other vessels around
B. operating in a narrow channel
C. the Master enters it in the ship's log
D. necessary to avoid immediate danger

04411. For the purpose of the Rules, except where otherwise required, the term:

A. "vessel" includes seaplanes
B. "seaplane" includes nondisplacement craft
C. "vessel engaged in fishing" includes a vessel fishing with trolling lines
D. "vessel restricted in her ability to maneuver" includes fishing vessels

04412. A vessel displaying the lights illustrated in DIAGRAM 44 is:

A. towing
B. conducting underwater survey operations
C. drifting
D. aground

04413. Which statement is true concerning a 75-m power-driven vessel underway at night?

A. She must exhibit an all-round white light at the stern.
B. She must exhibit forward and after masthead lights.
C. She must exhibit only a forward masthead light.
D. She may exhibit a red light over a green light forward.

04414. Every vessel which is directed by these Rules to keep out of the way of another vessel shall, if the circumstances of the case admit, avoid:

A. crossing ahead of the other
B. crossing astern of the other
C. passing port to port
D. passing starboard to starboard

04415. Which of the following is the danger signal?

A. a continuous sounding of the fog horn
B. firing a gun every minute
C. 5 or more short rapid blasts on the whistle
D. 1 long blast on the whistle

04416. Navigation lights must be displayed in all weathers from sunset to sunrise. They:

A. must be displayed when day signals are being used
B. must be displayed when moored to a pier
C. may be extinguished at night on open waters when no other vessels are in the area
D. may be displayed during daylight

04417. Which of the following would describe a head-on situation?

A. Seeing 1 red light of a vessel directly ahead.
B. Seeing 2 forward white towing identification lights in a vertical line on a towing vessel directly ahead.
C. Seeing both sidelights of a vessel directly off your starboard beam.
D. Seeing both sidelights of a vessel directly ahead.

04418. When 2 vessels are in immediate danger of collision, the stand-on vessel must:

A. abandon ship
B. assist in taking whatever action is necessary to avoid collision
C. hold course and speed
D. sound a distress signal

04419. A vessel 25 meters in length is required to have onboard which of the following sound signaling appliances?

A. none
B. whistle only
C. whistle and bell only
D. whistle, bell and gong

04420. A vessel transferring provisions or cargo at sea shall display during the day:

A. 2 black balls in a vertical line
B. 3 black balls in a vertical line
C. 3 shapes in a vertical line; the highest and lowest shall be red balls and the middle a white diamond
D. 3 black shapes in a vertical line; the highest and lowest shall be balls and the middle 1 a diamond

04421. You see a red sidelight bearing NW (315°). That vessel may be heading:

A. south (180°)
B. east (090°)
C. northeast (045°)
D. west (270°)

04422. The duration of each blast of whistle signals used by a power-driven vessel in fog whether making way or underway but making no way is:

A. about 1 second
B. 2 to 4 seconds
C. 4 to six seconds
D. eight to ten seconds

04423. Which statement is true concerning a "vessel engaged in fishing"?

A. The vessel may be using nets, lines, or trawls.
B. The vessel may be trolling.
C. The vessel is classified as "restricted in her ability to maneuver".
D. It sounds the same fog signal as a vessel underway but stopped.

04424. The Rules state that risk of collision shall be deemed to exist:

A. whenever 2 vessels approach from opposite directions
B. if the bearing of an approaching vessel does not appreciably change
C. whenever a vessel crosses ahead of the intended track of another vessel
D. if 1 vessel is overtaking another

04425. A power-driven vessel exhibits the same lights as a:

A. vessel towing, when not underway
B. vessel towing astern
C. sailing vessel
D. pushing vessel and a vessel being pushed, when they are in a composite unit

04426. Your vessel is underway in fog but stopped and making no way through the water. What fog signal should you sound?

A. 1 prolonged blast at 1 minute intervals
B. 2 prolonged blasts at 1 minute intervals
C. 1 prolonged blast at 2 minute intervals
D. 2 prolonged blasts at 2 minute intervals

04427. A towing light, according to the Rules, is a:

A. white light
B. red light
C. yellow light
D. blue light

04428. What signal shall a power-driven vessel sound when making way in fog?

A. 1 short blast every 2 minutes
B. 1 long blast every 2 minutes
C. 1 long and 2 short blasts every 2 minutes
D. 3 short blasts every 2 minutes

04429. 2 vessels are meeting head and head. How must the vessels pass?

A. One vessel must alter course while the other must continue on its course.
B. The vessels should determine which will alter course by sounding whistle signals.
C. Both vessels should alter course to port and pass starboard to starboard.
D. Both vessels should alter course to starboard and pass port to port.

04430. Which vessel does NOT sound a fog signal of 1 prolonged followed by 2 short blasts?

A. a vessel engaged in dredging
B. a sailing vessel
C. a vessel being towed
D. a vessel engaged in fishing

04431. A vessel 50 meters in length and at anchor is required to sound which of the following fog signals?

A. 5-second ringing of a bell every minute
B. 5-second ringing of a bell every 2 minutes
C. 5-second sounding of a gong every minute
D. 5-second sounding of both a bell and gong every 2 minutes

04432. A vessel displaying the lights shown in DIAGRAM 61 is:

A. fishing
B. a pilot vessel at anchor
C. a fishing vessel aground
D. fishing and hauling her nets

04433. Which vessel is NOT to be regarded as "restricted in her ability to maneuver"?

A. a vessel transferring provisions underway
B. a pushing vessel and a vessel being pushed when connected in a composite unit
C. a vessel servicing a navigation mark
D. a vessel launching aircraft

04434. Which statement correctly applies to a situation where a sailing vessel is overtaking a power-driven vessel?

A. The power-driven vessel must keep out of the way of the sailing vessel.
B. A "special circumstance" situation exists.
C. The sailing vessel must keep out of the way of the power-driven vessel.
D. The vessel which has the other vessel to the right must keep out of the way.

04435. Which procedure(s) shall be used to determine risk of collision?

A. watching the compass bearing of an approaching vessel
B. systematic observation of objects detected by radar
C. long-range radar scanning
D. all of the above

04436. As defined in the Navigation Rules, a white masthead light shows through an arc of how many degrees?

A. 90°
B. 112.5°
C. 225°
D. 360°

04437. What is the minimum length of an anchored vessel which is required to show a white light both forward and aft?

A. 50 meters
B. 100 meters
C. 150 meters
D. 200 meters

04438. At anchor in fog, the fog signal of another vessel underway has been steadily growing louder and the danger of collision appears to exist. In addition to the required fog signal, what signal may be used to indicate the presence of your vessel?

A. the danger signal, 5 or more rapid blasts on the whistle
B. 3 blasts on the whistle, 1 short, 1 prolonged, and 1 short
C. 3 blasts on the whistle, 1 prolonged followed by 2 short
D. No other signal may be used.

04439. Signals required for vessels aground include:

A. by night, the anchor lights for a vessel of her length, and 3 red lights in a vertical line
B. a short, a prolonged, and a short blast
C. by day, 3 black balls in a vertical line
D. all of the above

04440. Which craft would be considered a "power-driven vessel" under the Rules?

A. an auxiliary sail vessel, using her engine
B. a canoe being propelled by a small outboard motor
C. a tug powered by a diesel engine
D. all of the above

04441. A power-driven vessel less than 12 meters in length may, instead of the under-

way lights for vessels under 50 meters, at night, show which of the following?

A. sidelights and stern light
B. 1 all-round white light and sidelights
C. masthead light only
D. stern light only

04442. Which vessel shall not impede the passage of a vessel which can only navigate inside a narrow channel?

A. a vessel of less than 20 meters in length
B. a vessel not under command
C. a vessel engaged in surveying
D. all of the above

04443. Which statement is true in an overtaking situation?

A. One vessel is approaching another vessel from more than 20 degrees abaft the beam.
B. It is the duty of the vessel being overtaken to get out of the way.
C. Any later change of bearing between the 2 vessels shall not make the overtaking vessel a crossing vessel.
D. all of the above

04444. Which vessel must exhibit a conical shape, apex downwards?

A. a 10-meter vessel engaged in fishing
B. a 15-meter vessel proceeding under sail when also being propelled by machinery
C. a 20-meter vessel restricted in her ability to maneuver
D. all of the above

04445. Which vessel must show a towing light above the stern light?

A. a vessel pushing 3 barges ahead
B. a vessel towing alongside
C. a vessel with a 150-meter tow astern
D. none of the above

04446. Which is NOT a distress signal?

A. a continuous sounding with any fog signal apparatus
B. a signal sent by radiotelephone consisting of the spoken word "Mayday"
C. an International Code Signal of N. C.
D. the firing of green star rockets or shells

04447. A rigid replica of the International Code flag "A" may be shown by a vessel:

A. pulling a submarine cable
B. engaged in diving operations
C. engaged in underway replenishment
D. transferring explosives

04449. In a crossing situation, which vessel may sound the danger signal?

A. give-way vessel
B. stand-on vessel
C. either vessel
D. neither vessel

04450. At night, you sight the lights illustrated in DIAGRAM 55. What do the lights indicate?

A. a tug with a tow astern
B. a tug with a tow alongside
C. a tug not under command
D. a pipeline

04451. Every vessel should at all times proceed at a "safe speed". " Safe speed" is defined as that speed where:

A. you can stop within your visibility range
B. you can take proper and effective action to avoid collision
C. you are traveling slower than surrounding vessels
D. no wake comes from your vessel

04452. You are underway in fog and you hear 3 distinct bell strokes followed by 5 seconds of rapid bell ringing followed by 3 distinct bell strokes. This signal indicates a vessel:

A. aground
B. engaged in underwater construction
C. at anchor
D. in distress

04453. Vessels "A" and "B" are crossing as shown in DIAGRAM 30. Which statement is true?

A. The vessels should pass starboard to starboard.
B. Vessel "B" should pass under the stern of vessel "A".
C. Vessel "B" should alter course to the right.
D. Vessel "A" must keep clear of vessel "B".

04454. In a crossing situation, a stand-on vessel which is forced to take action in order to avoid collision shall, if possible, avoid:

A. turning to port
B. turning to starboard
C. decreasing speed
D. increasing speed

04455. Which vessel is "underway" within the meaning of the Rules?

A. a vessel at anchor with the engine turning
B. a vessel tied to an offshore mooring buoy
C. a vessel aground with the engine turning
D. a vessel drifting with the engine stopped

04456. What is the required fog signal for a manned vessel being towed at night?

A. 1 prolonged followed by 1 short blast
B. 1 prolonged followed by 3 short blasts
C. 1 prolonged followed by 2 short blasts
D. 2 prolonged blasts

04457. If you anchor your 25-meter vessel in a harbor, what light(s) must you show?

A. 1 all-round white light
B. 2 all-round white lights
C. 1 all-round red light
D. all the deck house lights

04458. While navigating a power-driven vessel at night, you sight the red sidelight of another vessel on your port bow. Its after masthead light is to the right of the forward masthead light. You should:

A. hold course and speed
B. alter course to port
C. stop engines
D. sound the danger signal

04459. 3 short blasts of the whistle means:

A. "danger"
B. "I am in distress"
C. "my vessel is towing"
D. "I am operating astern propulsion"

04460. Of the vessels listed, which must keep out of the way of all the others?

A. a sailing vessel
B. a vessel restricted in her ability to maneuver
C. a vessel not under command
D. a vessel fishing

04461. During the day, a vessel with a tow over 200 meters in length will show:

A. a black ball
B. a diamond shape
C. 2 cones, apexes together
D. 1 cone, apex upward

04462. A fog signal of 1 long blast followed by 4 short blasts would mean the presence of a:

A. vessel being towed
B. fishing vessel trawling
C. vessel at anchor warning of her location
D. power-driven pilot vessel on station underway

04463. You are underway on vessel "B" approaching vessel "A", as shown in DIAGRAM 38. You are unable to see any sidelights on vessel "A". This is a(n):

A. meeting situation
B. crossing situation
C. overtaking situation
D. special circumstances situation

04464. A vessel not under command, underway but not making way, would show:

A. 2 all-round red lights in a vertical line
B. sidelights
C. a stern light
D. all of the above

04465. Which statement is true, according to the Rules?

A. A fishing vessel has the right of way over a vessel constrained by her draft.
B. A vessel not under command shall avoid impeding the safe passage of a vessel constrained by her draft.
C. A vessel engaged in fishing shall, so far as possible, keep out of the way of a vessel restricted in her ability to maneuver.
D. A vessel restricted in her ability to maneuver shall keep out of the way of a vessel not under command.

04466. Which lights shall a 200-meter vessel exhibit when at anchor?

A. in the forepart of the vessel, a 225-degree white light
B. in the after part of the vessel, a 112.5-degree white light
C. any available working lights to illuminate the decks
D. in the forepart of the vessel, a 112.5-degree white light

04467. As defined in the rules, the term "vessel" would include a:

A. non-self-propelled raft
B. seaplane
C. hovercraft
D. all of the above

04468. You see a vessel displaying 3 lights in a vertical line. The highest and lowest lights are red and the middle light is white. She is also showing a white light at the stern, which is lower than the forward light. It could be a:

A. survey vessel
B. vessel not under command
C. vessel aground
D. pilot vessel with port side to you

04469. A pilot vessel may continue to sound an identity signal in fog if she is:

A. aground
B. at anchor
C. not under command
D. no longer on pilotage duty

04470. You are in charge of a stand-on vessel in a crossing situation. The other vessel is .5 miles to port. You have determined that risk of collision exists. You should:

A. take avoiding action immediately upon determining that risk of collision exists
B. immediately sound the danger signal, and change course
C. take avoiding action only after giving the give-way vessel time to take action, and determining that her action is not appropriate
D. hold course and speed until the point of extremis, and then sound the danger signal, taking whatever action will best avoid collision

04471. A vessel engaged in a towing operation which severely restricts the towing vessel and her tow in their ability to deviate from their course shall, when making way, show:

A. the lights for a towing vessel
B. the lights for a vessel restricted in its ability to maneuver
C. sidelights and stern light
D. all of the above

04472. Which statement is true concerning seaplanes on the water?

A. A seaplane must exhibit appropriate lights but need not exhibit shapes.
B. A seaplane should show the lights for a vessel constrained by her draft.
C. In situations where a risk of collision exists, a seaplane should always give way.
D. A seaplane on the water shall, in general, keep well clear of all vessels.

04473. A head-on situation at night would be 1 in which you see:

A. 1 sidelight of a vessel ahead of you
B. 1 sidelight and a masthead light of a vessel ahead of you
C. 1 sidelight, a masthead and range light of a vessel ahead of you
D. both sidelights of a vessel ahead of you

04474. In a crossing situation, the stand-on vessel should normally:

A. take action to cross ahead of the other vessel
B. take action to pass astern of the other vessel
C. maintain course and speed
D. change course and increase speed

04475. A dredge not engaged in dredging but proceeding to a dredging location at night would:

A. not be required to show any lights
B. be required to show the lights of an underway dredge
C. be required to show the lights of a stationary dredge
D. be required to show the lights of a power-driven vessel underway

04476. At night you sight a vessel displaying 1 green light. This light could indicate a:

A. vessel drifting
B. vessel at anchor
C. small motorboat underway
D. sailboat underway

04477. There is provision to depart from the Rules, if necessary, to avoid:

A. a close-quarters situation
B. an overtaking situation
C. immediate danger
D. any of the above

04478. Risk of collision exists when an approaching vessel has a(n):

A. generally steady bearing and decreasing range
B. generally steady range and increasing bearing
C. increasing range and bearing
D. decreasing bearing only

04479. What signal shall be used to indicate doubt that sufficient action is being taken by another vessel to avoid collision?

A. 5 short and rapid blasts of the whistle
B. 3 long blasts of the whistle
C. 3 short and rapid blasts of the whistle
D. 1 prolonged blast followed by 3 short blasts of the whistle

04480. A power-driven vessel when towing another vessel astern (tow less than 200 meters) shall show:

A. 2 masthead lights in a vertical line instead of the forward masthead light
B. 2 masthead lights in a vertical line instead of either the forward or after masthead lights
C. 2 towing lights in a vertical line at the stern
D. a small white light abaft the funnel

04481. While underway in fog, you hear the rapid ringing of a bell for about 5 seconds followed by the sounding of a gong for about 5 seconds. This signal came from a:

A. vessel fishing
B. seaplane anchored
C. vessel over 100 meters in length at anchor
D. vessel aground

04482. You are underway in a narrow channel and you are being overtaken by a vessel astern. The overtaking vessel sounds a signal indicating his intention to pass your vessel on your starboard side. If such an action appears dangerous you should sound:

A. 5 short and rapid blasts
B. 3 short and rapid blasts
C. 1 prolonged followed by 1 short blast
D. 1 prolonged, 1 short, 1 prolonged and 1 short blast in that order

04483. A vessel restricted in her ability to maneuver shall:

A. turn off her sidelights when not making way
B. when operating in restricted visibility, sound a whistle signal of 2 prolonged and 1 short blast
C. show a dayshape of 2 diamonds in a vertical line
D. keep out of the way of a vessel engaged in fishing

04484. A vessel at anchor sounds her fog signal at intervals of not:

A. more than 1 minute
B. more than 2 minutes
C. more than 3 minutes
D. less than 2 minutes

04485. Your vessel is underway in reduced visibility. You hear, about 20 degrees on the starboard bow, a fog signal of another vessel. Which of the following actions should you take?

A. Alter course to starboard to pass around the other vessel.
B. Slow your engines and let him pass ahead of you.
C. Reduce your speed to bare steerageway.
D. Alter course to port to pass him on his port side.

04486. What dayshape would a vessel at anchor show during daylight?

A. 1 black ball
B. 2 black balls
C. 3 black balls
D. No signal

04487. A vessel displaying the dayshape illustrated in DIAGRAM 34 is:

A. towing
B. fishing
C. anchored
D. being towed

04488. When approaching a bend in a channel where you cannot see around the other side because of the height of the bank, you should:

A. stop engines and navigate with caution
B. stay in the middle of the channel
C. sound passing signals to any other vessel that may be on the other side of the bend
D. sound a whistle blast of at least 4 to 6 seconds duration

04489. Which statement is true concerning a vessel of 150 meters in length, at anchor?

A. She may show an all-round white light where it can best be seen.
B. She must show an all-round white light forward and a second such light aft.
C. The showing of working lights is optional.
D. none of the above

04490. Which of the following vessels would be required to show a white light from a lantern exhibited in sufficient time to prevent collision?

A. a vessel sailing
B. a rowboat
C. a 6-meter motorboat
D. a small vessel fishing

04491. Barges being towed at night:

A. must be lighted at all times
B. must be lighted only if manned
C. must be lighted only if towed astern
D. need not be lighted

04492. When you sight another vessel ahead showing both the red and green sidelights, the most appropriate action you should take would be to:

A. carefully watch his compass bearing
B. start a radar plot in order to ascertain his course
C. alter your course to port
D. alter your course to starboard

04493. You are underway in fog and hear 1 short, 1 prolonged and 1 short blast in succession. What is the meaning of this signal?

A. A vessel is in distress.
B. A vessel is fishing.
C. A vessel is at anchor.
D. A vessel is towing.

04494. A vessel engaged on pilotage duty which is at anchor must show which of the following lights at night?

A. a stern light only
B. anchor lights only
C. an all-round white light over a red light only
D. an all-round white light over a red light and anchor lights

04495. You see a vessel displaying signals shown in DIAGRAM 4. Which of the following is it?

A. vessel under sail also being propelled by machinery
B. small tug with tow greater than 200 meters astern
C. a vessel trawling
D. small fisherman with nets out more than 150 meters

04496. A vessel which is fishing is required to show sidelights and a stern light only when:

A. anchored
B. underway
C. dead in the water
D. underway and making way

04497. Which of the following is a requirement for any action taken to avoid collision?

A. When in sight of another vessel, any action taken must be accompanied by sound signals.
B. The action taken must include changing the speed of the vessel.
C. The action must be positive and made in ample time.
D. all of the above

04498. In the daytime, you see a large sailing vessel on the beam. You know that she is also propelled by machinery if she shows:

A. a basket
B. a black ball
C. a black cone
D. 2 black cones

04499. At night, the lights illustrated in DIAGRAM 76 would indicate a vessel:

A. trawling
B. laying submarine cable
C. towing astern
D. dredging

04500. Your vessel is stopped and making no way, but is not in any way disabled. Another vessel is approaching you on your starboard beam. Which statement is true?

A. The other vessel must give way since your vessel is stopped.
B. Your vessel is the give-way vessel in a crossing situation.
C. You should be showing the lights or shapes for a vessel not under command.
D. You should be showing the lights or shapes for a vessel restricted in her ability to maneuver.

04501. For identification purposes at night, U.S. Navy submarines on the surface may display an intermittent flashing light of which color?

A. amber (yellow)
B. white
C. blue
D. red

04502. Vessels engaged in fishing may show the additional signals described in Annex II to the Rules when they:

A. desire to do so
B. are fishing in a traffic separation zone
C. are in a narrow channel
D. are in close proximity to other vessels engaged in fishing

04503. Which vessel must show a masthead light abaft of and higher than her identifying lights?

A. A 55-meter vessel fishing
B. A 55-meter vessel trawling
C. A 100-meter vessel not under command
D. A 20-meter vessel engaged on pilotage duty

04504. While underway in a narrow channel, a vessel should stay:

A. in the middle of the channel
B. to the starboard side of the channel
C. to the port side of the channel
D. to the side of the channel that has the widest bends

04505. Vessels of less than what length may not impede the passage of other vessels in a narrow fairway?

A. 10 meters
B. 20 meters
C. 30 meters
D. 40 meters

04506. A lantern combining the 2 sidelights of a vessel's running lights may be shown on a:

A. sailing vessel of 25 m in length
B. 20-m vessel fishing and making way
C. 25-m power-driven vessel trolling
D. 6-m vessel under oars

04507. The lights required by the Rules must be shown:

A. from sunrise to sunset in restricted visibility
B. at all times
C. only from sunset to sunrise
D. whenever a look-out is posted

04508. Which vessel may carry her sidelights and stern light in a combined lantern on the mast?

A. an 18-meter sailing vessel
B. a 10-meter sailing vessel also being propelled by machinery
C. a 25-meter sailing vessel
D. all of the above

04509. A vessel nearing a bend or an area of a channel or fairway where other vessels may be hidden by an obstruction shall:

A. set her engines on slow ahead
B. sound a prolonged blast
C. post a look-out
D. all of the above

04510. You are approaching a vessel dredging during the day and see 2 balls in a vertical line on the port side of the dredge. These shapes mean that:

A. you should pass on the port side of the dredge
B. there is an obstruction on the port side of the dredge
C. the dredge is not under command
D. the dredge is moored

04511. Which statement is true concerning the light used to accompany whistle signals?

A. It is mandatory to use such a light.
B. The light shall have the same characteristics as a masthead light.
C. It is only used to supplement short blasts of the whistle.
D. all of the above

04512. Which vessel must sound its fog signal at intervals not to exceed 1 minute?

A. a power-driven vessel underway, not making way
B. a vessel constrained by her draft
C. a sailing vessel
D. a vessel aground

04513. By day, you sight a vessel displaying 3 shapes in a vertical line. The top and bottom shapes are balls, and the middle shape is a diamond. It is a:

A. vessel trolling
B. mineclearing vessel
C. trawler
D. vessel engaged in replenishment at sea

04514. You are heading due east (090°) and observe a vessel's red sidelight on your port beam. The vessel may be heading:

A. northwest (315°)
B. north (000°)
C. southeast (135°)
D. southwest (225°)

04515. When 2 power-driven vessels are crossing, which vessel has the right of way?

A. the vessel which is to starboard of the other
B. the vessel which is to port of the other
C. the larger vessel
D. the vessel that sounds the first whistle signal

04516. Which vessel is, by definition, unable to keep out of the way of another vessel?

A. vessel engaged in fishing
B. vessel restricted in her ability to maneuver
C. sailing vessel
D. vessel towing

04517. Which vessel must exhibit forward and after masthead lights when underway?

A. a 200-meter sailing vessel
B. a 50-meter power-driven vessel
C. a 100-meter vessel engaged in fishing
D. all of the above

04518. As defined in the Rules, a towing light is a yellow light having the same characteristics as a(n):

A. masthead light
B. all-round light
C. sidelight
D. stern light

04519. A vessel underway and making way in fog shall sound every 2 minutes:

A. 1 prolonged blast
B. 2 prolonged blasts
C. 1 prolonged blast and 2 short blasts
D. 3 distinct blasts

04520. When anchoring a 20-meter vessel at night, you must show:

A. 1 all-round white light
B. 2 all-round white lights
C. 1 all-round white light and a stern light
D. 1 all-round white light and a flare up light

04521. According to the Rules, all of the following are engaged in fishing EXCEPT a vessel:

A. setting nets
B. trawling
C. using a dredge net
D. trolling

04522. When a vessel sounds 3 short blasts on the whistle, this indicates that:

A. danger is ahead
B. her engines are going astern
C. the vessel is not under command (broken down)
D. all other vessels should stand clear

04523. An overtaking situation occurs when 1 vessel approaches another from more than how many degrees abaft the beam?

A. 0.0 degrees
B. 1.25 degrees
C. 22.5 degrees
D. 45.0 degrees

04524. What equipment for fog signals is required for a vessel 20 meters in length?

A. whistle only
B. bell only
C. whistle and bell only
D. whistle, bell and gong

04525. Sailing vessels have the right of way over power-driven vessels except:

A. in a crossing situation
B. in a meeting situation
C. when they are the overtaking vessel
D. on the inland waters of the U.S.

04526. Which statement is true concerning risk of collision?

A. Risk of collision does not exist if the compass bearing of the other vessel is changing.
B. Proper use shall be made of radar equipment to determine risk of collision.
C. Risk of collision must be determined before any action can be taken by a vessel.
D. Risk of collision shall exist if the vessels will pass within half a mile of each other.

04527. You are fishing at night, and you sight a vessel showing 3 lights in a vertical line. The upper and lower lights are red and the middle light is white. Which statement is true?

A. You must keep out of the way of the other vessel.
B. The other vessel is responsible to keep out of your way.

C. The other vessel is at anchor.
D. The rule of special circumstances applies.

04528. Which vessel is to sound a fog signal of one prolonged followed by two short blasts?

A. a vessel not under command
B. a sailing vessel, underway
C. a vessel restricted in her ability to maneuver, at anchor
D. all of the above

04529. A vessel may exhibit lights other than those prescribed by the Rules as long as the additional lights:

A. do not interfere with the keeping of a proper look-out
B. are not the color of either sidelight
C. have a lesser range than the prescribed lights
D. all of the above

04530. Which statement is true concerning a partly submerged vessel being towed?

A. It must show a yellow light at each end.
B. It will show red lights along its length.
C. A diamond shape will be carried at the aftermost extremity of the tow.
D. all of the above

04531. Your vessel enters fog. You stop your engines, and the vessel is dead in the water. What fog signal should you sound?

A. 1 prolonged blast every 2 minutes
B. 2 prolonged blasts every 2 minutes
C. 3 short blasts every 2 minutes
D. 1 prolonged and 2 short blasts every 2 minutes

04532. The term "power-driven vessel" refers to any vessel:

A. with propelling machinery onboard whether in use or not
B. making way against the current
C. with propelling machinery in use
D. travelling at a speed greater than that of the current

04533. In which situation do the Rules require both vessels to change course?

A. 2 power-driven vessels meeting head on
B. 2 power-driven vessels crossing when it is apparent to the stand-on vessel that the give-way vessel is not taking appropriate action
C. 2 sailing vessels crossing with the wind on the same side
D. all of the above

04534. A vessel towing where the tow prevents her from changing course shall carry:

A. only the lights for a vessel towing
B. only the lights for a vessel restricted in her ability to maneuver
C. the lights for a towing vessel and the lights for a vessel restricted in her ability to maneuver
D. the lights for a towing vessel and the lights for a vessel not under command

04535. Which of the following statements is true concerning the danger signal?

A. May be sounded by the stand-on vessel only
B. Indicates that the vessel is in distress
C. Is used to indicate a course change
D. May be supplemented by an appropriate light signal

04536. If a sailing vessel with the wind on the port side sees a sailing vessel to windward and cannot tell whether the other vessel has the wind on the port or starboard side, she shall:

A. hold course and speed
B. sound the danger signal
C. keep out of the way of the other vessel
D. turn to port and come into the wind

04537. Vessel "A" is on course 000 True. Vessel "B" is on a head-on course and is bearing 355 True, 200 yards away from vessel "A". To ensure a safe passing, vessel "A" should:

A. maintain course
B. alter course to port
C. alter course to ensure a starboard to starboard passing
D. maneuver to ensure a port to port passing

04538. Which of the following is a vessel "restricted in her ability to maneuver"?

A. a vessel not under command
B. a vessel constrained by her draft
C. a vessel underway in fog
D. a vessel towing unable to deviate from her course

04539. All of the following are distress signals under the Rules EXCEPT:

A. a green star signal
B. orange-colored smoke
C. red flares
D. the repeated raising and lowering of outstretched arms

04540. The lights illustrated in DIAGRAM 58 are those of a:

A. vessel being towed
B. power-driven vessel of less than 50 meters in length
C. fishing vessel at anchor
D. sailboat

04541. The Rules state that vessels may depart from the Rules when:

A. there are no other vessels around
B. operating in a narrow channel
C. the Master enters it in the ship's log
D. necessary to avoid immediate danger

04542. A vessel is towing and carrying the required masthead lights aft. What is the visibility arc of these lights?

A. 112.5 degrees
B. 135.0 degrees
C. 225.0 degrees
D. 360.0 degrees

04543. Which of the following would be a "special circumstance" under the Rules?

A. vessel at anchor
B. more than 2 vessels meeting
C. speed in fog
D. 2 vessels crossing

04544. You are approaching another vessel on crossing courses. She is approximately half a mile distant and is presently on your starboard bow. You believe she will cross ahead of you. She then sounds a whistle signal of 5 short blasts. You should:

A. answer the signal and hold course and speed
B. reduce speed slightly to make sure she will have room to pass
C. make a large course change, accompanied by the appropriate whistle signal, and slow down if necessary
D. wait for another whistle signal from the other vessel

04545. The Rules state that if there is any doubt as to whether a certain situation exists, it shall be considered to exist by the vessel in doubt. This principle applies to which situation(s)?

A. risk of collision
B. a vessel overtaking another vessel
C. a vessel meeting another head on
D. all of the above

04546. Which vessel may use the danger signal?

A. the vessel to port when 2 power-driven vessels are crossing
B. a vessel engaged in fishing, crossing the course of a sailing vessel

C. either of 2 power-driven vessels meeting end on
D. any of the above

04547. What is the minimum sound signaling equipment required aboard a vessel 10 meters in length?

A. a bell only
B. a whistle only
C. a bell and a whistle
D. any means of making an efficient sound signal

04548. Which statement is true regarding equipment for sound signals?

A. A vessel of less than 12 meters in length need not have any sound signaling equipment.
B. Any vessel over 12 meters in length must be provided with a gong.
C. Manual sounding of the signals must always be possible.
D. Automatic sounding of the signals is not permitted.

04549. When 2 sailing vessels are approaching each other as shown in DIAGRAM 3, which of the following statements correctly describes the situation?

A. Vessel "I" should stand on because she has the wind on her port side.
B. Vessel "II" should stand on because she is on the starboard tack.
C. Neither vessel has the right of way because they are meeting end on.
D. The Rule of Special circumstances applies to these vessels.

04550. Which of the following statements concerning an overtaking situation is correct?

A. The overtaking vessel is the stand-on vessel.
B. Neither vessel is the stand-on vessel.
C. The overtaking vessel must maintain course and speed.
D. The overtaking vessel must keep out of the way of the other.

04551. The Rules state that a vessel overtaking another vessel is relieved of her duty to keep clear when:

A. she is forward of the other vessel's beam
B. the overtaking situation becomes a crossing situation
C. she is past and clear of the other vessel
D. the other vessel is no longer in sight

04552. Which statement is true concerning fog signals?

A. All fog signals for sailing vessels are to be given at intervals of not more than 1 minute.
B. A vessel not under command sounds the same fog signal as a vessel towed.
C. The identity signal of a pilot vessel is the only fog signal sounded by such a vessel.
D. A vessel aground may sound a whistle signal.

04553. What dayshape would a vessel aground show during daylight?

A. 1 black ball
B. 2 black balls
C. 3 black balls
D. 4 black balls

04554. Which vessel must have a gong, or other equipment which will make the sound of a gong?

A. a sailing vessel
B. any vessel over 50 meters
C. any vessel over 100 meters
D. a power-driven vessel over 75 meters

04555. A sailing vessel is meeting a vessel fishing in a narrow channel. Which statement is true?

A. The fishing vessel is directed not to impede the passage of the sailing vessel.
B. The fishing vessel has the right of way.
C. Each vessel should move to the edge of the channel on her port side.
D. Each vessel should be displaying signals for a vessel constrained by her draft.

04556. Dayshapes shall be shown:

A. during daylight hours
B. during daylight hours in restricted visibility
C. between 8 AM and 4 PM daily
D. between sunset and sunrise

04557. Rule 14 describes the action to be taken by vessels meeting head to head. Which of the following conditions must be true in order for this rule to apply?

A. Both vessels must be power-driven.
B. They must be meeting on reciprocal or nearly reciprocal courses.
C. The situation must involve risk of collision.
D. all of the above

04558. The stern light shall be positioned such that it will show from dead astern to how many degrees on each side of the stern of the vessel?

A. 22.5
B. 67.5
C. 112.5
D. 135.0

04559. A vessel aground at night is required to show 2 red lights in a vertical line as well as:

A. not under command lights
B. restricted in her ability to maneuver lights
C. anchor lights
D. sidelights and a stern light

04560. When towing more than 1 barge astern at night:

A. only the last barge on the tow must be lighted
B. only the first and the last barges in the tow must be lighted
C. each barge in the tow must be lighted
D. only manned barges must be lighted

04561. Your vessel is aground in fog. In addition to the regular anchor signals, you will be sounding:

A. 3 strokes of the gong before and after the rapid ringing of the gong
B. a blast on the whistle
C. 3 strokes of the bell before and after the rapid ringing of the bell
D. no additional signals

04562. In a crossing situation, the vessel which has the other on her own starboard side shall:

A. if the circumstances of the case admit, avoid crossing ahead of the other
B. change course to port to keep out of the way
C. reduce her speed
D. all of the above

04563. You are on vessel "A" in DIAGRAM 32 and hear vessel "B" sound a signal indicating her intention to overtake you. You feel it is not safe for vessel "B" to overtake you at the present time. You should:

A. sound 5 or more short rapid blasts
B. sound 2 short blasts
C. not answer the whistle signal from vessel "B"
D. sound 3 blasts of the whistle

04564. Which vessel sounds the same fog signal when underway or at anchor?

A. a sailing vessel
B. a vessel restricted in her ability to maneuver
C. a vessel constrained by her draft
D. a vessel not under command

04565. You are approaching a bend in a river where, due to the bank, you cannot see around the other side. A vessel on the other side of the bend sounds 1 prolonged blast. You should:

A. sound passing signals
B. not sound any signal until you sight the other vessel
C. sound a prolonged blast
D. sound the danger signal

04566. The Rules require that a stand-on vessel take action to avoid collision when she determines that:

A. risk of collision exists
B. the other vessel will cross ahead of her
C. the other vessel is not taking appropriate action
D. collision cannot be avoided by the give-way vessel's maneuver alone

04567. In DIAGRAM 5, Vessel "A", which is towing, and vessel "B" are crossing as shown. Which vessel is the stand-on vessel?

A. Vessel "A" is the stand-on vessel because it is to port of vessel "B".
B. Vessel "A" is the stand-on vessel because it is towing.
C. Vessel "B" is the stand-on vessel because it is to starboard of vessel "A".
D. Neither vessel is the stand-on vessel in this situation.

04568. Which vessel is "underway" according to the Rules?

A. a vessel made fast to a single point mooring buoy
B. a purse seiner hauling her nets
C. a pilot vessel at anchor
D. a vessel which has run aground

04569. When 2 power-driven vessels are crossing, the vessel which has the other to starboard must keep out of the way if:

A. she is the faster vessel
B. the situation involves risk of collision
C. the vessels will pass within half a mile of each other
D. whistle signals have been sounded

04570. Which of the following signals may at some time be exhibited by a vessel trawling?

A. 2 white lights in a vertical line
B. A white light over a red light in a vertical line
C. 2 red lights in a vertical line
D. any of the above

04571. Risk of collision is considered to exist if:

A. 4 vessels are nearby
B. a vessel has steady bearing at constant range
C. there is any doubt that risk of collision exists
D. a special circumstance situation is apparent

04572. You are underway in low visibility and sounding fog signals. What changes would you make in the fog signal immediately upon losing propulsion?

A. Begin sounding 2 prolonged blasts at 2-minute intervals.
B. Begin sounding 1 prolonged blast followed by 3 short blasts at 2-minute intervals.
C. Begin sounding 1 prolonged blast followed by 2 short blasts at 2-minute intervals.
D. No change should be made in the signal.

04573. A power-driven vessel shows the same lights as a:

A. vessel engaged in towing, when not underway
B. vessel towing astern
C. sailing vessel
D. pushing vessel and a vessel being pushed, when rigidly connected in a composite unit

04574. Which vessel shall not show her sidelights?

A. any vessel that is not under command
B. any fishing vessel that is not making way
C. any sailing vessel when becalmed
D. any vessel engaged in underwater operations

04575. A vessel is overtaking when she can see which lights of the vessel she is approaching?

A. only the stern light of the vessel
B. the stern light and 1 sidelight
C. only a sidelight of the vessel
D. the masthead lights of the vessel

04576. At night you sight the lights illustrated in DIAGRAM 66. What do the lights indicate?

A. a tug with a tow astern
B. a tug with a tow alongside
C. a ship being assisted by a tug
D. a vessel engaged in fishing

04577. You are underway and approaching a bend in the channel where vessels approaching from the opposite direction cannot be seen. You should sound:

A. 1 blast, 4 to 6 seconds in length
B. 3 blasts, 4 to 6 seconds in length
C. 1 continuous blast until you are able to see around the bend
D. 1 blast, 8 to 10 seconds in length

04578. The term "short blast" on the whistle or horn means a duration of:

A. 1 second
B. 4 to 6 seconds
C. 8 to 12 seconds
D. 12 to 15 seconds

04579. As defined in the Rules, the term "vessel" includes:

A. seaplanes
B. nondisplacement craft
C. barges
D. all of the above

04580. At night a vessel is sighted displaying the identification lights in DIAGRAM 45. This could indicate a:

A. pilot vessel less than 50 meters, underway and not engaged on pilotage duty
B. vessel engaged in fishing
C. vessel aground less than 50 meters
D. vessel engaged in dredging at anchor with an obstruction on 1 side

04581. Under the Rules, a vessel shall slacken her speed, stop, or reverse her engines to:

A. avoid collision
B. allow more time to assess the situation
C. be stopped in an appropriate distance
D. all of the above

04582. At night, a vessel displaying the lights in DIAGRAM 52 is:

A. towing by pushing ahead
B. underway
C. towing a submerged object
D. engaged in dredging

04583. An anchor ball need NOT be exhibited by a vessel if she is:

A. under 50 meters in length, and anchored in an anchorage
B. over 150 meters in length
C. rigged for sail
D. less than 7 meters in length, and not in or near an area where other vessels normally navigate

04585. While underway at night you are coming up on a vessel from astern. What lights would you expect to see?

A. red and green sidelights
B. 2 white lights
C. 1 white light and red and green sidelights
D. 1 white light

04586. Which of the following describes a head-on situation?

A. seeing 1 red light of a vessel directly ahead
B. seeing 2 forward white towing lights in a vertical line on a towing vessel directly ahead
C. seeing both sidelights of a vessel directly off your starboard beam
D. seeing both sidelights of a vessel directly ahead

04587. A vessel anchored in fog may warn an approaching vessel by sounding:

A. the whistle continuously
B. 1 short, 1 prolonged, and 1 short blast of the whistle
C. 5 or more short and rapid blasts of the whistle
D. 3 distinct strokes on the bell before and after sounding the anchor signal

04588. While underway in fog, you hear a vessel ahead sound 2 blasts on the whistle. You should:

A. sound 2 blasts and change course to the left
B. sound whistle signals only if you change course
C. sound only fog signals until the other vessel is sighted
D. not sound any whistle signals until the other vessel is sighted

04589. You are operating in restricted visibility and hear a signal of a rapidly ringing bell followed by the rapid sounding of a gong. It could be a:

A. 30-meter sail vessel at anchor
B. 150-meter power-driven vessel aground
C. vessel in distress
D. 300-meter power-driven vessel at anchor

04590. A vessel being towed, if manned, shall sound a fog signal of:

A. 2 short blasts
B. 3 short blasts
C. 1 prolonged and 2 short blasts
D. 1 prolonged and 3 short blasts

04591. Which of the following is the sound signal for a vessel 75 meters in length, restricted in her ability to maneuver when carrying out her work at anchor?

A. 5 second ringing of a bell at intervals of not more than 1 minute
B. 1 prolonged blast followed by 2 short blasts at intervals of not more than 2 minutes
C. 5 second ringing of a bell and 5 second sounding of a gong at intervals of not more than 1 minute
D. 4 short blasts at intervals of not more than 2 minutes

04592. A look-out shall be maintained:

A. only at night
B. only during restricted visibility
C. at night and during restricted visibility
D. at all times

04593. Risk of collision may be deemed to exist:

A. if the compass bearing of an approaching vessel does NOT appreciably change
B. even when an appreciable bearing change is evident, particularly when approaching a vessel at close range
C. if you observe both sidelights of a vessel ahead for an extended period of time
D. all of the above

04594. The Rules state that certain factors are to be taken into account when determining safe speed. 1 of the factors stated is the:

A. state of wind, sea and current, and the proximity of navigational hazards
B. maximum attainable speed of your vessel
C. temperature
D. aids to navigation that are available

04595. Which vessel, when anchored at night, would not be required to show anchor lights?

A. a power-driven vessel
B. a vessel on pilotage duty
C. a vessel dredging
D. a vessel restricted in her ability to maneuver

04596. A vessel displaying the dayshape in DIAGRAM 13 is:

A. fishing
B. towing
C. being towed
D. anchored

04597. A vessel not under command shall display:

A. 2 red lights at night and 2 black balls during daylight
B. 2 red lights at night and 3 black balls during daylight
C. 3 red lights at night and 2 black balls during daylight
D. 3 red lights at night and 3 black balls during daylight

04598. A vessel engaged in fishing while at anchor shall sound a fog signal of:

A. 1 prolonged and 2 short blasts at 2 minute intervals
B. 1 prolonged and 3 short blasts at 2 minute intervals

C. a rapid ringing of the bell for 5 seconds at 1 minute intervals
D. a sounding of the bell and gong at 1 minute intervals

04599. Underway at night you see the red sidelight of a vessel well off your port bow. Which statement is true?

A. You are required to alter course to the right.
B. You must stop engines.
C. You are on a collision course with the other vessel.
D. You may maintain course and speed.

04600. Which vessel would sound a fog signal consisting of the ringing of a bell for 5 seconds?

A. a vessel engaged in fishing, at anchor
B. a vessel restricted in its ability to maneuver, at anchor
C. a sailing vessel, at anchor
D. a sailing vessel becalmed

04601. A vessel towing a barge astern would show, at the stern:

A. only a stern light
B. a towing light above the stern light
C. 2 towing lights in a vertical line
D. 2 white lights in a vertical line

04602. A fog signal consisting of 1 prolonged blast followed by 4 short blasts would indicate the presence of a:

A. vessel being towed
B. fishing vessel engaged in trawling
C. vessel at anchor warning of her location
D. power-driven pilot vessel on station underway

04603. In addition to sidelights what light should a vessel being towed show?

A. a stern light
B. a masthead light
C. not under command lights
D. range lights

04604. A pilot vessel may continue to sound an identity signal if she is:

A. aground
B. at anchor
C. not under command
D. being towed

04605. When 2 power-driven vessels are meeting head-on and there is a risk of collision, each shall:

A. stop her engines
B. alter course to starboard
C. sound the danger signal
D. back down

04606. A vessel with a tow over 200 meters in length will, during the day, show:

A. a diamond shape
B. 2 cones, apexes together
C. a black ball
D. 1 cone, apex upward

04607. What is the minimum length of vessels required to show 2 anchor lights?

A. 40 meters
B. 50 meters
C. 60 meters
D. 70 meters

04608. A vessel showing a rigid replica of the International Code flag "A" is engaged in:

A. diving operations
B. dredging
C. fishing
D. mineclearance operations

04609. In determining "safe speed", all of the following must be taken into account EXCEPT the:

A. maximum horsepower of your vessel
B. presence of background lights at night
C. draft of your vessel
D. maneuverability of your vessel

04610. You are aboard the give-way vessel in a crossing situation. Which of the following should you NOT do in obeying the Rules?

A. Cross ahead of the stand-on vessel.
B. Make a large course change to starboard.
C. Slow your vessel.
D. Back your vessel.

04611. A vessel, which does not normally engage in towing operations, is towing a vessel in distress. She:

A. need not show the lights for a vessel engaged in towing, if it is impractical to do so
B. may show not under command lights
C. must show a yellow light above stern light
D. must show the lights for a vessel towing

04612. An all-round flashing yellow light may be exhibited by a(n):

A. vessel laying cable
B. vessel towing a submerged object
C. vessel not under command
D. air cushion vessel

04613. Working lights shall be used to illuminate the decks of a vessel:

A. over 100 meters at anchor
B. not under command
C. constrained by her draft
D. any of the above

04614. Which vessel may show identifying lights when not engaged in her occupation?

A. a fishing vessel
B. a pilot vessel
C. a mineclearance vessel
D. none of the above

04615. A pilot vessel may continue to sound an identity signal if she is:

A. underway, but not making way
B. aground
C. being towed
D. not engaged in pilotage duty

04616. If your vessel is the stand-on vessel in a crossing situation:

A. you must keep your course and speed
B. you may change course and speed as the other vessel must keep clear
C. the other vessel must keep course and speed
D. both vessels must keep course and speed

04617. A vessel proceeding along a narrow channel shall:

A. avoid crossing the channel at right angles
B. not overtake any vessels within the channel
C. keep as close as possible to the edge of the channel on her starboard side
D. when nearing a bend in the channel, sound a long blast of the whistle

04618. Which vessel would exhibit sidelights when underway and not making way?

A. a vessel towing astern
B. a vessel trawling
C. a vessel not under command
D. a vessel engaged in dredging operations

04619. Which vessel is not to impede the passage of a vessel which can only navigate safely within a narrow channel?

A. any vessel less than 20 meters in length
B. any sailing vessel
C. a vessel engaged in fishing
D. all of the above

04620. A tug is towing 3 manned barges in line in fog. The second vessel of the tow should sound:

A. no fog signal
B. 1 short blast
C. 1 prolonged and 3 short blasts
D. 1 prolonged and 2 short blasts

04621. The steering and sailing rules for vessels in restricted visibility apply to vessels:

A. in sight of one another in fog
B. navigating in or near restricted visibility area
C. only if showing special purpose lights
D. only if they have operational radar

04622. The Navigation Rules state that a vessel shall be operated at a safe speed at all times so that she can be stopped within:

A. the distance of visibility
B. 1/2 the distance of visibility
C. a distance appropriate to the existing circumstances and conditions
D. the distance that it would require for the propeller to go from full ahead to full astern

04623. A towing vessel 35 meters in length, with a tow 100 meters astern, must show a minimum of how many masthead lights?

A. 1
B. 2
C. 3
D. 4

04624. A vessel displaying the lights in DIAGRAM 56 could be a vessel:

A. towing a barge alongside
B. underway and laying cable
C. at anchor and dredging
D. underway and carrying dangerous cargo

04625. Which of the following must be true in order for a stand-on vessel to take action to avoid collision by her maneuver alone?

A. She must be in sight of the give-way vessel.
B. There must be risk of collision.
C. She must determine that the give-way vessel is not taking appropriate action.
D. all of the above

04626. A vessel being towed astern, where the length of the tow exceeds 200 meters, will exhibit:

A. 2 balls in a vertical line
B. a diamond shape where it can best be seen
C. a ball on each end of the tow
D. no dayshape

04627. While underway, you sight a vessel displaying the dayshapes in DIAGRAM 6. You should:

A. maintain course and speed
B. provide assistance, the other vessel is in distress
C. stay clear, the other vessel cannot get out of the way
D. stop your vessel and sound passing signals

04628. A sailing vessel displaying the dayshape in DIAGRAM 35 is indicating that she is:

A. being propelled by power as well as sail
B. on a starboard tack
C. close-hauled and has difficulty maneuvering
D. fishing as well as sailing

04629. For a stand-on vessel to take action to avoid collision she shall, if possible, not:

A. decrease speed
B. increase speed
C. turn to port for a vessel on her port side
D. turn to starboard for a vessel on port side

04630. Except where it has been determined that a risk of collision does not exist, every vessel which hears, apparently forward of her beam, the fog signal of another vessel shall:

A. if necessary, take all her way off
B. stop her engines
C. begin a radar plot
D. all of the above

04631. 2 barges are being pushed ahead by a towboat. Which statement is true concerning lights on the barges?

A. Each vessel should show sidelights.
B. Each vessel should show at least 1 white light.
C. The barges should be lighted as separate units.
D. The barges should be lighted as 1 vessel.

04632. The Rules state that a seaplane shall:

A. not be regarded as a vessel
B. in general, keep well clear of all vessels
C. proceed at a slower speed than surrounding vessels
D. when making way, show the lights for a vessel not under command

04633. If practical, when shall a manned vessel being towed sound her fog signal?

A. immediately before the towing vessel sounds hers
B. immediately after the towing vessel sounds hers
C. as close to the mid-cycle of the towing vessel's signals as possible
D. at any time as long as the interval is correct

04634. Your tug is underway at night and NOT towing. What light(s) should your vessel show aft to other vessels coming up from astern?

A. 1 white light
B. 2 white lights
C. 1 white light and 1 yellow light
D. 1 white light and 2 yellow lights

04635. A vessel conducting mineclearing operations will show:

A. 3 balls in a vertical line
B. 2 balls in a vertical line
C. 1 ball near the foremast and 1 ball at each fore yard
D. 1 diamond near the foremast head and 1 ball at each fore yard

04636. A vessel sailing shall keep out of the way of all of the following vessels except a vessel:

A. not under command
B. engaged on pilotage duty
C. restricted in her ability to maneuver
D. engaged in fishing

04637. Which statement is true concerning a vessel under oars?

A. She must show a stern light.
B. She is allowed to show the same lights as a sailing vessel.
C. She must show a fixed all-round white light.
D. She must show a dayshape of a black cone.

04638. A vessel is underway and fishing with trolling lines. This vessel:

A. must keep out of the way of sailing vessels
B. must sound a 1 prolonged, 2 short blasts signal in restricted visibility
C. is the stand-on vessel when overtaking power-driven vessels
D. all of the above

04639. At night you sight a vessel displaying a single green light. This is a:

A. vessel at anchor
B. small motorboat underway
C. vessel drifting
D. sailing vessel

04640. When 2 power-driven vessels are crossing, which vessel is the stand-on vessel?

A. the vessel which is to starboard of other vessel
B. the vessel which is to port of other vessel
C. the larger vessel
D. the vessel that sounds the first whistle signal

04641. Which vessel must exhibit forward and after masthead lights when making way?

A. a 75-meter vessel restricted in her ability to maneuver
B. a 100-meter sailing vessel
C. a 150-meter vessel engaged in fishing
D. a 45-meter vessel engaged in towing

04642. A vessel in fog has detected by radar alone a meeting vessel ahead on a collision course. In order to avoid a close quarters situation, the vessel should:

A. turn to port
B. turn to starboard
C. maintain course and speed and sound the danger signal
D. maintain course and speed and sound no signal

04643. A sailing vessel underway at night may show:

A. a red light over a green light at masthead
B. a green light over a red light at masthead
C. 2 white lights in a vertical line at the stern
D. an all-round white light at the bow

04644. A vessel engaged in trawling will show identification lights of:

A. a red light over a white light
B. a white light over a red light
C. a green light over a white light
D. 2 red lights in a vertical line

04645. Which of the following is a requirement for a vessel navigating near an area of restricted visibility?

A. A power-driven vessel shall have her engines ready for immediate maneuver.
B. She must sound appropriate sound signals.
C. If she detects another vessel by radar, she shall determine if risk of collision exists.
D. all of the above

04646. By night, you sight the lights of a vessel engaged in underwater operations. If an obstruction exists on the port side of the vessel, it will be marked by:

A. a floodlight
B. 2 red lights in a vertical line
C. a single red light
D. any visible lights

04647. At night, a vessel displaying the lights in DIAGRAM 65 is:

A. fishing
B. anchored

C. being towed
D. drifting

04648. You are in charge of a power-driven vessel in dense fog. You observe another vessel on radar who is half a mile distant on your port bow. You should:

A. sound the danger signal
B. exchange passing signals
C. sound 1 long blast
D. make no change in your fog signal

04649. Which vessel may carry her sidelights and stern light in 1 combined lantern?

A. A 10-meter power-driven vessel
B. A 15-meter vessel propelled by sail and machinery
C. A 10-meter sailing vessel
D. all of the above

04650. What lights would be shown at night by a vessel which is restricted in her ability to deviate from her course?

A. 3 red lights in a vertical line
B. 3 white lights in a vertical line
C. 3 lights in a vertical line, the highest and lowest white and the middle red
D. 3 lights in a vertical line, the highest and lowest red and the middle white

04651. Which vessel is the stand-on vessel when 2 vessels crossing in fog are not in sight of one another?

A. The vessel which has the other on her own starboard side
B. The vessel which has the other on her own port side
C. The 1 which hears the other's fog signal first
D. Neither vessel is the stand-on vessel.

04652. A vessel displaying the dayshapes in DIAGRAM 18 is a vessel:

A. towing astern with a tow greater than 200 meters in length
B. not under command
C. dredging
D. carrying dangerous cargo

04653. A vessel showing the dayshape in DIAGRAM 34:

A. has a tow which exceeds 200 meters
B. is engaged in surveying or underwater work
C. is not under command
D. is fishing

04654. A vessel engaged in fishing shall keep out of the way of a vessel:

A. under sail
B. restricted in her ability to maneuver
C. crossing a channel
D. all of the above

04655. Which vessel shall turn off her sidelights?

A. any vessel that is not under command
B. any fishing vessel that is not making way
C. any sailing vessel when becalmed
D. any vessel engaged in underwater operations

04656. A vessel fishing at night, with gear extending more than 150 meters horizontally outwards, will show in the direction of the gear:

A. 1 white light
B. 2 vertical white lights
C. 1 yellow light
D. 2 vertical yellow lights

04657. In restricted visibility, a vessel which detects by radar alone the presence of another vessel shall determine if a close quarters situation is developing or risk of collision exists. If so, she shall:

A. sound the danger signal
B. when taking action, make only course changes
C. avoid altering course toward a vessel abaft the beam
D. all of the above

04658. A 60-meter vessel which is trawling is required to show how many white masthead lights at night?

A. 1
B. 2
C. 3
D. 4

04659. A vessel servicing a pipeline during the day shall display:

A. 3 black shapes in a vertical line; the highest and lowest are balls, and the middle 1 is a diamond
B. 3 shapes in a vertical line; the highest and lowest are red balls, and the middle 1 is a white diamond
C. 3 black balls in a vertical line
D. 2 black balls in a vertical line

04660. In fog you observe your radar and determine that risk of collision exists with a vessel which is 2 miles off your port bow. You should:

A. stop your engines
B. sound danger signal at 2-minute intervals

C. hold course and speed until the other vessel is sighted
D. take proper avoiding action as soon as possible

04661. Which statement is true concerning a towing vessel which is unable to deviate from her course?

A. By day, she shall carry black cylinder shape.
B. By day, she shall carry 2 black balls in a vertical line.
C. By night, she would show the same lights as a vessel not under command.
D. By day, she would show the same shapes as a vessel restricted in her ability to maneuver.

04662. Vessel "A" (towing) and vessel "B" are meeting as shown in DIAGRAM 12. In this situation, which statement is true?

A. Both vessels should alter course to starboard and pass port to port.
B. Both vessels should alter course to port and pass starboard to starboard.
C. Vessel "A" should hold course while vessel "B" alters course to starboard.
D. Vessel "A" has the right of way.

04663. Which statement is true regarding equipment for sound signals?

A. A vessel of less than 12 meters in length need not have any sound signaling equipment.
B. Manual sounding of the signals must always be possible.
C. Any vessel over 12 meters in length must be provided with a gong.
D. Signals must be able to be sounded manually and automatically.

04664. You are approaching a narrow channel. You see a vessel that can only be navigated safely within the channel. You should:

A. hold your course and speed
B. sound the danger signal
C. not cross the channel if you might impede the other vessel
D. initiate an exchange of passing signals

04665. What is the minimum sound signaling equipment required aboard a vessel 10 meters in length?

A. any means of making efficient sound signal
B. a bell only
C. a whistle only
D. a bell and a whistle

04666. Which vessel must have a gong, or other equipment which will make the sound of a gong?

A. a sailing vessel
B. any vessel over 50 meters
C. a power driven vessel over 75 meters
D. any vessel over 100 meters

04667. While underway and in sight of another vessel, you put your engines on astern propulsion. Which statement concerning whistle signals is true?

A. You need not sound any whistle signals.
B. You must sound 1 blast if backing to starboard.
C. You must sound whistle signals only if the vessels are meeting.
D. You must sound 3 short blasts on the whistle.

04668. Two power-driven vessels are crossing as shown in DIAGRAM 42. Vessel "A" sounds 3 short blasts on the whistle. This signal means that vessel "A":

A. intends to hold course and speed
B. is uncertain about the actions of "B"
C. proposes to cross ahead of the other vessel
D. is backing engines

04669. Which statement is TRUE concerning the light used with whistle signals?

A. Use of such a light is required.
B. Its purpose is to supplement short blasts of the whistle.
C. The light shall have the same characteristics as a masthead light.
D. all of the above

04670. What determines if a vessel is "restricted in her ability to maneuver"?

A. whether or not all of the vessel's control equipment is in working order
B. the vessel's draft in relation to the available depth of water
C. whether the nature of the vessel's work limits maneuverability required by the Rules of the Road
D. whether or not the vessel is the give-way vessel in a meeting situation

04671. Which statement is true concerning the light used to accompany whistle signals?

A. It is only used to supplement short blasts of the whistle.
B. It is mandatory to use such a light.
C. The light shall have the same characteristics as a masthead light.
D. all of the above

04672. Which of the following statements is true concerning the danger signal?

A. Only the stand-on vessel can sound the danger signal.
B. Radio transmissions may be used in place of the danger signal.
C. Vessels must be in sight of each other in order to use the danger signal.
D. The danger signal consists of 5 or more prolonged blasts of the whistle.

04673. Which vessel may sound the danger signal?

A. either vessel in a meeting situation
B. the give-way vessel in a crossing situation
C. a vessel at anchor
D. all of the above

04674. You are on watch in fog. Which of the following vessels is "in sight"?

A. a vessel that you can see from the bridge
B. a radar target of which you have determined the course and speed
C. a vessel of which you can hear the fog signal
D. all of the above

04675. In a meeting situation, which vessel may sound the danger signal?

A. stand-on vessel
B. give-way vessel
C. either vessel
D. neither vessel

04676. You are underway in a narrow channel and are being overtaken by a vessel astern. The overtaking vessel sounds a signal indicating her intention to pass on your starboard side. If such an action appears dangerous, you should sound:

A. 1 prolonged followed by 1 short blast
B. 1 prolonged, 1 short, 1 prolonged and 1 short blast in that order
C. 5 short and rapid blasts
D. 3 short and rapid blasts

04677. You are on vessel "A", as shown in DIAGRAM 32, and hear vessel "B" sound a signal indicating his intention to overtake you. You feel it is not safe for vessel "B" to overtake you at the present time. You should:

A. sound 2 short blasts
B. sound 5 or more short rapid blasts
C. not answer the whistle signal from vessel "B"
D. sound 3 blasts of the whistle

04678. Which of the following is a light signal authorized by the Secretary of the Navy as an additional navigational light for a ship of war?

A. flashing amber beacon for submarines
B. green masthead and yardarm lights indicating mine clearance operations
C. red-white-red lights in a vertical line for a carrier launching aircraft
D. yellow flares indicating torpedo firing exercises

04679. Dayshapes shall be displayed:

A. from sunset to sunrise
B. at all times, whether underway or at anchor
C. by day
D. 1 hour before sunrise to 1 hour after sunset

04680. Dayshapes shall be displayed:

A. between sunset and sunrise
B. between 8 AM and 4 PM daily
C. during daylight hours in restricted visibility
D. during daylight hours only

04681. A vessel may exhibit lights other than those prescribed by the Rules as long as the additional lights:

A. are not the same color as either side light
B. have a lesser range of visibility than the prescribed lights
C. do not impair the visibility or distinctive character of the prescribed lights
D. all of the above

04682. A vessel may exhibit lights other than those prescribed by the Rules as long as the additional lights:

A. do not interfere with the keeping of a proper look-out
B. do not impair the visibility or distinctive character of the prescribed lights
C. cannot be mistaken for the lights specified elsewhere in the Rules
D. all of the above

04683. The stern light shall be positioned such that it will show from dead astern to how many degrees on each side of the stern of the vessel?

A. 135.0
B. 112.5
C. 67.5
D. 22.5

04684. You see a red sidelight bearing NW (315°). That vessel may be heading:

A. northwest (315°)
B. east (090°)
C. southwest (225°)
D. west (270°)

04685. What does the word "breadth" mean?

A. greatest breadth
B. molded breadth
C. breadth on the main deck
D. breadth at the load waterline

04686. If underway in low visibility and sounding fog signals, what changes would you make in the fog signal immediately upon losing the power plant?

A. Begin sounding 1 prolonged blast followed by 2 short blasts at 2-minute intervals.
B. Begin sounding 1 prolonged blast followed by 3 short blasts at 2-minute intervals.
C. Begin sounding 2 prolonged blasts at 2-minute intervals .
D. No change should be made in the signal.

04687. A vessel engaged in fishing while at anchor shall sound a fog signal of:

A. 1 prolonged and 3 short blasts at 1 minute intervals
B. a rapid ringing of the bell for 5 seconds at 1 minute intervals
C. 1 prolonged and 2 short blasts at 2 minute intervals
D. a sounding of the bell and gong at 1 minute intervals

04688. Which of the following is the sound signal for a vessel 75 meters in length, restricted in her ability to maneuver, at anchor?

A. 1 prolonged blast followed by 2 short blasts at intervals of not more than 2 minutes
B. 5 second ringing of a bell at intervals of not more than 1 minute
C. 4 short blasts at intervals of not more than 2 minutes
D. 5 second ringing of a bell and 5 second sounding of a gong at intervals of not more than 1 minute

04689. Which vessel sounds the same fog signal when underway or at anchor?

A. a sailing vessel
B. a vessel constrained by her draft
C. a vessel restricted in her ability to maneuver
D. a vessel not under command

04690. Which vessel would sound a fog signal consisting of the ringing of a bell for 5 seconds?

A. a vessel engaged in fishing at anchor
B. a vessel restricted in its ability to maneuver at anchor
C. a sailing vessel at anchor
D. all of the above

04691. A 200-meter vessel is aground in fog. Which signal is optional?

A. a bell signal
B. a whistle signal
C. a gong signal
D. all of the above are mandatory.

04692. Which of the following is NOT a vessel "restricted in her ability to maneuver"?

A. a vessel laying mat revetments for bank protection along a channel
B. a vessel towing with limited maneuverability due to a large unwieldy tow
C. a deep-draft vessel that can only navigate in a dredged channel
D. a towing vessel underway with a fuel barge alongside and taking on fuel

04693. A 200-meter vessel is aground in restricted visibility. Which signal is optional?

A. a whistle signal
B. a gong signal
C. a bell signal
D. all of the above are optional.

04694. Which statement is true concerning fog signals?

A. All fog signals for sailing vessels are to be given at intervals of not more than 1 minute.
B. A vessel aground may sound a whistle signal.
C. A vessel not under command sounds the same fog signal as a vessel towed.
D. The identity signal of a pilot vessel is the only fog signal sounded by such a vessel.

04695. Underway in fog, you hear a vessel ahead sound 2 whistle blasts. You should:

A. not sound any whistle signals until the other vessel is sighted
B. sound only fog signals until the other vessel is sighted
C. sound whistle signals only if you change course
D. sound 2 blasts and change course to the left

04696. You are underway in fog when you hear the rapid ringing of a bell for 5 seconds followed by the sounding of a gong for 5 seconds. This signal indicates a vessel:

A. engaged in pair trawling
B. fishing while making no way
C. more than 100 meters in length, at anchor
D. engaged on pilotage duty

04697. A tug is towing 3 barges in line in restricted visibility. The second vessel of the tow should sound:

A. 1 prolonged and 2 short blasts
B. 1 prolonged and 3 short blasts
C. 1 short blast
D. no fog signal

04698. Which of the following is true when operating in fog and other vessels are detected by radar?

A. The bearings should be repeatedly checked because a large bearing change will insure that you avoid collision.
B. You should determine the course and speed of all radar contacts.
C. You should maneuver before the other vessel is in sight if the CPA is close aboard.
D. Long-range scanning will provide early warning of all other vessels within the radar's range.

04699. What is the identity signal which may be sounded by a vessel engaged on pilotage duty in fog?

A. 2 short blasts
B. 3 short blasts
C. 4 short blasts
D. 5 short blasts

04700. What does the word "length" refer to?

A. length between the perpendiculars
B. length overall
C. waterline length
D. register length

04701. A fog signal of 1 prolonged blast followed by 4 short blasts would mean the presence of a:

A. vessel being towed
B. power-driven pilot vessel on station underway
C. fishing vessel trawling
D. vessel at anchor warning of her location

04702. You are heading due east (090°) and observe a vessel's red sidelight on your port beam. The vessel may be heading:

A. northwest (315°)
B. southeast (135°)
C. northeast (045°)
D. southwest (225°)

04703. As defined in the Rules, a towing light is a yellow light having the same characteristics as a(n):

A. special flashing light
B. anchor light
C. stern light
D. masthead light

04704. The masthead light may be located at other than the centerline on a vessel:

A. less than 50 meters in length
B. less than 20 meters in length
C. of special construction
D. engaged in trolling

04705. In complying with the Rules, of what must the mariner take due regard?

A. limited backing power of his vessel
B. radar information about nearby vessels
C. the occupation of the other vessel, if known
D. all of the above

04706. A "flashing light" is a light that:

A. flashes at regular intervals at a frequency of 120 flashes or more per minute
B. is yellow in color
C. is visible over an arc of the horizon of not less than 180° nor more than 225°
D. all of the above

04707. While underway at night you are coming up on a vessel from astern. What light(s) would you expect to see?

A. a stern light only
B. 2 masthead lights
C. both sidelights and the stern light
D. sidelights only

04708. At night, a vessel displaying the lights in DIAGRAM 52 is:

A. at anchor
B. aground
C. underway
D. dredging

04709. At night, a vessel displaying the lights in DIAGRAM 52 is:

A. aground
B. making way
C. at anchor
D. transferring dangerous cargo

04710. Which vessel would exhibit sidelights when underway and not making way?

A. a vessel engaged in fishing
B. a vessel not under command
C. a vessel engaged in dredging
D. a power-driven vessel

04711. Which vessel would exhibit sidelights when underway and not making way?

A. a vessel trawling
B. a vessel not under command

C. a pilot vessel
D. a vessel engaged in dredging

04712. You are on a vessel that cannot comply with the spacing requirement for masthead lights due to the nature of the vessel's function. What is required in this situation?

A. The vessel must carry only the lights that comply with the rules; others may be omitted.
B. The vessel's lights must comply as closely as possible, as determined by her government.
C. The vessel must be altered to permit full compliance with the rules.
D. An all-round light should be substituted for the after masthead light and the stern light.

04713. What equipment for fog signals is required for a vessel 20 meters in length?

A. whistle and bell only
B. whistle only
C. bell only
D. whistle, bell and gong

04714. Which vessel would exhibit sidelights when underway and not making way?

A. a vessel not under command
B. a vessel towing by pushing ahead
C. a vessel engaged in dredging
D. a vessel trawling

04715. Which of the following is a "vessel restricted in her ability to maneuver"?

A. a deep-draft vessel that can only navigate in a dredged channel
B. a vessel fishing with a bottom trawl that must remain on course
C. a large tanker that is being towed as a dead ship to drydock
D. a vessel laying revetment mats to provide bank protection along a channel

04716. What dayshape should a vessel being towed exhibit if the tow EXCEEDS 200 meters?

A. a cone, apex downward
B. a cone, apex upward
C. a diamond
D. a ball

04717. A sailing vessel underway at night may show:

A. a green light over a red light
B. a red light over a white light
C. 2 white lights at the stern
D. none of the above

04718. A vessel displaying the lights in DIAGRAM 56 could be a vessel:

A. transferring dangerous cargo
B. at anchor and dredging
C. restricted in her ability to maneuver, not making way
D. a dredge underway and dredging

04719. A vessel engaged in mineclearing is showing 3 green lights as shown in DIAGRAM 68. These lights indicate that an approaching vessel should pass no closer than:

A. 500 meters
B. 1000 meters
C. 1500 meters
D. 2000 meters

04720. A vessel displaying the light illustrated in DIAGRAM 56 could be a vessel:

A. towing a barge alongside
B. at anchor and dredging
C. underway and engaged in surveying operations
D. restricted in her ability to maneuver and not making way

04721. Which vessel when anchored at night, would not be required to show anchor lights?

A. a vessel engaged in underwater operations
B. a vessel not under command
C. a vessel engaged on pilotage duty
D. a vessel engaged in survey operations

04722. Which of the following vessels, when anchored at night, would not be required to show anchor lights?

A. a power-driven vessel
B. a vessel engaged in survey operations
C. a vessel engaged on pilotage duty
D. a vessel engaged in fishing

04723. At night, a vessel is sighted displaying the lights in DIAGRAM 45. This could be a:

A. vessel engaged in fishing at anchor
B. pilot vessel on pilotage duty
C. vessel engaged in launching or recovering aircraft
D. power-driven vessel at anchor

04724. At night, a vessel displaying the lights in DIAGRAM 65 is:

A. trawling
B. not under command
C. anchored
D. drifting

04725. What is the minimum sound signaling equipment required aboard a vessel 14 meters in length?

A. any means of making efficient sound signal
B. a bell only
C. a whistle only
D. a bell and a whistle

04726. A tug is towing 3 unmanned barges in line in fog. The third vessel of the tow should sound:

A. no fog signal
B. 1 short blast
C. 1 prolonged and 3 short blasts
D. 1 prolonged, 1 short and 1 prolonged blast

04728. Which statement is TRUE, according to the Rules?

A. A sailing vessel has the right of way over a vessel engaged in fishing.
B. A vessel not under command shall keep out of the way of a vessel engaged in fishing.
C. A vessel engaged in fishing shall, so far as possible, keep out of the way of a vessel restricted in her ability to maneuver.
D. A vessel restricted in her ability to maneuver shall keep out of the way of a vessel not under command.

04729. Which statement is TRUE, according to the Rules?

A. A sailing vessel has the right of way over a vessel engaged in fishing.
B. A vessel engaged in fishing shall, so far as possible, keep out of the way of a vessel restricted in her ability to maneuver.
C. A vessel restricted in her ability to maneuver shall keep out of the way of a vessel not under command.
D. A vessel not under command shall keep out of the way of a vessel engaged in fishing.

04730. Which of the following signals may at some time be exhibited by a vessel trawling?

A. 2 white lights in a vertical line
B. A red light over a white light in a vertical line
C. 2 fixed yellow lights in a vertical line
D. any of the above

04731. Additional light signals are provided in the Annexes to the Rules of the Road for vessels:

A. not under command
B. engaged in fishing
C. engaged in towing
D. under sail

04732. Vessels engaged in fishing may show the additional signals described in Annex II to the Rules when they are:

A. trolling
B. fishing in a traffic separation zone
C. close to other vessels engaged in fishing
D. in a narrow channel

04733. A distress signal:

A. consists of 5 or more short blasts of the fog signal apparatus
B. consists of the raising and lowering of a large white flag
C. may be used separately or with other distress signals
D. is used to indicate doubt about another vessel's intentions

04734. A vessel may use any sound or light signals to attract the attention of another vessel as long as:

A. white lights are not used
B. red and green lights are not used
C. the signal cannot be mistaken for a signal authorized by the Rules
D. the vessel signals such intentions over the radiotelephone

04735. 1 of the signals, other than a distress signal, that can be used by a vessel to attract attention is a(n):

A. red star shell
B. searchlight
C. burning barrel
D. orange smoke signal

04736. When should the fog signal of a vessel being towed be sounded?

A. When the vessel being towed is unmanned.
B. When the vessel being towed is manned.
C. All towed vessels, manned or unmanned, must sound fog signals.
D. Towed vessels are never required to sound fog signals.

04737. If another vessel can only be safely navigated in a narrow channel which you are approaching, you should:

A. not cross the channel if you might impede the other vessel
B. hold your course and speed if she is on your port bow
C. sound 3 short blasts, and take all way off your vessel
D. sound 2 prolonged blasts followed by 1 short blast

04738. You are the stand-on vessel in a crossing situation. If you think the give-way vessel is NOT taking sufficient action to avoid collision, you should sound:

A. 1 short blast and maintain course
B. the danger signal
C. no signal and maneuver at will
D. 2 short blasts, alter to port, and pass astern

04739. Which statement is TRUE, according to the Rules?

A. A vessel restricted in her ability to maneuver shall keep out of the way of a vessel not under command.
B. A vessel not under command shall keep out of the way of a vessel engaged in fishing.
C. A vessel engaged in fishing shall, so far as possible, keep out of the way of a vessel restricted in her ability to maneuver.
D. A sailing vessel has the right of way over a vessel engaged in fishing.

04745. If another vessel can only be safely navigated in a narrow channel which you are approaching, you should:

A. hold your course and speed if he is on your port bow
B. sound 3 short blasts, and take all way off your vessel
C. not cross the channel if you might impede the other vessel
D. sound 2 prolonged blasts followed by 1 short blast

04770. While underway in fog, you hear a vessel ahead sound 2 prolonged blasts on the whistle. You should:

A. sound 2 blasts and change course to left
B. sound whistle signals only if you change course
C. not sound any whistle signals until the other vessel is sighted
D. sound only fog signals until the other vessel is sighted

04780. You are the stand-on vessel in a crossing situation. If you think the give-way vessel is NOT taking sufficient action to avoid collision, you should sound:

A. the danger signal
B. 2 short blasts, alter to port, and pass astern
C. no signal and maneuver at will
D. 1 short blast and maintain course

04818. A vessel engaged in mineclearance operations shows special identity lights:

A. instead of the masthead lights
B. which mean that other vessels should not approach within 1000 meters
C. that are 225-degree green lights
D. all of the above

04819. Which of the breadths shown in DIAGRAM 87 represents the breadth in the Rules?

A. A
B. B
C. C
D. D

04820. You are about to cross a narrow channel when you see an approaching vessel that can only be navigated safely within the channel. You should:

A. cross the channel as you have right of way
B. cross only if the vessel in the channel is approaching on your port side
C. not cross the channel if you might impede the other vessel
D. sound the danger signal

04825. Which of the following is a light signal authorized by the Secretary of the Navy as an additional navigational light for a ship of war?

A. 2 yellow lights in a vertical line for a carrier launching aircraft
B. green masthead and yardarm lights for a vessel engaged in mineclearing operations
C. flashing amber beacon for submarines
D. yellow flares indicating torpedo firing exercises

04826. According to the Navigation Rules, you may depart from the Rules when:

A. you do so to avoid immediate danger
B. no vessels are visible on radar
C. you are in a close quarters situation
D. out of sight of land

04827. The Rules state that vessels may depart from the requirements of the Rules when:

A. operating in restricted visibility
B. operating in a narrow channel
C. necessary to avoid immediate danger
D. the Master enters it in the ship's log

04828. The Rules state that vessels may depart from the Rules when:

A. there are other vessels in the vicinity
B. operating in a traffic separation scheme
C. engaged in a situation involving more than 2 vessels
D. necessary to avoid immediate danger

04829. The term "restricted visibility", when used in the Rules, refers to:

A. situations when you can see vessels on radar that you cannot see visually
B. visibility of less than half a mile

C. any condition where visibility is restricted
D. visibility where you cannot see shore

04830. The Navigation Rules define a "vessel not under command" as a vessel which:

A. from the nature of her work is unable to keep out of the way of another vessel
B. does not have a proper look-out
C. by taking action contrary to the Rules has created a special circumstance situation
D. through some exceptional circumstance is unable to maneuver as required by the Rules

04831. Which craft is a "power-driven vessel" under the Rules of the Road?

A. an auxiliary sailing vessel, using her engine
B. a canoe propelled by a small outboard
C. a trawler on her way to fishing grounds
D. all of the above

04832. A vessel is "in sight" of another vessel when she:

A. can be observed visually or by radar
B. has determined that risk of collision exists
C. can be seen well enough to determine her heading
D. can be observed visually from the other vessel

04833. Which statement is true concerning a "vessel engaged in fishing"?

A. The vessel is classified as "restricted in her ability to maneuver".
B. Her gear will not affect the vessel's maneuverability.
C. The vessel may be using nets, lines, or trawls.
D. She sounds the same fog signal as a vessel underway but stopped and making no way.

04834. To be considered "engaged in fishing" under the Rules, a vessel must be:

A. power-driven
B. showing lights or shapes for a vessel restricted in its ability to maneuver
C. using nets
D. using fishing apparatus which restricts maneuverability

04835. The word "vessel", in the Rules, includes:

A. a barge permanently affixed to the shore
B. nondisplacement craft
C. a drilling unit attached to the Outer Continental Shelf
D. all of the above

04836. Which vessel is, by definition, unable to keep out of the way of another vessel?

A. vessel engaged in fishing
B. vessel not underway
C. sailing vessel
D. vessel restricted in her ability to maneuver

04837. A vessel "restricted in her ability to maneuver" is 1 which:

A. through some exceptional circumstance is unable to maneuver as required by the Rules
B. from the nature of her work is unable to maneuver as required by the Rules
C. due to adverse weather conditions is unable to maneuver as required by the Rules
D. has lost steering and is unable to maneuver

04838. What determines if a vessel is "restricted in her ability to maneuver"?

A. whether or not all of the vessel's control equipment is in working order
B. the vessel's draft in relation to the available depth of water
C. whether the vessel is operating in a narrow channel
D. the nature of the vessel's work, limiting maneuverability required by the Rules

04839. A vessel is considered to be "restricted in her ability to maneuver" under the Rules if she is:

A. at anchor
B. mineclearing
C. engaged in fishing
D. engaged in towing

04840. All of the following vessels are "restricted in their ability to maneuver" EXCEPT a vessel:

A. laying a pipeline
B. not under command
C. mineclearing
D. dredging

04841. A vessel transferring cargo while underway is classified by the Rules as a vessel:

A. restricted in her ability to maneuver
B. in special circumstances
C. not under command
D. constrained by her draft

04842. Which vessel is "underway" according to the Rules?

A. a vessel made fast to a single point mooring buoy
B. a vessel engaged in towing, not making way
C. a pilot vessel at anchor
D. a vessel which has run aground

04843. According to the Rules, to what does the word "length" refer?

A. length between the perpendiculars
B. length along the waterline
C. length overall
D. registered length

04844. What does the word "breadth" mean in the Rules?

A. breadth on the uppermost continuous deck
B. molded breadth
C. greatest breadth
D. breadth at the load waterline

04845. Which of the following represents the length of a vessel as defined by the Rules? (See DIAGRAM 86)

A. A
B. B
C. C
D. D

04846. In determining "safe speed", the Rules list all of the following as factors which must be taken into account EXCEPT the:

A. limitations of radar equipment
B. presence of background lights at night
C. maximum horsepower of your vessel
D. maneuverability of your vessel

04847. Which factor is listed in the Rules as 1 which must be taken into account when determining safe speed?

A. the construction of the vessel
B. the experience of vessel personnel
C. the location of vessels detected by radar
D. all of the above

04848. The Rules state that certain factors are to be taken into account when determining safe speed. 1 of the factors stated is the:

A. aids to navigation that are available
B. maximum attainable speed of your vessel
C. temperature
D. current

04849. "Safe speed" is defined as that speed where:

A. you can stop within your visibility range
B. the vessel is not subject to vibrations
C. you are travelling slower than surrounding vessels
D. you can take proper and effective action to avoid collision

04850. The Rules state that risk of collision shall be deemed to exist:

A. whenever 2 vessels are on opposite courses
B. whenever a vessel crosses ahead of the intended track of another vessel
C. if the bearing of an approaching vessel does not appreciably change
D. if 1 vessel approaches another so as to be overtaking

04851. In which situation would you consider a risk of collision to exist?

A. A vessel is 1 point on your starboard bow, range increasing, bearing changing slightly to the right.
B. A vessel is broad on your starboard beam, range decreasing, bearing changing rapidly to the right.
C. A vessel is 2 points abaft your port beam, range decreasing, bearing constant.
D. A vessel is on your starboard quarter, range increasing, bearing is constant.

04852. Which of the following is true when operating in fog and other vessels are detected by radar?

A. The bearings should be repeatedly checked because a large bearing change will insure that you avoid collision.
B. You should maneuver before another vessel is in sight if a close-quarters situation is developing.
C. You should determine the course and speed of all radar contacts at six minute intervals.
D. Long-range scanning will provide early warning of all other vessels within radar's range.

04853. You are approaching another vessel on crossing courses. She is about 1 mile distant and is on your starboard bow. You believe she will cross ahead of you but she sounds a whistle signal of 5 short blasts. You should:

A. answer the signal and hold course and speed
B. reduce speed slightly
C. initiate a passing signal that will allow for a half mile clearance
D. make a large course change, and slow down if necessary

04854. You are approaching another vessel on crossing courses. She is approximately half a mile distant and is presently on your starboard bow. You believe she will cross ahead of you but she sounds a whistle signal of 5 short blasts. You should:

A. sound a signal of 1 prolonged blast
B. make a large course change
C. reduce speed slightly to make sure she will have room to pass
D. wait for another whistle signal from the other vessel

04855. Under the Rules, any vessel may slacken her speed, stop, or reverse her engines to:

A. create a crossing situation
B. allow more time to assess the situation
C. attract the attention of another vessel
D. all of the above

04856. Which of the following is a requirement for any action taken to avoid collision?

A. When in sight of another vessel, any action taken must be accompanied by sound signals.
B. Any action taken must not result in another close quarters situation.
C. Any action taken must include speed change.
D. all of the above

04857. A vessel proceeding along a narrow channel shall:

A. avoid crossing the channel if it impedes another vessel navigating in the channel
B. not overtake any vessels within the channel
C. keep as close as possible to the edge of the channel on her port side
D. when nearing a bend in the channel, sound a long blast of the whistle

04858. Underway in a channel, you should:

A. stay near the middle of the channel
B. keep to the starboard side of any vessels you meet
C. exchange whistle signals with any other vessels in the channel
D. keep to the side of the channel which lies to starboard

04859. A sailing vessel is meeting a vessel engaged in fishing in a narrow channel. Which statement is true?

A. Each vessel should move to the edge of the channel on her port side.
B. The vessels are required to exchange signals.
C. The fishing vessel is directed not to impede the passage of the sailing vessel.
D. Each vessel should be displaying signals for a vessel constrained by her draft.

04860. A vessel engaged in mineclearance operations shows special identity lights:

A. in addition to the lights required for a power-driven vessel
B. which means that other vessels should not approach closer than 500 meters on either side of the vessel
C. that are green and show through an arc of the horizon of 225 degrees
D. all of the above

04861. When navigating in thick fog with the radar on, you should:

A. station the look-out in the wheelhouse to keep a continuous watch on the radar
B. secure the sounding of fog signals until a vessel closes within 5 miles
C. station a look-out as low down and far forward as possible
D. keep the radar on the shortest available range for early detection of approaching vessels

04862. You are underway in thick fog. Which of the following statements is true?

A. The radar must be on and used for scanning.
B. A look-out is not required if the radar is on.
C. Fog signals are only required when a vessel is detected by radar.
D. Radar should be kept on a short-range scale for maximum detection of vessels close aboard.

04863. A sailing vessel is meeting a vessel engaged in fishing in a narrow channel. Which statement is true?

A. The fishing vessel must sound the danger signal.
B. The fishing vessel shall not impede the passage of the sailing vessel.
C. Each vessel should move to the edge of the channel on her port side.
D. Both vessels should be displaying the signal for a vessel restricted in ability to maneuver.

04864. Which of the following vessels shall not impede the passage of a vessel which can safely navigate only within a narrow channel or fairway?

A. a vessel of less than 50 meters in length
B. a sailing vessel
C. a vessel servicing an aid to navigation
D. all of the above

04865. Your 15-meter vessel is crossing a narrow channel and a large cargo vessel to starboard is within the channel and crossing your course. You should:

A. hold your course and speed
B. sound the danger signal
C. keep out of the way of the cargo vessel
D. not cross the channel

04866. If 2 sailing vessels are running free with the wind on the same side, which 1 must keep clear of the other?

A. the 1 with the wind closest abeam
B. the 1 to windward
C. the 1 to leeward
D. the 1 that sounds the first whistle signal

04867. In many cases, the Rules state that if there is any doubt as to whether a certain situation exists, it shall be considered to exist by the vessel in doubt. This principle applies to which situation?

A. a designation as the stand-on vessel
B. a crossing situation
C. risk of collision
D. all of the above

04868. Which statement is true concerning 2 sailing vessels approaching each other?

A. The vessel making the most speed is the give-way vessel.
B. A sailing vessel overtaking another is the give-way vessel.
C. A sailing vessel seeing another to leeward on an undetermined tack shall hold her course.
D. all of the above

04869. Sailing vessels have the right of way over power-driven vessels except:

A. in a crossing situation
B. when they are making more speed than the power-driven vessel
C. when they are overtaking a power-driven vessel
D. on the Inland Waters of the United States

04870. In which situation do the Rules require both vessels to change course?

A. any time the danger signal is sounded
B. when 2 power-driven vessels are crossing and it is apparent to the stand-on vessel that the give-way vessel is not taking appropriate action
C. when 2 power-driven vessels are meeting head-on
D. all of the above

04871. Your vessel is NOT making way, but is not in any way disabled. Another vessel is approaching you on your starboard beam. Which statement is true?

A. Your vessel is obliged to stay out of the way.
B. The other vessel must give way, since your vessel is stopped.
C. You should be showing the lights or shapes for a vessel not under command.
D. You should be showing the lights or shapes for a vessel restricted in her ability to maneuver.

04872. If you are the stand-on vessel in a crossing situation, you may take action to avoid collision by your maneuver alone. When may this action be taken?

A. as soon as you determine that risk of collision exists
B. only when you have reached extremis
C. when it becomes apparent that the give-way vessel is not taking appropriate action
D. when you determine that your present course will cross ahead of the other vessel

04873. In a crossing situation on open waters, a sailing vessel shall keep out of the way of all the following vessels EXCEPT a vessel:

A. not under command
B. restricted in her ability to maneuver
C. engaged in towing
D. fishing

04874. Which of the following would be a "special circumstance" under the Rules?

A. vessel at anchor
B. 2 vessels meeting
C. speed in fog
D. more than 2 vessels crossing

04875. In restricted visibility, a vessel being towed, if manned, shall sound a signal of:

A. 1 prolonged and 3 short blasts
B. 1 prolonged and 2 short blasts
C. 3 short blasts
D. 2 short blasts

04877. You are the stand-on vessel in a crossing situation. If you think the give-way vessel is NOT taking sufficient action to avoid collision, you should sound:

A. 1 short blast and maintain course
B. 2 short blasts, alter to port, and pass astern
C. the danger signal
D. no signal and maneuver at will

05000. While underway in fog, you hear a vessel ahead sound 2 prolonged blasts on the whistle. You should:

A. sound only fog signals until the other vessel is sighted
B. not sound any whistle signals until the other vessel is sighted
C. sound 2 blasts and change course to left
D. sound whistle signals only if you change course

06000. While underway in fog, you hear a vessel ahead sound 2 prolonged blasts on the whistle. You should:

A. sound 2 blasts and change course to left
B. sound only fog signals until the other vessel is sighted
C. sound whistle signals only if you change course
D. not sound any whistle signals until the other vessel is sighted

INTERNATIONAL–ONLY QUESTIONS

08000. To indicate that a vessel is constrained by her draft, a vessel may display, in a vertical line:

A. 3 360° red lights
B. 2 225° red lights
C. 3 360° blue lights
D. 2 225° blue lights

08001. A power-driven vessel pushing ahead or towing alongside will display:

A. 2 all-round red lights where they can best be seen
B. 2 towing lights in a vertical line
C. 2 forward masthead lights in a vertical line
D. a single white light forward

08002. Which statement is true concerning a vessel "constrained by her draft"?

A. She must be a power-driven vessel.
B. She is not under command.
C. She may be a vessel being towed.
D. She is hampered because of her work.

08003. A vessel using a traffic separation scheme shall:

A. only anchor in the separation zone
B. if obliged to cross a traffic lane, do so at as small an angle as is practicable
C. avoid anchoring in areas near the termination of the scheme
D. utilize the separation zone for navigating through the scheme if she is impeding other traffic due to her slower speed

08004. When moving from a berth alongside a quay (wharf), a vessel must sound:

A. 3 short blasts
B. a long blast
C. a prolonged blast
D. No signal is required.

08005. You are in charge of a 250-meter freight vessel proceeding down a narrow channel. There is a vessel engaged in fishing on your starboard bow half a mile away. Which statement is true?

A. You are not to impede the fishing vessel.
B. If you are in doubt as to the fishing vessel's intentions, you may sound the danger signal.
C. You are to slow to bare steerageway until clear of the fishing vessel.
D. You must sound the danger signal.

08006. The International Rules apply:

A. to all waters which are not inland waters
B. only to waters outside the territorial waters of the United States

C. only to waters where foreign vessels travel
D. upon the high seas and connecting waters navigable by seagoing vessels

08007. A towing light is:

A. shown at the bow
B. white in color
C. shown in addition to the stern light
D. an all-round light

08008. In a narrow channel, an overtaking vessel which intends to pass on the other vessel's port side would sound:

A. 1 prolonged followed by 2 short blasts
B. 1 short blast
C. 2 short blasts
D. 2 prolonged followed by 2 short blasts

08009. While underway on the high seas in restricted visibility, you hear a fog signal of 1 prolonged and 2 short blasts. It could be any of the following EXCEPT a vessel:

A. minesweeping
B. engaged in fishing
C. constrained by her draft
D. being towed

08010. A vessel displaying 3 red lights in a vertical line is:

A. not under command
B. aground
C. dredging
D. constrained by her draft

08011. At night, a power-driven vessel underway of less than 7 meters in length where its maximum speed does not exceed 7 knots may show, as a minimum:

A. sidelights and a stern light
B. the lights required for a vessel more than 7 meters in length
C. sidelights only
D. 1 all-round white light

08012. A signal of intent, which must be answered by another vessel, is sounded in international waters by a vessel:

A. meeting another head and head
B. crossing the course of another
C. overtaking another
D. any of the above

08013. When 2 vessels are in sight of one another, all of the following signals may be given EXCEPT:

A. a light signal of at least 5 short and rapid flashes
B. 4 short whistle blasts
C. 1 prolonged, 1 short, 1 prolonged and 1 short whistle blasts
D. 2 short whistle blasts

08014. A power-driven vessel leaving a quay or wharf must sound what signal?

A. 3 short blasts
B. A long blast
C. A prolonged blast
D. No signal is required.

08015. Lighting requirements in inland waters are different from those on international waters for:

A. barges being pushed ahead
B. vessels constrained by their draft
C. vessels towing by pushing ahead
D. all of the above

08016. What whistle signal, if any, would be sounded when 2 vessels are meeting, but will pass clear starboard to starboard?

A. 1 short blast
B. 2 short blasts
C. 5 or more short blasts
D. No signal is required.

08017. In a narrow channel, a vessel trying to overtake another on the other vessel's port side, would sound a whistle signal of:

A. 1 short blast
B. 2 short blasts
C. 2 prolonged blasts followed by 1 short blast
D. 2 prolonged blasts followed by 2 short blasts

08018. On open water, a power-driven vessel coming up dead astern of another vessel and altering her course to starboard so as to pass on the starboard side of the vessel ahead would sound:

A. 2 short blasts
B. 1 short blast
C. 2 prolonged blasts followed by 1 short blast
D. 1 long and 1 short blast

08019. If a vessel displays 3 all-round red lights in a vertical line at night, during the day she may show:

A. 3 balls in a vertical line
B. a cylinder
C. 2 diamonds in a vertical line
D. 2 cones, apexes together

08020. A vessel not under command sounds the same fog signal as a vessel:

A. towing
B. constrained by her draft
C. under sail
D. all of the above

08021. Your vessel is crossing a narrow channel, and a vessel to port is within the channel and crossing your course. She is showing a black cylinder. What is your responsibility?

A. Hold your course and speed
B. Sound the danger signal
C. Begin an exchange of passing signals
D. Do not cross the channel if you might impede the other vessel

08022. You are approaching another vessel and will pass starboard to starboard without danger if no course changes are made. You should:

A. hold course and sound a 2 blast whistle
B. hold course and sound no whistle signal
C. change course to right and sound 1 blast
D. hold course and sound 1 blast

08023. A fishing vessel is approaching a vessel not under command. Which of the following statements is correct?

A. The fishing vessel must keep clear of the vessel not under command.
B. If the vessel not under command is a power-driven vessel, she must keep clear of the fishing vessel.
C. They must exchange whistle signals.
D. Both vessels are required to take action to stay clear of each other.

08024. Which signal is only sounded by a power-driven vessel?

A. a signal meaning "I am altering my course to starboard".
B. a signal meaning "I intend to overtake you on your starboard side".
C. a signal meaning that the vessel sounding it is in doubt as to the other vessel's actions.
D. a signal sounded when approaching a bend.

08025. The light which may be used with a vessel's whistle is to be:

A. used when the whistle is broken
B. used prior to sounding the whistle
C. used only at night
D. a white light

08026. You are in sight of another vessel in a crossing situation, and the other vessel sounds 1 short blast. You are going to hold course and speed. You should:

A. answer with 1 short blast
B. answer with 2 short blasts
C. sound the danger signal
D. sound no whistle signal

08027. 2 prolonged blasts followed by 1 short blast on the whistle is a signal which could be sounded by a:

A. fishing vessel
B. vessel anchored
C. mineclearing vessel
D. vessel overtaking another in a narrow channel

08028. In a crossing situation on International waters, a short blast by the give-way vessel indicates that the vessel:

A. is holding course and speed
B. is turning to starboard
C. intends to pass port to port
D. will keep out of the way of the stand-on vessel

08029. What dayshape is prescribed for a vessel constrained by her draft?

A. a black cone, apex upward
B. a black cone, apex downward
C. 2 vertical black balls
D. a cylinder

08030. A vessel not under command sounds the same fog signal as a vessel:

A. engaged in towing
B. constrained by her draft
C. under sail
D. all of the above

08031. Which statement(s) is(are) true concerning light signals?

A. The time between flashes shall be about 5 seconds.
B. The time between successive signals shall be not less than ten seconds.
C. The light signals are to be used when not using sound signals.
D. all of the above

08032. Under what circumstances would an overtaking vessel sound a whistle signal of 2 prolonged followed by 1 short blast?

A. when overtaking in restricted visibility
B. when overtaking in a narrow channel

C. when overtaking on open waters
D. when no other vessels are in the immediate area

08033. A vessel may enter a traffic separation zone:

A. in an emergency
B. to engage in fishing within the zone
C. to cross the traffic separation scheme
D. any of the above

08034. In a traffic separation scheme, when joining a traffic lane from the side, a vessel shall do so:

A. at as small an angle as possible
B. as nearly as practical at right angles to the general direction of traffic flow
C. only in case of an emergency or to engage in fishing within the zone
D. never

08035. There are 2 classes of vessels which, to the extent necessary to carry out their work, do not have to comply with the rule regarding traffic separation schemes. 1 of these is a vessel:

A. engaged in fishing in a traffic lane
B. servicing a submarine cable
C. towing another
D. engaged on pilotage duty

08036. A vessel using a traffic separation scheme is forbidden to:

A. proceed through an inappropriate traffic lane
B. engage in fishing in the separation zone
C. cross a traffic lane
D. enter the separation zone, even in an emergency

08037. A traffic separation zone is that part of a traffic separation scheme which:

A. is located between the separation scheme and the nearest land
B. contains all the traffic moving in 1 direction
C. is designated as an anchorage area
D. separates traffic proceeding in 1 direction from traffic proceeding in opposite direction

08038. In which case would an overtaking vessel sound a whistle signal of 2 prolonged followed by 1 short blast?

A. when overtaking in restricted visibility
B. when overtaking in a narrow channel
C. when overtaking on open waters
D. when no other vessels are in the immediate area

08039. When vessels are in sight of one another, 2 short blasts from 1 of the vessels means:

A. "I am altering my course to starboard"
B. "I am altering my course to port"
C. "I intend to change course to starboard"
D. "I intend to change course to port"

08040. Which vessel may NOT exhibit 2 red lights in a vertical line?

A. a vessel constrained by her draft
B. a trawler
C. a vessel aground
D. a dredge

08041. Vessel "A" is overtaking vessel "B" on open waters and will pass without changing course. Vessel "A":

A. should sound 2 short blasts
B. should sound the danger signal
C. should sound 1 long blast
D. need not sound any whistle signals

08042. Of the vessels listed, which must keep out of the way of all the others?

A. a vessel constrained by her draft
B. a vessel restricted in her ability to maneuver
C. a vessel on pilotage duty
D. a vessel engaged in fishing

08043. Which of the following vessels would NOT sound a fog signal of 1 prolonged and 2 short blasts?

A. a vessel not under command
B. a vessel constrained by her draft
C. a vessel being towed
D. a vessel sailing

08044. In international waters, you are on Vessel "I" in the situation shown in DIAGRAM 36. Vessel "II" sounds 1 short blast. What action should you take?

A. Sound 1 short blast and hold course and speed.
B. Hold course and speed without giving a signal.
C. Sound 1 short blast and slow down or turn to starboard.
D. Sound the danger signal and slow to moderate speed.

08045. You intend to overtake a vessel in a narrow channel, and you intend to pass along the vessel's port side. How should you signal your intention?

A. No signal is necessary.
B. 2 prolonged blasts

C. 2 short blasts
D. 2 prolonged followed by 2 short blasts

08046. A vessel sounds 2 short blasts. This signal indicates the vessel:

A. intends to alter course to port
B. intends to pass starboard to starboard
C. is altering course to port
D. will alter course to port

08047. A vessel sounds 1 short blast. This signal indicates the vessel:

A. intends to alter course to starboard
B. intends to pass starboard to starboard
C. is altering course to starboard
D. intends to pass port to port

08048. You are underway in a narrow channel, and you are being overtaken by a vessel astern. After the overtaking vessel sounds the proper signal indicating his intention to pass your vessel on your starboard side, you signal your agreement by sounding:

A. 1 short blast
B. 2 prolonged blasts
C. 2 prolonged followed by 2 short blasts
D. 1 prolonged, 1 short, 1 prolonged and 1 short blast in that order

08049. When 2 vessels are in sight of one another, all of the following signals are appropriate EXCEPT:

A. a light signal of at least 5 short and rapid flashes
B. 4 short blasts on the whistle
C. 1 prolonged, 1 short, 1 prolonged and 1 short blast on the whistle, in that order
D. 2 short blasts on the whistle

08050. A sailing vessel is overtaking a vessel in a narrow channel, so as to pass on the power-driven vessel's port side. The overtaken vessel will have to move to facilitate passage. The sailing vessel is the:

A. stand-on vessel and would sound 2 short blasts
B. give-way vessel and would sound no whistle signal
C. stand-on vessel and would sound no whistle signal
D. give-way vessel and would sound 2 prolonged blasts followed by 2 short blasts

08051. A vessel constrained by her draft may display:

A. 3 all-round red lights
B. 2 225° red lights

C. 3 all-round blue lights
D. 2 225° blue lights

08052. When 2 vessels meet, a 2 blast whistle signal by either of the vessels indicates:

A. "I intend to alter course to port"
B. "I desire to pass starboard to starboard"
C. "I desire to pass port to port"
D. "I am altering course to port"

08053. A 20-meter power-driven vessel pushing ahead or towing alongside will display:

A. a single white light forward
B. 2 masthead lights in a vertical line
C. 2 towing lights in a vertical line
D. 2 all-round red lights where they can best be seen

08054. Which statement applies to a vessel "constrained by her draft"?

A. She is severely restricted in her ability to change her course because of her draft in relation to the available depth of water.
B. The term applies only to vessels in marked channels.
C. She is designated as a "vessel restricted in her ability to maneuver".
D. The vessel must be over 100 m in length.

08055. A vessel using a traffic separation scheme shall:

A. only anchor in the separation zone
B. avoid crossing traffic lanes, but if obliged to do so, shall cross on a heading at as small an angle as is practical
C. avoid anchoring in areas near the termination of the scheme
D. use the separation zone for navigating through the scheme if she is hindering other traffic due to her slower speed

08056. A whistle signal of 1 prolonged, 1 short, 1 prolonged and 1 short blast, is sounded by a vessel:

A. at anchor
B. towing a submerged object
C. being overtaken in a narrow channel
D. in distress

08057. Your vessel is backing out of a slip in a harbor and you can see that other vessels are approaching. You should sound:

A. 3 short blasts when leaving the slip
B. 1 long blast followed by 3 short blasts when the last line is taken aboard
C. 1 prolonged blast only
D. the danger signal

08058. Which vessel is to keep out of the way of the others?

A. a vessel constrained by her draft
B. a vessel engaged in underwater operations
C. a vessel engaged in trawling
D. a vessel not under command

08059. You are in sight of a power-driven vessel that sounds 2 short blasts of the whistle. This signal means that the vessel:

A. is altering course to port
B. is altering course to starboard
C. intends to leave you on her port side
D. intends to leave you on her starboard side

08060. You are operating a vessel through a narrow channel and your vessel must stay within the channel to be navigated safely. Another vessel is crossing your course from starboard to port, and you are in doubt as to his intentions. You:

A. may sound the danger signal
B. may sound 1 prolonged and 2 short blasts
C. should sound 1 short blast to indicate that you are holding course and speed
D. are required to back down

08061. Vessel "A" is overtaking vessel "B" on open waters as shown in DIAGRAM 17, and will pass without changing course. Vessel "A":

A. should sound 2 short blasts
B. should sound the danger signal
C. should sound 1 long blast
D. need not sound any whistle signals

08062. If you sighted 3 red lights in a vertical line on another vessel at night, it would be a vessel:

A. aground
B. constrained by her draft
C. dredging
D. moored over a wreck

08063. On open water 2 vessels are in an overtaking situation. The overtaking vessel has just sounded 1 short blast on the whistle. What is the meaning of this whistle signal?

A. "I request permission to pass you on my port side."
B. "I will maintain course and speed and pass you on your starboard side."
C. "On which side should I pass?"
D. "I am changing course to starboard."

08064. You are underway in fog and hear a fog signal consisting of 1 prolonged and 2 short blasts. It could be any of the following EXCEPT a vessel:

A. engaged in minesweeping
B. engaged in fishing
C. constrained by her draft
D. being towed

08065. Vessel "A" and "B" are in a crossing situation on the high seas as shown in DIAGRAM 14. "B" blows 1 short blast. What is the proper action for "A" to take?

A. Answer with 1 blast and hold course and speed.
B. Hold course and speed.
C. Answer with 1 blast and keep clear of vessel "B".
D. Sound danger signal.

08066. Which signal may be sounded by 1 of 2 vessels in sight of each other?

A. 4 short blasts on the whistle
B. 1 prolonged blast on the whistle
C. 1 short blast on the whistle followed by 1 flash on a light
D. 1 short, 1 prolonged, and 1 short blast on the whistle

08067. Which vessel shall avoid impeding the safe passage of a vessel constrained by her draft?

A. a vessel not under command
B. a fishing vessel
C. a vessel restricted in her ability to maneuver
D. all of the above

08068. A signal of 1 prolonged, 1 short, 1 prolonged, and 1 short blast, in that order is given by a vessel :

A. engaged on pilotage duty
B. in distress
C. at anchor
D. being overtaken in a narrow channel

08069. Which signal is appropriate from 1 of 2 vessels in sight of each other?

A. 4 short blasts on the whistle
B. 1 prolonged blast on the whistle
C. 1 short blast on the whistle followed by 1 flash on a light
D. 1 short, 1 prolonged, and 1 short blast on the whistle

08070. In addition to her running lights, an underway vessel constrained by her draft shall carry in a vertical line:

A. a red light, a white light, and a red light
B. 2 red lights
C. 2 white lights
D. 3 red lights

08071. Which of the following vessels is NOT regarded as being "restricted in her ability to maneuver"?

A. a vessel servicing an aid to navigation
B. a vessel engaged in dredging
C. a towing vessel with tow unable to deviate from its course
D. a vessel constrained by her draft

08072. When 2 vessels are in sight of one another, all of the following signals may be given EXCEPT:

A. a light signal of at least 5 short and rapid flashes
B. 1 prolonged, 1 short, 1 prolonged and 1 short whistle blasts
C. 4 short whistle blasts
D. 2 short whistle blasts

08073. In a narrow channel, an overtaking vessel which intends to PASS on the other vessel's port side would sound:

A. 1 prolonged followed by 2 short blasts
B. 1 short blast
C. 2 prolonged followed by 2 short blasts
D. 2 short blasts

08074. 2 prolonged blasts followed by 1 short blast on the whistle is a signal which would be sounded by a vessel:

A. overtaking another in a narrow channel
B. anchored
C. engaged in mineclearance
D. engaged in fishing

08075. You intend to overtake a vessel in a narrow channel, and you intend to pass along the vessel's port side. How should you signal your intention?

A. 2 short blasts followed by 2 prolonged blasts
B. 2 prolonged followed by 2 short blasts
C. 2 prolonged blasts only
D. 2 short blasts only

08076. You are underway in a narrow channel, and you are being overtaken by a vessel astern. After the overtaking vessel sounds the proper signal indicating his intention to pass your vessel on your starboard side, you signal your agreement by sounding:

A. 2 prolonged followed by 2 short blasts
B. 1 prolonged, 1 short, 1 prolonged and 1 short blast
C. 1 short blast
D. 2 prolonged blasts

08077. Vessel "A" is overtaking vessel "B" on open waters and will pass without changing course. Vessel "A":

A. should sound 2 prolonged blasts followed by 2 short blasts
B. should sound the danger signal
C. need not sound any whistle signals
D. should sound 1 long blast

08078. Vessel "A" is overtaking vessel "B" on open waters as shown in DIAGRAM 17, and will pass without changing course. Vessel "A":

A. need not sound any whistle signals
B. should sound 2 short blasts
C. should sound the danger signal
D. should sound 1 long blast

08079. Which signal is only sounded by a power-driven vessel?

A. a signal meaning "I intend to overtake you on your starboard side".
B. a signal meaning that the vessel sounding it is in doubt as to the other vessel's actions.
C. a signal meaning "I am altering my course to starboard".
D. a signal sounded when approaching a bend.

08080. Which signal is appropriate from 1 of 2 vessels in sight of each other?

A. 1 short blast on the whistle followed by 1 flash on a light
B. 4 short blasts on the whistle
C. 1 prolonged blast on the whistle
D. 1 short, 1 prolonged, and 1 short blast on the whistle

08081. The light which may be used with a vessel's whistle must be:

A. used when the whistle is broken
B. a white light
C. used only at night
D. used prior to sounding the whistle

08082. Which statement is true concerning light signals?

A. The time between flashes shall be about 5 seconds.
B. The light signals are to be used when not using sound signals.
C. The time between successive signals shall be not less than ten seconds.
D. all of the above

08084. At night, a power-driven vessel less than 7 meters in length, with a maximum speed which does not exceed 7 knots, may show when underway:

A. a combination lantern
B. sidelights and a white stern light
C. 1 all-round white light
D. a lantern showing a white light exhibited in sufficient time to prevent collision

08085. At night, a power-driven vessel less than 7 meters in length, with a maximum speed which does not exceed 7 knots, must show when underway at least:

A. 1 white 360° light
B. a white light on the near approach of another vessel
C. sidelights and a stern light
D. the lights required of a vessel less than 12 meters in length

08086. Lighting requirements in inland waters are different from those for international waters for:

A. barges being towed astern
B. vessels not under command
C. vessels towing by pushing ahead
D. all of the above

08087. Lighting requirements in inland waters are different from those for international waters for:

A. barges being towed by pushing ahead
B. vessels restricted in their ability to maneuver
C. vessels towing astern
D. barges being towed astern

08088. A 20-meter power-driven vessel pushing ahead or towing alongside will display:

A. 2 towing lights in a vertical line
B. a towing light above the stern light
C. 2 all-round red lights at the masthead
D. 2 masthead lights in a vertical line

08089. A towing light:

A. flashes at regular intervals of 50-70 flashes per minute
B. is yellow in color
C. shows an unbroken light over an arc of the horizon of not less than 180° nor more than 225°
D. all of the above

08090. A towing light is:

A. shown below the stern light
B. white in color
C. displayed at the masthead
D. a light having the same characteristics as the stern light

08091. Systems of inbound and outbound lanes to promote the safe flow of vessel traffic in certain areas around the world are known as:

A. merchant vessel reporting systems
B. traffic separation schemes
C. collision avoidance fairways
D. restricted maneuverability channels

08092. A light used to signal passing intentions must be an:

A. alternating red and yellow light
B. alternating white and yellow light
C. all-round white or yellow light
D. all-round white light only

08093. Traffic separation schemes established by the International Maritime Organization:

A. provide inbound and outbound lanes to promote the safe flow of vessel traffic
B. provide vessel reporting systems to assist in search and rescue in the event of a vessel casualty
C. provide routing and scheduling procedures to reduce shipping delays
D. prohibit vessels carrying hazardous cargoes from entering waters that are environmentally sensitive

08096. A vessel constrained by her draft may display:

A. 3 all-round red lights instead of lights required for a power-driven vessel of her class
B. the same lights as a vessel restricted in her ability to maneuver
C. 3 all-round red lights in addition to lights required for a power-driven vessel of her class
D. the lights for a power-driven vessel which is not under command

08097. What dayshape is prescribed for a vessel constrained by her draft?

A. a black diamond
B. a cylinder
C. a black ball
D. a black cone, apex upward

08098. If at night a vessel displays 3 all-round red lights in a vertical line, during the day she may show:

A. 2 cones, base to base
B. 3 black balls in a vertical line
C. a cylinder
D. a cone, apex downward

08099. A vessel displaying 3 red lights in a vertical line is:

A. restricted in her ability to maneuver
B. not under command
C. engaged in mineclearing operations
D. constrained by her draft

08100. The International Rules of the Road apply:

A. to all waters
B. to any waters inside the territorial waters of the U. S.
C. only to waters where foreign vessels travel
D. upon the high seas and connecting waters navigable by seagoing vessels

08101. Which statement applies to a vessel "constrained by her draft"?

A. The term only applies to vessels in narrow channels.
B. She is severely restricted in her ability to change her course because of her draft in relation to the available depth and width of navigable water.
C. She is designated as a "vessel restricted in her ability to maneuver".
D. The vessel must be over 100 m in length.

08102. Which statement is true concerning a vessel "constrained by her draft"?

A. She is hampered because of her work.
B. She is unable to maneuver due to some exceptional circumstance.
C. She may be a vessel being towed.
D. She must be a power-driven vessel.

08103. Which of the following vessels is NOT "restricted in her ability to maneuver"?

A. a vessel servicing an aid to navigation
B. a vessel constrained by her draft
C. a towing vessel with tow, unable to deviate from its course
D. a vessel engaged in dredging

08104. Your vessel is constrained by draft and operating in a narrow channel. Another vessel is crossing your course from starboard to port, and you are in doubt as to her intentions. You:

A. should sound 1 short blast to indicate that you are holding course and speed
B. must sound 1 prolonged blast
C. may sound the danger signal
D. are required to back down

08105. Your vessel is crossing a narrow channel and a vessel to port is within the channel and crossing your course. She is showing a black cylinder. You should:

A. hold your course and speed
B. not impede the other vessel
C. exchange passing signals
D. sound the danger signal

08106. In a traffic separation scheme, when joining a traffic lane from the side, a vessel shall do so:

A. only in case of an emergency or to engage in fishing within the zone
B. as nearly as practical at right angles to the general direction of traffic flow
C. at as small an angle as possible
D. only to anchor within the zone

08107. A traffic separation zone is that part of a traffic separation scheme which:

A. is located between the scheme and the nearest land
B. separates traffic proceeding in 1 direction from traffic proceeding in opposite direction
C. is designated as an anchorage area
D. contains all the traffic moving in the same direction

08108. A vessel using a traffic separation scheme shall NOT:

A. cross a traffic lane
B. engage in fishing in the separation zone
C. proceed in an inappropriate traffic lane
D. enter the separation zone

08109. There are 2 classes of vessels which do not have to comply with the rule regarding traffic separation schemes, to the extent necessary to carry out their work. 1 of those is a vessel:

A. engaged in fishing
B. towing another
C. servicing a navigational aid
D. on pilotage duty

08110. A vessel using a traffic separation scheme shall:

A. avoid anchoring in areas near the termination of the scheme
B. avoid crossing traffic lanes, but if obliged to do so, shall cross on a heading at as small an angle as is practical
C. only anchor in the separation zone
D. use the separation zone for navigating through the scheme if she is hindering other traffic due to her slower speed

08111. Your vessel is backing out of a slip in a harbor, and visibility is restricted looking upstream. You should sound:

A. 1 prolonged blast only
B. 1 long blast followed by 3 short blasts when the last line is taken aboard
C. 1 prolonged blast followed by 3 short blasts when leaving the slip
D. the danger signal

08112. Traffic separation schemes established by the International Maritime Organization:

A. provide routing and scheduling procedures to reduce shipping delays
B. provide traffic patterns in congested areas, so that vessels can operate without having a separate lookout
C. provide inbound and outbound lanes to promote the safe flow of vessel traffic
D. prohibit vessels carrying hazardous cargoes from entering waters that are environmentally sensitive

08113. You are approaching another vessel and will pass starboard to starboard without danger if no course changes are made. You should:

A. hold course and sound no whistle signal
B. hold course and sound a 2 blast whistle signal
C. change course to starboard and sound 1 blast
D. hold course and sound 1 blast

08114. Which of the following statements is true concerning a situation involving a fishing vessel and a vessel not under command?

A. They are required to communicate by radiotelephone.
B. If the vessel not under command is a power-driven vessel, she must keep clear of the fishing vessel.
C. The fishing vessel must keep out of the way of the vessel not under command.
D. Both vessels are required to take action to stay clear of each other.

08115. Of the vessels listed, which must keep out of the way of all the others?

A. a vessel constrained by her draft
B. a vessel restricted in her ability to maneuver
C. a vessel pushing a barge
D. a vessel engaged in fishing

08116. Which vessel shall avoid impeding the safe passage of a vessel constrained by her draft?

A. a vessel not under command
B. a sailing vessel
C. a vessel restricted in her ability to maneuver
D. all of the above

08118. A signal of intent must be sounded in international waters by:

A. a vessel meeting another head and head
B. a vessel overtaking another in a narrow channel
C. a vessel crossing the course of another
D. the give-way vessel in a crossing situation

08119. Yellow lights are NOT used to identify:

A. towing vessels pushing ahead
B. air cushion vessels in a nondisplacement mode
C. purse seiners
D. U. S. submarines

08120. A light used to signal passing intentions must be an:

A. all-round yellow light only
B. all-round white light only
C. all-round blue light only
D. alternating red and yellow light

08121. Which statement is TRUE, according to the Rules?

A. A fishing vessel has the right of way over a vessel constrained by her draft.
B. A vessel not under command shall avoid impeding the safe passage of a vessel constrained by her draft.
C. A vessel engaged in fishing shall, so far as possible, keep out of the way of a vessel restricted in her ability to maneuver.
D. A vessel restricted in her ability to maneuver shall keep out of the way of a vessel not under command.

08126. A light used to signal passing intentions must be an:

A. all-round white or yellow light
B. all-round yellow light only
C. all-round white light only
D. Any colored light is acceptable

08127. Which statement is TRUE, according to the Rules?

A. A fishing vessel has the right of way over a vessel constrained by her draft.
B. A vessel engaged in fishing shall, so far as possible, keep out of the way of a vessel restricted in her ability to maneuver.
C. A vessel not under command shall avoid impeding the safe passage of a vessel constrained by her draft.
D. A vessel restricted in her ability to maneuver shall keep out of the way of a vessel not under command.

08128. Which statement is TRUE, according to the Rules?

A. A vessel engaged in fishing shall, so far as possible, keep out of the way of a vessel restricted in her ability to maneuver.
B. A vessel restricted in her ability to maneuver shall keep out of the way of a vessel not under command.
C. A vessel not under command shall avoid impeding the safe passage of a vessel constrained by her draft.
D. A fishing vessel has the right of way over a vessel constrained by her draft.

08129. Which statement is TRUE, according to the Rules?

A. A vessel restricted in her ability to maneuver shall keep out of the way of a vessel not under command.
B. A vessel not under command shall avoid impeding the safe passage of a vessel constrained by her draft.
C. A fishing vessel has the right of way over a vessel constrained by her draft.
D. A vessel engaged in fishing shall, so far as possible, keep out of the way of a vessel restricted in her ability to maneuver.

08131. What characteristic must a light have if used to signal passing intentions?

A. It must be an all-round white light.
B. It must be an alternating blue and white light.
C. It must be an all-round white and yellow light.
D. It must be an alternating red and yellow light.

08135. What characteristic must a light used to indicate passing intentions have?

A. It must be an alternating red and yellow light.
B. It must be an all-round white light.
C. It must be an all-round yellow light.
D. It must be an all-round blue light.

00001 C	00064 A	00127 D	04027 D	04091 B	04154 C	04217 D	04280 A
00002 B	00065 B	00128 C	04028 D	04092 D	04155 D	04218 A	04281 D
00003 B	00066 B	00129 B	04029 B	04093 A	04156 C	04219 D	04282 A
00004 B	00067 C	00130 D	04030 B	04094 C	04157 D	04220 B	04283 C
00005 A	00068 D	00131 B	04031 A	04095 B	04158 C	04221 D	04284 D
00006 B	00069 A	00132 C	04032 A	04096 A	04159 D	04222 B	04285 C
00007 A	00070 A	00133 A	04033 B	04097 B	04160 A	04223 A	04286 A
00008 A	00071 D	00134 B	04034 A	04098 D	04161 A	04224 B	04287 D
00009 B	00072 C	00135 C	04035 D	04099 B	04162 C	04225 A	04288 B
00010 D	00073 D	00136 D	04036 A	04100 B	04163 C	04226 C	04289 B
00011 C	00074 B	00137 C	04037 A	04101 A	04164 B	04227 B	04290 B
00012 D	00075 C	00138 B	04038 B	04102 B	04165 A	04228 B	04291 C
00013 C	00076 A	00139 D	04039 B	04103 C	04166 A	04229 B	04292 B
00014 C	00077 B	00140 A	04040 B	04104 B	04167 A	04230 C	04293 D
00015 C	00078 D	00141 C	04041 A	04105 A	04168 B	04231 B	04294 C
00016 D	00079 C	00142 B	04042 B	04106 B	04169 D	04232 C	04295 C
00017 D	00080 C	00143 C	04043 D	04107 B	04170 B	04233 A	04296 C
00018 C	00081 B	00144 C	04044 D	04108 C	04171 D	04234 D	04297 A
00019 D	00082 B	00145 A	04045 A	04109 C	04172 B	04235 A	04298 B
00020 B	00083 D	00146 C	04046 B	04110 C	04173 D	04236 D	04299 B
00021 D	00084 D	00147 D	04047 B	04111 B	04174 C	04237 C	04300 A
00022 D	00085 D	00148 C	04048 C	04112 C	04175 A	04238 C	04301 D
00023 C	00086 C	00149 C	04049 B	04113 A	04176 D	04239 B	04302 B
00024 C	00087 D	00150 C	04050 B	04114 C	04177 C	04240 B	04303 D
00025 A	00088 B	00163 D	04051 A	04115 C	04178 A	04241 A	04304 B
00026 B	00089 B	00216 B	04052 A	04116 B	04179 D	04242 C	04305 D
00027 B	00090 C	00220 C	04053 A	04117 B	04180 B	04243 A	04306 A
00028 B	00091 A	00221 C	04054 C	04118 A	04181 B	04244 B	04307 A
00029 C	00092 B	00222 D	04055 C	04119 A	04182 D	04245 D	04308 D
00030 C	00093 D	00223 A	04056 C	04120 D	04183 A	04246 A	04309 A
00031 D	00094 A	00224 B	04057 D	04121 A	04184 B	04247 D	04310 D
00032 B	00095 C	00225 D	04058 B	04122 D	04185 D	04248 D	04311 D
00033 A	00096 A	00227 A	04059 D	04123 A	04186 B	04249 A	04312 B
00034 A	00097 D	00262 C	04060 B	04124 C	04187 C	04250 A	04313 A
00035 C	00098 C	00352 B	04061 D	04125 B	04188 C	04251 C	04314 D
00036 D	00099 C	00727 C	04062 A	04126 D	04189 C	04252 D	04315 A
00037 B	00100 D	00821 D	04064 A	04127 C	04190 A	04253 D	04316 B
00038 C	00101 A	04000 B	04065 B	04128 C	04191 B	04254 D	04317 C
00039 D	00102 D	04002 C	04066 D	04129 A	04192 B	04255 C	04318 B
00040 C	00103 B	04003 D	04067 D	04130 A	04193 A	04256 D	04319 D
00041 B	00104 A	04004 C	04068 A	04131 D	04194 C	04257 D	04320 D
00042 A	00105 B	04005 B	04069 A	04132 A	04195 D	04258 C	04321 D
00043 B	00106 C	04006 C	04070 C	04133 C	04196 C	04259 C	04322 D
00044 C	00107 D	04007 C	04071 D	04134 B	04197 C	04260 B	04323 A
00045 B	00108 D	04008 D	04072 A	04135 D	04198 A	04261 D	04324 C
00046 A	00109 B	04009 C	04073 B	04136 C	04199 D	04262 D	04325 B
00047 A	00110 B	04010 C	04074 D	04137 D	04200 D	04263 A	04326 C
00048 A	00111 A	04011 C	04075 C	04138 D	04201 B	04264 C	04327 C
00049 C	00112 C	04012 A	04076 D	04139 B	04202 C	04265 C	04329 B
00050 C	00113 D	04013 D	04077 A	04140 D	04203 B	04266 D	04330 D
00051 D	00114 C	04014 B	04078 D	04141 C	04204 D	04267 C	04331 B
00052 A	00115 A	04015 D	04079 D	04142 A	04205 C	04268 B	04332 C
00053 C	00116 C	04016 A	04080 A	04143 D	04206 C	04269 A	04333 A
00054 B	00117 B	04017 C	04081 C	04144 A	04207 B	04270 C	04334 A
00055 B	00118 B	04018 D	04082 B	04145 C	04208 A	04271 C	04335 B
00056 C	00119 C	04019 A	04083 B	04146 A	04209 B	04272 B	04336 A
00057 A	00120 B	04020 D	04084 B	04147 D	04210 D	04273 C	04337 B
00058 D	00121 D	04021 D	04085 D	04148 D	04211 C	04274 D	04338 D
00059 A	00122 C	04022 A	04086 C	04149 A	04212 C	04275 C	04339 D
00060 C	00123 C	04023 C	04087 C	04150 B	04213 D	04276 B	04340 A
00061 A	00124 B	04024 D	04088 D	04151 A	04214 D	04277 A	04341 B
00062 A	00125 D	04025 C	04089 D	04152 B	04215 D	04278 D	04342 A
00063 B	00126 B	04026 D	04090 C	04153 C	04216 B	04279 B	04343 D

04344 B	04408 D	04472 D	04535 D	04599 D	04662 A	04725 D	04868 B
04345 D	04409 C	04473 D	04536 C	04600 C	04663 B	04726 A	04869 C
04346 B	04410 D	04474 C	04537 D	04601 B	04664 C	04728 C	04870 C
04347 D	04411 A	04475 D	04538 D	04602 D	04665 A	04729 B	04871 A
04348 A	04412 D	04476 D	04539 A	04603 A	04666 D	04730 A	04872 C
04349 B	04413 B	04477 C	04540 B	04604 B	04667 D	04731 B	04873 C
04350 C	04414 A	04478 A	04541 D	04605 B	04668 D	04732 C	04874 D
04351 B	04415 C	04479 A	04542 C	04606 B	04669 B	04733 C	04875 A
04352 C	04416 D	04480 B	04543 B	04607 B	04670 C	04734 C	04877 C
04353 A	04417 D	04481 C	04544 C	04608 A	04671 A	04735 B	05000 A
04354 A	04418 B	04482 A	04545 D	04609 A	04672 C	04736 B	06000 B
04355 B	04419 C	04483 A	04546 D	04610 A	04673 D	04737 A	08000 A
04356 C	04420 D	04484 A	04547 D	04611 A	04674 A	04738 B	08001 C
04357 C	04421 A	04485 C	04548 C	04612 D	04675 C	04739 D	08002 A
04358 D	04422 C	04486 A	04549 B	04613 A	04676 C	04745 C	08003 C
04359 C	04423 A	04487 B	04550 D	04614 D	04677 B	04770 D	08004 D
04360 C	04424 B	04488 D	04551 C	04615 A	04678 A	04780 A	08005 B
04361 B	04425 D	04489 B	04552 D	04616 A	04679 C	04818 B	08006 D
04362 B	04426 D	04490 B	04553 C	04617 C	04680 D	04819 A	08007 C
04363 C	04427 C	04491 A	04554 C	04618 A	04681 C	04820 C	08008 D
04364 C	04428 B	04492 D	04555 A	04619 D	04682 D	04825 C	08009 C
04365 A	04429 C	04493 C	04556 A	04620 A	04683 C	04826 A	08010 D
04366 A	04430 C	04494 D	04557 D	04621 B	04684 C	04827 C	08011 D
04367 C	04431 A	04495 D	04558 B	04622 C	04685 A	04828 D	08012 C
04368 B	04432 B	04496 D	04559 C	04623 B	04686 A	04829 C	08013 B
04369 D	04433 B	04497 C	04560 C	04624 B	04687 C	04830 D	08014 D
04370 C	04434 C	04498 C	04561 C	04625 D	04688 A	04831 D	08015 D
04371 D	04435 D	04499 A	04562 A	04626 B	04689 C	04832 D	08016 D
04372 D	04436 C	04500 B	04563 A	04627 C	04690 C	04833 C	08017 D
04373 A	04437 A	04501 A	04564 B	04628 A	04691 B	04834 D	08018 B
04374 D	04438 B	04502 D	04565 C	04629 C	04692 C	04835 B	08019 B
04375 B	04439 C	04503 B	04S66 D	04630 A	04693 A	04836 D	08020 D
04376 A	04440 D	04504 B	04567 C	04631 D	04694 B	04837 B	08021 B
04377 B	04441 B	04505 B	04568 B	04632 B	04695 B	04838 D	08022 B
04378 A	04442 A	04506 D	04569 B	04633 B	04696 C	04839 B	08023 A
04379 D	04443 C	04507 A	04570 D	04634 A	04697 D	04840 B	08024 A
04380 D	04444 B	04508 A	04571 C	04635 C	04698 C	04841 A	08025 D
04381 B	04445 C	04509 B	04572 C	04636 B	04699 C	04842 B	08026 D
04382 A	04446 D	04510 B	04573 D	04637 B	04700 B	04843 C	08027 D
04383 C	04447 B	04511 C	04574 B	04638 A	04701 B	04844 C	08028 B
04384 D	04449 C	04512 D	04575 A	04639 D	04702 D	04845 C	08029 D
04385 A	04450 B	04513 D	04576 B	04640 A	04703 C	04846 C	08030 D
04386 A	04451 B	04614 D	04577 A	04641 A	04704 C	04847 C	08031 B
04387 C	04452 A	04515 A	04578 A	04642 B	04705 D	04848 D	08032 B
04389 D	04453 D	04516 B	04579 D	04643 A	04706 A	04849 D	08033 D
04390 D	04454 A	04517 B	04580 A	04644 C	04707 A	04850 C	08034 A
04391 B	04455 D	04518 D	04581 D	04645 D	04708 C	04851 C	08035 B
04392 B	04456 B	04519 A	04582 B	04646 B	04709 B	04852 B	08036 A
04393 C	04457 A	04520 A	04583 D	04647 B	04710 D	04853 D	08037 D
04394 D	04458 A	04521 D	04585 D	04648 D	04711 C	04854 B	08038 B
04395 C	04459 D	04522 B	04586 D	04649 C	04712 B	04855 B	08039 B
04396 A	04460 A	04523 C	04587 B	04650 D	04713 A	04856 B	08040 A
04397 C	04461 B	04524 C	04588 C	04651 D	04714 B	04857 A	08041 D
04398 C	04462 D	04525 C	04589 D	04652 C	04715 D	04858 D	08042 C
04399 B	04463 C	04526 B	04590 D	04653 D	04716 C	04859 C	08043 C
04400 C	04464 A	04527 A	04591 B	04654 B	04717 D	04860 A	08044 B
04401 D	04465 C	04528 D	04592 D	04655 B	04718 D	04861 C	08045 D
04402 A	04466 C	04529 A	04593 D	04656 A	04719 B	04862 A	08046 C
04403 C	04467 D	04530 C	04594 A	04657 C	04720 C	04863 B	08047 C
04404 D	04468 A	04531 B	04595 C	04658 A	04721 A	04864 B	08048 D
04405 B	04469 B	04532 C	04596 D	04659 A	04722 D	04865 C	08049 B
04406 C	04470 C	04533 A	04597 A	04660 D	04723 B	04866 B	08050 D
04407 C	04471 D	04534 C	04598 A	04661 D	04724 C	04867 C	08051 A

08052 D   08119 A
08053 B   08120 B
08054 A   08121 C
08055 C   08126 C
08056 C   08127 B
08057 A   08128 A
08058 C   08129 D
08059 A   08131 A
08060 A   08135 B
08061 D
08062 B
08063 D
08064 D
08065 B
08066 C
08067 B
08068 D
08069 C
08070 D
08071 D
08072 C
08073 C
08074 A
08075 B
08076 B
08077 C
08078 A
08079 C
08080 A
08081 B
08082 C
08084 C
08085 A
08086 C
08087 A
08088 D
08089 B
08090 D
08091 B
08092 D
08093 A
08096 C
08097 B
08098 C
08099 D
08100 D
08101 B
08102 D
08103 B
08104 C
08105 B
08106 C
08107 B
08108 C
08109 C
08110 A
08111 A
08112 C
08113 A
08114 C
08115 C
08116 B
08118 B

DECK GENERAL

SHIP HANDLING

Propeller and Rudder Forces

To predict the motion of a power-driven vessel, you must consider three forces exerted at the stern:

• *Propeller thrust* is either forward (in forward gear) or aft (in reverse gear) and is maximum with the vessel dead in the water.

• *Side propeller thrust* is to starboard for an RH prop in forward gear and to port in reverse. Side thrusts are opposite for an LH prop.

• *Rudder force* depends on the flow of water over the rudder, due to both propeller action and motion through the water. It is in the direction opposite to the direction steered when the propeller is turning forward.

Combined Forces in Action

Single screw vessel with RH propeller

• *Getting underway* the rudder kicks stern to starboard, requiring right rudder.

• *Underway* at speed, side force diminishes, requiring less right rudder. Vessels requiring rudder action while on a constant course are said to possess "helm."

• *Stopping*, the propeller is reversed. Both propeller thrust and side propeller thrust reverse, kicking the stern to port.

• *Backing* is less predictable. Initially, side propeller thrust is strong and rudder force weak. Rudder force and response to rudder increase as the vessel gains way.

• *Casting* (kicking around) turns a vessel in a small space. To turn a vessel sharply to port:

  1. Go ahead with left full rudder until stern swings to starboard.

  2. As soon as vessel gains way, back prop with right full rudder until vessel stops.

  3. Repeat steps 1 and 2 until vessel is headed in desired direction.

Pivot Point

When turning sharply, a vessel acts as if it is pivoting about a point on the keel. For a powerboat the pivot point is usually about one-third of the length aft of the bow. For a sailboat with a fin keel, the pivot point is roughly centered on the keel. You should keep the pivot point in mind when maneuvering in close quarters in order to predict the path of the stern.

Propeller and Rudder Forces

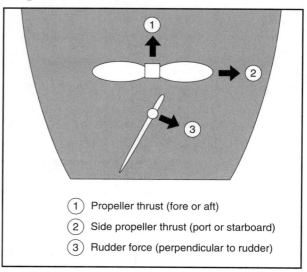

① Propeller thrust (fore or aft)

② Side propeller thrust (port or starboard)

③ Rudder force (perpendicular to rudder)

Twin Screws

A vessel with twin screws has two advantages in maneuvering:

1. Since the starboard propeller is RH and the port propeller LH, if both engines are turning at the same rpm, there will be no net side force.

2. Since starboard and port propellers are offset from the centerline, each individually exerts a turning force both in forward and reverse. By operating one in forward and the other in reverse, the vessel can be turned with little forward or aft movement.

Twin Screw Action

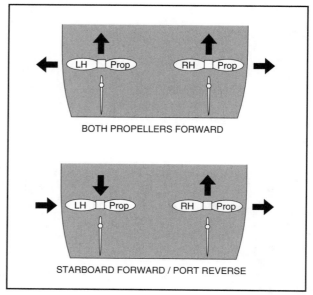

BOTH PROPELLERS FORWARD

STARBOARD FORWARD / PORT REVERSE

Dock Lines

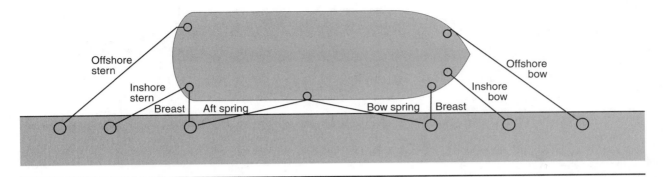

Offshore stern

Inshore stern

Breast Aft spring Bow spring Breast

Offshore bow

Inshore bow

Docking Procedures for a Single RH Prop

NO CURRENT, NO WIND

1. Forward slow
2. Back down
3. Stern swings to port

1. Forward slow in steep approach
2. Hard port; back slow

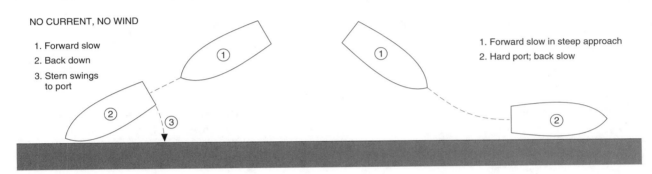

CURRENT, NO WIND

1. Forward slow
2. Attach forward spring
3. Current swings stern in

Current

1. Forward slow in steep approach
2. Hard port; back slow
3. Attach aft spring
4. Forward slow; hard left swings stern in

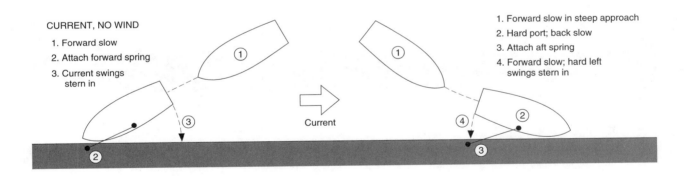

WIND, NO CURRENT

1. Forward slow
2. Back down; stern swings
3. Wind pushes to dock

Wind

Wind

1. Forward moderate, steep approach
2. Hard port; nose in
3. Attach bow and aft spring lines
4. Forward moderate; hard left pulls stern into wind

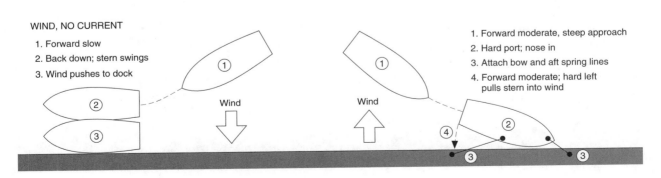

Getting Underway with a Single RH Prop

NO CURRENT, NO WIND

1. Forward slow on aft spring
2. Back, no rudder
3. Forward, right rudder

1. Back, left rudder
2. When clear, forward—hard left rudder

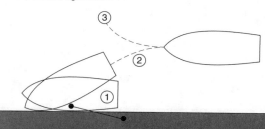

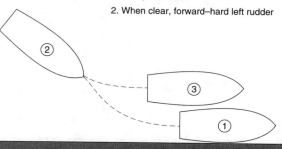

CURRENT, NO WIND

1. On stern line, let current push bow out
2. Retrieve stern line, power ahead

1. On bow line, let current push stern out
2. Back, right rudder
3. Forward, left rudder

Current

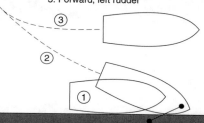

WIND, NO CURRENT

1. Double bow line
2. Forward slow, left rudder
3. Back, right rudder
4. Forward, right rudder

1. Cast off all lines
2. Drift away from dock
3. Forward, right rudder

Wind

Wind

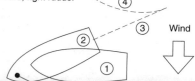

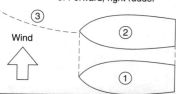

Vessel Motions

- *Roll* is motion about the length axis. It can be most uncomfortable for people who are prone to motion sickness due to its rhythmic, unceasing nature. It can be lessened by tacking—taking the waves on the bow or stern quarter in a zig-zag course.

- *Pitch* is motion about the width axis. It is made worse by speed and is punishing to the vessel. It can be lessened by slowing and tacking.

- *Yaw* is turning about the vertical axis. Following waves can make a vessel yaw by throwing the stern to the side. It can be lessened by increasing speed, by shifting weight to the stern, and by taking seas on the quarter rather than dead astern. However, when running a narrow inlet with following seas, it is best to keep the seas dead astern by quick reaction—even anticipation.

- *Broaching* is yawing out of control until the vessel lies parallel to the waves. Combined with the centrifugal force of the turn, it can capsize a marginally stable vessel. Avoiding a broach in extreme conditions is the ultimate test of helmsmanship, requiring judgment and anticipation of wave effects.

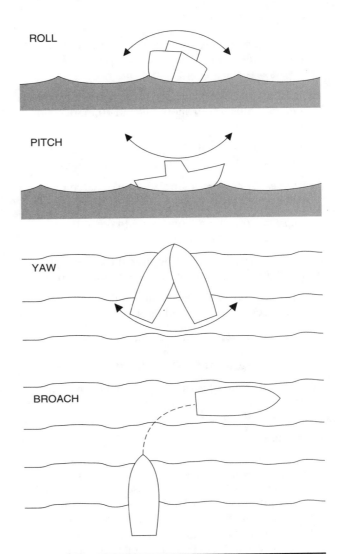

ROLL

PITCH

YAW

BROACH

Cushion and Suction Effects

- *Bank cushion* is the pushing of the bow of a vessel away from the bank of a narrow channel by water piled up between the bow and the bank by the vessel's bow wave.

- *Bank suction* is the pulling of the stern of a vessel toward the bank of a narrow channel by the lowering of pressure due to increased water velocity (the Bernoulli effect), as well as by the suction of the propellers.

- *Squat* is the pulling of the stern of a vessel toward the bottom of a shallow channel by the lowering of pressure due to increased water velocity (the Bernoulli effect), as well as by the suction of the propellers.

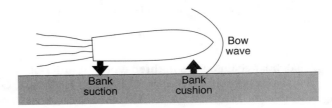

Bow wave

Bank suction

Bank cushion

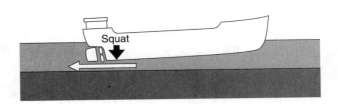

Squat

MOORING AND ANCHORING

Mooring

A mooring system is ground tackle designed for long-term tethering of a vessel. A typical mooring consists of—starting at the bottom:

- *Mushroom anchor* or *large concrete or granite block*. A mushroom should weigh 10 lb. per foot of boat length.

- *Heavy chain*. Chain length should equal that of the vessel. Typical chain diameter is 1 inch.

- *Swivel shackle*. Shackle size should match that of the heavy chain.

- *Light chain*. Chain length should equal the maximum depth of water.

- *Mooring ball*. Ball or buoy should easily support the light chain; material should be non-marring.

- *Nylon pennant*. The pennant should be of length 12-20 feet and be secured directly to the chain.

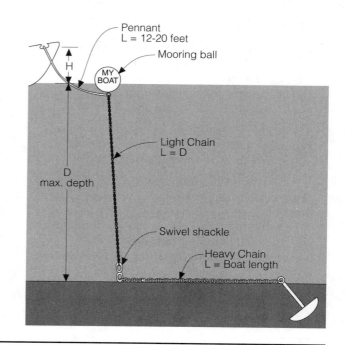

Anchoring and Ground Tackle

The term "ground tackle" refers to all of the equipment used in anchoring: windlass, rode (wire, rope or chain) and anchor.

Windlass

Windlasses may be horizontal (axle horizontal) or vertical. A typical horizontal anchor windlass is shown at right. The smooth gypsy is used to haul on rope; the socketed wildcat engages and hauls in chain. A riding pawl locks the wildcat, preventing chain from running out. A chain stripper disengages the chain links from the wildcat and feeds them down the hawsepipe to the chain locker below. A devil's claw (not shown) takes the strain of the deployed chain and acts as a preventer and/or snubber.

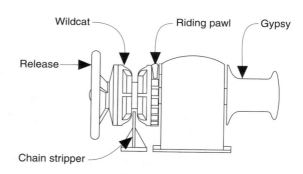

Chain

Small boat chain comes in three types (in order of increasing strength): Proof Coil, BBB, and High Test. Chain "size" is the nominal diameter of the material of the link. When new, the diameter of U.S. chain is actually about $1/32''$ greater than the nominal.

Chain links are either open or studded. Studding prevents the chain from kinking and increases the chain's strength by about 15%.

Chain is purchased—and measured—in 90' "shots." An all-chain rode is often marked with wire: 1 wire = 1 shot; 2 wires = 2 shots, etc.

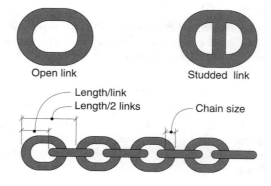

Anchor Terminology

Fluke: part that resists pulling out of the bottom.

Bill: point of the fluke.

Palm: flat face of the fluke.

Arm: arm that supports the flukes.

Shank: long member connecting arm to stock.

Crown: reinforced point at which arm and shank are joined.

Stock: member at right angles to shank and arm which tilts the anchor to engage the fluke.

Head: top of the shank which engages the stock.

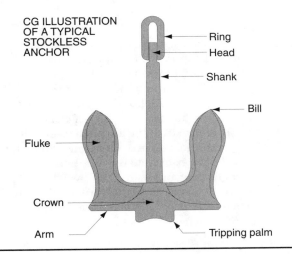

CG ILLUSTRATION OF A TYPICAL STOCKLESS ANCHOR

Ring
Head
Shank
Bill
Fluke
Crown
Arm
Tripping palm

Anchor Types

- *Fisherman:* also known as a Yachtsman and as a kedge. These anchors are not intended primarily to bury themselves in mud, but to catch on a rocky bottom. More than the other types, they depend on weight to hold them down.

- *Danforth:* the classic light-weight anchor, designed to dig into a soft bottom. It thus depends more on fluke area than on weight. A disadvantage is that when the wind shifts, the Danforth sometimes flips out, instead of pivoting to follow the rode. The Fortress is an ultra low-weight aluminum version of the Danforth. It is so light that it is sometimes difficult to lower in a strong current.

- *Plow:* This anchor literally plows itself into a soft bottom. An advantage is that, once set, it will turn to follow the rode without flipping out.

- *Bruce:* similar to the plow, but rigid and easier to handle. A disadvantage is that it can become fouled with a lump of clay and may not reset.

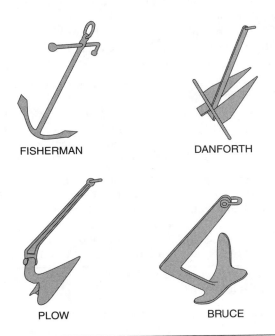

FISHERMAN
DANFORTH
PLOW
BRUCE

Sizing Ground Tackle

Vessel length	Chain size	Chain length	Rope size	Bruce pounds	Danforth model	Fisherman pounds	Plow pounds
0–20'	$3/16$"	10'	$5/16$"	5	8-S	—	6
20–25'	$1/4$"	20'	$3/8$"	11	13-S	40	15
25–30'	$5/16$"	25'	$7/16$"	16	22-S	50	25
30–35'	$3/8$"	30'	$1/2$"	22	40-S	50	35
35–40'	$7/16$"	35'	$5/8$"	33	65-S	70	45
40–50'	$7/16$"	40'	$5/8$"	44	130-S	70	60
50–60'	$1/2$"	50'	$3/4$"	66	180-S	—	75

Anchoring

Single anchor. Pick your spot and calculate the length of rode, L. Approach into the wind (or current, if stronger) and stop upwind the distance, L, from where you want your boat to ride. Put the engine into reverse, lower the anchor, and pay out rode for a 4:1 scope. Snub the rode on a cleat (if chain, tighten windlass brake). If the anchor digs in (indicated by the rode going taut), pay out more rode for a 6:1 scope. Power back until the rode goes taut again. When the anchor sets the bow will dip suddenly and the boat will spring forward. Finally, pay out rode to match the conditions: calm—6:1; average—7:1; heavy wind—up to 10:1.

Two anchors off the bow. Set the first anchor, as above, to port of the position you would place a single anchor. After setting the first anchor, power to starboard to a point equidistant on the other side and drop the second anchor. Carefully drop back, paying out a scope of 6:1, then set the anchor. Finally, pay out rode until the two rodes are of equal length.

Bahamian moor. Prepare two anchors on the bow and calculate final lengths of rode, L. Power upwind or up current. Drop the first anchor the distance, L, downwind of your desired spot. Feed out rode until you have let out 2L. Drop the second anchor and set as with a single anchor. Retrieve L of the first rode.

Mediterranean moor. Calculate the length of rode, L. Drop the anchor a distance of L plus one boat length out from fastening pont on shore. Back down toward the shore, setting the anchor, as in the single anchor. Adjust dock lines and rode for final position. If your boat backs poorly, run the anchor out in a dinghy.

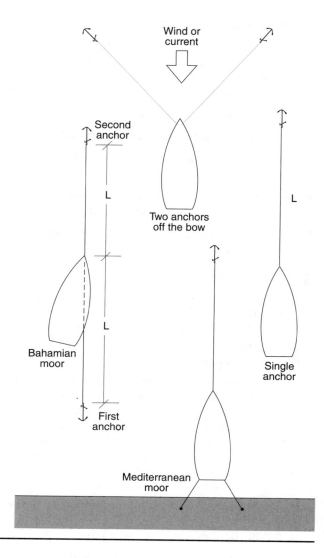

Breaking Out

Power the boat slowly forward in the direction of the anchor while the foredeck crew takes in the rode. Since the helmsman cannot see the rode, the crew should occasionally point in its direction for guidance.

As soon as the rode is vertical, the crew quickly snubs the rode around a cleat. The inertia and buoyancy of the boat will exert a great force straight up or slightly forward, breaking the anchor out of the bottom. You will know when the anchor is free because the bow will dip, then spring back as the anchor releases its grip. The anchor is then retrieved with the boat in neutral or slow ahead.

With a chain rode, have a snubber line with a chain hook already cleated. As the rode goes vertical, snub the chain with the hook. This will prevent the chain from jumping out of the wildcat.

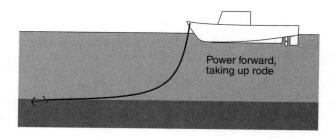

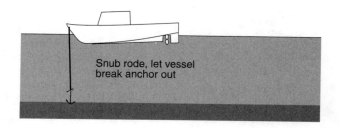

MARLINSPIKE

Rope

Rope is what you buy on spools at the chandlery. Rope becomes line as soon as it has a designated purpose, i.e. "dockline" or "halyard." Until recently, rope was made from natural fibers, usually hemp (sisal) or manila (wild banana plant). While less expensive and more "nautical," all of the natural fibers are inferior to synthetic rope in several important regards. Natural fibers are subject to rot, so must be dried before stowing. If used in salt water, they must first be rinsed in fresh water because salt attracts moisture. Last, natural fiber rope has about half the strength of the same size of nylon rope when new.

The three most used synthetics include:

- *nylon:* not capitalized because no longer a trade name, nylon is strong and easy to handle. It has a unique ability to stretch up to 50% and recover. It is thus well suited for use as dock lines and anchor rodes, but dangerous to use for towing.

- *Dacron:* one of a group of polyester fibers—others include Fortrel, Terylene, and Kodel—Dacron is also strong and easy to handle. It is used extensively for rigging because, unlike nylon, it stretches very little. Dacron rope can also be manufactured in a variety of finishes, from hard and slick to soft and fuzzy, and a wide variety of colors.

- *polypropylene:* not capitalized because generic, polypropylene is relatively weak, hard, stiff, subject to kinking, and just downright ornery. It is used only because it floats, thus keeping it from getting caught in propellers. The Coast Guard specifies its use in thrown lifelines.

The most significant advantage of synthetic fiber over natural fiber is ithat it doesn't rot and, therefore, retains its strength. The table below lists average strengths of *new* rope.

Rope is manufactured in three popular geometries:

- *3-strand* is the classic "rope," made up of material twisted into fibers, yarns, and strands. In the nearly universal right-hand laid rope, looking at the rope with the bitter end held away from you, the yarns consist of fibers twisted clockwise (CW), the strands of yarns twisted CCW, and the rope of strands twisted CW again. The twists are alternated to reduce the tendency of the rope to twist under tension and to build in a tension that holds the rope tightly together. The twists are not perfectly balanced, however, so that the line "wants to be" coiled CW to avoid kinking.

- *Single-braid* is a modern developement, made possible by braiding machines. Its chief advantage is that it has little tendency to twist and therefore kink. Coil braided halyards, sheets and docklines CW, just to develop the habit so you won't coil three-strand the wrong way. Braided anchor rode and tow lines can be faked down in a figure-eight pattern without kinking. Single-braid, being hollow, is reasonably simple to splice.

- *Double-braid* consists of a braided core inside a braided shell. The core and shell are often of different materials, giving the rope a range of characteristics. It is extremely flexible and easy on the hands, making it ideal for running rigging and dock lines. Double-braid is difficult to splice, however.

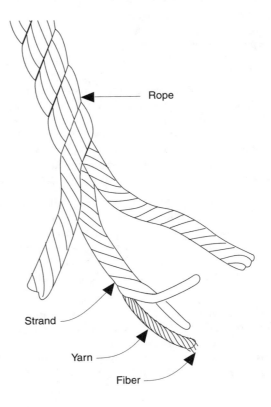

Ultimate Breaking Strength, lb.

Dia., in.	Hemp	Nylon	Dacron	Poly
$1/4$	800	1700	1500	1200
$3/8$	1800	3600	3200	2600
$1/2$	3300	6600	5800	4700
$5/8$	5000	10000	8800	7300
$3/4$	7000	15000	13000	10600
1	12000	25000	22000	18800
$1^1/2$	27000	56000	49000	42000

Wire Rope

Wire rope is made from either stainless or galvanized steel and consists of two geometries denoted by the number of strands and number of wires per strand:

- 1x19 is a single strand of 19 wires. Because the wires are large, 1x19 is very stiff. It is used mostly for standing rigging. Its disadvantage is stiffness; an advantage is resistance to wear.

- 7x19 has seven strands, each consisting of 19 wires. Due to the small wire, it is quite flexible and is used primarily for running rigging. The small wires are easily worn through, producing "meat hooks," or sharp, broken wires.

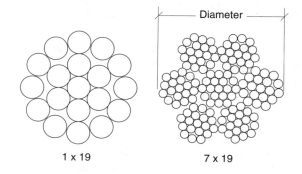

1 x 19   7 x 19

Coiling and Stowing

Rope should be coiled in the same direction as the lay, or twist, as seen looking along the rope with the bitter end held away. Nearly all three-strand rope has a clockwise lay. It is considered good practice to coil braided rope clockwise, as well.

Flemish is to make a Flemish coil—the end of a line laid in a tight spiral flat on the deck. It looks good, but serves no useful purpose.

Faking—or faking down—is to lay a rope on deck in a series of figure-eights, so that the rope will run free without tangling.

Flaking—often confused with "faking"—consists of laying out on deck in parallel rows.

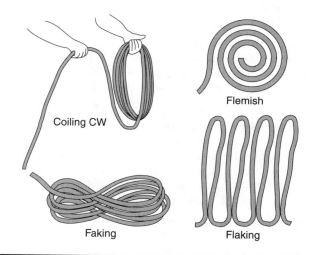

Coiling CW   Flemish

Faking   Flaking

Splices

- *Short splice:* the strongest way to connect two ropes. Because there are six strands in the cross section, the short splice is thick and may not run through a properly-sized block. The long splice—where each strand of one rope replaces a strand of the second—is uniform in diameter, so can run through blocks. The long splice is weaker, however.

- *Eye splice:* stronger than any knot in forming a loop, the eye splice is common on one end of dock lines, as well as at the anchor end of a rode. For the anchor rode, a metal or plastic thimble inserted in the eye eliminates chafe. Unless the eye is very tight around the thimble, the eye should be whipped tight.

- *Back splice:* a nautical way to prevent unravelling of the end of a line. As with the short splice, the cross-sectional area of the back splice is twice that of its rope, so it cannot be used where the rope has to be pulled through a block or fairlead.

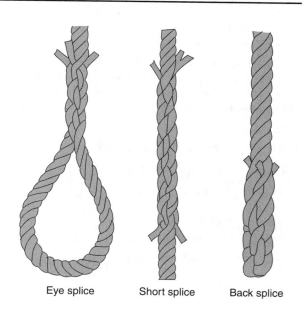

Eye splice   Short splice   Back splice

Terminology

- *Bitter end:* the free end of a line.

- *Standing part:* the longer part of a line which is fixed during the tying of a knot.

- *Bight:* a loop formed by crossing the bitter end over itself.

- *Turn:* a loop formed around a post, rail, or the rope itself.

- *Splice:* weaving strands of a rope to itself or to a second piece of rope.

- *Whipping:* wrapping twine or tape around a rope end to prevent unraveling.

- *Seizing:* wrapping twine or tape around rope to bind two ropes together or a rope to another object.

- *Worming:* laying smaller line in the spiral grooves (with the lay) between rope strands.

- *Parcelling:* winding strips of canvas over, and in the same direction as, worming.

- *Serving:* winding small line against the lay and over worming and parcelling to protect rope from chafe and water damage.

Worming, parcelling, and serving are anachronisms from the days of natural-fiber rope. The purpose of the process is to prevent water from penetrating between the strands of a rope and causing it to rot. Regardless, you should learn the terminology because you will probably see it in a question!

The difference between *worming, parcelling* and *serving* can be remembered from the ditty,

> *"Worm and parcel with the lay,*
> *Turn and serve the other way."*

Knots

- *Timber hitch and half hitch (A):* used for hauling timbers and starting lashings.

- *Round turn and double half hitch (B):* used to tie up when the length of line needs to be adjusted; faster but less secure than the bowline. If you want the adjustment to hold, add a third half hitch.

- *Fisherman's bend (C):* also known as an anchor bend, its primary use is in tying a rode to an anchor; more secure and less chafing than the bowline.

- *Becket or sheet bend (D):* used instead of square knot for tying lines of different diameter together.

- *Bowline on a bight (E):* used for rescue; a conscious victim puts one leg through each loop; if unconscious, put both legs through one loop and the chest and arms through the other.

- *Plain whipping (F):* a fast way to whip the end of a line, but more likely to slip off than the sailmaker's whip.

- *Sailmaker's whip (G):* requires a sailmaker's needle, but will not slip off, even with severe use.

- *Double blackwall hitch (H):* same as the single Blackwall hitch—for attaching a line to a cargo hook—but more secure.

- *Carrick bend (I):* for connecting two large hawsers; more secure than the square knot.

- *Stopper (J):* a short length of rope used to grab running rigging in a rolling hitch; a "stopper knot" is any knot at the end of a line to prevent its running out.

- *Barrel hitch (K):* used for lifting barrels upright.

- *Rolling hitch (L):* used for fastening a line to a spar.

- *Bowline (M):* the most useful knot aboard a boat; will not slip, but can always be untied.

- *Double sheet bend (N):* used to secure two lines of different diameter; more secure than the single sheet bend.

- *Blackwall hitch (O):* quick way to temporarily attach a line to a cargo hook.

- *French bowline (P):* also known as the "Portugese bowline" and the "caulkner's bowline"; used to support a person with the legs through one loop and the trunk through the second loop.

- *Half hitch (Q):* generally a turn of a line around an object with the bitter end being led back through the bight; the basis of many other knots.

- *Marline hitch (R):* The Coast Guard is wrong here; shown is the "marling hitch" used to lash canvas to a spar.

- *Square knot or reef knot (S):* used to connect two lines of equal diameter; easy to untie except when under strain.

- *Clove hitch (T):* used to attach line to a piling; more secure if followed with a single half hitch.

REGULATIONS

Laws vs. Regulations ("Regs")

Congress passes *laws*. By necessity, Congress cannot deal with the vast amount of detail required to administer the spirit of a law. For this reason, a regulatory agency, specified by the law, is charged with developing and enforcing the details as *regulations*.

Regulations are printed in the *Code of Federal Regulations*, a series of volumes, collectively known as the "CFRs." You can see the entire code at any major library that has a Government Documents section. The CFRs are broken down into topics by:

Title (the statute)

Subchapter (major topic)

Part (minor topic)

For up to 100 ton licenses, you may be asked questions from:

Title 33

Subchapter A

Part 26 (Bridge-to-bridge)

Subchapter O

Parts 151-159 (Pollution)

Title 46

Subchapter B

Parts 10-15 (Licensing of crew)

Subchapter C

Parts 24-26 (Uninspected vessels)

Subchapter S

Parts 170-174 (Subdivision & stability)

Subchapter T

Parts 175-187 (Small passenger vessels)

There is no use trying to memorize all of the CFRs you may be examined on, since they are available at the exam. Just knowing how they are organized and how to use the indices (listed at the end of each Subchapter) should suffice.

Since most under 100-ton master and mate licenses are used to operate inspected small passenger vessels ("T-boats"), most of your questions will come from Title 46, Subchapter T. So that you can familiarize yourself with the contents of Subchapter T, we reprint its index here on the following pages.

Looking Up an Answer

A simple example should suffice to demonstrate the process of finding an answer from the CFRs supplied at the exam.

Example:

How many paddles must accompany life floats on inspected passenger vessels of under 100 tons?

1. The vessel is a T boat and thus falls under Title 46, Subchapter T.

2. Look for key words in the index at the end of the Subchapter. (The index for Title 46, Subchapter T, appears on the following pages.) Key words for this question might be *paddles*, *life floats*, or *lifesaving equipment*.

3. Looking in the index, we score all three times.

Under "paddles":

Under "life floats":

Under "lifesaving equipment":

4. What do you think? Should we look at Part 180, Section 15? Looking through the book we find:

Subpart 180.15—Equipment for Life Floats and Buoyant Apparatus

§ 180.15-1 Equipment required.

(a) Each life float shall be fitted with a life line and shall be equipped with two paddles, a water light and a painter.

Answer: two paddles

INDEX

BLOCK AND TACKLE

Construction and Terminology

The figure at right shows the parts of a basic block. When a line is passed through a block (or blocks), the line is said to be *rove*. When rove, the block(s) and line are known as a *tackle*.

The end of the tackle which remains fixed is the *standing part*. The moving block is the *hauling part*. The end of the line you pull on is the *fall*.

To separate the blocks is to *overhaul*. To bring the blocks closer together is to *round in* or to *round up*. When the two blocks come together, they are *two-blocked* or *chock-a-block*.

To properly size a block and its line, use the following rules, where circumference = 3.14 × diameter:

- fiber: block diameter = 3 × rope circumference

    sheave diameter = 2 × rope circumference

- wire: sheave diameter = 20 × rope diameter

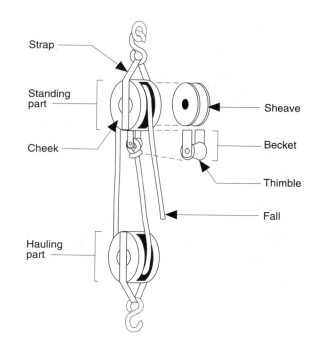

Strap
Standing part
Cheek
Hauling part
Sheave
Becket
Thimble
Fall

Operation

The figure at right shows the names of the tackles on which you will be examined.

The mechanical advantage of a tackle depends on two factors:

- the number of sheaves or pulleys
- whether the hauling line comes from the standing part or the hauling part.

Imagine the tackle to be lifting a weight against gravity. The numerical mechanical advantage is the *number of lines supporting, or pulling on, the weight*.

Obviously, the greatest advantage obtains when the hauling line is pulling on the weight; in such a case, the tackle is said to be *rove to advantage*. Counting the number of lines pulling up on the weight in the figure at right, you can see that the mechanical advantages of the tackles in the top row are 1-6, and those in the bottom row 2-7.

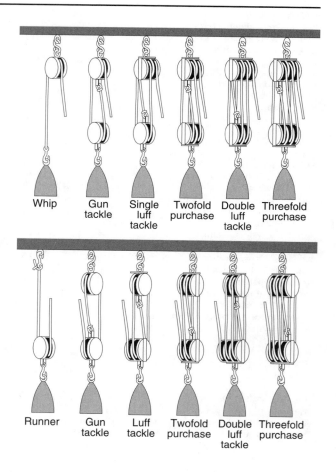

Whip Gun tackle Single luff tackle Twofold purchase Double luff tackle Threefold purchase

Runner Gun tackle Luff tackle Twofold purchase Double luff tackle Threefold purchase

TOWING

Equipment

A *bridle*, consisting of equal lengths of wire cable connected by a triangular *fishplate*, distributes the load on the tow and helps prevent yawing. The *main hawser* may be of wire (usually) or rope. The *catenary* form of the hawser reduces the shock load, but a *spring hawser* may be added between the bridle and main hawser to reduce shock further.

The length of the hawser may be adjusted to keep both tug and tow in phase with the waves.

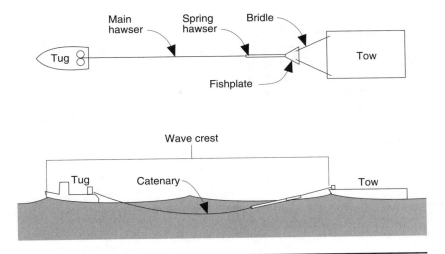

Yawing

Yawing (the tendency of a tow to veer side-to-side) is annoying because it makes the path of the tow unpredictable. Extreme yawing can even lead to tripping (capsizing) of the tug, as shown.

Yaw can be minimized by:

- trimming the tow down by the stern

- deploying a stern drogue

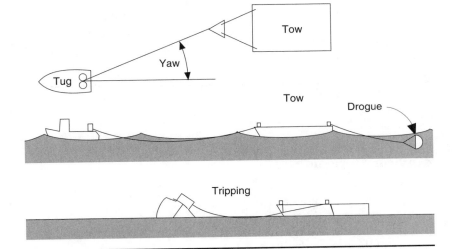

Towing Options

With more than one tug, the most powerful tug's hawser should be attached closer to the center of the tow. In a tandem tug, the smaller tug should tow the larger tug.

With multiple in-line tows, the hawser of the aft tow may be attached to the stern of the forward tow, or it may run under the forward tow and be attached to the forward tow fishplate.

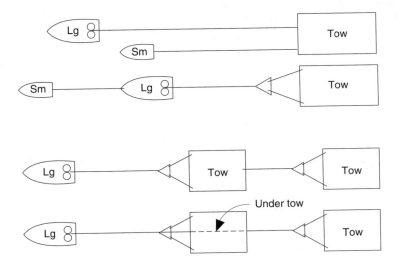

Pushing

When the tow is pushed ahead of the tug, it is imperative that the two be rigidly connected so that they act as a single vessel. Note the placement of lines to ensure immobility.

The same principle applies to tows made up of multiple barges.

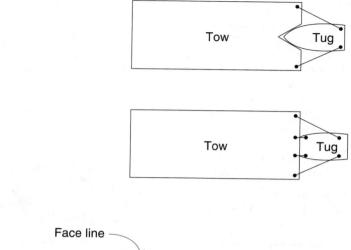

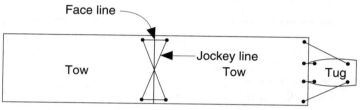

Towing Alongside

Towing alongside—also known as hip towing—requires a rigid connection between tug and tow. The tug is lashed to an aft quarter of the tow so that its propeller and rudder are well clear aft of the tow. Placing propulsion and steering aft also maximizes turning ability.

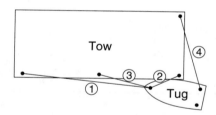

① Bow line

② Towing line

③ Backing line

④ Stern line

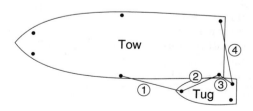

TRIM AND LOAD LINES

Displacement

According to Archimedes' Principle, a vessel displaces a weight of water equal to its own weight. Therefore, *displacement* is a measure of a vessel's weight.

Displacement is expressed in either:

- *short tons* (2,000 lb.), or
- *long tons* (2,240 lb.)

Displacement can also be calculated to indicate load-carrying capacity, where one ton of displacement equals 100 cubic feet of interior volume:

- *gross tons* = volume inside watertight bulkheads
- *net tons* = all volume inside watertight bulkheads except for the operational spaces.

Draft Marks

Draft marks at both bow and stern indicate the depth of the keel below the water line. A vessel that is neither trimmed down by the bow nor trimmed down by the stern can have different drafts fore and aft.

Draft marks are 6" high and spaced 12" from base to base. The base of a number indicates the number of feet exactly. If the waterline is at the top of a number, the draft is the number of feet, plus six inches.

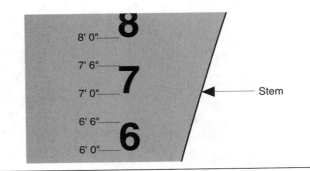

Loadlines (Plimsoll Mark)

Loadlines are painted at the midpoints on both sides of a vessel. The horizontal bars indicate the maximum depth to which the vessel may be loaded, depending on the season and whether the water is salt or fresh.

To one side is a circle with a horizontal bisecting bar, at the same level as the summer water line. There may be letters at the ends of the bisecting bar which indicate the vessel's registration society or agency. In the United States, the certificating agency is the American Bureau of Shipping (ABS).

The "freshwater allowance" allows a vessel, loading for an ocean voyage in a freshwater river or lake, to be trimmed below the fresh water line if it will later rise to the appropriate salt water line.

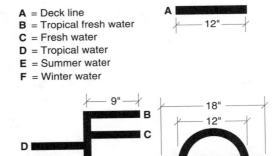

A = Deck line
B = Tropical fresh water
C = Fresh water
D = Tropical water
E = Summer water
F = Winter water

Great Lakes Loadlines

Great Lakes loadlines —for vessels registered in the Great Lakes—are similar to the Plimsoll Mark, but with more fresh water gradations.

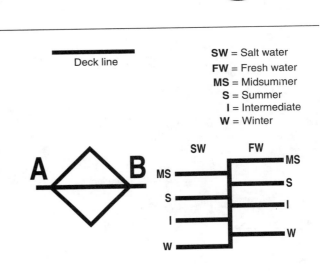

Deck line

SW = Salt water
FW = Fresh water
MS = Midsummer
S = Summer
I = Intermediate
W = Winter

CONSTRUCTION AND STABILITY

Construction

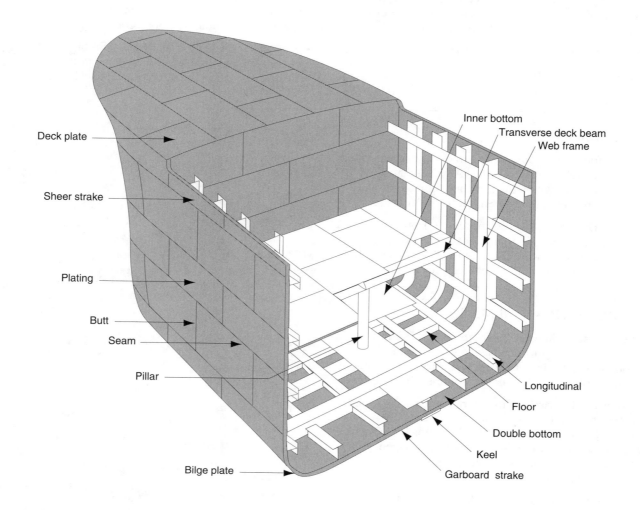

Deck plate

Sheer strake

Plating

Butt

Seam

Pillar

Bilge plate

Inner bottom

Transverse deck beam

Web frame

Longitudinal

Floor

Double bottom

Keel

Garboard strake

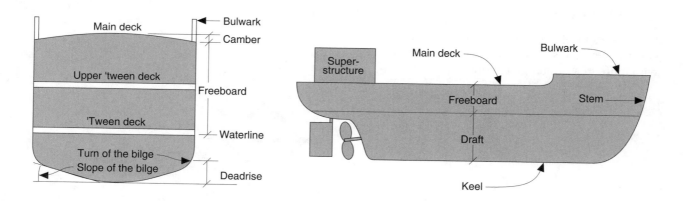

Main deck
Bulwark
Camber
Upper 'tween deck
Freeboard
'Tween deck
Waterline
Turn of the bilge
Slope of the bilge
Deadrise

Super-structure
Main deck
Bulwark
Freeboard
Stem
Draft
Keel

Center of Gravity (G)

Center of gravity is defined as "the point in a body around which its weight is evenly distributed and through which the force of gravity acts."

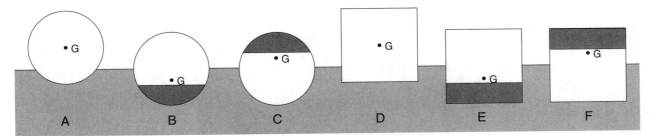

A. Homogeneous empty cylinder. Since the cylinder is uniform and empty, its center of gravity, G, is in the exact center. If set in motion, the cylinder will not stop at a predictable point, because it is neither stable nor unstable.

B. Same cylinder with weight in bottom. The heavy weight shifts the center of gravity, G, downward. Being stable, the cylinder will always return to its original position.

C. Same cylinder with weight concentrated at top. The heavy weight shifts the center of gravity, G, upward. The unstable cylinder will flip 180° to look like the stable cylinder B.

D. Homogeneous cube. Since the cube is empty, its center of gravity, G, is in the exact center. If tipped less than 45°, it will return to level. If tipped more than 45°, it will flip on its side.

E. Cube with weight concentrated in bottom. The heavy weight shifts the center of gravity, G, downward. The cube is more stable than either cylinder B or cube D and will nearly always return to its original position.

F. Cube with weight concentrated at top. The heavy weight shifts the center of gravity, G, upward. Has stability like D for small tilts, but flips like C for large tilts.

Note that if the weight in B had been a fluid, the fluid would always flow to the lowest point, therefore *contributing nothing to stability*.

The stability of a floating object is a function of:

• Shape—flatter is more stable

• Location of G—lower is more stable

• Weight—if location is low, more is more stable

Center of Buoyancy (B)

Since buoyancy is the weight of the water displaced by a floating (or submerged) object, the center of buoyancy, B, is the geometric center of the submerged portion of the object

Figure 1

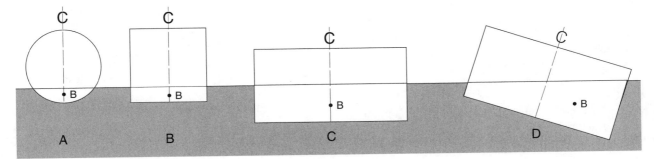

Interaction of G and B

In calculating the stability of a vessel, a floating object, it is useful to define two heights, as shown in Figure 2:

- KG—the height of G above the keel
- KB—the height of B above the keel

Observe that as the cylinders and cubes in Figure 1 are tilted, both G and KG remain fixed relative to the center lines of the objects. When the rectangular object, C, is tilted, D, the center of buoyancy, B, shifts away from the center line.

The same shift occurs in the vessel in Figure 3. At (a) the vessel is upright. Both G and B are on the vertical center line of the hull. Since the two forces at G and B are equal and opposite along the same line, the vessel is stable.

At (b) the vessel is heeled. The center of buoyancy, B, has shifted away from the center line. G and B are offset, producing a restoring torque. The measure of the torque is the "righting arm," GZ, the horizontal distance between G and the vertical projection of B. GZ increases as G is lowered and vice versa.

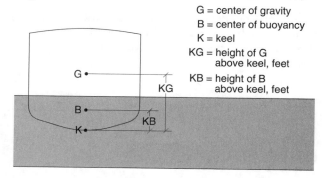

Figure 2

G = center of gravity
B = center of buoyancy
K = keel
KG = height of G above keel, feet
KB = height of B above keel, feet

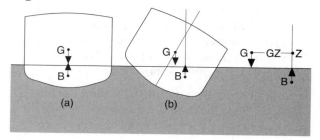

Figure 3

(a)　(b)

The Metacenter, M

In the figure at right, note the point, M, where the vertical projection of B and the centerline meet. If G were raised to M, the righting arm GZ would become zero, and there would be no stabilizing force. In fact, if G were raised above M, GZ would act to roll the vessel over!

You can see that the higher M and the lower G, the more stable the vessel. The metacentric height, GM, is defined as the vertical distance between G and M. As shown in the bottom figure, GM can be calculated as: GM = KM − KG.

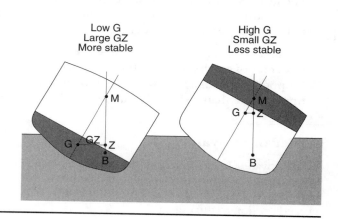

Low G
Large GZ
More stable

High G
Small GZ
Less stable

Rolling Period, T

A very stable, "stiff," vessel has a short rolling period; a marginally stable, "tender," vessel has a long period. The period, in seconds, can be calculated from the metacentric height, GM, and the beam, W, where both measurements are in feet:

$$T = 0.44W/(GM)^{1/2}$$

Example: a vessel has a beam of 15'3" and a metacentric height of 2'6".

$$T = 0.44 \times 15.25/(2.5)^{1/2}$$

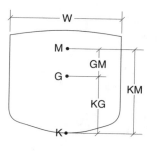

W = beam
M = metacenter
G = center of gravity
K = keel
KG = height of G above keel, feet
KM = height of metacenter above keel, feet
GM = metacentric height = KM − KG

00002. You are standing the wheelwatch when you hear the cry "Man overboard starboard side". You should be ready to:

A. give full right rudder
B. give full left rudder
C. put the rudder amidships
D. throw a life ring to mark the spot

00003. A stopper used in securing the ground tackle for sea that consists of a grab attached to a turnbuckle is a:

A. riding pawl
B. buckler
C. devil's claw
D. locking ring

00005. You are standing the wheelwatch when you hear the cry, "Man overboard starboard side". Y ou should be ready to:

A. give full left rudder
B. give full right rudder
C. put the rudder amidships
D. throw a life ring to mark the spot

00006. Which of the following statements about a tunnel bow thruster is TRUE?

A. It provides lateral control without affecting headway.
B. It is fully effective at speeds up to about 6 knots.
C. It can be used to slow the ship in addition to backing down.
D. It will allow you to hold a position when the current is from astern.

00007. In illustration D044DG, the mooring line labeled "F" is called a:

A. breast line
B. bow line
C. forward spring line
D. none of the above

00013. In illustration D044DG, the mooring line labeled "G" is called a(n):

A. inshore bow line
B. offshore bow line
C. forward breast line
D. forward spring line

00016. When underway and proceeding ahead, as the speed increases, the pivot point tends to:

A. move aft
B. move forward
C. move lower
D. remain stationary

00017. In illustration D044DG, the mooring line labeled "E" is called a(n):

A. bow spring line
B. aft spring line
C. forward breast line
D. bow line

00022. What is a wildcat?

A. A ring on the windlass with indentations to grab the anchor chain.
B. A winch that is running out of control due to a failure of the overspeed trips.
C. A line that has jumped off the gypsyhead while under strain.
D. A nylon line that parts under strain and whips back in a hazardous manner.

00025. The turning circle of a vessel making a turn over 360° is the path followed by the:

A. center of gravity
B. bow
C. bridge
D. centerline

00026. The pivoting point of a fully loaded vessel with normal trim proceeding ahead at sea speed is:

A. right at the bow
B. 1/3 the length of the vessel from the bow
C. 1/2 the length of the vessel from the bow
D. 2/3 the length of the vessel from the bow

00027. Under Title 46 of the United States Code, the person in charge of a documented vessel who fails to report a complaint of a sexual offense may be:

A. fined up to $5,000
B. imprisoned for up to one year
C. charged with accessory to sexual assault
D. all of the above

00029. You are in charge of a U. S. documented vessel. under Title 46 of the United States Code, if you fail to report a complaint of a sexual offense, you may be:

A. criminally charged and jailed
B. civilly charged and fined
C. held personally liable by the victim and sued
D. all of the above

00032. The explosive range of a fuel lies between the lower explosive limit and the:

A. flash point
B. ignition temperature
C. upper explosive limit
D. fire point

00036. The distance that a vessel travels from the time that the order to put engines full astern until the vessel is dead in the water is known as:

A. advance
B. head reach
C. surge
D. transfer

00037. What are the two main types of stud link chain?

A. chain and stud link chain
B. flash-butt welded chain and Di-Lok chain
C. flash-butt welded chain and rig chain
D. stud link chain and flash-butt welded chain

00043. In illustration D044DG, the mooring line labeled "D" is called a(n):

A. after spring line
B. forward spring line
C. waist breast line
D. stern line

00046. Which of the following statements concerning the handling qualities of a fully loaded vessel as compared with those of a light vessel is FALSE?

A. A fully loaded vessel will be slower to respond to the engines.
B. A fully loaded vessel will maintain her headway further.
C. A light vessel will be more affected by the wind.
D. A light vessel loses more rudder effect in shallow water.

00051. You are the licensed operator of a 100 GT towing vessel sailing coastwise. What percentage of the deck crew must be able to understand the language commonly used onboard the vessel?

A. 50%
B. 65%
C. 75%
D. 100%

00054. Your vessel has grounded on a bar. Which of the following should you do?

A. If you cannot get clear immediately, lighten the ship by pumping all ballast overboard.
B. Run the engine full astern to keep from being set further onto the bar.
C. Switch to the high suction for condenser circulating water, if it is submerged.
D. all of the above

00055. You are in charge of a U. S. documented vessel. Under Title 46 of the United States Code, if you fail to report a complaint of a sexual offense, you may be:

A. held personally liable by the victim and sued
B. criminally charged and jailed
C. civilly charged and fined
D. all of the above

00056. The effect of wind on exposed areas of the vessel is most noticeable when:

A. backing
B. going slow ahead
C. going full ahead
D. turning

00057. Under Title 46 of the United States Code, the person in charge of a documented vessel who fails to report a complaint of a sexual offense may be:

A. charged with accessory to sexual assault
B. fined up to $5,000
C. imprisoned for up to one year
D. all of the above

00063. Which space(s) is(are) deducted from gross tonnage to derive net tonnage?

A. boatswain's stores
B. chart room
C. spaces for the exclusive use of the officers or crew
D. all of the above

00065. Under Title 46 of the United States Code, the person in charge of a documented vessel who fails to report a complaint of a sexual offense may be:

A. charged with accessory to sexual assault
B. imprisoned for up to one year
C. fined up to $5,000
D. all of the above

00066. Your vessel has most of its superstructure forward. How will the vessel lie relative to the wind when drifting with no way on?

A. with the wind from ahead
B. with the wind off the port beam
C. with the wind off the starboard beam
D. with the wind from abaft the beam

00067. You are in charge of a U. S. documented vessel. under Title 46 of the United States Code, if you fail to report a complaint of a sexual offense, you may be:

A. civilly charged and fined
B. criminally charged and jailed

C. held personally liable by the victim and sued
D. all of the above

00076. Leeway is the:

A. difference between the true course and the compass course
B. momentum of a vessel after her engines have been stopped
C. lateral movement of a vessel downwind of her intended course
D. displacement of a vessel multiplied by her speed

00077. When steering a vessel, a good helmsman will:

A. use as much rudder as possible to keep the vessel on course
B. apply rudder to move the compass card towards the lubbers line when off course
C. repeat back to the watch officer any rudder commands before executing them
D. keep the rudder amidships except when changing course

00083. In illustration D044DG, the mooring line labeled "A" is called a(n):

A. offshore stern line
B. onshore stern line
C. after spring line
D. after breast line

00086. The turning circle of a ship making a turn of 360° or more is defined as the path followed by the:

A. bow
B. bridge
C. centerline
D. pivoting point

00093. A lookout can leave his station:

A. ONLY when properly relieved
B. at the end of the watch
C. 15 minutes before the end of the watch
D. at any time

00094. All of the following records are usually maintained by the watch- standing officers aboard a vessel EXCEPT the:

A. deck logbook
B. official logbook
C. compass record book
D. chronometer error book

00096. The distance a vessel moves at right angles to the original course, when a turn of 180° has been completed, is called the:

A. advance
B. pivoting point
C. tactical diameter
D. kick

00104. You are on watch at sea at night, and a fire breaks out in #3 hold just forward of the bridge. Which of the following would you NOT do immediately?

A. Call the Master.
B. Proceed to the space and inspect the extent of the fire.
C. Shut down the cargo hold ventilation.
D. Sound the fire alarm signal to rouse out all hands.

00105. Which of the following is the strongest mooring line?

A. Dacron
B. nylon
C. polyethylene
D. manila

00106. In relation to the turning circle of a ship, the term "kick" means the distance:

A. around the circumference of the turning circle
B. gained at right angles to the original course
C. gained in the direction of the original course
D. the ship moves sidewise from the original course after the rudder is first put over

00114. You are on watch at sea on course 090°T, and a man falls over your starboard side. You immediately start a Williamson Turn. Which of the following steps is out of sequence?

A. right full rudder until the vessel heads 150° T
B. shift the helm to left full rudder
C. continue with left full until on course 270° T
D. order engines ahead full

00116. In relation to the turning circle of a ship, the term "transfer" means the distance:

A. gained in the direction of the original course
B. gained at right angles to the original course
C. the ship moves sidewise from the original course away from the direction of the turn after the rudder is first put over
D. around the circumference of the turning circle

00117. If two mooring lines are to be placed on the same bollard, which method is BEST to use?

A. Place the eye from the forward line on the bollard and then place the eye from the second line directly over the first.
B. It makes no difference how the lines are placed.

C. Place the eye from either line on the bollard, and then bring the eye of the other line up through the eye of the first, and place it on the bollard.
D. Place both eyes on the bollard, in any manner, but lead both lines to the same winch head on the vessel and secure them on the winch.

00125. Chafing gear is normally used:

A. for portable fenders
B. for ground tackle
C. on the inside of the hawsepipe
D. on mooring lines

00126. The distance a vessel moves parallel to the original course from the point where the rudder is put over to any point on the turning circle is called the:

A. advance
B. drift angle
C. pivoting point
D. transfer

00127. In illustration D044DG, the mooring line labeled "C" is called a:

A. breast line
B. shore line
C. spring line
D. stern line

00134. Your ship is steaming at night with the gyropilot engaged when you notice that the vessel's course is slowly changing to the right. Which of the following actions should you take FIRST?

A. Call the Master.
B. Change to telemotor steering.
C. Notify the engine room of the steering malfunction.
D. Send the Quartermaster to the emergency steering station.

00136. You have your rudder right 20° and your engine running ahead slow. After making two complete circles, which of the following could you measure?

A. final diameter
B. kick
C. tactical diameter
D. transfer

00144. The lookout sights a vessel dead ahead. This should be reported on the bell with:

A. 1 bell
B. 2 bells
C. 3 bells
D. 4 bells

00146. When turning a ship in restricted space with a strong wind, it is normally best to:

A. go ahead on both engines with the rudder hard to one side if on a twin screw vessel
B. back down with the rudder hard to one side if on a single screw vessel
C. take advantage of the tendency to back to port if on a twin screw vessel
D. turn so that the tendency to back into the wind can be used if on a single-screw vessel

00147. In illustration D044DG, the mooring line labeled "B" is called a(n):

A. inshore stern line
B. offshore stern line
C. after spring line
D. after breast line

00153. The proper way to correct a mistake in the logbook is to:

A. erase the entry and rewrite
B. draw several lines through the entry, rewrite, and initial the correction
C. completely black out the entry, rewrite, and initial the correction
D. draw a line through the entry, rewrite, and initial the correction

00154. A bow lookout sights an object to port. How many bell strokes should he sound?

A. 1
B. 2
C. 3
D. 4

00156. When heading on a course, you put your rudder hard over. The distance traveled parallel to the direction of the original course from where you put your rudder over to any point on the turning circle is known as:

A. advance
B. head reach
C. tactical diameter
D. transfer

00157. The proper way to correct a mistake in the logbook is to:

A. draw a line through the entry, rewrite, and initial the correction
B. draw several lines through the entry, rewrite, and initial the correction
C. erase the entry and rewrite
D. completely black out the entry, rewrite, and initial the correction

00164. A lookout should report objects sighted using:

A. true bearings
B. magnetic bearings
C. gyro bearings
D. relative bearings

00166. The distance gained in the direction of the original course when turning is known as:

A. advance
B. drift
C. tactical diameter
D. transfer

00171. You have determined the maneuvering characteristics of your vessel by taking the radar ranges and bearings of an isolated light while making a turn. The results are listed in illustration D035DG. Based on this data what is the transfer for a turn of 30°?

A. 40 yards
B. 140 yards
C. 190 yards
D. 230 yards

00174. A lookout should be posted:

A. during all periods of low visibility
B. only between the hours of sunset and sunrise
C. only when entering and leaving port
D. at all times when the vessel is within sight of shore

00176. The turning circle of a ship is the path followed by the:

A. tipping center
B. bow
C. outermost part of the ship while making the circle
D. pivoting point

00177. The measurement of the amount of force a towing vessel is capable of applying to a motionless tow is called:

A. shaft horsepower
B. delivered horsepower
C. bollard pull
D. towrope pull

00179. The minimum temperature required to ignite gas or vapor without a spark or flame being present is called:

A. flash point
B. fire point
C. autoignition temperature
D. lower explosive limit

00182. What size of manila line is required to hold a weight of 932 lb., if you use a safety factor of 6?

A. 2.0"
B. 2.5"
C. 3.0"
D. 3.5"

00184. While standing lookout duty at night, a dim light on the horizon will be seen quickest by looking:

A. at an area just a little below the horizon
B. at the horizon, where the sky and water appear to meet
C. a little above the horizon
D. well below the horizon line

00185. You are under sail in a lifeboat and running free. the maximum drive of the sails is reached just before the:

A. lee shroud starts to go slack
B. luff of the mainsail starts to quiver
C. headsail is blanketed by the mainsail
D. tiller requires a constant angle to maintain course

00186. The pivoting point of a vessel is usually located:

A. near the bow
B. approximately 1/3 of the vessel's length from the bow
C. approximately 2/3 of the vessel's length from the bow
D. near the stern

00192. In illustration D044DG, the mooring line labeled "H" is called a(n):

A. offshore bow line
B. onshore bow line
C. offshore spring line
D. forward breast line

00194. A vessel spotted at 45° relative can be reported as:

A. on the starboard beam
B. broad on the starboard bow
C. 4 points forward of starboard bow
D. 4 points abaft the starboard beam

00197. Serving is:

A. marline or ratline wound along the grooves of a rope
B. narrow strips of light canvas or cotton cloth spiral-wrapped along the rope
C. marline tightly wound on the rope by means of a board or mallet
D. a splice made by laying the strand of one rope into the vacated grooves of another rope

00202. When making a mooring wire fast to bitts it is recommended that you:

A. use only figure eights
B. take 2 round turns around 1 bitt, then make figure eights
C. take 3 round turns around both bitts, then make figure eights
D. alternate round turns and figure eights around both bitts

00203. How does the effect known as "bank suction" act on a single-screw vessel proceeding along a narrow channel?

A. It pulls the bow toward the bank.
B. It pushes the entire vessel away from the bank.
C. It pulls the stern toward the bank.
D. It heels the vessel toward the bank.

00204. What does the helm command "shift the rudder" mean?

A. Put the rudder over to the opposite side, the same number of degrees it is now.
B. Put the rudder amidships and hold the heading steady as she goes.
C. Shift the rudder control to the alternate steering method.
D. Stop the swing of the ship.

00206. In stopping distances of vessels, HEAD REACH can best be described as the:

A. difference between the vessel's speed through the water at any instant and the new speed ordered on the telegraph
B. distance the vessel has actually run through the water since a change of speed was ordered
C. distance vessel will run between taking action and being stationary in the water
D. speed at which a vessel should proceed to ensure that she will run a predetermined distance, once her engines have been stopped

00207. A towing vessel's capability is BEST measured by horsepower, maneuverability, displacement and:

A. stability
B. propeller design
C. bollard pull
D. towing winch horsepower

00211. A seaman is entitled by law to his/her release when:

A. he/she is intoxicated
B. his/her vessel is overloaded
C. there is a change of home port
D. there is a change of Master

00214. The helm command "meet her" means:

A. use rudder to check the swing
B. decrease the rudder angle which is on
C. steer more carefully
D. note the course and steady on that heading

00215. How does effect known as "bank suction" act on a single-screw vessel proceeding along a narrow channel?

A. It pulls the bow toward the bank.
B. It heels the vessel toward the bank.
C. It pushes the entire vessel away from the bank.
D. It pulls the stern toward the bank.

00216. As a ship moves through the water, it drags with it a body of water called a wake. The ratio of the wake speed to the ship's speed is called:

A. propeller velocity
B. speed of advance
C. wake distribution
D. wake fraction

00224. The term "Shift the Rudder" means:

A. put the rudder amidships
B. use right or left rudder
C. check, but do not stop the vessel from swinging
D. change from right (left) to left (right) rudder an equal amount

00226. Which statement is TRUE concerning the vessel's slipstream?

A. It has no effect on the steering of the vessel.
B. It has no effect on the rudder when the helm is amidships.
C. Its velocity is the same as that of the wake.
D. The propeller gives it a helical motion.

00227. An ocean towing bridle should:

A. have equal legs of sufficient length
B. have a large angle between the legs
C. be formed on a bight of cable through a ring
D. never be made up of chain

00232. The angle at which the fluke penetrates the soil is called the:

A. fluke angle
B. tripping angle
C. penetration angle
D. holding angle

00234. The helm command "shift your rudder" means:

A. double your rudder angle or go to full rudder
B. bring your rudder amidships
C. change from right rudder to left rudder an equal number of degrees
D. check the swing of the vessel

00236. As the propeller turns, voids are formed on the trailing and leading edges of the propeller blades causing a low in propulsive efficiency, pitting of the blades, and vibration. These voids are known as:

A. advance
B. cavitation
C. edging
D. slip

00239. Flame screens are used to:

A. contain flammable fumes
B. protect firefighters from flames
C. prevent flames from entering tanks
D. keep flames and sparks from getting out of an engine's exhaust system

00243. A towing vessel becomes tripped while towing on a hawser astern. What factor is MOST important when assessing the risk of capsizing?

A. length of the towline
B. height of the towline connection
C. longitudinal position of the towline connection
D. direction of opposing force

00244. "Hard right rudder" means:

A. put the rudder over to the right all the way
B. jam the rudder against the stops
C. meet a swing to the right, then return to amidships
D. put the rudder over quickly to 15 right rudder

00245. The fitting that allows a boom to move freely both vertically and laterally is called the:

A. swivel
B. lizard
C. spider band
D. gooseneck

00246. The force exerted by a propeller which tends to throw the stern right or left is termed:

A. discharge current
B. sidewise current
C. suction current
D. wake current

00253. Which of the following terms describes the distance that a ship moves forward with each revolution of its propeller?

A. advance
B. head reach
C. pitch
D. propeller slip

00254. "Ease the rudder" means to:

A. move the rudder slowly in the direction of the most recent rudder command
B. bring the rudder amidships
C. decrease the rudder angle
D. steer the course which is your present heading

00264. The total weight of cargo, fuel, water, stores, passengers and crew, and their effects, that a ship can carry, is the:

A. bale cubic
B. deadweight
C. gross tonnage
D. loaded displacement

00265. Which of the following statements is TRUE about hooks and shackles?

A. Hooks are stronger than shackles of the same diameter.
B. Shackles are stronger than hooks of the same diameter.
C. Hooks and shackles of the same diameter are of equal strength.
D. All the above may be true, depending on the hook's or shackle's overall length.

00266. The distance that a ship moves forward with each revolution of its propeller is called:

A. advance
B. head reach
C. pitch
D. propeller slip

00271. Total responsibility of the shipment and discharge of seamen is that of the:

A. Master of the vessel
B. steamship company
C. U. S. Custom Service
D. U. S. Coast Guard

00274. What is the difference between net tonnage and gross tonnage?

A. Net tonnage is the gross tonnage less certain deductions.
B. Net tonnage is tonnage of cargo compared to tonnage of whole ship.
C. Net tonnage is gross tonnage minus engine and bunker spaces.
D. Net tonnage is the net weight of the ship.

00276. As a ship moves through the water, it causes a wake, which is also moving forward relative to the sea. In addition to a fore and aft motion, this wake also has a(n):

A. downward and inward flow
B. downward and outward flow
C. upward and inward flow
D. upward and outward flow

00282. The latch of a safety hook is installed to:

A. increase the strength of the hook
B. prevent the sling ring from coming out of the hook if the strain is abruptly eased
C. prevent the sling ring from coming out of the hook if there is a strain on the sling ring
D. all of the above

00284. The beam of a vessel refers to the:

A. depth between decks
B. internal cubic capacity
C. molded depth of the vessel
D. width of the vessel

00286. Sidewise pressure of the propeller tends to throw a ship's stern to the right or left, depending on rotation. The pressure is caused by:

A. back current from the rudder
B. greater pressure on the upper blades
C. lower pressure on the trailing edge of the blades
D. greater pressure on the lower blades

00291. You are the licensed operator of a 100 GT towing vessel making coastwise runs. Whenever a crew member is discharged from your vessel you must:

A. issue a Certificate of Discharge and make an entry in his Continuous Discharge Book
B. sign a Certificate of Discharge or make an entry in his Continuous Discharge Book
C. retain the crew member's Continuous Discharge Book onboard
D. retain the crew member's Certificate of Discharge onboard

00293. Which space(s) is(are) NOT exempt when measuring gross tonnage?

A. auxiliary machinery spaces above the deck
B. steering gear room
C. cargo holds
D. galley in a deckhouse

00294. Displacement refers to the:

A. cubic capacity of a vessel
B. deadweight carrying capacity of a vessel

C. gross tonnage of a vessel
D. number of long tons of water displaced by a vessel afloat

00296. You are on a course of 000°T and put the rudder right 30°. In what direction will the transfer be measured?

A. 000° T
B. 090° T
C. 180° T
D. 270° T

00304. To warp a vessel means to:

A. anchor the vessel
B. bring the head into the wind
C. clean the decks
D. move the vessel by hauling on lines

00306. Your single-screw vessel with a right-handed propeller is dead in the water, when you reverse your engine with your rudder amidships, you would expect your vessel to:

A. kick its stern to port
B. kick its stern to starboard
C. move astern without swinging
D. swing its stern to starboard, then to port

00314. "Avast" means:

A. let go
B. pull
C. slack off
D. stop

00316. On a single-screw vessel with a right-handed propeller, when you are going full speed astern with full right rudder, the bow will swing:

A. quickly to port, then more slowly to port
B. slowly to port, then quickly to starboard
C. to port
D. to starboard

00324. A "chock" is a:

A. deck fitting used to secure mooring lines
B. deck fitting used as a fairlead
C. sharp block of wood used to support hygroscopic cargo
D. smoke pipe for the galley stove

00326. In order to back a right-handed, single-screw vessel in a straight line, you will probably:

A. not need to use any rudder
B. need to use some left rudder
C. need to use some right rudder
D. need to use full left rudder

00332. The helm command "Meet her" means:

A. steer more carefully
B. use rudder to check the swing
C. decrease the existing rudder angle
D. note the course and steady on that heading

00334. The space above the engine room is called the:

A. fidley
B. gold locker
C. middle hatch
D. noble

00336. When a vessel with a single right-hand propeller backs to port, the:

A. bow falls off to starboard
B. vessel moves to port without changing heading
C. bow swings to port
D. vessel moves to starboard without changing heading

00344. The purpose of a bilge well is to:

A. afford access to the shell through the double bottoms
B. collect water to be pumped out
C. provide access for the pneumercator
D. provide a base line for sounding measurements

00345. What does the helm command "shift the rudder" mean?

A. Put the rudder amidships and hold the heading steady as she goes.
B. Put the rudder over to the opposite side, the same number of degrees it is now.
C. Shift the rudder control to the alternate steering method.
D. Stop the swing of the ship.

00346. A vessel is equipped with a single right-handed screw. With rudder amidships and calm wind, the vessel will most likely back:

A. straight astern
B. to port
C. to starboard
D. in no particular direction

00351. Which certificate is issued by the American Bureau of Shipping?

A. Certificate of Inspection
B. Load Line Certificate
C. Safety Equipment Certificate
D. Permit to Proceed for repairs

00354. A "stopper" is:

A. a short length of line used for temporarily holding another line
B. a snatch block for handling a topping lift
C. an engine telegraph
D. the brake on a cargo winch

00355. Generally speaking, you are best able to keep a vessel under steering control when the vessel has:

A. headway
B. sternway
C. no way on, with engines stopped
D. no way on, with engines full ahead

00357. What does the proof test load of an anchor chain demonstrate?

A. breaking strength of the chain
B. strength of the chain to a specified limit
C. adequate holding power for new bottom conditions
D. safe working load of the chain

00361. The strictest load line regulations apply to:

A. gas carriers
B. freighters (break-bulk)
C. passenger ships
D. tankers

00362. A towing vessel is tripped when:

A. it is overtaken by the tow
B. it is pulled sideways by the tow
C. the weight of the towing hawser causes loss of maneuverability
D. the propeller is fouled by the towing hawser

00363. Which space(s) is(are) deducted from gross tonnage to derive net tonnage?

A. steering gear room
B. chart room
C. open structures
D. all of the above

00364. A long ton contains:

A. 1,000 lb.
B. 2,000 lb.
C. 2,240 lb.
D. 2,400 lb.

00366. When backing down with sternway, the pivot point of a vessel is:

A. at the bow
B. about 1/3 of the vessel's length from the bow
C. about 1/4 of the vessel's length from the stern
D. aft of the propellers

00371. In the United States, the load line markings are determined for new ships by the:

A. American Bureau of Shipping
B. Coast Guard
C. Federal Maritime Board
D. IMO

00372. Keeping the draft at or below the load line mark will insure that the vessel has adequate:

A. ballast
B. reserve buoyancy
C. displacement
D. rolling periods

00374. Holes in the bulwark, which allow deck water to drain into the sea are:

A. doggers
B. fidleys
C. freeing ports
D. swash ports

00376. If the engines of a right-handed single-screw vessel with headway on are put full astern as the wheel is put hard left, what pattern will the bow follow?

A. It will swing to the left (and will swing left faster) as the vessel loses way.
B. It will swing to the left, straighten out and then swing to the right as the vessel loses way.
C. It will swing to the left without increasing or decreasing its swing.
D. The bow will swing to the right.

00384. A "strongback" refers to a:

A. bar securing a cargo port
B. centerline vertical bulkhead
C. deep beam
D. spanner stay

00386. When maneuvering a vessel with a right-hand screw and the rudder amidships, it should be remembered that the vessel will back:

A. to port
B. to starboard
C. in a straight line directly astern
D. downstream, the stern going in the direction of the current

00394. The rope which is rove from the truck to be used with a bosun chair is called a:

A. gantline
B. life line
C. strop
D. whip

00396. A vessel is equipped with twin propellers, both turning outboard with the engines half ahead. If there is no wind or current and the rudder is amidships, which of the following will happen?

A. The bow will swing to starboard.
B. The bow will swing to port.
C. The vessel will steer a zigzag course.
D. The vessel will steer a fairly straight course.

00401. The Tonnage Certificate indicates:

A. deadweight tons
B. displacement tons
C. measurement tons
D. power tons

00404. A vessel's "quarter" is that section which is:

A. abeam
B. dead astern
C. just aft the bow
D. on either side of the stern

00406. A twin-screw vessel with a single rudder is making headway with the engines full speed ahead. If there is no wind or current, which statement is FALSE?

A. If one screw is stopped, the ship will turn toward the side of the stopped screw.
B. The principal force which turns the ship is set up by the wake against the forward side of the rudder.
C. Turning response by use of the rudder only is greater than on a single-screw vessel.
D. With the rudder amidships, the ship will steer a fairly steady course.

00408. What is the meaning of the term "tare weight"?

A. pounds of force necessary to damage a container
B. total weight of a container and contents
C. weight of a container
D. weight of the contents of a container

00414. To "ease" a line means to:

A. cast off
B. double up so that one line does not take all the strain
C. pay out more line to remove most of the tension
D. slack it off quickly

00416. While moving ahead, a twin-screw ship has an advantage over a single-screw ship because:

A. correct trim will be obtained more easily
B. drag effect will be cancelled out
C. side forces will be eliminated
D. speed will be increased

00421. An International Tonnage Certificate will be issued to a vessel when it meets several requirements, one of which is that the vessel must:

A. admeasure over 100 GT
B. be 79 or more feet in length
C. engage in intercoastal or international trade
D. be issued a Certificate of Inspection

00424. Faking a line means to:

A. arrange it on deck in long bights
B. coil it down on deck
C. put a whipping on it
D. stow it below

00427. What is the greatest danger of an overriding tow?

A. fouling of the towing hawser
B. loss of steering
C. tripping
D. collision between the tow and the stern of the towing vessel

00431. Official proof of an American vessel's nationality is contained in the:

A. Certificate of Inspection
B. Official Log
C. Certificate of Documentation
D. Shipping Articles

00434. To "belay" a line means:

A. coil it down
B. heave it taut
C. stow it below
D. secure it to a cleat

00436. The rudder is amidships and both screws are going ahead. What will happen if the starboard screw is stopped?

A. The bow will go to port.
B. The bow will go to starboard.
C. The bow will remain steady.
D. The stern will go to starboard.

00437. Prior to getting underway in fresh or brackish water, the Master must:

A. log the density of the water
B. secure all overboard discharges
C. take on fresh water ballast
D. clean the sides with fresh water

00442. "Ease the rudder" means to:

A. move the rudder slowly in the direction of the most recent rudder command
B. decrease the rudder angle
C. bring the rudder amidships
D. steer the course which is your present heading

00444. A metal object on the pier resembling a tree stump and made to receive mooring lines, is a:

A. bight
B. bollard
C. chock
D. camel

00446. A twin-screw vessel can clear the inboard propeller and maneuver off a pier best by holding a(n):

A. after bow spring line and going slow ahead on the inboard engine
B. forward quarter spring line and going slow astern on the outboard engine
C. after bow spring line and going slow ahead on both engines
D. after bow spring line and going slow ahead on the outboard engine

00451. Which of the following is official proof of a vessel's ownership?

A. Certificate of Documentation
B. Bill of Sale
C. Transfer Certificate
D. Logbook

00454. A rope ladder with wooden rungs is a:

A. drop ladder
B. life ladder
C. Jacob's ladder
D. jury ladder

00455. A vessel having continuous closely spaced transverse strength members is:

A. longitudinally framed
B. transversely framed
C. cellular framed
D. web framed

00456. You are in charge of a twin-screw vessel going ahead with rudders amidships. If suddenly the port screw stops turning, the bow will:

A. go to port
B. go to starboard
C. not veer to either side
D. go first to port and then to starboard

00461. Except when surrendered to the issuing office, the Certificate of Documentation with a coastwise license endorsement of a towing vessel:

A. may be retained by the owner at the home port or kept on the vessel
B. must be posted under transparent material in the pilothouse
C. must be carried on board
D. must be kept on file at the corporate offices of the owner or operator

00466. You are going ahead on twin engines when you want to make a quick turn to starboard. What actions will turn the boat quickest?

A. reverse port engine, apply right rudder
B. reverse port engine, rudder amidships
C. reverse starboard engine, apply right rudder
D. reverse starboard engine, rudder amidships

00471. The official identification of a vessel is found in the:

A. Certificate of Inspection
B. Classification Certificate
C. Load Line Certificate
D. Certificate of Documentation

00472. On a long ocean tow, the bridle should be made up of two equal lengths of:

A. chain
B. wire
C. nylon
D. manila

00474. On an anchor windlass, the wheel over which the anchor chain passes is called a:

A. brake compressor wheel
B. devil's claw
C. wildcat
D. winch head

00475. In illustration D044DG, the mooring line labeled "F" is called a:

A. bow line
B. breast line
C. forward spring line
D. none of the above

00476. You are backing on twin engines with rudder amidships, when your port engine stalls. In order to continue backing on course, you should:

A. apply left rudder
B. apply right rudder
C. increase engine speed
D. keep your rudder amidships

00481. Which U. S. agency would assign an official number to a vessel?

A. American Bureau of Shipping
B. Collector of Customs
C. Treasury Department
D. Coast Guard

00484. On stud-link anchor chain it has been estimated that the addition of the stud increases the strength of the link by:

A. 10%
B. 15%
C. 20%
D. 50%

00486. You are backing on twin engines, with rudder amidships, when your starboard engine stalls. In order to continue backing on course, you should:

A. apply left rudder
B. apply right rudder
C. increase your engine speed
D. keep your rudder amidships

00491. A change of a U. S. vessel's name can only be made by which government agency?

A. American Bureau of Shipping
B. Commissioner of Customs
C. Treasury Department
D. Coast Guard

00494. What best describes an anchor buoy?

A. a black ball that is hoisted when the ship anchors
B. a buoy attached to the anchor
C. a buoy attached to the scope of an anchor chain
D. a mark of the number of fathoms in an anchor chain

00495. Which space(s) is (are) deducted from gross tonnage to derive net tonnage?

A. boatswain's stores
B. companions and booby hatches
C. passenger spaces
D. all of the above

00496. Your twin-screw vessel is moving ASTERN with rudder amidships when the starboard screw suddenly quits turning. Your vessel's head will:

A. go to port
B. go to starboard
C. remain stationary
D. suddenly drop down

00504. Anchors are prevented from running out when secured by the:

A. brake
B. devil's claw
C. pawls
D. all of the above

00506. With rudder amidships and negligible wind, a twin-screw vessel moving astern with both engines backing will back:

A. to port
B. to starboard
C. in a fairly straight line
D. in a circular motion

00514. The part of an anchor which takes hold on the bottom is the:

A. arm
B. base
C. fluke
D. stock

00516. You are going ahead on twin engines with rudder amidships when your starboard engine stalls. If you desire to continue your course, you should:

A. apply left rudder
B. apply right rudder
C. increase engine speed
D. keep your rudder amidships

00517. What is the purpose of the intermediate spring?

A. serves as a backup for the main tow hawser in case of failure
B. provides weight and flexibility to the total tow makeup
C. lengthens the main tow hawser to keep the tow in step
D. distributes the towing load

00521. A single heavy wire made up for the topping lift is called a:

A. bale
B. spanner wire
C. bull line
D. working guy

00524. The purpose of the stripping bar on an anchor windlass is to:

A. clean off any mud that may have accumulated on the chain
B. engage or disengage the wildcat
C. fairlead the chain from the hawsepipe to the wildcat
D. prevent the chain from fouling the wildcat

00526. You are going ahead on twin engines with rudder amidships, when your port engine stalls. If you desire to continue your course, you should:

A. apply right rudder
B. apply left rudder
C. keep your rudder amidships
D. increase engine speed

00534. What would be considered part of the ground tackle?

A. Charlie noble
B. devil's claw
C. gooseneck
D. rat's tail

00535. In illustration D044DG, the mooring line labeled "G" is called a(n):

A. offshore bow line
B. inshore bow line
C. forward breast line
D. forward spring line

00536. When a vessel is backing on the starboard screw, and going ahead on the port screw, the bow will:

A. back on a straight line
B. move ahead on a straight line
C. swing to port
D. swing to starboard

00541. The official number of a documented vessel is:

A. not required to be marked anywhere on the vessel
B. required to be permanently marked on the vessel's structure
C. required to be painted on the vessel's stern
D. required to be painted on the vessel's bow

00544. If the winch should fail while you are hauling in the anchor, what prevents the anchor cable from running out?

A. Chain stopper
B. Devil's claw
C. Hawse ratchet
D. Riding pawl

00546. A twin-screw ship going ahead on the starboard screw only tends to:

A. move in a straight line
B. veer to port
C. veer from side to side
D. veer to starboard

00551. The name and home port of a documented vessel is:

A. not required to be marked anywhere on the vessel
B. required to be marked on both bows and on the keel
C. required to be marked on the stern with the name of the vessel marked on both bows
D. required to be marked on the keel, stern, and both bows

00554. Which part of the patent anchor performs the same function as the stock of an old fashioned anchor; that is, forces the flukes to dig in?

A. bill or pea
B. arm
C. shank
D. tripping palm

00556. You may best turn a twin-screw vessel about to the right in a narrow channel by using:

A. both engines ahead and helm
B. one engine only
C. port engine ahead and the starboard engine astern
D. both engines astern and use helm

00557. A report of casualty to a vessel must include:

A. the estimated cost of damage
B. an evaluation of who was at fault
C. the amount of ballast on board
D. the name of the owner or agent of the vessel

00561. Which space CANNOT be deducted from gross tonnage when calculating net tonnage?

A. crew mess room
B. forepeak ballast tank
C. master's cabin
D. chain locker

00564. The anchors on the bow are known as:

A. bower anchors
B. kedge anchors
C. spare anchors
D. stream anchors

00566. The BEST way to steer a twin-screw vessel if you lose your rudder is by using:

A. one engine and a steering oar
B. both engines at the same speed
C. one engine at a time
D. one engine running at reduced speed and controlling the vessel with the other

00574. What type of link is generally used to connect shots of anchor chain?

A. detachable
B. open
C. pear shaped
D. stud link

00576. In twin-screw engine installations while going ahead, maneuvering qualities are most effective when the tops of the propeller blades both turn:

A. to starboard
B. outboard from the center
C. to port
D. inboard from the center

00577. You are signing on a crew. A man presents a Merchant Mariner's Document that you suspect has been tampered with. What action should you take?

A. Confiscate the document and deliver it to the Coast Guard.
B. Sign the man on and notify the Coast Guard at the first U. S. port of call.
C. Refuse to sign the man on articles until authorized by the Coast Guard.
D. Refuse to sign the man on and notify the FBI of unauthorized use of a federal document.

00582. In illustration D044DG, the mooring line labeled "E" is called a(n):

A. after spring line
B. bow spring line
C. forward breast line
D. bow line

00584. Which position in illustration D019DG is the MOST dangerous position when tying up a vessel?

A. I
B. II
C. III
D. IV

00586. With rudder amidships and negligible wind, a vessel moving forward with one engine ahead and the other backing will:

A. move in a straight line
B. turn in a direction away from the engine moving ahead
C. turn in a direction toward the engine moving ahead
D. move sideways through the water

00592. When a helmsman receives the command "Right 15 degrees rudder", the helmsman's immediate reply should be:

A. "Right 15 degrees rudder"
B. "Aye Aye Sir"
C. "Rudder is right 15 degrees"
D. No reply, just carry out the order.

00594. A bollard is found on the:

A. beach
B. deck
C. pier
D. towed vessel

00595. The turning circle of a vessel is the path followed by the:

A. outermost part of the ship while making the circle
B. center of gravity
C. bow
D. tipping center

00601. Your vessel has completed an inspection for certification and is issued a temporary certificate. This:

A. expires 6 months after it is issued
B. must be exchanged for a regular Certificate of Inspection before going foreign or out of state
C. has the full force of a regular Certificate of Inspection
D. must be posted in the vicinity of the officers' licenses

00604. The term "lee side" refers to the:

A. side of the vessel exposed to the wind
B. side of the vessel sheltered from the wind
C. port side
D. starboard side

00605. You would properly secure a bosun's chair to a gantline with a:

A. fisherman's bend
B. bowline
C. double sheetbend
D. double blackwall hitch

00612. When backing down with sternway, the pivot point of a vessel is:

A. at the bow
B. about 1/3 of the vessel's length from the bow
C. aft of the propellers
D. about 1/4 of the vessel's length from the stern

00613. A lookout can leave his station:

A. at the end of the watch
B. ONLY when properly relieved
C. at any time
D. 15 minutes before the end of the watch

00614. A fid is a:

A. mallet used when splicing wire rope
B. sharp pointed crow bar used to unlay wire rope
C. tapered steel pin used to separate wire rope
D. tapered wooden pin used when splicing heavy rope

00617. In illustration D044DG, the mooring line labeled "A" is called a(n):

A. onshore stern line
B. offshore stern line
C. after breast line
D. after spring line

00624. A serving mallet is used in:

A. covering wire or fiber rope
B. forcing fids into a line
C. dogging hatches
D. splicing lines

00627. Your ship is steaming at night with the gyropilot engaged when you notice that the vessel's course is slowly changing to the right. What action should you take FIRST?

A. Switch to telemotor steering.
B. Shift steering to the emergency steering station.
C. Call the master.
D. Notify the engine room.

00630. You are executing a Williamson turn. Your vessel has swung about 60° from the original course heading. What action should you take?

A. Put rudder amidships and check the swing.
B. Stop the engines and prepare to maneuver to pick up the man in the water.
C. Shift your rudder.
D. Increase to maximum speed.

00631. At least one reinspection shall be made on each vessel holding a Certificate of Inspection valid for 2 years. This inspection shall be held between the 10th and 14th months of the duration period of the certificate and shall be:

A. at the discretion of the inspector, but in no greater detail than required for original certification
B. at the discretion of the inspector, but in no lesser detail than required for original certification
C. generally similar in scope to the inspection required for certification, but in less detail
D. equivalent to the inspection required for certification

00632. What does the helm command "shift the rudder" mean?

A. Stop the swing of the ship.
B. Shift the rudder control to the alternate steering method.
C. Put the rudder over to the opposite side, the same number of degrees it is now.
D. Put the rudder amidships and hold the heading steady as she goes.

00634. The "iron mike" is a(n):
A. pilot
B. speaker
C. standby wheel
D. automatic pilot

00636. The use of an anchor to assist in turning in restricted waters is:

A. a last resort
B. good seamanship
C. the sign of a novice shiphandler
D. to be used only with a single-screw vessel

00637. A tow bridle is attached to the main tow hawser at the:

A. bight ring
B. tow hook
C. fishplate
D. swivel

00640. While underway, if one of your crew members falls overboard from the starboard side, you should IMMEDIATELY:

A. apply left rudder
B. throw the crew member a life preserver
C. begin backing your engines
D. position your vessel to windward and begin recovery

00641. What document shows the minimum required crew a vessel must have to navigate from one port in the United States to another?

A. Articles
B. Certificate of Inspection
C. Crew List
D. Register

00642. In illustration D044DG, the mooring line labeled "B" is called a(n):

A. offshore stern line
B. inshore stern line
C. after spring line
D. after breast line

00643. A vessel's tropical load line is 6" above her summer load line. Her TPI is 127 tons. She will arrive in the summer zone 8

days after departure. She will burn off about 47 tons/day and water consumption is 12 tons/day. How many tons may she load above her summer load line if she loads in the tropical zone?

A. 376
B. 472
C. 762
D. 1016

00644. The "lay" of a line refers to:

A. its normal location of stowage
B. the direction of twist in the strands
C. the manner in which it is coiled
D. the manner in which it is rigged

00650. A crew member has just fallen overboard off your port beam. Which of the following actions should you take?

A. Immediately put the rudder over hard right.
B. Immediately put the rudder over hard left.
C. Immediately put the engines astern.
D. Wait until the stern is well clear of the man and then put the rudder over hard right.

00651. Fire fighting equipment requirements for a particular vessel may be found on the:

A. Certificate of Inspection
B. Certificate of Seaworthiness
C. Classification Certificate
D. Certificate of Registry

00654. A rope made of a combination of wire and fiber is known as:

A. independent
B. lang lay
C. preformed
D. spring lay

00657. Which space(s) is(are) deducted from gross tonnage to derive net tonnage?

A. companions and booby hatches
B. open structures
C. spaces for the exclusive use of the officers or crew
D. water ballast spaces

00660. Your vessel is steaming at sea when you receive word that a member of the crew has fallen overboard on the starboard side. you should FIRST:

A. notify the Master
B. put the wheel hard right
C. put the engines full astern
D. sound the man overboard alarm

00661. The number of certificated lifeboatmen required for a vessel will be found on the:

A. Certificate of Inspection
B. Station Bill
C. lifeboats
D. Register or Enrollment

00662. You are signing on the Radio Officer. Which statement is TRUE?

A. He must have a Merchant Mariner's Document endorsed "See License as Radio Officer".
B. He must present either an FCC license or a Coast Guard license.
C. You must consult the "List of Qualifications" on the reverse of his FCC license to ensure that he is qualified to operate the radio equipment installed on board.
D. His Coast Guard license may have an added endorsement as "Electronics Repair Officer".

00664. To coil down a rope against the lay, bring the lower end up through the center of the coil, and coil down with the lay in order to straighten kinks from a new rope is known as:

A. coiling
B. faking
C. flemishing
D. thoroughfooting

00666. You are proceeding at a slow speed with your starboard side near the right bank of a channel. If your vessel suddenly sheers toward the opposite bank, the BEST maneuver would be:

A. full ahead, hard left rudder
B. full ahead, hard right rudder
C. full astern, hard left rudder
D. full astern, hard right rudder

00670. You must evacuate a seaman by helicopter lift. Which of the following statements is TRUE?

A. The ship should be stopped with the wind off the beam while the helicopter is hovering overhead.
B. The basket or stretcher must not be allowed to touch the deck.
C. The tending line of the litter basket should be secured to the ship beyond the radius of the helicopter blades.
D. The hoist line should be slack before the basket or stretcher is hooked on.

00672. When towing alongside (breasted tow), more forward movement will be imparted to the tow by:

A. increasing the angle of line pull to the keel axis of the tow
B. reducing the angle of line pull to the keel axis of the tow
C. positioning the towing vessel on the forward end of the tow
D. shortening the length of the tow line

00673. In illustration D044DG, the mooring line labeled "C" is called a:

A. shore line
B. breast line
C. spring line
D. stern line

00674. Stuffer-braid rope has:

A. a yarn core
B. no core
C. 3 strands
D. 12 threads

00676. Conditions for crossing a rough bar would be best at:

A. low water slack
B. high water slack
C. high water ebb
D. high water flood

00677. In illustration D044DG, the mooring line labeled "D" is called a(n):

A. forward spring line
B. after spring line
C. waist breast line
D. stern line

00680. You must medivac a critically injured seaman by helicopter hoist. Which of the following statements is TRUE?

A. The ship's relative wind should be from dead ahead at 10 to 30 knots.
B. The deck crew at the hoist point should not wear baseball hats.
C. The helicopter's drop line should be secured to the ship not more than 15' from the hoist position.
D. When using a "horsecollar", the bight of the loop should be around the chest of the injured seaman.

00682. In illustration D044DG, the mooring line labeled "H" is called a(n):

A. forward breast line
B. offshore bow line
C. offshore spring line
D. onshore bow line

00684. Right-laid line should be coiled:

A. clockwise
B. counterclockwise
C. either clockwise or counterclockwise
D. with the use of a reel

00686. The effect known as "bank cushion" acts in which of the following ways on a single-screw vessel proceeding along a narrow channel?

A. It forces the bow away from the bank.
B. It forces the stern away from the bank.
C. It forces the entire vessel away from the bank.
D. It heels the vessel toward the bank.

00690. A rescue helicopter hoist area would preferably have a minimum radius of at least:

A. 6 feet of clear deck
B. 10 feet of clear deck
C. 25 feet of clear deck
D. 50 feet of clear deck

00692. The tow makeup that is designed to keep the catenary of the tow hawser to a minimum is called the:

A. Christmas tree tow
B. tandem tow
C. British tow
D. tandem tug tow

00694. An advantage of nylon rope over manila rope is that nylon rope:

A. can be used in conjunction with wire or spring-lay rope
B. can be stored on decks exposed to sunlight
C. can hold a load even when a considerable amount of the yarns have been abraded
D. gives audible warning of overstress whereas manila does not

00696. A vessel travelling down a narrow channel, especially if the draft is nearly equal to the depth of the water, may set off the nearer side. This effect is known as:

A. smelling the bottom
B. squatting
C. bank suction
D. bank cushion

00700. A tug is approaching to take a broken down steamer in tow in moderately heavy weather. In most cases the:

A. steamer will drift stern downwind
B. tug will drift faster than the steamer
C. tug should approach stern to
D. tug should approach from downwind

00703. After a collision or accident, the operator of an uninspected vessel MUST assist people affected by the collision or accident if he or she can do so without:

A. serious danger to his or her own vessel
B. further damaging the other vessel
C. undue delay
D. creating a panic on either vessel

00704. Laying out a line in successive circles flat on deck with the bitter end in the center is known as:

A. coiling
B. faking
C. flemishing
D. lining

00706. The effect known as "bank suction" acts in which of the following ways on a single-screw vessel proceeding along a narrow channel?

A. It pulls the bow toward the bank.
B. It pulls the stern toward the bank.
C. It pulls the entire vessel toward the bank.
D. It heels the vessel toward the bank.

00710. Which of the following is NOT an advantage of the Williamson turn?

A. In a large vessel (VLCC) much of the headway will be lost thereby requiring little astern maneuvering.
B. When the turn is completed, the vessel will be on a reciprocal course and nearly on the original track line.
C. The initial actions are taken at well defined points and reduce the need for individual judgement.
D. The turn will return the vessel to the man's location in the shortest possible time.

00714. Using a safety factor of 6, determine the safe working load of manila line with a breaking stress of 8 tons.

A. 0.75 tons
B. 1.25 tons
C. 1.33 tons
D. 8.00 tons

00716. On a single-screw vessel proceeding along a narrow channel, the effect known as bank cushion has which of the following results on a vessel?

A. forces the bow away from the bank
B. forces the stern away from the bank
C. forces the entire vessel bodily away from the bank
D. decreases the draft at the bow

00717. It is the responsibility of the Master to ensure that:

A. the Station Bill is posted in each compartment
B. temporary personnel and visitors are advised of emergency stations
C. names of crew members are listed on the Station Bill
D. no changes are made to the Station Bill

00720. You suspect that a crewmember has fallen overboard during the night and immediately execute a Williamson turn. What is the PRIMARY advantage of this maneuver under these circumstances?

A. You will be on a reciprocal course and nearly on the track line run during the night.
B. The turn provides the maximum coverage of the area to be searched.
C. The turn enables you to reverse course in the shortest possible time.
D. You have extra time to maneuver in attempting to close in on the man for rescue.

00721. In illustration D044DG, the mooring line labeled "F" is called a:

A. bow line
B. forward spring line
C. breast line
D. none of the above

00724. Using a safety factor of 5, determine what is the safe working load for 3-1/2 inch manila line with a breaking stress of 4.9 tons.

A. 0.82 tons
B. 0.98 tons
C. 2.45 tons
D. 12.25 tons

00726. A common occurrence when a vessel is running into shallow water is that:

A. the wake is less pronounced
B. the vessel is more responsive to the rudder
C. "squat" will cause a decrease in bottom clearance and an increase in draft
D. all of the above

00727. Which space(s) is(are) deducted from gross tonnage to derive net tonnage?

A. galley fitted with range or oven
B. open structures
C. passenger spaces
D. boatswain's stores

00730. In a Williamson turn, the rudder is put over full until the:

A. vessel has turned 90° from its original course
B. vessel has turned 60° from its original course
C. vessel is on a reciprocal course
D. emergency turn signal sounds

00732. What action should be taken FIRST in the event of a sinking tow in shallow water?

A. Pay out the towline until the sunken tow reaches bottom.
B. Sever the towline.
C. Immediately head for the nearest shoreline.
D. Contact the Coast Guard.

00734. What is the computed breaking strength of a 4" manila line?

A. 5,280 lb.
B. 7,700 lb.
C. 12,200 lb.
D. 14,400 lb.

00736. You notice that your speed has decreased, the stern of your vessel has settled more into the water and that your rudder is sluggish in responding. What is the MOST likely cause for this?

A. mechanical problems with the steering gear
B. shallow water
C. loss of lubricating oil in the engine
D. current

00740. The extension of the after part of the keel in a single-screw vessel upon which the stern post rests is called the:

A. boss
B. knuckle
C. skeg
D. strut

00742. Lighter longitudinal stiffening frames on the vessel's side plating are called:

A. stringers
B. side frames
C. side stiffeners
D. intercostals

00744. When using natural-fiber rope, you should NEVER:

A. dry the line before stowing it
B. reverse turns on winches periodically to keep out kinks
C. try to lubricate the line
D. use chafing gear

00746. What effect does speed through the water have on a vessel which is underway in shallow water?

A. A decrease in the speed results in a decrease in steering response and maneuverability.
B. An increase in speed results in the stern sucking down lower than the bow.
C. An increase in speed results in the vessel rising on an even plane.
D. A decrease in speed results in the vessel sucking down on an even plane.

00750. On a single-screw vessel, a function of the stern frame is:

A. furnishing support to the rudder, propeller shaft, and transom frame
B. providing foundations for after mooring winches
C. providing foundations for the main propulsion engines
D. transferring the driving force of the propeller to the hull

00754. Which of the following methods is used to detect rot in manila lines?

A. feeling the surface of the line for broken fibers
B. measuring the reduction in circumference of the line
C. observing for the appearance of mildew on the outer surface
D. opening the strands and examining the inner fibers

00756. A vessel in shallow water might experience:

A. bank cushion
B. bank suction
C. squatting
D. yawing

00764. Roundline is a:

A. 4-stranded, left- or right-handed line
B. 3-stranded, right-handed line
C. 3-stranded, left-handed line
D. small tarred hempline of 3 strands laid left-handed

00766. Insufficient space between the hull and bottom in shallow water will prevent normal screw currents resulting in:

A. waste of power
B. sudden sheering to either side
C. sluggish rudder response
D. all of the above

00770. The ratio of the height of a vessels rudder to its width is referred to as the:

A. aspect ratio
B. constriction ratio

C. rudder ratio
D. steering ratio

00772. To reduce stress on the towing hawser when towing astern (ocean tow), the hawser should be:

A. secured to the aftermost fitting on the towing vessel
B. just touching the water
C. underwater
D. as short as possible

00774. The strongest of the natural fibers is:

A. cotton
B. hemp
C. manila
D. sisal

00776. In most cases, when a large merchant vessel enters shallow water at high speed the:

A. maneuverability will increase
B. speed will increase
C. bow will squat farther than the stern
D. vessel will rise slightly, on a level plane

00784. Marline is:

A. 4-stranded sisal line
B. 3-stranded cotton line
C. sail twine
D. 2-stranded hemp cord

00786. You are on a single-screw vessel with a right-handed propeller, and you are making headway. When you come upon shallow water:

A. you will have better rudder response
B. your speed will increase without a change in your throttle
C. your rudder response will become sluggish
D. your vessel will tend to ride higher

00794. "White Line" is made from:

A. cotton
B. hemp
C. manila
D. sisal

00796. When you enter shallow water, you would expect your rudder response to:

A. be sluggish, and your speed to decrease
B. be sluggish, and your speed to increase
C. improve, and your speed to decrease
D. improve, and your speed to increase

00799. Temporary Certificates of Inspection are effective until the:
A. SOLAS Certificate is issued

B. Load Line Certificate is renewed
C. Classification Society Approval is issued
D. Permanent Certificate of Inspection is issued

00800. A Kort nozzle refers to a(n):

A. hollow tube surrounding the propeller used to improve thrust
B. nozzle attached to a firefighting hose
C. intake valve on a diesel engine
D. piston cylinder on a diesel engine

00801. When oil is discharged overboard, an entry is required in the:

A. Engine Rough Log
B. Oil Record Book
C. Official Logbook
D. Deck Rough Log

00804. Line is called "small stuff" if its circumference is less than:

A. 1/2"
B. 3/4"
C. 1"
D. 1-3/4"

00806. Which of the following will MOST likely occur when entering shallow water?

A. Rudder action will become more effective.
B. The vessel's list will change.
C. The vessel's trim will change.
D. An increase in speed will occur.

00810. A "dog" is a:

A. crow bar
B. device to force a water tight door against the frame
C. heavy steel beam
D. wedge

00814. In the manufacture of line, plant fibers are twisted together to form:

A. cable
B. line
C. strands
D. yarns

00816. Water may boil up around the stern of a vessel in a channel due to:

A. slack water when upbound
B. shallow water
C. a cross current
D. a head current

00817. In illustration D044DG, the mooring

line labeled "G" is called a(n):

A. forward spring line
B. forward breast line
C. inshore bow line
D. offshore bow line

00822. You are on watch at sea, at night, and a fire breaks out in #3 hold. which of the following should be done IMMEDIATELY?

A. Shut down the cargo hold ventilation.
B. Proceed to the space and determine the extent of the fire.
C. Flood the space with C02 from the fixed fire fighting system.
D. Cool the deck to contain the fire.

00824. The larger sizes of manila line are normally indicated by their:

A. radius
B. diameter
C. circumference
D. weight per foot

00826. In order to reduce your wake in a narrow channel, you should:

A. apply enough rudder to counter the effect of the current
B. change your course to a zigzag course
C. reduce your speed
D. shift the weight to the stern

00827. The pitch of a propeller is a measure of the:

A. angle that the propeller makes with a free stream of water
B. angle that the propeller makes with the surface of the water
C. number of feet per revolution the propeller is designed to move in still water without slip
D. positive pressure resulting from the difference of the forces on both sides of the moving propeller in still water without slip

00834. A whipping on a fiber line:

A. keeps the ends from fraying
B. strengthens it
C. protects your hands
D. becomes part of a splice

00836. River currents have a basic tendency to:

A. pick up speed where the channel widens
B. run slower in the center of the channel
C. hug the inside of a bend
D. cause the greatest depth of water to be along the outside of a bend

00840. The terms "cant frame" and "counter" are associated with the vessel's:

A. cargo hatch
B. forecastle
C. steering engine
D. stern

00841. All entries in the Official Logbook must be signed by the Master and:

A. the Union Representative
B. the person about which the entry concerns
C. no one else
D. one other crew member

00844. Whipping the bitter end of a fiber rope is used to:

A. prevent moisture from entering the bitter end
B. increase the circumference of the rope
C. make for easier handling
D. prevent fraying of the bitter end

00846. A vessel proceeding along the bank of a river or channel has the tendency to:

A. continue in line with the bank
B. hug the bank
C. sheer away from the bank
D. increase speed

00847. When towing astern what equipment should be ready near the towing hawser?

A. first aid kit
B. axe or cutting torch
C. fire extinguisher
D. chafing gear

00850. Panting frames are located in the:

A. after double bottoms
B. centerline tanks on tankships
C. fore and after peaks
D. forward double bottoms

00854. A piece of small stuff (small line) secured to an object to prevent it from going adrift is a:

A. lanyard
B. keeper
C. noose
D. stopper

00856. A wedge of water building up between the bow and nearer bank which forces the bow out and away describes:

A. bank cushion
B. bank suction
C. combined effect
D. bend effect

00861. every entry required to be made in the Official Logbook shall be signed by the:

A. Mate on watch
B. Master and Chief Mate or other member of the crew
C. Master only
D. Purser, one of the Mates, and some other member of the crew

00862. The terms "pintle" and "gudgeon" are associated with the:

A. anchor windlass
B. jumbo boom
C. rudder
D. steering engine

00864. During the manufacture of line, yarns are twisted together in the:

A. opposite direction from which the fibers are twisted together to form strands
B. same directions the fibers are twisted to form strands
C. opposite direction from which the fibers are twisted together to form the line
D. opposite direction from which the fibers are twisted together forming cables

00866. For the deepest water when negotiating a bend in a river, you should navigate your vessel:

A. toward the inside bend of the river
B. toward the outside bend of the river
C. toward the center of the river just before the bend, then change course for the river's center after the bend
D. in the river's center

00870. The terms "ceiling" and "margin plate" are associated with the:

A. crew's quarters
B. engine room
C. main deck
D. tank top

00871. In writing up the logbook at the end of your watch, you make an error in writing an entry. What is the proper means of correcting this error?

A. Cross out the error with a single line, and write the correct entry, then initial it.
B. Carefully and neatly erase the entry and rewrite it correctly.
C. Remove this page of the log book, and rewrite all entries on a clean page.
D. Blot out the error completely and rewrite the entry correctly.

00874. Which of the following types of line would have the LEAST resistance to mildew and rot?

A. manila
B. nylon
C. Dacron
D. polypropylene

00876. Your intention is to overtake a vessel moving in a narrow channel. As you approach the other vessel's stern to pass alongside:

A. you will gain speed
B. both vessels will gain speed
C. the vessels will drift together
D. the vessels will drift apart

00880. The projecting lugs of the rudderpost which furnish support to the rudder are called:

A. bases
B. gudgeons
C. pintles
D. rudder lugs

00881. The proper way to correct a mistake in the logbook is to:

A. erase the entry and rewrite
B. completely black out the entry and rewrite
C. draw a line through the entry and rewrite
D. draw several lines through the entry and rewrite

00884. In order to clean a mooring line that is full of mud and sand, the line should be:

A. hosed down with fresh water
B. hosed down with salt water
C. scrubbed with detergent and water
D. steam cleaned with high pressure steam

00886. Two vessels are abreast of each other and passing port to port in a confined waterway. What would you expect as you approach the screws of the other vessel?

A. your speed would significantly increase.
B. your draft would significantly decrease.
C. your bow would sheer towards the other vessel.
D. your bow would sheer away from the other vessel.

00890. A term applied to the bottom shell plating in a double-bottom ship is:

A. bottom floor
B. outer bottom
C. shear plating
D. tank top

00892. On a shallow water tow, the catenary of the towline should be:

A. large
B. small
C. eliminated
D. adjusted frequently

00894. When taking a length of new manila rope from the coil, you should:

A. mount the coil so it will turn like a spool and unreel from the outside
B. roll the coil along the deck and allow the rope to fall off the coil
C. lay the coil on end with the inside end down, then pull the inside end up through the middle of the coil
D. lay the coil on end with the inside end up then unwind the rope from the outside of the coil

00896. A V-shaped ripple with the point of the V pointing upstream in a river indicates a:

A. submerged rock, not dangerous to navigation
B. sunken wreck, not dangerous to navigation
C. towed-under buoy
D. all of the above

00900. Camber, in a ship, is usually measured in:

A. feet per feet of breadth
B. feet per feet of length
C. inches per feet of breadth
D. inches per feet of length

00901. Which of the following is required to be entered into the Official Logbook?

A. opening a side-port at sea to renew a gasket
B. the annual required stripping and cleaning of the lifeboats
C. the biennial weight test of the lifeboats and falls
D. the drafts on entering port

00902. The number of Able Seamen required on board is stated in the:

A. American Bureau of Shipping code
B. SOLAS Certificate
C. Classification Certificate
D. Certificate of Inspection

00904. In order to help protect fiber rope from rotting, the line must be:

A. dried, and stowed in a place with adequate ventilation
B. stowed in a hot, moist compartment
C. stowed on deck at all times
D. washed and stowed in any compartment

00906. A snag or other underwater obstruction may be detected in a current by a:

A. V-shaped ripple with the point of the V pointing upstream
B. V-shaped ripple with the point of the V pointing downstream
C. small patch of smooth water on a windy day
D. smoothing out of the vessel's wake

00910. The purpose of sheer in ship construction is to:

A. allow the ship to ride waves with drier decks
B. eliminate the need for butt straps
C. eliminate the need for margin plates
D. give greater strength at the deck edge

00914. When natural fiber rope gets wet, the:

A. overall strength of the line will decrease
B. line shrinks in length
C. line will become more elastic
D. line will be easier to handle

00916. A condition where two currents meet at the downstream end of a middle bar can be determined by a:

A. small whirlpool
B. smooth patch of water
C. V-shaped ripple with the point of the V pointing downstream
D. V-shaped ripple with the point of the V pointing upstream

00922. You are on watch at sea at night, and a fire breaks out in #3 hold. Which of the following would you NOT do immediately?

A. shut down the cargo hold ventilation
B. sound the fire alarm signal to rouse out all hands
C. call the Master
D. proceed to the space and inspect the extent of the fire

00924. Before stowing wet manila mooring lines, you should:

A. wash them with salt water and stow immediately
B. dry them out without washing
C. wash them with fresh water, dry and stow
D. stow immediately after use so air will not cause dry rot

00925. In illustration D044DG, the mooring line labeled "E" is called a(n):

A. bow line
B. after spring line

C. bow spring line
D. forward breast line

00926. Usually, the most gentle way of riding out a severe storm is:

A. head on at slow speeds
B. hove to
C. running before the wind
D. to rig a sea anchor

00932. A vessel's "quarter" is that section:

A. abeam
B. dead astern
C. just forward of the beam
D. on either side of the stern

00934. Which of the following methods is used to detect rot in manila lines?

A. opening the strands and examining the inner fibers
B. measuring the reduction in circumference of the line
C. observing for the appearance of mildew on the outer surface
D. feeling the surface of the line for broken fibers

00936. When there is plenty of sea room a vessel with a relatively small GM will ride easiest in a heavy gale with the:

A. vessel drifting, engines stopped
B. seas on the quarter, engines slow astern
C. ship's head to the wind and sea, engines slow ahead
D. wind 2 to 3 points on the bow, engines slow ahead

00937. On an ocean tow, you notice that another vessel is about to pass between the towing vessel and the tow. you should IMMEDIATELY:

A. turn away from the approaching vessel
B. shine a spotlight in the direction of the tow
C. sever the towline
D. slow down and pay out the main tow hawser

00941. Which of the following logbooks is required to be submitted to the Coast Guard?

A. Official Log
B. Smooth Log
C. Rough Log
D. Bell Log

00944. When caring for natural-fiber line, you should NEVER:

A. dry the line before stowing it
B. lubricate the line

C. protect the line from weather
D. slack off taut lines when it rains

00946. Which measure should NOT be taken to reduce the pounding of a vessel in a head sea?

A. add ballast in the after peak
B. add ballast forward
C. alter course
D. reduce speed

00950. The upward slope of a ship's bottom from the keel to the bilge is known as:

A. camber
B. slope
C. deadrise
D. keel height

00951. The responsibility for maintaining the Official Logbook on voyages between the Atlantic and Pacific coasts of the United States rests with the:

A. Chief Mate of the vessel
B. Master of the vessel
C. Deck Officer of the Watch at the time of the occurrence
D. Purser of the vessel

00954. In order to correctly open a new coil of manila line, you should:

A. pull the tagged end from the top of the coil
B. pull the tagged end through the eye of the coil
C. secure the outside end and unroll the coil
D. unreel the coil from a spool

00956. When a vessel is swinging from side to side off course due to quartering seas, the vessel is:

A. broaching
B. pitchpoling
C. rolling
D. yawing

00957. Your vessel has completed an inspection for certification and is issued a Temporary Certificate of Inspection. The Temporary Certificate:

A. has the full force of the regular Certificate of Inspection
B. expires 6 months after it is issued
C. must be exchanged for a regular Certificate of Inspection within 3 months
D. is retained in the custody of the Master

00960. Gross tonnage indicates the vessel's:

A. displacement in metric tons
B. total weight including cargo
C. volume in cubic feet
D. draft in feet

00961. Which logbook includes a statement of conduct, ability, and character of each crew member on the completion of a voyage?

A. Official Logbook
B. Department Logbook
C. Crew Logbook
D. Smooth Log

00964. To coil a left-hand laid rope, you should coil the line in:

A. a clockwise direction only
B. a counterclockwise direction only
C. an alternating clockwise and counterclockwise direction
D. either a clockwise or a counterclockwise direction

00966. When a boat turns broadside to heavy seas and winds, thus exposing the boat to the danger of capsizing, the boat has:

A. broached
B. pitchpoled
C. trimmed
D. yawed

00968. The Master, upon satisfactory proof of failure to comply with a law intended to promote marine safety:

A. shall be fined or imprisoned
B. shall be subject to termination
C. may have his license suspended or revoked
D. shall receive a reprimand from the U. S. Coast Guard

00970. What is the difference between net tonnage and gross tonnage?

A. net tonnage is the gross tonnage less certain deductions for machinery and other areas
B. net tonnage is tonnage of cargo compared to tonnage of whole ship
C. net tonnage is the net weight of the ship
D. there is no difference

00974. Right-laid line should be coiled:

A. clockwise
B. counterclockwise
C. either clockwise or counterclockwise
D. with the use of a reel

00976. When the period of beam seas equals the natural rolling period of a vessel, which of the following will MOST likely occur?

A. excessive pitching
B. excessive yawing
C. excessive rolling
D. no change should be evident

00977. An ocean tow is sinking in deep water. Attempts to sever the towing hawser are unsuccessful. what action should now be taken?

A. abandon the towing vessel
B. radio for emergency assistance
C. slip the towline and allow it to run off the drum
D. secure all watertight openings on the towing vessel

00978. When a person voluntarily surrenders his license to a U. S. Coast Guard investigating officer, he signs a statement indicating that:

A. all title to the license is given up for 5 years
B. his rights to a hearing are waived
C. he may be issued a new license in 5 years after passing another written examination
D. all of the above

00980. The perforated elevated bottom of the chain locker which prevents the chains from touching the main locker bottom, and allows seepage water to flow to the drains is called a:

A. cradle
B. draft
C. harping
D. manger

00982. The Station Bill must be posted in conspicuous locations and signed by the:

A. Safety Officer
B. Coast Guard Officer approving the bill
C. owner
D. Master

00984. To coil a right-laid rope, you should coil the line in:

A. a clockwise direction
B. a counterclockwise direction
C. alternating clockwise and counterclockwise directions
D. either a clockwise or counterclockwise direction

00986. When running before a heavy sea, moving weights aft will affect the handling of a vessel by:

A. reducing rolling
B. increasing rolling
C. reducing yawing
D. increasing yawing

00987. What does the helm command "shift the rudder" mean?

A. Stop the swing of the ship.
B. Shift the rudder control to the alternate steering method.
C. Put the rudder amidships and hold the heading steady as she goes.
D. Put the rudder over to the opposite side, the same number of degrees it is now.

00990. Freeboard is measured from the upper edge of the:

A. bulwark
B. deck line
C. gunwale bar
D. sheer strake

00991. When the azimuth of the Sun has been taken and the deviation of the standard compass computed, the watch officer should record the results:

A. in the vessel's Official Logbook
B. on the Compass Deviation Card
C. in the Compass Deviation Log
D. on a Napier diagram

00993. Your vessel is to dock bow in at a pier. Which line will be the most useful when maneuvering the vessel alongside the pier?

A. bow breast line
B. bow spring line
C. inshore head line
D. stern breast line

00994. Manila lines in which the strands are right-hand laid:

A. should be coiled in a clockwise direction
B. should be coiled counterclockwise
C. may be coiled either clockwise or counterclockwise
D. should never be coiled

00996. With a following sea, a vessel will tend to:

A. heave to
B. pound
C. reduce speed
D. yaw

00998. Which of the following offenses shall result in an administrative law judge revoking all licenses, certificates and documents held by a person?

A. sale of narcotic drugs
B. serious neglect of duty
C. serious theft of vessel's property
D. all of the above

01004. Failure to uncoil manila line properly could result in a(n):

A. excessive number of fishhooks
B. excessive number of kinks
C. 50% loss of efficiency of the line
D. increase in deterioration of the line

01005. What device is designed to automatically hold the load if power should fail to an electric winch?

A. pneumatic brake
B. electromagnetic brake
C. hand brake
D. motor controller

01006. Which of the following actions will reduce the yawing of a vessel in a following sea?

A. increasing speed
B. pumping out tanks aft
C. shifting weights to the bow
D. shifting weights to the stern

01007. When using the term "limber system" one is referring to a:

A. cleaning system
B. drainage system
C. strengthening system
D. weight reduction system

01008. When a person voluntarily deposits his license or document with a Coast Guard investigating officer:

A. he permanently gives up his rights to the license or document
B. it may be for reasons of mental or physical incompetence
C. it must be for reason of addiction to narcotics
D. all of the above

01010. When the longitudinal strength members of a vessel are continuous and closely spaced, the vessel is:

A. transversely framed
B. longitudinally framed
C. intermittently framed
D. web framed

01011. After your vessel has been involved in a casualty, you are required to make your logbooks, bell books, etc., available to:

A. attorneys for opposition parties
B. marine surveyors
C. U. S. Coast Guard officials
D. all of the above

01012. In illustration D044DG, the mooring line labeled "A" is called a(n):

A. after breast line
B. after spring line
C. offshore stern line
D. onshore stern line

01014. In order to detect rot in manila lines, you should:

A. feel the surface of the line for broken fibers
B. measure the reduction in circumference of the line
C. observe any mildew on the outer surface
D. open the strands and exam the inner fibers

01016. Your vessel is off a lee shore in heavy weather and laboring. Which one of the following actions should you take?

A. put the sea and wind about 2 points on either bow and reduce speed
B. heave to in the trough of the sea
C. put the sea and wind on either quarter and proceed at increased speed
D. put the bow directly into the sea and proceed at full speed

01018. What agency of the U. S. Government can initiate a suspension or revocation action against a licensed merchant mariner for violation of any load line acts?

A. American Bureau of Shipping
B. U. S. Coast Guard
C. U. S. Customs Department
D. U. S. Maritime Administration

01020. The Plimsoll mark on a vessel is used to:

A. align the vessel's tailshaft
B. determine the vessel's trim
C. determine the vessel's freeboard
D. locate the vessel's centerline

01024. A fiber rope can be ruined by dampness because of:

A. rotting
B. shrinking
C. stretching
D. unlaying

01026. When making way in heavy seas, you notice that your vessel's screw is being lifted clear of the water and racing. One way to correct this would be to:

A. increase speed
B. decrease speed
C. move more weight forward
D. shift the rudder back and forth several times

01028. By law, a user of marijuana may be subject to:

A. loss of pay during the period of such use
B. reprimand by the Coast Guard
C. revocation of license or certificate
D. termination of employment

01030. If an attempt is made to hoist a load that exceeds the capacity of an electric winch, an overload safety device causes a circuit breaker to cut off the current to the winch motor:

A. when the line pull reaches the rated winch capacity
B. after the line pull exceeds the rated winch capacity
C. after a short build-up of torque
D. immediately

01031. Which certificate is NOT issued by the Coast Guard?

A. Award of Official Number
B. Certificate of Inspection
C. Classification of Hull and Machinery
D. Safety Equipment Certificate

01032. A flanged plate fitted over an air port on the ship's outside shell to prevent water from entering the port is a:

A. brow
B. copper plate
C. cover plate
D. shade

01033. Each person has a designated area to proceed to in the event of a fire. This assignment is shown clearly on the:

A. fire fighting plan
B. shipping articles
C. certificate of Inspection
D. station bill

01034. You are the licensed operator of a 100 GT towing vessel sailing coastwise. What percentage of the deck crew must be able to understand the language commonly used onboard the vessel?

A. 100%
B. 75%
C. 65%
D. 50%

01036. What is meant by "broaching to"?

A. having the vessel head toward the sea
B. running before a sea
C. being turned broadside to the sea
D. having the vessel filled with water

01041. The document on a vessel, annually endorsed by an American Bureau of Shipping surveyor, is called the:

A. Certificate of Inspection
B. Classification Certificate
C. Load Line certificate
D. Seaworthy Certificate

01044. Using a safety factor of 6, determine the safe working load of a line with a breaking strain of 30,000 pounds.

A. 4,000 lb.
B. 5,000 lb.
C. 20,000 lb.
D. 100,000 lb.

01045. If a hydraulic pump on a winch accidentally stops while hoisting, the load will stay suspended because:

A. a check valve will close that prevents reverse circulation
B. a friction brake will automatically engage
C. the electric pump motor will cut out
D. the control lever will move to the stop position

01046. In a following sea, a wave has overtaken your vessel and thrown the stern to starboard. To continue along your original course, you should:

A. use more right rudder
B. use more left rudder
C. increase speed
D. decrease speed

01048. It is the duty of the owner, agent, Master, or person in charge of a vessel involved in a marine casualty to give notice as soon as possible to the nearest marine inspection office of the U. S. Coast Guard if the property damage is in excess of:

A. $1,500
B. $10,000
C. $25,000
D. $50,000

01050. The "margin plate" is the:

A. outboard strake of plating on each side of an inner bottom
B. outer strake of plating on each side of the main deck of a vessel
C. plate which sits atop the center vertical keel
D. uppermost continuous strake of plating on the shell of a vessel

01054. Which mooring line has the least elasticity?

A. Dacron
B. nylon
C. esterlene
D. polypropylene

01056. In which of the following situations could a vessel MOST easily capsize?

A. running into head seas
B. running in the trough
C. running with following seas
D. anchored with your bow into the seas

01058. Who shall, as soon as possible, notify the nearest U. S. Coast Guard Marine Safety or Marine Inspection Office when a vessel has been damaged in excess of $25,000?

A. the owner of the vessel
B. the Master of the vessel
C. the person in charge of the vessel at the time of casualty
D. any of the above

01064. Which factor is MOST likely to impair the strength and durability of synthetic line?

A. dry rot
B. mildew
C. sunlight
D. washing with mild soap

01066. If you notice that you're racing your propeller in rough weather, you should:

A. decrease your engine speed
B. ignore it
C. increase your engine speed
D. stop your engine, until the rough weather passes

01068. You shall notify the nearest U. S. Coast Guard Marine Inspection Office as soon as possible when your vessel has been damaged in excess of:

A. $1,000
B. $1,500
C. $10,000
D. $25,000

01074. A new coil of nylon line should be opened by:

A. pulling the end up through the eye of the coil
B. taking a strain on both ends
C. uncoiling from the outside with the coil standing on end
D. unreeling from a spool

01076. You are proceeding in heavy weather and you have your bow meeting the seas. To prevent pounding, you should:

A. change course, in order to take the seas at an 85° angle from the bow
B. decrease speed
C. increase speed
D. secure all loose gear

01078. The penalty for failing to give aid without reasonable cause in the case of collision is:

A. 1 year imprisonment or $500
B. 2 years imprisonment or $1000
C. 2 years imprisonment or $1500
D. 2 years imprisonment or $2000

01080. The "inner bottom" is the:

A. tank top
B. compartment between the tank top and shell of the vessel
C. inner side of the vessel's shell
D. space between two transverse bottom frames

01084. A normal safe working load for nylon rope is:

A. 20% of its breaking strain
B. 40% of its breaking strain
C. 50% of its breaking strain
D. 66% of its breaking strain

01087. The turning circle of a vessel is the path followed by the:

A. center of gravity
B. outermost part of the ship while making the circle
C. bow
D. tipping center

01088. You shall notify the nearest U. S. Coast Guard Marine Inspection Office as soon as possible when one of your crew members remains incapacitated from an injury for over:

A. 24 hours
B. 48 hours
C. 60 hours
D. 72 hours

01090. The function of a chock on a vessel with solid bulwarks is to:

A. allow water shipped on deck to flow off rapidly
B. permit easy jettison of deck cargo in an emergency
C. prevent stress concentration in the bulwark
D. provide openings through the bulwarks for mooring lines

01092. When a helmsman receives the command "Right 15 degrees rudder", the helmsman's immediate reply should be:

A. "Rudder is right 15 degrees"
B. "Aye Aye Sir"
C. "Right 15 degrees rudder"
D. No reply is necessary, just carry out the order.

01094. Which statement is TRUE with respect to the elasticity of nylon mooring lines?

A. Nylon can stretch over 40% without being in danger of parting.
B. Nylon can be elongated by 100% before it will part.
C. Nylon will part if it is stretched any more than 20%.
D. Under load, nylon will stretch and thin out but will return to normal size when free of tension.

01098. During the course of a voyage, a seaman falls on the main deck and injures his ankle. The Master should submit a Report of Marine Accident, Injury or Death if the:

A. injured is incapacitated more than 72 hours
B. injured is incapacitated more than 24 hours
C. injury results in loss of life only
D. injury is the result of misconduct

01100. What is the purpose of the freeing ports on a vessel with solid bulwarks?

A. allow water which may be shipped on deck to flow off rapidly
B. permit easy jettisoning of deck cargo in an emergency
C. prevent the formation of any unusual stress concentration points
D. lighten the above deck weight caused by a solid bulwark

01102. In illustration D044DG, the mooring line labeled "B" is called a(n):

A. after breast line
B. after spring line
C. inshore stern line
D. offshore stern line

01104. The quality that makes nylon line dangerous is that it:

A. breaks down when wet
B. kinks when wet
C. is not elastic
D. stretches

01108. In which casualty case would it be UNNECESSARY to notify the local Coast Guard Marine Safety Office?

A. a seaman is injured and in the hospital 4 days.
B. nylon mooring line parts while the vessel is tied up and kills a harbor worker who was on the pier.

C. your vessel is backing from a dock and runs aground, but is pulled off by tugs in 30 minutes.
D. your vessel strikes a pier and does $1,500 damage to the pier but none to the vessel.

01110. One function of a bulwark is to:

A. help keep the deck dry
B. prevent stress concentrations on the stringer plate
C. protect against twisting forces exerted on the frame of the vessel
D. reinforce the side stringers

01112. What is an advantage of the 6x37 class of wire rope over the 6x19 class of wire rope of the same diameter?

A. greater flexibility
B. more resistance to corrosion
C. more resistance to elongation
D. lower weight per foot

01114. What type of stopper would you use on a nylon mooring line?

A. chain
B. nylon
C. manila
D. wire

01115. The proper way to correct a mistake in the Logbook is to:

A. draw several lines through the entry, rewrite, and initial the correction
B. draw a line through the entry, rewrite, and initial the correction
C. completely black out the entry, rewrite, and initial the correction
D. erase the entry and rewrite

01116. On a single-screw vessel, when coming port side to a pier and being set off the pier, you should:

A. swing wide and approach the pier so as to land starboard side to
B. approach the pier on a parallel course at reduced speed
C. make your approach at a greater angle than in calm weather
D. point the vessel's head well up into the pier and decrease your speed

01118. Which of the following would require you to furnish a notice of marine casualty to the Coast Guard?

A. You collide with a buoy and drag it off station with no apparent damage to the vessel or the buoy.

B. A seaman slips on deck and is bedridden for 2 days before returning to duty.
C. Your vessel is at anchor and grounds at low tide with no apparent damage.
D. Storm damage to the cargo winch motors requiring repairs costing $19,000.

01122. The function of the freeing ports on a vessel with solid bulwarks is to:

A. prevent stress concentration in the bulwark
B. permit easy jettison of deck cargo in an emergency
C. provide openings through the bulwarks for mooring lines
D. allow water shipped on deck to flow off rapidly

01124. Which material makes the strongest mooring line?

A. Dacron
B. manila
C. nylon
D. polyethylene

01125. The pivoting point of a vessel going ahead is :

A. about 1/3 of the vessel's length from the bow
B. about 2/3 of the vessel's length from the bow
C. at the hawsepipe
D. near the stern

01126. You are approaching a pier and intend to use an anchor to assist in docking port side to. You would NOT use the port anchor if:

A. a tug is made up to the starboard bow
B. another vessel is berthed ahead of your position
C. the wind was blowing from the starboard side
D. there is shallow water en route to the berth

01130. The fittings used to secure a water-tight door are known as:

A. clamps
B. clasps
C. dogs
D. latches

01132. A lookout can leave his station:

A. at the end of the watch
B. at any time
C. ONLY when properly relieved
D. 15 minutes before the end of the watch

01134. The critical point in nylon line elongation is considered to be:

A. 20%
B. 30%
C. 40%
D. 50%

01136. Your vessel is to dock bow in at a pier without the assistance of tugboats. Which line will be the most useful when maneuvering the vessel alongside the pier?

A. bow breast line
B. bow spring line
C. inshore head line
D. stern breast line

01139. The pivoting point of a vessel going ahead is:

A. near the stern
B. at the hawsepipe
C. about 1/3 of the vessel's length from the bow
D. about 2/3 of the vessel's length from the bow

01140. In a transversely framed ship, the transverse frames are supported by all of the following EXCEPT:

A. girders
B. longitudinals
C. side stringers
D. web plates

01144. Which rope has the greatest breaking strength?

A. manila
B. nylon
C. polyester
D. polypropylene

01146. While your vessel is docked port side to a wharf, a sudden gale force wind causes the vessel's bow lines to part. The bow begins to fall away from the dock, and no tugs are immediately available. Which measures should you take FIRST?

A. Call the Master and the deck gang.
B. Slip the stern lines, let the vessel drift into the river, and then anchor.
C. Let go the starboard anchor.
D. Obtain assistance and attempt to put some new bow lines out.

01150. In ship construction, frame spacing is:

A. greater at the bow and stern
B. reduced at the bow and stern
C. uniform over the length of the vessel
D. uniform over the length of the vessel, with the exception of the machinery spaces, where it is reduced due to increased stresses

01154. Which of the following lines would be least likely to kink?

A. braided
B. left-handed laid
C. right-handed laid
D. straight laid

01156. The BEST time to work a boat into a slip would be:

A. when the wind is against you
B. with the current setting against you
C. at slack water
D. with a cross current

01160. In a longitudinally-framed ship, the longitudinal frames are held in place and supported by athwartship members called:

A. floors
B. margin plates
C. stringers
D. web frames

01164. Which of the following types of line has the GREATEST floatability characteristics?

A. Dacron
B. nylon
C. old manila
D. polypropylene

01165. The station bill shows each hand's lifeboat station, duties during abandonment, basic instructions and:

A. all emergency signals
B. instructions for lowering the lifeboats
C. the time each weekly drill will be held
D. work schedule

01166. You are 15' off a pier and docking a vessel using only a bow and stern line. Once the slack is out of both lines, you begin to haul in on the bow line. What is the effect on the vessel?

A. the bow will come in and the stern will go out.
B. the bow will come in and the stern will remain the same distance off the pier.
C. the bow and stern will both come in.
D. the stern will come in and the bow will remain the same distance off the pier.

01170. Transverse frames are more widely spaced on a ship that is designed with the:

A. centerline system of framing
B. isometric system of framing
C. longitudinal system of framing
D. transverse system of framing

01174. Compared to manila line, size for size, nylon line:

A. has less strength than manila line
B. has more strength than manila line
C. is equivalent to manila line
D. will rot quicker than manila line

01176. Your vessel is lying next to a pier with a spring line led aft from the bow. With no other forces acting on the vessel, putting the engines ahead should bring:

A. the bow in and the stern out
B. both the bow and stern in
C. the bow out and the stern in
D. both the bow and stern out

01184. A new coil of nylon line should be opened by:

A. pulling the end up through the eye of the coil
B. uncoiling from the outside with the coil standing on end
C. taking a strain on both ends
D. unreeling from a spool

01185. In illustration D044DG, the mooring line labeled "C" is called a:

A. stern line
B. spring line
C. breast line
D. shore line

01192. A person has fallen overboard and is being picked up with a lifeboat. If the person appears in danger of drowning, the lifeboat should be maneuvered to make:

A. an approach from leeward
B. an approach from windward
C. the most direct approach
D. an approach from across the wind

01193. The main advantage of a Chinese stopper over the one line stopper is that it:

A. will not jam on the mooring line
B. is stronger
C. is easier to use when under heavy tension
D. is safer to use when under heavy tension

01194. What type of line is LEAST heat resistant?

A. wire
B. Dacron
C. nylon
D. polypropylene

01196. You are landing a single-screw vessel, with a right-hand propeller, starboard side to the dock. When you have approached the

desired position and backed the engine, you would expect the vessel to:

A. lose headway without swinging
B. turn her bow toward the dock
C. turn her bow away from the dock
D. head into the wind, regardless of the side the wind is on

01204. An advantage of nylon rope over manila rope is that nylon rope:

A. can hold a load even when a considerable number of the yarns have been abraded
B. can be stored on decks exposed to sunlight
C. can be used in conjunction with wire or spring-lay rope
D. gives audible warning of overstress whereas manila does not

01206. You are landing a single-screw, left-handed propeller vessel, starboard side to the dock. When you have approached your desired position off the dock, you back your engines with your rudder amidships. You would expect the vessel to:

A. lose headway without swinging
B. turn its bow towards the dock
C. turn its stern towards the dock
D. drift away from the dock

01210. To rigidly fasten together the peak frames, the stem, and the outside framing, a horizontal plate is fitted across the forepeak of a vessel. This plate is known as a(n):

A. apron plate
B. breast hook
C. intercostal plate
D. joiner

01214. Which of the following statements is TRUE concerning nylon line?

A. manila line will usually last longer than nylon line.
B. nylon line is excellent for use in alongside towing.
C. a normal safe working load (SWL) will stretch nylon 50%.
D. nylon stoppers should be used with nylon line.

01216. It is easier to dock a right-hand, single-screw vessel:

A. starboard side to the wharf
B. either side to the wharf
C. port side to the wharf
D. stern to the wharf

01217. The proper way to correct a mistake in the Logbook is to:

A. erase the entry and rewrite
B. draw a line through the entry, rewrite, and initial the correction
C. draw several lines through the entry, rewrite, and initial the correction
D. completely black out the entry, rewrite, and initial the correction

01224. Which of the following is NOT a recommended practice when handling nylon line?

A. nylon lines which become slippery because of oil or grease should be scrubbed down.
B. manila line stoppers should be used for holding nylon hawsers.
C. when easing out nylon line, keep an extra turn on the bitt to prevent slipping.
D. iced-over nylon lines should be thawed and drained before stowing.

01226. You are docking a vessel starboard side to with the assistance of two tugs. You are attempting to hold the vessel off by operating both tugs at right angles to the vessel and at full power. You must ensure that:

A. steerageway is not taken off
B. the bow doesn't close the dock first
C. the bow closes the dock first
D. the ship has no headway at the time

01230. Which statement concerning solid floors is TRUE?

A. They must be watertight.
B. They may have lightening, limber, or air holes cut into them.
C. They are built of structural frames connected by angle struts and stiffeners, with flanged plate brackets at each end.
D. They are lighter than open floors.

01234. Which of the following types of line will stretch the MOST when under strain?

A. polypropylene
B. Dacron
C. nylon
D. manila

01240. Bilge keels are fitted on ships to:

A. assist in drydock alignment
B. improve the vessel's stability
C. protect the vessel from slamming against piers
D. reduce the rolling of the vessel

01244. Nylon line is NOT suitable for:

A. towing
B. lashings
C. boat falls
D. mooring lines

01250. The floors in a vessel's hull structure are kept from tripping, or folding over, by:

A. face plates
B. bottom longitudinals
C. longitudinal deck beams
D. transverse deck beams

01252. Control of flooding should be addressed:

A. first
B. following control of fire
C. following restoration of vital services
D. only if a threat exists

01254. Under identical load conditions, nylon, when compared with natural fiber line, will stretch:

A. less and have less strength
B. more and have less strength
C. more and have greater strength
D. less and have greater strength

01260. The function of the bilge keel is to:

A. reduce the rolling of the vessel
B. serve as the vessel's main strength member
C. add strength to the bilge
D. protect the vessel's hull when alongside a dock

01264. Which of the following types of line would BEST be able to withstand sudden shock loads?

A. polypropylene
B. nylon
C. Dacron
D. manila

01270. The floors in a vessel's hull structure are kept from tripping, or rolling over, by:

A. transverse deck beams
B. bottom longitudinals
C. longitudinal deck beams
D. face plates

01272. With a man overboard, the maneuver which will return your vessel to the man in the shortest time is:

A. a Williamson Turn
B. engine(s) crash astern, no turn
C. two 180° turns
D. a single turn with hard rudder

01274. If given equal care, nylon line should last how many times longer than manila line?

A. 3
B. 4
C. 5
D. 6

01275. The tension on an anchor cable increases so that the angle of the catenary to the seabed at the anchor reaches 10. How will this affect the anchor in sandy soil?

A. It will have no effect.
B. It will increase the holding power.
C. It will reduce the holding power.
D. It will cause the anchor to snag.

01276. When moored with a Mediterranean moor, the ship should be secured to the pier by having:

A. a stern line and 2 quarter lines crossing under the stern
B. a stern line, 2 bow lines, and 2 quarter lines leading aft to the pier
C. all regular lines leading to the pier in opposition to the anchor
D. 2 bow lines and 2 midships lines leading aft to the pier

01280. Vertical structural members attached to the floors that add strength to the floors are called:

A. boss plates
B. buckler plates
C. stiffeners
D. breast hooks

01282. When evacuating a seaman by helicopter lift, the vessel should be:

A. stopped with the wind dead ahead
B. stopped with the wind on the beam
C. underway with the wind 30° on the bow
D. underway on a course to provide no apparent wind

01284. Using a safety factor of 5, determine the safe working load of a line with a breaking strain of 20,000 pounds.

A. 4,000 lb.
B. 5,000 lb.
C. 20,000 lb.
D. 100,000 lb.

01285. What information must be entered on the station bill?

A. names of all crew members
B. use and application of special equipment

C. listing of approved emergency equipment
D. duties and station of each person during emergencies

01286. The anchors should be dropped well out from the pier while at a Mediterranean moor to:

A. eliminate navigational hazards by allowing the chain to lie along the harbor bottom
B. increase the anchor's reliability by providing a large catenary in the chain
C. permit the ship to maneuver in the stream while weighing anchors
D. prevent damage to the stern caused by swinging against the pier in the approach

01287. The term "shift the rudder" means:

A. change from right (left) to left (right) rudder an equal amount
B. use right or left rudder
C. check, but do not stop the vessel from swinging
D. put the rudder amidships

01290. Which is NOT an advantage of double bottoms?

A. The tank top forms a second skin for the vessel.
B. The center of gravity of a loaded bulk cargo ship may be raised to produce a more comfortable roll.
C. The floors and longitudinals distribute the upward push of the water on the ship's bottom.
D. They are less expensive to construct because of increased access space.

01294. A nylon line is rated at 15,000 lb. breaking strain. Using a safety factor of 5, what is the safe working load (SWL)?

A. 3000 lb.
B. 5000 lb.
C. 15000 lb.
D. 65000 lb.

01296. To ensure the best results during the Mediterranean moor, the chains should:

A. be crossed around the bow
B. tend out at right angles to the bow
C. tend aft 60° from each bow
D. tend forward 30° on either bow

01302. Reinforcing frames attached to a bulkhead on a vessel are called:

A. side longitudinals
B. intercostals
C. stiffeners
D. brackets

01304. A nylon line is rated at 12,000 lb. breaking strain. Using a safety factor of 5, what is the safe working load (SWL)?

A. 2,000 lb.
B. 2,400 lb.
C. 12,000 lb.
D. 60,000 lb.

01305. What is an advantage of the 6x19 class of wire rope over the 6x37 class of wire rope of the same diameter?

A. greater holding power
B. better fatigue life
C. more resistance to elongation
D. more resistance to corrosion

01306. In making fast stern to, as in some Mediterranean ports where a swell is liable to make in resulting in a surge, how would you tie up?

A. Use manila or fiber hawsers only.
B. Use wires only from stern and each quarter.
C. Use wires and manila hawsers as required.
D. Use wires from each quarter and manila hawsers from stern.

01312. In illustration D044DG, the mooring line labeled "D" is called a(n):

A. stern line
B. forward spring line
C. after spring line
D. waist breast line

01314. A wire rope rove through 2 single blocks with 2 parts at the moving block is used for a boat fall. The weight of the 100-person boat is 5 tons. Compute the required breaking strain. Safety Factor - 6, weight per person - 165 lb., 10% friction per sheave (2 sheaves).

A. 18.30 tons B. S.
B. 20.29 tons B. S.
C. 22.27 tons B. S.
D. 24.31 tons B. S.

01316. The anchor chain should be kept moderately taut during a Mediterranean moor to:

A. facilitate speed of recovery during the weighing process
B. indicate the anchor's location to passing or mooring ships
C. prevent damage to the stern in the event of a head wind
D. provide a steady platform for the gangway between the fantail and pier

01320. A cofferdam is:

A. any deck below the main deck and above the lowest deck
B. a member that gives fore-and-aft strength
C. made by placing 2 bulkheads a few feet apart
D. a heavy fore-and-aft beam under the deck

01323. "Ease the rudder" means to:

A. decrease the rudder angle
B. move the rudder slowly in the direction of the most recent rudder command
C. bring the rudder amidships
D. steer the course which is your present heading

01326. After casting off moorings at a mooring buoy in calm weather, you should:

A. go full ahead on the engine(s)
B. back away a few lengths to clear the buoy and then go ahead on the engines
C. go half ahead on the engines and put the rudder hard right
D. go half ahead on the engines and pass to windward of the buoy

01329. A pelican hook:

A. can be released while under strain
B. is used for boat falls
C. is used for extra heavy loads
D. is used for light loads only

01330. Beams are cambered to:

A. increase their strength
B. provide drainage from the decks
C. relieve deck stress
D. all of the above

01336. When picking up your mooring at the buoy, the correct method is to:

A. approach the buoy with the wind and current astern
B. approach the buoy with the wind and current ahead
C. approach the buoy with wind and sea abeam
D. stop upwind and up current and drift down on the buoy

01339. Backstays are:

A. running rigging leading aft from the masts
B. running rigging leading forward from the masts
C. standing rigging leading aft from the masts
D. standing rigging from the cross trees to the mast head

01340. The usual depth of a beam bracket is:

A. 2-1/2 times the depth of the beam
B. 5 times the depth of the beam
C. 10 times the depth of the beam
D. same depth as the beam

01344. When working with wire rope, which must be considered?

A. Metal sheaves should be lined with wood or leather.
B. It needs better care than hemp or manila.
C. It should be lubricated annually.
D. The diameter of a sheave over which a rope is worked should be 10 times that of the rope.

01346. The best method of determining if a vessel is dragging anchor is to note:

A. the amount of line paid out
B. how much the vessel sheers while at anchor
C. a change in the tautness of the anchor chain
D. changes in bearings of fixed objects onshore

01349. A shroud is:

A. any wire running fore-and-aft on a ship
B. any wire with a fiber core
C. a heavy wire extending from the trunk of the mast to the head of the boom
D. a heavy wire extending from the mast, athwartships to the deck, to support the mast

01350. A deck beam does NOT:

A. act as a beam to support vertical deck loads
B. lessen the longitudinal stiffness of the vessel
C. tie the sides of the ship in place
D. act as a web to prevent plate wrinkling due to twisting action on the vessel

01354. A 6x19 wire rope would be:

A. 6 inches in diameter and 19 fathoms long
B. 6 inches in circumference with 19 strands
C. 6 strands with 19 wires in each strand
D. 19 strands with 6 wires in each strand

01356. If your vessel is dragging her anchor in a strong wind, you should:

A. shorten the scope of anchor cable
B. increase the scope of anchor cable
C. put over the sea anchor
D. put over a stern anchor

01358. Seeing that all hands are familiar with their duties, as specified in the Station Bill, is the responsibility of the:

A. Master
B. Chief Mate
C. Safety Officer
D. department heads

01359. The term "standing rigging" refers to:

A. booms and king posts
B. guys and vangs
C. stays and shrouds
D. topping lifts and cargo runners

01364. Which molten substance is poured into the basket of a wire rope socket being fitted to the end of a wire rope?

A. babbitt
B. bronze
C. lead
D. zinc

01365. A person who sees someone fall overboard should:

A. call for help and keep the individual in sight
B. run to the radio room to send an emergency message
C. immediately jump in the water to assist the individual
D. go to the bridge for the distress flares

01366. The best method to stop a vessel which is dragging anchor in a sand bottom is to:

A. reduce the length of the cable
B. pay out more cable
C. back the engines
D. swing the rudder several times to work the anchor into the bottom

01368. Fire and abandon ship stations and duties may be found on the:

A. Crewman's Duty List
B. Certificate of Inspection
C. Shipping Articles
D. Station Bill

01370. The strength of a deck will be increased by adding:

A. camber
B. deck beam brackets
C. hatch beams
D. sheer

01374. Which type of stopper should be used to stop off wire rope?

A. chain
B. manila
C. polypropylene
D. wire

01375. A chain stripper is used to:

A. prevent chain from clinging to the wildcat
B. clean the marine debris from the chain

C. flake chain from a boat's chain locker
D. clean chain prior to an X-ray inspection

01376. Generally speaking, the most favorable bottom for anchoring is:

A. very soft mud
B. rocky
C. a mixture of mud and clay
D. loose sand

01380. The deck beam brackets of a transversely framed vessel resist:

A. hogging stresses
B. sagging stresses
C. racking stresses
D. shearing stresses

01384. The wire rope used for cargo handling on board your vessel has a safe working load of 8 tons. It shall be able to withstand a breaking test load of:

A. 32 tons
B. 40 tons
C. 48 tons
D. 64 tons

01386. The holding capabilities of an anchor are determined by the:

A. anchor's abilities to bury itself in the bottom
B. anchor's weight only
C. scope of the anchor line only
D. size of the vessel

01392. In illustration D044DG, the mooring line labeled "H" is called a(n):

A. forward breast line
B. offshore spring line
C. offshore bow line
D. onshore bow line

01394. Galvanizing would be suitable for protecting wire rope which is used for:

A. cargo runners
B. stays
C. topping lifts
D. any of the above

01396. Lifting the anchor from the bottom is called:

A. broaching the anchor
B. shifting the anchor
C. walking the anchor
D. weighing the anchor

01406. How many fathoms are in a shot of anchor cable?

A. 6
B. 15
C. 20
D. 30

01410. The result of two forces acting in opposite directions and along parallel lines, is an example of what type of stress?

A. tensile
B. compression
C. shear
D. strain

01414. A wire rope that has been over-strained will show:

A. a bulge in the wire where the strain occurred
B. a decrease in diameter where the strain occurred
C. a kink in the wire where the strain occurred
D. no visible effects of an overstrain

01416. What is meant by veering the anchor chain?

A. bringing the anchor to short stay
B. heaving in all the chain
C. locking the windlass to prevent more chain from running out
D. paying out more chain

01420. Tensile stress is a result of two forces acting in:

A. opposite directions on the same line, tending to pull the material apart
B. opposite directions on the same line, tending to compress the object
C. opposite directions along parallel lines
D. the same direction along parallel lines

01426. Forty-five fathoms is marked on the anchor chain by:

A. one turn of wire on the first stud from each side of the detachable link
B. two turns of wire on the second stud from each side of the detachable link
C. 3 turns of wire on the third stud from each side of the detachable link
D. 4 turns of wire on the fourth stud from each side of the detachable link

01427. Which letter in illustration DO30DG represents a plain whipping?

A. e
B. f
C. j
D. v

01430. A vessel's bottom will be subjected to tension when weight is concentrated:

A. amidships
B. aft
C. at both ends of the vessel
D. forward

01434. In the manufacture of wire rope, if the wires are shaped to conform to the curvature of the finished rope before they are laid up, the rope is called:

A. composite
B. left-lay
C. improved
D. preformed

01435. Which letter in illustration DO30DG represents a clove hitch?

A. x
B. u
C. t
D. r

01436. How many feet are there in 2 shots of anchor chain?

A. 50
B. 60
C. 180
D. 360

01440. If a vessel is loaded in such a manner that she is said to be sagging, what kind of stress is placed on the sheer strake?

A. compression
B. racking
C. tension
D. thrust

01443. The Safety of Life at Sea Convention was developed by the:

A. U. S. Coast Guard
B. American Bureau of Shipping
C. International Maritime Organization
D. American Institute of Maritime Shipping

01444. If kinking results while wire rope is being coiled clockwise, you should:

A. coil it counterclockwise
B. not coil it
C. take a turn under
D. twist out the kinks under a strain

01446. The marking on an anchor chain for 30 fathoms is:

A. 2 links on each side of the 30 fathom detachable link are painted white
B. 1 link on each side of the 30 fathom detachable link is painted white
C. 3 links on each side of the 30 fathom detachable link are painted white
D. only the detachable link is painted red

01448. Nylon line is better than manila for:

A. towing alongside
B. towing astern
C. holding knots and splices
D. resisting damage from chemicals

01450. When a vessel is stationary and in a hogging condition, the main deck is under:

A. compression stresses
B. racking stress
C. shear stress
D. tension stress

01455. Which letter in illustration DO30DG represents a bowline on a bight?

A. h
B. i
C. m
D. w

01456. How many turns of wire normally mark either side of the shackle 45 fathoms from the anchor?

A. 1
B. 2
C. 3
D. 4

01458. The catenary in a towline is:

A. a short bridle
B. the downward curvature of the hawser
C. another name for a pelican hook
D. used to hold it amidships

01460. Weight concentration in which of the following areas will cause a vessel's bottom to be subjected to tension stresses?

A. aft
B. amidships
C. at both ends
D. forward

01462. Two mooring lines may be placed on the same bollard and be cast off if:

A. the eye of the second line is dipped
B. the mooring lines are doubled
C. the bollard has 2 horns
D. one of the lines is a breast line

01463. On a small boat, which of the following knots is BEST suited for attaching a line to the ring of an anchor?

A. clove hitch
B. figure-8 knot
C. fisherman's bend
D. overhand knot

01464. When talking about wire rope, the lay of the wire is the:

A. direction wires and strands are twisted together
B. number of strands in the wire
C. direction the core is twisted
D. material used in the core

01468. Which of the following will NOT reduce yawing of a tow?

A. increasing the length of the towing hawser
B. trimming the tow by the stern
C. stowing deck loads so the sail area is aft
D. drogues put over the stern

01470. Signs of racking stresses generally appear at the:

A. bow and stern shell frames and plating
B. junction of the frames with the beams and floors
C. garboard strake, at each side of the keel
D. thrust bearing of the main shaft

01472. Which of the pictures in illustration DO30DG represents a single becket bend?

A. e
B. f
C. g
D. h

01473. The "carrick bend" is used to:

A. add strength to a weak spot in a line
B. join 2 hawsers
C. be a stopper to transfer a line under strain
D. join lines of different sizes

01474. To find the distance the strands should be unlaid for an eye splice, multiply the diameter of the wire in inches by:

A. 12
B. 24
C. 36
D. 48

01475. In illustration D044DG, the mooring line labeled "G" is called a(n):

A. forward spring line
B. offshore bow line
C. forward breast line
D. inshore bow line

01476. How is the size of chain determined?

A. length of link in inches
B. diameter of metal in link in inches
C. links per fathom
D. weight of stud cable in pounds

01478. What does "in step" refer to in regards to towing?

A. the towed vessel follows exactly in the wake of the towing vessel.
B. there is no catenary in the towing hawser.
C. when turning, both the towed and towing vessels turn at the same time.
D. both the towed and towing vessels reach a wave crest or trough at the same time.

01480. When a vessel is stationary and in a hogging condition, the main deck is under:

A. compression stress
B. tension stress
C. shear stress
D. racking stress

01483. The knot used to join 2 lines or 2 large hawsers for towing is called a:

A. square knot
B. carrick bend
C. sheet bend
D. bowline

01484. A metal eye spliced into a wire is called a:

A. cyclops
B. fish eye
C. thimble
D. chip

01486. Which is NOT a part of an anchor?

A. bill
B. devil's claw
C. palm
D. crown

01487. You are approaching a wrecked vessel in order to remove survivors from it. If your vessel drifts faster than the wrecked vessel, how should you make your approach?

A. to windward of the wrecked vessel
B. to leeward of the wrecked vessel
C. directly astern of the wrecked vessel
D. at 3 times the drifting speed of the wrecked vessel

01488. What does the term "end-for-end" refer to in regards to a wire towing hawser?

A. cutting off the bitter and towing ends of the wire rope
B. splicing 2 wire ropes together
C. removing the wire rope from the drum and reversing it so that the towing end becomes the bitter end
D. removing the wire rope from the drum and turning it over so that the wire bends in the opposite direction when rolled on a drum

01490. If a vessel is loaded in such a manner that she is said to be sagging, what kind of stress is placed on the sheer strake?

A. compression
B. tension
C. thrust
D. racking

01492. Which of the pictures in illustration DO30DG represents a fisherman's bend?

A. f
B. g
C. k
D. l

01493. The knot used to join 2 lines of different diameter is a:

A. square knot
B. carrick bend
C. becket bend
D. sheepshank

01494. After splicing an eye in a piece of wire rope, the splice should be parceled and served to:

A. strengthen the line
B. increase its efficiency
C. prevent hand injury covering loose ends
D. make the line more flexible

01495. A common class of wire rope is the 6x37 class. What does the 37 represent?

A. number of wires in the inner core
B. number of strands per wire rope
C. tensile strength of the wire
D. number of wires per strand

01496. The purpose of the devil's claw is to:

A. act as a chain stopper
B. prevent the windlass from engaging
C. prevent the chain from fouling on deck
D. control the wildcat

01497. Which of the pictures in illustration DO30DG represents a round turn and 2 half hitches?

A. e
B. f
C. q
D. s

01498. The biggest problem you generally encounter while towing a single tow astern is:

A. the catenary dragging on the bottom
B. swamping of the tow
C. the tow tending to dive
D. yaw

01499. In illustration D044DG, the mooring line labeled "E" is called a(n):

A. bow line
B. forward breast line
C. after spring line
D. bow spring line

01500. Sometimes it is desirable to connect a member both by riveting and welding. Which statement is TRUE concerning this procedure?

A. Tearing through the member is more likely in this type connection.
B. The weld may be broken by the stresses caused by riveting.
C. The weld increases the tensile stress on the rivet heads.
D. The welding must be completed before the riveting commences.

01503. Which of the following knots should be used to send a man over the side when he may have to use both hands?

A. bowline
B. french bowline
C. bowline on a bight
D. running bowline

01504. A 6-strand composite rope made up of alternate fiber and wire strands around a fiber core is called:

A. spring lay
B. lang lay
C. cable lay
D. alternate lay

01506. The sprocket wheel in a windlass, used for heaving in the anchor, is termed a:

A. capstan
B. dog wheel
C. fairlead
D. wildcat

01508. While towing, sudden shock-loading caused during heavy weather can be reduced by:

A. using a short tow hawser
B. using a non-elastic type hawser
C. using a heavier hawser
D. decreasing the catenary in the hawser

01513. Which of the followings knots is suitable for hoisting an unconscious person?

A. bowline in a bight
B. French bowline
C. fisherman's loop
D. spider hitch

01514. A 6x12, 2-inch wire rope has:

A. 12 strands and a 2-inch diameter
B. 12 strands and a 2-inch circumference
C. 6 strands and a 2-inch diameter
D. 6 strands and a 2-inch circumference

01516. The length of a standard "shot" of chain is:

A. 12 fathoms
B. 15 fathoms
C. 18 fathoms
D. 20 fathoms

01517. Which of the pictures in illustration DO30DG represents a timber hitch?

A. e
B. f
C. n
D. u

01523. When making a short splice in wire rope:

A. all tucks go against the lay
B. all tucks go with the lay
C. the first 3 wires are tucked against the lay and the last 3 go with the lay
D. the first 3 wires are tucked with the lay and the last 3 go against the lay

01524. A mooring line is described as being 6x24, 1-3/4 inch wire rope. What do the above numbers refer to?

A. strands, yarns, circumference
B. strands, wires, diameter
C. wires, yarns, diameter
D. strands, circumference, wires

01525. The term "shift the rudder" means:

A. use right or left rudder
B. change from right (left) to left (right) rudder an equal amount

C. check, but do not stop the vessel from swinging
D. put the rudder amidship

01526. One shot of anchor chain is equal to how many feet?

A. 6
B. 15
C. 45
D. 90

01528. You are being towed by one tug. As you lengthen the bridle legs, you:

A. increase your chances of breaking the towing hawser
B. reduce the yawing of your vessel
C. reduce spring effect of the tow connection
D. increase chances of breaking the bridle legs

01529. When a winch breaks down, or some similar occurrence makes only one winch available at a hatch, which alternate rig would provide a temporary solution while repairs are made?

A. Frisco Rig
B. split fall rig
C. West Coast Rig
D. yard and stay jury rig

01530. Shell plating is:

A. the galvanizing on steel
B. a hatch cover
C. the outer plating of a vessel
D. synonymous with decking

01532. To determine the number of portable fire extinguishers required on an inspected vessel, you should check the:

A. Hot Work permit
B. Certificate of Inspection
C. Safety of Life at Sea Certificate
D. Station Bill

01533. What is the BEST splice for repairing a parted synthetic fiber mooring line?

A. Liverpool splice
B. locking long splice
C. long splice
D. short splice

01534. Which statement(s) is(are) TRUE concerning wire rope?

A. wire rope should be condemned if the outside wires are worn to 1/2 the original diameter.
B. wire rope should be condemned if the fiber core appears moist.

C. wire rope which is right-hand laid should be coiled counterclockwise to prevent kinking.
D. all of the above

01536. When anchoring, it is a common rule of thumb to use a length of chain:

A. 5 to 7 times the depth of water
B. 7 to 10 times the depth of water
C. twice the depth of water
D. twice the depth of water plus the range of tide

01538. Your vessel is being towed, and you are using a tripping rope. A tripping rope of fiber or wire is used to:

A. give added strength to the main tow hawser
B. retrieve the main tow hawser
C. retrieve the outboard legs of the bridle where they are connected to the fishplate
D. open the pelican hook at the fishplate

01543. Which is normally used to hold wire rope for splicing?

A. come along
B. jigger
C. rigger's screw
D. sealing clamp

01544. The main function of the core of a wire rope is to:

A. give flexibility
B. keep the outer strands in position
C. allow some circulation around the strands
D. allow lubrication inside the rope

01546. Which of the following would be the BEST guide for determining the proper scope of anchor chain to use for anchoring in normal conditions?

A. 1 shot of chain for every 10 feet of water
B. 1 shot of chain for every 15 feet of water
C. 1 shot of chain for every 30 feet of water
D. 1 shot of chain for every 90 feet of water

01548. Which of the following could be used as fairleads on a towed vessel?

A. chocks
B. double bitts
C. roller chocks
D. all of the above

01550. Keel scantlings of any vessel are greatest amidships because:

A. connections between forebody and afterbody are most crucial
B. of maximum longitudinal bending moments

C. of severest racking stresses
D. resistance to grounding is at a maximum amidships

01552. Which of the pictures in illustration DO30DG represents a stopper hitch?

A. m
B. p
C. r
D. v

01553. The correct way to make an eye in a wire rope with clips is to place the clips with the:

A. first and third U-bolts on the bitter end and the second U-bolt on the standing part
B. first and third U-bolts on the standing part and the second U-bolt on the bitter end
C. U-bolts of all clips on the bitter end
D. U-bolts of all clips on the standing part

01554. Wire ropes are classified by the:

A. number of strands and the number of wires per strand
B. diameter
C. circumference
D. wire diameter compared to core diameter

01555. When carrying out a parallel track search pattern, the course of the search units should normally be which of the following?

A. in the same direction as anticipated drift
B. in the opposite direction of anticipated drift
C. perpendicular to the line of anticipated drift
D. downwind

01556. When anchoring, good practice requires 5 to 7 fathoms of chain for each fathom of depth. In deep water you should use:

A. the same ratio
B. more chain for each fathom of depth
C. less chain for each fathom of depth
D. 2 anchors with the same ratio of chain

01557. When relieving the helm, the new helmsman should find it handy to know the:

A. amount of helm carried for a steady course
B. variation in the area
C. leeway
D. deviation on that heading

01558. When making up a tow connection, you should use:

A. safety hooks
B. plain eye hooks
C. round pin shackles
D. screw pin shackles

01560. Which arrangement of shell plating is used MOST in modern shipbuilding?

A. clinker
B. flush
C. in-and-out
D. joggled

01563. Which of the following statements concerning 2 lines spliced together is TRUE?

A. Splicing is used to increase the circumference of each line.
B. Splicing 2 lines together is stronger than knotting 2 lines together.
C. Splicing is used to increase the overall strength of the line.
D. Splicing is used to prevent rotting of the line's bitter end.

01564. What is the main reason to slush a wire rope?

A. keep the wire soft and manageable
B. lubricate the inner wires and prevent wear
C. prevent kinking
D. prevent rotting

01565. While in drydock your vessel will be belt-gauged. This process involves:

A. measuring the thickness of the tail shaft liner
B. taking the vessel's offsets to check for hull deformation
C. testing and examining the anchor cables for defective links
D. drilling or sonic-testing the hull to determine the plate thickness

01566. In illustration D044DG, the mooring line labeled "A" is called a(n):

A. after breast line
B. after spring line
C. onshore stern line
D. offshore stern line

01568. A tackle is "two blocked" when the blocks are:

A. equally sharing the load
B. jammed together
C. as far apart as possible
D. rove to the highest mechanical advantage

01569. Which of the following endings is NOT acceptable in a wire rope that is free to rotate when hoisting?

A. poured socket
B. Liverpool eye slice
C. eye formed with a pressure clamped sleeve
D. eye formed by clips

01570. Which of the following is NOT an advantage of ship construction using welded butt joints in the shell plating?

A. keeps practically 100% of tensile strength at the joints
B. reduces frictional resistance
C. reduces plate stress
D. reduces weight

01573. Which of the following statements concerning splices is TRUE?

A. a back splice is used to permanently connect 2 lines together.
B. a long splice is used to connect 2 lines that will pass through narrow openings.
C. a short splice is used to temporarily connect 2 lines.
D. in splicing fiber rope, you would splice with the lay of the line.

01574. Wire rope is galvanized to:

A. protect it from corrosion due to salt water
B. make it bend more easily
C. increase its strength
D. increase its circumference

01575. The key to rescuing a man overboard is:

A. good communication
B. a dedicated crew
C. good equipment
D. well-conducted drills

01576. Using a scope of 5, determine how many shots of chain you should put out to anchor in 5 fathoms of water?

A. 1
B. 2
C. 3
D. 5

01578. That portion of the screw current moving with the propeller is known as:

A. discharge current
B. forward current
C. propeller current
D. suction current

01580. Shell plating that has curvature in 2 directions and must be heated and hammered to shape over specially prepared forms is called:

A. compound plate
B. furnaced plate
C. flat plate
D. rolled plate

01583. Which statement concerning a short splice is TRUE?

A. It is used to temporarily join 2 lines together.
B. A short splice is stronger than 2 lines joined by a knot.
C. A short splice decreases the diameter of the line.
D. none of the above

01584. The size of wire rope is determined by the:

A. number of strands
B. number of wires in each strand
C. circumference
D. diameter

01586. If you pay out more anchor cable, you:

A. decrease the holding power of your anchor
B. decrease the swing of your boat while at anchor
C. increase the holding power of your anchor
D. increase the possibility that your boat will drag anchor

01588. On a single-screw vessel (right-hand propeller) going full ahead with good headway, the engine is put astern, and the rudder is placed hard left. Which statement indicates how the stern of the vessel will swing?

A. Swing to starboard until headway is lost and then to port.
B. Immediately swing to port.
C. Swing to port until headway is lost and then may possibly swing to starboard.
D. Swing slowly to port at first and then quickly to port.

01590. A 30-pound plate would be:

A. 5/8" thick
B. 11/16" thick
C. 3/4" thick
D. 1" thick

01593. A long splice in a line:

A. is used in running rigging
B. doubles the size of the line
C. is only used on fiber rope
D. is very weak

01594. What is the breaking strain of steel wire rope with a 5/8" diameter?

A. 1.0 tons
B. 6.6 tons
C. 9.6 tons
D. 15.6 tons

01595. Which of the pictures in illustration DO30DG represents a barrel hitch?

A. o
B. u
C. v
D. w

01596. Using a scope of 5, determine how many feet of chain you should put out to anchor in 12 fathoms of water.

A. 60 feet
B. 72 feet
C. 360 feet
D. 450 feet

01597. At the required fire drill, all persons must report to their stations and demonstrate their ability to perform the duties assigned to them:

A. by the Coast Guard Regulations
B. in the Station Bill
C. by the person conducting the drill
D. at the previous safety meeting

01598. On a vessel equipped with a single propeller, propeller action alone has the MOST effect on directional control when the engines are put:

A. full ahead
B. full astern
C. half ahead
D. slow astern

01600. A person who sees an individual fall overboard should:

A. immediately jump in the water to assist the individual
B. call for help and keep the individual in sight
C. run to the radio room to send an emergency message
D. go to the bridge for the distress flares

01603. Which of the following would be the strongest when placed in a line?

A. clove hitch
B. long splice
C. short splice
D. square knot

01604. Which knot would serve BEST as a safety sling for a person working over the side?

A. bowline on a bight
B. French bowline
C. jug sling
D. lifting hitch

01605. The pivoting point of a vessel going ahead is:

A. near the stern
B. about 2/3 of the vessel's length from the bow
C. at the hawsepipe
D. about 1/3 of the vessel's length from the bow

01606. To safely anchor a vessel, there must be sufficient "scope" in the anchor cable. Scope is the ratio of:

A. weight of cable to weight of vessel
B. weight of cable to weight of anchor
C. length of anchor to depth of water
D. length of cable to depth of water

01607. Using a scope of 6, how much cable would have to be used in order to anchor in 24' of water?

A. 4'
B. 18'
C. 30'
D. 144'

01608. With a ship dead in the water and the rudder amidships, as the right-handed screw starts to turn ahead, the bow will tend to go:

A. right because of sidewise pressure
B. left because of sidewise pressure
C. straight ahead
D. as influenced by tide and sea

01610. The joint formed when 2 steel shell plates are placed longitudinally side to side is called a:

A. bevel
B. bond
C. butt
D. seam

01612. Which of the pictures in illustration DO30DG represents a stopper?

A. e
B. n
C. r
D. s

01613. Which splice should you use in order to make a permanent loop in a line?

A. back splice
B. eye splice
C. long splice
D. short splice

01614. What bend or knot is used to tie a small line to a larger one?

A. becket bend
B. bowline
C. clove hitch
D. lark's head

01616. In moderate wind and current what should be the length of chain with a single anchor?

A. 5 times the depth of the water in good holding ground
B. 10 times the depth of the water in shallow water
C. 2 times the depth of the water in poor holding ground
D. 8 times the depth of the water in deep water

01618. A twin-screw vessel is easier to maneuver than a single-screw vessel because the former:

A. permits the rudder to move faster
B. generates more power
C. can turn without using her rudder
D. can suck the water away from the rudder

01620. Owing to the greater girth of a ship amidships than at the ends, certain strakes are dropped as they approach the bow and stern to reduce the amount of plating at the ends. These strakes are called:

A. drop strakes
B. stealers
C. throughs
D. voids

01623. A short splice in a line:

A. decreases the size of the line
B. should be used if the line is going through a block
C. should only be used in wire rope
D. doubles the size of the line

01624. What kind of hitch should you use to secure a spar?

A. blackwall hitch
B. stage hitch
C. timber hitch
D. 2 half hitches

01626. Using a scope of 6, determine how many feet of anchor cable you should put out to anchor in 12' of water.

A. 2'
B. 18'
C. 48'
D. 72'

01628. You are going ahead on twin engines when you want to make a quick turn to port. Which actions will turn your boat the fastest?

A. reverse port engine; apply left rudder
B. reverse port engine; rudder amidships
C. reverse starboard engine; apply left rudder
D. reverse starboard engine; rudder amidships

01630. The fore and aft run of deck plating which strengthens the connection between the beams and the frames and keeps the beams square to the shell is called the:

A. garboard strake
B. limber strake
C. sheer strake
D. stringer strake

01631. Which of the following is required to be posted in the pilothouse of a vessel?

A. Certificate of Inspection
B. officer's licenses
C. Station Bill
D. Vessel's Maneuvering Characteristics

01633. The strongest way to join the ends of 2 ropes is with a:

A. back splice
B. short splice
C. square knot
D. carrick bend

01634. A monkey fist is found on a:

A. heaving line
B. lead line
C. manrope
D. mooring line

01635. In illustration D044DG, the mooring line labeled "B" is called a(n):

A. after breast line
B. after spring line
C. offshore stern line
D. inshore stern line

01636. When anchoring a vessel under normal conditions, what scope of chain is recommended?

A. 4 times the depth of water
B. 2 1/2 times the depth of water
C. 5 to 7 times the depth of water
D. 15 times the depth of water

01638. On a twin-screw, twin-rudder vessel, the most effective way to turn in your own water, with no way on, is to put:

A. one engine ahead and one engine astern, with full rudder
B. one engine ahead and one engine astern, with rudder amidships
C. both engines ahead, with full rudder
D. both engines astern, with full rudder

01640. The garboard strake is the:

A. raised flange at the main deck edge
B. riveted crack arrester strap on all-welded ships
C. riveting pattern most commonly used in ship construction
D. row of plating nearest the keel

01642. Which of the pictures in illustration DO30DG represents a carrick bend?

A. h
B. j
C. l
D. m

01643. The splice designed to pass easily through a block is called a(n):

A. eye splice
B. short splice
C. long splice
D. block splice

01644. A rolling hitch can be used to:

A. make a temporary eye
B. mouse a hook
C. secure a line around a spar
D. shorten a line

01645. Class C EPIRBs are:

A. manually activated and operate on maritime (VHF) channels
B. automatically activated and operate on maritime (VHF) channels
C. manually operated and detected by satellite
D. automatically operated and detected by satellite

01646. What is the normal length of anchor cable used to anchor a vessel?

A. an amount equal to the depth of the water
B. 2 times the depth of water
C. 3 to 4 times the depth of water
D. 5 to 7 times the depth of water

01648. When steaming through an anchorage, a Shipmaster should:

A. avoid crossing close astern of the anchored ships
B. avoid crossing close ahead of the anchored ships

C. keep the ship moving at a good speed to reduce set
D. transit only on a flood tide

01650. To reduce the number of strakes at the bow, 2 strakes are tapered and joined at their ends by a single plate. This plate is known as a:

A. cover plate
B. joiner
C. lap strake
D. stealer plate

01651. A placard containing instructions for use of the breeches buoy (Form CG-811) shall be placed:

A. in the pilothouse and engine room
B. in the messroom(s)
C. where available to the watch officer
D. where best visible in the officer's and crew's quarters

01653. Which tool is used to open the strands of fiber lines when making an eye splice?

A. belaying spike
B. fid
C. heaver
D. pricker

01654. What knot should be used to bend 2 hawsers together for towing?

A. double carrick bend
B. fisherman's bend
C. heaving line bend
D. rolling hitch

01655. Which of the pictures in illustration DO30DG represents a double blackwall hitch?

A. f
B. g
C. l
D. r

01657. What is the perimeter of a circle with a radius of 5.1 feet?

A. 81.71 ft
B. 64.08 ft
C. 40.85 ft
D. 32.04 ft

01660. The strake on each side of the keel is called a:

A. sheer strake
B. gatewood strake
C. insulation strake
D. garboard strake

01661. Which of the following is NOT required by law to be posted aboard a vessel?

A. Certificate of Inspection
B. Official Crew List
C. officer's licenses
D. Station Bill

01663. A bench hook is used for:

A. handling of cargo cases
B. hanging oilskins
C. sewing canvas
D. splicing small stuff

01664. A method used to make an eye in a bight of line where it cannot be spliced is known as:

A. braiding
B. plaiting
C. seizing
D. serving

01665. Which of the pictures in illustration DO30DG represents a sailmaker's whipping?

A. e
B. f
C. j
D. k

01666. While anchoring your vessel, the BEST time to let go of the anchor is when your vessel is:

A. dead in the water
B. moving slowly astern over the ground
C. moving fast ahead over the ground
D. moving fast astern over the ground

01670. The term "strake" is used in reference to:

A. rudder mountings
B. anchor gear
C. hull plating
D. vessel framing

01671. The number of certificated able seamen and lifeboatmen required on a vessel is determined by the:

A. International Maritime Organization
B. Corps of Engineers
C. Coast Guard
D. American Bureau of Shipping

01673. A sail hook is used for:

A. hoisting a windsail
B. parceling
C. sewing canvas
D. testing canvas

01674. Which is NOT a type of seizing?

A. flat seizing
B. racking seizing
C. throat seizing
D. tube seizing

01675. What is the name of the mark indicated by the letter D in illustration DOO3DG?

A. tropical water line
B. summer water line
C. fresh water line
D. winter water line

01676. When preparing to hoist the anchor, the FIRST step should be to:

A. engage the wildcat
B. put the brake in the off position
C. take off the chain stopper
D. take the riding pawl off the chain

01680. In vessel construction, the garboard strake is:

A. located next to and parallel to the keel
B. located next to and parallel to the gunwale
C. another term for the bilge keel
D. another term for the rub rail

01683. "Herringbone" is a term associated with:

A. anchoring
B. mooring
C. sewing
D. splicing

01684. Temporary seizings on wire rope are made with:

A. marline
B. sail twine
C. tape
D. wire

01685. Which of the pictures in illustration DO30DG represents a marline hitch?

A. w
B. v
C. s
D. h

01686. When weighing anchor in a rough sea, how would you avoid damaging bow plating?

A. heave it home as fast as you can
B. heave it home intermittently, between swells
C. leave the anchor under foot, until the vessel may be brought before the sea
D. wait for a calm spot between seas, then house it

01687. What is the perimeter of a circle with a radius of 4.2 feet?

A. 26.39 ft
B. 21.19 ft
C. 17.81 ft
D. 13.20 ft

01689. In illustration D044DG, the mooring line labeled "C" is called a:

A. stern line
B. spring line
C. shore line
D. breast line

01693. What is the stress on the hauling part when lifting a 4900 lb. weight using a twofold purchase rove to least advantage?

A. 980 lb.
B. 1225 lb.
C. 1715 lb.
D. 1837 lb.

01694. A "whipping" is:

A. a messenger
B. a stopper for nylon line
C. a U-bolt for securing a cargo whip to the winch drum
D. twine tied around a rope end

01695. What is the perimeter of a circle with a radius of 3.7 feet?

A. 11.62 ft
B. 17.49 ft
C. 23.25 ft
D. 25.72 ft

01696. Mooring with 2 anchors has what major advantage over anchoring with one anchor?

A. The vessel will not reverse direction in a tidal current.
B. The radius of the vessel's swing will be shortened.
C. A mooring approach may be made from any direction.
D. The vessel will not swing with a change in wind.

01700. Which letter designates the bilge strake of the vessel shown in illustration D001DG?

A. a
B. b
C. c
D. d

01703. What is the stress on the hauling part when lifting a 4,200 lb. weight using a three-fold purchase rove to advantage?

A. 571.4 lb.
B. 715.2 lb.
C. 960.0 lb.
D. 1066.7 lb.

01704. Whipping the bitter end of a fiber rope is used to:

A. increase the circumference of the rope
B. make for easier handling
C. prevent fraying of the bitter end
D. prevent moisture from entering the bitter end

01706. Your vessel is anchored in an open roadstead with 3 shots of chain out on the port anchor. The wind freshens considerably and the anchor begins to drag. Which of the following actions should you take FIRST?

A. Drop the starboard anchor short with about one shot of chain.
B. Sheer out to starboard using the rudder, and drop the starboard anchor with about 4 shots of chain.
C. Put the engines slow ahead to help the anchor.
D. Veer out more chain on the port anchor.

01711. You are bound from port A governed by the summer load line mark to port B also governed by the summer mark. The great circle track will take you into a zone governed by the winter mark. Which statement is TRUE?

A. You cannot load beyond the summer mark at port A and must be at the winter mark upon arrival at port B.
B. You can only load to the winter mark plus any fresh water allowance and burnout to sea at port A.
C. You must be at the winter mark when you enter the winter zone and cannot exceed the summer mark after departing port A.
D. You can load so that upon arrival at the pier at port B your freeboard is equal to the summer mark less any fresh water allowance.

01713. The cheek length of a block in inches should be about:

A. 3 times the circumference of a manila line
B. 5 times the diameter of a manila line
C. 2 times the diameter of its sheaves for manila line
D. 20 times the diameter of a manila line

01714. A "sheepshank" is used to:

A. keep a line from fraying
B. join lines of unequal size
C. be a stopper
D. shorten a line

01716. Which is the correct procedure for anchoring a small to medium size vessel in deep water?

A. Let the anchor fall free from the hawsepipe, but apply the brake at intervals to check the rate of fall.
B. Back the anchor slowly out of the hawsepipe a few feet, and then let it fall in the normal fashion.
C. Let the anchor fall off the brake right from the hawsepipe, but keep a slight strain on the brake.
D. Under power, back the anchor out until it is near, but clear of, the bottom before letting it fall.

01717. With a large tow astern, there is immediate danger to the tug in the event of the:

A. tug losing power
B. tow line parting
C. bridle twisting
D. tow broaching

01720. Your vessel is to dock bow in at a pier. Which line will be the most useful when maneuvering the vessel alongside the pier?

A. bow spring line
B. bow breast line
C. stern breast line
D. inshore head line

01723. What is meant by the term "two-blocked"?

A. the bottom block touches the top block
B. the line has jumped the sheaves
C. there are turns in the fall
D. you have 2 blocks

01724. A "bowline" is used to:

A. join lines of equal size
B. form a temporary eye (loop) at the end of a line
C. be a stopper
D. keep a line from fraying

01725. The term "shift the rudder" means:

A. use right or left rudder
B. check, but do not stop the vessel from swinging
C. change from right (left) to left (right) rudder an equal amount
D. put the rudder amidships

01726. When attempting to free an anchor jammed in the hawsepipe, the simplest method of freeing it may be:

A. a simple kick, such as starting the windlass at full power
B. rigging a bull rope to pull it out
C. to grease the hawsepipe
D. to pry it loose with a short piece of pipe

01728. You are approaching a wrecked vessel which is on fire in order to remove survivors. Your approach should be:

A. to leeward of the wrecked vessel
B. at a speed of at most 1/2 that of the wrecked vessel
C. at a speed of at least that of the wrecked vessel
D. to windward of the wrecked vessel

01730. A disk with a horizontal line through its center, equivalent to the summer load line, is called the:

A. deadrise mark
B. maximum allowable draft mark
C. plimsol mark
D. tonnage mark

01732. Which of the pictures in illustration DO30DG represents a half hitch?

A. u
B. s
C. k
D. h

01733. To draw both blocks of a tackle apart is called:

A. chockablocking
B. fleeting
C. overhauling
D. two blocking

01734. Which of the following knots would reduce the strength of a line by the LEAST amount?

A. bowline
B. clove hitch
C. sheet bend
D. 2 half hitches

01736. Which precautions should be used before letting the anchor go?

A. see that the chain is all clear
B. see that the anchor is clear of obstructions
C. see that the wildcat is disengaged
D. all of the above

01737. When evacuating a seaman by helicopter lift, what course should the ship take?

A. downwind so that the apparent wind is close to nil.
B. a course that will keep a free flow of air, clear of smoke, over the hoist area.
C. a course that will have the hoist area in the lee of the superstructure.
D. with the wind dead ahead because the helicopter is more maneuverable when going into the wind.

01739. If 2 falls are attached to lift a 1-ton load, what angle between the falls will result in the stress on each fall being equal to the load being lifted?

A. 60°
B. 75°
C. 120°
D. 150°

01740. The group of markings shown in illustration D003DG is called a:

A. loft mark
B. load line mark
C. test mark
D. water mark

01741. The Load Line Regulations are administered by the:

A. U. S. Coast Guard
B. Maritime Administration
C. Loyd's Register of Shipping
D. National Cargo Bureau

01743. A mooring line leading at nearly right angles to the keel is a:

A. bow line
B. breast line
C. spring line
D. stern line

01744. Which of the following knots will reduce the strength of a rope by the greatest amount?

A. fisherman's bend
B. 2 half hitches
C. bowline
D. square knot

01746. Which of the following would NOT be used to describe the amount of anchor chain out? "Three shots":

A. at the water's edge
B. on deck
C. on the bottom
D. well in the water

01748. An Official Logbook is required on which of the following vessels?

A. 150 GT tug from Boston to New Orleans.
B. 100 GT tug going from New York to San Pedro, California.
C. 50 GT tug going from Miami to Seattle.
D. 199 GT tug on a coastwise trip of 650 miles.

01749. A sling is rigged on a piece of pipe weighing 1000 lb. The angle between the sling legs is 140 and the legs are of equal length. What stress is exerted on each sling leg when the pipe is lifted?

A. 1318 lb.
B. 1366 lb.
C. 1414 lb.
D. 1469 lb.

01750. A grapnel is a:

A. device for securing a chain topping lift
B. hook to prevent the anchor cable from slipping
C. device used to drag for a submerged cable or line
D. type of clam bucket used for discharging bulk cargo

01751. The load line certificate is issued by:

A. the American Bureau of Shipping
B. the National Cargo Bureau
C. the United States Coast Guard
D. United States Customs

01753. To reeve a right-angle threefold purchase start with the:

A. left sheave bottom block
B. left sheave top block
C. middle sheave top block
D. right sheave bottom block

01754. The best method for tying 2 lines of the same size together is by using a:

A. becket bend
B. 2 bowlines
C. single carrick bend
D. square knot

01755. Which of the pictures in illustration DO30DG represents a French bowline?

A. o
B. t
C. v
D. w

01756. When anchoring a vessel, it is best to release the anchor when:

A. going full astern
B. going full ahead
C. going slow astern
D. dead in the water

01760. A hook that will release quickly is a:

A. longshore hook
B. margin hook
C. marginal hook
D. pelican hook

01761. The assigning authority for load lines for U. S. vessels is:

A. the U. S. Coast Guard
B. the American Bureau of Shipping
C. Lloyd's Register of Shipping
D. the National Cargo Bureau

01762. What is the perimeter of a circle with a radius of 2.5 feet?

A. 7.86 ft
B. 15.71 ft
C. 19.63 ft
D. 22.71 ft

01763. You are in charge while handling a synthetic hawser on a capstan. The hawser has a heavy strain and you wish to avoid the hawser's slipping on the capstan drum. Which action should you take?

A. Back off on the capstan a bit and have the seaman take several more turns on the drum.
B. Have the seaman take a strain on the hawser and carefully have several turns added on the drum.
C. Have more than one seaman hold a strain on the hawser and continue to heave easy.
D. While continuing to heave slowly on the capstan, have the seaman take several more turns on the drum.

01764. The "square knot" is used for:

A. forming temporary eyes in lines
B. joining 2 lines of equal size
C. keeping line from unlaying or fraying
D. joining 2 lines of different size

01765. The annual survey for endorsement of a load line certificate must be held within:

A. the 3 month period immediately following the certificate's anniversary date
B. the 3 month period immediately preceding the certificate's anniversary date
C. 3 months either way of the certificate's anniversary date
D. the 3 month period centered on the certificate's anniversary date

01766. When anchoring in a current, you should:

A. drop the anchor with the bow headed downstream
B. back your vessel into the current
C. anchor while stemming the current
D. all of the above

01767. What is the name of the mark indicated by the letter E in illustration DOO3DG?

A. fresh water line
B. winter water line
C. tropical water line
D. summer water line

01768. As a general rule, if your vessel is drifting in calm water with negligible current, the wind will maneuver your vessel until it strikes the vessel:

A. on or near the beam
B. within 5° of the bow
C. directly on the bow
D. directly on the stern

01769. Two falls are supporting a 1.5 ton load. The port fall is at an angle of 40° from the vertical. The starboard fall is at an angle of 70° from the vertical. What is the stress on each fall?

A. port 1.5 tons, starboard 1.0 tons
B. port 1.5 tons, starboard 1.5 tons
C. port 1.7 tons, starboard 1.3 tons
D. port 1.7 tons, starboard 2.0 tons

01771. The agency which assigns load lines and issues Load Line Certificates is:

A. the American Bureau of Shipping
B. the Secretary of Commerce
C. U. S. Customs
D. the U. S. Coast Guard

01772. What is the volume in a cone with a base diameter of 32' and a height of 21'?

A. 8,444.60 cubic ft.
B. 7,732.81 cubic ft.
C. 5,629.73 cubic ft.
D. 703.72 cubic ft.

01773. What size block shell should be used with a 4" manila line?

A. 8"
B. 12"
C. 16"
D. 24"

01774. Which of the following knots is used to attach 2 different sized lines together?

A. granny knot
B. sheet bend
C. square knot
D. thief knot

01776. When anchoring in calm water, it is best to:

A. maintain slight headway when letting go the anchor
B. wait until the vessel is dead in the water before letting go the anchor
C. have slight sternway on the vessel while letting go the anchor
D. let the anchor go from the stern with the anchor cable leading from the bow

01777. What is the volume in a cone with a base diameter of 23' and a height of 14'?

A. 1,648.05 cubic ft.
B. 1,938.89 cubic ft.
C. 2,908.33 cubic ft.
D. 7,755.55 cubic ft.

01778. You are landing a single-screw vessel with a right-handed propeller port side to a dock. When you have approached your desired position off the dock, you back down on your engines, with rudder amidships. You would expect the vessel to:

A. drift away from the dock
B. lose headway without swinging
C. turn its stern towards the dock
D. turn its stern away from the dock

01781. Which organization usually assigns load lines to U. S. vessels?

A. National Load-Line Agency
B. National Shipping Bureau
C. American Bureau of Shipping
D. American Regulations Council

01782. When evacuating a seaman by helicopter lift, which of the following statements is TRUE?

A. The vessel should be stopped with the wind dead ahead during the hoisting operation.
B. Flags should be flown to provide a visual reference as to the direction of the apparent wind.
C. The drop line should be grounded first then secured as close to the hoist point as possible.
D. The hoist area should be located as far aft as possible so the pilot will have a visual reference while approaching.

01783. Which mooring line is likely to undergo the most strain when docking a ship under normal conditions?

A. bow line
B. breast line
C. spring line
D. stern line

01784. The "rolling hitch" could be used to:

A. join 2 lines of different sizes
B. join 2 lines of equal sizes
C. add strength to a weak spot in a line
D. act as a stopper to transfer a line under strain

01786. When anchoring in a river where the current is from one direction only, the best way to lay out 2 anchors is to have them:

A. directly in line with the bow
B. side by side, with their lines on the port and starboard side
C. so that their lines form an angle
D. on top of one another

01787. Which of the pictures in illustration DO30DG represents a blackwall hitch?

A. f
B. h
C. p
D. s

01788. Which position shown in illustration D019DG is the most dangerous when tying up?

A. I
B. II
C. III
D. IV

01790. Which space(s) is(are) exempt when measuring gross tonnage?

A. auxiliary machinery spaces above the uppermost continuous deck
B. steering gear room
C. chart room, if it is part of the wheelhouse
D. all of the above

01792. What is the name of the mark indicated by the letter F in illustration D003DG?

A. fresh water line
B. summer water line
C. winter water line
D. tropical water line

01793. The lines led forward from the bow and aft from the stern when a vessel is moored to the dock are:

A. bow and stern lines
B. breast lines
C. halyards
D. warps

01794. A "figure-8" knot is used to:

A. be a stopper
B. shorten a line
C. join lines of equal size
D. keep a line from passing through a sheave

01795. Which of the pictures in illustration DO30DG represents a double sheet bend?

A. f
B. l
C. r
D. t

01796. Which safety check(s) should be made before letting the anchor go?

A. see that the anchor is clear of obstructions
B. see that the chain is all clear
C. see that the wildcat is disengaged
D. all of the above

01798. You are on a single-screw vessel with a left-handed propeller making no way in the water. How would your vessel react when you apply right rudder?

A. bow will kick to starboard
B. bow will kick to port
C. rudder has no effect on the vessel
D. stern will kick to port, then slowly swing to starboard

01800. The figure obtained by dividing the total volume of the ship in cubic feet (after omission of exempted spaces) by 100 is the:

A. bale cubic
B. gross tonnage
C. light displacement
D. net tonnage

01802. Which of the pictures in illustration DO30DG represents a bowline?

A. g
B. h
C. l
D. q

01803. A snatch block is a:

A. block used only with manila rope
B. chock roller
C. hinged block
D. strong block used for short, sharp pulls

01804. Instead of whipping an end of a line, a temporary means of preventing the line from unraveling is to tie a:

A. becket bend
B. blackwall hitch
C. figure-8 knot
D. square knot

01805. In towing it is desirable for the tug and tow to ride crests simultaneously because:

A. shock loading on the tow line is reduced
B. towing speed is improved
C. the tow is more visible from the tug
D. the catenary of the tow line is reduced

01806. If the situation arose where it became necessary to tow a disabled vessel, which statement is TRUE concerning the towing line?

A. The towing line between the 2 vessels should be clear of the water.
B. The towing line should be taut at all times between the vessels.
C. There should be a catenary so the line dips into the water.
D. none of the above

01807. When evacuating a seaman by helicopter lift, which of the following statements is TRUE?

A. When lifting from an area forward of the bridge, the apparent wind should be about 30° on the port bow.
B. The vessel should be slowed to bare steerageway.
C. If the hoist is at the stern, booms extending aft at the stern should be lowered and cradled with the topping lifts hove taut.
D. The litter should not be touched until it has been grounded.

01809. When relieving the helm, the new helmsman should find it handy to know the:

A. leeway
B. variation in the area
C. amount of helm carried for a steady course
D. deviation on that heading

01811. You are towing a large barge on a hawser. Your main engine suddenly fails. What is the greatest danger?

A. tug and tow will go aground
B. tow will endanger other traffic
C. tow will overrun tug
D. tow will block the channel

01813. A snatch block would most likely be used as a:

A. boat fall
B. fairlead
C. riding pawl
D. topping lift

01814. In illustration D044DG, the mooring line labeled "D" is called a(n):

A. stern line
B. forward spring line
C. waist breast line
D. after spring line

01815. "Ease the rudder" means to:

A. steer the course which is your present heading
B. move the rudder slowly in the direction of the most recent rudder command
C. bring the rudder amidships
D. decrease the rudder angle

01816. Which of the pictures in illustration DO30DG represents a square knot?

A. w
B. r
C. p
D. h

01818. Compare a twin-screw tug to a single-screw tug. Which of the following concerning the twin-screw tug is FALSE?

A. The failure of one engine does not mean loss of control of the tow.
B. It is more maneuverable.
C. It develops more bollard pull for the same horsepower.
D. It is generally subject to more propeller damage from debris in the water.

01819. The stringer plate is represented by what letter in illustration D033DG?

A. a
B. c
C. i
D. n

01820. If a drill required by regulations is not completed, the Master or person in charge must:

A. report this immediately to the Commandant of the Coast Guard
B. log the reason for not completing the drill
C. conduct 2 of the required drills at the next opportunity
D. all of the above

01821. What is the principal danger in attempting to swing a barge on a hawser in order to slow the barge's speed?

A. Dangerous wakes may result from the swinging barge and capsize the tug.
B. The barge may swing too quickly and run over the tug.

C. Free surface effect of liquid inside the barge may rupture the barge bulkheads if the turn is too quick.
D. The barge may pass under the hawser and capsize the tug.

01822. The knot lettered V in illustration DO30DG is a:

A. bowline
B. clove hitch
C. marline hitch
D. carrick bend

01823. The purpose of chafing gear is to:

A. prevent corrosion of standing rigging
B. prevent corrosion of running rigging
C. prevent wear caused by the rubbing of one object against another
D. protect the body against extreme cold

01824. What is the volume in a cone with a base diameter of 4.5 feet and a height of 3 feet?

A. 4.50 cu. ft.
B. 7.12 cu. ft.
C. 9.81 cu. ft.
D. 15.90 cu. ft.

01826. The knot lettered X in illustration DO30DG is a:

A. timber hitch
B. becket bend
C. clove hitch
D. blackwall hitch

01827. What is the volume in a cone with a base diameter of 8 ft. and a height of 6 ft.?

A. 100.53 ft.
B. 131.39 ft.
C. 172.72 ft.
D. 197.39 ft.

01828. If your vessel is broken down and rolling in heavy seas, you can reduce the possibility of capsizing by:

A. constantly shifting the rudder
B. moving all passengers to one side of the boat
C. rigging a sea anchor
D. moving all passengers to the stern

01829. The term "shift your rudder" means:

A. change from right rudder to left rudder an equal number of degrees
B. double your rudder angle or go to full rudder
C. bring your rudder amidships
D. check the swing of the vessel

01831. A "loose" tow may cause all of the following EXCEPT:

A. loss of maneuverability
B. lines to part
C. damage to the tug and tow
D. a saving in the transit time

01832. The run of plating labeled A in illustration D033DG is known as the:

A. sheer strake
B. stringer plate
C. deck strake
D. deck longitudinal

01833. The standing part of a tackle is:

A. all the fall except the hauling part
B. the hook that engages the weight to be moved
C. that part to which power is applied
D. that part of the falls made fast to one of the blocks

01836. While towing, what is the principal danger in attempting to swing a barge on a hawser in order to slow the barge's speed?

A. The barge may pass under the hawser and capsize the tug.
B. The barge may swing too quickly and run over the tug.
C. Free surface effect of liquid inside the barge may rupture the barge bulkheads when turning too quickly.
D. Dangerous wakes may result from the swinging barge and capsize the tug.

01838. When mooring a vessel alongside a dock, you should, if possible:

A. go in with the current
B. go in against the current
C. approach the dock at a 90° angle and swing to
D. pass a mooring line to the dock with a heaving line and let the crew pull the vessel in

01840. You are approaching a steamer that is broken down and are preparing to take her in tow. Before positioning your vessel to pass the towline, you must:

A. compare the rate of drift between the ships
B. install chafing gear on the towline
C. secure the bitter end of the towing hawser to prevent loss if the tow is slipped
D. have traveling lizards rigged to guide the towline while it is paid-out

01841. If a tow sinks in shallow water, you should:

A. release it immediately
B. attempt to beach it before it goes under
C. pay out cable until it's on the bottom and buoy the upper end
D. shorten cable to keep it off the bottom

01842. The knot lettered W in illustration DO30DG is a:

A. clove hitch
B. square knot
C. barrel hitch
D. stopper knot

01843. The sheave diameter to be used with a 3" manila rope is:

A. 3"
B. 6"
C. 9"
D. 12"

01844. A wooden float placed between a ship and a dock to prevent damage to both is a:

A. camel
B. dolphin
C. rat guard
D. wedge

01848. The most favorable condition to encounter when you dock your vessel is when the wind and current are:

A. crossing your course in the same direction
B. crossing your course in opposite directions
C. parallel to the pier from ahead
D. setting you on the pier

01849. The knot lettered U in illustration DO30DG is a:

A. half hitch
B. round knot
C. becket bend
D. plain whipping

01852. What is normally used to pass a mooring line to a dock?

A. distance line
B. gantline
C. heaving line
D. tag line

01853. A breeches buoy is being rigged from the shore to a stranded vessel. The initial shot line passed to the vessel is normally made fast to a:

A. hawser which is used to pass a tail-block and whip to the vessel
B. hawser with breeches buoy and harness attached

C. hawser which should be made fast to the vessel below the intended location of the tail-block
D. tail-block and whip which may be used to pass a hawser to the vessel

01854. The structural member indicated by the letter F in illustration D033DG is known as a(n):

A. erection
B. pillar
C. girder
D. deck support

01855. Which problem is virtually impossible to detect during an in-service inspection of used anchor chain?

A. cracks
B. elongation
C. loose studs
D. fatigue

01856. When passing a hawser to the dock you would FIRST use what line?

A. gantline
B. heaving line
C. preventer
D. warp

01857. The knot lettered T in illustration DO30DG is a:

A. round turn and 2 half hitches
B. French bowline
C. carrick bend
D. stopper hitch

01858. The easiest way to anchor a vessel in a current is to:

A. stem the current and make very slow headway when the anchor is dropped
B. stem the current and be falling aft very slowly when the anchor is dropped
C. stem the current and endeavor to make neither headway nor sternway when the anchor is dropped
D. stop all headway through the water and keep the current astern when the anchor is dropped

01859. You are attempting to take a dead ship in tow. All lines have been passed and secured. How should you get underway?

A. Order minimum turns until the towing hawser is just clear of the water, then reduce speed to that necessary to keep the line clear of the water.
B. If the towline is properly adjusted and weighted you can order slow or dead slow and the towline will act as a spring to absorb the initial shock.

C. Order minimum turns until the towing hawser is taut and then continue at that speed until towing speed is attained.
D. Order minimum turns until the catenary almost breaks the water, then stop. Order more turns as the hawser slackens but keep the catenary in the water.

01862. How much force would be required to lift a weight of 200 pounds using a gun tackle rigged to disadvantage (do not consider friction)?

A. 50 lb.
B. 100 lb.
C. 150 lb.
D. 200 lb.

01863. If a mooring line should part while you are tying up at a dock, you should make a temporary eye by tying a:

A. becket bend
B. clove hitch
C. bowline
D. square knot

01864. Progressive flooding may be indicated by:

A. ballast control alarms
B. excessive draft
C. excessive list or trim
D. a continual worsening of list or trim

01868. When being towed by one tug, the towing bridle should be connected to towing:

A. bitts with figure-eights
B. pad eyes with a pelican hook
C. pad eyes with a safety hook
D. all of the above

01869. You are using tackle number 10 in illustration DO29DG to lift a weight of 120 pounds. If you include 10 percent of the weight for each sheave for friction, what is the pull on the hauling part required to lift the weight?

A. 57 lb.
B. 42 lb.
C. 39 lb.
D. 34 lb.

01870. The knot lettered S in illustration DO30DG is a:

A. bowline
B. blackwall hitch
C. half hitch
D. hook hitch

01873. How much weight can you lift by applying 100 lb. of force to a twofold purchase rigged to disadvantage (do not consider friction)?

A. 200 lb.
B. 300 lb.
C. 400 lb.
D. 500 lb.

01875. A seam is indicated by what letter in illustration D033DG?

A. e
B. h
C. l
D. m

01878. When being towed, a fairlead is a:

A. fabricated shape used to change the direction of a flexible member of the tow hookup
B. fabricated shape used to secure the tow hookup to the towed vessel
C. line connecting the fishplate to the bridle legs
D. line connecting the tow bridle to the towed vessel

01879. What is the mechanical advantage of a threefold purchase when rove to disadvantage and neglecting friction?

A. 3
B. 4
C. 5
D. 6

01880. You are using tackle number 11 in illustration DO29DG to lift a weight of 300 lb. If you include 10% of the weight for each sheave for friction, what is the pull on the hauling part required to lift the weight?

A. 75 lb.
B. 90 lb.
C. 110 lb.
D. 117 lb.

01883. The most common method of securing a line to a cleat is a:

A. half hitch, then round turns
B. round turn, then figure-8s
C. figure-8, then round turns
D. figure-8, then half hitches

01886. The knot lettered R in illustration DO30DG is a:

A. double becket bend
B. bowline
C. fisherman's bend
D. round turn and 2 half hitches

01887. A small light tackle with blocks of steel or wood that is used for miscellaneous small jobs is called a:

A. snatch block
B. threefold purchase
C. handy-billy
D. chockablock

01888. The bridle for ocean tows consists of how many legs?

A. 1
B. 2
C. 3
D. 4

01893. When a block and tackle is "rove to advantage", this means that the:

A. blocks have been overhauled
B. hauling parts of 2 tackles are attached
C. hauling part leads through the movable block
D. hauling part leads through the standing block

01894. A load line is assigned by:

A. U. S. Customs
B. the Department of Energy
C. the Corps of Engineers
D. a recognized classification society approved by the U. S. Coast Guard

01895. The knot lettered Q in illustration DO30DG is a:

A. square knot
B. clove hitch
C. bowline
D. round knot

01898. Back-up wires on a towed vessel provide:

A. a factor of safety
B. additional strength
C. a distribution of the towing load
D. all of the above

01902. The joint indicated by letter D in illustration D033DG is a:

A. seam
B. butt
C. span
D. sheet line

01903. When securing a manila line to a bitt, what is the minimum number of round turns you should take before figure-eighting the line?

A. 0
B. 1
C. 2-3
D. 4-5

01905. You have a large, broken-down vessel in tow with a wire rope and anchor cable towline. Both vessels have made provision for slipping the tow in an emergency; however, unless there are special circumstances:

A. the towing vessel should slip first
B. the vessel towed should slip first
C. they should slip simultaneously
D. either vessel may slip first

01908. When towing astern, increased catenary serves to:

A. increase control of the tow
B. prevent the towing vessel from going in irons
C. make the towing vessel less maneuverable
D. reduce shock stress on the towing hawser

01910. The knot lettered J in illustration DO30DG is a:

A. plain whipping
B. bowline
C. marline hitch
D. becket bend

01913. An example of a messenger is a:

A. fairlead
B. heaving line
C. stay
D. warp

01914. You need to make a fixed loop at the end of a line in order to use the line as a mooring line. You have no time to make a splice. Which knot should you use?

A. bowline
B. figure-8
C. overhand
D. round-turn and 2 half hitches

01915. A butt is indicated by what letter in illustration D033DG?

A. j
B. f
C. e
D. d

01917. How many tons of salt water can be loaded into a flat-ended cylindrical tank with a diameter of 5 feet and a length of 14 feet?

A. 31.42
B. 15.71

C. 7.85
D. 6.25

01918. Which statement is TRUE concerning hawser towing?

A. The catenary in a hawser should be sufficient so that the hawser just touches the bottom.
B. The hawser is of sufficient length for towing when taut between tug and tow.
C. Increasing speed usually increases the catenary in the hawser.
D. Shortening the tow hawser generally decreases the maneuverability of the tug.

01923. Disregarding friction, a twofold purchase when rove to disadvantage has a mechanical advantage of:

A. 2
B. 3
C. 4
D. 5

01924. The knot lettered I in illustration DO30DG is a:

A. square knot
B. round knot
C. bowline on a bight
D. timber hitch

01926. How many tons of salt water can be loaded into a flat-ended cylindrical tank with a diameter of 5' and a length of 12'?

A. 6.73
B. 7.85
C. 13.46
D. 26.93

01928. Which towing method maintains the MOST control over the tow?

A. tandem towing
B. Honolulu towing
C. tandem tug towing
D. breasted tug towing

01929. How many tons of salt water can be loaded into a flat-ended cylindrical tank with a diameter of 5 feet and a length of 10 feet?

A. 22.44
B. 11.22
C. 7.48
D. 5.61

01931. You are using tackle number 12 in illustration DO29DG to lift a weight of 300 lb. If you include 10% of the weight for each sheave for friction, what is the pull on the hauling part required to lift the weight?

A. 80 lb.
B. 69 lb.
C. 55 lb.
D. 50 lb.

01933. When checking a mooring line, you should:

A. ensure the bight is not fouled between the ship and the dock by taking up slack
B. pay out slack and keep free for running
C. secure more turns to hold the line against any strain, then clear the area
D. surge the line so that it maintains a strain without parting

01935. The knot H in illustration DO30DG is a:

A. becket bend
B. bowline
C. plain whipping
D. crown knot

01936. A "gypsy" is a:

A. punt used for painting over the side
B. small, reciprocating steam engine
C. spool-shaped drum fitted on a winch
D. swinging derrick

01938. Towing a structure using 2 tugs approximately side by side, each using one hawser, is referred to as a:

A. tandem tow
B. Honolulu tow
C. breasted tug tow
D. tandem tug tow

01939. You are on a vessel that has broken down and are preparing to be taken in tow. You will use your anchor cable as part of the towline. Which of the following statements is TRUE?

A. The anchor cable should be veered enough to allow the towline connection to be just forward of your bow.
B. The anchor cable should be veered enough to allow the towline connection to be immediately astern of the towing vessel.
C. The strain of the tow is taken by the riding pawl, chain stopper, and anchor windlass brake.
D. The anchor cable should be led out through a chock if possible to avoid a sharp nip at the hawsepipe lip.

01943. In order to pay out or slack a mooring line which is under strain, you should.

A. sluice the line
B. surge the line
C. stopper the line
D. slip the line

01944. The garboard strake is indicated by what letter in illustration D033DG?

A. a
B. b
C. g
D. h

01946. The revolving drum of a winch used to haul lines is called a:

A. bull gear
B. gypsyhead
C. spanner
D. wildcat

01948. The Honolulu (Christmas Tree) tow was devised to:

A. keep the catenary to a minimum
B. allow easy removal of a center tow
C. reduce hawser length
D. increase the catenary

01949. Using a scope of 5, determine how many feet of cable you should put out to anchor in 5 fathoms of water.

A. 100
B. 150
C. 200
D. 250

01950. You are proceeding to a distress site and expect large numbers of people in the water. Which of the following is TRUE?

A. You should stop to windward of the survivors in the water and only use the ship's boats to recover the survivors.
B. If the survivors are in inflatable rafts you should approach from windward to create a lee for the survivors.
C. An inflatable life raft secured alongside can be an effective boarding station for transfer of survivors from the boats.
D. Survivors in the water should never be permitted alongside due to the possibility of injury from the vessel.

01953. Which of the following is likely to occur when you are surging synthetic mooring lines on the gypsyhead during mooring operations?

A. The lines may jam and then jump off the gypsyhead.
B. If there is sudden strain on the line, the man tending the line may be pulled into the gypsyhead.
C. The line's surging may caused the vessel to surge.
D. The heat generated may cause the lines to temporarily fuse to the gypsyhead.

01957. The strake of shell plating indicated by letter H in illustration D033DG is known as the:

A. sheer strake
B. outboard keel plate
C. garboard strake
D. bilge strake

01958. When tandem tug towing, the more powerful of the 2 tugs should be:

A. the lead tug
B. behind the lead tug
C. towing at a right angle to the smaller tug
D. towing at a faster speed than the smaller tug

01960. The knot lettered G in illustration DO30DG is a:

A. round turn and 2 half hitches
B. fisherman's bend
C. timber hitch
D. barrel hitch

01961. Why is it necessary to veer a sufficient amount of chain when anchoring a vessel?

A. to insure that the vessel has enough room to swing while at anchor
B. to insure that the anchor flukes bite into the ocean bottom
C. to insure that there is sufficient weight from the anchor and chain to prevent dragging
D. to insure that there is more chain out than there is in the chain locker

01962. The maximum draft to which a vessel can legally be submerged is indicated by the:

A. load line mark
B. Certificate of Inspection
C. Station Bill
D. tonnage mark

01963. What should you do to a line to prevent fraying where it passes over the side of the vessel?

A. worm that part of the line
B. splice that part of the line
C. cover it with chafing gear
D. install a cleat

01964. You have taken another vessel in tow. You can tell that the towing speed is too fast when the:

A. vessels are not in step
B. towline feels like it is "jumping" when touched
C. catenary comes clear of the water
D. towed vessel yaws excessively

01966. The turning circle of a vessel making a turn of over 360° is the path followed by the:

A. bow
B. bridge
C. center of gravity
D. centerline

01969. If you shorten the scope of anchor cable, your anchor's holding power:

A. decreases
B. increases
C. remains the same
D. the scope has no relation to an anchor's holding power

01970. The structural member indicated by the letter L in illustration D033DG is known as a(n):

A. web frame
B. bilge keel
C. side keel
D. longitudinal

01973. Which statement is TRUE about placing the eyes of 2 mooring lines on the same bollard?

A. Put one line at the low point and one at the high point of the bollard so they don't touch.
B. Take the eye of the second line up through the eye of the first line before putting the second line on the bollard.
C. Never put 2 mooring lines on the same bollard.
D. The mooring line forward should be put on the bollard first.

01975. The knot lettered F in illustration DO30DG is a:

A. becket bend
B. square knot
C. fisherman's bend
D. round turn and 2 half hitches

01976. A longitudinal is indicated by what letter in illustration D033DG?

A. c
B. e
C. l
D. m

01978. When towing, the least amount of tension will be on each bridle leg when the 2 legs:

A. form a large angle with each other
B. form a small angle with each other
C. are of unequal length
D. are joined by a fishplate

01979. Which is a proper size block to use with a 3-inch circumference manila line?

A. 6-inch cheek, 4-inch sheave
B. 8-inch cheek, any size sheave
C. 9-inch cheek, 6-inch sheave
D. at least 12-inch sheave

01980. What is the name of the mark indicated by the letter C in illustration DOO3DG?

A. fresh water line
B. tropical water line
C. summer water line
D. winter North Atlantic water line

01981. The boom stops are installed on a crane to:

A. prevent the boom from being raised too high
B. prevent the boom from swinging
C. support the boom when not in use
D. prevent the boom from being lowered

01982. You are using tackle number 8 in illustration DO29DG to lift a weight of 100 lb. If you include 10% of the weight for each sheave for friction, what is the pull on the hauling part required to lift the weight?

A. 120 lb.
B. 55 lb.
C. 40 lb.
D. 37 lb.

01983. When a line is subject to wear where it passes through a mooring chock, it should be:

A. wormed, parceled and served
B. wrapped with heavy tape
C. wrapped with chafing gear
D. wrapped in leather

01984. Your load line certificate expires on 27 May 1988. The vessel is surveyed on that date and is found satisfactory. You are sailing foreign the same day. Which of the following statements is TRUE?

A. A new certificate must be issued before you sail.
B. The existing certificate is endorsed as valid for a 5 year period commencing 27 May 1988.
C. The existing certificate is extended for a period of up to 150 days.
D. The existing certificate is extended until the first foreign port of call where a new certificate will be issued by the local surveyor.

01985. You are on a 165' long vessel with a draft of 9' and twin screws. Which of the following statements about rescuing a survivor in the water with ship pickup is TRUE?

should stop to windward of the man
...rift down on him.
...ou should stop with the man on your
...ather beam and twist the ship up to him.
...A pickup off the weather bow gives maxi-
...ium maneuverability with the least possibil-
ty of injury to the man.
D. Ship pickup should never be used with a
shallow draft vessel.

01988. When towing, what is the advantage
of using a chain bridle on a wire hawser?

A. It makes for an easy connection.
B. It gives a spring effect to cushion the shock.
C. It eliminates the necessity of a swivel.
D. It doesn't require chafing gear.

01989. If you were to pass a stopper on a wire
rope, what should the stopper be made of?

A. wire
B. manila
C. nylon
D. chain

01993. The usual method of arranging a line
on deck so that it will run out easily without
kinking or fouling is:

A. coiling the line
B. faking down the line
C. flemishing the line
D. racking the line

01994. The space indicated by the letter J in
illustration D033DG is known as the:

A. double bottom
B. flooding barrier
C. floor space
D. bilge tank

01995. The single turn method of returning
to a man overboard should be used only if:

A. the man is reported missing rather than
immediately seen as he falls overboard
B. the vessel is very maneuverable
C. the conning officer is inexperienced
D. a boat will be used to recover the man

01996. Which of the following methods should
be used to secure a manila line to a bitt?

A. a round turn on the bitt farthest from the
strain and then figure-eights
B. a round turn on the bitt closest to the
strain and then figure-eights
C. figure-eights and then a round turn at the
top of both bitts
D. only figure-eights are necessary on both bitts

01997. What is the name of tackle number 12
in illustration DO29DG?

A. threefold purchase
B. davit tackle
C. deck tackle
D. gin tackle

01998. When towing in an open seaway, it is
important to use a towing line:

A. made only of wire rope, due to possible
weather conditions
B. that will have the tow on a crest while your
vessel is in a trough
C. that will have the tow on a crest while your
vessel is on a crest
D. with little dip to gain maximum control of
the tow

02000. The vessel in illustration D025DG has
broken down and you are going to take her in
tow. The wind is coming from her starboard
beam. Both vessels are making the same
amount of leeway. Where should you position
your vessel when you start running lines?

A. a
B. b
C. c
D. d

02001. You are using tackle number 9 in illustration DO29DG to lift a weight of 120 lb. If
you include 10% of the weight for each
sheave for friction, what is the pull on the
hauling part required to lift the weight?

A. 52 lb.
B. 39 lb.
C. 30 lb.
D. 27 lb.

02002. The structural member indicated by
the letter K in illustration D033DG was fitted
in segments between continuous longitudinals. It is known as what type of floor?

A. intercostal
B. open
C. lightened
D. nonwatertight

02003. Chafing gear is used to:

A. anchor the boat
B. pick up heavy loads
C. protect fiber rope from abrasion
D. strengthen mooring lines

02004. Which of the following statements concerning a man overboard emergency is FALSE?

A. In small, shallow-draft vessels, the man
overboard should be picked up on the
weather bow.
B. The ship pickup is difficult with very large
vessels due to the lack of maneuverability.
C. You should always place your vessel upwind
of a survivor in the water to create a lee.
D. The ship pickup is faster than using a small
boat.

02005. A block that can be opened at the
hook or shackle end to receive a bight of the
line is a:

A. bight block
B. gin block
C. heel block
D. snatch block

02007. The command "shift your rudder" means:

A. double your rudder angle or go to full rudder
B. change from right rudder to left rudder an
equal number of degrees
C. bring your rudder amidships
D. check the swing of the vessel

02008. When towing another vessel, the
length of the towing line should be:

A. as long as possible
B. as short as possible under the circum-
stances and not over 2 wave lengths
C. such that one vessel will be on a crest while
the other is in a trough
D. such that the vessels will be in step

02011. The structural member indicated by
the letter K in illustration D033DG is a:

A. longitudinal frame
B. stringer
C. girder
D. floor

02013. A mooring line that checks forward
motion of a vessel at a pier is a:

A. bow line
B. forward bow line
C. stern line
D. stern breast line

02014. From illustration DO29DG, you are
using tackle number 12 to lift a weight. The
hauling part of this tackle is bent to the
weight hook (w) of tackle number 2. What is
the mechanical advantage of this rig?

A. 9
B. 10
C. 14
D. 21

02016. The revolving drum of a winch used to haul lines is called a:

A. bull gear
B. gypsyhead
C. spanner
D. wildcat

02018. When towing astern, one way to reduce yawing of the tow is to:

A. trim the tow by the stern
B. trim the tow by the head
C. have the tow on an even keel
D. list the tow on the side it is yawing

02020. To facilitate passing the end of a large rope through a block, you could use a:

A. gantline
B. head line
C. reeving line
D. sail line

02022. In determining the scope of cable to be used when anchoring, which of the following should NOT be considered?

A. depth of the water
B. character of the holding ground
C. advance and transfer at low speeds
D. type of anchor cable

02023. A mooring line leading at nearly right angles to the keel is a:

A. spring line
B. bow line
C. stern line
D. breast line

02025. What is the chief hazard encountered when surging synthetic mooring lines on the gypsyhead during operations?

A. If there is sudden strain, the man tending the line may be pulled into the gypsyhead.
B. The lines may jam and then jump off the gypsyhead.
C. The lines' surging may cause the vessel to surge.
D. The heat generated may cause the lines to temporarily fuse to the gypsyhead.

02027. Your vessel is issued a load line certificate dated 27 May 1987. Which of the following is NOT an acceptable date for one of the surveys for endorsements?

A. 28 February 1988
B. 27 November 1988
C. 26 August 1989
D. 27 May 1990

02028. When making up a long, large coastwise tow, which of the following procedures is INCORRECT?

A. a chain towing bridle is generally preferred
B. safety shackles should be used when connecting to the fishplate
C. rig tripping ropes (retrieving lines)
D. back-up wires are left slack

02029. When anchored, increasing the scope of the anchor chain normally serves to:

A. prevent fouling of the anchor
B. decrease swing of the vessel
C. prevent dragging of the anchor
D. reduce strain on the windlass

02030. Safety equipment on board vessels must be approved by the:

A. U. S. Coast Guard
B. Safety Standards Bureau
C. Occupational Health and Safety Agency (OSHA)
D. National Safety Council

02033. A spring line would lead:

A. fore and aft from the ship's side
B. to the dock at a right angle to the vessel
C. through the bull nose or chock at the bow
D. through the chock at the stern

02034. You are ordering a new block to use with a 3-inch circumference manila line. Which of the following represents a proper size block for this line?

A. 6-inch cheek, 4-inch sheave
B. 8-inch cheek, any size sheave
C. 9-inch cheek, 6-inch sheave
D. block with at least a 12-inch sheave

02037. You are riding to a single anchor. The vessel is yawing excessively. Which action should be taken to reduce the yawing?

A. Veer chain to the riding anchor.
B. Heave to a shorter scope of chain on the riding anchor.
C. Drop the second anchor at the extreme end of the yaw and veer to a short scope on that anchor.
D. Drop the second anchor at the extreme end of the yaw, then adjust the cables until the scope is equal.

02038. With a large ocean tow in heavy weather, you should NOT:

A. keep the stern of the tug well down in the water
B. adjust the towline so the tug is on the crest when the tow is in the trough
C. keep the low point of the catenary in the water
D. use a long towing hawser

02040. The plating indicated by the letter N in illustration D033DG is known as the:

A. inner bottom
B. floor riders
C. tank-top rider plating
D. ceiling

02041. Which tackle arrangement has the LEAST mechanical advantage?

A. single whip
B. gun tackle
C. luff tackle
D. twofold purchase

02043. A mooring line that prevents a boat from moving sideways away from the dock is a:

A. bow line
B. breast line
C. stern line
D. spring line

02045. When relieving the helm, the new helmsman should find it handy to know the:

A. deviation on that heading
B. variation in the area
C. leeway
D. amount of helm carried for a steady course

02046. The structural member indicated by the letter I in illustration D033DG is the:

A. garboard strake
B. center pillar
C. keel
D. girder

02048. The MINIMUM acceptable size for a towing bridle would be that size in which the safe working load (SWL) of each leg of the bridle is equal to:

A. 1/2 the SWL of the main towing hawser
B. 3/4 the SWL of the main towing hawser
C. that of the main towing hawser
D. twice that of the main towing hawser

02050. In illustration D044DG, the mooring line labeled "H" is called a(n):

A. forward breast line
B. offshore spring line
C. onshore bow line
D. offshore bow line

02053. A mooring line leading 45° to the keel, used to check forward or astern movement of a vessel, is called a:

A. spring line
B. warp line
C. bow line
D. breast line

02054. What is the name of the mark indicated by the letter B in illustration D003DG?

A. timber summer mark
B. tropical fresh water line
C. tropical water line
D. summer water line

02058. Which of the following is NOT suitable for use in making up the towing rig for a heavy, long ocean tow?

A. chain
B. ring
C. solid thimble
D. a fishplate

02059. You are handling a mooring line and you are instructed to "Check the line". What should be done?

A. You should ensure the bight is not fouled between ship and dock by taking up slack.
B. The line is paid out smartly and kept free for running.
C. The line should be secured by adding more turns and then the area should be cleared.
D. The line is surged so that it maintains a strain without parting.

02061. A sheave is a:

A. grooved wheel in a block
B. line to hold a lifeboat next to the embarkation deck
C. partial load of grain
D. seaman's knife

02062. The vessel in illustration D025DG has broken down, and you are going to take her in tow. The wind is coming from her starboard beam. She is making more leeway than you. Where should you position your vessel when you start running lines?

A. a
B. b
C. c
D. d

02063. A "spring line" is:

A. any wire rope used for mooring
B. a fire-warp
C. a mooring line running diagonally to the keel
D. a mooring line perpendicular to the keel

02064. While underway in thick fog you are on watch and hear the cry "man overboard". What type of maneuver should you make?

A. be sure the man is clear, back down until stopped, then send a boat
B. round turn
C. racetrack turn
D. Williamson turn

02065. A continual worsening of the list or trim indicates:

A. negative GM
B. progressive flooding
C. structural failure
D. an immediate need to ballast

02067. What is the mechanical advantage of tackle number 12 in illustration DO29DG?

A. 3.0
B. 5.5
C. 6.0
D. 7.0

02068. You intend to tow a barge with 1 tug and expect continuous high winds from the north. To reduce the yaw of your tow, you should:

A. reduce the draft of the barge
B. shorten one leg of the bridle
C. place bulky deck loads as far aft as possible
D. trim the barge down by the bow

02069. A "spring line" is a:

A. mooring line made of spring lay wire rope
B. mooring line running diagonally to the keel
C. mooring line parallel to the keel
D. wire rope used for securing an anchor buoy

02070. Which of the following statements about the Williamson turn is FALSE?

A. It requires the highest degree of shiphandling skills to accomplish.
B. It is the slowest of methods used in turning the vessel.
C. It is the best turn to use when the victim is not in sight due to reduced visibility.
D. It returns the vessel to the original track line on a reciprocal course.

02073. When rigging a bosun's chair on a stay with a shackle:

A. mouse the shackle to the chair
B. never allow the shackle pin to ride on the stay
C. secure it with small stuff
D. seize the end of the shackle

02075. The knot E in illustration DO30DG is a:

A. stopper hitch
B. blackwall hitch
C. timber hitch and half hitch
D. bowline on a bight

02076. A person who sees someone fall overboard should:

A. immediately jump in the water to assist the individual
B. go to the bridge for the distress flares
C. run to the radio room to send an emergency message
D. call for help and keep the individual in sight

02078. While towing, bridle legs of unequal lengths may cause:

A. the bridle to foul
B. the shorter leg to fail
C. chafing on the fairlead or bitts
D. a bent swivel

02081. A seaman is reported missing in the morning and was last seen after coming off the mid-watch. What type of turn would you use to return to the track line?

A. Williamson
B. racetrack
C. 180° turn
D. Anderson

02083. You are in a lifeboat with a standing lugsail set. In order to reef the sail, you must NOT:

A. shift the sheet to the reef cringle
B. gather the loose part of the foot of the sail before passing the reef points
C. shift the tack to the side opposite to where it is presently set
D. secure the reef points under the sail

02086. What is the mechanical advantage of tackle number 11 in illustration DO29DG?

A. 7.0
B. 6.0
C. 5.5
D. 5.0

02088. You have been towing on a hawser astern and have just let go the tow. Your deckhands are pulling in and faking the towing hawser by hand on the stern. The most dangerous action to take at this time would be to:

A. continue ahead at slow speed
B. continue ahead at half speed
C. stop your engines
D. back down on your engines

02093. What is the mechanical advantage of tackle number 10 in illustration DO29DG?

A. 4.0
B. 4.5
C. 5.0
D. 5.5

02095. You are using a racetrack turn to recover a man overboard. The vessel is first steadied when how many degrees away from the original heading?

A. 60° to 70°
B. 90°
C. 135°
D. 180°

02097. What is the name of tackle number 11 in illustration DO29DG?

A. 3-2 purchase
B. double luff tackle
C. gun tackle
D. topping lift

02098. Snow has obliterated surface features and the sky is covered with uniform, altostratus clouds. There are no shadows and the horizon has disappeared. What is this condition called?

A. ice blink
B. whiteout
C. water sky
D. aurora reflection

02100. The primary purpose of a load line is to establish required:

A. freeboard
B. drafts
C. transverse stability
D. fresh water allowances

02102. A seaman deserts the vessel in a foreign port. What should the Master do with any of the deserter's personal effects remaining on board?

A. sell them at auction and deposit the money in the ship's morale or welfare fund
B. donate them to a local charity upon return to the United States
C. transfer them to the custody of the Secretary of the Dept. of Transportation
D. inventory them, make an appropriate entry in the Official Logbook and dispose of them at sea

02104. You are proceeding to a distress site where the survivors are in life rafts. Which of the following actions will assist in making your ship more visible to survivors?

A. steering a zigzag course with 5 to 10 minutes on each leg
B. steering a sinuous course
C. hoisting all the code flags
D. making smoke in daylight

02106. Under which of the following conditions would a racetrack turn be superior to a Williamson turn in a man overboard situation?

A. The man has been missing for a period of time.
B. The sea water is very cold and the man is visible.
C. There is thick fog.
D. The wind was from astern on the original course.

02107. What is the name of the mark indicated by the letter A in illustration D003DG?

A. Winter North Atlantic water line
B. fresh water line
C. deck line
D. Plimsoll mark

02111. You are coming to anchor in 16 fathoms of water. In this case, on a small to medium size vessel, the:

A. anchor may be dropped from the hawsepipe
B. anchor should be lowered to within 2 fathoms of the bottom before being dropped
C. scope should always be at least 10 times the depth of the water.
D. scope should always be less than 5 times the depth of the water

02112. Which of the following is NOT surveyed at an annual load line survey?

A. the overall structure and layout of the vessel for alterations to the superstructure
B. the bilge pumping system
C. main deck hatch covers
D. portholes and deadlights in the side plating

02113. One major advantage of the round turn in a man overboard situation is that it:

A. is the fastest method
B. is easy for a single-screw vessel to perform
C. requires the least shiphandling skills to perform
D. can be used in reduced visibility

02116. What is the name of tackle number 10 in illustration DO29DG?

A. 2-2 purchase
B. deck purchase
C. twofold purchase
D. double runner

02117. When a vessel is involved in a casualty, the cost of property damage includes the:

A. cost of labor and material to restore the vessel to the service condition which existed prior to the casualty
B. loss of revenues while the vessel is being repaired, up to a maximum of $50,000
C. damage claims awarded to individuals or companies involved in the casualty, up to a maximum of $50,000
D. all of the above

02119. You are coming to anchor in 8 fathoms of water. In this case, the:

A. anchor may be dropped from the hawsepipe
B. anchor should be lowered to within 2 fathoms of the bottom before being dropped
C. anchor should be lowered to the bottom then the ship backed and the remainder of the cable veered
D. scope should be less than 3 times the depth of the water

02122. What is the name of tackle number 9 in illustration DO29DG?

A. single purchase
B. 1-2 tackle
C. double whip
D. luff tackle

02124. You are on watch aboard a vessel heading NW with the wind from dead ahead, in heavy seas. You notice a man fall overboard from the starboard bow. Which of the following actions would NOT be appropriate?

A. hard right rudder
B. throw a life buoy to the man, if possible
C. send a man aloft
D. get the port boat ready

02126. You have anchored in a mud and clay bottom. The anchor appears to be dragging in a storm. What action should you take?

A. Shorten the scope of the cable.
B. Veer cable to the anchor.
C. Drop the other anchor underfoot.
D. Drop the second anchor, veer to a good scope, then weigh the first anchor.

02127. With a man overboard, the type of maneuver to use to return your vessel to the man in the shortest time is:

A. a Williamson Turn
B. engine(s) crash astern, no turn
C. a single turn with hard rudder
D. two 180° turns

02130. In a racetrack turn, to recover a man overboard, the vessel is steadied for the second time after a turn of how many degrees from the original heading?

A. 60
B. 135
C. 180
D. 360

02135. A load line certificate is valid for how many years?

A. 1
B. 2
C. 3
D. 5

02144. "Hard right rudder" means:

A. jam the rudder against the stops
B. put the rudder over quickly to 15° right rudder
C. meet a swing to the right, then return to amidships
D. put the rudder over to the right all the way

02146. On a single-screw vessel with a right-handed propeller, when the vessel is going full speed astern with full right rudder, the bow will swing:

A. quickly to port, then more slowly to port
B. to port
C. slowly to port, then quickly to starboard
D. to starboard

02147. What is the name of tackle number 8 in illustration DO29DG?

A. parbuckle
B. gun tackle
C. single purchase
D. single luff tackle

02149. When anchoring in a clay bottom, what is one hazard that may cause the anchor to drag?

A. The flukes may dig in unevenly and capsize the anchor when under stress.
B. The flukes may not dig in.
C. The anchor may get shod with clay and not develop full holding power.
D. The anchor will tend to dig in and come to rest near the vertical.

02150. The vessel in illustration D025DG has broken down and you are going to take her in tow. The wind is coming from her starboard beam. You are making more leeway than she. Where should you position your vessel when you start running lines?

A. a
B. b
C. c
D. d

02157. You are in a fresh water port loading logs with gear rated at 5 tons, and suspect the weight of the logs exceeds the SWL of the gear. The logs are floating in the water alongside the vessel and have 95% of their volume submerged. The average length of the logs is 15 feet and the average diameter is 4.4 feet. What is the nearest average weight of the logs, based on these average measurements?

A. 5.5 tons
B. 6.0 tons
C. 7.7 tons
D. 24.1 tons

02159. What is the mechanical advantage of tackle number 9 in illustration DO29DG?

A. 1
B. 2
C. 3
D. 4

02163. What is the name of tackle number 7 in illustration DO29DG?

A. runner
B. inverted whip
C. whip
D. single purchase

02168. What is the name of tackle number 6 in illustration DO29DG?

A. triple purchase
B. clew garnet tackle
C. boat falls
D. threefold purchase

02169. What is the mechanical advantage of tackle number 8 in illustration DO29DG?

A. 3.0
B. 1.5
C. 1.0
D. 0.5

02173. What is the name of tackle number 5 in illustration DO29DG?

A. 3-2 purchase
B. double luff tackle
C. twofold purchase
D. fourfold whip

02179. A design modification of an anchor chain which prevents kinking is the:

A. detachable link
B. stud link
C. kenter link
D. connecting link

02181. When relieving the helm, the new helmsman should know the:

A. course per magnetic steering compass
B. gyro error
C. variation
D. maximum rudder angle previously used

02182. What is the name of tackle number 4 in illustration DO29DG?

A. double whip
B. luff tackle
C. twofold purchase
D. 2-2 tackle

02185. You are using tackle number 7 in illustration DO29DG to lift a weight of 100 lb. If you include 10% of the weight for each sheave for friction, what is the pull on the hauling part required to lift the weight?

A. 200 lb.
B. 150 lb.
C. 110 lb.
D. 55 lb.

02186. What is the mechanical advantage of tackle number 7 in illustration DO29DG?

A. 0.0
B. 0.5
C. 1.0
D. 2.0

02187. From illustration DO29DG, you are using tackle number 10 to lift a weight. The hauling part of this tackle is bent to the weight hook (w) of tackle number 5. What is the mechanical advantage of this rig?

A. 25
B. 20
C. 15
D. 10

02189. You are conducting trials to determine the maneuvering characteristics of your vessel. While making a turn you take the ranges and bearings of an isolated light with the results shown in illustration D034DG. Based on this information, what is the transfer for a turn of 75°?

A. 340 yards
B. 280 yards
C. 230 yards
D. 190 yards

02190. What is the name of tackle number 3 in illustration DO29DG?

A. 1-2 purchase
B. gun tackle
C. single luff tackle
D. double whip

02191. A wooden deck installed on top of the plating, N, in illustration D033DG is known as:

A. spar decking
B. furring
C. ceiling
D. flooring

02192. The component on a windlass which physically engages the chain during haul in or pay out is the:

A. devil's claw
B. bull gear
C. wildcat
D. cat head

02193. You have determined the maneuvering characteristics of your vessel by taking the radar ranges and bearings of an isolated light while making a turn. The results are listed in illustration D035DG. Based on this data what is the tactical diameter of the turning circle?

A. 755 yards
B. 780 yards
C. 820 yards
D. 880 yards

02194. What is the mechanical advantage of tackle number 6 in illustration DO29DG?

A. 6.0
B. 5.5
C. 5.0
D. 3.0

02195. You have determined the maneuvering characteristics of your vessel by taking the radar ranges and bearings of an isolated light while making a turn. The results are listed in illustration D035DG. Based on this data what is the transfer for a turn of 180°?

A. 745 yards
B. 770 yards

C. 840 yards
D. 890 yards

02196. From illustration DO29DG, you are using tackle number 10 to lift a weight. The hauling part of this tackle is bent to the weight hook (w) of tackle number 4. What is the mechanical advantage of this rig?

A. 24
B. 20
C. 13
D. 9

02198. You are conducting trials to determine the maneuvering characteristics of your vessel. While making a turn, you take ranges and bearings of an isolated light with the results shown in illustration D034DG. Based on this information, what is the transfer for a turn of 90°?

A. 355 yards
B. 380 yards
C. 410 yards
D. 455 yards

02199. What is the name of tackle number 2 in illustration DO29DG?

A. whip
B. onefold purchase
C. single purchase
D. gun tackle

02203. A Chinese stopper (2 lines) will hold best when you:

A. fasten the bitter ends to the mooring line with half hitches
B. twist the ends together and hold them in the direction of the pull
C. twist the ends together and hold them in the direction opposite to the pull
D. twist the ends together and hold them at right angles to the mooring line

02204. In writing up the logbook at the end of your watch, you make an error in writing an entry. What is the proper means of correcting this error?

A. Blot out the error completely and rewrite the entry correctly.
B. Carefully and neatly erase the entry and rewrite it correctly.
C. Cross out the error with a single line, and write the correct entry, then initial it.
D. Remove this page of the log book, and rewrite all entries on a clean page.

02206. You are using tackle number 6 in illustration DO29DG to lift a weight of 300 lb. If you include 10% of the weight for each

sheave for friction, what is the pull on the hauling part required to lift the weight?

A. 80 lb.
B. 69 lb.
C. 55 lb.
D. 50 lb.

02211. What is the mechanical advantage of tackle number 5 in illustration DO29DG?

A. 2.0
B. 4.0
C. 5.0
D. 5.5

02212. You have determined the maneuvering characteristics of your vessel by taking the radar ranges and bearings of an isolated light while making a turn. The results are listed in illustration D035DG. Based on this data what is the advance for a turn of 30°?

A. 380 yards
B. 420 yards
C. 470 yards
D. 525 yards

02213. From illustration DO29DG, you are using tackle number 6 to lift a weight. The hauling part of this tackle is bent to the weight hook (w) of tackle number 8. What is the mechanical advantage of this rig?

A. 11
B. 16
C. 18
D. 24

02214. You are conducting trials to determine the maneuvering characteristics of your vessel. While making a turn, you take ranges and bearings of an isolated light with the results shown in illustration D034DG. Based on this information, what is the advance for a turn of 90°?

A. 820 yards
B. 870 yards
C. 930 yards
D. 975 yards

02216. What is the mechanical advantage of tackle number 4 in illustration DO29DG?

A. 1
B. 2
C. 3
D. 4

02217. The knot lettered P in illustration DO30DG is a:

A. rolling hitch
B. clove hitch
C. round turn and 2 half hitches
D. marline hitch

02219. You are using tackle number 5 in illustration DO29DG to lift a weight of 300 lb. If you include 10% of the weight for each sheave for friction, what is the pull on the hauling part required to lift the weight?

A. 50 lb.
B. 75 lb.
C. 90 lb.
D. 112 lb.

02221. From illustration D029DG, you are using tackle number 5 to lift a weight. The hauling part of this tackle is bent to the weight hook (w) of tackle number 8. What is the mechanical advantage of this rig?

A. 20
B. 15
C. 10
D. 5

02222. The lower seam of the strake indicated by the letter B in illustration D033DG is sometimes riveted. This is done to:

A. increase the strength in a highly stressed area
B. provide the flexibility inherent in a riveted seam
C. serve as a crack arrestor and prevent hull girder failure
D. reduce construction costs

02223. What is the mechanical advantage of tackle number 3 in illustration DO29DG?

A. 1
B. 2
C. 3
D. 4

02224. When improperly tied, what knot shown in illustration DO30DG is called a granny or thief's knot?

A. f
B. m
C. r
D. w

02225. Which of the knots in illustration DO30DG should be used to secure a line to a spar when the pull is perpendicular to the spar?

A. e
B. f
C. n
D. p

02226. The knot lettered O in illustration DO30DG is a:

A. timber hitch
B. barrel hitch
C. carrick bend
D. blackwall hitch

02227. You are using tackle number 4 in illustration DO29DG to lift a weight of 120 lb. If you include 10% of the weight for each sheave for friction, what is the pull on the hauling part required to lift the weight?

A. 20 lb.
B. 30 lb.
C. 42 lb.
D. 57 lb.

02228. You have determined the maneuvering characteristics of your vessel by taking the radar ranges and bearings of an isolated light while making a turn. The results are listed in illustration D035DG. Based on this data what is the transfer for a turn of 60°?

A. 140 yards
B. 180 yards
C. 225 yards
D. 270 yards

02229. From illustration DO29DG, you are using tackle number 5 to lift a weight. The hauling part of this tackle is bent to the weight hook (w) of tackle number 9. What is the mechanical advantage of this rig?

A. 20
B. 9
C. 5
D. 4

02230. What is the name of tackle number 1 in illustration DO29DG?

A. whip
B. onefold purchase
C. gun tackle
D. runner

02231. What is the mechanical advantage of tackle number 2 in illustration DO29DG?

A. 0.5
B. 1.0
C. 2.0
D. 3.0

02232. The main use of the knot lettered M in illustration DO30DG is to:

A. marry 2 hawsers
B. form a temporary eye in the end of a line

C. secure a heaving line to a hawser
D. provide a seat for a man to work over the side

02233. The knot lettered N in illustration DO30DG is a:

A. timber hitch
B. rolling bowline
C. stopper
D. heaving line hitch

02235. You are conducting trials to determine the maneuvering characteristics of your vessel. While making a turn, you take ranges and bearings of an isolated light with the results shown in illustration D034DG. Based on this information, what is the advance for a turn of 75°?

A. 800 yards
B. 860 yards
C. 910 yards
D. 955 yards

02236. Another name for the garboard strake is the:

A. A strake
B. Z strake
C. side keel plate
D. stringer plate

02238. What is the area of a circle with a radius of 12 feet after a sector of 60° has been removed?

A. 18.85 sq. ft.
B. 75.40 sq. ft.
C. 94.25 sq. ft.
D. 376.99 sq. ft.

02239. You are using tackle number 3 in illustration DO29DG to lift a weight of 120 lb. If you include 10% of the weight for each sheave for friction, what is the pull on the hauling part required to lift the weight?

A. 52 lb.
B. 49 lb.
C. 40 lb.
D. 27 lb.

02240. What is the mechanical advantage of tackle number 1 in illustration DO29DG?

A. 0.5
B. 1.0
C. 1.5
D. 2.0

02241. The letter M in illustration D033DG indicates a(n):

A. web frame
B. intercostal
C. stringer
D. cant frame

02242. What is the area of a circle with a radius of 21' after a sector of 120° has been removed?

A. 115.45 sq. ft.
B. 230.91 sq. ft.
C. 461.81 sq. ft.
D. 923.63 sq. ft.

02243. From illustration DO29DG, you are using tackle number 4 to lift a weight. The hauling part of this tackle is bent to the weight hook (w) of tackle number 11. What is the mechanical advantage of this rig?

A. 4
B. 6
C. 10
D. 24

02247. The knot lettered M in illustration DO30DG is a:

A. stopper
B. lashing
C. becket bend
D. carrick bend

02249. Which of the knots in illustration DO30DG should be used to secure a line to a spar when the pull is parallel to the spar?

A. g
B. f
C. p
D. q

02250. You have determined the maneuvering characteristics of your vessel by taking radar ranges and bearings of an isolated light while making a turn. The results are listed in illustration D035DG. Based on this data what is the transfer for a turn of 90°?

A. 380 yards
B. 430 yards
C. 485 yards
D. 525 yards

02251. In illustration D033DG, letter I indicates the keel. Which of the following plates is NOT part of the keel?

A. center vertical keel
B. rider plate
C. longitudinal girder
D. flat plate keel

02253. What is the area of a circle with a radius of 17 ft. after a sector of 57° has been removed?

A. 764.17 sq. ft.
B. 190.66 sq. ft.
C. 145.27 sq. ft.
D. 36.85 sq. ft.

02254. From illustration DO29DG, you are using tackle number 4 to lift a weight. The hauling part of this tackle is bent to the weight hook (w) of tackle number 10. What is the mechanical advantage of this rig?

A. 4
B. 5
C. 9
D. 20

02255. You are using tackle number 2 in illustration DO29DG to lift a weight of 100 lb. If you include 10% of the weight for each sheave for friction, what is the pull on the hauling part required to lift the weight?

A. 50 lb.
B. 55 lb.
C. 60 lb.
D. 110 lb.

02256. You are conducting trials to determine the maneuvering characteristics of your vessel. While making a turn, you take ranges and bearings of an isolated light with the results shown in illustration D034DG. Based on this information, what is the transfer for a turn of 180°?

A. 875 yards
B. 910 yards
C. 975 yards
D. 1015 yards

02258. The knot lettered L in illustration DO30DG is a:

A. square knot
B. double blackwall hitch
C. fisherman's bend
D. timber hitch

02259. You have determined the maneuvering characteristics of your vessel by taking radar ranges and bearings of an isolated light while making a turn. The results are listed in illustration D035DG. Based on this data what is the advance for a turn of 90°?

A. 490 yards
B. 350 yards
C. 800 yards
D. 885 yards

02261. The machinery associated with heaving in and running out anchor chain is the:

A. winch
B. windlass
C. draw works
D. dynamic pay out system

02263. You are using tackle number 1 in illustration DO29DG to lift a weight of 100 lb. If you include 10% of the weight for each sheave for friction, what is the pull on the hauling part required to lift the weight?

A. 50 lb.
B. 55 lb.
C. 100 lb.
D. 110 lb.

02264. When you "end for end" a wire rope, you:

A. cut off the free end and bitter end of the rope
B. splice 2 wire ropes together
C. remove the wire rope from the drum and reverse it so that the free end becomes the bitter end
D. remove the wire rope from the drum and turn it over, so the wire bends in the opposite direction

02265. You are conducting trials to determine the maneuvering characteristics of your vessel. While making a turn, you take ranges and bearings of an isolated light with the results shown in illustration D034DG. Based on this information, what is the transfer for a turn of 45°?

A. 130 yards
B. 165 yards
C. 195 yards
D. 230 yards

02267. The knot lettered K in illustration DO30DG is a:

A. sailmaker's whipping
B. carrick bend
C. barrel hitch
D. stopper

02268. The helm command "shift your rudder" means:

A. check the swing of the vessel
B. double your rudder angle or go to full rudder
C. bring your rudder amidships
D. change from right rudder to left rudder an equal number of degrees

02269. You are on a single-screw left-handed propeller vessel. When you have full sternway with left full rudder, you should expect the stern to swing:

A. quickly to starboard, then slowly to port
B. slowly to port, then quickly to starboard
C. to port
D. to starboard

02272. Which of the knots shown in illustration D030DG is secure only when there is a strain on the line?

A. h
B. i
C. l
D. p

02273. What is the area of a circle with a radius of 4 ft. after a sector of 111° has been removed?

A. 3.90 sq. ft.
B. 8.67 sq. ft.
C. 34.77 sq. ft.
D. 50.27 sq. ft.

02275. When inspecting wire rope before a hoisting operation, one must look for:

A. fishhooks
B. kinks
C. worn spots
D. all of the above

02276. You have determined the maneuvering characteristics of your vessel by taking the radar ranges and bearings of an isolated light while making a turn. The results are listed in illustration D035DG. Based on this data what is the advance for a turn of 60°?

A. 665 yards
B. 710 yards
C. 745 yards
D. 780 yards

02280. You are conducting trials to determine the maneuvering characteristics of your vessel. While making a turn, you take ranges and bearings of an isolated light with the results shown in illustration D034DG. Based on this information, what is the advance for a turn of 45°?

A. 590 yards
B. 635 yards
C. 690 yards
D. 740 yards

02283. What is the area of a circle with a radius of 2 ft. after a sector of 86° has been removed?

A. 2.39 sq. ft.
B. 3.02 sq. ft.
C. 9.55 sq. ft.
D. 12.57 sq. ft.

02284. In determining the scope of anchor line to pay out when anchoring a small boat, one must consider the:

A. charted depth of water only
B. depth of water, including tidal differences
C. type of line being used for the anchor rope
D. type of anchor being used

02285. In writing up the logbook at the end of your watch, you make an error in writing an entry. What is the proper means of correcting this error?

A. Remove this page of the log book, and rewrite all entries on a clean page.
B. Carefully and neatly erase the entry and rewrite it correctly.
C. Blot out the error completely and rewrite the entry correctly.
D. Cross out the error with a single line, and write the correct entry, then initial it.

02288. Which of the following will cause wire rope to fail?

A. operating the winch too fast
B. using a sheave of 9 times the wire's diameter
C. kinking
D. all of the above

02290. The sprocket teeth on a wildcat are known as the:

A. pawls
B. devil's claws
C. whelps
D. pockets

02292. The biggest problem encountered when towing bridle legs are too short is:

A. retrieval
B. adjusting tension
C. excessive strain
D. hookup to main tow line

02301. In towing, chocks are used to:

A. protect the tow line from chafing
B. secure the end of the tow line on the tug
C. stop off the tow line while retrieving it
D. absorb shock loading on the tow line

02302. Which of the following is NOT required to be approved or certified by the U. S. Coast Guard before being used on inspected vessels?

A. lifesaving equipment that is in excess of the regulatory minimum
B. ship's stores that are hazardous in nature
C. steel plate used in hull construction
D. EPIRBs

02305. Which of the following will cause a wire rope to fail?

A. using a medium graphite grease as a lubricant
B. operating a winch too slow
C. using a sheave with an undersized throat
D. a sheave diameter of 24 times the wire's diameter

02315. Which of the following splices should you use to connect 2 separate lines together?

A. back splice
B. chain splice
C. eye splice
D. long splice

02316. A lookout can leave his station:

A. at any time
B. at the end of the watch
C. 15 minutes before the end of the watch
D. ONLY when properly relieved

02325. Which line cannot be spliced?

A. braided line with a hollow core
B. double-braided line
C. braided line with a solid core
D. any line can be spliced

02335. When 2 lines are spliced together:

A. the size of the lines at the splice decreases
B. they are stronger than if knotted together
C. the overall strength of each line is increased
D. the bitter ends will resist rotting

02341. The grooved wheel inside a block is called a:

A. cheek
B. gypsy
C. sheave
D. drum

02342. How many tons of salt water can be loaded into a flat ended cylindrical tank with a diameter of 3 feet and a length of 8 feet?

A. 1.62
B. 1.98
C. 3.23
D. 6.46

02343. When securing a hook to the end of a wire rope you should use:

A. a bowline knot
B. a long splice
C. an overhand knot with a wire rope clip
D. wire rope clips with a thimble eye

02344. An example of a stock anchor is a:

A. bruce anchor
B. flipper Delta anchor
C. hook anchor
D. IWT anchor

02345. A splice that can be used in running rigging, where the line will pass through blocks, is a:

A. short splice
B. long splice
C. back splice
D. spindle splice

02346. What is the volume of a sphere with a radius of 11 feet?

A. 506.75 cu. ft.
B. 696.78 cu. ft.
C. 5,575.28 cu. ft.
D. 44,593.82 cu. ft.

02347. What is an advantage of having wire rope with a fiber core over that of a wire rope of the same size with a wire core?

A. Fiber core rope offers greater strength.
B. Fiber core rope offers greater flexibility.
C. Fiber core rope can be used at higher operating temperatures.
D. Fiber core rope is the only type authorized for cargo runners.

02349. What is the volume of a sphere with a radius of 7 feet?

A. 11,491.87 cu. ft.
B. 1,436.76 cu. ft.
C. 963.72 cu. ft.
D. 205.21 cu. ft.

02350. A temporary wire eye splice made with 3 wire rope clamps will hold to approximately what percentage of the total rope strength?

A. 20%
B. 50%
C. 80%
D. 99%

02351. What is the area of a circle with a diameter of 12 ft. after a sector of 86° has been removed?

A. 108.57 sq. ft.
B. 86.08 sq. ft.
C. 28.65 sq. ft.
D. 27.14 sq. ft.

02352. The recessed areas on a wildcat are called:

A. pawls
B. sockets
C. pockets
D. whelps

02353. Which of the following mooring lines would be used to prevent sideways motion of a vessel moored to a pier?

A. a line led forward from the bow
B. a line led aft from the bow
C. a line led in the same direction as the keel
D. a line led at a right angle to the keel

02354. What is the area of a circle with a diameter of 21 ft. after a sector of 72° has been removed?

A. 277.09 sq. ft.
B. 149.43 sq. ft.
C. 69.27 sq. ft.
D. 52.78 sq. ft.

02355. The metal, teardrop-shaped object sometimes used within an eye splice is a:

A. grommet
B. reinforcement
C. splice form
D. thimble

02356. "Hard right rudder" means:

A. jam the rudder against the stops
B. meet a swing to the right, then return to amidships
C. put the rudder over to the right all the way
D. put the rudder over quickly to 15° right rudder

02358. Which is the heaviest grade of canvas?

A. no. 1
B. no. 5
C. no. 7
D. no. 12

02360. Splices made in nylon should:

A. be long splices only
B. have extra tucks taken
C. be short splices only
D. be around a thimble

02365. A 6-strand composite rope made up of alternate fiber and wire strands around a fiber core is called:

A. spring lay
B. lang lay
C. cable lay
D. alternate lay

02367. What is the volume of a sphere with a radius of 5 ft.?

A. 4,188.00 cu. ft.
B. 523.60 cu. ft.
C. 129.62 cu. ft.
D. 65.44 cu. ft.

02384. What is the volume of a sphere with a radius of 3 feet?

A. 113.08 cu. ft.
B. 96.57 cu. ft.
C. 37.69 cu. ft.
D. 28.23 cu. ft.

02387. What is the area of a circle with a diameter of 2 ft. after a sector of 60° has been removed?

A. 0.25 sq. ft.
B. 0.52 sq. ft.
C. 2.09 sq. ft.
D. 2.62 sq. ft.

02388. What is the area of a circle with a diameter of 4 ft. after a sector of 120° has been removed?

A. 2.67 square ft.
B. 4.19 square ft.
C. 8.38 square ft.
D. 10.67 square ft.

02389. What is the area of a circle with a diameter of 17 ft. after a sector of 111° has been removed?

A. 36.94 sq. ft.
B. 156.99 sq. ft.
C. 226.98 sq. ft.
D. 627.47 sq. ft.

02390. Determine the weight of a rectangular piece of 20.4 lb. steel measuring 4 ft. by 6 ft.

A. 204.0 lb.
B. 489.6 lb.
C. 734.4 lb.
D. 979.2 lb.

02391. Determine the weight of a rectangular piece of 40.8 lb. steel measuring 3 ft. by 5 ft.

A. 326.4 lb.
B. 453.6 lb.
C. 612.0 lb.
D. 1224.0 lb.

02392. Determine the weight of a rectangular piece of 12.75 pound steel measuring 5 feet by 8 feet.

A. 510.00 lb.
B. 255.00 lb.
C. 198.89 lb.
D. 165.75 lb.

02393. Determine the weight of a rectangular piece of 25.5 lb. steel measuring 4.5 ft. by 6.7 ft.

A. 285.6 lb.
B. 329.7 lb.
C. 591.2 lb.
D. 768.8 lb.

02394. Determine the area of a triangle with a base of 3.5 ft. and a height of 4.0 ft.

A. 7.0 sq. ft.
B. 7.5 sq. ft.
C. 11.5 sq. ft.
D. 14.0 sq. ft.

02395. Determine the area of a triangle with a base of 4.7 ft. and a height of 6.3 ft.

A. 29.6 sq. ft.
B. 26.2 sq. ft.
C. 18.5 sq. ft.
D. 14.8 sq. ft.

02396. Determine the area of a triangle with a base of 5.8 ft. and a height of 2.1 ft.

A. 12.2 sq. ft.
B. 7.9 sq. ft.
C. 6.1 sq. ft.
D. 3.0 sq. ft.

02397. Determine the area of a triangle with a base of 6.7 ft. and a height of 9.1 ft.

A. 61.0 sq. ft.
B. 30.5 sq. ft.
C. 22.9 sq. ft.
D. 15.8 sq. ft.

02398. how many tons of salt water can be loaded into a flat ended cylindrical tank with a diameter of 4.5 ft. and a length of 8 ft.?

A. 1.82
B. 3.64
C. 7.27
D. 14.54

02400. The turning circle of a vessel is the path followed by the:

A. bow
B. outermost part of the ship while making the circle
C. center of gravity
D. tipping center

02450. Which of the following statements is NOT true concerning precautions during fueling operations?

A. All engines, motors, fans, etc. should be shut down when fueling.
B. All windows, doors, hatches, etc. should be closed.
C. A fire extinguisher should be kept nearby.
D. Fuel tanks should be topped off with no room for expansion.

02451. A safety shackle is identified by its:

A. shape
B. pin
C. certification stamp
D. color code

02454. You are going astern (single-screw, right-handed propeller) with the anchor down at a scope of twice the depth of the water. As the anchor dredges, you should expect the:

A. stern to walk to the same side as the anchor being used
B. vessel to back in a straight line
C. stern to walk to port but at a reduced rate
D. stern to walk to port at a faster rate than normal

02456. Which term describes a part of a natural fiber line?

A. lacings
B. lays
C. strands
D. twines

02459. Tripping defects in anchors frequently occur in:

A. deep water
B. shallow water
C. stiff soils
D. soft soils

02460. You are operating a twin-screw vessel and lose your port engine. You continue to operate on your starboard engine only. What action would you take to move your vessel ahead in a straight line?

A. compensate with right rudder
B. compensate with left rudder
C. surging the starboard engine
D. rudder amidships - no compensation necessary on twin-screw vessel

02461. In writing up the logbook at the end of your watch, you make an error in writing an entry. What is the proper means of correcting this error?

A. Carefully and neatly erase the entry and rewrite it correctly.
B. Cross out the error with a single line, and write the correct entry, then initial it.
C. Blot out the error completely and rewrite the entry correctly.
D. Remove this page of the log book, and rewrite all entries on a clean page.

02462. Which term describes a part of a natural fiber line?

A. twines
B. fibers
C. lays
D. lacings

02464. Which term describes a part of a natural fiber line?

A. yarns
B. twines
C. lacings
D. lays

02470. Which type of bottom provides most anchors with the BEST holding ability?

A. clay and rocks
B. soft mud
C. sandy mud
D. soft sand

02471. To determine the number of Able Seamen required on an inspected vessel, you should check the:

A. Load Line Certificate
B. operations manual
C. Safety of Life at Sea Certificate
D. Certificate of Inspection

02472. A "liner" in riveted construction of a vessel is a(n):

A. small plate which fills the aperture between riveted strakes and the vessel framing
B. backing plate which is used to level the strakes while riveting, and then removed
C. internal frame to which the side shell is riveted
D. seam welded after riveting is completed

02474. Generally speaking, the more destructive storms occurring on the Great Lakes usually come from the:

A. northeast or east
B. southwest or west
C. northwest or north
D. southeast or south

02475. The use of liners in riveted construction is eliminated by using:

A. lapped construction
B. strapped construction
C. joggled construction
D. belted construction

02480. A Danforth lightweight anchor does NOT hold well in which type of bottom?

A. mud
B. grass
C. sand
D. clay

02489. A fitting, used to secure line or wire rope, consisting of a single body and 2 protruding horns is called a:

A. bitt
B. bollard
C. capstan
D. cleat

02490. The BEST method of protecting that portion of a fiber anchor cable nearest the anchor from chafing on the bottom is:

A. using a small scope ratio
B. replacing that portion with a short length of chain
C. using a hockle to keep that portion of the anchor line off the bottom
D. using a synthetic line

02491. Before being certified by the American Bureau of Shipping, anchor chain must undergo:

A. USCG inspection
B. a breaking test
C. X-ray inspection
D. spectroanalysis

02492. When a tug makes up to a large vessel, the spring line should lead from the forward most part of the tug so that:

A. friction on the spring line is minimized
B. the length of the spring line is minimized
C. the head line and spring line can be worked simultaneously
D. your tug can pivot freely

02494. The major components which determine the length of a catenary in a deployed anchor cable are water depth, cable weight, and:

A. cable tension
B. water temperature
C. bottom conditions
D. water density

02499. Single hull vessels operating exclusively on the Great Lakes must be drydocked at intervals not to exceed:

A. 12 months
B. 24 months
C. 48 months
D. 60 months

02500. Which part of an anchor actually digs into the bottom?

A. stock
B. fluke
C. shank
D. crown

02510. It is recommended that lines be turned end-for-end occasionally. The reason is:

A. a line is weakened by constantly pulling on it in one direction
B. normal wear on the line is thus distributed to different areas
C. it prevents the line from kinking or unlaying
D. it prevents permanent misalignment of the line's internal strands

02519. If a vessel navigating the Great Lakes is required to carry 12 ring life buoys, how many of these buoys must have water lights attached?

A. 2
B. 4
C. 6
D. 9

02520. When a line is secured on deck by laying it down in close concentric coils, one against the other, in the form of a flat mat, with the free end at the center, it is said to be:

A. coiled
B. faked
C. flemished
D. seized

02521. The period of roll is the time difference between:

A. zero inclination to full inclination on one side
B. full inclination on one side to full inclination on the other side
C. full inclination on one side to the next full inclination on the same side
D. zero inclination to the next zero inclination

02530. If your vessel has gone aground in waters where the tide is falling, the BEST action you can take is to:

A. set out a kedge anchor
B. shift the vessel's load aft and repeatedly surge the engine(s) in reverse
C. shift the vessel's load forward and wait until the next high tide
D. slowly bring the engines to full speed reverse

02537. Small passenger vessels certified for operation on the Great Lakes are required to have on board one: (small passenger vessel regulations)

A. class A EPIRB
B. class C EPIRB
C. class S EPIRB
D. satellite EPIRB

02539. The distance between rivets in a row is known as the:

A. arm
B. pitch
C. gage
D. rivet distance

02540. In small craft terminology, all of the anchor gear between a boat and her anchor is called the:

A. stock
B. chock
C. scope
D. rode

02549. An example of a stock anchor is a(n):

A. articulated anchor
B. flipper Delta anchor
C. hook anchor
D. Danforth anchor

02550. When a small craft's anchor fouls in a rocky bottom, the FIRST attempt to clear it should be made by:

A. hauling vertically on the line
B. making the line fast to the bitt and bringing the vessel further forward
C. reversing the angle and direction of pull, with moderate scope
D. increasing the scope and running slowly in a wide circle with the anchor line taut

02552. When using a Mediterranean Moor, the vessel is moored with her:

A. bow to the pier
B. anchors crossed
C. anchor chains forward, side to the pier
D. stern to the pier

02553. The key to rescuing a man overboard is:

A. good equipment
B. a dedicated crew
C. well-conducted drills
D. good communication

02558. A sling is a device used in:

A. hoisting cargo aboard a vessel
B. hoisting personnel aboard a vessel
C. securing a small boat to a large vessel
D. hoisting the anchor

02559. A vessel in Great Lakes service shall carry anchors in accordance with standards established by the:

A. American Bureau of Shipping
B. Canadian Coast Guard
C. U. S. Coast Guard
D. underwriter of the vessel

02562. As you hold a piece of manila line vertically in front of you, the strands run from the lower left to the upper right. What type of line is this?

A. right-hand laid
B. cable-laid
C. sennet-laid
D. water-laid

02564. The major components which determine the length of catenary in a deployed anchor cable are water depth, cable tension, and:

A. environmental forces
B. bottom conditions
C. cable weight
D. water density

02567. When relieving the helm, the new helmsman should know the:

A. variation
B. gyro error
C. course per magnetic steering compass
D. maximum rudder angle previously used

02568. You are proceeding through a narrow channel on a right-handed single- screw vessel. The vessel starts to sheer due to bank suction/cushion effect. What action should you take?

A. stop engines with right full rudder
B. back full with rudder amidships
C. dead slow ahead with right full rudder
D. drop the anchor to short stay and right rudder

02570. When a line is laid down in loose, looping figure-eights, it is said to be:

A. faked
B. flemished
C. coiled
D. chined

02572. A tug would NOT assist a ship to steer if the tug is made up to the large vessel:

A. by a towline ahead of the vessel
B. forward on either bow of the vessel
C. approximately amidships of the vessel
D. on the vessel's quarter

02573. On a single-screw vessel with a right-handed propeller, when the vessel is going full speed astern with full right rudder, the bow will swing:

A. to port
B. to starboard
C. slowly to port then quickly to starboard
D. quickly to port, then more slowly to port

02574. You are proceeding down a channel and lose the engine(s). You must use the anchors to stop the ship. Which statement is TRUE?

A. Pay out all of the cable before setting up on the brake to insure the anchors dig in and hold.
B. For a mud, mud and clay, or sandy bottom pay out a scope of 5 to 7 times the depth before setting up on the brake.
C. Use one or both anchors with a scope of twice the depth before setting the brake.
D. Drop the anchor to short stay and hold that scope.

02580. You want to double the strength of a mooring line by using 2 lines. One requirement in obtaining this goal is that the second line must:

A. be 1 times the diameter of the first
B. be married to the first
C. not cross the first
D. be of the same length

02581. How does effect known as "bank suction" act on a single-screw vessel proceeding along a narrow channel?

A. it pulls the stern toward the bank.
B. it heels the vessel toward the bank.
C. it pushes the vessel away from the bank.
D. it pulls the bow toward the bank.

02589. The angle at which the anchor flukes penetrate the soil is the:

A. tripping angle
B. holding angle
C. penetration angle
D. acute angle

02590. Which method of adjusting mooring lines is most useful for leaving a boat free to rise and fall with the tide?

A. crossing the spring lines
B. slacking all forward running lines while keeping all after running lines taut

C. doubling up on spring or breast lines
D. slacking bow and stern lines

02591. When a tow astern veers from side to side on its tow line, the BEST way of controlling the action is to:

A. trim the tow by the bow
B. trim the tow by the stern
C. list the tow to windward
D. adjust the length of the towing bridle

02595. Yawing can be described as:

A. jumping on the tow line as the tow pitches
B. jumping on the tow line as the tow slams into waves
C. veering from side to side on the end of the tow line
D. corkscrew motion of the tow due to wave action

02596. A person who sees an individual fall overboard should:

A. immediately jump into the water to assist the individual
B. call for help and keep the individual in sight
C. run to the radio room to send an emergency message
D. go to the bridge for the distress flares

02597. On a small boat, if someone fell overboard and you did not know over which side the person fell, you should:

A. immediately reverse the engines
B. stop the propellers from turning and throw a ring buoy over the side
C. increase speed to full to get the vessel away from the person
D. first put the rudder hard over in either direction

02600. A smooth, tapered pin, usually of wood, used to open up the strands of a rope for splicing is referred to as a(n):

A. batten
B. bench hook
C. awl
D. fid

02601. To determine the number of inflatable life rafts required on a vessel, you should check the:

A. Load Line Certificate
B. SOLAS Certificate
C. Stability Letter
D. Certificate of Inspection

02602. As you hold a piece of manila line vertically in front of you, the strands run from the lower right to the upper left. What type of line is this?

A. plain-laid
B. shroud-laid
C. left-hand laid
D. water-laid

02604. The joint formed when 2 steel plates are placed end-to-end is called a:

A. bevel
B. seam
C. butt
D. bond

02607. Which statement is TRUE concerning lifeboat installations on Great Lakes vessels?

A. All davit installations shall have 3 lifelines fitted to a davit span.
B. All vessels over 3,000 gross tons must be fitted with gravity davits.
C. All lifelines shall be able to reach the water at the vessel's lightest draft with a 15 list.
D. all of the above

02612. When using the anchor to steady the bow while approaching a dock you must be aware of the fact that:

A. the vessel will tend to take a large sheer towards the side where the anchor is down
B. steering control is ineffective in trying to turn to the side opposite to that of the anchor being used
C. the anchor cable must never lead under the hull
D. using an offshore anchor decreases the chances of the anchor holding

02617. After a collision or accident, the operator of an uninspected vessel MUST assist people affected if he or she can do so without:

A. undue delay
B. serious danger to his or her own vessel
C. creating a panic on either vessel
D. further damaging the other vessel

02619. On the Great Lakes, the term "controlling depth" means the:

A. designed dredging depth of a channel constructed by the Corps of Engineers
B. minimum amount of tail water available behind a dam
C. distance in units of the chart from the reference datum to the bottom
D. least depth within the limits of the channel which restricts the navigation

02624. The Certificate of Loading required by each vessel carrying grain in bulk is issued by the:

A. owner or charterer of the vessel
B. American Bureau of Shipping
C. shipper of the cargo
D. National Cargo Bureau

02632. The horizontal flat surfaces where the upper stock joins the rudder are the:

A. rudder keys
B. rudder palms
C. lifting flanges
D. shoes of the rudder

02642. Which of the following is 2-stranded, left-handed small stuff?

A. houseline
B. marline
C. ratline
D. lagline

02652. When using the anchor to steady the bow in a maneuvering situation, you have the proper scope of anchor cable when the:

A. bow is held in position with the engines coming ahead slowly
B. anchor is at short stay
C. scope is not more than 5 times the depth of the water
D. cable enters the water at an angle between 60° and 85° from the horizontal

02658. A Kip is equal to:

A. 1000 lb.
B. 1000 kg.
C. 2000 lb.
D. 2240 lb.

02665. With a man overboard, the maneuver which will return your vessel to the man in the shortest time is:

A. a Williamson Turn
B. a single turn with hard rudder
C. engine(s) crash astern, no turn
D. two 180° turns

02666. On the Great Lakes, short-term fluctuations in water levels may be a result of any of the following EXCEPT:

A. strong winds
B. sudden changes in barometric pressure
C. seiches
D. below normal rain fall

02667. On a single-screw vessel with a right-handed propeller, when the vessel is going full speed astern with full right rudder, the bow will swing:

A. quickly to port, then more slowly to port
B. slowly to port, then quickly to starboard
C. to starboard
D. to port

02672. The term "scantlings" refers to the:

A. draft of a vessel
B. measurements of structural members
C. requirements for ship's gear
D. placement of a vessel's loadline

02674. You operate a towing vessel on inland waters exclusively. If you regularly service or contact foreign flag vessels in the course of business, which of the following is TRUE?

A. your vessel must be inspected.
B. your crew must have identification credentials.
C. a customs official must be on board when contacting a foreign flag vessel.
D. all contacts with a foreign flag vessel must be reported to the U. S. Coast Guard.

02678. What happens to the pulling power of a winch when retrieving wire rope?

A. it increases
B. it decreases
C. it remains the same
D. it fluctuates, depending on the gearing system

02682. What term describes a 3-strand rope laid up right- or left-handed?

A. soft-laid
B. hard-laid
C. sennet-laid
D. hawser-laid

02690. When must the Master of a vessel log the position of load line marks in relation to the surface of the water in the logbook?

A. once a day
B. at the change of every watch
C. only when in fresh or brackish water
D. prior to getting underway

02692. Your vessel is on a voyage from Ogdensburg, NY to Chicago, IL via the Great Lakes. The date is October 3rd of the current year. If your vessel is subject to the load line requirements, to which of her marks should she be loaded? (See illustration D0031DG.)

A. Fresh water - Winter
B. Salt water - Intermediate
C. Fresh water - Intermediate
D. Salt water - Winter

02694. When relieving the helm, the new helmsman should know the:

A. gyro error
B. course per magnetic steering compass
C. variation
D. maximum rudder angle previously used

02696. You are on a power-driven vessel proceeding down a channel, with the current, on a river on the Great Lakes System. If you meet another power-driven vessel who is upbound, your responsibilities include:

A. backing down to get out of the way
B. waiting for the other vessel to signal her intentions, and then answering promptly
C. proposing a safe way to pass
D. all of the above

02704. The legs of a tow bridle are joined together with a:

A. bridle plate
B. shackle
C. fishplate
D. tri-link

02708. Which of the following statements is TRUE with respect to the load line markings shown in illustration D031DG?

A. A vessel displaying these marks may load in the salt waters of the St. Lawrence River.
B. Vessels engaged solely on Great Lakes voyages are not required to show these marks.
C. U. S. flag vessels less than 100 feet in length and less than 200 gross tons are not required to show these marks.
D. U. S. flag vessels of 100 gross tons and upward must show these marks.

02712. Which two Great Lakes are considered hydraulically as one?

A. Lakes Superior - Huron
B. Lakes Michigan - Huron
C. Lakes Erie - St. Clair
D. Lakes Erie - Ontario

02714. The major components which determine the length of catenary in a deployed anchor cable are cable tension, cable weight, and:

A. water density
B. bottom conditions
C. environmental forces
D. water depth

02716. A channel is stated as having a controlling depth of 38 feet. Which is TRUE?

A. At least 80% of the channel is cleared to the charted depth.
B. At least 50% of the channel is cleared to the charted depth.
C. 100% of the channel width is clear to 38 feet.
D. The sides of the channel conform to at least 50% of the controlling depth.

02718. On Great Lakes vessels, midsummer load lines apply:

A. April 16 through April 30 and September 16 through September 30
B. May 1 through September 15
C. July 16 through August 30
D. June 16 through September 16

02729. The load line markings shown in illustration D031DG are inscribed on the vessel's:

A. port side
B. starboard side
C. sides
D. stern

02732. Flanking rudders affect a vessel's heading because of the:

A. effect of the propeller flow on the rudder
B. water flow due to the vessel's movement through the water
C. tunnel affect of the water flow past opposing rudders
D. discharge current being channeled to impinge on the vessel's deadwood

02735. Periodic surveys to renew the load line assignment must be made at intervals not exceeding:

A. 18 months
B. 2 years
C. 3 years
D. 5 years

02736. Distances on the Great Lakes System are generally expressed in:

A. miles above the entrance to the St. Lawrence Seaway (MASLW)
B. miles above the head of the passes (AHP)
C. nautical miles
D. statute miles

02738. Assume that your vessel has just entered Lake Michigan via the Straits of Mackinac and is proceeding south to Chicago. Which of the following statements is TRUE with respect to the aids to navigation you will encounter along this route?

A. Aids to navigation are serviced jointly by the U. S. and Canadian Coast Guard.
B. Red buoys should be passed down your starboard side.
C. Green buoys mark the location of wrecks or obstructions which must be passed by keeping the buoy on the right hand.
D. All solid colored buoys are numbered, the red buoys bearing odd numbers and green buoys bearing even numbers.

02739. What is the period of validity of a Cargo Ship Radiotelegraphy or Radiotelephony Certificate?

A. 6 months
B. 12 months
C. 24 months
D. 60 months

02745. While standing lookout duty at night a dim light on the horizon will be seen quickest by looking:

A. a little above the horizon
B. directly towards the light
C. a little below the horizon
D. quickly above then quickly below the horizon

02746. Which of the Great Lakes experiences the LEAST amount of water level fluctuation between seasonal high and low water marks?

A. Lake Huron
B. Lake Erie
C. Lake Superior
D. Lake Michigan

02748. The Lake Carriers Association and the Dominion Marine Association prescribe separation routes for upbound and downbound vessels on the Great Lakes. The recommended courses for these routes are shown on the Great Lakes Charts in the form of:

A. red or magenta figures over a segmented course line track
B. red figures over a solid course line track
C. black figures over a segmented course line track
D. green figures over a solid course line track

02759. Which of the Great Lakes is MOST affected by short-term lake level fluctuations?

A. Lake Superior
B. Lake Michigan
C. Lake Huron
D. Lake Erie

02760. When the wave period and the apparent rolling period are the same:

A. synchronous rolling occurs
B. roll period decreases
C. roll period increases
D. roll amplitude is dampened

02761. A short ton is a unit of weight consisting of:

A. 1,000 lb.
B. 2,000 lb.
C. 2,205 lb.
D. 2,240 lb.

02768. Which of the Great Lakes lies entirely within the United States?

A. Lake Ontario
B. Lake St. Clair
C. Lake Michigan
D. Lake Superior

02774. There are basically 3 categories of water level fluctuations on the Great Lakes. Which of the following is NOT included as one of these?

A. long-term fluctuations
B. controlled outflow fluctuations
C. seasonal fluctuations
D. short-term fluctuations

02776. How are aids to navigation on the Great Lakes arranged geographically?

A. in a westerly and northerly direction, except on Lake St. Clair
B. in an easterly and southerly direction, except on Lake Erie
C. in a westerly and northerly direction, except on Lake Michigan
D. in an easterly and southerly direction, except on the New York State Barge Canal

02778. Assume that your vessel has just entered Lake Erie by way of the Welland Canal and is proceeding in a Southwesterly direction. Which of the following statements about the aids to navigation you can expect to encounter along the route is TRUE?

A. The characteristics of buoys and other aids are as if "returning from seaward" when proceeding in this direction.
B. All aids are maintained by the U. S. Coast Guard, 9th Coast Guard District, Cleveland, Ohio.
C. All red, even-numbered buoys should be kept on your port side when proceeding in this direction.
D. Lighted aids, fog signals, and radiobeacons maintained by Canada are not included in the Great Lakes Light List.

02783. The effect of ocean current is usually more evident on a tug and tow than on a tug navigating independently because the:

A. speed of the tow is less
B. tow line catches the current
C. current causes yawing
D. current will offset the tow

02784. Which of the Great Lakes generally has the shorter navigation season?

A. Lake Erie
B. Lake Huron
C. Lake Michigan
D. Lake Superior

02789. Your vessel is approaching the International Bridge on the St. Marys River. If the gage on the bridge, read from top to bottom, indicates 124 ft. and the IGLD (1955) is 600 ft., determine the actual vertical clearances between the existing water level and the lowest point of the bridge over the channel.

A. 124 ft.
B. 476 ft.
C. 724 ft.
D. 840 ft.

02792. When relieving the helm, the new helmsman should find it handy to know the:

A. variation in the area
B. amount of helm carried for a steady course
C. leeway
D. deviation on that heading

02794. The Great Lakes Edition of the Notice to Mariners is published:

A. weekly by the 9th Coast Guard District
B. monthly by the Army Corps of Engineers
C. monthly by the Naval Oceanographic office
D. biweekly by the Commandant, U. S. Coast Guard

02798. The primary purpose of the stud is to prevent the anchor chain from:

A. kinking
B. distorting
C. elongating
D. breaking

02799. Who publishes the "Canadian List of Lights, Buoys and Fog Signals"?

A. the U. S. Coast Guard
B. the Canadian Coast Guard
C. the U. S. Hydrographic Service
D. the Canadian Hydrographic Service

02802. In illustration D031DG, the single line located directly above the diamond is the:

A. load line
B. water line
C. freeboard line
D. deck line

02805. "Hard right rudder" means:

A. jam the rudder against the stops
B. put the rudder over to the right all the way
C. meet a swing to the right, then return to amidships
D. put the rudder over quickly to 15 degrees right rudder

02808. Under the forces of its own weight, the suspended length of line will fall into a shape known as a:

A. polygon
B. holding arc
C. catenary curve
D. parabolic curve

02812. A tug equipped with flanking rudders is backing down with sternway. The stern will move to port the fastest if:

A. the rudder is hard to port and the flanking rudders are hard to port
B. the rudder is amidships and the flanking rudders are hard to port
C. the rudder is hard to port and the flanking rudders are hard to starboard
D. all rudders are hard to starboard

02814. Your vessel is crossing a river on the Great Lakes System. A power-driven vessel is ascending the river, crossing your course from port to starboard. Which statement is TRUE?

A. The vessel ascending the river has the right of way.
B. Your vessel has the right of way, but you are directed not to impede the other vessel.
C. The other vessel must hold as necessary to allow you to pass.
D. You are required to propose the manner of passage.

02816. Which statement is TRUE concerning lighting requirements for Great Lakes vessels?

A. The showing of a forward masthead light is optional for vessels under 150 meters.
B. An all-round white light may be carried in lieu of the second masthead light and sternlight.
C. Sidelights for vessels over 50 meters are required to have only a 2-mile range of visibility.
D. Great Lakes vessels are exempted from the requirement to show yellow towing lights.

02817. The command "meet her" means the helmsman should:

A. decrease the rudder angle
B. steer more carefully
C. use rudder to slow the vessel's swing
D. note the course and steady on that heading

02822. Which of the following statements about stopping a vessel is TRUE?

A. A lightly laden vessel requires as much stopping distance as a fully laden vessel when the current is from astern.
B. A vessel is dead in the water when the back wash from astern operation reaches the bow.
C. A tunnel bow thruster can be used in emergency situations to reduce the stopping distance.
D. When a vessel is dead in the water any speed displayed by doppler log reflects the current.

02832. You are transiting the Straits of Mackinac by way of an improved channel. You have information which indicates that the channel's Federal project depth is 28 ft. Which of the following statements is TRUE with regards to this channel?

A. The least depth within the limits of the channel is 28 ft.
B. The design dredging depth of the channel is 28 ft.
C. The channel has 28 ft. in the center but lesser depths may exist in the remainder of the channel.
D. The maximum depth which may be expected within the limits of the channel is 28 ft.

02836. Which of the Great Lakes is generally the LAST to reach its seasonal low and seasonal high water marks?

A. Lake Superior
B. Lake Michigan
C. Lake Huron
D. Lake Ontario

02848. Nautical charts published by the Canadian Hydrographic service which are referenced in the United States Coast Pilot are identified by:

A. the abbreviation "can" preceding the chart number
B. the letter "C" in parentheses following the chart number
C. an asterisk preceding the chart number
D. a footnote number

02854. The term "Great Lakes", as defined by the Inland Rules of the Road, does NOT include:

A. portions of the Chicago River
B. portions of the Calumet River
C. the St. Lawrence River to Trois Rivieres
D. Saginaw Bay

02855. A 150-meter vessel is proceeding down the course of a narrow channel in the Great Lakes System. A 60-meter vessel is starting to cross the channel. Which statement is TRUE?

A. If the smaller vessel is engaged in fishing, he shall not impede the passage of the other vessel.
B. The crossing vessel has the right of way.
C. The vessel in the channel must slow to her steerageway.
D. The larger vessel is considered to be a vessel restricted in her ability to maneuver.

02858. Which characteristic is a disadvantage of a controllable-pitch propeller as compared to a fixed-pitch propeller?

A. slightly higher fuel consumption
B. lack of directional control when backing
C. inefficient at high shaft RPM
D. some unusual handling characteristics

02866. A person found operating a vessel while intoxicated is liable for all of the following EXCEPT .

A. imprisonment for up to 1 year
B. a fine of not more than $5,000
C. seizure of his vessel and forfeiture of the title
D. a civil penalty of not more than $1,000

02870. A single-screw vessel going ahead tends to turn more rapidly to port because of propeller:

A. discharge current
B. suction current
C. sidewise force
D. thrust

02872. The Sheer Plan:

A. shows a longitudinal side elevation
B. is an endwise view of the ship's molded form
C. is usually drawn for the port side only
D. has the forebody to the right of centerline and afterbody to the left of centerline

02879. The vertical reference for all water levels and bench marks on the Great Lakes - St. Lawrence River System is known as:

A. Mean Sea Level Datum
B. International Great Lakes Datum
C. Great Lakes Low Water Datum
D. North Central Reference Datum

02882. What does the line labeled "MS" denote on the Great Lakes load line model in illustration D031DG?

A. mean sea level
B. mid season
C. maximum submergence
D. mid summer

02889. What is the minimum size required before a vessel can be documented?

A. 5 net tons
B. 100 gross tons
C. 26'; end to end over the deck excluding sheer
D. 40'; end to end over the deck excluding sheer

02894. The term "Great Lakes", as defined by the Inland Rules of the Road, includes part of the:

A. Calumet River
B. Chicago River
C. St. Lawrence River
D. all of the above

02896. You are proceeding against the current on a river in the Great Lakes System. You are meeting a downbound vessel. Both vessels are power-driven. The other vessel sounds 1 short blast. Your obligation is to:

A. change course to port
B. hold course and speed
C. sound 3 short blasts
D. hold to permit safe passing

02902. Which of the following basic categories of water level fluctuations on the Great Lakes is the MOST regular?

A. seasonal fluctuations
B. outflow fluctuations
C. short-term fluctuations
D. long-term fluctuations

02906. What might you do to aid in retrieving an anchor, if you are planning to anchor in an area where several anchors have been lost due to fouling?

A. anchor using both anchors
B. anchor with scope of 8 or more to 1
C. use a stern anchor
D. fit a crown strap and work wire to the anchor

02910. If your vessel is a single-screw ship with a right-handed propeller, the easiest way to make a landing, if there is no current present, is:

A. port side to
B. starboard side to

C. dropping anchor and swinging the ship in to the pier
D. either port or starboard side to, with no difference in degree of difficulty

02911. The wooden plug inserted in the vent of a damaged tank should be removed in case it is decided to:

A. pump from the damaged tank
B. fight a fire
C. abandon ship
D. use the crossover system

02915. The key to a rapid and effective response to a man overboard situation is:

A. well-conducted drills
B. a dedicated crew
C. good equipment
D. good communication

02920. You are on a large vessel fitted with a right-handed controllable-pitch propeller. When making large speed changes while decreasing pitch, which of the following is TRUE?

A. You will probably have full directional control throughout the speed change.
B. You may lose rudder control until the ship's speed has dropped to correspond to propeller speed.
C. The stern will immediately slew to starboard due to unbalanced forces acting on the propeller.
D. The stern will immediately slew to port due to unbalanced forces acting on the propeller.

02922. A long pole with a hook at one end, used to reach for lines, is known as a:

A. pike pole
B. jack staff
C. line rod
D. hooker

02924. You are on a large vessel fitted with a right-handed controllable-pitch propeller set at maximum forward pitch. Which of the following statements about reversing is TRUE?

A. When the pitch is reversed, the stern will slew to port even with headway.
B. The vessel will respond to the rudder until sternway is developed, then the stern will slew to starboard.
C. There will probably be a loss of steering control.
D. The vessel will have full rudder control throughout the speed change from ahead to astern.

02929. A vessel is loaded to her summer marks for a voyage from Montreal, Canada to Duluth, MN via the Great Lakes System. The voyage has been estimated to take 9 days. If the vessel departs Montreal on September 28th, which of the following statements is TRUE?

A. The vessel must be at her summer marks when she arrives at Duluth.
B. The vessel is in violation of the load line requirements.
C. The vessel's intermediate load line marks may not be submerged after September 30.
D. The vessel must be at her winter marks by the evening of the third day.

02930. A large vessel is equipped with a controllable-pitch propeller. Which statement is TRUE?

A. When dead in the water, it is often difficult to find the neutral position and slight headway or sternway may result.
B. When going directly from full ahead to full astern, there is complete steering control.
C. When the vessel has headway and the propeller is in neutral, there is no effect on rudder control.
D. When maneuvering in port, full ahead or astern power can usually be obtained without changing shaft RPM.

02932. What type of rudder may lose its effectiveness at angles of 10 or more degrees?

A. contra-guide
B. balanced spade
C. unbalanced
D. flat plate

02933. Your vessel is to dock bow in at a pier. Which line will be the most useful when maneuvering the vessel alongside the pier?

A. stern breast line
B. bow spring line
C. bow breast line
D. inshore head line

02936. Storms that enter the Great Lakes Basin from the west and northwest at a peak in October are the products of pressure systems known as:

A. northwesters
B. Alberta lows
C. fata Morgana
D. polar highs

02938. Which of the following statements concerning storm surges on the Great Lakes is FALSE?

A. They are common along the deeper areas of the lakes.
B. They cause rapid differences in levels between one end of the lake and the other.
C. The greatest water level difference occurs when the wind is blowing along the axis of the lake.
D. If the wind subsides rapidly, a seiche effect will most likely occur.

02939. A vessel operating on the Great Lakes, and whose position is south of an eastward-moving storm center, would NOT experience:

A. a falling barometer
B. lowering clouds and drizzle
C. a southwest to west wind
D. rain or snow

02940. When a tanker reduces speed without backing, the rate of change of speed is rapid initially but becomes less and less so, and ultimately very slow as the final speed is approached. This rate of change of speed through the water depends on many factors. The factor which has the GREATEST effect is the:

A. horsepower
B. wind force, direction and state of sea
C. number of propellers
D. displacement of the particular tanker involved

02950. In relation to the turning circle of a ship, the term "advance" means the distance:

A. gained at right angles to the original course
B. gained in the direction of the original course
C. moved sidewise from the original course when the rudder is first put over
D. around the circumference of the turning circle

02951. The helm command "meet her" means:

A. decrease the rudder angle
B. note the course and steady on that heading
C. steer more carefully
D. use rudder to check the swing

02954. An intermediate spring is:

A. fitted in each leg of the towing bridle
B. generally located between the "fishplate" and the main towing hawser
C. secured at the "H" bitts
D. usually made of manila hawser

02955. Yawing can be described as:

A. jumping on the tow line as the tow pitches
B. jumping on the tow line as the tow slams into waves

C. veering from side to side on the end of the tow line

D. corkscrew motion of the tow due to wave action

02957. Your vessel is to dock bow in at a pier without the assistance of tugboats. Which line will be the most useful when maneuvering the vessel alongside the pier?

A. bow breast line
B. inshore head line
C. stern breast line
D. bow spring line

02958. Ordinarily, the use of the bow thruster becomes ineffective:

A. over 3 knots headway
B. at any speed astern
C. at any speed ahead
D. over 1 knot sternway

02959. A metal ring on the bottom of a block, to which the standing part of a tackle is spliced, is known as a(n):

A. becket
B. loop
C. swivel
D. eye

02960. When cutting wire rope, seizings are put on each side of the cut. The seizings prevent the wire from unlaying and also:

A. maintain the original balance of the tension in the wires and strands
B. prevent moisture from entering between the wires at the cut end
C. force lubricant from the core to protect the raw, cut end
D. all of the above

02964. "Seiche" is defined as a(n):

A. unusually strong storm system which approaches the Great Lakes System generally from the Northeast
B. lake current which is predominant during the spring and fall navigation season on the Great Lakes
C. oscillation caused by the diminishing of forces which cause lake level fluctuations
D. higher than normal high water or lower than normal low water

02969. Fog can form in any season on the Great Lakes, but it is MOST likely to occur over open waters in:

A. summer and early autumn
B. autumn and early winter

C. winter and early spring
D. spring and early summer

02970. What material may be substituted for zinc when making a poured metal socket ending to a wire rope?

A. lead
B. babbitt
C. solder
D. nothing

02980. Which of the following is a step in attaching a poured metal socket to a wire rope?

A. Etch the wire with acid.
B. Install a wire seizing on the wire that will be inside the socket.
C. Ensure the fiber core is well lubricated.
D. Pour molten babbitt metal into the socket.

02981. When the anchor is brought to and holding, the horizontal component of anchor cable tensions should equal the:

A. displacement tonnage
B. weight forces
C. buoyancy forces
D. environmental forces

02988. It is desirable, when mooring to a buoy, to approach the buoy with the current from:

A. ahead
B. broad on the bow
C. abeam
D. astern

02990. When cutting regular-lay wire rope, what is the minimum number of seizings to be placed on each side of the cut?

A. 1
B. 2, and 3 on rope diameters over 1 inch
C. 3, and more on larger diameter wire ropes
D. 4

02994. Nearly half of all storms that enter the Great Lakes Basin during the period from October through May come from:

A. highs which originate in the east and east central USA
B. lows which originate in north central and western Canada
C. highs which originate in northeastern and eastern Canada
D. lows which originate in parts of the central and western USA

02996. Advection fog, a common occurrence on the Great Lakes, forms when:

A. air comes in contact with a rapidly cooling land surface
B. frigid arctic air moves across the lakes and becomes saturated
C. relatively warm air flows over cooler water
D. cool air contacts warm river currents

02999. Which of the following is NOT characteristic of the conditions which would be experienced by a vessel located south of an eastward-moving storm center on the Great Lakes?

A. falling barometer
B. a southwest to west wind
C. lowering clouds
D. rain or snow

03011. Shifting weight aft in heavy weather will reduce the tendency to yaw, but may increase the tendency to:

A. be pooped
B. pitchpole
C. broach
D. squat

03012. Which of the following will NOT reduce yawing of a tow?

A. increasing the length of the towing hawser
B. trimming the tow by the bow
C. trimming the tow by the stern
D. drogues put over the stern

03016. To obtain better steering control when you are towing a tow alongside, your vessel should be positioned with its:

A. bow extending forward of the tow
B. stern amidships of the tow
C. stern extending aft of the tow
D. bow even with the bow of the tow

03018. When turning a vessel in shallow water, which of the following statements is TRUE?

A. the rate of turn is increased
B. the rate of turn is decreased
C. the turning diameter increases
D. the turning diameter remains the same

03026. Which type of fog is the most dense and widely spread of those that occur on the Great Lakes?

A. steam fog
B. advection fog
C. radiation fog
D. lake effect fog

03028. The term "inland waters", as defined in the Rules of the Road, includes:

A. the Great Lakes in their entirety
B. the Mississippi River System
C. U. S. waters out to 3 miles offshore
D. the St. Lawrence River to Anticosti Island

03044. When you have a tow alongside, your stern should extend aft of the tow in order to:

A. avoid shading your stern light
B. provide a better lead for your lines
C. obtain better steering control
D. let the barge deflect floating objects from your propeller

03054. The phenomenon known as a "seiche" is most likely to occur on Lake Erie:

A. in passage of a rapidly moving warm front
B. when strong winds from the Northeast suddenly diminish
C. during the months of January thru March
D. when the moon and sun are in alignment

03056. Advection fog is particularly tenacious over which portions of the lakes?

A. northwest
B. southeast
C. northeast
D. southwest

03074. In securing a towing cable, consideration must be given to letting go in an emergency. The possible whip of towlines when released can be overcome by:

A. increasing the shaft RPM prior to release
B. using a pelican hook for quick release
C. using preventers
D. using a short chain for the lead through the stern chock

03076. The part of the anchor indicated by the letter K in illustration D038DG is the:

A. crown
B. ring
C. shank
D. bending shot

03082. Which of the following is NOT true with regards to the Great Lakes Light List?

A. The Light List does not contain information on any of the navigational aids maintained by Canada.
B. Volume VII does not include information on Class III private aids to navigation.
C. The Light List does not include Coast Guard mooring buoys, special purpose buoys, or buoys marking fish net areas.
D. The Light List should be corrected each week from the appropriate Notice to Mariners.

03083. You are signing on a crew. You can determine the number and qualifications of the crew that you are required to carry by consulting what document?

A. Certificate of Inspection
B. Crew List
C. Articles of Agreement
D. Fo'c'sle Card

03088. A "check" line is:

A. a safety line attached to a man working over the side
B. used to measure water depth
C. used to slow the headway of a barge
D. used to measure the overhead height of a bridge

03094. Your vessel is underway and approaching an overhead obstruction on Lake Superior. Given the following information, determine the clearance between your vessel and the obstruction. Highest point on vessel: 74 ft. Lowest point of obstruction: 126 (LWD) Monthly lake level: +2 (LWD) International Great Lakes Datum: 600.0 (182.88 meters)

A. 474 feet
B. 400 feet
C. 175 feet
D. 50 feet

03095. You are standing the wheelwatch when you hear the cry, "Man overboard starboard side". You should be ready to:

A. give full left rudder
B. put the rudder amidships
C. give full right rudder
D. throw a life ring to mark the spot

03098. A weight of 1,000 short tons is equivalent to:

A. 1,500 foot-pounds
B. 2,240 long tons
C. 2,000 pounds
D. 2,000 kips

03099. A lashing used to secure 2 barges side by side, lashed in a "X" fashion, is called a:

A. quarter line
B. back line
C. peg line
D. jockey line

03100. A holder of a license as Operator of Uninspected Towing Vessels may navigate a towing vessel each day for a period NOT to exceed:

A. 6 hours
B. 12 hours
C. 18 hours
D. 24 hours

03102. When hip towing, a line led from the stern of the towboat forward to the barge provides the towing pull when:

A. going ahead
B. dead in the water
C. in a following current
D. backing

03104. When maneuvering a heavy barge up a wide channel with a tug, the tow may be most closely controlled by making up to the barge:

A. with a short tow astern
B. nearly bow to bow, at a small angle
C. amidships, parallel to the barge
D. nearly stern to stern, at a small angle to barge

03106. You have a tow of 6 standard barges made up 2 abreast and 3 long. How long is your tow?

A. 350 feet
B. 390 feet
C. 525 feet
D. 585 feet

03109. When hip towing, a line led from the bow of the towing vessel aft to the vessel being towed would be a:

A. backing line
B. towing line
C. stern line
D. breast line

03110. The number or name of a tank barge shall be:

A. displayed in at least 4 different positions on the barge
B. carved on a wooden board and attached to the barge's hull
C. displayed as close to the navigation lights as possible
D. displayed at the highest point of the barge's hull such that it can be seen from either side

03112. A tug is to assist in docking an ocean-going vessel on a hawser. The greatest danger to the tug is:

A. from the ship's propeller when making up aft
B. from being overrun if making up forward
C. hull damage while alongside passing a hawser
D. getting in a tripping position

03114. Which item in illustration D024DG is rigged to transmit the thrust from one barge to another barge when going ahead?

A. i
B. h
C. e
D. b

03122. When a tug is "in irons", she:

A. is made fast to the dock with engines secured
B. is in dry dock
C. may be in danger of being overrun by her tow
D. should pay out more towline

03124. You attach a line to a stationary barge lying off your starboard beam in order to maneuver it into position to make up tow. The line used to do this is a:

A. jockey line
B. fore and aft line
C. check line
D. swing line

03128. The length of a single link of 3-inch anchor chain is 18 inches. What is the length of a 500 link section of chain?

A. 500 feet
B. 600 feet
C. 625 feet
D. 750 feet

03130. Which of the following is NOT required on an uninspected towing vessel?

A. Certificate of Documentation
B. Certificate of Inspection
C. Operators Merchant Marine License
D. FCC Radio Certificate

03132. Which of the following may prevent a tug from tripping or capsizing when towing a large vessel?

A. surge lines
B. stern towing pins
C. under riders
D. safety shackles

03134. When using 2 tugs to assist in mooring a large, deeply laden ship, the most powerful tug is usually placed:

A. forward to control the bow
B. amidships to move the entire vessel evenly
C. aft to assist the ship's rudder and propeller
D. anywhere, since the maneuverability of the tug governs the placement not the power

03138. When pushing ahead, wires leading from the quarters of the after outboard barges to the after part of a towboat:

A. prevent the towboat from sliding when the rudder is moved
B. prevent the barges from spreading out when backing down
C. hold the towboat securely to the barges
D. prevent the sidewise movement of the face barges

03142. Why are stern towing bitts placed well forward of the rudder when hawser towing?

A. to keep the hawser from fouling the rudder
B. to keep the towing bitts as far away as possible from the tugs pivoting point
C. to allow the stern to swing more freely when using rudder
D. to have as much of the towing hawser in use as possible

03144. Your tow consists of 8 barges. You have 6 jumbo barges made up 3 abreast and 2 long, with 2 standards abreast as lead barges. How long is your tow?

A. 525 feet
B. 545 feet
C. 565 feet
D. 595 feet

03148. The part of the anchor indicated by the letter H in illustration D038DG is the:

A. fluke
B. shank
C. tripping palm
D. crown

03152. The danger of a towing vessel tripping is increased the closer the towline is secured to:

A. the stern
B. amidships
C. the bow
D. the quarter

03162. When maneuvering from pull towing to breasted (alongside) towing, a twin-screw tug is more likely than a single-screw tug of equal horsepower to:

A. trip or capsize
B. foul the towline
C. go into irons
D. part the towing strap

03165. When steering a vessel, a good helmsman does NOT:

A. consider steering a vessel a highly responsible job
B. use as much rudder as possible to keep the vessel on course
C. use as little rudder as possible to keep the vessel on course
D. advise his relief of the course being steered

03168. Which item in illustration DO24DG is rigged to transmit the thrust from one barge to another when backing down?

A. i
B. h
C. c
D. b

03170. A license for Operator of Uninspected Towing Vessels shall be renewed within:

A. 90 days before date of expiration
B. 90 days after date of expiration
C. 12 months before date of expiration
D. 12 months after date of expiration

03176. The part of the anchor indicated by the letter G in illustration D038DG is the:

A. fluke
B. shank
C. tripping palm
D. crown

03180. A license issued by the U. S. Coast Guard for Operator of Uninspected Towing Vessel is valid for:

A. 2 years and must be renewed
B. 3 years and must be renewed
C. 5 years and must be renewed
D. life and need not be renewed

03204. What term indicates the immersed body of the vessel forward of the parallel mid-body?

A. run
B. flare
C. entrance
D. sheer

03218. The term "bollard pull" refers to a towing vessel's:

A. propulsion horsepower available
B. pulling ability at cruise power
C. towing winch capability
D. pulling ability under static conditions

03230. In case of a collision or accident involving an uninspected vessel, regulations require that the operator render assistance to persons affected by the collision or accident only if the operator can do so without:

A. further damaging the other vessel
B. undue delay
C. serious danger to his or her own vessel
D. creating a panic on either vessel

03234. Rolling is angular motion of the vessel about what axis?

A. longitudinal
B. transverse
C. vertical
D. centerline

03239. What term is the rise in height of the bottom plating from the plane of the base line?

A. deadrise
B. camber
C. molded height
D. sheer

03240. You are the operator of a towing vessel which becomes involved in a collision. By law it is your duty to render assistance:

A. if your vessel is at fault
B. if you can do so without excessive delay
C. if you can do so without serious danger to your vessel
D. regardless of the circumstances

03242. What term indicates the line drawn at the top of the flat plate keel?

A. base line
B. molded line
C. designer's waterline
D. keel line

03244. The shank is indicated by what letter in illustration D038DG?

A. k
B. j
C. h
D. f

03248. The rope which is the lightest is:

A. manila
B. nylon
C. polypropylene
D. Dacron

03250. You are operator in charge of a towing vessel that collides with a buoy and drags it off station. Which of the following actions should you take if the damage to your vessel was not serious?

A. If the buoy is afloat, no action is necessary.
B. Wait 1 week and submit CG form 2692 to the nearest Coast Guard Marine Inspection Office.

C. Immediately notify the nearest Coast Guard Marine Inspection Office and no further action is necessary.
D. Immediately notify the nearest Marine Inspection Office and then submit CG Form 2692.

03260. When underway with a tow, you are required to notify the Coast Guard in which of the following casualty situations?

A. damage to property amounting to $1,500
B. loss of bridge-to-bridge radio capability
C. an injury incapacitates a person for 60 hours
D. loss of main propulsion

03262. Fracture damage to the end links of the anchor cable, or to the Jews' harp may be eliminated by:

A. using a small diameter connecting shackle
B. ensuring the swivel is well lubricated and free to turn
C. installing the connecting shackle with the bow towards the anchor
D. securing a piece of wood to the Jews' harp

03269. Which of the following provides little or no indication that a vessel is dragging?

A. changing radar range to an object abeam
B. drift lead with the line tending forward
C. the cable alternately slackening and then tightening
D. changing bearings to fixed distant objects abeam

03270. A vessel is tide rode when it is:

A. carrying extra rudder to compensate for the current
B. necessary to adjust the course steered to allow for the current
C. at anchor and stemming the current
D. being forced off of a pier by the hydraulic effect of the current

03275. When underway with a tow, you are required to notify the Coast Guard in which of the following casualty situations?

A. damage to property amounting to $12,500
B. loss of bridge-to-bridge radio capability
C. an injury incapacitates a person for 50 hours
D. stranding or grounding

03282. What term indicates the immersed body of the vessel aft of the parallel midbody?

A. run
B. stern
C. counter
D. flow

03284. A vessel will moor port side to a wharf at a berth limited by vessels ahead and astern. Your tug should be made up to the vessel's:

A. stern on a hawser
B. quarter
C. waist
D. bow

03288. The angular movement of a vessel about a horizontal line drawn from its bow to its stern is:

A. pitching
B. rolling
C. heaving
D. swaying

03291. The riding pawl is:

A. a safety interlock in a cargo winch that prevents the runner from overspeeding
B. a stopper that prevents the anchor cable from running free if the cable jumps the wildcat
C. the device that locks the deck lashings of the Peck and Hale system
D. the lug that rides on the eccentric rib and engages the locking ring on the windlass

03294. Your vessel is to dock bow in at a pier without the assistance of tugboats. Which line will be the most useful when maneuvering the vessel alongside the pier?

A. bow breast line
B. stern breast line
C. bow spring line
D. inshore head line

03300. You are heading into the sea during rough weather. Having too much weight forward can cause your small boat to:

A. broach
B. plunge into the wave
C. rise rapidly over the wave
D. list

03308. What term indicates a curvature of the decks in a longitudinal direction?

A. deadrise
B. camber
C. sheer
D. flare

03309. Catenary as applied to tow lines denotes the:

A. dip of the line
B. stretch of the line
C. strain on the line
D. length of the line

03320. Which of the following types of bottoms is BEST suited for holding an anchor of a small boat?

A. mud and clay
B. rocky
C. sandy
D. gravel

03322. The fluke is indicated by what letter in illustration D038DG?

A. f
B. g
C. h
D. i

03324. When steering a vessel, a good helmsman does NOT:

A. consider steering a vessel a highly responsible job
B. use as little rudder as possible to maintain course
C. use as much rudder as possible to keep the vessel on course
D. advise his relief of the course being steered

03328. The vertical motion of a floating vessel is known as:

A. surge
B. sway
C. heave
D. pitch

03329. What term indicates the vertical distance between the bottom at the centerline and the bottom at any given point?

A. camber
B. sheer
C. rake
D. rise of bottom

03330. When towing astern, chafing gear should NOT be used on a hawser which is:

A. attached to an "H" bitt
B. attached to an automatic towing engine
C. held amidships by a gob rope
D. connected to a swivel

03338. What is used to prevent wear on tow lines that bear on hard surfaces?

A. chafing gear
B. chocks
C. grease
D. boots

03339. Pitching is angular motion of the vessel about what axis?

A. longitudinal
B. transverse
C. vertical
D. centerline

03340. It is NOT advisable to use nylon for alongside towing because it:

A. stretches too much
B. is too difficult to make fast
C. parts too readily
D. is too susceptible to mildew

03342. What term indicates a transverse curvature of the deck?

A. deadrise
B. camber
C. freeboard
D. flare

03346. When connecting the tow bridle to a tug, the end of the bridle is passed with a:

A. heaving line
B. shot line
C. high line
D. messenger line

03347. The opening in the deck underneath the anchor windlass that leads to the chain locker is the:

A. hawsepipe
B. fallpipe
C. drop-pipe
D. spill pipe

03350. It is NOT advisable to use nylon for alongside towing because it:

A. stretches too much
B. is too expensive for everyday towing usage
C. binds on the cleats
D. parts too readily

03360. On a light tow, which of the following could you substitute for a fishplate?

A. heart-shaped shackle
B. pelican hook
C. swivel
D. ring

03370. A tow span or tow bar is used to:

A. insure that the hawser leads directly aft as it passes over the stern of the towing vessel
B. increase the stability of the towing vessel by raising the hawser off the deck
C. reduce chafing of the towing hawser
D. prevent fouling of the hawser on deck gear located on the stern of the towing vessel

03372. The lead of a tow bridle can be redirected with a:

A. bollard
B. chock
C. pad eye
D. bitt

03374. Angular motion about the longitudinal axis of a vessel is known as:

A. pitch
B. surge
C. sway
D. roll

03378. The part of the anchor indicated by the letter F in illustration D038DG is the:

A. shank
B. bar
C. stock
D. shot

03380. When hip towing, a line led from the stern of the towboat forward to the barge provides the towing pull when:

A. going ahead
B. dead in the water
C. in a following current
D. backing

03390. When towing, a tow hook is used to:

A. provide quick release of the hawser
B. "gaff-on" a tow when it is coming alongside
C. attach a hawser to a tow which has no bitts or pad eyes
D. join 2 hawsers for lengthening a tow

03392. What term indicates the midships portion of a vessel that has a constant cross section?

A. half length
B. amidships
C. middle body
D. molded length

03394. The crown is indicated by what letter in illustration D038DG?

A. k
B. j
C. h
D. g

03395. The holding power of an anchor at a given scope of cable increases when the:

A. amount of chain lying along the bottom increases
B. length of the catenary is reduced
C. mooring line tension is increased
D. amount of chain lying along the bottom decreases

03396. A tow that veers to the side on the end of the tow line is said to:

A. yaw
B. surge
C. sway
D. swing

03400. In a tow made up astern, the fishplate:

A. connects the hawser to the bridle
B. connects the bridle to the tow
C. keeps the hawser amidships on the tug
D. is the capping piece on the "H" bitt

03410. When "checking down" a barge using a check line you should use:

A. 1 round turn and at least 2 figure-eights around the timber heads
B. at least 3 figure-eights around the timber heads
C. a clove hitch around 1 timber head
D. at least 3 round turns around 1 timber head

03420. A face line is used to:

A. prevent barge movement in a lock
B. secure 2 barges end-to-end
C. secure barges to the towboat
D. secure barges side-by-side

03430. Which of the following is NOT considered "jewelry"?

A. steamboat ratchets
B. manila lines
C. buttons
D. shackles

03432. A vessel is wind rode when it is:

A. at anchor and heading into the wind
B. backing into the wind
C. carrying lee rudder
D. necessary to apply a leeway correction to the course

03434. The Scharnow turn should be used in a man overboard situation only when:

A. the man can be kept in sight from the bridge while maneuvering
B. the turn is started immediately when the man goes over

C. there has been sufficient time elapsed since the man went over to complete the maneuver
D. the vessel has twin screws to assist in making the turn

03438. One advantage of chain over wire rope for a tow bridle is that it:

A. is stronger than wire
B. resists damage from chafing
C. handles more easily
D. equalizes towing forces better

03439. Horizontal fore or aft motion of a vessel is known as:

A. pitch
B. surge
C. sway
D. roll

03440. The circular steel structures installed around the propeller of a towboat are the:

A. nozzles
B. shrouds
C. struts
D. hoods

03442. The part of the anchor indicated by the letter J in illustration D038DG is the:

A. crown
B. shank
C. bill
D. tip

03448. What part of the ground tackle is the MOST likely to develop fractures due to extensive anchor use?

A. anchor shank
B. end links
C. swivel
D. fluke

03449. What term indicates an inward curvature of the ship's hull above the waterline?

A. camber
B. tumble home
C. deadrise
D. flare

03450. Kort nozzles are installed around the propellers of some vessels to:

A. increase the thrust of the propeller
B. protect the wheel from striking sawyers
C. prevent the wheel from striking barges towed on the hip
D. prevent the wheel from touching bottom in low water

03452. A drift lead indicates that the vessel is dragging anchor when the line is:

A. taut and leading forward
B. slack
C. leading out perpendicular to the centerline
D. leading under the hull

03456. The vertical movement of a vessel in the water is called:

A. pitch
B. sway
C. heave
D. roll

03459. The pea is indicated by what letter in illustration D038DG?

A. j
B. h
C. g
D. f

03460. Which of the following is NOT a device for securing a line to?

A. kevel
B. standpipe
C. button
D. timber head

03462. What is the penalty for assaulting the Master?

A. fine of not more than $1000
B. fine of not more than $500 and/or imprisonment for not more than 1 year
C. imprisonment for not more than 2 years
D. revocation of the Merchant Mariner's Document (and license if applicable)

03463. Deckhands onboard towing vessels shall be divided into 3 watches when on a trip exceeding what minimum length?

A. 1000 miles
B. 800 miles
C. 700 miles
D. 600 miles

03464. The ultimate or maximum strength of a wire rope is referred to as the:

A. operating strength
B. working load
C. breaking strength
D. lifting load

03465. Illustration DO38DG depicts what type of anchor?

A. stockless
B. Danforth
C. old fashioned
D. kedge

03466. What is a spill pipe?

A. a drainage pipe that carries rain or spray from an upper deck to a lower deck.
B. a pipe under the anchor windlass leading to the chain locker.
C. a chute, usually over the stern, to lead dumped garbage clear of the hull.
D. an opening in the deck leading outside the hull.

03470. The section of each end of a barge which is heavily reinforced to take the pressure of pushing is called the:

A. headlog
B. towhead
C. collision bulkhead
D. bullnose

03476. The strongest method of forming an eye in wire rope is:

A. 3 wire rope clamps
B. an eye splice with 4 or 5 tucks
C. a thimble fastened with 4 or 5 tucks
D. a wire rope socket attached with zinc

03480. When barge headlogs do not meet or are not even with one another, the void or opening between them is called a:

A. notch
B. hole
C. spacing
D. gap

03484. You are on watch and see a man fall overboard. Which of the following man overboard turns should NOT be used in this situation?

A. Scharnow
B. single turn
C. racetrack
D. Williamson

03487. The opening in the deck that leads the anchor cable outside the hull is the:

A. hawsepipe
B. fallpipe
C. drop-pipe
D. spill pipe

03488. Angular motion about the vertical axis of a vessel is known as:

A. yaw
B. surge
C. sway
D. roll

03490. A device used to tighten up remaining slack in wire rope when you are making up to a tow is a:

A. tripping line
B. tripping bracket
C. norman pin
D. steamboat ratchet

03492. The Master of a passenger vessel which is not required to maintain an Official Logbook must keep a record of the number of passengers received and delivered from day to day. This record must be available for a period of:

A. 6 months
B. 12 months
C. 24 months
D. 36 months

03494. Nylon rope is often used in the makeup of a tow line because it:

A. floats
B. stretches
C. handles easily
D. resists rot

03500. Hull leaks can be temporarily repaired by:

A. parceling
B. parbuckling
C. caulking
D. seizing

03502. The point that is halfway between the forward and after perpendicular and is a reference point for vessel construction is the:

A. half length
B. mid-body
C. center line
D. amidships

03504. Metal plates that cover the top of the hawsepipe are called:

A. footings
B. plugs
C. buckler plates
D. stop waters

03508. A situation has occurred in which your vessel must be towed. When the towing vessel passes the towing line to you, you should secure the line:

A. to the base of the foremast
B. to the forwardmost bitts
C. to the forward part of the deckhouse
D. at the stern

03510. If a small vessel springs a leak, the first thing to do, if possible, before making temporary repairs, is to bring the leak above the water, while avoiding:

A. a list toward the wind and sea or current
B. a list away from the wind and sea or current
C. the jettisoning of cargo
D. any adverse effects on stability

03511. The wheel on the windlass with indentations for the anchor chain is the:

A. grabber
B. wildcat
C. locking ring
D. pawl

03514. Illustration D038DG depicts what type of anchor?

A. stock
B. Danforth
C. patent
D. old-fashioned

03518. A tug's horsepower available at the shaft is:

A. indicated horsepower
B. brake horsepower
C. dynamic horsepower
D. net horsepower

03520. A situation has occurred where it becomes necessary for you to be towed. What action should be taken to prevent your vessel from yawing?

A. shift weight to the bow
B. shift weight to the center of the boat
C. shift weight to the stern
D. throw excess weight overboard

03530. Which of the following is NOT a duty of a look-out?

A. Refuse to talk to others, except as required by duty.
B. Remain standing during your watch.
C. Report every sighting.
D. Supervise any deck work going on in the area.

03544. Wire rope should be renewed when the:

A. outer wires are rusted
B. outer wires are worn to half their original diameter

C. inner core appears dry
D. certification period expires

03550. When can a look-out leave his duty station?

A. 15 minutes before the end of the watch
B. at the end of the watch
C. when properly relieved
D. at any time

03556. The choice of length of tow bridle legs is governed by the:

A. expected towing forces
B. capability of retrieving gear
C. freeboard of the unit being towed
D. need to reduce yaw

03560. Which of the following should look-outs report?

A. discolored water
B. shoals
C. floating objects
D. all of the above

03561. A holder of a license as Operator of Uninspected Towing Vessels may navigate a towing vessel each day for a period not to exceed:

A. 24 hours
B. 18 hours
C. 12 hours
D. 6 hours

03565. The safety stopper that prevents the anchor cable from running free if the cable jumps the wildcat is the:

A. riding pawl
B. devil's claw
C. buckler plate
D. spill pipe

03570. As look-out, you spot an object 45° off your port bow. You should report the object as:

A. broad on the port bow
B. 3 points on the port bow
C. 3 points forward of the port beam
D. on the port beam

03576. Heave is motion along the:

A. longitudinal axis
B. transverse axis
C. vertical axis
D. centerline axis

03582. What term indicates the length measured along the summer load line from the intersection of that load line with foreside of the stem and the intersection of that load line with after side of the rudder post?

A. length overall
B. register length
C. length between perpendiculars
D. length on the waterline

03583. Indicated horsepower refers to a towing vessel's power:

A. theoretically available
B. measured on a test bed
C. developed at the shaft
D. measured by dynamometer

03584. The tripping palm is indicated by what letter in illustration D038DG?

A. f
B. g
C. h
D. j

03586. The last shot of an anchor cable is usually painted:

A. white
B. international orange
C. yellow
D. red

03588. Conventional anchors are LEAST likely to "dig-in" to a bottom consisting of:

A. soft clay
B. hard mud
C. sand
D. rock

03590. When steering a vessel, a good helmsman does NOT:

A. use as much rudder as possible to maintain course
B. consider steering a vessel a highly responsible job
C. use as little rudder as possible to maintain course
D. advise his relief of the course being steered

03599. What term indicates the outward curvature of the hull above the waterline?

A. sheer
B. tumble home
C. deadrise
D. flare

03600. When a helmsman receives the command "Right 15 degrees rudder", the helmsman's immediate reply should be:

A. "Aye Aye Sir"
B. "Right 15 degrees rudder"
C. "Rudder is right 15 degrees"
D. No reply is necessary, just carry out the order

03606. A spreader bar is used to:

A. increase the lifting capacity
B. increase the lifting radius
C. protect the slings
D. protect the upper part of a load

03608. The horizontal port or starboard movement of a vessel is called:

A. yaw
B. sway
C. surge
D. heave

03614. While you are on watch, you learn that a crewman has not been seen on board for the past 3 hours. What type of turn is BEST in this man overboard situation?

A. round
B. Scharnow
C. racetrack
D. single turn of 180°

03616. A tug in irons is:

A. rudder bound
B. being tripped by the tow line
C. unable to maneuver
D. broached

03631. The number of certificated able seamen and lifeboatmen required on board is stated in the:

A. Certificate of Inspection
B. American Bureau of Shipping Code
C. Station Bill
D. Safety of Life at Sea Convention

03645. Conventional anchors are LEAST likely to "dig in" to a bottom consisting of:

A. soft clay
B. hard mud
C. very soft mud
D. sand

03654. Horizontal transverse motion of a vessel is known as:

A. pitch
B. surge

C. sway
D. heave

03662. Unless extremely flexible wire rope is used, the sheave diameter should always be as large as possible, but should NEVER be less than:

A. 20 times the rope diameter
B. 10 times the rope diameter
C. 2 times the rope diameter
D. the rope diameter

03684. In towing, heaving lines are used for:

A. passing a tow bridle to the tug
B. passing a messenger line
C. heaving in the tow bridle
D. service lines with rocket line throwers

03686. In the event of a parted tow line, action should be taken to:

A. prevent the tow from overriding the tug
B. abandon the unit
C. retrieve the tow bridle
D. relieve strain on the retrieving line

03689. The wildcat is linked to the central drive shaft on most windlasses by:

A. an electromagnetic brake
B. a hydraulic coupling
C. aligning the keyways on both and inserting a key
D. a mechanical coupling where lugs engage detents

03690. The part of the anchor indicated by the letter I in illustration D038DG is the:

A. tripping palm
B. fluke
C. bill
D. stock

03692. Which of following provides little or no indication that a vessel is dragging anchor?

A. increasing radar range to a fixed object ahead
B. drift lead with the line leading perpendicular to the centerline
C. vibrations felt by placing a hand on the cable
D. changing bearings to distant fixed objects abeam

03719. There are 2 advantages to the Scharnow turn in a man overboard situation: One is that it saves distance along the track line when compared to the Williamson turn, and the other is that:

A. it is usually the fastest of man overboard turns
B. it can be used in both the immediate action and the delayed action situations
C. in fog, if the turn is started as soon as the man goes over, the vessel will be at the point where he went over when the turn is completed
D. it returns the vessel to the original track line on a reciprocal course

03722. The next-to-last shot of an anchor cable is usually painted:

A. white
B. international orange
C. yellow
D. red

03724. What part of the ground tackle is the MOST likely to develop fractures due to extensive anchor use?

A. anchor shank
B. swivel
C. Jews' harp
D. fluke

03728. A long tow line is always used during an ocean tow because:

A. a margin of safety is provided should the line part
B. the tow line will wear more evenly
C. there will be less stress on the tow line
D. a slight increase in speed will be realized

03742. It is good practice to use long tow lines for ocean tows because the:

A. wear on the tow line is equalized
B. weight of the tow line increases towing force
C. dip in the tow line absorbs shock loads
D. danger of overriding is reduced

03743. With a man overboard, the maneuver which will return your vessel to the man in the shortest time is:

A. a single turn with hard rudder
B. engine(s) crash astern, no turn
C. a Williamson Turn
D. two 180° turns

03780. Which of the following provides little or no indication that a vessel is dragging anchor?

A. decreasing radar range to a fixed object astern
B. drift lead with the line leading forward
C. the cable alternately slackening and then tightening
D. changing bearing to a fixed object ahead

03790. The locking pin that joins the parts of a detachable link is held in position by:

A. a tack weld
B. the self-locking characteristics of its taper
C. a cotter pin
D. a lead plug

03820. When making a Scharnow turn, the:

A. rudder must be put over towards the side the man went over
B. initial turn direction is away from the side the man went over
C. rudder is put hard over and the initial turn is maintained until about 240° from the original course
D. man overboard must be not more than 300 feet astern when starting the turn

03960. The line with the most stretch is:

A. manila
B. nylon
C. polypropylene
D. Dacron

03982. Fairleads perform the same function as:

A. deadeyes
B. bollards
C. bitts
D. chocks

04004. A vessel certificated for Great Lakes service and NOT required to have a Class A EPIRB, must have:

A. a portable radio apparatus
B. 2 Class C EPIRBs
C. a radio direction finder
D. 50% additional life raft capacity on each side of the vessel

04005. The key to rescuing a man overboard is:

A. a dedicated crew
B. well-conducted drills
C. good equipment
D. good communication

04009. What is used to prevent twisting of a towing bridle?

A. bitt
B. bulkhead
C. V-spring
D. fishplate

04012. The purpose of item G in illustration D024DG is to:

A. distribute the vessel's thrust over a wider area
B. prevent the towboat from capsizing if item I should part
C. prevent the knee from shifting when the rudder is put hard over
D. keep the barges from shifting fore and aft

04013. What is the MINIMUM size required before a vessel can be documented?

A. 26 feet; end-to-end over the deck excluding sheer
B. 100 gross tons
C. 5 net tons
D. 26 feet between perpendiculars

04014. In illustration D024DG, the facewire refers to item:

A. i
B. h
C. b
D. a

04016. Which of the following statements is TRUE concerning weather conditions on the Great Lakes?

A. When a vessel is south of an eastward-moving storm center, the approach of the low is evidenced by winds from the north to northeast.
B. When a vessel is north of an eastward-moving storm center, changes in the weather are less distinctive than when sailing south of the center.
C. The most destructive storms usually come from the northwest or north.
D. Thunderstorms are most likely to develop from March through July.

04018. Conventional anchors are most likely to "dig in" to a bottom consisting of:

A. sand
B. very soft mud
C. shale
D. rock

04019. How many life preservers are required to be permanently stowed in a lifeboat which carries 25 persons, on a cargo vessel engaged in Great Lakes service?

A. 1
B. 2
C. 12
D. 25

04026. One of the greatest hazards of towing by pushing ahead is parting what item in illustration D024DG?

A. a
B. b

C. f
D. i

04040. When towing another vessel astern, the length of the towing line should be:

A. as long as possible
B. such that one vessel will be on a crest while the other is in a trough
C. such that the vessels will be "in step"
D. not over two wave lengths in seas up to 10 feet

04043. When backing down with sternway, the pivot point of a vessel is:

A. aft of the propellers
B. about 1/4 of the vessel's length from the stern
C. about 1/3 of the vessel's length from the bow
D. at the bow

04044. You are arriving in port and are assigned to anchor in anchorage circle B-4. It has a diameter of 500 yards and your vessel's LOA is 484 feet. If you anchor in 8 fathoms at the center of the circle, what is the maximum number of shots of chain you can use and still remain in the circle?

A. 6 shots
B. 5 shots
C. 4 shots
D. 3 shots

04047. Your vessel is to dock bow in at a pier. Which line will be the most useful when maneuvering the vessel alongside the pier?

A. inshore head line
B. bow spring line
C. stern breast line
D. bow breast line

04051. In case of a collision or accident involving an uninspected vessel, regulations state that an operator would NOT be required to render assistance to persons affected by the accident if:

A. the other vessel did not appear to be sinking
B. it would cause undue delay to his voyage
C. the other vessel was at fault
D. it would cause serious danger to his or her own vessel

04052. You are arriving in port and are assigned to anchor in anchorage circle B-4. It has a diameter of 700 yards and your vessel's LOA is 600 feet. If you anchor in 11 fathoms at the center of the circle, what is the maximum number of shots of chain you can use and still remain in the circle?

A. 4 shots
B. 5 shots
C. 6 shots
D. 7 shots

04054. "Hanging a barge off" means to:

A. moor the barge to the bank and leave
B. remove and deliver a barge from a multiple tow
C. remove a barge while locking through
D. tow a barge astern

04057. Your vessel is to dock bow in at a pier without the assistance of tugboats. Which line will be the most useful when maneuvering the vessel alongside the pier?

A. bow spring line
B. inshore head line
C. stern breast line
D. bow breast line

04060. You are arriving in port and are assigned to anchor in anchorage circle B-4. It has a diameter of 550 yards and your vessel's LOA is 449 feet. If you anchor in 9 fathoms at the center of the circle, what is the maximum number of shots of chain you can use and still remain in the circle?

A. 6 shots
B. 5 shots
C. 4 shots
D. 3 shots

04067. When steering a vessel, a good helmsman does NOT:

A. use as little rudder as possible to maintain course
B. advise his relief of the course being steered
C. consider steering a vessel a highly responsible job
D. use as much rudder as possible to maintain course

04069. The horizontal fore-and-aft movement of a vessel is called:

A. yaw
B. sway
C. heave
D. surge

04090. Conventional anchors are most likely to "dig in" to a bottom consisting of:

A. very soft mud
B. hard mud
C. shale
D. rock

00002 A	00192 A	00384 A	00584 A	00734 D	00910 A	01045 A	01216 C
00003 C	00194 B	00386 A	00586 B	00736 B	00914 B	01046 A	01217 B
00005 B	00197 C	00394 A	00592 A	00740 C	00916 C	01048 C	01224 B
00006 A	00202 B	00396 D	00594 C	00742 A	00922 D	01050 A	01226 D
00007 A	00203 C	00401 C	00595 B	00744 C	00924 C	01054 A	01230 B
00013 A	00204 A	00404 D	00601 C	00746 B	00925 C	01056 B	01234 C
00016 B	00206 C	00406 C	00604 B	00750 A	00926 C	01058 D	01240 D
00017 A	00207 C	00408 C	00605 C	00754 D	00932 D	01064 C	01244 B
00022 A	00211 B	00414 C	00612 D	00756 C	00934 A	01066 A	01250 B
00025 A	00214 A	00416 C	00613 B	00764 B	00936 A	01068 D	01252 B
00026 B	00215 D	00421 B	00614 D	00766 D	00937 D	01074 D	01254 C
00027 A	00216 D	00424 A	00617 B	00770 A	00941 A	01076 B	01260 A
00029 B	00224 D	00427 D	00624 A	00772 C	00944 B	01078 B	01264 B
00032 C	00226 D	00431 C	00627 A	00774 C	00946 A	01080 A	01270 B
00036 B	00227 A	00434 D	00630 C	00776 C	00950 C	01084 A	01272 D
00037 B	00232 A	00436 B	00631 C	00784 D	00951 B	01087 A	01274 C
00043 A	00234 C	00437 A	00632 C	00786 C	00954 B	01088 D	01275 C
00046 D	00236 B	00442 B	00634 D	00794 A	00956 D	01090 D	01276 A
00051 C	00239 C	00444 B	00636 B	00796 A	00957 A	01092 C	01280 C
00054 C	00243 B	00446 D	00637 C	00799 D	00960 C	01094 D	01282 C
00055 C	00244 A	00451 A	00640 B	00800 A	00961 A	01098 A	01284 A
00056 A	00245 D	00454 C	00641 B	00801 B	00964 B	01100 A	01285 D
00057 B	00246 B	00455 B	00642 B	00804 D	00966 A	01102 C	01286 C
00063 D	00253 C	00456 A	00643 B	00806 C	00968 C	01104 D	01287 A
00065 C	00254 C	00461 C	00644 B	00810 B	00970 A	01108 D	01290 D
00066 D	00264 B	00466 C	00650 B	00814 D	00974 A	01110 A	01294 A
00067 A	00265 B	00471 D	00651 A	00816 B	00976 C	01112 A	01296 D
00076 C	00266 C	00472 A	00654 D	00817 C	00977 C	01114 B	01302 C
00077 C	00271 A	00474 C	00657 C	00822 A	00978 B	01115 B	01304 B
00083 A	00274 A	00475 B	00660 B	00824 C	00980 D	01116 C	01305 D
00086 D	00276 C	00476 B	00661 B	00826 C	00982 D	01118 C	01306 A
00093 A	00282 B	00481 D	00662 A	00827 C	00984 A	01122 D	01312 C
00094 B	00284 D	00484 B	00664 D	00834 A	00986 C	01124 C	01314 C
00096 C	00286 D	00486 A	00666 B	00836 D	00987 D	01125 A	01316 C
00104 B	00291 B	00491 D	00670 D	00840 D	00990 B	01126 D	01320 C
00105 B	00293 C	00494 B	00672 B	00841 D	00991 C	01130 C	01323 A
00106 D	00294 D	00495 A	00673 B	00844 D	00993 A	01132 C	01326 B
00114 D	00296 B	00496 A	00674 A	00846 C	00994 A	01134 C	01329 A
00116 B	00304 D	00504 D	00676 B	00847 B	00996 D	01136 B	01330 B
00117 C	00306 A	00506 C	00677 B	00850 C	00998 A	01139 C	01336 B
00125 D	00314 D	00514 C	00680 B	00854 A	01004 B	01140 D	01339 C
00126 A	00316 C	00516 A	00682 B	00856 A	01005 B	01144 B	01340 A
00127 A	00324 B	00517 B	00684 A	00861 B	01006 D	01146 C	01344 B
00134 B	00326 C	00521 A	00686 A	00862 C	01007 B	01150 B	01346 D
00136 A	00332 B	00524 D	00690 D	00864 A	01008 B	01154 A	01349 D
00144 C	00334 A	00526 A	00692 A	00866 B	01010 B	01156 C	01350 B
00146 D	00336 A	00534 B	00694 C	00870 D	01011 C	01160 D	01354 C
00147 A	00344 B	00535 B	00696 D	00871 A	01012 C	01164 D	01356 B
00153 D	00345 B	00536 D	00700 D	00874 A	01014 D	01165 A	01358 A
00154 B	00346 B	00541 B	00703 A	00876 C	01016 A	01166 C	01359 C
00156 A	00351 B	00544 D	00704 C	00880 B	01018 B	01170 C	01364 D
00157 A	00354 A	00546 B	00706 B	00881 C	01020 C	01174 B	01365 A
00164 D	00355 A	00551 C	00710 D	00884 A	01024 A	01176 A	01366 B
00166 A	00357 B	00554 D	00714 C	00886 C	01026 B	01184 D	01368 D
00171 A	00361 C	00556 C	00716 A	00890 B	01028 C	01185 C	01370 B
00174 A	00362 B	00557 D	00717 B	00892 B	01030 B	01192 C	01374 A
00176 D	00363 B	00561 B	00720 A	00894 C	01031 C	01193 A	01375 A
00177 C	00364 C	00564 A	00721 C	00896 C	01032 A	01194 D	01376 C
00179 C	00366 C	00566 D	00724 B	00900 C	01033 D	01196 B	01380 C
00182 B	00371 A	00574 A	00726 C	00901 A	01034 B	01204 A	01384 B
00184 C	00372 B	00576 B	00727 D	00902 D	01036 C	01206 C	01386 A
00185 B	00374 C	00577 C	00730 B	00904 A	01041 C	01210 B	01392 C
00186 B	00376 B	00582 B	00732 A	00906 A	01044 B	01214 D	01394 B

01396 D	01530 C	01633 B	01740 B	01824 D	01938 C	02040 A	02185 D
01406 B	01532 B	01634 A	01741 A	01826 C	01939 C	02041 A	02186 D
01410 C	01533 D	01635 D	01743 B	01827 A	01943 B	02043 B	02187 A
01414 B	01534 A	01636 C	01744 D	01828 C	01944 D	02045 D	02189 B
01416 D	01536 A	01638 A	01746 C	01829 A	01946 B	02046 C	02190 C
01420 A	01538 C	01640 D	01748 B	01831 D	01948 A	02048 C	02191 C
01426 C	01543 C	01642 D	01749 D	01832 B	01949 B	02050 D	02192 C
01427 C	01544 B	01643 C	01750 C	01833 D	01950 C	02053 A	02193 D
01430 A	01546 B	01644 C	01751 A	01836 A	01953 D	02054 B	02194 A
01434 D	01548 D	01645 B	01753 C	01838 B	01957 C	02058 B	02195 C
01435 A	01550 B	01646 D	01754 D	01840 A	01958 B	02059 D	02196 B
01436 C	01552 B	01648 B	01755 B	01841 C	01960 B	02061 A	02198 B
01440 A	01553 C	01650 D	01756 C	01842 B	01961 B	02062 D	02199 D
01443 C	01554 A	01651 C	01760 D	01843 B	01962 A	02063 C	02203 B
01444 C	01555 A	01653 B	01761 B	01844 A	01963 C	02064 D	02204 C
01446 A	01556 C	01654 A	01762 B	01848 C	01964 C	02065 B	02206 A
01448 B	01557 A	01655 C	01763 A	01849 A	01966 C	02067 D	02211 C
01450 D	01558 D	01657 D	01764 B	01852 C	01969 A	02068 B	02212 C
01455 B	01560 B	01660 D	01765 C	01853 D	01970 D	02069 B	02213 C
01456 C	01563 B	01661 B	01766 C	01854 B	01973 B	02070 A	02214 B
01458 B	01564 B	01663 C	01767 D	01855 D	01975 D	02073 B	02216 D
01460 B	01565 D	01664 C	01768 A	01856 B	01976 C	02075 C	02217 A
01462 A	01566 D	01665 D	01769 A	01857 B	01978 B	02076 D	02219 C
01463 C	01568 B	01666 B	01771 A	01858 B	01979 C	02078 B	02221 B
01464 A	01569 B	01670 C	01772 C	01859 D	01980 A	02081 A	02222 C
01468 C	01570 C	01671 C	01773 B	01862 B	01981 A	02083 C	02223 C
01470 B	01573 B	01673 C	01774 B	01863 C	01982 C	02086 B	02224 D
01472 D	01574 A	01674 D	01776 C	01864 D	01983 C	02088 D	02225 B
01473 B	01575 D	01675 A	01777 B	01868 A	01984 C	02093 C	02226 B
01474 C	01576 B	01676 A	01778 C	01869 D	01985 C	02095 D	02227 C
01475 D	01578 D	01680 A	01781 C	01870 B	01988 B	02097 B	02228 A
01476 B	01580 B	01683 C	01782 B	01873 C	01989 D	02098 B	02229 A
01478 D	01583 B	01684 D	01783 C	01875 A	01993 B	02100 A	02230 A
01480 B	01584 D	01685 B	01784 D	01878 A	01994 A	02102 C	02231 C
01483 B	01586 C	01686 C	01786 C	01879 D	01995 B	02104 D	02232 A
01484 C	01588 A	01687 A	01787 D	01880 A	01996 B	02106 B	02233 C
01486 B	01590 C	01689 D	01788 A	01883 B	01997 A	02107 C	02235 A
01487 A	01593 A	01693 C	01790 D	01886 A	01998 C	02111 B	02236 A
01488 C	01594 C	01694 D	01792 C	01887 C	02000 C	02112 B	02238 D
01490 A	01595 A	01695 C	01793 A	01888 B	02001 B	02113 A	02239 A
01492 B	01596 C	01696 B	01794 D	01893 C	02002 A	02116 C	02240 B
01493 C	01597 B	01700 D	01795 C	01894 D	02003 C	02117 A	02241 A
01494 C	01598 B	01703 C	01796 D	01895 C	02004 C	02119 A	02242 D
01495 D	01600 B	01704 C	01798 C	01898 D	02005 D	02122 D	02243 D
01496 A	01603 C	01706 D	01800 B	01902 B	02007 B	02124 D	02247 D
01497 B	01604 B	01711 C	01802 D	01903 B	02008 D	02126 D	02249 C
01498 D	01605 D	01713 A	01803 C	01905 A	02011 D	02127 C	02250 A
01499 D	01606 D	01714 D	01804 C	01908 D	02013 C	02130 D	02251 C
01500 D	01607 D	01716 D	01805 A	01910 A	02014 C	02135 D	02253 A
01503 B	01608 B	01717 A	01806 C	01913 B	02016 B	02144 D	02254 D
01504 A	01610 D	01720 B	01807 D	01914 A	02018 A	02146 B	02255 C
01506 D	01612 B	01723 A	01809 C	01915 D	02020 C	02147 B	02256 B
01508 C	01613 B	01724 B	01811 C	01917 C	02022 C	02149 C	02258 B
01513 B	01614 A	01725 C	01813 B	01918 D	02023 D	02150 A	02259 A
01514 C	01616 A	01726 A	01814 D	01923 C	02025 D	02157 B	02261 B
01516 B	01618 C	01728 D	01815 D	01924 C	02027 B	02159 D	02263 D
01517 A	01620 A	01730 C	01816 A	01926 A	02028 D	02163 A	02264 C
01523 A	01623 D	01732 A	01818 C	01928 D	02029 C	02168 D	02265 A
01524 B	01624 C	01733 B	01819 A	01929 D	02030 A	02169 A	02267 A
01525 B	01626 D	01734 D	01820 B	01931 B	02033 A	02173 B	02268 D
01526 D	01628 A	01736 D	01821 D	01933 D	02034 C	02179 B	02269 C
01528 B	01630 D	01737 B	01822 C	01935 A	02037 C	02181 A	02272 C
01529 D	01631 D	01739 C	01823 C	01936 C	02038 B	02182 C	02273 C

02275 D	02480 B	02708 A	02938 A	03180 C	03459 A	03820 C
02276 A	02489 B	02712 B	02939 C	03204 C	03460 B	03960 B
02280 C	02490 B	02714 D	02940 D	03218 D	03462 C	03982 D
02283 C	02491 B	02716 C	02950 B	03230 C	03463 D	04004 B
02284 B	02492 D	02718 B	02951 D	03234 A	03464 C	04005 B
02285 D	02494 A	02729 C	02954 B	03239 A	03465 A	04009 D
02288 D	02499 D	02732 A	02955 C	03240 C	03466 B	04012 C
02290 C	02500 B	02735 D	02957 D	03242 A	03470 A	04013 C
02292 C	02510 B	02736 D	02958 A	03244 D	03476 D	04014 A
02301 A	02519 B	02738 B	02959 A	03248 C	03480 A	04016 B
02302 C	02520 C	02739 B	02960 A	03250 C	03484 A	04018 A
02305 C	02521 C	02745 A	02964 C	03260 D	03487 A	04019 B
02315 D	02530 A	02746 C	02968 C	03262 D	03488 A	04026 D
02316 D	02537 B	02748 A	02970 D	03269 A	03490 D	04040 C
02325 C	02539 B	02759 D	02980 A	03270 C	03492 B	04043 B
02335 B	02540 D	02760 A	02981 D	03275 D	03494 B	04044 D
02341 C	02549 D	02761 B	02988 A	03282 A	03500 C	04047 C
02342 A	02550 C	02768 C	02990 C	03284 D	03502 D	04051 D
02343 D	02552 D	02774 B	02994 D	03288 B	03504 C	04052 B
02344 D	02553 C	02776 C	02996 C	03291 B	03508 B	04054 A
02345 B	02558 A	02778 A	02999 B	03294 C	03510 D	04057 A
02346 C	02559 A	02783 A	03011 A	03300 B	03511 B	04060 C
02347 B	02562 A	02784 D	03012 B	03308 C	03514 C	04067 D
02349 B	02564 C	02789 A	03016 C	03309 A	03518 B	04069 D
02350 C	02567 C	02792 B	03018 C	03320 A	03520 C	04090 B
02351 B	02568 D	02794 A	03026 B	03322 D	03530 D	
02352 C	02570 A	02798 A	03028 B	03324 A	03544 B	
02353 D	02572 C	02799 B	03044 C	03328 C	03550 C	
02354 A	02573 A	02802 D	03054 B	03329 D	03556 D	
02355 D	02574 C	02805 B	03056 A	03330 B	03560 D	
02356 C	02580 D	02808 C	03074 C	03338 A	03561 C	
02358 A	02581 A	02812 A	03076 B	03339 B	03565 A	
02360 B	02589 A	02814 A	03082 A	03340 A	03570 A	
02365 A	02590 A	02816 B	03083 A	03342 B	03576 C	
02367 B	02591 B	02817 C	03088 C	03346 D	03582 C	
02384 A	02595 C	02822 D	03094 D	03347 D	03583 A	
02387 D	02596 B	02832 B	03095 C	03350 A	03584 B	
02388 C	02597 B	02836 A	03098 D	03360 A	03586 D	
02389 B	02600 D	02848 C	03099 D	03370 D	03588 D	
02390 B	02601 D	02854 C	03100 B	03372 B	03590 A	
02391 C	02602 C	02855 A	03102 D	03374 D	03599 D	
02392 A	02604 C	02858 D	03104 D	03378 A	03600 B	
02393 D	02607 C	02866 C	03106 C	03380 D	03606 D	
02394 A	02612 D	02870 C	03109 B	03390 A	03608 B	
02395 D	02617 B	02872 A	03110 D	03392 C	03614 B	
02396 C	02619 D	02879 B	03112 D	03394 C	03616 C	
02397 B	02624 D	02882 D	03114 C	03395 A	03631 A	
02398 B	02632 B	02889 A	03122 C	03396 A	03645 C	
02400 C	02642 B	02894 D	03124 D	03400 A	03654 C	
02450 D	02652 A	02896 D	03128 A	03410 D	03662 A	
02451 B	02658 A	02902 A	03130 B	03420 C	03684 B	
02454 C	02665 B	02906 D	03132 B	03430 C	03686 C	
02456 C	02666 D	02910 A	03134 A	03432 A	03689 D	
02459 D	02667 D	02911 A	03138 B	03434 C	03690 B	
02460 A	02672 B	02915 A	03142 C	03438 B	03692 B	
02461 B	02674 B	02920 B	03144 C	03439 B	03719 D	
02462 B	02678 B	02922 A	03148 D	03440 A	03722 C	
02464 A	02682 D	02924 C	03152 B	03442 C	03724 C	
02470 C	02690 D	02929 C	03162 B	03448 B	03728 C	
02471 D	02692 C	02930 A	03165 B	03449 B	03742 C	
02472 A	02694 B	02932 B	03168 C	03450 A	03743 A	
02474 B	02696 C	02933 C	03170 D	03452 A	03780 D	
02475 C	02704 C	02936 B	03176 C	03456 C	03790 D	

NAVIGATION GENERAL

WEATHER

Prevailing or General Winds

All weather, including the wind, is driven by the sun. Warm air is light and rises; cold air is dense and falls. Because more solar energy falls on equatorial regions than on polar regions, warmed air rises over the Equator and falls over the Poles. Actually, due to a variety of complicating factors, the circulation in each hemisphere breaks into three cells.

Where warm air rises, air (wind) moves in horizontally to replace it. Conversely, wind blows away from where air is falling. Due to the rotation of the earth (the Coriolis Force), wind in the Northern Hemisphere is deflected to the right; wind in the Southern Hemisphere is deflected to the left.

Study the action of the rising and falling air masses and the generation of winds in the iullustration at right. Memorize the names of the zones and their locations.

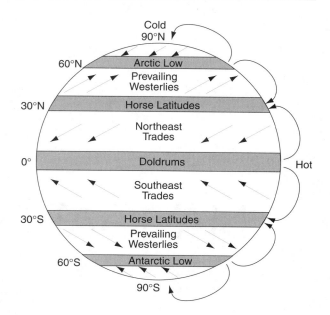

Local Effects

Prevailing winds are generated all year long, modified seasonally by the tilt of the earth. The same engine also works on a diurnal (daily) basis, particularly at a boundary between land and water. While the sun is up, the surface temperature of the land rises above that of the water. The land warms the air, which then rises. The rising air leaves a vacuum which draws more air in from over the water. The inflow of cool air from over the water is called a sea breeze.

After the sun sets, the engine runs in reverse. This time the land cools faster than the water. The relatively warmer air over the water now rises, drawing in replacement air from the adjacent land. This reverse air flow is called a land breeze.

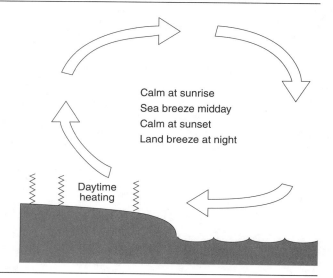

Continental Scale Effects

On a much larger scale, air masses tend to take on the temperature and humidity characteristics of the earth beneath them.

For example, the air over Northern Canada in winter becomes cooler and dryer than the air over the ocean. These cold, dense, high-pressure arctic air masses spill down over North America in winter, dramatically modifying weather as far south as Florida.

During summer, the air over the relatively cool North Atlantic generates the Azores High, a persistent high pressure region characterized by cool dry air and light winds.

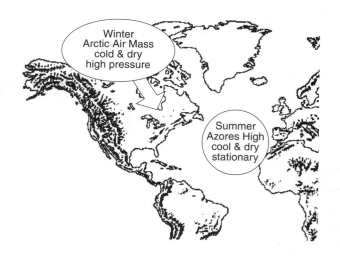

Cyclones

Wind is the result of pressure differences. The speed of the wind is proportional to the pressure gradient —the horizontal rate of change of pressure. The illustration at right shows a low pressure area surrounded by isobars—lines of equal pressure—measured in millibars. As the air moves toward the center of the "low," it is deflected to the right by the Coriolis force. If there were no friction, the wind would flow exactly along the isobars, but friction with the surface causes it to spiral in at about a 30° angle.

The winds around a low blow counter-clockwise. Such a wind system is called a cyclone.

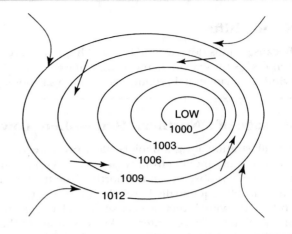

Anticlones

Winds blowing outward from the center of a high pressure area are similarly deflected to the right in the Northern Hemisphere. Again, rather than following the isobars exactly, the winds spiral outward at about a 30° inclination. The defection causes winds around a high to spin clockwise. The wind system is called an anti-cyclone because the winds are opposite to those of a cyclone.

To remember wind direction, just remember that as wind moves from higher pressure to lower pressure it is always deflected to the right in the Northern Hemisphere. In the Southern Hemisphere, the deflection and resulting spins are just the opposite.

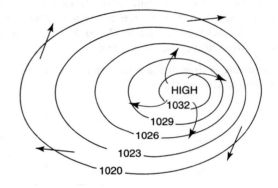

Buys Ballot's Law

According to Buys Ballot's law, if you face the wind around a low in the Northern Hemisphere, the center of the low will be about 30° aft of your outstretched right arm. This is an extremely useful law, and one you will probably confront in the exam, since it helps you evade the path of a hurricane.

In the case of a hurricane, the precision of the law can be slightly improved by changing the 30° inclination to 20° ahead of the storm and 45° behind the storm. The differences are due to the fact that the wind vector is the resultant of the cyclonic wind speed plus the speed of advance of the storm.

Anticyclonic winds—the winds around a high—are not nearly so dangerous. You will probably not be asked a similar question about them. However, in case you are curious, you can invert Buys Ballot's law to deduce the location of the center of a high as well. Facing the wind around a high, the center of the high will be about 30° forward of your outstretched left arm.

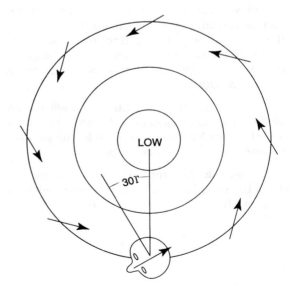

Wind Shifts

Because winds flow around low and high pressure centers, as these centers move we can expect local winds to change in direction. As with Buys Ballot's law, understanding the direction of flow around lows and highs will allow you to picture the movement of the centers as they pass by.

Passage of a Northern Hemisphere Low

The illustration at right depicts a low pressure system (cyclone) moving from west to east. As the center moves, an observer to the north of the track will find himself sequentially in relative positions 1, 2, and 3. The wind directions are seen to change from SE to NE to N. This counterclockwise shifting of the wind is called *backing*. (Remember, *counter*-clockwise = *backing*.)

An observer to the south of the track will experience the wind shift sequence 4, 5, and 6. The wind will shift clockwise from S to SW to W. A clockwise shift of the wind is called *veering*.

The rule is thus: if the wind backs, the center will pass to the south.

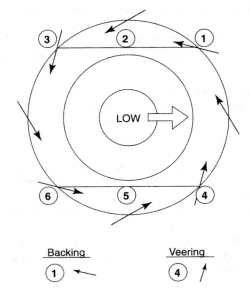

Passage of a Northern Hemisphere High

The illustration at right depicts a high pressure system (anticyclone) moving from west to east. As the center moves, an observer to the north of the track will find himself sequentially in relative positions 1, 2, and 3. The wind directions are seen to change from NW to W to SW. The shift is counterclockwise and so is *backing*.

An observer to the south of the track will experience the wind shift sequence 4, 5, and 6. The wind will shift clockwise from N to NE to E. The shift is clockwise, so the wind is *veering*.

The same rule then applies to both lows and highs: if the wind backs, a pressure center will pass to your south.

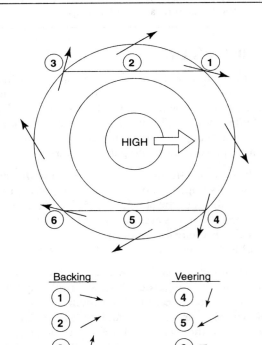

Humidity and Condensation

Air holds water vapor (the gaseous form of water) like a sponge—when it holds all it can (100% relative humidity), any excess will be forced out as liquid water. The amount of vapor air can hold decreases as temperature drops. When air is cooled by contact with a cold drink, for example, excess water vapor condenses on the glass as liquid water.

This is what happens when fog forms. Humid air cools and the excess water vapor is squeezed out. The tiny water droplets can cling to a surface and form dew. They can also be suspended in air as fog.

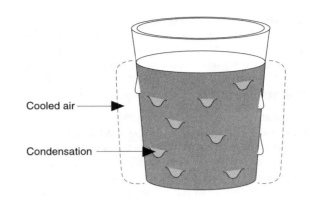

Cooled air

Condensation

Radiation Fog

When the night sky is clear, the surface of the earth is "looking at" deep space where the temperature is a mighty cold -459°F!

It is as if you stood naked in front of an open refrigerator. Got the picture? Anyway, the earth loses heat, the air contacting the earth cools, and water vapor condenses from the air as a *radiation fog*. Wind, mixing the air, will dissipate radiation fog.

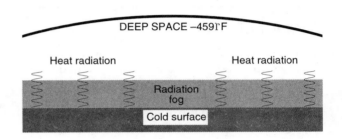

DEEP SPACE –459°F

Heat radiation   Heat radiation

Radiation fog

Cold surface

Advection Fog

Advection is air motion. When warm moist air formed over a large water body advects (moves) over colder land, the air will cool. If the original humidity is high enough, or if the temperature drop is great enough, an advection fog will form over the land. This is common along coastal land areas in winter.

A similar effect takes place when warm moist air moves from an area of warm water across an area of cooler water. This is the cause of the famous fogs on the Grand Banks, where air from the very warm Gulf Stream area encounters the cold Laborador Current.

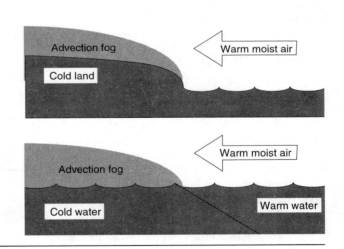

Advection fog

Cold land

Warm moist air

Advection fog

Cold water

Warm moist air

Warm water

Sea Smoke

On bitter cold winter days, the surfaces of water bodies seem to "smoke." As you no doubt suspect, the smoke is actually fog. Very cold air in contact with the water picks up warmth and humidity. But the warmed air is now buoyant, and so rises. As it rises, however, it cools again, condensing out the water vapor it just absorbed.

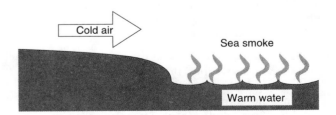

Cold air

Sea smoke

Warm water

Air Masses and Fronts

Air masses of different temperature do not readily mix. Cold air masses are heavier than warm air masses, so, when they meet, the warm air mass rises over the cold. A boundary between air masses is a frontal surface. The line where a frontal surface touches the earth is a front.

As air masses move, the front is named for the advancing mass, i.e. for the mass which will be in place after passage of the front.

Warm Front

As an advancing warm air mass rides over a cold air mass, the warm humid air is very gradually forced upward where it cools. A warm front is, therefore, preceded by high thin clouds which gradually lower and thicken. Often rain falls for a day or more. Since warm air is lighter, the pressure also falls as a warm front approaches. After frontal passage, temperature and humidity rise, pressure steadies and wind drops.

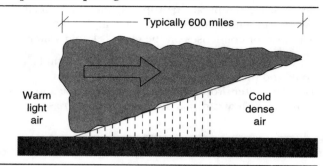

Cold Front

As an advancing cold air mass forces its way under a warm air mass, the warm air is forced upward quickly along the steep frontal boundary, often producing cumulonimbus clouds (thunderheads). When the wind is higher behind the front, gusty squalls can be expected. Since the frontal boundary is steep, passage of the front typically takes only a few hours. After frontal passage, pressure increases, temperature drops and humidity and cloudiness decrease.

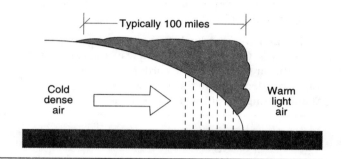

Symbols for Fronts

The weather map symbols for fronts (see right) are easy to remember. The warm front looks warm and soft, while the cold front looks spiky and cold. A stationary front is where neither the warm nor the cold air mass is advancing. The occluded front looks like the warm and cold fronts overprinted.

Frontal Waves

Cold fronts tend to move more rapidly than warm fronts. This leads to the development of frontal waves that sweep across the U.S. from west to east. The illustration at right shows a fully developed frontal wave. Note that the wind shifts clockwise as the warm front passes and shifts clockwise again when the cold front passes.

As the cold front closes in on the warm front, the wave becomes steeper, pressure at the crest decreases (the low "deepens") and wind and rain become more intense. Ultimately, the two fronts merge as an occluded front. After occlusion, the cold air lifts the entire warm air mass, the fronts disappear and weather settles down.

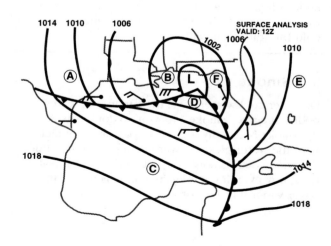

Clouds

Clouds are grouped by height; named by description.

Height Groups

High clouds—mean lower level above 20,000 feet

Middle clouds—mean level 6,500 to 20,000 feet

Low clouds—mean lower level below 6,500 feet

Name Descriptors

Cirrus—curl, lock, tuft of hair

Cumulus—heap, pile, accumulation

Stratus—spread out, flatten, cover with a layer

Alto—high, upper air

Nimbus—rain cloud

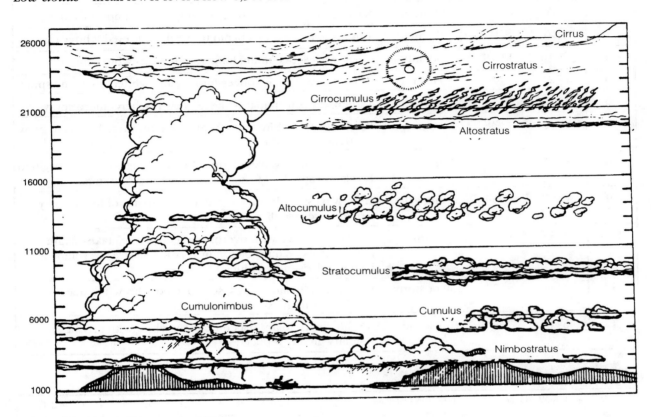

Names of Principle Cloud Types

Cirrus (Ci)—detached, delicate and fibrous high clouds. Generally associated with fair weather. If followed by lower clouds, however, they foretell rain.

Cirrostratus (Cs)—thin, whitish veil, that produces halos around sun and moon. Also, "mare's tails." Both effects foretell rain or snow in 24-48 hours.

Cirrocumulus (Cc)—white scales, arranged in rows, known as "mackerel sky." Associated with fair weather. Followed by lower clouds, they foretell rain.

Altostratus (As)—gray veil. The sun appears out of focus with corona. When nimbostratus appear below them, expect continuous rain within a few hours.

Altocumulus (Ac)—cottony masses, usually uniformly distributed with blue sky between. May lead to thunderstorms, but of short duration.

Stratocumulus (Sc)—low, soft, grayish, roll-shaped masses. Usually form after altocumulus and are followed by a clear night.

Cumulus (Cu)—dense with flat base and much vertical development. They never cover the entire sky. Usually associated with fair weather.

Nimbostratus (Ns)—low, dark, shapeless layer. The "rain cloud." Rain is steady or intermittent, but not showery.

Cumulonimbus (Cb)—tremendous vertical development. Top may spread out horizontally in form of an anvil. Typically results in lightning and rain.

Stratus (St)—uniform low cloud with base often below 1,000 feet. If thick, makes the sky dark. Often produces steady mist.

Wind

Beaufort Force	Knots	Miles per Hr	WMO Description	Observed Effects
0	0-1	0-1	Calm	Sea like a mirror
1	1-3	1-3	Light air	Ripples with the appearance of scales
2	4-6	4-7	Light breeze	Small wavelets; crests of glassy appearance, not breaking
3	7-10	8-12	Gentle breeze	Large wavelets; crests begin to break, scattered whitecaps
4	11-16	13-18	Moderate	Small waves, becoming longer; numerous whitecaps
5	17-21	19-24	Fresh	Moderate waves of longer form; many whitecaps; some spray
6	22-27	25-31	Strong	Larger waves forming; whitecaps everywhere; more spray
7	28-33	32-38	Near gale	Sea heaps up; white foam from breaking waves begins to blow in streaks
8	34-40	39-46	Gale	Moderately high waves of greater length; edges of crests begin to break into spindrift; foam blown in well-marked streaks
9	41-47	47-54	Strong gale	High waves; sea begins to roll; dense streaks of foam; spray may reduce visibility
10	48-55	55-63	Storm	Very high waves with overhanging crests; sea takes white appearances; foam is blown in very dense streaks; rolling is heavy and visibility reduced.
11	56-63	64-73	Violent storm	Exceptionally high waves; sea covered with white foam patches; visibility still more reduced
12	64+	74+	Hurricane	Air filled with foam; sea completely white with driving spray; visibility greatly reduced

Beaufort Wind Scale

Storm Warnings

SMALL CRAFT ADVISORY Wind to 33 kn (38 mph)	GALE WARNING Wind 34–47 kn (39–54 mph)	STORM WARNING Wind 48–63 kn (55–73 mph)	HURRICANE WARNING Wind over 63 kn (over 73 mph)
DAYTIME SIGNALS (FLAGS)			
RED	RED RED	RED/ BLACK	RED/ BLACK
NIGHT SIGNALS (LIGHTS)			
RED WHITE	WHITE RED	RED RED	RED WHITE RED

Maneuvering in a Hurricane

The force wind exerts is proportional to the square of the wind speed. The force exerted by a 120 mph wind is, thus, more than twice as great as that of a 80 mph wind. This is important because, if you know the approximate location and direction of advance of a hurricane, you can maneuver to your advantage.

In the Northern Hemisphere, hurricane winds blow counterclockwise around the eye. At any point in a hurricane, local wind is the sum of the anticyclonic circulation plus the speed of advance of the eye. In the illustration at right, where the eye is advancing northward, wind speed to the east is increased, and wind speed to the west is decreased, by the speed of advance. For example, if the average wind speed at the outer circle is 100 mph and the speed of advance is 20 mph, the wind speed at B is 100 + 20 = 120 mph, while the wind speed at A is 100 - 20 = 80 mph.

The area to the right of the hurricane's track is called the *danger semicircle*. The area to the left of the track is the *navigable semicircle,* for obvious reasons. If you find yourself at sea, in the path of a hurricane, sketch the illustration as shown. If directly on or to the left of the track, put the wind on your starboard quarter. If to the right in the danger semicircle, put the wind on your starboard bow. Do not sit still or run directly ahead of the track.

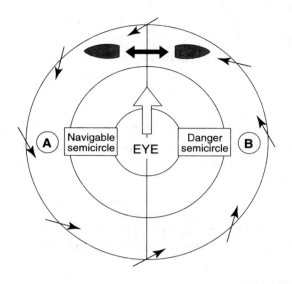

Synoptic Maps

Weather maps received by facsimile recorders are synoptic maps, meaning that they show simultaneous weather conditions at many weather stations. To avoid the necessity of words, conditions at each weather station are shown by symbols.

You will probably not be asked to interpret a full station report, but you may be asked to identify one or more weather symbols. The illustration at right shows the most likely symbols.

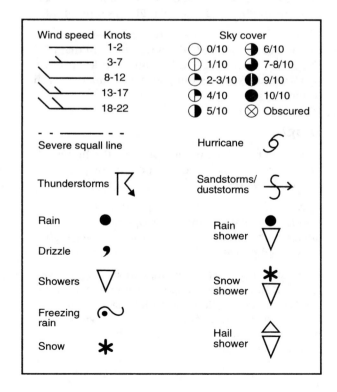

TIDES AND CURRENTS

The Causes of Tides

The periodic rise and fall of ocean waters experienced along most of the earth's coasts is due to a combination of factors:

- *Gravitational attraction* between the water and the moon and sun. Due to its proximity, the moon exerts the largest force.

- *Centrifugal force* on water opposite the moon, as the earth and moon turn about a common center.

- *Geometry* of water bodies, resulting in resonant oscillations and in piling up at the ends of funnel-shaped bodies.

The earth rotates once per 24 hours. The moon, however, revolves about the earth once per month and rises 50 minutes later each day. High tides, therefore, occur about 50 minutes later each day.

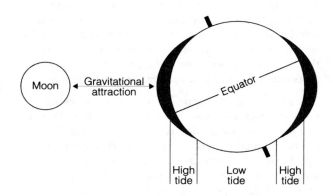

Types of Tides

All coasts are effected by tides. Due to the tilt of the earth and basin shapes, however, some areas get two highs and lows per day, others get one high and one low, while others get uneven tides.

Semi-diurnal tides have two tides per day of roughly equal amplitude. The U.S. East Coast has this type of tide.

Diurnal tides occur just once a day and are usually of small amplitude. Pensacola, FL, has diurnal tides.

Mixed tides occur twice daily, with the amplitude of one tide being markedly different from that of the other. Galveston, TX, has diurnal tides, followed by mixed tides, depending on the declination of the moon.

Heights

Where there is just one tide per day, the highest point is called high water, while the low point is called low water.

Where there are two tides per day, the four stands—times when the tide stops rising or falling—are called higher high water, lower high water, higher low water and lower low water.

Mean sea level is the average of all heights over the year. Because the danger of running aground is greatest when the tide is at its lowest, however, both charts and tide tables use mean lower low water as the datum (reference height) for both depth and tide tables.

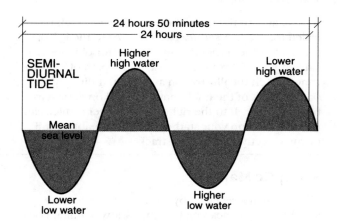

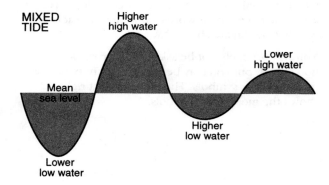

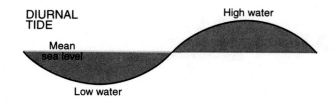

Tide Tables

Tide tables were published by National Ocean Service (NOS) until 1995. Since then NOS has made the information available to private publishers who offer the data to the public in book form. Four annual volumes are available:

- *Tide Tables: Europe & West Coast of Africa*
- *Tide Tables: East Coast of North & South America*
- *Tide Tables: West Coast of North & South America*
- *Tide Tables: Central & Western Pacific Ocean and Indian Ocean*

Each volume consists mostly of two tables. The following two pages contain a sample page of each table from the volume *Tide Tables 1995, East Coast of North and South America*.

Table 1 contains the times and heights of high and low waters for the entire year for 50 reference ports, including the one shown, Portland, ME.

Table 2 contains tidal differences to be applied to the data in Table 1 for approximately 2,500 subordinate stations. The example page contains stations subordinate to Portland, ME.

Table 1—Reference Stations

Table 1 is in geographic order of reference port. Once you have found the port of interest, find the page containing the month and day. The data for 8 and 9 May, 1995, is shaded on the sample page.

After the month and day, the first column lists the times of high and low water in Standard Time. To convert to Daylight Savings Time, add one hour. The next column shows the height in feet above datum, which for Portland, ME, is mean lower low water. Obviously, the higher numbers refer to high tides. The third column lists the same tide heights in centimeters.

On 8 May, 1995, the first high water is 8.7 feet above datum at 0439 (4:39 AM). The low water that follows is 1.1 feet above datum at 1058. Since low water is above the 0.0-foot datum by 1.1 feet, the depth of water at low tide at this time will be 1.1 foot greater than that shown on local charts.

Tidal data for May 9 is shown because there are only three tides shown for the date. Three-tide days occur about once every seven days because the four-tide semidiurnal cycle takes 24 hours and 50 minutes.

Table 2—Subordinate Station Differences

Table 2 is listed in the geographic order from north to south of subordinate stations. You can find subordinate stations either by paging through Table 2 or by looking up the name of the station location in the index at the back of the book. Let's look up Station 861, Peaks Island, ME.

Following the number and name of the station, the next two columns list the latitude and longitude of the station. The next two columns show time corrections for high and low waters to be applied to the corresponding times for the reference station in Table 1. The next pair of columns list height corrections for high and low waters. Height corrections indicated by an asterisk (*) are multipliers. If there is no asterisk, the correction is in feet to be added or subtracted. The last three columns show the mean range (mean high water - mean low water), mean spring range (average range at the times of spring tides), and mean tide (the average of mean high and mean low). The mean tide isn't halfway between datum and mean high water because datum in this case is NOT mean low water, but mean *lower* low water.

For Peaks Island, ME, we find differences to be applied to Portland, ME, of:

- time of high water (-0 04)
- time of low water (-0 08)
- height of high water (*0.99)
- height of low water (*0.99)

Using Table 1 and Table 2 Together

Using both Table 1 and Table 2, we can find the heights and times of tides at any subordinate stations for any day.

Example: Find the height and time of the second high tide on 8 May, 1995, at Peaks Island, ME.

Solution: Find Peaks Island, ME, either in the index or directly in Table 2. In Table 2 we find that Peaks Island is Station 861 and is based on Portland, ME.

In Table 1, find Portland, ME, and the date 8 May, 1995. The second high tide for that date is 8.5 feet at 1719.

In Table 2 find Station 861, Peaks Island. The height correction is *0.99 and the time of high water correction is -0 04 minutes. The answer is, therefore:

$$(8.5 \times 0.99) = 8.4 \text{ feet}$$

$$\text{at } (1719 - 0\ 04) = 1715.$$

Table 1. Tides— Portland, Maine, 1995

Times and Heights of High and Low Waters

April

Day	Time	ft	cm	Day	Time	ft	cm
1 Sa	0547	-0.5	-15	16 Su	0509	-1.5	-46
	1159	9.8	299		1123	10.5	320
	1800	0.1	3		1724	-0.8	-24
					2337	11.4	347
2 Su	0011	10.1	308	17 M	0558	-1.7	-52
	0625	-0.4	-12		1213	10.5	320
	1238	9.5	290		1813	-0.8	-24
	1837	0.4	12				
3 M	0046	9.9	302	18 Tu	0026	11.5	351
	0704	-0.1	-3		0649	-1.6	-49
	1316	9.1	277		1305	10.3	314
	1913	0.7	21		1904	-0.6	-18
4 Tu	0123	9.6	293	19 W	0119	11.3	344
	0743	0.2	6		0743	-1.4	-43
	1356	8.8	268		1401	10.0	305
	1952	1.1	34		1959	-0.2	-6
5 W	0203	9.3	283	20 Th	0215	10.9	332
	0824	0.6	18		0841	-1.0	-30
	1438	8.4	256		1501	9.7	296
	2034	1.4	43		2100	0.2	6
6 Th	0246	9.0	274	21 F	0316	10.5	320
	0909	0.9	27		0944	-0.5	-15
	1525	8.1	247		1605	9.4	287
	2120	1.7	52		2206	0.5	15
7 F	0334	8.7	265	22 Sa	0423	10.0	305
	0958	1.2	37		1050	-0.1	-3
	1616	7.9	241		1713	9.3	283
	2212	1.9	58		2316	0.7	21
8 Sa	0427	8.5	259	23 Su	0534	9.7	296
	1052	1.4	43		1157	0.1	3
	1711	7.8	238		1820	9.3	283
	2308	1.9	58				
9 Su	0524	8.5	259	24 M	0027	0.7	21
	1149	1.4	43		0643	9.5	290
	1808	8.0	244		1301	0.2	6
					1923	9.5	290
10 M	0008	1.8	55	25 Tu	0132	0.5	15
	0623	8.6	262		0747	9.5	290
	1244	1.2	37		1400	0.2	6
	1902	8.3	253		2018	9.7	296
11 Tu	0105	1.4	43	26 W	0230	0.2	6
	0719	8.8	268		0844	9.5	290
	1335	0.9	27		1451	0.2	6
	1952	8.8	268		2108	9.9	302
12 W	0158	0.8	24	27 Th	0321	0.0	0
	0812	9.2	280		0934	9.6	293
	1423	0.5	15		1538	0.3	9
	2038	9.4	287		2152	10.1	308
13 Th	0248	0.2	6	28 F	0406	-0.2	-6
	0901	9.7	296		1019	9.6	293
	1509	0.0	0		1619	0.3	9
	2122	10.1	308		2231	10.1	308
14 F	0335	-0.5	-15	29 Sa	0448	-0.3	-9
	0948	10.1	308		1100	9.5	290
	1553	-0.4	-12		1657	0.5	15
	2206	10.7	326		2308	10.1	308
15 Sa	0422	-1.1	-34	30 Su	0526	-0.2	-6
	1035	10.4	317		1138	9.3	283
	1638	-0.7	-21		1733	0.7	21
	2251	11.2	341		2343	10.0	305

May

Day	Time	ft	cm	Day	Time	ft	cm
1 M	0602	-0.1	-3	16 Tu	0542	-1.9	-58
	1215	9.2	280		1158	10.5	320
	1808	0.9	27		1755	-0.7	-21
2 Tu	0017	9.9	302	17 W	0009	11.8	360
	0638	0.0	0		0635	-1.8	-55
	1251	9.0	274		1252	10.4	317
	1843	1.1	34		1849	-0.5	-15
3 W	0053	9.7	296	18 Th	0104	11.6	354
	0715	0.3	9		0730	-1.6	-49
	1329	8.8	268		1349	10.2	311
	1921	1.3	40		1947	-0.2	-6
4 Th	0131	9.5	290	19 F	0202	11.1	338
	0753	0.5	15		0828	-1.1	-34
	1409	8.6	262		1449	10.0	305
	2001	1.5	46		2048	0.1	3
5 F	0212	9.3	283	20 Sa	0303	10.6	323
	0834	0.7	21		0928	-0.7	-21
	1452	8.4	256		1551	9.8	299
	2045	1.6	49		2153	0.4	12
6 Sa	0256	9.0	274	21 Su	0408	10.1	308
	0919	0.9	27		1030	-0.2	-6
	1538	8.3	253		1654	9.7	296
	2134	1.8	55		2300	0.7	21
7 Su	0345	8.8	268	22 M	0515	9.6	293
	1007	1.1	34		1133	0.2	6
	1627	8.3	253		1756	9.6	293
	2227	1.7	52				
8 M	0439	8.7	265	23 Tu	0008	0.7	21
	1058	1.1	34		0621	9.3	283
	1719	8.5	259		1234	0.5	15
	2324	1.6	49		1856	9.7	296
9 Tu	0535	8.7	265	24 W	0111	0.6	18
	1152	1.0	30		0723	9.1	277
	1812	8.9	271		1331	0.7	21
					1951	9.8	299
10 W	0022	1.2	37	25 Th	0208	0.4	12
	0634	8.9	271		0820	9.0	274
	1246	0.8	24		1423	0.8	24
	1905	9.4	287		2040	9.8	299
11 Th	0119	0.7	21	26 F	0259	0.3	9
	0731	9.2	280		0911	9.0	274
	1339	0.5	15		1510	0.9	27
	1956	10.0	305		2125	9.9	302
12 F	0214	0.0	0	27 Sa	0345	0.1	3
	0827	9.6	293		0957	9.0	274
	1430	0.1	3		1552	0.9	27
	2046	10.6	323		2205	10.0	305
13 Sa	0307	-0.7	-21	28 Su	0426	0.1	3
	0920	10.0	305		1038	9.0	274
	1521	-0.3	-9		1630	1.0	30
	2136	11.2	341		2242	10.0	305
14 Su	0358	-1.3	-40	29 M	0504	0.0	0
	1012	10.3	314		1116	9.0	274
	1611	-0.6	-18		1707	1.1	34
	2226	11.6	354		2317	9.9	302
15 M	0450	-1.7	-52	30 Tu	0540	0.1	3
	1105	10.5	320		1153	8.9	271
	1702	-0.7	-21		1742	1.2	37
	2317	11.9	363		2352	9.9	302
				31 W	0615	0.2	6
					1229	8.8	268
					1817	1.2	37

June

Day	Time	ft	cm	Day	Time	ft	cm
1 Th	0027	9.8	299	16 F	0050	11.6	354
	0650	0.3	9		0715	-1.6	-49
	1305	8.8	268		1334	10.4	317
	1854	1.3	40		1933	-0.3	-9
2 F	0104	9.6	293	17 Sa	0147	11.2	341
	0726	0.4	12		0810	-1.2	-37
	1342	8.7	265		1430	10.3	314
	1933	1.4	43		2032	0.0	0
3 Sa	0143	9.5	290	18 Su	0246	10.6	323
	0804	0.5	15		0906	-0.7	-21
	1422	8.7	265		1528	10.1	308
	2015	1.4	43		2133	0.3	9
4 Su	0225	9.3	283	19 M	0346	10.0	305
	0845	0.6	18		1003	-0.2	-6
	1504	8.7	265		1626	9.9	302
	2101	1.4	43		2237	0.6	18
5 M	0311	9.1	277	20 Tu	0448	9.4	287
	0929	0.7	21		1102	0.3	9
	1549	8.9	271		1725	9.7	296
	2152	1.4	43		2340	0.7	21
6 Tu	0401	9.0	274	21 W	0551	9.0	274
	1017	0.7	21		1200	0.8	24
	1638	9.1	277		1822	9.6	293
	2247	1.2	37				
7 W	0456	8.9	271	22 Th	0042	0.8	24
	1109	0.7	21		0653	8.7	265
	1730	9.4	287		1256	1.0	30
	2345	0.9	27		1917	9.6	293
8 Th	0555	9.0	274	23 F	0140	0.7	21
	1204	0.6	18		0750	8.6	262
	1824	9.8	299		1349	1.2	37
					2008	9.6	293
9 F	0045	0.4	12	24 Sa	0232	0.6	18
	0656	9.1	277		0843	8.5	259
	1301	0.4	12		1438	1.3	40
	1920	10.4	317		2054	9.6	293
10 Sa	0145	-0.2	-6	25 Su	0319	0.5	15
	0757	9.4	287		0930	8.6	262
	1358	0.1	3		1523	1.3	40
	2016	10.9	332		2137	9.7	296
11 Su	0243	-0.8	-24	26 M	0402	0.4	12
	0855	9.7	296		1013	8.6	262
	1454	-0.2	-6		1603	1.3	40
	2111	11.4	347		2216	9.8	299
12 M	0338	-1.3	-40	27 Tu	0441	0.3	9
	0952	10.1	308		1052	8.7	265
	1549	-0.4	-12		1641	1.2	37
	2206	11.8	360		2252	9.8	299
13 Tu	0433	-1.7	-52	28 W	0517	0.2	6
	1048	10.3	314		1129	8.8	268
	1644	-0.6	-18		1717	1.2	37
	2300	11.9	363		2328	9.9	302
14 W	0527	-1.9	-58	29 Th	0551	0.2	6
	1143	10.5	320		1204	8.8	268
	1739	-0.7	-21		1752	1.2	37
	2355	11.9	363				
15 Th	0621	-1.8	-55	30 F	0003	9.8	299
	1238	10.5	320		0624	0.2	6
	1835	-0.6	-18		1239	8.9	271
					1829	1.1	34

TABLE 2 – TIDAL DIFFERENCES AND OTHER CONSTANTS

No.	PLACE	POSITION		DIFFERENCES				RANGES		Mean Tide Level
				Time		Height				
		Latitude	Longitude	High Water	Low Water	High Water	Low Water	Mean	Spring	
		North	**West**	h m	h m	ft	ft	ft	ft	ft
	MAINE, Casco Bay–cont. Time meridian, 75° W			on Portland, p.32						
833	Little Flying Point, Maquoit Bay	43° 50'	70° 03'	–0 01	–0 01	*0.99	*0.99	9.0	10.3	4.8
835	South Freeport	43° 49'	70° 06'	+0 12	+0 10	*0.99	*0.99	9.0	10.3	4.8
837	Chebeague Point, Great Chebeague Island.	43° 46'	70° 06'	–0 04	–0 09	*0.99	*0.99	9.0	10.4	4.8
839	Prince Point	43° 46'	70° 10'	0 00	0 00	*1.01	*1.00	9.2	10.6	4.9
841	Doyle Point	43° 45'	70° 08'	–0 02	–0 03	*1.00	*0.88	9.2	10.5	4.9
843	Falmouth Foreside	43° 44'	70° 12'	+0 01	0 00	*1.00	*1.03	9.1	10.5	4.9
845	Great Chebeague Island	43° 43'	70° 08'	+0 03	+0 03	*1.00	*1.00	9.1	10.5	4.9
847	Cliff Island, Luckse Sound	43° 42'	70° 07'	–0 02	–0 02	*1.00	*1.00	9.1	10.4	4.9
849	Vaill Island	43° 41'	70° 09'	+0 05	+0 01	*0.98	*1.03	9.0	10.3	4.8
851	Long Island	43° 41'	70° 10'	–0 01	0 00	*1.00	*1.00	9.1	10.4	4.9
853	Cow Island	43° 41'	70° 11'	–0 01	0 00	*1.00	*1.00	9.1	10.5	4.9
855	Presumpscot River Bridge	43° 41'	70° 15'	+0 01	+0 04	*1.01	*1.06	9.2	10.6	5.0
857	Back Cove	43° 41'	70° 15'	+0 02	+0 06	*0.97	*0.97	9.1	10.5	4.9
859	Great Diamond Island	43° 40'	70° 12'	–0 01	0 00	*0.99	*1.00	9.0	10.4	4.9
861	Peaks Island	43° 39'	70° 12'	–0 04	–0 08	*0.99	*0.99	9.0	10.4	4.8
863	Cushing Island	43° 39'	70° 12'	+0 01	0 00	*0.99	*1.00	9.0	10.4	4.9
865	PORTLAND	43° 40'	70° 15'	Daily predictions				9.1	10.4	4.9
867	Fore River	43° 38'	70° 17'	+0 02	+0 02	*1.00	*1.00	9.1	10.5	4.9
869	Portland Head Light	43° 37'	70° 12'	–0 02	–0 02	*0.97	*0.97	8.9	10.2	4.8
	MAINE, outer coast–cont.									
871	Richmond Island	43° 33'	70° 14'	–0 03	–0 03	*0.98	*0.98	8.9	10.1	4.8
873	Old Orchard Beach	43° 31'	70° 22'	0 00	–0 06	*0.97	*0.97	8.8	10.1	4.7
875	Wood Island Harbor	43° 27'	70° 21'	+0 02	–0 04	*0.96	*0.96	8.7	9.9	4.7
877	Cape Porpoise	43° 22'	70° 26'	+0 12	+0 14	*0.95	*0.95	8.7	9.9	4.7
879	Kennebunkport	43° 21'	70° 28'	+0 16	+0 16	*0.94	*0.94	8.6	9.9	4.6
881	York Harbor	43° 08'	70° 38'	+0 03	+0 13	*0.95	*0.95	8.6	9.9	4.6
883	Seapoint, Cutts Island	43° 05'	70° 40'	+0 01	–0 04	*0.96	*0.96	8.8	10.1	4.7
	MAINE and NEW HAMPSHIRE									
	Portsmouth Harbor									
885	Jaffrey Point	43° 03'	70° 43'	–0 03	–0 05	*0.95	*0.95	8.7	10.0	4.7
887	Gerrish Island	43° 04'	70° 42'	–0 02	–0 03	*0.95	*0.95	8.7	10.0	4.7
889	Fort Point	43° 04'	70° 43'	+0 03	+0 07	*0.94	*0.94	8.6	9.9	4.6
891	Kittery Point	43° 05'	70° 42'	–0 07	+0 01	*0.96	*0.96	8.7	10.0	4.7
893	Seavey Island	43° 05'	70° 45'	+0 20	+0 18	*0.89	*0.89	8.1	9.4	4.4
895	Portsmouth	43° 05'	70° 45'	+0 22	+0 17	*0.86	*0.86	7.8	9.0	4.2
	Piscataqua River									
897	Atlantic Heights	43° 05'	70° 46'	+0 37	+0 28	*0.82	*0.82	7.5	8.6	4.0
899	Dover Point	43° 07'	70° 50'	+1 33	+1 37	*0.70	*0.70	6.4	7.4	3.4
901	Salmon Falls River entrance	43° 11'	70° 50'	+1 35	+1 52	*0.75	*0.75	6.8	7.8	3.6
903	Squamscott River RR. Bridge	43° 03'	70° 55'	+2 19	+2 41	*0.75	*0.75	6.8	7.8	3.6
905	Gosport Harbor, Isles of Shoals	42° 59'	70° 37'	+0 02	–0 02	*0.93	*0.93	8.5	9.8	4.5
907	Hampton Harbor	42° 54'	70° 49'	+0 14	+0 32	*0.91	*0.91	8.3	9.5	4.5
	MASSACHUSETTS, outer coast									
909	Merrimack River entrance	42° 49'	70° 49'	+0 20	+0 24	*0.91	*0.91	8.3	9.5	4.4
911	Newburyport, Merrimack River	42° 49'	70° 52'	+0 31	+1 11	*0.86	*0.86	7.8	9.0	4.2
913	Plum Island Sound (south end)	42° 43'	70° 47'	+0 12	+0 37	*0.94	*0.94	8.6	9.9	4.6
915	Annisquam	42° 39'	70° 41'	0 00	–0 07	*0.96	*0.96	8.7	10.1	4.7
917	Rockport	42° 40'	70° 37'	+0 04	+0 02	*0.94	*0.94	8.6	10.0	4.6
				on Boston, p.36						
919	Gloucester Harbor	42° 36'	70° 40'	–0 01	–0 04	*0.91	*0.91	8.7	10.1	4.6
921	Manchester Harbor	42° 34'	70° 47'	0 00	–0 04	*0.92	*0.92	8.8	10.2	4.7
923	Beverly	42° 32'	70° 53'	+0 02	–0 03	*0.94	*0.94	9.0	10.4	4.7
925	Salem	42° 31'	70° 53'	+0 04	+0 03	*0.92	*0.92	8.8	10.2	4.7
927	Marblehead	42° 30'	70° 51'	0 00	–0 04	*0.95	*0.95	9.1	10.6	4.8
	Broad Sound									
929	Nahant	42° 25'	70° 55'	+0 01	0 00	*0.94	*0.94	9.0	10.4	4.8
931	Lynn Harbor	42° 27'	70° 58'	+0 10	+0 06	*0.96	*0.96	9.2	10.7	4.9
	Boston Harbor									
933	Boston Light	42° 20'	70° 53'	+0 02	+0 03	*0.94	*0.94	9.0	10.4	4.8
935	Lovell Island, The Narrows	42° 20'	70° 56'	+0 04	+0 03	*0.95	*0.95	9.1	10.6	4.8
937	Deer Island (south end)	42° 21'	70° 58'	+0 01	0 00	*0.97	*0.97	9.3	10.8	4.9
939	Belle Isle Inlet entrance	42° 23'	71° 01'	+0 20	+0 17	*1.00	*1.00	9.5	11.0	5.0
941	Castle Island	42° 20'	71° 01'	0 00	+0 02	*0.99	*0.99	9.4	10.9	5.0
943	BOSTON	42° 21'	71° 03'	Daily predictions				9.5	11.0	5.1
945	Dover St. Bridge, Fort Point Channel	42° 21'	71° 04'	+0 06	+0 08	*1.01	*1.01	9.6	11.0	5.1
	Charles River									
947	Charlestown Bridge	42° 22'	71° 04'	+0 04	+0 04	*1.00	*1.00	9.5	11.0	5.0
949	Charles River Dam	42° 22'	71° 04'	+0 07	+0 06	*1.00	*1.00	9.5	11.0	5.0
951	Charlestown	42° 22'	71° 03'	0 00	+0 01	*1.00	*1.00	9.5	11.0	5.0
953	Chelsea St. Bridge, Chelsea River	42° 23'	71° 01'	+0 01	+0 06	*1.01	*1.01	9.6	11.1	5.1
955	Neponset, Neponset River	42° 17'	71° 02'	–0 02	+0 03	*1.00	*1.00	9.5	11.0	5.0
957	Moon Head	42° 19'	70° 59'	+0 01	+0 04	*0.99	*0.99	9.4	10.9	5.0
959	Rainsford Island, Nantasket Roads	42° 19'	70° 57'	0 00	+0 02	*0.95	*0.95	9.1	10.6	4.8

Types of Tidal Current

Tidal currents in the open ocean are *rotary*, i.e. the direction of the water flow rotates 360° during a full tidal period. Rotary currents tend to be small and have little effect on navigation. You may be asked a rotary-current question, however, so we will explain them at the end of this section.

The type of tidal current you definitely will be examined on is the *periodic ebb and flood* in constricted water bodies, such as estuaries. This type of flow is nearly linear because the shape of the water body constrains it to be so.

Tidal Current Terminology

- *Flood* is the movement of tidal current into or up a tidal river or estuary.

- *Ebb* is the movement of tidal current out of or down a tidal river or estuary.

- *Slack water* is the state of the tide when its current is zero, or as close to zero as it gets.

Tidal Current Tables

Tidal current tables are published in three annual volumes:

- *Tidal Current Tables: Atlantic Coast of North America*

- *Tidal Current Tables: Pacific Coast of North America and Asia*

- *Regional Tide and Tidal Current Tables: New York Harbor to Chesapeake Bay*

Like tide tables, each volume consists mostly of two tables. The following two-pages contain a sample page of each table from the volume *Tidal Current Tables—Atlantic Coast of North America.*

Table 1 contains the times of slack water and the times and magnitudes of maximum flood and maximum ebb for the entire year for 25 reference stations, including the sample, Chesapeake Bay Entrance.

Table 2 contains current differences to be applied to the currents in Table 1 for approximately 1,200 subordinate stations. The example page contains stations subordinate to Chesapeake Bay Entrance.

Table 1—Reference Stations

Find the reference station nearest your location and the page covering the month and day. The data for Chesapeake Bay Entrance, 3 June, 1995, is shaded on the sample page.

After the month and day, the first column lists the times of slack water in Standard Time. To convert to Daylight Savings Time add one hour. The next column shows the times of maximum current. The third column shows the magnitude of the maximum current in knots and whether it is an ebb or a flood.

On 3 June, 1995, the first slack water is at 0216 (2:16 AM). The next maximum current is an ebb of 1.0 knots occurring at 0553. Following the ebb the current goes slack again at 0934.

Table 2—Subordinate Station Differences

You can find subordinate stations by paging through Table 2 or by looking up the station name in the index. Let's look up Station 4556, York Spit Channel, N of Buoy "26."

Following the number and name of the station, the next three columns list the water depth, latitude and longitude of the station. The next four columns show time corrections for minimum (slack) before flood, maximum flood, slack before ebb, and maximum ebb. The next pair of columns list speed ratios (multipliers) to apply to maximum flood and ebb currents.

Using Table 1 and Table 2 Together

Using Table 1 and Table 2, we can find the maximum currents and slack waters at any subordinate stations for any day.

Example: Find the time and maximum speed of the first ebb on 3 June, 1995, at York Spit Channel.

Solution: Find the time and speed of first maximum ebb at the reference station, Chesapeake Bay Entrance (found above as 1.0 knots at 0553). Next find the time difference and speed multiplier for maximum ebb at York Spit Channel (+ 1 26 and 0.9). Finally, apply the difference factors to find the answers:

time of maximum ebb 05 53 + 1 26 = 07 19

speed of maximum ebb 1.0 kn × 0.9 = 0.9 kn

Current Diagrams

The time of maximum flood increases as you proceed further into an estuary. You can take advantage of this phenomenon to "go with the flow" and minimize transit time between locations in the diagram. The example diagram below is one of five in the Atlantic Coast tidal current volume.

Select a sloped line from the two sets below, according to your vessel's speed through the water and whether northbound or southbound. Using a parallel rule, transfer the chosen line to the flood (shaded) or ebb (unshaded) zone, keeping the line as close to the center of the zone as possible between your departure and destination points.

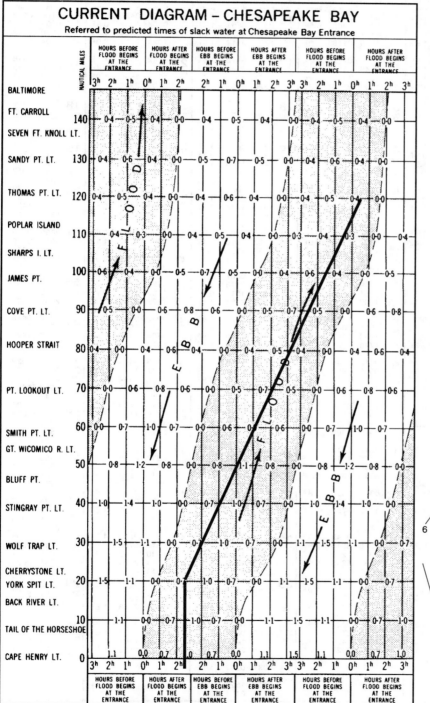

Example: You wish to go from York Split Light to Thomas Point Light on the flood tide. Your vessel's cruising speed is 10 knots. At what time should you leave to derive maximum benefit from the flood current?

Solution: Transfer the 10 knot northbound slope to the flood (shaded) zone between York Spit (nm 20 on the left scale) to Thomas Point Light (nm 120). Move the slope line until it is centered in the zone. From the intersection of the slope line to the horizontal line at 20 nm, draw a vertical line down to read the optimum departure time. The answer is 2.5 hours after slack before flood at Chesapeake Bay Entrance. To get the actual time, find the time of slack before flood from Table 1, as shown on the previous page, and add two hours and 30 minutes.

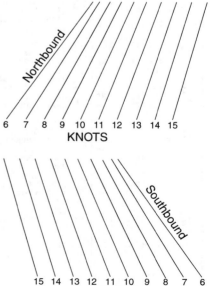

Table 1—Daily Current Predictions

Chesapeake Bay Entrance, Virginia, 1995

F–Flood, Dir. 300° True   E–Ebb, Dir. 129° True

April

Day	Slack h m	Max h m	knots		Day	Slack h m	Max h m	knots
1 Sa		0323	1.4E		**16** Su		0249	1.7E
	0632	0852	0.8F			0557	0821	1.0F
	1141	1514	1.4E			1115	1454	1.8E
	1820	2105	1.1F			1754	2044	1.6F
2 Su	0032	0400	1.3E		**17** M	0017	0336	1.8E
	0719	0932	0.8F			0649	0909	0.8F
	1215	1544	1.3E			1203	1541	1.7E
	1900	2142	1.0F			1843	2131	1.5F
3 M	0110	0439	1.2E		**18** Tu	0107	0428	1.7E
	0805	1013	0.6F			0743	1000	1.0F
	1249	1617	1.2E			1256	1633	1.6E
	1940	2222	0.9F			1938	2222	1.4F
4 Tu	0148	0523	1.1E		**19** W	0158	0527	1.6E
	0852	1058	0.5F			0840	1055	0.9F
	1324	1657	1.0E			1350	1734	1.5E
	2023	2305	0.8F			2035	2318	1.3F
5 W	0227	0612	0.9E		**20** Th	0252	0629	1.5E
	0944	1148	0.4F			0942	1157	0.8F
	1401	1746	0.9E			1453	1840	1.3E
	2109	2353	0.7F			2138		
6 Th	0310	0700	0.8E		**21** F		0018	1.1F
	1042	1239	0.3F			0354	0732	1.4E
	1442	1839	0.9E			1049	1301	0.7F
	2202					1610	1947	1.2E
						2249		
7 F		0041	0.6F		**22** Sa		0121	0.9F
	0404	0748	0.8E			0502	0836	1.3E
	1146	1333	0.3F			1156	1411	0.6F
	1539	1931	0.8E			1735	2100	1.1E
	2303							
8 Sa		0134	0.5F		**23** Su	0001	0231	0.7F
	0505	0843	0.8E			0607	0944	1.3E
	1242	1442	0.3F			1259	1547	0.7F
	1703	2030	0.8E			1848	2215	1.2E
9 Su	0005	0238	0.5F		**24** M	0115	0356	0.7F
	0600	0943	0.9E			0705	1045	1.3E
	1329	1557	0.4F			1356	1653	0.8F
	1816	2138	0.8E			1954	2317	1.2E
10 M	0102	0347	0.5F		**25** Tu	0221	0457	0.7F
	0649	1033	1.0E			0758	1136	1.3E
	1407	1641	0.5F			1445	1735	0.9F
	1919	2240	1.0E			2052		
11 Tu	0158	0437	0.6F		**26** W		0012	1.3E
	0735	1115	1.2E			0319	0541	0.7F
	1440	1716	0.7F			0844	1222	1.3E
	2016	2332	1.1E			1528	1811	1.0F
						2140		
12 W	0248	0517	0.8F		**27** Th		0104	1.4E
	0819	1156	1.3E			0408	0622	0.7F
	1513	1751	1.0F			0924	1305	1.3E
	2107					1604	1847	1.0F
						2222		
13 Th		0022	1.3E		**28** F		0150	1.4E
	0334	0558	0.9F			0451	0703	0.7F
	0903	1239	1.5E			0959	1342	1.3E
	1549	1830	1.2F			1639	1925	1.1F
	2155					2300		
14 F		0113	1.5E		**29** Sa		0231	1.4E
	0420	0643	1.0F			0534	0748	0.7F
	0946	1324	1.6E			1033	1416	1.3E
	1628	1913	1.4F			1714	2003	1.1F
	2241					2337		
15 Sa		0202	1.6E		**30** Su		0308	1.3E
	0508	0731	1.0F			0618	0829	0.7F
	1029	1410	1.7E			1106	1445	1.3E
	1709	1958	1.5F			1751	2041	1.1F
	2328							

May

Day	Slack h m	Max h m	knots		Day	Slack h m	Max h m	knots
1 M	0013	0341	1.3E		**16** Tu	0000	0321	1.8E
	0701	0909	0.6F			0631	0851	1.0F
	1141	1515	1.2E			1144	1524	1.8E
	1829	2118	1.0F			1824	2114	1.6F
2 Tu	0050	0415	1.2E		**17** W	0051	0412	1.8E
	0745	0950	0.6F			0727	0944	1.0F
	1219	1548	1.2E			1241	1617	1.7E
	1909	2156	0.9F			1920	2206	1.5F
3 W	0126	0452	1.1E		**18** Th	0142	0509	1.7E
	0830	1032	0.5F			0823	1040	0.9F
	1257	1627	1.1E			1342	1719	1.5E
	1951	2236	0.8F			2019	2302	1.3F
4 Th	0203	0538	1.0E		**19** F	0236	0611	1.6E
	0918	1120	0.4F			0923	1142	0.8F
	1337	1714	1.0E			1447	1826	1.4E
	2034	2320	0.7F			2122		
5 F	0240	0625	0.9E		**20** Sa		0002	1.1F
	1009	1210	0.3F			0332	0711	1.5E
	1419	1809	0.9E			1027	1246	0.8F
	2121					1601	1932	1.2E
						2230		
6 Sa		0006	0.6F		**21** Su		0103	0.9F
	0322	0710	0.9E			0433	0810	1.4E
	1102	1301	0.3F			1130	1352	0.7F
	1513	1902	0.8E			1720	2041	1.1E
	2215					2342		
7 Su		0055	0.6F		**22** M		0207	0.7F
	0409	0755	0.9E			0533	0913	1.3E
	1151	1354	0.3F			1230	1517	0.7F
	1632	1957	0.8E			1832	2154	1.1E
	2316							
8 M		0144	0.5F		**23** Tu	0055	0323	0.6F
	0501	0845	1.0E			0628	1015	1.3E
	1233	1457	0.4F			1327	1633	0.8F
	1748	2059	0.8E			1937	2259	1.1E
9 Tu	0018	0244	0.5F		**24** W	0204	0431	0.6F
	0550	0939	1.1E			0717	1107	1.2E
	1312	1554	0.6F			1417	1718	0.9F
	1850	2206	1.0E			2035	2355	1.2E
10 W	0118	0348	0.6F		**25** Th	0304	0517	0.6F
	0637	1029	1.2E			0802	1152	1.2E
	1350	1637	0.8F			1500	1751	0.9F
	1948	2303	1.1E			2124		
11 Th	0215	0440	0.7F		**26** F		0046	1.2E
	0725	1116	1.4E			0354	0557	0.6F
	1430	1716	1.1F			0843	1232	1.2E
	2041	2356	1.3E			1539	1825	0.9F
						2206		
12 F	0308	0525	0.8F		**27** Sa		0133	1.2E
	0815	1203	1.5E			0438	0638	0.5F
	1512	1757	1.3F			0920	1311	1.2E
	2132					1615	1901	1.0F
						2243		
13 Sa		0049	1.5E		**28** Su		0214	1.2E
	0358	0613	0.9F			0518	0721	0.5F
	0906	1252	1.7E			0957	1346	1.2E
	1557	1843	1.5F			1650	1940	1.0F
	2220					2319		
14 Su		0142	1.7E		**29** M		0249	1.2E
	0447	0704	1.0F			0559	0805	0.5F
	0958	1344	1.8E			1033	1418	1.2E
	1641	1932	1.6F			1727	2019	1.0F
	2309					2355		
15 M		0232	1.8E		**30** Tu		0321	1.2E
	0538	0758	1.0F			0640	0847	0.5F
	1049	1434	1.8E			1112	1451	1.2E
	1731	2023	1.6F			1804	2057	1.0F
					31 W	0031	0352	1.1E
						0723	0928	0.5F
						1153	1526	1.2E
						1843	2134	0.9F

June

Day	Slack h m	Max h m	knots		Day	Slack h m	Max h m	knots
1 Th	0107	0427	1.1E		**16** F	0126	0449	1.7E
	0808	1009	0.5F			0803	1023	1.0F
	1236	1604	1.1E			1330	1702	1.6E
	1924	2211	0.9F			2004	2245	1.3F
2 F	0142	0507	1.1E		**17** Sa	0216	0548	1.6E
	0850	1053	0.4F			0900	1123	0.9F
	1319	1650	1.0E			1433	1808	1.4E
	2005	2251	0.8F			2105	2343	1.1F
3 Sa	0216	0553	1.0E		**18** Su	0306	0645	1.5E
	0934	1141	0.4F			0959	1225	0.8F
	1403	1742	0.9E			1541	1912	1.3E
	2049	2335	0.7F			2210		
4 Su	0250	0637	1.1E		**19** M		0041	0.9F
	1019	1229	0.4F			0359	0740	1.4E
	1455	1837	0.9E			1059	1324	0.8F
	2139					1655	2017	1.1E
						2320		
5 M		0019	0.7F		**20** Tu		0139	0.7F
	0326	0720	1.1E			0453	0837	1.3E
	1101	1314	0.5F			1157	1432	0.7F
	1605	1930	0.9E			1805	2127	1.1E
	2238							
6 Tu		0107	0.6F		**21** W	0030	0243	0.6F
	0408	0804	1.1E			0545	0936	1.2E
	1142	1404	0.5F			1251	1555	0.7F
	1719	2028	0.9E			1908	2234	1.0E
	2340							
7 W		0200	0.6F		**22** Th	0139	0355	0.5F
	0457	0855	1.2E			0631	1031	1.1E
	1223	1501	0.7F			1343	1650	0.8F
	1822	2133	1.0E			2007	2331	1.0E
8 Th	0042	0302	0.6F		**23** F	0242	0448	0.4F
	0548	0949	1.3E			0715	1117	1.1E
	1308	1556	0.9F			1430	1728	0.8F
	1920	2237	1.1E			2059		
9 F	0145	0404	0.7F		**24** Sa		0022	1.1E
	0641	1042	1.4E			0333	0529	0.4F
	1354	1644	1.2F			0758	1158	1.1E
	2016	2332	1.3E			1513	1801	0.9F
						2143		
10 Sa	0242	0458	0.8F		**25** Su		0109	1.1E
	0736	1134	1.6E			0416	0609	0.5F
	1442	1730	1.4F			0840	1237	1.1E
	2110					1551	1837	0.9F
						2221		
11 Su		0027	1.5E		**26** M		0151	1.1E
	0337	0548	0.9F			0455	0652	0.5F
	0834	1227	1.7E			0923	1314	1.2E
	1531	1818	1.5F			1628	1917	0.9F
	2201					2257		
12 M		0122	1.6E		**27** Tu		0226	1.1E
	0428	0640	1.0F			0534	0738	0.5F
	0932	1322	1.8E			1006	1352	1.2E
	1621	1910	1.6F			1704	1958	0.9F
	2252					2332		
13 Tu		0215	1.7E		**28** W		0258	1.1E
	0519	0736	1.0F			0614	0823	0.5F
	1030	1417	1.8E			1048	1429	1.2E
	1714	2004	1.6F			1741	2036	1.0F
	2343							
14 W		0305	1.8E		**29** Th	0008	0327	1.2E
	0611	0833	1.0F			0657	0905	0.5F
	1129	1509	1.8E			1132	1506	1.2E
	1809	2058	1.6F			1819	2112	1.0F
15 Th	0035	0355	1.8E		**30** F	0044	0400	1.2E
	0708	0927	1.0F			0737	0945	0.5F
	1229	1603	1.7E			1218	1545	1.2E
	1906	2150	1.5F			1859	2148	0.9F

Table 2—Current Differences

CHESAPEAKE BAY
Time meridian, 75° W

No.	PLACE	Position — Latitude North	Position — Longitude West	Meter Depth (ft)	Time Diff. Min. before Flood	Time Diff. Flood	Time Diff. Min. before Ebb	Time Diff. Ebb	Speed Ratio Flood	Speed Ratio Ebb	Min. before Flood (knots)	Min. before Flood Dir.	Max. Flood (knots)	Max. Flood Dir.	Min. before Ebb (knots)	Min. before Ebb Dir.	Max. Ebb (knots)	Max. Ebb Dir.
					h m	h m	h m	h m			knots		knots		knots		knots	
4441	Cape Henry Light, 1.1 n.mi. NNE of	36°56.33'	75°59.98'	15d	+0 26	+0 03	−0 04	+0 10	1.3	1.3	–	–	1.0	298°	–	–	1.7	113°
	...do.	36°56.33'	75°59.98'	38d	+1 42	−1 41	−1 36	−1 52	1.4	1.0	0.2	003°	1.1	275°	0.2	189°	1.2	106°
4446	Cape Henry Light, 2.0 n.mi. north of	36°57.53'	78°00.63'	15d	+0 12	+0 25	−1 00	−0 20	1.5	0.9	0.1	210°	1.2	289°	0.1	190°	1.1	110°
	...do.	36°57.53'	76°00.63'	39d	−0 23	+0 10	+0 55	−0 17	1.5	0.5	0.1	012°	1.2	277°	–	–	0.7	110°
	...do.	36°57.53'	76°00.63'	54d	−1 03	+0 07	+0 34	−1 05	1.1	0.4	0.1	002°	0.9	263°	0.2	177°	0.5	111°
4451	CHESAPEAKE BAY ENTRANCE	36°58.80'	75°59.88'	15d	on Chesapeake Bay Entrance, p.44 — Daily predictions						0.0	–	0.8	300°	0.0	–	0.8	129°
4456	Cape Henry Light, 4.6 miles north of	37°00.1'	75°59.3'	14d	−0 27	−0 09	+0 19	+0 23	1.6	1.0	–	–	1.3	294°	–	–	1.3	104°
4461	Cape Henry Light, 5.9 n.mi. north of	37°01.40'	75°59.55'		−0 59	−0 09	−0 26	−0 36	0.8	0.5	0.1	228°	0.6	307°	0.1	229°	0.7	140°
4466	Lynnhaven Roads	36°55.1'	76°04.9'		−0 20	+0 15	−0 10	−0 10	1.0	0.7	–	–	0.8	280°	0.1	232°	0.9	070°
4471	Lynnhaven Inlet bridge	36°54.4'	76°05.6'		−1 18	−1 10	−1 43	−2 30	0.7	1.1	–	–	0.6	180°	–	–	1.4	000°
	Chesapeake Bay Bridge Tunnel																	
4476	Chesapeake Beach, 1.5 miles north of	36°56.69'	76°07.33'	15d	+0 29	+0 48	+0 06	+0 00	1.0	0.7	0.1	228°	0.8	305°	–	–	0.9	100°
4481	Thimble Shoal Channel (Buoy "10")	36°58.73'	76°07.57'	45d	−0 04	+0 30	+0 45	+0 16	1.4	0.6	–	–	1.1	302°	–	–	0.7	122°
	...do.	36°58.73'	76°07.57'		−0 55	+0 15	+1 25	−0 17	0.8	0.2	0.1	228°	0.7	285°	–	–	0.3	105°
4486	Tail of the Horseshoe	36°59.57'	76°06.20'	12	+0 05	+0 30	+0 16	+0 28	1.1	0.8	–	–	0.9	300°	–	–	1.0	110°
4491	Cape Henry Light, 8.3 mi. NW of	37°02.20'	76°06.60'		+0 16	+0 43	+0 45	+0 26	1.2	0.9	–	–	1.0	329°	–	–	1.0	133°
4496	Chesapeake Channel (bridge tunnel)	37°02.50'	76°04.33'	13d	+0 05	+0 38	+0 32	+0 19	2.2	1.2	–	–	1.8	335°	0.1	229°	1.5	145°
4501	Chesapeake Channel (Buoy "15")	37°03.40'	76°05.58'		−0 30	+0 33	+0 50	+0 38	0.8	0.4	0.2	037°	0.6	311°	–	–	0.4	125°
	...do.	37°03.40'	76°05.58'	34d	−0 21	+0 27	+0 57	−0 07	0.7	0.3	0.2	032°	0.6	309°	0.1	232°	0.4	139°
4506	Fishermans Island, 3.2 miles WSW of	37°04.00'	78°02.25'		−0 22	−0 12	−0 17	−0 36	1.5	1.3	–	–	1.2	330°	–	–	1.6	135°
4511	Fishermans Island, 1.4 miles WSW of	37°04.78'	78°00.25'		−1 09	−0 02	−0 12	−1 02	2.2	1.3	–	–	1.8	330°	–	–	1.1	140°
4516	Fishermans I Bridge 1.4 n.mi. S of	37°03.37'	75°58.33'	16d	−0 19	−0 29	−0 15	−0 26	1.2	1.1	0.2	218°	1.0	297°	–	–	1.4	126°
	...do.	37°03.37'	75°58.33'	26d	−0 37	−0 19	−0 16	−0 34	1.0	0.8	–	–	0.8	290°	–	–	1.0	120°
4521	Fishermans I. Bridge, 0.7 n.mi. S of	37°04.85'	75°59.33'	15d	−0 57	−0 15	−0 24	−0 35	1.9	1.5	0.2	223°	1.5	306°	0.1	218°	1.9	140°
4526	Fishermans I., 0.4 mile west of	37°05.57'	76°00.33'		−0 21	−0 08	−0 06	−0 42	2.5	1.6	–	–	2.0	005°	–	–	2.0	175°
4531	Fishermans I., 1.4 n.mi. WNW of	37°06.10'	76°00.00'	16d	−0 28	−0 14	−0 12	−0 27	1.4	1.0	0.1	060°	1.2	333°	0.1	247°	1.2	155°
4536	Fishermans I., 1.1 miles northwest of	37°06.50'	75°58.30'		−0 39	+0 20	+0 23	−0 19	2.2	1.3	–	–	1.8	355°	–	–	1.6	165°
4541	Cape Charles, off Wise Point	37°06.88'	75°58.30'	5	+0 09	+0 37	+0 56	+1 20	0.9	0.2	–	–	0.7	305°	–	–	0.3	075°
4546	Little Creek, 0.2 n.mi. N of east jetty	36°56.05'	76°01.60'	15d	−1 01	−1 18	−0 39	−1 01	0.4	0.3	–	–	0.3	278°	–	–	0.3	092°
4551	Butler Bluff, 2.1 n.mi. WSW of	37°09.37'	76°01.60'	14d	+0 02	+0 14	+0 57	+0 02	0.9	0.7	–	–	0.8	348°	–	–	0.8	164°
4556	York Spit Channel, N of Buoy "26"	37°12.90'	76°08.50'	7	+1 33	+1 50	+1 24	+1 26	1.0	0.9	–	–	0.8	010°	–	–	1.1	195°
4561	Old Plantation Flats Lt., 0.5 mi. W of	37°14.00'	76°04.10'	15d	+1 31	+2 01	+1 55	+1 06	1.5	1.0	0.2	280°	1.2	005°	0.1	094°	1.3	175°
4566	Cape Charles City, 3.3 n.mi. west of	37°15.87'	76°05.62'	40d	+0 38	+1 18	+1 03	+1 01	1.2	0.8	–	–	1.0	355°	0.1	284°	1.0	187°
	...do.	37°15.87'	76°05.62'	95d	+0 16	+0 43	+1 10	+0 30	1.1	0.7	–	–	0.9	356°	–	–	0.8	182°
4571	New Point Comfort, 4.1 n.mi. ESE of	37°17.40'	76°11.45'	15d	+0 29	+1 00	+1 37	+1 24	1.0	0.8	0.1	223°	1.0	322°	0.3	098°	0.8	138°
4576	Wolf Trap Light, 5.8 mile west of	37°23.4'	76°11.9'		+1 07	+1 22	+0 46	+0 46	1.0	1.0	0.3	296°	0.8	018°	–	–	1.2	202°
4581	Wolf Trap Light, 5.8 miles east of	37°23.1'	76°04.3'		+1 43	+2 00	+1 34	+1 36	1.2	1.0	–	–	1.0	015°	–	–	1.2	190°
4586	Church Neck Point, 1.9 n.mi. W of	37°24.20'	76°00.78'		+2 23	+2 40	+2 14	+2 16	1.1	0.9	–	–	0.9	015°	–	–	1.3	175°
4591	Wolf Trap Light, 6.1 n.mi. ENE of	37°24.50'	76°03.83'	15d	+0 46	+1 37	+1 36	+0 50	0.6	0.3	–	–	0.4	003°	0.2	098°	0.4	177°
4596	Wolf Trap Light, 5.2 n.mi. ENE of	37°24.50'	76°03.83'	14d	+1 40	+1 58	+2 28	+2 11	1.6	0.9	0.2	275°	1.3	006°	0.2	279°	1.1	191°
	...do.	37°24.50'	76°03.83'	29d	+0 26	+0 55	+1 27	+1 07	0.8	0.5	0.2	099°	0.7	012°	0.2	098°	0.7	173°
	...do.	37°24.50'	76°05.00'	15d	+1 43	+2 34	+2 41	+2 09	1.6	0.9	0.2	283°	1.3	010°	0.2	098°	1.1	183°
	...do.	37°24.50'	76°05.00'	40d	+1 07	+2 24	+2 43	+1 19	1.3	0.5	0.2	089°	1.0	352°	0.2	266°	0.7	183°
4601	Wolf Trap Light, 1.4 n.mi. NNE of	37°24.67'	76°05.00'	63d	+0 24	+2 16	+2 05	+1 11	1.4	0.9	–	–	0.8	343°	–	–	0.6	158°
4606	Wolf Trap Light, 2.0 n.mi. NW of	37°25.00'	76°12.90'	15d	+1 38	+2 16	+1 52	+1 19	0.7	0.4	0.2	088°	1.1	005°	0.2	088°	1.2	166°
4611	Nassawadox Point, 1.9 n.mi. NW of	37°29.97'	75°59.37'	14d	+0 03	+0 33	+1 05	+0 08	0.8	0.5	–	–	0.6	345°	0.1	270°	0.6	178°
4616	Gwynn Island, 8.0 n.mi. east of	37°29.70'	76°06.50'	13d	+1 16	+1 43	+1 56	+1 36	1.2	0.9	0.2	267°	0.6	352°	0.2	270°	1.0	175°
4621	Gwynn Island, 1.5 n.mi. east of	37°30.03'	76°10.4'	14d	+2 03	+3 03	+2 48	+2 33	0.7	0.4	0.2	102°	1.0	357°	0.1	090°	0.5	209°
4626	Stingray Point, 5.5 miles east of	37°35.0'	76°02.3'	28d	+0 33	+1 07	+1 46	+0 23	0.6	0.4	–	–	0.6	013°	0.1	281°	0.5	159°
4631	Stingray Point, 12.5 miles east of	37°33.8'	76°03.80'	16d	+0 59	+0 54	+0 54	+0 22	1.2	0.6	–	–	0.5	331°	0.1	227°	0.9	179°
4636	Powells Bluff, 2.2 n.mi. NW of	37°35.45'	76°08.10'	17d	+2 28	+3 36	+3 21	+2 32	1.2	0.6	–	–	1.0	343°	–	–	0.9	175°
4641	Windmill Point Light, 8.3 n.mi. ESE of	37°34.60'	76°03.80'	14d	+2 18	+3 00	+2 09	+2 36	0.8	0.5	0.1	101°	1.0	030°	–	–	0.6	201°
	...do.	37°34.60'	76°03.80'	33d	+1 21	+2 57	+1 54	+2 46	1.1	0.7	0.1	270°	0.6	015°	0.1	284°	0.8	182°
	...do.				+1 06	+1 22	+3 07	+2 14	0.6	0.3	0.2	099°	0.5	017°	0.2	255°	0.4	172°

Rotary Currents

Most open ocean tidal currents rotate in direction through the tidal period of 12 hours 25 minutes. The tidal current volumes contain information on rotary currents for a few dozen offshore locations (former lightship stations). The illustration at right was drawn from the data listed for Frying Pan Shoal, off Cape Hatteras. The arrows show the direction the current is flowing at the number of hours after the time of maximum flood at Charleston (listed in Table 1). The speeds are monthly averages. Speeds increase by 15-20% at times of full and new moons, and decrease by the same amount at quadrature.

Note that there is no slack water in a rotary current. Instead, there is a minimum current and a maximum current, separated by three hours, thus corresponding to low and high tides.

Wind Driven Current

Wind will cause a surface current due to friction. Just as in the atmosphere, the wind-driven current will be deflected to the right in the Northern Hemisphere. Observed current vs wind speed at most light ships averaged:

Wind, mph	10	20	30	40	50
Current, kn	0.2	0.3	0.4	0.5	0.6

While the Coriolis force causes an average current deflection of 30° to the right of the wind, the configuration of the coast can alter the direction. The Atlantic Coast tidal current volume lists data for 20 lightship stations. Here are the deflections for Frying Pan Shoals, where + means to the right and - means to the left of the wind direction. Wind from:

N (34°)	NE (18°)	E (2°)	SE (48°)
S (48°)	SW (26°)	W (-7°)	NW (-27°)

Combined Effects

Rotary and wind-driven currents combine the same way as vessel speed through the water and current. *Example:* the wind at Frying Pan shoals has been northwesterly at an average velocity of 22 knots. The predicted set and drift of the rotary current are 125° at 0.6 knot. What current should you expect?

Solution: plot the rotary current vector of 0.6 kn @ 125°T. The 22 knot wind should produce a 0.3 kn wind-driven current. With the wind from the NW, the deflection is -27°, so the wind driven vector is 0.3 kn @ (135° - 27°) = 108°, which we add to the rotary vector. The resultant current is 0.9 kn @ 119°.

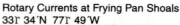

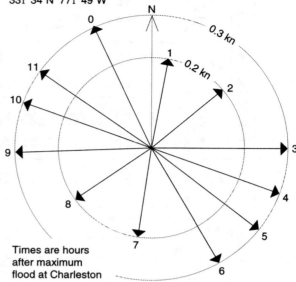

Rotary Currents at Frying Pan Shoals
33Γ 34′N 77Γ 49′W

Times are hours after maximum flood at Charleston

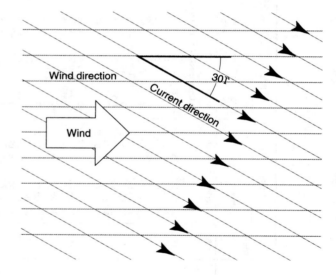

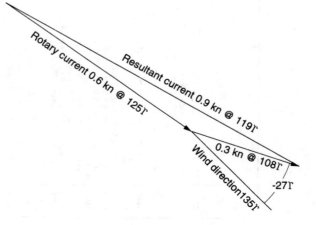

Charts

A nautical chart projects part of the spherical earth onto a flat surface. It shows information needed to pilot a vessel safely from point to point. It is also a plotting surface on which the navigator can work problems.

The most common nautical projection for small areas is the Mercator, where the surface of the earth (imagine it to be a transparent globe) is projected onto a cylinder, tangent to the earth at the Equator, from a point source of light at the earth's center. The Mercator projection is used for two very good reasons: 1) rhumb lines plot as straight lines; 2) the vertical scale is 1´ of latitude = 1 nautical mile.

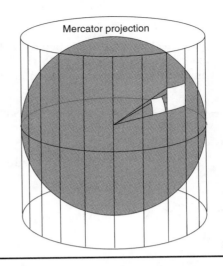
Mercator projection

Chart Scales

Chart scale is the ratio of a unit of distance on the chart to the distance represented on the earth in the same units. Scale is represented in two ways:

- a fraction, such as 1/80,000. Note that a larger denominator indicates a smaller scale.

- a scale—a subdivided bar—indicating nautical miles, statute miles and sometimes yards. The vertical scale of 1´ = 1 nm is also commonly used.

Four common NOS classifications by scale are:

Sailing charts—>600,000 for long ocean voyaging

General charts—150,000–600,000 for cruising outside the major buoys

Coastal charts—50,000–150,000 for inside buoys

Harbor charts—<50,000 for inside harbors

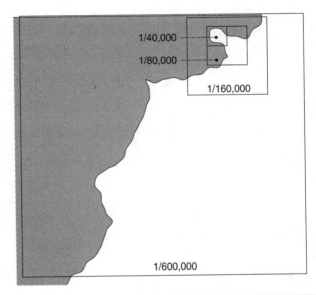

Chart Numbering System

NOS and DMAHTC share a common numbering system, where North America is designated as Region 1. South and Central America fall in Region 2.

The illustration at right shows the subdivisions of Region 1. Learn these subdivisions. You may see them on the exam.

All chart numbers within a subregion start with the subregion number. For example, within subregion 12, Chart 12200 is the general chart (scale 1/400,000) for Cape May to Cape Hatteras.

NOS offers chart catalogs (free through chart dealers) which show the numbering system in detail. Get the catalog for your area.

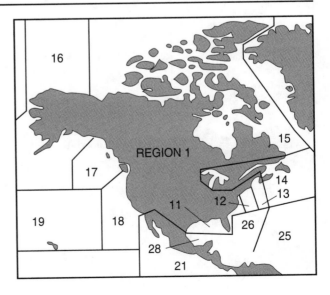

Chart No. 1

Chart No. 1 is not a chart at all. Published by NOS, it is a collaboration between NOS and DMAHTC, listing all of the symbols (in color), abbreviations and terms used on NOS and DMAHTC charts. Below and on the next page are the more common symbols. Navigation aids are covered later in this chapter.

Relief

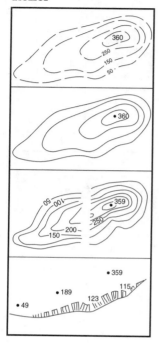

Approximate contour lines with approximate height

Form lines with spot height

Contour lines with spot height

Spot heights

Water Features

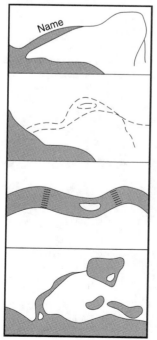

River, Stream

Intermittent river

Rapids, Waterfalls

Lakes

Bridges

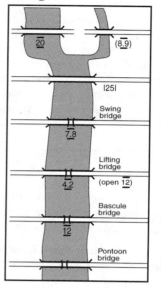

Vertical clearance above high water

Horizontal clearance

Swing bridge

Lifting bridge

Bascule bridge

Pontoon bridge

Ports

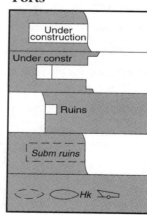

Works at sea

Works under construction

Ruins

Submerged ruins

Hulk

Canals

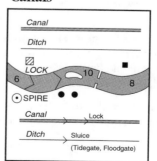

Canal

Lock (on large-scale chart)

Lock (on small-scale chart)

Tidal Levels and Charted Data

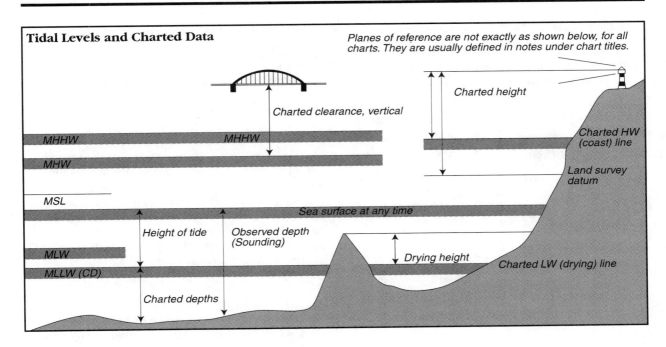

Planes of reference are not exactly as shown below, for all charts. They are usually defined in notes under chart titles.

Charted clearance, vertical

Charted height

MHHW   MHHW

Charted HW (coast) line

MHW

Land survey datum

MSL

Sea surface at any time

Height of tide   Observed depth (Sounding)

MLW

Drying height

MLLW (CD)

Charted LW (drying) line

Charted depths

Depth Contours

Feet	Fm/m	▨ Green ▨ Blue
0	0	
6	1	
12	2	
18	3	
24	4	
30	5	
36	6	
60	10	
120	20	
180	30	
240	40	
300	50	
600	100	
1200	200	
1800	300	
2400	400	
3000	500	
6000	1000	

Types of Seabed, Intertidal Areas

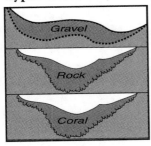

Area with stones, gravel or shingle

Rocky area, which covers and uncovers

Coral reef, which covers and uncovers

Obstructions

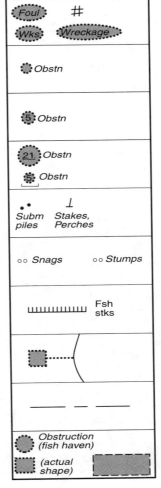

Remains, not dangerous to navigation

Obstruction, depth unknown

Obstruction, least depth known

Obstruction, swept by wire or diver

Stumps of posts or piles, submerged

Submerged pile, stump or snag (with exact position)

Fishing stakes

Fish trap, fish weirs, tunny nets

Fish trap area, tunny nets area

Fish haven (artificial fishing reef)

Publications Other Than Charts

Tide Tables (four volumes) are prepared annually by the National Ocean Service (NOS) and were covered earlier in this chapter.

Tidal Current Tables (two volumes) are also prepared annually by NOS and covered in an earlier section.

Tidal Current Charts

Published for 11 bodies of water, each set contains 11 hourly chartlets showing tidal current vectors. The vectors show both direction and speed in knots at the time of spring tides.

Coast Pilot

NOS publishes nine annual *United States Coast Pilots* to supplement nautical charts of U.S. waters. The nine volumes are:

1. *Eastport to Cape Cod*

2. *Cape Cod to Sandy Hook*

3. *Sandy Hook to Cape Henry*

4. *Cape Henry to Key West*

5. *Gulf of Mexico, Puerto Rico, Virgin Islands*

6. *Great Lakes and Connecting Waterways*

7. *California, Oregon, Washington and Hawaii*

8. *Alaska–Dixon Entrance to Cape Spencer*

9. *Cape Spencer to Beaufort Sea*

Information is derived from field inspections, survey vessels and harbor authorities. An excerpt from *Volume 1, Atlantic Coast: Eastport to Cape Cod* is shown in the box below.

> (463) **New Meadows River,** at the northeastern end of Casco Bay, is about 8.5 miles long from **Bear Island** at the entrance to the highway bridge on a dam at the head of navigation. A lighted buoy off **Fort Point** (43°46.8′ N., 69°53.6′W.) marks the entrance to the river. It has a deep water channel for the first 6 miles, and a draft of about 12 feet can be carried to within 0.5 mile of the dam. The principal dangers are buoyed.
> (464) Above **Howard Point,** about 1.5 miles south of the dam, the channel is narrow and unmarked, and has a depth of about 7 feet to the dam. Local knowledge is necessary to carry the best water above **Foster Point,** 3 miles from the head.
> (465) The river is seldom used except by local fishing boats and small pleasure craft. Small craft can enter New Meadows River from westward 6 miles above its entrance through Gurnet Strait.
> (466) **Cundy Harbor** is a good anchorage for small vessels on the west side of New Meadows River, 1 mile above its mouth. The harbor is clear and has depths of 22 to 31 feet. A buoy marks the south end of the bare ledges on the northeast side of the harbor.

American Practical Navigator (Bowditch)

DMAHTC publishes the reference known simply as "Bowditch." Subjects covered include piloting, electronic navigation, celestial navigation, navigational mathematics, navigational safety, oceanography and marine meteorology.

Sailing Directions

DMAHTC publishes *Sailing Directions*, which consist of 37 *Enroutes* and 10 *Planning Guides* for foreign waters. *Planning Guides* describe general features of ocean basins; *Enroutes* describe features of coastlines, ports and harbors. The Planning Guides are relatively permanent and the Enroutes are frequently updated. Between updates, both are corrected by *Notice to Mariners*.

List of Lights, Radio Aids and Fog Signals

DMAHTC publishes *List of Lights,* not to be confused with the Coast Guard *Light Lists* (see below). This volume is very similar in content to *Light Lists*, but covers foreign waters. It does not, however, cover lighted buoys inside harbors.

Notice to Mariners

DMAHTC publishes the weekly *Notice to Mariners* prepared jointly by NOS and the Coast Guard. The information is for the correction of charts, light lists and sailing directions. The semi-annual *Summary of Corrections* makes updating simpler. Each Coast Guard District also publishes a weekly *Local Notice to Mariners*, free for the asking.

Light Lists

The U.S. Coast Guard publishes seven annual *Light Lists* which list complete information about U.S. navigation lights and other navigation aids. They are intended to be used in conjunction with nautical charts, and are corrected by *Notice to Mariners*. The seven volumes are:

1. *Atlantic Coast–St. Croix River, ME to Toms River, NJ*

2. *Atlantic Coast–Toms River, NJ to Little River Inlet, SC*

3. *Atlantic Coast–Little River Inlet, SC to Econfina, FL plus Greater Antilles*

4. *Gulf of Mexico–Econfina River, FL to Rio Grande, TX*

5. *Mississippi River System*

6. *Pacific Coast and Pacific Islands*

7. *Great Lakes*

The following page contains an excerpt from *Vol. I.*

Light Lists

(1) No.	(2) Name and location	(3) Position	(4) Characteristic	(5) Height	(6) Range	(7) Structure	(8) Remarks
		N/W				**MAINE – First District**	
	CASCO BAY (Chart 13290)						
	PORTLAND HARBOR (Chart 13292)						
	Portland Harbor						
7565	**Portland Head Light**	43 37.4 70 12.5	Fl W 4^s	101	24	White conical tower, connected dwelling. 80	HORN: 1 blast ev 15^s (2^s bl). Lighted throughout 24 hours.
7570	**Portland Head Directional Light**	43 37.4 70 12.5	F W (R+G sector)	23	W 15 R 11 G 11	At base of Portland Head Light.	Shows red from 271.3° to 274.3°; white from 274.3° to 275.8°, green from 275.8° to 279.3°.
7575	**Ram Island Ledge Light**	43 37.9 70 11.3	Fl (2) W 6^s 1^s fl 1.0^s ec. 1^s fl 3.0^s ec.	77	12	Light-gray, conical, granite tower.	Emergency light of reduced intensity when main light is extinguished. HORN: 1 blast ev 10^s (1^s bl).
7580	– **Main Approach** Lighted Bell Buoy 12	43 38.0 70 12.5	Fl R 4^s		4	Red.	
7590	– **Midchannel** Lighted Gong Buoy PH	43 38.4 70 13.0	Mo (A) W		6	Red and white stripes with red spherical topmark.	
7595	Portland Main Approach Buoy 14					Red nun.	

Description of Columns

1. Light List number

2. Name of the aid. When preceded by a dash (–) the bold heading is part of the name of the aid.

3. Geographic position in latitude and longitude. Note: position is approximate and is listed only to facilitate locating the aid on the chart.

4. Light characteristic for a lighted aid. Morse characteristic for a radiobeacon.

5. Height above water from mean high water to the focal plane of a fixed light.

6. Nominal range of lighted aids, in nm, listed by color for alternating lights. Effective range for radio beacons in nautical miles. Not listed for ranges, directional lights or private aids to navigation.

7. Structural characteristic of the aid, including dayboard, description of fixed structure, color and type of buoy and height above ground.

8. General remarks, including fog signal and RACON characteristics, light sector arc of visibility, radar reflector if installed on fixed structure, emergency lights, seasonal remarks, and private aid identification.

Abbreviations

Al	Alternating	LNB	Large Nav Buoy
bl	blast	MHz	Megahertz
C	Canadian	Mo	Morse Code
ec	Eclipse	Oc	Occulting
ev	Every	ODAS	Anch. Ocean. Data Buoy
F	Fixed	Q	Quick Flashing
fl	flash	Ra ref	Radar reflector
Fl	Flashing	RBN	Radiobeacon
FS	Fog Signal	R	Red
Fl(2)	Group flashing	s	seconds
G	Green	si	silent
I	Interrupted	SPM	Single Point Mooring Buoy
Iso	Isophase	W	White
kHz	Kilohertz	Y	Yellow
LFl	Long Flash		
lt	Lighted		

Determining the Range of a Light

The range of a light is the distance at which it can be seen. This is a function of three variables: heights of the light and observer (geographic range), intensity of the light (nominal range), and meteorological visibility (luminous range). Any one of the variables can prove to be the limiting factor. We find the solution by calculating geographic range and luminous range and picking the smaller of the two.

Geographic Range

The illustration at top right shows how the earth's curvature limits range. The distance, D_E, from the height of the eye, H_E, to the tangent to the earth's surface is called the distance to the horizon.

D_E (and D_L) can be found from the Geographic Range Table at right (found in the *Light Lists*). It can also be calculated using a simple 4-function calculator as:

$$D_E = 1.17 \sqrt{H_E}$$

Example: $H_E = 20$ feet. $D_E = 1.17 \sqrt{20} = 5.2$ feet.

Don't forget, Geographic Range = $D_E + D_L$!

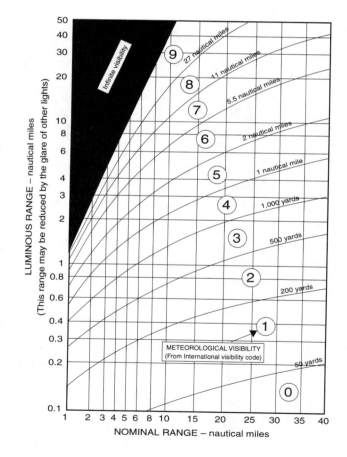

Geographic Range Table

Height Feet	Distance nm	Height Feet	Distance nm	Height Feet	Distance nm
5	2.6	70	9.8	250	18.5
10	3.7	75	10.1	300	20.3
15	4.5	80	10.5	350	21.9
20	5.2	85	10.8	400	23.4
25	5.9	90	11.1	450	24.8
30	6.4	95	11.4	500	26.2
35	6.9	100	11.7	550	27.4
40	7.4	110	12.3	600	28.7
45	7.8	120	12.8	650	29.8
50	8.3	130	13.3	700	31.0
55	8.7	140	13.8	800	33.1
60	9.1	150	14.3	900	35.1
65	9.4	200	16.5	1000	37.0

Nominal Range

The range listed in the Light Lists (column 6) *is* the nominal range of the light, simple as that.

Luminous Range

The nominal range of a light in the *Light Lists* assumes a meteorological visibility of 10 nm. The Luminous Range Diagram at right (found in the front of the *Light Lists*) allows you to find luminous range, given nominal range and the actual meteorological visibility. To use the diagram, enter at the bottom with nominal range, follow the vertical line to where it intersects the meteorological visibilty curve, then run horizontally to find luminous range.

Example: The *Light List* shows that a navigational light has a nominal range of 10 miles and a height above water of 38 feet. Your height of eye is 52 feet and the visibility is 11.0 miles. At what approximate range will you first sight the light?

Solution:

Geographic range = D_E (8.4 nm) + D_L (7.2 nm) = 15.6 nm

Nominal range = 10 nm

Luminous range = 10.5 nm

Answer: 10.5 nm

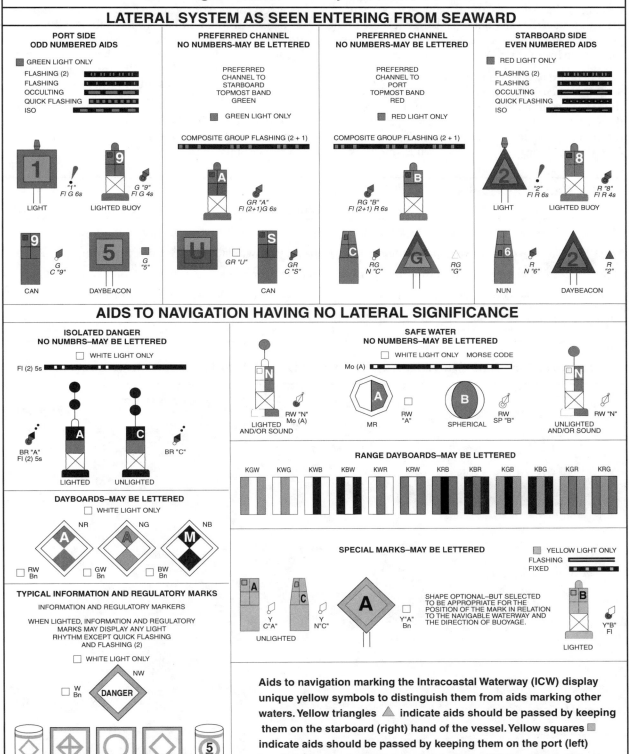

Lateral Systems

Lateral buoyage systems are suited for narrow channels and for coastlines without many islands. Each buoy indicates the direction of a danger relative to the course of the channel or coastline. The United States Aids to Navigation System is a lateral system.

There are two world lateral systems. North and South America, Japan, Korea and the Phillipines use the IALA B system (red, right, returning). The rest of the world uses the IALA A system (green, right, returning). Most buoyage questions will involve the U.S. Aids to Navigation System shown in this book.

Cardinal Systems

Cardinal systems are suited for areas with many isolated rocks, shoals and islands. A cardinal mark is used with the compass to indicate the direction to navigable water. It takes its name from the quadrant in which it is placed. There is deep water to the north of a north mark, to the east of an east mark, to the south of a south mark, and to the west of a west mark.

You may get a question or two on the cardinal system. The table below summarizes the characteristics of cardinal marks.

IALA Cardinal Marks

Quadrant	Topmarks	Color Bands	Quick Flash Light Pattern
North	Two cones with both points up	Black over yellow	Uninterrupted quick
East	Two cones with bases together	Black, yellow, black	3 quick in a group
South	Two cones with both points down	Yellow over black	6 quick followed by 1 long
West	Two cones with points together	Yellow, black, yellow	9 flashes in a group

Memory aids: Topmarks, "West is a Wine glass."
Lights–associate with a clock, i.e. East is 3, South is 6, West is 9.

A Fictitious Nautical Chart Demonstrating the IALA–B Lateral System

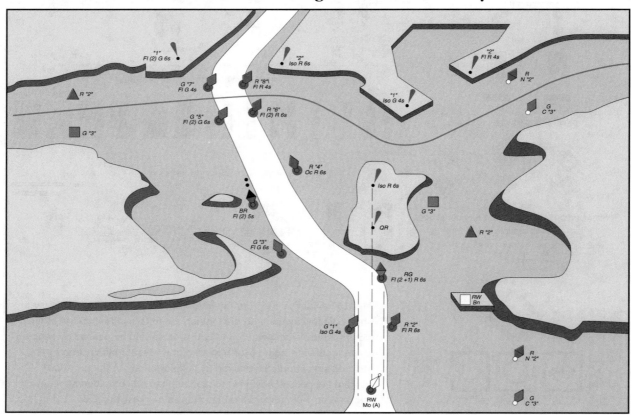

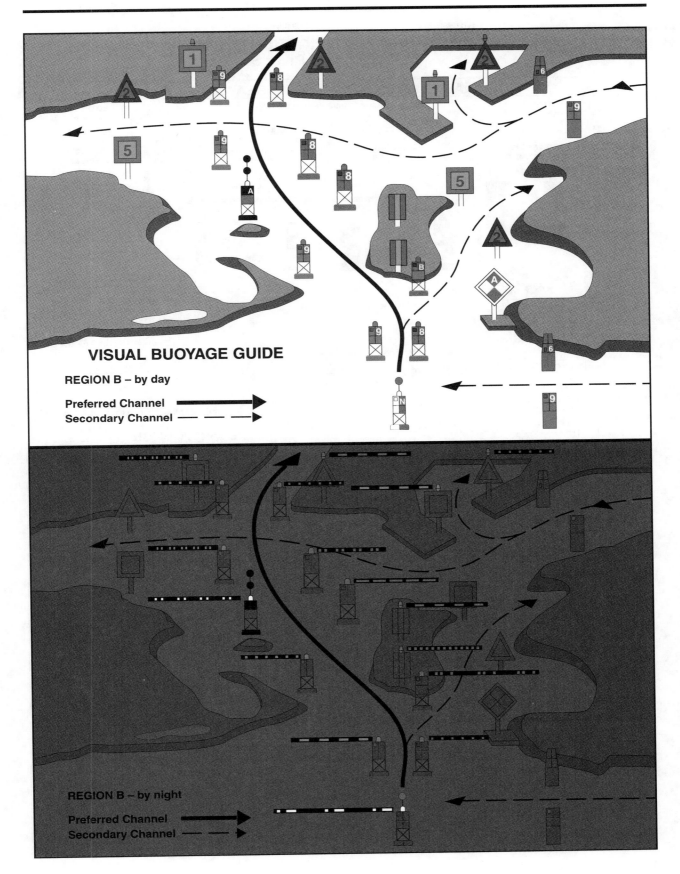

VISUAL BUOYAGE GUIDE

REGION B – by day

Preferred Channel

Secondary Channel

REGION B – by night

Preferred Channel

Secondary Channel

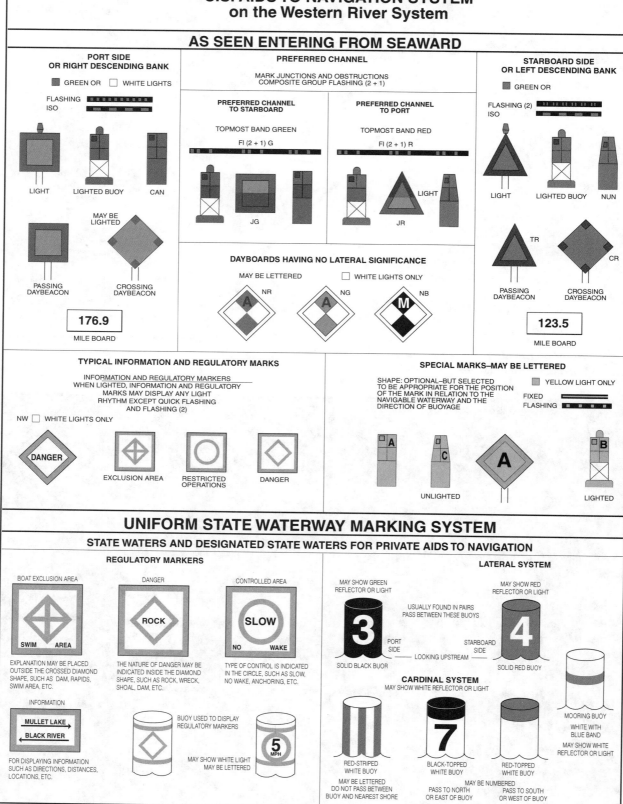

U.S. AIDS TO NAVIGATION SYSTEM
on the Western River System

AS SEEN ENTERING FROM SEAWARD

PORT SIDE OR RIGHT DESCENDING BANK

GREEN OR WHITE LIGHTS

FLASHING
ISO

LIGHT · LIGHTED BUOY · CAN

MAY BE LIGHTED

PASSING DAYBEACON · CROSSING DAYBEACON

176.9 MILE BOARD

PREFERRED CHANNEL

MARK JUNCTIONS AND OBSTRUCTIONS
COMPOSITE GROUP FLASHING (2 + 1)

PREFERRED CHANNEL TO STARBOARD
TOPMOST BAND GREEN
Fl (2 + 1) G
JG

PREFERRED CHANNEL TO PORT
TOPMOST BAND RED
Fl (2 + 1) R
LIGHT
JR

DAYBOARDS HAVING NO LATERAL SIGNIFICANCE

MAY BE LETTERED · WHITE LIGHTS ONLY

A NR · A NG · M NB

STARBOARD SIDE OR LEFT DESCENDING BANK

GREEN OR

FLASHING (2)
ISO

LIGHT · LIGHTED BUOY · NUN

TR · CR

PASSING DAYBEACON · CROSSING DAYBEACON

123.5 MILE BOARD

TYPICAL INFORMATION AND REGULATORY MARKS

INFORMATION AND REGULATORY MARKERS
WHEN LIGHTED, INFORMATION AND REGULATORY
MARKS MAY DISPLAY ANY LIGHT
RHYTHM EXCEPT QUICK FLASHING
AND FLASHING (2)

NW WHITE LIGHTS ONLY

DANGER · EXCLUSION AREA · RESTRICTED OPERATIONS · DANGER

SPECIAL MARKS—MAY BE LETTERED

SHAPE: OPTIONAL–BUT SELECTED
TO BE APPROPRIATE FOR THE POSITION
OF THE MARK IN RELATION TO THE
NAVIGABLE WATERWAY AND THE
DIRECTION OF BUOYAGE

YELLOW LIGHT ONLY

FIXED
FLASHING

A · C · A UNLIGHTED · B LIGHTED

UNIFORM STATE WATERWAY MARKING SYSTEM

STATE WATERS AND DESIGNATED STATE WATERS FOR PRIVATE AIDS TO NAVIGATION

REGULATORY MARKERS

BOAT EXCLUSION AREA
SWIM AREA

EXPLANATION MAY BE PLACED
OUTSIDE THE CROSSED DIAMOND
SHAPE, SUCH AS DAM, RAPIDS,
SWIM AREA, ETC.

DANGER
ROCK

THE NATURE OF DANGER MAY BE
INDICATED INSIDE THE DIAMOND
SHAPE, SUCH AS ROCK, WRECK,
SHOAL, DAM, ETC.

CONTROLLED AREA
SLOW
NO WAKE

TYPE OF CONTROL IS INDICATED
IN THE CIRCLE, SUCH AS SLOW,
NO WAKE, ANCHORING, ETC.

INFORMATION
MULLET LAKE
BLACK RIVER

FOR DISPLAYING INFORMATION
SUCH AS DIRECTIONS, DISTANCES,
LOCATIONS, ETC.

BUOY USED TO DISPLAY
REGULATORY MARKERS

MAY SHOW WHITE LIGHT
MAY BE LETTERED

5 MPH

LATERAL SYSTEM

MAY SHOW GREEN
REFLECTOR OR LIGHT

3
PORT SIDE

SOLID BLACK BUOR

USUALLY FOUND IN PAIRS
PASS BETWEEN THESE BUOYS

LOOKING UPSTREAM

MAY SHOW RED
REFLECTOR OR LIGHT

4
STARBOARD SIDE

SOLID RED BUOY

CARDINAL SYSTEM
MAY SHOW WHITE REFLECTOR OR LIGHT

RED-STRIPED
WHITE BUOY
MAY BE LETTERED
DO NOT PASS BETWEEN
BUOY AND NEAREST SHORE

7
BLACK-TOPPED
WHITE BUOY
PASS TO NORTH
OR EAST OF BUOY

RED-TOPPED
WHITE BUOY
MAY BE NUMBERED
PASS TO SOUTH
OR WEST OF BUOY

MOORING BUOY
WHITE WITH
BLUE BAND
MAY SHOW WHITE
REFLECTOR OR LIGHT

Compass Errors

There are two reasons why a magnetic compass does not always point to True North (the North Pole):

Variation—the difference between the direction toward the North Pole and the direction toward the Earth's North Magnetic Pole. (The map at right shows variation.)

Deviation—the difference between the direction to magnetic north and the direction the compass points.

Variation is said to be "west" when the compass points to the west of True North. The compass at right shows a compass rotated 11° to the west by a variation of 11°W. Similarly, deviation is said to be "west" if it causes the compass to rotate even further to the west.

Correcting and Uncorrecting

Correcting—starting with compass reading and working toward True—is simple if you can remember just one mnemonic: *Correcting Add East (CAE)*.

A simple example will demonstrate. Suppose the compass reads 180°, the variation (from the chart) is 11°W, and compass deviation on a heading of 180° is 6°E (from the vessel's deviation table). Using C-A-E:

$$\text{True} = \text{Compass} + \text{Variation} + \text{Deviation}$$
$$= 180° + 11°W + 6°E$$
$$= 180° + (-11°) + (6°)$$
$$= 175°T$$

The examples below show how easy it is to find true, compass, variation or deviation, given the other three quantities. Practice!

Correcting Add East (Subtract West)

Compass Reading	Variation →	Deviation	True Direction
45°	6W(-6)	3E(+3)	45-6+3=42°T
90°	11W(-11)	5W(-5)	90-11-5=74°T
110°	17W(-17)	3E(+3)	110-17+3=96°T
284°	6E(+6)	5W(-5)	284+6-5=285°T

Uncorrecting Add West (Subtract East)

Compass Reading	← Variation	Deviation	True Direction
117-4+11=124	11°W(+11)	4°E(-4)	117°T
245+6+7=258	7°W(+7)	6°W(+6)	245°T
93-2-2=89	2°E(-2)	2°E(-2)	093°T
13+3+14=30	14°W(+14)	3°W(+3)	013°T

Correcting Add East (Subtract West)

Compass Reading	Variation →	Deviation	True Direction
45°	6W(-6)	45-6+x=42 x=+3 (3E)	42°T
90°	90+x-5=74 x=-11 (11W)	5W(-5)	74°T
110°	17W(-17)	110-17+x=96 x=+3 (3E)	96°T
284°	284+x-5=285 x=+6 (6E)	5W(-5)	285°T

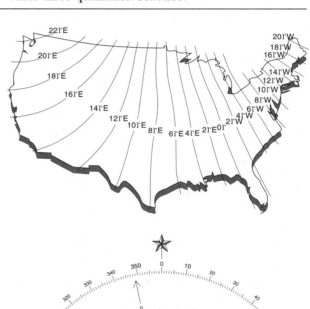

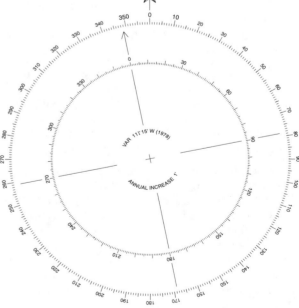

LORAN

Loran

The Loran C system consists of chains of radio transmitting stations, operating on a carrier frequency of 100 kHz, and separated by hundreds of miles. Within a chain, one station is designated as the master and the others as secondaries. There are a minimum of two and a maximum of four secondaries for each master.

Masters and secondaries transmit pulses at precise time intervals (controlled by Cesium atomic clocks). A shipboard Loran receiver measures the time differences (TDs) between arrival of the master and secondary pulse pairs. The receiver displays either the TDs in microseconds, or latitude and longitude, which it computes from the TDs.

The time difference between arrival of master and secondary pulses is a measure of the difference in distances between the receiver and the two transmitters. Locations with constant time differences (TDs) fall along hyperbolic curves, as shown in the chart at right. That is why Loran is known as a hyperbolic radio navigation system.

By comparing the overall pulse envelopes, Loran receivers can measure TDs to about .01 microseconds—equivalent to 10 feet. Using the radio waves that travel along the ground (the ground wave), Loran is very *repeatable* to about 1,200 miles. Reception of sky waves, which bounce off the earth's ionosphere, allows degraded reception to about 3,000 miles.

Unfortunately, topography and variations in the earth's conductivity affect travel times and so distort the hyperbolae. Uncorrected *accuracy* is more like ±0.25 mile. Sophisticated Loran receivers store correction factors (ASFs) which they use to improve the latitude/longitude conversion.

At turn-on Loran receivers acquire signals and match cycles automatically. Most receivers will be "tracking" (producing reliable positions) within five minutes. When a secondary station becomes unreliable, it transmits a coded signal which causes the receiver to "blink" and alert the operator.

All of North America is blanketed by a series of overlapping Loran chains, each having its own Group Repetition Interval (GRI). It is up to the operator to select the best GRI for his area. "Best" involves distance from the chain—which controls signal strength and spacing of hyperbola—and crossing angle of the LOPs. The figure at right shows that, for a given TD uncertainty, the area of position uncertainty is much less for steep crossing angles than for shallow angles. As a rule of thumb any angle >30° is acceptable.

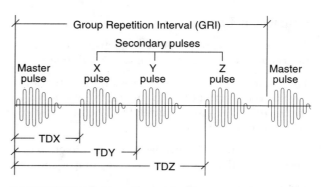

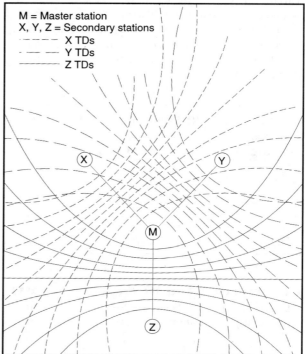

M = Master station
X, Y, Z = Secondary stations
------ X TDs
-·-·- Y TDs
——— Z TDs

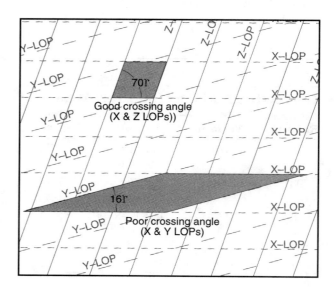

Good crossing angle
(X & Z LOPs))

Poor crossing angle
(X & Y LOPs)

RADAR

How Radar Works

Radar is the only navigation system in which the signals originate at the vessel (unless you consider a depth sounder a navigation system). The radar system sends out extremely high frequency pulses from a rotating antenna, the direction of which is indicated by a rotating line on the screen called the cursor. When a pulse strikes an object, a portion of the energy is reflected back to the antenna where it is received, amplified and displayed in the direction of the cursor as a "pip." The distance of the pip from the center of the screen indicates its range; the direction of the cursor when the pip occurs is its bearing.

Limitations

The strength of the reflected pulse depends not only on target size, but material and orientation:

- Metals reflect best, followed by water, rock, wood, and plastics. Wood and plastic vessels require metal radar reflectors.

- Assuming the same material and size, targets with flat surfaces perpendicular to the bearing reflect better.

Radar transmission is line-of-sight, i.e. it cannot see over the horizon. The maximum range of a radar system is therefore calculated in the same way as the visible range of a light (see page 222).

Radar cannot resolve (present as separate) targets which are closer together than the radar antenna's horizontal beam width. Beam width for a 30" antenna is 3.8°, for a 48" antenna 1.9°.

Displays and Tracking Targets

Figure A at top right shows the components of a typical display. The fixed vertical line is the ship's heading for a "relative display" or north for a "stabilized display" connected to a gyrocompass. Range and bearing of the target is indicated by variable range and bearing markers which the operator controls.

Figure B shows a sequence of reflections with decreasing range but constant bearing. The radar plot shows that the vessel and the target are on collision courses and must take avoiding action.

Figure C shows a sequence of reflections where both range and bearing are changing. By drawing a line between successive reflections, you can tell that risk of collision does not exist. In fact, you can measure the projected distance of closest approach.

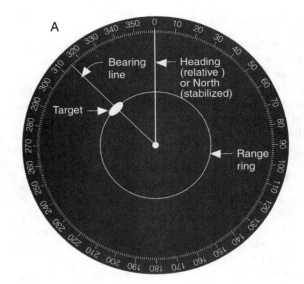

A

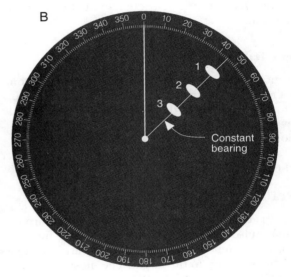

B

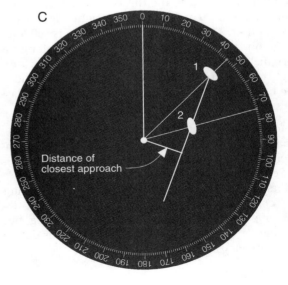

C

LOP from Range Only

Due to beam width, range determined by radar is generally more accurate than bearing. A single range reading establishes a circle of position centered on the nearest point of the target. Figure D shows a series of such circles of position centered on the edge of a coastline. The vessel must be on the line of position (LOP) tangent to all of the circles of position.

Fix from Single Range and Bearing

Figure E shows a target of known position on a chart. The vessel is known to be somewhere along the circle of position centered on the target and of radius equal to the range. At the same time, the vessel must be somewhere along the bearing line drawn through the target. The location of the vessel is, therefore, at the intersection of the two lines of position.

Fix from Two or Three Ranges

Figure F shows three separate charted targets along a shoreline. The range of each is drawn as a circle of position centered on the respective targets. Only two circles of position are required to fix the location of the vessel, but three circles are better. The best estimate of the vessel's position is at the center of the "cocked hat" formed by the three circles.

Reflectors and Racons

Several devices are used to enhance the return of radar pulses. *Radar reflectors* are passive metal objects designed to maximize the return regardless of the direction to the target. The most common reflector is similar to the three-corned mirror, i.e. three flat metal (or foil) plates at right angles to each other. Theoretically, a radar pulse is reflected from one surface to a another, then back along the original path to the antenna. These reflectors are lightweight, sturdy and inexpensive, and should be hung from the mast of every wood or fiberglass vessel.

Racons are active transponders (RACON = RAdar transponder beaCON) placed on some large navigational buoys. When the racon detects a radar pulse, it sends out a coded pulse of its own, such as a Morse Code letter. On a radar screen a buoy having a racon will appear as the normal buoy pip, but accompanied by a pattern on the same bearing, but at slightly greater range. The greater range is due to a slight delay in sending out the code.

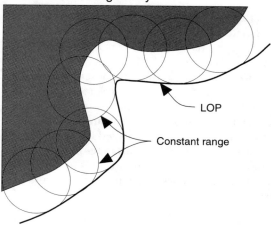

D. LOP from Range Only

LOP

Constant range

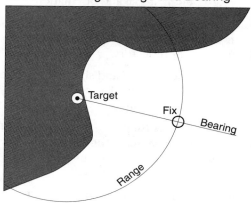

E. Fix from Single Range and Bearing

Target

Fix

Bearing

Range

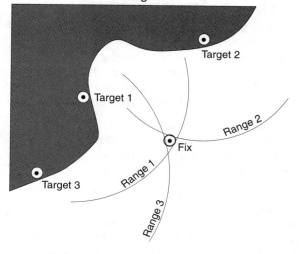

F. Fix from Three Ranges

Target 2

Target 1

Range 2

Fix

Range 1

Target 3

Range 3

00000. In plotting a running fix, how many fixed objects are needed to take your line of position from?

A. none
B. 1
C. 2
D. 3

00001. Unlighted, red and green, horizontally-banded buoys with the topmost band red:

A. are cylindrical in shape and called can buoys
B. are conical in shape and called nun buoys
C. may either be cylindrical or conical since the shape has no significance
D. are triangular in shape to indicate that it may not be possible to pass on either side of the buoy

00002. On an isomagnetic chart, the line of zero variation is the:

A. zero variation line
B. isogonic line
C. variation line
D. agonic line

00003. Blinking of a Loran-C signal indicates:

A. the signal is in proper sequence
B. there will be no increase or decrease in kHz
C. there is an error in the transmission of that signal
D. that it has the proper GRI

00006. Wind velocity varies:

A. directly with the temperature of the air mass
B. directly with the pressure gradient
C. inversely with the barometric pressure
D. inversely with the absolute humidity

00007. The period at high or low tide during which there is no change in the height of the water is called the:

A. range of the tide
B. plane of the tide
C. stand of the tide
D. reversing of the tide

00008. When you are steering on a pair of range lights and find the upper light is above the lower light you should:

A. come left
B. come right
C. continue on the present course
D. wait until the lights are no longer in a vertical line

00009. When displayed under a single-span fixed bridge, red lights indicate:

A. the channel boundaries
B. that vessels must stop
C. the bridge is about to open
D. that traffic is approaching from the other side

00010. The wind at Frying Pan shoals has been northwesterly at an average velocity of 22 knots. The predicted set and drift of the rotary current are 125° at 0.6 knot. What current should you expect?

A. 119° at 0.9 knot
B. 172° at 1.1 knots
C. 225° at 0.6 knot
D. 340° at 0.4 knot

00011. A buoy having red and green horizontal bands would have a light characteristic of:

A. interrupted quick-flashing
B. composite group-flashing
C. Morse (A)
D. quick flashing

00012. Lines on a chart which connect points of equal magnetic variation are called:

A. magnetic latitudes
B. magnetic declinations
C. dip
D. isogonic lines

00013. Most modern Loran-C receivers, when not tracking properly, have a(n):

A. bell alarm to warn the user
B. lighted alarm signal to warn the user
C. alternate signal keying system
D. view finder for each station

00014. You have replaced the chart paper in the course recorder. Which of the following is NOT required to ensure that a correct trace is recorded?

A. test the electrical gain to the thermograph pens
B. set the zone pen on the correct quadrant
C. line the course pen up on the exact heading of the ship
D. adjust the chart paper to indicate the correct time

00015. What is the length of a nautical mile?

A. 1,850 m
B. 2,000 yd.
C. 6,076 ft.
D. 6,080 ft.

00016. The direction of the surface wind is:

A. directly from high toward low pressure
B. directly from low toward high pressure
C. from high pressure toward low pressure deflected by the earth's rotation
D. from low pressure toward high pressure deflected by the earth's rotation

00017. "Stand" of the tide is that time when:

A. the vertical rise or fall of the tide has stopped
B. slack water occurs
C. tidal current is at a maximum
D. the actual depth of the water equals the charted depth

00018. If possible, a vessel's position should be plotted by bearings of:

A. buoys close at hand
B. fixed known objects on shore
C. buoys at a distance
D. any of the above

00019. You are approaching a swing bridge at night. You will know that the bridge is open for river traffic when:

A. the fixed, green light starts to flash
B. the amber light changes to green
C. the red light is extinguished
D. the red light changes to green

00020. You are underway on course 050° T and your maximum speed is 12 knots. The eye of a hurricane bears 120° T, 110 miles from your position. The hurricane is moving towards 285° T at 25 knots. If you maneuver at 12 knots to avoid the hurricane, what could be the maximum CPA?

A. 77 miles
B. 82 miles
C. 87 miles
D. 93 miles

00021. Which buoy is lettered?

A. green can buoy
B. preferred channel buoy
C. red lighted buoy
D. green gong buoy

00022. A chart showing the coast of Mexico is produced by, and could be ordered from, the United States:

A. Defense Mapping Agency Hydrographic Center
B. Coast Guard
C. Naval Observatory
D. National Ocean Service

00023. If Loran-C signals become unsynchronized, the receiver operator is warned because:

A. signals begin to blink
B. signals begin to shift
C. stations discontinue transmission
D. stations transmit grass

00025. You are in LONG 144° E. The date is 6 February, and the zone time is 0800. The Greenwich date and time are:

A. 2200, 5 February
B. 2300, 5 February
C. 1700, 6 February
D. 1800, 6 February

00026. Wind direction may be determined by observing all of the following EXCEPT:

A. low clouds
B. waves
C. whitecaps
D. swells

00027. Spring tides are tides that:

A. have lows lower than normal and highs higher than normal
B. have lows higher than normal and highs lower than normal
C. are unpredictable
D. occur in the spring of the year

00028. When using a buoy as an aid to navigation which of the following should be considered?

A. The buoy should be considered to always be in the charted location.
B. If the light is flashing, the buoy should be considered to be in the charted location.
C. The buoy may not be in the charted position.
D. The buoy should be considered to be in the charted position if it has been freshly painted.

00029. You are approaching a multiple-span bridge at night. The main navigational channel span will be indicated by:

A. a red light on the bridge pier on each side of the channel
B. a steady blue light in the center of the span
C. three white lights in a vertical line in the center of the span
D. a flashing green light in the center of the span

00031. When approaching a preferred-channel buoy, the best channel is NOT indicated by the:

A. light characteristic
B. color of the uppermost band

C. shape of an unlighted buoy
D. color of the light

00032. The datum used for soundings on charts of the Atlantic Coast of the United States is:

A. mean low water
B. mean lower low water
C. mean high water springs
D. mean high water

00033. Most modern Loran-C receivers automatically detect station blink which:

A. indicates the station is transmitting normally
B. triggers alarm indicators to warn the operator
C. automatically shuts down the receiver
D. causes the receiver to shift automatically to another Loran chain

00034. The normal variation between the actual depth of water and the indicated depth on an electronic depth sounder due to water conditions is on the side of safety. This would NOT be true in a case when the water:

A. has high salinity
B. is unusually warm
C. is fresh
D. is extremely cold

00037. What does the term "tide" refer to?

A. horizontal movement of the water
B. vertical movement of the water
C. mixing tendency of the water
D. salinity content of the water

00038. When navigating a vessel, you:

A. can always rely on a buoy to be on station
B. can always rely on a buoy to show proper light characteristics
C. should assume a wreck buoy is directly over the wreck
D. should never rely on a floating aid to maintain its exact position

00041. Mean high water is the reference plane used for:

A. all vertical measurements
B. heights above water of land features such as lights
C. soundings on the East and West Coasts
D. water depths on the East Coast only

00042. The datum used for soundings on charts of the East Coast of the United States is:

A. mean low water springs
B. mean low water

C. mean lower low water
D. half tide level

00043. A buoy with a composite group-flashing light indicates a(n):

A. anchorage area
B. fish net area
C. bifurcation
D. dredging area

00044. The speed of sound through ocean water is nearly always:

A. faster than the speed of calibration for the fathometer
B. the same speed as the speed of calibration for the fathometer
C. slower than the speed of calibration for the fathometer
D. faster than the speed of calibration for the fathometer, unless the water is very warm

00047. The range of tide is the:

A. distance the tide moves out from the shore
B. duration of time between high and low tide
C. difference between the heights of high and low tide
D. maximum depth of the water at high tide

00048. When should a navigator rely on the position of floating aids to navigation?

A. during calm weather only
B. during daylight only
C. only when inside a harbor
D. only when fixed aids are not available

00050. The difference between the heights of low and high tide is the:

A. period
B. range
C. distance
D. depth

00051. In the U. S. Aids to Navigation System, red and green horizontally-banded buoys mark:

A. channels for shallow draft vessels
B. general anchorage areas
C. fishing grounds
D. junctions or bifurcations

00052. The reference datum used in determining the heights of land features on most charts is:

A. mean sea level
B. mean high water
C. mean low water
D. half-tide level

00053. Loran-C may be used for safe navigation in harbor areas due to:

A. multipulse grouping
B. repeatability of readings
C. synchronization control
D. using secondary vs. slave stations

00054. The elapsed time of a fathometer signal (from sound generation to the return of the echo) is 1 second. What is the depth of the water at the point sounded?

A. 400 ft.
B. 400 fm.
C. 800 ft.
D. 800 fm.

00057. The height of tide is the:

A. depth of water at a specific time due to tidal effect
B. difference between the depth of the water and the area's tidal datum
C. difference between the depth of the water and the high water tidal level
D. difference between the depth of the water at high tide and the depth of the water at low tide

00058. In calculating a running fix position, what is the minimum number of fixed objects needed to take your lines of position from?

A. 1
B. 2
C. 3
D. none

00061. Red lights may appear on:

A. horizontally-banded buoys
B. vertically-striped buoys
C. yellow buoys
D. spherical buoys

00062. Charted depth is the:

A. vertical distance from the chart sounding datum to the ocean bottom, plus height of tide
B. vertical distance from the chart sounding datum to the ocean bottom
C. average height of water over a specified period of time
D. average height of all low waters at a place

00063. A "full service" Loran-C receiver provides:

A. matching pulse rates of at least 20 stations
B. an automatic on-and-off switch
C. a horizontal matching of all delayed hyperbolic signals
D. automatic signal acquisition and cycle matching

00064. Your vessel's fathometer transmits a signal which is returned 1.5 seconds later. Your vessel is in how much water?

A. 1,800 ft.
B. 3,600 ft.
C. 5,400 ft.
D. 7,200 ft.

00066. A veering wind will do which?

A. change direction in a clockwise manner in the Northern Hemisphere
B. circulate about a low pressure center in a counterclockwise manner in the Northern Hemisphere
C. vary in strength constantly and unpredictably
D. circulate about a high pressure center in a clockwise manner in the Southern Hemisphere

00067. Which of the following is the correct definition of height of tide?

A. the vertical distance from the tidal datum to the level of the water at any time
B. the vertical difference between the heights of low and high water
C. the vertical difference between a datum plane and the ocean bottom
D. the vertical distance from the surface of the water to the ocean floor

00068. A position obtained by taking lines of position from 1 object at different times and advancing them to a common time is a(n):

A. dead reckoning position
B. estimated position
C. fix
D. running fix

00070. Mean lower low water is the reference plane used for:

A. all vertical measurements
B. heights above water for lights, mountains, etc.
C. soundings on the east and west coasts
D. water depths on the east coast only

00071. A preferred-channel buoy may be:

A. lettered
B. spherical
C. showing a white light
D. all of the above

00072. The datum from which the predicted heights of tides are reckoned in the Tide Tables is:

A. mean low water
B. the same as that used for the charts of the locality

C. the highest possible level
D. given in Table 3 of the Tide Tables

00073. After initial turn-on, most modern Loran-C receivers will be automatically tracking within:

A. 1 minute
B. 3 minutes
C. 5 minutes
D. 10 minutes

00074. When operated over a muddy bottom, a fathometer may indicate:

A. a shallow depth reading
B. a zero depth reading
C. no depth reading
D. 2 depth readings

00076. In the Northern Hemisphere, a wind that shifts counterclockwise is a:

A. veering wind
B. backing wind
C. reverse wind
D. chinook wind

00077. When there are small differences between the heights of 2 successive high tides or 2 successive low tides, the tides are called:

A. diurnal
B. semi-diurnal
C. solar
D. mixed

00078. A single line of position combined with a dead reckoning position results in a(n):

A. assumed position
B. estimated position
C. fix
D. running fix

00080. When the Moon is at first quarter or third quarter phase, what type of tides will occur?

A. apogean
B. perigean
C. neap
D. spring

00081. A buoy with a composite group-flashing light indicates a(n):

A. bifurcation
B. fish net area
C. anchorage area
D. dredging area

00082. On the West Coast of North America, charted depths are taken from:

A. high water
B. mean tide level
C. mean low water
D. mean lower low water

00083. All Loran-C transmitting stations are equipped with cesium frequency standards which permit:

A. every station in 1 chain to transmit at the same time
B. each station to transmit without reference to another station
C. on-line transmission of single-line transmitters at the same time
D. each station to only depend on the master for synchronization and signal ratio

00084. When using an echo sounder in deep water, it is NOT unusual to:

A. receive a strong return at about 200 fathoms during the day, and 1 nearer the surface at night
B. receive a first return near the surface during the day, and a strong return at about 200 fathoms at night
C. receive false echoes at a constant depth day and night
D. have to recalibrate every couple of days due to inaccurate readings

00086. A weather forecast states that the wind will commence backing. In the Northern Hemisphere, this would indicate that it will:

A. shift in a clockwise manner
B. shift in a counterclockwise manner
C. continue blowing from the same direction
D. decrease in velocity

00087. A tide is called diurnal when:

A. only 1 high and 1 low water occur during a lunar day
B. the high tide is higher and the low tide is lower than usual
C. the high tide and low tide are exactly 6 hours apart
D. two high tides occur during a lunar day

00088. Which of the following positions includes the effects of wind and current?

A. dead reckoning position
B. leeway position
C. estimated position
D. set position

00090. When the Moon is new or full, what type of tides occur?

A. neap
B. spring
C. diurnal
D. apogean

00091. A preferred-channel buoy will show a:

A. white light whose characteristic is Morse (A)
B. group-occulting white light
C. composite group-flashing (2 + 1) white light
D. composite group-flashing (2 + 1) red or green light

00092. When utilizing a Pacific Coast chart, the reference plane of soundings is:

A. mean low water springs
B. mean low water
C. mean lower low water
D. lowest normal low water

00093. The time interval between the transmission of signals from a pair of Loran-C stations is very closely controlled and operates with:

A. an atomic time standard
B. Daylight Savings Time
C. Eastern Standard Time
D. Greenwich Mean Time

00094. When using a recording depth finder in the open ocean, what phenomena is most likely to produce a continuous trace that may not be from the actual ocean bottom?

A. echoes from a deep scattering layer
B. echoes from schools of fish
C. multiple returns reflected from the bottom to the surface and to the bottom again
D. poor placement of the transducer on the hull

00096. A weather forecast states that the wind will commence veering. In the Northern Hemisphere this indicates that the wind will:

A. shift in a clockwise manner
B. shift in a counterclockwise manner
C. continue blowing from the same direction
D. increase in velocity

00097. The lunar or tidal day is:

A. about 50 minutes shorter than the solar day
B. about 50 minutes longer than the solar day
C. about 10 minutes longer than the solar day
D. the same length as the solar day

00098. A position that is obtained by applying estimated current and wind to your vessel's course and speed is a(n):

A. dead reckoning position
B. estimated position
C. fix
D. none of the above

00100. You are underway on course 050° T and your maximum speed is 12 knots. The eye of a hurricane bears 080° T, 100 miles from your position. The hurricane is moving towards 265° T at 22 knots. What course should you steer at 12 knots to have the maximum CPA?

A. 219°
B. 208°
C. 199°
D. 190°

00101. A lighted preferred-channel buoy may show a:

A. fixed red light
B. Morse (A) white light
C. composite group-flashing light
D. yellow light

00103. In Loran-C the high accuracy of atomic time and frequency controls allows each station to operate:

A. at higher frequencies
B. on schedule, independently
C. at 1,975 kHz
D. in a multiplex phase

00104. What should you apply to a fathometer reading to determine the depth of water?

A. subtract the draft of the vessel
B. add the draft of the vessel
C. subtract the sea water correction
D. add the sea water correction

00106. A local wind which occurs during the daytime and is caused by the different rates of warming of land and water is a:

A. foehn
B. chinook
C. land breeze
D. sea breeze

00107. The average height of the surface of the sea for all stages of the tide over a 19 year period is called:

A. mean high water
B. mean low water
C. half-tide level
D. mean sea level

00108. A position that is obtained by using 2 or more intersecting lines of position taken at nearly the same time, is a(n):

A. dead-reckoning position
B. estimated position
C. fix
D. running fix

00110. A millibar is a unit of:

A. humidity
B. precipitation
C. pressure
D. temperature

00111. Green lights may appear on:

A. horizontally-banded buoys
B. vertically-striped buoys
C. yellow buoys
D. spherical buoys

00113. The type of transmission used in Loran-C is a:

A. single pulse
B. wide pulse
C. multipulse
D. narrow pulse

00114. The readings from most fathometers indicate the:

A. actual depth of water
B. actual depth of water below keel
C. average depth from waterline to hard bottom
D. average depth of water to soft bottom

00116. What wind results from a land mass cooling more quickly at night than an adjacent water area?

A. coastal breeze
B. sea breeze
C. land breeze
D. mistral

00117. Mean high water is the average height of:

A. the higher high waters
B. the lower high waters
C. the lower of the 2 daily tides
D. all high waters

00118. Which of the following describes an accurate position that is NOT based on any prior position?

A. dead reckoning position
B. estimated position
C. fix
D. running fix

00120. You are underway on course 050° T and your maximum speed is 13 knots. The eye of a hurricane bears 100° T, 120 miles

from your position. The hurricane is moving towards 275° T at 25 knots. If you maneuver at 13 knots to avoid the hurricane, what could be the maximum CPA?

A. 72 miles
B. 78 miles
C. 83 miles
D. 89 miles

00121. A safe water mark may be:

A. vertically striped
B. spherical
C. showing a white light
D. all of the above

00122. The subregions of the United States Gulf and East Coasts are numbered 11, 12, and 13 within the chart numbering system. Which of the following chart numbers indicates a chart for either the Gulf or East Coast?

A. 11250
B. 18411
C. 21228
D. 17136

00123. If the radio signal ground wave extends out for less distance than the minimum skywave distance, there is an area in which no signal is received. This is called the:

A. skip zone
B. blackout zone
C. diffraction zone
D. shadow zone

00124. An electronic depth finder operates on the principle that:

A. radio signals reflect from a solid surface
B. sound waves travel at a constant speed through water
C. radar signals travel at a constant speed through water
D. pressure increases with depth

00126. A katabatic wind blows:

A. up an incline due to surface heating
B. in a circular pattern
C. down an incline due to cooling of the air
D. horizontally between a high and a low pressure area

00127. Mean low water is the average height of:

A. the surface of the sea
B. high waters and low waters
C. all low waters
D. the lower of the 2 daily tides

00128. A position obtained by applying only your vessel's course and speed to a known position is a:

A. dead reckoning position
B. fix
C. probable position
D. running fix

00130. The distance between the surface of the water and the tidal datum is the:

A. range of tide
B. height of tide
C. charted depth
D. actual water depth

00131. A vertically-striped buoy may be:

A. striped black and green
B. striped black and yellow
C. lighted with a red light
D. lighted with a white light

00133. The line connecting the Loran-C master station with a secondary station is called the:

A. focus line
B. base line
C. side line
D. center line

00134. The recording fathometer produces a graphic record of the:

A. bottom contour only up to depths of 100 fathoms
B. depth under the keel against a time base
C. contour of the bottom against a distance base
D. depth of water against a distance base

00136. Which Beaufort force indicates a wind speed of 65 knots?

A. Beaufort force 0
B. Beaufort force 6.5
C. Beaufort force 12
D. Beaufort force 15

00137. Priming of the tides occurs:

A. at times of new and full Moon
B. when the Earth, Moon, and Sun are lying approximately on the same line
C. when the Moon is between first quarter and full and between third quarter and new
D. when the Moon is between new and first quarter and between full and third quarter

00138. The path that a vessel is expected to follow, represented on a chart by a line drawn from the point of departure to the point of arrival, is the:

A. DR plot
B. track line
C. heading
D. estimated course

00140. You are underway on course 050° T and your maximum speed is 12 knots. The eye of a hurricane bears 080° T, 100 miles from your position. The hurricane is moving towards 265° T at 22 knots. If you maneuver at 12 knots to avoid the hurricane, what could be the maximum CPA?

A. 76 miles
B. 69 miles
C. 63 miles
D. 56 miles

00141. You are en route to assist vessel A. Vessel A is underway at 6 knots on course 133° T, and bears 042° T, 105 miles from you. What is the time to intercept if you make 10 knots?

A. 17h 03m
B. 17h 19m
C. 17h 30m
D. 17h 49m

00142. Which of the following nautical charts is intended for coastwise navigation outside of outlying reefs and shoals?

A. approach charts
B. general charts
C. sailing charts
D. coast charts

00144. In modern fathometers the sonic or ultrasonic sound waves are produced electrically by means of a(n):

A. transmitter
B. transducer
C. transceiver
D. amplifier

00147. Which statement is TRUE concerning equatorial tides?

A. They occur when the Sun is at minimum declination north or south.
B. They occur when the Moon is at maximum declination north or south.
C. The difference in height between consecutive high or low tides is at a minimum.
D. They are used as the basis for the vulgar establishment of the port.

00148. When possible, a DR plot should always be started from which of the following?

A. any position
B. a known position

C. an assumed position
D. none of the above

00149. You are underway on course 050° T and your maximum speed is 13 knots. The eye of a hurricane bears 100° T, 120 miles from your position. The hurricane is moving towards 275° T at 25 knots. What course should you steer at 13 knots to have the maximum CPA?

A. 339°
B. 333°
C. 326°
D. 320°

00150. An alternating light:

A. shows a light with varying lengths of the lighted period
B. shows a light that changes color
C. marks an alternate lesser-used channel
D. is used as a replacement for another light

00151. Under the U. S. Aids to Navigation System, spherical buoys may be:

A. numbered
B. lettered
C. lighted
D. all of the above

00152. A chart with a natural scale of 1:160,000 is classified as a:

A. sailing chart
B. general chart
C. coast chart
D. harbor chart

00153. In illustration D004NG, the line extending beyond the stations at A and B is referred to as the:

A. slave line
B. zero line
C. baseline extension
D. centerline

00154. What factor has the greatest effect on the amount of gain required to obtain a fathometer reading?

A. salinity of water
B. temperature of water
C. atmospheric pressure
D. type of bottom

00155. The velocity of the current in large coastal harbors is:

A. predicted in Tidal Current Tables
B. unpredictable

C. generally constant
D. generally too weak to be of concern

00156. In reading a weather map, closely spaced pressure gradient lines would indicate:

A. high winds
B. high overcast clouds
C. calm or light winds
D. fog or steady rain

00157. Tropic tides are caused by the:

A. Moon being at its maximum declination
B. Moon crossing the Equator
C. Sun and Moon both being near 0° declination
D. Moon being at perigee

00158. Discounting slip, if your vessel is turning RPM for 10 knots and making good a speed of 10 knots, the current could be:

A. with you at 10 knots
B. against you at 10 knots
C. slack
D. with you at 2 knots

00160. Loran-C ground waves provide position information of reasonable accuracy out to a maximum of:

A. 800 miles
B. 1,000 miles
C. 1,200 miles
D. 1,500 miles

00161. How is a safe water mark, that can be passed close aboard on either side, painted and lighted?

A. black and white stripes with an interrupted quick flashing light
B. black and red stripes with a Morse (A) light
C. black and red stripes with an interrupted quick flashing light
D. red and white stripes with a Morse (A) light

00162. A chart with a scale of 1:80,000 would fall into the category of a:

A. sailing chart
B. general chart
C. coast chart
D. harbor chart

00163. Loran-C sky waves provide position information of reasonable accuracy out to more than:

A. Loran-C sky waves cannot be used.
B. 1,000 miles
C. 1,500 miles
D. 2,000 miles

00166. On the pole side of the high pressure belt in each hemisphere, the pressure diminishes. The winds along these gradients are diverted by the Earth's rotation toward the east and are known as the:

A. geostrophic winds
B. doldrums
C. horse latitudes
D. prevailing westerlies

00167. When the Moon's declination is maximum north, which of the following will occur?

A. mixed-type tides
B. higher high tides and lower low tides
C. tropic tides
D. equatorial tides

00168. Your vessel is making way through the water at a speed of 12 knots. Your vessel traveled 30 nautical miles in 2 hours 20 minutes. What current are you experiencing?

A. a following current at 2.0 knots
B. a head current of 2.0 knots
C. a following current of 0.9 knot
D. a head current of 0.9 knot

00170. Which of the buoy symbols in illustration D032NG indicates a safe water mark?

A. d
B. c
C. b
D. a

00171. Under the U. S. Aids to Navigation System, a lighted buoy with a spherical topmark marks:

A. safe water
B. the port side of the channel
C. a hazard to navigation
D. the position of underwater cables

00172. A chart with a scale of 1:45,000 is a:

A. harbor chart
B. coast chart
C. general chart
D. sailing chart

00173. The usable range of Loran-C is:

A. limited to under 500 miles
B. as much as 3,000 miles, using sky waves
C. less than that of Loran-A
D. limited to sky waves

00176. What wind pattern has the most influence over the movement of frontal weather systems over the North American Continent?

A. subpolar easterlies
B. northeast trades
C. prevailing westerlies
D. dominant southwesterly flow

00177. How many high waters usually occur each day on the East Coast of the United States?

A. 1
B. 2
C. 3
D. 4

00178. You are steering a southerly course, and you note that the chart predicts an easterly current. Without considering wind, how may you allow for the set?

A. head your vessel slightly to the right
B. head your vessel slightly to the left
C. decrease your speed
D. increase your speed

00179. You are proceeding up a channel at night. It is marked by a range which bears 185° T. You steady up on a compass course of 180° with the range in line dead ahead. This indicates that you(r):

A. must come right to get on the range
B. course is in error
C. compass has some easterly error
D. are being affected by a southerly current

00180. What is a lighted safe water mark fitted with to aid in its identification?

A. a spherical topmark
B. red and white retroreflective material
C. a sequential number
D. a red and white octagon

00181. Which navigational mark may be lettered?

A. an unlighted, green, can buoy
B. a spherical buoy
C. a red buoy
D. a port side dayshape

00182. The scale on a chart is given as 1:5,000,000. This means that:

A. 1 inch is equal to 5,000 inches on the Earth's surface
B. 1 nautical mile on the chart is equal to 5,000 inches on the Earth's surface
C. 1 inch is equal to 5,000,000 inches on the Earth's surface
D. 1 nautical mile on the chart is equal to 5,000,000 inches on the Earth's surface

00183. The maximum reliable ground wave range of Loran-C is approximately:

A. 700 miles
B. 900 miles
C. 1,200 miles
D. 2,300 miles

00186. In the doldrums, you will NOT have:

A. high relative humidity
B. frequent showers and thunderstorms
C. steep pressure gradients
D. frequent calms

00187. Which statement is TRUE concerning apogean tides?

A. They occur only at quadrature.
B. They occur when the Moon is nearest Earth.
C. They cause diurnal tides to become mixed.
D. They have a decreased range from normal.

00191. Safe water buoys may show:

A. flashing red lights only
B. flashing green lights only
C. white lights only
D. yellow lights only

00192. The description "Racon" beside an illustration on a chart would mean a:

A. radar conspicuous beacon
B. circular radiobeacon
C. radar transponder beacon
D. radar calibration beacon

00193. In using Loran-C, skywave reception gives greater range but is:

A. only accurate during daylight hours
B. less accurate
C. only accurate at twilight
D. more accurate than using ground waves

00196. The area of strong westerly winds occurring between 40° S and 60° S latitude is called the:

A. polar easterlies
B. prevailing westerlies
C. roaring forties
D. jet streams

00197. Chart legends printed in capital letters show that the associated landmark is:

A. conspicuous
B. inconspicuous
C. a government facility or station
D. a radio transmitter

00198. You are en route to assist vessel A. vessel A is underway at 6 knots on course 133° T, and bears 343° T at 92 miles from you. What is the time to intercept if you make 9 knots?

A. 7h 44m
B. 7h 12m
C. 6h 40m
D. 6h 08m

00201. What is a lighted safe water mark fitted with to aid in its identification?

A. red and white retroreflective material
B. a spherical topmark
C. a sequential number
D. a red and white octagon

00202. On charts of U. S. Waters, a magenta marking is NOT used for marking a:

A. radiobeacon
B. lighted buoy
C. prohibited area
D. 5 fathom curve

00203. In any Loran-C chain, there are 3 or more stations transmitting pulses which radiate in all directions. One of the stations is the master station, and the others in the chain are the:

A. radio stations
B. secondary stations
C. monitor stations
D. pulse stations

00206. The winds you would expect to encounter in the North Atlantic between latitudes 5° and 30° are known as the:

A. doldrums
B. westerlies
C. trades
D. easterlies

00207. An important lunar cycle affecting the tidal cycle is called the nodal period. How long is this cycle?

A. 16 days
B. 18 days
C. 6 years
D. 19 years

00211. The light rhythm of Morse (A) is shown on:

A. preferred-channel buoys
B. starboard- or port-side buoys
C. special marks
D. safe water buoys

00212. Which aid is NOT marked on a chart with a magenta circle?

A. radar station
B. radar transponder beacon
C. radiobeacon
D. aero light

00213. In illustration D001NG, the station located at "A" is the:

A. on station
B. off station
C. master station
D. slave station

00216. The prevailing winds in the band of latitude from approximately 5° N to 30° N are the:

A. prevailing westerlies
B. northeast trade winds
C. southeast trade winds
D. doldrums

00217. In certain areas of the world there is often a slight fall in tide during the middle of the high water period. The practical effect is to create a longer period of stand at higher water. This special feature is called a(n):

A. apogean tide
B. double high water
C. perigean tide
D. bore

00218. A line of position may be a(n):

A. irregular line
B. straight line
C. arc
D. any of the above

00220. At 0000 you fix your position and plot a new DR track line. At 0200 you again fix your position and it is 0.5 mile east of your DR. Which statement is TRUE?

A. the current is westerly at 0.5 knot.
B. you must increase speed to compensate for the current.
C. the current cannot be determined.
D. the drift is 0.25 knot.

00221. In the United States, a buoy having red and white vertical stripes would have a light characteristic of:

A. group occulting
B. Morse (A)
C. interrupted quick flashing
D. quick flashing

00222. Which of the following statements concerning illustration D010NG is correct? (Soundings and heights are in m.)

A. Maury Lightship swings about her anchor on a circle with a 21-m diameter.
B. The position of the lightship is indicated by the center of the star on the symbol's mast.
C. There is a 12-m deep hole inside the 5-m curve just west of Beito Island.
D. The sunken wreck southwest of Beito Island shows the hull or superstructure above the sounding datum.

00223. In the Loran-C configuration shown in illustration D003NG, the stations located at X, Y, and Z are called:

A. repeater stations
B. secondary stations
C. composite stations
D. alternate stations

00226. What winds blow towards the Equator from the area about 30° north?

A. prevailing westerlies
B. roaring thirties
C. equatorial flow
D. northeast trades

00227. The class of tide that prevails in the greatest number of important harbors on the Atlantic Coast is:

A. interval
B. mixed
C. diurnal
D. semidiurnal

00228. Illustration D042NG represents the symbols used on radiofacsimile weather charts. Which of these symbols indicates a convergence line?

A. l
B. f
C. m
D. q

00229. The level of mean high water is used to indicate the shoreline:

A. when there is a large tidal fluctuation
B. on all U. S. Charts
C. only on charts showing offshore coasts
D. where the coastline does not change significantly between high and low water

00230. If the Loran-C ground wave does NOT extend out as far as the skywave skip distance, there will be a skip zone in which:

A. no Loran-C signal is received
B. only ground waves are received
C. only skywaves are received
D. both ground waves and skywaves are received

00231. You are outbound in a buoyed channel on course 015° T. You sight a white light showing a Morse (A) characteristic bearing 359° relative. For safety, you should:

A. change course to 359° T to pass near buoy
B. continue on course and pass near the buoy
C. alter course to 000° T and leave the buoy well clear to starboard
D. check the chart to see where the marked danger lies in relation to the buoy

00232. Which of the following statements concerning the chartlet in illustration DO10NG is TRUE? (Soundings and heights are in m.)

A. Maury Lightship is visible for 17 miles.
B. The bottom to the south-southeast of the lightship is soft coral.
C. There is a 12-m deep hole west of Beito Island and inside the 5-m line.
D. There is a dangerous eddy southeast of Beito Island.

00233. To determine which Loran-C signal to use, examine the chart and find a set of LOP's which result in a good crossing angle. A good crossing angle should be at least:

A. 10°
B. 15°
C. 25°
D. 30°

00234. When the declination of the Moon is 0°12.5' S, you can expect some tidal currents in Gulf Coast ports to:

A. exceed the predicted velocities
B. become reversing currents
C. have either a double ebb or a double flood
D. become weak and variable

00236. The winds with the greatest effect on the set, drift, and depth of the equatorial currents are the:

A. doldrums
B. horse latitudes
C. trade winds
D. prevailing westerlies

00237. Neap tides occur when the:

A. Moon is in its first quarter and third quarter phases
B. Sun and Moon are on opposite sides of Earth

C. Moon's declination is maximum and opposite to that of the Sun
D. Sun and Moon are in conjunction

00239. As you enter a channel from seaward in a U. S. Port, the numbers on the starboard side buoys:

A. decrease and the buoys are black
B. increase and the buoys are green
C. decrease and the buoys are red
D. increase and the buoys are red

00240. In a river subject to tidal currents, the best time to dock a ship without the assistance of tugs is:

A. at high water
B. when there is a following current
C. at slack water
D. at stand

00241. A spherical buoy may be:

A. numbered
B. lettered
C. lighted
D. all of the above

00242. The difference between the heights of low and high tide is the:

A. range
B. period
C. depth
D. distance

00243. The Loran lines drawn on navigation charts represent which of the following?

A. ground waves
B. skywaves
C. either ground waves or skywaves interchangeably
D. an average between ground wave and skywave positions

00244. To make sure of getting the full advantage of a favorable current, you should reach an entrance or strait at what time in relation to the predicted time of the favorable current?

A. 1 hour after the predicted time
B. at the predicted time
C. 30 minutes before flood, 1 hour after ebb
D. 30 minutes before the predicted time

00246. The consistent winds blowing from the horse latitudes to the doldrums are called the:

A. prevailing westerlies
B. polar easterlies

C. trade winds
D. roaring forties

00247. Neap tides occur:

A. at the start of spring, when the Sun is nearly over the Equator
B. only when the Sun and Moon are on the same sides of the Earth and are nearly in line
C. when the Sun and Moon are at approximately 90° to each other, as seen from Earth
D. when the Sun, Moon, and Earth are nearly in line, regardless of alignment order

00251. A mid-channel buoy, if lighted, will show a:

A. fixed red light
B. Morse (A) white light
C. green light
D. flashing red light

00252. A large automated navigational buoy, such as those that have replaced some lightships, would be shown on a chart by which symbol in illustration D015NG?

A. a
B. b
C. c
D. d

00253. Loran-C is what type of system?

A. reflected electron
B. electrical radiation
C. quarterpoint electrical navigation
D. hyperbolic radio navigation

00254. The range of tide is the:

A. difference between the heights of high and low tide
B. distance the tide moves out from the shore
C. duration of time between high and low tide
D. maximum depth of the water at high tide

00256. The belt of light and variable winds between the westerly wind belt and the northeast trade winds is called the:

A. subtropical high pressure belt
B. intertropical convergence zone
C. doldrum belt
D. polar frontal zone

00257. Spring tides occur:

A. at the start of spring, when the Sun is nearly over the Equator
B. only when the Sun and Moon are on the same side of the Earth and nearly in line

C. when the Sun and Moon are at approximately 90° to each other as seen from the Earth
D. when the Sun, Moon, and Earth are nearly in line, in any order

00259. Illustration D042NG represents the symbols used on radiofacsimile weather charts. The symbol indicated at letter "Q" represents a:

A. convergence zone
B. squall line
C. convergence line
D. weather boundary

00260. The National Ocean Service publishes:

A. Light Lists
B. Coast Pilots
C. Pilot Charts
D. Sailing Directions

00261. You are heading out to sea in a buoyed channel and see a quick-flashing green light on a buoy ahead of you. In U. S. waters, you should leave the buoy:

A. well clear on either side
B. about 50 yd. off on either side
C. to port
D. to starboard

00262. Which of the buoy symbols in illustration D032NG indicates a safe water mark?

A. a
B. b
C. c
D. d

00263. Loran-C uses the multiple pulse system because:

A. less signal energy is necessary for receiver operation
B. more signal energy is available at the receiver
C. it significantly increases the peak power
D. it increases the signal capacity

00266. The horse latitudes are characterized by:

A. weak pressure gradients and light, variable winds
B. the formation of typhoons or hurricanes in certain seasons
C. steady winds in 1 direction for 6 months followed by wind reversal for the next 6 months
D. steady winds generally from the southeast in the Southern Hemisphere

00267. You are inbound in a channel marked by a range. The range line is 309° T. You are steering 306° T and have the range in sight as indicated

in illustration D047NG. The range continues to open. What action should you take?

A. Alter course to the right to 309° T or more to bring the range in line.
B. Come left until the range closes, then steer to the left of 306° T.
C. Alter course to the left to close the range, then alter course to 309° T.
D. Continue on course but be prepared to come left if the range continues to open.

00268. Illustration D042NG represents the symbols used on radiofacsimile weather charts. The symbol indicated at letter "L" represents a:

A. convergence line
B. maritime air mass
C. warm front
D. convergence zone

00269. You are taking bearings on two known objects ashore. The BEST fix is obtained when the angle between the lines of position is:

A. 90°
B. 30°
C. 45°
D. 60°

00270. You are entering port and have been instructed to anchor, as your berth is not yet available. You are on a SW'ly heading, preparing to drop anchor, when you observe the range lights depicted in illustration D047NG on your starboard beam. You should:

A. drop the anchor immediately as the range lights mark an area free of obstructions
B. drop the anchor immediately as a change in the position of the range lights will be an indication of dragging anchor
C. ensure your ship will NOT block the channel or obstruct the range while at anchor
D. NOT drop the anchor until the lights are in line

00271. Your vessel is leaving New York Harbor in dense fog. As the vessel slowly proceeds toward sea, you sight a green can buoy on the starboard bow. Which of the following actions should you take?

A. Turn hard right to get back into the channel.
B. Pass the buoy close to, leaving it to your port.
C. Stop and fix your position.
D. Stand on, leaving the buoy to your starboard.

00272. What does the symbol in illustration DO33NG indicate on a chart?

A. a sunken vessel marked by a buoy
B. a safe water beacon

C. a red and white can buoy
D. a can buoy with a rotating white light

00273. Loran-C is which type of navigation system?

A. hyperbolic, long-range navigation system
B. short-range electronic
C. long-range, high frequency navigation system
D. long-range, with a frequency of 1950 kHz

00275. Which of the following statements concerning illustration D010NG is correct? (Soundings and heights are in m.)

A. The sunken wreck southwest of Beito Island shows the hull or superstructure above the sounding datum.
B. There is a 12-m deep hole inside the 5-m curve just west of Beito Island.
C. The position of the lightship is indicated by the center of the star on the symbol's mast.
D. Maury Lightship swings about her anchor on a circle with a 21-m diameter.

00276. The region of high pressure extending around the Earth at about 35° N latitude is called the:

A. prevailing westerlies
B. horse latitudes
C. troposphere
D. doldrums

00277. Your vessel goes aground in soft mud. You would have the best chance of refloating it on the next tide if it grounded at:

A. low water neap
B. low water spring
C. high water neap
D. high water spring

00278. You are underway on course 050° T and your maximum speed is 11 knots. The eye of a hurricane bears 070° T, 80 miles from your position. The hurricane is moving towards 270° T at 19 knots. If you maneuver at 11 knots to avoid the hurricane, what could be the maximum CPA?

A. 84 miles
B. 79 miles
C. 74 miles
D. 66 miles

00279. As a vessel changes course to starboard, the compass card in a magnetic compass:

A. remains aligned with compass north
B. also turns to starboard

C. first turns to starboard then counterclock-wise to port
D. remains aligned with compass north

00280. Under the U. S. Aids to Navigation System, a lighted buoy with a spherical top-mark marks:

A. the port side of the channel
B. safe water
C. a hazard to navigation
D. the position of underwater cables

00281. A lighted buoy to be left to starboard, when entering a U. S. port from seaward, shall have a:

A. white light
B. red light
C. green light
D. light characteristic of Morse (A)

00282. The symbol which appears beside a light on a chart reads "Gp Fl R (2) 10 sec 160 ft 19M". Which of the following describes the light?

A. It is visible 10 miles.
B. Its distinguishing number is "19M".
C. It has a radar reflector.
D. none of the above

00283. Loran-C operates on a single frequency centered on:

A. 100 kHz
B. 500 kHz
C. 1,850 kHz
D. 1,950 kHz

00286. On the pole side of the trade wind belt, there is an area of high pressure with weak pressure gradients and light, variable winds. This area is called the:

A. prevailing westerlies
B. geostrophic winds
C. doldrums
D. horse latitudes

00289. A position obtained by crossing lines of position taken at different times and advanced to a common time is a(n):

A. running fix
B. dead-reckoning position
C. fix
D. estimated position

00290. The true wind is from 330° T, speed 6 knots. You want the apparent wind to be 30 knots from 10° on your port bow. To what course and speed must you change?

A. cn 240°, 28.0 knots
B. cn 270°, 28.0 knots
C. cn 180°, 30.0 knots
D. cn 090°, 32.5 knots

00291. A buoy marking a wreck may be:

A. showing a green light
B. lettered with an occulting light
C. numbered and showing a yellow light
D. numbered and showing a white light

00292. The symbol which appears beside a light on a chart reads "Gp Fl R (2) 10 sec 160 ft 19M". Which characteristic does the light possess?

A. it is visible 2 nautical miles.
B. its distinguishing number is "19M".
C. it has a red light.
D. it flashes once every 10 seconds.

00293. The use of pulse groups and extremely precise timing at each Loran-C station makes possible the use of:

A. high frequency pulses
B. combinations of high and low frequency pulses
C. the same frequency for all stations in a chain
D. varied long and short pulses

00296. The wind flow from the horse lati-tudes to the doldrums is deflected due to:

A. Coriolis force
B. the mid-latitude, semi-permanent high
C. differing atmospheric pressures
D. the prevailing westerlies

00299. Steady precipitation is typical of:

A. coming cold weather conditions
B. a warm front weather condition
C. high pressure conditions
D. scattered cumulus clouds

00300. Which of the symbols in illustration D018NG represents a warm front?

A. a
B. b
C. c
D. d

00301. In the U. S. Aids to Navigation System, lateral aids as seen entering from seaward will display lights with which characteristic?

A. flashing
B. occulting
C. quick flashing
D. any of the above

00302. Which symbol represents a 20-fathom curve?

A. -..-..-..-..
B. - — — — -
C. - -:- -:- -:- -:
D. - - - - - - - -

00303. A Loran-C receiver in operation first receives pulses from the:

A. slave station
B. master station
C. multiple stations
D. secondary stations

00306. Weather conditions in the middle lati-tudes generally move:

A. eastward
B. westward
C. northward
D. southward

00308. The wind at Frying Pan Shoals has been west-northwesterly at an average veloc-ity of 40 knots. The predicted set and drift of the rotary current are 323° at 0.6 knot. What current should you expect?

A. 001° at 0.7 knot
B. 018° at 0.4 knot
C. 052° at 0.6 knot
D. 089° at 0.9 knot

00309. You are underway on course 050° T and your maximum speed is 12 knots. The eye of a hurricane bears 120° T, 110 miles from your position. The hurricane is moving towards 285° T at 25 knots. What course should you steer at 12 knots to have the maximum CPA?

A. 332°
B. 339°
C. 346°
D. 357°

00311. You are steaming southward along the West Coast of the United States when you encounter a buoy showing a flashing red light. The buoy should be left on:

A. the vessel's starboard side
B. the vessel's port side
C. either side close aboard
D. either side well clear

00312. The depth of water on a chart is indi-cated as 23 m. This is equal to:

A. 11.5 fm.
B. 12.6 fm.

C. 69.0 ft.
D. 78.6 ft.

00313. The Loran-C receiver:

A. is not bothered by interference
B. can be used at any distance with accuracy
C. can be bothered by interference
D. is reliable only from sunrise to sunset

00316. According to Buys Ballot's law, when an observer in the Northern Hemisphere experiences a northwest wind, the center of low pressure is located to the:

A. northeast
B. west-southwest
C. northwest
D. south-southeast

00319. Illustration D042NG represents the symbols used by radiofacsimile weather charts. The symbol indicated at letter "F" represents a:

A. maritime air mass
B. weather boundary
C. convergence zone
D. squall line

00321. Which buoy may be even numbered?

A. mid-channel buoy
B. unlighted nun buoy
C. lighted green buoy
D. any of the above

00322. The chart symbol indicating that the bottom is coral is:

A. C
B. Cl
C. Co
D. C

00323. The position accuracy of Loran-C degrades with increasing distance from the transmitting stations as:

A. gains are made over the signal path
B. a result of variation in propagation conditions
C. the frequency of the pulses increases
D. the stations shift pulses

00326. You are steaming west in the North Atlantic in an extratropical cyclonic storm, and the wind is dead ahead. According to the law of Buys Ballot, the center of low pressure lies:

A. to the north of you
B. to the south of you
C. ahead of you
D. astern of you

00327. When Daylight Savings Time is kept the times of tide and current calculations must be adjusted. One way of doing this is to:

A. subtract 1 hour from the times listed under the reference stations
B. add 1 hour to the times listed under the reference stations
C. apply no correction, as the times in the reference stations are adjusted for Daylight Savings Time
D. add 15° to the standard meridian when calculating the time difference

00328. The direction of prevailing winds in the Northern Hemisphere is caused by the:

A. magnetic field at the North Pole
B. Gulf Stream
C. earth's rotation
D. arctic cold fronts

00329. Illustration D042NG represents the symbols used on radiofacsimile weather charts. Which of these symbols indicates a weather boundary?

A. i
B. h
C. g
D. f

00331. Which of the following indicates a buoy that should be left to port when entering from seaward? (U. S. Aids to Navigation System)

A. white light
B. group flashing characteristic
C. nun shape
D. odd number

00332. Which chart symbol indicates the bottom is clay?

A. Cly
B. Cla
C. Cl
D. C

00333. Loran-C stations transmit groups of pulses at specific times. The time interval between transmissions from the master station is the:

A. coding delay
B. group repetition interval
C. pulse interval
D. phase code

00336. You are steaming eastward in the North Atlantic in an extratropical cyclonic storm and the wind is dead ahead. According to the law of Buys Ballot, the center of the low pressure lies:

A. ahead of you
B. astern of you
C. to the north
D. to the south

00337. In order to predict the actual depth of water using the Tide Tables, the number obtained from the Tide Tables:

A. is the actual depth
B. should be added to or subtracted from the charted depth
C. should be multiplied by the charted depth
D. should be divided by the charted depth

00338. Illustration D042NG represents the symbols used on radiofacsimile weather charts. The symbol indicated at letter "N" represents:

A. hail
B. freezing rain
C. rain
D. snow

00339. The wind at Frying Pan Shoals has been north-northeasterly at an average velocity of 30 knots. The predicted set and drift of the rotary current are 355° at 0.8 knot. What current should you expect?

A. 010° at 1.1 knots
B. 047° at 0.3 knot
C. 325° at 0.7 knot
D. 279° at 1.0 knot

00340. Data relating to the direction and velocity of rotary tidal currents can be found in the:

A. Mariner's Guide
B. Nautical Almanac
C. Tide Tables
D. Tidal Current Tables

00341. Buoys which only mark the port or starboard side of the channel will never exhibit a light with which characteristic?

A. flashing
B. quick flashing
C. composite group flashing
D. equal interval (isophase)

00345. A navigator fixing a vessel's position by radar:

A. should never use radar bearings
B. should only use radar bearings when the range exceeds the distance to the horizon
C. can use radar information from 1 object to fix the position
D. must use information from targets forward of the beam

00346. If your weather bulletin shows the center of a low pressure area to be 100 miles due east of your position, what winds can you expect in the Northern Hemisphere?

A. east to northeast
B. east to southeast
C. north to northwest
D. south to southeast

00347. Illustration D042NG represents the symbols used on radiofacsimile weather charts. Which of these symbols indicates rain?

A. n
B. m
C. i
D. g

00349. The direction of the southeast trade winds is a result of the:

A. equatorial current
B. humidity
C. rotation of the earth
D. change of seasons

00350. When making landfall at night, the light from a powerful lighthouse may sometimes be seen before the lantern breaks the horizon. This light is called the:

A. diffusion
B. backscatter
C. loom
D. elevation

00351. Which buoy may be odd numbered?

A. a spherical buoy
B. an unlighted can buoy
C. a red buoy
D. a yellow buoy

00356. When facing into the wind in the Northern Hemisphere the center of low pressure lies:

A. directly in front of you
B. directly behind you
C. to your left and behind you
D. to your right and behind you

00359. You are en route to assist vessel A. Vessel A is underway at 4.5 knots on course 233° T, and bears 264° T, 68 miles from you. What is the time to intercept if you make 13 knots?

A. 6h 31m
B. 6h 47m
C. 7h 03m
D. 7h 34m

00360. Illustration D042NG represents the symbols used on radiofacsimile weather charts. The symbol indicated at letter "M" represents:

A. rain
B. snow
C. hail
D. ice

00361. As your vessel is heading southward along the East Coast of the United States, you encounter a buoy showing a red flashing light. How should you pass this buoy?

A. Pass it about 50 yd. off on either side.
B. Leave it to your starboard.
C. Leave it to your port.
D. Pass it well clear on either side.

00366. If an observer in the Northern Hemisphere faces the surface wind, the center of low pressure is towards his:

A. left, slightly behind him
B. right, slightly behind him
C. left, slightly in front of him
D. right, slightly in front of him

00369. You are underway on course 050° T and your maximum speed is 11 knots. The eye of a hurricane bears 070° T, 80 miles from your position. The hurricane is moving towards 270° T at 19 knots. What course should you steer at 11 knots to have the maximum CPA?

A. 250°
B. 234°
C. 227°
D. 215°

00370. Prevailing winds between 30° N and 60° N latitude are from the:

A. north
B. south
C. east
D. west

00371. Which buoy may be odd numbered?

A. mid-channel buoy
B. unlighted nun buoy
C. lighted green buoy
D. any of the above

00376. According to Buys Ballot's law, when an observer in the Northern Hemisphere experiences a northeast wind the center of low pressure is located to the:

A. northeast
B. west-southwest

C. northwest
D. south-southeast

00378. A navigator fixing position by radar:

A. should never use radar bearings
B. can use radar information from 1 object to fix the position
C. should only use radar bearings when the range exceeds the distance to the horizon
D. must use information from targets forward of the beam

00380. Prevailing winds between 30° N and 60° N latitude are from the:

A. east
B. west
C. north
D. south

00381. A nun buoy will:

A. be green in color
B. have an even number
C. be left to port when entering from seaward
D. be cylindrical in shape

00386. Your vessel is on course 180° T speed 22 knots. The apparent wind is from 70° off the port bow, speed 20 knots. The true direction and speed of the true wind are:

A. 45° T, 21.0 knots
B. 51° T, 24.2 knots
C. 58° T, 21.2 knots
D. 64° T, 26.0 knots

00388. You are underway on course 120° T and your maximum speed is 12 knots. The eye of a hurricane bears 150° T, 120 miles from your position. The hurricane is moving towards 295° T at 20 knots. If you maneuver at 12 knots to avoid the hurricane, what could be the maximum CPA?

A. 89 miles
B. 96 miles
C. 105 miles
D. 117 miles

00389. The edge of a hurricane has overtaken your vessel in the Gulf of Mexico, and the northwest wind of a few hours ago has shifted to the west. This is an indication that you are located in the:

A. navigable semicircle
B. dangerous semicircle
C. low pressure area
D. eye of the storm

00390. During winter, SE trade winds are:

A. stronger than during the summer months
B. weaker than during the summer months
C. drier than during the summer months
D. wetter than during the summer months

00391. When outbound from a U. S. port, a buoy displaying a flashing red light indicates:

A. a junction with preferred channel to the left
B. a sharp turn in the channel to the right
C. the port side of the channel
D. a wreck to be left on vessel's starboard side

00392. A pilot chart does NOT contain information about:

A. average wind conditions
B. tidal currents
C. magnetic variation
D. average limits of field ice

00394. An instrument designed to maintain a continuous record of atmospheric pressure is a:

A. mercurial barometer
B. aneroid barometer
C. barograph
D. thermograph

00396. Your vessel is on course 150° T, speed 17 knots. The apparent wind is from 40° off the starboard bow, speed 15 knots. What is the speed of the true wind?

A. 9.0 knots
B. 10.2 knots
C. 11.0 knots
D. 12.0 knots

00398. The velocity of the apparent wind can be less than the true wind and from the same direction, if certain conditions are present. 1 condition is that the:

A. ship's speed is less than the true wind velocity
B. true wind is from dead astern
C. true wind is on the beam
D. true wind is from dead ahead

00399. Where would you find information concerning the duration of slack water?

A. American Practical Navigator
B. Sailing Directions
C. Tide Tables
D. Tidal Current Tables

00401. You are steaming in a westerly direction along the Gulf Coast. You see ahead of you a lighted buoy showing a red isophase light. What action should you take?

A. Alter course to port and leave the buoy to starboard.
B. Alter course to starboard and leave the buoy to port.
C. Alter course and leave the buoy nearby on either side.
D. Alter course and pass the buoy well-off on either side.

00402. All of the following can be found on a Pilot Chart EXCEPT information concerning the:

A. percentage of frequency of wave heights
B. visibility conditions
C. sea surface temperatures
D. amounts of precipitation

00404. An aneroid barometer is an instrument:

A. used to measure the speed of wind
B. in which the pressure of the air is measured
C. that tells which direction a storm is coming from
D. used to measure the height of waves

00406. Your vessel is on course 135° T speed 18 knots. From the appearance of the sea you estimate the speed of the true wind as 24.5 knots. The apparent wind is 40° on the starboard bow. Determine the speed of the apparent wind.

A. 24.2 knots
B. 28.4 knots
C. 32.2 knots
D. 35.5 knots

00408. A buoy bears 176° T at 3000 yd. What is the course to make good to leave the buoy 100 yd. to port?

A. 174° T
B. 176° T
C. 178° T
D. 180° T

00410. The height of the tide at low water is 0.0 ft. The range is 9.0 ft. The duration is 06h 00m. The height of the tide 02h 12m before high water will be:

A. 8.3 ft.
B. 6.3 ft.
C. 4.7 ft.
D. 2.7 ft.

00411. When entering from seaward, a buoy displaying a single-flashing red light would indicate:

A. a junction with preferred channel to the left
B. a sharp turn in the channel to the right
C. the starboard side of the channel
D. a wreck to be left on the vessel's port side

00412. If you were sailing in the North Pacific and were interested in the ice and iceberg limits, you could find this information in the:

A. Pilot Chart
B. Coast Pilot
C. Notice to Mariners
D. none of the above

00414. The barometer is an instrument for measuring the:

A. temperature
B. relative humidity
C. dew point
D. atmospheric pressure

00416. A ship is on course 195° at a speed of 15 knots. The apparent wind is from 40° on the port bow, speed 30 knots. The direction and speed of the true wind are:

A. 068° T, 30 knots
B. 127° T, 21 knots
C. 263° T, 42 knots
D. 292° T, 42 knots

00418. In most cases, the direction of the apparent wind lies between the bow and:

A. the direction of the true wind
B. true north
C. the beam on the windward side
D. the beam on the lee side

00419. The ocean bottom that extends from the shoreline out to an area where there is a marked change in slope to a greater depth is the:

A. abyssal plain
B. continental shelf
C. borderland
D. offshore terrace

00420. You are inbound in a channel marked by a range. The range line is 309° T. You are steering 306° T and have the range in sight as indicated in illustration D047NG. The range continues to open. What action should you take?

A. Come left until the range closes then steer to the left of 306° T.
B. Continue on course but be prepared to come left if the range continues to open.
C. Alter course to the left to close the range, then alter course to 309° T.
D. Alter course to the right to 309° T or more to bring the range in line.

00421. Daylight Savings Time is a form of zone time that adopts the time:

A. 1 zone to the west
B. 1 zone to the east
C. 2 zones to the west
D. 2 zones to the east

00422. If you are sailing from the East Coast of the United States to the Caribbean Sea, which of the following publications would contain information on weather, currents, and storms?

A. Sailing Charts of the Caribbean Sea
B. Pilot Charts of the North Atlantic
C. Light Lists, Atlantic and Gulf Coast
D. Tidal Current Tables

00423. You have calibrated your RDF. When compiling the calibration table, the correction to be applied to any future RDF bearings is listed against the:

A. true bearing of the transmitter
B. relative bearing of the transmitter
C. heading of the vessel
D. time of reception

00424. For an accurate barometer check, you would:

A. check it with a barometer on another vessel
B. take readings from several barometers and average them
C. check it with the barometer at the ship chandlery
D. check it against radio or Weather Bureau reports of the immediate vicinity

00426. The wind speed and direction observed from a moving vessel is known as:

A. coordinate wind
B. true wind
C. apparent wind
D. anemometer wind

00428. A buoy bears 178° T at 3000 yd. What is the course to make good to leave the buoy 100 yd. to starboard?

A. 174° T
B. 176° T
C. 178° T
D. 180° T

00430. The southeast trade winds actually blow toward the:

A. southeast
B. south
C. east
D. northwest

00431. When a buoy marks a channel bifurcation, the preferred channel is NOT indicated by:

A. the shape of an unlighted buoy
B. the light color of a lighted buoy
C. the color of the topmost band
D. whether the number is odd or even

00434. The purpose of the "set" hand on an aneroid barometer is to:

A. adjust the barometer
B. indicate any change in the reading of the barometer
C. provide a correction for height above sea level
D. provide a correction for temperature changes

00436. A wind vane on a moving vessel shows:

A. dead reckoning wind direction
B. true wind direction
C. apparent wind direction
D. estimated wind direction

00439. If a weather bulletin shows the center of a low pressure system to be 100 miles due east of you, what winds can you expect in the Southern Hemisphere?

A. south-southwesterly
B. north-northwesterly
C. south-southeasterly
D. north-northeasterly

00440. You are inbound in a channel marked by a range. The range line is 309° T. You are steering 306° T and have the range in sight as indicated in illustration D047NG. What action should you take?

A. Continue on the present heading until the range is in line, then alter course to the left.
B. Immediately alter course to the right to bring the range in line.
C. Immediately alter course to 309° T.
D. Continue on course if the range is closing, otherwise alter course to the left.

00441. A yellow buoy may exhibit a(n):

A. fixed red light
B. flashing light
C. white light
D. occulting light

00444. A sylphon cell is a part of a:

A. maximum thermometer
B. barograph
C. thermograph
D. hygrometer

00446. The usual sequence of directions in which a tropical cyclone moves in the Southern Hemisphere is:

A. northwest, west, and south
B. southwest, south and southeast
C. north, northwest and east
D. west, northwest and north

00448. Mean high water is the reference datum used to measure:

A. soundings on the East Coast of the U. S.
B. soundings in European waters
C. heights of topographical features in the U. S.
D. both heights and soundings worldwide

00449. You are en route to assist vessel A. vessel A is underway at 5 knots on course 063° T, and bears 136° T at 78 miles from you. What is the course to steer at 13 knots to intercept vessel A?

A. 096°
B. 092°
C. 088°
D. 085°

00450. You are en route to Jacksonville, FL, from San Juan, P. R. There is a fresh N'ly wind blowing. As you cross the axis of the Gulf Stream you would expect to encounter:

A. cirrus clouds
B. smoother seas and warmer water
C. steeper waves, closer together
D. long swells

00451. Which light characteristic can be used on a special purpose mark?

A. fixed
B. occulting
C. equal interval
D. quick flashing

00454. On what does the operation of an aneroid barometer depend?

A. thin, metal, air tight cell
B. curved tube containing alcohol
C. column of mercury supported by atmospheric pressure
D. expansion of mercury in a closed tube

00456. Which of the following conditions exists in the eye of a hurricane?

A. wind rapidly changing in direction
B. a temperature much lower than that outside the eye
C. towering cumulonimbus clouds
D. an extremely low barometric pressure

00458. The prevailing westerlies of the Southern Hemisphere blow 18-30 knots:

A. all year long
B. during the summer months only
C. during the winter only
D. during spring only

00459. A buoy bears 178° T at 3000 yd. What is the course to make good to leave the buoy 100 yd. to port?

A. 174° T
B. 176° T
C. 178° T
D. 180° T

00460. When using horizontal sextant angles of 3 objects to fix your position, an indeterminate position will result in which of the following situations?

A. the objects lie in a straight line.
B. the vessel is inside of a triangle formed by the objects.
C. the vessel is outside of a triangle formed by the objects.
D. a circle will pass through your position and the 3 objects.

00461. Under the U. S. Aids to Navigation System, a yellow buoy may:

A. mark a fish net area
B. be lighted with a white light
C. show a fixed red light
D. any of the above

00463. The signal transmitted by a radio beacon station is referred to as its:

A. group sequence
B. frequency
C. directional signal
D. characteristic signal

00464. Prior to reading an aneroid barometer, you should tap the face lightly with your finger to:

A. expose any loose connections
B. demagnetize the metal elements
C. bring the pointer to its true position
D. contract and expand the glass face

00466. In the relatively calm area near the hurricane center, the seas are:

A. moderate but easily navigated
B. calm
C. mountainous and confused
D. mountainous but fairly regular as far as direction is concerned

00468. Which of the symbols in illustration D018NG represents a cold front?

A. a
B. b
C. c
D. d

00469. Where are the prevailing westerlies of the Southern Hemisphere located?

A. between the Equator and 10° latitude
B. between 10° and 20° latitude
C. between 30° and 60° latitude
D. between 60° and 90° latitude

00470. You are underway on course 120° T and your maximum speed is 12 knots. The eye of a hurricane bears 150° T at 120 miles. The hurricane is moving towards 295° at 20 knots. What course should you steer at 12 knots to have the maximum CPA?

A. 312°
B. 330°
C. 348°
D. 001°

00471. Yellow lights may appear on:

A. special purpose buoys
B. vertically-striped buoys
C. horizontally-banded buoys
D. spherical buoys

00474. Which of the following indications, afforded by the barometer, are most meaningful in forecasting weather?

A. the words "Fair — Change — Rain"
B. the direction and rate of change of barometric pressure
C. the actual barometric pressure
D. the relative humidity

00476. Tropical cyclones normally form within which of the following belts of latitude?

A. 0° to 15°
B. 15° to 30°
C. 30° to 45°
D. 45° to 60°

00478. The velocity of the apparent wind can be more than the true wind, and come from the same direction, if certain conditions are present. One condition is that the:

A. ship's speed must be less than the true wind velocity
B. true wind must be from dead astern

C. true wind velocity must be faster than the ship's speed
D. true wind must be from dead ahead

00479. You are en route to assist vessel A. Vessel A is underway at 5 knots on course 063° T, and bears 136° T at 78 miles from you. What is the course to steer at 13 knots to intercept vessel A?

A. 114°
B. 158°
C. 295°
D. 340°

00480. What kind of pressure systems travel in tropical waves?

A. high pressure
B. low pressure
C. subsurface pressure
D. terrastatic pressure

00481. A special mark (yellow buoy), if lighted, may exhibit which light rhythm?

A. flashing
B. Morse "A"
C. equal interval
D. occulting

00484. The needle of an aneroid barometer points to 30.05 on the dial. This indicates that the barometric pressure is:

A. 30.05 inches of mercury
B. 30.05 millimeters of mercury
C. 30.05 millibars
D. falling

00486. Tropical cyclones do not form within 5° of the Equator because:

A. there are no fronts in that area
B. it is too hot
C. it is too humid
D. of negligible Coriolis force

00489. You are anchored in the Aleutian Island chain and receive word that a tsunami is expected to strike the islands in 6 hours. What is the safest action?

A. Get underway and be in deep, open-ocean water when the tsunami arrives.
B. Increase the scope of the anchor cable and drop the second anchor underfoot at short stay.
C. Get underway and be close inshore on the side of the island away from the tsunami.
D. Plant both anchors with about a 60° angle between them, and let out a long scope to each anchor.

00490. You are underway on course 050° T and your maximum speed is 10 knots. The eye of a hurricane bears 100° T, 90 miles from your position. The hurricane is moving towards 285° T at 19 knots. What course should you steer at 10 knots to have the maximum CPA?

A. 221°
B. 226°
C. 233°
D. 238°

00491. A special purpose buoy shall be:

A. lighted with a white light
B. striped black and red
C. lighted with a red light
D. yellow

00493. The pictures shown in illustration D011NG represent the geographic location of a vessel and the radar presentation at the same time. Which of the following statements is TRUE?

A. Ship No. 1 is not detected due to the shadow effect of the headland.
B. The small island is not detected due to the effect of beam width.
C. A tangent bearing of the headland to the south-southeast should be corrected by adding one-half of the beam width.
D. Ship No. 2 is not detected due to the reflective mass of the background mountain overpowering the ship's reflective signals.

00494. Barometers are usually calibrated to indicate atmospheric pressure in:

A. inches of mercury and centimeters
B. ft. of mercury and millibars
C. inches of mercury and millimeters
D. inches of mercury and millibars

00496. Severe tropical cyclones (hurricanes, typhoons) occur in all warm-water oceans except the:

A. Indian Ocean
B. North Pacific Ocean
C. South Pacific Ocean
D. South Atlantic Ocean

00498. What is an advantage of the magnetic compass aboard vessels?

A. Compass error is negligible at or near the earth's magnetic poles.
B. It does not have to be checked as often.
C. It is reliable due to its essential simplicity.
D. All points on the compass rose are readily visible.

00499. Which of the symbols in illustration D018NG represents an occluded front?

A. a
B. b
C. c
D. d

00501. Which of the buoys listed below could be used to mark an anchorage?

A. white buoy numbered "3"
B. white buoy with a green top
C. white buoy with orange bands
D. yellow buoy lettered "N"

00503. You are approaching a light with a RACON. The light may be identified on radar by:

A. a dashed line running from the center of the scope to the light
B. an audible signal when the sweep crosses the light
C. a circle appearing on the scope surrounding the light
D. a coded signal appearing on the same bearing at a greater range than the light

00504. Barometer readings in weather reports are given in terms of pressure at:

A. sea level
B. Washington, DC
C. the weather station
D. the broadcasting station

00508. Which of the following statements concerning the chartlet in illustration D010NG is TRUE? (Soundings and heights are in m.)

A. There is a dangerous eddy southeast of Beito Island.
B. Maury Lightship is visible for 17 miles.
C. The bottom to the south-southeast of the lightship is soft coral.
D. There is a 12-m deep hole west of Beito Island and inside the 5-m line.

00509. A line of position derived by radar range from an undetermined point on a coast will be a:

A. straight line
B. arc
C. parabola
D. line parallel to the coast

00510. Which aid is NOT marked on a chart with a magenta circle?

A. aero light
B. radar station
C. radar transponder beacon
D. radiobeacon

00511. A survey (special purpose mark) buoy:

A. must be lighted
B. may have a flashing red light
C. may have a fixed white light
D. none of the above

00513. You are radar scanning for a buoy fitted with a racon. Which radar screen in illustration D017NG represents the presentation you should expect on the PPI?

A. a
B. b
C. c
D. d

00514. What instrument measures wind velocity?

A. hydrometer
B. barometer
C. psychrometer
D. anemometer

00516. A hurricane moving northeast out of the Gulf passes west of your position. You could expect all of the following EXCEPT:

A. higher than normal tides
B. high winds
C. winds veering from S, through W, to NW
D. light showers

00518. The apparent wind's speed and the true wind's speed will be equal when:

A. the true wind is dead ahead
B. the true wind is dead astern
C. the true wind's speed is equal to ship's speed
D. the true wind's speed is zero

00519. The chart of a beach area shows a very flat slope to the underwater beach bottom. What type of breakers can be expected when trying to land a boat on this beach?

A. surging
B. spilling
C. plunging
D. converging

00520. On charts of U. S. waters, a magenta marking is NOT used for marking a:

A. 5-fathom curve
B. prohibited area
C. lighted buoy
D. radiobeacon

00523. A radar display in which north is always at the top of the screen is a(n):

A. unstabilized display
B. stabilized display
C. composition display
D. relative display

00524. An anemometer on a moving vessel measures:

A. apparent wind speed only
B. true wind speed and true wind direction
C. true wind speed only
D. apparent wind speed and true wind direction

00526. When a hurricane passes over colder water or land and loses the source of heat, the storm assumes the characteristics of a(n):

A. high pressure area
B. extratropical cyclone
C. tropical storm
D. easterly wave

00528. Which of the following should you expect when you encounter a tsunami in the open ocean?

A. violent seas from mixed directions
B. no noticeable change from existing sea state
C. winds increasing to gale force from the northwest in the Northern Hemisphere
D. a major wave of extreme height and length

00529. In some river mouths and estuaries the incoming high-tide wave crest overtakes the preceding low-tide trough. This results in a wall of water proceeding upstream, and is called a:

A. seiche
B. bore
C. boundary wave
D. surge

00530. Under the U. S. Aids to Navigation System, a lighted buoy with a spherical top-mark marks:

A. the port side of the channel
B. the position of underwater cables
C. safe water
D. a hazard to navigation

00531. You have been informed that dredging operations may be underway in your vicinity. Which of the following buoys would indicate the area?

A. white buoy with a green top
B. white and international orange buoy
C. yellow buoy
D. yellow and black vertically-striped buoy

00532. In a river subject to tidal currents, the best time to dock a ship without tugs is:

A. at high water
B. at slack water
C. at stand
D. when there is a following current

00533. You are using a radar in which your own ship is shown at the center, and the heading flash always points to 0°. If bearings are measured in relation to the flash, what type of bearings are produced?

A. relative
B. true
C. compass
D. magnetic

00534. Which of the following is TRUE concerning an anemometer on a moving vessel?

A. It measures true wind speed.
B. It measures true wind speed and true wind direction.
C. It measures apparent wind speed.
D. It measures apparent wind speed and true wind direction.

00536. You are en route from Puerto Rico to New York. A hurricane makes up and is approaching. If the wind veers steadily, this indicates that your vessel is:

A. in the dangerous semicircle
B. in the navigable semicircle
C. directly in the path of the storm
D. in the storm center

00538. Which of the symbols in illustration D018NG represents a stationary front?

A. a
B. b
C. c
D. d

00539. You are underway on course 050° T and your maximum speed is 13 knots. The eye of a hurricane bears 120° T, 100 miles from your position. The hurricane is moving towards 265° T at 25 knots. What course should you steer at 13 knots to have the maximum CPA?

A. 324° T
B. 306° T
C. 299° T
D. 276° T

00540. An orange and white buoy with a rectangle on it is used to indicate:

A. danger
B. a controlled area
C. an exclusion area
D. general information

00541. A yellow buoy may mark:

A. a wreck
B. a shoal area
C. an anchorage area
D. a middle ground

00542. The only cylindrical projection widely used for chart navigation is the:

A. Lambert conformal
B. Mercator
C. azimuthal
D. gnomonic

00543. A radar display in which the orientation of the display is fixed, so that the north is always at the top of the screen, is called a(n):

A. relative display
B. composite display
C. stabilized display
D. unstabilized display

00544. The instrument most commonly used to gather the data for determining the relative humidity is the:

A. hydrometer
B. psychrometer
C. barometer
D. anemometer

00546. If it is impossible to avoid a hurricane in the Northern Hemisphere, the most favorable place to be when the storm passes is in:

A. the dangerous semicircle
B. the eye (center) of the storm
C. that half of the storm lying to the right of the storm's path
D. that half of the storm lying to the left of the storm's path

00548. When the declination of the Moon is 0°12.5' S, you can expect some tidal currents in Gulf Coast ports to:

A. have either a double ebb or a double flood
B. become reversing currents
C. become weak and variable
D. exceed the predicted velocities

00549. On a working copy of a weather map, an occluded front is represented by what color line?

A. red
B. blue
C. alternating red and blue
D. purple

00550. The description "Racon" beside an illustration on a chart would mean a:

A. radar transponder beacon
B. radar conspicuous beacon
C. radar calibration beacon
D. circular radiobeacon

00551. Spoil grounds, anchorage areas, cable areas, and military exercise areas are all marked by yellow buoys. What special mark on the buoy will indicate the specific area you are in?

A. a topmark triangular in shape
B. a topmark spherical in shape
C. lettering on the buoy
D. a topmark consisting of 2 cones with the points up

00554. A sling psychrometer is a(n):

A. type of cargo gear
B. instrument used in celestial navigation
C. instrument used to measure temperatures
D. instrument used to measure specific gravity

00556. In a tropical cyclone in the Northern Hemisphere, a vessel hove to with the wind shifting counterclockwise would be:

A. in the navigable semicircle
B. in the dangerous semicircle
C. directly in the path of the center
D. ahead of the storm

00558. A buoy bears 176° T at 3000 yd. What is the course to make good to leave the buoy 100 yd. to starboard?

A. 174° T
B. 176° T
C. 178° T
D. 180° T

00561. Buoys which mark dredging areas are painted:

A. black
B. yellow
C. green
D. red

00564. A hygrometer is a device used for determining:

A. the absolute temperature
B. atmospheric pressure
C. wind velocity
D. relative humidity

00566. You are attempting to locate your position with reference to a hurricane center

in the Northern Hemisphere. If the wind direction remains steady, but with diminishing velocity, you are most likely:

A. in the right semicircle
B. in the left semicircle
C. on the storm track ahead of the center
D. on the storm track behind the center

00568. The chart of a beach area shows a very steep slope to the underwater beach bottom. What type of breakers can be expected when trying to land a boat on this beach?

A. surging
B. converging
C. spilling
D. plunging

00569. A line of position formed by sighting 2 charted objects in line is called a(n):

A. relative bearing
B. range line
C. track line
D. estimated position

00570. Chart legends printed in capital letters show that the associated landmark is:

A. inconspicuous
B. conspicuous
C. a government facility or station
D. a radio transmitter

00571. The Coast Guard Captain of the Port has excluded all traffic from a section of a port, while a regatta is taking place. The buoys marking this exclusion area will be:

A. nun or can-shaped to conform to the overall direction of navigation
B. yellow
C. orange and white
D. marked with a spherical topmark

00573. What is the name of the movable, radial guide line used to measure direction on a radar?

A. compass rose
B. cursor
C. plan position indicator
D. variable range marker

00574. If your mercurial barometer reads 30.50 inches and the temperature is 56° F, what is the correct reading at 55° N, 150° W?

A. 30.42
B. 30.45
C. 30.50
D. 30.53

00576. In a tropical cyclone in the Southern Hemisphere, a vessel hove to with the wind shifting clockwise would be:

A. ahead of the storm center
B. in the dangerous semicircle
C. directly behind the storm center
D. in the navigable semicircle

00579. Low pressure disturbances, which travel along the intertropical convergence zone, are called:

A. permanent waves
B. tidal waves
C. tropical waves
D. tropical storms

00581. The Captain of the Port has closed to navigation, and buoyed, a section of a harbor. These buoys would be painted:

A. red or green to conform with the other lateral aids
B. red and green horizontally-striped
C. solid yellow
D. white with orange marks

00583. The radar control used to reduce sea return at close ranges is the:

A. gain control
B. sensitivity time control
C. fast time constant
D. pulse length control

00584. The correction(s) which must be applied to an aneroid barometer reading include(s):

A. height error
B. gravity error
C. temperature error
D. all of the above

00586. The approximate distance to a storm center can be determined by noting the hourly rate of fall of the barometer. If the rate of fall is 0.08 - 0.12 inches, what is the approximate distance to the storm center?

A. 50 to 80 miles
B. 80 to 100 miles
C. 100 to 150 miles
D. 150 to 250 miles

00588. You are underway on course 050° T and your maximum speed is 10 knots. The eye of a hurricane bears 100° T, 90 miles from your position. The hurricane is moving towards 285° T at 19 knots. If you maneuver at 10 knots to avoid the hurricane, what could be the maximum CPA?

A. 39 miles
B. 45 miles
C. 53 miles
D. 59 miles

00591. White lights may be found on:

A. special purpose buoys
B. spherical buoys
C. information and regulatory buoys
D. numbered buoys

00593. Radar makes the most accurate determination of the:

A. direction of a target
B. distance to a target
C. size of a target
D. shape of a target

00594. Barometers are calibrated at a standard temperature of:

A. 0° F
B. 32° F
C. 60° F
D. 70° F

00596. Which condition would NOT indicate the approach of a tropical storm?

A. long, high swells
B. cirrus clouds
C. halos about the Sun or Moon
D. decrease in wind velocity

00599. Magnetic compass deviation:

A. varies depending upon the bearing used
B. is the angular difference between magnetic north and compass north
C. is published on the compass rose on most nautical charts
D. is the angular difference between geographic and magnetic meridians

00600. The dangerous semicircle of a typhoon in the Southern Hemisphere is that area:

A. measured from due south clockwise 180°
B. measured from due south counterclockwise 180°
C. to the left of the storm's track
D. ahead of the typhoon measured from the storm's track to 90° on each side

00601. White and orange buoys, if lighted, shall show which color of light?

A. white
B. orange
C. red
D. alternating yellow and white

00602. Between the Equator and the 46th parallel of latitude, there are 3099 meridional parts. How many degrees of equatorial longitude does 3099 meridional parts represent?

A. 35°52'45"
B. 51°39'00"
C. 74°21'11"
D. 82°36'12"

00606. Early indications of the approach of a hurricane may be all of the following EXCEPT:

A. short confused swells
B. gradually increasing white clouds (mare's tails)
C. pumping barometer
D. continuous fine mist-like rain

00609. A tropical wave is located 200 miles due west of your position, which is north of the Equator. Where will the wave be in 24 hours?

A. farther away to the west
B. farther away to the east
C. in the same place
D. closer and to the west

00610. The apparent wind's speed can be zero only when 2 conditions are present. One condition is that the true wind:

A. must be from dead ahead
B. speed must be zero
C. must be from dead astern
D. must be on the beam

00611. Lighted information markers display:

A. yellow lights
B. green lights
C. white lights
D. red lights

00613. Your radar indicates a target; however, there is no visible object at the point indicated. A large mountain, approximately 50 miles away on the same bearing as the target, is breaking the horizon. You should suspect the radar target is caused by:

A. a submerged submarine
B. ducting
C. sub-refraction
D. ionospheric skip waves

00616. Which of the following indicates that a tropical cyclone can be expected at your position within 24 to 48 hours?

A. a daily fluctuation of over 6 millibars in the barometric reading
B. a sudden wind shift from southwest to northwest followed by steadily increasing winds

C. the normal swell pattern becoming confused, with the length of the swell increasing
D. an overcast sky with steadily increasing rain from nimbostratus clouds

00618. What is the mark on a lead line indicating 13 fathoms?

A. white linen rag
B. red woolen rag
C. 3 knots
D. 3 strips of leather

00619. According to Buys Ballot's Law, when an observer in the Southern Hemisphere experiences a northwest wind, the center of the low pressure is located to the:

A. east-northeast
B. south-southwest
C. east-southeast
D. west-southwest

00620. Chart legends which indicate a conspicuous landmark are printed in:

A. capital letters
B. italics
C. boldface print
D. underlined letters

00621. Navigational marks used for informational or regulatory purposes are:

A. solid yellow
B. white with orange geometric shapes
C. red and white vertically-striped
D. green and red horizontally-banded

00626. What indicates the arrival of a hurricane within 24 to 36 hours?

A. the normal swell becoming lower and from a steady direction
B. long bands of nimbostratus clouds radiating from a point over the horizon
C. the barometer drops 2 millibars between 1000 and 1600
D. unusually good weather with above average pressures followed by a slow fall of 4 millibars in 6 hours

00628. What is the mark on a lead line indicating 17 fathoms?

A. wooden toggle
B. white linen rag
C. red woolen rag
D. no marking

00629. The rise and fall of the ocean's surface due to a distant storm is known as:

A. sea
B. waves
C. fetch
D. swell

00630. What kind of weather would you expect to accompany the passage of a tropical wave?

A. heavy rain and cloudiness
B. good weather
C. a tropical storm
D. dense fog

00631. A light characteristic of composite group-flashing indicates that there is a(n):

A. sharp turn in the channel
B. narrowing in the channel at that point
C. junction in the channel
D. obstruction that must be left to port

00633. You have another ship overtaking you close aboard to starboard. You have 3 radar targets bearing 090° relative at ranges of: 5 miles, 1 mile and 1.5 miles. In this case, the unwanted echoes are called:

A. multiple echoes
B. spoking
C. indirect echoes
D. side-lobe echoes

00635. As a vessel changes to starboard, the compass card in a magnetic compass:

A. first turns to starboard then counterclockwise to port
B. remains aligned with compass north
C. turns counterclockwise to port
D. also turns to starboard

00636. Tropical cyclones are classified by form and intensity. Which of the four mentioned disturbances does not have closed isobars?

A. hurricane
B. tropical disturbance
C. tropical depression
D. cyclone

00638. Swell is the rise and fall of the ocean's surface due to:

A. fetch
B. distant winds
C. local storms
D. the pull of the Moon

00639. In the Northern Hemisphere, what type of cloud formations would you expect to see to the west of an approaching tropical wave?

A. cumulus clouds lined up in rows extending in a northeast to southwest direction
B. high altostratus clouds in the morning hours
C. cirrostratus clouds lined up in rows extending in a northeast to southwest direction
D. cirrostratus clouds lined up in rows extending in a north to south direction

00640. What is the mark on a lead line indicating 20 fathoms?

A. line with 2 knots
B. 2 strips of leather
C. 2 pieces of rag
D. 2 lengths of line

00641. Buoys which mark isolated dangers are painted with alternating :

A. red and black bands
B. green and black bands
C. red and white stripes
D. green and white bands

00642. Which government agency publishes the U. S. Coast Pilot?

A. Army Corps of Engineers
B. Defense Mapping Agency
C. National Ocean Service
D. U. S. Coast Guard

00643. When using the radar for navigating:

A. the best fix is obtained by using a tangent bearing and a range
B. and using 2 radar ranges for a fix, the objects of the ranges should be close to reciprocal bearings
C. and using ranges, the most rapidly changing range should be measured last
D. and crossing a radar range of 1 object with the visual bearing of a second object, the two objects should be 80° to 110° apart

00646. You have determined that you are in the right semicircle of a tropical cyclone in the Northern Hemisphere. What action should you take to avoid the storm?

A. place the wind on the starboard quarter and hold that course
B. place the wind on the port quarter and hold that course
C. place the wind on the port bow and hold that course
D. place the wind on the starboard bow and hold that course

00649. You are on course 226° T. In order to check the latitude of your vessel, you should observe a celestial body on which bearing?

A. 226°
B. 270°
C. 000°
D. 026°

00650. What classification of tropical cyclone would have closed isobars, counterclockwise rotary circulation, and sustained winds between 34 and 63 knots?

A. a tropical disturbance
B. a tropical depression
C. a tropical storm
D. a hurricane

00651. Which topmark in illustration D023NG identifies an isolated danger?

A. a
B. b
C. c
D. d

00652. What agency of the U. S. Government issues charts of U. S. waters and Coast Pilots?

A. National Ocean Service
B. Defense Mapping Agency
C. U. S. Coast Guard
D. U. S. Naval Observatory

00653. You have been observing your radar screen and notice that a contact on the screen has remained in the same position for several minutes. Your vessel is making 10 knots through the water. Which of the following statements is TRUE?

A. The contact is dead in the water.
B. The contact is on the same course and speed as your vessel.
C. The contact is on a reciprocal course at the same speed as your vessel.
D. The radar is showing false echoes and is probably defective.

00655. The Equator is:

A. the primary great circle of the Earth perpendicular to the axis
B. the line to which all celestial observations are reduced
C. the line from which a celestial body's altitude is measured
D. all of the above

00656. In the Northern Hemisphere you are caught in the dangerous semicircle with plenty of sea room available. The best course of action is to bring the wind on the:

A. starboard bow and make as much headway as possible
B. starboard quarter, and make as much headway as possible
C. port quarter, and make as much headway as possible
D. port bow, and make as much headway as possible

00657. Current refers to the:

A. vertical movement of the water
B. horizontal movement of the water
C. density changes in the water
D. none of the above

00658. Monsoons are characterized by:

A. light, variable winds with little or no humidity
B. strong, gusty winds that blow from the same general direction all year
C. steady winds that reverse direction semi-annually
D. strong, cyclonic winds that change direction to conform to the passage of an extreme low pressure system

00659. What is the mark on a lead line indicating 25 fathoms?

A. leather with 2 holes
B. white linen rag
C. red woolen rag
D. line with 1 knot

00660. What is the length of a nautical mile?

A. 1,850 m
B. 6,080 ft.
C. 2,000 yd.
D. 6,076 ft.

00661. Under the IALA Buoyage Systems, safe water marks may show a:

A. composite group-flashing, Fl(2 + 1), red light
B. composite group-flashing, Fl(2 + 1), green light
C. quick-flashing, Q(9)15s, white light
D. white Morse (A) light

00663. You are underway at 10 knots. At 1800 you note a radar contact dead ahead at a range of 10 miles. At 1812 the contact is dead ahead at a range of 8 miles. The estimated speed of the contact is:

A. dead in the water
B. 5 knots
C. 10 knots
D. 15 knots

00665. 17 degrees of latitude is equal to:

A. 68 miles
B. 510 miles
C. 1020 miles
D. 4080 miles

00666. In the Northern Hemisphere, your vessel is believed to be in the direct path of a hurricane, and plenty of sea room is available. The best course of action is to bring the wind on the:

A. starboard bow, note the course, and head in that direction
B. starboard quarter, note the course, and head in that direction
C. port quarter, note the course, and head in that direction
D. port bow, note the course, and head in that direction

00667. The navigable semicircle of a typhoon in the Southern Hemisphere is the area:

A. behind the typhoon, measured from 90° to 180° from each side of the storm's track
B. to the right of the storm's track
C. ahead of the typhoon, measured from the storm's track to 90° on each side
D. measured from due south, counterclockwise 180°

00668. You are en route to assist vessel A. Vessel A is underway at 6 knots on course 133° T, and bears 042° T at 105 miles from you. What is the course to steer at 10 knots to intercept vessel A?

A. 083°
B. 088°
C. 093°
D. 099°

00669. A vessel encountering hurricane or typhoon conditions is required to transmit reports to the closest meteorological service every:

A. hour
B. 3 hours
C. 6 hours
D. 8 hours

00671. You sight a buoy fitted with a double-sphere topmark. If sighted at night, this buoy would show:

A. a quick-flashing red light
B. a quick-flashing green light
C. a white flashing light showing a group of 2 flashes
D. a red flashing light showing a group of 3 flashes

00672. You are planning to enter an unfamiliar U. S. port. What publication provides information about channel depths, dangers, obstructions, anchorages and marine facilities available in that port?

A. American Practical Navigator
B. Notice to Mariners
C. United States Coast Pilot
D. Sailing Guide

00673. You are underway at 5 knots and see on your radar a contact 10 miles directly astern of you. Twelve minutes later, the contact is 8 miles directly astern of you. What is the estimated speed of the contact?

A. dead in the water
B. 1 knot
C. 10 knots
D. 15 knots

00675. Fifteen degrees of latitude is equal to:

A. 600 miles
B. 900 miles
C. 1200 miles
D. 1500 miles

00676. If you are caught in the left semicircle of a tropical storm, in the Southern Hemisphere, you should bring the wind:

A. on the starboard quarter, hold course and make as much way as possible
B. 2 points on the port quarter, and make as much way as possible
C. on the port bow, and make as much way as possible
D. dead ahead and heave to

00677. A swift current occurring in a narrow passage connecting two large bodies of water, which is produced by the continuously changing difference in height of tide at the two ends of the passage, is called a:

A. hydraulic current
B. rectilinear current
C. rotary current
D. harmonic current

00679. A tropical wave is usually preceded by:

A. tropical storms
B. good weather
C. heavy rain and cloudiness
D. heavy seas

00680. The apparent wind's speed can be zero only when two conditions are present. One condition is that the true:

A. wind must be on the beam
B. wind's speed must be zero
C. wind must be from dead ahead
D. wind's speed equals the ship's speed

00681. You sight a spar buoy with the top mark shown in illustration D027NG. You must:

A. pass to the east of the buoy
B. pass to the south of the buoy
C. pass to the north of the buoy
D. keep well clear of the buoy and pass on either side

00682. Which of the following tables is NOT found in the U. S. Coast Pilots?

A. climatological table
B. luminous range table
C. meteorological table
D. coastwise distance table

00683. A radar contact will remain stationary on a relative motion radar display only when it is:

A. on the same course as your vessel
B. at the same speed as your vessel
C. on the same course and speed as your vessel
D. on a reciprocal course at the same speed as your vessel

00685. Thirty-two meters equals:

A. 17.50 ft.
B. 58.52 ft.
C. 96.00 ft.
D. 104.99 ft.

00686. The pressure gradient between the horse latitudes and doldrums runs:

A. east-west
B. north-south
C. northeast-southeast
D. northwest-southwest

00687. The drift and set of tidal, river, and ocean currents refer to the:

A. position and area of the current
B. speed and direction toward which current flows
C. type and characteristic of the current's flow
D. none of the above

00688. In mid-ocean, the characteristics of a wave are determined by three factors. Which of the following is NOT one of these factors?

A. effect of the Moon's gravity
B. fetch
C. wind velocity
D. length of time a wind has been blowing

00690. What level of development of a tropical cyclone has a 100 mile radius of circulation, gale force winds, less than 990 millibars of pressure and vertically formed cumulonimbus clouds?

A. a tropical disturbance
B. a tropical depression
C. a tropical storm
D. a typhoon

00691. Of the four light characteristics shown in illustration D019NG, which one does NOT represent a safe water mark of the IALA Buoyage Systems?

A. a
B. b
C. c
D. d

00693. Which general statement concerning radar is NOT true?

A. Raising the antenna height increases the radar range.
B. The ability of radar to detect objects is unaffected by weather conditions.
C. Radar bearings are less accurate than radar ranges.
D. Radar should be checked regularly during clear weather to ensure that it is operating properly.

00696. The diurnal pressure variation is most noticeable in the:

A. polar regions
B. horse latitudes
C. roaring forties
D. doldrums

00697. The set of the current is the:

A. speed of the current at a particular time
B. maximum speed of the current
C. direction from which the current flows
D. direction in which the current flows

00699. You are en route to assist vessel A. Vessel A is underway at 6 knots on course 133° T, and bears 343° T at 92 miles from you. What is the course to steer at 9 knots to intercept vessel A?

A. 033°
B. 038°
C. 042°
D. 047°

00701. In the IALA Buoyage Systems, buoys with alternating red and green horizontal bands are used to indicate:

A. fishing areas
B. spoil grounds
C. the preferred channel
D. isolated dangers

00702. What publication contains information on navigation regulations, landmarks, channels, anchorages, tides, currents, and clearances of bridges for Chesapeake Bay?

A. Coast Pilot
B. Light List
C. Sailing Directions
D. Pilot Charts

00703. Which of the following statements concerning the operation of radar in fog is TRUE?

A. Radar ranges are less accurate in fog.
B. Navigation buoys will always show on radar.
C. A sandy beach will show up clearer on radar than a rocky cliff.
D. Small wooden boats may not show on radar.

00706. A steep barometric gradient indicates:

A. calms
B. light winds
C. strong winds
D. precipitation

00707. Set of the current is:

A. its velocity in knots
B. direction from which it flows
C. estimated current
D. direction towards which it flows

00709. A sea breeze is a wind:

A. that blows towards the sea at night
B. that blows towards an island during the day
C. caused by cold air descending a coastal incline
D. caused by the distant approach of a hurricane

00710. What is the FIRST sign of the existence of a well developed tropical cyclone?

A. gale force winds from the north
B. an unusually long ocean swell
C. steep, short-period waves and light wind
D. thunderstorms and higher than usual humidity

00711. In the IALA Maritime Buoyage Systems, a red and white vertically-striped buoy is used as a(n):

A. safe water mark
B. cardinal mark
C. isolated danger mark
D. special mark not primarily used for navigation

00712. Information about the pilotage available at Miami Harbor may best be obtained from which of the following publications?

A. World Port Index
B. Sailing Directions
C. Pilot Chart
D. United States Coast Pilot

00713. The closest point of approach (CPA) of a contact on a relative motion radar may be determined:

A. immediately when contact is noted on radar
B. only if the radar scope is watched constantly
C. after contact has been marked at least twice
D. by an occasional glance at the radar

00716. Standard atmospheric pressure in inches of mercury is:

A. 30.00
B. 28.92
C. 29.92
D. 29.00

00717. Which term refers to the direction a current is flowing?

A. set
B. drift
C. vector direction
D. stand

00720. What change in the condition of the seas could indicate the formation of a tropical storm or hurricane several hundred miles from your location?

A. a long swell from an unusual direction
B. a lengthy lull in the wind and seas
C. large seas coming from different directions
D. a brisk chop from the southeast

00721. Under the IALA Buoyage Systems, a red and white vertically-striped buoy would NOT indicate:

A. a landfall
B. the extreme end of an islet
C. a mid-channel
D. a center line

00722. Which of the following would describe the explosive anchorages in the ports on the East Coast of the United States?

A. Sailing Directions
B. Pilot Rules for Inland Waters
C. Coast Pilot
D. Notice to Mariners

00726. Sea-level atmospheric pressure equals:

A. 14.7 pounds per square inch
B. 29.92 inches of mercury
C. 1013.25 millibars
D. all of the above

00727. What is an ebb current?

A. a current at minimum flow
B. a current coming in
C. a current going out
D. a current at maximum flow

00729. The doldrums are characterized by:

A. steady, light to moderate winds
B. frequent calms
C. clear skies
D. low humidity

00730. The largest waves or swells created by a typhoon or hurricane will be located:

A. in the southeast quadrant of the storm
B. directly behind the storm center
C. forward and to the right of its course
D. behind and to the left of its course

00731. Under the IALA Buoyage Systems, a vertically-striped buoy may be striped red and:

A. green
B. black
C. white
D. yellow

00732. What publication has information on the climate, distances, navigation regulations, outstanding landmarks, channels and anchorages of Long Island Sound?

A. Light List
B. Coast Pilot
C. Sailing Directions
D. Pilot Chart

00733. Which of the following would give the best radar echo?

A. the beam of a three-masted sailing vessel with all sails set
B. a 110' fishing vessel with a radar reflector in its rigging
C. a 300' tanker, bow on
D. a 600' freighter, beam on

00734. You are approaching Chatham Strait from the south in foggy weather. You have Coronation Island and Hazy Islands on the radar. Suddenly the radar malfunctions. You then resort to using whistle echoes to determine your distance off Coronation Island. Your stopwatch reads 16.3 seconds for the echo to be heard. How far are you off Coronation Island?

A. 1.0 mile
B. 1.5 miles
C. 2.0 miles
D. 2.5 miles

00735. The period of the Earth's revolution from perihelion to perihelion is the:

A. astronomical year
B. anomalistic year
C. solar year
D. sidereal year

00736. A line on a weather chart connecting places which have the same barometric pressure is called an:

A. isotherm
B. isallobar
C. isobar
D. isotope

00737. Which of the following describes an ebb current?

A. horizontal movement of the water away from the land following low tide
B. horizontal movement of the water toward the land following low tide
C. horizontal movement of the water away from the land following high tide
D. horizontal movement of the water toward the land following high tide

00740. A very light breeze that causes ripples on a small area of still water is a:

A. cat's paw
B. hog's breath
C. williwaw
D. chinook

00741. What is the light phase characteristic of a lighted isolated-danger mark (IALA Buoyage Systems)?

A. interrupted quick flashing
B. very quick flashing
C. long flashing
D. group flashing

00742. You are preparing to take a tow from San Diego to Portland, OR. Good seamanship would require that you have on board, available for reference and use, all of the following EXCEPT the:

A. Coast Pilot
B. Harbor and Coastal Charts for ports of refuge en route
C. Sailing Directions (En route)
D. Light List

00743. The Consol navigation system, used in Russian and Northern European waters, can be used:

A. for precise navigation in coastal waters
B. by measuring the phase difference of the dots and dashes
C. as an aid to ocean navigation
D. if the vessel is fitted with a special Consol receiver

00744. A handheld instrument used to measure distances between objects and the ship is a:

A. vernier
B. psychrometer
C. hygrometer
D. stadimeter

00745. Retrograde motion is the:

A. movement of the points of intersection of the planes of the ecliptic and the Equator
B. apparent westerly motion of a planet with respect to stars
C. movement of a superior planet in its orbit about the Sun
D. movement of the celestial north pole in an elliptical pattern in space

00746. Lines drawn through points on the Earth having the same atmospheric pressure are known as:

A. isothermal
B. millibars
C. isobars
D. seismics

00747. The movement of water away from shore or downstream is called a(n):

A. reversing current
B. ebb current
C. flood current
D. slack current

00748. You are steaming west in the South Atlantic in an extratropical cyclonic storm, and the wind is dead ahead. According to the law of Buys Ballot, the center of low pressure lies:

A. to the north of you
B. to the south of you
C. dead ahead of you
D. dead astern of you

00749. You are en route to assist vessel A. Vessel A is underway at 4.5 knots on course 233° T, and bears 264° T at 68 miles from you. What is the course to steer at 13 knots to intercept vessel A?

A. 249°
B. 256°
C. 262°
D. 268°

00750. On a working copy of a weather map, a cold front is represented by what color line?

A. red
B. blue
C. alternating red and blue
D. purple

00751. Under the IALA Buoyage Systems, a yellow buoy may mark:

A. fish net areas
B. spoil areas
C. military exercise zones
D. all of the above

00752. What publication would NOT be used on a voyage from Houston to New York?

A. Coast Pilot
B. Light List
C. Radio Navigational Aids
D. Sailing Directions (En route)

00754. Deviation in a compass is caused by the:

A. vessel's geographic position
B. vessel's heading
C. earth's magnetic field
D. influence of the magnetic materials of the vessel

00756. Which of the following is a common unit of measure for atmospheric pressure?

A. knots
B. inches
C. degrees
D. feet

00757. The term "flood current" refers to that time when the water:

A. is flowing towards the land
B. is moving towards the ocean
C. level is not changing
D. level is rising because of heavy rains

00758. A tropical cyclone has recurved and entered temperate latitudes. In the Northern Hemisphere when a large high pressure system lies north of the storm, what situation may occur?

A. The low may suddenly deepen, and the cyclone intensify and pick up speed.
B. The left semicircle may become the dangerous semicircle.

C. The low and the high may merge and cancel out the weather characteristics of each.
D. The high may force the cyclone to reverse its track.

00759. At 0000 you fix your position and plot a new DR track line. At 0200 you again fix your position and it is 0.5 mile west of your DR. Which of the following statements is TRUE?

A. The set is 090°, drift 0.5 knot.
B. The set is 270°, drift 0.25 knot.
C. The set is 270°, drift 0.5 knot.
D. The set is 270°, drift 1.0 knot.

00760. As a vessel changes course to starboard, the compass card in a magnetic compass:

A. first turns to starboard then counterclockwise to port
B. also turns to starboard
C. remains aligned with compass north
D. turns counterclockwise to port

00761. Under the IALA Buoyage Systems, a safe water mark may NOT:

A. be spherical
B. display a white light
C. be lettered
D. show a quick flashing light

00762. In addition to the Notice to Mariners, chart correction information may be disseminated through all of the following except the:

A. Summary of Corrections
B. Local Notice to Mariners
C. Daily Memorandum
D. Chart Correction Card

00763. Time signals broadcast by WWV and WWVH are transmitted:

A. every 15 minutes
B. every 30 minutes
C. every hour
D. continuously throughout day

00764. Magnetic variation changes with a change in:

A. the vessel's heading
B. sea conditions
C. seasons
D. the vessel's position

00766. Which of the following positions includes the effects of wind and current?

A. dead reckoning position
B. leeway position

C. set position
D. estimated position

00767. Which of the following describes a flood current?

A. horizontal movement of the water toward the land after high tide
B. horizontal movement of the water toward the land after low tide
C. horizontal movement of the water away from the land following high tide
D. horizontal movement of the water away from the land following low tide

00770. You are plotting a running fix in an area where there is a determinable current. How should this current be treated in determining the position?

A. The course and speed made good should be determined and used to advance the LOP.
B. The drift should be added to ship's speed.
C. The current should be ignored.
D. The set should be applied to second bearing.

00771. Under the IALA Buoyage Systems, a spherical buoy will mark the:

A. safe water
B. port side of the channel
C. a hazard to navigation
D. the position of an underwater cable

00772. The Local Notice to Mariners is published by the U. S. Coast Guard:

A. daily
B. weekly
C. monthly
D. semiannually

00773. What is the basic principle of the magnetic compass?

A. Magnetic materials of the same polarity repel each other and those of opposite polarity attract.
B. The Earth's magnetic lines of force are parallel to the surface of the Earth.
C. Magnetic meridians connect points of equal magnetic variation.
D. The compass needle(s) will, when properly compensated, lie parallel to the isogonic lines of the Earth.

00774. Variation is not constant; it is different with every change in:

A. speed
B. vessel heading
C. geographical location
D. cargo

00776. You are navigating in pilotage waters using running fixes. The maximum time between fixes should be about:

A. 4 hours
B. 1 hour
C. 30 minutes
D. 5 minutes

00777. Slack water occurs when there is:

A. no horizontal motion of the water
B. no vertical motion of the water
C. a weak ebb or flood current
D. neither a vertical nor a horizontal motion

00778. The navigable semicircle of a hurricane in the Northern Hemisphere is that area of the storm measured:

A. from true north clockwise to 180° T
B. from true north counterclockwise to 180° T
C. from the bow counterclockwise to 180° relative
D. from the direction of the storm's movement counterclockwise 180°

00780. Apparent wind speed blowing across your vessel while underway can be measured by a(n):

A. barometer
B. wind vane
C. anemometer
D. thermometer

00781. The IALA Buoyage Systems do NOT apply to:

A. the sides and centerlines of navigable channels
B. natural dangers and other obstructions, such as wrecks
C. lighthouses and lightships
D. areas in which navigation may be subject to regulation

00782. Mariners are FIRST warned of serious defects or important changes to aids to navigation by means of:

A. Marine Broadcast Notice to Mariners
B. Weekly Notices to Mariners
C. corrected editions of charts
D. Light Lists

00783. Magnetism which is present only when the material is under the influence of an external field is called:

A. permanent magnetism
B. induced magnetism

C. residual magnetism
D. terrestrial magnetism

00784. Variation is the angular measurement between:

A. compass north and magnetic north
B. compass north and true north
C. magnetic meridian and the geographic meridian
D. your vessel's heading and the magnetic meridian

00786. The greater the pressure difference between a high and a low pressure center, the:

A. dryer the air mass will be
B. cooler the temperature will be
C. greater the force of the wind will be
D. warmer the temperature will be

00789. The dangerous semicircle of a hurricane in the Northern Hemisphere is that area of the storm:

A. to the right of the storm's track
B. measured from true north clockwise to 180° T
C. measured from true north counterclockwise to 180° T
D. between the ship's heading and the bearing to the eye

00790. At 0000 you fix your position and plot a new DR track line. At 0030 you again fix your position and it is 0.5 mile from your 0030 DR. Which statement is TRUE?

A. The current is westerly.
B. The drift is 0.5 knot.
C. You must alter course to the left to regain the track line.
D. none of the above

00791. Under the IALA Buoyage Systems, the topmark of a red and white vertically-striped buoy shall be:

A. X-shaped
B. 2 black spheres
C. a single red sphere
D. a single red cone

00792. Information about temporary, short term changes affecting the safety of navigation in U. S. waters is disseminated to navigational interests by the:

A. Daily Memorandum
B. HYDROLANT or HYDROPAC broadcasts
C. Local Notice to Mariners
D. Summary of Corrections

00793. The permanent magnetism of a vessel may change in strength due to:

A. a collision with another vessel
B. being moored on a constant heading for a long period of time
C. being struck by lightning
D. any of the above

00796. Cyclones tend to move:

A. perpendicular to the isobars in their warm sectors
B. parallel to the isobars in their warm sectors
C. parallel to the line of the cold front
D. perpendicular to the line of the cold front

00798. A HYDROLANT warning would normally be sent for all of the following EXCEPT:

A. extinguishment of Robbins Reef Light in New York City's Upper Bay
B. unexploded ordnance in ocean waters at a depth of 78 fathoms
C. the presence of a large unwieldy tow in congested offshore water
D. a report of an overdue ship

00799. In Region A of the IALA Buoyage System, when entering from seaward, the starboard side of a channel would be marked by a:

A. green can buoy
B. red can buoy
C. green conical buoy
D. red conical buoy

00801. You are entering an African port and see ahead of you a red can-shaped buoy. What action should you take?

A. alter course to leave the buoy to port
B. alter course to leave the buoy to starboard
C. pass the buoy close aboard on either side
D. pass the buoy well clear on either side

00802. Which of the following is a weekly publication advising mariners of important matters affecting navigational safety?

A. Light List
B. Notice to Mariners
C. Coast Pilot
D. Sailing Directions

00803. Which of the following buoys will NOT display white retroreflective material?

A. safe water mark
B. isolated danger mark
C. preferred channel mark
D. daymark of no lateral significance

00804. A relative bearing is always measured from:

A. true north
B. magnetic north
C. the vessel's beam
D. the vessel's head

00806. Temperature and moisture characteristics are modified in a warm or cold air mass due to:

A. pressure changes in the air mass
B. movement of the air mass
C. the heterogeneous nature of the air mass
D. upper level atmospheric changes

00808. On a working copy of a weather map, a stationary front is represented by what color line?

A. red
B. blue
C. alternating red and blue
D. purple

00809. The compass rose on a nautical chart indicates both variation and:

A. deviation
B. annual rate of variation change
C. precession
D. compass error

00812. Defects and/or changes in aids to navigation are published by means of:

A. Local Notice to Mariners
B. Weekly Notice to Mariners
C. marine broadcasts
D. all of the above

00813. At the magnetic Equator there is no induced magnetism in the vertical soft iron because:

A. The lines of force cross the Equator on a 0°-180° alignment
B. The quadrantal error is 0°
C. There is no vertical component of the Earth's magnetic field
D. The intercardinal headings have less than 1° error

00814. Frost smoke will occur when:

A. extremely cold air from shore passes over warmer water
B. warm dry air from shore passes over cooler water
C. cold ocean water evaporates into warm air
D. cool rain passes through a warm air mass

00816. Cyclones that have warm sectors usually move:

A. westerly
B. parallel to the isobars in the warm sector
C. toward the nearest high pressure area
D. faster than the accompanying cold front

00818. Ocean swells originating from a typhoon can move ahead of it at speeds near:

A. 10 knots
B. 20 knots
C. 30 knots
D. 50 knots

00820. A position obtained by crossing lines of position taken at different times and advanced to a common time is a(n):

A. dead-reckoning position
B. running fix
C. estimated position
D. fix

00822. Charts should be corrected by using information published in (the):

A. Light List
B. American Practical Navigator
C. Notice to Mariners
D. Coast Pilot

00823. The greatest directive force is exerted on the magnetic compass when the:

A. needles are nearly in line with the meridian
B. vessel is near the magnetic poles
C. variation is near zero
D. vessel is near the magnetic Equator

00824. An "atoll cloud" forming over an island due to heating of the land during the daytime would be what type?

A. cirrus
B. cumulus
C. stratus
D. nimbus

00826. In the U. S., which direction do air masses usually move?

A. easterly
B. southerly
C. northerly
D. southwesterly

00828. The true wind has been determined to be from 210° T, speed 12 knots. You desire the apparent wind to be 30 knots from 10° on the port bow. What course must you steer, and what speed must you make for this to occur?

A. 235° T, 18.6 knots
B. 245° T, 20.0 knots
C. 325° T, 22.4 knots
D. 335° T, 23.6 knots

00829. You are plotting a running fix in an area where there is a determinable current. How should this current be treated in determining the position?

A. The drift should be added to the ship's speed.
B. The set should be applied to the second bearing.
C. The current should be ignored.
D. The course and speed made good should be determined and used to advance the LOP.

00830. The highest frequency of tropical cyclones in the North Atlantic Ocean occurs during:

A. January, February and March
B. April, May and June
C. August, September and October
D. July, November and December

00832. What is the most important source of information to be used in correcting charts and keeping them up to date?

A. Fleet Guides
B. Notice to Mariners
C. Sailing Directions
D. Pilot Charts

00833. The magnetic compass magnets are acted on by the horizontal component of the Earth's total magnetic force. This magnetic force is GREATEST at the:

A. north magnetic pole
B. south magnetic pole
C. magnetic prime vertical meridian
D. magnetic Equator

00834. In many areas "atoll" clouds (clouds of vertical development) are produced over small islands. These are the result of:

A. rising air currents produced by the warm islands
B. warm air from the sea rising over higher land areas
C. cool land air mixing with warm sea air
D. descending air over the islands

00836. In North America the majority of the weather systems move from:

A. north to south
B. south to north
C. east to west
D. west to east

00838. A navigator fixing a vessel's position by radar:

A. must use information from targets forward of the beam
B. should never use radar bearings
C. should only use radar bearings when the range exceeds the distance to the horizon
D. can use radar information from 1 object to fix the position

00840. Which of the following positions includes the effects of wind and current?

A. estimated position
B. set position
C. leeway position
D. dead reckoning position

00842. Coast Pilots and navigational charts are kept corrected and up-to-date by using the:

A. Pilot Charts
B. Notices to Mariners
C. Tide Tables
D. Current Tables

00843. The line which connects the points of zero magnetic dip is:

A. an agonic line
B. the magnetic Equator
C. a magnetic meridian
D. any of the above

00844. A cloud of marked vertical development (often anvil-shaped) would be classified as:

A. cirrus
B. cirrocumulus
C. altocumulus
D. cumulonimbus

00846. Weather in the middle latitudes generally travels from:

A. east to west
B. north to south
C. west to east
D. none of the above

00848. The difference between the DR position and a fix, both of which have the same time, is known as:

A. the estimated position
B. drift
C. current
D. leeway

00849. The Light List shows that a navigational light has a nominal range of 12 miles and a height above water of 25 ft. Your height of eye is 30 ft. and the visibility is 0.5 mile. At what approximate range will you first sight the light?

A. 0.5 mile
B. 1.4 miles
C. 5.2 miles
D. 12.0 miles

00850. When is the peak of the hurricane season in the Western North Pacific?

A. January through March
B. April through June
C. July through October
D. November through December

00852. Which of the following is published by the U. S. Coast Guard?

A. Light List
B. Nautical Charts
C. Tide Tables
D. U. S. Coast Pilot

00853. The standard magnetic compass heading differs from the true heading by:

A. compass error
B. latitude
C. variation
D. deviation

00854. The appearance of nimbostratus clouds in the immediate vicinity of a ship at sea would be accompanied by which of the following conditions?

A. rain and poor visibility
B. dropping barometric pressure and backing wind in the Northern Hemisphere
C. high winds and rising sea
D. severe thunderstorms

00855. Which condition exists at the summer solstice in the Northern Hemisphere?

A. the north polar regions are in continual darkness.
B. the Northern Hemisphere is having short days and long nights.
C. the Southern Hemisphere is having winter.
D. the Sun shines equally on both hemispheres.

00856. The flow of air around an anticyclone in the Southern Hemisphere is:

A. clockwise and outward
B. counterclockwise and outward
C. clockwise and inward
D. counterclockwise and inward

00858. Your ship is proceeding on course 320° T at a speed of 25 knots. The apparent wind is from 30° off the starboard bow, speed 32 knots. What is the relative direction, true direction and speed of the true wind?

A. relative 80°, true 040° T, 16.2 knots
B. relative 40°, true 080° T, 16.4 knots
C. relative 80°, true 060° T, 15.2 knots
D. relative 60°, true 040° T, 18.6 knots

00860. The Light List shows that a navigational light has a nominal range of 10 miles and a height above water of 38 ft. Your height of eye is 52 ft. and the visibility is 11.0 miles. At what approximate range will you first sight the light?

A. 10.5 miles
B. 13.6 miles
C. 14.2 miles
D. 15.3 miles

00862. The U. S. Coast Guard publishes:

A. Light Lists
B. U. S. Coast Pilots
C. Radio Navigational Aids
D. all of the above

00863. The compass heading of a vessel differs from the true heading by:

A. compass error
B. variation
C. magnetic dip
D. deviation

00864. Uniform, grayish-white cloud sheets that cover large portions of the sky, and are responsible for a large percentage of the precipitation in the temperate latitudes, are called:

A. altostratus
B. altocumulus
C. cirrostratus
D. cirrocumulus

00866. Anticylones are usually characterized by:

A. dry, fair weather
B. high winds and cloudiness
C. gustiness and continuous precipitation
D. overcast skies

00869. Tropical storms and hurricanes are most likely to form in the Southern Hemisphere during:

A. January through March
B. April through May
C. June through August
D. September through November

00872. What agency publishes the Light Lists?

A. United States Coast Guard
B. National Ocean Service
C. Oceanographic Office
D. Army Corps of Engineers

00873. Compass error is equal to the:

A. deviation minus variation
B. variation plus compass course
C. algebraic sum of the variation and deviation
D. difference between true and magnetic compass

00874. Altostratus clouds are defined as:

A. high clouds
B. middle clouds
C. low clouds
D. vertical development clouds

00876. A generally circular low pressure area is called a(n):

A. cyclone
B. anticyclone
C. cold front
D. occluded front

00879. You are en route to assist vessel A. Vessel A is underway at 4.5 knots on course 233° T, and bears 346° T at 68 miles from you. What is the course to steer at 13 knots to intercept vessel A?

A. 328°
B. 323°
C. 318°
D. 314°

00880. You are taking bearings on two known objects ashore. The BEST fix is obtained when the angle between the lines of position is:

A. 60°
B. 90°
C. 45°
D. 30°

00882. Some lights used as aids to marine navigation have a red sector to indicate a danger area. The limits of a colored sector of a light are listed in the Light List in which of the following manners?

A. geographical positions outlining the area of the sector
B. true bearings as observed from the ship toward the light
C. an outline of the area of the sector
D. true bearings as observed from the light toward the ship

00883. In changing from a magnetic compass course to a true course, you should apply:

A. variation
B. deviation
C. variation and deviation
D. a correction for the direction of current set

00884. Which of the following cloud types is normally associated with thunderstorms?

A. cirrus
B. stratus
C. cumulus
D. cumulonimbus

00886. The circulation around a low pressure center in the Northern Hemisphere is:

A. counterclockwise
B. variable
C. clockwise
D. anticyclonic

00888. Recurvature of a hurricane's track usually results in the forward speed:

A. increasing
B. decreasing
C. remaining the same
D. varying during the day

00889. The Light List shows that a navigational light has a nominal range of 6 miles and a height above water of 18 ft. Your height of eye is 47 ft. and the visibility is 1.5 miles. At what approximate range will you first sight the light?

A. 1.5 miles
B. 2.0 miles
C. 6.0 miles
D. 12.7 miles

00890. If several fixed navigational lights are visible at the same time, each one may be positively identified by checking all of the following EXCEPT what against the Light List?

A. rhythm
B. period
C. intensity
D. color

00892. When a buoy is in position only during a certain period of the year, where may the dates when the buoy is in position be determined?

A. Light List
B. Notice to Mariners
C. on the chart
D. Coast Pilot

00893. One point of a compass is equal to how many degrees?

A. 7.5
B. 11.25
C. 17.5
D. 22.5

00894. On a clear, warm day, you notice the approach of a tall cumulus cloud. The cloud top has hard well defined edges and rain is falling from the dark lower edge. Should this cloud pass directly overhead:

A. it will be preceded by a sudden increase in wind speed
B. it will be preceded by a sudden decrease in wind speed
C. the wind speed will not change as it passes
D. the wind will back rapidly to left in a counterclockwise direction as it passes

00896. The wind direction around a low pressure area in the Northern Hemisphere is:

A. clockwise and inward
B. clockwise and outward
C. counterclockwise and inward
D. counterclockwise and outward

00900. An orange and white buoy with a rectangle on it is a(n):

A. informational buoy
B. junction buoy
C. safe water buoy
D. all of the above

00902. All of the following information concerning lighted aids to navigation may be read directly from the Light List EXCEPT the:

A. location
B. height of light above water
C. luminous range
D. light characteristics

00903. Eight points of a compass are equal to how many degrees?

A. 45
B. 90
C. 180
D. 360

00904. All of the following are associated with cumulonimbus clouds EXCEPT:

A. steady rainfall
B. hail storms
C. thunderstorms
D. tornadoes or waterspouts

00906. In the Northern Hemisphere, an area of counterclockwise wind circulation surrounded by higher pressure is a:

A. low
B. high
C. warm front
D. cold front

00909. What is the average speed of movement of a hurricane prior to recurvature?

A. 4 to 6 knots
B. 6 to 8 knots
C. 10 to 12 knots
D. 15 to 20 knots

00910. The Light List shows that a navigational light has a nominal range of 12 miles and a height above water of 25 ft. Your height of eye is 38 ft. and the visibility is 5.5 miles. At what approximate range will you first sight the light?

A. 5.5 miles
B. 6.8 miles
C. 8.0 miles
D. 12.0 miles

00911. Under the IALA-B Buoyage System, a buoy displaying a red light will:

A. be left to starboard entering from seaward
B. show a light characteristic of Morse Code "A"
C. be lettered
D. have a radar reflector

00912. The Light List Does NOT contain information on:

A. Loran-C station systems
B. aeronautical lights useful for marine navigation
C. radiobeacon systems
D. radio direction finder calibration stations

00913. How many points are there in a compass card?

A. 4
B. 8
C. 24
D. 32

00914. If the sky was clear, with the exception of a few cumulus clouds, it would indicate:

A. rain
B. hurricane weather
C. fair weather
D. fog setting in

00916. Bad weather is usually associated with regions of:

A. low barometric pressure
B. high barometric pressure
C. steady barometric pressure
D. changing barometric pressure

00919. You are plotting a running fix in an area where there is a determinable current. How should this current be treated in determining the position?

A. The drift should be added to ship's speed.
B. The course and speed made good should be determined and used to advance LOP.
C. The current should be ignored.
D. The set should be applied to second bearing.

00920. What is the average speed of the movement of a hurricane following the recurvature of its track?

A. 5 to 10 knots
B. 20 to 30 knots
C. 40 to 50 knots
D. over 60 knots

00921. Under the IALA-B Buoyage System, a conical buoy will be:

A. red in color
B. numbered with an odd number
C. left to port when entering from seaward
D. all of the above

00922. How is the intensity of a light expressed in the Light Lists?

A. luminous range
B. geographic range
C. nominal range
D. meteorological range

00923. A magnetic compass is marked in how many degrees?

A. 90
B. 180
C. 360
D. 400

00924. The form of cloud often known as "mackerel sky" which is generally associated with fair weather is:

A. nimbostratus
B. stratus
C. cirrocumulus
D. cumulonimbus

00926. When a low pressure area is approaching, the weather generally:

A. improves
B. gets worse

C. remains the same
D. is unpredictable

00929. Which of the following errors is NOT included in the term "current" when used in relation to a fix?

A. poor steering
B. leeway
C. known compass error
D. ocean currents

00930. Which of the following statements about radio navigational warnings is TRUE?

A. The topics for warnings included in HYDROLANTS, HYDROPACS, and NAVAREA warnings are the same.
B. NAVAREA warnings concern only coastal navigation and inland navigation in large bays or sounds such as Puget Sound.
C. The United States is responsible for NAVAREA warnings in the North Atlantic north of 7° N, and west of 15° W.
D. Long range radio navigational warnings are usually broadcast by radiotelephone, radiotelegraph, and radio-teletypewriter.

00931. Under the IALA-B Buoyage System, when entering from seaward, a buoy that should be left to port will be:

A. black
B. red
C. green
D. yellow

00932. To find the specific phase characteristic of a lighthouse on a sound of the United States you would use the:

A. American Practical Navigator
B. Light List
C. Nautical Chart Catalog
D. U. S. Coast Pilot

00933. How many degrees are there on a compass card?

A. 360
B. 380
C. 390
D. 420

00934. Clouds that form as small white flakes or scaly globular masses covering either small or large portions of the sky are:

A. cirrus
B. cirrostratus
C. altostratus
D. cirrocumulus

00935. The Light List shows that a navigational light has a nominal range of 5 miles and a height above water of 21 ft. Your height of eye is 32 ft. and the visibility is 1.0 mile. At what approximate range will you first sight the light?

A. 1.0 mile
B. 1.5 miles
C. 5.0 miles
D. 11.7 miles

00936. A cyclone in its final stage of development is called a(n):

A. tornado
B. anticyclone
C. occluded cyclone or occluded front
D. polar cyclone

00939. That half of the hurricane to the right hand side of its track (as you face the same direction that the storm is moving) in the Northern Hemisphere is called the:

A. windward side
B. leeward side
C. safe semicircle
D. dangerous semicircle

00940. What is the length of a nautical mile?

A. 6,076 ft.
B. 6,080 ft.
C. 2,000 yd.
D. 1,850 m

00942. Light Lists for coastal waters are:

A. published annually and require no corrections
B. published every second year and must be corrected
C. published every 5 years and require no correction
D. correct only to the date of publication

00944. High clouds, composed of small white flakes or scaly globular masses, and often banded together to form a "mackerel sky", would be classified as:

A. cirrus
B. cirrocumulus
C. altocumulus
D. cumulonimbus

00946. The wind circulation around a high pressure center in the Northern Hemisphere is:

A. counterclockwise and moving towards high
B. counterclockwise and moving outward from the high
C. clockwise and moving towards the high
D. clockwise and moving outward from high

00949. In Region A of the IALA Buoyage System, when entering from seaward, the port side of a channel would be marked by a:

A. black can buoy
B. red can buoy
C. black conical buoy
D. red conical buoy

00950. Where is the dangerous semicircle located on a hurricane in the Southern Hemisphere?

A. to the left of the storm's track
B. to the right of the storm's track
C. in the high pressure area
D. on the south side

00952. Which of the following is TRUE concerning new editions of Light Lists?

A. Supplements to new editions are issued monthly by the U. S. Coast Guard.
B. New editions are published by the National Ocean Survey.
C. New editions are corrected through the date shown on the title page.
D. none of the above

00953. The magnetic compass operates on the principle that:

A. like magnetic poles attract
B. unlike magnetic poles repel
C. unlike poles attract
D. the poles of the compass line up with the geographic poles of the earth

00954. A thin, whitish, high cloud popularly known as "mare's tails" is:

A. altostratus
B. stratus
C. cumulus
D. cirrus

00956. Good weather is usually associated with a region of:

A. low barometric pressure
B. high barometric pressure
C. falling barometric pressure
D. pumping barometric pressure

00960. The Light List shows that a navigational light has a nominal range of 15 miles and a height above water of 29 ft. Your height of eye is 52 ft. and visibility is 6.0 miles. At what approximate range will you first sight the light?

A. 9.0 miles
B. 11.0 miles

C. 14.5 miles
D. 15.0 miles

00962. Chart legends which indicate a conspicuous landmark are printed in:

A. underlined letters
B. boldfaced print
C. italics
D. capital letters

00964. The thin, whitish, high clouds composed of ice crystals, popularly known as "mare's tails" are:

A. cirrostratus
B. cirrocumulus
C. cumulonimbus
D. nimbostratus

00966. Most high pressure areas in the United States are accompanied by:

A. precipitation
B. clear, cool weather
C. humid, sticky weather
D. cool fogs

00972. In which of the following sources could you find the number of a chart for a certain geographic area?

A. Chart No. 1
B. Catalog of Nautical Charts
C. American Practical Navigator
D. U. S. Coast Guard Light List

00973. The heading of a vessel is indicated by what part of the compass?

A. card
B. needle
C. lubber's line
D. gimbals

00974. Which of the following clouds commonly produce a halo about the Sun or Moon?

A. cirrostratus
B. cirrocumulus
C. altostratus
D. altocumulus

00976. The atmosphere in the vicinity of a high pressure area is called a(n):

A. anticyclone
B. cold front
C. occluded front
D. cyclone

00977. In the Sargasso Sea there are large quantities of seaweed and no well defined currents. This area is located in the:

A. Central North Atlantic Ocean
B. Caribbean Sea
C. Western North Pacific Ocean
D. area off the West Coast of South America

00978. The wind velocity is higher in the dangerous semicircle of a typhoon because of the:

A. recurvature effect
B. extension of the low pressure ridge
C. wind circulation and forward motion of storm
D. direction of circulation and pressure gradient

00979. What kind of conditions would you observe as the eye of a storm passes over your vessel's position?

A. huge waves approaching from all directions, clearing skies, light winds and an extremely low barometer
B. flat calm seas, heavy rain, light winds and an extremely low barometer
C. flat calm seas, heavy rain, light winds and high pressure
D. huge waves approaching from all directions, clearing skies, light winds and high pressure

00980. When the declination of the Moon is 0°12.5' S, you can expect some tidal currents in Gulf Coast ports to:

A. have either a double ebb or a double flood
B. become weak and variable
C. become reversing currents
D. exceed the predicted velocities

00981. The characteristic of a lighted cardinal mark may be:

A. very quick flashing
B. flashing
C. fixed
D. occulting

00982. The Defense Mapping Agency Hydrographic Center's List of Lights for coasts other than the United States and its possessions does NOT provide information on:

A. lighted buoys in harbors
B. storm signal stations
C. radio direction finder stations at or near lights
D. radio beacons located at or near lights

00983. Error may be introduced into a magnetic compass by:

A. making a structural change to the vessel
B. a short circuit near the compass

C. nylon clothing
D. any of the above

00984. The bases of middle clouds are located at altitudes of between:

A. 3,000 to 6,500 ft.
B. 6,500 to 20,000 ft.
C. 10,000 to 35,000 ft.
D. 20,000 to 60,000 ft.

00986. A warm air mass is characterized by:

A. stability
B. instability
C. gusty winds
D. good visibility

00989. The Light List shows that a navigational light has a nominal range of 18 miles and height above water of 22 ft. Your height of eye is 16 ft. and the visibility is 2.0 miles. At what approximate range will you first sight the light?

A. 2.0 miles
B. 2.7 miles
C. 4.2 miles
D. 5.8 miles

00994. Which of the following lists clouds, in sequence, from highest in the sky to lowest in the sky?

A. altostratus, cirrostratus, stratus
B. cirrostratus, altostratus, stratus
C. stratus, cirrostratus, altostratus
D. altostratus, stratus, cirrostratus

00996. Warm air masses will generally have:

A. turbulence within the mass
B. stratiform clouds
C. heavy precipitation
D. good visibility

00997. A coastal current:

A. is generated by waves striking the beach
B. flows outside the surf zone
C. flows in a circular pattern
D. is also known as a longshore current

00998. The navigable semicircle of a tropical storm in the South Indian Ocean is located on which side of the storm's track?

A. rear
B. front
C. left
D. right

01000. You are inbound in a channel marked by a range. The range line is 309° T. You are steering 306° T and have the range in sight as indicated in illustration D047NG. What action should you take?

A. Continue on course if the range is closing, otherwise alter course to the left.
B. Continue on the present heading until the range is in line, then alter course to the left.
C. Immediately alter course to the right to bring the range in line.
D. Immediately alter course to 309° T.

01002. What publication contains information about the port facilities in Cadiz, Spain?

A. World Port Index
B. United States Coast Pilot
C. Nautical Index
D. Sailing Directions

01004. A low, uniform layer of cloud resembling fog, but not resting on the ground, is called:

A. cumulus
B. nimbus
C. stratus
D. cirrus

01006. An air mass is termed "warm" if:

A. it is above 70° F
B. the ground over which it moves is cooler than the mass
C. it originated in a high pressure area
D. it originated in a low pressure area

01007. When a current flows in the opposite direction to the waves, the wave:

A. length is increased
B. height is increased
C. velocity increases
D. length is unchanged

01008. The Light List indicates that a light has a nominal range of 18 miles and is 38 ft. high. If the visibility is 6 miles and your height of eye is 15 ft., at what distance will you sight the light?

A. 18.0 miles
B. 12.8 miles
C. 11.7 miles
D. 6.0 miles

01012. General information about the location, characteristics, facilities and services for U. S. and foreign ports may be obtained from which of the following publications?

A. World Port Index
B. Sailing Directions

C. Distances Between Ports
D. Coast Pilot

01014. Relative humidity is the percentage of water vapor that is in the air as compared to the maximum amount it can hold at:

A. a specific barometric pressure
B. a specific temperature
C. a specific wind speed
D. any time

01016. A source of an air mass labeled mTw is:

A. the Equator
B. the Gulf of Mexico
C. Alaska
D. Canada

01018. An aneroid barometer reading should be corrected for differences in :

A. elevation
B. temperature
C. wind speed
D. latitude

01020. The Light List shows that a navigational light has a nominal range of 6 miles and a height above water of 18 ft. Your height of eye is 40 ft. and the visibility is 27.0 miles. At what approximate range will you first sight the light?

A. 5.6 miles
B. 6.0 miles
C. 9.0 miles
D. 12.1 miles

01024. The dew point is reached when the:

A. temperature of the air equals the temperature of the seawater
B. atmospheric pressure is 14.7 lbs. per sq. in.
C. relative humidity reaches 50%
D. air becomes saturated with water vapor

01025. A first magnitude star is:

A. 2.5 times as bright as a second magnitude star
B. 3 times as bright as a second magnitude star
C. 5 times as bright as a second magnitude star
D. 10 times as bright as a second magnitude star

01026. An air mass that has moved down from Canada would most likely have the symbols:

A. mPk
B. cPk
C. cTk
D. cTw

01028. At what angle to the isobars do surface winds blow over the open sea?

A. about 90°
B. about 50°
C. about 25°
D. about 15°

01029. Which of the following would be the subject of a NAVAREA warning?

A. a drifting buoy sighted in mid-ocean
B. extinguishment of Wolf Trap Light located inside Chesapeake Bay
C. all military exercises on the high seas involving 4 or more vessels
D. off-air times of radio beacons when scheduled for routine maintenance

01034. The expression "the air is saturated" means:

A. the relative humidity is 100%
B. the vapor pressure is at its minimum for the prevailing temperature
C. precipitation has commenced
D. cloud cover is 100%

01036. A frontal thunderstorm is caused by:

A. pronounced local heating
B. wind being pushed up a mountain
C. a warm air mass rising over a cold air mass
D. an increased lapse rate caused by advection of warm surface air

01039. While taking weather observations, you determine that the wind is coming from the west. In the weather log, you would record the wind direction as:

A. 000°
B. 090°
C. 180°
D. 270°

01040. An occluded front is usually caused by a:

A. cold front becoming stationary
B. warm front becoming stationary
C. cold front overtaking a warm front
D. warm front dissipating

01045. The Light List shows that a navigational light has a nominal range of 15 miles and a height above water of 40 ft. Your height of eye is 25 ft. and the visibility is 5.0 miles. At what approximate range will you first sight the light?

A. 6.2 miles
B. 9. 5 miles
C. 12.9 miles
D. 14.2 miles

01046. The probability of a sudden wind may be foretold by:

A. a partly cloudy sky
B. an overcast sky
C. a fast approaching line of dark clouds
D. the formation of cumulus clouds in the sky

01048. The velocity of the current in large coastal harbors is:

A. unpredictable
B. generally too weak to be of concern
C. predicted in Tidal Current Tables
D. generally constant

01049. At 0000 you fix your position and change course to 270° T. At 0030 you again fix your position, and it is 0.5 mile east of your DR. Which of the following statements is TRUE?

A. the set is 090°, drift 0.5 knot.
B. the set is 090°, drift 1.0 knot.
C. the set is 270°, drift 0.5 knot.
D. the set is 270°, drift 1.0 knot.

01050. The passing of a low pressure system can be determined by periodically checking the:

A. thermometer
B. hygrometer
C. barometer
D. anemometer

01051. Under the IALA-A and B Buoyage Systems, a cardinal mark may NOT be used to:

A. indicate that the deepest water in an area is on the named side of the mark
B. indicate the safe side on which to pass a danger
C. draw attention to a feature in the channel such as a bend, junction, bifurcation, or end of a shoal
D. indicate the port and starboard sides of well-defined channels

01056. The steepness of a cold front depends on:

A. the direction of wind around the front
B. its velocity
C. the temperature of the air behind the front
D. the precipitation generated by the front

01059. The Light List shows that a navigational light has a nominal range of 17 miles and a height above water of 28 ft. Your height of eye is 32 ft. and the visibility is 11.0 miles. At what approximate range will you first sight the light?

A. 11.0 miles
B. 12.6 miles
C. 15.7 miles
D. 18.0 miles

01060. Isobars on a synoptic chart are useful in predicting:

A. temperature
B. dew point
C. wind velocity
D. relative humidity

01061. In waters where the IALA Cardinal System is used you would expect to find danger:

A. lying to the south of an eastern quadrant buoy
B. lying to the south of a northern quadrant buoy
C. lying to the east of an eastern quadrant buoy
D. beneath or directly adjacent to the buoy

01064. The dew point temperature is:

A. always higher than the air temperature
B. always lower than the air temperature
C. equal to the difference between the wet and dry bulb temperatures
D. the temperature at which the air is saturated with water vapor

01065. You are in the Northern Hemisphere and a tropical wave is located 200 miles due east of your position. Where will the wave be located 12 hours later?

A. farther away to the east
B. in the same position
C. nearby to the east
D. farther away to the west

01066. The slope of a warm front is about:

A. 1 mile vertically to 10 miles horizontally
B. 1 mile vertically to 50 miles horizontally
C. 1 mile vertically to 150 miles horizontally
D. 1 mile vertically to 500 miles horizontally

01069. What do the numbers on isobars indicate?

A. barometric pressure
B. temperature
C. rain in inches
D. wind speed

01070. Chart legends which indicate a conspicuous landmark are printed in:

A. underlined letters
B. capital letters

C. italics
D. boldface print

01071. A cardinal mark showing an uninterrupted quick-flashing white light indicates the deepest water in the area is on the:

A. north side of the mark
B. west side of the mark
C. east side of the mark
D. south side of the mark

01073. Chart legends printed in capital letters show that the associated landmark is:

A. inconspicuous
B. a radio transmitter
C. conspicuous
D. a government facility or station

01074. As the temperature for a given mass of air increases, the:

A. dew point increases
B. dew point decreases
C. relative humidity increases
D. relative humidity decreases

01075. The expression "first magnitude" is usually used to refer only to bodies of magnitude:

A. 1.5 and greater
B. 1.25 and greater
C. 1.0 and greater
D. 0.5 and greater

01076. Which is TRUE concerning the speed of fronts?

A. Cold fronts move faster than warm fronts.
B. Cold fronts move slower than warm fronts.
C. Cold fronts and warm fronts move with equal speed.
D. Cold fronts move slower at the northern end and faster at the southern end.

01078. The description "Racon" beside an illustration on a chart would mean a:

A. radar conspicuous beacon
B. radar transponder beacon
C. radar calibration beacon
D. circular radiobeacon

01084. As the temperature of a given mass of air decreases, the:

A. absolute humidity decreases
B. relative humidity increases
C. specific humidity decreases
D. dew point rises

01086. When crossing a front isobars tend to:

A. change from smooth curves within the air mass to sharp bends at the front
B. change from sharp bends within the air mass to smooth curves at the front
C. pass smoothly across the front with no change
D. become closer together at the front and pass through in straight lines

01087. The velocity of a rotary tidal current will increase when the Moon is:

A. new
B. full
C. at perigee
D. all of the above

01088. Which of the following statements about an estimated position is TRUE?

A. It is more reliable than a fix based on radar bearings.
B. It may be based on a single LOP or questionable data.
C. When a 3-LOP fix plots in a triangle, the center of the triangle is the estimated position.
D. It is usually based on soundings.

01089. You are en route to assist vessel A. Vessel A is underway at 5.5 knots on course 033° T, and bears 248° T at 64 miles from you. What is the course to steer at 13 knots to intercept vessel A?

A. 262°
B. 269°
C. 276°
D. 281°

01090. Referring to illustration D049NG, what weather conditions would you expect to find at position A?

A. winds NW-W at 20 knots, heavy rain, and high seas
B. light northerly winds, partly cloudy, and high seas
C. winds calm, light rain, and calm seas
D. winds NE-E at 20 knots, heavy rain, and high seas

01091. The cardinal mark topmark shown in illustration D024NG represents which quadrant?

A. northern
B. eastern
C. southern
D. western

01094. A light, feathery deposit of ice caused by the sublimation of water vapor directly into the crystalline form, on objects whose temperatures are below freezing, is known as:

A. dew
B. frost
C. glaze
D. snow

01096. With the passage of an occluded front the temperature:

A. rises rapidly
B. remains about the same
C. drops rapidly
D. depends on whether warm type or cold type occlusion

01097. The velocity of a rotary tidal current will be decreased when the Moon is:

A. at apogee
B. new
C. full
D. any of the above

01104. Which condition(s) is(are) necessary for the formation of dew?

A. clear skies
B. calm air
C. earth's surface cooler than the air
D. all of the above

01105. The Light List shows that a navigational light has a nominal range of 22 miles and height above water of 48 ft. Your height of eye is 35 ft. and the visibility is 20.0 miles. At what approximate range will you first sight the light?

A. 10.5
B. 13.2
C. 14.7
D. 32.0

01106. The legend symbol which designates an occluded front is represented by a:

A. red line
B. purple line
C. blue line
D. dashed blue line

01107. A rotary current sets through all directions of the compass. The time it takes to complete one of these cycles is approximately:

A. 2 1/2 hours
B. 3 1/2 hours
C. 6 1/2 hours
D. 12 1/2 hours

01108. Preferred channel buoys indicate the preferred channel to transit by:

A. odd or even numbers
B. the color of their top band
C. the location of the buoy in the channel junction
D. the characteristic of the buoy's light

01110. To make sure of getting the full advantage of a favorable current, you should reach an entrance or strait at what time in relation to the predicted time of the favorable current?

A. at the predicted time
B. 30 minutes before the predicted time
C. 1 hour after the predicted time
D. 30 minutes before flood, 1 hour after an ebb

01111. Black double-cone topmarks are the most important feature, by day, of cardinal marks. Which of the four topmarks shown in illustration D030NG indicates the best navigable water lies to the west of the buoy?

A. a
B. b
C. c
D. d

01114. Mechanical lifting of air by the upslope slant of the terrain is called:

A. vertical lifting
B. convective lifting
C. advective lifting
D. topographic lifting

01116. When a cold air mass and a warm air mass meet, and there is no horizontal motion of either air mass, it is called a(n):

A. cold front
B. occluded front
C. stationary front
D. warm front

01117. A rotary current sets through all directions of the compass. The time it takes to complete one of these cycles is approximately:

A. 3 hours
B. 6-1/2 hours
C. 12-1/2 hours
D. 25 hours

01121. The articulated light is superior to other types of buoys because:

A. the radar reflectors reflect better signals
B. fog horn signals travel farther to sea
C. they are equipped with strobe lights
D. it has a reduced watch circle

01122. A barometer showing falling pressure would indicate the approach of a:

A. high pressure system
B. low pressure system
C. high dew point
D. low dew point

01124. The region containing 3/4 of the mass of the atmosphere and the region to which are confined such phenomena as clouds, storms, precipitation and changing weather conditions is called:

A. stratosphere
B. troposphere
C. stratopause
D. tropopause

01125. The Light List shows that a navigational light has a nominal range of 19 miles and a height above water of 52 ft. Your height of eye is 42 ft. and the visibility is 10.0 miles. At what approximate range will you first sight the light?

A. 10.0 miles
B. 15.7 miles
C. 16.5 miles
D. 19.0 miles

01126. When a warm air mass is adjacent to a cold air mass, the separation line between the two is called a(n):

A. front
B. isobar
C. isotherm
D. equipotential line

01127. In a river subject to tidal currents, the best time to dock a ship without the assistance of tugs is:

A. at slack water
B. at stand
C. when there is a following current
D. at high water

01129. When running free in light airs, the personnel in a lifeboat under sail should be distributed so that:

A. the boat is trimmed by the bow
B. the boat has no trim
C. the boat is trimmed by the stern
D. the trim, either by the bow or stern, is not excessive

01131. What is the meaning of "Fl (2+1)" in conjunction with navigational aids?

A. a flashing light varied at regular intervals by a fixed light of greater brilliance
B. light flashes are combined in alternating groups, with a different number of flashes in each group
C. a light showing groups of 2 or more flashes at regular intervals
D. a fixed light varied at regular intervals by groups of 2 or more flashes of greater brilliance

01132. On charts of U. S. waters, a magenta marking is NOT used for marking a:

A. radiobeacon
B. 5-fathom curve
C. prohibited area
D. lighted buoy

01134. The Earth's irregular heating is caused by:

A. the time of day
B. the seasons
C. geography
D. all of the above

01136. When a warm air mass overtakes a retreating cold air mass, the contact surface is called a(n):

A. warm front
B. cold front
C. line squall
D. occluded front

01137. When the declination of the Moon is 0°12.5' S, you can expect some tidal currents in Gulf Coast ports to:

A. become weak and variable
B. exceed the predicted velocities
C. become reversing currents
D. have either a double ebb or a double flood

01140. What is the light characteristic of a lighted, preferred-channel buoy?

A. group-flashing
B. composite group-flashing
C. interrupted quick-flashing
D. fixed and flashing

01141. Which of the following is characteristic of an isophase light?

A. 4 sec. Flash, 2 sec. Eclipse, 3 sec. Flash, 2 sec. Eclipse
B. 2 sec. Flash, 5 sec. Eclipse
C. 1 sec. Flash, 1 sec. Eclipse
D. 6 sec. Flash, 3 sec. Eclipse

01142. Referring to illustration D049NG, what weather conditions would you expect to find at position B?

A. winds NW at 20.5 knots, steady warm temperatures, high seas
B. winds calm, falling temperatures, clear skies, high seas
C. winds S-SE at 25 knots, falling temperatures, squally, high seas
D. none of the above

01144. Freezing salt water spray should be anticipated when the air temperature drops below what maximum value?

A. 32° F
B. 28° F
C. 0° F
D. -40° F

01146. Which of the following about a front is TRUE?

A. It is a boundary between 2 air masses.
B. There are temperature differences on opposite sides of a front.
C. There are abrupt pressure differences across a front.
D. all of the above

01147. To make sure of getting the full advantage of a favorable current, you should reach an entrance or strait at what time in relation to the predicted time of the favorable current?

A. 1 hour after
B. at the predicted time
C. 30 minutes before
D. 30 minutes before flood, 1 hour after an ebb

01148. The numeral in the center of a wind rose circle on a pilot chart indicates the:

A. total number of observations
B. average wind force on the Beaufort scale
C. average wind force in knots
D. percentage of calms

01149. You are entering port and have been instructed to anchor, as your berth is not yet available. You are on a SW'ly heading, preparing to drop anchor, when you observe the range lights depicted in illustration D047NG on your starboard beam. You should:

A. ensure your ship will NOT block the channel or obstruct the range while at anchor
B. drop the anchor immediately as the range lights mark an area free of obstructions
C. drop the anchor immediately as a change in the position of the range lights will be an indication of dragging anchor
D. not drop the anchor until the lights are in line

01151. Buoys are marked with reflective material to assist in their detection by searchlight. Which of the following statements is TRUE?

A. A safe-water buoy will display red and white vertical stripes of reflective material.
B. All reflective material is white because it is the most visible at night.
C. A special-purpose mark will display either red or green reflective material to agree with its shape.
D. A preferred-channel buoy displays either red or green reflective material to agree with the top band of color.

01154. The speed at which an ocean wave system advances is called:

A. wave length
B. ripple length
C. group velocity
D. wave velocity

01155. Which aid is NOT marked on a chart with a magenta circle?

A. radar station
B. aero light
C. radiobeacon
D. radar transponder beacon

01156. When cold air displaces warm air you have a(n):

A. cold front
B. occluded front
C. stationary front
D. warm front

01157. How many slack tidal currents usually occur each day?

A. 1
B. 2
C. 3
D. 4

01158. What type of cloud is indicated by the number 5 in illustration D039NG?

A. cirrostratus
B. cirrocumulus
C. altocumulus
D. nimbostratus

01159. Two navigational hazards are located near to each other, but each is marked by an individual cardinal buoyage system. The buoys of one Cardinal System may be identified from the other system by:

A. the differing light colors
B. one system having odd numbers while the other system has even numbers
C. one system using horizontal bands while the other system uses vertical stripes
D. the difference in the periods of the light

01160. Referring to illustration D049NG, what change in the wind could be expected at position C if the flow of high pressure was in a northerly direction?

A. decreasing and shifting to the east
B. decreasing and shifting to the north
C. increasing with no change of direction
D. increasing and shifting to the east

01161. Which of the following is characteristic of an occulting light?

A. 1 sec. Flash, 2 sec. Eclipse, 1 sec. Flash, 5 sec. Eclipse
B. 5 sec. Flash, 5 sec. Eclipse
C. 4 sec. Flash, 2 sec. Eclipse, 3 sec. Flash, 2 sec. Eclipse
D. 6 sec. Flash, 6 sec. Eclipse

01162. A line of all possible positions of your vessel at any given time is a:

A. longitude line
B. latitude line
C. line of position
D. fix

01164. The largest waves (heaviest chop) will usually develop where the wind blows:

A. at right angles to the flow of the current
B. against the flow of the current
C. in the same direction as the flow of the current
D. over slack water

01165. Which of the following statements concerning the chartlet in illustration D010NG is TRUE? (Soundings and heights are in m.)

A. Maury Lightship is visible for 17 miles.
B. There is a dangerous eddy southeast of Beito Island.
C. There is a 12-m deep hole west of Beito Island and inside the 5-m line.
D. The bottom to the south-southeast of the lightship is soft coral.

01166. A series of brief showers accompanied by strong, shifting winds may occur along or some distance ahead of a(n):

A. upper front aloft
B. cyclone
C. occluded front
D. cold front

01167. The velocity of the current in large coastal harbors is:

A. unpredictable
B. predicted in Tidal Current Tables
C. generally constant
D. generally too weak to be of concern

01168. What type of cloud is indicated by the number 4 in illustration D039NG?

A. altocumulus
B. cirrostratus
C. cumulus
D. altostratus

01169. Illustration D042NG represents the symbols used on radiofacsimile weather charts. The symbol indicated at letter "O" represents:

A. sandstorms
B. thunderstorms
C. snow
D. rain showers

01170. Which of the following statements concerning illustration D010NG is correct? (Soundings and heights are in m.)

A. Maury Lightship swings about her anchor on a circle with a 21-m diameter.
B. The sunken wreck southwest of Beito Island shows the hull or superstructure above the sounding datum.
C. There is a 12-m deep hole inside the 5-m curve just west of Beito Island.
D. The position of the lightship is indicated by the center of the star on the symbol's mast.

01171. A light that has a light period shorter than its dark period is described as:

A. flashing
B. pulsating
C. occulting
D. alternating

01172. What position on illustration D049NG would likely have stratus or stratocumulus clouds, occasional light drizzle, steady westerlies around 10 knots, and steady temperatures?

A. b
B. c
C. d
D. e

01174. Your vessel is en route from Japan to Seattle and is located at position I on the weather map in illustration D013NG. You should experience which of the following weather conditions?

A. clear skies with warm temperatures
B. steady precipitation
C. overcast skies with rising temperature
D. thundershowers

01175. Solid green arrows on the main body of a pilot chart indicate:

A. prevailing wind directions
B. prevailing ocean current directions
C. probable surface current flow
D. shortest great circle routes

01176. After the passage of a cold front, the barometric pressure:

A. drops, and the temperature drops
B. drops, and the temperature rises
C. rises, and the temperature drops
D. rises, and the temperature rises

01178. The range of tide is the:

A. distance the tide moves out from the shore
B. difference between the heights of high and low tide
C. duration of time between high and low tide
D. maximum depth of the water at high tide

01179. What type of cloud is indicated by the number 3 in illustration D039NG?

A. cirrocumulus
B. altocumulus
C. nimbostratus
D. cumulus

01181. An occulting light is one in which:

A. the period of darkness exceeds the period of light
B. there is only a partial eclipse of the light
C. the periods of light and darkness are equal
D. the period of light exceeds the period of darkness

01182. Referring to illustration D049NG, what wind speeds are reported in position C?

A. 3 knots
B. 10 knots
C. 20 knots
D. 30 knots

01184. Your position, X, in illustration D009NG is at LAT 35° S. What winds are you experiencing?

A. northeasterly
B. northwesterly
C. southeasterly
D. southwesterly

01185. An orange and white buoy with a rectangle on it displays:

A. directions
B. distances
C. locations
D. all of the above

01186. As a cold front passes an observer, pressure:

A. drops and winds become variable
B. rises and winds become gusty
C. drops and winds become gusty
D. rises and winds become variable

01190. What type of cloud is indicated by the number 2 in illustration D039NG?

A. cumulus
B. cirrostratus
C. stratocumulus
D. altostratus

01191. You plot a fix using 3 lines of position and find they intersect in a triangle. The actual position of the vessel:

A. is outside of the triangle
B. may be anywhere in the triangle
C. may be inside or outside of the triangle
D. is the geometric center of the triangle

01192. You are en route to assist vessel A. Vessel A is underway at 5.5 knots on course 033° T, and bears 284° T at 43 miles from you. What is the course to steer at 16 knots to intercept vessel A?

A. 284°
B. 303°
C. 329°
D. 342°

01194. In the Northern Hemisphere, an observer at point II in the weather system in illustration D014NG should experience a wind shift from the:

A. southwest, clockwise to northwest
B. northeast, clockwise to west-southwest
C. northeast, counterclockwise to northwest
D. east, counterclockwise to south-southwest

01195. A position that is obtained by applying estimated current and wind to your vessel's course and speed is a(n):

A. dead reckoning position
B. fix
C. estimated position
D. none of the above

01196. In the Northern Hemisphere, gusty winds shifting clockwise, a rapid drop in temperature, thunderstorms or rain squalls in summer (frequent rain/snow squalls in winter) then a rise in pressure followed by clearing skies, indicate the passage of a(n):

A. warm front
B. tropical cyclone
C. anticyclone
D. cold front

01198. Illustration D042NG represents the symbols used on radiofacsimile weather charts. Which of these symbols indicates a dust storm?

A. i
B. h
C. o
D. p

01199. The Sailing Directions (En route) contain information on which of the following?

A. well-charted inner dangers
B. port facilities
C. coastal anchorages
D. offshore traffic separation schemes

01201. Which of the following is NOT true concerning color sectors of lights?

A. Color sectors are expressed in degrees from the light toward the vessel.
B. Color sectors may indicate dangerous waters.
C. Color sectors may indicate the best water across a shoal.
D. Color sectors may indicate a turning point in a channel.

01202. Referring to illustration D049NG, what wind speeds are reported at position A?

A. 10 knots
B. 15 knots
C. 20 knots
D. 25 knots

01203. If the compass heading and the magnetic heading are the same then:

A. the deviation has been offset by the variation
B. there is something wrong with the compass
C. the compass is influenced by nearby metals
D. there is no deviation on that heading

01204. Which of the symbols in illustration DO18NG designates a stationary front?

A. a
B. b
C. c
D. d

01205. How is the annual rate of change for magnetic variation shown on a pilot chart?

A. gray lines on the uppermost inset chart
B. red lines on the main body of the chart
C. in parenthesis on the lines of equal magnetic variation
D. annual rate of change is not shown

01206. Brief, violent showers frequently accompanied by thunder and lightning are usually associated with:

A. passage of a warm front
B. passage of a cold front
C. winds shifting counterclockwise in the Northern Hemisphere
D. stationary high pressure systems

01208. What type of cloud is indicated by the number 1 in illustration D039NG?

A. cirrus
B. altostratus
C. altocumulus
D. nimbostratus

01210. You are inbound in a channel marked by a range. The range line is 309° T. You are steering 306° T and have the range in sight as indicated in illustration D047NG. The range continues to open. What action should you take?

A. Alter course to the right to 309° T or more to bring the range in line.
B. Continue on course but be prepared to come left if the range continues to open.
C. Come left until the range closes, then steer to the left of 306° T.
D. Alter course to the left to close the range, then alter course to 309° T.

01211. Red sectors of navigation lights warn mariners of:

A. floating debris
B. heavily trafficked areas
C. recently sunken vessels
D. shoals or nearby land

01212. Range daymarks may be painted any of the following colors EXCEPT:

A. red
B. green
C. yellow
D. black

01213. If the magnetic heading is greater than the compass heading, the deviation is:

A. east
B. west

C. north
D. south

01215. Daylight Savings Time is a form of zone time that adopts the time:

A. 2 zones to the east
B. 2 zones to the west
C. 1 zone to the east
D. 1 zone to the west

01216. In the Northern Hemisphere, winds veering sharply to the west or northwest with increasing speed are indications that a:

A. cold front has passed
B. low pressure center is approaching
C. stationary front exists
D. high pressure center has passed

01220. Under the U. S. Aids to Navigation System, a lighted buoy with a spherical top-mark marks:

A. the position of underwater cables
B. a hazard to navigation
C. the port side of the channel
D. safe water

01221. On a chart, the characteristic of the light on a lighthouse is shown as flashing white with a red sector. The red sector:

A. indicates limits of the navigable channel
B. indicates a danger area
C. is used to identify the characteristics of light
D. serves no significant purpose

01222. On entering from seaward, a starboard side daymark will:

A. show a fixed red light if lighted
B. show a Morse (A) white light
C. be square in shape
D. have an even number if numbered

01223. The difference between magnetic heading and compass heading is called:

A. variation
B. deviation
C. compass error
D. drift

01224. DMAHTC charts are adopting the metric system. In order to change a charted depth in m to ft. you should use the conversion table found:

A. in the Light List
B. in Bowditch Vol. II
C. on the chart
D. all of the above

01226. Cumulonimbus clouds are most likely to accompany a(n):

A. high pressure system
B. cold front
C. warm front
D. occluded front

01231. Some lights used as aids to marine navigation have a red sector to indicate a danger area. The limits of a colored sector of light are listed in the Light List in which of the following manners?

A. geographical positions outlining the area of the sector
B. true bearings as observed from the light toward a vessel
C. true bearings as observed from a vessel toward the light
D. bearings given in the Light List are always magnetic

01232. Entering from sea, triangular shaped daymarks are used to mark:

A. the starboard side of the channel
B. the centerline of the channel
C. an obstruction where the preferred channel is to starboard
D. special purpose areas

01233. Deviation is the angle between the:

A. true meridian and axis of the compass card
B. true meridian and the magnetic meridian
C. magnetic meridian and axis of compass card
D. axis of the compass card and the degaussing meridian

01234. What information does the outer ring of a compass rose on a nautical chart provide?

A. variation
B. true directions
C. magnetic directions
D. annual rate of variation change

01236. After the passage of a cold front the visibility:

A. does not change
B. improves rapidly
C. improves only slightly
D. becomes poor

01239. While taking weather observations, you determine that the wind is blowing from the northeast. You would record the wind direction in the weather log as:

A. 045°
B. 090°

C. 135°
D. 225°

01241. Which picture in illustration D034NG shows a fixed and flashing light?

A. a
B. b
C. c
D. d

01242. Daymarks marking the starboard side of the channel when going towards the sea are:

A. green squares
B. green triangles
C. red squares
D. red triangles

01243. Magnetic heading differs from compass heading by:

A. compass error
B. true heading
C. variation
D. deviation

01244. What is the mark on a lead line indicating 5 fathoms?

A. leather with a hole
B. white linen rag
C. red woolen rag
D. line with 5 knots

01246. What change accompanies the passage of a cold front in the Northern Hemisphere?

A. wind shift from northeast clockwise to SW
B. steady dropping of barometric pressure
C. steady precipitation, gradually increasing in intensity
D. a line of cumulonimbus clouds

01249. What is the light characteristic of a lighted, preferred-channel buoy?

A. fixed and flashing
B. continuous quick
C. isophase
D. composite group-flashing

01250. Daylight Savings Time is a form of zone time that adopts the time:

A. 1 zone to the east
B. 1 zone to the west
C. 2 zones to the east
D. 2 zones to the west

01251. A List of Lights entry (L Fl) is a single flashing light which shows a long flash of not less than:

A. 1.0 second duration
B. 1.5 seconds duration
C. 2.0 seconds duration
D. 3.0 seconds duration

01252. Port side daymarks may be:

A. numbered
B. octagonal
C. black and white
D. of any shape

01253. The horizontal angle between the magnetic meridian and the north-south line of the compass is the:

A. deviation
B. variation
C. compass error
D. dip

01256. A cold front moving in from the northwest can produce:

A. thunderstorms, hail, and then rapid clearing
B. increasing cloud cover lasting for several days
C. lengthy wet weather
D. low ceilings with thick cirrus clouds

01261. A light having characteristics which include color variations is defined as:

A. switching
B. alternating
C. oscillating
D. fluctuating

01262. A safe water daymark has what shape?

A. triangle
B. diamond
C. sphere
D. octagon

01263. The compass deviation changes as the vessel changes:

A. geographical position
B. speed
C. heading
D. longitude

01265. When reporting wind direction, you should give the direction in:

A. true degrees
B. magnetic compass degrees
C. relative degrees
D. isobaric degrees

01266. A line of clouds, sharp changes in wind direction, and squalls are most frequently associated with a(n):

A. occluded front
B. warm front
C. cold front
D. warm sector

01268. On a nautical chart, the inner ring of a compass rose indicates:

A. true directions
B. compass error
C. deviation
D. magnetic directions

01269. The Light List indicates that a light has a nominal range of 14 miles and is 42 ft. high. If the visibility is 16 miles and your height of eye is 20 ft., at what approximate distance will you sight the light?

A. 20.1 miles
B. 16.0 miles
C. 12.8 miles
D. 7.6 miles

01270. What is the mark on a lead line indicating 7 fathoms?

A. wooden toggle
B. white linen rag
C. red woolen rag
D. 2 strips of leather

01271. What word indicates color variation in the characteristics of a light?

A. opposing
B. changing
C. reversing
D. alternating

01272. What are the colors of a midchannel daymark?

A. black and red
B. red and white
C. green and red
D. green and white

01273. Deviation changes with a change in:

A. latitude
B. heading
C. longitude
D. sea conditions

01274. Illustration D042NG represents the symbols used on radiofacsimile weather charts. Which of these symbols indicates a sandstorm?

A. h
B. o
C. p
D. k

01275. How is variation indicated on a small-scale nautical chart?

A. magnetic compass table
B. magnetic meridians
C. isogonic lines
D. Variation is not indicated on small-scale nautical charts.

01276. Which of the following weather changes accompanies the passage of a cold front in the Northern Hemisphere?

A. wind shift from northeast, clockwise to SW
B. steady dropping of barometric pressure
C. steady precipitation, gradually increasing in intensity
D. a line of cumulonimbus clouds

01278. The difference between the heights of low and high tide is the:

A. depth
B. distance
C. range
D. period

01280. A current perpendicular to a vessel's track has the greatest affect on the vessel's course made good:

A. at high vessel speeds
B. at low vessel speeds
C. in shallow water
D. in deep water

01281. The time required for a lighted aid to complete a full cycle of light changes is listed in the Light List as the:

A. set
B. frequency
C. period
D. function

01282. Entering from sea, a daymark on the port side of the channel would be indicated on a chart by a:

A. red triangle with the letter R
B. white triangle with the letters RG
C. green square with the letter G
D. white square with the letters GR

01283. The error in a magnetic compass caused by the vessel's magnetism is called:

A. variation
B. deviation
C. compass error
D. bearing error

01284. The Sailing Directions (En route) contain information on all of the following EXCEPT:

A. ocean currents
B. outer dangers to navigation
C. tidal currents
D. major port anchorages

01285. You are en route to assist vessel A. Vessel A is underway at 5.5 knots on course 033° T, and bears 248° T at 64 miles from you. What is the time to intercept if you make 13 knots?

A. 4h 55m
B. 4h 36m
C. 3h 59m
D. 3h 44m

01286. Which condition will occur after a cold front passes?

A. temperature rises
B. stratus clouds form
C. pressure decreases
D. humidity decreases

01290. In addition to the National Weather Service, what agency provides plain-language radio weather advisories for the coastal waters of the United States?

A. U. S. Defense Mapping Agency
B. U. S. Hydrological Survey
C. U. S. Coast Guard
D. American Meteorological Service

01291. The period of a lighted aid to navigation refers to the:

A. date of construction or establishment
B. length of time between flashes of the light
C. time required for the longest flash of each cycle
D. time required for the light to complete each cycle

01292. A triangular daymark would be colored:

A. red
B. red and white
C. green
D. green and white

01293. Deviation is caused by:

A. changes in the earth's magnetic field
B. nearby magnetic land masses or mineral deposits
C. magnetic influence inherent to that particular vessel
D. the magnetic lines of force not coinciding with the lines of longitude

01294. What is the mark on a lead line indicating 10 fathoms?

A. 1 knot
B. 1 strip of leather
C. leather with a hole
D. no marking

01295. The best estimate of the wind direction at sea level can be obtained from observing the direction of the:

A. cloud movement
B. vessel heading
C. waves
D. swells

01296. After a cold front passes the barometric pressure usually:

A. fluctuates
B. remains the same
C. remains the same, with clouds forming rapidly
D. rises, often quite rapidly, with clearing skies

01301. The four standard light colors used for lighted aids to navigation are red, green, white and:

A. purple
B. orange
C. blue
D. yellow

01302. What feature(s) of a daymark is (are) used to identify the beacon upon which it is mounted?

A. color and shape
B. size
C. method of construction
D. signal characteristics

01303. Compass deviation is caused by:

A. magnetism from the earth's magnetic field
B. misalignment of the compass
C. magnetism within the vessel
D. a dirty compass housing

01306. What type of clouds are associated with a cold front?

A. altostratus and fracto-cumulus
B. altostratus and cirrus
C. cirrus and cirrostratus
D. cumulus and cumulonimbus

01310. An urgent marine storm warning message would be broadcast on:

A. 2670 KHz

B. 156.80 MHz (VHF-FM Ch. 16)
C. 157.10 MHz (VHF-FM Ch. 22A)
D. none of the above

01311. Which of the following is the characteristic of a quick light?

A. shows groups of 2 or more flashes at regular intervals
B. durations of light and darkness are equal
C. shows not less than 50 flashes per minute
D. shows quick flashes for about 5 seconds followed by a 1 second dark period

01312. What factor(s) determine(s) the charted visibility of a lighthouse's light in clear visibility?

A. height and intensity of the light
B. height of the light and the observer
C. height of the observer and the intensity of the light
D. height of the light only

01313. Variation in a compass is caused by:

A. worn gears in the compass housing
B. magnetism from the earth's magnetic field
C. magnetism within the vessel
D. lack of oil in the compass bearings

01314. Illustration D042NG represents the symbols used on radiofacsimile weather charts. Which of these symbols indicates hail?

A. n
B. h
C. q
D. f

01315. What is a lighted safe water mark fitted with to aid in its identification?

A. red and white retroreflective material
B. a sequential number
C. a spherical topmark
D. a red and white octagon

01316. When a warm air mass overtakes a cold air mass, the contact surface is called a:

A. line squall
B. water spout
C. cold front
D. warm front

01319. The Sailing Directions (Planning Guide) contain information on all of the following EXCEPT:

A. coastal features
B. ocean basin environment
C. ocean routes
D. military operating areas

01321. A lighthouse can be identified by:

A. its painted color
B. its light color and phase characteristic
C. its type of structure
D. all of the above

01323. The magnetic compass error which changes with the geographical location of your vessel is called:

A. deviation
B. variation
C. compensation
D. differentiation

01324. When Daylight Savings Time is kept, the time of tide and current calculations must be adjusted. One way of doing this is to:

A. add 1 hour to the times listed under the reference stations
B. subtract 1 hour from the time differences listed for the subordinate stations
C. apply no correction as the times in the reference stations are adjusted for Daylight Savings Time
D. add 15° to the standard meridian when calculating the time difference

01325. You change course entering port and steady up on a range with the lights in line. After a few minutes you observe the range lights as shown in illustration D047NG. You should alter your heading to the:

A. left, and when the range lights are in line again, steer to keep them dead ahead
B. right, and when the range lights are in line again, steer to keep them dead ahead
C. left, and when the range lights are in line again, steer to keep them in line fine on the starboard bow
D. right, and when the range lights are in line, steer to keep them in line fine on the port bow

01326. A cloud sequence of cirrus, cirrostratus, and altostratus clouds followed by rain usually signifies the approach of a(n):

A. occluded front
B. stationary front
C. warm front
D. cold front

01330. If you are located within a stationary high pressure area and your aneroid barometer is falling very slowly, what would this indicate?

A. a wind shift of 180°
B. a large increase in wind velocity
C. a decrease in the intensity of the system

D. an increase in the intensity of the system
01331. When trying to sight a lighthouse you notice a glare from a town in the background. The range at which the light may be sighted due to this glare is:

A. considerably reduced
B. increased slightly due to extra lighting
C. unchanged
D. increased if the light is red or green due to contrast with the glare

01333. If a magnetic compass is not affected by any magnetic field other than the Earth's, which statement is TRUE?

A. compass error and variation are equal
B. compass north will be true north
C. variation will equal deviation
D. there will be no compass error

01334. Illustration D042NG represents the symbols used on radiofacsimile weather charts. The symbol indicated at letter "H" represents:

A. ice
B. snow
C. rain
D. hail

01336. On the approach of a warm front, barometric pressure usually:

A. falls
B. is steady
C. is uncertain
D. rises

01338. What type of cloud is indicated by the number 6 in illustration D039NG?

A. altocumulus
B. stratocumulus
C. altostratus
D. cirrus

01340. The annual change in variation for an area can be found in:

A. the handbook for Magnetic Compass Adjustment, Pub 226
B. the center of the compass rose on a chart of the area
C. the compass deviation table
D. variation does not change.

01341. The height of a light is measured from what reference point?

A. mean low water
B. mean high water
C. average water level
D. geographical sea level

01342. The coloring of an occluded front on a weather map is a(n):

A. blue line
B. purple line
C. dashed blue line
D. alternate red and blue line

01343. Variation is a compass error that you:

A. can correct by adjusting the compass card
B. can correct by adjusting the compensating magnets
C. can correct by changing the vessel's heading
D. cannot correct

01344. Which of the buoy symbols in illustration D032NG indicates a safe water mark?

A. d
B. c
C. b
D. a

01345. A large automated navigational buoy, such as those that have replaced some light-ships, would be shown on a chart by which symbol in illustration D015NG?

A. d
B. c
C. b
D. a

01346. Cirrus clouds followed by cirrostratus then altostratus, stratus, and occasionally nimbostratus indicate the approach of a(n):

A. cold front
B. warm front
C. tropical front
D. occluded front

01349. Illustration D042NG represents the symbols used on radiofacsimile weather charts. Which of these symbols indicates a severe squall line?

A. f
B. i
C. g
D. h

01350. You are running parallel to the coast and plotting running fixes using bearing of the same object. You are making more speed than assumed for the running fix. In relation to the position indicated by the fix you will be:

A. closer to the coast
B. farther from the coast
C. on the track line ahead of the fix

D. on the track line behind the fix

01351. Luminous range is the:

A. maximum distance at which a light may be seen in clear weather
B. maximum distance at which a light may be seen under existing visibility conditions
C. maximum distance at which a light may be seen considering the height of the light and the height of the observer
D. average distance of visibility of light

01353. The difference in degrees between true north and magnetic north is called:

A. variation
B. deviation
C. drift
D. compass error

01356. The first indications a mariner will have of the approach of a warm front will be:

A. large cumulonimbus (thunderclouds) building up
B. high cirrus clouds gradually changing to cirrostratus and then to altostratus
C. fog caused by the warm air passing over the cooler water
D. low dark clouds accompanied by intermittent rain

01360. What kind of clouds are composed entirely of ice crystals and are found at very high altitudes?

A. cumulus
B. cirrus
C. stratus
D. nimbostratus

01361. The luminous range of a light takes into account the:

A. glare from background lighting
B. existing visibility conditions
C. elevation of the light
D. observer's height of eye

01362. What type of cloud is indicated by the number 7 in illustration D039NG?

A. cirrostratus
B. altocumulus
C. cumulus
D. cumulonimbus

01363. True heading differs from magnetic heading by:

A. deviation
B. variation
C. compass error

D. northerly error

01364. The Sailing Directions are published in the En route format and the:

A. coastal editions
B. World Port Index
C. Pilot Format
D. Planning Guide

01366. Clouds appearing in the following order: cirrus, cirrostratus, altostratus, status, and nimbostratus usually indicate the approach of a(n):

A. warm front
B. occluded front
C. medium front
D. cold front

01370. What type of cloud is indicated by the number 8 in illustration D039NG?

A. cumulonimbus
B. altostratus
C. cirrostratus
D. nimbostratus

01374. On a working copy of a weather map, a warm front is represented by what color line?

A. red
B. blue
C. alternating red and blue
D. purple

01376. Which of the following is typical of warm front weather conditions?

A. a steady barometer
B. a wind shift from southwest to northwest
C. scattered cumulus clouds
D. steady precipitation

01379. The lubber's line on a magnetic compass indicates:

A. compass north
B. the direction of the vessel's head
C. magnetic north
D. a relative bearing taken with an azimuth circle

01380. What kind of weather could you expect soon after seeing hook or comma shaped cirrus clouds?

A. rain with the approach of a warm front
B. clearing with the approach of a cold front
C. continuing fog and rain
D. the formation of a tropical depression

01381. Geographic range is the maximum distance at which a light may be seen under:

A. existing visibility conditions, limited only by the curvature of the Earth
B. perfect visibility conditions, limited only by the curvature of the Earth
C. existing visibility conditions, limited only by the intensity of the light
D. perfect visibility conditions, limited only by interference from background lighting

01382. The chart indicates the variation was 3°45' W in 1988, and the annual change is increasing 6'. If you use the chart in 1991 how much variation should you apply?

A. 3°27' W
B. 3°27' E
C. 4°03' W
D. 4°03' E

01384. What type of cloud is indicated by the number 9 in illustration D039NG?

A. cumulus
B. cumulonimbus
C. altostratus
D. stratocumulus

01385. What is the length of the lunar day?

A. 24h 50m 00s
B. 24h 00m 00s
C. 23h 56m 04s
D. 23h 03m 56s

01386. The FIRST indications a mariner will have of the approach of a warm front will be:

A. large cumulonimbus clouds building up
B. low dark clouds with intermittent rain
C. fog caused by the warm air passing over the cooler water
D. high clouds gradually followed by lower thicker clouds

01389. A boundary between 2 air masses is a:

A. lapse rate
B. isobar
C. front
D. continent

01390. The fog most commonly encountered at sea is called:

A. conduction fog
B. radiation fog
C. frontal fog
D. advection fog

01391. When a light is first seen on the horizon it will disappear again if the eye is immediately lowered several ft. When the eye is raised the

light will again be visible. This is called:
A. checking a light
B. luminous range
C. obscuring a light
D. bobbing a light

01392. Cumulonimbus clouds are indicated by what number in illustration D039NG?

A. 9
B. 7
C. 5
D. 3

01395. The lunar day is:

A. longer than a solar day
B. shorter than a solar day
C. the same length as the solar day
D. longer than a solar day during the summer months and shorter in winter months

01396. On the approach of a warm front barometric pressure usually:

A. falls
B. rises
C. is steady
D. is unreliable

01398. Nimbostratus clouds are indicated by what number in illustration D039NG?

A. 8
B. 6
C. 4
D. 1

01400. What type of clouds are among the most dependable for giving an indication of an approaching weather system?

A. cumulus
B. altostratus
C. cumulostratus
D. nimbus

01401. The maximum distance at which a light may be seen under the existing visibility conditions is called:

A. nominal range
B. luminous range
C. charted range
D. geographic range

01402. As a vessel changes course to starboard, the compass card in a magnetic compass:

A. first turns to starboard then counterclockwise to port
B. also turns to starboard
C. turns counterclockwise to port

D. remains aligned with compass north
01406. Which of the following will act to dissipate fog?

A. upwelling cold water
B. advection of warm air over a colder surface
C. rain that is warmer than air
D. downslope motion of an air mass along a coast

01408. An occluded front is caused by a(n):

A. low pressure area
B. high pressure area
C. area of calm air
D. cold front overtaking a warm front

01409. You are en route to assist vessel A. Vessel A is underway at 5.5 knots on course 033° T, and bears 284° T, 43 miles from you. What is the time to intercept if you make 16 knots?

A. 2h 16m
B. 2h 22m
C. 2h 34m
D. 2h 42m

01410. An orange and white buoy marked with a rectangle indicates:

A. a fish net area
B. general information
C. an anchorage
D. midchannel

01411. The nominal range of a light may be accurately defined as the maximum distance at which a light may be seen:

A. under existing visibility conditions
B. under perfect visibility
C. with 10 miles visibility
D. with 15 miles visibility

01412. The distance between the surface of the water and the tidal datum is the:

A. actual water depth
B. range of tide
C. charted depth
D. height of tide

01416. Radiation fog:

A. always forms over water
B. is formed by a temperature inversion
C. is thinnest at the surface
D. dissipates during the evening

01419. The MOST important feature of the material used for making the binnacle of a standard magnetic compass is that it is:

A. nonmagnetic
B. weatherproof
C. corrosion resistant
D. capable of being permanently affixed to the vessel

01421. What is the approximate geographic visibility of an object with a height above the water of 70 ft., for an observer with a height of eye of 65 ft.?

A. 16.8 nm
B. 19.0 nm
C. 20.6 nm
D. 22.4 nm

01422. Cumulus clouds are indicated by what number in illustration D039NG?

A. 3
B. 5
C. 6
D. 7

01426. Fog is most commonly associated with a(n):

A. warm front at night
B. low pressure area
C. anticyclone
D. lack of frontal activity

01428. The speed of sound in water is approximately:

A. 1.5 times its speed in air
B. 2.5 times its speed in air
C. 3.5 times its speed in air
D. 4.5 times its speed in air

01430. The Light List indicates that a light has a nominal range of 14 miles and is 42 ft. high. If the visibility is 6 miles and your height of eye is 20 ft., at what approximate distance will you sight the light?

A. 20.1 miles
B. 10.0 miles
C. 7.6 miles
D. 6.0 miles

01431. A lighthouse is 120 ft. high and the light has a nominal range of 18 miles. Your height of eye is 42 ft. If the visibility is 11 miles, approximately how far off the light will you be when the light becomes visible?

A. 12.5 miles
B. 16.0 miles
C. 19.0 miles
D. 23.5 miles

01434. Which of the following is NOT a characteristic of cardinal marks?

A. yellow and black bands
B. white lights
C. square or triangular topmarks
D. directional orientation to a hazard

01436. Fog forms when the air:

A. is 50% water saturated
B. is 90% water saturated
C. temperature is greater than the dew point temperature
D. temperature equals or is below the dew point temperature

01438. In the Northern Hemisphere you are caught in the dangerous semicircle of a storm with plenty of sea room available. The best course of action is to bring the wind on the:

A. port quarter and make as much headway as possible
B. starboard quarter and make as much headway as possible
C. starboard bow and make as much headway as possible
D. port bow and make as much headway as possible

01439. Illustration D042NG represents the symbols used on radiofacsimile weather charts. The symbol indicated at letter "G" represents a:

A. weather boundary
B. thunderstorm
C. wide spread sandstorm
D. severe line squall

01440. A mercurial barometer at sea is subject to rapid variations in height ("pumping") due to the pitch and roll of the vessel. To avoid this error, measurements of atmospheric pressure at sea are usually measured with a(n):

A. syphon barometer
B. cistern barometer
C. aneroid barometer
D. fortin barometer

01444. Stratocumulus clouds are indicated by what number in illustration D039NG?

A. 1
B. 4
C. 6
D. 7

01445. The planet Mars will have its greatest magnitude when at:

A. conjunction
B. opposition
C. east quadrature
D. west quadrature

01446. When compared to air temperature, which of the following factors is most useful in predicting fog?

A. vapor pressure
B. dew point
C. barometric pressure
D. absolute humidity

01448. Spring tides occur when the:

A. Moon is in its first quarter or third quarter phase
B. Sun and Moon oppose each other
C. Moon's declination is maximum and opposite to that of the Sun
D. Moon is new or full

01449. The presence of stratus clouds and a dying wind will usually result in:

A. heavy rain
B. heavy snow
C. thick fog
D. clearing skies

01450. The distance between the surface of the water and the tidal datum is the:

A. range of tide
B. charted depth
C. height of tide
D. actual water depth

01456. The fog produced by warm moist air passing over a cold surface is called:

A. conduction fog
B. radiation fog
C. frontal fog
D. advection fog

01459. In a tropical cyclone, in the Northern Hemisphere, a vessel hove to with the wind shifting counterclockwise would be:

A. ahead of the storm center
B. in the dangerous semicircle
C. in the navigable semicircle
D. directly in the approach path of the storm

01461. The chart indicates the variation was 3°45' W in 1988, and the annual change is decreasing 6'. If you use the chart in 1991 how much variation should you apply?

A. 3°27' W

NAVIGATION GENERAL QUESTIONS   275

B. 3°27' E
C. 4°03' W
D. 4°03' E

01462. Altocumulus clouds are indicated by what number in illustration D039NG?

A. 1
B. 3
C. 4
D. 5

01464. A line of position derived from a Loran reading is a section of a(n):

A. straight line
B. arc
C. parabola
D. hyperbola

01466. Advection fog is most commonly caused by:

A. air being warmed above the dew point
B. saturation of cold air by rain
C. a rapid cooling of the air near the surface of the Earth at night
D. warm moist air being blown over a colder surface

01470. Illustration D042NG represents the symbols used on radiofacsimile weather charts. Which of these symbols indicates a hurricane?

A. m
B. i
C. l
D. k

01471. A mountain peak charted at 700 ft. breaks the horizon, and your height of eye is 12 ft. What is your approximate distance off (choose closest answer)?

A. 34.7 nm
B. 40.3 nm
C. 55.3 nm
D. 61.6 nm

01472. What is the mark on a lead line indicating 4 fathoms?

A. no marking
B. 4 knots
C. red woolen rag
D. white linen rag

01474. You are on course 061° T. To check the longitude of your vessel you should observe a celestial body on which bearing?

A. 090°

B. 180°
C. 241°
D. 061°

01475. What kind of cloud is the classic "thunderhead"?

A. cumulonimbus
B. stratus
C. cirrus
D. altostratus

01476. When warm moist air blows over a colder surface and is cooled below its dew point it causes:

A. radiation fog
B. ice fog
C. advection fog
D. frost smoke

01478. Altostratus clouds are indicated by what number in illustration D039NG?

A. 1
B. 4
C. 6
D. 8

01479. A microbarograph is a precision instrument that provides a:

A. charted record of atmospheric temperature over time
B. charted record of atmospheric pressure over time
C. graphic record of combustible gases measured in an atmosphere
D. graphic record of vapor pressure from a flammable/combustible liquid

01480. What is the definition of height of tide?

A. the vertical difference between the heights of low and high water
B. the vertical difference between a datum plane and the ocean bottom
C. the vertical distance from the surface of the water to the ocean floor
D. the vertical distance from the tidal datum to the level of the water at any time

01482. Which statement concerning current is TRUE?

A. current can be determined by measuring the direction and distance between simultaneous EP and DR positions.
B. the drift of the current should be averaged out on a 1 hour basis.
C. after the current is determined, it should not be used for further plotting because it is an unknown variable.

D. the distance between a simultaneous DR position and fix is equal to the drift of the current.

01486. Which condition would most likely result in fog?

A. warm moist air blowing over cold water
B. airborne dust particles
C. warm moist air blowing over warm water
D. dew point falling below the air temperature

01489. Cumulonimbus clouds can produce:

A. dense fog and high humidity
B. gusty winds, thunder, rain/hail, and lightning
C. clear skies with the approach of a cold front
D. a rapid drop in barometric pressure followed by darkness

01490. In the IALA-B Buoyage System, preferred-channel-to-port or preferred-channel-to-starboard buoys, when fitted with lights, will show a:

A. quick flashing light
B. long flashing light
C. composite group flashing (2 + 1) light
D. group flashing

01493. You are running parallel to the coast and estimate that the current is against you. In plotting a running fix using bearings from the same object on the coast, the greatest safety margin from inshore dangers will result if what speed is used to determine the fix?

A. minimum speed estimate
B. maximum speed estimate
C. average speed estimate
D. a running fix should not be used under these conditions.

01494. Cirrocumulus clouds are indicated by what number in illustration D039NG?

A. 7
B. 5
C. 3
D. 1

01496. In a microbarograph, the pen should be checked and the inkwell filled:

A. each time the chart is changed
B. once per month
C. once per week
D. daily

01497. When drawing a weather map and an isobar crosses a front, the isobar is drawn:

A. perpendicular to the front
B. kinked and pointing away from the low
C. kinked and pointing towards the low
D. kinked and pointing towards the high for a warm front only

01498. A true bearing of a charted object, when plotted on a chart, will establish a:

A. fix
B. line of position
C. relative bearing
D. range

01501. What is the distance from the bottom of a wave trough to the top of a wave crest?

A. wave length
B. wave height
C. wave breadth
D. wave depth

01502. You are running parallel to the coast and take a running fix using bearings of the same object. If you are making less speed than used for the running fix, in relation to the position indicated by the fix, you will be:

A. closer to the coast
B. farther from the coast
C. on the track line ahead of the fix
D. on the track line behind the fix

01503. A radar range to a small, charted object such as a light will provide a line of position in what form?

A. straight line
B. arc
C. parabola
D. hyperbola

01505. At 0000 you fix your position and change course to 090° T. At 0030 you again fix your position and it is 0.5 mile east of your DR. Which of the following statements is TRUE?

A. the current is easterly.
B. the drift is 0.5 knot.
C. you should alter course to the right to regain the track line.
D. the current is perpendicular to your track line.

01506. You are steaming southward along the West Coast of the United States when you sight a buoy showing a flashing green light. How should you pass this buoy?

A. leave it to your port
B. leave it to your starboard
C. pass it close aboard on either side
D. pass it on either side but well clear of it

01507. When you are steering on a pair of range lights and find the upper light is above the lower light you should:

A. come right
B. come left
C. wait until the lights are no longer in a vertical line
D. continue on the present course

01508. A line of position is:

A. a line connecting 2 charted objects
B. a line on some point of which the vessel may be presumed to be located
C. the position of your vessel
D. not used in a running fix

01509. Your facsimile prognostic chart indicates that you will cross the cold front of a low pressure system in about 24 hours. You should:

A. expect to see cirrus clouds followed by altostratus and nimbostratus clouds
B. alter course to remain in navigable semicircle
C. prepare for gusty winds, thunderstorms, and a sudden wind shift
D. expect clear weather, with steady winds and pressure, until the front passes

01511. A vessel encountering hurricane or typhoon conditions is required to transmit reports to closest meteorological service every:

A. 8 hours
B. 6 hours
C. 3 hours
D. hour

01514. The compass error of a magnetic compass that has no deviation is:

A. zero
B. equal to variation
C. eliminated by adjusting the compass
D. constant at any geographical location

01518. Which of the following publications requires infrequent corrections?

A. list of Lights
B. Coast Pilot
C. Sailing Directions (Planning Guide)
D. radio Navigational Aids

01520. The diurnal inequality of the tides is caused by:

A. the declination of the Moon
B. changing weather conditions
C. the Moon being at apogee
D. the Moon being at perigee

01523. Which of the following is a characteristic of the weather preceding an approaching warm front?

A. gusty winds
B. steadily falling barometric pressure
C. decreasing relative humidity
D. clearing skies

01525. You are in LAT 50° S and obtain an RDF bearing on a vessel 400 miles due west of you. You should expect to receive the bearing from the:

A. southeast quadrant
B. northeast quadrant
C. northwest quadrant
D. southwest quadrant

01527. Your vessel is on course 270° T, speed 10 knots. The apparent wind is from 10° off the port bow, speed 30 knots. What is the direction of the true wind?

A. 345° T
B. 255° T
C. 165° T
D. 075° T

01528. Cirrostratus clouds are indicated by what number in illustration D039NG?

A. 1
B. 2
C. 8
D. 9

01530. In shallow water, waves too steep to be stable, causing the crests to move forward faster than the rest of the wave, are called:

A. rollers
B. breakers
C. white caps
D. surfers

01536. What will NOT induce errors into a doppler sonar log?

A. increased draft
B. pitch
C. roll
D. change in trim

01538. The winds of the roaring forties are strongest near:

A. 40° N
B. 50° N
C. 40° S
D. 50° S

01539. You are steaming in the open ocean of the North Pacific between the Aleutian Chain and Hawaii. A warning broadcast indicates that an earthquake has occurred in the Aleutians and has generated a tsunami that is predicted to hit Hawaii. What action is necessary for the ship's safety?

A. calculate the tsunami's ETA at your position and turn to a course that will head into the Tsunami
B. securely stow all loose gear, check deck lashings, and prepare for extreme rolls
C. no special action as tsunamis are inconspicuous in the open ocean
D. prepare for sudden, high-velocity wind gusts from rapidly changing directions

01540. You are sailing south on the ICW when you sight a green can buoy with a yellow square painted on it. Which of the following is TRUE?

A. you should pass the buoy close aboard on either side.
B. the buoy marks end of the ICW in that area.
C. you should leave the buoy to port.
D. the yellow square is retroreflective material used to assist in sighting the buoy at night.

01542. To find a magnetic course from a true course you must apply:

A. magnetic anomalies (local disturbances)
B. deviation
C. variation
D. deviation and variation

01543. The distance between the surface of the water and the tidal datum is the:

A. height of tide
B. charted depth
C. actual water depth
D. range of tide

01544. The height of wave crests can be increased by:

A. a storm surge
B. a high pressure area
C. the jet stream
D. a cold front

01545. The change in the length of day becomes greater as latitude increases because of the:

A. inclination of the diurnal circle to the Equator
B. decreasing distance between the terrestrial meridians
C. increased obliquity of the celestial sphere
D. changing distance between the earth and the Sun

01546. You are sailing south on the ICW when you sight a red nun buoy with a yellow triangle painted on it. Which of the following is TRUE?

A. geometric symbols such as squares and triangles replace letters and numbers on ICW aids to navigation.
B. the ICW and another waterway coincide in this geographical area.
C. the yellow triangle identifies a sharp turn (over 60°) in the channel.
D. this is an information or regulatory buoy that also has lateral significance.

01547. Which of the following light combinations is NOT used to indicate a navigational channel passing under a fixed bridge?

A. red lights on the LDB and green lights on the RDB
B. 3 white lights in a vertical line
C. 2 green lights in a range under the span
D. a fixed red light on each pier at the channel edge

01548. Illustration D042NG represents the symbols used on radiofacsimile weather charts. The symbol indicated at letter "K" represents a:

A. hurricane
B. thunderstorm
C. convergence zone
D. convergence line

01549. What is the mark on a lead line indicating 3 fathoms?

A. white linen rag
B. red woolen rag
C. 3 knots
D. 3 strips of leather

01550. Cirrus clouds are indicated by what number in illustration D039NG?

A. 1
B. 4
C. 5
D. 7

01553. Your DR position is LAT 20° N, LONG 50° W. From this position you take an RDF bearing on a vessel in LAT 25° N, LONG 45° W. The RDF bearing is 041.8°. The rhumb line bearing of the vessel is:

A. 41.8° T
B. 42.9° T
C. 44.0° T
D. 44.8° T

01555. Under the U. S. Aids to Navigation

System, a yellow buoy is a:
A. safe water buoy
B. junction buoy
C. cardinal mark
D. special purpose mark

01556. The vertical distance from the tidal datum to the level of the water is the:

A. range of tide
B. charted depth
C. height of tide
D. actual water depth

01557. A doppler log in the volume reverberation mode indicates:

A. speed being made good
B. speed through the water
C. the set of the current
D. the depth of the water

01560. Under the IALA-A and B Buoyage Systems, a buoy with alternating red and white vertical stripes indicates:

A. that there is navigable water all around
B. an isolated danger exists
C. that the preferred channel is to port
D. that the preferred channel is to starboard

01561. You are sailing south on the ICW when you sight a red nun buoy with a yellow square painted on it. Which of the following is TRUE?

A. the buoy is off station and should be ignored as a navigational mark.
B. the waterway in that area has shoaled and the available depth of water is less than the project depth.
C. ICW traffic should not proceed beyond the buoy unless the crossing waterway is clear of all traffic.
D. you should leave the buoy to port.

01562. What is the mark on a lead line indicating 2 fathoms?

A. 2 knots
B. 2 strips of leather
C. 2 pieces of rope
D. no marking

01563. Neap tides occur only:

A. at a new or full Moon
B. when the Sun, Moon and Earth are in line
C. at approximately 28-day intervals
D. when the Moon is at quadrature

01564. Which of the following is a characteristic of cardinal marks?

A. light rhythms indicating directional orientation
B. vertical stripes
C. square or triangular topmarks
D. number - letter combinations for identification

01565. Determine the approximate geographic visibility of an object, with a height above the water of 85 ft., for an observer with a height of eye of 60 ft.

A. 18.4 nm
B. 19.7 nm
C. 20.8 nm
D. 21.5 nm

01566. Illustration D042NG represents the symbols used on radiofacsimile weather charts. Which of these symbols indicates thunderstorms?

A. i
B. k
C. l
D. m

01567. Buoys and day beacons exhibiting a yellow triangle or square painted on them are used:

A. in minor harbors where the controlling depth is 10 ft. or less
B. on isolated stretches of the ICW to mark undredged areas
C. where the ICW and other waterways coincide
D. at particularly hazardous turns of the channel

01568. You are approaching a vertical lift bridge. You know the span is fully open when:

A. 3 white lights in a vertical line are lit
B. a red light starts to flash at about 60 times a minute
C. a yellow light is illuminated on the bridge pier
D. there is a range of green lights under the lift span

01569. 3 or 4 ft. of the total height of a storm surge in a hurricane can be attributed to:

A. an increase in temperature
B. an increase in the wave period
C. the wind velocity
D. the decrease in atmospheric pressure

01573. Which of the following statements about satellite navigation is TRUE?

A. while a fix can be generated by signals received from 2 satellites, 3 satellites are necessary for reliable accuracy.
B. the satellites are in equatorial orbits around

the earth about 60° of longitude apart.
C. the satellite navigation system determines a fix by measuring the doppler shift of the radio signals from the satellite.
D. the ship's receiver cannot begin processing data until the antenna locks onto the satellite and starts continuous tracking.

01575. Which statement is TRUE concerning "night effect" and the reception of radio signals?

A. "Night effect" is most prevalent late at night.
B. During "night effect", polarization is at a minimum.
C. "Night effect" is caused by rapid changes in the ionosphere.
D. "Night effect" is caused by all of the polarized ground waves being vertical.

01576. You are entering an east coast port and see a buoy with a yellow triangle painted on it. This indicates:

A. you are in the vicinity of the ICW
B. the buoy is a special mark
C. the buoy is off station
D. a sharp turn in the channel

01580. What is the mark on a lead line indicating 1 fathom?

A. 1 strip of leather
B. 1 knot
C. leather with a hole
D. no marking

01581. Illustration D042NG represents the symbols used on radiofacsimile weather charts. The symbol indicated at letter "I" represents:

A. rain showers
B. thunderstorms
C. snow storms
D. sand storms

01586. A green buoy has a yellow triangle on it. This is a(n):

A. information or regulatory buoy that has lateral significance
B. buoy that is off-station and is marked to warn mariners of its wrong position
C. dual purpose marking used where the ICW and other waterways coincide
D. buoy that was set in error and will be replaced with a red nun buoy

01592. An orange and white buoy marked with a rectangle indicates:

A. an anchorage
B. a fish net area
C. midchannel

D. general information

01594. Illustration D042NG represents the symbols used on radiofacsimile weather charts. The symbol indicated at letter "P" represents:

A. snow
B. hail
C. freezing rain
D. sleet

01595. The Light List indicates that a light has a nominal range of 8 miles and is 48 ft. high. If the visibility is 6 miles and your height of eye is 35 ft., at what approximate distance will you sight the light?

A. 15.0 miles
B. 12.4 miles
C. 8.0 miles
D. 5.9 miles

01596. You are sailing south on the ICW when you sight a red nun buoy with a yellow square painted on it. Which of the following is TRUE?

A. you should leave the buoy on your port hand.
B. this buoy marks the end of the ICW in that geographic area.
C. the yellow is retroreflective material used to assist in sighting the buoy at night.
D. the yellow square is in error and it should be a yellow triangle.

01597. The dense black cumulonimbus clouds surrounding the eye of a hurricane are called:

A. spiral rainbands
B. cloud walls
C. funnel clouds
D. cyclonic spirals

01599. The time interval between successive wave crests is called the:

A. trough
B. period
C. frequency
D. epoch

01602. Most modern Loran-C receivers automatically detect station blink which:

A. indicates the station is transmitting normally
B. automatically shuts down the receiver
C. triggers alarm indicators to warn the operator
D. causes the receiver to shift automatically to another Loran chain

01603. A position that is obtained by using 2 or more intersecting lines of position, taken at nearly the same time, is a(n):

A. estimated position

B. fix
C. running fix
D. dead-reckoning position

01604. Illustration D042NG represents the symbols used on radiofacsimile weather charts. Which of these symbols indicates freezing rain?

A. m
B. n
C. o
D. p

01605. Which of the following is NOT a unit of a satellite navigation set aboard ship?

A. transmitter to trigger the satellite to broadcast
B. data processor to process signals from satellite
C. video display or printer to show generated data
D. antenna to receive satellite signals

01606. Aids to navigation marking the Intracoastal Waterway can be identified by:

A. the letters ICW after the aid's number or letter
B. yellow stripes, squares or triangles marked on them
C. white retroreflective material
D. the light characteristic and color for lighted aids

01608. When using a buoy as an aid to navigation which of the following should be considered?

A. if the light is flashing the buoy should be considered to be in the charted location.
B. the buoy may not be in the charted position.
C. the buoy should be considered to be in the charted position if it has been freshly painted.
D. the buoy should be considered to always be in the charted position.

01610. When the navigational channel passes under a fixed bridge, the edges of the channel are marked on the bridge with what lights?

A. red lights
B. 3 white lights in a vertical line
C. red lights on the LDB and green lights on the RDB
D. yellow lights

01611. Which of the following indicates a dual purpose buoy?

A. red buoy with a horizontal yellow band
B. red and white vertically-striped buoy with a

vertical yellow stripe
C. red and white vertically-striped buoy with a red spherical topmark
D. green buoy with a yellow square

01612. The strongest winds and heaviest rains in a hurricane are found in the:

A. outer bands
B. eye
C. cloud walls
D. spiral rainbands

01613. Where would you find information concerning the duration of slack water?

A. Tide Tables
B. Tidal Current Tables
C. American Practical Navigator
D. Sailing Directions

01615. Illustration D042NG represents the symbols used on radiofacsimile weather charts. Which of these symbols indicates snow?

A. g
B. h
C. m
D. n

01616. Which picture in illustration D034NG shows a Morse (A) light?

A. a
B. b
C. c
D. d

01617. The inner cloud bands of a hurricane, when viewed from a distance, form a mass of dense, black cumulonimbus clouds called the:

A. bar of the storm
B. eye of the storm
C. funnel
D. front

01618. The Light List indicates that a light has a nominal range of 14 miles and is 26 ft. high. If the visibility is 4 miles and your height of eye is 20 ft., at what approximate distance will you sight the light?

A. 7.5 miles
B. 9.6 miles
C. 11.2 miles
D. 14.0 miles

01622. The correction to be applied to a Loran-C reading when matching a skywave to a ground wave may be found:

A. printed on Loran charts covering areas where skywaves are used
B. in the Radio Aids to Navigation, PUB 117
C. in the Loran-C Correction Tables
D. skywaves cannot be matched to ground waves in Loran-C to produce a usable reading.

01631. Which picture in illustration D034NG shows an occulting light?

A. a
B. b
C. c
D. d

01645. The navigation data broadcast of a navigational satellite does NOT include information:

A. about variation in the Doppler count
B. to enable the receiver to identify the satellite
C. on time according to the satellite clock
D. on the location of the satellite

01646. Which picture in illustration D034NG shows a flashing light?

A. a
B. b
C. c
D. d

01670. At extended distances from a pair of Loran stations:

A. skywaves should not be used with Loran-C
B. a skywave may be used only when matched to another skywave
C. a skywave may be matched to a ground wave
D. a skywave may be matched to a ground wave providing the ground wave comes from the master station

01671. Cirrus clouds are composed primarily of:

A. ice crystals
B. water droplets
C. snow crystals
D. nitrogen

01672. Data relating to the direction and velocity of rotary tidal currents can be found in the:

A. Mariner's Guide
B. Tidal Current Tables
C. Nautical Almanac
D. Tide Tables

01675. You are entering port and have been instructed to anchor, as your berth is not yet available. You are on a SW'ly heading, preparing to drop anchor, when you observe the range lights depicted in illustration D047NG

on your starboard beam. You should:
A. not drop the anchor until the lights are in line
B. ensure your ship will NOT block the channel or obstruct the range while at anchor
C. drop the anchor immediately as the range lights mark an area free of obstructions
D. drop the anchor immediately as a change in the position of the range lights will be an indication of dragging anchor

01750. Clearance gauges at bridges indicate:

A. the height of the tide
B. depth of water under the bridge
C. charted vertical clearance at mean low water
D. distance from the water to low steel of the bridge

01754. The dumping of refuse in a lock is permitted:

A. when approved by the lockmaster
B. when locking downbound
C. at no time
D. during high water only

01760. A doppler log in the bottom return mode indicates the:

A. velocity of the current
B. bottom characteristics
C. depth of the water
D. speed over the ground

01761. Chart legends which indicate a conspicuous landmark are printed in:

A. italics
B. underlined letters
C. capital letters
D. boldfaced print

01766. You are approaching a lock and see a flashing amber light located on the lock wall. You should:

A. stand clear of the lock entrance
B. approach the lock under full control
C. enter the lock as quickly as possible
D. hang off your tow on the lock wall

01768. A flashing red light displayed at a single lock means that the lock:

A. is ready to use, but vessels must stand clear
B. is ready to use, and vessels may approach
C. cannot be made ready immediately, and vessels shall stand clear
D. cannot be made ready immediately, but vessels may approach

01770. A doppler speed log indicates speed over ground:

A. at all times
B. in the bottom return mode
C. in the volume reverberation mode
D. only when there is no current

01771. What type of precipitation is a product of the violent convection found in thunderstorms?

A. snow
B. freezing rain
C. hail
D. rain

01774. Restricted areas at locks and dams are indicated by:

A. flashing red lights upstream and fixed red lights downstream
B. yellow unlighted buoys
C. signs and/or flashing red lights
D. red daymarks upstream and green daymarks downstream

01778. Illustration D037NG represents a movable dam. If the wickets are down and there are open weirs due to high water, what light(s) will be shown at A if the lock walls and piers are not awash?

A. 1 red light
B. 2 red lights
C. 3 red lights
D. 1 green light

01779. The Light List indicates that a light has a nominal range of 14 miles and is 26 ft. high. If the visibility is 14 miles and your height of eye is 20 ft., at what approximate distance will you sight the light?

A. 7.5 miles
B. 11.2 miles
C. 14.0 miles
D. 18.1 miles

01782. You are on course 027° T and take a relative bearing to a lighthouse of 220°. What is the true bearing to the lighthouse?

A. 113°
B. 193°
C. 247°
D. 279°

01784. If your vessel were proceeding down river (descending), a green square marker with a green reflector border on the right bank would be a:

A. mile board
B. dredging mark
C. passing daymark

D. crossing daymark

01786. You are downbound approaching a lock and see 3 green lights in a vertical line. This indicates:

A. that the lock chamber is open and ready to receive your tow
B. that you should hold up until the signal changes to 2 green lights
C. the upstream end of the river wall
D. the upstream end of the land wall

01789. Illustration D036NG represents a fixed C of E lock and dam. What navigational light(s) is(are) exhibited at the position indicated by the letter F in the illustration?

A. 1 red light
B. 2 green lights
C. 3 green lights
D. no light

01790. A Doppler speed log indicates speed through the water:

A. at all times
B. in the bottom return mode
C. in the volume reverberation mode
D. only when there is no current

01800. In order to insure that a RACON signal is displayed on the radar, you should:

A. increase the brilliance of the PPI scope
B. turn off the interference controls on the radar
C. use the maximum available range setting
D. increase the radar signal output

01804. Magnetic information on a chart may be:

A. found in the center(s) of the compass rose(s)
B. indicated by isogonic lines
C. found in a note on the chart
D. any of the above

01806. Sometimes foreign charts are reproduced by DMA. on such a chart a wire dragged (swept) area may be shown in purple or:

A. green
B. red
C. magenta
D. yellow

01808. An orange and white buoy with an open-faced orange diamond on it indicates:

A. danger
B. vessels are excluded from the area
C. the buoy is a mooring buoy
D. operating restrictions are in effect

01809. What occurs when rising air cools to

the dew point?
A. advection fog
B. humidity decreases
C. winds increase
D. clouds form

01810. Where would you find information concerning the duration of slack water?

A. Tide Tables
B. Sailing Directions
C. Tidal Current Tables
D. American Practical Navigator

01816. An orange and white buoy with a circle marked on it indicates:

A. danger
B. vessels are excluded from the area
C. a mooring buoy
D. operating restrictions are in effect

01818. In order to utilize the capacity of a lock to its maximum, pleasure craft are locked through with all of the following EXCEPT:

A. coal barges
B. oil barges
C. sand barges
D. cement barges

01820. Information on the operating times and characteristics of foreign radiobeacons can be found in what publication?

A. List of Lights
B. Coast Pilot
C. Sailing Directions
D. List of Radiobeacons

01822. What is the relative bearing of an object broad on the port bow?

A. 315°
B. 330°
C. 345°
D. 360°

01824. Illustration D036NG represents a fixed C of E lock and dam. What navigational light(s) is(are) exhibited at the position indicated by the letter C in the illustration?

A. 1 red light
B. 2 green lights
C. 3 green lights
D. no light

01826. Illustration D036NG represents a fixed C of E lock and dam. What navigational light(s) is(are) exhibited at the position indicated by the letter D in the illustration?

A. 1 red light
B. 2 green lights
C. 3 green lights
D. no light

01829. Illustration D036NG represents a fixed C of E lock and dam. What navigational light(s) is(are) exhibited at the position indicated by the letter E in the illustration?

A. 1 red light
B. 2 green lights
C. 3 green lights
D. no light

01830. A vessel heading NNW is on a course of:

A. 274.5°
B. 292.0°
C. 315.5°
D. 337.5°

01838. The Light List shows a lighted aid to navigation on the left bank. This means that the light can be seen on the right side of a vessel:

A. ascending the river
B. descending the river
C. crossing the river
D. proceeding towards sea

01840. A vessel heading NW is on a course of:

A. 274.5°
B. 292.5°
C. 315.0°
D. 337.5°

01844. What is the relative bearing of an object sighted dead ahead?

A. 015°
B. 090°
C. 180°
D. 360°

01848. The buoy symbol printed on your chart is leaning to the northeast. This indicates:

A. you should stay to the north or east of the buoy
B. you should stay to the west or south of the buoy
C. the buoy is a major lighted buoy
D. nothing special for navigational purposes

01850. A vessel heading WNW is on a course of:

A. 270.0°
B. 292.5°
C. 315.0°
D. 337.5°

01858. An orange and white buoy with a cross within a diamond marked on it indicates:

A. danger
B. vessels are excluded from the area
C. an anchorage area
D. operating restrictions are in effect

01859. While proceeding downriver (descending) you sight a red diamond-shaped panel with small, red reflector squares in each corner on the left bank. Under the U. S. Aids to Navigation System on the Western Rivers this is a:

A. special purpose signal
B. passing daymark
C. crossing daymark
D. cable crossing

01860. A vessel heading WSW is on a course of:

A. 202.5°
B. 225.0°
C. 247.5°
D. 271.0°

01862. What is the relative bearing of an object broad on the starboard quarter?

A. 090°
B. 105°
C. 135°
D. 150°

01868. Illustration D036NG represents a fixed C of E lock and dam. What navigational light(s) is(are) exhibited at the position indicated by the letter A in the illustration?

A. 1 red light
B. 2 red lights
C. 2 green lights
D. 3 green lights

01869. Illustration D036NG represents a fixed C of E lock and dam. What navigational light(s) is(are) exhibited at the position indicated by the letter B in the illustration?

A. 1 red light
B. 2 green lights
C. 3 green lights
D. no light

01870. A vessel heading SW is on a course of:

A. 202.5°
B. 225.0°
C. 247.5°
D. 270.0°

01880. A vessel heading SSW is on a course of:

A. 202.5°
B. 225.0°
C. 247.5°
D. 270.0°

01883. Pressure gradient is a measure of:

A. a high-pressure area
B. pressure difference over horizontal distance
C. pressure difference over time
D. vertical pressure variation

01884. If a sound signal is emitted from the oscillator of a fathometer, and 2 seconds elapse before the returning signal is picked up, what depth of water is indicated?

A. 1648 fathoms
B. 1248 fathoms
C. 1048 fathoms
D. 824 fathoms

01885. A mooring buoy is painted:

A. white with a blue band
B. yellow
C. any color that does not conflict with the lateral system
D. white with a green top

01886. What is the relative bearing of an object dead astern?

A. 000°
B. 090°
C. 180°
D. 270°

01887. The Light List indicates that a light has a nominal range of 10 miles and is 11 ft. high. If the visibility is 15 miles and your height of eye is 20 ft., at what approximate distance will you sight the light?

A. 12.0 miles
B. 11.0 miles
C. 10.0 miles
D. 9.0 miles

01888. What is the relative bearing of an object broad on the starboard bow?

A. 030°
B. 045°
C. 060°
D. 075°

01890. A vessel heading SSE is on a course of:

A. 112.5°
B. 135.0°

C. 157.5°
D. 180.0°

01892. The shoreline shown on nautical charts of areas affected by large tidal fluctuations is usually the line of mean:

A. lower-low water
B. low water
C. tide level
D. high water

01898. The subregions of the United States Gulf and East Coasts are numbered 11, 12 and 13 within the chart numbering system. Which of the following chart numbers indicates a chart for either the Gulf or East Coast?

A. 14312
B. 25134
C. 21105
D. 11032

01899. What is the relative bearing of an object broad on the starboard beam?

A. 045°
B. 060°
C. 075°
D. 090°

01902. Under the numbering system used by DMA, a 4 digit number may be used for:

A. large scale charts of infrequently navigated areas such as the polar regions
B. charts of rivers or canal systems such as the Ohio River or Erie Canal
C. non-navigational materials, such as a chart correction template or maneuvering board
D. foreign charts reproduced by DMA

01907. Data relating to the direction and velocity of rotary tidal currents can be found in the:

A. Tide Tables
B. Nautical Almanac
C. Tidal Current Tables
D. Mariner's Guide

01923. Little or no change in the barometric reading over a twelve hour period indicates:

A. stormy weather is imminent
B. that present weather conditions will continue
C. a defect in the barometer
D. increasing wind strength

01936. The parallel of latitude at 66°33' N is the:

A. Tropic of Cancer
B. Tropic of Capricorn

C. Arctic Circle
D. Ecliptic

01946. When making landfall at night, you can determine if a light is a major light or an offshore buoy by:

A. the intensity of the light
B. checking the period and characteristics against the Light List
C. the color, because the buoy will have only a red or a green light
D. any of the above can be used to identify the light.

01951. Spring tides occur:

A. when the Moon is new or full
B. when the Moon and Sun have declination of the same name
C. only when the Moon and Sun are on the same sides of the earth
D. at the beginning of spring when the Sun is over the Equator

01961. What kind of pressure systems travel in tropical waves?

A. subsurface pressure
B. terrastatic pressure
C. high pressure
D. low pressure

01984. When a dual purpose marking is used, the mariner following the Intracoastal Waterway should be guided by the:

A. color of the aid
B. shape of the aid
C. color of the top band
D. shape of the yellow mark

01986. The Moon is farthest from the Earth at:

A. the full Moon
B. apogee
C. the lunar solstice
D. quadrature

01987. An instrument useful in predicting fog is the:

A. sling psychrometer
B. microbarograph
C. anemometer
D. aneroid barometer

01988. The parallel of latitude at 23°27' N is the:

A. Tropic of Cancer
B. Tropic of Capricorn
C. Arctic Circle
D. Ecliptic

01992. The parallel of latitude at 23°27′ S is the:

A. Tropic of Cancer
B. Tropic of Capricorn
C. Arctic Circle
D. Ecliptic

01996. When approaching a lock entrance, the visual signal displayed when a single lock is ready for entrance is a flashing:

A. red light
B. green light
C. amber light
D. white light

02000. A vessel heading SE is on a course of:

A. 112.5°
B. 135.0°
C. 157.5°
D. 180.0°

02001. You have changed course and steadied up on a range. Your heading is 285° T, same as the charted range, and it appears as in illustration D048NG. After several minutes the range appears as in illustration D047NG and your heading is still 285° T. This indicates a:

A. southerly current
B. northerly current
C. leeway caused by a NE'Ly wind
D. course made good to the left of the true course

02002. What term is used to describe a river barge designed to carry coal or any similar cargo not requiring weather protection?

A. single skin
B. double skin
C. open hopper
D. deck barge

02004. The velocity of the wind, its steady direction, and the amount of time it has blown determines a wind driven current's:

A. temperature
B. density
C. deflection
D. speed

02006. What is the relative bearing of an object broad on the port beam?

A. 315°
B. 300°
C. 270°
D. 235°

02007. Data relating to the direction and velocity of rotary tidal currents can be found in the:

A. Mariner's Guide
B. Tidal Current Tables
C. Nautical Almanac
D. Tide Tables

02010. A vessel heading ESE is on a course of:

A. 112.5°
B. 135.0°
C. 157.5°
D. 180.0°

02014. Which stock number indicates a DMAHTC chart designed for coastwise navigation outside of outlying reefs and shoals?

A. 19BCO19243
B. WOPGN530
C. ICORR5873
D. 14XCO14902

02020. A vessel heading ENE is on a course of:

A. 022.5°
B. 045.0°
C. 067.5°
D. 090.0°

02021. While on watch, you notice that the air temperature is dropping and is approaching the dew point. What type of weather should be forecasted?

A. hail
B. heavy rain
C. sleet
D. fog

02028. Which of the following stock numbers indicates a DMAHTC chart designed for navigation and anchorage in a small waterway?

A. wOAZC17
B. ICORR5876
C. 15XHA15883
D. pILOT55

02030. A vessel heading NE is on a course of:

A. 022.5°
B. 045.0°
C. 067.5°
D. 090.0°

02032. The subregions of the United States Gulf and East Coasts are numbered 11, 12, 13 within the chart numbering system. Which of the following chart numbers indicates a chart for either the Gulf or East Coast?

A. 31301
B. 14311
C. 13305
D. 11121

02040. A vessel heading NNE is on a course of:

A. 022.5°
B. 045.0°
C. 067.5°
D. 090.0°

02041. Information on radiobeacons used for marine navigation in foreign waters will be found in the:

A. List of Lights
B. Radio Navigational Aids
C. Sailing Directions (En route)
D. Directory of Radiobeacons, Radio Direction Finders and Radar Stations

02043. Stormy weather is usually associated with regions of:

A. changing barometric pressure
B. high barometric pressure
C. steady barometric pressure
D. low barometric pressure

02044. What is the relative bearing of an object broad on the port quarter?

A. 195°
B. 225°
C. 240°
D. 265°

02048. You are upbound approaching a lock and dam and see 2 green lights in a vertical line. This indicates:

A. the downstream end of an intermediate wall
B. that a double lockage is in progress
C. the downstream end of the land wall
D. the navigable pass of a fixed weir dam

02050. The point where the vertical rise or fall of tide has stopped is referred to as:

A. slack water
B. the riptide
C. the stand of the tide
D. the reverse of the tide

02052. Under the chart numbering system used by DMA, the first digit of a multi-digit number indicates:

A. the general geographic area
B. the general scale of the chart
C. whether it is a major or minor chart
D. the projection used to construct the chart

02054. Illustration D038NG represents a fixed C of E lock and dam. What navigational light(s) is(are) exhibited at the position indicated by the letter B in the illustration?

A. 1 red light
B. 2 green lights
C. 3 green lights
D. no lights

02056. Illustration D038NG represents a fixed C of E lock and dam. What navigational light(s) is(are) exhibited at the position indicated by the letter C in the illustration?

A. 1 red light
B. 2 green lights
C. 3 green lights
D. no lights

02058. Illustration D038NG represents a fixed C of E lock and dam. What navigational light(s) is(are) exhibited at the position indicated by the letter D in the illustration?

A. 1 red light
B. 2 green lights
C. 3 green lights
D. no lights

02059. Illustration D038NG represents a fixed C of E lock and dam. What navigational light(s) is(are) exhibited at the position indicated by the letter E in the illustration?

A. 1 red light
B. 2 red lights
C. 2 green lights
D. 3 green lights

02060. What is the relative bearing of an object broad on the starboard quarter?

A. 045°
B. 090°
C. 135°
D. 225°

02061. Fog is likely to occur when there is little difference between the dew point and the:

A. relative humidity
B. air temperature
C. barometric pressure
D. absolute humidity

02062. Illustration D038NG represents a fixed C of E lock and dam. What navigational light(s) is(are) exhibited at the position indicated by the letter F in the illustration?

A. 1 red light
B. 2 red lights

C. 2 green lights
D. 3 green lights

02066. Diagram number D037NG represents a movable dam. If there is high water and the wickets are down so that there is an unobstructed navigable pass through the dam, what light(s) will be shown at B if the lock walls and piers are not awash?

A. 1 red light
B. 2 red lights
C. 3 red lights
D. no lights

02067. The Light List indicates that a light has a nominal range of 10 miles and is 11 ft. high. If the visibility is 5 miles and your height of eye is 20 ft., at what approximate distance will you sight the light?

A. 6.3 miles
B. 7.4 miles
C. 8.4 miles
D. 9.0 miles

02068. Diagram number D037NG represents a movable dam. If there is high water and the wickets are down so that there is an unobstructed navigable pass through the dam, what light(s) will be shown at D if the lock walls and piers are not awash?

A. 1 red light
B. 2 red lights
C. 3 red lights
D. 1 amber light

02069. Illustration D037NG represents a moveable dam. If a bear trap is open what will be displayed at the lock to indicate this condition?

A. a flashing amber light
B. a white circular disc
C. a red diamond
D. 2 amber lights

02070. What is the relative bearing of an object on the port beam?

A. 045°
B. 090°
C. 180°
D. 270°

02072. Illustration D037NG represents a movable dam. If a bear trap is open what will be displayed at the lock to indicate this condition?

A. an amber light under a red light
B. a white square
C. a green triangle
D. a yellow pentagon

02073. Chart legends printed in capital letters show that the associated landmark is:

A. a radio transmitter
B. a government facility or station
C. inconspicuous
D. conspicuous

02074. When approaching a lock and at a distance of not more than a mile, vessels desiring a single lockage shall sound which signal?

A. 1 long blast followed by 1 short blast
B. 1 short blast followed by 1 long blast
C. 2 short blasts
D. 2 long blasts

02075. Information about major breakdowns, repairs, or other emergency operations with regard to weirs and (or) wicket dams, on the western rivers, may be obtained by consulting the:

A. Light List Vol. V
B. U. S. Coast Pilot
C. Broadcast Notice to Mariners
D. Sailing Directions

02078. If a towboat requires a double lockage it shall give which sound signal at a distance of not more than 1 mile from the lock?

A. 1 short blast followed by 2 long blasts
B. 1 long blast followed by 1 short blast
C. 2 long blasts followed by 1 short blast
D. 1 long blast followed by 2 short blasts

02079. Permission to enter the riverward chamber of twin locks is given by the lockmaster and consists of which sound signal?

A. 1 short blast
B. 2 short blasts
C. 1 long blast
D. 2 long blasts

02080. Your are on course 030° T. The relative bearing of a lighthouse is 45°. What is the true bearing?

A. 015°
B. 075°
C. 255°
D. 345°

02081. You are taking bearings on two known objects ashore. The BEST fix is obtained when the angle between the lines of position is:

A. 30°
B. 45°
C. 60°
D. 90°

02082. You are holding position above Gallipolis Lock and Dam when you hear 2 long blasts of the horn from the lock. This indicates that you should:

A. enter the riverward lock
B. hold position until 2 more upbound tows have locked through
C. enter the landward lock
D. hold position until the lower gates are closed

02083. Information about major breakdowns, repairs, or other emergency operations with regard to weirs and (or) wicket dams, on the western rivers, may be obtained by consulting the:

A. U. S. Coast Pilot
B. Broadcast Notice to Mariners
C. Sailing Directions
D. Light List Vol. V

02084. You are approaching Gallipolis Lock and Dam. The traffic signal light is flashing red. You should:

A. hold your position and not attempt to enter the lock
B. approach the lock slowly under full control
C. proceed at normal speed to enter the lock
D. none of the above

02085. Information about major breakdowns, repairs, or other emergency operations with regard to weirs and (or) wicket dams, on the western rivers, may be obtained by consulting the:

A. Broadcast Notice to Mariners
B. Light List Vol. V
C. U. S. Coast Pilot
D. Sailing Directions

02086. You are downbound on the Ohio River locking through Greenup. The chamber has been emptied and the lower gates are open. You hear one short blast of the whistle from the lock. You should:

A. leave the lock
B. hold up until another tow enters the adjacent lock
C. tie off to the guide wall until the river is clear of traffic
D. hold in the lock chamber due to a malfunction with the gate

02087. The Light List indicates that a light has a nominal range of 20 miles and is 52 ft. high. If the visibility is 20 miles and your height of eye is 20 ft., at what approximate distance will you sight the light?

A. 33.0 nm
B. 20.0 nm
C. 13.5 nm
D. 8.5 nm

02088. Information about major breakdowns, repairs, or other emergency operations with regard to weirs and (or) wicket dams, on the western rivers, may be obtained by consulting the:

A. Sailing Directions
B. Light List Vol. V
C. U. S. Coast Pilot
D. Broadcast Notice to Mariners

02089. Permission to leave the riverward chamber of twin locks is given by the lockmaster and consists of which sound signal?

A. 1 short blast
B. 2 short blasts
C. 1 long blast
D. 2 long blasts

02090. You are underway in an area where the charted depth is 8 fathoms. You compute the height of tide to be -4.0 ft. The draft of your vessel is 5.0 ft. You determine the depth of the water beneath your keel to be:

A. 39 ft.
B. 43 ft.
C. 47 ft.
D. 57 ft.

02091. The velocity of the current in large coastal harbors is:

A. unpredictable
B. generally constant
C. generally too weak to be of concern
D. predicted in Tidal Current Tables

02092. Descending boats, while awaiting their turn to enter a lock, shall NOT block traffic from the lock. They shall be above the lock by at LEAST:

A. 100 ft.
B. 200 ft.
C. 300 ft.
D. 400 ft.

02093. Information about major breakdowns, repairs, or other emergency operations with regard to weirs and (or) wicket dams, on the western rivers, may be obtained by consulting the:

A. Light List Vol. V
B. List of Lights

C. Broadcast Notice to Mariners
D. Sailing Directions

02097. Information about major breakdowns, repairs, or other emergency operations with regard to weirs and (or) wicket dams, on the western rivers, may be obtained by consulting the:

A. Sailing Directions
B. Broadcast Notice to Mariners
C. Light List Vol. V
D. none of the above

02099. You are inbound in a channel marked by a range. The range line is 309° T. You are steering 306° T and have the range in sight as indicated in illustration D047NG. What action should you take?

A. continue on the present heading until the range is in line, then alter course to the left.
B. continue on course if the range is closing, otherwise alter course to the left.
C. immediately alter course to the right to bring the range in line.
D. immediately alter course to 309° T.

02100. You are underway in a vessel with a draft of 7.0 ft. The charted depth for your position is 9 fathoms. You compute the height of tide to be +3.0 ft. You determine the depth of the water beneath your keel to be:

A. 32 ft.
B. 41 ft.
C. 50 ft.
D. 64 ft.

02101. Information about major breakdowns, repairs, or other emergency operations with regard to weirs and (or) wicket dams, on the western rivers, may be obtained by consulting the:

A. Broadcast Notice to Mariners
B. Light List Vol. V
C. U. S. Coast Pilot
D. all of the above

02102. The subregions of the United States Gulf and East Coasts are numbered 11, 12, 13 within the chart numbering system. Which of the following chart numbers indicates a chart for either the Gulf or East Coast?

A. 21214
B. 11314
C. 14313
D. 14114

02103. The description "Racon" beside an illustration on a chart would mean a:

A. radar calibration beacon
B. circular radiobeacon
C. radar conspicuous beacon
D. radar transponder beacon

02104. An orange and white buoy giving location information will be marked with what symbol?

A. open-faced diamond
B. diamond with a cross
C. circle
D. square or rectangle

02105. An orange and white buoy with a rectangle on it is used to indicate:

A. danger
B. a controlled area
C. an exclusion area
D. general information

02110. You are underway in a vessel with a draft of 6.0 ft. You are in an area where the charted depth of the water is 4 fathoms. You would expect the depth of water beneath your keel to be approximately:

A. 12 ft.
B. 18 ft.
C. 24 ft.
D. 30 ft.

02111. Vessels regularly navigating rivers above Cairo, Illinois, shall at all times have on board a copy of:

A. Light List Vol. V
B. U. S. Coast Pilot
C. U. S. Army Corps of Engineers Regulations (Blue Book)
D. Sailing Directions

02112. Vessels regularly navigating rivers above Cairo, Illinois, shall at all times have on board a copy of:

A. U. S. Coast Pilot
B. U. S. Army Corps of Engineers Regulations (Blue Book)
C. Nautical Almanac for the year
D. Light List Vol. V

02113. Vessels regularly navigating rivers above Cairo, Illinois, shall at all times have on board a copy of:

A. U. S. Army Corps of Engineers Regulations (Blue Book)
B. Nautical Almanac for the year
C. Sailing Directions
D. Light List Vol. V

02114. Vessels regularly navigating rivers above Cairo, Illinois, shall at all times have on board a copy of:

A. Sailing Directions
B. Nautical Almanac for the year
C. U. S. Coast Pilot
D. U. S. Army Corps of Engineers Regulations (Blue Book)

02115. Vessels regularly navigating rivers above Cairo, Illinois, shall at all times have on board a copy of:

A. U. S. Army Corps of Engineers Regulations (Blue Book)
B. Light List Vol. V
C. U. S. Coast Pilot
D. none of the above

02116. Vessels regularly navigating rivers above Cairo, Illinois, shall at all times have on board a copy of:

A. Nautical Almanac for the year
B. U. S. Army Corps of Engineers Regulations (Blue Book)
C. Sailing Directions
D. all of the above

02120. If a chart indicates the depth of water to be 6 fathoms and your draft is 6.0 ft., what is the depth of the water under your keel? (Assume the actual depth and charted depth to be the same.)

A. 6.0 ft.
B. 26.5 ft.
C. 30.0 ft.
D. 56.5 ft.

02121. In plotting a running fix, how many fixed objects are needed to take your lines of position from?

A. 3
B. 2
C. 1
D. none

02122. A position that is obtained by using two or more intersecting lines of position taken at nearly the same time, is a(n):

A. fix
B. running fix
C. estimated position
D. dead-reckoning position

02125. On charts of U. S. waters, a magenta marking is NOT used for marking a:

A. radiobeacon
B. lighted buoy
C. 5-fathom curve
D. prohibited area

02126. Your chart indicates that there is an isolated rock and names the rock using vertical letters. This indicates the:

A. rock is visible at low water springs only
B. rock is a hazard to deep draft vessels only
C. rock is dry at high water
D. exact position of the rock is doubtful

02127. Diagram number D037NG represents a movable dam. If there is high water and the wickets are down so that there is an unobstructed navigable pass through the dam, what light(s) will be shown at B if the lock walls and piers are not awash?

A. no lights
B. 1 red light
C. 2 red lights
D. 3 red lights

02128. Diagram number D037NG represents a movable dam. If there is high water and the wickets are down so that there is an unobstructed navigable pass through the dam, what light(s) will be shown at B if the lock walls and piers are not awash?

A. 3 red lights
B. 2 red lights
C. 1 red light
D. no lights

02129. Diagram number D037NG represents a movable dam. If there is high water and the wickets are down so that there is an unobstructed navigable pass through the dam, what light(s) will be shown at B if the lock walls and piers are not awash?

A. no lights
B. 3 red lights
C. 2 red lights
D. 1 red light

02130. You are underway and pass by a lighthouse. Its light, which was white since you first sighted it, changes to red. This indicates:

A. the light is characterized as alternating flashing
B. the lighthouse has lost power and has switched to emergency lighting
C. the identifying light characteristic of the lighthouse
D. you have entered an area of shoal water or other hazard

02131. The white lights in a vertical line on a multiple-span bridge indicate:

A. the main channel
B. the draw span is inoperable
C. the river is obstructed under that span
D. scaffolding under the span is reducing the vertical clearance

02132. What is the definition of height of tide?

A. the vertical difference between the heights of low and high water
B. the vertical difference between a datum plane and the ocean bottom
C. the vertical distance from the tidal datum to the level of the water at any time
D. the vertical distance from the surface of the water to the ocean floor

02133. From May through September a row of flashing amber (yellow) lights across the Illinois River at Peoria would indicate that:

A. dredging is in progress
B. wicket dams are lowered
C. wicket dams are raised
D. none of the above

02135. From May through September a row of flashing amber (yellow) lights across the Illinois River at Peoria would indicate that:

A. wicket dams are raised
B. wicket dams are lowered
C. construction is in progress
D. dredging is in progress

02136. From May through September a row of flashing amber (yellow) lights across the Illinois River at Peoria would indicate that:

A. wicket dams are lowered
B. wicket dams are raised
C. dredging is in progress
D. construction is in progress

02137. From May through September a row of flashing amber (yellow) lights across the Illinois River at Peoria would indicate that:

A. construction is in progress
B. dredging is in progress
C. wicket dams are raised
D. wicket dams are lowered

02138. From May through September a row of flashing amber (yellow) lights across the Illinois River at Peoria would indicate that:

A. dredging is in progress
B. wicket dams are lowered

C. construction is in progress
D. wicket dams are raised

02139. From May through September a row of flashing amber (yellow) lights across the Illinois River at Peoria would indicate that:

A. wicket dams are lowered
B. wicket dams are raised
C. construction is in progress
D. none of the above

02140. The visible range marked on charts for lights is the:

A. minimum distance at which the light may be seen with infinite visibility
B. minimum distance the light may be seen based on a 12 mile distance to visible horizon
C. maximum distance the light may be seen restricted by the height of the light and the curvature of the earth
D. maximum distance at which a light may be seen in clear weather with 10 miles visibility

02141. What lights would you see on the Illinois Water Way when any wickets of the dam or bear traps are open, or partially open, which may cause a set in the current conditions in the upper lock approach?

A. red over green
B. green over red
C. red over amber (yellow)
D. green over amber (yellow)

02142. What lights would you see on the Illinois Water Way when any wickets of the dam or bear traps are open, or partially open, which may cause a set in the current conditions in the upper lock approach?

A. green over amber (yellow)
B. red over amber (yellow)
C. red over blue
D. green over red

02143. What lights would you see on the Illinois Water Way when any wickets of the dam or bear traps are open, or partially open, which may cause a set in the current conditions in the upper lock approach?

A. red over amber (yellow)
B. green over amber (yellow)
C. red over green
D. green over red

02145. What lights would you see on the Illinois Water Way when any wickets of the dam or bear traps are open, or partially open, which may cause a set in the current conditions in the upper lock approach?

A. green over red
B. red over blue
C. green over amber (yellow)
D. red over amber (yellow)

02146. What lights would you see on the Illinois Water Way when any wickets of the dam or bear traps are open, or partially open, which may cause a set in the current conditions in the upper lock approach?

A. green over red
B. red over blue
C. red over amber (yellow)
D. none of the above

02147. What lights would you see on the Illinois Water Way when any wickets of the dam or bear traps are open, or partially open, which may cause a set in the current conditions in the upper lock approach?

A. green over blue
B. red over amber (yellow)
C. red over green
D. none of the above

02150. On a Mercator chart, 1 nm is equal to:

A. 1 minute of longitude
B. 1 degree of longitude
C. 1 minute of latitude
D. 1 degree of latitude

02152. Permanent magnetism is found in:

A. hard iron
B. soft iron
C. vertical iron only
D. horizontal iron only

02160. Information for updating nautical charts is primarily found in the:

A. Notice to Mariners
B. Coast Pilots
C. nautical chart catalogs
D. Sailing Directions

02164. The line connecting the points of the earth's surface where there is no dip is the:

A. agonic line
B. magnetic Equator
C. isodynamic
D. isopor

02165. Diagram number D037NG represents a movable dam. If there is high water and the wickets are down so that there is an unobstructed navigable pass through the dam, what light(s) will be shown at B if the lock walls and piers are not awash?

A. 3 red lights
B. 2 red lights
C. 1 red light
D. 1 amber light

02166. Diagram number D037NG represents a movable dam. If there is high water and the wickets are down so that there is an unobstructed navigable pass through the dam, what light(s) will be shown at B if the lock walls and piers are not awash?

A. 1 amber light
B. 3 red lights
C. 2 red lights
D. 1 red light

02167. Diagram number D037NG represents a movable dam. If there is high water and the wickets are down so that there is an unobstructed navigable pass through the dam, what light(s) will be shown at B if the lock walls and piers are not awash?

A. 1 red light
B. 2 red lights
C. 3 red lights
D. 1 amber light

02169. To make sure of getting the full advantage of a favorable current, you should reach an entrance or strait at what time in relation to the predicted time of the favorable current?

A. 30 minutes before the predicted time
B. 1 hour after the predicted time
C. at the predicted time
D. 30 minutes before flood, 1 hour after ebb

02170. The temperature at which the air is saturated with water vapor and below which condensation of water vapor will occur is referred to as:

A. precipitation point
B. vapor point
C. dew point
D. absolute humidity

02171. Diagram number D037NG represents a movable dam. If there is high water and the wickets are down so that there is an unobstructed navigable pass through the dam, what light(s) will be shown at B if the lock walls and piers are not awash?

A. 1 amber light
B. 1 red light
C. 2 red lights
D. 3 red lights

02172. The shoreline on charts of confined coastal waters, where there is little tidal influence, may be the line of mean:

A. lower-low water
B. low water
C. water level
D. low-water springs

02175. Diagram Number D037NG represents a movable dam. If there is high water and the wickets are down so that there is an unobstructed navigable pass through the dam, what light(s) will be shown at D if the lock walls and piers are not awash?

A. 1 amber light
B. 1 red light
C. 2 red lights
D. 3 red lights

02176. Diagram Number D037NG represents a movable dam. If there is high water and the wickets are down so that there is an unobstructed navigable pass through the dam, what light(s) will be shown at D if the lock walls and piers are not awash?

A. 3 red lights
B. 2 red lights
C. 1 red light
D. 1 amber light

02177. Diagram Number D037NG represents a movable dam. If there is high water and the wickets are down so that there is an unobstructed navigable pass through the dam, what light(s) will be shown at D if the lock walls and piers are not awash?

A. 1 amber light
B. 3 red lights
C. 2 red lights
D. 1 red light

02180. Relative humidity is defined as:

A. the maximum vapor content the air is capable of holding
B. the minimum vapor content the air is capable of holding
C. the ratio of the actual vapor content at the current temperature to the air's vapor holding capability
D. the relation of the moisture content of the air to barometric pressure

02181. Diagram Number D037NG represents a movable dam. If there is high water and the wickets are down so that there is an unobstructed navigable pass through the dam, what light(s) will be shown at D if the lock walls and piers are not awash?

A. 1 red light
B. 2 red lights
C. 3 red lights
D. no lights

02182. Diagram Number D037NG represents a movable dam. If there is high water and the wickets are down so that there is an unobstructed navigable pass through the dam, what light(s) will be shown at D if the lock walls and piers are not awash?

A. no lights
B. 1 red light
C. 2 red lights
D. 3 red lights

02183. Diagram number D037NG represents a movable dam. If there is high water and the wickets are down so that there is an unobstructed navigable pass through the dam, what light(s) will be shown at D if the lock walls and piers are not awash?

A. 3 red lights
B. 2 red lights
C. 1 red light
D. no light

02187. Diagram number D037NG represents a movable dam. If there is high water and the wickets are down so that there is an unobstructed navigable pass through the dam, what light(s) will be shown at D if the lock walls and piers are not awash?

A. no lights
B. 3 red lights
C. 2 red lights
D. 1 red lights

02190. Clouds are classified according to their:

A. size
B. moisture content
C. altitude and how they were formed
D. location in a front

02191. The chart indicates the variation was 3°45' E in 1988, and the annual change is increasing 6'. If you use the chart in 1991 how much variation should you apply?

A. 3°27' E
B. 3°27' W
C. 3°45' E
D. 4°03' E

02200. Cloud formations are minimal when the:

A. surface temperature and temperature aloft are equal

B. surface temperature and temperature aloft differ greatly
C. barometric pressure is very low
D. relative humidity is very high

02210. A dead reckoning (DR) plot:

A. ignores the effect of surface currents
B. is most useful when in sight of land
C. must be plotted using magnetic courses
D. may be started at an assumed position

02211. What is the length of a nautical mile?

A. 1,850 m
B. 6,076 ft.
C. 6,080 ft.
D. 2,000 yd.

02212. What information is found in the chart title?

A. number of the chart
B. edition date
C. variation information
D. survey information

02215. You are required to enter a lock on your voyage. Information on the lock regulations, signals, and radio communications can be found in:

A. the publication "Key to the Locks"
B. Bowditch
C. Corps of Engineers Information Bulletin
D. Coast Pilot

02220. A dead reckoning (DR) plot:

A. must utilize magnetic courses
B. must take set and drift into account
C. should be replotted hourly
D. should be started each time the vessel's position is fixed

02230. A nautical mile is a distance of approximately how much greater than or less than a statute mile?

A. 1/4 less
B. 1/7 less
C. 1/4 greater
D. 1/7 greater

02236. Which is true of a downbound power-driven vessel, when meeting an upbound vessel on the Western Rivers?

A. She has the right of way.
B. She shall propose the manner of passage.
C. She shall propose the place of passage.
D. all of the above

02239. A flashing green light displayed at a single lock means that the lock is:

A. ready for entrance
B. ready for entrance, but gates cannot be closed completely
C. being made ready for entrance
D. not ready for entrance

02240. If you observe a buoy off station:

A. fill out and mail CG Form 2692 to the nearest Coast Guard office
B. appear in person at the nearest Coast Guard office
C. notify Coast Guard Headquarters in Washington, DC
D. immediately contact the nearest Coast Guard office by radiotelephone

02243. Which aid is NOT marked on a chart with a magenta circle?

A. radar station
B. radar transponder beacon
C. aero light
D. radiobeacon

02246. The speed of an ocean current Is dependent on:

A. the density of the water
B. the air temperature
C. the presence of a high pressure area near it
D. underwater soil conditions

02250. The most important information to be obtained from a barometer is the:

A. difference between the reading of the two pointers, which shows wind direction
B. last two figures of the reading of the pointer, such as 87, 76, or 92
C. present reading of the pressure, combined with the changes in pressure observed in the recent past
D. weather indications printed on the dial (such as "cold, wet," etc.) under the pointer

02251. Which of the following statements concerning the chartlet in illustration D010NG is TRUE? (Soundings and heights are in m.)

A. Maury Lightship is visible for 17 miles.
B. The bottom to the south-southeast of the lightship is soft coral.
C. There is a dangerous eddy southeast of Beito Island.
D. There is a 12-m deep hole west of Beito Island and inside the 5-m line.

02252. The vertical angle between the horizontal and the magnetic line of force is the:

A. elevation
B. magnetic angle
C. vertical angle
D. dip

02254. A rock and sand structure extending from the bank of the river toward the channel is known as a:

A. wingdam
B. towhead
C. cutoff
D. landwall

02255. The height of tide is the:

A. depth of water at a specific time due to tidal effect
B. difference between the depth of the water at high tide and the depth of the water at low tide
C. difference between the depth of the water and the high water tidal level
D. difference between the depth of the water and the area's tidal datum

02260. A device trailed astern of a vessel to measure distance traveled through the water is a(n):

A. ammeter
B. patent log
C. trim tab
D. drogue

02261. You determine your vessel's position by taking a range and bearing to a buoy. Your position will be plotted as a(n):

A. running fix
B. fix
C. dead-reckoning position
D. estimated position

02264. The revision date of a chart is printed on what area of the chart?

A. top center
B. lower-left corner
C. part of the chart title
D. any clear area around the neat line

02269. One of the factors which affects the circulation of ocean currents is:

A. humidity
B. varying densities of water
C. vessel traffic
D. the jet stream

02270. The lubber's line of a magnetic compass:

A. always shows true north direction
B. indicates the vessel's heading

C. is always parallel to the vessel's transom
D. is located on the compass card

02271. What is the definition of height of tide?

A. the vertical distance from the surface of the water to the ocean floor
B. the vertical distance from the tidal datum to the level of the water at any time
C. the vertical difference between a datum plane and the ocean bottom
D. the vertical difference between the heights of low and high water

02277. The Light List indicates that a light has a nominal range of 20 miles and is 52 ft. high. If the visibility is 12.0 miles and your height of eye is 20 ft., at what approximate distance will you sight the light?

A. 21.5 miles
B. 20.0 miles
C. 13.7 miles
D. 12.0 miles

02280. Which of the following would influence a magnetic compass?

A. electrical wiring
B. iron pipe
C. radio
D. all of the above

02286. Which of the following light signals indicates that you have permission to enter a lock on the Ohio River?

A. steady red
B. flashing amber
C. steady green
D. flashing green

02292. The points on the earth's surface where the magnetic dip is 90° are:

A. along the magnetic Equator
B. connected by the isoclinal line
C. the isopors
D. the magnetic poles

02310. Which weather instrument measures atmospheric pressure?

A. Beaufort scale
B. anemometer
C. sling psychrometer
D. barometer

02317. The Light List indicates that a light has a nominal range of 13 miles and is 36 ft. high. If the visibility is 7.0 miles and your height of eye is 25 ft., at what approximate distance will you sight the light?

A. 10.0 miles
B. 12.9 miles
C. 14.2 miles
D. 17.0 miles

02320. The type of current which will have the greatest effect on the course made good for your vessel is:

A. one flowing in the same direction as your course steered
B. one flowing in the opposite direction as your course steered
C. one that flows at nearly right angles to your course steered
D. a rotary current in which the direction of current flow constantly changes

02328. Universal Time (UTI) is another name for:

A. sidereal time
B. Greenwich Mean Time
C. ephemeris time
D. atomic time

02330. Your are heading in a northerly direction when you come across an easterly current. Your vessel will:

A. be pushed to starboard
B. be pushed to port
C. decrease in engine speed
D. remain on course

02332. Magnetic dip is a measurement of the angle between the:

A. geographic pole and the magnetic pole
B. lubber's line and true north
C. horizontal and the magnetic line of force
D. compass heading and the magnetic heading

02335. The Light List indicates that a light has a nominal range of 13 miles and is 36 ft. high. If the visibility is 17 miles and your height of eye is 25 ft., at what approximate distance will you sight the light?

A. 10.0 miles
B. 12.9 miles
C. 14.2 miles
D. 17.0 miles

02340. What is a "Special Warning"?

A. an urgent message concerning a vessel in distress
B. a weather advisory about unusual meteorological or oceanographic phenomena hazardous to vessels

C. a broadcast disseminating an official government proclamation affecting shipping
D. a radio navigational warning concerning a particularly hazardous condition affecting navigation

02341. Which of the following statements concerning illustration D010NG is correct? (Soundings and heights are in m.)

A. Maury Lightship swings about her anchor on a circle with a 21-m diameter.
B. The position of the lightship is indicated by the center of the star on the symbol's mast.
C. The sunken wreck southwest of Beito Island shows the hull or superstructure above the sounding datum.
D. There is a 12-m deep hole inside the 5-m curve just west of Beito Island.

02348. Under the IALA Cardinal System, a mark with a quick light showing 9 flashes every 15 seconds indicates that the safest water is on the:

A. north side of the mark
B. west side of the mark
C. east side of the mark
D. south side of the mark

02349. The summer solstice is the point where the Sun is at:

A. maximum declination north
B. maximum declination south
C. 0° declination going to northerly declinations
D. 0° declination going to southerly declinations

02350. The principal advantage of NAVTEX radio warnings is that:

A. they can be used by mariners who do not know Morse code
B. only an ordinary FM radio is necessary to receive these warnings
C. information on a given topic is only broadcast at specified times
D. they cover a broad spectrum of the radio band allowing reception on almost any type of receiver

02351. A position obtained by applying ONLY your vessel's course and speed to a known position is a:

A. running fix
B. probable position
C. fix
D. dead-reckoning position

02353. A single line of position combined with a dead-reckoning position results in a(n):

A. estimated position
B. assumed position
C. fix
D. running fix

02360. What U. S. Agency is responsible for NAVAREA warnings?

A. Coast Guard
B. National Oceanic and Atmospheric Administration
C. National Ocean Service
D. Defense Mapping Agency

02361. The range of tide is the:

A. maximum depth of the water at high tide
B. duration of time between high and low tide
C. distance the tide moves out from the shore
D. difference between the heights of high and low tide

02363. In illustration D051NG, the position labeled C was plotted because:

A. the vessel's speed changed
B. the vessel's course changed from due North to due East
C. running fixes are better estimates of true position than dead-reckoning positions
D. all of the above are correct

02370. In the United States, short-range radio navigational warnings are broadcast by the:

A. Coast Guard
B. Corps of Engineers
C. NOAA
D. harbor master of the nearest port

02373. The vertical distance from the tidal datum to the level of the water is the:

A. actual water depth
B. range of tide
C. charted depth
D. height of tide

02378. Which of the following light signals indicates that you may approach the lock?

A. flashing red
B. flashing amber
C. steady amber
D. steady green

02379. The winter solstice is the point where the Sun is at:

A. maximum declination north
B. maximum declination south
C. 0° declination going to northerly declinations
D. 0° declination going to southerly declinations

02380. The navigation regulations applicable to a U. S. inland waterway can be found in the:

A. Notices to Mariners
B. Channel Reports
C. Sailing Directions
D. Coast Pilots

02381. The difference between the heights of low and high tide is the:

A. period
B. distance
C. depth
D. range

02384. On U. S. Charts, you can tell if a named feature such as a rock (i. e. Great Eastern Rock in Block Island Sound) is submerged by the:

A. color of ink used to print the name
B. style of type used to print the name
C. dashed circle around the feature
D. magenta circle around the feature

02389. The autumnal equinox is the point where the Sun is at:

A. maximum declination north
B. maximum declination south
C. 0° declination going to northerly declinations
D. 0° declination going to southerly declinations

02390. You are in a channel in U. S. waters near an industrial plant with a load/discharge facility for barges. You hear a siren being sounded at the facility. What does this indicate?

A. There is danger at the facility due to a fire or cargo release.
B. A towboat with a hazardous cargo barge is being moved to or from the facility.
C. The facility is warning a barge to shut down transfer operations due to weather conditions (electrical storms, tornado, etc.).
D. A barge at the facility has commenced loading or discharging operations.

02392. The point where the Sun is at maximum declination north or south is:

A. aphelion
B. perihelion
C. an equinox
D. a solstice

02396. Perihelion is the point where the Sun:

A. is nearest to the Earth
B. is farthest from the Earth
C. is on the opposite side of the Earth from the Moon
D. and Moon and Earth are in line

02400. You are in a channel in U. S. waters near an industrial plant with a load/discharge facility for barges. You see an emergency rotating flashing light on the facility light up. What does this indicate?

A. A barge at the facility has commenced transferring a hazardous cargo.
B. A barge carrying a hazardous cargo is mooring or unmooring at the facility.
C. The facility is warning a barge to shut down transfer operations due to weather conditions (electrical storm, tornado, hurricane, etc.).
D. There is danger at the facility due to a fire or cargo release.

02409. You are approaching the first of 2 drawbridges that span a narrow channel. The second drawbridge is close to the first. What signals should you sound?

A. Sound the request-for-opening signal for the first bridge only, who will notify the second bridge of your approach.
B. Sound the request-for-opening signal twice in succession to indicate you must pass through both bridges.
C. Sound the request-for-opening signal, pause for about 10 seconds, then sound 2 prolonged blasts.
D. Sound the request-for-opening signal and, after the bridge acknowledges it, sound the request-for-opening signal for second bridge.

02416. An orange and white buoy indicating a vessel-exclusion area will be marked with what symbol?

A. open-faced diamond
B. diamond with a cross
C. circle
D. square

02417. Most modern Loran-C receivers automatically detect station blink which:

A. triggers alarm indicators to warn the operator
B. indicates the station is transmitting normally
C. causes the receiver to shift automatically to another Loran chain
D. automatically shuts down the receiver

02418. While proceeding downriver, you sight a red triangular-shaped daymark on the left bank. Under the U. S. Aids to Navigation System on the Western Rivers this is a:

A. special purpose signal
B. passing daymark
C. mark with no lateral significance
D. crossing daymark

02419. A backlash below a lock is defined as a:

A. current setting your vessel on the wall
B. current setting into the lock chamber
C. an eddy working along the lower guide wall
D. current setting counterclockwise

02420. You are on course 355° T and take a relative bearing of a lighthouse of 275°. What is the true bearing to the lighthouse?

A. 080°
B. 085°
C. 280°
D. 270°

02424. Under the IALA-B Buoyage System, when entering from seaward a lateral system buoy to be left to starboard may display which topmark in illustration D046NG?

A. a
B. b
C. c
D. d

02426. You are in charge of a power-driven vessel crossing a river on the Western Rivers. You must keep out of the way of:

A. a sail vessel descending the river
B. a power-driven vessel ascending the river
C. a vessel restricted in its ability to maneuver crossing the river
D. any of the above

02428. If your vessel were proceeding up river (ascending), the port side of the channel would be marked according to the U. S. Aids to Navigation System on the Western Rivers by:

A. green can buoys
B. red can buoys
C. green nun buoys
D. red nun buoys

02430. You are on course 222° T and take a relative bearing of a lighthouse of 025°. What is the true bearing to the lighthouse?

A. 197°
B. 247°
C. 315°
D. 335°

02435. What is a lighted safe water mark fitted with to aid in its identification?

A. a red and white octagon
B. red and white retroreflective material
C. a sequential number
D. a spherical topmark

02436. Aphelion is the point where the Sun:

A. and Moon and Earth form a right angle
B. and Moon and Earth are in line
C. crosses the celestial Equator
D. is farthest from the Earth

02437. When Daylight Savings Time is kept, the times of tide and current calculations must be adjusted. One way of doing this is to:

A. add 15° to the standard meridian when calculating the time differences
B. apply no correction as the times at the reference stations are adjusted for Daylight Savings Time
C. add 1 hour to the times listed for the reference stations
D. subtract 1 hour from the times listed for the subordinate stations

02438. The radar control that reduces weak echoes out to a limited distance from the ship is the:

A. sensitivity time control (sea-clutter control)
B. receiver gain control
C. brilliance control
D. fast time constant (differentiator)

02440. You are on course 357° T and take a relative bearing of a lighthouse of 180°. What is the true bearing to the lighthouse?

A. 003°
B. 227°
C. 177°
D. 363°

02449. You are approaching a drawbridge that will open at any time upon request. What signal should you sound to request the bridge be opened?

A. 2 short blasts
B. 1 short, 1 prolonged, 1 short blast
C. 1 prolonged, 1 short blast
D. 2 prolonged blasts

02450. You are on course 180° T and take a relative bearing of a lighthouse of 225°. What is the true bearing to the lighthouse?

A. 045°
B. 135°
C. 180°
D. 270°

02454. Illustration D037NG represents a moveable dam. If the wickets are down and there are open weirs due to high water, what light(s) will be shown at C if the lock walls and piers are not awash?

A. 1 red light
B. 2 red lights
C. 3 red lights
D. 1 amber light

02456. An orange and white buoy marking an area where operating restrictions are in effect will be marked with what symbol?

A. open-faced diamond
B. diamond with a cross
C. circle
D. rectangle

02458. In the U. S. Aids to Navigation System on the Western Rivers, the light characteristic of group flashing (2) is used for lights on:

A. the right descending bank
B. the left descending bank
C. preferred channel buoys
D. daymarks with no lateral significance

02459. The controlling depth of the river is:

A. the minimum depth of the river prescribed in the channel maintenance program
B. the edge of a dredged channel
C. the highest level to which the river may rise without flooding
D. the least available water in a channel which limits the draft of boats and tows

02460. You are on course 344° T and take a relative bearing of a lighthouse of 270°. What is the true bearing to the lighthouse?

A. 016°
B. 074°
C. 090°
D. 254°

02466. On the Western Rivers, a vessel crossing a river must:

A. only keep out of the way of a power-driven vessel descending the river
B. keep out of the way of any vessel descending the river
C. keep out of the way of a power-driven vessel ascending or descending the river
D. keep out of the way of any vessel ascending or descending the river

02468. Under the U. S. Aids to Navigation System on the Western Rivers, the buoys marking the starboard side of the channel when going upstream will be:

A. black
B. red
C. green
D. yellow

02470. You are on course 344° T and take a relative bearing of a lighthouse of 090°. What is the true bearing to the lighthouse?

A. 016°
B. 074°
C. 254°
D. 270°

02480. You are on course 277° T and take a relative bearing of a lighthouse of 045°. What is the true bearing to the lighthouse?

A. 038°
B. 232°
C. 315°
D. 322°

02483. An orange and white buoy with a rectangle on it is used to indicate:

A. general information
B. an exclusion area
C. danger
D. a controlled area

02488. In which publication could you find information concerning the minimum lighting required for bridges on U. S. waters?

A. Chart No. 1.
B. Code of Federal Regulations
C. Mississippi River Systems Light List
D. Notice to Mariners

02489. You are approaching a drawbridge and must pass through during a scheduled closure period. What signal should you sound?

A. 5 short blasts
B. 2 prolonged, 2 short blasts
C. 3 prolonged blasts
D. 3 short blasts, 2 prolonged blasts

02496. An orange and white buoy marking a danger area will have what symbol on it?

A. open-faced diamond
B. diamond with a cross
C. circle
D. square

02498. The light characteristic of flashing is used in the Aids to Navigation System on the Western Rivers for lights on:

A. the right descending bank
B. the left descending bank
C. preferred channel buoys
D. daymarks with no lateral significance

02499. The "head of the bend" is the:

A. top or upstream beginning of a bend
B. bottom or downstream beginning of a bend
C. midpoint or center radius of a bend
D. center line or apex of a bend

02506. Which is TRUE of a downbound vessel when meeting an upbound vessel on the Western Rivers?

A. She has the right of way only if she is a power-driven vessel.
B. She has the right of way only if she has a tow.
C. She does not have the right of way, since the other vessel is not crossing the river.
D. She must wait for a whistle signal from the upbound vessel.

02508. Normal pool elevation is the height in ft. of the section of river above a dam. This height is measured from:

A. low steel on the Huey P. Long Bridge
B. mean sea level
C. the local water table
D. the minimum dam control level

02509. All persons or vessels within the lock area, including the lock approach channels, come under the authority of the:

A. dockmaster
B. dock captain
C. lockmaster
D. lock foreman

02513. Most modern Loran-C receivers automatically detect station blink which:

A. indicates the station is transmitting normally
B. automatically shuts down the receiver
C. causes the receiver to shift automatically to another Loran chain
D. triggers alarm indicators to warn the operator

02525. Daylight Savings Time is a form of zone time that adopts the time:

A. 2 zones to the west
B. 2 zones to the east
C. 1 zone to the west
D. 1 zone to the east

02527. In the doldrums you can expect:

A. steady, constant winds
B. frequent rain showers and thunderstorms
C. steep pressure gradients
D. low relative humidity

02528. Illustration D038NG represents a fixed C of E lock and dam. What navigational light(s) is(are) exhibited at the position indicated by the letter A in the illustration?

A. 1 red light
B. 2 red lights
C. 2 green lights
D. no light

02529. A bridge over a navigable waterway is being repaired. There is a traveller platform under the bridge's deck that significantly reduces the vertical clearance. If required by the CG district commander, how will this be indicated at night?

A. illumination by flood lights
B. a quick flashing red light at each lower corner
C. a strobe light visible both up and downstream
D. fixed amber lights under the extreme outer edges of the traveller

02530. The distance between any 2 meridians measured along a parallel of latitude:

A. increases in north latitude and decreases in south latitude
B. decreases as DLO increases
C. increases with increased latitude
D. decreases with increased latitude

02536. A revised print of a chart is made:

A. after every major hydrographic survey of the area covered by the chart
B. when there are numerous corrections to be made or the corrections are extensive
C. when a low-stock situation occurs and minor corrections are made
D. every 2 years to update the magnetic variation information

02538. The light characteristic of composite group flashing (2 + 1) is used in the Aids to Navigation System on the Western Rivers for lights on:

A. the right descending bank
B. the left descending bank
C. preferred channel buoys
D. daymarks with no lateral significance

02539. Under the IALA Cardinal System, a mark with quick white light showing 3 flashes every 10 seconds indicates that the safest water in the area is on the:

A. north side of the mark
B. west side of the mark
C. east side of the mark
D. south side of the mark

02540. The distance between any 2 meridians measured along a parallel of latitude and expressed in miles is the:

A. difference in longitude
B. mid-longitude
C. departure
D. meridian angle

02544. At McAlpine L & D, normal upper pool elevation is 420.0 ft. MSL, equal to 12.0 ft. on the upper gage. The vertical clearance at the Clark Memorial Highway bridge is 72.6 ft. above normal pool. What is the clearance if the gage reads 27.2 ft.?

A. 25.4 ft.
B. 57.4 ft.
C. 60.6 ft.
D. 72.6 ft.

02546. A structure usually made of stone ore cement pilings which extend from the bank at approximately right angles to the current is called a:

A. dike
B. revetment
C. cutoff
D. crib

02548. On the Mississippi River, gage zero is the gage reading measured from the:

A. National Geodetic Vertical Datum
B. low water reference plane
C. the lowest recorded river depth
D. the highest recorded river depth

02549. Corps of Engineer locks monitor which frequency for initial calls to the locks?

A. 156.6 MHz (channel 12)
B. 156.65 MHz (channel 13)
C. 156.7 MHz (channel 14)
D. 156.8 MHz (channel 16)

02583. You are in the Northern Hemisphere and a tropical wave is located 200 miles due west of your position. Where will the wave be located 24 hours later?

A. in the same place
B. closer and to the west
C. closer and to the east
D. farther away to the west

02586. A chart has extensive corrections to be made to it. When these are made and the chart is again printed, the chart issue is a:

A. first edition
B. new edition
C. revised edition
D. reprint

02588. You are approaching an open draw-bridge and sound the proper signal. You receive no acknowledgment from the bridge. What action should you take?

A. Approach with caution and proceed through the open draw.
B. Approach under full control to a position no closer than 400 yd. from the bridge and await a signal from the bridge.
C. Hold in the channel as a vessel is closing the bridge from the other direction.
D. Resound the opening signal and do not pass through the bridge until signals have been exchanged.

02589. Under the IALA Cardinal System, a mark with a quick white light showing 6 flashes followed by 1 long flash indicates that the safest water is on the:

A. north side of the mark
B. west side of the mark
C. east side of the mark
D. south side of the mark

02592. A deadhead is a(n):

A. tree or log awash in a nearly vertical position
B. crew member who refuses to work
C. upstream end of a land wall
D. buoy that is adrift

02594. At McAlpine L & D, normal upper pool elevation is 420.0 ft. MSL, equal to 12.0 ft. on the upper gage. The vertical clearance at the Clark Memorial Highway bridge is 72.6 ft. above normal pool. What is the clearance if the gage reads 10.6 ft.?

A. 84.6 ft.
B. 83.2 ft.
C. 74.0 ft.
D. 62.0 ft.

02596. The abbreviation L. W. R. P. On the navigation maps means:

A. low water reference plane
B. low winter runoff point
C. least water river plane
D. land wall reference point

02597. You determine your vessel's position by taking a range and bearing to a buoy. Your position will be plotted as a(n):

A. fix
B. running fix
C. estimated position
D. dead-reckoning position

02598. A vessel is proceeding downstream in a narrow channel on the Western Rivers when another vessel is sighted moving upstream. Which vessel has the right of way?

A. the vessel moving upstream against the current.
B. the vessel moving downstream with a following current.
C. the vessel located more towards the channel centerline.
D. the vessel with the least amount of maneuverability.

02600. A parallel of latitude other than the Equator is a:

A. great circle
B. loxodromic curve
C. small circle
D. gnomonic curve

02625. Stormy weather is usually associated with regions of:

A. high barometric pressure
B. changing barometric pressure
C. low barometric pressure
D. steady barometric pressure

02626. What information is found in the chart title?

A. date of the first edition
B. date of the edition and, if applicable, the revision
C. information on the sounding datum
D. information on which IALA buoyage system applies

02628. A drawbridge may use visual signals to acknowledge a vessel's request to open the draw. Which of the following signals does NOT indicate that the draw will be opened immediately?

A. a flashing amber light
B. a fixed red light
C. a white flag raised and lowered vertically
D. a flashing white light

02629. Under the IALA Buoyage Systems, which topmark in illustration D022NG is used on a special mark?

A. a
B. b
C. c
D. d

02632. A section of the river that is narrower than usual and is often navigable from bank to bank is a:

A. chute
B. stabilized channel
C. slough
D. navigable pass

02634. Under the U. S. Aids to Navigation System on the Western Rivers, a preferred channel buoy is:

A. horizontally-banded red and green
B. vertically-striped red and white
C. solid red
D. solid green

02636. You are ascending a river and exchanging navigational information via radiotelephone with a descending vessel. If the descending vessel advises you to "watch for the set" above point X, what would you expect to encounter above point X?

A. an increase in current velocity
B. slack water
C. shallow water
D. a sideways movement of your vessel

02638. A vessel crossing a river on the Western Rivers has the right of way over:

A. vessels ascending the river
B. vessels descending the river
C. all vessels ascending and descending river
D. none of the above

02639. Under the U. S. Aids to Navigation System used on the Western Rivers, aids to navigation lights on the right descending bank show:

A. white or green lights
B. white or red lights
C. green lights only
D. white lights only

02646. During Daylight Savings Time the meridian used for determining the time is located farther:

A. east
B. west
C. east in west longitude and west in east longitude
D. west in west longitude and east in east longitude

02651. Low pressure disturbances which travel along the intertropical convergence zone are called:

A. tropical waves
B. tropical disturbances
C. permanent waves
D. tidal waves

02664. The Light List shows a lighted aid to navigation on the right bank. This means that the light can be seen on the left side of a vessel:

A. crossing the river
B. descending the river
C. ascending the river
D. proceeding towards sea

02666. The following boats are approaching a lock. Which has priority for locking?

A. an 85' yacht
B. Corps of Engineer towboat running empty-headed
C. "Delta Queen" (passenger vessel)
D. an integrated chemical tow

02668. You are approaching a drawbridge and have sounded the request-for-opening signal. The bridge has responded with 5 short blasts. What reply should you sound?

A. none; no reply is required
B. 5 short blasts
C. 2 prolonged blasts
D. 1 prolonged, 1 short blast

02669. Under the IALA Buoyage System, which topmark in illustration D023NG will be displayed on a safe water mark?

A. a
B. b
C. c
D. d

02672. When you are steering on a pair of range lights and find the upper light is in line above the lower light, you should:

A. continue on the present course
B. come left
C. come right
D. wait until the lights are no longer in a vertical line

02673. A bluff bar is a bar:

A. extending out from a bluff alongside the river
B. that tends to give a false indication of its position
C. that has a sharp drop off into deep water
D. that is perpendicular to the current

02674. In the U. S. Aid to Navigation System on the Western Rivers, a preferred channel buoy to be left to port while proceeding downstream will:

A. have the upper band red
B. show a red or white light if lighted

C. have a characteristic of composite group flashing if lighted
D. all of the above

02675. When you are steering on a pair of range lights and find the upper light is in line above the lower light, you should:

A. come left
B. continue on the present course
C. come right
D. wait until the lights are no longer in a vertical line

02676. The place where a channel moves from along 1 bank of the river over to the other bank of the river is called a:

A. draft
B. cutoff
C. draw
D. crossing

02678. A vessel crossing a river on the Western Rivers, must keep out of the way of a power-driven vessel:

A. descending the river with a tow
B. ascending the river with a tow
C. ascending the river without a tow
D. all of the above

02679. Under the U. S. Aids to Navigation System on the Western Rivers, a daymark on the right descending bank will:

A. be green
B. have an odd number
C. indicate the gage reading
D. have yellow retroreflective markings

02695. You are plotting a running fix in an area where there is a determinable current. How should this current be treated in determining the position?

A. The drift should be added to the ship's speed.
B. The current should be ignored.
C. The course and speed made good should be determined and used to advance the LOP.
D. The set should be applied to the second bearing.

02703. What publication indicates the HYDROLANTS or HYDROPACS issued since the previous working day?

A. Broadcast Notice to Mariners
B. Local Notice to Mariners
C. Daily Memorandum
D. Summary of Corrections

02704. The Light List shows a lighted aid to navigation on the right bank. This means that the light can be seen on the right side of a vessel:

A. proceeding from seaward
B. crossing the river
C. ascending the river
D. descending the river

02705. Data relating to the direction and velocity of rotary tidal currents can be found in the:

A. Tidal Current Tables
B. Mariner's Guide
C. Tide Tables
D. Nautical Almanac

02706. The following types of vessels are awaiting lockage on the upper Mississippi. Which type of vessel is normally passed through the lock first?

A. pleasure craft
B. commercial towboats
C. commercial passenger vessels
D. commercial fishing vessels

02707. Where would you find information concerning the duration of slack water?

A. Tidal Current Tables
B. Tide Tables
C. American Practical Navigator
D. Sailing Directions

02708. You are approaching a drawbridge and have sounded the proper whistle signal requesting it to open. You hear a signal of 1 prolonged and 1 short blast from the bridge. What action should you take?

A. anchor or use an alternate route because the bridge is out of service for an extended period of time.
B. approach to a point not closer than 400 yd. from the bridge and await further signals.
C. hold in the channel as the bridge will open within 15 minutes.
D. approach under full control to pass through the bridge.

02709. Under the IALA-B Buoyage System, when entering from seaward a lateral system buoy to be left to port may display which topmark in illustration D046NG?

A. a
B. b
C. c
D. d

02712. A bold reef is a reef:

A. with part of it extending above the water
B. that can be detected by water turbulence
C. that drops off sharply
D. perpendicular to the current

02714. A current moving across a lock entrance toward the river or toward the dam is called a(n):

A. cutoff
B. outdraft
C. lockwash
D. springpool

02716. Under the U. S. Aids to Navigation System on the Western Rivers, passing daymarks on the left descending bank are:

A. green squares
B. green diamonds
C. red diamonds
D. red triangles

02718. A power-driven vessel operating in a narrow channel, with a following current, on the Western Rivers, is meeting an upbound vessel. Which statement is TRUE?

A. The downbound vessel has the right-of-way.
B. The downbound vessel must initiate the required maneuvering signals.
C. The downbound vessel must propose the manner and place of passage.
D. all of the above

02719. Under the U. S. Aids to Navigation System on the Western Rivers, passing daymarks on the right descending bank are:

A. red diamond-shaped panels with red reflector borders
B. red triangular-shaped panels with red reflector borders
C. green square-shaped panels with green reflector borders
D. green triangular-shaped panels with green reflector borders

02720. When pushing barges ahead close to a steep revetment where there is no current, which of the following is MOST likely to occur?

A. The stern of the towboat will tend to sheer away from the revetment.
B. Your speed over the ground will increase.
C. The head of the tow will tend to sheer away from the revetment.
D. all of the above

02721. In plotting a running fix, how many fixed objects are needed to take your lines of position from?

A. 1
B. 2
C. 3
D. none

02722. The paths of intended travel between 3 or more points is the:

A. course
B. track
C. bearing
D. course over the ground

02725. A position that is obtained by using 2 or more intersecting lines of position taken at nearly the same time, is a(n):

A. estimated position
B. dead-reckoning position
C. running fix
D. fix

02726. A daymark used as a special mark is indicated by what letter in illustration D045NG?

A. a
B. b
C. c
D. d

02729. While navigating in fog off a coastline of steep cliffs, you hear the echo of the ship's fog horn 5.5 seconds after the signal was sounded. What is the distance to the shore?

A. 1275 yd.
B. 1150 yd.
C. 1000 yd.
D. 825 yd.

02730. When attempting an upstream landing while pushing empty barges ahead in a hard onshore wind, the approach is best made:

A. with bow out, stern in
B. with bow in, stern out
C. parallel to the dock, as close in as possible
D. parallel to the dock, as far out as possible

02737. A lateral system buoy displaying a quick light:

A. should be passed close aboard on either side
B. indicates that special caution is required
C. is used at a channel bifurcation or junction
D. is painted with red and white vertical stripes

02738. While navigating in fog off a coastline of steep cliffs, you hear the echo of the ship's fog horn 3 seconds after the signal was sounded. What is the distance to the shore?

A. 1100 yd.
B. 872 yd.
C. 550 yd.
D. 792 yd.

02739. A daymark used to indicate the starboard side of the channel when approaching from seaward will have the shape indicated by what letter in illustration D045NG?

A. a
B. b
C. c
D. d

02740. When one upbound vessel is overtaking another vessel and both are pushing a tow ahead, what reaction may you expect?

A. Both towheads will tend to drift apart, and the overtaking vessel will be slowed down.
B. Both towheads will tend to drift together, and the overtaking vessel will be slowed down.
C. Both towheads will tend to drift apart, and the overtaken vessel will be slowed down.
D. Both towheads will tend to drift together, and the overtaken vessel will be slowed down.

02741. A general chart could have a scale of:

A. 1:200,000
B. 1:1,000,000
C. 1:50,000
D. not more than 1:25,000

02742. A white diamond daymark with an orange border is used:

A. as a special mark
B. for information or regulatory purposes
C. for a lateral aid on the Intracoastal Waterway
D. as a safe water mark

02744. The standard atmospheric pressure measured in inches of mercury is:

A. 29.92
B. 500.0
C. 760.0
D. 1013.2

02746. What is used to measure wind velocity?

A. psychrometer
B. barometer
C. wind sock
D. anemometer

02748. You are inbound in a channel marked by a range. The range line is 309° T. You are steering 306° T and have the range in sight as indicated in illustration D047NG. The range continues to open. What actions should you take?

A. Alter course to the right to 309° T or more to bring the range in line.
B. Continue on course but be ready to come right if the range continues to open.
C. Alter course to the left until the range is in line then alter course to 309° T.
D. Come left until the range closes then steer to the left of 306° T.

02750. When pushing a tow and approaching barges tied off to the shore, you should:

A. increase speed so you will pass faster
B. decrease speed while passing so you won't create a suction
C. do nothing different as the barges should be tied off properly
D. move to the opposite side of the channel from the barges and increase speed

02752. A daymark used to indicate the safe water in a channel will have the shape indicated by what letter in illustration D045NG?

A. a
B. b
C. c
D. d

02760. You are pushing a tow, at high speed, near the right hand bank of a canal. The forces affecting your towboat and tow will tend to:

A. push both the head of the tow and the stern of the towboat away from the right hand bank
B. push the head of the tow away from, and pull the stern of the towboat into, the right hand bank
C. pull both the head of the tow and the stern of the towboat into the right hand bank
D. pull the head of the tow into, and push the stern of the towboat away from, the right hand bank

02762. If you take a bearing of 176° to a lighthouse, what other bearing of another prominent object would give the best fix?

A. 079°
B. 151°
C. 176°
D. 292°

02764. You are in a channel inbound from sea. A daymark used to mark a channel junction when the preferred channel is to port will have the shape indicated by what letter in illustration D045NG?

A. a
B. b
C. c
D. d

02766. In low latitudes, the high(s) of the diurnal variation of pressure occur(s) at:

A. noon
B. noon and midnight
C. 1000 and 2200
D. 1600

02768. What type of daymark is used to mark the starboard side of the channel when entering from sea?

A. red and white octagon
B. black and white diamond
C. red triangle
D. green square

02769. If your vessel must pass through a draw during a scheduled closure period, what signal should you sound to request the opening of the draw?

A. 1 prolonged blast followed by 1 short blast
B. 3 short blasts
C. 1 prolonged blast followed by 3 short blasts
D. 5 short blasts

02770. What is most likely to happen when you push a tow into an eddy?

A. Going upstream you will make better speed with no danger involved.
B. Going downstream you will be slowed down.
C. There is a good chance you will break up the tow.
D. No danger exists as long as you steer a straight course through the eddy.

02772. The direction in which a vessel should be steered between two points is the:

A. course
B. heading
C. bearing
D. course over the ground

02777. A sailing chart could have a scale of:

A. not more than 1:25,000
B. 1:35,000
C. 1:100,000
D. 1:700,000

02778. A special daymark is a:

A. red-and-white octagon
B. daymark with a yellow stripe on it
C. green square
D. yellow diamond

02779. The buoy indicated by the letter B in illustration D044NG is a:

A. nun
B. can
C. spar
D. pillar

02780. You are pushing a tow ahead and passing close to another towboat which is pushing ahead in the same direction (you are overtaking). After the towheads pass close alongside:

A. you will gain speed
B. both boats will gain speed
C. the tows will tend to drift apart
D. the tows will tend to drift together

02782. Your radar is set on a true motion display. Which of the following will appear to move across the PPI scope.

A. own ship's marker
B. echo from a ship at anchor
C. echoes from land masses
D. all of the above

02784. Some Loran-C receivers automatically compute and read out the latitude and longitude of a vessel's position. This indicated position may be in error if:

A. the crossing angle of the selected LOP's is less than 48°
B. there is signal distortion due to skywave contamination
C. the signal travels a significant distance over land
D. there is excessive super-refraction due to ducting

02788. The Light List indicates that a dayboard is a type KGW. You should:

A. see a green and white diamond
B. leave it to port when southbound on the Atlantic Coast ICW
C. pass it close aboard on either side
D. look for another daymark to form the range

02789. In fog, when homing on a radiobeacon from a large navigational buoy, you should:

A. alter course as soon as the fog signal is heard
B. apply the conversion angle to the received signal's bearing
C. disconnect the calibration cam (if so equipped)
D. ensure that the bearing moves aft

02790. A towboat has the same draft as the barges it is pushing ahead. If the distance from the stern of the towboat to the head of the tow is 800 ft., where is the approximate location of the pivot point of the unit?

A. at the head of the tow
B. 250 ft. from the head of the tow
C. 400 ft. from the head of the tow
D. 600 ft. from the head of the tow

02792. If you take a bearing of 142° and 259° to two prominent objects, what bearing of a third object will provide the best fix?

A. 081°
B. 238°
C. 201°
D. 234°

02794. The standard atmospheric pressure in millibars is:

A. 760.0
B. 938.9
C. 1000.0
D. 1013.2

02798. A can buoy is indicated by what letter in illustration D044NG?

A. a
B. b
C. c
D. d

02799. A sequenced radiobeacon is one that:

A. transmits for 1 minute at 1 frequency and then shifts to another frequency for the next minute
B. shares the same transmitting frequency with other stations and transmits intermittently
C. provides a range and a bearing when used with a calibrated RDF receiver
D. must be used in conjunction with a continuous radiobeacon to obtain an LOP

02800. The pivot point of a towboat with a tow ahead is usually which of the following?

A. one third the length of the combined unit forward of the towboat
B. one third the length of the combined unit back from the head
C. at the head of the towboat
D. one half the length of the combined unit

02801. Mean high water is used:

A. as the reference for soundings on the Gulf Coast of the U. S.
B. to indicate the shoreline where there is a large tidal fluctuation
C. as the reference plane for bottom contour lines
D. as the sounding datum for rivers, lakes, etc. regulated by locks

02805. You are entering port and have been instructed to anchor, as your berth is not yet available. You are on a SW'ly heading, preparing to drop anchor, when you observe the range lights depicted in illustration D047NG on your starboard beam. You should:

A. drop the anchor immediately as the range lights mark an area free of obstructions
B. drop the anchor immediately as a change in the position of the range lights will be an indication of dragging anchor
C. not drop the anchor until the lights are in line
D. ensure your ship will NOT block the channel or obstruct the range while at anchor

02809. The diurnal variation of pressure is not visible in the middle latitudes in winter because:

A. it is masked by the pressure changes of moving weather systems
B. the decreased gravitational effect from the Sun causes the variation to fade
C. the decreased average temperature is less than the critical temperature
D. the increased Coriolis force disperses the pressure variation

02810. When steering a tow downstream around the shape of a sand bar, and staying on the proper side of the buoys, an operator should be cautious of:

A. eddies under the bar
B. swift current under the bar causing loss of control
C. cross-currents pushing the tow away from the bar
D. cross-currents pushing the tow into the bar

02814. In low latitudes the range of the diurnal variation of pressure is up to:

A. 0.5 millibar
B. 3.0 millibars
C. 6.0 millibars
D. 10.0 millibars

02816. The length of a wave is the length:

A. of the wave's crest
B. of the wave's trough
C. measured from crest to trough
D. measured from crest to crest

02818. If you take bearings of 313° T and 076° T to two prominent objects, what bearing of a third object will provide the best fix?

A. 048° T
B. 101° T
C. 142° T
D. 187° T

02819. The time interval between successive wave crests is called:

A. wave period
B. wavelength
C. frequency
D. significant wave height

02820. A towboat is pushing barges ahead at a dangerously fast speed when:

A. the towboat vibrates when backing down
B. the roostertail exceeds the height of the main deck
C. a strain is placed on the face wires
D. water comes over the foredeck of the lead barges

02821. The height of tide is the:

A. difference between the depth of the water at high tide and the depth of the water at low tide
B. depth of water at a specific time due to tidal effect
C. difference between the depth of the water and the area's tidal datum
D. difference between the depth of the water and the high water tidal level

02822. While navigating in fog off a coastline of steep cliffs, you hear the echo of the ship's fog horn 2 seconds after the signal was sounded. What is the distance to the shore?

A. 360 yd.
B. 320 yd.
C. 280 yd.
D. 140 yd.

02826. If you take a bearing of 043° and 169° to two prominent objects, what bearing of a third object will provide the best fix?

A. 356°
B. 102°
C. 144°
D. 201°

02828. The daily recurring pattern of pressure changes most noticeable in low latitudes is the:

A. daily lapse reading
B. diurnal variation of pressure
C. pressure tendency
D. synoptic pressure

02829. A spar buoy is indicated by what letter in illustration D044NG?

A. a
B. b
C. c
D. d

02830. The proper way to approach a downstream lock where there is an outdraft is to be:

A. wide out from the land wall, keeping the stern in at all times
B. wide out from the land wall, keeping the stern out at all times
C. close in to the land wall, keeping the stern in at all times
D. close in to the land wall, keeping the stern out at all times

02831. A coastal chart could have a scale of:

A. not more than 1:25,000
B. 1:35,000
C. 1:100,000
D. 1:500,000

02832. The Light List indicates that a dayboard is a type MR. You should:

A. leave it on either side
B. look for the other dayboard forming the range
C. look for an all red daymark
D. check to enter the correct channel at this junction daymark

02834. Mariners should be careful about taking RDF bearings on commercial stations broadcasting entertainment programs. What condition would probably NOT affect such a bearing?

A. The actual broadcast antenna may be remote from the broadcast station.
B. The shorter wave length of the broadcast band tends to re-radiate from the vessel's structure.
C. Many of these stations are inland causing land effect when the signal crosses the coastline.
D. The operating frequency may differ from the calibrated frequency of the RDF.

02838. If you take a bearing of 191° and 313° to two prominent objects, what bearing of a third object will provide the best fix?

A. 001°
B. 069°
C. 209°
D. 356°

02839. Privately maintained aids to navigation:

A. are painted white and must use a white light if lighted
B. must be conspicuously marked by a signboard with the words "PRIVATE AID"
C. must conform to the standards of the U. S. Aids to Navigation System
D. are not permitted in or along first-class waterways and may be authorized for second- and third-class waterways

02840. The lockmaster has given you permission to tie off on the lower guide wall to wait your turn to lock through. What should you be most concerned with?

A. a downbound vessel
B. an upbound vessel
C. current reaction when the lock chamber is being emptied
D. current reaction when the lock chamber is being filled

02841. You are required to enter a lock on your voyage. Information on the lock regulations, signals, and radio communications can be found in:

A. the publication "Key to the Locks"
B. Bowditch
C. Corps of Engineer Information Bulletin
D. Coast Pilot

02842. The drawspan of a floating drawbridge may be marked with:

A. 2 white lights
B. a yellow diamond
C. flashing blue lights
D. 3 red lights on each side of the draw

02843. A position obtained by applying ONLY your vessel's course and speed to a known position is a:

A. fix
B. running fix
C. dead-reckoning position
D. probable position

02844. The signal from a ramark will show on the PPI as a:

A. coded signal on the same bearing and at a greater range than the transponder
B. circle surrounding the transponder
C. radial line from the transponder to the center of the PPI
D. dashed circle at the same range as the transponder

02846. What type of daymark is used to mark the port side of the channel when entering from sea?

A. red and white octagon
B. black and white diamond
C. red triangle
D. green square

02848. While navigating in fog off a coastline of steep cliffs, you hear the echo of the ship's fog horn 6 seconds after the signal was sounded. What is the distance to the shore?

A. 1200 yd.
B. 1100 yd.
C. 1000 yd.
D. 900 yd.

02849. If you take a bearing of 086° to a light-house, what other bearing of another prominent object would give the best fix?

A. 000°
B. 066°
C. 112°
D. 271°

02850. What is used to help prevent damage to barges, locks, and landings when you are locking or landing a tow?

A. dock cushions
B. springers
C. landing bars
D. bumpers (fenders)

02851. You determine your vessel's position by taking a range and bearing to a buoy. Your position will be plotted as a(n):

A. dead-reckoning position
B. estimated position
C. running fix
D. fix

02852. A daymark used as a regulatory or information mark will have the shape indicated by what item in illustration D045NG?

A. a
B. b
C. c
D. d

02858. While navigating in fog off a coastline of steep cliffs, you hear the echo of the ship's fog horn 2 1/2 seconds after the signal was sounded. What is the distance to the shore?

A. 225 yd.
B. 460 yd.
C. 750 yd.
D. 910 yd.

02859. The buoy indicated by the letter C in illustration D044NG is a:

A. nun
B. can
C. spar
D. pillar

02860. On the Mississippi and Ohio Rivers, there is a special type of fog known as steam fog. It is caused by:

A. warm air passing over much colder water
B. cold air passing over much warmer water
C. a rapid cooling of the ground on a clear night
D. rain coming out of a warm air mass aloft

02862. When slanted letters are used to spell the name of a charted object you know the:

A. object is only a hazard to vessels drawing in excess of 20'
B. position is approximate or doubtful
C. object is always visible
D. object may cover and uncover with the tide

02868. You are inbound in a channel marked by a range. The range line is 309° T. You are steering 306° T and have the range in sight as indicated in illustration D048NG. What action should you take?

A. Continue on the present heading until the range is in line then alter course to the right.
B. Immediately alter course to the right to bring range in line.
C. Continue on course if the range is closing otherwise alter course to the left.
D. Immediately alter course to 309° T if the range is closing.

02869. A pillar buoy is indicated by what letter in illustration D044NG?

A. a
B. b
C. c
D. d

02870. Steam fog is most likely to occur on the Mississippi and Ohio Rivers in:

A. spring, around late evening
B. spring, around early evening
C. fall, around early morning
D. fall, around midday

02872. When using a directional loop antenna to take an RDF bearing, the sense antenna is used to:

A. determine which station of a group of sequenced stations is transmitting
B. increase the sensitivity of the receiver
C. resolve the 180° ambiguity
D. eliminate the induced currents caused by signal re-radiation from the vessel's structure

02874. What daymark has no lateral significance?

A. red triangle
B. red and white octagon
C. green and white diamond
D. green square

02875. A harbor chart could have a scale of:

A. not more than 1:25,000
B. 1:35,000
C. 1:150,000
D. not less than 1:500,000

02877. All private aids to navigation in or along navigable waters of the United States are listed in the:

A. Sailing Directions
B. Light List
C. List of Private Aids
D. Aids to Navigation Manual

02880. While upbound through Memphis, the weather report on the TV news indicates that a cold front will cross western Kentucky and Tennessee the next morning. What weather should accompany this front?

A. light, southerly winds; high humidity and possibly fog
B. overcast with steady, light rain or drizzle
C. gusting winds shifting to the northwest with thunderstorms
D. scattered clouds with light to moderate southeasterly winds and possibly fog

02882. While upbound through Memphis, the weather report on TV news indicates that a warm front is stationary over the Kentucky - Missouri - Tennessee areas. What weather conditions should you expect?

A. strong, gusting winds from the NW with thundershowers
B. light winds from the northeast with clear skies
C. a "blue norther"
D. southerly winds with steady rain; fog or overcast

02886. On mid-ocean waters, the height of a wind-generated wave is not affected by the:

A. water depth exceeding 100 ft.
B. fetch
C. wind's velocity
D. duration of the wind

02890. While passing through Memphis, the weather report on the TV news indicates that a cold front is crossing western Kentucky and Tennessee. Tomorrow's weather will be dominated by a high pressure area. What weather should you expect tomorrow?

A. light, southerly winds; high humidity and possibly fog
B. moderate winds from the northwest, clear visibility and cooler temperatures

C. low overcast; mild temperatures with light, steady rain or drizzle

D. scattered clouds with light, southeasterly winds; high humidity and possibly fog

02891. Twenty-three meters equal:

A. 17.50 ft.
B. 75.46 ft.
C. 96.00 ft.
D. 104.99 ft.

02892. The Light List indicates that a day-board is a type NB. You should:

A. see a black triangle
B. look for another daymark forming a range
C. expect a daymark of no lateral significance
D. check to enter the correct channel at the junction daymark

02894. Fetch is the:

A. distance a wave travels between formation and decay
B. stretch of water over which a wave-forming wind blows
C. time in seconds required for two crests to pass a given point
D. measurement of a wave's steepness

02895. An orange and white buoy with a rectangle on it is a(n):

A. junction buoy
B. safe water buoy
C. informational buoy
D. all of the above

02896. You are navigating in pilotage waters using running fixes. The maximum time between fixes should be about:

A. 5 minutes
B. 30 minutes
C. 1 hour
D. 4 hours

02899. If you take a bearing of 043° and 169° to two prominent objects, what bearing of a third object will provide the best fix?

A. 356°
B. 073°
C. 192°
D. 309°

02900. Who should be consulted for changing conditions of controlling depths in major channels?

A. U. S. Coast Guard
B. Defense Mapping Agency

C. National Ocean Survey
D. U. S. Army Corps of Engineers

02902. The direction a vessel is pointed at any given time is the:

A. course
B. track
C. heading
D. course over the ground

02908. A daymark used to indicate the port side of the channel when approaching from seaward is indicated by what letter in illustration D045NG?

A. a
B. b
C. c
D. d

02909. A nun buoy is indicated by what letter in illustration D044NG?

A. a
B. b
C. c
D. d

02910. You are taking bearings on two known objects ashore. The BEST fix is obtained when the angle between the lines of position is:

A. 60°
B. 45°
C. 90°
D. 30°

02912. Error in RDF bearings may be induced by various conditions. Which of the following would probably NOT affect an RDF bearing?

A. the great circle radio wave path to the transmitter being parallel to a coastline.
B. a skywave contaminating the ground wave.
C. the ground wave crossing a land mass between the transmitter and your vessel.
D. sunspot effect on bearings taken around noon.

02914. A daymark with red and green bands and a red band on top will have the shape indicated by what letter in illustration D045NG?

A. a
B. b
C. c
D. d

02916. If you take a bearing of 191° and 313° to 2 prominent objects, what bearing of a third object will provide the best fix?

A. 022°
B. 131°
C. 211°
D. 249°

02918. What agency maintains federal aids to navigation?

A. Corps of Engineers
B. Coast Guard
C. National Ocean Service
D. Maritime Administration

02919. You are using a radiobeacon for an RDF bearing. It is part of a 6-station sequence and just ceased transmitting. How long must you wait before that particular beacon starts transmitting again?

A. 50 seconds
B. 1 minute
C. 5 minutes
D. 50 minutes

02920. Navigation charts of the Upper Mississippi River are published by:

A. National Ocean Survey
B. Lake Survey
C. Corps of Engineers, U. S. Army
D. U. S. Coast Guard

02922. The Light List indicates that a day-board is a type TR-SY. You should:

A. look for a TR-TY dayboard to form a range
B. leave it port when southbound on the Atlantic portions of the ICW
C. pass it close aboard on either side
D. expect a daymark with no lateral significance

02924. If you take a bearing of 264° to a lighthouse, what other bearing of another object would give the best fix?

A. 289°
B. 350°
C. 081°
D. 120°

02925. A single line of position combined with a dead-reckoning position results in a(n):

A. running fix
B. fix
C. assumed position
D. estimated position

02926. You are inbound in a channel marked by a range. The range line is 309° T. You are steering 306° T and have the range in sight as indicated in illustration D047NG. The range continues to open. What action should you take?

A. Come left until the range closes then steer to the left of 306° T.
B. Alter course to the right to 309° T or more to bring the range in line.
C. Continue on course but be prepared to come right if the range continues to open.
D. Alter course to the left to close the range, then alter course to 309° T.

02927. In illustration D051NG, the position labeled C was plotted because:

A. the vessel's course changed from due North to due East
B. running fixes are better estimates of true position than dead-reckoning positions
C. the vessel's speed changed
D. all of the above are correct

02928. You are in a buoyed channel at night and pass a lighted buoy with an irregular characteristic. You should report this to the:

A. Coast Guard
B. harbor master
C. Corps of Engineers
D. National Ocean Service

02931. The vertical distance from the tidal datum to the level of the water is the:

A. range of tide
B. height of tide
C. actual water depth
D. charted depth

02932. The channel under a bridge is marked with lights of the lateral system. The bridge piers adjacent to the channel shall be marked with:

A. occulting white lights
B. yellow lights
C. fixed white lights
D. flashing blue lights

02937. The depth of the water is indicated on a chart as 32 m. This is equal to:

A. 11.50 fathoms
B. 12.62 fathoms
C. 17.50 fathoms
D. 104.99 fathoms

02938. If you take a bearing of 176° to a lighthouse, what other bearing of another prominent object would give the best fix?

A. 000°
B. 021°
C. 189°
D. 272°

02939. The buoy indicated by the letter D in illustration D044NG is a:

A. nun
B. can
C. spar
D. pillar

02940. On the Corps of Engineer's Navigation Maps, the channel is:

A. midway between the banks
B. indicated by depths (in ft.)
C. indicated by a broken line
D. not indicated

02941. During Daylight Savings Time the meridian used for determining the time is located farther:

A. west in west longitude and east in east longitude
B. east in west longitude and west in east longitude
C. east
D. west

02942. Which statement about sequenced radiobeacon operation is TRUE?

A. Each station broadcasts for 6 minutes and is silent for 54 minutes.
B. The distance between stations must be at least 250 miles to prevent confusion of signals.
C. In a 6 station group, each station broadcasts for 1 minute and is silent for 5 minutes.
D. Only minor radiobeacons (20 miles or less range) are sequenced.

02944. The height of a wave is the vertical distance:

A. from the still water plane to the crest
B. from the still water plane to the trough
C. from crest to trough
D. between water levels at 1-quarter of the wave's length

02945. A position that is obtained by applying estimated current and wind to your vessel's course and speed is a(n):

A. estimated position
B. dead reckoning position
C. fix
D. none of the above

02946. You are inbound in a channel marked by a range. The range line is 309° T. You are steering 306° T and have the range in sight as indicated in illustration DO48NG. The range is closing. What action should you take?

A. Alter course to the right to 309° T or move to close the range then steer 309° T.
B. Continue on 306° T until the range closes then change course to 309° T.
C. Steer 306° T until on the range then steer to the left of 306° T to stay on the range.
D. Come left until the range closes, then steer to the right of 309° T.

02947. A position obtained by crossing lines of position taken at different times and advanced to a common time is a(n):

A. fix
B. dead-reckoning position
C. running fix
D. estimated position

02948. What is used to eliminate the 180° ambiguity when taking an RDF bearing with a rotating loop antenna?

A. the null
B. sense antenna
C. calibration cam
D. signal strength meter

02950. On an Army Corps of Engineers navigation map, each mile A. h. P. Is marked by a:

A. dashed red line
B. number showing mileage
C. navigation light
D. red circle

02952. The channel under a bridge is marked with lights of the lateral system. The centerline of the channel shall be marked on the bridge by:

A. an occulting white light
B. a yellow light
C. 3 fixed white lights
D. a flashing blue light

02954. You are inbound in a channel marked by a range. The range line is 309° T. You are steering 306° T and have the range in sight as indicated in illustration D047NG. What action should you take?

A. Continue on the present heading until the range is in line then alter course to the left.
B. Immediately alter course to the right to bring the range in line.
C. Continue on course if the range is closing, otherwise alter course to the left.
D. Immediately alter course to 309° T.

02960. Which of the following is NOT found in the Mississippi River System Light List?

A. distance that a lighted aid to navigation can be seen at night
B. distance between major points on the Mississippi River
C. a color plate showing the details of the aids to navigation used on the Mississippi River
D. times of Coast Guard broadcasts concerning river stages

02961. Which of the following positions includes the effects of wind and current?

A. dead reckoning positions
B. estimated positions
C. leeway position
D. set position

02962. While navigating in fog off a coastline of steep cliffs, you hear the echo of the ship's fog horn 4 1/2 seconds after the signal was sounded. What is the distance to the shore?

A. 405 yd.
B. 628 yd.
C. 730 yd.
D. 825 yd.

02965. Which symbol represents a 10-fathom curve?

A.
B.... :..
C.: : :
D.........

02966. If you take a bearing of 264° to a lighthouse, what other bearing of another prominent object would give the best fix?

A. 291°
B. 059°
C. 182°
D. 239°

02969. A red triangular daymark is used to mark:

A. the centerline of a navigable channel
B. the starboard side (when entering from sea) of a waterway
C. a prominent object of navigational interest that has no lateral significance
D. area of a channel where passing another vessel is permitted

02970. The Light List shows a lighted aid to navigation on the left bank. This means that the light can be seen on the left side of a vessel:

A. ascending the river
B. descending the river
C. crossing the river
D. proceeding from seaward

02972. You are in a channel inbound from sea. A daymark used to mark a channel junction when the preferred channel is to starboard will have the shape indicated by what letter in illustration D045NG?

A. a
B. b
C. c
D. d

02974. What daymark shape is used in the lateral system?

A. semicircle
B. triangle
C. pentagon
D. diamond

02976. A large navigational buoy (LNB) is painted:

A. red
B. yellow
C. with red and white vertical stripes
D. with a distinct color and pattern unique to each buoy

02977. Which symbol represents a 2-fathom curve?

A.— — —
B... :. :.
C.: : :
D........

02979. If you take a bearing of 356° to a lighthouse, what other bearing of another prominent object would give the best fix?

A. 013°
B. 082°
C. 176°
D. 201°

02980. What volume of the Coast Guard Light List is used for the Mississippi River system?

A. I
B. II
C. IV
D. V

02981. The radio navigational warning system that provides information on navigational and meteorological hazards on coastal waters near the broadcasting station is known as:

A. NAVTEX
B. HYDROLANT/HYDROPAC
C. NAVAREA
D. SAFESEA

02982. If you take a bearing of 142° and 259° to two prominent objects, what bearing of a third object will provide the best fix?

A. 019°
B. 084°
C. 166°
D. 281°

02984. What two shapes indicated in illustration D045NG are used to indicate a preferred channel?

A. A and B
B. B and C
C. C and D
D. A and D

02986. Some places maintain a zone time of -13. What are the time and date at Greenwich if the zone time and date are 2152, 10 January?

A. 1052, 9 January
B. 0852, 10 January
C. 1052, 10 January
D. 1052, 11 January

02988. The buoy indicated by the letter A in illustration D044NG is a:

A. nun
B. can
C. spar
D. pillar

02990. In which of the following sources could you find the vertical clearance of a bridge on the Ohio River?

A. Notice to Mariners
B. Light List of the Mississippi River System
C. Great Lakes Pilot
D. Coast Pilot of the Gulf of Mexico

02992. The radar echo from an overhead power line will usually appear on the PPI scope as:

A. a contact on a collision course
B. a weak echo showing the length of the power line
C. a contact located at the low point of sag
D. overhead power lines usually do not provide enough signal return to provide an echo

02994. If you take a bearing of 313° and 076° of two prominent objects, what bearing of a third object will provide the best fix?

A. 014°
B. 133°
C. 255°
D. 339°

02998. While navigating in fog off a coastline of steep cliffs, you hear the echo of the ship's fog horn 3 1/2 seconds after the signal was sounded. What is the distance to the shore?

A. 640 yd.
B. 480 yd.
C. 315 yd.
D. 143 yd.

02999. When entering a channel from seaward, the numbers on buoys:

A. are the same as the Light List number
B. are marked in 6 inch figures with retroreflective material
C. increase with the even numbers to starboard
D. decrease with the odd numbers to starboard

03000. All aids to navigation listed in the Mississippi River System Light List are shown as miles from a reference point and on the:

A. east or west bank
B. left or right descending bank
C. port or starboard side of the vessel
D. left or right ascending bank

03002. The diurnal variation of pressure is most noticeable:

A. above the polar circles
B. in a low pressure area
C. during periods of low temperatures
D. in the doldrums

03003. The height of tide is the:

A. difference between the depth of the water and the area's tidal datum
B. depth of water at a specific time due to tidal effect
C. difference between the depth of the water and the high water tidal level
D. difference between the depth of the water at high tide and the depth of the water at low tide

03004. While navigating in fog off a coastline of steep cliffs, you hear the echo of the ship's fog horn 4 seconds after the signal was sounded. What is the distance to the shore?

A. 209 yd.
B. 363 yd.
C. 480 yd.
D. 730 yd.

03005. The agonic line on an isomagnetic chart indicates the:

A. magnetic Equator
B. magnetic longitude reference line

C. points where there is no variation
D. points where there is no annual change in variation

03006. You are outbound in a channel marked by a range astern. The range line is 309° T. You are steering 127° T and have the range in sight as indicated in illustration D047NG. What action should you take?

A. Come right to 129° T.
B. Continue on course until the range comes in line then alter course to 129° T.
C. Continue on course until the range comes in line then alter course to 125° T.
D. Come right to close the range then when on the range steer 129° T.

03008. If you take a bearing of 086° to a lighthouse, what other bearing of another prominent object would give the best fix?

A. 291°
B. 261°
C. 242°
D. 196°

03009. "Proceeding from seaward" for the purpose of the direction of buoying offshore, lateral system buoys would be proceeding:

A. northerly on the Atlantic Coast
B. easterly on the Gulf Coast
C. northerly on the Pacific Coast
D. none of the above

03010. A white buoy with a blue band is:

A. an isolated danger mark
B. a hydrographic data collection buoy
C. a mooring buoy
D. marking a restricted area

03011. The survey information upon which a chart is based is found:

A. at the top center of the next line
B. near the chart title
C. at the lower left corner
D. at any convenient location

03012. The drawspan of a floating drawbridge may be marked with:

A. a yellow light showing Morse (B)
B. a yellow and white diamond
C. flashing blue lights
D. 3 red lights on each side of the draw

03013. An orange and white buoy with a rectangle on it displays:

A. directions
B. dangers
C. exclusion areas
D. all of the above

03016. The control that shortens all echoes on the display and reduces clutter caused by rain or snow is the:

A. sensitivity time control (sea clutter control)
B. receiver gain control
C. brilliance control
D. fast time constant (differentiator)

03018. If you take a bearing of 356° to a lighthouse, what other bearing of another prominent object would give the best fix?

A. 013°
B. 178°
C. 256°
D. 342°

03019. Where would you find information about the time of high tide at a specific location on a particular day of the year?

A. Tide Tables
B. Tidal Current Tables
C. Coast Pilot
D. Nautical Almanac

03020. A mooring buoy, if lighted, must show what color light?

A. yellow
B. white
C. blue
D. any color except red or green

03021. What information is found in the chart title?

A. chart number
B. chart sounding datum
C. revision and edition date
D. variation information

03022. A daymark with red and green bands and a green band on top will have the shape indicated by what letter in illustration D045NG?

A. a
B. b
C. c
D. d

03023. You have steadied up on a range dead ahead in line with your keel. After a few minutes the range, still dead ahead, appears as shown in illustration D047NG. What action do you take?

A. alter heading to the left
B. alter heading to the right
C. increase speed
D. maintain heading, keeping the range dead ahead

03025. You determine your vessel's position by taking a range and bearing to a buoy. Your position will be plotted as a(n):

A. estimated position
B. dead-reckoning position
C. fix
D. running fix

03026. A compass card without north-seeking capability that is used for relative bearings is a(n):

A. bearing circle
B. pelorus
C. bearing bar
D. alidade

03028. The channel under a bridge is marked with aids from the lateral system. The centerline of the channel is marked on the bridge with:

A. a yellow triangle
B. 3 white lights
C. a black and white diamond
D. a red and white octagon

03030. Isogonic lines are lines on a chart indicating:

A. points of equal variation
B. points of zero variation
C. the magnetic latitude
D. magnetic dip

03031. Which symbol in illustration D015NG would indicate a large automated navigational buoy, such as those that have replaced some lightships?

A. a
B. b
C. c
D. d

03032. The direction in which a vessel is steered is the course. The path actually followed is the:

A. route
B. track
C. heading
D. course over the ground

03033. A navigator fixing a vessel's position by radar:

A. can use radar information from one object to fix the position
B. should never use radar bearings
C. should only use radar bearings when the range exceeds the distance to the horizon
D. must use information from targets forward of the beam

03034. You are outbound in a channel marked by a range astern. The range line is 309° T. You are steering 127° T and have the range in sight as indicated in illustration D048NG. Assuming there is no set and drift, what action should you take?

A. Come right to 131° T and check to see if the range closes.
B. Continue on course until the range comes in line then alter course to 129° T.
C. Continue on course until the range comes in line then alter to 125° T.
D. Come left to close the range then when on the range steer 127° T.

03035. A major advantage of the NAVTEX system when compared to other systems is that:

A. the information can be received on an ordinary FM radio
B. warnings are printed out for reading when convenient
C. broadcasts are at scheduled times
D. a low frequency band is used for long distance transmission

03036. What daymark has no lateral significance?

A. square; top half green and bottom half red
B. black and white diamond
C. red triangle
D. green square

03038. In low latitudes, the low(s) of the diurnal variation of pressure occur(s) at:

A. noon
B. noon and midnight
C. 1000 and 2200
D. 0400 and 1600

03039. As you enter a U. S. channel from seaward the numbers on the buoys:

A. increase with the can buoys being even numbered
B. increase with the can buoys being odd numbered
C. decrease with the can buoys being even numbered
D. increase in channels going to the N or W, and decrease in channels going S or E

03040. What type of instrument would be used to help predict the approach of a low pressure system?

A. anemometer
B. fathometer
C. barometer
D. thermometer

03042. How long would a steady wind need to blow in order to create a wind driven current?

A. 2 hours
B. 6 hours
C. 12 hours
D. 18 hours

03052. The Sailing Directions contain information on:

A. required navigation lights
B. lifesaving equipment standards
C. casualty reporting procedures
D. currents in various locations

03053. The vertical distance from the tidal datum to the level of the water is the:

A. height of tide
B. range of tide
C. actual water depth
D. charted depth

03054. In illustration D051NG, the position labeled C was plotted because:

A. running fixes are better estimates of true position than dead-reckoning positions are
B. the vessel's course changed from due North to due East
C. the vessel's speed changed
D. all of the above are correct

03055. A single line of position combined with a dead-reckoning position results in a(n):

A. running fix
B. fix
C. estimated position
D. assumed position

03056. A position obtained by applying ONLY your vessel's course and speed to a known position is a:

A. fix
B. dead-reckoning position
C. running fix
D. probable position

03060. What information is NOT found in the chart title?

A. survey information
B. scale
C. date of first edition
D. projection

03061. In a river subject to tidal currents, the best time to dock a ship without the assistance of tugs is:

A. at stand
B. at high water
C. when there is a following current
D. at slack water

00000 B	00084 A	00171 A	00267 B	00371 C	00481 A	00588 C	00687 B
00001 B	00086 B	00172 A	00268 D	00376 D	00484 A	00591 C	00688 A
00002 D	00087 A	00173 B	00269 A	00378 B	00486 D	00593 B	00690 C
00003 C	00088 C	00176 C	00270 C	00380 B	00489 A	00594 B	00691 A
00006 B	00090 B	00177 B	00271 D	00381 B	00490 B	00596 D	00693 B
00007 C	00091 D	00178 A	00272 B	00386 B	00491 D	00599 B	00696 D
00008 C	00092 C	00179 C	00273 A	00388 D	00493 C	00600 C	00697 D
00009 A	00093 A	00180 A	00275 A	00389 A	00494 D	00601 A	00699 B
00010 A	00094 A	00181 B	00276 B	00390 A	00496 D	00602 B	00701 C
00011 B	00096 A	00182 C	00277 B	00391 C	00498 C	00606 A	00702 A
00012 D	00097 B	00183 C	00278 D	00392 B	00499 D	00609 A	00703 D
00013 B	00098 B	00186 C	00279 A	00394 C	00501 D	00610 C	00706 C
00014 A	00100 B	00187 D	00280 B	00396 C	00503 D	00611 C	00707 D
00015 C	00101 C	00191 C	00281 B	00398 B	00504 A	00613 B	00709 B
00016 C	00103 B	00192 C	00282 D	00399 D	00508 A	00616 A	00710 B
00017 A	00104 B	00193 B	00283 A	00401 A	00509 D	00618 D	00711 A
00018 B	00106 D	00196 C	00286 D	00402 D	00510 A	00619 B	00712 D
00019 D	00107 D	00197 A	00289 A	00404 B	00511 D	00620 C	00713 C
00020 A	00108 C	00198 B	00290 D	00406 D	00513 B	00621 B	00716 C
00021 B	00110 C	00201 B	00291 A	00408 C	00514 D	00626 D	00717 A
00022 A	00111 A	00202 D	00292 C	00410 B	00516 D	00628 C	00720 A
00023 A	00113 C	00203 B	00293 C	00411 C	00518 D	00629 D	00721 B
00025 A	00114 B	00206 C	00296 A	00412 A	00519 B	00630 A	00722 C
00026 D	00116 C	00207 D	00299 B	00414 D	00520 A	00631 C	00726 D
00027 A	00117 D	00211 D	00300 C	00416 B	00523 B	00633 A	00727 C
00028 C	00118 C	00212 D	00301 D	00418 A	00524 A	00635 B	00729 B
00029 C	00120 A	00213 C	00302 A	00419 B	00526 B	00636 B	00730 C
00031 A	00121 D	00216 B	00303 B	00420 A	00528 B	00638 C	00731 C
00032 B	00122 A	00217 B	00306 A	00421 B	00529 B	00639 A	00732 B
00033 B	00123 A	00218 D	00308 B	00422 B	00530 C	00640 A	00733 D
00034 D	00124 B	00220 D	00309 C	00423 B	00531 C	00641 A	00734 B
00037 B	00126 C	00221 B	00311 B	00424 D	00532 B	00642 C	00735 B
00038 D	00127 C	00222 D	00312 B	00426 C	00533 A	00643 C	00736 C
00041 B	00128 A	00223 B	00313 C	00428 B	00534 C	00646 D	00737 C
00042 C	00130 B	00226 D	00316 A	00430 D	00536 A	00649 C	00740 A
00043 C	00131 D	00227 D	00319 B	00431 D	00538 A	00650 C	00741 D
00044 A	00133 B	00228 D	00321 B	00434 B	00539 A	00651 B	00742 C
00047 C	00134 B	00229 A	00322 C	00436 C	00540 D	00652 A	00743 C
00048 D	00136 C	00230 A	00323 B	00439 A	00541 C	00653 B	00744 D
00050 B	00137 D	00231 B	00326 A	00440 D	00542 B	00655 A	00745 B
00051 D	00138 B	00232 D	00327 B	00441 B	00543 C	00656 A	00746 C
00052 B	00140 C	00233 D	00328 C	00444 B	00544 B	00657 B	00747 B
00053 B	00141 C	00234 D	00329 D	00446 B	00546 D	00658 C	00748 B
00054 B	00142 B	00236 C	00331 D	00448 C	00548 C	00659 D	00749 B
00057 B	00144 B	00237 A	00332 C	00449 A	00549 D	00660 D	00750 B
00058 A	00147 C	00239 D	00333 B	00450 C	00550 A	00661 D	00751 D
00061 A	00148 B	00240 C	00336 D	00451 A	00551 C	00663 A	00752 D
00062 B	00149 B	00241 B	00337 B	00454 A	00554 C	00665 C	00754 D
00063 D	00150 B	00242 A	00338 C	00456 D	00556 A	00666 B	00756 B
00064 B	00151 B	00243 A	00339 C	00458 A	00558 A	00667 B	00757 A
00066 A	00152 B	00244 D	00340 D	00459 D	00561 B	00668 D	00758 B
00067 A	00153 C	00246 C	00341 C	00460 D	00564 D	00669 B	00759 B
00068 D	00154 D	00247 C	00345 C	00461 A	00566 D	00671 C	00760 C
00070 C	00155 A	00251 B	00346 C	00463 D	00568 A	00672 C	00761 D
00071 A	00156 A	00252 B	00347 A	00464 C	00569 B	00673 D	00762 D
00072 B	00157 A	00253 D	00349 C	00466 C	00570 B	00675 B	00763 D
00073 C	00158 C	00254 A	00350 C	00468 B	00571 C	00676 C	00764 D
00074 D	00160 C	00256 A	00351 B	00469 C	00573 B	00677 A	00766 D
00076 B	00161 D	00257 D	00356 D	00470 C	00574 B	00679 B	00767 B
00077 B	00162 C	00259 C	00359 D	00471 A	00576 D	00680 D	00770 A
00078 B	00163 D	00260 B	00360 B	00474 B	00579 C	00681 D	00771 A
00080 C	00166 D	00261 D	00361 B	00476 A	00581 D	00682 B	00772 B
00081 C	00167 C	00262 D	00366 B	00478 D	00583 B	00683 C	00773 A
00082 D	00168 C	00263 B	00369 D	00479 A	00584 A	00685 D	00774 C
00083 B	00170 A	00266 A	00370 D	00480 B	00586 B	00686 B	00776 C

00777 A	00879 A	00983 D	01111 C	01205 A	01310 B	01421 B	01545 C
00778 D	00880 B	00984 B	01114 D	01206 B	01311 C	01422 D	01546 B
00780 C	00882 B	00986 A	01116 C	01208 A	01312 A	01426 A	01547 A
00781 C	00883 C	00989 D	01117 C	01210 C	01313 B	01428 D	01548 A
00782 A	00884 D	00994 B	01121 D	01211 D	01314 B	01430 B	01549 D
00783 B	00886 A	00996 B	01122 B	01212 C	01315 C	01431 C	01550 A
00784 C	00888 A	00997 B	01124 B	01213 A	01316 D	01434 C	01553 B
00786 C	00889 B	00998 D	01125 B	01215 C	01319 A	01436 D	01555 D
00789 A	00890 C	01000 A	01126 A	01216 A	01321 D	01438 C	01556 C
00790 A	00892 A	01002 A	01127 A	01220 D	01323 B	01439 D	01557 B
00791 C	00893 B	01004 C	01129 C	01221 B	01324 A	01440 C	01560 A
00792 C	00894 A	01006 B	01131 B	01222 D	01325 C	01444 C	01561 D
00793 D	00896 C	01007 B	01132 B	01223 B	01326 C	01445 B	01562 B
00796 B	00900 A	01008 C	01134 D	01224 D	01330 C	01446 B	01563 D
00798 A	00902 C	01012 A	01136 A	01226 B	01331 A	01448 D	01564 A
00799 C	00903 B	01014 B	01137 A	01231 C	01333 A	01449 C	01565 B
00801 A	00904 A	01016 B	01140 B	01232 A	01334 D	01450 C	01566 A
00802 B	00906 A	01018 A	01141 C	01233 C	01336 A	01456 D	01567 C
00803 C	00909 C	01020 C	01142 C	01234 B	01338 B	01459 C	01568 D
00804 D	00910 C	01024 D	01144 B	01236 B	01340 B	01461 A	01569 D
00806 B	00911 A	01025 A	01146 D	01239 A	01341 B	01462 D	01573 C
00808 C	00912 B	01026 B	01147 C	01241 A	01342 B	01464 D	01575 C
00809 B	00913 D	01028 D	01148 D	01242 A	01343 D	01466 D	01576 A
00812 D	00914 C	01029 D	01149 A	01243 D	01344 A	01470 D	01580 D
00813 C	00916 A	01034 A	01151 D	01244 B	01345 C	01471 A	01581 B
00814 A	00919 B	01036 C	01154 C	01246 D	01346 B	01472 A	01586 C
00816 B	00920 B	01039 D	01155 B	01249 D	01349 C	01474 A	01592 D
00818 D	00921 A	01040 C	01156 A	01250 A	01350 B	01475 A	01594 C
00820 B	00922 C	01045 B	01157 D	01251 C	01351 B	01476 C	01595 D
00822 C	00923 C	01046 C	01158 C	01252 A	01353 A	01478 B	01596 A
00823 D	00924 C	01048 C	01159 D	01253 A	01356 B	01479 B	01597 B
00824 B	00926 B	01049 B	01160 A	01256 A	01360 B	01480 D	01599 B
00826 A	00929 C	01050 C	01161 C	01261 B	01361 B	01482 B	01602 C
00828 A	00930 A	01051 D	01162 C	01262 D	01362 C	01486 A	01603 B
00829 C	00931 C	01056 B	01164 B	01263 C	01363 B	01489 B	01604 D
00830 C	00932 B	01059 B	01165 B	01265 A	01364 D	01490 C	01605 A
00832 B	00933 A	01060 C	01166 D	01266 C	01366 A	01493 A	01606 B
00833 D	00934 D	01061 B	01167 B	01268 D	01370 D	01494 C	01608 B
00834 A	00935 B	01064 D	01168 D	01269 C	01374 A	01496 A	01610 A
00836 D	00936 C	01065 C	01169 A	01270 C	01376 D	01497 B	01611 D
00838 D	00939 D	01066 C	01170 B	01271 D	01379 B	01498 B	01612 C
00840 A	00940 A	01069 A	01171 A	01272 B	01380 A	01501 B	01613 B
00842 B	00942 D	01070 B	01172 C	01273 B	01381 B	01502 A	01615 C
00843 B	00944 B	01071 A	01174 D	01274 B	01382 C	01503 B	01616 D
00844 D	00946 D	01073 C	01175 B	01275 C	01384 B	01505 A	01617 A
00846 C	00949 B	01074 D	01176 C	01276 D	01385 A	01506 B	01618 A
00848 C	00950 A	01075 A	01178 B	01278 C	01386 D	01507 D	01622 A
00849 B	00952 C	01076 A	01179 A	01280 B	01389 C	01508 B	01631 B
00850 C	00953 C	01078 B	01181 D	01281 C	01390 D	01509 C	01645 A
00852 A	00954 D	01084 B	01182 D	01282 C	01391 D	01511 C	01646 C
00853 A	00956 B	01086 A	01184 A	01283 B	01392 A	01514 B	01670 C
00854 A	00960 B	01087 D	01185 D	01284 A	01395 A	01518 C	01671 A
00855 C	00962 D	01088 B	01186 B	01285 D	01396 A	01520 A	01672 B
00856 B	00964 A	01089 A	01190 B	01286 D	01398 A	01523 B	01675 B
00858 A	00966 B	01090 A	01191 C	01290 C	01400 B	01525 D	01750 D
00860 A	00972 B	01091 D	01192 B	01291 D	01401 B	01527 B	01754 C
00862 A	00973 C	01094 B	01194 A	01292 A	01402 D	01528 B	01760 D
00863 A	00974 A	01096 D	01195 C	01293 C	01406 D	01530 B	01761 C
00864 A	00976 A	01097 A	01196 D	01294 C	01408 D	01536 A	01766 B
00866 A	00977 A	01104 D	01198 C	01295 C	01409 C	01538 D	01768 C
00869 A	00978 C	01105 C	01199 C	01296 D	01410 B	01539 C	01770 B
00872 A	00979 A	01106 B	01201 A	01301 D	01411 C	01540 C	01771 C
00873 C	00980 B	01107 D	01202 B	01302 A	01412 D	01542 C	01774 C
00874 B	00981 A	01108 B	01203 D	01303 C	01416 B	01543 A	01778 A
00876 A	00982 A	01110 B	01204 A	01306 D	01419 A	01544 A	01779 B

01782 C	02028 C	02130 D	02317 A	02527 B	02738 C	02860 B	02981 A
01784 C	02030 B	02131 A	02320 C	02528 D	02739 D	02862 D	02982 A
01786 C	02032 D	02132 C	02328 B	02529 B	02740 C	02868 B	02984 D
01789 A	02040 A	02133 C	02330 A	02530 D	02741 A	02869 C	02986 B
01790 A	02041 A	02135 A	02332 C	02536 C	02742 B	02870 C	02988 B
01800 B	02043 D	02136 B	02335 B	02538 C	02744 D	02872 C	02990 B
01804 D	02044 B	02137 C	02340 C	02539 C	02746 D	02874 C	02992 A
01806 A	02048 A	02138 D	02341 C	02540 C	02748 D	02875 B	02994 A
01808 A	02050 C	02139 B	02348 B	02544 B	02750 B	02877 B	02998 A
01809 D	02052 A	02140 D	02349 A	02546 A	02752 C	02880 C	02999 C
01810 C	02054 D	02141 C	02350 A	02548 A	02760 B	02882 D	03000 B
01816 D	02056 B	02142 B	02351 D	02549 D	02762 A	02886 A	03002 D
01818 B	02058 C	02143 A	02353 A	02583 D	02764 D	02890 B	03003 A
01820 A	02059 A	02145 D	02360 D	02586 B	02766 C	02891 B	03004 D
01822 A	02060 C	02146 C	02361 D	02588 A	02768 C	02892 C	03005 C
01824 C	02061 B	02147 B	02363 C	02589 D	02769 D	02894 B	03006 D
01826 B	02062 A	02150 C	02370 A	02592 A	02770 C	02895 A	03008 D
01829 D	02066 C	02152 A	02373 D	02594 C	02772 A	02896 B	03009 C
01830 D	02067 A	02160 A	02378 B	02596 A	02777 D	02899 D	03010 C
01838 A	02068 A	02164 B	02379 B	02597 C	02778 D	02900 D	03011 B
01840 C	02069 B	02165 A	02380 D	02598 B	02779 C	02902 C	03012 A
01844 D	02070 D	02166 B	02381 D	02600 C	02780 D	02908 A	03013 A
01848 D	02072 A	02167 C	02384 B	02625 C	02782 A	02909 D	03016 D
01850 B	02073 D	02169 A	02389 D	02626 C	02784 C	02910 C	03018 C
01858 B	02074 A	02170 C	02390 A	02628 B	02788 D	02912 D	03019 A
01859 C	02075 C	02171 D	02392 D	02629 D	02789 D	02914 D	03020 B
01860 C	02078 D	02172 C	02396 A	02632 A	02790 B	02916 D	03021 B
01862 C	02079 D	02175 B	02400 D	02634 A	02792 C	02918 B	03022 A
01868 A	02080 B	02176 C	02409 D	02636 D	02794 D	02919 C	03023 A
01869 D	02081 D	02177 D	02416 B	02638 D	02798 A	02920 C	03025 A
01870 B	02082 A	02180 C	02417 A	02639 A	02799 B	02922 B	03026 B
01880 A	02083 B	02181 A	02418 B	02646 A	02800 B	02924 B	03028 D
01883 B	02084 A	02182 B	02419 C	02651 A	02801 B	02925 D	03030 A
01884 D	02085 A	02183 C	02420 D	02664 C	02805 D	02926 A	03031 B
01885 A	02086 A	02187 D	02424 A	02666 B	02809 A	02927 B	03032 D
01886 C	02087 C	02190 C	02426 D	02668 B	02810 A	02928 A	03033 A
01887 D	02088 D	02191 D	02428 A	02669 A	02814 C	02931 B	03034 B
01888 B	02089 B	02200 A	02430 B	02672 A	02816 D	02932 B	03035 B
01890 C	02090 A	02210 A	02435 D	02673 C	02818 D	02937 C	03036 B
01892 D	02091 D	02211 B	02436 D	02674 D	02819 A	02938 D	03038 D
01898 D	02092 D	02212 D	02437 C	02675 B	02820 D	02939 A	03039 B
01899 D	02093 C	02215 D	02438 A	02676 D	02821 C	02940 C	03040 C
01902 C	02097 B	02220 D	02440 C	02678 D	02822 A	02941 C	03042 C
01907 C	02099 B	02230 D	02449 C	02679 A	02826 B	02942 C	03052 D
01923 B	02100 C	02236 D	02450 A	02695 C	02828 B	02944 C	03053 A
01936 C	02101 A	02239 A	02454 B	02703 C	02829 B	02945 A	03054 A
01946 B	02102 B	02240 D	02456 C	02704 D	02830 C	02946 A	03055 C
01951 A	02103 D	02243 C	02458 B	02705 A	02831 C	02947 C	03056 B
01961 D	02104 D	02246 A	02459 D	02706 C	02832 A	02948 B	03060 C
01984 D	02105 D	02250 C	02460 D	02707 A	02834 B	02950 D	03061 D
01986 B	02110 B	02251 C	02466 C	02708 D	02838 B	02952 A	
01987 A	02111 C	02252 D	02468 B	02709 D	02839 C	02954 C	
01988 A	02112 B	02254 A	02470 B	02712 B	02840 C	02960 A	
01992 B	02113 A	02255 D	02480 D	02714 B	02841 D	02961 B	
01996 B	02114 D	02260 B	02483 A	02716 D	02842 B	02962 D	
02000 B	02115 A	02261 D	02488 B	02718 D	02843 C	02965 C	
02001 B	02116 B	02264 B	02489 A	02719 C	02844 C	02966 C	
02002 C	02120 C	02269 B	02496 A	02720 C	02846 D	02969 B	
02004 D	02121 C	02270 B	02498 A	02721 A	02848 B	02970 B	
02006 C	02122 A	02271 B	02499 A	02722 B	02849 A	02972 A	
02007 B	02125 C	02277 A	02506 A	02725 D	02850 D	02974 B	
02010 A	02126 C	02280 D	02508 B	02726 B	02851 B	02976 A	
02014 B	02127 D	02286 D	02509 C	02729 C	02852 B	02977 D	
02020 C	02128 A	02292 D	02513 D	02730 A	02858 B	02979 B	
02021 D	02129 B	02310 D	02525 D	02737 B	02859 D	02980 D	

SAFETY

FIRST AID

WOUNDS

Types

- *Punctures* are holes produced by pointed objects such as bullets, nails, or sharp sticks. Surface bleeding may be minor, but hidden, internal bleeding may occur if the puncture is deep. Infection is a major concern since the wound is not easily cleaned.

- *Incisions* are cuts such as would be produced by a knife or broken glass. Arteries and veins may be severed, so bleeding can be extensive. Extensive incisions require stitches to close the wound.

- *Abrasions* are a wearing away of the skin, as by sandpaper. Bleeding is usually a minor oozing, but the wound should be thoroughly cleaned because the skin's primary defensive layer has been worn away.

- *Lacerations* are irregular breaks in the skin—as opposed to incisions. Tissue damage is often greater than with incisions. Lacerations should be thoroughly cleansed and usually require stitches.

- *Avulsions* are a tearing away of the flesh, such as a torn ear or severed limb. Bleeding is extensive when veins and arteries are severed as well.

Stopping Bleeding

- *Direct pressure* is the preferred blood-stopping method for a nonprofessional. The object is to slow blood flow enough for clotting to take place by compressing the veins and arteries against muscle or bone. The wound should be covered with a sterile bandage or clean cloth if possible, while the pressure is being applied. Even if the bandage becomes soaked, do not remove the pressure until bleeding stops.

- *Elevation* of the wounded part reduces the blood pressure and rate of bleeding. It is not a substitute for direct pressure.

- *Arterial pressure* is pressure applied directly to an artery where it passes over a bone. The *brachial pressure point* is inside the upper arm, midway between shoulder and elbow, and between the biceps and triceps muscles. The *femoral pressure point* is inside the thigh at the middle of the crease of the groin. Since pressure at these points cuts off blood flow to the entire arm or leg, it should be used only when direct pressure and elevation prove insufficient.

- *Tourniquets* are bands of cloth tightened around a limb just above a wound to stop all blood flow. Releasing pressure on a tourniquet resumes blood flow and may actually increase the chances of shock and death. They are, thus, last resort measures where the decision is to risk losing the limb to save the life.

Removing Foreign Objects

- *Splinters* are normally more irritants than dangers. Remove shallow splinters with sterilized—held over an open flame or boiled—tweezers or needles. Deep splinters should be removed only by a doctor.

- *Fish hooks* may be simply backed out if the barb has not engaged. If the barb is deep, however, the least damage is usually caused by pushing it out the other side, clipping it off, then backing the hook out. A tetanus shot should be given for the latter case.

- *Large objects* that are deeply embedded—even knives— should not be removed! While in place they likely minimize internal bleeding. Immobilize the object and rush the victim to the hospital.

Preventing Infection

- *Cleansing* the wound is the most important step in preventing infection. Antibacterial agents may be used but are not required. Simply wash your hands and the skin area around the wound with soap and water. Flush the wound—opening it wide—with running tap water. Blot the wound dry with sterile gauze and cover with a sterile bandage.

- *Symptoms* of an infected wound include: redness (particularly if the redness spreads), swelling of the area, tenderness or pain, pus draining from the wound and elevated temperature (fever).

- *Infected wounds* require the attention of a doctor. Until then, immobilize and elevate the wound and apply dry or wet heat to the area, 30 minutes on and 30 minutes off.

BONES AND JOINTS

Fractures

- *Simple fractures* are those where the bone is not exposed.

- *Compound fractures* are those where the fracture is compounded by the bone being exposed. The wound is usually caused by the jagged edge of the broken bone. Compound fractures are more serious due to the likelihood of infection.

- *Symptoms* of a fracture include: an audible snap, difficulty moving the member, pain or tenderness at the fracture location, asymmetry (difference in length or shape between like members), swelling and discoloration and an obvious crookedness.

- *First aid* consists of immobilizing the fractured member to prevent further damage before being attended by a doctor. If the wait will be long, apply a splint.

Joints

- *Sprains* are damage to tendons, ligaments and blood vessels due to overextension of a joint. Severe sprains should be x-rayed to see if a fracture is also involved. First aid consists of immobilization, elevation and the application of ice packs over several days.

- *Strains* are damage to muscles due to overexertion. The muscles are stretched and may be partially torn. First aid consists of rest and application of moist heat.

- *Dislocation* is the separation of a joint. Reduction—restoring the bones to their proper places—should not be attempted except by a doctor or other trained person, due to the possibility of further damage to the joint. First aid until the doctor attends is immobilization.

SHOCK

Definition and Causes

Traumatic shock, as opposed to electrical or insulin shock, is a depression of the body's vital functions (principally blood flow and respiration) as a result of injury. If untreated, it often leads to death even when the injury itself is not life-threatening. The causes are many, including: loss of blood, loss of body fluids other than blood, chemical poisoning, anaphylaxis (allergic reaction) and respiratory difficulty.

Symptoms

- *Early* signs of traumatic shock include: pale, cool, and possibly clammy skin, dizziness, faint rapid pulse and abnormal breathing.

- *Late (advanced)* signs include apathy, mottled skin and, especially, wide dilation of the pupils of the eye.

First Aid

- *Improve circulation.* Blood pressure and flow to the head are most important and are improved by laying the victim flat on the ground and raising the feet. A single exception to the feet-up rule is the case of a victim with a head injury, where increased blood pressure to the brain may prove dangerous.

- *Aid respiration.* If the victim is having difficulty breathing, make sure the airway is clear, then place him on his back with the chest and head slightly elevated.

- *Regulate temperature.* Make sure the victim is neither too cold nor too hot.

- *Administer fluids.* If and only if: 1) medical assistance will be delayed for more than an hour; 2) the victim is fully conscious and having no respiratory problem; and 3) there is no likelihood of head injury. Fluids may be given orally. The recommended fluid is room-temperature water with one teaspoon of salt per quart, administered at the rate of one half cup (4 oz.) every 15 minutes.

RESPIRATORY FAILURE

The ABCs

The three critical requirements to get oxygen to the brain are the ABCs:

- *(A)irway* —unobstructed mouth and throat.

- *(B)reathing* —air heard or felt flowing in and out of the mouth or nose.

- *(C)irculation* —flow of blood, evidenced by a pulse felt at the carotid artery beside the Adam's apple.

CPR

To administer CPR to a victim:

1. Check the ABCs.

2. Clean the mouth of any obstruction.

3. Raise the chin and pinch the nose shut.

4. Place your mouth over the victim's and give two breaths.

5. Place the heel of one hand 2" above the bottom of the breastbone and the other hand on top of the bottom hand, and depress the chest $1^1/2$" to 2" for $1/2$ second. Repeat 15 times at the rate of 80-100 compressions per minute.

6. Repeat Steps 4 and 5 until victim resumes breathing. Check the ABCs every two minutes.

7. If two people are available to administer CPR, one gives one breath, the other gives five compressions, etc.

Heimlich Maneuver

To clear an airway obstruction when it cannot be reached through the mouth:

1. Stand behind the victim.

2. Hold arms around the victim below the rib cage.

3. Make a fist with one hand and grip the fist with your other hand. Place the thumb of the fist against the chest hollow just below the ribs and thrust it rapidly and forcefully up against the chest up to four times.

4. If the victim is already unconscious, lay him flat on his back and apply the chest thrusts from the front. Be prepared to remove whatever comes up.

5. If the obstruction is dislodged, start CPR.

BURNS

Degrees

- *First degree*—skin is red.

- *Second degree*—skin red and blistered .

- *Third degree*—skin charred (brown or black).

First Aid

1. Check breathing. Apply CPR, if necessary.

2. Apply cold, wet cloths for 5-10 minutes.

3. Administer strong pain medication.

4. Flush the burned area with fresh water (salt water, if fresh is not available) for a full 30 minutes. DO NOT apply Vaseline or any type of cooking oil or butter.

5. DO apply an antibacterial ointment, if available.

6. Cover with a loose sterile bandage. Do not puncture blisters.

POISONING

Ingested

- *Corrosive substances* such as acids, alkalis, ammonia and petroleum distillates (gasoline, diesel fuel, paint thinner, etc.) typically burn the lips, mouth and throat and lead to breathing difficulty. Do NOT induce vomiting, as this will just lead to further exposure of the esophagus to corrosion. All you can do is dilute the substance with several glasses of milk.

- *Noncorrosive substances* should be gotten up as soon as possible. Induce vomiting by sticking the finger down the throat or by swallowing 30 cc syrup of Ipecac diluted with four glasses of water.

- *Bacterial food* results in abdominal pain, vomiting and diarrhea. If vomiting has not yet occurred, hasten it with the finger or syrup of Ipecac. Fluids will be helpful, but only well after vomiting has ceased.

Inhaled

Carbon monoxide and the fumes of many petroleum distillates may cause headaches, dizziness and disorientation. Treatment consists of fresh air. Administer CPR, if necessary.

Contact with Skin

Poisons, such as acids and alkalis, on the skin or in the eyes should be flushed with plenty of fresh water.

HEAT EFFECTS

Heatstroke (Sunstroke)

- *Symptoms include* red, hot and dry skin, strong and rapid pulse and very high body temperature.

- *Treatment* consists of lowering the body temperature by immersion in cold water (not ice), or sponging with a cold, wet towel or rubbing alcohol until the temperatures drops to less than 102°F.

Heat Exhaustion

- *Symptoms* include pale, cool and clammy skin, dizziness, nausea and sometimes cramps.

- *Treatment* consists of laying the victim down with feet elevated and giving salted water (1 teaspoon per quart) at the rate of 8 ounces every 15 minutes for one hour.

Heat Cramps

- *Symptoms* include cramping of legs and abdomen.

- *Treatment* consists of giving salted water (1 teaspoon per quart) at the rate of 8 ounces every 15 minutes for one hour, and gentle massage of the cramped muscles.

COLD EFFECTS

Frostbite

- *Symptoms include* glossy, white skin which is hard on the surface but soft underneath. In extreme cases, large blisters may appear.

- *Treatment* consists of rapid warming in running or circulating warm water (102-105°F). Do not massage frozen area. Discontinue warming as soon as color returns. If frozen area is a limb or member, exercise it gently.

Hypothermia

- *Symptoms* include shivering, muscular weakness and numbness and low body temperature. In extreme cases, the victim becomes unconscious.

- *Treatment* consists of warming the entire body quickly. Remove clothing and immerse the victim fully in water at 102-105°F. If the victim is conscious, give him hot liquids, but not alcohol. Discontinue treatment as soon as body temperature returns to normal.

SUDDEN ILLNESS

Heart Attack

- *Symptoms* include pain described as pressure on the chest , pain radiating to the neck, shoulders and possibly down one or both arms, shortness of breath, sweating, nausea and mild indigestion.

- *Treatment* consists of 1) calling for an ambulance, 2) CPR if necessary, 3) loosening clothing, having victim sit quietly in a comfortable position, and administering three nitroglycerine tablets, if available, under the tongue at 10-minute intervals.

Stroke

- *Symptoms of a major stroke* include unconsciousness, paralysis or weakness on one side of the body, unequal pupil size, slurred speech, respiratory difficulty and loss of bowel and/or bladder control.

- *Symptoms of a minor stroke* include headache, dizziness, confusion, weakness in an arm or leg, some memory and speech loss and personality change.

- *Treatment* consists of 1) calling for an ambulance, 2) CPR if necessary, and 3) placing the victim on his side to maintain an open airway.

Fainting

- *Symptoms* include paleness, sweating, dizziness, coldness of the skin and unconsciousness.

- *Treatment* consists of laying victim down and loosening clothing. If victim recovers consciousness quickly, give him fluids. If recovery is not quick, call for an ambulance.

Seizure (Convulsions)

- *Symptoms* include unconsciousness and convulsions.

- *Treatment* consists of protecting the victim from injuring himself until the seizure passes. Insert a padded stick—not your fingers— between the teeth to prevent biting of the tongue and remove furniture or otherwise protect the victim's head from injury. When victim recovers, encourage rest.

Hyperglycemia (Too Much Blood Sugar)

- *Symptoms* include drowsiness, confusion and a fruity breath odor.

- *Treatment* consists of immediate hospitalization.

Hypoglycemia (Insulin Shock or Too Little Blood Sugar)

- *Symptoms* include gnawing hunger, dizziness, weakness, cold sweat, tremor and ultimately unconsciousness.

- *Treatment (conscious victim)* consists of increasing the victim's blood sugar content by administering candy, fruit juice, a soft drink or anything that contains real sugar.

- *Treatment (unconscious victim)* consists of taking the patient to the emergency room ASAP for intravenous dextrose.

Anaphylactic Shock (Severe Allergic Reaction)

- *Symptoms* include respiratory distress (the most dangerous aspect), burning and itching of the skin, particularly around head and neck, possible nausea, vomiting and/or diarrhea.

- *Treatment* consists of injecting epinephrine (every vessel should carry a kit). If epinephrine is not available, administer an antihistamine such as Benadryl.

FIRE FIGHTING

THE FIRE TRIANGLE

Fires require three elements. Remove one and the fire goes out (the basic principle of fire fighting).

- *Fuel*—any combustible material, such as wood, paper, oil, plastic, gasoline, paint.

- *Oxygen*—a minimum of 16% by volume of air (the normal concentration of oxygen in air is 21%).

- *Heat*—temperature high enough to ignite the fuel.

CLASSIFICATION OF FIRES

Fires are grouped into four classes depending primarily on the type of fuel:

- *Class A*—wood, cloth, paper, rubber, some plastics.

- *Class B*—petroleum products, alcohols, paints.

- *Class C*—energized electrical components.

- *Class D*—combustible metals such as magnesium.

Fire Extinguisher Characteristics

Type	Fire Class	How It Works	Comments
Water	A	Removes heat	Conducts electricity.
CO_2	ABC	Displaces oxygen	Doesn't lower temperature, so fire can reignite. Easily dissipated by wind. Suffocating to fire fighter.
Halon	ABC	Displaces oxygen	Being discontinued due to ozone depletion.
Dry Chemical	ABC BC	Reacts with fuel to inhibit combustion	Powder residue harmful to engines and electronics.
Foam	AB	Cuts off oxygen. Removes heat.	Conducts electricity.

Required Contents of Fire Extinguishers

Extinguisher Class	CO_2, lb.	Halon, lb.	Dry Chemical, lb.	Foam, gal.
B-I	4	2.5	2	1.25
B-II	15	10	10	2.5

Coast Guard Requirements

Boat Size	Fire Extinguishers Required	Extinguishers Required if Fixed Extinguisher in Engine Space
Under 26´	(1) B-I, unless construction does not allow	Not applicable
26´ to <40´	(2) B-I or (1) B-II	(1) B-I
40´ to 65´	(3) B-I, or (1) B-I plus (1) B-II	(2) B-I or (1) B-II

THE ALL-PURPOSE FIRE NOZZLE

Large vessels have fixed fire-fighting systems consisting of hydrant stations, hoses and nozzles. The all-purpose nozzle can spray water in three patterns:

1. *Straight stream (handle pulled back)*—for maximum range and force.

2. *High-velocity fog (handle straight up)*—for a wide, coarse spray with a range of 20-30 feet.

3. *Low-velocity fog (handle straight up with special applicator nozzle)*—for a fine fog which absorbs the maximum amount of heat.

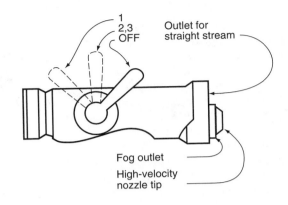

FIGHTING A FIRE

The Coast Guard encourages an organized approach to fire fighting. The recommended procedure is:

1. Sound the general alarm bell for 10 seconds. Simultaneously, turn the vessel so any smoke and flames are downwind.

2. Issue a PAN-PAN distress call on VHF CH16.

3. Have the crew assemble any passengers far from the fire and have them don life preservers.

4. Use your head—remember the fire triangle.

- *Fuel*— If the fuel is an easily handled object, throw it overboard!

- *Oxygen*— If the fire is in an enclosed space, deprive it of oxygen by sealing off the space.

- *Heat*—If there is a fixed fire extinguisher in the space, activate it. If not, and the fire is accessible, use the appropriate type of extinguisher to cool the fire.

Once you have extinguished a fire in an enclosed space, do not open the space for at least 15 minutes to avoid reignition.

If you have extinguished an electrical fire by turning off the battery switch or the main circuit breaker, do not turn on again until you have isolated or disconnected the circuit involved in the fire.

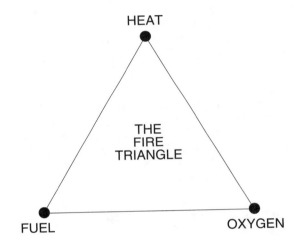

OIL DISCHARGE

From an oil-discharge placard (required to be posted in or near the engine):

"The Federal Water Pollution Control Act prohibits the discharge of oily waste into or upon the navigable waters of the United States, or the waters of the contiguous zone, or which may affect natural resources belonging to, appertaining to, or under the exclusive management authority of the United States. If such discharge causes a film or discoloration of the surface of the water or causes a sludge or emulsion beneath the surface of the water, violators are subject to substantial civil penalty and/or criminal sanctions including fines and imprisonment."

Spills of heavy oil are worse than those of gasoline and diesel because they don't evaporate, but the spill of *any* form of oil is a serious offense. Be aware of the following points:

1. When a spill is discovered, fueling or other operations should be discontinued and containment and removal initiated ASAP.

2. When a spill occurs, no matter how small, the *person in charge of the vessel* must report the spill *immediately* to the *Coast Guard.* Give your name, the vessel name, the owner's name, the type of discharge, the location and any weather/current/tide conditions that might affect the spread of the oil. Failure to supply these facts may be considered in any subsequent hearing.

3. *Anyone* associated with the spill—not just the owner, master, or person in charge—may be held responsible under the law.

4. The maximum fine for a small spill is $5,000. In addition, the owner or operator of the vessel is responsible for all cleanup costs.

5. The maximum penalty for *not reporting a spill immediately* is a fine of $10,000, a year in jail, or both.

6. Penalties are assessed only after someone has been charged and a hearing held.

7. The use of dispersants (detergents) is generally *not allowed* since they merely mix the oil with water and allow the oil to sink to the bottom where it is more harmful to the environment. The only exception is when authorized by a Federal On-Scene Coordinator.

8. The proper method of dealing with waste oil is collection and disposal in a proper disposal facility.

OVERBOARD SEWAGE DISCHARGE

The Federal Water Pollution Control Act also mandates that marine sanitation devices (MSDs) be installed on all vessels which have fixed toilets. Type I MSDs treat the waste before discharge. Type III systems use holding tanks. Vessels built after January, 1980, must have Type III systems.

Overboard discharge of untreated waste is prohibited on lakes, rivers, and within three nm of shore. In addition, no discharge, even of treated waste, is permitted in "no discharge zones."

WASTE DISCHARGE

From a waste-discharge placard (required to be posted on any vessel 26 or more feet in length):

"It is illegal for any vessel to dump plastic trash anywhere in the ocean or navigable waters of the United States. Annex V of the MARPOL (Marine Pollution) 73/78 Treaty is an International Law for a cleaner, safer environment. Violations of these requirements may result in civil penalty up to $25,000 fine and imprisonment."

PROHIBITED WASTE BY ZONES

U.S. Lakes (Including all of Great Lakes), Rivers, Bays, Sounds and within 3 nm of shore (Territorial Sea)

Plastic	Dunnage	Paper
Rags	Food	Garbage
Metals	Glass	Crockery

3 to 12 nm from Shore

Plastic	Dunnage, lining and floating packing materials	

If not ground to < 1"

Paper	Rags	Food
Metals	Glass	Crockery

12 to 25 nm from Shore

Plastic	Dunnage, lining and floating packing materials

Beyond 25 nm from Shore

Plastic

DISTRESS SIGNALS

Flares and Smoke Signals Required for Uninspected Vessels:

- *Day:*   3 floating orange smoke, or

  3 hand-held orange smoke, or

  1 orange flag with black square and circle.

- *Day/Night:*   3 rocket parachute red flares, or

  3 aerial pyrotechnic red flares, or

  3 hand-held red flares.

Inspected Vessels–Lakes, Bays, Sounds & Rivers:

- *Day:*   3 hand-held orange smoke and

  3 hand-held red flares, or

  3 rocket parachute red flares.

- *Night*   3 hand-held red flares, or

  3 rocket parachute red flares.

Inspected Vessels–Oceans and Coastwise:

- *Day:*   6 hand-held orange smoke and

  6 hand-held red flares, or

  6 rocket parachute red flares.

- *Night:*   6 hand-held red flares, or

  6 rocket parachute red flares.

EPIRB
(Emergency Position Indicating Radio Beacon)

Inspected Vessels operating beyond three nm from shore must carry a Category I (float free and automatic transmit) 406 MHz EPIRB, which sends a registered code indicating the name, type and owner of the vessel in distress.

All Category I EPIRBs must have their hexadecimal code registered with the NOAA data base (required by 47 CFR 80.1061).

EPIRBs must be tested monthly and the test recorded in a log. The test can be monitored by both an indicating light and by hearing an oscillating tone on an FM radio at 99.5 MHz. All testing must be performed between 00 and 05 minutes past the hour.

Class A EPIRBs (121.5 and 248 MHz) also float free and automatically transmit to SARSAT satellites, but do not send identification information. These EPIRBs are being phased out on inspected vessels.

Official COLREGS 72 Distress Signals

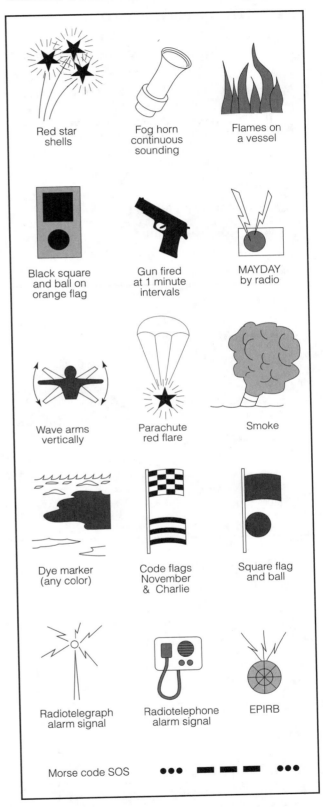

Red star shells

Fog horn continuous sounding

Flames on a vessel

Black square and ball on orange flag

Gun fired at 1 minute intervals

MAYDAY by radio

Wave arms vertically

Parachute red flare

Smoke

Dye marker (any color)

Code flags November & Charlie

Square flag and ball

Radiotelegraph alarm signal

Radiotelephone alarm signal

EPIRB

Morse code SOS   ••• ▬▬ ▬▬ ▬▬ •••

FLOTATION DEVICES

Personal Flotation Devices (PFDs)

- *Uninspected:* 1 Type I, II, III, or V PFD for each person aboard. The Type V must be worn on deck to count.

- *Inspected:* 1 Type I for each person aboard, plus child-size PFDs for 10% of the vessel capacity. In any case, child-size PFDs must be provided for every child aboard. All PFDs must be marked with the vessel name.

Ring Buoys

- *Inspected ≤65':* 1-24" life ring buoy.

- *Inspected >65':* 3-24" life ring buoys.

At least one ring buoy must have a 60' line of 5/16", buoyant, non-kinking, and dark/UV-resistant material.

Life Floats

The number and sizes of life floats for inspected vessels depends on the vessel's operating area, water temperature, and construction. However, all life floats must be readily accessible, be both manually and automatically deployable on sinking and include a lifeline, pendant, painter, 2 paddles and a floating light.

Life Rafts

Wood inspected vessels with no subdivision operating coastwise routes must have inflatable buoyant apparatus (life rafts) for 67% of capacity.

All inspected vessels operating warm-water ocean routes must have inflatable buoyant apparatus for 67% of capacity.

All vessels with no subdivision operating cold-water ocean routes must have inflatable buoyant apparatus for 100% of capacity.

Life Raft

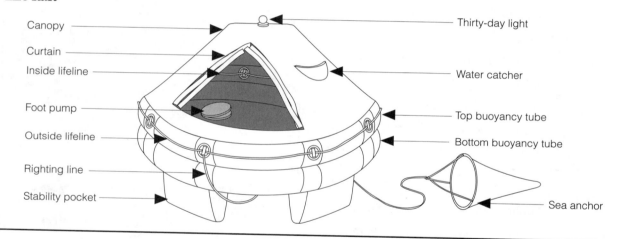

Installation of Hydrostatic Release Units

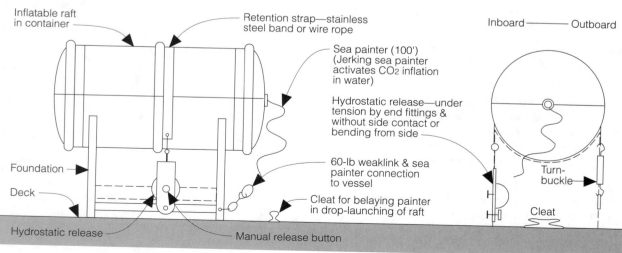

PROCEDURE

In the case of a "man overboard" (MOB), the person who observes the incident should shout, "Man overboard (starboard or port) side!" and throw a life ring or PFD toward the victim. This will mark the location, as well as provide assurance to the victim. The crew should then point continuously toward the person in the water. If there is another person on board, he/she can be designated to point, as well, while the crew dons a life vest and lifeline.

On hearing the man-overboard alert, the helmsman should immediately put the helm hard to the same side as the victim in order to swing the stern away from the victim, then initiate a turn to retrieve the victim as quickly as possible. At the same time a PAN PAN should be sent, giving the vessel location to all other vessels in the area.

- The *single (or round) turn*, although the fastest, will generally not result in a good approach to the victim unless the vessel is small and extremely maneuverable.

- If the victim is still visible, the quickest turn for larger vessels is the *race track*.

- If the location of the victim is unknown, the *Scharnow turn* (turn until headed 240° from the original course, then swing back until headed 180° from the original course) should be executed in order to most quickly retrace the original track to where the victim is most likely to be found.

- The *Williamson turn* (turn until headed 60° from the original course, then swing back until headed 180° from the original course) is similar to the Scharnow in returning to the original track, but takes slightly longer to execute.

Generally the victim should be taken aboard midships on the leeward side. This will keep the victim away from the propellers, give the victim some protection from waves and ensure that the vessel will not be blown out of reach. A step ladder is the best way to retrieve the victim, with a life-jacketed and tethered crew in the water to assist, if necessary.

TYPES OF TURNS

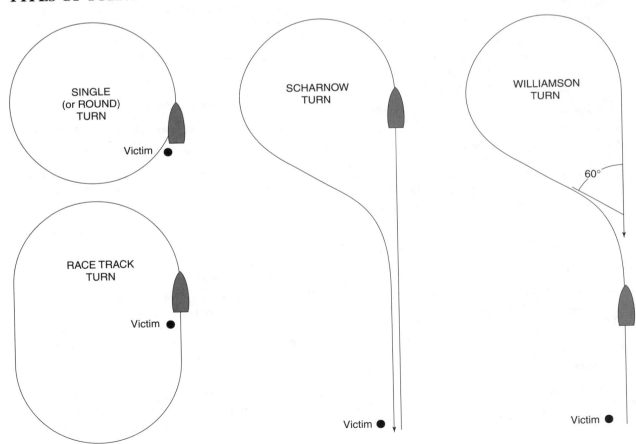

SMALL ENGINE OPERATION

GASOLINE ENGINES

Principle

Fuel is brought to the carburetor from the fuel tank by a fuel pump. On the intake stroke of a piston, air and vaporized fuel are drawn through the intake valve into the cylinder. On the compression stroke, the air/fuel mixture is compressed to about $1/8$ of its original volume (compression ratio of eight). Near the top of the compression stroke a spark, induced across the gap of the spark plug, ignites the air/fuel mixture. The combustion and expansion of gas forces the piston down in a power stroke. In the following exhaust stroke, the combustion gases are vented out through the exhaust valve.

Troubleshooting

If a gasoline engine won't start, it probably isn't getting one of two things:

1. Fuel—check in order:

  • Is there fuel in the tank?

  • Is the fuel shutoff valve open?

  • Is fuel getting to the carburetor?

  • Is the choke in the proper position (on, or closed, if the engine is cold/off if warm)?

2. Spark—remove a spark plug and, holding the threaded portion against the engine, see if a blue spark jumps the gap as the engine is cranked. If not, check the distributor, coil and power to the coil.

Ventilation

Gasoline engines and fuel tank spaces must be positively ventilated. The blower should be wired so that the engine can't be started until the blower has run. The engine space must be equipped with a flammable vapor detector which operates 30 seconds before engine startup and while the engine is running.

DIESEL ENGINES

Principle

Fuel is pulled through a fuel filter (usually primary and secondary fuel filters) to remove particulates and water. From the fuel filter the fuel enters an injection pump which increases the fuel pressure to thousands of pounds per square inch and delivers a timed pulse of fuel to each of the fuel injectors in turn.

On the intake stroke, air is drawn through the intake valve, filling the cylinder. On the compression stroke, the air is compressed to about $1/20$ its original volume (compression ratio of 20), which heats the air to about 1,000°F. The fuel injector then delivers a fine spray of diesel fuel which ignites, since its ignition temperature is around 750°F. The controlled injection/burn results in a power stroke. When the piston returns on its exhaust stroke, the combustion gases are flushed out through the exhaust valve.

Troubleshooting

Since the diesel fuel is ignited simply by the high temperature resulting from the high compression, a diesel engine has no electrical ignition system, making it much more reliable in the marine environment. If a diesel engine won't start, it probably isn't getting fuel (air in the fuel line is a likely reason).

Check in order:

  • Is there fuel in the tank?

  • Is the fuel shutoff valve open?

  • Is the primary fuel filter clogged or full of water?

  • Is there fuel at the outlet of the fuel pump?

  • With the engine cranking, does clear fuel (no bubbles) flow from the injection pump bleed screw(s), indicating air in the line?

BOTH GASOLINE AND DIESEL ENGINES

Engine Cooling

Both gasoline and diesel propulsion engines must be water cooled. The engine head, block, and exhaust manifold must be water jacketed and cooled by water from a pump which operates whenever the engine is running. Fresh water systems (with heat exchangers) may also be used.

Outboard engines and auxiliary engines with self-contained fuel systems may be air cooled, if they are installed on an open deck.

Fuel Shutoff Valves

Fuel supply lines must have fuel shutoff valves—one at the tank connection, and one at the engine end of the fuel line. The shutoff valve at the tank must be manually operable from outside the compartment in which the valve is located, preferably from the weather deck.

If suitably protected from flames, the valve handle may be located so that the operator doesn't have to reach more than 12" into the valve space.

REQUIRED EQUIPMENT FOR T-BOATS

All Small Passenger Vessels (T-boats) that operate more than 1,000' from land must be equipped with a VHF-FM radio. All vessels operating more than 20 nm offshore (oceans) must be equipped with an SSB radio.

REQUIRED LICENSES FOR T-BOATS

Any vessel operating outside of the headlands is required to have an FCC Safety Radio Telephone Certificate, Radio Operator's License and a Ship's Station License. Note that the Radio Operator's License requires an exam and is not the same as the common Restricted Radiotelephone Operator Permit required to operate radios on recreational vessels. The FCC inspection interval for the Safety Radio Telephone Certificate is five years.

BRIDGE TO BRIDGE

Passenger vessels over 100 tons, any vessel over 300 tons, dredges, commercial tugs over 26´ and any vessel over 20 meters in inland waters is required to monitor CH13 (one watt maximum) whenever underway. Transmissions are exclusively for bridge to bridge (vessel bridges or steering stations) conversations regarding maneuvering and for communication with operable highway and railroad bridges.

RADIO LOGS

Every inspected vessel is required to maintain a radio log. The log must list the hours of operation, the operating condition of the radio, any radio checks performed, all radio tests and maintenance performed by a licensed radio technician, all MAYDAY messages received and all MAYDAY, PAN PAN or SECURITE messages sent.

Entries in the log may never be erased. If a change is required, the error should be crossed out and accompanied by the initials of the person making the correction.

Maintenance and repair performed by a licensed radio technician not part of the crew must be logged with the repair person's name, license number and issue date of the license.

PRIORITY MESSAGES

There are three levels of radio traffic which have priority over ordinary traffic. In decreasing order:

- *MAYDAY*—a vessel in immediate danger (fire, sinking, grounded and breaking up, etc.).
- *PAN-PAN*—urgent situation requiring assistance (man overboard, medical evacuation required, etc.).
- *SECURITE*—information regarding vessel movement, navigation safety, or severe weather warning (examples: large tug and tow in narrow channel, missing navigation aid, tornado warning).

VHF PROTOCOL

- *Priority Messages.* Call and remain on CH 16, unless directed by the Coast Guard to CH 22A. No other vessel should use CH 16 while the emergency exists. A vessel receiving a distress signal should respond, "Received" or "Romeo, Romeo, Romeo." If the vessel in distress or the Coast Guard is having difficulty with interfering traffic, either may transmit a "Seelonce distress" message which should silence all other traffic until the rescinding "Prudence distress" is given.

- *Non-Priority Messages.* Initiate contact on CH 09 (some areas still use CH 16). Upon contact, immediately switch to a working channel. Limit all calls to two minutes. A marine radio is not a telephone!

PHONETIC PRONUNCIATION

When VHF transmission is poor, you are encouraged to use phonetic pronunciation. In the case of the alphabet, pronunciation is fairly evident. Numbers are a different matter. Here is how the Coast Guard interprets numbers (the number 8 doesn't appear in any of the exam questions):

1	OFF-NAH-WUN
2	BEE-SOH-TOO
3	TAY-RAH-TREE
4	KAR-TAY-FOWER
5	PAN-TAH-FIVE
6	SOK-SEE-SIX
7	SAY-TAY-SEVEN
9	NO-VAY-NINER

	Range, ship-to-ship	Power	Distress Frequency	Calling Frequency	Bridge-to-Bridge
VHF	line-of-sight (20-30 nm)	low 1 Watt high 25 Watt	CH 16 156.8 MHz	CH 9	CH 13 1 Watt maximum
SSB	up to 10,000 nm	150 Watt	2,182 kHz	any	NA

SAFETY QUESTIONS

00002. An airplane wants a vessel to change course and proceed towards a vessel in distress. The actions of the aircraft to convey this message will NOT include:

A. circling the vessel at least once
B. heading in the direction of the distress location
C. flashing the navigation lights on and off
D. crossing ahead and rocking the wings

00003. To turn over an inflatable life raft that is upside down, you should pull on the:

A. canopy
B. manropes
C. sea painter
D. righting line

00004. A green signal, floating in the air from a parachute, about 300 feet above the water, indicates that a submarine:

A. has fired a torpedo during a drill
B. will be coming to the surface
C. is on the bottom in distress
D. is in distress and will try to surface

00005. Pollution of the waterways may result from the discharge of:

A. sewage
B. the galley trash can
C. an oily mixture of one part per million
D. all of the above

00008. You are alone and administering CPR to a an adult victim. How many chest compressions and how many inflations should you administer in each sequence?

A. 5 compressions then 1 inflation
B. 15 compressions then 2 inflations
C. 20 compressions then 3 inflations
D. 30 compressions then 4 inflations

00009. The International Regulations for Preventing Collisions at Sea contain the requirements for:

A. signals that must be sounded when being towed in restricted visibility
B. minimum hawser lengths when being towed
C. lights that must be displayed on anchor buoys
D. mooring procedures for support vessels when transferring cargo

00010. Which of the following is the correct definition of transverse metacenter?

A. The distance between the actual center of gravity and the maximum center of gravity that will still allow a positive stability.

B. The point to which G may rise and still permit the vessel to possess positive stability.
C. The sum of the center of buoyancy and the center of gravity.
D. The transverse shift of the center of buoyancy as a vessel rolls.

00011. A patient in shock should NOT be placed in which position?

A. on their side if unconscious
B. head down and feet up, no injuries to face or head
C. flat ontheir back with head and feet at the same level
D. arms above their head

00013. If your life raft is to leeward of a fire on the water, you should first:

A. cut the line to the sea anchor
B. paddle away from the fire
C. splash water over the liferaft to cool it
D. get out of the raft and swim to safety

00014. A yellow signal floating in the air from a small parachute, about 300 feet above the water, would indicate that a submarine:

A. has fired a torpedo during a drill
B. is about to rise to periscope depth
C. is on the bottom in distress
D. is disabled and unable to surface

00018. When administering mouth to mouth resuscitation to an adult, you should breathe at the rate of how many breaths per minute?

A. 4
B. 8
C. 12
D. 20

00019. The operator of the ship's radiotelephone, if the radiotelephone is carried voluntarily, must hold at least a:

A. mate's license
B. restricted radiotelephone operator permit
C. second-class radio operator's license
D. seaman's document

00020. If the VCG of a ship rises 1.7 feet, the GZ for the various angles of inclination will:

A. decrease
B. increase
C. remain unchanged
D. be changed by the amount of GG' x cosine of the angle

00021. Coast Guard regulations require that all of the following emergencies be covered at the periodic drills on a fishing vessel EXCEPT:

A. minimizing the affects of unintentional flooding
B. fire on board
C. rescuing an individual from the water
D. emergency towing

00023. An inflatable life raft is in the water, still in its container and attached to the ship by the painter line. You see that the ship is sinking rapidly. What action should you take with respect to the life raft container?

A. Cut the painter line so it will not pull the life raft container down.
B. Swim away from the container so you will not be in danger as it goes down.
C. Take no action because the painter will cause the life raft to inflate and open the container.
D. Manually open the container and inflate the life raft with the hand pump.

00024. Which single-letter sound signal may be made only in compliance with the International Rules of the Road?

A. D
B. F
C. Q
D. U

00028. The rescuer can best provide an airtight seal during mouth-to-mouth ventilation by pinching the victim's nostrils and:

A. cupping a hand around the patient's mouth
B. keeping the head elevated
C. applying his mouth tightly over the victim's mouth
D. holding the jaw down firmly

00029. In order to discharge a CO_2 portable extinguisher, the operator must first:

A. invert the CO_2 extinguisher
B. squeeze the two trigger handles together
C. remove the locking pin
D. open the discharge valve

00030. Transverse stability calculations require the use of:

A. hog or sag calculations or tables
B. hydrostatic curves
C. general arrangement plans
D. cross-sectional views of the vessel

00031. All of the following are part of the fire triangle EXCEPT:

A. electricity
B. fuel
C. oxygen
D. heat

00033. Liferafts are less maneuverable than lifeboats due to their:

A. shape
B. shallow draft
C. large sail area
D. all of the above

00034. Which single-letter sound signal may only be made in compliance with the Rules?

A. D
B. E
C. S
D. all of the above

00035. Which statement is TRUE of a gasoline spill?

A. It is visible for a shorter time than a fuel oil spill.
B. It is not covered by the pollution laws.
C. It does little harm to marine life.
D. It will sink more rapidly than crude oil.

00038. When applying chest compressions on an adult victim during CPR, the sternum should be depressed about:

A. 1/2 inch or less
B. 1/2 to 1 inch
C. 1 to 1-1/2 inches
D. 1-1/2 to 2 inches

00040. The principal danger from ice collecting on the upper works is the:

A. decrease in capabilities of radar
B. decrease in displacement
C. adverse effect on trim
D. loss of stability

00041. Before using a fixed CO_2 system to fight an engine room fire, you must:

A. secure the engine room ventilation
B. secure the machinery in the engine room
C. evacuate all engine room personnel
D. all of the above

00043. If an inflatable life raft is overturned, it may be righted by:

A. filling the stabilizers on one side with water
B. releasing the CO_2 cylinder
C. pushing up from under one end
D. standing on the inflating cylinder and pulling on the straps on the underside of the raft

00044. The spread of fire is prevented by:

A. heating surfaces adjacent to the fire
B. removing combustibles from the endangered area
C. increasing the oxygen supply
D. all of the above

00045. Which statement is TRUE concerning small oil spills?

A. They usually disappear quickly.
B. They usually stay in a small area.
C. They may cause serious pollution as the effect tends to be cumulative.
D. A small spill is not dangerous to sea life in the area.

00048. When administering chest compression during CPR, at what part of the victim's body should the pressure be applied?

A. lower half of the sternum
B. tip of the sternum
C. top half of the sternum
D. left chest over the heart

00049. The best procedure to follow in fighting a fire in the electrical switchboard in the engine room would be to secure the power then:

A. use a portable foam extinguisher
B. use a low velocity fog adapter with the fire hose
C. use a portable CO_2 extinguisher
D. determine the cause of the fire

00053. If an inflatable life raft inflates upside down, you can right it by:

A. pushing up on one side
B. standing on the CO_2 bottle, holding the bottom straps, and throwing your weight backwards
C. getting at least three or four men to push down on the side containing the CO_2 cylinder
D. doing nothing; it will right itself after the canopy supports inflate

00055. Most minor spills of oil products are caused by:

A. equipment failure
B. human error
C. major casualties
D. unforeseeable circumstances

00058. Changing rescuers while carrying out artificial respiration should be done:

A. without losing the rhythm of respiration
B. only with the help of two other people

C. by not stopping the respiration for more than 5 minutes
D. at 10-minute intervals

00060. If a vessel rolls slowly and sluggishly in a seaway, this condition indicates that the vessel:

A. has offcenter weights
B. is taking on water
C. has a greater draft forward than aft
D. has poor stability

00063. You have abandoned ship and are in an inflatable raft that has just inflated. You hear a continuous hissing coming from a fitting in a buoyancy tube. What is the cause of this?

A. The salt water is activating the batteries of the marker lights on the canopy.
B. The inflation pump is in automatic operation to keep the tubes fully inflated.
C. A deflation plug is partially open allowing the escape of CO_2.
D. Excess inflation pressure is bleeding off and should soon stop.

00065. You are on a containership steaming 8 miles off the Florida Keys. Which of the following statements concerning the discharge of oil is correct?

A. The discharge of oil is prohibited except in an emergency.
B. The bilges may be pumped if the discharge is first circulated through an approved oily water separator.
C. The engineroom bilges may be pumped provided the discharge does not exceed 20 ppm of oil.
D. You must be within an area "specially designated for oil" before you can discharge inside the 12-mile limit.

00068. The most essential element in the administration of CPR is:

A. to have the proper equipment for the process
B. the speed of treatment
C. the administration of oxygen
D. the treatment for traumatic shock

00070. Referring to illustration D001SA, which of the following represents the center of gravity?

A. GZ
B. M
C. B
D. G

00071. Each hand portable fire extinguisher must be marked with:

A. the name of the vessel on which it is located
B. the date that it was installed
C. the names of the individuals qualified to use it
D. an identification number

00072. To disengage a survival craft suspended from the cable above the water, you must pull the safety pin and:

A. pull the hook release handle
B. pull the hook release handle and use the ratchet bar
C. use the ratchet bar and depress the retainer
D. pull the hook release handle and depress the retainer

00073. A life raft which has inflated bottom-up on the water:

A. should be righted by standing on the carbon dioxide cylinder, holding the righting straps and leaning backwards
B. should be righted by standing on the life line, holding the righting straps and leaning backwards
C. will right itself when the canopy tubes inflate
D. must be cleared of the buoyant equipment before it will right itself

00075. If you must abandon a rig in VERY HEAVY SEAS, in a survival craft, when should you remove the safety pin and pull the hook release?

A. immediately upon launching
B. one to three feet before first wave contact
C. upon first wave contact
D. only when waterborne

00077. Normally, the percentage of oxygen in air is:

A. 16%
B. 18%
C. 21%
D. 25%

00078. Before CPR is started, you should:

A. establish an open airway
B. treat any bleeding wounds
C. insure the victim is conscious
D. make the victim comfortable

00079. A squeeze-grip type carbon dioxide portable fire extinguisher has been partially discharged. It should be:

A. labeled empty and recharged as soon as possible
B. replaced in its proper location if weight loss is no more than 25%

C. replaced in its proper location regardless of weight
D. replaced in its proper location if weight loss is no more than 15%

00080. Referring to illustration D001SA, which of the following represents metacentric height?

A. M
B. GM
C. BM
D. GZ

00081. Which extinguishing agent is most likely to allow reflash as a result of not cooling the fuel below its ignition temperature?

A. CO_2
B. water stream
C. water spray
D. foam

00082. You are fighting a class "B" fire with a portable dry chemical extinguisher. The discharge should be directed:

A. to bank off a bulkhead onto the fire
B. at the seat of the fire, starting at the near edge
C. over the top of the fire
D. at the main body of the fire

00083. If more than one raft is manned after the vessel has sunk:

A. each raft should go in a different direction in search of land
B. the possibility of a search aircraft finding you is increased by spreading out
C. reduce the number of rafts by getting as many people as possible into as few rafts as possible
D. tie the rafts together and try to stay in a single group

00084. After using a CO_2 portable extinguisher, it should be:

A. put back in service if some CO_2 remains
B. hydrostatically tested
C. retagged
D. recharged

00088. You are attempting to administer CPR to a victim. When you blow into his mouth it is apparent that no air is getting into the lungs. What should you do?

A. Blow harder to force the air past the tongue.
B. Raise the victim's head higher than his feet.
C. Press on the victim's lungs so that air pressure will blow out any obstruction.
D. Re-tip the head and try again.

00090. Referring to illustration D001SA, which of the following represents the righting arm?

A. GM
B. GZ
C. BM
D. Angle MGZ

00091. Except in rare cases, it is impossible to extinguish a shipboard fire by:

A. removing the fuel
B. interrupting the chain reaction
C. removing the oxygen
D. removing the heat

00093. If, for any reason, it is necessary to abandon ship while far out at sea, it is important that the crew members should:

A. separate from each other as this will increase the chances of being rescued
B. get away from the area because sharks will be attracted to the vessel
C. immediately head for the nearest land
D. remain together in the area because rescuers will start searching at the vessel's last known position

00097. The only portable electrical equipment permitted in a compartment which is not gas free is a lamp that is:

A. battery fed
B. self-contained
C. approved explosion proof
D. all of the above

00098. When two people are administering CPR to a victim, how many times per minute should the chest be compressed?

A. 30
B. 45
C. 60
D. 80

00099. Annex V to MARPOL 73/78 contains requirements pertaining to the discharge into the marine environment of:

A. oil
B. garbage
C. noxious liquid substances
D. none of the above

00100. When a vessel has positive stability, the distance between the line of force through B and the line of force through G is called the:

A. metacentric height
B. righting arm

C. righting moment
D. metacentric radius

00102. You are underway when a fire breaks out in the forward part of your vessel. If possible, you should:

A. put the vessel's stern into the wind
B. abandon ship to windward
C. call for assistance
D. keep going at half speed

00103. You have just abandoned ship and boarded a raft. After the raft is completely inflated you hear a whistling noise coming from a safety valve. You should:

A. not become alarmed unless it continues for a long period of time
B. plug the safety valve
C. unscrew the deflation plugs
D. remove the safety valve and replace it with a soft patch

00105. The International Regulations for Preventing Collisions at Sea contain the requirements for:

A. lights that must be displayed on anchor buoys
B. the display of load line markings
C. minimum horsepower for tugs involved in rig moves
D. lighting of mobile offshore drilling units being towed

00106. A B-II fire extinguisher has a minimum capacity of:

A. 3 gallons of foam
B. 20 pounds of CO_2
C. 10 pounds of dry chemical
D. any of the above

00108. Antiseptics are used principally to:

A. promote healing
B. prevent infection
C. reduce inflammation
D. increase blood circulation

00110. A vertical shift of weight to a position above the vessel's center of gravity will:

A. increase reserve buoyancy
B. decrease the righting moments
C. decrease KG
D. increase KM

00112. Your vessel is broken down and rolling in heavy seas. You can reduce the possibility of capsizing by:

A. rigging a sea anchor
B. constantly shifting the rudder
C. moving all personnel forward and low
D. moving all personnel aft

00113. If you hear air escaping from the liferaft just after it has inflated, you should:

A. quickly hunt for the hole before the raft deflates
B. check the sea anchor line for a tear if the seas are rough
C. check the painter line attachment for a tear caused by the initial opening
D. not panic since the safety valves allow excess pressure to escape

00115. Class C EPIRBs are required to be carried on board:

A. deep draft vessels on the high seas
B. fishing vessels
C. small passenger vessels on the Great Lakes
D. deep draft vessels in coastwise service

00116. Which of the following hand portable or semi-portable fire extinguishers is classified as a B-II extinguisher?

A. A 2-1/2 gallon soda acid and water
B. A 1-1/4 gallon foam
C. A 2-1/2 gallon foam
D. A 15 pound dry chemical

00118. A tourniquet should be used to control bleeding only:

A. with puncture wounds
B. when all other means have failed
C. when the victim is unconscious
D. to prevent bleeding from minor wounds

00119. Which of the following would be considered a vessel under the International Rules of the Road?

A. a jack-up rig under tow
B. a semisubmersible drilling rig under tow
C. a semisubmersible drilling rig drifting after breaking a tow line
D. all of the above

00120. The point to which G may rise and still permit the vessel to have positive stability is called the:

A. metacentric point
B. metacenter
C. metacentric radius
D. tipping center

00123. If you are forced to abandon ship in a lifeboat, you should:

A. remain in the immediate vicinity
B. head for the nearest land
C. head for the closest sea-lanes
D. vote on what to do, so all hands will have a part in the decision

00125. The requirements for reporting oil spills may vary geographically; however, all oil spills must be reported to the:

A. U. S. Corps of Engineers
B. U. S. Coast Guard
C. local police
D. local fire department

00128. A seaman has sustained a small, gaping laceration of the arm that would require sutures to close if medical facilities were available. What can be done as an alternative to temporarily close the wound?

A. Wrap a tight bandage around the wound.
B. Gently close the wound and while holding it closed apply a compression bandage.
C. Use temporary stitches of sail twine.
D. Apply butterfly strips under a sterile dressing.

00129. A life float on a fishing vessel must be equipped with:

A. a righting line
B. red hand flares
C. pendants
D. drinking water

00130. When making a turn on most merchant ships, the vessel will heel outwards if:

A. the vessel has very little draft
B. G is above the center of lateral resistance
C. G is below the center of lateral resistance
D. the vessel is deeply laden

00133. You have abandoned ship and are in charge of a life raft. How much water per day should you permit each occupant to drink after the first 24 hours?

A. 1 can
B. 1 pint
C. 1 quart
D. 1 gallon

00135. Which of the following statements concerning an accidental oil spill in the navigable waters of the U. S. is FALSE?

A. The person in charge must report the spill to the Coast Guard.
B. Failure to report the spill may result in a fine.
C. The company can be fined for the spill.
D. The Corps of Engineers is responsible for the cleanup of the spill.

00136. Which item is NOT required to be marked with the vessel's name?

A. hand-portable fire extinguisher
B. life preserver
C. fire hose
D. lifeboat oar

00138. A person reports to you with a fish-hook in his thumb. To remove it you should:

A. pull it out with pliers
B. cut the skin from around the hook
C. push the barb through, cut it off, then remove the hook
D. have a surgeon remove it

00139. When fighting a fire in an enclosed space, the hose team should crouch as low as possible to:

A. protect themselves from smoke
B. obtain the best available air
C. allow the heat and steam to pass overhead
D. all of the above

00140. Which statement is TRUE of a stiff vessel?

A. She will have a large metacentric height.
B. Her period of roll will be large due to her large metacentric height.
C. She will have an unusually high center of gravity.
D. She will pitch heavily.

00141. Which emergency is required to be covered at the required periodic drills on a fishing vessel?

A. recovering an individual from the water
B. steering casualty
C. emergency towing
D. loss of propulsion power

00143. You have abandoned ship in tropical waters. Which procedure(s) should be used during a prolonged period in a raft?

A. Wet clothes during the day to decrease perspiration.
B. Get plenty of rest.
C. Keep the entrance curtains open.
D. all of the above

00145. Which of the following statements concerning an accidental oil spill in the navigable waters of the U. S. is TRUE?

A. The Corps of Engineers is responsible for the cleanup of the spill.
B. The Department of Interior is responsible for the cleanup of the spill.

C. A warning broadcast must be made by radiotelephone.
D. The person in charge must report the spill to the Coast Guard.

00148. First aid treatment for small cuts and open wounds would be to:

A. have the patient lie down and cover the wound when the bleeding stops
B. stop the bleeding, clean, medicate, and cover the wound
C. apply an ice pack to the wound and cover it when the bleeding stops
D. apply a hot towel to purge the wound, then medicate and cover it

00153. If you reach shore in a life raft, the first thing to do is:

A. drag the raft ashore and lash it down for a shelter
B. find some wood for a fire
C. get the provisions out of the raft
D. set the raft back out to sea so someone may spot it

00155. When oil is accidentally discharged into the water, what should you do after reporting the discharge?

A. Prevent spreading and remove as much of the oil as possible from the water.
B. Throw chemicals on the water to disperse oil.
C. Throw sand on the water to sink the oil.
D. Request the Coast Guard take care of cleaning up the oil.

00156. Annually, all carbon dioxide fire extinguishers aboard a vessel are:

A. weighed
B. discharged and recharged
C. checked for pressure loss
D. sent ashore to an approved service facility

00158. A person has suffered a laceration of the arm. Severe bleeding has been controlled by using a sterile dressing and direct pressure. What is the next action to be taken?

A. Apply a tourniquet to prevent the bleeding from restarting.
B. Apply a pressure bandage over the dressing.
C. Remove any small foreign matter and apply antiseptic.
D. Administer fluids to assist the body in replacing the lost blood.

00159. The class A EPIRB transmits a signal:

A. that follows the curvature of the earth
B. that can be picked up by SARSAT satellite

C. that activates an alarm on nearby aircraft
D. to alert shore stations and then transmits a homing signal

00163. The greatest danger in cold temperatures, when at sea in an inflatable life raft, is:

A. asphyxiation due to keeping the canopy closed
B. hypothermia caused by the cold temperature
C. collapsing of the raft due to the cold temperatures
D. starvation

00165. Which of the following is FALSE regarding halon fire extinguishers?

A. They are more effective than CO2 extinguishers.
B. They leave no residue.
C. They are noncorrosive.
D. They are nontoxic.

00168. In all but the most severe cases, bleeding from a wound should be controlled by:

A. applying direct pressure to the wound
B. submerging the wound in lukewarm water
C. cooling the wound with ice
D. applying a tourniquet

00171. You are underway when a fire breaks out in the forward part of your vessel. If practicable, the first thing you should do is to:

A. call for assistance
B. abandon ship to windward
C. put the vessel's stern into the wind
D. keep going at half speed

00172. As Master of an inspected small passenger vessel, you have a question regarding a proposed modification to a watertight bulkhead. In which subchapter of Title 46 of the Code of Federal Regulations would you find the answer?

A. Subchapter B
B. Subchapter S
C. Subchapter T
D. Subchapter F

00173. While adrift in an inflatable life raft in hot, tropical weather:

A. the canopy should be deflated so that it will not block cooling breezes
B. the pressure valve may be periodically opened to prevent excessive air pressure
C. deflating the floor panels may help to cool personnel
D. the entrance curtains should never be opened

00175. The pollution prevention regulations derived from MARPOL are applicable on which of the following waters?

A. inland waters of the U. S. only
B. Great Lakes waters of the U. S. only
C. western rivers of the U. S. only
D. navigable waters, adjoining shorelines and contiguous zone of the U. S.

00177. Before taking drinking water on board in the U. S. or its possessions, the responsible person from the vessel should determine that the source:

A. is used by a city
B. has been treated with chlorine
C. is approved by the Public Health Service
D. is not from surface water

00178. Bleeding from a vein may be ordinarily controlled by:

A. applying direct pressure to the wound
B. heavy application of a disinfectant
C. pouring ice water directly onto the wound
D. pinching the wound closed

00180. Which of the following is TRUE of a "stiff" vessel?

A. It has a small GM.
B. It pitches heavily.
C. It has an unusually high center of gravity.
D. Its period of roll is short.

00183. Which statement is TRUE concerning an inflatable life raft?

A. The floor may be inflated for insulation from cold water.
B. Crew members can jump into the raft without damaging it.
C. The raft may be boarded before it is fully inflated.
D. all of the above

00185. Which substance is not considered to be "Oil" under the pollution prevention regulations?

A. petroleum and fuel oil
B. sludge
C. oil mixed with dredge spoil
D. oil refuse and oil mixed with wastes

00187. Which of the following represents poor sanitary procedures?

A. Keep and use a separate filling hose for potable (drinking) water.
B. Locate potable (drinking) water tanks as low as possible in the bilge.

C. Eliminate enclosed spaces in which trash, food particles, dirt may gather.
D. After washing dishes with soap and warm water, sterilize them in water of at least 170° F.

00188. The preferred method of controlling external bleeding is by:

A. direct pressure on the wound
B. elevating the wounded area
C. pressure on a pressure point
D. a tourniquet above the wound

00189. The purpose of the inclining experiment is to:

A. determine the location of the metacenter
B. determine the lightweight center of gravity location
C. verify the hydrostatic data
D. verify data in the vessel's operating manual

00191. Where will you find the requirements for the lights that must be displayed on a mobile offshore drilling unit that is being towed?

A. Notice to Mariners
B. COLREGS
C. Coast Pilot
D. Light List

00195. As soon as the officer in charge of the vessel has taken steps to stop the discharge of oil or oily mixture into a U. S. harbor, which of the following must he do FIRST?

A. rig a boom for recovery
B. call the Coast Guard
C. alert the fire department
D. inform the Environmental Protection Agency

00198. A person suffering from possible broken bones and internal injuries should:

A. be assisted in walking around
B. be examined then walked to a bunk
C. not be moved but made comfortable until medical assistance arrives
D. not be allowed to lie down where injured but moved to a chair or bunk

00200. Which is TRUE of a tender ship?

A. It has a large GM.
B. Its period of roll is long.
C. It has a very low center of gravity.
D. It has a good transverse stability.

00205. When a vessel violates the oil pollution laws, who may be held responsible?

A. Master only
B. owners only

C. licensed officers only
D. any individual connected with the vessel involved in the operation

00207. What chemical is used to treat water in order to ensure its safety for drinking?

A. nitrogen
B. chlorine
C. carbon
D. oxygen

00208. What is the primary purpose of a splint applied in first aid?

A. control bleeding
B. reduce pain
C. immobilize the fracture
D. reset the bone

00212. In the navigable waters of the United States, Annex V to MARPOL 73/78 is NOT applicable to a(n):

A. recreational yacht
B. uninspected towing vessel
C. uninspected passenger vessel under 100 GT
D. U. S. government vessel

00215. What is the maximum civil penalty for discharging oil in U. S. waters in violation of the Federal Water Pollution Control Act?

A. $500
B. $1,000
C. $5,000
D. $10,000

00218. A compound fracture is a fracture:

A. in which more than one bone is broken
B. in which the same bone is broken in more than one place
C. which is accompanied by internal bleeding
D. which causes external bleeding at the site of the fracture

00220. Metacentric height is a measure of:

A. initial stability only
B. stability through all angles
C. maximum righting arm
D. all of the above

00225. The Federal Water Pollution Control Act requires the person in charge of a vessel to immediately notify the Coast Guard as soon as he knows of any oil discharge. Failure to notify the Coast Guard can lead to a fine of:

A. $500 or 30 days in jail, or both
B. $1,000 or 60 days in jail, or both

C. $10,000 or 1 year in jail, or both
D. $50,000 or 5 years in jail, or both

00228. Which of the following is the most serious type of fracture?

A. compound
B. greenstick
C. closed
D. crack

00229. Fuel oil tank vents are fitted with a screen which will stop:

A. oil from flowing out of the tank vent
B. air from entering the tank vent
C. vapors from leaving the tank vent
D. flames on deck from entering the tank vent

00230. Initial stability of a vessel may be improved by:

A. removing loose water
B. adding weight low in the vessel
C. closing crossover valves between partly filled double bottom tanks
D. any of the above

00231. If a fire starts on your vessel while refueling you should first:

A. stop refueling
B. sound the general alarm
C. determine the source of the fire
D. attempt to extinguish the fire

00235. If you fail to notify the Coast Guard of an oil spill, you may be subject to a fine of up to:

A. $500
B. $1,000
C. $5,000
D. $10,000

00237. Where must an EPIRB be stowed?

A. under lock and key
B. where it can float free
C. in the engine room
D. in the pilothouse

00238. Unless there is danger of further injury, a person with a compound fracture should not be moved until bleeding is controlled and:

A. the bone has been set
B. the fracture is immobilized
C. radio advice has been obtained
D. the wound has been washed

00240. Addition of weight above the center of gravity of a vessel will always:

A. reduce reserve buoyancy
B. reduce righting moments
C. increase GM
D. all of the above

00243. Which is correct about storm oil?

A. It has a moderate effect in surf.
B. It is most effective in shallow water.
C. It reduces friction between wind and water.
D. Mineral oil is the most effective type.

00245. Storage batteries should be charged in a well ventilated area because:

A. they generate heat
B. they emit hydrogen
C. of the toxic fumes they emit
D. they recharge faster in a well ventilated space

00247. All self-propelled vessels on an international voyage must be equipped with how many Emergency Position Indicating Radiobeacons (EPIRB)?

A. 1 approved Category I EPIRB
B. 2 approved Category I EPIRBs
C. 3 approved Category II EPIRBs
D. 4 Category II EPIRBs

00248. You are treating a shipmate with a compound fracture of the lower arm. What action should you take?

A. Apply a tourniquet to control bleeding then align the bones and splint.
B. Apply traction to the hand to keep the bones in line, splint and apply a pressure dressing.
C. Force the ends of the bones back into line, treat the bleeding, and splint.
D. Apply a bulky, sterile, pressure dressing to control bleeding, then apply a temporary splint and place the victim in bed.

00252. Which of the following, when removed, will result in the extinguishment of a fire?

A. nitrogen
B. sodium
C. oxygen
D. carbon dioxide

00253. In order to benefit from the use of storm oil in heavy seas, the storm oil should be:

A. around the rudder and screws
B. completely around the vessel
C. to leeward of the vessel
D. to windward of the vessel

00257. A coastwise vessel is not required to carry an EPIRB when its route does not extend more than 20 miles from a harbor of safe refuge, and:

A. its route does not extend more than 25 miles from the nearest land
B. it carries an FCC approved VHF radiotelephone
C. at least 1 lifeboat on each side of the vessel is fitted with a fixed radio installation
D. a self-activating smoke signal is mounted at each bridge wing

00258. In any major injury to a person, the first aid includes the treatment for the injury and what other treatment?

A. application of CPR
B. removal of any foreign objects
C. administration of oxygen
D. treatment for traumatic shock

00261. A person who willfully violates safety regulations may be fined up to $5,000 and:

A. imprisoned for up to a year
B. imprisoned for up to 5 years
C. forbidden to work in the fishing industry
D. no other penalty may be applied

00262. Which fire detection system is actuated by sensing a heat rise in a compartment?

A. manual fire detection system
B. automatic fire detection system
C. smoke detection system
D. watchman's supervisory system

00263. Which of the following listed oils is not suitable for storm oil?

A. fish oil
B. vegetable oil
C. mineral oil
D. animal oil

00265. The term "discharge", as it applies to the pollution regulations, means:

A. spilling
B. leaking
C. dumping
D. all of the above

00267. How often should the "EPIRB" battery be checked?

A. every 2 years
B. it doesn't matter
C. every 3 years
D. monthly

00268. Which of the following is NOT a treatment for traumatic shock?

A. Keep the patient warm but not hot.
B. Have the injured person lie down.
C. Massage the arms and legs to restore circulation.
D. Relieve the pain of the injury.

00269. To remedy a leaking fire hose connection at the hydrant, secure the valve and:

A. replace the gasket in the male coupling
B. reduce fire pump pressure
C. replace the gasket in the female coupling
D. rethread the male coupling

00270. When cargo is shifted from the lower hold to the main deck:

A. the center of gravity will move upwards
B. the GM will increase
C. the center of buoyancy will move downward
D. all of the above

00271. A fishing vessel casualty must be reported to the Coast Guard if it involves:

A. loss of life
B. an injury requiring only first aid
C. $10,000 in property damage
D. loss of equipment which doesn't reduce the vessel's maneuverability

00272. Fire alarm system thermostats are actuated by:

A. smoke sensors
B. the difference in thermal expansion of two dissimilar metals
C. pressure loss due to air being heated
D. an electric eye which actuates when smoke interferes with the beam

00273. Which type of oil is suitable for use as storm oil?

A. fish oil
B. crude oil
C. lube oil
D. mineral oil

00275. A method NOT usually allowed in cleaning up oil spills in the United States is:

A. skimmers
B. straw
C. dispersants
D. sawdust

00277. The vessel's Emergency Position Indicating Radiobeacon (EPIRB) must be tested:

A. weekly
B. monthly

C. every 2 months
D. every 3 months

00278. Which of the following is a treatment for traumatic shock?

A. Administer CPR.
B. Administer fluids.
C. Open clothing to allow cooling of the body.
D. Keep the victim in a sitting position.

00279. The purpose of storm oil in a sea anchor is to:

A. weigh down the anchor
B. lubricate the anchor
C. repel dangerous fish
D. smooth the sea

00281. The gross weight of a fully charged CO_2 bottle in a fixed CO_2 system is 220 lbs. When the bottle is empty it weighs 110 lbs. What is the minimum acceptable gross weight of the CO_2 bottle before it should be recharged by the manufacturer?

A. 200 lbs
B. 205 lbs
C. 210 lbs
D. 220 lbs

00282. The difference in water spray pattern between the high-velocity tip and low-velocity applicator on the all-purpose nozzle is due to:

A. a difference in water pressure
B. the method of breaking up the water stream
C. the length of the applicator
D. all of the above

00283. Spreading oil on the open sea has the effect of:

A. diminishing the height of the seas
B. lengthening the distance between successive crests
C. increasing the height of the seas
D. preventing the wave crests from breaking

00285. The use of sinking and dispersing agents for removal of surface oil is:

A. the most common method used in the United States
B. too expensive for common use
C. generally safe to sea life
D. generally harmful to sea life

00287. The Master shall insure that the Emergency Position Indicating Radiobeacon (EPIRB) is:

A. secured inside the wheelhouse
B. tested annually
C. tested monthly
D. secured in the emergency locker

00288. When a person is in shock, what is the condition of the skin?

A. warm and dry
B. warm and damp
C. cold and dry
D. cold and damp

00290. When cargo is shifted from the main deck into the lower hold of a vessel, which of the following will happen?

A. The GM will increase.
B. The metacenter will move upward.
C. The center of buoyancy will move upward.
D. all of the above

00291. A U. S. merchant vessel is NOT subject to the requirements of Annex V to MARPOL 73/78:

A. outside of 25 nautical miles from nearest land
B. outside of the navigable waters of the United States
C. in the waters of those countries not signatory to MARPOL
D. none of the above

00292. High-velocity fog:

A. is a finer, more diffuse water spray than low velocity fog
B. requires that the water pressure be no greater than 60 psi
C. produces an effective fog pattern no more than 6 feet beyond the nozzle
D. extinguishes a fire by absorbing heat and reducing the supply of oxygen

00293. Which of the following is TRUE concerning life preservers which are severely damaged?

A. They must be replaced.
B. They must be tested for buoyancy before being continued in use.
C. They can be repaired by a reliable seamstress.
D. They can be used for children.

00295. The most common type of containment device(s) for spilled oil on the water is(are):

A. straw
B. booms
C. skimmers
D. chemical dispersants

00296. In weighing CO_2 cylinders, they must be recharged if weight loss exceeds:

A. 10% of weight of full bottle
B. 15% of weight of full bottle
C. 20% of weight of charge
D. 10% of weight of charge

00297. Which of the following information is NOT required to be posted in or near the wheelhouse?

A. stopping time and distance from full speed while maintaining course with minimum rudder
B. a diagram of advance and transfer for turns of 30°, 60°, 90° and 120° at full speed with maximum rudder and constant power
C. for vessels with a fixed propeller, a table of shaft RPMs for a representative range of speeds
D. operating instructions for change-over procedures for remote steering gear systems

00298. Which of the following is NOT a symptom of traumatic shock?

A. slow, deep breathing
B. pale, cold skin
C. weak, rapid pulse
D. restlessness and anxiety

00300. Shifting a weight in a cargo vessel from the upper tween deck to the lower hold will:

A. make the vessel more tender
B. make the vessel stiffer
C. increase the rolling period
D. decrease the metacentric height

00302. If you are fighting a fire below the main deck of your vessel, which action is most important concerning the stability of the vessel?

A. shutting off electricity to damaged cables
B. draining fire-fighting water and pumping it overboard
C. maneuvering the vessel so the fire is on the lee side
D. removing burned debris from the cargo hold

00303. Plastic material may be discharged overboard from a vessel if it is:

A. nowhere while afloat
B. 25 miles from shore
C. 12 miles from shore
D. 3 miles from shore

00305. Which method of oil cleanup is usually NOT allowed?

A. employing a boom
B. using suction equipment
C. sinking agents
D. skimmers

00308. When you are treating a person for shock, you should wrap him in warm coverings to:

A. increase body heat
B. preserve present body heat
C. avoid self-inflicted wounds caused by spastic movement
D. protect the person from injury during transportation

00309. Life preservers must be stenciled with the:

A. maximum weight allowed
B. stowage space assigned
C. vessel's home port
D. vessel's name

00311. Spontaneous ignition can result from:

A. an unprotected drop-light bulb
B. careless disposal or storage of material
C. smoking in bed
D. worn electrical wires on power tools

00312. The spray of water in low-velocity fog will have:

A. greater range than high-velocity fog
B. lesser range than high-velocity fog
C. about the same range as high-velocity fog
D. greater range than a solid stream

00313. Kapok life preservers require proper care, and should NOT be:

A. stowed near open flame or where smoking is permitted
B. used as seats, pillows, or foot rests
C. left on open decks
D. any of the above

00317. Your vessel will be entering the navigable waters of the United States. You are required by regulations to:

A. test the primary and secondary steering systems no more than 8 hours before entering
B. correct the charts of the area to be transited using the Notice(s) to Mariners or foreign equivalent reasonably available
C. have a copy of, or an extract of the List of Lights
D. check the magnetic compass for the correct deviation

00318. The fundamental treatment for preventing traumatic shock following an accident is to:

A. have victim exercise to increase circulation
B. keep victim from electrical equipment
C. keep victim warm and dry while lying down
D. apply ice packs and avoid excitement

00319. Foam is effective in combating what class(es) of fire?

A. A
B. B
C. A and B
D. B and C

00322. A definite advantage of using water as a fire extinguishing agent is its characteristic:

A. alternate expansion and contraction as water in liquid state becomes vapor
B. absorption of smoke and gases as water is converted from liquid to vapor
C. rapid contraction as water is converted from a liquid to a vapor
D. rapid expansion as water absorbs heat and changes to steam

00323. Which of the following statements is FALSE concerning life preservers?

A. They come in two sizes, child and adult.
B. They are required to be of highly visible color.
C. The "bib" life preserver will not support an unconscious wearer in an upright position.
D. They must be able to support the wearer in an upright position.

00324. The national distress, safety, and calling frequency is channel:

A. 13
B. 16
C. 18
D. 22

00328. A man has suffered a burn on the arm. There is extensive damage to the skin with charring present. How would this injury be classified using standard medical terminology?

A. dermal burn
B. third-degree burn
C. major burn
D. lethal burn

00331. One of the limitations of foam as an extinguishing agent is that foam:

A. cannot be made with salt water
B. is heavier than oil and sinks below its surface
C. is corrosive and a hazard to fire fighters
D. conducts electricity

00332. When using a high-velocity fog stream in a passageway, the possibility of a blow back must be guarded against. Blow back is most likely to occur when:

A. pressure builds up in the nozzle which causes a surge of water
B. the only opening in a passageway is the one from which the nozzle is being advanced
C. pressure in the fire hose drops below 100 psi
D. a bulkhead collapses due to heat and pressure

00333. Which statement is TRUE concerning life preservers?

A. Buoyant vests may be substituted for life preservers.
B. Life preservers are designed to turn an unconscious person's face clear of the water.
C. Life preservers must always be worn with the same side facing outwards to float properly.
D. Lightly stained or faded life preservers will fail in the water and should not be used.

00337. You are sailing the navigable waters of the United States. You must have a currently corrected copy (or extract) of the:

A. List of Lights
B. Tide Tables
C. Sailing Directions
D. Pollution Prevention Regulations

00338. A man has suffered a burn on the arm. There is reddening of the skin, blistering and swelling. How would this injury be classified using standard medical terminology?

A. major burn
B. secondary burn
C. second-degree burn
D. blister burn

00339. If a firefighting situation calls for low-velocity fog you would:

A. order the engine room to reduce pressure on the fire pump
B. put the lever on an all-purpose fire nozzle all the way forward
C. attach a low-velocity fog applicator with the nozzle shut down
D. put the lever on an all-purpose fire nozzle all the way back

00341. The Master or other vessel representative must contact the nearest Coast Guard Marine Safety Office within 5 days of a(n):

A. grounding
B. injury which requires first aid
C. accident which requires $2500 of repairs
D. All of the above are correct.

00342. Every injury aboard a commercial fishing industry vessel must be reported to the:

A. Coast Guard
B. vessel owner or owner's agent
C. Occupational Safety and Health Administration
D. National Fisheries Service

00343. An emergency sea anchor may be constructed by using:

A. a boat bucket
B. an air tank filled with water
C. an oar and canvas weighted down
D. any of the above

00344. The signal that actuates the radio auto-alarms on a vessel is a series of:

A. 6 dashes sent in 1 minute
B. 6 dashes sent in 2 minutes
C. 12 dashes sent in 1 minute
D. 12 dashes sent in 2 minutes

00348. A man has suffered a burn on the arm. There is a reddening of the skin but no other apparent damage. How would this injury be classified using standard medical terminology?

A. minor burn
B. superficial burn
C. extremity burn
D. first-degree burn

00352. Which of the following is an advantage of water fog over a straight stream of water in fighting an oil fire?

A. It has a smothering effect on the fire.
B. It removes combustible vapors from the air.
C. It gives more protection to fire fighting personnel.
D. all of the above

00353. When a sea anchor is used in landing in a heavy surf, headway is checked by:

A. slacking the tripping line and towing the apex end forward
B. slacking the tripping line and towing the mouth forward by the holding line
C. towing with the tripping line and the holding line slack
D. towing the apex end forward with the tripping line

00354. The distress message of a ship in distress should include considerable information, which might facilitate the rescue. This information should:

A. always be included in the initial distress message
B. be transmitted using the International Code of Signals

C. be transmitted as a series of short messages, if time allows
D. include the vessel's draft

00355. The center of flotation of a vessel is the point in the waterplane:

A. about which the vessel lists and trims
B. which coincides with the center of buoyancy
C. which, in the absence of external forces, is always vertically aligned with the center of gravity
D. which is shown in the hydrostatic tables as VCB

00357. The operator of a vessel's radiotelephone must hold at least a:

A. third class radiotelegraph operator certificate
B. restricted radiotelephone operator permit
C. general radiotelephone operator license
D. mate's license

00358. When treating a person for third-degree burns, you should:

A. submerge the burn area in cold water
B. make the person stand up and walk to increase circulation
C. cover the burns with thick, sterile dressings
D. break blisters and remove dead tissue

00362. Water fog from an all-purpose nozzle may be effectively used to:

A. fight an electrical fire
B. fight a magnesium fire
C. eliminate smoke from a compartment
D. all of the above

00363. You are in a lifeboat in a heavy sea. Your boat is dead in the water, unable to make way. To prevent broaching to, you should:

A. take no action, broaching is recommended in a heavy sea
B. put out the sea anchor
C. put out the sea painter
D. fill the bottom of the boat with about 1 foot of water to make it ride better

00367. A ship's radiotelephone station license is issued by the:

A. U. S. Coast Guard
B. Federal Communications Commission
C. Radio Technical Commission for Marine Services
D. Maritime Mobile Service Commission

00368. The FIRST concern in treating a person for an extensive burn is to prevent or reduce:

A. disfigurement
B. infection
C. pain
D. asphyxia

00373. If your vessel is broken down and rolling in heavy seas, you can reduce the possibility of capsizing by:

A. constantly shifting the rudder
B. moving all personnel forward and low
C. moving all personnel aft
D. rigging a sea anchor

00374. A vessel operating outside of coastal waters must carry an automatically activated Emergency Position Indicating Radio Beacon (EPIRB) if she:

A. does not have berthing facilities
B. has berthing and galley facilities
C. is a workboat and her mothership carries an EPIRB
D. none of the above are correct.

00375. Normal fueling results in the collection of waste oil in drip pans and containers. Which procedure is an approved method of disposing of the waste oil?

A. draining it overboard when the vessel gets underway
B. placing it in proper disposal facilities
C. adding sinking agents and discharging it into the water
D. mixing it with dispersants before draining it overboard

00377. The regulations governing the frequencies of the bridge-to-bridge radiotelephone are promulgated by the:

A. Department of Transportation
B. Federal Communications Commission
C. U. S. Coast Guard
D. Department of Defense

00378. Surface burns should first be treated by:

A. washing the area with a warm soap and water solution
B. flooding, bathing, or immersing the area in cold water
C. covering the area with talcum power and bandaging tightly
D. leaving them exposed to the atmosphere

00379. Plastic material may be discharged overboard from a vessel if it is:

A. 3 miles from shore
B. 12 miles from shore

C. 25 miles from shore
D. nowhere while afloat

C00382. Having the handle of an all-purpose nozzle in the vertical position, with an applicator attached, will:

A. produce high-velocity fog
B. produce low-velocity fog
C. produce a straight stream
D. shut off the water

00383. The purpose of the tripping line on a sea anchor is to:

A. aid in casting off
B. direct the drift of the vessel
C. aid in its recovery
D. maintain maximum resistance to broaching

00387. If your vessel is equipped with a radiotelephone, what must also be aboard?

A. Certificate of Inspection
B. copy of Part 83 of FCC regulations
C. copy of ship to shore channels
D. radio station license

00388. A victim has suffered a second-degree burn to a small area of the lower arm. What is the proper treatment for this injury?

A. Immerse the arm in cold water for 1 to 2 hours, apply burn ointment, and bandage.
B. Open any blisters with a sterile needle, apply burn ointment and bandage.
C. Apply burn ointment, remove any foreign material and insure that nothing is in contact with the burn.
D. Immerse the arm in cold water for 1 to 2 hours, open any blister and apply burn ointment.

00391. Foam is a very effective smothering agent and:

A. it provides cooling as a secondary effect
B. works well on extinguishing electrical fires
C. can be used to combat combustible metal fires
D. all of the above

00393. A sea anchor is:

A. a heavy anchor with extra long line used to anchor in deep water
B. a cone shaped bag used to slow down the wind drift effect
C. a pad eye to which the sea painter is made fast
D. made of wood if it is of an approved type

00394. If you are transmitting a distress message by radiotelephone you should:

A. use plain language if possible
B. always use the International Code
C. preface it by the word "interco"
D. follow the transmission with the radio alarm signal

00397. When maintenance work is performed on the radiotelephone equipment by a licensed operator who is not employed aboard the vessel on a full time basis, the entry in the radiotelephone log is not required to include:

A. his mailing address
B. the class of his license
C. the issue date of his license
D. the serial number of his license

00398. For small, first-degree burns the quickest method to relieve pain is to:

A. immerse the burn in cold water
B. administer aspirin
C. apply petroleum jelly
D. apply a bandage to exclude air

00400. To remove the effects of free communication flooding, it would usually be most advantageous to:

A. close the cross-connection valve between the off-center tanks
B. completely flood high center tanks
C. ballast double bottom wing tanks
D. close any opening to the sea in an off-center tank

00402. To lubricate the swivel or remove corrosion from a fire hose coupling, you should use:

A. glycerine
B. graphite
C. kerosene
D. fresh water and soap

00403. Due to the shape of the sea anchor, the best way to haul it back aboard is by:

A. hauling in on the anchor line as you would any anchor
B. getting all hands to assist
C. its trip line
D. cutting the line, as you cannot haul it back in

00407. Any person maintaining a listening watch on a bridge-to-bridge radiotelephone must be able to:

A. speak English
B. repair the unit

C. send Morse Code
D. speak a language the vessel's crew will understand

00408. If a person is unconscious from electric shock, you should first remove him from the electrical source and then:

A. administer ammonia smelling salts
B. check for serious burns on the body
C. determine if he is breathing
D. massage vigorously to restore circulation

00411. Under Annex V to MARPOL 73/78, garbage discharged from vessels that are located between 3 and 12 nautical miles from nearest land must be ground to less than:

A. 1"
B. 1-1/4"
C. 1-1/2"
D. 2"

00412. To get low-velocity fog from an all-purpose nozzle, you would:

A. attach the bronze nozzle tip to the fog outlet of the nozzle
B. attach an applicator to the nozzle in place of the bronze nozzle tip
C. attach an applicator to the solid stream outlet on the nozzle
D. simply move the handle to the vertical position on the nozzle

00413. The part of a sea anchor that allows it to be easily brought back aboard a life raft is the:

A. drag line
B. bridle
C. trip line
D. iron ring

00414. In a distress situation, the two tone alarm signal should be followed immediately by the:

A. distress position
B. spoken words "Mayday, Mayday, Mayday"
C. ship's name
D. ship's call letters

00415. What must ocean going vessels of 100 GT be fitted with for oily mixtures?

A. a fixed system to discharge the slops overboard
B. a fixed system to discharge oily mixtures to a reception facility
C. a portable system to discharge the slops overboard
D. a portable system to discharge oily mixtures to a reception facility

00417. According to the regulations, you are required to retain a record of the use of your radiotelephone for a period of not less than:

A. 1 month
B. 4 months
C. 6 months
D. 1 year

00418. Treatments of heat exhaustion consist of:

A. moving to a shaded area and laying down
B. bathing with rubbing alcohol
C. placing the patient in a tub of cold water
D. all of the above

00421. After the initial AMVER Position Report, sent by a vessel sailing foreign, subsequent Position Reports must be sent no less frequently than every:

A. 24 hours
B. 36 hours
C. 48 hours
D. Monday, Wednesday, and Friday

00422. The all-purpose nozzle will produce a fog stream by:

A. pulling the nozzle handle all the way back toward the operator
B. pulling the nozzle handle back to a position where the handle is perpendicular to the plane of the nozzle
C. pushing the nozzle handle forward as far as it will go
D. inserting a fog applicator between the fire hose and nozzle

00423. When you stream a sea anchor, you should make sure that the holding line is:

A. long enough to cause the pull to be more horizontal than downward
B. long enough to reach bottom
C. short enough to cause the pull to be downward
D. short enough to avoid tangling

00424. Which of the following would be used to call all stations in your vicinity by radiotelephone?

A. calling all stations
B. Charlie Quebec
C. Alpha Alpha
D. Kilo

00427. Radio station logs involving communications incident to a disaster shall be retained by the station licensee for a period of:

A. 4 years from date of entry
B. 3 years from date of entry
C. 2 years from date of entry
D. 1 year from date of entry

00428. Physical exertion on the part of a person who has fallen into cold water would:

A. be the best thing to try if there was no rescue in sight
B. increase survival time in the water
C. increase the rate of heat loss from the body
D. not affect the heat loss from the body

00429. You are at sea and not in a special area as defined in ANNEX V of MARPOL. How many nautical miles from land must you be to discharge ground garbage (that will pass through a 1-inch screen) into the sea?

A. 3 nm
B. 6 nm
C. 12 nm
D. 25 nm

00432. One advantage of the "all-purpose nozzle" is that it:

A. can fit any size hose
B. converts a stream of water into a fog
C. increases the amount of water reaching the fire
D. can spray two streams of water at the same time

00434. You are underway in the Gulf of Mexico when you hear a distress message over the VHF radio. The position of the sender is about 20 miles south of Galveston, TX, and you are about 80 miles ESE of Galveston. What action should you take?

A. Immediately acknowledge receipt of the distress message.
B. Defer acknowledgment for a short interval so that a coast station may acknowledge receipt.
C. Do not acknowledge receipt until other ships nearer to the distress have acknowledged.
D. Do not acknowledge receipt because you are too far away to take action.

00437. A statement concerning the operating condition of the required radiotelephone equipment shall be made in the radiotelephone log each:

A. hour
B. watch
C. day
D. week

00438. A crew member has suffered frostbite to the toes of both feet. You should:

A. immerse the feet in warm water
B. warm the feet with a heat lamp
C. warm the feet at room temperature
D. rub the feet

00439. Fixed CO2 systems would not be used on crew's quarters or:

A. the paint locker
B. spaces open to the atmosphere
C. cargo holds
D. the engine room

00441. Your vessel is broken down and rolling in heavy seas. You can reduce the possibility of capsizing by:

A. moving all personnel aft
B. constantly shifting the rudder
C. rigging a sea anchor
D. moving all personnel forward and low

00442. On the all-purpose nozzle, the position of the valve when the handle is all the way forward is:

A. shut
B. fog
C. solid stream
D. spray

00443. What does "EPIRB" stand for?

A. Emergency Position Indicating Radar Buoy
B. Electronic Pulse Indicating Radiobeacon
C. Emergency Position Indicating Radiobeacon
D. none of the above

00444. A call between any two ship stations on an intership working frequency shall have a maximum duration of:

A. 2 minutes
B. 3 minutes
C. 4 minutes
D. 5 minutes

00447. According to the "Vessel Bridge-to-Bridge Radiotelephone Act", which is NOT required in the radiotelephone log?

A. distress and alarm signals transmitted or intercepted
B. times of beginning and end of watch period
C. routine navigational traffic
D. daily statement about the condition of the required radiotelephone equipment

00448. Treatment of frostbite includes:

A. rubbing affected area with ice or snow
B. rubbing affected area briskly to restore circulation
C. wrapping area tightly in warm cloths
D. warming exposed parts rapidly

00450. Which type of portable fire extinguisher is best suited for putting out a Class D fire?

A. dry chemical
B. CO2
C. foam
D. dry powder

00452. When the handle of an all-purpose nozzle is in the forward position, the nozzle will:

A. produce high-velocity fog
B. produce low-velocity fog
C. produce a straight stream
D. shut off the water

00453. Which statement is TRUE concerning lifesaving equipment?

A. The Master may assign an officer to keep the lifesaving equipment in good condition.
B. All lifeboat winch control apparati are required to be examined every month.
C. Nothing may be stowed in a lifeboat other than the required equipment.
D. all of the above

00454. When calling a ship on VHF-FM frequencies, Bell System coast stations normally call on channel:

A. 13
B. 16
C. 19
D. 23

00457. According to the "Vessel Bridge-to-Bridge Radiotelephone Act", your radiotelephone log must contain:

A. a record of all routine calls
B. a record of your transmissions only
C. home address of the vessel's Master or owner
D. a summary of all distress calls and messages

00458. Which of the following procedures should be followed when individuals are rescued in cold climates and suffer from hypothermia?

A. Give them brandy.
B. Get them to a hot room.
C. Immerse in a hot bath (105°F, 40°C).
D. Cover with an electric blanket set for maximum temperature.

00462. When the handle of an all-purpose nozzle is in the vertical position and without an applicator, the all-purpose nozzle will:

A. produce high-velocity fog
B. produce low-velocity fog
C. produce a straight stream
D. shut off the water

00463. Which of the following documents would list all the lifesaving equipment required for a vessel?

A. Certificate of Inspection
B. American Bureau of Shipping Classification Certificate
C. International Convention for the Safety of Life at Sea Certificate
D. Certificate of Registry

00464. If you are calling ship-to-shore using the VHF-FM service, you can tell that the working channel of the desired coast station is busy if you hear:

A. speech
B. signalling tones
C. a busy signal
D. any of the above

00467. Which of the following is the required location of the radiotelephone station aboard a vessel to which the Vessel Bridge-to-Bridge Radiotelephone Act applies?

A. on the bridge or in the wheelhouse
B. in a separate radio compartment
C. adjacent to the main power source
D. as high as possible on the vessel

00468. The most effective warming treatment for a crew member suffering from hypothermia is:

A. running or jumping to create heat
B. lying in the sun
C. a warm water bath
D. mouth-to-mouth resuscitation

00469. A low-velocity fog applicator attached to the all-purpose nozzle is required to produce a fog pattern diameter of at LEAST:

A. 8 feet
B. 22 feet
C. 25 feet
D. 65 feet

00470. A squeeze-grip type carbon dioxide portable fire extinguisher has been partially discharged. It should be:

A. replaced in its proper location if weight loss is no more than 15%
B. labeled empty and recharged as soon as possible
C. replaced in its proper location regardless of weight
D. replaced in its proper location if weight loss is no more than 25%

00472. When the handle of an all-purpose nozzle is pulled all the way back, it will:

A. produce high-velocity fog
B. produce low-velocity fog
C. produce a straight stream
D. shut off the water

00473. Which of the following knots is suitable for hoisting an unconscious person?

A. bowline in a bight
B. French bowline
C. fisherman's loop
D. spider hitch

00474. If possible, when making ship-to-shore calls on VHF, you should use the:

A. VHF-FM service
B. coastal harbor service
C. high seas service
D. emergency broadcast service

00477. The radiotelephone required by the Vessel Bridge-to-Bridge Radiotelephone Act is for the exclusive use of:

A. the Master or person in charge of the vessel
B. a person designated by the Master
C. a person on board to pilot the vessel
D. all of the above

00478. If a crew member faints, and the face is flushed, you should:

A. lay the crew member down with the head and shoulders slightly raised
B. administer a liquid stimulant
C. lay the crew member down with the head lower than the feet
D. attempt to stand the crew member upright to restore consciousness

00481. The "fly" refers to the:

A. horizontal dimension of a flag
B. sea state in a hurricane
C. loose end of a line
D. keeper ring of a pelican hook

00482. The high velocity fog tip used with the all-purpose fire fighting nozzle should always be:

A. attached by a chain
B. coated with heavy grease to prevent corrosion
C. painted red for identity as emergency equipment
D. stored in the clip at each fire station

00483. Which of the following is considered primary lifesaving equipment?

A. life preservers
B. lifeboats
C. ring life buoys
D. personal flotation devices

00484. A message warning of a tropical storm should be sent as a(n):

A. routine message
B. urgent message
C. distress message
D. safety message

00487. Which of the following statements is TRUE concerning radiotelephones on board towing vessels?

A. There cannot be a radiotelephone located anywhere except in the wheelhouse.
B. The officer in charge of the wheelhouse is considered to have the radiotelephone watch.
C. Only distress messages may be transmitted over channel 13.
D. Only the Master of the vessel is allowed to speak over the radiotelephone.

00488. To determine whether or not an adult victim has a pulse, the rescuer should check the pulse at the:

A. carotid artery in the neck
B. femoral artery in the groin
C. brachial artery in the arm
D. radial artery in the wrist

00489. An extinguisher with 15 lbs. of CO_2 or 10 lbs. of dry chemical is a size:

A. I
B. II
C. III
D. IV

00492. The spray of water produced by using the high-velocity fog position on an all-purpose nozzle will have:

A. greater range than low-velocity fog
B. lesser range than low-velocity fog
C. about the same range as low-velocity fog
D. greater range than a solid stream

00494. A message giving warning of a hurricane should have which of the following prefixes when sent by radiotelephone?

A. Pan-Pan (3 times)
B. Securite Securite Securite
C. TTT TTT TTT
D. no special prefix

00497. What VHF channel does the Coast Guard use to broadcast routine weather reports?

A. 13 or 14
B. 16 or 17
C. 21 or 22
D. 44 or 45

00498. An unconscious person should NOT be:

A. placed in a position with the head lower than the body
B. given an inhalation stimulant
C. given something to drink
D. treated for injuries until conscious

00500. Safety shackles are fitted with:

A. a threaded bolt
B. a round pin, with a cotter pin
C. a threaded bolt, locknuts, and cotter pins
D. round pins and locknuts

00504. If you wished to transmit a message by voice concerning the safety of navigation, you would preface it by the word:

A. Mayday
B. Pan-pan
C. Securite
D. Safety

00505. Which of the following vessels is NOT required to have a Pollution Placard posted on board?

A. 15-foot passenger vessel
B. 75-foot towing vessel
C. 50-foot cabin cruiser used for pleasure only
D. 150-foot unmanned tank barge

00507. You are required to maintain a continuous listening watch on channel:

A. 6 (156.3 MHz)
B. 12 (156.6 MHz)
C. 14 (156.7 MHz)
D. 16 (156.8 MHz)

00508. Which of the following should NOT be a treatment for a person who has received a head injury and is groggy or unconscious?

A. give a stimulant
B. elevate his head
C. stop severe bleeding
D. treat for shock

00509. Placing a lashing across a hook to prevent a fitting from slipping out of the hook is called:

A. faking
B. flemishing down
C. mousing
D. worming

00510. A new crew member, who has not received any safety instructions or participated in any drills, reports on board. The Master must provide a safety orientation:

A. within 1 week
B. within 24 hours
C. on reporting day if it occurs within normal work hours
D. before sailing

00514. You hear on the radiotelephone the word "Securite" spoken three times. This indicates that:

A. a message about the safety of navigation will follow
B. a message of an urgent nature about the safety of a ship will follow
C. the sender is in distress and requests immediate assistance
D. you should secure your radiotelephone

00515. Which statement is TRUE concerning the placard entitled "Discharge of Oil Prohibited"?

A. It is required on all vessels.
B. It may be located in a conspicuous place in the wheelhouse.
C. It may be located at the bilge and ballast pump control station.
D. all of the above

00516. Which toxic gas is a product of incomplete combustion, and is often present when a fire burns in a closed compartment?

A. carbon dioxide
B. hydrogen sulfide
C. carbon monoxide
D. nitric oxide

00517. The VHF radiotelephone calling/safety/distress frequency is:

A. 156.8 MHz (channel 16)
B. 156.7 MHz (channel 14)
C. 156.65 MHz (channel 13)
D. 156.6 MHz (channel 12)

00518. If a person gets battery acid in his eye while filling a battery, he should FIRST wash the eye with:

A. boric acid solution
B. water
C. baking soda solution
D. ammonia

00522. A spanner is a:

A. cross connection line between two main fire lines
B. special wrench for tightening couplings in a fire hose line
C. tackle rigged to support a fire hose
D. none of the above

00524. The radiotelephone safety message urgently concerned with safety of a person would be prefixed by the word:

A. Mayday
B. Pan-Pan
C. Safety
D. Interco

00527. The VHF radiotelephone frequency designated to be used only to transmit or receive information pertaining to the safe navigation of a vessel is:

A. 156.8 MHz (channel 16)
B. 156.7 MHz (channel 14)
C. 156.65 MHz (channel 13)
D. 156.6 MHz (channel 12)

00528. If a person gets something in his eye and you see that it is not embedded, you can:

A. get him to rub his eye until the object is gone
B. remove it with a match or toothpick
C. remove it with a piece of dry sterile cotton
D. remove it with a moist, cotton-tipped applicator

00531. A CO2 portable extinguisher is annually checked by:

A. reading the gage pressure
B. weighing the extinguisher
C. discharging a small amount of CO2
D. seeing if the seal has been broken

00532. Fire hose should be washed with:

A. salt water and a wire brush
B. caustic soap
C. mild soap and fresh water
D. a holystone

00533. What is the purpose of limber holes?

A. to allow for air circulation
B. to allow for stress and strain in rough waters
C. to allow water in the boat to drain overboard
D. to allow water in the bilge to get to the boat drain

00534. Your vessel has been damaged and is taking on water, but you do not require immediate assistance. Which of the following radiotelephone signals would you use to preface a message advising other vessels of your situation?

A. Mayday-Mayday-Mayday
B. Pan-Pan (3 times)
C. Securite-Securite-Securite
D. SOS-SOS-SOS

00537. What frequency has the FCC designated for the use of bridge-to-bridge radiotelephone stations?

A. 156.275 MHz channel 65
B. 156.65 MHz channel 13
C. 157.00 MHz channel 28
D. 157.00 MHz channel 20

00538. For a victim who is coughing and wheezing from a partial obstruction of the airway by a foreign body, a potential rescuer should:

A. perform the Heimlich maneuver
B. immediately start CPR
C. give back blows and something to drink
D. bend the victim over and give back blows

00542. Before inserting a low-velocity fog applicator into an all-purpose nozzle, you must: (See illustration D004SA.)

A. install the high-velocity nozzle tip
B. move the handle to position 2
C. move the handle to position 1
D. remove the high-velocity nozzle tip

00544. In radiotelephone communications, the prefix PAN-PAN indicates that:

A. a ship is threatened by grave and imminent danger and requests immediate assistance
B. a calling station has an urgent message about the safety of a person
C. the message following the prefix will be about the safety of navigation
D. the calling station requests immediate medical assistance

00547. Channel 13 (156.65 MHz), the designated bridge-to-bridge channel, may NOT be used for which of the following?

A. To exchange navigational information between vessels
B. To exchange navigational information between a vessel and a shore station
C. to conduct necessary tests
D. to exchange operating schedules with company dispatcher

00548. A shipmate chokes suddenly, cannot speak, and starts to turn blue. What action should you take?

A. Administer the Heimlich maneuver.
B. Make the victim lie down with the feet elevated to get blood to the brain.
C. Immediately administer CPR.
D. Do nothing until the victim becomes unconscious.

00549. If a vessel takes a sudden, severe list or trim from an unknown cause, you should first:

A. determine the cause before taking counter-measures
B. assume the shift is due to off-center loading
C. counterflood
D. assume the cause is environmental forces

00553. Which of the following is TRUE concerning lifeboat gripes?

A. They must be released by freeing a safety shackle.
B. They should not be released until the boat is in lowering position.
C. They may be adjusted by a turnbuckle.
D. They are normally used only with radial davits.

00557. The Vessel Bridge-to-Bridge Radiotelephone Act establishes the frequency for bridge-to-bridge communications as 156.65 MHz or channel:

A. 12
B. 13
C. 14
D. 16

00558. If someone suffers a heart attack and has ceased breathing, you should:

A. immediately give a stimulant, by force if necessary
B. make the victim comfortable in a bunk
C. immediately start CPR
D. administer oxygen

00561. The 12 foot low velocity fog applicator:

A. has a spray pattern 12 feet in diameter
B. can be used in conjunction with both 1-1/2 inch and 2-1/2 inch all-purpose nozzles

C. has a 90° bend at its discharge end
D. has a screw thread end which connects to the all-purpose nozzle

00565. Small oil spills on deck can be kept from going overboard by:

A. driving wooden plugs into the vents
B. closing the lids on the vents
C. plugging the scuppers
D. plugging the sounding pipes

00567. Channel 13 is primarily used for ship to ship communication. On a secondary basis, channel 13 can be used for:

A. coast to aircraft operational communications
B. aircraft to ship operational communications
C. coast to ship navigational communications
D. aircraft to ship navigational communications

00568. A person suffering from a heart attack may show which of the following symptoms?

A. shortness of breath
B. pain in the left arm
C. nausea
D. all of the above

00571. To increase the extent of flooding your vessel can suffer without foundering, you could:

A. ballast the vessel
B. increase reserve buoyancy
C. lower the center of gravity
D. raise the center of gravity

00575. Pollution regulations require that each scupper in an enclosed deck area have a:

A. wooden plug
B. soft rubber plug
C. two-piece soft patch
D. mechanical means of closing

00577. All towing vessels of 26 feet or over in length while navigating are required to carry which of the following items?

A. at least 2 lifeboats
B. a radiotelephone
C. a loran receiver
D. none of the above

00578. When fighting fires in spaces containing bottles of LPG (liquefied petroleum gas), you should:

A. attempt to isolate the fire from the LPG
B. cool the bottles or remove them from the fire area
C. see that valves on all LPG bottles are closed
D. place insulating material over the bottles

00580. Freeboard is measured from the upper edge of the:

A. bulwark
B. deck line
C. gunwale bar
D. sheer strake

00585. For how long must a "Declaration of Inspection" be maintained?

A. 1 week
B. 2 weeks
C. 1 month
D. 3 months

00587. Which vessel would NOT be required to have a radiotelephone?

A. A 34-foot vessel engaged in towing
B. A dredge operating in a channel
C. A vessel of 100 GT carrying 50 passengers for hire
D. A 12-meter private yacht

00589. Fires are grouped into what categories?

A. Class A, B, C and D
B. Type 1, 2, 3, and 4
C. combustible solids, liquids, and gases
D. flammable solids, liquids, and gases

00590. The distance between the waterline of a vessel and the main deck is called:

A. draft
B. freeboard
C. buoyancy
D. camber

00592. A foam-type portable fire extinguisher would be most useful in combating a fire in:

A. solid materials such as wood or bales of fiber
B. flammable liquids
C. a piece of electrical equipment
D. combustible metallic solids

00597. The "Vessel Bridge-to-Bridge Radiotelephone Act" applies to:

A. every towing vessel of 16 feet or over in length while navigating
B. every vessel of 50 GT and upward, carrying one or more persons for hire
C. all aircraft operating on the water
D. every power-driven vessel of 20 meters and upward while navigating

00598. A fire must be ventilated:

A. when using an indirect attack on the fire such as flooding with water

B. to prevent the gases of combustion from surrounding the firefighters
C. to minimize heat buildup in adjacent compartments
D. if compressed gas cylinders are stowed in the compartment on fire

00599. In order to initiate CPR on a drowning victim:

A. start chest compressions before the victim is removed from the water
B. drain water from the lungs before ventilating
C. begin mouth-to-mouth ventilations in the water if possible
D. do not tilt the head back since it may cause vomiting

00600. The amount of freeboard which a ship possesses has a tremendous effect on its:

A. initial stability
B. free surface
C. stability at large angles of inclination
D. permeability

00604. If the batteries for the portable radio are of a type that require recharging, they shall be brought to a full charge at least once:

A. a week
B. every 2 weeks
C. a month
D. every 3 months

00605. The owner of a vessel subject to the pollution regulations shall keep a written record, available for inspection by the COTP, of:

A. the name of each person currently designated as a person in charge
B. the date and result of the most recent test on the system relief valves
C. the date and location of each inspection of the bilge overboard discharge valves
D. all of the above

00607. The "Vessel Bridge-to-Bridge Radiotelephone Act" applies to which of the following towboats?

A. a 100 GT towboat, 24 feet in length
B. a 90-foot towboat tied to the pier
C. a 60-foot towboat towing by pushing ahead
D. a 400 GT towboat anchored

00608. Where possible, a fire of escaping liquefied flammable gas should be extinguished by:

A. cooling the gas below the ignition point
B. cutting off the supply of oxygen
C. stopping the flow of gas
D. interrupting the chain reaction

00610. The amount of freeboard which a ship possesses has a tremendous effect on its:

A. initial stability
B. free surface
C. permeability
D. stability at large angles of inclination

00611. The maximum draft to which a vessel may be safely loaded is called:

A. mean draft
B. calculated draft
C. deep draft
D. load line draft

00612. A shipmate suffers a heart attack and stops breathing. You should:

A. immediately give a stimulant, by force if necessary
B. immediately start CPR
C. make the victim comfortable in a bunk
D. administer oxygen

00614. The batteries for all fixed and portable radio apparatus on lifeboats shall, if the batteries are of a type which requires recharging, be brought to full charge at least once:

A. a week
B. every 2 weeks
C. a month
D. every 2 months

00615. The owner or operator of each vessel subject to the pollution regulations is NOT required to keep written records of:

A. the name of each person designated as a person in charge
B. the date and results of the most recent equipment inspection
C. cargoes carried and dates delivered, including destinations
D. dates and locations of valve inspections

00617. All entries in the radiotelephone log of vessels engaged on international voyages, except on the Great Lakes or Inland Waters, shall be kept in:

A. local standard time (LST)
B. eastern standard time (EST)
C. Greenwich mean time (GMT)
D. central standard time (CST)

00619. Fighting a fire in the galley poses the additional threat of:

A. contaminating food with extinguishing agent
B. spreading through the engineering space
C. loss of stability
D. a grease fire in the ventilation system

00621. The color of the signal flare sent up by a submarine about to surface is:

A. white
B. green
C. yellow
D. red

00627. The time kept in the radiotelephone log shall be counted:

A. from 0000 to 1200 beginning at midnight and noon
B. from 0000 to 2400 beginning at midnight
C. from 12:01 am to 12:00 beginning at midnight
D. in any convenient system

00629. The necessity for administering artificial respiration may be recognized by:

A. vomiting
B. blue color and lack of breathing
C. irregular breathing
D. unconsciousness

00630. Reserve buoyancy is measured by:

A. GM
B. the void portion of the ship below the waterline which is enclosed and watertight
C. transverse watertight bulkheads
D. the part of the enclosed and watertight portion of a vessel above the waterline

00632. Portable foam type fire extinguishers are most effective on:

A. mattress fires
B. oil fires
C. wood fires
D. all of the above

00637. The date and time kept in the radiotelephone log shall commence at:

A. midnight
B. noon
C. beginning of the watch
D. any convenient time

00640. The volume of all intact and watertight spaces of a vessel above its waterline is the vessel's:

A. free surface
B. marginal stability
C. reserve buoyancy
D. freeboard

00642. As an extinguishing agent, foam:

A. conducts electricity
B. should be directed at the source of the fire
C. is most effective on burning liquids which are flowing
D. extinguishes by cooling the fire below ignition temperature

00647. As specified by the "Vessel Bridge-to-Bridge Radiotelephone Act", after 1 January 1974, the maximum power of all transmitters used shall be not more than:

A. 25 watts
B. 50 watts
C. 75 watts
D. 100 watts

00649. Which of the following, when removed, will result in the extinguishment of a fire?

A. nitrogen
B. oxygen
C. sodium
D. carbon dioxide

00650. Which of the following may be an indication of reserve buoyancy?

A. metacentric height
B. righting moment
C. rolling period
D. freeboard

00651. Artificial respiration may be necessary in cases of:

A. drowning
B. electrocution
C. poisoning
D. all of the above

00652. How does foam extinguish an oil fire?

A. by cooling the oil below the ignition temperature
B. by removing the fuel source from the fire
C. by excluding the oxygen from the fire
D. by increasing the weight of the oil

00654. Which of the following statements about transmitting distress messages by radiotelephone is INCORRECT?

A. Distress messages should first be transmitted on 2182 kHz.
B. Channel 16 (156.8 mHz) is especially effective for distress signals when operating far offshore.
C. If no answer is received on the designated distress frequencies, repeat the distress call on any frequency available.

D. It is advisable to follow a distress message on 2182 kHz by a long count or a continued repetition of the vessel's name or call letters.

00655. The spread of fire is NOT prevented by:

A. shutting off the oxygen supply
B. cooling surfaces adjacent to the fire
C. removing combustibles from the endangered area
D. Each of the above choices prevents the spread of fire.

00657. What is the normal operating power for ship-to-ship communications on channel 13?

A. 1 watt or less
B. 5 watts
C. 10 watts
D. 20 watts

00660. Reserve buoyancy is:

A. the enclosed watertight part of a vessel above the waterline
B. the void portion of the ship below the waterline which is enclosed and watertight
C. transverse watertight bulkheads
D. a measure of metacentric height

00661. The Master of a fishing vessel must hold drills at a minimum of once every:

A. day
B. week
C. month
D. 3 months

00662. Foam extinguishes a fire by:

A. cooling
B. chemical action
C. smothering
D. inerting the air

00664. Your vessel is in distress and you have made radiotelephone contact with a U. S. Coast Guard vessel. The Coast Guard vessel requests that you give him a long count. This indicates that:

A. your radio transmitter is not working properly
B. the Coast Guard vessel is testing its receiver
C. the Coast Guard vessel is taking a radio direction finder bearing on your vessel
D. the Coast Guard vessel is requesting your position in latitude and longitude

00666. On vessels equipped with electric power operated lifeboat winches, the Master is responsible that such winches and associated equipment are examined at least once in each period of:

A. 2 months
B. 3 months
C. 4 months
D. 5 months

00667. Failure to comply with the provisions of the "Vessel Bridge-to-Bridge Radio-Telephone Act" can result in a:

A. $500 civil penalty charged against the Master
B. $1500 civil penalty charged against the Master
C. $500 criminal penalty charged against the Master
D. $1500 criminal penalty charged against the Master

00670. Which action will affect the trim of a vessel?

A. moving high weights lower
B. adding weight at the tipping center
C. moving a weight forward
D. any of the above

00672. A foam-type portable fire extinguisher would be most useful in combating a fire in:

A. generators
B. oil drums
C. the bridge controls
D. combustible metals

00674. A distress frequency used on radiotelephone is:

A. 400 kilohertz
B. 2182 kilohertz
C. 2728 kilohertz
D. 8221 kilohertz

00677. Every vessel navigated in violation of the Vessel Bridge-to-Bridge Radiotelephone Act or the regulations thereunder is subject to a penalty of not more than:

A. $100
B. $500
C. $1000
D. $1500

00678. Fire may be spread by which of the following means?

A. conduction of heat to adjacent surfaces
B. direct radiation
C. convection
D. all of the above

00679. All of the following are part of the fire triangle EXCEPT:

A. heat
B. oxygen

C. electricity
D. fuel

00684. The Coast Guard emergency radiotelephone frequency is:

A. 2132 kilohertz
B. 2182 kilohertz
C. 2670 kilohertz
D. 2750 kilohertz

00687. A Master of a vessel subject to the Vessel Bridge-to-Bridge Radiotelephone Act who fails to comply with the Act or the regulations thereunder may be fined not more than:

A. $2,000
B. $1,500
C. $1,000
D. $500

00688. Which of the following may ignite fuel vapors?

A. static electricity
B. an open and running motor
C. loose wiring
D. all of the above

00689. After a person has been revived by artificiial respiration, he should be:

A. walked around until he is back to normal
B. given several shots of whiskey
C. kept lying down and warm
D. allowed to do as he wishes

00692. Why should foam be banked off a bulkhead when extinguishing an oil fire?

A. to coat the surrounding bulkheads with foam in case the fire spreads
B. to cool the bulkhead closest to the fire
C. to prevent any oil on the bulkheads from igniting
D. to prevent agitation of the oil and spreading the fire

00694. What is the international distress frequency for radiotelephones?

A. 500 kHz
B. 1347 kHz
C. 2182 kHz
D. 2738 kHz

00697. A violation of the Vessel Bridge-to-Bridge Radiotelephone Act may result in a:

A. civil penalty of $500 against the Master or person in charge of a vessel
B. civil penalty of $1,000 against the vessel itself

C. suspension and/or revocation of an operator's FCC license
D. all of the above

00698. The spread of fire is prevented by:

A. cooling surfaces adjacent to the fire
B. removing combustibles from the endangered area
C. shutting off the oxygen supply
D. all of the above

00699. When administering artificial respiration, it is of utmost importance to:

A. use the mouth-to-mouth method
B. clear airways
C. use the rhythmic pressure method
D. know all approved methods

00700. Intact buoyancy is a term used to describe:

A. the volume of all intact spaces above the waterline
B. an intact space below the surface of a flooded area
C. an intact space which can be flooded without causing a ship to sink
D. the space at which all the vertical upward forces of buoyancy are considered to be concentrated

00702. Which of the following statements concerning foam as an extinguishing agent is TRUE?

A. Foam conducts electricity.
B. To be most effective, foam should be directed at the source of the fire.
C. Foam is most effective on burning liquids which are flowing.
D. Foam can ONLY be used to extinguish class A fires.

00704. Which radiotelephone transmission may be sent over channel 16?

A. Distress signal MAYDAY
B. Call to a particular station
C. A meteorological warning
D. any of the above

00707. If your bridge-to-bridge radiotelephone ceases to operate, you must:

A. immediately anchor your vessel and arrange for repairs to the system
B. moor your vessel at the nearest dock available and arrange for repairs to the system
C. arrange for the repair of the system so that repairs are completed within 48 hours
D. exercise due diligence to restore the system at the earliest practicable time

00708. Which of the following elements of the fire triangle, when removed, will result in the extinguishment of a fire?

A. fuel
B. heat
C. oxygen
D. any of the above

00710. Buoyancy is a measure of the ship's:

A. ability to float
B. deadweight
C. freeboard
D. midships strength

00711. When administering artificial respiration to an adult, the breathing cycle should be repeated about:

A. 12 to 15 times per minute
B. 18 to 20 times per minute
C. 20 to 25 times per minute
D. as fast as possible

00712. Which of the following statements is TRUE concerning the application of foam on an oil fire?

A. It cools the surface of the liquid.
B. It gives protection to fire fighting personnel against the heat of the fire.
C. It forms a smothering blanket on the surface of the oil.
D. It should be used at the same time a solid stream of water is being applied.

00714. A Coast Guard radiotelephone message concerning an aid to navigation being off station would be preceded by the word:

A. "PAN-PAN"
B. "MAYDAY"
C. "SOS"
D. "SECURITY"

00715. Your vessel is taking on fuel when a small leak develops in the hose. You order the pumping stopped. Before you resume pumping, you should:

A. notify the terminal superintendent
B. place a large drip pan under the leak and plug the scuppers
C. repair the hose with a patch
D. replace the hose

00717. If your radiotelephone fails underway:

A. visual signals must be given to oncoming vessels
B. you must immediately tie up in the nearest port until the radiotelephone is repaired

C. you must anchor until the radiotelephone is repaired
D. the loss of the radiotelephone must be considered in navigating the vessel

00719. A fire hose has a:

A. male coupling at both ends
B. female coupling at both ends
C. female coupling at the nozzle end and a male coupling at the hydrant end
D. male coupling at the nozzle end and a female coupling at the hydrant end

00720. The center of volume of the immersed portion of the hull is called the:

A. center of buoyancy
B. center of flotation
C. center of gravity
D. tipping center

00721. Forces within a vessel have caused a difference between the starboard and port drafts. This difference is:

A. list
B. heel
C. trim
D. flotation

00724. Messages concerning weather conditions transmitted by radiotelephone are preceded by:

A. MAYDAY
B. PAN-PAN
C. SECURITE
D. SOS

00725. When you notice oil on the water near your vessel while taking on fuel, you should FIRST:

A. stop loading
B. notify the senior deck officer
C. notify the terminal superintendent
D. determine whether your vessel is the source

00727. Under the Vessel Bridge-to-Bridge Radiotelephone Act, failure of a vessel's radiotelephone equipment:

A. constitutes a violation of the Act
B. obligates the operator to moor or anchor the vessel immediately
C. requires immediate, emergency repairs
D. does not, in itself, constitute a violation of the Act

00729. At what rate would you render artificial respiration to an adult?

A. 4 to 6 times per minute
B. 12 to 15 times per minute
C. 20 to 30 times per minute
D. At least 30 times per minute

00731. At sea, no person on board any vessel to which Annex V to MARPOL 73/78 applies may discharge:

A. plastic
B. metal
C. glass
D. paper

00732. Which of the following statements is(are) TRUE concerning the use of dry chemical extinguishers?

A. You should direct the spray at the base of the fire.
B. You should direct the spray directly into the fire.
C. You should direct the spray at a vertical bulkhead and allow it to flow over the fire.
D. any of the above

00735. You are fueling your vessel when you notice oil in the water around your vessel. You should immediately stop fueling and:

A. begin cleanup operations
B. notify the U. S. Coast Guard
C. leave the area
D. notify the Corps of Engineers

00738. If there is a fire aft aboard your vessel, which maneuver will be most effective in fighting the fire?

A. Put the wind off either beam.
B. Head the bow into the wind and decrease speed.
C. Put the stern into the wind and increase speed.
D. Put the stern into the wind and decrease speed.

00740. Which of the following does NOT indicate motion of the vessel?

A. pitch
B. roll
C. trim
D. yaw

00742. An advantage of an ABC dry chemical over a carbon dioxide extinguisher is:

A. lack of toxicity
B. the multipurpose extinguishing ability
C. burn-back protection
D. cooling ability

00744. When using VHF channel 16 (156.8 mHz) or 2182 kHz, and you need help, but are not in danger, you should use the urgent signal:

A. "ASSISTANCE NEEDED"
B. "PAN-PAN"
C. "MAYDAY"
D. "SECURITE"

00745. If you detect oil around your vessel while in the discharging process, the first thing to do is:

A. try to find out where the oil is coming from
B. call the Master
C. have the pumpman check discharge piping
D. shut down operations

00748. A fire has broken out on the stern of your vessel. To help fight the fire you should maneuver your vessel so that the wind:

A. blows the fire back toward the vessel
B. comes over the bow
C. comes over the stern
D. comes over either beam

00749. The "hoist" refers to the:

A. gangway when alongside a pier
B. vertical motion of a vessel in a seaway
C. vertical dimension of a flag
D. wire rope used as a runner as part of the cargo gear

00750. The center of flotation of a vessel is defined as:

A. the center of volume of the immersed portion of the vessel
B. the center of gravity of the water plane
C. that point at which all the vertical downward forces of weight are considered to be concentrated
D. that point at which all the vertical upward forces of buoyancy are considered to be concentrated

00752. Which of the following statements describes the primary process by which fires are extinguished by dry chemical?

A. The stream of dry chemical powder cools the fire.
B. The dry chemical powder attacks the fuel and oxygen chain reaction.
C. The powder forms a solid coating over the surface.
D. The dry chemical smothers the fire.

00753. How should signal flares be used after you have abandoned ship and are adrift in a life raft?

A. Immediately use all the signals at once.
B. Use all the signals during the first night.
C. Employ a signal every hour after abandoning ship until they are gone.
D. Use them only when you are aware of a ship or plane in the area.

00754. "PAN-PAN" repeated three times over the radiotelephone indicates what type of message will follow?

A. Distress
B. Safety
C. All clear
D. Urgency

00755. While taking fuel on your vessel, you notice oil on the water around the vessel. What should you do FIRST?

A. stop fueling
B. notify the dispatcher
C. notify the terminal superintendent
D. determine if your vessel is the source

00758. In handling a vessel at sea in which a fire in the forepeak has been discovered, and wind is from ahead at 35 knots, you should:

A. remain on course and hold speed
B. change course and put stern to wind
C. change course to put wind on either beam and increase speed
D. remain on course but slack speed

00760. When dry chemical extinguishers are used to put out class B fires, there is a danger of reflash because:

A. dry chemical is not an effective agent on Class B fires
B. little or no cooling occurs
C. dry chemical dissipates quickly
D. Class B fires have an inherent tendency to reflash

00761. Which of the following, when removed, will result in the extinguishment of a fire?

A. oxygen
B. carbon dioxide
C. sodium
D. nitrogen

00762. The most effective extinguishing action of dry chemical is:

A. breaking the chain reaction
B. the CO2 that is formed when heated
C. smothering
D. shielding of radiant heat

00764. What word is an international distress signal when sent by radiotelephone?

A. Securite
B. Mayday
C. Breaker
D. Pan

00768. Which of the following statements is/are TRUE concerning carbon dioxide?

A. It is heavier than air.
B. It is an inert gas.
C. It is used on class B and C fires.
D. all of the above

00769. A life float on a fishing vessel must be equipped with:

A. a painter
B. red smoke flares
C. a jacknife
D. a signal mirror

00772. A dry chemical fire extinguisher is not as desirable as CO2 for fighting a class "C" fire because:

A. the dry chemical is a conductor
B. the dry chemical leaves a residue
C. CO2 will not dissipate in air
D. it takes smaller amounts of CO2 to cover the same area

00778. An aluminum powder fire would be classified as class:

A. A
B. B
C. C
D. D

00782. As compared to carbon dioxide, dry chemical has which advantage(s)?

A. compatible with all foam agents
B. cleaner
C. more protective against re-flash
D. all of the above

00785. Part 156 of the Pollution Prevention Regulations concerns:

A. transfer operations and procedures
B. vessel design
C. large oil transfer facilities
D. equipment

00788. Fires in which of the following classes would most likely occur in the engine room of a vessel?

A. Classes A and B
B. Classes B and C
C. Classes C and D
D. Classes A and D

00790. Which would NOT provide extra buoyancy for a vessel with no sheer?

A. lighter draft
B. raised fo'c'sle head
C. raised poop
D. higher bulwark

00791. During a training exercise a submarine wishing to indicate that a torpedo has been fired will send up what color smoke from a float?

A. black
B. red
C. orange
D. yellow

00792. Which of the following is NOT an advantage of a dry chemical extinguisher as compared to a carbon dioxide extinguisher?

A. It has a greater range.
B. It provides a heat shield for the operator.
C. It is nontoxic.
D. It offers lasting, effective protection against burn-back.

00798. A fire starts in a switchboard due to a short circuit. This would be which class of fire?

A. A
B. B
C. C
D. D

00799. Lines or gear NOT in use should be:

A. conspicuously marked
B. stowed anywhere
C. left on deck
D. secured or stowed out of the way

00800. The "trimming arm" of a vessel is the horizontal distance between the:

A. LCB and LCF
B. LCF and LCB
C. forward perpendicular and LCG
D. LCB and LCG

00801. No person on board any vessel to which Annex V to MARPOL 73/78 applies may discharge garbage of any type when:

A. less than 12 nautical miles from the United States
B. less than 12 nautical miles from nearest land

C. in the navigable waters of the United States
D. less than 25 nautical miles from nearest land

00802. A portable dry chemical fire extinguisher discharges by:

A. gravity when the extinguisher is turned upside down
B. pressure from a small CO_2 cartridge on the extinguisher
C. air pressure from the hand pump attached to the extinguisher
D. pressure from the reaction when water is mixed with the chemical

00803. The abandon ship signal on the ship's whistle is:

A. 6 short blasts and 1 long blast
B. more than 6 short blasts
C. more than 6 short blasts and 1 long blast
D. 1 long blast of at least 10 seconds

00808. A fire in a pile of canvas would be classified as class:

A. A
B. B
C. C
D. D

00809. If vomiting occurs during a mouth-to-mouth resuscitation effort, the best immediate procedure to follow is:

A. ignore it and continue mouth-to-mouth ventilation
B. pause for a moment until the patient appears quiet again, then resume ventilation mouth-to-mouth
C. switch to mouth-to-nose ventilation
D. turn the patient's body to the side, sweep out the mouth and resume mouth-to-mouth ventilation

00810. When a vessel's LCG is aft of her LCB, the vessel will:

A. trim by the stern
B. trim by the head
C. be on an even keel
D. be tender

00811. Your vessel is broken down and rolling in heavy seas. You can reduce the possibility of capsizing by:

A. constantly shifting the rudder
B. rigging a sea anchor
C. moving all personnel aft
D. moving all personnel forward and low

00812. When extinguishing a class "B" fire with a portable dry chemical extinguisher, the discharge should be directed:

A. at the seat of the fire, starting at the near edge
B. to bank off a bulkhead onto the fire
C. over the top of the fire
D. at the main body of the fire

00813. The continuous sounding of the general alarm bells and the whistle for a period of at least 10 seconds is the signal for:

A. abandon ship
B. dismissal from fire and emergency stations
C. fire and emergency
D. man overboard

00818. A fire in a transformer terminal would be classified as class:

A. A
B. B
C. C
D. D

00819. Providing you are not in a special area, such as the Mediterranean or Red Sea, how many nautical miles from land must you be to throw wooden dunnage into the sea?

A. 25 nm
B. 12 nm
C. 6 nm
D. 3 nm

00820. The two points that act together to trim a ship are the:

A. LCF and LCB
B. LCG and LCB
C. metacenter and LCG
D. VCG and LCG

00821. Bleeding from a vein is:

A. dark red and slow
B. bright red and slow
C. bright red and spurting
D. dark red and spurting

00822. When electrical equipment is involved in a fire, the stream of dry chemicals should be:

A. aimed at the source of the flames
B. fogged above the equipment
C. shot off a flat surface onto the flames
D. used to shield against electrical shock

00823. The signal for fire aboard ship is:

A. more than 6 short blasts and 1 long blast on the whistle, and the same signal on the general alarm
B. continuous sounding of the ship's whistle and general alarm for at least 10 seconds
C. 1 short blast on the whistle
D. continuous blowing of the ship's whistle for a period of 10 seconds

00828. A fire in a pile of dunnage would be classified as class:

A. A
B. B
C. C
D. D

00829. A fire starting by spontaneous combustion can be expected in which of the following conditions?

A. Paints, varnish or other liquid flammables are stowed in a dry stores locker.
B. Inert cargoes such as pig iron are loaded in a wet condition.
C. Oily rags are stowed in a metal pail.
D. Clean mattresses are stored in contact with an electric light bulb.

00831. The spread of fire is prevented by:

A. heating surfaces adjacent to the fire
B. leaving combustibles in the endangered area
C. shutting off the oxygen supply
D. all of the above

00832. Which statement is TRUE concerning the use of a dry chemical extinguisher?

A. You should direct the stream at the base of the fire.
B. You should direct the stream directly into the fire.
C. You should direct the stream at a vertical bulkhead and allow it to flow over the fire.
D. any of the above

00833. After reading the station bill, you see that "3 short blasts on the whistle and 3 short rings on the general alarm bells," is the signal for:

A. abandon ship
B. dismissal from fire and emergency stations
C. fire and emergency
D. man overboard

00838. A class C fire would be burning:

A. fuel oil
B. wood
C. celluloid
D. electrical insulation

00840. If a vessel is loaded in such a manner that she is said to be sagging, what kind of stress is placed on the sheer strake?

A. compression
B. tension
C. thrust
D. racking

00841. Blood flowing from a cut artery appears:

A. dark red with a steady flow
B. bright red with a steady flow
C. bright red and in spurts
D. dark red and in spurts

00842. As compared to carbon dioxide, dry chemical has which advantage?

A. cleaner
B. effective on metal fires
C. greater range
D. more cooling effect

00848. The class of fire on which a blanketing effect is essential is class:

A. A
B. B
C. C
D. D

00850. When a vessel is stationary and in a hogging condition, the main deck is under:

A. compression stress
B. tension stress
C. shear stress
D. racking stress

00851. The preferred agent used in fighting a helicopter crash fire is:

A. CO2
B. dry chemical
C. water
D. foam

00852. Which of the following statements concerning the application of dry chemical powder is NOT true?

A. At temperatures of less than 32° F, the extinguisher must be recharged more often.
B. When possible, the fire should be attacked from windward.
C. The stream should be directed at the base of the fire.
D. Directing the stream into burning flammable liquid may cause splashing.

00858. A fire in trash and paper waste would be classified as class:

A. A
B. B
C. C
D. D

00860. A ship's forward draft is 22'-04" and its after draft is 24'-00". The draft amidships is 23'-04". This indicates a concentration of weight:

A. at the bow
B. in the lower holds
C. amidships
D. at the ends

00862. Dry chemical extinguishers extinguish class B fires to the greatest extent by:

A. cooling
B. smothering
C. oxygen dilution
D. breaking the chain reaction

00868. Burning wood is what class of fire?

A. A
B. B
C. C
D. D

00869. As a last resort, a tourniquet can be used to:

A. hold a victim in a stretcher
B. stop uncontrolled bleeding
C. hold a large bandage in place
D. restrain a delirious victim

00870. The forward draft of your ship is 27'-11" and the after draft is 29'-03". The draft amidships is 28'-05". Your vessel is:

A. hogged
B. sagged
C. listed
D. trimmed by the head

00871. The bilge pump on a fishing vessel:

A. must be fixed if the vessel exceeds 12 meters in length
B. may be used as a fire pump
C. must be portable if there are more than 4 watertight compartments
D. must be capable of pumping at least 450 gpm

00873. At the required fire drill, all persons must report to their stations and demonstrate their ability to perform the duties assigned to them:

A. by the Coast Guard regulations
B. in the station bill

C. by the person conducting the drill
D. at the previous safety meeting

00878. A fire in a pile of linen is a class:

A. A
B. B
C. C
D. D

00879. To operate a portable CO2 extinguisher continuously in the discharge mode:

A. slip the "D yoke" ring in the lower handle over the upper handle
B. remove the locking pin
C. open the discharge valve
D. invert the CO2 extinguisher

00880. A ship's forward draft is 22'-04" and its after draft is 23'-00". The draft amidships is 23'-04". This indicates a concentration of weight:

A. at the bow
B. in the lower holds
C. amidships
D. at the ends

00881. If a person suffers a simple fracture of a limb, you should:

A. attempt to set the fracture
B. prevent further movement of the bone
C. apply a tourniquet without delay
D. alternately apply hot and cold compresses

00882. Fire in an engine compartment is best extinguished with carbon dioxide gas (CO2) and by:

A. closing the compartment except for the ventilators
B. completely closing the compartment
C. leaving the compartment open to the air
D. increasing the air flow to the compartment by blowers

00885. Which type of marine sanitation device (MSD) is used solely for the storage of sewage and flushwater at ambient air pressure and temperature?

A. Type I
B. Type II
C. Type III
D. Type IV

00887. Carbon dioxide as a fire fighting agent has which of the following advantages over other agents?

A. It causes minimal damage.
B. It is safer for personnel.

C. It is cheaper.
D. It is most effective on a per unit basis.

00888. An oil fire would be classified as class:

A. A
B. B
C. C
D. D

00889. Small quantities of flammable liquids needed at a work site should be:

A. used only under the supervision and direction of a ship's officer
B. tightly capped and stowed with other tools near the job site when securing at the end of the day
C. used only when a pressurized fire hose is laid out ready for immediate use
D. in a metal container with a tight cap

00891. To prevent the spread of fire by convection you should:

A. shut off all electrical power
B. remove combustibles from direct exposure
C. cool the bulkhead around the fire
D. close all openings to the area

00892. While you are working in a space, the fixed CO2 system is accidentally activated. You should:

A. secure the applicators to preserve the charge in the cylinders
B. continue with your work as there is nothing you can do to stop the flow of CO2
C. retreat to fresh air and ventilate the compartment before returning
D. make sure all doors and vents are secured

00895. Which type of Marine Sanitation Device (MSD) treats sewage to the minimum acceptable level for overboard discharge?

A. Type I
B. Type II
C. Type III
D. Type IV

00896. Your cargo vessel's Certification of Inspection expires 30 April 1992. One of your inflatable life rafts was last serviced in January 1992. The raft must be reinspected no later than:

A. April 1992
B. July 1992
C. January 1992
D. April 1993

00897. Which statement is TRUE concerning carbon dioxide?

A. It is lighter than air.
B. It is an inert gas.
C. It is used mostly on class A fires.
D. all of the above

00898. A galley grease fire would be classified as which class of fire?

A. A
B. B
C. C
D. D

00899. EXCEPT when suffering from a head or chest injury a patient in shock should be placed in which position?

A. head up and feet down
B. head down and feet up
C. flat on back with head and feet elevated
D. arms above the head

00901. A squeeze-grip type carbon dioxide portable fire extinguisher has been partially discharged. It should be:

A. replaced in its proper location if weight loss is no more than 15%
B. replaced in its proper location if weight loss is no more than 25%
C. labeled empty and recharged as soon as possible
D. replaced in its proper location regardless of weight

00902. Your vessel is equipped with a fixed CO2 system and a fire main system. In the event of an electrical fire in the engine room, what is the correct procedure for fighting the fire?

A. Use the CO2 system and evacuate the engine room.
B. Use the fire main system and evacuate the engine room.
C. Evacuate the engine room and use the CO2 system.
D. Evacuate the engine room and use the fire main system.

00904. If you are on the beach and are signalling to a small boat in distress that your present location is dangerous and they should land to the left, you would:

A. fire a green star to the left
B. send the letter K by light and point to the left
C. place an orange signal to your left as you signal with a white light
D. send the code signal S followed by L

00905. The color of the signal flare sent up by a submarine coming to periscope depth is:

A. white
B. green
C. yellow
D. red

00906. Inflatable life rafts shall be serviced at a U. S. C. G. servicing facility every 12 months or not later than the next vessel inspection for certification. However, the total elapsed time between servicing cannot exceed:

A. 12 months
B. 14 months
C. 15 months
D. 16 months

00907. An advantage of a dry chemical over a carbon dioxide fire extinguisher is its:

A. greater range
B. effectiveness on all types of fires
C. cleanliness
D. all of the above

00908. If ignited, which material would be a class B fire?

A. magnesium
B. paper
C. wood
D. diesel oil

00912. A "15-pound" CO2 extinguisher is so called because:

A. there are 15 pounds of CO2 in the container
B. the container, when full, weighs 15 pounds
C. the pressure at the discharge nozzle is 15 psi
D. the empty container weighs 15 pounds

00914. Which of the following is the lifesaving signal for "You are seen -assistance will be given as soon as possible"?

A. red star rocket
B. orange smoke signal
C. green star rocket
D. vertical motion of a flag

00915. Which condition is NOT necessary for a substance to burn?

A. The temperature of the substance must be equal to or above its fire point.
B. The air must contain oxygen in sufficient quantity.
C. The mixture of vapors with air must be within the "explosive range".
D. All of the above are necessary for a substance to burn.

00916. Who should inspect and test an inflatable life raft?

A. the Chief Mate
B. the manufacturer or authorized representative
C. shipyard personnel
D. a certificated lifeboatman

00917. Foam-type portable fire extinguishers are most useful in combating fires involving:

A. solid materials such as wood or bales of fiber
B. inflammable liquids
C. electrical equipment
D. metallic solids

00918. Fires which occur in energized electrical equipment, such as switchboard insulation, are classified as class:

A. A
B. B
C. C
D. D

00919. After an accident, the victim may go into shock and die. What should be done to help prevent shock?

A. Slightly elevate the head and feet.
B. Keep the person awake.
C. Keep the person lying down and at a comfortable temperature.
D. Give the person a stimulant to increase blood flow.

00920. If a vessel lists to the port side, the center of buoyancy will:

A. move to port
B. move to starboard
C. move directly down
D. stay in the same position

00921. You can determine that a CO2 fire extinguisher is fully charged by:

A. looking at the gage
B. checking the nameplate data
C. weighing by hand
D. weighing with a properly calibrated scale

00922. An upright vessel has negative GM. GM becomes positive at the angle of loll because the:

A. free surface effects are reduced due to pocketing
B. KG is reduced as the vessel seeks the angle of loll
C. effective beam is increased causing BM to increase
D. underwater volume of the hull is increased

00924. Which of the following is the lifesaving signal for "You are seen - assistance will be given as soon as possible"?

A. 3 white star signals
B. horizontal motion with a white flag
C. vertical motion of a white light
D. code letter "K" by blinker light

00925. The center of flotation of a vessel is located at the geometric center of the:

A. underwater volume
B. above water volume
C. amidships section
D. waterplane area

00926. Life rafts of the inflatable type must be overhauled and inspected at a U. S. Coast Guard approved service facility every:

A. 6 months
B. 12 months
C. 18 months
D. 24 months

00927. The extinguishing agent most effective for combating wood fires is:

A. water
B. carbon dioxide
C. foam
D. dry chemical

00928. A fire in the Loran gear would be of what class?

A. A
B. B
C. C
D. D

00929. According to Annex V to MARPOL 73/78, garbage containing plastic is permitted to be disposed of by:

A. incinerating offshore
B. discharging when at least 12 nautical miles from nearest land
C. grinding to less than 1" and discharging at least 12 nautical miles from nearest land
D. grinding to less than 1" and discharging at least 25 nautical miles from nearest land

00930. Semi-portable extinguishers used on inspected vessels are sizes:

A. II, III, and IV
B. I, II, and III
C. III, IV, and V
D. IV and V

00931. The major cause of shock in burn victims is the:

A. high level of pain
B. emotional stress
C. increase in body temperature and pulse rate
D. massive loss of fluid through the burned area

00932. Portable CO2 fire extinguishers should NOT be used to inert a space containing flammable liquids due to the danger of:

A. the CO2 being inhaled by personnel
B. reflash of burning liquids
C. vapor condensation on the extinguisher
D. the discharge causing a static spark

00934. The signal employed in connection with the use of shore lifesaving apparatus to signify, in general, "Affirmative" is:

A. vertical motion of the arms
B. code signal "C" sent by light or sound signaling apparatus
C. firing of a red star signal
D. none of the above

00935. If an airplane circles a vessel 3 times, crosses the vessel's course close ahead while rocking the wings and heads off in a certain direction, what does this indicate?

A. The plane is in distress and will have to ditch.
B. The plane is going to drop a package and wishes the vessel to recover it.
C. Someone is in distress in that direction and the vessel should follow and assist.
D. There is danger ahead and the best course is indicated by the direction of the aircraft.

00936. If your vessel is equipped with inflatable life rafts, how should they be maintained?

A. Have your crew check them annually.
B. They do not need any maintenance.
C. Have them sent ashore to an approved maintenance facility annually.
D. Have them serviced by the shipyard annually.

00937. On a class "B" fire, which portable fire extinguisher would be the LEAST desirable?

A. carbon dioxide
B. soda-acid
C. dry chemical
D. foam

00938. A magnesium fire is class:

A. A
B. B
C. C
D. D

00939. CO2 cylinders forming part of a fixed fire extinguishing system must be pressure tested at least every:

A. year
B. 2 years
C. 6 years
D. 12 years

00940. When a vessel is inclined due to some external force, the:

A. shape of the vessel's underwater hull remains the same
B. vessel's center of gravity shifts to the center of the vessel's underwater hull
C. vessel's center of buoyancy shifts to the center of the vessel's underwater hull
D. vessel's mean draft increases

00942. A 15-pound CO2 extinguisher:

A. contains 15 pounds of CO2
B. weighs 15 pounds when full of CO2
C. has 15 pounds of pressure at the nozzle
D. weighs 15 pounds when empty

00944. The manual lifesaving signal indicating "You are seen - assistance will be given as soon as possible" is the:

A. vertical motion of white flags
B. vertical motion of a white light or flare
C. firing of a green star signal
D. none of the above

00945. The color of rockets, shells or rocket parachute flares used to indicate that the vessel is in distress and requires immediate assistance is:

A. white
B. green
C. red
D. yellow

00946. Who is required to provide approved placards containing instructions for the launching and inflation of an approved inflatable life raft?

A. Officer in Charge, Marine Inspection
B. the manufacturer of the life raft
C. Maritime Administration
D. the owner of the vessel on which the life rafts are carried

00947. When fighting an oil or gasoline fire in the bilge, which of the following should NOT be used?

A. foam
B. solid stream water nozzle

C. all-purpose nozzle
D. carbon dioxide

00948. Fires in combustible metals such as sodium or magnesium are classified as class:

A. A
B. B
C. C
D. D

00950. If your vessel has taken a slight list from the off-center loading of material on deck, the:

A. list should be easily removed
B. mean draft is affected
C. vessel may flop
D. vessel is trimmed

00951. If a crewman suffers a second-degree burn on the arm, you should:

A. drain any blisters
B. apply antiseptic ointment
C. scrub the arm thoroughly to prevent infection
D. immerse the arm in cold water

00952. What is the proper method of determining whether a portable CO2 fire extinguisher needs recharging?

A. Check the tag to see when the extinguisher was last charged.
B. Release a small amount of CO2; if the CO2 discharges, the extinguisher is acceptable.
C. Weigh the extinguisher and compare the weight against that stamped on the valve.
D. Recharge the extinguisher at least once each year.

00954. Which is the lifesaving signal for, "This is the best place to land"?

A. red star rocket
B. orange smoke signal
C. green star rocket
D. horizontal motion of a flag

00957. Fires in an engine compartment where gasoline is burning require which of the following types of extinguishers?

A. carbon dioxide
B. dry chemical
C. foam
D. any of the above

00958. Which substance might be subject to spontaneous combustion?

A. coal
B. scrap rubber

C. leather
D. any of the above

00961. Safety is increased if:

A. extra line and wire are laid out on deck for emergency use
B. all lashings are made up, and the decks are clean and clear
C. power tools are kept plugged in for immediate use
D. spare parts are kept on deck for ready access

00962. A carbon dioxide fire extinguisher should be recharged:

A. at least annually
B. whenever it is below its required weight
C. only if the extinguisher has been used
D. before every safety inspection

00964. Which of the following signals is used by a rescue unit to indicate, "Avast hauling"?

A. firing of a green star signal
B. firing of a red star signal
C. an orange smoke signal
D. 3 white star rockets fired at 1-minute intervals

00967. Which of the following fire extinguishers should NOT be used in fighting a Class "B" fire?

A. carbon dioxide
B. dry chemical
C. foam (stored pressure type)
D. soda-acid

00968. Which condition is necessary for a substance to burn?

A. The temperature of the substance must be equal to or above its fire point.
B. The air must contain oxygen in sufficient quantity.
C. The mixture of vapors with air must be within the "explosive range".
D. all of the above

00969. That center around which a vessel trims is called a:

A. tipping center
B. center of buoyancy
C. center of gravity
D. turning center

00970. During cargo operations, your vessel has developed a list due to the center of gravity rising above the transverse metacenter. To correct the list, you should:

A. shift weight to the high side
B. shift weight to the centerline

C. add weight in the lower holds or double bottoms
D. remove weight from the lower holds or double bottoms

00971. When should you first have any food or water after boarding a lifeboat or life raft?

A. after 12 hours
B. after 24 hours
C. within 48 hours
D. some food and water should be consumed immediately and then not until 48 hours later

00972. Which of the following statements concerning carbon dioxide is FALSE?

A. It displaces the oxygen in the air.
B. It cannot be seen.
C. It cannot be smelled.
D. It is safe to use near personnel in a confined space.

00974. Which of the following signals is used by a rescue unit to indicate, "Hawser is made fast"?

A. firing of a green star signal
B. firing of a red star signal
C. an orange smoke signal
D. 3 white star rockets at 1-minute intervals

00976. Inflatable life rafts carried on passenger vessels must be maintained annually in which of the following ways?

A. They must be overhauled by the ship's crew.
B. They must be sent to the Coast Guard for servicing.
C. They must be sent to the steamship company shore repair facility.
D. They must be sent to a Coast Guard approved service facility.

00977. What type of fire is the foam (stored-pressure type) fire extinguisher effective on?

A. Classes A & B
B. Classes A & C
C. Classes B & C
D. all of the above

00979. When should you first have any food or water after boarding a lifeboat or life raft?

A. after 12 hours
B. after 24 hours
C. within 48 hours
D. some food and water should be consumed immediately and then not until 48 hours later

00980. Assuming an even transverse distribution of weight in a vessel, which condition could cause a list?

A. empty double-bottoms and lower holds, and a heavy deck cargo
B. flooding the forepeak to correct the vessel's trim
C. having KG smaller than KM
D. having a small positive righting arm

00981. Oily rags stored in a pile that is open to the atmosphere are a hazard because they will:

A. deteriorate and give off noxious gasses
B. spontaneously heat and catch fire
C. attract lice and other vermin and serve as a breeding ground
D. none of the above

00982. In continuous operation, the effective range of the 15 pound CO_2 extinguisher is limited to:

A. 2 to 4 feet
B. 3 to 8 feet
C. 9 to 12 feet
D. 10 to 15 feet

00984. The lifesaving signal indicated by a horizontal motion of a white light or white flare means:

A. "Landing here highly dangerous"
B. "Negative"
C. "Avast hauling"
D. all of the above

00986. The capacity of any life raft on board a vessel can be determined by:

A. examining the Certificate of Inspection
B. examining the plate on the outside of the raft container
C. referring to the station bill
D. referring to the shipping articles

00987. Which of the following extinguishing agents will cool down a heated bulkhead in the least amount of time?

A. water stream
B. water fog
C. steam
D. dry chemical

00988. Which of the following portable fire extinguishers should be used on a class C fire on board a vessel?

A. carbon dioxide
B. soda acid
C. foam
D. carbon tetrachloride

00989. First-, second-, and third-degree burns are classified according to the:

A. area of the body burned
B. source of heat causing the burn
C. layers of skin affected
D. size of the burned area

00990. If a vessel will list with equal readiness to either side, the list is most likely caused by:

A. negative GM
B. off-center weight
C. pocketing of free surface
D. excessive freeboard

00991. Fire extinguishing agents used on Class C fires must be:

A. able to absorb heat
B. water based
C. nonconducting
D. nontoxic

00992. When discharging a portable CO_2 fire extinguisher, you should not hold the horn of the extinguisher because:

A. the horn becomes extremely hot
B. the horn becomes extremely cold
C. caustic chemicals could burn your hands
D. the horn is placed directly in the fire when discharging

00994. The signal to guide vessels in distress, which indicates, "This is the best place to land" is the:

A. horizontal motion of a white flag
B. letter K in Morse code given by light
C. code flag S as a hoist
D. firing of a white star signal

00996. What is the penalty for failure to enforce, or comply with, the vessel bridge-to-bridge radiotelephone regulations?

A. civil penalty of no more than $500
B. civil penalty of no more than $5,000
C. $5,000 fine and imprisonment for not more than 1 year, or both
D. $1,000 fine or imprisonment for not more than 2 years

00997. Which fire-fighting agent is most effective at removing heat?

A. water spray
B. foam
C. carbon dioxide
D. dry chemical

00999. A documented vessel operating over 50 miles offshore must carry an inflatable life raft with a:

A. SOLAS A pack
B. SOLAS B pack
C. coastal pack
D. small vessel pack

01000. A vessel continually lists to one side and has a normal rolling period. Which of the following statements is TRUE?

A. The vessel has negative GM.
B. The center of gravity is on the centerline.
C. The list can be corrected by reducing KM.
D. The vessel has asymmetrical weight distribution.

01002. How do you operate a portable CO2 fire extinguisher?

A. Point the horn down.
B. Turn cylinder upside-down.
C. Break the rupture disc.
D. Pull pin, squeeze grip.

01004. The lifesaving signal used to indicate, "Landing here highly dangerous" is:

A. firing of a white star signal
B. firing of a red star signal
C. vertical motion of a red light
D. code letter "K" given by light or sound signaling apparatus

01006. According to regulations, the combination flare and smoke distress signals on a life raft shall remain in service no longer than:

A. 1 year
B. 3 years
C. 5 years
D. 6 years

01007. Which of the following is the best conductor of electricity?

A. carbon dioxide
B. distilled water
C. fresh water
D. salt water

01008. A minor heat burn of the eye should be treated by:

A. gently flooding with water
B. warming the eye with moist warm packs
C. laying the person flat on his back
D. mineral oil drops directly on the eye

01010. Which of the following actions would best increase the transverse stability of a merchant vessel at sea?

A. ballasting the double bottom tanks
B. deballasting the deep tanks

C. positioning a heavy lift cargo on the main deck
D. raising the cargo booms to the upright position

01011. Which vessel(s) is(are) required to comply with the vessel bridge-to-bridge radiotelephone regulations while navigating?

A. towing vessels 25 feet or less in length
B. passenger vessels of 50 gross tons or less, carrying 1 or more passengers
C. power-driven vessels 20 meters in length or greater
D. an intermittently manned floating plant under the control of a dredge

01012. The discharge from a carbon dioxide fire extinguisher should be directed:

A. at the base of the flames
B. at the center of the flames
C. to the lee side of the flames
D. over the tops of the flames

01013. A shipmate suffers a heart attack and stops breathing. You should:

A. immediately give a stimulant, by force if necessary
B. administer oxygen
C. make the victim comfortable in a bunk
D. immediately start CPR

01014. Which of the following signals for the guidance of small boats would be used by a shore rescue unit to indicate "Landing here highly dangerous"?

A. the firing of a white star signal
B. horizontal motion with a white flag
C. vertical motion of a white light
D. code letter "K" by blinker light

01016. For how long are distress flares approved?

A. 1 year
B. 2 years
C. 3 years
D. 5 years

01017. The extinguishing agent most likely to allow reignition of a fire is:

A. carbon dioxide
B. foam
C. water fog
D. water stream

01019. You are operating 10 miles offshore with 3 people aboard. What kind of survival craft must you carry?

A. an inflatable life raft with a coastal pack
B. a life float
C. an inflatable buoyant apparatus
D. No survival craft is required.

01020. Which vessels must comply with the vessel bridge-to-bridge radiotelephone regulations while navigating?

A. towing vessels 25 feet in length or less
B. passenger vessels of 100 gross tons or greater, carrying 1 or more passengers for hire
C. power-driven vessels 12 meters or less in length
D. all of the above

01021. Which vessel(s) is(are) required to comply with the vessel bridge-to-bridge radiotelephone regulations while navigating?

A. towing vessel 25 feet or less in length
B. passenger vessel of 50 GT or less, carrying one or more passengers for hire
C. power-driven vessels 12 meters or less in length, operating on inland waters
D. dredges engaged in operations likely to restrict navigation of other vessels in or near a channel or fairway

01022. When fighting a fire on a bulkhead using a portable carbon dioxide extinguisher, the stream should be directed at the:

A. base of the flames, moving the horn from side to side, following the flames upward as they diminish
B. top of the flaming area, moving the horn from side to side, following the flames downward as they diminish
C. center of the flaming area, moving the horn vertically from top to bottom
D. bottom of the flaming area, moving the horn vertically to the top following the flames upward as they diminish

01023. Providing you are not in a special area, such as the Mediterranean or Red Sea, how many nautical miles from land must you be to throw packing materials that will float into the sea?

A. 3 nm
B. 6 nm
C. 12 nm
D. 25 nm

01024. The firing of a red star signal may mean:

A. "This is the best place to land"
B. "You are seen - assistance will be given as soon as possible"
C. "Tail block is made fast"
D. "Slack away"

01027. What is the most important characteristic of the extinguishing agent in fighting a class "C" fire?

A. weight
B. temperature
C. electrical conductivity
D. cost

01028. Symptoms of heat stroke are:

A. cold and moist skin, high body temperature
B. cold and dry skin, low body temperature
C. hot and moist skin, high body temperature
D. hot and dry skin, high body temperature

01029. Which vessel(s) is(are) required to comply with the vessel bridge-to-bridge radiotelephone regulations while navigating?

A. towing vessel 26 feet in length or greater
B. passenger vessels of 100 gross tons or greater, carrying 1 or more passengers for hire
C. power-driven vessels 20 meters in length or greater
D. all of the above

01030. Which vessel(s) is(are) required to comply with the vessel bridge-to-bridge radiotelephone regulations while navigating?

A. towing vessels 25 feet or less in length, engaged in towing operations
B. passenger vessel 50 gross tons or less, carrying passengers for hire
C. dredges engaged in operations likely to restrict navigation of other vessels in or near a channel or fairway
D. an intermittently manned floating plant under the control of a dredge

01032. When used to fight fire, carbon dioxide:

A. is effective if used promptly on an oil fire
B. has a greater cooling effect than water
C. is lighter than air
D. is harmless to cargo and crew

01033. After a collision, your vessel begins flooding. This will cause the KB to do which of the following?

A. fall
B. remain stationary
C. rise
D. shift to the high side

01034. Which vessels must comply with the vessel bridge-to-bridge radiotelephone regulations while navigating?

A. towing vessels 26 feet in length or greater
B. passenger vessels less than 100 gross tons

C. power-driven vessels 12 meters or less in length
D. all of the above

01036. Life preservers must be marked with the:

A. stowage space assigned
B. vessel's name
C. vessel's home port
D. maximum weight allowed

01037. What is the minimum size power-driven vessel, not engaged in towing, required to comply with the vessel bridge-to-bridge radiotelephone regulations?

A. 50 meters
B. 25 meters
C. 20 meters
D. 12 meters

01038. The operator, or whomever is designated to pilot the vessel, while underway on the navigable waters of the United States, must:

A. maintain a listening watch, and must communicate in English
B. use the bridge-to-bridge VHF-FM designated frequency only to exchange navigational information or necessary tests
C. have on board an operator who holds a restricted radiotelephone operator permit or higher license, as well as a FCC ship station license
D. all of the above

01040. General requirements for a vessel's radiotelephone station log are that:

A. logs must be kept in an orderly manner
B. erasures are not allowed
C. it must identify the vessel's name and official number
D. all of the above

01042. What danger exists to people when CO2 is discharged in a small enclosed space?

A. damaged eardrums
B. electric shock
C. frostbite
D. respiratory arrest

01044. What is the lifesaving signal for, "You are seen - assistance will be given as soon as possible"?

A. green star rocket
B. red star rocket
C. orange smoke signal
D. horizontal motion of a flag

01047. The main advantage of a steady stream of water on a class "A" fire is that it:

A. breaks up and cools the fire
B. protects the firefighting crew
C. removes the oxygen
D. washes the fire away

01052. The danger associated with using carbon dioxide in an enclosed space is:

A. frostbite
B. skin burns
C. asphyxiation
D. an explosive reaction

01053. Your vessel is damaged and listing to port. The rolling period is long, and the vessel will occasionally assume a starboard list. What action should you take first?

A. Fill an empty double bottom tank on the starboard side.
B. Transfer all possible movable weights from port to starboard.
C. Pump out ballast from the port and starboard double bottom tanks.
D. Press up a slack centerline double bottom tank.

01054. By day, the signal meaning, "This is the best place to land" is a:

A. vertical motion of a red flag
B. vertical motion of a white flag or the arms
C. white smoke signal
D. white star rocket

01056. U. S. C. G. approved buoyant work vests are considered to be items of safety equipment and may be worn by members of the crew:

A. in lieu of life preservers during fire drills
B. in lieu of life preservers during boat drills
C. in lieu of life preservers during an actual emergency
D. when carrying out duties near a weather deck's edge

01057. The primary method by which water fog puts out fires is by:

A. removing the oxygen
B. cooling the fire below the ignition temperature
C. removing combustible material
D. diluting combustible vapors

01058. Which of the following describes a relationship between flash point and ignition temperature?

A. Both are higher than normal burning temperatures.
B. The flash point is always higher.
C. The ignition temperature is always higher.
D. They are not necessarily related.

01059. Provided every effort is made to preserve body moisture content by avoiding perspiration, how long is it normally possible to survive without water?

A. Up to 3 days
B. 8 to 14 days
C. 15 to 20 days
D. 25 to 30 days

01061. What are the symptoms of sun stroke?

A. Temperature falls below normal, pulse is rapid and feeble, skin is cold and clammy.
B. Temperature is high, pulse is strong and rapid, skin is hot and dry.
C. Temperature is high, pulse is slow and feeble, skin is clammy.
D. Temperature falls below normal, pulse is rapid, skin is clammy.

01062. Weight is considered during the periodic required inspection and servicing of:

A. CO_2 (carbon dioxide) fire extinguishers
B. foam fire extinguishers
C. water (stored pressure) fire extinguishers
D. all of the above

01064. By day, the horizontal motion of a white flag, or arms extended horizontally, by a person on the beach would indicate:

A. "Haul away"
B. "Tail block is made fast"
C. "Negative"
D. "Affirmative"

01066. Coast Guard approved buoyant work vests:

A. may be substituted for 10 percent of the required life preservers
B. should be stowed adjacent to lifeboats and emergency stations
C. may be used by boat crews and line handlers during lifeboat drills
D. should be used when carrying out duties near a weather deck's edge

01067. A large oil fire on the deck of a ship can be fought most effectively with:

A. dry chemical
B. foam
C. high-velocity fog
D. soda acid

01074. Which one of the following signals is made at night by a lifesaving station to indicate "Landing here highly dangerous"?

A. horizontal motion of a white light or flare
B. vertical motion of a white light or flare
C. white star rocket
D. vertical motion of a red light or flare

01076. The lifesaving equipment on all vessels shall be:

A. inspected weekly
B. worn at all times
C. readily accessible
D. tested yearly

01077. A vessel's KG is determined by:

A. dividing the total longitudinal moment summations by displacement
B. dividing the total vertical moment summations by displacement
C. multiplying the MT1 by the longitudinal moments
D. subtracting LCF from LCB

01080. A vessel to which Annex V to MARPOL 73/78 applies is located in a MARPOL designated special area, 14 nautical miles from nearest land. What type of garbage is permitted to be discharged?

A. paper products
B. glass ground to less than 1"
C. metal ground to less than 1"
D. food waste

01081. All of the following are part of the fire triangle EXCEPT:

A. heat
B. oxygen
C. fuel
D. electricity

01086. Required lifesaving equipment shall be:

A. kept on board no more than 2 years
B. inspected and serviced every 6 months
C. destroyed if more than 5 years old
D. maintained in good and serviceable condition

01087. A combination or all-purpose nozzle could be used to produce:

A. low velocity fog only
B. a solid stream only
C. a solid stream and foam
D. a solid stream and fog

01088. The flash point of a liquid means the temperature:

A. at which a liquid will give off inflammable vapors
B. at which a liquid will burn steadily
C. at which a liquid will explode
D. that a liquid must reach before it will flow readily

01089. During counterflooding to correct a severe list aggravated by an off-center load, your vessel suddenly takes a list or trim to the opposite side. You should:

A. continue counterflooding in the same direction
B. continue counterflooding, but in the opposite direction
C. immediately stop counterflooding
D. deballast from the low side

01094. A small craft advisory forecasts winds of up to what speed?

A. 16 kts.
B. 24 kts.
C. 33 kts.
D. 48 kts.

01097. Foam extinguishes a fire by:

A. shutting off the air supply
B. cooling the fuel to below ignition temperature
C. dispersing the fuel
D. removing the source of ignition

01098. Which statement is TRUE concerning the "flash point" of a substance?

A. It is lower than the ignition temperature.
B. It is the temperature at which a substance will spontaneously ignite.
C. It is the temperature at which a substance, when ignited, will continue to burn.
D. It is the temperature at which the released vapors will fall within the explosive range.

01101. A crew member has suffered frost bite to the toes of his right foot. Which of the following is NOT an acceptable first aid measure?

A. Rub the toes briskly.
B. Elevate the foot slightly.
C. Thaw the frozen toes slowly.
D. Give aspirin or other medication for pain if necessary.

01103. A vessel is "listed" when it is:

A. inclined due to an off-center weight
B. inclined due to the wind

C. down by the head
D. down by the stern

01104. When there is a small craft advisory, winds are predicted up to:

A. 15 knots
B. 24 knots
C. 33 knots
D. 42 knots

01107. In the production of chemical foam by a continuous-type generator:

A. the maximum water pressure to be used is 50 psi
B. the speed of foam production is slower at lower water temperatures
C. each pound of foam powder produces about 800 gallons of chemical foam
D. fresh water only should be used

01108. The vapor pressure of a substance:

A. increases with the temperature
B. decreases as temperature increases
C. is not affected by temperature
D. may increase or decrease as the temperature rises

01113. Releasing oil from the sea anchor of a lifeboat may:

A. keep the propeller from being fouled
B. increase propeller speed
C. help calm the waves in the vicinity of the craft
D. increase the holding power of the sea anchor

01114. The National Weather Service differentiates between small craft, gale, whole gale and hurricane warnings by the:

A. amount of rain forecasted
B. wave heights forecasted
C. amount of cloud cover forecasted
D. wind speed forecasted

01118. The tendency of a flammable liquid to vaporize is indicated by its:

A. ignition temperature
B. flash point
C. flammable range
D. convection index

01121. As Master of an inspected small passenger vessel, you have a question regarding a proposed modification to a watertight bulkhead. In which subchapter of Title 46 of the Code of Federal Regulations would you find the answer?

A. Subchapter F
B. Subchapter T

C. Subchapter S
D. Subchapter B

01127. Compared to the amount of concentrated foam liquid used, the amount of low expansion mechanical foam produced is:

A. 97 times greater
B. 94 times greater
C. 10 times greater
D. 2 times greater

01128. Most fire and explosions occur in a fuel tank:

A. during fueling when the fuel first strikes the tank bottom
B. during fueling when fuel strikes fuel already in the tank
C. when underway as the fuel is moved by wave action
D. shortly after fueling when fuel vapors gather

01131. If you observe any situation which presents a safety or pollution hazard during fuel transfer operations, what action should you take FIRST?

A. Close the valves at the transfer manifold.
B. Notify the person in charge of the shore facility.
C. Shut down the transfer operation.
D. Sound the fire alarm.

01133. If you must enter water on which there is an oil fire, you should:

A. protect your life preserver by holding it above your head
B. enter the water on the windward side of the vessel
C. keep both hands in front of your face to break the water surface when diving head first
D. wear very light clothing

01137. One gallon of low expansion foam solution will produce about:

A. 10 gallons of foam
B. 25 gallons of foam
C. 100 gallons of foam
D. 500 gallons of foam

01138. Which of the following is LEAST likely to cause ignition of fuel vapors?

A. static electricity
B. an open running electric motor
C. loose wiring
D. explosion proof lights

01147. A carbon dioxide fire extinguisher is required to be recharged if weight loss exceeds:

A. 1 percent of weight of charge
B. 5 percent of weight of charge
C. 7 percent of weight of charge
D. 10 percent of weight of charge

01148. Spontaneous combustion is most likely to occur in:

A. rags soaked in linseed oil
B. overloaded electrical circuits
C. dirty swabs and cleaning gear
D. partially loaded fuel tanks

01149. If the metacentric height is small, a vessel will:

A. be tender
B. have a quick and rapid motion
C. be stiff
D. yaw

01151. Treatment of sunstroke consists principally of:

A. cooling, removing to shaded area, and lying down
B. bathing with rubbing alcohol
C. drinking ice water
D. all of the above

01158. Spontaneous combustion is caused by:

A. an outside heat source heating a substance until it ignites
B. conduction of heat through a wall of material to the substance
C. chemical action within a substance
D. any of the above

01162. Which of the following instruments is suitable for determining the presence of explosive concentrations of fuel oil vapors in tanks?

A. a flame safety lamp
B. a combustible gas indicator
C. a liquid cargo meter
D. any of the above

01168. What is the maximum oxygen content below which flaming combustion will no longer occur?

A. 1%
B. 10%
C. 15%
D. 21%

01178. The lowest temperature required to cause self-sustained combustion of a substance independent of any outside source of ignition is called:

A. explosive range
B. flash point
C. ignition temperature
D. combustion temperature

01184. If a raft is to be released manually, where should the operating cord be attached before throwing the raft overboard?

A. Do not attach the cord to anything but throw it overboard with the raft container.
B. to some fixed object on the ship
C. Stand on it with your foot.
D. to the special pad eye on the "raft davit launcher"

01186. On a rigid life raft which is equipped with all of the required equipment you may NOT find a:

A. boathook
B. fishing kit
C. lifeline or grab rail
D. sea painter

01188. The most effective way to apply a foam stream if the fire is on deck or is a running fire, is to direct the stream:

A. onto the surface of the burning liquid
B. ahead of the burning liquid and bounce it on the fire
C. at the base of the burning liquid in a sweeping motion
D. just above the surface of the burning liquid

01194. Which operation should be done when launching an inflatable life raft by hand?

A. Open the life raft casing.
B. Turn the valve on the CO2 cylinder to start inflation.
C. Make sure the operating cord is secured to the vessel before throwing it over the side.
D. After inflation, detach operating cord from life raft.

01196. The jackknife on an inflatable life raft will always be located:

A. in one of the equipment bags
B. in a special pocket near the forward entrance
C. on a cord hanging from the canopy
D. in a pocket on the first aid kit

01197. After a squeeze-grip type carbon dioxide portable fire extinguisher has been partially discharged on a fire, it should be:

A. replaced in its proper location if weight loss is no more than 15%
B. replaced in its proper location if weight loss is no more than 25%

C. replaced in its proper location regardless of weight
D. labeled empty and recharged as soon as possible

01201. While taking on fuel oil, the transfer hose leaks causing a sheen in the water. You should:

A. apply dispersants to the sheen
B. repair the leak with duct tape
C. reduce the rate of transfer
D. shut down operations

01204. Generally, when lifting an inflatable life raft back aboard ship you would use the:

A. towing bridle
B. main weather cover
C. external lifelines
D. righting strap

01206. Inflatable life rafts are provided with a:

A. jackknife
B. towing connection
C. lifeline
D. all of the above

01207. Which extinguishing agent is most effective on a mattress fire?

A. CO2
B. foam
C. dry chemical
D. water

01208. A vessel aground may have negative GM since the:

A. decrease in KM is equal to the loss of draft
B. virtual rise of G is directly proportional to the remaining draft
C. lost buoyancy method is used to calculate KM, and KB is reduced
D. displacement lost acts at the point where the ship is aground

01211. A crew member suffering from generalized hypothermia should be given:

A. a small dose of alcohol
B. treatment for shock
C. a large meal
D. a brisk rub down

01212. Ambient air, which you normally breathe, contains what percent of oxygen?

A. 6%
B. 10%
C. 15%
D. 21%

01213. When a wind force causes a vessel to heel to a static angle, the:

A. centers of buoyancy and gravity are in the same vertical line
B. righting moment equals the wind-heeling moment
C. center of buoyancy remains the same
D. deck-edge immersion occurs

01214. An inflatable life raft should be lifted back aboard the ship by using:

A. the single hook at the top of the raft
B. two lines passed under the raft
C. the towing bridle
D. any of the above

01216. After launching, an inflatable raft should be kept dry inside by:

A. opening the automatic drain plugs
B. draining the water pockets
C. using the electric bilge pump
D. using the bailers and cellulose sponge

01217. What types of portable fire extinguishers are designed for use on electrical fires?

A. dry chemical and carbon dioxide
B. foam (stored pressure) and soda-acid
C. carbon dioxide and foam (stored pressure)
D. dry chemical and soda-acid

01223. The survival craft carried aboard a commercial fishing vessel must safely accommodate:

A. all of the people aboard
B. the number of people required by the certificate of inspection
C. the entire crew
D. none of the above are correct.

01224. In order to retrieve an inflatable life raft and place it on deck, you should heave on the:

A. lifelines
B. righting strap
C. sea anchor
D. towing bridle

01226. When making a permanent repair in an inflatable life raft using a repair kit, how long after the repair is made should you hold off "topping up" the lost air?

A. You do not have to hold off.
B. 12 hours
C. 24 hours
D. 2 hours

01227. Which of the following types of portable fire extinguishers is NOT designed for use on flammable liquid fires?

A. foam (stored pressure)
B. soda-acid
C. dry chemical
D. carbon dioxide

01228. When approaching a fire from leeward, you should shield firefighters from the fire by using:

A. low-velocity fog
B. high-velocity fog
C. a straight stream of water
D. foam spray

01231. After a life raft is launched, the operating cord:

A. serves as a sea painter
B. detaches automatically
C. is used to rig the boarding ladder
D. is cut immediately as it is of no further use

01235. Which of the following should NOT be done for a person who has fainted?

A. Revive the person with smelling salts.
B. Loosen the clothing.
C. Lay the person horizontally.
D. Dash cold water in the face.

01236. Inflatable life rafts are provided with:

A. a portable radio
B. an oil lantern
C. canned milk
D. a towing bridle

01237. Portable-foam fire extinguishers are designed for use on what classes of fires?

A. A and B
B. A and C
C. B and C
D. A, B, and C

01238. When attempting to enter a compartment containing a fire, which method of applying water is most appropriate?

A. high-velocity fog stream directed toward the overhead
B. straight stream directed into the center of the fire
C. sweeping the compartment with a fog stream
D. solid steam directed toward the overhead

01244. The painter on a rigid life raft shall be of:

A. nylon line not less than 2 in. in circumference
B. hemp line not less than 2-1/4 in. in circumference
C. cotton cord not less than 2-1/2 in. in circumference
D. manila line not less than 2-3/4 in. in circumference

01246. Inflatable life rafts are provided with:

A. a Very pistol
B. a towing connection
C. a portable radio
D. canned milk

01247. The recommended method of effectively applying foam on a fire is to:

A. spray directly on the base of the fire
B. flow the foam down a nearby vertical surface
C. sweep the fire with the foam
D. spray directly on the surface of the fire

01248. In the event of fire in a machinery space:

A. the fixed carbon dioxide system should be used only when all other means of extinguishment have failed
B. the fixed carbon dioxide system should be used immediately, as it is the most efficient means of extinguishment
C. water in any form should not be used as it will spread the fire
D. the space should be opened 5 minutes after flooding CO_2 to prevent injury to personnel

01249. Which area is designated a special area by Annex V to MARPOL 73/78?

A. Gulf of Mexico
B. Caribbean Sea
C. Red Sea
D. Great Lakes

01251. The proper stimulant for an unconscious person is:

A. tea
B. coffee
C. whiskey and water
D. ammonia inhalant

01252. When fighting a fire with a portable dry chemical fire extinguisher, the stream should be directed:

A. over the top of the flames
B. off a bulkhead into the fire
C. in front of the fire
D. at the base of the fire

01254. The painter of the inflatable life raft has a length of:

A. 6 fathoms
B. 50 feet
C. 100 feet
D. 300 feet

01255. The color of the signal flare sent up by a submarine indicating that a torpedo has been fired in a training exercise is:

A. white
B. green
C. yellow
D. red

01256. The purpose of the 4 water pockets, located on the underside at each corner of the raft, is to:

A. stow rainwater; these 4 spaces will not take up valuable space
B. act as stabilizers by filling with sea water as soon as the raft is inflated and in an upright position
C. hold the freshwater required by regulation to be provided in the raft when packed
D. none of the above

01257. Providing you are not sailing in the Red Sea or another special area as listed in ANNEX V of MARPOL, how many miles from land must you be to throw garbage including bottles, rags, and glass that has not been ground up into the sea?

A. 3 nm
B. 6 nm
C. 12 nm
D. 25 nm

01262. Which portable fire extinguisher is normally recharged in a shore facility?

A. dry chemical (cartridge-operated)
B. water (cartridge-operated)
C. water (pump tank)
D. carbon dioxide

01263. When chipping rust on a vessel, the most important piece of safety gear is:

A. a hard hat
B. gloves
C. goggles
D. a long sleeve shirt

01264. The operating cord on an inflatable life raft should be renewed by:

A. removing the top half of the shell, cutting the line at its source, and renewing completely
B. cutting the line where it enters the case and replacing that portion

C. leaving the original line and tying another one to it so the two lines will take the strain
D. an approved servicing facility ashore

01265. You are picking up a person that has fallen overboard. A small craft should approach the victim with the:

A. victim to leeward
B. victim to windward
C. wind on your port side
D. wind on your starboard side

01266. A life line must be connected to the life raft:

A. at the bow
B. at the stern
C. in the middle
D. all around

01268. A soda-acid extinguisher is most effective against fires of class:

A. A
B. B
C. C
D. D

01272. When approaching a fire from windward, you should shield firefighters from the fire by using:

A. low-velocity fog
B. high-velocity fog
C. a straight stream of water
D. foam spray

01274. On inflatable life rafts, the operating cord should be renewed by:

A. cutting the old line off and renewing same
B. an approved servicing facility ashore
C. opening the case and replacing the entire line
D. one of the ship's officers

01275. When a man who has fallen overboard is being picked up by a lifeboat, the boat should approach with the wind:

A. astern and the victim just off the bow
B. ahead and the victim just off the bow
C. just off the bow and the victim to windward
D. just off the bow and the victim to leeward

01276. The lights on the outside of the canopy on an inflatable life raft operate:

A. by turning the globe clockwise
B. by a switch at each light
C. by a light sensor
D. automatically when the raft is inflated

01277. When possible, what is the FIRST step in combating an engine fuel-pump fire which results from a broken fuel line?

A. Secure all engine room doors, hatches, and vents.
B. Close the fuel line valve.
C. Check the spread of the fire with foam.
D. Cast the barge off the wharf.

01278. An extinguishing agent which effectively cools, dilutes combustible vapors, removes oxygen and provides a heat and smoke screen is:

A. carbon dioxide
B. Halon 1301
C. dry chemical
D. water fog

01279. A crewman has suffered a blow to the head and various symptoms indicate a concussion. Proper treatment includes:

A. turning the victim's head to the side to keep his airway open
B. positioning the victim so the head is lower than the body
C. giving the victim water if he is thirsty, but no food
D. placing a pillow only under the victim's head

01281. You are in the process of righting an inflatable life raft that has inflated in an upside down position. Which of the following is TRUE?

A. As the raft flips to the upright position, you will be thrown clear.
B. After the raft is in the upright position on top of you, dive down to prevent your life preservers from fouling as you come out.
C. Swim out from under the raft in a face up position to keep your life preservers clear of the raft.
D. You should remove your life preservers before attempting to right an inflatable raft.

01282. When approaching a fire from leeward you should shield fire fighters from the fire by using:

A. a straight stream of water
B. foam spray
C. high-velocity fog
D. low-velocity fog

01284. The operating cord on an inflatable life raft also serves as a:

A. lifeline
B. painter
C. drogue
D. marker

01286. The inside light in an inflatable life raft is turned on:

A. automatically as the life raft inflates
B. with a switch near the boarding handle
C. at night because the light has a photosensitive switch
D. by screwing the bulb in after the raft is inflated

01288. Which extinguishing agent is the best for use on electrical fires?

A. foam
B. CO_2
C. dry chemical
D. water fog

01289. An undocumented vessel with 10 people aboard and operating 25 miles off the seacoast must carry a survival craft of the:

A. inflatable buoyant apparatus type
B. buoyant apparatus type
C. life float type
D. any of the above types are acceptable.

01292. What is the most important consideration when determining how to fight an electrical fire?

A. whether the fire is in machinery or passenger spaces
B. danger of shock to personnel
C. the amount of toxic fumes created by the extinguisher
D. maintaining electrical power

01294. Prior to the ship's sailing, the operating cord on each inflatable life raft should be:

A. attached to the raft stowage cradle or to a secure object nearby with a weak link
B. checked to see that it's unattached
C. coiled neatly on the raft container
D. faked on deck and led through a chock

01296. Hand holds or straps on the underside of an inflatable life raft are provided:

A. to right the raft if it capsizes
B. to carry the raft around on deck
C. for crewmen to hang on to
D. to hang the raft for drying

01298. If a powdered aluminum fire is being fought, the correct extinguishing agent would be:

A. dry powder
B. water fog
C. CO_2
D. steam

01299. In reviving a person who has been overcome by gas fumes, which of the following would you AVOID doing?

A. giving stimulants
B. prompt removal of the patient from the suffocating atmosphere
C. applying artificial respiration and massage
D. keeping him warm and comfortable

01301. A vessel to which Annex V to MARPOL 73/78 applies is located 24 nautical miles from the nearest land. What type of garbage is prohibited from being discharged?

A. glass
B. crockery
C. metal
D. dunnage

01302. A class B fire is most successfully fought by:

A. preventing oxygen from reaching the burning material
B. cooling the burning material below its ignition temperature
C. using the extinguishing agent to make the burning material fire-resistant
D. using the extinguishing agent to absorb the heat

01304. The painter line of an inflatable life raft should be:

A. free running on the deck
B. faked out next to the case
C. secured to a permanent object on deck
D. stowed near the raft

01306. Water pockets on the underside of an inflatable life raft are for:

A. catching rain water
B. stability
C. easy drainage
D. maneuverability

01307. Firefighting foam is only effective when the foam:

A. penetrates to the bottom of the fire
B. is kept saturated with low velocity water fog
C. mixes with the burning fuel oil
D. completely covers the top of burning liquid

01308. Which of the following would be the most effective agent to use to extinguish a fire in drums of inflammable liquids stowed on the weather deck of a vessel?

A. carbon dioxide
B. foam

C. steam
D. water fog

01311. Which of the following statements about pneumatic chipping tools is TRUE?

A. The operator must wear safety goggles or glasses.
B. The equipment must be grounded to prevent shock hazard.
C. The chipping mechanism is made of a nonsparking material that is safe to use near explosive atmospheres.
D. The needles of the needle-type chipping gun must be replaced when they have been blunted more than 1/2 of their diameter.

01312. The best method of extinguishing a class A fire is to:

A. remove oxygen from the area
B. cool fuel below ignition temperature
C. smother with CO2
D. smother fire with foam

01314. If you wish to remove an inflatable life raft from its cradle, the best way to free it is by:

A. cutting the restraining strap
B. unscrewing the turnbuckle on the back of the cradle
C. lifting one end of the raft
D. pushing the plunger on the center of the hydrostatic release

01316. The air spaces in the floor of an inflatable raft will provide protection against:

A. warm water temperatures
B. cold water temperatures
C. tears in the outside skin of the bottom of the raft
D. all of the above

01317. The most effective way of applying carbon dioxide from a portable extinguisher to a fire is by:

A. forming a cloud cover over the flames
B. directing the gas at the base of the flames in a slow sweeping motion
C. discharging the carbon dioxide into the heart of the flames
D. bouncing the discharge off an adjacent bulkhead just above the burning surface

01318. The most effective fire extinguishing agent to use on burning linen is:

A. water
B. carbon dioxide
C. dry chemical
D. foam

01319. Where should station bills be posted?

A. crew's quarters
B. dining areas
C. passageways adjacent to living areas
D. all of the above

01320. Fire extinguishers on inspected vessels are numbered by size I through V, with I being:

A. used for electrical fires only
B. the smallest
C. the most accessible
D. the most effective

01324. A hydrostatic release mechanism for a life raft:

A. must be wet before it will release
B. should be kept in a watertight cover except in an emergency
C. will inflate the raft in its cradle if operated manually
D. must be submerged to a certain depth to release automatically

01326. A feature on all inflatable life rafts is:

A. safety straps from the overhead
B. built in seats
C. releasing hooks at each end
D. water stabilizing pockets

01327. If you are forced to abandon ship in a life raft, your course of action should be to:

A. remain in the immediate vicinity
B. head for the nearest land
C. head for the closest sea-lanes
D. let the persons in the boat vote on what to do

01328. Any extinguishing agent used on a Class "C" fire must have what important property?

A. cooling ability
B. leaves no residue
C. penetrating power
D. nonconductivity

01332. An important step in fighting any electrical fire is to:

A. stop ventilation
B. stop the vessel
C. de-energize the circuit
D. apply water to extinguish the fire

01334. A raft should be manually released from its cradle by:

A. cutting the straps that enclose the container
B. removing the rubber sealing strip from the container

C. loosening the turnbuckle on the securing strap
D. pushing the button on the hydrostatic release

01335. What prevents an inflated life raft from being pulled under by a vessel which sinks in water over 100 feet in depth?

A. the hydrostatic release
B. nothing
C. a Rottmer release
D. the weak link in the painter line

01336. A feature of an inflatable raft which helps keep people stationary in rough weather is:

A. lashings on the floor of the raft for the passenger's feet
B. straps from the overhead
C. safety straps on the inside of the raft
D. ridges in the floor of the raft

01337. It is desirable to have screens on the vents of potable water tanks to:

A. filter the incoming air
B. prevent explosions
C. prevent backups
D. stop insects from entering

01338. Regular foam can be used on all but which of the following flammable liquids?

A. motor gasoline
B. jet fuel
C. crude petroleum
D. alcohol

01340. When compared to a high-expansion foam, a low-expansion foam will:

A. be dryer
B. be lighter
C. be less heat resistant
D. not cling to vertical surfaces

01341. Persons who have swallowed a non-petroleum based poison are given large quantities of warm, soapy water or warm salt water to:

A. induce vomiting
B. absorb the poison from the blood
C. neutralize the poison in the blood
D. increase the digestive process and eliminate the poison

01342. The first action which should be taken in event of fire on your vessel is to:

A. notify the Coast Guard
B. sound the alarm
C. have passengers put on life preservers
D. cut off air supply to the fire

01344. What is the purpose of the hydrostatic release?

A. to release the raft from the cradle automatically as the ship sinks
B. to inflate the raft automatically
C. to test the rafts hydrostatically
D. none of the above

01345. An inflatable life raft can be launched by:

A. the float-free method only
B. kicking the hydrostatic release
C. throwing the entire container overboard then pulling on the operating cord to inflate the raft
D. removing the securing straps

01346. The canopy of your life raft should:

A. go into place as the raft is inflated
B. be put up after everyone is aboard
C. be put up only in severe weather
D. be used as a sail if the wind is blowing

01347. A quick and rapid motion of a vessel in a seaway is an indication of a(n):

A. large GM
B. high center of gravity
C. excessive free surface
D. small GZ

01348. Dry chemical fire extinguishers would be effective for which type of fire?

A. burning oil
B. electrical
C. paint
D. all of the above

01352. If you have a fire in the engine room, your FIRST act should be to:

A. discharge the fixed CO_2 system into the engine room
B. secure the fuel supply and ventilation to the engine room
C. maneuver your vessel into the wind
D. have all of your crew get in the life raft

01354. If the hydrostatic release mechanism for an inflatable life raft is not periodically serviced and becomes inoperative, it will fail to:

A. set the water lights on immersion
B. release the dye-marker from the life raft
C. free the life raft from the vessel
D. break the seal on the carbon dioxide cylinder

01355. As a vessel sinks to a depth of 15 feet, the hydrostatic trip releases the life raft container from its cradle by:

A. breaking the weak link
B. releasing the tie-down strap
C. pulling the operating cord
D. releasing the CO_2 canister

01356. What is placed on the under side of an inflatable life raft to help prevent it from being skidded by the wind or overturned?

A. ballast bags
B. a keel
C. strikes
D. sea anchor

01358. Which extinguishing agent is best for use on a magnesium fire?

A. water
B. sand
C. CO2
D. dry chemical

01361. The area indicated by the letter G in illustration D033DG is known as the:

A. entrance
B. stringer plate
C. turn of the bilge
D. garboard

01362. In the event of fire in the crew's quarters of your vessel, one of your first acts should be to:

A. ventilate the quarters as much as possible
B. prepare to abandon ship
C. close all ventilation to the quarters if possible
D. attempt to put the fire out yourself without sounding the alarm

01363. Before entering the chain locker, you should:

A. have someone standing by
B. make sure there is sufficient air within the locker
C. de-energize the windlass
D. all of the above

01364. Signaling devices provided on inflatable life rafts include:

A. a Very pistol
B. orange smoke signals
C. an air horn
D. a lantern

01365. The most important thing to remember when launching an inflatable life raft by hand is to:

A. open the CO_2 inflation valve
B. open the raft container

C. ensure that the operating cord is secured to the vessel
D. inflate the raft on the vessel, then lower it over the side

01366. The air spaces in the floor of an inflatable life raft will provide protection against:

A. asphyxiation from CO2
B. loss of air in the sides of the raft
C. rough seas
D. cold water temperatures

01368. A fire in electrical equipment should be extinguished by using:

A. salt water
B. foam
C. low velocity fog
D. CO2

01370. What portable extinguisher should be protected from cold temperature?

A. foam
B. C02
C. dry chemical
D. all of the above

01371. What statement about immersion suits is TRUE?

A. All models will automatically turn an unconscious person face-up in the water.
B. The exposure suit seals in body heat and provides protection against hypothermia for weeks.
C. The suit is flameproof and provides protection to the wearer while swimming through burning oil.
D. The suits provide for limited body movement such as walking, climbing a ladder and picking up small objects like a pencil.

01372. It is necessary to secure the forced ventilation to a compartment where there is a fire to:

A. allow the exhaust fans to remove smoke
B. extinguish the fire by carbon monoxide smothering
C. prevent additional oxygen from reaching the fire
D. protect fire fighting personnel from smoke

01373. You are reading draft marks on a vessel and you observe that the water level is halfway between the bottom of the number 5 and the top of the number 5. What is the draft of the vessel?

A. 4'-09"
B. 5'-09"
C. 5'-03"
D. 5'-06"

01374. Puncture leaks in the lower tubes or bottom of an inflatable life raft should first be stopped by using:

A. sealing clamps
B. repair tape
C. a tube patch
D. sail twine and vulcanizing kit

01375. To launch a life raft by hand, you should:

A. cut the casing bands, throw the life raft over the side and it will then inflate
B. detach the operating cord, throw the raft over the side and it will then inflate
C. cut the casing bands, throw the raft over the side and pull the operating cord
D. throw the life raft over the side and pull the operating cord

01376. Which of the following distress signals is required for a life raft in ocean service and could be effectively used to attract the attention of aircraft at night?

A. the water light
B. smoke marker
C. red hand-held flares
D. orange dye marker

01378. The most effective cooling agent among those normally used to fight fires is:

A. water fog
B. chemical foam
C. mechanical foam
D. carbon dioxide

01381. Large volumes of carbon dioxide are safe and effective for fighting fires in enclosed spaces, such as in a pumproom, provided that the:

A. persons in the space wear gas masks
B. persons in the space wear damp cloths over their mouths and nostrils
C. ventilation system is secured and all persons leave the space
D. ventilation system is kept operating

01382. Ventilation systems connected to a compartment in which a fire is burning are normally closed to prevent the rapid spread of the fire by:

A. convection
B. conduction
C. radiation
D. spontaneous combustion

01384. On most makes of inflatable rafts you can make the batteries that operate the light on the inside of these rafts last longer by:

A. unscrewing the bulb during the daylight
B. operating the switch for the light
C. taking no action as there is no way of preserving power
D. taking no action as they shut off automatically in daylight

01385. An inflatable life raft is hand-launched by:

A. pulling a cord
B. cutting the wire restraining bands
C. removing the rubber packing strip
D. throwing the entire container overboard

01386. If the metacentric height is large, a vessel will:

A. be tender
B. have a slow and easy motion
C. be stiff
D. have a tendency to yaw

01387. A vessel is "listed" when it is:

A. down by the head
B. down by the stern
C. inclined due to off-center weight
D. inclined by the head

01388. Which agent will absorb the most heat?

A. CO2
B. foam
C. water
D. dry chemical

01391. Halon extinguishes fire primarily by:

A. cooling
B. smothering
C. shielding of radiant heat
D. chain breaking

01392. Except in rare cases, it is impossible to extinguish a shipboard fire by:

A. removing the heat
B. removing the oxygen
C. removing the fuel
D. interrupting the chain reaction

01393. When reading the draft marks in illustration D032DG, you note the water level is about 4 inches below the bottom of the number 11. What is the draft?

A. 10'-08"
B. 10'-10"
C. 11'-04"
D. 11'-08"

01394. In each inflatable raft, what piece of equipment is provided to make quick, emergency, temporary repairs to a cut or rip in a raft?

A. none
B. glue and rubber patches
C. several various-sized repair clamps
D. self-adhesive rubberized canvas patches

01395. After you have thrown the life raft and stowage container into the water, you inflate the life raft by:

A. pulling on the painter line
B. forcing open the container which operates the CO2
C. hitting the hydrostatic release
D. using the hand pump provided

01396. If you find an inflatable life raft container with steel bands around the case, you should:

A. tell the Master
B. leave the bands in place
C. tell the Mate
D. remove the bands yourself

01397. To reduce mild fever the MOST useful drug is:

A. bicarbonate of soda
B. paregoric
C. aspirin
D. aromatic spirits of ammonia

01402. When using carbon dioxide to fight a fire on a bulkhead, The CO2 should be applied:

A. first to the bottom of the flaming area, sweeping from side to side, and following the flames upward
B. in a circular motion from the middle of the bulkhead outward
C. to the top of the flaming area, sweeping from side to side, and working toward the bottom
D. in an up-and-down motion from one side of the bulkhead to the other

01404. Signaling devices which are provided on inflatable life rafts include:

A. rocket shoulder rifle
B. an oil lantern
C. hand-held red flares
D. an air horn

01405. When launching an inflatable life raft, you should make sure that the operating cord is:

A. fastened to some substantial part of the vessel
B. not fastened to anything

C. secured to the hydrostatic release
D. fastened to the raft container

01406. When a ship is abandoned and there are several rafts in the water, one of the first things to be done is:

A. separate the rafts as much as possible to increase chances of detection
B. transfer all supplies to one raft
C. transfer all the injured to one raft
D. secure the rafts together to keep them from drifting apart

01408. Which of the following is NOT a characteristic of carbon dioxide fire-extinguishing agents?

A. effective even if ventilation is not shut down
B. will not deteriorate in storage
C. non-corrosive
D. effective on electrical equipment

01414. What statement about immersion suits is TRUE?

A. All models will automatically turn an unconscious person face-up in the water.
B. The immersion suit seals in body heat and provides protection against hypothermia for weeks.
C. The suit will still be serviceable after a brief (2-6 seconds) exposure to flame and burning.
D. The wearer of the suit is not restricted in body movement and the suit may be donned well in advance of abandoning ship.

01415. When reading the draft marks in illustration D032DG, you note the water level forward is at the top of the 8, and the water level aft is at the top of the 8. What is the mean draft?

A. 8'-06"
B. 8'-03"
C. 8'-00"
D. 7'-06"

01416. Which of the following is NOT a characteristic of Halon (1301)?

A. It is colorless.
B. It is sweet smelling.
C. It may cause dizziness when inhaled.
D. It does not conduct electricity.

01422. Mechanical gearing of deck machinery such as the windlass or boat hoists should:

A. be open to view so, if a foreign object gets in the gearing, the operator can immediately stop the machinery
B. have a guard over the gearing

C. be painted a contrasting color from the base color in order to call attention to the gearing
D. not be operated if there is any crew within 10 feet of the machinery

01424. Halon gas will decompose and may form very hazardous toxic fumes when discharged:

A. directly on flames
B. at room temperature
C. in an extreme cold climate
D. none of the above

01426. A vessel aground may have negative GM since the:

A. decrease in KM is equal to the loss of draft
B. virtual rise of G is directly proportional to the remaining draft
C. displacement lost acts at the point where the ship is aground
D. lost buoyancy method is used to calculate KM, and KB is reduced

01428. A Halon 1301 cylinder contains 100 pounds of liquid at 360 psi. It must be recharged when the pressure drops below how many psi?

A. 360
B. 352
C. 336
D. 324

01429. When collecting condensation for drinking water:

A. a sponge used to mop up and store condensation must be kept salt free
B. only condensation on the bottom of the canopy should be collected
C. it should be strained through a finely woven cloth
D. chlorine tablets should be used to make it drinkable

01432. When reading the draft marks in illustration D032DG, you note that 2 inches of the 9 forward is visible above the water level, and the water level is 4 inches below the 10 aft. What is the mean draft?

A. 9'-10"
B. 9'-06"
C. 9'-04"
D. 9'-02"

01433. You should NOT use a power tool if:

A. it has a 3-prong plug
B. the insulation of the power wires is worn
C. hand tools can be used instead
D. the power source is alternating current

01434. Halon fire extinguishers are NOT effective when used on which of the following types of fires?

A. fires in electrical equipment
B. flammable oils and greases
C. Class "A" fires in ordinary combustibles
D. materials containing their own oxygen

01438. The color of the signal flare sent up by a submarine to indicate an emergency condition within the submarine is:

A. white
B. green
C. yellow
D. red

01439. Safety goggles or glasses are NOT normally worn when doing which of the following?

A. using a rotary grinder with an installed shield
B. letting go the anchor
C. handling wire rope or natural fiber line
D. painting with a spray gun

01443. When jumping into water upon which there is an oil-fire, you should:

A. break the water surface with your hands when diving head-first
B. use your hands to hold your knees to your chest
C. cover your eyes with one hand while pinching your nose shut and covering your mouth with the other
D. enter the water at the bow or stern on the windward side of the vessel

01445. When instructing a crew member concerning the right way to lift a weight, you would instruct him to:

A. arch the back to add strength to the muscles
B. bend his knees and lift with his legs
C. bend his back and stoop
D. bend his back and stoop with arms straight

01448. After making the required notification that a large oil spill into the water has occurred, the FIRST action should be to:

A. apply straw or sawdust on the oil
B. contain the spread of the oil
C. throw grains of sand into the oil
D. have the vessel move out of the spill area

01449. A vessel to which Annex V to MARPOL 73/78 applies is located 10 nautical miles from the nearest land. What type of garbage is prohibited from being discharged?

A. food waste
B. rags ground to less than 1"
C. paper ground to less than 1"
D. none of the above

01452. First aid means:

A. medical treatment of accident
B. setting of broken bones
C. emergency treatment at the scene of the injury
D. dosage of medications

01453. The hoods over galley ranges present what major hazard?

A. Grease collects in the duct and filter and if it catches fire is difficult to extinguish.
B. In order to effectively draw off cooking heat they present a head-injury hazard to a person of average or more height.
C. They inhibit the effective operation of fire fighting systems in combatting deep fat fryer or range fires.
D. They concentrate the heat of cooking and may raise surrounding flammable material to the ignition point.

01456. When reading the draft marks in illustration D032DG, you note the water level is at the bottom of number 11. What is the draft?

A. 11'-06"
B. 11'-00"
C. 10'-09"
D. 10'-06"

01462. In cleaning up an oil spill, chemical agents would:

A. absorb the oil for easy removal
B. remove the oil from the water
C. disperse or dissolve the oil into the water
D. not affect the oil

01463. To prevent the spread of fire by convection you should:

A. cool the bulkhead around the fire
B. close all openings to the area
C. shut off all electrical power
D. remove combustibles from direct exposure

01469. What statement about immersion suits is TRUE?

A. All models will automatically turn an unconscious person face-up in the water.
B. The immersion suit reduces the rate of body cooling and increases the survival time in cold water to hours or days.

C. The suit is flameproof and provides protection to a wearer swimming in burning oil.
D. The suit provides a full range of body movement and is suitable for routine wear on deck.

01471. Which of the following do regulations allow to be marked with EITHER the name of the fishing vessel OR the name of the person to whom it is assigned?

A. immersion suit
B. buoyant apparatus
C. ring buoy
D. life float

01472. When reading the draft marks in illustration D032DG, you note the water level forward is 4 inches below the 11, and the water level aft is 2 inches below the top of the 11. What is the mean draft?

A. 11'-08"
B. 11'-06"
C. 11'-04"
D. 11'-00"

01474. In cleaning up an oil spill, the use of straw or reclaimed paper fibers would be an example of what type of oil removal?

A. chemical agent removal
B. mechanical removal
C. absorbent removal
D. none of the above

01479. If your vessel is aground at the bow, it would be preferable that any weight removals be made from the:

A. bow
B. mid-section
C. stern
D. any of the above

01481. When reading the draft marks in illustration D032DG, you note that the water level is at the top of number 8. What is the draft?

A. 7'-09"
B. 8'-00"
C. 8'-03"
D. 8'-06"

01482. Which extinguishing agent is most effective on a mattress fire?

A. CO2
B. foam
C. dry chemical
D. water

01488. When compared to a high-expansion foam, a low-expansion foam will:

A. be dryer
B. be lighter
C. be more heat resistant
D. cling to vertical surfaces

01490. When reading the draft marks in illustration D032DG, you note the water level forward leaves about 4 inches of the 11 visible, and the water level aft is at the top of the 10. What is the mean draft?

A. 10'-06"
B. 10'-08"
C. 10'-10"
D. 11'-02"

01498. The spread of fire is prevented by:

A. cooling surfaces adjacent to the fire
B. leaving combustibles in the endangered area
C. increasing the oxygen supply
D. all of the above

01502. A portable foam (stored-pressure type) fire extinguisher would be most useful in combating a fire in:

A. generators
B. oil drums
C. the bridge controls
D. combustible metals

01503. If you have to jump in the water when abandoning ship, your legs should be:

A. spread apart as far as possible
B. held as tightly against your chest as possible
C. in a kneeling position
D. extended straight down and crossed at the ankles

01504. When reading the draft marks in illustration D032DG, you note the water level is about 4 inches below the bottom of 10. What is the draft?

A. 10'-04"
B. 10'-02"
C. 9'-08"
D. 9'-04"

01507. A thrust block is designed to:

A. absorb the shock of wave pressure at the bow
B. be placed between the engines and the foundation to absorb the vibration
C. transmit the thrust of the engine to the propeller
D. transmit the thrust of the propeller to the vessel

01508. Portable foam fire extinguishers are designed for use on class:

A. A and class B fires
B. A and class C fires
C. B and class C fires
D. A, class B, and class C fires

01512. Where would you find the draft marks on a ship?

A. deep tanks
B. voids
C. midships near the waterline
D. area of water line near stem and stern

01523. The term "oil" as used in the Oil Pollution Regulations means:

A. fuel oil
B. sludge
C. oil refuse
D. all of the above

01525. When reading the draft marks in illustration D032DG, you note that 2 inches of the top of number 9 are visible above the waterline. What is the draft?

A. 8'-10"
B. 9'-02"
C. 9'-04"
D. 9'-08"

01526. Which of the following types of portable fire extinguishers is NOT designed for use on flammable liquid fires?

A. foam
B. dry chemical
C. water (cartridge-operated)
D. carbon dioxide

01536. What types of portable fire extinguishers are designed for putting out electrical fires?

A. foam and soda-acid
B. foam and carbon dioxide
C. foam and dry chemical
D. dry chemical and carbon dioxide

01540. Which statement concerning the collection of fresh water is FALSE?

A. Fresh water may be obtained from fish.
B. Lifeboat covers or canopies should be washed with rain before drinking water is collected.
C. Fresh water may be collected from condensation inside the life raft.
D. Seawater should never be consumed.

01541. Which would be considered pollution under the U. S. water pollution laws?

A. garbage
B. hazardous substances

C. oil
D. all of the above

01543. Which of the following is TRUE concerning immersion suits and their use?

A. Only a light layer of clothing may be worn underneath.
B. They provide sufficient flotation to do away with the necessity of wearing a life jacket.
C. They should be tight fitting.
D. A puncture in the suit will not appreciably reduce its value.

01546. What are the most important reasons for using water fog to fight fires?

A. smothers burning surfaces, organically destroys fuel
B. cools fire and adjacent surfaces, provides protective barrier
C. reaches areas not protected by steam or CO2 smothering systems
D. allows fire to be attacked from leeward, saturates liquid surfaces

01547. Which of the following procedures is NOT recommended when it is necessary to swim through an oil fire?

A. Wear as much clothing as possible.
B. Enter the water feet first.
C. Swim with the wind.
D. Cover your eyes with one hand when entering the water.

01553. What is an advantage of using foam in fire fighting?

A. It is effective in controlling fire in flowing oil such as coming from a broken fuel line.
B. It absorbs heat from materials that could cause reignition.
C. Most foams can be used jointly with dry chemical extinguishing agents to attack a fire by two methods of extinguishment.
D. Once the surface is blanketed with foam and the fire is extinguished, no further foam is required.

01555. Seawater may be used for drinking:

A. at a maximum rate of 2 ounces per day
B. mixed with an equal quantity of fresh water
C. if gathered during or immediately after a hard rain
D. under no conditions

01556. Which fire extinguishing agent has the greatest capacity for absorbing heat?

A. water
B. foam

C. dry chemical
D. carbon Dioxide

01558. A Halon 1301 cylinder is periodically tested for weight loss and pressure loss. What minimum percentage of the full pressure can be lost before the cylinder must be recharged?

A. 3%
B. 5%
C. 10%
D. 15%

01559. The capacity of any life raft on board a vessel can be determined by:

A. examining the Certificate of Inspection
B. examining the plate on the outside of the raft container
C. referring to the station bill
D. referring to the shipping articles

01560. The most important reason for taking anti-seasickness pills as soon as possible after entering a life raft is to:

A. assist in sleeping
B. reduce appetite by decreasing nausea
C. prevent loss of body moisture by vomiting
D. prevent impaired judgement due to motion-induced deliriousness

01563. Who should inspect and test an inflatable life raft?

A. the person in charge
B. the manufacturer or authorized representative
C. shipyard personnel
D. a certificated lifeboatman

01564. What action is routinely performed at the annual servicing and inspection of a dry-chemical cartridge-operated portable fire extinguisher?

A. insure the chemical is powdery
B. replace the cartridge
C. pressure test the discharge hose
D. test the pressure gauge for proper operation

01566. CO2 extinguishes a fire by:

A. cooling
B. smothering
C. chemical action
D. all of the above

01569. What statement about immersion suits is FALSE?

A. The suit should be worn only when abandoning ship.
B. The suit is received from the manufacturer in an outer storage bag that should be used aboard ship for storing the suit.
C. The front zipper should be lubricated with beeswax or paraffin.
D. Immersion suits provide protection against hypothermia even if there is a small leak or tear.

01571. A Halon 1301 cylinder is periodically tested for weight loss and pressure loss. It must be recharged if it has lost more than what minimum percentage of its weight?

A. 3%
B. 5%
C. 10%
D. 15%

01572. Your fishing vessel operates more than 25 miles from the coastline on the Great Lakes. Which of the following distress signals is NOT required to be on board?

A. 3 red parachute flares
B. 6 red hand flares
C. 1 electric distress light
D. 3 orange smoke signals

01575. Foam extinguishes a fire by:

A. smothering the burning material
B. chemical combination with burning material
C. absorbing the burning material
D. organic destruction of the burning material

01584. What data is NOT painted on the bow of a lifeboat?

A. Number of persons allowed
B. Capacity in cubic feet
C. Weight of the boat
D. Home port

01586. What does the success of an indirect attack on a fire depend on?

A. size of the fire when initially observed
B. complete containment of the fire
C. cooling ability of the firefighting agent
D. class of the fire

01590. After a vessel transmits the original distress message, what signal should be sent to allow ships to take RDF bearings?

A. SOS 3 times
B. MO for 3 minutes
C. E for 1 minute
D. ET for 3 minutes

01597. What characteristic is an advantage of Halon as a fire extinguishing medium?

A. electrically non-conductive
B. relatively inexpensive
C. effective against chemicals containing an oxidizer
D. all of the above

01602. What statement about immersion suits is FALSE?

A. They should be worn while working on deck when you could be washed overboard.
B. The suit is received from the manufacturer in a bag intended to be used for storage of the suit on board ship.
C. During the annual inspection and maintenance, the zipper should be lubricated with beeswax or paraffin.
D. A small leak of water into the suit will destroy its protective qualities against hypothermia.

01610. An "ABC" dry chemical fire extinguisher would be least effective against a fire in:

A. a mattress
B. spilled liquids such as oil or paint
C. high voltage electrical gear
D. a trash can

01612. What action is routinely performed at the annual servicing and inspection of a dry-chemical cartridge-operated portable fire extinguisher?

A. Test the pressure gauge for correct reading.
B. Weigh the cartridge.
C. Replace the dry chemical.
D. Pressure test the discharge hose.

01617. When compared to low-expansion foam, a high-expansion foam will:

A. be wetter
B. be lighter
C. be more heat resistant
D. not cling to vertical surfaces

01618. What characteristic of Halon is a disadvantage when it is used as a fire extinguishing medium?

A. leaves a residue
B. cost, relative to other agents
C. breaks down while under prolonged storage
D. conducts electricity

01620. One disadvantage of using regular dry chemical (sodium bicarbonate) in firefighting is that:

A. it can break down under high heat and emit noxious fumes
B. it will decompose under prolonged storage and lose its effectiveness
C. fire has been known to flash back over the surface of an oil fire
D. it is ineffective in fighting fires in high-voltage electrical equipment

01621. Why is spare fire hose rolled for storage?

A. Water in the hose is forced out the end in the rolling process.
B. The threads on the male end are protected by the hose.
C. Rolling provides maximum protection against entry of foreign objects into the couplings.
D. Rolling provides maximum protection to the outer covering of the hose.

01623. When testing a class A EPIRB, you need to use:

A. nothing other than the test indicator on the top of the EPIRB
B. an ordinary FM radio
C. the test meter supplied by the manufacturer
D. a voltage meter indicating in the 0.5 to 12 volt range

01627. The canvas covering of fire hose is called the:

A. casing
B. outer hose
C. line cover
D. jacket

01629. What is an advantage of using foam in fire fighting?

A. The air bubbles in foam act as an insulator in fighting a class C fire.
B. The effectiveness of foam in forming a blanket over a burning liquid increases as the temperature of the liquid increases.
C. Foam can be used to control gases escaping from compressed gas cylinders.
D. Foam sets up a vapor barrier over a flammable liquid preventing flammable gases from rising.

01631. What statement about immersion suits is TRUE?

A. Some models will not automatically turn an unconscious person face-up in the water.
B. The immersion suit seals in body heat and provides protection against hypothermia for weeks.
C. The suit is flameproof and provides protection to the wearer while swimming through burning oil.

D. The wearer of the suit is severely restricted in body movement and the suit should be donned just before abandoning ship.

01632. When joining the female coupling of the fire hose to the male outlet of the hydrant, you should make sure that the:

A. threads are lubricated
B. nozzle is attached to the hose
C. female coupling has a gasket
D. hose is led out

01634. To prevent the spread of fire by convection you should:

A. close all openings to the area
B. shut off all electrical power
C. remove combustibles from direct exposure
D. cool the bulkhead around the fire

01635. What firefighting method is an example of an indirect attack on a fire?

A. bouncing a straight stream of water off the overhead to create spray effect
B. spraying foam on a bulkhead and letting it flow down and over a pool of burning oil
C. flooding a paint locker with CO2 and sealing the compartment
D. cooling adjacent bulkheads with water to prevent the spread of the fire by conduction

01637. What characteristic is a disadvantage of Halon as a fire extinguishing medium?

A. conducts electricity
B. difficult to store
C. large volume necessary to be effective
D. ineffective in powdered metal fires

01640. A Halon 1301 cylinder contains 100 pounds of liquid at 360 psi. It must be recharged when the weight drops below how many pounds of liquid?

A. 90
B. 92
C. 95
D. 98

01645. What action is routinely performed at the annual servicing and inspection of a dry chemical cartridge operated portable fire extinguisher?

A. Replace the dry chemical.
B. Replace the cartridge.
C. Test the pressure gauge for correct reading.
D. Check the squeeze grip for operation.

01648. What is an advantage of using foam in fire fighting?

A. It is particularly effective on oil fires where the temperatures of the liquid are over 100° C (212° F).
B. Most foams can be used in conjunction with dry chemicals to attack a fire by two methods.
C. Foam is effective on combustible metal fires.
D. Foam can be made with seawater or fresh water.

01650. When compared to low-expansion foam, a high-expansion foam will:

A. be drier
B. be heavier
C. be more heat resistant
D. not cling to vertical surfaces

01665. Which statement about stowing spare hose is TRUE?

A. Fold the hose so that the male coupling is about 4 feet from the female coupling, then roll it up.
B. Roll the hose starting at the female end.
C. Roll the hose starting at the male end.
D. Fold the hose into lengths about 6 feet long and then lash the folds together.

01669. You have abandoned ship and after two days in a raft you can see an aircraft near the horizon apparently carrying out a search pattern. You should:

A. switch the EPIRB to the homing signal mode
B. use the voice transmission capability of the EPIRB to guide the aircraft to your raft
C. turn on the strobe light on top of the EPIRB
D. use visual distress signals in conjunction with the EPIRB

01670. You are testing a class A EPIRB. You will know the EPIRB is working properly when the indicator light comes on, and you hear over the test frequency:

A. an oscillating tone
B. the Morse Code for SOS
C. a computerized voice saying Mayday
D. the Morse signal for your vessel's call letters

01671. When should the full power test of a class A EPIRB be made?

A. at any time
B. minute 00 to 05 of any hour
C. minute 15 to 18 or 45 to 48 of any hour
D. any day between 0700 to 0800 GMT

01686. How many B-II fire extinguishers must be in the machinery space of a 175-foot long fishing vessel propelled by engines with 2300 brake horsepower?

A. 2
B. 3
C. 4
D. 5

01687. What statement about immersion suits is TRUE?

A. Immersion suits should be worn while performing routine work on deck.
B. After purchasing, the suit should be stowed in the storage bag in which it was received.
C. During the annual maintenance, the front zipper should be lubricated using light machine oil or mineral oil.
D. Any tear or leak will render the suit unserviceable and it must be replaced.

01688. Each commercial fishing vessel must have at least one immersion suit, exposure suit, or life preserver for each:

A. person aboard
B. person working on deck
C. crew member
D. none of the above are correct.

01697. The difference between a class A and a class B EPIRB is that the class A EPIRB:

A. operates on both military and civilian aircraft distress frequencies
B. transmits both an alerting signal and a homing signal
C. must be of the float free type and automatically activated
D. operates with a greater signal power

01701. Movement of liquid in a tank when a vessel inclines causes an increase in:

A. righting arm
B. metacentric height
C. height of the uncorrected KG
D. natural rolling period

01705. What statement about immersion suits is TRUE?

A. Immersion suits should be worn during routine work on deck to provide maximum protection.
B. After purchasing, the suit should be removed from its storage bag and hung on a hanger where readily accessible.
C. During annual maintenance, the front zipper should be lubricated with paraffin or beeswax.
D. Small leaks or tears may be repaired using the repair kit packed with the suit.

01810. Halon extinguishes a fire by:

A. breaking the chain reaction
B. smothering the fire
C. cooling the fire
D. coating the fuel with a nonflammable surface

01811. What should be your FIRST action if you discover a fire aboard ship?

A. Sound the alarm.
B. Attempt to put out the fire.
C. Confine it by closing doors, ports, vents, etc.
D. Call the Master.

01823. What is the MINIMUM distance a vessel subject to the requirements of Annex V to MARPOL 73/78 must be located from nearest land to legally discharge paper trash?

A. 5 nautical miles
B. 10 nautical miles
C. 12 nautical miles
D. 25 nautical miles

01831. A slow and easy motion of a vessel in a seaway is an indication of a:

A. small GM
B. low center of gravity
C. stiff vessel
D. large GZ

01837. Each life raft on a unit which is launched from a position more than 10 feet above the water must be:

A. limited to carry no more than 10 persons
B. launched by a davit mechanism
C. stowed in quick release racks
D. inspected every 6 months

01851. When using a handheld smoke signal from a lifeboat, you should activate the signal:

A. on the downwind side
B. on the upwind side
C. inside the boat
D. at the stern

01860. You are underway at sea when a fire is reported in the forward part of the vessel. If the wind is from dead ahead at 20 knots, you should:

A. remain on course and hold speed
B. change course to put the wind on either beam and increase speed
C. change course and put the stern to the wind
D. remain on course but decrease speed

01862. All electrical appliances aboard a vessel should be grounded to:

A. prevent them from falling when vessel rolls
B. protect personnel from electrical shock
C. increase their operating efficiency
D. prevent unauthorized personnel from operating them

01870. When should a fire be ventilated?

A. when attacking the fire directly
B. when using a steam smothering system
C. when using the fixed CO2 system
D. all of the above

01880. The primary reason for placing covers over storage batteries is to:

A. prevent the accumulation of explosive gases
B. protect the hull from leaking electrolyte
C. prevent movement in rough waters
D. protect against accidental shorting across terminals

01890. Spaces containing batteries require good ventilation because:

A. ventilation avoids CO2 build up
B. ventilation supplies extra oxygen for charging the battery
C. ventilation avoids flammable gas accumulation
D. less electrolyte is required to maintain the batteries' charge

01900. The accumulation of dangerous fumes generated by the storage batteries is best prevented by:

A. covering the batteries in a nonconducting, solid enclosure
B. mounting the batteries in a position as high as possible
C. natural or mechanical ventilation
D. securing the batteries to vibration reducing mounting brackets

01909. On a passenger vessel, the vessel's name must appear on:

A. rigid type life rafts
B. lifeboats
C. lifeboat oars
D. all of the above

01910. Which of the following visual distress signals is acceptable for daylight use only?

A. hand-held red flare
B. self-contained rocket-propelled parachute red flare
C. hand-held orange smoke distress flare
D. red aerial pyrotechnic flare

01920. Which statement is TRUE concerning life preservers?

A. Buoyant vests may be substituted for life preservers.
B. Kapok life preservers must have plastic-covered pad inserts.
C. Life preservers must always be worn with the same side facing outwards.
D. Life preservers are not designed to turn a person's face clear of the water when unconscious.

01930. Lifesaving equipment shall be stowed so that it will be:

A. locked up
B. readily accessible for use
C. inaccessible to passengers
D. on the topmost deck of the vessel at all times

01938. A wobbling tail shaft is an indication of:

A. shallow water
B. an engine that is misfiring
C. a tight tail shaft gland
D. worn stern bearing or misalignment

01940. Life preservers should be stowed in:

A. the forepeak
B. the wheelhouse
C. convenient protected topside locations
D. locked watertight containers

01950. The lifesaving equipment on all vessels shall be:

A. inspected weekly
B. stowed in locked compartments
C. readily accessible
D. tested yearly

01951. With no alternative but to jump from a vessel, the correct posture should include:

A. holding down the life preserver against the chest with one arm crossing the other, covering the mouth and nose with a hand, and feet together
B. knees bent and held close to the body with both arms around legs
C. body straight and arms held tightly at the sides for feet first entry into the water
D. both hands holding the life preserver below the chin with knees bent and legs crossed

01954. After machinery is put in motion, you should:

A. look to see that it is running
B. pay no attention as long as it runs

C. check for water, fuel or oil leaks; check operating pressures and temperatures; check cooling water system operation
D. keep the engine space closed so that in case a failure occurs, the damage will be confined to the engine space only

01979. A documented oceangoing fishing vessel is required to have emergency instructions posted if it:

A. exceeds 49 feet in length
B. is over 25 gross tons
C. carries more than 16 persons
D. has sleeping accommodations

01983. What is required in addition to the heat, fuel and oxygen of the fire triangle to have a fire?

A. electricity
B. chain reaction
C. pressure
D. smoke

01997. Vessels to which Annex V to MARPOL 73/78 applies may discharge garbage containing plastics:

A. 5 nautical miles from nearest land
B. 12 nautical miles from nearest land
C. 25 nautical miles from nearest land
D. none of the above

02032. What is the primary hazard, other than fire damage, associated with a class C fire?

A. susceptible to reflash
B. electrocution or shock
C. explosion
D. deep seated fire

02053. What is the international calling and distress channel found on all VHF-FM equipped drilling rigs?

A. Channel 1
B. Channel 10
C. Channel 16
D. Channel 68

02055. What agency issues the Ship Station License for the VHF marine radio on a mobile offshore drilling unit?

A. U. S. Coast Guard
B. Department of Transportation
C. Federal Broadcast Authority
D. Federal Communications Commission

02057. You cannot operate a VHF or SSB radiotelephone aboard a rig unless that station is licensed by the:

A. Federal Communications Commission
B. U. S. Coast Guard
C. Minerals Management Service
D. Department of Energy

02061. Where would you find the "call sign" or "call letters" of the radio station on your rig?

A. In the rig Safety Manual
B. On the Certificate of Inspection
C. On the Ship Station License
D. On the rig Watch Bill

02063. If there are a number of survivors in the water after abandoning ship, they should:

A. tie themselves to the unit so they won't drift with the current
B. form a small circle group to create a warmer pocket of water in the center of the circle
C. send the strongest swimmer to shore for assistance
D. form a raft by lashing their life preservers together

02073. If your rig is equipped with an SSB radio, what frequency would you use to initiate a distress call?

A. 1982 kHz
B. 2082 kHz
C. 2182 kHz
D. 2282 kHz

02109. A fire is discovered in the forepeak of a vessel at sea. The wind is from ahead at 35 knots. You should:

A. change course and put the stern to the wind
B. remain on course and hold speed
C. change course to put the wind on either beam and increase speed
D. remain on course but slack the speed

02121. A life float on a fishing vessel must be equipped with:

A. smoke flares
B. a life line
C. a hydrostatic release
D. a signal mirror

02137. Where would you find the FCC authorization for transmitting on your rig's EPIRB?

A. on the Ship Station License
B. on the side of the EPIRB transmitter
C. in the Radio Log
D. on the Certificate of Inspection

02138. A class C EPIRB:

A. is primarily designed for vessels operating up to 50 miles offshore or on the Great Lakes
B. transmits a signal that can be detected by SARSAT satellite
C. must be manually activated
D. operates in the medium and low frequency bands

02142. What is meant by the term "overhaul" in firefighting?

A. Slow down the spread of fire by cooling adjacent structures.
B. Cover the fire with foam.
C. Smother fire with a blanket or similar object.
D. Break up solid objects to ensure that any deep seated fires are extinguished.

02144. A class C EPIRB:

A. should be used on board vessels operating not more than 200 miles offshore
B. transmits an alerting signal on channel 16 followed by a homing signal on channel 15
C. is automatically activated when it floats free of a sinking vessel
D. transmits a swept tone signal on the aviation distress frequency

02147. Each life preserver must be readily accessible to the person for whom it is intended while he or she is:

A. at work
B. in his or her berthing area
C. BOTH at work and in his or her berthing area
D. None of the above are correct.

02166. A class C EPIRB:

A. is designed for use by vessels operating up to 20 miles offshore or on large protected waters
B. is automatically activated after floating free of a sinking vessel
C. can be detected by SARSAT satellite
D. transmits on VLF frequencies

02175. To keep injured survivors warm in the water after abandoning ship, they should:

A. be placed in the middle of a small circle formed by the other survivors in the water
B. float on their backs with their arms extended for maximum exposure to the air
C. remove their life preservers and hold on to the uninjured survivors
D. sip water at intervals of 15 minutes

02181. To prevent the spread of fire by conduction you should:

A. shut off all electrical power
B. close all openings to the area

C. remove combustibles from direct exposure
D. cool the bulkheads around the fire

02201. The name of the fishing vessel is NOT required to be marked on a(n):

A. EPIRB
B. inflatable life raft
C. lifefloat
D. buoyant apparatus

02202. Which of the following approved lifesaving devices is required for each person on board a motor vessel carrying passengers?

A. buoyant cushion
B. buoyant vest
C. life preserver
D. ring life buoy

02219. Each buoyant work vest must be:

A. U. S. Coast Guard approved
B. marked with the name of the vessel
C. equipped with a water light
D. all of the above

02233. You are underway when a fire breaks out in the forward part of your vessel. If possible, you should:

A. call for assistance
B. abandon ship to windward
C. keep going at half speed
D. put the vessel's stern into the wind

02237. Topside icing decreases vessel stability because it reduces initial stability and:

A. increases displacement
B. increases free surface
C. increases draft
D. is usually offcenter

02251. Which of the following will NOT decrease the stability of a vessel?

A. topside icing
B. running with a following sea
C. using 35% of the fuel in a full tank
D. lowering a weight suspended by a boom onto the deck

02253. Using a sea anchor with the survival craft will:

A. reduce your drift rate
B. keep the survival craft from turning over
C. aid in recovering the survival craft
D. increase your visibility

02264. Where a propeller shaft passes through the hull, water is prevented from entering by means of a:

A. stuffing box
B. propeller boss
C. seacock
D. stop-water

02265. A right-handed propeller will cause the survival craft to:

A. walk the stern to starboard in reverse
B. walk the stern to port in reverse
C. run faster than a left-handed propeller
D. right it if capsized

02270. When a vessel is inclined at a small angle the center of buoyancy will:

A. remain stationary
B. move toward the low side
C. move toward the high side
D. move to the height of the metacenter

02282. Class A EPIRBs are required on:

A. self-propelled, inspected vessels
B. towing vessels
C. recreational vessels
D. uninspected passenger vessels

02290. In order to calculate the TPI of a vessel, for any given draft, it is necessary to divide the area of the waterplane by:

A. 35
B. 120
C. 240
D. 420

02293. Releasing oil from the sea anchor of a survival craft may:

A. keep the propeller from being fouled
B. increase propeller speed
C. help calm the waves in the vicinity of the craft
D. increase the holding power of the sea anchor

02299. The first treatment given to a person overcome by benzene vapor should be to:

A. remove them to fresh air
B. flush their face with water for about 5 minutes
C. stand them up and walk them around
D. remove their clothing and wrap them in blankets

02307. Why does a centrifugal bilge pump require priming?

A. to lubricate shaft seals
B. lack of ability to lift water level to impellers

C. head pressure must equal discharge pressure
D. to overcome resistance of water in the discharge line

02321. A Class A EPIRB is NOT:

A. approved by the Coast Guard
B. designed for float free, automatic activation
C. operated on 121.5/243 MHz
D. operated manually

02327. How many B-II fire extinguishers must be in the machinery space of a 75-foot long fishing vessel propelled by engines with 600 brake horsepower?

A. 5
B. 4
C. 3
D. 2

02331. How is water running along the shaft of a leaking centrifugal pump prevented from entering the shaft bearing?

A. shaft seal
B. water flinger
C. drain hole
D. lantern ring

02335. What is required in addition to the heat, fuel and oxygen of the fire triangle to have a fire?

A. chain reaction
B. electricity
C. pressure
D. smoke

02336. While loading bulk oil, you notice oil on the water near the barge. What should you do first?

A. Search the vessel for leaks.
B. Notify terminal superintendent.
C. Stop loading.
D. Notify the Coast Guard.

02351. How many B-II fire extinguishers must be in the machinery space of a 75-foot long fishing vessel propelled by engines with 2200 brake horsepower?

A. 5
B. 4
C. 3
D. 2

02362. A tankerman who permits or causes oil to go into a navigable waterway may be punished federally by:

A. fine
B. imprisonment

C. suspension or revocation of tankerman's document
D. all of the above

02371. What does the term "head" mean when applied to a fire pump?

A. length of the discharge pipe
B. height of the discharge pipe
C. difference between the discharge and suction pressures
D. sum of discharge and suction pressures

02401. A high velocity fog stream can be used in fire fighting situations to drive heat and smoke ahead of the fire fighters in a passageway. This technique should only be used when:

A. using a 2-1/2 inch hose
B. there is an outlet for the smoke and heat
C. the fire is totally contained by the ship's structure
D. at least two fog streams can be used

02439. If you observe any situation which presents a safety or pollution hazard during fuel transfer operations what action should you take first?

A. Close the valves at the transfer manifold.
B. Notify the person in charge of the shore facility.
C. Shut down the transfer operation.
D. Sound the fire alarm.

02448. A person on a fixed or floating platform engaged in oil exploration MAY discharge food waste into the sea when the distance from nearest land is at least:

A. 3 nautical miles
B. 5 nautical miles
C. 12 nautical miles
D. 25 nautical miles

02475. Your fishing vessel is required to have a compass. It must also have a(n):

A. deviation table
B. radar reflector
C. electronic position-fixing device
D. copy of the Sailing Directions

02488. If a crew member is exposed to phenol by way of skin or eye contact, you should IMMEDIATELY:

A. administer oxygen
B. treat victim for shock
C. flush skin and eyes with water
D. give victim stimulant

02504. A reinspection of the vessel shall be made between which of the following months while the Certificate of Inspection is valid?

A. 8 - 12 months
B. 10 - 12 months
C. 10 - 14 months
D. 12 - 14 months

02523. How many B-II fire extinguishers must be in the machinery space of a 75-foot long fishing vessel propelled by engines with 2000 brake horsepower?

A. 2
B. 3
C. 4
D. 5

02536. To prevent the spread of fire by conduction you should:

A. shut off all electrical power
B. close all openings to the area
C. cool the bulkheads around the fire
D. remove combustibles from direct exposure

02541. When lifting loads from a boat in heavy weather, the load should be taken when the boat:

A. reaches the crest
B. begins to fall
C. begins to rise
D. reaches the trough

02549. Vessels A and B are identical; however, "A" is more tender than "B". This means that "A" relative to "B" has a:

A. lower KG
B. smaller GM
C. smaller roll angle
D. larger GZ

02562. How many B-II fire extinguishers must be in the machinery space of a 175-foot long fishing vessel propelled by engines with 4000 brake horsepower?

A. 2
B. 3
C. 4
D. 5

02582. When the height of the metacenter is the same as the height of the center of gravity, the metacentric height is equal to:

A. the height of the metacenter
B. the height of the center of gravity
C. half the height of the metacenter
D. zero

02599. Oil fires are best extinguished by:

A. cutting off the supply of oxygen
B. removing the fuel
C. cooling below the ignition temperature
D. spraying with water

02606. The angle at which the fluke penetrates the soil is called the:

A. fluke angle
B. tripping angle
C. penetration angle
D. holding angle

02613. What is required in addition to the heat, fuel and oxygen of the fire triangle to have a fire?

A. smoke
B. electricity
C. chain reaction
D. pressure

02614. What is required in addition to the heat, fuel and oxygen of the fire triangle to have a fire?

A. smoke
B. electricity
C. pressure
D. chain reaction

02617. Which circumstance below is an exception to the garbage discharge requirements in Annex V to MARPOL 73/78?

A. The garbage to be discharged will sink.
B. Garbage accumulation on board has exceeded storage space.
C. A person falls overboard, and a plastic ice chest is thrown for flotation.
D. The destination port or terminal cannot receive garbage.

02636. When providing first aid to a victim of gas poisoning, the MOST important symptom to check for is:

A. suspension of breathing
B. unconsciousness
C. slow and weak pulse
D. cold and moist skin

02644. When working on a tow, a good safety precaution is to:

A. carry loads on your inside shoulder when walking along the outside of a barge
B. tighten ratchets outboard
C. walk on the top of covered barges when possible to avoid narrow gunwales
D. always remove the toothpick after tightening the ratchet

02646. How many B-II fire extinguishers must be in the machinery space of a 175-foot long fishing vessel propelled by engines with 3200 brake horsepower?

A. 2
B. 3
C. 4
D. 5

02648. Flames from small leaks of LFG may be extinguished by:

A. utilizing carbon dioxide or dry chemical fire extinguishers
B. utilizing soda and acid fire extinguishers
C. blowing the flames out
D. letting it burn itself out

02658. Drains or outlets for drawing off fuel from a fuel tank should:

A. be located at the lowest portion of the tank
B. have only a gravity-forced flow
C. extend to an external area of the hull
D. not be installed

02662. A vessel with a large GM will:

A. have a small amplitude roll in heavy weather
B. tend to ship water on deck in heavy weather
C. be subject to severe racking stresses
D. be less likely to have cargo shift

02664. Gasoline fumes tend to:

A. settle near the bottom of the bilge
B. settle near the top of the bilge
C. settle evenly throughout all levels of the bilge by mixing with air
D. disperse to atmosphere

02665. You are in the North Sea, which is a special area listed in ANNEX V of MARPOL. How many miles from land must you be to throw broken plywood dunnage over the side?

A. 6 nm
B. 12 nm
C. 25 nm
D. must be retained aboard

02682. The purpose of fuses in wiring is to:

A. allow for cutting out branch circuits
B. prevent overloading the circuits
C. reduce voltage to the branch circuits
D. permit the use of smaller wiring for lighting circuits

02689. A vessel with a large GM will:

A. have more resistance to listing in case of damage
B. have less tendency for synchronous rolling
C. be less likely to have cargo shift
D. ride more comfortably

02690. Heavy fuel oils when spilled are:

A. more harmful to sea life than lighter oils
B. easier to clean up than lighter refined oils
C. less harmful to sea life than lighter oils
D. not a real threat to marine life

02698. Using a sea anchor will:

A. reduce your drift rate
B. keep the life raft from turning over
C. aid in recovering the life raft
D. increase your visibility

02712. A vessel with a small GM will:

A. be more subject to synchronous rolling
B. have a short rolling period
C. provide an uncomfortable ride for personnel
D. have a smaller amplitude of roll in heavy weather

02716. A life float on a fishing vessel must be equipped with:

A. red parachute flares
B. drinking water
C. a jacknife
D. a light

02742. A vessel with a small GM will:

A. have a large amplitude of roll
B. provide a comfortable ride for the crew and passengers
C. have drier decks in heavy weather
D. be likely to have cargo shift in heavy weather

02754. Which of the following lifesaving equipment must be tested monthly?

A. inflatable PFD's
B. EPIRB
C. hydrostatic releases
D. dated batteries

02764. If you wear extra clothing when entering the water after abandoning ship it will:

A. weigh you down
B. preserve body heat
C. reduce your body heat
D. make it more difficult to breathe

02766. How do you know how many passengers you may carry? (Small Passenger Vessel Regulations)

A. as many as possible
B. the amount on the Certificate of Inspection
C. use your own judgement
D. no more than 40 passengers

02768. Passenger vessels of less than 65 ft. in length must be inspected by the Coast Guard when they carry more than: (Small Passenger Vessel Regulations)

A. 12 passengers
B. 50 passengers
C. 6 passengers
D. 1 passenger

02769. Starting motors, generators, and any other spark producing devices shall be: (Small Passenger Vessel Regulations)

A. of the alternating current type
B. mounted as high as practicable above the bilges
C. rated for at least 12 volts
D. all of the above

02784. When abandoning ship and jumping into the water from a substantial height without a life jacket, you should:

A. dive head first, using your hands to break the surface of the water
B. hold your arms firmly at your sides and jump feet first
C. jump feet first, covering your nose and mouth with one hand and grasping the opposing upper arm with the other
D. jump feet first, holding your knees to your chest

02786. Certain equipment aboard vessels, inspected under the Small Passenger Vessel Regulations is required to be marked with the vessel's name. This includes: (Small Passenger Vessel Regulations)

A. bunks, silverware, china, and glassware
B. anchors, line, paint cans, and fuel drums
C. life preservers, life floats, oars and paddles
D. whistle, searchlights, navigation lights, and ship's bell

02789. As appropriate for the intended voyage, all vessels must carry adequate and up-to-date: (Small Passenger Vessel Regulations)

A. charts
B. Coast Pilots
C. Light Lists
D. all of the above

02790. The weight of liquefied petroleum gas vapors as compared to air is:

A. variable
B. the same
C. lighter
D. heavier

02791. Seawater may be used for drinking:

A. under no conditions
B. at a maximum rate of 2 ounces per day
C. if gathered during or immediately after a hard rain
D. after mixing with an equal quantity of fresh water

02796. Aboard vessels subject to the "Rules and Regulations for Small Passenger Vessels", cooking and heating equipment: (Small Passenger Vessel Regulations)

A. shall be suitable for marine use
B. may use liquefied petroleum gas
C. cannot employ gasoline
D. must meet all three requirements above

02799. One of the principal dangers inherent in liquefied petroleum gas is:

A. as it warms up it becomes heavier than air
B. the way it reacts with sea water
C. the strong odor it produces
D. its low temperature causes frostbite or freezing

02801. How many B-II fire extinguishers must be in the machinery space of a 175-foot long fishing vessel propelled by engines with 2000 brake horsepower?

A. 2
B. 3
C. 4
D. 5

02808. A Certificate of Inspection for vessels not more than 65 feet in length and of less than 100 gross tons carrying more than 6 passengers will be issued for a period of: (Small Passenger Vessel Regulations)

A. 6 months
B. 1 year
C. 2 years
D. 3 years

02809. Acid batteries shall be located in a: (Small Passenger Vessel Regulations)

A. lead-lined tray
B. tin-lined tray
C. copper- or brass-lined tray
D. wooden box

02812. Which of the following is correct with respect to required watertight bulkheads? (Small Passenger Vessel Regulations)

A. Penetrations are prohibited.
B. Sluice valves are not permitted.
C. Each bulkhead must be "stepped" at the midpoint.
D. all of the above

02816. The length of a line which is required to be attached to a ring life buoy must be at least: (Small Passenger Vessel Regulations)

A. 30 feet
B. 60 feet
C. 90 feet
D. 120 feet

02819. Pyrotechnic distress signals are not required on vessels operating on "short runs". A "short run" is limited to: (Small Passenger Vessel Regulations)

A. water of less than 20 foot depth
B. where land is always in sight
C. no more than 5 miles
D. about 30 minutes away from the dock

02822. Life floats required by Small Passenger Vessel Regulations must be:

A. of a sufficient number for all persons on board for vessels in ocean service
B. of a sufficient number for at least 50% of all persons on board for vessels in ocean service
C. used on board as primary lifesaving equipment for vessels in coastwise service
D. international orange in color only for vessels in lakes, bays and sounds service

02825. The purpose of the inclining experiment is to:

A. determine the location of the metacenter
B. determine the lightweight center of gravity location
C. verify the hydrostatic data
D. verify data in the vessel's operating manual

02826. To prevent the spread of fire by convection:

A. cool the bulkhead around the fire
B. remove combustibles from direct exposure
C. close all openings to the area
D. shut off all electrical power

02828. How often shall the steering gear of each vessel be tested by the Master or Mate? (Small Passenger Vessel Regulations)

A. once a week
B. prior to getting underway for the day's operation
C. every 72 operating hours while underway
D. once a month

02829. The vessel's steering gear, signaling whistle, controls or communication systems shall be tested by the operator: (Small Passenger Vessel Regulations)

A. once a week
B. before getting underway for day's operation
C. at every inspection and reinspection
D. at least once in every 48 hours

02832. Which of the following fuels cannot be used for cooking on vessels carrying passengers for hire? (Small Passenger Vessel Regulations)

A. kerosene
B. coal
C. wood
D. gasoline

02836. The remote control for a fixed fire extinguishing system should be:

A. painted red and labeled
B. concealed from the crew
C. protected by plexiglass
D. padlocked

02839. What type of cooking equipment is acceptable aboard vessels subject to Rules and Regulations for Small Passenger Vessels? (Small Passenger Vessel Regulations)

A. gasoline
B. propane
C. butane
D. LPG

02842. Any vessel of 65 feet or less in length, however propelled, must not be operated with more than 6 passengers aboard: (Small Passenger Vessel Regulations)

A. unless the operator has a Master's License
B. unless the vessel has a valid Permit to Proceed
C. until a boarding officer has checked the papers
D. until a permit is obtained from the collector of customs

02848. The inspection of a 50 ft. vessel of 65 GT carrying more than 6 passengers is required by the Coast Guard once in every: (Small Passenger Vessel Regulations)

A. 4 years with a minimum of three reinspections during the 4 year period
B. 3 years

C. 4 years
D. 3 years with a minimum of two reinspections during the 3 year period

02852. The collision bulkhead is: (Small Passenger Vessel Regulations)

A. amidships forward of the engine room
B. just forward of the steering compartment
C. in the engine room
D. 5% to 15% of the waterline length abaft the stem at the load water line

02858. Vessels not limited to daylight operation are required to be fitted with at least: (Small Passenger Vessel Regulations)

A. 2 ring life buoys and 1 water light attached
B. 1 ring life buoy and 1 water light attached
C. 3 ring life buoys and 2 water lights attached
D. 2 ring life buoys and 2 water lights attached

02859. For signaling, vessels operating on runs of more than 30 minutes shall carry in the pilot house or other suitable location: (Small Passenger Vessel Regulations)

A. 6 orange hand smoke distress signals
B. 6 red hand flare distress signals
C. 1 3-cell flashlight
D. 6 red hand flare distress signals and 6 orange hand smoke distress signals or twelve combination signals

02862. Small passenger vessels in coastwise service shall carry sufficient life floats or buoyant apparatus for: (Small Passenger Vessel Regulations)

A. all persons aboard
B. 75% of all persons aboard
C. 50% of all persons aboard
D. 30% of all persons aboard

02866. If a vessel is not equipped with an automatically activated emergency lighting system, the vessel must be: (Small Passenger Vessel Regulations)

A. operated only in daylight hours
B. provided with gasoline or kerosene lights
C. equipped with luminous tape markings on emergency equipment
D. equipped with individual storage battery powered lights

02867. In illustration D041DG, the symbol for amidships is:

A. 2
B. 3
C. 4
D. 5

02870. To prevent the spread of fire by conduction you should:

A. remove combustibles from direct exposure
B. cool the bulkheads around the fire
C. close all openings to the area
D. shut off all electrical power

02871. In illustration D041DG, the symbol 3 represents:

A. displacement
B. amidships
C. forward perpendicular
D. baseline

02873. In illustration D041DG, the symbol for the reference from which transverse measurements are made is:

A. 5
B. 4
C. 3
D. 1

02875. In illustration D041DG, 5 represents:

A. displacement
B. leverage center
C. centerline
D. counterflood limits

02877. In illustration D041DG, the symbol for the vertical plane midway between the fore and aft perpendiculars is:

A. 2
B. 3
C. 4
D. 5

02882. Whenever any vessel having a Certificate of Inspection is dry-docked for major repairs, the person in charge of the vessel, the owner, or the agent should report this to the: (Small Passenger Vessel Regulations)

A. Officer in Charge, Marine Inspection
B. National Cargo Bureau, Inc.
C. American Boat and Yacht Council, Inc.
D. all of the above

02886. A vessel operated in salt water for 6 months or less in a 12 month period shall be dry docked at intervals not to exceed:

A. 24 months
B. 36 months
C. 48 months
D. 60 months

02887. Seawater may be used for drinking:

A. at a maximum rate of 2 ounces per day
B. under no conditions
C. after mixing with an equal quantity of fresh water
D. if gathered during or immediately after a hard rain

02888. The inspection of small passenger vessels of 60 feet in length carrying more than 6 persons is required by the Coast Guard: (Small Passenger Vessel Regulations)

A. once in every 4 years with a minimum of 3 reinspections during the 4 year period
B. once in every 3 years with a minimum of 2 reinspections during the 3 year period
C. once in every 2 years with a minimum of one reinspection during the 2 year period
D. once every 6 months

02889. Switchboards which are accessible to passengers shall be: (Small Passenger Vessel Regulations)

A. equipped with handrails and rubber matting
B. grounded to the main engine on a wooden hulled boat
C. the dead front type, totally enclosed
D. equipped with switch locks

02896. Your vessel is certificated to carry 50 persons. You are required to have: (Small Passenger Vessel Regulations)

A. 50 adult life jackets
B. 40 adult life jackets and 10 children's
C. 50 adult life jackets and 5 children's
D. 50 adult life jackets and 2 children's

02897. If the result of loading a vessel is an increase in the height of the center of gravity, there will always be an increase in the:

A. metacentric height
B. righting arm
C. righting moment
D. vertical moments

02898. Painters fitted to life floats shall be not less than: (Small Passenger Vessel Regulations)

A. 20 meters in length
B. 30 meters in length
C. 70 meters in length
D. 100 meters in length

02899. All small passenger vessels operating on runs more than 30 minutes are required to carry: (Small Passenger Vessel Regulations)

A. 3 red hand flare distress signals and 3 orange hand smoke distress signals or 6 hand combination flare and smoke distress signals
B. 8 red hand flare distress signals and 8 orange hand smoke distress signals or 16 hand combination flare and smoke distress signals
C. 6 red hand flare distress signals and 6 orange hand smoke distress signals, or 12 hand combination flare and smoke distress signals
D. none of the above

02902. Vessels in ocean service shall carry sufficient life floats for: (Small Passenger Vessel Regulations)

A. 25% of all persons on board
B. 50% of all persons on board
C. 75% of all persons on board
D. 100% of all persons on board

02905. Each emergency light must be marked with:

A. the letter "E"
B. an arrow pointing to the nearest exit
C. a no-smoking symbol
D. the word "DANGER"

02906. Which of the following small passenger vessels is required to carry a compass on board? (Small Passenger Vessel Regulations)

A. a non-self-propelled vessel
B. a vessel operating in protected waters with a short restricted route
C. a vessel operating on the Ohio River
D. a vessel operating on the Gulf of Mexico

02908. A C. G. issued license must be renewed within how many months after the expiration date of the old license? (Small Passenger Vessel Regulations)

A. 1 month
B. 6 months
C. 12 months
D. 24 months

02909. Following a collision or accident, the Master of each vessel involved must render assistance to persons affected by the collision or accident: (Small Passenger Vessel Regulations)

A. if he can do so without any risk to his vessel
B. if he can do so without undue delay
C. if he can do so without serious danger to his vessel
D. without regard to any danger to his vessel

02911. In the event of a fire, the doors to a stairtower must be closed to prevent the spread of fire by:

A. ventilation
B. convection
C. radiation
D. conduction

02918. Which of the following statements is TRUE concerning the ventilation of engine and fuel tank compartments on uninspected towing vessels using fuel with a flash point of 100° F?

A. There shall be at least 3 ventilator ducts open to the atmosphere.
B. At least 1 exhaust duct shall extend from the atmosphere to the lower portion of the bilge.
C. At least 1 intake duct shall extend from the atmosphere to the lower portion of the bilge.
D. Only vessels using fuel with a flash point above 100° F need ventilate engine and fuel compartments.

02919. All of the following are part of the fire triangle EXCEPT:

A. fuel
B. electricity
C. oxygen
D. heat

02922. Whenever practicable, the Certificate of Inspection must be posted: (Small Passenger Vessel Regulations)

A. as high as feasible in the pilot house
B. near the area where passengers embark
C. in any location desired
D. in a conspicuous place where it will be most likely to be observed by the passengers

02927. If the metacentric height is small, a floating MODU will:

A. be tender
B. have a quick and rapid motion
C. be stiff
D. yaw

02928. It is recommended that drip collectors required on all carburetors, except those of down draft type, be drained by: (Small Passenger Vessel Regulations)

A. a device for automatic return of all drip to the engine air intakes
B. no means whatsoever
C. a separate pipe leading to the bilges
D. a pump leading over the edge of the collector to a point outside the hull by the most direct means feasible

02929. Switches other than those mounted on the switchboard shall be of the: (Small Passenger Vessel Regulations)

A. enclosed type
B. knife type
C. push button type
D. rotary type

02932. Which of the following is FALSE concerning the use of unicellular plastic foam work vests on board vessels? (Small Passenger Vessel Regulations)

A. They may be substituted for up to 50% of the required life preservers.
B. They shall be of an approved type.
C. They shall be stowed separately from required lifesaving equipment.
D. They may be worn by crew members when working near or over the water.

02938. What equipment is required on a life float? (Small Passenger Vessel Regulations)

A. 2 paddles, water-light, and painter
B. water-light, painter, and signal mirror
C. water-light and painter only
D. 2 paddles, painter, and 6 red flares

02939. All vessels subject to the Rules and Regulations for Small Passenger Vessels except those on short runs must carry which of the following in the pilot house? (Small Passenger Vessel Regulations)

A. 6 red hand flares and 6 orange smoke signals in a watertight container
B. 2 ring buoys with attached water lights
C. a battery operated red-flasher lantern
D. all of the above

02942. Vessels in ocean service shall carry: (Small Passenger Vessel Regulations)

A. lifefloats for 50% of all persons on board
B. buoyant apparatus for all persons on board
C. sufficient lifefloats for all persons on board
D. life preservers for 50% of all persons on board

02948. Licenses are issued for a term of: (Small Passenger Vessel Regulations)

A. 3 years
B. 5 years
C. 1 year
D. 2 years

02949. What information are you required to report to the Coast Guard when an accident occurs in which loss of life results? (Small Passenger Vessel Regulations)

A. location of the occurrence
B. number and name of vessel
C. names of owners
D. all of the above

02953. When the height of the metacenter has the same value as the height of the center of gravity, the metacentric height is equal to:

A. the height of the metacenter
B. the height of the center of gravity
C. the same as half the height of the metacenter
D. zero

02958. The discharge side of every fire pump must be equipped with a:

A. gate valve
B. pressure gauge
C. check valve
D. strainer

02961. The Certificate of Inspection issued to a vessel carrying more than 6 passengers must be: (Small Passenger Vessel Regulations)

A. posted on board under glass, if practical
B. posted on the dock where passengers are embarked
C. retained at the owner's principal place of business
D. kept on file by the Collector of Customs

02966. Each vessel shall be dry-docked or hauled out at intervals not to exceed 18 months if operated in salt water a total of more than: (Small Passenger Vessel Regulations)

A. 6 months in the 18 month period since it was last dry-docked or hauled out
B. 9 months in the 18 month period since it was last dry-docked or hauled out
C. 12 months in the 18 month period since it was last dry-docked or hauled out
D. 15 months in the 18 month period since it was last dry-docked or hauled out

02968. Air-cooled radiators for gasoline propulsion engine cooling: (Small Passenger Vessel Regulations)

A. must be approved for marine use
B. must have a double fan installation
C. must be filled with fresh water
D. are not permitted

02969. All inlets and discharges led through the vessel's hull below a line drawn parallel to and not less than 6 inches above the load waterline shall be fitted with: (Small Passenger Vessel Regulations)

A. cast-iron shut-off valves
B. a wooden plug
C. an efficient and accessible means of closing
D. a blank-off flange

02972. Regulations require that approved buoyant work vests: (Small Passenger Vessel Regulations)

A. may not be carried on inspected vessels
B. may be substituted for 10% of the required life preservers
C. shall be stowed in a place inaccessible to passengers
D. shall be stowed separately from the required life preservers

02976. The number of children's life preservers carried on board must be at least what percentage of the total? (Small Passenger Vessel Regulations)

A. 5%
B. 7.5%
C. 10%
D. 15%

02978. Which of the following equipment is not required for a life float? (Small Passenger Vessel Regulations)

A. paddles
B. water light
C. painter
D. compass

02979. Which of the following vessels is required to carry an Emergency Position Indicating Radio Beacon (EPIRB) on board? (Small Passenger Vessel Regulations)

A. a vessel operating exclusively on inland waters
B. a vessel limited to 20 miles offshore, which carries a radiotelephone on board
C. a vessel limited to 100 miles offshore
D. none of the above

02983. The height of the metacenter above the keel will vary depending on the:

A. draft and beam of the drilling unit
B. displacement and deadweight of the drilling unit
C. buoyancy and trim of the drilling unit
D. tonnage and deadweight of the drilling unit

02986. The person in charge of a vessel is required to prepare and post which of the following, in a conspicuous place accessible to the crew and passengers? (Small Passenger Vessel Regulations)

A. emergency checkoff lists
B. a tide table for the area
C. instructions on artificial respiration
D. the location of the first aid kit

02988. No person whose license has been revoked shall be issued another license except upon: (Small Passenger Vessel Regulations)

A. approval of the Commandant
B. taking a new examination
C. approval of the Officer-in-Charge, Marine Inspection
D. approval of an administrative law judge

02989. In which of the following marine casualty situations would it NOT be necessary to immediately notify the U. S. Coast Guard? (Small Passenger Vessel Regulations)

A. loss of life
B. major damage affecting the seaworthiness of a vessel
C. damage amounting to $2,000.00
D. injury to a person which requires medical treatment beyond first aid

02992. A 98 GT uninspected towing vessel with a 1500 B. H. P. engine capability would be required to carry how many type B-II hand portable fire extinguishers on board?

A. 2
B. 4
C. 6
D. 8

02993. Convection spreads a fire by:

A. the transfer of heat across an unobstructed space
B. burning liquids flowing into another space
C. transmitting the heat of a fire through the ship's metal
D. heated gases flowing through ventilation systems

02998. The minimum amount of lifesaving equipment required aboard an 85 foot uninspected towing vessel consists of:

A. 1 approved flotation cushion for each person on board
B. 1 approved life preserver for each person on board and 1 life ring
C. 1 approved inflatable vest for each person on board
D. lifeboat capacity equal to 1 1/2 times the number of persons on board

03002. A Certificate of Inspection issued to a vessel will show the: (Small Passenger Vessel Regulations)

A. crew requirements
B. minimum fire fighting and lifesaving equipment

C. route permitted
D. all of the above

03005. All vessels having a Certificate of Inspection and operating exclusively in salt water shall be dry-docked or hauled out: (Small Passenger Vessel Regulations)

A. once in each calendar year
B. once in each fiscal year
C. at the time of each inspection
D. at intervals not to exceed 18 months

03009. Enclosed spaces containing gasoline, machinery, or fuel tanks shall have which of the following types of ventilation? (Small Passenger Vessel Regulations)

A. natural supply and mechanical exhaust
B. mechanical supply and natural exhaust
C. mechanical supply and mechanical exhaust
D. natural supply and natural exhaust

03016. Pyrotechnic distress signals are required to be renewed no later than the first inspection after a certain period of time after the date of manufacture. What is this period of time? (Small Passenger Vessel Regulations)

A. 18 months
B. 2 years
C. 3 years
D. 4 years

03018. Each lifefloat on an inspected vessel shall be fitted and equipped with: (Small Passenger Vessel Regulations)

A. a lifeline, a painter, and 1 paddle
B. a lifeline, a painter, and a water light
C. 2 paddles, a water light, and a lifeline
D. 2 paddles, a water light, a lifeline, and a painter

03019. All vessels not limited to daylight service shall be fitted with a ring life buoy: (Small Passenger Vessel Regulations)

A. on the stern of the vessel
B. with a 20 fathom line attached
C. with no line attached
D. with 10 fathoms of line and a water light close by to be attached

03022. Vessels whose routes are restricted to 20 miles from a harbor of safe refuge shall carry life floats or buoyant apparatus for not less than: (Small Passenger Vessel Regulations)

A. 25% of all persons on board
B. 50% of all persons on board
C. 75% of all persons on board
D. 100% of all persons on board

03026. Who has the responsibility to prepare and post emergency checkoff lists in a conspicuous place accessible to crew and passengers? (Small Passenger Vessel Regulations)

A. The owner of the vessel
B. The Master of the vessel
C. The U. S. Coast Guard Inspector
D. The American Boat and Yacht Council, Inc.

03028. You are underway as Master on board your vessel. Your license must be: (Small Passenger Vessel Regulations)

A. displayed in the company office on shore
B. displayed in your home
C. in your possession on board the vessel
D. kept in the Coast Guard office where you sat for your license

03029. The Small Passenger Vessel Regulations require a stability test, under the supervision of the Coast Guard, conducted by the owner, builder or his representative when: (Small Passenger Vessel Regulations)

A. carrying more than 49 passengers
B. the vessel's stability is questioned
C. an increased passenger allowance is authorized above the original passenger allowance
D. all of the above

03032. Controls for a fixed carbon dioxide system shall be mounted:

A. directly outside the space protected by the system
B. as near the gas cylinders as possible
C. in the pilothouse
D. on the main deck near the bow

03046. What is the period of validity of a Certificate of Inspection issued to a 50 GT, passenger carrying vessel which is 60 feet in length? (Small Passenger Vessel Regulations)

A. 1 year
B. 2 years
C. 3 years
D. 4 years

03047. Automatic fire dampers in ventilation systems are operated by use of:

A. remotely operated valves
B. fusible links
C. C02 system pressure switches
D. heat or smoke detectors

03048. Which of the following is required for a vertical dry exhaust system? (Small Passenger Vessel Regulations)

A. a spark arrestor
B. a silencer
C. an automatic damper
D. a rain and spray cap

03049. Except as otherwise provided, vessels permitted to carry not more than 49 passengers shall be fitted with at least: (Small Passenger Vessel Regulations)

A. 1 wash basin
B. 1 toilet
C. 2 toilets
D. 2 toilets and 1 wash basin

03052. Which of the following statements is TRUE concerning work vests on board a vessel? (Small Passenger Vessel Regulations)

A. They may be worn during drills.
B. They may be substituted for up to 10% of the required lifesaving gear on board.
C. They need not be of an approved type.
D. They must be stowed separately from approved life preservers.

03056. The service use of pyrotechnic distress signals measured from the date of manufacture shall be limited to a period of: (Small Passenger Vessel Regulations)

A. 1 year
B. 2 years
C. 3 years
D. 4 years

03058. Life floats and buoyant apparatus shall be marked: (Small Passenger Vessel Regulations)

A. with the vessel's name
B. conspicuously in 1-1/2" letters with the number of persons allowed
C. with the vessel's name on all paddles and oars contained therein
D. all of the above

03059. A small passenger vessel with an "S" designator is required to carry how many ring life buoys? (Small Passenger Vessel Regulations)

A. 1
B. 2
C. 3
D. 4

03062. The licensed operator of a vessel shall make sure the EPIRB is tested: (Small Passenger Vessel Regulations)

A. daily
B. weekly
C. every 2 weeks
D. monthly

03066. Every vessel shall have its steering gear tested by the Master or Mate: (Small Passenger Vessel Regulations)

A. once a week
B. prior to getting under way for the day's operation
C. every 72 operating hours while underway
D. once a month

03068. In the case of collision, accident or other casualty involving a small passenger vessel, it shall be the duty of the Master to: (Small Passenger Vessel Regulations)

A. render assistance at the scene of the accident, if possible
B. notify the Coast Guard in the case of serious vessel damage
C. exchange information as to name, address etc. with the other vessel
D. all of the above

03069. Unless otherwise stated, the term "approved" applied to a vessel's equipment, means approved by the: (Small Passenger Vessel Regulations)

A. American Bureau of Shipping
B. Congress of the United States
C. Commandant of the Coast Guard
D. Board of Fire Underwriters

03082. Life preservers shall be stowed so they will be: (Small Passenger Vessel Regulations)

A. locked up
B. in various parts of the vessel, readily accessible for use
C. inaccessible to passengers
D. on the topmost deck of the vessel at all times

03084. All lifefloats and buoyant apparatus shall be conspicuously marked with the: (Small Passenger Vessel Regulations)

A. manufacturer's price, stock number, and inspection date
B. vessel's name, tonnage, and horsepower
C. vessel's name, and number of persons allowed, in at least 1-1/2 inch high letters and numbers
D. vessel's name, and number of persons allowed, in at least 3-1/2 inch high letters and numbers

03091. When will the float-free emergency position indicating radiobeacon be activated after abandoning ship?

A. immediately after floating free
B. after about 1 hour when the salt water activates the battery

C. only when keyed by radar of another vessel
D. only when daylight activates the photocell

03096. The purpose of the shut off valve at the gasoline tank operable from outside the tank space is to:

A. control the amount of gasoline to the engine
B. shut off the gasoline supply at the tank in case of fire
C. be used if the gasoline tank leaks
D. all of the above

03102. Which type of fixed fire extinguishing systems is approved for use on board uninspected vessels?

A. carbon dioxide
B. steam smothering
C. chemical foam
D. all of the above

03104. The emergency check-off list required on vessels carrying 6 or fewer passengers for hire must contain information on all of the following EXCEPT:

A. precautions for rough weather
B. actions required in the event of accident
C. procedures for man overboard emergencies
D. emergency procedures for fire at sea

03108. A CO2 extinguisher which has lost 10% of its charge must be:

A. used at the earliest opportunity
B. hydrotested
C. recharged
D. weighed again in 1 month

03110. If the Certificate of Inspection of a damaged 75 ft. passenger vessel has expired, which of the following certificates may be issued to allow its movement to a repair facility? (Small Passenger Vessel Regulations)

A. Change of Employment
B. Permit to Proceed
C. Application for Inspection
D. Temporary Certificate of Inspection

03112. An 85 foot uninspected towing vessel with a crew of 10 persons on board must carry at LEAST:

A. 10 approved ring life buoys and 10 approved life preservers
B. 10 approved work vests
C. 10 approved life jackets and 1 approved ring life buoy
D. 11 approved life preservers

03119. Life floats and buoyant apparatus may be stowed in tiers, or one above the other, to a height of not more than: (Small Passenger Vessel Regulations)

A. 3 feet
B. 4 feet
C. 5 feet
D. 6 feet

03120. Prior to the issuance of an initial Certificate of Inspection, the construction arrangement and equipment of a vessel must be acceptable to the: (Small Passenger Vessel Regulations)

A. American Bureau of Shipping surveyor
B. U. S. Salvage Marine surveyor
C. Officer in Charge, Marine Inspection
D. U. S. Customs Collector

03121. To prevent the spread of fire by conduction:

A. cool the bulkheads around the fire
B. remove combustibles from direct exposure
C. close all openings to the area
D. shut off all electric power

03122. All life preservers carried on board small passenger vessels are required to be marked: (Small Passenger Vessel Regulations)

A. with the vessel's name
B. whether it's an adult or child life preserver
C. with the maximum weight to be held by the life preserver
D. with the maximum serviceable life of the life preserver

03123. You are monitoring VHF Channel 16 when you receive a call to your vessel, TEXAS PRIDE. What is the proper way to answer the call?

A. "This is TEXAS PRIDE. Pick a channel. "
B. "This is TEXAS PRIDE on Channel 16. Come back. "
C. "This is TEXAS PRIDE, WSR 1234, reply Channel 10. "
D. "Please stand by. We're busy right now. "

03124. On a life float or buoyant apparatus, the life line is: (Small Passenger Vessel Regulations)

A. secured around the sides and ends in bights of not longer than 3 feet
B. woven into a net and secured in the center of the float
C. used for securing unconscious persons to the sides
D. the lanyard for securing provisions

03127. Automatic fire dampers in ventilation systems are operated by use of a:

A. fusible link
B. remote operated valve
C. C02 system pressure switch
D. heat or smoke detector

03130. What is the minimum height of rails on passenger decks of ferryboats, excursion vessels, and vessels of a similar type? (Small Passenger Vessel Regulations)

A. 18 inches high
B. 24 inches high
C. 39-1/2 inches high
D. 42 inches high

03132. Prior to starting any enclosed engine, you should:

A. check the flame arrester
B. check the gasoline tank
C. check the battery
D. ventilate bilges and check for gasoline leaks

03134. Which of the following is a B-II fire extinguisher? (Uninspected Vessel Regulations)

A. a 2-1/2 gallon water (stored pressure) extinguisher
B. a 15 lb. CO2 extinguisher
C. a 2 lb. dry chemical extinguisher
D. a 1-1/4 gallon foam extinguisher

03136. Where should the tops of vents from gasoline tanks terminate?

A. in open air
B. inside cabins near the overhead
C. in the machinery space near the engine air intake
D. underwater

03137. With damaged floating vessels, the most important consideration is the preservation of:

A. bilge pumping capacity
B. reserve buoyancy
C. level attitude
D. instability

03140. Escape hatches and other hatches in weather decks on passengers vessels operating on other than protected waters: (Small Passenger Vessel Regulations)

A. must be watertight
B. must be open at all times
C. need not be watertight
D. none of the above

03149. If a gasoline engine fails to start, the procedure to find the cause is to:

A. break the joint in the fuel line at the engine and let the gas run in the bilges
B. disconnect the wires at the spark plugs and make the spark jump the gap
C. prime the engine with ether through spark plug openings
D. ventilate the space, then check the battery, spark plugs, carburetor and fuel line

03150. You are required to have a B-II fire extinguisher. What extinguisher fits that requirement? (Small Passenger Vessel Regulations)

A. 2 lb. dry chemical
B. 15 lb. dry chemical
C. 15 lb. carbon dioxide
D. 12 gallon foam

03152. U. S. Coast Guard approved work vests may be substituted for personnel flotation devices (life preservers):

A. aboard work vessels
B. aboard towing vessels
C. aboard sailing vessels
D. under no circumstances

03154. Except as otherwise provided in the regulations, escapes from all general areas accessible to the passengers or where the crew may be quartered or normally employed shall not be less than: (Small Passenger Vessel Regulations)

A. 2
B. 3
C. 4
D. 5

03158. Electric generators can be protected against overload:

A. with switches
B. with a governor on the engine
C. with fuses or circuit breakers
D. by using heavy wire

03159. Fusible-link fire dampers are operated by:

A. a break-glass and pull-cable system
B. electrical controls on the bridge
C. a mechanical arm outside the vent duct
D. the heat of a fire melting the link

03160. Fixed ballast, if used, may be: (Small Passenger Vessel Regulations)

A. discharged or moved at anytime
B. moved temporarily for examination or repair of the vessel, when done under the supervision of an inspector

C. moved under the supervision of the owner, Master or shipyard
D. moved under any condition except extreme emergency

03161. The wooden plug fitted tightly in the vent of a damaged tank may prevent the tank from:

A. filling completely
B. developing free surfaces
C. developing free surface moments
D. collapsing

03162. All life preservers and ring buoys shall be marked with the vessel's name in letters at least: (Small Passenger Vessel Regulations)

A. 1/2 inch high
B. 1 inch high
C. height not specified
D. 1-1/2 inches high

03167. Topside icing that blocks freeing ports and scuppers:

A. is usually below the center of gravity and has little effect on stability
B. will cause water on deck to pocket and increase stability
C. may decrease stability by increasing free surface effect due to water on deck
D. increases the effective freeboard and increases the wind-heel affect

03170. Which of the following would be a B-I extinguisher? (Small Passenger Vessel Regulations)

A. 2.5 gallon foam
B. 10 pound carbon dioxide
C. 2 pound dry chemical
D. 5 pound foam

03171. Automatic fire dampers in ventilation systems are operated by use of:

A. fusible links
B. remotely operated valves
C. CO2 system pressure switches
D. heat or smoke detectors

03172. Where a mechanical exhaust ventilation system is used with gasoline engines, before starting the engine(s), the exhaust blower should be run a sufficient time to:

A. warm up the exhaust blower motor
B. provide a proper supply of fresh air for the engine(s)
C. see the system is in good operating condition
D. insure at least 1 complete change of air in the compartments concerned

03173. Which of the following is considered to be a B-II portable fire extinguisher?

A. 2 pound dry chemical
B. 2-1/2 gallon foam
C. 4 pound carbon dioxide
D. all of the above

03174. Which of the following is considered to be a B-II portable fire extinguisher?

A. 2-1/2 gallon foam
B. 4 pound carbon dioxide
C. 2 pound dry chemical
D. all of the above

03176. The tops of vents from gasoline tanks should terminate?

A. in open air
B. inside cabins
C. in machinery space
D. underwater

03182. What is the minimum number of portable fire extinguishers required on board a Class 3 motorboat having a fixed fire system on board? (Uninspected Vessel Regulations)

A. 1 B-I
B. 2 B-I or 1 B-II
C. 3 B-I or 2 B-II
D. 4 B-I

03184. The center of buoyancy and the metacenter are in the line of action of the buoyant force:

A. only when there is positive stability
B. only when there is negative stability
C. only when there is neutral stability
D. at all times

03189. If a gasoline engine turns over but is hard to start, the cause is generally:

A. a defective ignition
B. low lube oil level
C. weak valve springs
D. too heavy a load

03190. Your 75 GT vessel is 80 feet in length and carrying passengers for hire. You are required to have on board a minimum of how many fire pumps? (Small Passenger Vessel Regulations)

A. 1 fixed hand pump and 1 portable hand pump
B. 1 power pump and 1 portable hand pump
C. 2 fixed hand pumps
D. 2 power pumps

03192. Which of the following statements is FALSE concerning the use of unicellular plastic foam work vests on board towboats?

A. They may be substituted for up to 50% of the required life preservers.
B. They shall be of an approved type.
C. They shall be stowed separately from required lifesaving equipment.
D. They may be worn by crew members when working near or over the water.

03194. Generally, which of the following is used to inflate life rafts?

A. CO2
B. oxygen
C. hydrogen
D. compressed air

03196. Which of the following shall be conducted during a fire and boat drill?

A. All watertight doors which are in use while the vessel is underway shall be operated.
B. All lifeboat equipment shall be examined.
C. Fire pumps shall be started and all exterior outlets opened.
D. all of the above

03198. The principal reason for mounting starting motors, generators, and other spark producing devices as high above the bilges as practicable is to:

A. keep them dry when the bilges are full of water
B. keep them cool when the vessel is underway
C. make them more accessible for repairs
D. prevent accidental ignition of any gasoline vapors that may have accumulated in the bilges

03200. Which of the following circumstances concerning an inspected passenger vessel would require knowledge and approval of the Officer in Charge, Marine Inspection? (Small Passenger Vessel Regulations)

A. the removal of a watertight bulkhead
B. a minor overhaul of the propulsion machinery
C. renewal of an FCC Certificate for a radiotelephone
D. all of the above

03201. The stamped full weight of a 100 lb. CO2 bottle is 314 lbs. What is the minimum weight of the bottle before it has to be recharged?

A. 282 lbs.
B. 294 lbs.
C. 300 lbs.
D. 304 lbs.

03202. Motor vessels carrying passengers for hire must carry one of which of these approved lifesaving devices for each person aboard? (Small Passenger Vessel Regulations)

A. buoyant cushion
B. life preserver
C. ring buoy
D. buoyant vest

03210. The fire pump required for a 75 GT mechanically propelled vessel, 58 feet in length, carrying 52 passengers shall be capable of: (Small Passenger Vessel Regulations)

A. a minimum pumping capacity of 10 gallons per minute
B. a minimum pumping capacity of 25 gallons per minute
C. a minimum pumping capacity of 50 gallons per minute
D. discharging an effective stream from a hose connected to the highest outlet

03212. Before starting a gasoline engine on a motorboat, you should make sure for safety that:

A. the gasoline tank is full
B. the bilges, cabins, etc. are thoroughly ventilated
C. you have fresh water on board
D. each of the above is followed

03214. What does the "B" on a "B-II" fire extinguisher refer to? (Uninspected Vessel Regulations)

A. size of the applicator
B. size of the nozzle
C. size of the extinguisher
D. class of fire that the extinguisher should be used on

03216. Gasoline fuel tank vents should terminate:

A. in the engine compartment
B. in the fuel tank space
C. above or outside the hull
D. at the most convenient location

03220. All vessels shall carry: (Small Passenger Vessel Regulations)

A. no fire equipment other than the main fire pump
B. an emergency hand fire and bilge pump
C. not less than 3 fire pumps
D. some suitable and detachable pump for fire fighting purposes

03223. After 1 September 1992, in the North Pacific area, a documented 75-foot fishing vessel operating in cold waters 25 miles off the coast must have at least a(n):

A. buoyant cushion for each person on board
B. inflatable life raft with a SOLAS pack
C. inflatable buoyant apparatus with EPIRB attached
D. approved rescue boat

03228. A fuel line breaks, sprays fuel on the hot exhaust manifold, and catches fire. Your FIRST action should be to:

A. batten down the engine room
B. start the fire pump
C. apply carbon dioxide to the fire
D. shut off the fuel supply

03229. The engine head, block, and exhaust manifold shall be: (Small Passenger Vessel Regulations)

A. water jacketed
B. air cooled
C. preheated prior to starting
D. drained weekly

03230. Which of the following statements is TRUE concerning a hand fire pump on board a vessel? (Small Passenger Vessel Regulations)

A. The hand fire pump shall be located adjacent to the main engine spaces.
B. It shall be of at least 2 gallons per minute capacity.
C. It shall be painted red.
D. It may also serve as a bilge pump.

03232. Which of the following statements is TRUE concerning work vests on board a vessel?

A. They may be worn during drills.
B. They may be substituted for up to 10% of the required lifesaving gear onboard.
C. They need not be of an approved type.
D. They must be stowed separately from approved life preservers.

03234. The abandon ship signal is:

A. a continuous ringing of general alarm bells for at least 10 seconds
B. a continuous ringing of the general alarm, and sounding of the ship's whistle
C. more than 6 short blasts and 1 long blast of the ship's whistle and the same signal on the general alarm bells
D. a continuous sounding of the ship's whistle

03238. During fueling, all doors, hatches, and ports:

A. to windward should be opened and the ones to leeward should be closed
B. to leeward should be opened and the ones to windward should be closed
C. should be opened
D. should be closed

03240. When a vessel is required to have a power-driven fire pump, this may also be used for: (Small Passenger Vessel Regulations)

A. drinking water supply system
B. bilge pump
C. engine cooling water
D. none of the above

03242. Every vessel carrying passengers for hire shall have on board an approved life preserver: (Small Passenger Vessel Regulations)

A. for every passenger on board
B. for every person on board, plus 10% children's life preservers
C. for every person on board, plus 10% additional on upper deck in box
D. or buoyant cushion for every person on board plus 10% for children

03243. If there's a fire aboard your vessel, you should FIRST:

A. notify the Coast Guard
B. cut off air supply to the fire
C. have passengers put on life preservers
D. sound the alarm

03250. Which statement is TRUE concerning fire hose on a small passenger vessel? (Small Passenger Vessel Regulations)

A. Fire hose on "L" designated vessels shall be at least 3/4" outside diameter.
B. 1 length of fire hose shall be provided for every 2 fire hydrants on board.
C. All fittings on hoses shall be of steel or other ferrous metal.
D. A length of hose shall be attached to each fire hydrant at all times.

03252. Before any machinery is put in operation, you should:

A. ventilate all compartments, see that the machinery is clean and there are no obstructions
B. just turn the key and start up
C. take for granted that there are no fuel leaks
D. assume there are no volatile fumes in the engine space

03254. All uninspected motor vessels constructed after 25 April 1940, which use fuel with a flash point of 110° F or less, shall have at least what number of ventilator ducts for the removal of explosive or flammable gases from every engine and fuel tank compartment? (Uninspected Vessel Regulations)

A. 1
B. 2
C. 3
D. 4

03256. Gasoline vapor is of such weight relative to air that it will tend to collect:

A. above the floor plates of the bilges
B. above the carburetor level
C. at the lowest point of the bilge areas
D. at no particular level

03260. A length of fire hose shall be: (Small Passenger Vessel Regulations)

A. attached to each fire hydrant at all times
B. equipped with a rotary sprinkler head
C. marked with lot number and wholesale price
D. not more than 10 feet in length

03268. Diesel engines are considered safer than gasoline engines because:

A. they are more heavily built
B. the fuel used is less volatile
C. they can be easily reversed
D. they operate at a lower speed

03269. Which of the following exhausts should be carefully inspected at regular intervals?

A. engine
B. galley
C. heater
D. all of the above

03270. Which of the following portable fire extinguishers would be permitted in the propulsion machinery spaces of a gasoline fueled vessel not having a fixed CO2 system on board? (Small Passenger Vessel Regulations)

A. 2-1/2 gallon foam extinguisher
B. 4 lb. CO2 extinguisher
C. 2 lb. dry chemical extinguisher
D. none of the above

03272. Where should life preservers be stowed?

A. in the forepeak
B. in the wheelhouse
C. topside in protected locations convenient to personnel
D. in locked watertight and fireproof containers on or above the main deck

03274. Vessels required to be equipped with an approved backfire flame arrester are:

A. those with diesel engines
B. all those with gasoline engines
C. those with large engines only
D. none of the above

03278. Gasoline tanks should be filled:

A. to the top to expel all vapors from the tanks
B. to the top so the operator is certain how much fuel he has aboard
C. with only sufficient fuel for the planned trip so excess gasoline is not carried
D. to near the top with some space allowed for gasoline expansion

03280. What type of fire extinguishers are permitted on inspected vessels? (Small Passenger Vessel Regulations)

A. foam
B. carbon dioxide
C. dry chemical
D. all of the above

03284. In vessels that normally carry children, there shall be provided a number of approved life preservers suitable for children equal to at least: (Small Passenger Vessel Regulations)

A. 20% of the passengers carried
B. 10% of the total number of persons carried
C. 10% of the passengers carried
D. 20% of the total number of persons carried

03290. On vessels that are required to have fixed carbon dioxide fire extinguishing systems, the controls to operate the system shall be installed in an accessible location: (Small Passenger Vessel Regulations)

A. outside the space protected
B. inside the space protected
C. at the carbon dioxide cylinders
D. in a padlocked waterproof metal box

03292. Upon completion of fueling a gasoline driven vessel it is necessary to:

A. keep ports, doors, windows, and hatches closed
B. start engines immediately
C. ventilate before starting engine
D. none of the above

03294. The number of fire extinguishers required on uninspected motor vessels (over 65 feet in length) is based on a vessel's:

A. length and brake horsepower
B. gross tonnage and brake horsepower
C. draft and gross tonnage
D. crew list and trade

03296. Which statement is TRUE concerning fuel vapors on a vessel?

A. Fuel vapors gather in the lowest portions of the vessel.
B. Fuel vapors can only be ignited by an open flame.
C. Vent outlets should be located above the level of the carburetor air intake.
D. none of the above

03300. How many portable fire extinguishers are required in the propulsion machinery space of a vessel which uses diesel oil if there is a fixed CO2 system installed on board? (Small Passenger Vessel Regulations)

A. none
B. 1 B-I extinguisher
C. 1 B-I and 1 B-II extinguishers
D. 2 B-II extinguishers

03304. If your passenger vessel has been issued a stability letter, it must be:

A. filed in the ship's office
B. posted in a passenger area
C. posted adjacent to the Certificate of Inspection
D. posted in the pilothouse

03308. The quickest method to stop a small diesel engine whose throttle or governor has become stuck open is to:

A. close the fuel supply valve
B. turn off the ignition switch
C. smother the air intake
D. apply the shaft brake

03309. The exhaust pipe shall be kept gas tight throughout its entire length because:

A. bilge water may enter the exhaust pipe
B. entry of air may cause vapor lock
C. carbon monoxide may enter the internal portions of the vessel
D. the joint gaskets may be blown

03310. Fixed carbon dioxide fire extinguishing systems shall be installed to protect enclosed machinery and fuel tank spaces of all vessels using gasoline or other fuel having a flash point of: (Small Passenger Vessel Regulations)

A. 50° F or lower
B. 75° F or lower
C. 90° F or lower
D. 110° F or lower

03312. To comply with regulations, the life preservers aboard an uninspected towing vessel must be:

A. readily accessible
B. securely stowed
C. stored in sealed containers
D. stowed with the emergency provisions

03314. Which of the following devices is required to be installed under the carburetor of a gasoline engine?

A. box of sawdust
B. drip collector
C. vent
D. flame arrestor

03318. Should you discover a leak in the gasoline line to the engine, the best thing to do is:

A. activate the CO2 system
B. make a temporary repair with canvas or tape
C. start the bilge pump
D. close the fuel valve at the tank

03320. If your vessel is required to have a fire ax on board, where would it be located? (Small Passenger Vessel Regulations)

A. in or next to the pilothouse
B. in below decks passenger accommodations
C. just outside the engine room access
D. in the galley near the stove

03322. If your vessel is certificated to carry 10 persons, among which are adults and children, how many life preservers are you required to carry on board? (Small Passenger Vessel Regulations)

A. 11 adult
B. 10 adult and 1 child
C. 10 adult and 5 child
D. 10 adult

03326. The nozzle of a gasoline hose or can should be kept:

A. in contact with the fill opening to guard against static spark
B. from making contact with the fill opening to guard against static spark
C. in contact with the fill opening to allow proper venting
D. none of the above

03329. A fire is discovered in the forepeak of a vessel at sea. The wind is from ahead at 35 knots. You should ,

A. remain on course and hold speed
B. remain on course but slack the speed
C. change course and put the stern to the wind
D. change course to put the wind on either beam and increase speed

03330. A carbon dioxide fire extinguisher is required to be recharged if the weight loss exceeds what percentage of the weight of the charge? (Small Passenger Vessel Regulations)

A. 1 percent
B. 5 percent
C. 7 percent
D. 10 percent

03331. The stability which exists after the unintentional flooding of a compartment is called:

A. intact stability
B. initial stability
C. immersion stability
D. damage stability

03332. When fueling has been completed:

A. the fuel tank fill pipe should be left open to allow gasoline vapors to vent from the tank
B. the engine should be started immediately to prevent vapor lock in the fuel line
C. all hatches should be opened and all compartments should be ventilated
D. open the fuel line and drain a small amount of gasoline into the bilge to clear the line of sediment

03334. The number of fire extinguishers required on uninspected motor vessels is based on a vessel's:

A. length
B. gross tonnage
C. draft
D. crew list

03336. Which of the following statements is TRUE concerning gasoline vapors on board a vessel?

A. They are heavier than air and will settle in the lowest part of the vessel.
B. They are lighter than air and will settle in the highest part of the vessel.
C. They should be vented into the engine to improve combustion.
D. They should be vented into the wheelhouse.

03339. Which of the following is acceptable flame screening?

A. a fitted single brass screen of 10 x 10 mesh
B. a fitted stainless steel screen of 30 x 30 mesh
C. a fitted single stainless steel screen of 15 x 15 mesh
D. two fitted brass screens of 10 x 15 mesh spaced 1/2 inch apart

03340. When a fixed fire extinguishing system is installed, it shall be of an approved: (Small Passenger Vessel Regulations)

A. carbon tetrachloride type
B. liquid foam type
C. light water type
D. carbon dioxide type

03348. Generally speaking, the fuel injected into a diesel engine combustion chamber is ignited by:

A. spark plugs
B. glow plugs
C. heat of compression
D. a magneto

03349. Which of the following devices is required in the fuel supply line at the engine?

A. flow meter
B. shut-off valve
C. pressure gauge
D. filter

03350. Which statement is TRUE concerning the number of portable fire extinguishers required in the wheelhouse of a small passenger vessel? (Small Passenger Vessel Regulations)

A. None are required.
B. One B-I extinguisher is required.
C. One B-II extinguisher is required.
D. Two B-I extinguishers are required.

03352. Which of the following personnel life-saving devices is/are approved for use on a towboat 150 feet in length?

A. life preserver
B. buoyant vest or cushion
C. special purpose safety device
D. all of the above

03354. Backfire flame arrestors are installed on:

A. fuel tanks
B. spark plugs
C. carburetors
D. distributors

03358. Spaces containing batteries require good ventilation because:

A. ventilation avoids CO2 buildup
B. ventilation supplies extra oxygen for the battery
C. ventilation avoids flammable gas accumulation
D. less water would be used

03360. Foam portable extinguishers should be discharged and refilled: (Small Passenger Vessel Regulations)

A. every 6 months
B. every 3 months
C. at each inspection and reinspection
D. only when used

03361. The moment created by a force of 12,000 tons and a moment arm of 0.25 foot is:

A. 48,000 ft-tons
B. 6,000 ft-tons
C. 3,000 ft-tons
D. 0 ft-tons

03362. The number of approved adult life preservers that shall be carried is equal to: (Small Passenger Vessel Regulations)

A. the amount of persons listed in the vessel's Certificate of Inspection
B. 50% of the amount of persons listed in the vessel's Certificate of Inspection
C. the amount of persons on board at the time
D. 50% of the amount of persons on board at the time

03370. The carbon dioxide cylinders of all portable and semi-portable extinguishers and fixed systems shall be retested and remarked whenever a cylinder remains in place on a vessel for: (Small Passenger Vessel Regulations)

A. 5 years from the latest test date stamped on the cylinder
B. 7 years from the latest test date stamped on the cylinder
C. 10 years from the latest test date stamped on the cylinder
D. 12 years from the latest test date stamped on the cylinder

03372. Which of the following statements is FALSE concerning precautions during fueling operations?

A. All engines, motors, fans, etc. should be shut down when fueling.
B. All windows, doors, hatches, etc. should be closed.
C. A fire extinguisher should be kept nearby.
D. Fuel tanks should be topped off with no room for expansion.

03374. Which of the following is NOT contained on the metallic name plate required to be attached to hand portable fire extinguishers?

A. the rated capacity in gallons, quarts, or pounds
B. the hydrostatic test date of the cylinder

C. the name of the item
D. an identifying mark of the actual manufacturer

03376. Outlets in fuel lines are:

A. permitted for drawing fuel
B. permitted for draining lines
C. permitted for bleeding lines
D. prohibited

03380. Annually, all carbon dioxide fire extinguishers aboard a vessel are: (Small Passenger Vessel Regulations)

A. checked for pressure loss
B. discharged and recharged
C. sent ashore to an approved service facility
D. weighed

03386. While proceeding towards a distress site you hear the message PRU-DONCE over the radiotelephone. What action should you take?

A. Advise the sender of your course, speed, position, and ETA at the distress site.
B. Resume base course and speed because the distress is terminated.
C. Shift your radio guard to the working frequency that will be indicated in the message.
D. Use that frequency only for restricted working communications.

03388. A carburetor is required to have a safety device called a(n):

A. pressure release
B. backfire flame arrestor
C. automatic shut off
D. flow valve

03390. Non-required lifesaving equipment such as water-ski vests: (Small Passenger Vessel Regulations)

A. must be removed from the vessel when carrying passengers
B. may be carried as excess equipment if of the approved type
C. may be carried as a substitute of not more than 5% of the required life jackets
D. may be carried regardless of approval or condition if in excess of required lifesaving equipment

03394. The carburetor is placed on the engine to:

A. distribute the gasoline
B. mix the fuel and air
C. properly lubricate the engine
D. assist in priming the cylinders

03398. Before starting any diesel or gasoline engine, which of the following must be checked?

A. oil level
B. flow of cooling water
C. exhaust discharge
D. all of the above

03399. Which sizes of fire extinguishers are considered to be semi-portable? (Uninspected Vessel Regulation)

A. I, II, III, IV, and V
B. I, II, and III only
C. II, III, and IV only
D. III, IV, and V only

03400. How should the number "9" be pronounced when spoken on the radiotelephone?

A. NEW-MER-AL-NINER
B. NUM-BER-NINE
C. NO-VAY-NINER
D. OK-TOH-NINE

03404. Convection spreads a fire by:

A. transmitting the heat of a fire through the ship's metal
B. heated gases flowing through ventilation systems
C. burning liquids flowing into another space
D. the transfer of heat across an unobstructed space

03410. How should the letter "I" be pronounced when spoken on the radiotelephone?

A. IN DEE GO
B. IN DEE AH
C. I EE
D. I VAN HO

03414. A rigid lifesaving device designed to support survivors partially in the water is a:

A. rigid life raft
B. life float
C. inflatable life raft
D. buoyant apparatus

03415. A vessel has a strong wind on the port beam. This has the same affect on stability as:

A. weight that is off-center to starboard
B. increasing the draft
C. reducing the freeboard
D. increasing the trim

03420. How should the number "1" be pronounced when spoken on the radiotelephone?

A. OO-NO
B. OO-NAH-WUN
C. NUM-EV-WUN
D. NEW-MAL-WON

03430. How should the letter "Q" be pronounced when spoken on the radiotelephone?

A. QWE BEC
B. QUE BACH
C. KEH BECK
D. QU UE

03435. Small passenger vessels whose routes are restricted to 20 miles from a harbor or safe refuge must carry approved lifefloats or buoyant apparatus for: (Small Passenger Vessel Regulations)

A. all persons on board
B. not less than 75% of all persons on board
C. not less than 50% of all persons on board
D. Small passenger vessels on such restricted routes may substitute ring life buoys for all required life floats or buoyant apparatus.

03440. How should the number "7" be pronounced when spoken on the radiotelephone?

A. SAY-TAY-SEVEN
B. SEE-ETA-SEVEN
C. NUM-BER-SEVEN
D. NEW-MER-AL-SEVEN

03460. How should the letter "T" be pronounced when spoken on the radiotelephone?

A. TEE
B. TA HO
C. TANG GO
D. TU TU

03462. A rigid lifesaving device only designed for survivors to hold on to while in the water is a:

A. life raft
B. life float
C. life preserver
D. buoyant apparatus

03472. Which of the following is considered "primary lifesaving equipment" for the purposes of the Passenger Vessel Regulations?

A. ring buoy
B. personal flotation device
C. lifeboat
D. all of the above

03474. The radiotelegraph alarm signal may be used to announce:

A. that a distress message will follow
B. a request for assistance in searching for a man overboard
C. an urgent warning about a cyclone
D. all of the above

03480. How should the number "6" be pronounced when spoken on the radiotelephone?

A. SOX-SIX
B. NUM-BER-SIX
C. SOK-SEE-SIX
D. NEW-MER-AL-SIX

03494. A passenger vessel in river service which operates exclusively in fresh water must be dry-docked or hauled out at intervals not to exceed:

A. 12 months
B. 24 months
C. 48 months
D. 60 months

03496. In general, how often are sanitary inspections of passenger and crew quarters made aboard passenger vessels in river service?

A. once each day
B. once each week
C. once each month
D. once each trip

03500. How should the letter "Z" be pronounced when spoken on the radiotelephone?

A. ZEE BR AH
B. ZEE ZE
C. ZE HE
D. ZOO LOO

03508. Except in rare cases, it is impossible to extinguish a shipboard fire by:

A. interrupting the chain reaction
B. removing the heat
C. removing the oxygen
D. removing the fuel

03510. When required, the steering gear, whistle, and the means of communication between the pilothouse and the engine room on a passenger vessel shall be tested by an officer of the vessel within a period of not more than how many hours prior to departure?

A. 4
B. 8
C. 12
D. 24

03512. You have sent a visual signal to an aircraft. The aircraft then flies over your position on a straight course and level altitude. What should you do?

A. Repeat your signal.
B. Send any more signals necessary.
C. Change course to follow the airplane.
D. Prepare for a helicopter pickup.

03520. How should the number "5" be pronounced when spoken on the radiotelephone?

A. FIVE-ER
B. NEW-MARL-FIVE
C. NUM-ERL-FIVE
D. PAN-TAH-FIVE

03536. There are two disadvantages to CO_2 as a total-flooding firefighting agent. One of these is the limited quantity available, and the other is:

A. the lack of cooling effect on heated materials
B. that it cannot be used in a dead ship situation with no electrical power to the CO_2 pump
C. that it breaks down under extreme heat to form poisonous gases
D. there is no effect on a class A fire even in an enclosed space

03540. How should the letter "R" be pronounced when spoken on the radiotelephone?

A. ROW ME OH
B. AR AH
C. ROA MA O
D. AR EE

03542. An aircraft has indicated that he wants you to change course and follow him. You cannot comply because of an emergency on board. What signal should you make?

A. Fire a red flare at night or a red smoke signal by day.
B. Send the Morse signal "N" by flashing light.
C. Make a round turn (360°) and resume course.
D. Make an "S" turn (hard right then hard left) and resume course.

03546. According to the regulations for passenger vessels, a "motor vessel" is one which is propelled by machinery other than steam and is more than:

A. 16 ft. in length
B. 34 ft. in length
C. 45 ft. in length
D. 65 ft. in length

03550. A passenger vessel must have an emergency squad when:

A. certificated for over 30 passengers
B. the size of the crew permits
C. more than 50 passengers are on board
D. on a voyage in excess of 12 hours duration

03551. Which toxic gas is a product of incomplete combustion, and is often present when a fire burns in a closed compartment?

A. carbon monoxide
B. carbon dioxide
C. hydrogen sulfide
D. nitric oxide

03554. You are underway in mid-ocean, when you hear a distress message over the VHF radio. The position of the sender is 20 miles away. What action should you take?

A. Immediately acknowledge receipt of the distress message.
B. Defer acknowledgment for a short interval so that a coast station may acknowledge receipt.
C. Do not acknowledge receipt until other ships nearer to the distress have acknowledged.
D. Do not acknowledge because you are too far away to take action.

03560. How should the number "4" be pronounced when spoken on the radiotelephone?

A. QUAD-ROS-FOOR
B. NUM-ERL-FOUR
C. NUMB-ER-FOWER
D. KAR-TAY-FOWER

03580. How should the letter "V" be pronounced when spoken on the radiotelephone?

A. VIK TAH
B. VIC TO RE
C. VIX TOO RE
D. VEE

03596. The light on a personal flotation device must be replaced:

A. when the power source is replaced
B. each year after installation
C. every 6 months
D. when it is no longer serviceable

03600. How should the number "3" be pronounced when spoken on the radiotelephone?

A. TAY-RAH-TREE
B. BEES-SOH-THREE
C. NUM-ERL-THREE
D. TRIC-THREE

03604. You are the first vessel to arrive at the scene of a distress. Due to the volume of traffic on the radio, you are unable to communicate with the vessel in distress. What action should you take?

A. Switch to flag hoists.
B. Broadcast "Seelonce Distress".
C. Broadcast "Charlie Quebec-Mayday-Quiet".
D. Key the microphone 3 times in quick succession.

03606. What radiotelephone signal indicates receipt of a distress message?

A. Roger wilco.
B. Romeo, Romeo, Romeo.
C. SOS acknowledged.
D. Mayday Roger.

03608. A fire has broken out on the stern of your vessel. You should maneuver your vessel so the wind:

A. comes over the bow
B. blows the fire back toward the vessel
C. comes over the stern
D. comes over either beam

03610. While a passenger vessel is underway, when may passengers visit the pilothouse?

A. Passengers are excluded from the pilothouse while underway.
B. Passengers are permitted in the pilothouse during daylight hours only.
C. Passengers are permitted to visit the pilothouse when authorized by the Master and officer of the watch.
D. Passengers are permitted in the pilothouse when they are escorted by a ship's officer.

03611. Each life preserver light that has a non-replaceable power source must be replaced:

A. every 6 months after initial installation
B. every 12 months after initial installation
C. every 24 months after initial installation
D. on or before the expiration date of the power source

03614. While proceeding towards a distress site you hear the message "Seelonce Feenee" over the radiotelephone. What action should you take?

A. Resume base course and speed because the distress situation is over.
B. Do not transmit over the radiotelephone.
C. Relay the initial distress message to the nearest shore station.
D. Resume normal communications on the guarded frequency.

03616. What radiotelephone signal indicates receipt of a distress message?

A. Received
B. Roger wilco
C. Seelonce
D. Mayday wilco

03620. How should the letter "O" be pronounced when spoken on the radiotelephone?

A. OCK TOW BER
B. O RI AN
C. OSS CAH
D. OA KAM

03634. You are underway in mid-ocean when you hear a distress message. The position of the sender is 150 miles away. No other vessel has acknowledged the distress. Your maximum speed is 5 knots and due to the seriousness of the distress, you cannot arrive on scene to provide effective assistance. What action should you take?

A. Do not acknowledge the distress message.
B. Send an urgency message about the distress.
C. Use the signal MAYDAY RELAY and transmit the distress message.
D. Transmit a message as though your vessel was in distress.

03640. How should the number "2" be pronounced when spoken on the radiotelephone?

A. NUM-BER-TOO
B. BEES-SOH-TOO
C. DOS-SOH-TU
D. NEM-MARL-TWO

03642. When communicating on the radiotelephone using plain English, what procedure word indicates the end of my transmission and that a response is necessary?

A. Out
B. Over
C. Roger
D. Wilco

03650. If your passenger vessel is fitted with a loudspeaker system, it must be tested at least:

A. once every week
B. once a day
C. once every trip
D. once a watch or once a trip, whichever is shorter

03654. When communicating on the radiotelephone using plain English, what procedure indicates that you have received another vessels transmission?

A. Out
B. Over
C. Roger
D. Wilco

03660. How should the letter "W" be pronounced when spoken on the radiotelephone?

A. DUB A U
B. WISS KEY
C. WI NE
D. WOO LF

03838. Fire dampers prevent spread of fire by:

A. convection
B. conduction
C. radiation
D. direct contact

03839. As Master of a small passenger vessel, you have a question regarding a proposed modification to a watertight bulkhead. In which subchapter of Title 46 of the Code of Federal Regulations would you find the answer?

A. Subchapter S
B. Subchapter B
C. Subchapter T
D. Subchapter F

03968. Each EPIRB shall be stowed in a manner which will permit:

A. easy access to its storage compartment
B. replacement of the battery without exposure to the weather
C. it to float free if the vessel sinks
D. it to remain attached to the vessel

04042. How many B-II fire extinguishers must be in the machinery space of a 75-foot long fishing vessel propelled by engines with 1200 brake horsepower?

A. 1
B. 2
C. 3
D. 4

04044. Convection spreads a fire by:

A. heated gases flowing through ventilation systems
B. the transfer of heat across an unobstructed space
C. burning liquids flowing into another space
D. transmitting the heat of a fire through the ship's metal

04106. In the event of a fire, the doors to a stairtower must be closed to prevent the spread of fire by:

A. conduction
B. ventilation
C. radiation
D. convection

04112. A fire is discovered in the forepeak of a vessel at sea. The wind is from ahead at 35 knots. You should:

A. remain on course and hold speed
B. remain on course but slack the speed
C. change course to put the wind on either beam and increase speed
D. change course and put the stern to the wind

04138. Multiple fire pumps may be used for other purposes provided that one pump is:

A. on line to the fire main
B. kept available for use on the fire main at all times
C. capable of being connected to the fire main
D. rated at or above 125 psi

04142. You are underway at sea when a fire is reported in the forward part of the vessel. The wind is from dead ahead at 20 knots. You should :

A. change course and put the stern to the wind
B. change course to put the wind on either beam and increase speed
C. remain on course and hold speed
D. remain on course but decrease speed

04174. Each EPIRB shall be tested using the integrated test circuit and output indicator every:

A. week
B. 2 weeks
C. month
D. quarter

04246. Radiation spreads a fire by:

A. transferring heat across an unobstructed space
B. heated gases flowing through ventilation systems
C. burning liquids flowing into another space
D. transmitting the heat of a fire through the ship's metal

04346. The EPIRB on board your vessel is required to be tested:

A. weekly
B. monthly
C. quarterly
D. yearly

04404. The letter and number symbols, such as B II, used to classify portable fire extinguishers indicate the:

A. class of fire and relative size of the extinguisher
B. class of fire and location aboard vessel
C. extinguishing agent and relative size of the extinguisher
D. extinguishing agent and location aboard vessel

04458. Any firefighting equipment that is carried in addition to the minimum required number must:

A. meet the applicable standards
B. be marked as additional equipment
C. be stowed in a separate area
D. all of the above

04486. The international body responsible for drafting the convention prohibiting marine pollution (MARPOL) is the:

A. Maritime Advisory Council
B. International Maritime Organization
C. International Association of Shipping
D. Association of Seafaring Nations

04506. A Class S EPIRB is a:

A. satellite EPIRB
B. safety EPIRB
C. ship EPIRB
D. survival craft EPIRB

04546. Fire dampers prevent the spread of fire by:

A. direct contact
B. radiation
C. conduction
D. convection

04562. After you activate your emergency position indicating radiobeacon, you should:

A. turn it off for 5 minutes every half-hour
B. turn it off and on at 5 minute intervals
C. turn it off during daylight hours
D. leave it on continuously

04572. You are underway at sea when a fire is reported in the forward part of the vessel. The wind is from dead ahead at 20 knots. You should:

A. remain on course and hold speed
B. change course and put the stern to the wind
C. change course to put the wind on either beam and increase speed
D. remain on course but decrease speed

04701. After you activate your emergency position indicating radiobeacon, you should:

A. turn it off for 5 minutes every half-hour
B. turn it off and on at 5-minute intervals
C. turn it off during daylight hours
D. leave it on continuously

04734. Seawater may be used for drinking:

A. if gathered during or immediately after a hard rain
B. at a maximum rate of 2 ounces per day
C. under no conditions
D. after mixing with an equal quantity of fresh water

04784. If there's a fire aboard your vessel, you should FIRST:

A. sound the alarm
B. notify the Coast Guard
C. have passengers put on life preservers
D. cut off air supply to the fire

04785. What should you do with your emergency position indicating radiobeacon if you are in a life raft in a storm?

A. Bring it inside the life raft and leave it on.
B. Bring it inside the life raft and turn it off until the storm passes.
C. Leave it outside the life raft and leave it on.
D. Leave it outside the life raft but turn it off.

04786. In illustration DO15SA, which number indicates the hydrostatic release?

A. 3
B. 6
C. 7
D. 10

05065. Under what condition are you allowed to depart from the Rules of the Road?

A. to avoid immediate danger
B. when authorized by the rig superintendent
C. to comply with an operator's requirement
D. under no conditions

05072. In illustration DO11SA, number 1 operates the:

A. releasing gear
B. pelican hook
C. sea painter
D. Fleming gear

05127. In illustration D041DG, the symbol for displacement is:

A. 1
B. 2
C. 3
D. 4

05131. In illustration D041DG symbol 1 refers to:

A. change of draft
B. centerline
C. angle of inclination
D. displacement

05133. In illustration D041DG, the symbol for the reference from which the height of the center of gravity is measured is:

A. 5
B. 4
C. 3
D. 2

05135. In illustration D041DG symbol 2 represents:

A. displacement
B. beam limit
C. bilge level
D. baseline

05154. The sea anchor shown in illustration DO14SA, number 14, will NOT:

A. check the life raft's way
B. keep the life raft end on to the sea
C. reduce the possibility of broaching or capsizing
D. right the raft if it inflates inverted

05192. There is a fire aft aboard your vessel. To help fight the fire, you should:

A. put the wind off either beam
B. put the stern into wind and decrease speed
C. put the stern into wind and increase speed
D. head the bow into wind and decrease speed

05232. Fusible-link fire dampers are operated by:

A. a mechanical arm outside the vent duct
B. electrical controls on the bridge
C. the heat of a fire melting the link
D. a break-glass and pull-cable system

05286. A vessel is inclined at an angle of loll. In the absence of external forces, the righting arm (GZ) is:

A. positive
B. negative
C. zero
D. vertical

05312. In illustration DO16SA, the line indicated by number 4 is connected to the:

A. releasing gear
B. sea painter
C. pelican hook
D. Fleming gear

05386. Which toxic gas is a product of incomplete combustion, and is often present when a fire burns in a closed compartment?

A. carbon dioxide
B. carbon monoxide
C. nitric oxide
D. hydrogen sulfide

05387. Which toxic gas is a product of incomplete combustion, and is often present when a fire burns in a closed compartment?

A. nitric oxide
B. carbon dioxide
C. hydrogen sulfide
D. carbon monoxide

05408. One of the first actions to be taken by survivors when they have boarded an inflatable life raft is to:

A. stream the sea anchor
B. take an anti-seasickness pill
C. open the pressure relief valve
D. drink at least 1 can of water

05418. Small passenger vessels in coastwise service must carry approved: (Small Passenger Vessel Regulations)

A. life floats
B. buoyant apparatus
C. inflatable life rafts
D. any of the above

05455. What percentage of the breaking strength is the generally accepted safe operating load of an anchor cable?

A. 10%
B. 25%
C. 35%
D. 50%

05457. The only wire rope termination which may be made in the field is:

A. swaged socket
B. thimbled mechanical splice
C. hand splice
D. spelter poured and resin sockets

5461. Thirty-five percent of the breaking strength of an anchor cable is generally accepted as the:

A. safe operating load
B. normal operating tension
C. emergency working load
D. allowable storm load

05463. A common class of wire rope used for mooring is the 6 x 19 class. What does the 6 represent?

A. factor of safety
B. number of wires per strand
C. number of strands per wire rope
D. number of wires in the core

05465. A common class of wire rope used for mooring is the 6 x 37 class. What does the 37 represent?

A. number of wires in the inner core
B. number of strands per wire rope
C. tensile strength of the wire
D. number of wires per strand

05467. What is an advantage of the 6 x 19 class of wire rope over the 6 x 37 class of wire rope of the same diameter?

A. greater holding power
B. better fatigue life
C. resistance to elongation
D. resistance to corrosion

05471. What is an advantage of the 6 x 37 class of wire rope over the 6 x 19 class of wire rope of the same diameter?

A. flexibility
B. resistance to corrosion
C. resistance to elongation
D. lower weight per foot

05473. Where do fatigue failures of wire rope mooring lines usually occur?

A. in the middle part of the line length
B. near the socketed end fitting adjacent to the anchor
C. at the point where the line touches the bottom
D. at the place the anchor buoy is attached to the line

05475. The primary advantage for using stud link chain in a mooring system on a rig is the:

A. stud link is more economical
B. stud keeps the chain from kinking
C. stud link chain is the strongest design
D. stud link improves anchor holding power

05479. The purpose of the inclining experiment on a vessel is to determine:

A. lightweight and lightweight center of gravity location
B. the position of the center of buoyancy
C. the position of the metacenter
D. the maximum load line

05481. A common means of connecting shots of anchor chain in the field is to use a:

A. sprocket
B. Kenter link
C. swivel
D. end shackle

05485. The maximum angular tolerance for a bent link of an anchor chain is:

A. 1 degree
B. 3 degrees
C. 5 degrees
D. 7 degrees

05486. Illustration DO09SA shows the correct method of securing a:

A. man-rope
B. frapping line
C. sea painter
D. lifeline

05487. A measurement device for inspecting anchor chain is the:

A. slide rule
B. go-no-go gauge
C. derrick tape
D. amp probe

05491. The American Petroleum Institute recommends that a new anchor chain should be inspected after being in service for:

A. 1 year
B. 3 years
C. 5 years
D. 10 years

05493. The American Petroleum Institute recommends that connecting links and anchor shackles be inspected using:

A. visual examinations
B. magnetic particle inspection
C. dye penetrant inspection
D. X-ray inspection

05495. Extended cyclical variations in tensions will cause an anchor chain to break due to:

A. fatigue
B. corrosion
C. distortion
D. abrasion

05505. Which problem is virtually impossible to detect during an in-service inspection of used mooring chain?

A. cracks
B. elongation
C. loose studs
D. fatigue

05507. The American Petroleum Institute recommends magnetic particle inspection for:

A. anchor chain
B. wire rope
C. connecting links
D. pendant wires

05511. When inspecting anchor chain, the American Petroleum Institute recommends checking the length over 5 links every:

A. 10 feet
B. 100 feet
C. 250 feet
D. 500 feet

05513. A link on an anchor chain should be replaced when wear or grinding of surface cracks has reduced the cross section area by:

A. 4%
B. 6%
C. 8%
D. 10%

05515. What should be done after repairing a surface crack on a link of anchor chain by grinding?

A. Examine the area by magnetic particle inspection.
B. Replace the chain in service.
C. Galvanize the area.
D. Post heat the area.

05517. Grinding to eliminate shallow surface defects should be done:

A. parallel to the longitudinal direction of the chain
B. perpendicular to the direction of the anchor chain
C. diagonally across the link of the anchor chain
D. around the circumference of the chain link

05521. Prior to magnetic particle inspection of anchor chain, the chain should be:

A. degaussed
B. demagnetized
C. soaked
D. sandblasted

05522. Radiation spreads a fire by:

A. transmitting the heat of a fire through the ship's metal
B. transferring heat across unobstructed space
C. burning liquids flowing into another space
D. heated gases flowing through ventilation systems

05523. Before being certified by the American Bureau of Shipping, anchor chain must undergo:

A. USCG inspection
B. a breaking test
C. X-ray inspection
D. spectroanalysis

05525. What does the proof test load of an anchor chain demonstrate?

A. the breaking strength of the anchor chain
B. strength of the anchor chain to a specified limit
C. adequate holding power for new bottom conditions
D. safe working load of the anchor chain

05527. With adaptor blocks/chocks in place on an LWT stock anchor, the trip angle will be:

A. 20°
B. 30°
C. 40°
D. 50°

05531. With adaptor blocks/chocks removed from an LWT stock anchor, the trip angle will be:

A. 20°
B. 30°
C. 40°
D. 50°

05533. Connecting elements of a mooring system should be fabricated from:

A. cast iron
B. forged steel
C. stainless steel
D. cast steel

05535. What effect is achieved from soaking an anchor?

A. It allows the bottom soil to consolidate.
B. It gives the palms time to trip the anchor.
C. It stabilizes the mooring system.
D. It lubricates the anchor for better tripping.

05541. What is the "holding power ratio" of an anchor?

A. maximum mooring line tension divided by the anchor's weight in air
B. anchor's weight in air divided by the maximum mooring line tension
C. preloading tension divided by the anchor's weight in air
D. operating tension divided by the anchor's weight in air

05543. What happens to the efficiency of an anchor when it is moved from sand to mud?

A. The efficiency increases.
B. The efficiency decreases.
C. The efficiency remains the same.
D. The efficiency cannot be determined.

05545. When a combination chain and wire rope mooring line is used, the chain is deployed:

A. at the anchor end of the line
B. at the wildcat end of the line
C. midway between the anchor and the wildcat
D. through the anchor buoy

05547. In a combination chain and wire rope mooring system, the chain is deployed at the anchor end of the line to:

A. increase fatigue life
B. eliminate the need for mooring buoys
C. prevent the anchor from fouling
D. increase the catenary

05551. Anchor shackles should have a breaking strength that is:

A. equal to the chains they are connecting
B. 25% more than the chains they connect
C. 50% more than the chains they connect
D. 100% more than the chains they connect

05553. The angle between the flukes and the shank of an anchor is called the:

A. holding angle
B. fleet angle
C. fluke angle
D. shank angle

05555. The fluke angle of an anchor system is the angle between the:

A. flukes and the shank
B. shank and the sea bottom
C. mooring line and the sea bottom
D. flukes and the shackle

05557. The holding power of an anchor is the:

A. maximum sustained vertical load an anchor will resist before dragging
B. maximum sustained horizontal load an anchor will resist before dragging
C. maximum sustained vertical load an anchor will resist before the mooring line breaks
D. maximum sustained horizontal load an anchor will resist before the mooring line breaks

05561. What line receives the hardest service in the mooring system?

A. guy wire
B. joining pendant
C. wildcat leader
D. anchor pendant

05563. Most large anchors are made with a:

A. bow type shackle
B. D-type shackle
C. U-type shackle
D. Kenter shackle

05565. What is the bow type anchor shackle primarily used for?

A. chain to chain connections
B. chain to anchor connections
C. Kenter link to anchor connections
D. wire rope connections

05567. What is the most important difference between the bow type anchor shackle and the D-type anchor shackle?

A. bow type provides a superior connection
B. D-type is weaker than the bow type
C. bow type is weaker than the D-type
D. D-type provides an inferior connection

05571. Which two components pass through the shank of an LWT anchor?

A. anchor shackle and stock
B. tripping palm and flukes
C. crown and chocks
D. swivel and stabilizer bar

05573. To develop maximum anchor holding power, the optimum angle between the anchor's shank and the mooring lines is:

A. 0 degrees
B. 10 degrees
C. 20 degrees
D. 30 degrees

05575. Increasing the area of the anchor flukes will:

A. increase holding power
B. decrease holding power

C. make penetration more complete
D. not effect holding power

05577. What is the advantage of a single streamlined fluke anchor over a double fluked anchor of similar weight?

A. It has multiple fluke angle settings.
B. It has increased holding power.
C. It holds well with either side down.
D. It is easier to handle on an anchor boat.

05585. Cable tension for catenary calculations is taken at the:

A. chain locker
B. fairlead
C. anchor
D. contact point of chain with seabed

05591. The major cause of anchor buoy pendant wire failures is:

A. corrosion
B. rough weather
C. defective sockets
D. mishandling

05595. An anchor winch should be equipped with mechanical brakes capable of holding:

A. half the breaking strength of the mooring line
B. the full breaking strength of the mooring line
C. the maximum expected tension of the mooring line
D. 50% over the working tension of the mooring line

05597. A chain stripper is used to:

A. prevent chain from clinging to the wildcat
B. clean the marine debris from the chain
C. flake chain from a boat's chain locker
D. clean chain prior to an X-ray inspection

05598. Fire dampers prevent the spread of fire by:

A. direct contact
B. radiation
C. convection
D. conduction

05648. The hydrostatic release on the inflatable life rafts on a fishing vessel must be:

A. replaced annually
B. tested monthly
C. serviced annually
D. overhauled quarterly

05655. When the air temperature is just below 32° F, freezing rain and snow adhere to:

A. surfaces near the waterline
B. on vertical windward surfaces
C. on horizontal windward surfaces
D. on vertical leeward surfaces

05657. Freezing rain and snow are most likely to adhere to horizontal surfaces when the air temperature is:

A. slightly above 32° F
B. at 32° F
C. just below 32° F
D. all of the above

05697. The motion that can significantly increase mooring line tension is:

A. pitch
B. roll
C. yaw
D. sway

05711. Installing tandem anchors on the same mooring line is referred to as:

A. doubling
B. pretensioning
C. piggybacking
D. paralleling

05751. When piggybacking anchors, the distance between the primary anchor and the secondary anchor is determined by:

A. bottom conditions
B. anchor types
C. water depth
D. workboat winch capacity

05753. The length of chain between the anchor and the end of the pendant line is called the:

A. pigtail chain
B. thrash chain
C. crown chain
D. wear chain

05763. What is the purpose of a chain stopper?

A. stops the chain during pay out
B. secures the chain after is has been stopped
C. stops off a 6 foot section for inspection
D. hydraulically cuts anchor chain

05824. The vertical distance between G and M is used as a measure of:

A. stability at all angles of inclination
B. initial stability
C. stability at angles less than the limit of positive stability
D. stability at angles less than the downflooding angle

05825. The tension on an anchor cable increases so that the angle of the catenary to the seabed at the anchor reaches 10 degrees. How will this affect the anchor in sandy soil?

A. It will have no effect.
B. It will increase the holding power.
C. It will reduce the holding power.
D. It will cause the anchor to snag.

05845. Yawing can be described as:

A. jumping on the tow line as the rig pitches
B. jumping on the tow line as the rig slams into waves
C. veering from side to side on the end of the tow line
D. corkscrew motion due to wave action

05901. With a rig in tow, there is immediate danger to the tug in the event of the:

A. tug losing power
B. tow line parting
C. bridle twisting
D. rig broaching

05917. What must be located on the discharge side of the pump in a fire main system?

A. pressure gauge
B. strainer
C. reduction valve
D. international shore connection

05921. Multiple fire pumps may be used for other purposes provided that one pump is:

A. on line to the fire main
B. available for use on the fire main at all times
C. capable of being connected to the fire main
D. rated at or above 125 psi

05923. The relief valve on a fire pump is set at 25 psi above the pressure necessary to maintain required fire streams, or:

A. 50 psi
B. 75 psi
C. 125 psi
D. 150 psi

05951. Control valves of a CO_2 system may be located within the protected space when:

A. it is impractical to locate them outside
B. there is also a control valve outside
C. the CO_2 cylinders are also in the space
D. an automatic heat-sensing trip is installed

05953. The stamped full weight of a 100 lb. CO_2 bottle is 314 lbs. What is the minimum weight of the bottle before it has to be recharged?

A. 282 lbs.
B. 294 lbs.
C. 300 lbs.
D. 304 lbs.

06049. While proceeding to a distress site, you hear the words "Seelonce mayday" on the radiotelephone. What action should you take?

A. Resume base course and speed as your assistance is no longer required.
B. Acknowledge receipt and advise your course, speed and ETA.
C. Relay the original distress message as no other vessel has acknowledged it.
D. Monitor the radiotelephone but do not transmit.

06246. The ventilation system of your ship has fire dampers restrained by fusible links. Which of the following statements is TRUE?

A. A fusible link will automatically open after a fire is extinguished and reset the damper.
B. Fusible links must be replaced at every inspection for certification.
C. Fusible links must be replaced if a damper is activated.
D. Fusible links are tested by applying a source of heat to them.

06249. Automatic fire dampers in ventilation systems are operated by use of:

A. heat or smoke detectors
B. CO2 system pressure switches
C. remotely operated valves
D. fusible links

06274. You are fighting a class "B" fire with a portable dry chemical extinguisher. The discharge should be directed:

A. at the main body of the fire
B. to bank off a bulkhead onto the fire
C. over the top of the fire
D. at the seat of the fire, starting at the near edge

06306. An inflatable life raft is thrown into the water from a sinking vessel. Which of the following occurs automatically after the painter trips the CO2 bottles to inflate the raft?

A. The sea anchor deploys.
B. The floor inflates.
C. If upside down, the craft rights itself.
D. The painter detaches from the raft.

06308. You are underway at sea when a fire is reported in the forward part of the vessel. The wind is from dead ahead at 20 knots. You should:

A. remain on course and hold speed
B. change course to put the wind on either beam and increase speed
C. remain on course but decrease speed
D. change course and put the stern to the wind

06313. The holding power of an anchor increases when the:

A. amount of chain lying along the bottom increases
B. length of the catenary is reduced
C. mooring line tension is increased
D. amount of chain lying along the bottom decreases

06402. Small passenger vessels in ocean service must carry approved: (Small Passenger Vessel Regulations)

A. life floats
B. buoyant apparatus
C. class C EPIRBs
D. any of the above

06604. Fusible-link fire dampers are operated by:

A. the heat of a fire melting the link
B. a break-glass and pull-cable system
C. electrical controls on the bridge
D. a mechanical arm outside the vent duct

06631. All portable fire extinguishers must be capable of being:

A. carried by hand to a fire
B. carried or rolled to a fire
C. recharged in the field
D. used on class "B" fires

06646. Fire in an engine compartment is best extinguished with carbon dioxide gas (CO2) and by:

A. closing the compartment except for the ventilators
B. increasing the air flow to the compartment by blowers
C. leaving the compartment open to the air
D. completely closing the compartment

06742. Low-velocity fog is produced by:

A. inserting an applicator in the combination nozzle
B. putting the handle of the combination nozzle in the vertical position
C. directing a straight stream of water against the ship's structure
D. the combination nozzle only when the water pressure exceeds 125 psi

06761. Each distress signal and self-activated smoke signal must be replaced not later than the marked date of expiration, or, from the date of manufacture, not later than:

A. 6 months
B. 12 months
C. 24 months
D. 36 months

06792. All portable fire extinguishers must be capable of being:

A. carried by hand to a fire
B. carried or rolled to a fire
C. recharged in the field
D. used on class "B" fires

06806. A fire has broken out on the stern of your vessel. You should maneuver your vessel so the wind:

A. blows the fire back toward the vessel
B. comes over the stern
C. comes over the bow
D. comes over either beam

06856. Fire dampers prevent spread of fire by:

A. conduction
B. convection
C. radiation
D. direct contact

06908. Topside icing decreases vessel stability because it is usually off-center and:

A. increases displacement
B. increases the height of the center of gravity
C. increases draft
D. reduces the pocketing of free surface

06936. Where must a Class A EPIRB be stowed?

A. under lock and key
B. in the engine room
C. where it can float free
D. inside the fo'c'sle head

06987. Severe airway burns would cause:

A. nausea
B. reddening of cheeks
C. complete obstruction of respiratory passages
D. nosebleed

06991. The first treatment of a person suspected of having airway burns is to:

A. move him to a cool location
B. confirm and maintain an open airway
C. apply cool damp dressing to his neck
D. have him drink cool liquids

07003. When treating a chemical burn, you should flood the burned area for at least:

A. 5 minutes
B. 10 minutes
C. 15 minutes
D. 20 minutes

07005. Chemical burns are caused by the skin coming in contact with:

A. acids or alkalies
B. diesel oil
C. acids, but not alkalies
D. alkalies, but not acids

07007. What precaution should be taken when treating burns caused by contact with dry lime?

A. Water should be applied in a fine spray.
B. The burned area should be immersed in water.
C. The entire burn area should be covered with ointment.
D. Before washing, the lime should be brushed away gently.

07021. The symptoms of heat exhaustion are:

A. slow and strong pulse
B. flushed and dry skin
C. slow and deep breathing
D. pale and clammy skin

07023. Heat exhaustion is caused by excessive:

A. loss of body temperature
B. loss of water and salt from the body
C. gain in body temperature
D. intake of water when working or exercising

07025. A patient suffering from heat exhaustion should FIRST be:

A. placed in a sitting position with the head lowered to the knees
B. kept standing and encouraged to walk slowly and continuously
C. given a glass of water and told to return to work after 15 minutes of rest
D. moved to a cool room and told to lie down

07027. To effectively treat a person suffering from heat exhaustion, you should:

A. administer artificial respiration
B. put him in a tub of ice water
C. give him sips of salty water
D. take his blood pressure

07031. Symptoms of sugar diabetes include:

A. increased appetite and thirst
B. decreased appetite and thirst
C. gain in weight
D. elevated temperature

07033. If a person with diabetes has been injured, the symptoms of the onset of a diabetic coma would include:

A. reduced appetite and thirst
B. sneezing and coughing
C. excessive thirst and fever
D. slurred speech and loss of coordination

07035. If a diabetic suffers an insulin reaction and is conscious, he should be given:

A. soda crackers and water
B. orange juice or a candy bar
C. an ounce of whiskey
D. a glass of milk

07037. Epilepsy is a chronic nervous disorder characterized by:

A. severe nausea and cramps
B. muscular convulsions with partial or complete loss of consciousness
C. sudden thirst and craving for candy
D. severe agitation and desire to get out of close spaces

07041. The most beneficial assistance for a person having an epileptic convulsion is to:

A. give the victim artificial respiration
B. completely restrain the victim
C. give the victim one 30 mg. tablet of phenobarbital
D. keep the victim from injuring him or herself

07043. While providing assistance to a victim of an epileptic seizure, it is most important to:

A. move the patient to a comfortable bed
B. get professional medical advice for further medical care
C. keep the patient awake and make him or her walk if necessary to keep him/her awake
D. remove any soiled clothing and put the patient in a clean bed

07045. Appendicitis symptoms include cramps or pain in the abdomen located in the:

A. lower left side
B. lower right side
C. upper left side
D. upper right side

07046. A fire has broken out on the stern of your vessel. You should maneuver your vessel so the wind:

A. blows the fire back toward the vessel
B. comes over either beam
C. comes over the stern
D. comes over the bow

07047. What would be the symptom if a person's appendix ruptured?

A. dilated pupils and shallow breathing
B. diarrhea and frequent urination
C. muscle tenseness in almost the entire abdomen
D. extreme sweating and reddening skin

07051. When a patient is suspected of having appendicitis, the primary action is to:

A. give patient a laxative to relieve pain
B. give patient morphine sulfate to relieve pain
C. evacuate patient to a hospital
D. give patient aspirin with a glass of water

07053. When a patient is suspected of having appendicitis, the pain should be relieved by:

A. keeping an ice bag over the appendix area
B. giving the patient a laxative
C. giving the patient morphine sulfate
D. giving the patient aspirin with a glass of water

07055. Seasickness is caused by rolling or rocking motions which affect fluids in the:

A. stomach
B. lower intestines
C. inner ear
D. bladder

07057. Symptoms of seasickness include:

A. fever and thirst
B. nausea and dizziness
C. stomach cramps and diarrhea
D. reddening of skin and hives

07058. Blocking open or removing fire dampers can cause:

A. fixed foam systems to be ineffective
B. faster cooling of the fire
C. the accumulation of explosive gases
D. the fire to spread through the ventilation system

07061. The primary concern in aiding a back injury patient is:

A. relieving the patient's pain by giving aspirin or stronger medication
B. avoiding possible injury to the spinal cord by incorrect handling

C. preventing convulsions and muscle spasms caused by the pain
D. providing enough fluids to prevent dehydration

07062. What should you do with your emergency position indicating radiobeacon if you are in a life raft in storm conditions?

A. Bring it inside the life raft and leave it on.
B. Bring it inside the life raft and turn it off until the storm passes.
C. Leave it outside the life raft and leave it on.
D. Leave it outside the life raft but turn it off.

07063. The symptoms of a fractured back are:

A. leg cramps in the muscles in one or both legs
B. pain and uncontrolled jerking of the legs and arms
C. vomiting and involuntary urination or bowel movement
D. pain at the site of the fracture and possible numbness or paralysis below the injury

07065. What is the procedure for checking for spinal cord damage to an unconscious patient?

A. Beginning at the back of the neck, and proceeding to the buttocks, press the spine to find where it hurts.
B. Prick the skin of the hands and the soles of the feet with a sharp object to check for reaction.
C. Selectively raise each arm and each leg and watch patient's face to see if he registers pain.
D. Roll patient onto his stomach and prick along the length of his spine to check reaction.

07067. An effective method for lifting and carrying patients with spinal injuries is known as the:

A. pack-strap carry
B. two man extremities carry
C. fireman's drag
D. four man log roll

07068. Deballasting a double bottom has what affect on KG?

A. KG is increased.
B. KG is decreased.
C. KG is not affected.
D. KG increases at light drafts and decreases at deep drafts.

07071. The sorting of accident victims according to the severity of their injuries is called:

A. evaluation
B. triage
C. surveying
D. prioritizing

07073. Where there are multiple accident victims, which condition should be the first to receive emergency treatment?

A. back injuries
B. major multiple fractures
C. suspension of breathing
D. burns

07075. Where there are multiple accident victims, which injuries should be the FIRST to receive emergency treatment?

A. major multiple fractures
B. eye injuries
C. back injuries with spinal-cord damage
D. airway and breathing difficulties

07077. Where there are multiple accident victims, which type of injury should be the first to receive emergency treatment?

A. severe shock
B. eye injuries
C. burns
D. major multiple fractures

07081. In managing a situation involving multiple injuries, the rescuer must be able to:

A. provide the necessary medication
B. rapidly evaluate the seriousness of obvious injuries
C. accurately diagnose the ailment or injury
D. prescribe treatment for the victim

07083. What can be determined about an injury from examining the condition of a victim's pupils?

A. The degree of pain being suffered
B. The degree of vision impairment
C. Whether the brain is functioning properly
D. Whether the victim's blood pressure is normal

07093. Normal mouth temperature is:

A. 96.4° F
B. 97.5° F
C. 98.6° F
D. 99.7° F

07095. When examining for possible neck injury, you should first check for spinal injury. Then the patient's head should be lifted gently, bending the neck so that his chin will touch his chest, and observe for:

A. uncontrolled knee jerking
B. unnatural stiffness of the neck
C. rapid blinking of the eyes
D. increased pulse rate

07096. Convection spreads a fire by:

A. transmitting the heat of a fire through the ship's metal
B. burning liquids flowing into another space
C. heated gases flowing through ventilation systems
D. the transfer of heat across an unobstructed space

07097. What is a convenient and effective system of examining the body of an injury victim?

A. Check the corresponding (left versus right) parts of the body.
B. Watch the patient's eyes as you probe parts of the body.
C. Look for discoloration of the patient's skin.
D. Look for uncontrolled vibration or twitching of parts of the body.

07121. CO_2 cylinders equipped with pressure actuated discharge heads will discharge automatically when:

A. the discharge valve is open
B. the control box glass is broken
C. pressure from the control cylinders is detected
D. the control cylinders have been completely discharged

07127. Spaces protected by a fixed CO_2 system must be equipped with an alarm which sounds:

A. for the first 20 seconds CO_2 is being released into the space
B. for at least 20 seconds prior to release of CO_2
C. during the entire period that CO_2 is being released
D. if all doors and ventilation are not secured

07131. A safety outlet is provided on the CO_2 discharge piping to prevent:

A. over pressurization of the space being flooded
B. rupture of cylinder due to temperature increase
C. over pressurization of the CO_2 discharge piping
D. flooding of a space where personnel are present

07143. Actuating the CO_2 fixed system causes the shutdown of the:

A. fuel supply
B. exhaust ventilation
C. supply and exhaust ventilation
D. mechanical and natural ventilation

07147. What should you do if you have transmitted a distress call a number of times on channel 16 and have received no reply?

A. Repeat the message using any other channel on which you might attract attention.
B. Key the microphone several times before transmitting again.
C. Turn up the volume on the receiver before transmitting again.
D. Report the problem to the head electrician.

07305. The use of obscene, indecent, or profane words in radio transmissions is punishable by:

A. a fine not to exceed $5,000 or imprisonment not more than 1 year, or both
B. a fine not to exceed $10,000 or imprisonment not more than 5 years, or both
C. a fine not to exceed $20,000
D. imprisonment not more than 30 days

07307. All VHF marine band radios operate in the simplex mode, which means that:

A. only one person may talk at a time
B. only two persons may talk at the same time
C. the radio only transmits
D. the radio only receives

07311. What is the calling and distress frequency on a single side band (SSB) marine radiotelephone?

A. 1492 kHz
B. 1892 kHz
C. 2082 kHz
D. 2182 kHz

07313. What is the most important thing to do before transmitting on a marine radio?

A. Ask for permission.
B. Record the time in your radio log.
C. Press the "push to talk" button 3 times.
D. Monitor the channel to insure that it is clear.

07317. When sending and receiving messages on the marine radio, confusion over unusual words can be avoided by using the:

A. delimiter switch
B. standard phonetic alphabet
C. low power switch
D. high power switch

07318. A cabinet or space containing the controls or valves for the fixed firefighting system must be:

A. posted with instructions on the operation of the system

B. ventilated and equipped with explosion-proof switches
C. painted with red and black diagonal stripes
D. equipped with a battery powered source of emergency lighting

07321. The reception of weak radio signals may be improved by "opening up" the squelch control. What is the normal setting of the squelch control?

A. just past the point where background noise is cut off
B. completely closed with the volume at the highest level
C. completely open with the volume at the lowest level
D. none of the above

07323. Whenever your marine radio is on, FCC Rules require you to monitor:

A. a commercial ship-to-ship channel
B. the last frequency that was used
C. the distress and calling frequency
D. the radio only if expecting a call

07325. One method of reducing the length of radio transmissions without distorting the meaning of your words is by using:

A. slang
B. secret codes
C. procedure words
D. analogies

07327. How long is a ship station license for a radiotelephone valid?

A. 1 year
B. 3 years
C. 5 years
D. 6 years

07331. Routine radio communications should be limited to no more than:

A. 1 minute
B. 3 minutes
C. 5 minutes
D. 8 minutes

07333. You have just tried calling another vessel on the VHF, and they have not replied. How long should you wait before calling that station again?

A. 1 minute
B. 2 minutes
C. 5 minutes
D. 7 minutes

07335. When making VHF radio calls to nearby stations, what level of transmitting power should you use?

A. low power
B. medium power
C. high power
D. extra high power

07337. If you log a distress message, it must include the:

A. sea state
B. names of witnesses
C. time of its occurrence
D. wind direction and velocity

07341. If you know that the vessel you are about to call on the VHF radio maintains a radio watch on both the working and the calling frequencies, what frequency should you call on?

A. calling frequency
B. distress frequency
C. urgency frequency
D. working frequency

07343. What is maximum power allowed by the FCC for VHF-FM radio transmissions?

A. 1 watt
B. 5 watts
C. 15 watts
D. 25 watts

07345. What is the average vessel-to-vessel range of VHF-FM radio communications?

A. 10 to 15 miles
B. 60 to 90 miles
C. 90 to 120 miles
D. 120 to 150 miles

07351. The most important factors affecting the range of SSB transmissions are:

A. atmospheric noise and radiated power
B. the frequency band selected and time of day or night
C. interference and position of the moon
D. radiated power and nearness to shore

07353. The height of a VHF radio antenna is more important than the power output wattage of the radio because:

A. VHF communications are "line of sight"
B. the air is more dense the higher you go
C. salt water is a poor conductor of sound
D. sea water absorbs the radiated energy

07355. When do you use your FCC call sign?

A. only at the beginning of a transmission
B. only in an emergency
C. only if asked by the U. S. Coast Guard
D. always at the beginning and ending of a transmission

07388. All marine low-speed diesels are of what design?

A. four-stroke
B. two-stroke
C. electronic ignition
D. forced exhaust

07405. VHF Channel 6 is used exclusively for what kind of communications?

A. radio checks and time checks
B. inter-vessel safety and search and rescue
C. working with helicopters
D. radio direction finding

07407. Which VHF channel should you avoid using as a working channel?

A. 7A
B. 8
C. 9
D. 16

07411. What is the spoken emergency signal for a distress signal over a VHF radio?

A. Red Alert
B. Security
C. Mayday
D. Pan

07412. In the event of a fire, the doors to a stairtower must be closed to prevent the spread of fire by:

A. ventilation
B. radiation
C. convection
D. conduction

07413. Which emergency signal would you use to call a boat to come assist a man overboard?

A. Distress signal
B. Urgency signal
C. Safety signal
D. none of the above

07415. What is the spoken emergency signal for a "man overboard" on the VHF radio?

A. Man Overboard
B. Security

C. Mayday
D. Pan-Pan

07417. You receive a call from the U. S. Coast Guard addressed to all stations. The call begins with the words "Pan-Pan" (3 times). What type of emergency signal would this be?

A. safety signal
B. urgency signal
C. distress signal
D. red alert signal

07421. After receiving your distress call, the U. S. C. G. will ask you to switch to which SSB frequency?

A. 2570
B. 2670
C. 2770
D. 2870

07423. On which frequencies do Class A EPIRBs operate?

A. 118.5 MHz and 240 MHz
B. 119.5 MHz and 241 MHz
C. 120.5 MHz and 242 MHz
D. 121.5 MHz and 243 MHz

07431. What time of day would an SSB radio have the longest transmitting range?

A. daylight before noon
B. at noon
C. daylight after noon
D. during darkness

07575. The upward pressure of displaced water is called:

A. buoyancy
B. deadweight
C. draft
D. freeboard

07577. The value of the maximum righting arm depends on the position of the center of buoyancy and the:

A. longitudinal center of gravity
B. transverse center of gravity
C. downflooding angle
D. vertical location of the center of gravity

07581. For a given displacement, the righting arm has its maximum value when:

A. KG is minimum
B. angle of inclination is a maximum
C. small-angle stability applies
D. KM is a minimum

07583. Stability is determined by the relationship of the center of gravity and the:

A. water depth
B. keel
C. center of flotation
D. center of buoyancy

07587. The geometric center of the underwater volume is known as the:

A. center of flotation
B. tipping center
C. center of gravity
D. center of buoyancy

07591. Stability is determined principally by the location of the center of gravity and the:

A. aft perpendicular
B. center of buoyancy
C. keel
D. center of flotation

07593. The horizontal distance between the vertical lines of action of gravity and the buoyant forces is called the:

A. righting arm
B. metacentric height
C. metacentric radius
D. height of the center of buoyancy

07595. For a vessel inclined by the wind, multiplying the buoyant force by the horizontal distance between the lines of action of the buoyant and gravity forces gives the:

A. righting moment
B. vertical moment
C. longitudinal moment
D. transverse moment

07597. In small angle stability theory, the metacenter is located at the intersection of the inclined vertical centerline and a vertical line through:

A. G
B. F
C. B
D. K

07601. At all angles of inclination, the true measure of a vessel's stability is the:

A. metacentric height
B. displacement
C. righting moment
D. inclining moment

07603. Initial stability refers to stability:

A. at small angles of inclination
B. when loaded with minimum deck load
C. when at transit draft
D. when GZ is zero

07605. For small angles of inclination, if the KG were equal to the KM, then the vessel would have:

A. positive stability
B. negative stability
C. neutral stability
D. maximum stability

07607. The difference between the height of the metacenter and the metacentric height is known as:

A. righting arm
B. metacentric radius
C. height of the center of buoyancy
D. height of the center of gravity

07613. GM cannot be used as an indicator of stability at all angles of inclination because:

A. M is not fixed at large angles
B. there is no M at large angles
C. G is not fixed at large angles
D. there is no G at large angles

07621. With regard to the metacentric height, which of the following is TRUE?

A. It is used to indicate the quality of initial stability.
B. It is located above the center of buoyancy.
C. It is measured vertically above the center of buoyancy.
D. Its determination is the objective of the inclining experiment.

07623. The weight of the liquid displaced by a vessel floating in sea water is equal to the:

A. weight required to sink the vessel
B. total weight of the vessel
C. displaced volume
D. reserve buoyancy

07625. The original equilibrium position is always unstable when:

A. metacentric height is negative
B. KM is higher than KG
C. KG exceeds maximum allowable limits
D. free surfaces are excessive

07631. At an angle of loll, the capsizing moment is:

A. maximum
B. negative
C. positive
D. zero

07635. At an angle of loll, the righting arm (GZ) is:

A. maximum
B. negative
C. positive, but reflexive
D. zero

07641. In small-angle stability, when external forces exist, the buoyant force is assumed to act vertically upwards through the center of buoyancy and through the:

A. center of gravity
B. center of flotation
C. metacenter
D. metacentric height

07643. When a vessel is floating upright, the distance from the keel to he metacenter is called the:

A. metacentric height
B. height of the baseline
C. height of the metacenter
D. righting arm

07645. What abbreviation represents the height of the center of buoyancy?

A. BK
B. KB
C. CB
D. BM

07647. The abbreviation GM is used to represent the:

A. height of the metacenter
B. righting arm
C. righting moment
D. metacentric height

07648. Buoyant apparatus are required to be fitted with all of the following equipment EXCEPT: (Small Passenger Vessel Regulations)

A. life lines
B. paddles
C. water lights
D. painters

07651. When positive stability exists, GZ represents the:

A. righting moment
B. center of gravity

C. righting arm
D. metacentric height

07655. In small angle stability, the metacentric height:

A. is found in the hydrostatic tables for a level vessel
B. multiplied by the displacement yields the righting moment
C. is always positive
D. is calculated by subtracting KG from KM

07657. The righting moment can be determined by multiplying the displacement by the:

A. vertical center of gravity (KG)
B. longitudinal center of gravity (LCG)
C. righting arm (GZ)
D. center of gravity (CG)

07663. Subtracting KGT from KMT yields:

A. BL
B. GMT
C. FSCT
D. KG

07665. Subtracting KGL from KML yields:

A. BL
B. GML
C. FSCL
D. KG

07667. Subtracting GMT from KMT yields:

A. BL
B. GMT
C. FSCT
D. KGT

07695. Adding the FSCL to KG yields:

A. KM
B. GM
C. KGT
D. KGL

07697. The distance between the bottom of the hull and the waterline is called:

A. tonnage
B. reserve buoyancy
C. draft
D. freeboard

07701. After transferring a weight forward on a vessel, the draft at the center of flotation will:

A. change, depending on location of the LCG
B. increase

C. decrease
D. remain constant

07713. It is determined that a vessel has taken up a list because of a negative GM. To lower G below M, a proper course of action is to:

A. deballast
B. transfer weight to the high side
C. ballast on the high side
D. add weight symmetrically below G

07725. Reserve buoyancy is the:

A. unoccupied space below the waterline
B. volume of intact space above the waterline
C. excess of the buoyant force over the gravity force
D. difference in the buoyant force in salt and fresh waters

07727. When flooding occurs in a damaged vessel, reserve buoyancy:

A. decreases
B. remains the same
C. increases
D. shifts to the low side

07737. The geometric center of the waterplane area is called the:

A. center of buoyancy
B. center of gravity
C. metacenter
D. center of flotation

07747. In the absence of external forces, the center of gravity of a floating vessel is located directly above the:

A. metacenter
B. amidships
C. center of flotation
D. geometric center of the displaced volume

07785. The result of multiplying a weight by a distance is a:

A. moment
B. force
C. couple
D. center of gravity location

07786. The straight stream capability of an all-purpose nozzle is used in fighting a class A fire to:

A. shield fire fighters from radiant heat
B. break up burning material
C. get the most water possible on the fire
D. drive heat and smoke ahead of the fire fighters

07787. A moment is obtained by multiplying a force by its:

A. couple
B. lever arm
C. moment of inertia
D. point of application

07841. In a combination chain and wire rope mooring system, the anchor chain is deployed at the anchor end of the line to:

A. increase fatigue life of the system
B. reduce the time to retrieve the line
C. increase the holding power
D. reduce the catenary

08036. Radiation spreads a fire by:

A. transmitting the heat of a fire through the ship's metal
B. burning liquids flowing into another space
C. transferring heat across an unobstructed space
D. heated gases flowing through ventilation systems

08045. At an angle of loll, the righting moment is:

A. maximum
B. negative
C. positive
D. zero

08054. A thrust block is designed to:

A. transmit the thrust of the engine to the propeller
B. transmit the thrust of the propeller to the vessel
C. absorb the shock of wave pressure at the bow
D. be placed between the engines and the foundation to absorb the vibration

08155. The moment created by a force of 12,000 tons and a moment arm of 0.25 foot is:

A. 48,000 ft-tons
B. 6,000 ft-tons
C. 3,000 ft-tons
D. 0 ft-tons

08156. Category 1 EPIRBs are required to be carried on board:

A. small passenger vessels on the Great Lakes
B. all deep draft vessels
C. fishing industry vessels
D. small passenger vessels

08157. A moment of 300 ft-tons is created by a force of 15,000 tons. What is the moment arm?

A. 50.00 feet
B. 25.00 feet
C. 0.04 foot
D. 0.02 foot

08222. Which of the following will improve stability?

A. closing watertight doors
B. pumping the bilges
C. loading cargo on deck
D. consuming fuel from a full tank

08223. What is the purpose of a check valve?

A. passes air but not liquid
B. regulates liquid flow
C. permits flow in one direction only
D. passes liquid but not air

08225. On what type of pump would you find an impeller?

A. centrifugal
B. gear
C. piston
D. vane

08235. What is the proper direction of flow through a globe valve when the valve is installed to be in a normally open position?

A. direction is unimportant
B. depends on seat configuration
C. from below the seat
D. from above the seat

08287. Automatic mechanical ventilation shutdown is required for CO2 systems protecting the:

A. machinery spaces
B. cargo compartments
C. living quarters
D. galley

08332. What type of stern tube bearing has the least friction?

A. oil-lubricated bearings
B. lignum vitae
C. hard rubber
D. bronze bushings

08337. What is the percentage of oxygen in a typical sample of uncontaminated air?

A. 12 percent
B. 15 percent
C. 18 percent
D. 21 percent

08342. Blocking open or removing fire dampers can cause:

A. the accumulation of explosive gases
B. the fire to spread through the ventilation system
C. faster cooling of the fire
D. fixed foam systems to be ineffective

08347. All diesel engines are classified as:

A. four cycle
B. compression ignition
C. vacuum ignition
D. external combustion

08353. What power source actuates a solenoid valve?

A. air pressure
B. hydraulic pressure
C. electric current
D. mechanical force

08355. What quality of a diesel fuel is most significant for efficient combustion?

A. volatility
B. viscosity
C. flash point
D. specific heat

08361. What is the effect of heated intake air on a diesel engine?

A. increases efficiency
B. increases engine horsepower
C. increases engine life
D. reduces engine horsepower

08363. Lubricating oil should be changed on a heavy duty diesel engine when:

A. it gets dark in color
B. a sample rubbed between fingers feels thin
C. it has been in use for a specified interval
D. it no longer supports combustion

08365. How should you warm up a diesel engine that has not been run for some time?

A. Run it at minimum speed for a period of time.
B. Run it at half speed for a period of time.
C. Bring it to top speed immediately.
D. Inject ether into the air intake.

08367. How would the exhaust of a properly operating diesel engine appear?

A. light blue haze
B. light brown haze
C. light gray haze
D. perfectly clear

08371. Each cylinder in a two stroke cycle engine experiences combustion:

A. once each crankshaft revolution
B. twice each crankshaft revolution
C. every other crankshaft revolution
D. every fourth stroke

08373. How does combustion air enter the cylinder of a two-cycle diesel engine?

A. cylinder head valves
B. ports
C. turbo chargers
D. bleeder valves

08375. Maintaining the close tolerances in diesel fuel pumps and injectors requires the use of:

A. fuel/water separators
B. day tanks
C. injector test stand
D. fuel filters

08377. What factor is essential to the proper operation of a radiator cooled engine?

A. cooling water pressure
B. jacket water treatment
C. air flow through the radiator
D. low heat of combustion

08381. What are the 3 basic types of engine starters?

A. air, water, electric
B. air, hydraulic, electric
C. metered, hydraulic, automatic
D. air, emergency, hydraulic

08383. What does a pyrometer measure on a diesel engine?

A. water temperature
B. water pressure
C. exhaust temperature
D. air box pressure

08384. A moment of 300 ft-tons is created by a force of 15,000 tons. What is the moment arm?

A. 50.00 feet
B. 25.00 feet
C. 0.04 foot
D. 0.02 foot

08385. What condition will result in the automatic shutdown of a diesel engine?

A. high jacket water pressure
B. high lube oil pressure
C. low lube oil pressure
D. excessive turbo charger speed

08391. What monitoring device best indicates the load being carried by a diesel engine?

A. lube oil pressure gauge
B. jacket water temperature gauge
C. tachometer
D. exhaust pyrometer

08393. Diesel engines obtain combustion air through turbo chargers, blowers, or:

A. air starters
B. carburetors
C. natural aspiration
D. air receivers

08395. What is the purpose of the intake/exhaust valves in a diesel engine?

A. They regulate the combustion cycle.
B. They supply cooling water.
C. They synchronize the ignition spark.
D. They supply and regulate the lubricant flow.

08397. What is the best indication of the loading of a diesel engine?

A. oil temperature
B. manifold pressure
C. exhaust gas temperature
D. fuel consumption

08405. The most serious effect of air in a diesel engine jacket water cooling system is that it:

A. causes corrosion
B. reduces the effectiveness of the coolant
C. can form pockets which exclude coolant
D. accelerates formation of mineral deposits

08407. If you are unable to stop a diesel engine by any other means, you should:

A. discharge a CO_2 extinguisher in the air inlet
B. pull off the distributor cap
C. secure the jacket water
D. secure the starting air supply valve

08411. What is one effect of running a diesel engine at too cool a temperature?

A. buildup of sludge in the lubricating system
B. excessive fuel consumption
C. severe heat stresses on mechanical parts
D. foaming of the lubricating oil

08412. When abandoning ship and jumping into the water from a substantial height:

A. dive head first, using your hands to break the surface of the water
B. hold your arms firmly at your sides and jump feet first

C. throw your life jacket into the water first and then jump feet first into the water next to it
D. jump feet first, holding onto your life jacket with one hand while covering your nose and mouth with the other

08413. What would white exhaust smoke from a diesel engine probably mean?

A. late fuel injection
B. excess combustion air
C. dribbling injector tips
D. excessive lube oil consumption

08415. The three conditions which cause engine shutdown are overspeed, low lube oil pressure, and:

A. high lube oil pressure
B. high jacket water pressure
C. high jacket water temperature
D. low jacket water pressure

08417. Sudden unloading of a diesel engine can cause:

A. decreased fuel efficiency
B. increased exhaust temperature
C. black smoke
D. overspeed trip

08421. If an engine shuts down due to high jacket water temperature, what action should be taken?

A. Open crankcase explosion covers.
B. Allow engine to cool gradually.
C. Slowly add cool water to the expansion tank.
D. Back flush the cooling water system.

08547. What does the term "head" mean when applied to a pump?

A. length of its discharge pipe
B. height of its discharge pipe
C. difference between the discharge and suction pressures
D. sum of discharge and suction pressures

08563. How often must CO2 systems be inspected to confirm cylinders are within 10% of the stamped full weight of the charge?

A. quarterly
B. semiannually
C. annually
D. biannually

08576. The ventilation system of your ship has fire dampers restrained by fusible links. Which of the following statements is TRUE?

A. A fusible link will automatically open after a fire is extinguished and reset the damper.
B. Fusible links must be replaced if a damper is activated.
C. Fusible links are tested by applying a source of heat to them.
D. Fusible links must be replaced at every inspection for certification.

08635. A weight of 1,000 kips is equivalent to:

A. 1,000 pounds
B. 2,000 short tons
C. 2,240 pounds
D. 500 short tons

08662. When may a work vest be substituted for a required life preserver?

A. to replace a damaged life preserver
B. for use during fire drills
C. for use during boat drills
D. at no time

08688. Life floats must be equipped with: (Small Passenger Vessel Regulations)

A. a sea anchor
B. a signal mirror
C. a class A EPIRB
D. paddles

08702. An oil fire is classified as class:

A. D
B. C
C. B
D. A

08782. Control of fire should be addressed:

A. immediately after restoring vital services
B. immediately
C. following control of flooding
D. following establishment of fire boundaries

08807. The prohibition against displaying lights which may be confused with required navigation lights applies:

A. from sunset to sunrise and during restricted visibility
B. only when other vessels are in the area
C. only when operating in a traffic separation scheme
D. only when under tow

08811. The center of the underwater volume of a floating vessel is the:

A. center of buoyancy
B. center of flotation

C. uncorrected height of the center of gravity of the vessel
D. center of gravity of the vessel corrected for free surface effects

08897. The international body responsible for drafting the convention prohibiting marine pollution (MARPOL) is the:

A. Maritime Advisory Council
B. International Maritime Organization
C. International Association of Shipping
D. Association of Seafaring Nations

08901. The Safety of Life at Sea Convention was developed by the:

A. U. S. Coast Guard
B. American Bureau of Shipping
C. International Maritime Organization
D. American Institute of Maritime Shipping

08902. A centrifugal pump must be primed to:

A. lubricate the shaft seals
B. lift water level to impellers
C. make pressure equal to discharge pressure
D. overcome pressure of water in discharge line

08903. The most effective first aid treatment for chemical burns is to immediately:

A. apply ointment to the burned area
B. flood the affected area with water
C. wrap the burn with sterile dressing
D. apply an ice pack to the burned area

08905. When it is necessary to remove a victim from a life threatening situation, the person giving first aid must:

A. pull the victim by the feet
B. avoid subjecting the victim to any unnecessary disturbance
C. carry the victim to a location where injuries can be assessed
D. place the victim on a stretcher before attempting removal

08907. When giving first aid, you should understand how to conduct primary and secondary surveys and know:

A. which medications to prescribe
B. how to diagnose an illness from symptoms
C. the limits of your capabilities
D. how to set broken bones

08911. If a victim is unconscious, you should first look for evidence of:

A. high fever
B. head injury

C. broken limbs
D. irregular breathing

08925. A vessel behaves as if all of its weight is acting downward through the center of gravity, and all its support is acting upward through the:

A. keel
B. center of buoyancy
C. tipping center
D. amidships section

08971. The change in weight (measured in tons) which causes a draft change of 1 inch is:

A. MT1 inch
B. ML1 inch
C. MH1 inch
D. TPI

08973. For a floating vessel, the result of subtracting KG from KM is the:

A. height of the metacenter
B. height of the righting arm
C. height of the center of buoyancy
D. metacentric height

08977. The important stability parameter, KG, is defined as the:

A. metacentric height
B. height of the metacenter above keel
C. height of the center of buoyancy above keel
D. height of the center of gravity above keel

08981. The important initial stability parameter, GM, is the:

A. metacentric height
B. height of the metacenter above keel
C. height of the center of buoyancy above keel
D. height of the center of gravity above keel

08983. The time required to incline from port to starboard and back to port again is called:

A. initial stability
B. range of stability
C. inclining moment
D. rolling period

08985. The time required to incline from bow down to stern down and return to bow down again is called:

A. rolling period
B. amplitude moment
C. inclining moment
D. pitching period

08987. The tendency of a vessel to return to its original trim after being inclined by an external force is:

A. equilibrium
B. buoyancy
C. transverse stability
D. longitudinal stability

08991. The enclosed area defined as the intersection of the surface of the water and the hull of a vessel is the:

A. amidships plane
B. longitudinal reference plane
C. baseline
D. waterplane

08993. The waterplane area is described as the intersection of the surface of the water in which a vessel floats and the:

A. baseline
B. vertical reference plane
C. hull
D. horizontal reference plane

08994. Two types of anchor shackles which are currently available are:

A. U-Type and posilok shackles
B. C-Type and wedge shackles
C. D-Type and bow shackles
D. wedge and kenter shackles

08997. Aboard a vessel, multiplying a load's weight by the distance of the load's center of gravity from the centerline results in the load's:

A. TCG
B. transverse moment
C. righting moment
D. transverse free surface moment

09001. The difference between the starboard and port drafts caused by shifting a weight transversely is:

A. list
B. heel
C. trim
D. flotation

09021. Aboard a vessel, dividing the sum of the longitudinal moments by the total weight yields the vessel's:

A. inclining moments
B. righting moments
C. vertical moments
D. longitudinal position of the center of gravity

09067. The TCG of a vessel may be found by dividing the displacement of the vessel into the:

A. transverse center of gravity of the vessel
B. sum of the vertical moments of the vessel
C. sum of the transverse moments of the vessel
D. transverse baseline of the vessel

09093. In addition to weighing the cartridge, what other maintenance is required for a cartridge-operated dry chemical extinguisher?

A. Weigh the powder in the canister.
B. Discharge a small amount to see that it works.
C. Check the hose and nozzle for clogs.
D. Check the external pressure gage.

09097. When must a dry chemical fire extinguisher be recharged?

A. after each use
B. when the air temperature exceeds 90° F
C. every 6 months
D. every 12 months

09101. Recharging a previously used cartridge-operated dry chemical extinguisher is accomplished by:

A. authorized fire equipment servicing personnel only
B. replacing the propellant cartridge and refilling with powder
C. puncturing the cartridge seal after installation
D. recharging the cartridge and refilling it with powder

09107. The amount of Halon remaining in an extinguisher is determined by:

A. internal inspection
B. checking the gage
C. weighing the cylinder
D. checking the tag

09111. Inspection of a Halon extinguisher involves checking the hose, handle, nozzle, and:

A. sight glass
B. weighing the extinguisher
C. service technician's report
D. the last date it was charged

09113. After using a Halon extinguisher, it should be:

A. put back in service if more than 50% of the charge remains
B. repainted
C. discarded
D. recharged

09115. An airplane should NOT send which signal in reply to a surface craft?

A. opening and closing the throttle
B. rocking the wings
C. flashing the navigational lights off and on
D. flashing Morse T

09121. The blocking or absence of fire dampers can cause:

A. the accumulation of explosive gases
B. faster cooling of the fire
C. the fire to spread through ventilation system
D. fixed foam systems to be ineffective

09125. Automatic fire dampers in ventilation systems are operated by use of a:

A. remote operated valve
B. fusible link
C. CO2 system pressure switch
D. heat or smoke detector

09129. Automatic fire dampers in ventilation systems are operated by use of a:

A. heat or smoke detector
B. fusible link
C. remote operated valve
D. C02 system pressure switch

09130. When administering first aid you should avoid:

A. any conversation with the patient
B. instructing bystanders
C. unnecessary haste and appearance of uncertainty
D. touching the patient before washing your hands

09137. Fighting a fire in the galley poses the additional threat of:

A. contaminating food with extinguishing agent
B. spreading through the engineering space
C. loss of stability
D. a grease fire in the ventilation system

09181. An immersion suit should be equipped with a(n):

A. air bottle for breathing
B. whistle and light
C. whistle, light, and reflective tape
D. whistle, light, and sea dye marker

09183. The zipper of an immersion suit should be lubricated with:

A. paraffin
B. oil

C. graphite
D. vegetable oil

09185. The external flotation bladder of a survival unit should be inflated:

A. only after 2 hours in the water
B. only after 4 hours in the water
C. before entry into the water
D. upon entry into the water

09187. The external flotation bladder on an immersion suit should be inflated:

A. before you enter the water
B. after you enter the water
C. after 1 hour in the water
D. after you notice that your suit is losing buoyancy

09191. After abandoning a vessel, water that is consumed within the first 24 hours:

A. will pass through the body with little absorbed by the system
B. will help to prevent fatigue
C. will quench thirst for only 2 hours
D. help to prevent seasickness

09193. Drinking salt water will:

A. be safe if mixed with fresh water
B. prevent seasickness
C. promote dehydration
D. protect against heat cramps

09195. When using the rain water collection tubes on a marine life raft, the first collection should be:

A. passed around so all can drink
B. poured overboard because of salt washed off the canopy
C. saved to be used at a later time
D. used to boil food

09197. In the first 24 hours after abandoning a vessel, water should be given only to personnel who are:

A. thirsty
B. sick or injured
C. wet
D. awake

09205. When you are firing a pyrotechnic distress signal, it should be aimed:

A. straight overhead
B. at the vessel whose attention you want to attract
C. into the wind
D. at about 60 degrees above the horizon

09246. Fighting a fire in a watertight compartment with hoses could reduce stability by:

A. progressive downflooding
B. reducing the level of potable water from the storage tanks
C. causing a list due to the water in the compartment
D. reducing the KG to minimum allowable

09276. You are underway when a fire breaks out in the forward part of your vessel. If possible, you should:

A. call for assistance
B. put the vessel's stern into the wind
C. abandon ship to windward
D. keep going at half speed

09282. There is a fire aft aboard your vessel. To help fight the fire, you should:

A. put the wind off either beam
B. put stern into the wind and increase speed
C. head bow into the wind and decrease speed
D. put stern into the wind and decrease speed

09307. When a rescuer finds an electrical burn victim in the vicinity of live electrical equipment or wiring, his first step is to:

A. flush water over any burned area of patient
B. apply ointment to burned areas on patient
C. get assistance to shut down electrical power in the area
D. remove the patient from the vicinity of the live electrical equipment or wiring

09311. Basic emergency care for an electrical burn is to:

A. flood the burn with water for 2 minutes
B. brush away the charred skin and wrap the burned area
C. cover the burned area with a clean cloth and transport the patient to a medical facility
D. apply ointment or spray to the burned area and wrap with a clean cloth

09313. When a patient has an electrical burn, it is important to:

A. look for a second burn, which may have been caused by the current passing through the body
B. locate the nearest water source and flood the burn with water for 5 minutes
C. remove any dirt or charred skin from the area of the burn
D. apply ointment to the burn area and wrap with clean cloth

09315. Since electrical burn victims are subjected to shock, the first medical response is to check for:

A. indication of broken bones
B. breathing and heartbeat
C. symptoms of concussion
D. bleeding injuries

09317. Which is a correct statement with respect to inserting an airway tube?

A. Only a trained person should attempt to insert an airway tube.
B. A size 2 airway tube is the correct size for an adult.
C. The airway tube will not damage the victim's throat.
D. Inserting airway tube will prevent vomiting.

09321. In battery charging rooms, ventilation should be provided:

A. at the lowest point
B. near the batteries
C. at the highest point
D. only when charging is in progress

09323. A fuel-air mixture below the lower explosive limit is too:

A. rich to burn
B. lean to burn
C. cool to burn
D. dense to burn

09325. Good housekeeping on a vessel prevents fires by:

A. allowing better access in an emergency
B. eliminating potential fuel sources
C. eliminating trip hazards
D. improving personnel qualifications

09327. Accumulations of oily rags should be:

A. kept in nonmetal containers
B. discarded as soon as possible
C. cleaned thoroughly for reuse
D. kept in the paint locker

09331. Paints and solvents on a vessel should be:

A. stored safely at the work site until work is completed
B. returned to the paint locker after each use
C. covered at all times to protect from ignition sources
D. stored in a suitable gear locker

09333. After extinguishing a fire with CO2, it is advisable to:

A. use all CO2 available to cool surrounding area
B. stand by with water or other agents
C. thoroughly ventilate the space of CO2
D. jettison all burning materials

09335. The disadvantage of using CO2 is that the:

A. CO2 does not cool the fire
B. cylinders are regulated pressure vessels
C. CO2 is not effective on class "B" fires
D. CO2 is not effective on class "C" fires

09337. Size I and II fire extinguishers are designated as:

A. portable
B. semi-portable
C. fixed
D. compact

09341. Dry chemical extinguishers may be used on what class of fires?

A. A only
B. B only
C. B and C only
D. A, B or C as marked on the extinguisher

09343. The device installed on Halon cylinders to prevent overpressurization is usually a:

A. safety valve
B. relief valve
C. rupture disc
D. control head

09347. CO2 cylinders must be recharged when the weight of the charge in the cylinder is less than what percent of the stamped full weight of the charge?

A. 80
B. 85
C. 90
D. 95

09351. Halon extinguishers used on a class B fire should be directed:

A. at the top of the flames
B. at the base of the fire near the edge
C. in short quick bursts
D. toward the upwind side of the fire

09357. Halon extinguishers used on a class C fire should be directed at the:

A. base of the equipment
B. top of the equipment
C. power source
D. source of the fire

09361. The principle personnel hazard unique to Halon extinguishers is:

A. displacement of oxygen
B. skin irritation
C. inhaling toxic vapors
D. eye irritation

09362. Fire in an engine compartment is best extinguished with carbon dioxide gas (CO2) and by:

A. closing the compartment except for the ventilators
B. leaving the compartment open to the air
C. completely closing the compartment
D. increasing the air flow to the compartment with blowers

09363. The primary function(s) of an automatic sprinkler system is(are) to:

A. extinguish the fire which triggers it
B. limit the spread of fire and control the amount of heat produced
C. protect people in the areas which have sprinkler heads
D. alert the crew to the fire

09365. When flammable liquids are handled in a compartment on a vessel, the ventilation for that area should be:

A. operated continuously while vapors may be present
B. operated intermittently to remove vapors
C. available on standby for immediate use
D. shut down if an explosive mixture is present

09367. A galley grease fire may be extinguished using:

A. water
B. foam
C. the range hood extinguishing system
D. fire dampers

09371. Overhauling a fire in the living quarters on a vessel must include:

A. opening dead spaces to check for heat or fire
B. evacuation of the vessel
C. sounding the "all clear" signal
D. operation of the emergency generator

09373. If heavy smoke is coming from the paint locker, the FIRST firefighting response should be to:

A. release the CO2 flooding system
B. open the door to evaluate extent of the fire
C. enter and use a portable extinguisher
D. secure the ventilation

09375. After extinguishing a paint locker fire using the fixed CO_2 system, the next action is to have the space:

A. opened and burned material removed
B. left closed with vents off until all boundaries are cool
C. checked for oxygen content
D. doused with water to prevent reflash

09377. You should deploy the sea anchor from a life raft to:

A. keep the life raft from capsizing
B. navigate against the current
C. to keep personnel from getting seasick
D. to stay in the general location

09381. If the life raft should capsize, all personnel should leave the raft and:

A. climb onto the bottom
B. swim away from the raft
C. right the raft using the righting straps
D. inflate the righting bag

09382. Fire in an engine compartment is best extinguished with carbon dioxide gas (CO_2) and:

A. completely closing the compartment
B. closing the compartment except for the ventilators
C. leaving the compartment open to the air
D. increasing the air flow to the compartment by blowers

09383. Immediately after abandoning a vessel, lookouts should be posted aboard life rafts to look for:

A. survivors in the water
B. food and water
C. land
D. bad weather

09385. When personnel are lifted by a helicopter from an inflatable life raft, the personnel on the raft should:

A. deflate the floor of the raft to reduce the danger of the raft overturning
B. inflate the floor of the raft to provide for additional stability
C. remove their life preservers to prepare for the transfer
D. take in the sea anchor to prevent fouling of the rescue sling

09387. When should you use distress flares and rockets?

A. only when there is a chance of their being seen by rescue vessels

B. at half-hour intervals
C. at 1-hour intervals
D. immediately upon abandoning the vessel

09391. Once you have established the daily ration of drinking water in a survival situation, how should you drink it?

A. small sips at regular intervals during the day
B. the complete daily ration at one time during the day
C. one-third the daily ration 3 times daily
D. small sips only after sunset

09397. CAT I EPIRBs transmit on frequencies that are monitored by:

A. orbiting satellites in space
B. commercial radio stations
C. private, commercial, and military aircraft
D. both A & C

09411. When anchoring in an area with a soft bottom, the fluke angle of an anchor should be set at:

A. 20°
B. 30°
C. 40°
D. 50°

09412. Radiation spreads a fire by:

A. transmitting the heat of a fire through the ship's metal
B. burning liquids flowing into another space
C. heated gases flowing through ventilation systems
D. the transfer of heat across an unobstructed space

09413. When anchoring in an area with a hard bottom, the fluke angle of an anchor should be set at:

A. 20°
B. 30°
C. 40°
D. 50°

09414. Blocking open or removing fire dampers can cause:

A. the fire to spread through the ventilation system
B. fixed foam systems to be ineffective
C. faster cooling of the fire
D. the accumulation of explosive gases

09415. A solution to overcome tripping defects is an arrangement of special plates on either side of the flukes, designed to set them in the correct tripping position. These special plates are called:

A. trippers
B. stocks
C. stabilizers
D. palms

09425. Which formula can be used to calculate metacentric height?

A. KM + GM
B. KM - GM
C. KM - KG
D. KB + BM

09427. In the absence of external forces, adding weight on one side of a floating vessel causes the vessel to:

A. heel until the angle of loll is reached
B. list until the center of buoyancy is aligned vertically with the center of gravity
C. trim to the side opposite TCG until all moments are equal
D. decrease draft at the center of flotation

09431. Subtracting FSCT from KGT yields:

A. BL
B. GMT
C. FSCT
D. KG

09435. For an upright vessel, draft is the vertical distance between the keel and the:

A. waterline
B. freeboard deck
C. plimsoll mark
D. amidships section

09437. A wind has caused a difference between drafts starboard and port. This difference is:

A. list
B. heel
C. trim
D. flotation

09441. The moment of a force is a measure of the:

A. turning effect of the force about a point
B. instantaneous value of the force
C. stability characteristics of the vessel
D. center of gravity location

09443. The magnitude of a moment is the product of the force and:

A. time
B. lever arm
C. displacement
D. angle of inclination

09445. The difference between the height of the metacenter and the height of the center of gravity is known as the:

A. metacentric height
B. height of the righting arm
C. fore and aft perpendicular
D. height of the center of buoyancy

09447. When initial stability applies, the height of the center of gravity plus the metacentric height equals the:

A. free surface moments
B. righting arm
C. height of the metacenter
D. corrected height of the center of gravity

09451. Initial stability is indicated by:

A. GM
B. KM
C. deck load
D. maximum allowed KG

09453. At all angles of inclination, the metacenter is located:

A. vertically above the center of buoyancy
B. vertically above the center of gravity
C. at the intersection of the upright vertical centerline and the line of action of the buoyant force
D. at the geometric center of the underwater volume

09454. If water is rising in the bilge of a life raft, you should first:

A. abandon the survival craft
B. check for cracks in the hull
C. shift all personnel to the stern
D. check the bilge drain plug

09455. The original equilibrium position is stable when:

A. metacentric height is positive
B. metacentric radius is positive
C. KG exceeds maximum allowable limits
D. free surfaces are excessive

09457. The center of buoyancy is located at the:

A. geometric center of the waterplane area
B. intersection of the vertical centerline and line of action of the buoyant force
C. center of gravity of the vessel corrected for free surface effects
D. geometric center of the displaced volume

09463. The value of the righting arm at an angle of loll is:

A. negative
B. zero
C. positive
D. equal to GM

09465. When inclined to an angle of list, the value of the righting arm is:

A. negative
B. zero
C. positive
D. maximum

09467. When inclined to an angle of list, the value of the righting moment is:

A. negative
B. zero
C. positive
D. maximum

09471. Which of the following is used as an indicator of initial stability?

A. GM
B. KG
C. KM
D. GZ

09473. What is the stability term for the distance from the center of gravity (G) to the Metacenter (M), when small-angle stability applies?

A. metacentric height
B. metacentric radius
C. height of the metacenter
D. righting arm

09477. The water in which a vessel floats provides vertical upward support. The point through which this support is assumed to act is known as the center of:

A. effort
B. flotation
C. gravity
D. buoyancy

09481. The difference between the initial trim and the trim after a loading change is known as:

A. trim
B. change of trim
C. final trim
D. change of draft

09485. The difference between the starboard and port drafts due to wind or seas is called:

A. list
B. heel
C. trim
D. flotation

09487. The geometric center of the underwater volume of a floating vessel is the center of:

A. hydrodynamic forces
B. flotation
C. gravity
D. buoyancy

09491. The difference between the height of the metacenter and the height of the center of gravity is:

A. KB
B. KG
C. KM
D. GM

09493. On a vessel, multiplying a load's weight by the distance of the load's center of gravity above the baseline results in a(n):

A. transverse moment
B. vertical moment
C. righting moment
D. inclining moment

09497. Stability is determined principally by the location of the point of application of two forces: the upward-acting buoyant force and the:

A. upward-acting weight force
B. downward-acting weight force
C. downward-acting buoyant force
D. environmental force

09501. Stability is determined principally by the location of the point of application of two forces: the downward-acting gravity force and the:

A. upward-acting weight force
B. downward-acting weight force
C. upward-acting buoyant force
D. environmental force

09503. Stability is determined principally by the location of two points in a vessel: the center of buoyancy and the:

A. metacenter
B. geometric center of the waterplane area
C. center of gravity
D. center of flotation

09505. With no environmental forces acting on the vessel, the center of gravity of an inclined vessel is vertically aligned with the:

A. longitudinal centerline
B. center of flotation
C. original vertical centerline
D. metacenter

09507. With no environmental forces, the center of gravity of an inclined vessel is vertically aligned with the:

A. longitudinal centerline
B. center of flotation
C. original vertical centerline
D. center of buoyancy

09511. In the absence of external forces, the center of buoyancy of an inclined vessel is vertically aligned directly below the:

A. center of gravity
B. amidships station
C. center of flotation
D. geometric center of the waterplane area

09513. In the presence of external forces, the center of buoyancy of an inclined vessel is vertically aligned with the:

A. center of gravity
B. metacenter
C. center of flotation
D. keel

09515. With no environmental forces, the center of gravity of an inclined vessel is vertically aligned directly above the:

A. longitudinal centerline
B. center of buoyancy
C. original vertical centerline
D. center of flotation

09517. Aboard a vessel, dividing the sum of the transverse moments by the total weight yields the vessel's:

A. vertical moments
B. transverse position of the center of gravity
C. inclining moments
D. righting moments

09521. Aboard a vessel, dividing the sum of the vertical moments by the total weight yields the vessel's:

A. height of the center of gravity
B. vertical moments
C. righting moments
D. inclining moments

09523. When the height of the metacenter is the same as the height of the center of gravity, the upright equilibrium position is:

A. stable
B. neutral
C. unstable
D. negative

09525. When the height of the metacenter is greater than the height of the center of gravity, a vessel has what type of stability?

A. stable
B. neutral
C. unstable
D. negative

09527. When the height of the metacenter is less than the height of the center of gravity, a vessel has what type of stability?

A. stable
B. neutral
C. negative
D. positive

09531. When the height of the metacenter is greater than the height of the center of gravity, the upright equilibrium position is stable and stability is:

A. unstable
B. neutral
C. negative
D. positive

09533. Unstable equilibrium exists at small angles of inclination when:

A. G is above M
B. G is off the centerline
C. B is off the centerline
D. B is above G

09535. When stability of a vessel is neutral, the value of GM:

A. only depends on the height of the center of gravity
B. only depends on the height of the metacenter
C. is greater when G is low
D. is zero

09537. When the height of the metacenter is less than the height of the center of gravity of a vessel, the upright equilibrium position is:

A. stable
B. neutral
C. unstable
D. negative

09541. When the height of the metacenter is the same as the height of the center of gravity of a vessel, the upright equilibrium position is:

A. stable
B. neutral
C. unstable
D. negative

09543. A stable upright equilibrium position for a vessel means that the metacenter is:

A. at a lower level than the baseline
B. on the longitudinal centerline
C. higher than the center of gravity
D. at amidships

09545. An unstable upright equilibrium position on a vessel means that the metacenter is:

A. lower than the center of gravity
B. at the same height as the center of gravity
C. higher than the baseline
D. on the longitudinal centerline

09547. A neutral equilibrium position for a vessel means that the metacenter is:

A. lower than the keel
B. at the same height as the center of gravity
C. exactly at midships
D. at the center of the waterplane area

09551. When the height of the metacenter is less than the height of the center of gravity, a vessel has what type of stability?

A. stable
B. neutral
C. unstable
D. positive

09553. When the height of the metacenter is greater than the height of the center of gravity, a vessel is in:

A. stable equilibrium
B. neutral equilibrium
C. unstable equilibrium
D. negative equilibrium

09557. Longitudinal moments are obtained by multiplying a vessel's weight and its:

A. VCG or KG
B. LCB
C. LCG
D. TCG

09561. Vertical moments are obtained by multiplying a vessel's weight and its:

A. VCG or KG
B. LCB
C. LCG
D. TCG

09563. The KG of a vessel is found by dividing the displacement into the:

A. height of the center of gravity of the vessel
B. sum of the vertical moments of the vessel

C. sum of the free surface moments of the vessel
D. sum of the longitudinal moments of the vessel

09564. Automatic fire dampers in ventilation systems are operated by use of:

A. remotely operated valves
B. CO2 system pressure switches
C. fusible links
D. heat or smoke detectors

09565. The LCG of a vessel may be found by dividing displacement into the:

A. longitudinal center of gravity of the vessel
B. sum of vertical moments of the vessel
C. sum of longitudinal moments of the vessel
D. longitudinal baseline of the vessel

09567. The correction to KG for transverse free surface effects may be found by dividing the vessel's displacement into the:

A. transverse free surface correction for the vessel
B. sum of the vertical moments of the vessel
C. sum of the transverse free surface moments of the vessel
D. transverse baseline of the vessel

09571. The correction to KG for longitudinal free surface effects for a vessel can be found by dividing the vessel's displacement into the:

A. transverse free surface correction for the vessel
B. sum of the vertical moments of the vessel
C. sum of the longitudinal free surface moments of the vessel
D. longitudinal centerline of the vessel

09573. A floating vessel will behave as if all of its weight is acting downward through the:

A. center of gravity
B. center of buoyancy
C. center of flotation
D. metacenter

09581. The CO2 flooding system is actuated by a sequence of steps which are:

A. break glass, pull valve, break glass, pull cylinder control
B. sound evacuation alarm, pull handle
C. open bypass valve, break glass, pull handle
D. open stop valve, open control valve, trip alarm

09602. What causes cavitation in a centrifugal pump?

A. vapor pockets in the flow stream
B. rough impeller surfaces
C. worn wearing rings
D. heavy fluid in the flow stream

09604. Except in rare cases, it is impossible to extinguish a shipboard fire by:

A. removing the oxygen
B. removing the fuel
C. interrupting the chain reaction
D. removing the heat

09606. You are fighting a Class B fire with a portable dry chemical extinguisher. The discharge should be directed:

A. over the top of the fire
B. to bank off a bulkhead onto the fire
C. at the seat of the fire, starting at the near edge
D. at the main body of the fire

09607. There is a fire aft aboard your vessel. To help fight the fire, you should:

A. head bow into the wind and decrease speed
B. put wind off either beam
C. put stern into the wind and increase speed
D. put stern into the wind and decrease speed

00002 C	00119 D	00268 C	00388 A	00509 C	00660 A	00798 C	00921 D
00003 D	00120 B	00269 C	00391 A	00510 D	00661 C	00799 D	00922 C
00004 A	00123 A	00270 A	00393 B	00514 A	00662 C	00800 D	00924 A
00005 D	00125 B	00271 A	00394 A	00515 C	00664 C	00801 C	00925 D
00008 B	00128 D	00272 B	00397 C	00516 C	00666 B	00802 B	00926 B
00009 A	00129 C	00273 A	00398 A	00517 A	00667 A	00803 D	00927 A
00010 B	00130 B	00275 C	00400 D	00518 B	00670 C	00808 A	00928 C
00011 D	00133 B	00277 B	00402 D	00522 B	00672 B	00809 D	00929 A
00013 A	00135 D	00278 B	00403 C	00524 B	00674 B	00810 A	00930 C
00014 B	00136 A	00279 D	00407 A	00527 C	00677 B	00811 B	00931 D
00018 C	00138 C	00281 C	00408 C	00528 D	00678 D	00812 A	00932 D
00019 B	00139 D	00282 B	00411 A	00531 B	00679 C	00813 C	00934 A
00020 A	00140 A	00283 D	00412 B	00532 C	00684 B	00818 C	00935 C
00021 D	00141 A	00285 D	00413 C	00533 D	00687 D	00819 A	00936 C
00023 C	00143 D	00287 D	00414 B	00534 B	00688 D	00820 B	00937 B
00024 A	00145 D	00288 D	00415 B	00537 B	00689 C	00821 A	00938 D
00028 C	00148 B	00290 A	00417 D	00538 D	00692 D	00822 A	00939 D
00029 C	00153 A	00291 D	00418 A	00542 D	00694 C	00823 B	00940 A
00030 B	00155 A	00292 D	00421 C	00544 B	00697 A	00828 C	00942 A
00031 A	00156 A	00293 A	00422 B	00547 D	00698 D	00829 C	00944 A
00033 D	00158 B	00295 B	00423 A	00548 A	00699 B	00831 C	00945 C
00034 D	00159 B	00296 D	00424 B	00549 A	00700 B	00832 A	00946 B
00035 A	00163 B	00297 B	00427 B	00553 C	00702 A	00833 B	00947 B
00038 D	00165 D	00298 A	00428 C	00557 B	00704 D	00838 D	00948 D
00040 D	00168 A	00300 B	00429 A	00558 C	00707 B	00840 C	00950 A
00041 D	00171 C	00302 B	00432 B	00561 C	00708 D	00841 C	00951 D
00043 D	00172 B	00303 D	00434 B	00565 C	00710 A	00842 C	00952 C
00044 B	00173 C	00305 C	00437 C	00567 D	00711 A	00848 B	00954 C
00045 C	00175 D	00308 B	00438 A	00568 D	00712 C	00850 B	00957 D
00048 A	00177 C	00309 D	00439 B	00571 B	00714 D	00851 D	00958 D
00049 C	00178 A	00311 B	00441 C	00575 D	00715 D	00852 A	00961 B
00053 B	00180 D	00312 B	00442 A	00577 B	00717 D	00858 A	00962 A
00055 B	00183 D	00313 D	00443 C	00578 B	00719 D	00860 C	00964 B
00058 A	00185 C	00317 B	00444 B	00580 B	00720 A	00862 D	00967 D
00060 D	00187 B	00318 C	00447 C	00585 C	00721 A	00868 A	00968 D
00063 D	00188 A	00319 C	00448 D	00587 D	00724 A	00869 B	00969 A
00065 B	00189 B	00322 D	00450 D	00589 A	00725 A	00870 A	00970 C
00068 B	00191 B	00323 C	00452 D	00590 B	00727 D	00871 B	00971 B
00070 D	00195 B	00324 B	00453 A	00592 B	00729 B	00873 B	00972 D
00071 D	00198 C	00328 B	00454 B	00597 D	00731 A	00878 A	00974 A
00072 B	00200 B	00331 D	00457 D	00598 B	00732 A	00879 A	00976 D
00073 A	00205 D	00332 B	00458 C	00599 C	00735 B	00880 C	00977 A
00075 A	00207 B	00333 B	00462 A	00600 C	00738 B	00881 B	00978 B
00077 C	00208 C	00337 B	00463 A	00604 A	00740 C	00882 B	00979 B
00078 A	00212 D	00338 C	00464 C	00605 D	00742 B	00885 C	00980 A
00079 A	00215 C	00339 C	00467 A	00607 C	00744 B	00887 A	00981 B
00080 B	00218 D	00341 A	00468 C	00608 C	00745 D	00888 D	00982 B
00081 A	00220 A	00342 B	00469 B	00610 D	00748 B	00889 D	00984 D
00082 B	00225 C	00343 D	00470 B	00611 D	00749 C	00891 D	00986 B
00083 D	00228 A	00344 C	00472 C	00612 B	00750 B	00892 C	00987 B
00084 D	00229 D	00348 D	00473 B	00614 A	00752 B	00895 A	00988 A
00088 D	00230 D	00352 D	00474 A	00615 C	00753 D	00896 C	00989 C
00090 B	00231 B	00353 B	00477 D	00617 C	00754 D	00897 B	00990 A
00091 A	00235 D	00354 C	00478 A	00619 D	00755 A	00898 B	00991 C
00093 D	00237 B	00355 A	00481 A	00621 A	00758 B	00899 B	00992 B
00097 D	00238 B	00357 C	00482 A	00627 B	00760 B	00901 C	00994 B
00098 C	00240 A	00358 C	00483 B	00629 B	00761 A	00902 C	00996 A
00099 B	00243 C	00362 C	00484 D	00630 D	00762 A	00904 D	00997 A
00100 B	00245 B	00363 B	00487 B	00632 B	00764 A	00905 C	00999 A
00102 A	00247 A	00367 B	00488 A	00637 A	00768 D	00906 C	01000 D
00103 A	00248 D	00368 C	00489 B	00640 C	00769 A	00907 A	01002 D
00105 D	00252 C	00373 B	00492 A	00642 A	00772 B	00908 D	01004 B
00106 C	00253 D	00374 B	00494 B	00647 A	00778 D	00912 A	01006 B
00108 B	00257 B	00375 B	00497 C	00649 B	00782 C	00914 B	01007 D
00110 B	00258 D	00377 B	00498 C	00650 D	00785 A	00915 D	01008 A
00112 A	00261 A	00378 B	00500 C	00651 D	00788 B	00916 B	01010 A
00113 D	00262 B	00379 B	00504 C	00652 C	00789 A	00917 B	01011 C
00115 C	00263 C	00382 B	00505 A	00654 D	00790 D	00918 C	01012 A
00116 C	00265 D	00383 C	00507 D	00655 D	00791 A	00919 C	01013 D
00118 B	00267 D	00387 D	00508 A	00657 A	00792 D	00920 A	01014 B

01016 C	01186 B	01316 D	01432 B	01637 D	02307 B	02858 B	03056 C
01017 A	01188 B	01317 B	01433 B	01640 C	02321 D	02859 D	03058 D
01019 D	01194 C	01318 A	01434 D	01645 D	02327 D	02862 A	03059 A
01020 B	01196 B	01319 D	01438 D	01648 D	02331 B	02866 D	03062 D
01021 D	01197 D	01320 B	01439 C	01650 A	02335 A	02867 B	03066 B
01022 A	01201 D	01324 D	01443 D	01665 A	02336 C	02870 B	03068 A
01023 D	01204 A	01326 D	01445 B	01669 D	02351 C	02871 B	03069 C
01024 D	01206 D	01327 A	01448 B	01670 B	02362 D	02873 A	03082 B
01027 C	01207 D	01328 D	01449 A	01671 B	02371 C	02875 C	03084 C
01028 D	01208 D	01332 C	01452 C	01686 B	02401 B	02877 B	03091 A
01029 D	01211 B	01334 D	01453 A	01687 B	02439 C	02882 A	03096 B
01030 C	01212 D	01335 D	01456 B	01688 A	02448 C	02886 B	03102 A
01032 A	01213 B	01336 C	01462 C	01697 C	02475 A	02887 B	03104 B
01033 C	01214 C	01337 D	01463 B	01701 D	02488 C	02888 B	03108 C
01034 A	01216 D	01338 D	01469 B	01705 A	02504 C	02889 C	03110 B
01036 B	01217 A	01340 D	01471 A	01810 A	02523 A	02896 C	03112 C
01037 C	01223 A	01341 A	01472 D	01811 A	02536 C	02897 D	03119 B
01038 D	01224 D	01342 B	01474 C	01823 C	02541 C	02898 B	03120 C
01040 D	01226 C	01344 A	01479 A	01831 A	02549 B	02899 C	03121 A
01042 D	01227 B	01345 C	01481 D	01837 B	02562 C	02902 D	03122 A
01044 C	01228 B	01346 A	01482 D	01851 A	02582 D	02905 A	03123 C
01047 A	01231 A	01347 A	01488 C	01860 C	02599 A	02906 D	03124 A
01052 C	01235 C	01348 D	01490 C	01862 B	02606 A	02908 C	03127 A
01053 D	01236 D	01352 B	01498 A	01870 A	02613 C	02909 C	03130 D
01054 B	01237 A	01354 C	01502 B	01880 D	02614 D	02911 B	03132 D
01056 D	01238 C	01355 B	01503 D	01890 C	02617 C	02918 B	03134 B
01057 B	01244 D	01356 A	01504 C	01900 C	02636 A	02919 B	03136 A
01058 C	01246 B	01358 B	01507 D	01909 D	02644 D	02922 D	03137 B
01059 B	01247 B	01361 C	01508 A	01910 C	02646 C	02927 A	03140 A
01061 B	01248 A	01362 C	01512 D	01920 B	02648 D	02928 A	03149 D
01062 A	01249 C	01363 D	01523 D	01930 B	02658 D	02929 A	03150 C
01064 C	01251 D	01364 B	01525 C	01938 D	02662 C	02932 A	03152 D
01066 D	01252 D	01365 C	01526 C	01940 C	02664 A	02938 A	03154 A
01067 B	01254 C	01366 D	01536 D	01950 C	02665 D	02939 A	03158 C
01074 A	01255 B	01368 D	01540 A	01951 A	02682 B	02942 C	03159 D
01076 C	01256 B	01370 A	01541 D	01954 C	02689 A	02948 B	03160 B
01077 B	01257 C	01371 D	01543 B	01979 C	02690 C	02949 D	03161 A
01080 D	01262 D	01372 C	01546 B	01983 B	02698 A	02953 D	03162 C
01081 D	01263 C	01373 C	01547 C	01997 D	02712 D	02958 B	03167 C
01086 D	01264 D	01374 A	01553 B	02032 B	02716 D	02961 A	03170 C
01087 D	01265 B	01375 D	01555 D	02053 C	02742 B	02966 B	03171 A
01088 A	01266 D	01376 C	01556 A	02055 D	02754 B	02968 D	03172 D
01089 C	01268 A	01378 A	01558 C	02057 A	02764 B	02969 C	03173 B
01094 C	01272 A	01381 C	01559 B	02061 C	02766 B	02972 D	03174 A
01097 A	01274 A	01382 A	01560 C	02063 B	02768 C	02976 C	03176 A
01098 A	01275 D	01384 B	01563 B	02073 C	02769 B	02978 D	03182 B
01101 A	01276 D	01385 D	01564 A	02109 A	02784 C	02979 C	03184 A
01103 A	01277 B	01386 C	01566 B	02121 B	02786 C	02983 A	03189 A
01104 C	01278 D	01387 C	01569 A	02137 A	02789 D	02986 A	03190 B
01107 B	01279 A	01388 C	01571 B	02138 C	02790 D	02988 A	03192 A
01108 A	01281 C	01391 D	01572 C	02142 D	02791 A	02989 C	03194 A
01113 C	01282 C	01392 C	01575 A	02144 B	02796 D	02992 B	03196 A
01114 D	01284 B	01393 A	01584 C	02147 C	02799 D	02993 D	03198 D
01118 B	01286 A	01394 C	01586 B	02166 A	02801 A	02998 B	03200 A
01121 C	01288 B	01395 B	01590 B	02175 A	02808 D	03002 D	03201 D
01127 C	01289 A	01396 B	01597 A	02181 D	02809 A	03005 D	03202 B
01128 A	01292 B	01397 C	01602 D	02201 B	02812 B	03009 A	03210 D
01131 C	01294 A	01402 A	01610 A	02202 C	02816 B	03016 C	03212 B
01133 B	01296 A	01404 C	01612 B	02219 A	02819 D	03018 D	03214 D
01137 A	01298 A	01405 A	01617 D	02233 D	02822 A	03019 D	03216 C
01138 D	01299 A	01406 D	01618 B	02237 D	02825 B	03022 B	03220 B
01147 D	01301 D	01408 A	01620 C	02251 D	02826 C	03026 B	03223 B
01148 A	01302 A	01414 C	01621 B	02253 A	02828 B	03028 C	03228 D
01149 A	01304 C	01415 A	01623 B	02264 A	02829 B	03029 D	03229 A
01151 A	01306 B	01416 B	01627 D	02265 B	02832 D	03032 A	03230 D
01158 C	01307 D	01422 B	01629 D	02270 C	02836 A	03046 C	03232 D
01162 B	01308 B	01424 A	01631 A	02282 A	02839 D	03047 B	03234 C
01168 C	01311 A	01426 C	01632 C	02290 D	02842 A	03048 A	03238 D
01178 C	01312 B	01428 D	01634 A	02293 C	02848 D	03049 B	03240 B
01184 B	01314 D	01429 A	01635 C	02299 A	02852 D	03052 D	03242 B

03243 D	03480 C	05408 B	05953 D	07323 C	08156 C	09097 A	09447 C
03250 D	03494 D	05418 D	06049 D	07325 C	08157 D	09101 B	09451 A
03252 A	03496 C	05455 C	06246 D	07327 C	08222 B	09107 C	09453 A
03254 B	03500 D	05457 D	06249 D	07331 B	08223 C	09111 B	09454 D
03256 C	03508 D	05461 A	06274 D	07333 B	08225 A	09113 D	09455 D
03260 A	03510 C	05463 C	06306 A	07335 A	08235 C	09115 A	09457 D
03268 B	03512 A	05465 D	06308 D	07337 C	08287 A	09121 C	09463 B
03269 D	03520 D	05467 A	06313 A	07341 D	08332 A	09125 B	09465 B
03270 A	03536 A	05471 A	06402 A	07343 D	08337 D	09129 B	09467 B
03272 C	03540 A	05473 B	06604 A	07345 A	08342 B	09130 C	09471 A
03274 B	03542 B	05475 B	06631 A	07351 B	08347 B	09137 D	09473 D
03278 D	03546 D	05479 A	06646 D	07353 A	08353 C	09181 B	09477 D
03280 D	03550 B	05481 B	06742 A	07355 D	08355 A	09183 A	09481 B
03284 B	03551 A	05485 B	06761 D	07388 B	08361 D	09185 D	09485 B
03290 A	03554 A	05486 C	06792 D	07405 B	08363 C	09187 B	09487 D
03292 C	03560 D	05487 B	06806 C	07407 D	08365 B	09191 A	09491 D
03294 B	03580 A	05491 B	06856 B	07411 C	08367 D	09193 C	09493 B
03296 A	03596 D	05493 D	06908 B	07412 C	08371 A	09195 B	09497 C
03300 A	03600 A	05495 A	06936 C	07413 B	08373 B	09197 B	09501 C
03304 D	03604 B	05505 D	06987 C	07415 D	08375 D	09205 D	09503 D
03308 C	03606 B	05507 C	06991 B	07417 B	08377 C	09246 C	09505 D
03309 C	03608 A	05511 B	07003 A	07421 B	08381 B	09276 B	09507 D
03310 D	03610 A	05513 D	07005 A	07423 D	08383 C	09282 C	09511 A
03312 A	03611 D	05515 A	07007 D	07431 D	08384 D	09307 C	09513 B
03314 B	03614 A	05517 A	07021 D	07575 A	08385 C	09311 C	09515 B
03318 D	03616 A	05521 D	07023 B	07577 D	08391 D	09313 A	09517 B
03320 A	03620 C	05522 B	07025 C	07581 A	08393 C	09315 B	09521 A
03322 B	03634 C	05523 B	07027 C	07583 D	08395 A	09317 A	09523 B
03326 A	03640 B	05525 B	07031 A	07587 D	08397 C	09321 C	09525 A
03329 C	03642 B	05527 B	07033 C	07591 B	08405 A	09323 B	09527 C
03330 D	03650 A	05531 D	07035 A	07593 A	08407 A	09325 B	09531 D
03331 D	03654 C	05533 B	07037 B	07595 A	08411 A	09327 B	09533 A
03332 C	03660 B	05535 A	07041 D	07597 C	08412 D	09331 B	09535 D
03334 B	03838 A	05541 A	07043 B	07601 C	08413 A	09333 B	09537 C
03336 A	03839 A	05543 B	07045 B	07603 A	08415 C	09335 A	09541 B
03339 B	03968 C	05545 A	07046 D	07605 C	08417 D	09337 A	09543 C
03340 D	04042 B	05547 D	07047 C	07607 C	08421 B	09341 D	09545 A
03348 C	04044 A	05551 A	07051 C	07613 A	08547 C	09343 C	09547 B
03349 B	04106 D	05553 C	07053 A	07621 A	08563 C	09347 C	09551 C
03350 B	04112 D	05555 A	07055 C	07623 B	08576 B	09351 B	09553 A
03352 A	04138 B	05557 B	07057 B	07625 A	08635 D	09357 D	09557 C
03354 C	04142 A	05561 D	07058 D	07631 D	08662 D	09361 C	09561 A
03358 C	04174 C	05563 A	07061 B	07635 D	08688 D	09362 C	09563 B
03360 C	04246 A	05565 D	07062 A	07641 C	08702 C	09363 B	09564 C
03361 C	04346 B	05567 C	07063 D	07643 C	08782 C	09365 A	09565 C
03362 A	04404 A	05571 A	07065 B	07645 B	08807 A	09367 C	09567 C
03370 D	04458 A	05573 A	07067 D	07647 D	08811 A	09371 A	09571 C
03372 D	04486 B	05575 A	07068 A	07648 B	08897 B	09373 D	09573 A
03374 B	04506 D	05577 B	07071 B	07651 C	08901 C	09375 B	09581 A
03376 D	04546 D	05585 B	07073 C	07655 D	08902 B	09377 D	09602 A
03380 D	04562 D	05591 B	07075 D	07657 C	08903 B	09381 C	09604 B
03386 D	04572 B	05595 B	07077 A	07663 B	08905 B	09382 A	09606 C
03388 B	04701 D	05597 A	07081 B	07665 B	08907 C	09383 A	09607 A
03390 B	04734 C	05598 C	07083 C	07667 D	08911 D	09385 A	
03394 B	04784 A	05648 C	07093 C	07695 D	08925 B	09387 A	
03398 A	04785 A	05655 C	07095 B	07697 C	08971 D	09391 C	
03399 D	04786 B	05657 C	07096 C	07701 D	08973 D	09397 A	
03400 C	05065 A	05697 D	07097 A	07713 D	08977 D	09411 D	
03404 B	05072 D	05711 C	07121 C	07725 B	08981 A	09412 D	
03410 B	05127 A	05751 C	07127 B	07727 A	08983 D	09413 B	
03414 B	05131 D	05753 C	07131 C	07737 D	08985 D	09414 A	
03415 A	05133 D	05763 B	07143 C	07747 D	08987 D	09415 D	
03420 B	05135 D	05824 B	07147 A	07785 A	08991 D	09425 C	
03430 C	05154 D	05825 C	07305 B	07786 B	08993 C	09427 B	
03435 C	05192 D	05845 C	07307 A	07787 B	08994 C	09431 D	
03440 A	05232 C	05901 A	07311 D	07841 C	08997 B	09435 A	
03460 C	05286 C	05917 A	07313 D	08036 C	09001 A	09437 B	
03462 D	05312 C	05921 B	07317 B	08045 D	09021 D	09441 A	
03472 C	05386 B	05923 C	07318 A	08054 B	09067 C	09443 B	
03474 D	05387 D	05951 C	07321 A	08155 C	09093 C	09445 A	

NAVIGATION
PROBLEMS

LATITUDE, LONGITUDE, DISTANCE AND COURSE

Latitude and Longitude

The earth approximates a sphere. Ignoring topography and irregularities due to density differences in the crust, the earth is actually an *oblate spheroid*, meaning that it is slightly fat around its middle. Leaving the fine points of the earth's shape and dimensions to cartographers, we will assume that the earth is a sphere.

A position on a flat piece of paper can be specified by its vertical distance from a horizontal edge of the paper and its horizontal distance from a vertical edge. Likewise, a position on a sphere can be specified by the vertical angle, or arc, from a horizontal reference plane through the sphere and the horizontal angle from a vertical reference plane through the sphere.

Latitude is the distance in degrees North or South of the Equator. *Longitude* is the distance, in degrees East or West of the Prime Meridian (also known as the Greenwich Meridian because it passes through Greenwich, England, where it was first defined).

The length of one degree of latitude is approximately the circumference of the earth around a meridian, divided by 360. The nautical mile (nm) was chosen to be the length of one minute of latitude (1´ = 1/60°). At the Equator, where the earth's horizontal circumference approximately equals its vertical circumference, the lengths of latitude and longitude degrees are nearly the same. At any other latitude, however, the length of a degree of longitude is less than that of a degree of latitude, and diminishes to zero at the poles.

Most charts used for coastal navigation are Mercator projections—what the earth would look like if projected from the center of the earth (imagine a tiny light at the center of a transparent earth) onto a cylinder tangent to the earth at the Equator. Since most charts cover a small area (typically a degree or less), the longitudinal distortion is tolerable. If you compare the lengths of latitude (vertical scale) and longitude (horizontal scale) minutes on the chart on the facing page, you will find that the longitude minute is shorter.

Find the latitude of a point by aligning a parallel rule horizontally, walking it to the point, and reading degrees, minutes, and tenths of minutes from the nearest vertical scale. Find longitude by aligning the rule vertically, walking it to the point, and reading degrees, minutes, and tenths of minutes from the nearest horizontal scale . Do this to confirm that the position of buoy "A" in the chart on the facing page is: Latitude 44° 13.8´ N and Longitude 70° 07.5´ W.

Distance

As pointed out above, distances on a nautical chart are usually measured in nautical miles (nm), where 1 nm equates to 1´of latitude. (Inland and Waterway charts are most often in statute miles, requiring the use of distance scales printed on the charts.) In the Mercator projection longitude scales are adjusted so that all distances, regardless of direction, can be measured off the vertical latitude scale. On charts covering very large areas the latitude scale does vary a small amount, so it is a good idea to use the portion of the latitude scale centered on where you are measuring.

To measure the distance between two points, hold your dividers to the vertical scale and adjust the points to exactly 1 nm (or other convenient exact distance, such as 2, 5, 10, etc. nm), then "walk" the dividers from point A to point B, counting as you go. When you get to the point where the remaining distance is less than the span of the dividers, adjust the dividers down to the remaining span, then measure the smaller span against the latitude scale to get the fraction of a nm. The total distance is the count (steps) plus the fraction.

Practice this technique to confirm the distances, D, plotted on the chart. For example, the distance between buoys "A" and "B" measures 5.3´ of latitude on the latitude scale along the right edge of the chart. The distance, D, is therefore 5.3 nm. It is customary to write the distance under the course.

Course

Charts are overprinted with one or more compass roses. The compass rose shows two sets of directions:

True—direction relative to the direction to the Geographic North Pole, indicated by the outer circle.

Magnetic—direction relative to the local lines of magnetic force, indicated by the inner circle.

Converting from magnetic to true and the reverse is covered in the chapter *Navigation General*. In this chapter we will use only true directions.

Course is the direction you intend to steer, in degrees clockwise from north. First draw a course line from a fix, or other position, in the direction you intend to steer. Using parallel rules, transfer the course line to the center of the nearest compass rose and read the direction in degrees. Write the course above the course line, as shown, preceded by C and followed by T (true) or M (magnetic). Do this to confirm that the course from buoy "A" to buoy "B" in the chart on the facing page is 082°T.

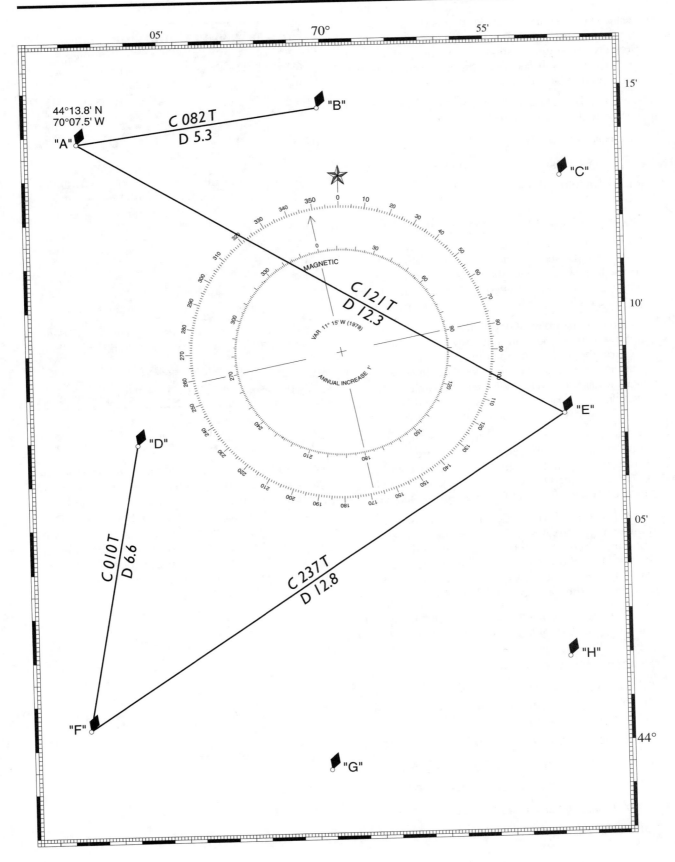

44°13.8' N
70°07.5' W

"A"

C 082 T
D 5.3

"B"

"C"

C 121 T
D 12.3

MAGNETIC

VAR 11° 15' W (1978)

ANNUAL INCREASE 1'

"D"

C 010 T
D 6.6

"E"

C 237 T
D 12.8

"H"

"F"

"G"

05'   70°   55'   15'   10'   05'   44°

DEAD RECKONING

Dead (from "deduced") reckoning is the projection of courses and speeds from a known position. The projected position is estimated, as opposed to fixed, because it doesn't take account of current, leeway, helmsman error, or unknown compass errors.

The dead reckoning (DR) plot should be drawn on a chart with pencil and updated:

• at least once per hour

• at every change of course or speed

• after any plotted line of position

Constructing a Dead Reckoning Plot

Draw a course line from the point of departure in the direction to be steered. Place the course above the course line, starting with the letter C, followed by the number of degrees, followed by T or M. Place the letter S and the speed in knots below the course line.

Indicate the point of departure by a small circle and dot—unless the point is a buoy or other obvious point on the chart—and the time horizontally with four digits. Time can be either local or Universal (formerly known as GMT). Indicate a fix from two or more lines of position (explained later in this chapter) by a similar circle and dot and the time horizontally.

Determine the first DR position by multiplying the speed by the time elapsed since departure. Transfer this distance from the latitude scale to the course line. Indicate the DR position by a small semicircle and dot, labeled with the four-digit time diagonally.

If the course changes at this point, draw a new course line in the new direction. Otherwise, extend the original course line in the same direction. Repeat the process, from DR to DR, each time using the speed and time elapsed since the previous DR to calculate the distance travelled.

Indicate an estimated position (explained later in this chapter) by a small square and dot, also labeled with a diagonal time.

Practice Problem

Copy the blank plotting sheet on Page 424 and use the following information to plot the DR shown in the chart on the next page:

0800 Depart Buoy "F" at Course 090T, Speed 10 kn

0816 Change Course to 028T, Speed to 8.5 kn

0841 Change Course to 090T, Speed to 10 kn

0904 Change Course to 042T, Speed to 8.5 kn

0929 Plot DR position

Speed, Distance and Time

Some navigators find the relationship between (S)peed, (D)istance and (T)ime to be obvious. For those not so blessed, try the following trick: Just remember the term DTs, then picture the D over the TS:

$$\frac{D}{TS}$$

To find one quantity from the other two, cover up the one you seek and what remains will be the answer. To find D, for example, cover the D and see the answer: TS.

D = TS

To find elapsed time, T, cover T and see :D/S

T = D/S

Remember to always convert fractional hours to a decimal value by dividing minutes by 60 before using it in a calculation. For example:

37 min = 37/60 = 0.62 hr

1hr 45min = 1 + 45/60 = 1.75 hr

Transfer and Advance

Large ships don't "turn on a dime." In fact, the distance travelled during a change of course can be so great that it must be figured into the DR plot—particularly when maneuvering in tight quarters. The transfer and advance characteristics of a vessel are determined and recorded by trial and then used in maneuvering. You will probably not get such questions, but just in case, here's the geometry.

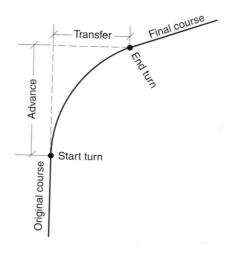

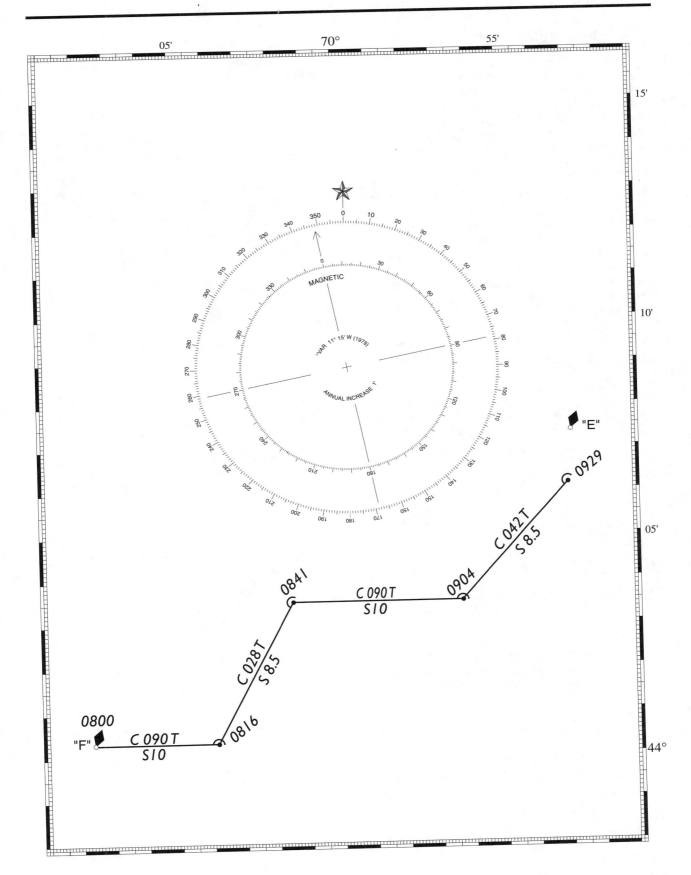

FIXES BY BEARINGS

Single Bearing

A bearing is the direction from a vessel to an object of known position, measured in degrees clockwise from north. Since there is only one line with that bearing which can be drawn through the known object, the vessel must be along the bearing line. The bearing line is, therefore, a line of position (LOP).

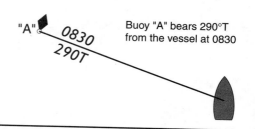

Buoy "A" bears 290°T from the vessel at 0830

Two-Bearing Fix

When you have two different LOPs, obtained by taking simultaneous (as nearly as possible) bearings on two different objects of known position, you know that you must be on both LOPs at the same time, i.e. at their intersection. The intersection of two LOPs is known as a two-bearing fix. We indicate such a fix with a small circle and dot at the intersection of the LOPs. Since this is a fix—not a DR or estimated position—we label it with the four-digit time, written horizontally.

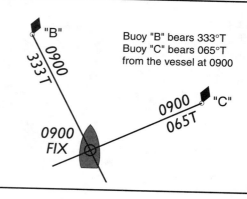

Buoy "B" bears 333°T
Buoy "C" bears 065°T
from the vessel at 0900

Three-Bearing Fix

When you have three different LOPs, obtained by taking bearings on three different objects of known position, you know that you should be at the intersection of all three LOPs. Since bearings taken from a vessel underway are subject to a few degrees uncertainty, however, the "intersection" will usually be a triangle (called the "cocked hat") formed by the three LOPs. In this case we place the circle and dot at the geometric center of the triangle, this being the most likely position. Again, label the fix with a horizontal, four-digit time.

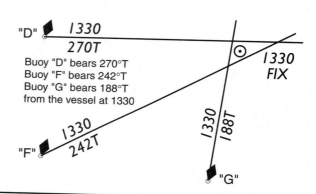

Buoy "D" bears 270°T
Buoy "F" bears 242°T
Buoy "G" bears 188°T
from the vessel at 1330

Radar Range as LOP

The distance, or range, to an object is easily and accurately obtained with radar. With this known distance from vessel to object, we can turn the range around and use it as the radius of a circular LOP centered on the known object. Circular LOPs may be combined with each other or with LOPs from bearings to obtain two-LOP and three-LOP fixes.

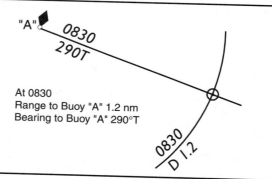

At 0830
Range to Buoy "A" 1.2 nm
Bearing to Buoy "A" 290°T

Practice Problem

Find the latitudes and longitudes of the 0900 and 1000 fixes shown on the chart on the next page. You should get, ±0.1´:

0900	44° 12.5´N	069° 55.8´W
1000	44° 03.1´N	069° 59.0´W

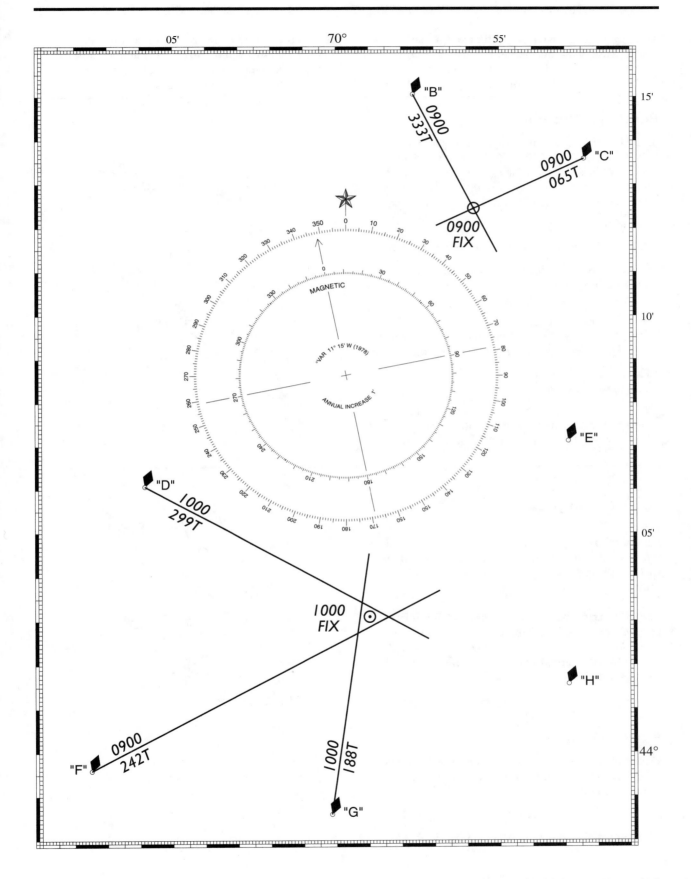

RUNNING FIXES

A running fix is a two-bearing fix except that the two bearings are taken on the same body at different times. The first bearing is taken, then advanced by DR to the time of the second bearing. Since the position of the advanced bearing is subject to the uncertainties of leeway and current during the elapsed time, the accuracy of the running fix is somewhat less than that of a simultaneous-bearing fix.

Plotting a Running Fix

In the illustration at right a bearing of 050°T is taken from the vessel to the buoy at 0900. At 0915 a bearing of 100°T is taken on the same buoy. During the time between bearing sights (0900 to 0915), the vessel remains on course 020°T at speed 6.0 knots.

To plot the fix:

• Plot the first bearing; label it with bearing and time.

• Calculate the advance of the vessel in the time elapsed between the first and second bearings (D= S x T = 6.0 x 15/60 = 1.5).

• Advance the first bearing this distance along the vessel's course—not at right angles to the bearing! Label the advanced bearing with both times.

• Plot the second bearing and label it with bearing and the second time.

• The fix is the intersection of the advanced and second bearings. Indicate the fix with a circle and dot, accompanied by "R FIX" and the four-digit time.

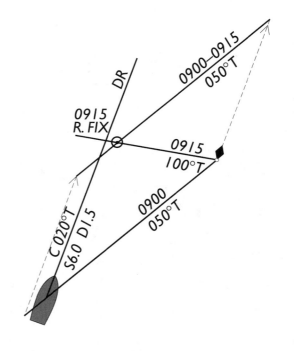

Track Not Important

One of the reasons a running fix is considered a fix, rather than a DR position or estimated position, is that the precise location of the vessel's track is not important.

In the illustration at right two parallel DR tracks are plotted. It makes no difference to the final solution which track—DR1 or DR2—we use to advance bearing 1. Only the direction of bearing one is important to the solution.

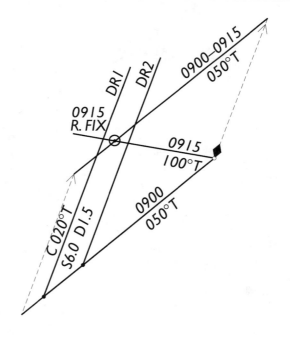

Practice Problem

Find the latitudes and longitudes of the 0900 and 1000 fixes shown on the chart on the next page. You should get, ±0.1´:

| 0411/1440 | 44° 13.0´N | 070° 03.6´W |
| 0630/0707 | 43° 59.6´N | 069° 58.7´W |

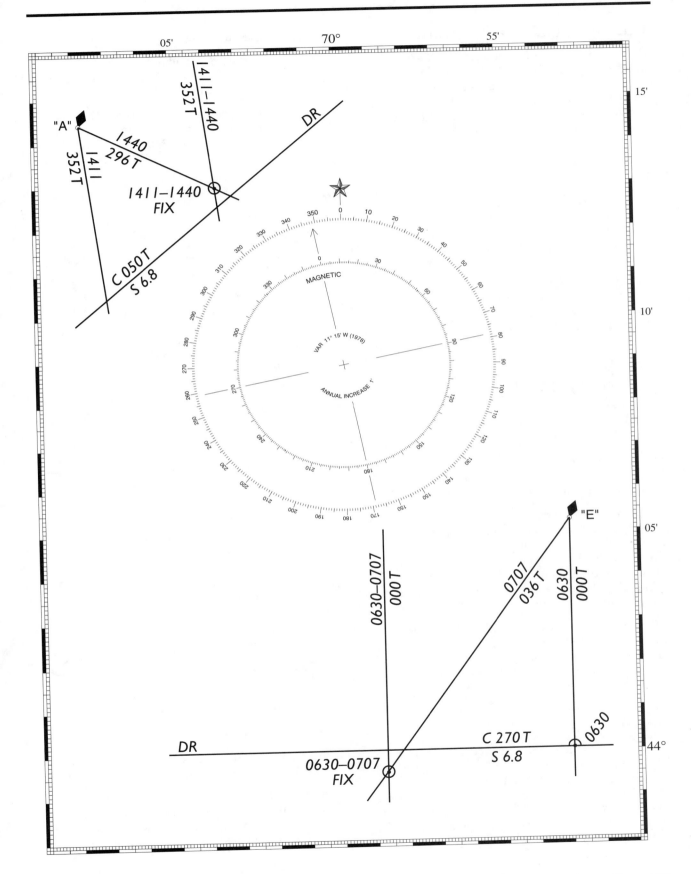

RELATIVE BEARINGS AND DISTANCE OFF

Relative Angles/Relative Bearings

Courses and bearings are measured clockwise, 0–360°, from either True North or Magnetic North. Relative angles and relative bearings are taken relative to the course or vessel's fore-and-aft line. Relative angles are 0–180° to port or starboard of the bow. Relative bearing are 0–360° clockwise from the bow.

In the illustration below:

Vessel 1: Course 020°T ; buoy "A" bears 050°T
              Relative angle = 030° to starboard
              Relative bearing = 030°

Vessel 2: Course 340°T; buoy "A" bears 310°T
              Relative angle = 30° to port
              Relative bearing = 330°

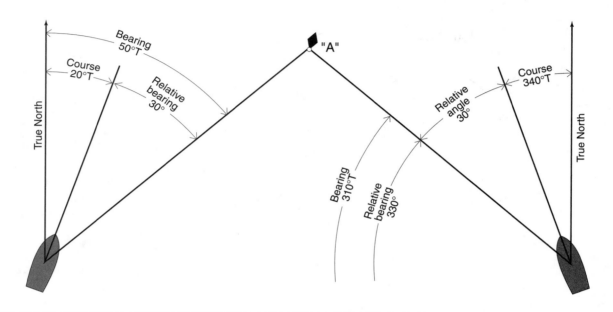

Doubling the Angle on the Bow

Relative angles have a valuable property. If a vessel maintains a steady course, and the relative angle to a fixed point doubles, then the distance from the vessel to the point at the time of the second sight equals the distance travelled between first and second sights. The trick works for all relative angles from 0° to 90°.

The trick also also works in reverse for relative angles from 90° to 180°, where the distance off is from the first sight. The special case of the relative angle pair of 45°/90° is called taking "bow-and-beam bearings."

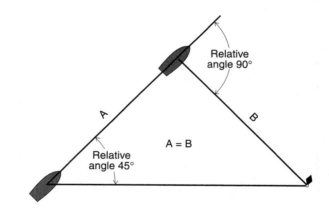

Distance Off

Distance off is the distance from the vessel to a fixed object. Most "distance off" problems are really nothing more than running fixes (see previous page) where the distance from the sighted object is measured with dividers from the fix position or at right angles from the extended course line. The practice problem offers an example.

Practice Problem

Use a blank plotting sheet to solve the problem below. Our solution is shown on the chart at right.

Your vessel is on a course of 297°T at 11 knots. At 0019 a light bears 274.5°T, and at 0048 the light bears 252°T. At what time and at what distance off will your vessel be when abeam of the light?

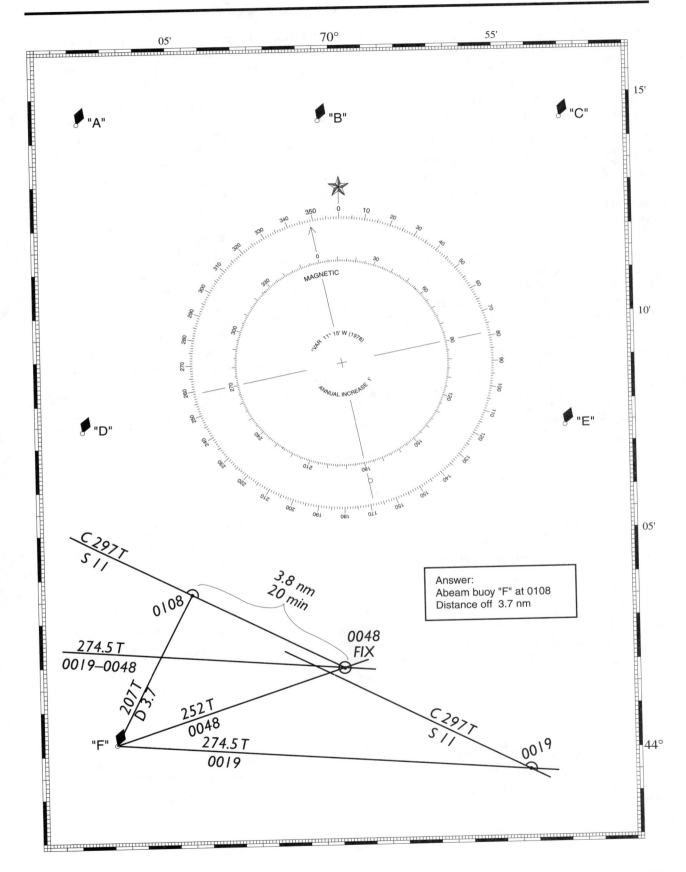

05'   70°   55'

15'

"A"

"B"

"C"

340   350   0   10
330   20
320   30
310   40
300   MAGNETIC   50
300   30   60
330   70
290   10'
280   VAR 11° 15' W (1978)   80
270   90   90
270   90
260   ANNUAL INCREASE 1'   100
250   120
240   110
230   120
220   130
210   140
200   180   170   150
210 190   160

"D"

"E"

05'

C 297 T
S 11

0108

3.8 nm
20 min

0048
FIX

274.5 T
0019–0048

Answer:
Abeam buoy "F" at 0108
Distance off 3.7 nm

207 T
D 3.7

252 T
0048

C 297 T
S 11

"F"

274.5 T
0019

0019

44°

CURRENT SET AND DRIFT

Current is horizontal flow of water. In bays and estuaries, current is most often tidal; offshore it is more often caused by steady winds. Current is described by two terms:

- *Set* is the direction toward which it is flowing, i.e. a set of 090°T is "setting to the east."

- *Drift* is the speed of the flow over the bottom

A vessel has course and speed. A current has set and drift. The motion of the water can be calculated in the same way we calculate motion of a vessel. The motion of the vessel over ground is thus the motion of the vessel through the water plus the motion of the water over ground.

When a vessel's course is parallel to the current's set, calculating vessel speed over the ground (SOG) is simple: just add or subtract current drift to or from vessel speed, depending on whether the current is with or against the vessel.

Example: A vessel is on course 270°T at 10 knots. There is a current setting 090°T at 2 knots. The vessel's SOG is thus 10 knots - 2 knots = 8 knots.

The illustration below shows the general effects of current on a vessel's track.

Quantities having both magnitude and direction are called vectors. Vessel speed and current are both vectors. The great thing about vectors is that they can be added by plotting them head-to-tail.

The top example on the chart at right demonstrates the concept. A vessel departs buoy "A" at 1330 on course 082°T at speed 9.8 knots. At 1417 (47 minutes after departure) the vessel has advanced 9.8 × 47/60 = 7.7 nm along the course line. During the same 47 minutes the current has been setting 135°T at 2.0 knots. The water has thus shifted 2.0 × 47/60 = 1.6 nm on a course of 135°T. The net effect is exactly as if the vessel sailed both legs, and the problem is solved in the same manner.

The bottom example turns the problem around to determine the set and drift of a current which would cause the observed offset between a DR position and a fix. The vessel departs buoy "F" at 1330 on course 082°T at speed 9.8 knots. At 1417 (47 minutes after departure) the vessel has, absent any current, advanced 9.8 × 47/60 = 7.7 nm along the course line. At the same time a fix is obtained from bearings on buoys "G" and "H". The set is measured to be 339°T; the drift is calculated as distance/time, 2.0 nm/(47/60 hr) = 2.6 knots.

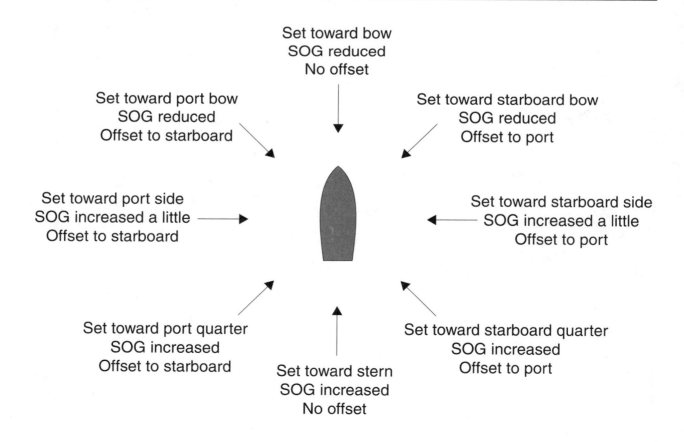

Set toward bow
SOG reduced
No offset

Set toward port bow
SOG reduced
Offset to starboard

Set toward starboard bow
SOG reduced
Offset to port

Set toward port side
SOG increased a little
Offset to starboard

Set toward starboard side
SOG increased a little
Offset to port

Set toward port quarter
SOG increased
Offset to starboard

Set toward starboard quarter
SOG increased
Offset to port

Set toward stern
SOG increased
No offset

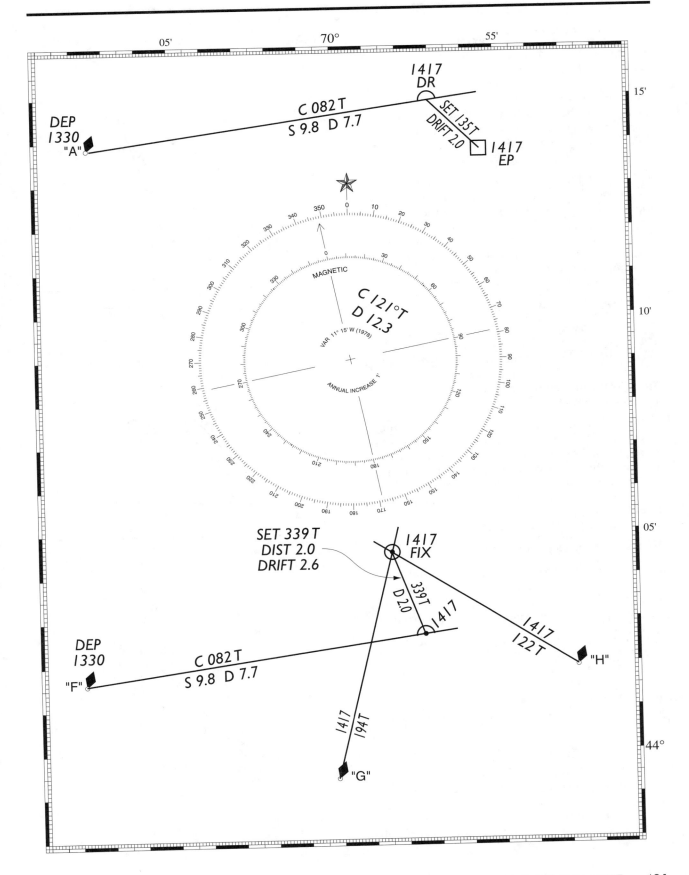

CURRENT VECTORS/COURSE TO STEER

Current Vectors

As we saw in the previous section, any motion which can be specified by a speed and a direction is a vector. Both vessel speed through the water and current are such motions. Here we will refine the concept by adding arrow heads to the vectors to show their directions and to remind us that vectors can be added, tail to head, to find net, or resultant, motion.

In illustration 1 a vessel is steering course 020°T at speed 5.0 knots. It is subject to a current of set 082°T and drift 2.9 knots. The resultant motion over the bottom is the vector drawn from the tail of the first vector, A, to the head of the second vector, C. The direction of the resultant motion is called the *track*. The speed over the bottom is called the *speed over ground (SOG)*.

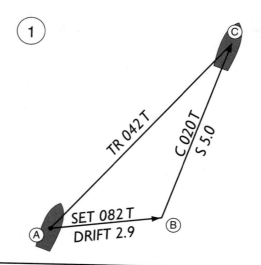

Finding Track and SOG

The simplest way to determine the track and SOG is to plot motion for one hour. Since distance is proportional to speed, and since distance advanced in one hour is numerically the same as speed, we can read the length of the resultant vector directly as SOG.

In illustration 2 draw the current vector in the direction of the set, 082°T, and of length equal to the drift, 2.9 nm. From the head of the current vector, draw the vessel's course vector of length equal to the distance travelled through the water in one hour, 5.0 nm. Connect points A and C and read the track and SOG, 042°T and 6.8 knots.

Finding Course to Steer

Use current vectors to determine course to steer to make good a course to a destination. We use the same vector triangle as above except now the known vectors are track (course made good) and current.

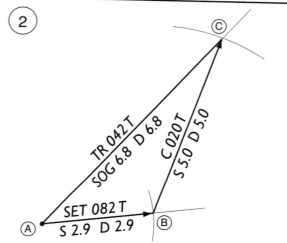

In illustration 3 draw the track from point of departure, A, to destination, D. Next draw the 1-hour current vector, A-B. From the head of the current vector, B, swing an arc of radius equal to speed to intersect the track. The length of vector A-C is SOG. The direction of vector B-C is course to steer (CTS).

Practice Problem

Using a blank plotting sheet (photocopy the blank plotting sheet on Page 424), find the course to steer through a current of set 114°T and drift 2.9 knots if the destination bears 073°T and your vessel's speed is 5.0 knots. Our solution is plotted on the chart at right.

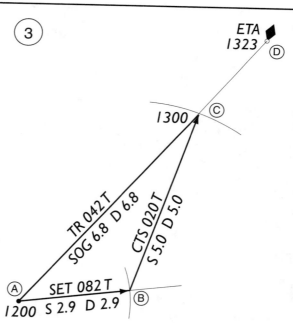

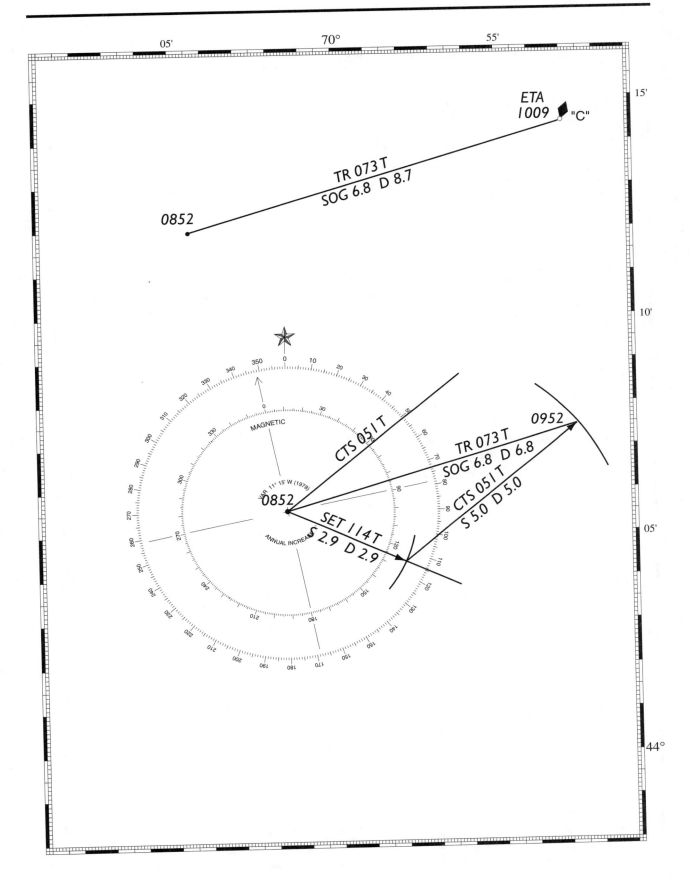

ETA 1009 ◆ "C"

TR 073 T
SOG 6.8 D 8.7

0852

CTS 051 T

MAGNETIC

VAR 11° 15' W (1978)

ANNUAL INCREASE

SET 114 T
S 2.9 D 2.9

0952

TR 073 T
SOG 6.8 D 6.8

CTS 051 T
S 5.0 D 5.0

0852

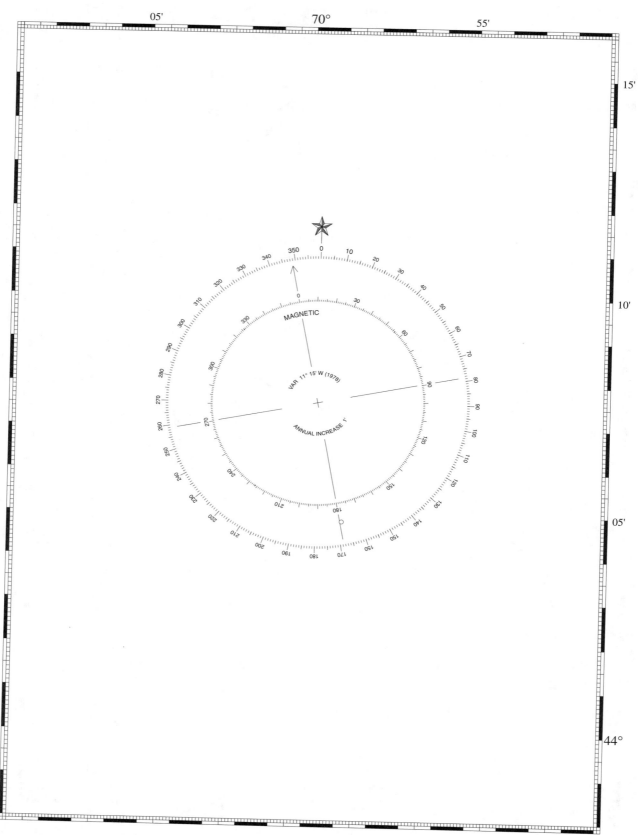

NAVIGATION PROBLEM QUESTIONS

02651. You are steering 246° T, and a light is picked up dead ahead at a distance of 14 miles at 1037. You change course to pass the light 2.5 miles off abeam to port. If you are making 12 knots, what is your ETA at the position 2.5 miles off the light?

A. 1143
B. 1146
C. 1149
D. 1152

02652. You are steering 163° T, and a light is picked up dead ahead at a distance of 11 miles at 0142. You change course to pass the light 2 miles off abeam to starboard. If you are making 13 knots, what is your ETA at the position 2 miles off the light?

A. 0226
B. 0229
C. 0232
D. 0235

02653. You are steering 019° T, and a light is picked up dead ahead at a distance of 11.6 miles at 0216. You change course to pass the light 3 miles off abeam to port. If you are making 14 knots, what is your ETA at the position 3 miles off the light?

A. 0258
B. 0301
C. 0304
D. 0307

02654. You are steering 231° T, and a light is picked up dead ahead at a distance of 12.3 miles at 0338. You change course to pass the light 4 miles off abeam to starboard. If you are making 16.5 knots, what is your ETA at the position 4 miles off the light?

A. 0420
B. 0423
C. 0426
D. 0429

02655. You are steering 078° T, and a light is picked up dead ahead at a distance of 15.6 miles at 2316. You change course to pass the light 4.5 miles off abeam to port. If you are making 17 knots, what is your ETA at the position 4.5 miles off the light?

A. 0006
B. 0009
C. 0012
D. 0015

02656. You are steering 257° T, and a light is picked up dead ahead at a distance of 13.3 miles at 2016. You change course to pass the

light 4 miles off abeam to starboard. If you are making 18.5 knots, what is your ETA at the position 4 miles off the light?

A. 2057
B. 2100
C. 2103
D. 2113

02657. You are steering 349° T, and a light is picked up dead ahead at a distance of 17.2 miles at 2122. You change course to pass the light 4.5 miles off abeam to port. If you are making 19.5 knots, what is your ETA at the position 4.5 miles off the light?

A. 2207
B. 2210
C. 2213
D. 2216

02658. You are steering 202° T, and a light is picked up dead ahead at a distance of 14.6 miles at 2234. You change course to pass the light 5 miles off abeam to starboard. If you are making 21 knots, what is your ETA at the position 5 miles off the light?

A. 2310
B. 2313
C. 2316
D. 2319

02659. You are steering 115° T, and a light is picked up dead ahead at a distance of 16.7 miles at 0522. You change course to pass the light 3.5 miles off abeam to port. If you are making 12 knots, what is your ETA at the position 3.5 miles off the light?

A. 0644
B. 0647
C. 0650
D. 0653

02660. You are steering 287° T, and a light is picked up dead ahead at a distance of 19.4 miles at 0419. You change course to pass the light 4 miles off abeam to starboard. If you are making 13 knots, what is your ETA at the position 4 miles off the light?

A. 0541
B. 0544
C. 0547
D. 0550

02661. You are steering 143° T, and a light is picked up dead ahead at a distance of 18.2 miles at 2006. You change course to pass the light 5.5 miles off abeam to port. If you are making 14.5 knots, what is your ETA at the position 5.5 miles off the light?

A. 2115
B. 2118
C. 2121
D. 2124

02662. You are on course 006° T, speed 16.6 knots. At 0516 you see a light bearing 008° T at a range of 10.2. If you change course at 0528 to leave the light abeam to port at 1.0 mile, at what time will the light be abeam?

A. 0553
B. 0556
C. 0604
D. 0607

02663. You are on course 035° T, speed 18.3 knots. At 0719 you see a buoy bearing 036° T at a range of 4.1. If you change course at 0725 to leave the buoy abeam to port at 1.0 mile, at what time will the buoy be abeam?

A. 0740
B. 0738
C. 0735
D. 0732

02664. You are on course 061° T, speed 12.4 knots. At 0839 you see a rock bearing 059° T at a range of 4.4 miles. If you change course at 0845 to leave the rock abeam to starboard at 1.5 mile, at what time will the rock be abeam?

A. 0854
B. 0859
C. 0903
D. 0906

02665. You are on course 079° T, speed 11.2 knots. At 0904 you see a daymark bearing 078° T at a range of 4.6. If you change course at 0910 to leave the daymark abeam to starboard at 0.5 mile, at what time will the daymark be abeam?

A. 0918
B. 0923
C. 0928
D. 0935

02666. You are on course 086° T, speed 11.7 knots. At 1013 you see a buoy bearing 088° T at a range of 4.8 miles. If you change course at 1019 to leave the buoy abeam to port at 1.0 mile, at what time will the buoy be abeam?

A. 1037
B. 1040
C. 1043
D. 1052

02667. Your vessel is on a course of 255° T, at 14 knots. At 2126 a lighthouse is sighted dead ahead at a distance of 11 miles. You change course at this time to pass the lighthouse 3 miles abeam to port. What will be your ETA at this position off the lighthouse?

A. 2149
B. 2201
C. 2211
D. 2228

02668. Your vessel is on a course of 255° T, at 14 knots. At 2116 a lighthouse is sighted dead ahead at a distance of 11 miles. You change course at this time to pass the lighthouse 3 miles abeam to port. What will be your ETA at this position off the lighthouse?

A. 2149
B. 2201
C. 2212
D. 2228

02669. You are steering 143° T, and a light is picked up dead ahead at a distance of 18.2 miles at 2006. You change course to pass the light 5.5 miles off abeam to port. If you are making 14.5 knots, what is your ETA at a position 5.5 miles off the light?

A. 2115
B. 2118
C. 2121
D. 2124

02670. You are steering 173° T, and a light is picked up dead ahead at a distance of 13.9 miles at 0054. You change course to pass the light 4.5 miles off abeam to port. If you are making 21 knots, what is your ETA at the position 4.5 miles off the light?

A. 0122
B. 0125
C. 0131
D. 0134

02671. While on a course of 349° T, a light bears 13° on the starboard bow at a distance of 10.8 miles. What course should you steer to pass 2.5 miles abeam of the light leaving it to starboard?

A. 346° T
B. 349° T
C. 352° T
D. 355° T

02672. While on a course of 283° pgc, a light bears 10° on the port bow at a distance of 8.3 miles. What course should you steer to pass 3.5 miles abeam of the light leaving it to port?

A. 289° pgc
B. 294° pgc
C. 298° pgc
D. 302° pgc

02673. At 2221 your course is 222° pgc at a speed of 11.2 knots, when radar detects a buoy bearing 355° relative, at a range of 5.8 miles. The gyro error is 2° E. If you change course at 2226, what course should you steer to leave the buoy 1.0 mile abeam to port?

A. 206° pgc
B. 210° pgc
C. 228° pgc
D. 231° pgc

02674. You are stearing on course 126° T at 14.8 knots. At 1022 you sight a buoy bearing 128° T, at a range of 4.8 miles. If you change course at 1026, what true course will you steer to leave the buoy 0.5 mile abeam to port?

A. 136°
B. 133°
C. 122°
D. 119°

02675. At 1423 you are on course 072° T, at 12.2 knots, when you sight a rock awash bearing 070° T at a range of 3.6 miles. If you change course at 1427, what course would you steer to leave the rock 1.0 mile abeam to port?

A. 049°
B. 054°
C. 086°
D. 091°

02676. While on a course of 019° pgc, a light bears 14° on the port bow at a distance of 15.3 miles. What course should you steer to pass 1.5 miles abeam of the light, leaving it to port?

A. 006° pgc
B. 011° pgc
C. 013° pgc
D. 015° pgc

02677. You sight a light 9° on your starboard bow at a distance of 21 miles. Assuming you make good your course, what will be your distance off the light when abeam?

A. 3.3 miles
B. 3.7 miles
C. 4.0 miles
D. 4.3 miles

02678. You are running coastwise on a course of 323° T, and you have a buoy bearing 11° on your port bow at a distance of 7 miles. You desire to leave the buoy abeam to port at a distance of 2.5 miles. What course should you steer?

A. 291° T
B. 312° T
C. 333° T
D. 344° T

02679. You are underway on a course of 135° pgc at 15 knots, and you sight a lighthouse dead ahead at a range of 12.5 miles at 1145. What course would you steer to leave the lighthouse 3.0 miles off your port beam?

A. 117° pgc
B. 121° pgc
C. 149° pgc
D. 154° pgc

02680. While on course 321° pgc with a 1° W gyro error, you pick up a buoy on radar bearing 001° relative at 5.2 miles. What will be the course to pass the buoy by 1 mile abeam to starboard, if you change course when the buoy is 4.5 miles away?

A. 305° T
B. 310° pgc
C. 316° T
D. 336° pgc

02681. Your vessel is on course 312° pgc and you sight a lighthouse dead ahead at a range of 10 miles. The gyro error is 3° E. What course would you steer to leave the lighthouse 1.5 miles abeam to starboard?

A. 309° pgc
B. 304° pgc
C. 309° T
D. 304° T

02682. While on a course of 066° pgc, a light bears 18° on the port bow at a distance of 12.3 miles. What course should you steer to leave the light 4 miles abeam to port?

A. 067° pgc
B. 072° pgc
C. 079° pgc
D. 085° pgc

02683. You are underway on a course of 135° pgc at 15 knots, and you sight a lighthouse dead ahead at a range of 12.5 miles at 1145. What course would you steer to leave the lighthouse 3.0 miles off your port beam?

A. 117° pgc
B. 121° pgc
C. 149° pgc
D. 154° pgc

02684. You are steering 173° T, and a light is picked up dead ahead at a distance of 13.9 miles at 0054. You change course to pass the light 4.5 miles off abeam to port. If you are making 21 knots, what is your ETA at the position 4.5 miles off the light?

A. 0122
B. 0125
C. 0131
D. 0134

02685. You are steering 031° T, and a light is picked up dead ahead at a distance of 12.7 miles at 0017. You change course to pass the light 3.5 miles off abeam to starboard. If you are making 11 knots, what is your ETA at the position 3.5 miles off the light?

A. 0118
B. 0121
C. 0124
D. 0127

02686. While on a course of 034° pgc, a light bears 8° on the port bow at a distance of 8.8 miles. What course should you steer to pass 2.5 miles abeam of the light leaving it to port?

A. 039° pgc
B. 043° pgc
C. 051° pgc
D. 059° pgc

02687. While on a course of 321° T, a light bears 7° on the starboard bow at a distance of 9.7 miles. What course should you steer to pass 3.5 miles abeam of the light leaving it to starboard?

A. 297° T
B. 300° T
C. 303° T
D. 307° T

02688. While on a course of 214° pgc, a light bears 9° on the port bow at a distance of 7.4 miles. What course should you steer to pass 2 miles abeam of the light leaving it to port?

A. 189° pgc
B. 209° pgc
C. 221° pgc
D. 229° pgc

02689. You are steering 107° T, and a light is picked up dead ahead at a distance of 11 miles at 0847. You change course to leave the light 3 miles off to starboard. If you are making 15.5 knots, what is your ETA at the position 3 miles off the light?

A. 0928
B. 0931
C. 0934
D. 0937

02690. While on a course of 066° pgc, a light bears 13° on the port bow at a distance of 12.3 miles. What course should you steer to pass 4 miles abeam of the light leaving it to port?

A. 067° pgc
B. 072° pgc
C. 079° pgc
D. 085° pgc

02691. While on a course of 159° T, a light bears 11° on the starboard bow at a distance of 10.6 miles. What course should you steer to pass 2 miles abeam of the light leaving it to starboard?

A. 159° T
B. 163° T
C. 167° T
D. 171° T

02692. While on a course of 097° pgc, a light bears 8° on the port bow at a distance of 11.7 miles. What course should you steer to pass 3 miles abeam of the light leaving it to port?

A. 082° pgc
B. 091° pgc
C. 104° pgc
D. 112° pgc

02693. While on a course of 279° T, a light bears 12° on the starboard bow at a distance of 9.3 miles. What course should you steer to pass 4 miles abeam of the light leaving it to starboard?

A. 253° T
B. 265° T
C. 291° T
D. 305° T

02694. While on a course of 152° T, a light bears 9° on the port bow at a distance of 11.6 miles. What course should you steer to pass 3 miles abeam of the light leaving it to port?

A. 153°
B. 158°
C. 163°
D. 167°

02695. You are underway on course 017° T at a speed of 14.2 knots. You sight a buoy bearing 025° T at a radar range of 3.7 miles at 1947. If you change course at 1953, what is the course to steer to leave the buoy abeam to starboard at 0.1 mile?

A. 021° T
B. 024° T
C. 027° T
D. 030° T

02696. You are underway on course 059° T at a speed of 13.8 knots. You sight a light bearing 064° T at a radar range of 5.1 miles at 1839. If you change course at 1845, what is the course to steer to leave the light abeam to starboard at 1.0 mile?

A. 047° T
B. 050° T
C. 052° T
D. 058° T

02697. You are underway on course 106° T at a speed of 15.3 knots. You sight a buoy bearing 109° T at a radar range of 3.6 miles at 1725. If you change course at 1728, what is the course to steer to leave the buoy abeam to port at 0.5 mile?

A. 100° T
B. 117° T
C. 120° T
D. 125° T

02698. While on a course of 138° T, a light bears 14° on the starboard bow at a distance of 8.6 miles. What course should you steer to pass 3 miles abeam of the light leaving it to starboard?

A. 132° T
B. 135° T
C. 138° T
D. 141° T

02699. You are underway on course 137° T at a speed of 16.2 knots. You sight a rock bearing 134° T at a radar range of 4.6 miles at 1508. If you change course at 1514, what is the course to steer to leave the rock abeam to port at 1.5 miles?

A. 162° T
B. 160° T
C. 158° T
D. 154° T

02700. You are underway on course 163° T at a speed of 15.8 knots. You sight a buoy bearing 161° T at a radar range of 5.5 miles at 1319. If you change course at 1325, what is the course to steer to leave the buoy abeam to starboard at 1.0 mile?

A. 145° T
B. 148° T
C. 151° T
D. 175° T

02701. You are underway on course 204° T at a speed of 17.3 knots. You sight a light bearing 205° T at a radar range of 4.7 miles at 1222. If you change course at 1228, what is the course to steer to leave the light abeam to port at 1.5 miles?

A. 223° T
B. 229° T
C. 236° T
D. 240° T

02702. You are underway on course 241° T at a speed of 18.2 knots. You sight a daymark bearing 241° T at a radar range of 3.9 miles at 1006. If you change course at 1009, what is the course to steer to leave the daymark abeam to starboard at 1.0 mile?

A. 220° T
B. 223° T
C. 257° T
D. 260° T

02703. You are underway on course 254° T at a speed of 16.5 knots. You sight a rock bearing 255° T at a radar range of 6.1 miles at 0916. If you change course at 0922, what is the course to steer to leave the rock abeam to starboard at 1.5 miles?

A. 268° T
B. 239° T
C. 236° T
D. 233° T

02704. You are underway on course 340° T at a speed of 14.8 knots. You sight a buoy bearing 342° T at a radar range of 4.8 miles at 1422. If you change course at 1428, what is the course to steer to leave the buoy abeam to port at 1.0 mile?

A. 327° T
B. 354° T
C. 357° T
D. 001° T

02705. While on a course of 192° T, a light bears 11° on the starboard bow at a distance of 12.7 miles. What course should you steer to pass 3 miles abeam of the light leaving it to starboard?

A. 167° T
B. 173° T
C. 185° T
D. 189° T

02706. While on a course of 216° pgc, a light bears 12° on the port bow at a distance of 11.2 miles. What course should you steer to pass 2 miles abeam of the light leaving it to port?

A. 208° pgc
B. 210° pgc
C. 212° pgc
D. 214° pgc

02707. You are underway on course 128° T at a speed of 17.6 knots. You sight a daymark bearing 126° T at a radar range of 4.3 miles at 1649. If you change course at 1654, what is the course to steer to leave the daymark abeam to starboard at 0.5 mile?

A. 113° T
B. 116° T
C. 119° T
D. 136° T

02851. Your vessel is on a course of 297° T at 11 knots. At 0019 a light bears 274.5° T, and at 0048 the light bears 252° T. At what time and at what distance off will your vessel be when abeam of the light?

A. 0102, 2.6 miles
B. 0108, 3.7 miles
C. 0057, 4.6 miles
D. 0117, 5.0 miles

02852. Your vessel is on a course of 129° T at 13 knots. At 1937 a light bears 151.5° T, and at 2003 the light bears 174° T. At what time and at what distance off will your vessel be when abeam of the light?

A. 2016, 2.8 miles
B. 2016, 3.9 miles
C. 2021, 3.9 miles
D. 2021, 2.8 miles

02853. Your vessel is on a course of 343° T at 14 knots. At 2156 a light bears 320.5° T, and at 2217 the light bears 298° T. At what time and at what distance off will your vessel be when abeam of the light?

A. 2232, 3.4 miles
B. 2235, 4.3 miles
C. 2228, 4.9 miles
D. 2241, 6.9 miles

02854. Your vessel is on a course of 221° T at 15 knots. At 0319 a light bears 198.5° T, and at 0353 the light bears 176° T. At what time and at what distance off will your vessel be when abeam of the light?

A. 0407, 4.3 miles
B. 0410, 5.2 miles
C. 0417, 6.0 miles
D. 0427, 7.4 miles

02855. Your vessel is on a course of 107° T at 16 knots. At 0403 a light bears 129.5° T, and at

0426 the light bears 152° T. At what time and at what distance off will your vessel be when abeam of the light?

A. 0434, 3.2 miles
B. 0442, 4.3 miles
C. 0434, 4.3 miles
D. 0442, 3.4 miles

02856. Your vessel is on a course of 034° T at 17 knots. At 0551 a light bears 056.5° T, and at 0623 the light bears 079° T. At what time and at what distance off will your vessel be when abeam of the light?

A. 0636, 5.9 miles
B. 0645, 5.9 miles
C. 0636, 6.4 miles
D. 0645, 6.4 miles

02857. Your vessel is on a course of 253° T at 18 knots. At 2027 a light bears 275.5° T, and at 2055 the light bears 298° T. At what time and at what distance off will your vessel be when abeam of the light?

A. 2115, 5.9 miles
B. 2109, 6.4 miles
C. 2123, 7.3 miles
D. 2104, 7.7 miles

02858. Your vessel is on a course of 082° T at 19 knots. At 0255 a light bears 059.5° T, and at 0312 the light bears 037° T. At what time and at what distance off will your vessel be when abeam of the light?

A. 0333, 5.1 miles
B. 0321, 4.7 miles
C. 0327, 4.3 miles
D. 0324, 3.8 miles

02859. Your vessel is on a course of 307° T at 20 knots. At 0914 a light bears 284.5° T, and at 0937 the light bears 262° T. At what time and at what distance off will your vessel be when abeam of the light?

A. 0950, 4.4 miles
B. 0953, 5.4 miles
C. 0957, 6.6 miles
D. 1002, 7.1 miles

02860. Your vessel is on a course of 144° T at 16 knots. At 0126 a light bears 166.5° T, and at 0152 the light bears 189° T. At what time and at what distance off will your vessel be when abeam of the light?

A. 0205, 4.1 miles
B. 0210, 4.8 miles
C. 0215, 6.0 miles
D. 0220, 6.4 miles

02861. Your vessel is on a course of 196° T at 17 knots. At 0417 a light bears 218.5° T, and at 0442 the light bears 241° T. At what time and at what distance off will your vessel be when abeam of the light?

A. 0500, 5.0 miles
B. 0504, 6.2 miles
C. 0500, 6.2 miles
D. 0504, 5.0 miles

02862. Your are on course 317° T at 13 knots. A light is bearing 22.5° relative at 0640. At 0659 the same light is bearing 45° relative. At what time should the light be abeam?

A. 0709
B. 0712
C. 0718
D. 0721

02863. Your vessel is underway on a course of 115° T at 18 knots. At 1850 a lighthouse bears 137.5° T. At 1920 the same lighthouse bears 160° T. What time will the lighthouse pass abeam to starboard?

A. 1929
B. 1941
C. 1949
D. 1955

02864. You are steering a course of 316° T, and a light bears 34° on the port bow at 2053. At 2126 the same light bears 68° on the port bow, and you have run 5 miles since the first bearing. What is the ETA when the lighthouse is abeam?

A. 2139
B. 2143
C. 2149
D. 2159

02865. You are steering a course of 240° T, and a lighthouse bears 025° on the starboard bow at 2116. At 2144 the same lighthouse bears 050° on the starboard bow, and you have run 6 miles since the first bearing. What is the ETA when the lighthouse is abeam?

A. 2156
B. 2159
C. 2202
D. 2205

02866. Your vessel is on a course of 311° T at 21 knots. At 1957 a light bears 337.5° T, and at 2018 the light bears 356° T. At what time and at what distance off will your vessel be when abeam of the light?

A. 2027, 5.2 miles
B. 2033, 6.8 miles
C. 2039, 7.4 miles
D. 2043, 10.3 miles

02867. Your vessel is on a course of 144° T at 20 knots. At 0022 a light bears 117.5° T, and at 0035 the light bears 099° T. At what time and at what distance off will your vessel be when abeam of the light?

A. 0044, 3.2 miles
B. 0048, 4.3 miles
C. 0052, 5.1 miles
D. 0056, 6.0 miles

02868. Your vessel is on a course of 358° T at 19 knots. At 0316 a light bears 024.5° T, and at 0334 the light bears 043° T. At what time and at what distance off will your vessel be when abeam of the light?

A. 0352, 5.7 miles
B. 0355, 6.2 miles
C. 0359, 7.1 miles
D. 0403, 8.0 miles

02869. Your vessel is on a course of 237° T at 18 knots. At 0404 a light bears 263.5° T, and at 0430 the light bears 282° T. At what time and at what distance off will your vessel be when abeam of the light?

A. 0448, 6.8 miles
B. 0452, 7.2 miles
C. 0456, 7.8 miles
D. 0500, 8.4 miles

02870. Your vessel is on a course of 126° T at 17 knots. At 0251 a light bears 099.5° T, and at 0313 the light bears 081° T. At what time and at what distance off will your vessel be when abeam of the light?

A. 0327, 4.4 miles
B. 0335, 6.2 miles
C. 0345, 6.8 miles
D. 0351, 7.4 miles

02871. Your vessel is on a course of 052° T at 16 knots. At 0916 a light bears 078.5° T, and at 0927 the light bears 097° T. At what time and at what distance off will your vessel be when abeam of the light?

A. 0929, 2.0 miles
B. 0932, 2.3 miles
C. 0935, 2.6 miles
D. 0938, 2.9 miles

02872. Your vessel is on a course of 272° T at 15 knots. At 2113 a light bears 245.5° T, and at 2120 the light bears 227° T. At what time and

at what distance off will your vessel be when abeam of the light?

A. 2124, 1.3 miles
B. 2127, 1.8 miles
C. 2131, 2.3 miles
D. 2135, 2.7 miles

02873. Your vessel is on a course of 103° T at 14 knots. At 1918 a light bears 129.5° T, and at 1937 the light bears 148° T. At what time and at what distance off will your vessel be when abeam of the light?

A. 1947, 2.8 miles
B. 1950, 3.2 miles
C. 1953, 3.8 miles
D. 1956, 4.4 miles

02874. Your vessel is on a course of 207° T at 13 knots. At 0539 a light bears 180.5° T, and at 0620 the light bears 162° T. At what time and at what distance off will your vessel be when abeam of the light?

A. 0633, 5.9 miles
B. 0641, 6.5 miles
C. 0653, 7.6 miles
D. 0701, 8.9 miles

02875. Your vessel is on a course of 316° T at 12 knots. At 2326 a light bears 289.5° T, and at 2354 the light bears 271° T. At what time and at what distance off will your vessel be when abeam of the light?

A. 0014, 4.8 miles
B. 0018, 5.2 miles
C. 0022, 5.6 miles
D. 0026, 6.4 miles

02877. Your vessel is steering 263° T at 22 knots. At 0413 a light bears 294° T, and at 0421 the same light bears 312° T. What will be your distance off abeam?

A. 3.4 miles
B. 3.7 miles
C. 4.3 miles
D. 4.9 miles

02878. Your vessel is steering 143° T at 16 knots. At 2147 a light bears 106° T, and at 2206 the same light bears 078° T. What will be your distance off abeam?

A. 5.1 miles
B. 5.4 miles
C. 5.9 miles
D. 6.5 miles

02879. Your vessel is steering 354° T at 14 knots. At 0317 a light bears 049° T, and at

0342 the same light bears 071° T. What will be your distance off abeam?

A. 12.4 miles
B. 12.7 miles
C. 13.0 miles
D. 13.3 miles

02880. Your vessel is steering 218° T at 19 knots. At 2223 a light bears 261° T, and at 2234 the same light bears 289° T. What will be your distance off abeam?

A. 4.3 miles
B. 4.8 miles
C. 5.1 miles
D. 5.4 miles

02881. Your vessel is steering 049° T at 15 knots. At 1914 a light bears 078° T, and at 1951 the same light bears 116° T. What will be your distance off abeam?

A. 6.7 miles
B. 7.1 miles
C. 7.5 miles
D. 8.3 miles

02882. Your vessel is steering 096° T at 17 knots. At 1847 a light bears 057° T, and at 1916 the same light bears 033° T. What will be your distance off abeam?

A. 9.9 miles
B. 10.7 miles
C. 11.4 miles
D. 11.9 miles

02883. Your vessel is steering 157° T at 18 knots. At 2018 a light bears 208° T, and at 2044 the same light bears 232° T. What will be your distance off abeam?

A. 12.8 miles
B. 14.4 miles
C. 15.2 miles
D. 16.7 miles

02884. Your vessel is steering 238° T at 11 knots. At 2304 a light bears 176° T, and at 2323 the same light bears 155° T. What will be your distance off abeam?

A. 7.6 miles
B. 8.1 miles
C. 8.6 miles
D. 9.1 miles

02885. Your vessel is steering 194° T at 13 knots. At 0116 a light bears 243° T, and at 0147 the same light bears 267° T. What will be your distance off abeam?

A. 11.2 miles
B. 11.6 miles
C. 12.0 miles
D. 12.5 miles

02886. Your vessel is steering 074° T at 12 knots. At 0214 a light bears 115° T, and at 0223 the same light bears 135° T. What will be your distance off abeam?

A. 2.4 miles
B. 3.0 miles
C. 3.5 miles
D. 4.2 miles

02887. Your vessel is steering 283° T at 10 knots. At 0538 a light bears 350° T, and at 0552 the same light bears 002° T. What will be your distance off abeam?

A. 9.6 miles
B. 10.1 miles
C. 10.7 miles
D. 11.3 miles

02888. Your vessel is underway on a course of 323.5° T at a speed of 16 knots. At 1945 a light bears 350° T. At 2010 the light bears 008.5° T. What will be your distance off when abeam of the light?

A. 3.3 miles
B. 4.8 miles
C. 6.7 miles
D. 8.7 miles

02889. While underway you sight a light 11° on your port bow at a distance of 12 miles. Assuming you make good your course, what will be your distance off the light when abeam?

A. 2.3 miles
B. 3.1 miles
C. 3.9 miles
D. 4.5 miles

02890. You are steaming on a course of 084° T at a speed of 13 knots. At 1919 a lighthouse bears 106.5° T. At 1957 the same lighthouse bears 129° T. What will be your distance off the lighthouse when abeam?

A. 4.3 miles
B. 5.7 miles
C. 7.1 miles
D. 8.2 miles

02891. You are steaming on course 168° T at a speed of 18 knots. At 1426 you sight a buoy bearing 144° T. At 1435 you sight the same buoy bearing 116° T. What is your distance off at the second bearing and predicted distance when abeam?

A. 2.3 miles 2nd bearing, 1.8 miles abeam
B. 2.5 miles 2nd bearing, 2.8 miles abeam
C. 2.8 miles 2nd bearing, 1.8 miles abeam
D. 3.3 miles 2nd bearing, 2.8 miles abeam

02892. You are steaming on a course of 114° T at 17 knots. At 1122 you observe a lighthouse bearing 077° T. At 1133 the lighthouse bears 051° T. What is distance off at second bearing?

A. 3.3 miles
B. 3.9 miles
C. 4.3 miles
D. 4.9 miles

02893. You are steaming on a course of 253° T at 14 knots. At 2329 you observe a lighthouse bearing 282° T. At 2345 the lighthouse bears 300° T. What is distance off at second bearing?

A. 3.7 miles
B. 4.3 miles
C. 5.2 miles
D. 5.9 miles

02894. You are steaming on a course of 071° T at 19 knots. At 1907 you observe a lighthouse bearing 122° T. At 1915 the lighthouse bears 154° T. What is your distance off at the second bearing?

A. 3.4 miles
B. 3.7 miles
C. 4.0 miles
D. 4.3 miles

02895. You are steaming on a course of 246° T at 17 knots. At 2107 you observe a lighthouse bearing 207° T. At 2119 the lighthouse bears 179° T. What is your distance off at the second bearing?

A. 3.9 miles
B. 4.2 miles
C. 4.6 miles
D. 5.1 miles

02896. You are steaming on a course of 133° T at 16 knots. At 2216 you observe a lighthouse bearing 086° T. At 2223 the lighthouse bears 054° T. What is your distance off at the second bearing?

A. 1.7 miles
B. 2.0 miles
C. 2.3 miles
D. 2.6 miles

02897. You are steaming on a course of 327° T at 13 knots. At 0207 you observe a lighthouse bearing 020° T. At 0226 the lighthouse bears 042° T. What is your distance off at the second bearing?

A. 8.5 miles
B. 8.9 miles
C. 9.2 miles
D. 9.7 miles

02898. You are steaming on a course of 267° T at 22 knots. At 0433 you observe a lighthouse bearing 290° T. At 0452 the lighthouse bears 328° T. What is distance off at second bearing?

A. 4.5 miles
B. 5.9 miles
C. 6.6 miles
D. 7.2 miles

02899. You are steaming on a course of 208° T at 21 knots. At 2019 you observe a lighthouse bearing 129° T. At 2030 the lighthouse bears 103° T. What is distance off at second bearing?

A. 8.2 miles
B. 8.6 miles
C. 8.9 miles
D. 9.3 miles

02900. You are steaming on a course of 167° T at 19.5 knots. At 1837 you observe a lighthouse bearing 224° T. At 1904 the lighthouse bears 268° T. What is your distance off at the second bearing?

A. 8.8 miles
B. 9.5 miles
C. 10.6 miles
D. 11.3 miles

02901. You are steaming on a course of 198° T at 18.5 knots. At 0316 you observe a lighthouse bearing 235° T. At 0348 the lighthouse bears 259° T. What is your distance off at the second bearing?

A. 14.8 miles
B. 15.3 miles
C. 15.8 miles
D. 16.3 miles

02902. You are steaming on a course of 058° T at 11.5 knots. At 0209 you observe a lighthouse bearing 129° T. At 0252 the lighthouse bears 173° T. What is your distance off at the second bearing?

A. 9.4 miles
B. 10.7 miles
C. 11.2 miles
D. 12.8 miles

02903. You are steaming on a course of 025° T at 15.5 knots. At 0645 you observe a lighthouse bearing 059° T. At 0655 the same lighthouse bears 075° T. What is your distance off at the second bearing?

A. 1.5 miles
B. 2.6 miles
C. 4.0 miles
D. 5.3 miles

02904. Your vessel is on course 093° T at 15 knots. At 1835 a light bears 136° T, and at 1857 the same light bears 170° T. What was your distance off the light at 1857?

A. 6.0 miles
B. 6.4 miles
C. 6.8 miles
D. 7.2 miles

02905. You are steaming on a course of 215° T at 14 knots. At 1841 you observe a lighthouse bearing 178° T. At 1904 the same lighthouse bears 156° T. What is your distance off at the second bearing?

A. 5.4 miles
B. 6.6 miles
C. 7.5 miles
D. 8.7 miles

02906. You are steaming on a course of 211° T at 17 knots. At 0417 a light bears 184° T, and at 0428 the same light bears 168° T. What is the distance off the light at 0428?

A. 3.4 miles
B. 4.6 miles
C. 5.1 miles
D. 5.6 miles

02907. You are running coastwise in hazy weather; the visibility improves just before you pass a lighthouse abeam. Your speed is 15 knots, and the lighthouse was abeam at 1015. At 1037 the lighthouse is 4 points abaft the beam. What is your distance off at the second bearing?

A. 3.9 miles
B. 5.5 miles
C. 6.6 miles
D. 7.8 miles

02908. Your vessel is on a course of 223° T at 17 knots. At 1323 a lighthouse bears 318° relative. At 1341 the same lighthouse bears 287° relative. What is your distance off the lighthouse at 1341?

A. 4.3 miles
B. 5.1 miles
C. 6.6 miles
D. 7.8 miles

02909. You are running coastwise in hazy weather; the visibility improves just before you pass a lighthouse abeam. Your speed is

14 knots, and the lighthouse was abeam at 0912. At 0939 the lighthouse is 4 points abaft the beam. What is your distance off at the second bearing?

A. 5.5 miles
B. 6.3 miles
C. 7.8 miles
D. 8.9 miles

02910. Your vessel is steaming on a course of 140° T at 15 knots. At 1530 a lighthouse bears 200° T. At 1550 it bears 249° T. What is your distance from the lighthouse at 1550?

A. 1.15 miles
B. 4.60 miles
C. 5.45 miles
D. 5.75 miles

02912. Your vessel is on a course of 079° T at 11 knots. At 0152 a light bears 105.5° T, and at 0209 the light bears 124° T. At what time and at what distance off will your vessel be when abeam of the light?

A. 0219, 2.3 miles
B. 0226, 3.1 miles
C. 0233, 3.9 miles
D. 0242, 4.7 miles

03050. The propeller on a vessel has a diameter of 23.7 feet and a pitch of 24.8 feet. What would be the apparent slip if the vessel cruised 442 miles in a 23 hour day (observed distance) at an average RPM of 89?

A. -7.6%
B. +7.6%
C. -11.8%
D. +11.8%

03051. The propeller on a vessel has a diameter of 20.6 feet and a pitch of 23.4 feet. What would be the apparent slip if the vessel cruised 538 miles in a 24 hour day (observed distance) at an average RPM of 87?

A. -11.6%
B. +11.6%
C. -10.3%
D. +10.3%

03052. The propeller on a vessel has a diameter of 21.2 feet and a pitch of 20.0 feet. What would be the apparent slip if the vessel cruised 391 miles in a 24 hour day (observed distance) at an average RPM of 88?

A. -11.5%
B. +11.5%
C. -6.2%
D. +6.2%

03053. The propeller on a vessel has a diameter of 19.9 feet and a pitch of 21.6 feet. What would be the apparent slip if the vessel cruised 395 miles in a 23 hour day (observed distance) at an average RPM of 78?

A. -3.2%
B. +3.2%
C. -12.0%
D. +12.0%

03054. The propeller on a vessel has a diameter of 22.8 feet and a pitch of 19.3 feet. What would be the apparent slip if the vessel cruised 287 miles in a 24 hour day (observed distance) at an average RPM of 67?

A. -6.3%
B. +6.3%
C. -24.0%
D. +24.0%

03055. The propeller on a vessel has a diameter of 24.6 feet and a pitch of 26.1 feet. What would be the apparent slip if the vessel cruised 462 miles in a 24 hour day (observed distance) at an average RPM of 72?

A. -2.7%
B. +2.7%
C. -3.8%
D. +3.8%

03056. The propeller on a vessel has a diameter of 18.8 feet and a pitch of 21.4 feet. What would be the apparent slip if the vessel cruised 378 miles in a 24 hour day (observed distance) at an average RPM of 76?

A. +1.9%
B. -1.9%
C. +4.7%
D. -4.7%

03057. The propeller on a vessel has a diameter of 25.3 feet and a pitch of 23.2 feet. What would be the apparent slip if the vessel cruised 515 miles in a 23 hour day (observed distance) at an average RPM of 93?

A. -3.6%
B. +3.6%
C. -5.2%
D. +5.2%

03058. The propeller on a vessel has a diameter of 20.9 feet and a pitch of 19.6 feet. What would be the apparent slip if the vessel cruised 447 miles in a 23 hour day (observed distance) at an average RPM of 108?

A. -5.6%
B. +5.6%

C. -7.0%
D. +7.0%

03059. The propeller on a vessel has a diameter of 21.5 feet and a pitch of 24.5 feet. What would be the apparent slip if the vessel cruised 458 miles in a 23 hour day (observed distance) at an average RPM of 78?

A. +5.6%
B. -5.6%
C. +12.3%
D. -12.3%

03060. The propeller on a vessel has a diameter of 24.0 feet and a pitch of 21.3 feet. What would be the apparent slip if the vessel cruised 510 miles in a 24 hour day (observed distance) at an average RPM of 86?

A. -12.2%
B. +12.2%
C. -17.5%
D. +17.5%

03061. The propeller on a vessel has a diameter of 20.2 feet and a pitch of 19.0 feet. What would be the apparent slip if the vessel cruised 367 miles in a 24 hour day (observed distance) at an average RPM of 84?

A. +2.9%
B. -2.9%
C. +5.2%
D. -5.2%

03062. The propeller on your vessel has a pitch of 22.8 feet. From 0800, 18 April, to 1020, 19 April, you steamed an observed distance of 403.6 miles. If your average RPM was 74, what was the slip?

A. +7.0%
B. -7.0%
C. +8.0%
D. -8.0%

03063. The observed distance for a day's run was 302.7 miles. The propeller had a pitch of 20'06", and the average RPM was 67. What was the slip?

A. +0.7%
B. -0.7%
C. +7.0%
D. -7.0%

03064. The propeller of a vessel has a pitch of 19.0 feet. If the vessel traveled 183.5 miles (observed distance) in 24 hours at an average of 44 RPM, what was the slip?

A. +7.4%
B. -7.4%

C. +11.6%
D. -11.6%

03065. The propeller on your vessel has a pitch of 18'09". If the observed distance for a day's run was 399.4 miles and the average RPM was 86, which of the following statements is TRUE?

A. The slip is a positive 5%.
B. The day's run by engine RPM was 404.5 miles.
C. The slip is a negative 5%.
D. The day's run by engine RPM was 390.6 miles.

03066. The observed noon to noon run for a 24 hour period is 489 miles. The average RPM for the day was 95. The pitch of the wheel is 22.5 feet. What is the slip of the wheel?

A. 3.3%
B. 3.5%
C. 3.9%
D. 3.8%

03067. From 1020, 3 March, to 1845, 5 March, your vessel steamed an observed distance of 845.6 miles. The average RPM was 78, and the pitch of the propeller was 20'03". What was the slip?

A. -4%
B. +4%
C. -8%
D. +8%

03068. Your vessel's propeller has a pitch of 22'06". From 0530, on 19 March, to 1930, 20 March, the average RPM was 82. The distance run by observation was 721.5 miles. What was the slip?

A. +4%
B. -4%
C. +7%
D. -7%

03069. If the speed necessary for reaching port at a designated time is 18.5 knots and the pitch of the propeller is 21.7 feet, how many revolutions per minute will the shaft have to turn, assuming a 4% negative slip?

A. 83
B. 90
C. 97
D. 114

03070. If the speed necessary for reaching port at a designated time is 19.6 knots and the pitch of the propeller is 24.6 feet, how many revolutions per minute will the shaft have to turn, assuming a 5% positive slip?

A. 76
B. 85
C. 97
D. 106

03071. If the speed necessary for reaching port at a designated time is 20.7 knots and the pitch of the propeller is 23.8 feet, how many revolutions per minute will the shaft have to turn, assuming a 3% negative slip?

A. 74
B. 79
C. 86
D. 98

03072. If the speed necessary for reaching port at a designated time is 17.4 knots and the pitch of the propeller is 25.6 feet, how many revolutions per minute will the shaft have to turn, assuming a 3% positive slip?

A. 63
B. 67
C. 71
D. 75

03073. If the speed necessary for reaching port at a designated time is 16.8 knots and the pitch of the propeller is 22.3 feet, how many revolutions per minute will the shaft have to turn, assuming a 4% negative slip?

A. 61
B. 66
C. 73
D. 80

03074. If the speed necessary for reaching port at a designated time is 19.2 knots and the pitch of the propeller is 22.7 feet, how many revolutions per minute will the shaft have to turn, assuming a 4% positive slip?

A. 82
B. 89
C. 96
D. 103

03075. If the speed necessary for reaching port at a designated time is 15.7 knots and the pitch of the propeller is 23.4 feet, how many revolutions per minute will the shaft have to turn, assuming a 6% negative slip?

A. 64
B. 68
C. 72
D. 76

03076. If the speed necessary for reaching port at a designated time is 16.4 knots and the pitch of the propeller is 23.8 feet, how

many revolutions per minute will the shaft have to turn, assuming a 6% positive slip?

A. 66
B. 74
C. 82
D. 90

03077. If the speed necessary for reaching port at a designated time is 23.7 knots and the pitch of the propeller is 20.8 feet, how many revolutions per minute will the shaft have to turn, assuming a 7% negative slip?

A. 108
B. 112
C. 116
D. 124

03078. If the speed necessary for reaching port at a designated time is 17.8 knots and the pitch of the propeller is 24.7 feet, how many revolutions per minute will the shaft have to turn, assuming a 7% positive slip?

A. 67
B. 71
C. 75
D. 79

03079. If the speed necessary for reaching port at a designated time is 18.2 knots and the pitch of the propeller is 23.9 feet, how many revolutions per minute will the shaft have to turn, assuming a 2% negative slip?

A. 70
B. 73
C. 76
D. 79

03080. If the speed necessary for reaching port at a designated time is 21.6 knots and the pitch of the propeller is 22.5 feet, how many revolutions per minute will the shaft have to turn, assuming a 2% positive slip?

A. 81
B. 87
C. 95
D. 99

03081. If the speed necessary for reaching port at a designated time is 12.6 knots and the pitch of the propeller is 13.6 feet, how many revolutions per minute will the shaft have to turn, assuming no slip?

A. 81
B. 85
C. 90
D. 94

03082. The speed of advance necessary to arrive in port at a designated time is 15.8 knots. The pitch of the propeller is 20.75 feet. You estimate 5% positive slip. How many RPM must you turn to make the necessary speed?

A. 73.5
B. 76.2
C. 79.9
D. 81.2

03083. The speed necessary to reach port at a designated time is 18.7 knots. The propeller pitch is 24'03", and you estimate 3% positive slip. How many RPM's will the shaft have to turn?

A. 81 RPM
B. 87 RPM
C. 98 RPM
D. 104 RPM

03084. If the speed necessary for reaching port at a designated time is 18.6 knots, and the pitch of the propeller is 26.2 feet, how many revolutions per minute will the shaft have to turn, assuming a 4% negative slip.

A. 69
B. 72
C. 75
D. 78

03085. You must average 16.25 knots to reach port at a designated time. Your propeller has a pitch of 21'08", and you estimate 4% negative slip. How many RPM's must you average to arrive on time?

A. 73 RPM
B. 77 RPM
C. 82 RPM
D. 88 RPM

03086. If the pitch of the propeller is 19.7 feet, and the revolutions per day are 86,178, calculate the day's run allowing 3% negative slip.

A. 279.2 miles
B. 287.6 miles
C. 311.4 miles
D. 326.2 miles

03087. If the pitch of the propeller is 20.6 feet, and the revolutions per day are 107,341, calculate the day's run allowing 3% positive slip.

A. 352.7 miles
B. 363.6 miles
C. 374.5 miles
D. 389.1 miles

03088. If the pitch of the propeller is 21.5 feet, and the revolutions per day are 96,666, calculate the day's run allowing 9% negative slip.

A. 311.1 miles
B. 341.8 miles
C. 357.9 miles
D. 372.6 miles

03089. If the pitch of the propeller is 22.4 feet, and the revolutions per day are 103,690, calculate the day's run allowing 9% positive slip.

A. 321.7 miles
B. 347.6 miles
C. 382.0 miles
D. 416.4 miles

03090. If the pitch of the propeller is 26.3 feet, and the revolutions per day are 87,421, calculate the day's run allowing 7% negative slip.

A. 351.7 miles
B. 378.1 miles
C. 404.6 miles
D. 419.3 miles

03091. If the pitch of the propeller is 25.1 feet, and the revolutions per day are 91,591, calculate the day's run allowing 7% positive slip.

A. 351.6 miles
B. 378.1 miles
C. 390.0 miles
D. 404.6 miles

03092. If the pitch of the propeller is 24.8 feet, and the revolutions per day are 93,373, calculate the day's run allowing 11% positive slip.

A. 307.3 miles
B. 339.0 miles
C. 380.9 miles
D. 422.8 miles

03093. If the pitch of the propeller is 23.2 feet, and the revolutions per day are 94,910, calculate the day's run allowing 11% negative slip.

A. 322.3 miles
B. 362.3 miles
C. 382.0 miles
D. 402.0 miles

03094. If the pitch of the propeller is 26.7 feet, and the revolutions per day are 131,717, calculate the day's run allowing 4% negative slip.

A. 555.2 miles
B. 578.4 miles
C. 601.6 miles
D. 649.4 miles

03095. If the pitch of the propeller is 21.3 feet, and the revolutions per day are 126,214, calculate the day's run allowing 4% positive slip.

A. 424.5 miles
B. 442.1 miles
C. 459.9 miles
D. 477.3 miles

03096. If the pitch of the propeller is 20.1 feet, and the revolutions per day are 118,178, calculate the day's run allowing 6% negative slip.

A. 367.2 miles
B. 381.6 miles
C. 398.4 miles
D. 414.1 miles

03097. If the pitch of the propeller is 19.4 feet, and the revolutions per day are 96,713, calculate the day's run allowing 6% positive slip.

A. 266.4 miles
B. 290.1 miles
C. 308.6 miles
D. 327.1 miles

03098. If the pitch of the propeller is 21.2 feet, and the revolutions per day are 93,660, calculate the day's run allowing 5% positive slip.

A. 163.3 miles
B. 217.8 miles
C. 310.3 miles
D. 342.9 miles

03099. The propellers on your twin screw vessel have a pitch of 16'04". What is the distance in a day's run if the average RPM is 94, and you estimate 7% positive slip?

A. 338.3 miles
B. 389.3 miles
C. 676.6 miles
D. 778.6 miles

03100. The pitch of the propeller on your vessel is 19'09". You estimate the slip at -3%. If you averaged 82 RPM for the day's run, how many miles did you steam?

A. 370.8
B. 373.6
C. 393.7
D. 395.3

03101. You are turning 100 RPM, with a propeller pitch of 25 feet, and an estimated slip of -5%. What is the speed of advance?

A. 24.7 knots

B. 23.5 knots
C. 25.9 knots
D. 22.3 knots

03102. You are turning 88 RPM, with a propeller pitch of 19 feet, and an estimated slip of 0%. What is the speed of advance?

A. 16.5 knots
B. 16.9 knots
C. 17.3 knots
D. 18.1 knots

03103. You are turning 93 RPM, with a propeller pitch of 25 feet, and an estimated slip of 0%. What is the speed of advance?

A. 20.2 knots
B. 21.9 knots
C. 22.4 knots
D. 22.9 knots

03104. You are turning 84 RPM, with a propeller pitch of 22 feet, and an estimated slip of 0%. What is the speed of advance?

A. 16.8 knots
B. 17.7 knots
C. 18.0 knots
D. 18.2 knots

03105. You are turning 82 RPM, with a propeller pitch of 23 feet, and an estimated slip of +6%. What is the speed of advance?

A. 17.5 knots
B. 17.9 knots
C. 18.4 knots
D. 19.7 knots

03106. You are turning 85 RPM, with a propeller pitch of 19 feet, and an estimated slip of +3%. What is the speed of advance?

A. 14.7 knots
B. 15.5 knots
C. 16.4 knots
D. 17.1 knots

03107. You are turning 68 RPM, with a propeller pitch of 18 feet, and an estimated slip of +2%. What is the speed of advance?

A. 10.7 knots
B. 11.5 knots
C. 11.8 knots
D. 12.3 knots

03108. You are turning 105 RPM, with a propeller pitch of 17 feet, and an estimated slip of -1%. What is the speed of advance?

A. 15.3 knots

B. 16.9 knots
C. 17.4 knots
D. 17.8 knots

03109. You are turning 90 RPM, with a propeller pitch of 24 feet, and an estimated slip of -3%. What is the speed of advance?

A. 18.8 knots
B. 19.2 knots
C. 20.6 knots
D. 21.9 knots

03110. You are turning 78 RPM, with a propeller pitch of 21 feet, and an estimated slip of -7%. What is the speed of advance?

A. 14.9 knots
B. 15.7 knots
C. 17.3 knots
D. 17.8 knots

03111. You are turning 100 RPM, with propeller pitch of 25 feet, and an estimated negative slip of 5%. What is the speed of advance?

A. 23.4 knots
B. 24.7 knots
C. 25.9 knots
D. 26.3 knots

03299. You have steamed 174 miles and consumed 18 tons of fuel. If you maintain the same speed, how many tons of fuel will you consume while steaming 416 miles?

A. 34.9 tons
B. 38.4 tons
C. 43.0 tons
D. 46.2 tons

03300. You have steamed 156 miles and consumed 19 tons of fuel. If you maintain the same speed, how many tons of fuel will you consume while steaming 273 miles?

A. 23.6 tons
B. 27.9 tons
C. 33.3 tons
D. 37.2 tons

03301. You have steamed 217 miles and consumed 23.0 tons of fuel. If you maintain the same speed, how many tons of fuel will you consume while steaming 362 miles?

A. 33.8 tons
B. 38.4 tons
C. 42.6 tons
D. 45.7 tons

03302. You have steamed 132 miles and consumed 14.0 tons of fuel. If you maintain the

same speed, how many tons of fuel will you consume while steaming 289 miles?

A. 21.6 tons
B. 24.5 tons
C. 27.9 tons
D. 30.7 tons

03303. You have steamed 174 miles and consumed 18.0 tons of fuel. If you maintain the same speed, how many tons of fuel will you consume while steaming 416 miles?

A. 34.9 tons
B. 38.4 tons
C. 43.0 tons
D. 46.2 tons

03304. You have steamed 265 miles and consumed 25.0 tons of fuel. If you maintain the same speed, how many tons of fuel will you consume while steaming 346 miles?

A. 32.6 tons
B. 37.4 tons
C. 42.6 tons
D. 49.5 tons

03305. You have steamed 201 miles and consumed 18.0 tons of fuel. If you maintain the same speed, how many tons of fuel will you consume while steaming 482 miles?

A. 25.2 tons
B. 43.2 tons
C. 52.6 tons
D. 103.5 tons

03306. You have steamed 264 miles and consumed 22.0 tons of fuel. If you maintain the same speed, how many tons of fuel will you consume while steaming 521 miles?

A. 31.7 tons
B. 38.6 tons
C. 43.4 tons
D. 85.7 tons

03307. You have steamed 182 miles and consumed 16.0 tons of fuel. If you maintain the same speed, how many tons of fuel will you consume while steaming 392 miles?

A. 28.3 tons
B. 34.5 tons
C. 49.6 tons
D. 74.2 tons

03308. You have steamed 142 miles and consumed 21.0 tons of fuel. If you maintain the same speed, how many tons of fuel will you consume while steaming 465 miles?

A. 43.4 tons
B. 57.6 tons
C. 68.8 tons
D. 72.8 tons

03309. You have steamed 142 miles and consumed 15.0 tons of fuel. If you maintain the same speed, how many tons of fuel will you consume while steaming 472 miles?

A. 36.5 tons
B. 49.9 tons
C. 53.8 tons
D. 61.4 tons

03310. You have steamed 216 miles and consumed 19.0 tons of fuel. If you maintain the same speed, how many tons of fuel will you consume while steaming 315 miles?

A. 27.7 tons
B. 32.3 tons
C. 36.9 tons
D. 40.4 tons

03311. You have steamed 162 miles and consumed 14.0 tons of fuel. If you maintain the same speed, how many tons of fuel will you consume while steaming 285 miles?

A. 24.6 tons
B. 34.7 tons
C. 43.3 tons
D. 54.8 tons

03312. You have steamed 199 miles and consumed 23.0 tons of fuel. If you maintain the same speed, how many tons of fuel will you consume while steaming 410 miles?

A. 32.6 tons
B. 39.9 tons
C. 47.4 tons
D. 97.6 tons

03313. You have steamed 300 miles and consumed 34 tons of fuel. If you maintain the same speed, how many tons of fuel will you consume while steaming 700 miles?

A. 79.3 tons
B. 74.3 tons
C. 68.4 tons
D. 66.2 tons

03314. You have steamed 150 miles and consumed 17 tons of fuel. If you maintain the same speed, how many tons of fuel will you consume while steaming 350 miles?

A. 12.82 tons
B. 29.41 tons

C. 34.00 tons
D. 39.66 tons

03451. You are underway and intend to make good a course of 040° T. You experience a current with a set and drift of 190° T at 1.4 knots, and a northwest wind produces a leeway of 3°. You adjust your course to compensate for the current and leeway, while maintaining an engine speed of 10 knots. What will be your speed made good over your intended course of 040° T?

A. 7.8 knots
B. 8.8 knots
C. 9.8 knots
D. 11.0 knots

03452. You wish to make good a course of 035° T while turning for an engine speed of 12 knots. The set is 340° T, and the drift is 2 knots. What course should you steer?

A. 027° T
B. 037° T
C. 044° T
D. 054° T

03453. You wish to make good a course of 350° T while turning for an engine speed of 10 knots. The set is 070° T, and the drift is 1.5 knots. What course should you steer?

A. 332° T
B. 341° T
C. 345° T
D. 359° T

03454. You wish to make good a course of 300° T while turning for an engine speed of 11 knots. The set is 350° T, and the drift is 2.1 knots. What course should you steer?

A. 278° T
B. 288° T
C. 292° T
D. 308° T

03455. You wish to make good a course of 230° T while turning for an engine speed of 12.5 knots. The set is 180° T, and the drift is 1.7 knots. What course should you steer?

A. 244° T
B. 236° T
C. 231° T
D. 222° T

03456. You wish to make good a course of 053° T while turning for an engine speed of 16 knots. The set is 345° T, and the drift is 2.4 knots. What course should you steer?

A. 047° T
B. 051° T
C. 055° T
D. 061° T

03457. You wish to make good a course of 035° T while turning for an engine speed of 12 knots. The set is 340° T, and the drift is 2 knots. What speed will you make good along the track line?

A. 12.2 knots
B. 12.7 knots
C. 13.0 knots
D. 13.3 knots

03458. You wish to make good a course of 350° T while turning for an engine speed of 10 knots. The set is 070° T, and the drift is 1.5 knots. What speed will you make good along the track line?

A. 9.7 knots
B. 10.2 knots
C. 10.5 knots
D. 11.0 knots

03459. You wish to make good a course of 300° T while turning for an engine speed of 11 knots. The set is 350° T, and the drift is 2.1 knots. What speed will you make good along the track line?

A. 12.2 knots
B. 12.7 knots
C. 12.9 knots
D. 13.4 knots

03460. You wish to make good a course of 230° T while turning for an engine speed of 12.5 knots. The set is 180° T, and the drift is 1.7 knots. What speed will you make good along the track line?

A. 11.5 knots
B. 12.5 knots
C. 13.6 knots
D. 14.0 knots

03461. You wish to make good a course of 053° T while turning for an engine speed of 16 knots. The set is 345° T, and the drift is 2.4 knots. What speed will you make good along the track line?

A. 14.1 knots
B. 15.2 knots
C. 16.1 knots
D. 16.8 knots

03462. You are underway on course 160° T at 10 knots. The current is 210° T at 0.9 knot. What is the course being made good?

A. 156° T
B. 160° T
C. 164° T
D. 169° T

03463. You are underway on course 215° T at 12 knots. The current is 000° T at 2.3 knots. What is the course being made good?

A. 209° T
B. 217° T
C. 222° T
D. 232° T

03464. You are underway on course 315° T at 14 knots. The current is 135° T at 1.9 knots. What is the course being made good?

A. 130° T
B. 315° T
C. 317° T
D. 322° T

03465. You are underway on course 000° T at 9.5 knots. The current is 082° T at 1.1 knots. What is the course being made good?

A. 007° T
B. 009° T
C. 021° T
D. 353° T

03466. You are underway on course 172° T at 18.5 knots. The current is 078° T at 2.8 knots. What is the course being made good?

A. 114° T
B. 163° T
C. 175° T
D. 181° T

03467. You are underway on course 160° T at 10 knots. The current is 210° T at 0.9 knot. What is the speed being made good?

A. 10.7 knots
B. 11.0 knots
C. 11.6 knots
D. 12.3 knots

03468. You are underway on course 215° T at 12 knots. The current is 000° T at 2.3 knots. What is the speed being made good?

A. 08.5 knots
B. 10.2 knots
C. 10.9 knots
D. 11.2 knots

03469. You are underway on course 315° T at 14 knots. The current is 135° T at 1.9 knots. What is the speed being made good?

A. 12.1 knots
B. 13.5 knots
C. 14.0 knots
D. 15.9 knots

03470. You are underway on course 000° T at 9.5 knots. The current is 082° T at 1.1 knots. What is the speed being made good?

A. 9.2 knots
B. 9.5 knots
C. 9.8 knots
D. 10.1 knots

03471. You are underway on course 172° T at 18.5 knots. The current is 078° T at 2.8 knots. What is the speed being made good?

A. 18.5 knots
B. 18.9 knots
C. 19.4 knots
D. 19.9 knots

03605. The true course from point A to point B is 317°. A SSW wind causes a 4° leeway, variation is 6° W and deviation is 1° E. What is the compass course to steer to make good the true course?

A. 326°
B. 318°
C. 313°
D. 308°

03606. You are steering 154° pgc. The wind is southwest causing 4° leeway. The gyro error is 3° E, variation is 11° W and deviation is 7° E. What is the true course made good?

A. 153° T
B. 158° T
C. 161° T
D. 164° T

03607. You desire to make good 152° T. The magnetic compass deviation is 4° E, the variation is 5° E, and the gyro error is 3° E. A southwesterly wind produces a 4° leeway. What course would you steer per standard compass to make good the true course?

A. 137° psc
B. 141° psc
C. 143° psc
D. 147° psc

03608. You are steering 125° pgc. The wind is southwest by south causing a 3° leeway. The variation is 6° E, the deviation is 2° W, and gyro error is 1° W. What is the true course made good?

A. 121° T
B. 123° T

C. 127° T
D. 129° T

03609. Enroute from Rio to Montevideo, the true course is 215°; the gyro error is 2° west. A north wind causes 3° leeway. What course would you steer per gyrocompass to make good the true course?

A. 220° pgc
B. 214° pgc
C. 216° pgc
D. 210° pgc

03610. While enroute from Sydney to the Panama Canal a vessel's true course is 071°. Variation is 14° E. Deviation is 4° W. A north breeze causes 2° leeway. What course would you steer psc in order to make good the true course?

A. 059° psc
B. 063° psc
C. 079° psc
D. 061° psc

03611. The track line on the chart is 274° T. Variation is 4° E, and deviation is 2° E. The gyro error is 1.5° E. What course would be steered by gyrocompass to make good the desired course?

A. 280.5° pgc
B. 278.0° pgc
C. 275.5° pgc
D. 272.5° pgc

03612. Your vessel is steering 195° per standard magnetic compass. Variation for the area is 13° W, and the deviation is 4° E. The wind is from the west-southwest, producing a 2° leeway. What true course are you making good?

A. 178° T
B. 180° T
C. 182° T
D. 184° T

03613. You are steering a magnetic compass course of 075°. The variation for the area is 10° W, and the compass deviation is 5° E. What is the true course you are steering?

A. 060° T
B. 070° T
C. 080° T
D. 090° T

03614. The true course between two points is 057°. Your gyrocompass has an error of 3° east and you make an allowance of 1° leeway for a north-northwest wind. What gyro course should be steered to make the true course good?

A. 053° pgc
B. 056° pgc
C. 059° pgc
D. 060° pgc

03615. You want to make good a true course of 137°. A north-northeast wind produces a 3° leeway. The variation is 11° west, deviation is 5° east, and gyrocompass error is 2° east. What course must you steer per gyrocompass to make the true course good?

A. 132° pgc
B. 134° pgc
C. 136° pgc
D. 138° pgc

03616. You desire to make good a true course of 046°. The variation is 6° E, magnetic compass deviation is 12° W, and the gyrocompass error is 3° W. A northerly wind produces a 5° leeway. What is the course to steer per standard magnetic compass to make good the true course?

A. 047° psc
B. 049° psc
C. 052° psc
D. 057° psc

03617. Your vessel is steering course 299° psc, variation for the area is 7° W, and deviation is 4° W. The wind is from the southwest, producing a 3° leeway. What true course are you making good?

A. 291° T
B. 296° T
C. 299° T
D. 313° T

03618. Your vessel is steering course 027° psc, variation for the area is 19° W, and deviation is 2° E. The wind is from the north-northwest, producing a 5° leeway. What true course are you making good?

A. 005° T
B. 015° T
C. 044° T
D. 049° T

03619. Your vessel is steering course 149° psc, variation for the area is 13° E, and deviation is 4° E. The wind is from the north, producing a 4° leeway. What true course are you making good?

A. 128° T
B. 136° T
C. 162° T
D. 170° T

03620. Your vessel is steering course 197° psc, variation for the area is 7° E, and deviation is 4° W. The wind is from the west, producing a 2° leeway. What true course are you making good?

A. 192° T
B. 196° T
C. 198° T
D. 202° T

03621. Your vessel is steering course 216° psc, variation for the area is 9° W, and deviation is 2° E. The wind is from the east, producing a 5° leeway. What true course are you making good?

A. 204° T
B. 214° T
C. 223° T
D. 227° T

03622. Your vessel is steering course 337° psc. Variation for the area is 13° W, and deviation is 4° E. The wind is from the south, producing a 3° leeway. What true course are you making good?

A. 325° T
B. 328° T
C. 331° T
D. 349° T

03623. Your vessel is steering course 166° psc, variation for the area is 8° W, and deviation is 3° W. The wind is from the west-southwest, producing a 2° leeway. What true course are you making good?

A. 153° T
B. 157° T
C. 175° T
D. 179° T

03624. Your vessel is steering course 073° psc, variation for the area is 15° E, and deviation is 4° E. The wind is from the southeast, producing a 4° leeway. What true course are you making good?

A. 050° T
B. 058° T
C. 088° T
D. 096° T

03625. Your vessel is steering course 111° psc, variation for the area is 5° E, and deviation is 3° W. The wind is from the northwest, producing a 1° leeway. What true course are you making good?

A. 108° T
B. 110° T
C. 112° T
D. 114° T

03626. Your vessel is steering course 284° psc, variation for the area is 6° W, and deviation is 3° E. The wind is from the north-northeast, producing a 3° leeway. What true course are you making good?

A. 275° T
B. 278° T
C. 284° T
D. 290° T

03627. Your vessel is steering course 243° psc. Variation for the area is 5° E, and deviation is 2° W. The wind is from the south-southeast, producing a 2° leeway. What true course are you making good?

A. 242° T
B. 244° T
C. 246° T
D. 248° T

03628. Your vessel is steering course 352° psc, variation for the area is 11° E, and deviation is 9° W. The wind is from the northeast, producing a 1° leeway. What true course are you making good?

A. 349° T
B. 351° T
C. 353° T
D. 355° T

03629. You desire to make good a true course of 129°. The variation is 7° E, magnetic compass deviation is 4° E, and gyrocompass error is 2° W. An easterly wind produces a 4° leeway. What is the course to steer per standard magnetic compass to make the true course good?

A. 114° psc
B. 116° psc
C. 122° psc
D. 126° psc

03630. You desire to make good a true course of 203°. The variation is 19° E, magnetic compass deviation is 2° W, and gyrocompass error is 1° E. A westerly wind produces a 3° leeway. What is the course to steer per standard magnetic compass to make the true course good?

A. 183° psc
B. 189° psc
C. 210° psc
D. 223° psc

03631. You desire to make good a true course of 329°. The variation is 13° W, magnetic compass deviation is 4° E, and gyrocompass error is 2° W. A southerly wind produces a 1° leeway. What is the course to steer per standard magnetic compass to make the true course good?

A. 319° psc
B. 321° psc
C. 337° psc
D. 339° psc

03632. You desire to make good a true course of 157°. The variation is 15° E, magnetic compass deviation is 9° W, and gyrocompass error is 3° E. A southwesterly wind produces a 2° leeway. What is the course to steer per standard magnetic compass to make the true course good?

A. 145° psc
B. 147° psc
C. 150° psc
D. 153° psc

03633. You desire to make good a true course of 067°. The variation is 11° W, magnetic compass deviation is 3° E, and gyrocompass error is 1° W. A northwesterly wind produces a 5° leeway. What is the course to steer per standard magnetic compass to make the true course good?

A. 054° psc
B. 064° psc
C. 070° psc
D. 074° psc

03634. You desire to make good a true course of 038°. The variation is 5° E, magnetic compass deviation is 4° W, and gyrocompass error is 4° W. A southeasterly wind produces a 4° leeway. What is the course to steer per standard magnetic compass to make the true course good?

A. 033° psc
B. 041° psc
C. 043° psc
D. 047° psc

03635. You desire to make good a true course of 236°. The variation is 8° E, magnetic compass deviation is 1° E, and gyrocompass error is 3° W. A south-southeasterly wind produces a 1° leeway. What is the course to steer per standard magnetic compass to make the true course good?

A. 226° psc
B. 228° psc
C. 244° psc
D. 246° psc

03636. You desire to make good a true course of 279°. The variation is 8° W, magnetic compass deviation is 3° E, and gyrocompass error is 1° E. A north-northwesterly wind produces a 3° leeway. What is the course to steer per standard magnetic compass to make the true course good?

A. 281° psc
B. 284° psc

C. 287° psc
D. 290° psc

03637. You desire to make good a true course of 347°. The variation is 11° E, magnetic compass deviation is 7° W, and gyrocompass error is 4° W. A north by east wind produces a 4° leeway. What is the course to steer per standard magnetic compass to make the true course good?

A. 339° psc
B. 343° psc
C. 347° psc
D. 351° psc

03638. You desire to make good a true course of 007°. The variation is 5° E, magnetic compass deviation is 3° W, and gyrocompass error is 2° E. A southwest by west wind produces a 2° leeway. What is the course to steer per standard magnetic compass to make the true course good?

A. 003° psc
B. 005° psc
C. 007° psc
D. 009° psc

03639. You desire to make good a true course of 132°. The variation is 10° W, magnetic compass deviation is 5° E, and gyrocompass error is 5° W. A northeast by east wind produces a 5° leeway. What is the course to steer per standard magnetic compass to make the true course good?

A. 132° psc
B. 135° psc
C. 137° psc
D. 142° psc

03640. You desire to make good a true course of 223°. The variation is 2° E, magnetic compass deviation is 2° E, and gyrocompass error is 1° W. An east-southeast wind produces a 3° leeway. What is the course to steer per standard magnetic compass to make the true course good?

A. 213° psc
B. 216° psc
C. 220° psc
D. 223° psc

03641. You desire to make good a true course of 174°. The variation is 17° W, magnetic compass deviation is 4° W, and gyrocompass error is 4° E. A west-southwest wind produces a 4° leeway. What is the course to steer per standard magnetic compass to make the true course good?

A. 195° psc
B. 197° psc
C. 199° psc
D. 203° psc

03642. You are steering 154° per gyrocompass. The wind is northeast by east, causing 4° leeway. The gyro error is 3.0° east, variation is 11° west, and deviation is 7.0° E. What is the true course made good?

A. 151° T
B. 158° T
C. 161° T
D. 164° T

03643. While en route from Montevideo to Walvis Bay a vessel's course is 116° psc. If the variation for the locality is 25° W and the deviation is 6° W, what is the true course made good if a west wind produces 1° leeway.

A. 084° T
B. 086° T
C. 148° T
D. 085° T

03644. While en route from Capetown to Rio a vessel's course is 281° pgc. If the variation for the locality is 24° W, the deviation is 4° E, and the gyro error 2° W, what is the true course made good?

A. 279° T
B. 261° T
C. 301° T
D. 283° T

03645. The true course between two points is 119°. Your gyrocompass has an error of 3° E and you make an allowance of 4° leeway for a south-southwest wind. What gyro course should be steered to make the true course good?

A. 112° pgc
B. 118° pgc
C. 120° pgc
D. 126° pgc

03646. The true course between two points is 041°. Your gyrocompass has an error of 1° W and you make an allowance of 2° leeway for an east-southeast wind. What gyro course should be steered to make the true course good?

A. 040° pgc
B. 042° pgc
C. 043° pgc
D. 044° pgc

03647. The true course between two points is 220°. Your gyrocompass has an error of 1° E and you make an allowance of 1° leeway for a north-northwest wind. What gyro course should be steered to make the true course good?

A. 220° pgc
B. 221° pgc
C. 222° pgc
D. 223° pgc

03648. The true course between two points is 312°. Your gyrocompass has an error of 3° W and you make an allowance of 4° leeway for a west by south wind. What gyro course should be steered to make the true course good?

A. 305° pgc
B. 311° pgc
C. 315° pgc
D. 318° pgc

03649. The true course between two points is 078°. Your gyrocompass has an error of 2° E and you make an allowance of 3° leeway for a north wind. What gyro course should be steered to make the true course good?

A. 073° pgc
B. 075° pgc
C. 077° pgc
D. 079° pgc

03650. The true course between two points is 194°. Your gyrocompass has an error of 2° W and you make an allowance of 1° leeway for a southwest wind. What gyro course should you steer to make the true course good?

A. 193° pgc
B. 195° pgc
C. 197° pgc
D. 199° pgc

03751. While proceeding up a channel on course 010° per gyrocompass, you notice a pair of range lights in alignment with the masts of your vessel when viewed forward. A check of the chart shows the range to be 009° T and the variation to be 15° W. If the ship's course is 026° psc, what is the deviation for the present heading?

A. 2° W
B. 2° E
C. 1° W
D. 1° E

03752. While your vessel is proceeding down a channel you notice a range of lights in line with your vessel's mast. If your vessel is on course 001° per gyrocompass and the charted value of the range of lights is 359° T, what is the gyrocompass error?

A. 2° W
B. 2° E
C. 1° E
D. 1° W

NAVIGATION PROBLEM ANSWERS

02651 B	02857 A	03059 B	03309 B	03641 C
02652 C	02858 D	03060 C	03310 A	03642 C
02653 C	02859 B	03061 A	03311 A	03643 A
02654 A	02860 B	03062 C	03312 C	03644 A
02655 B	02861 A	03063 C	03313 A	03645 C
02656 A	02862 B	03064 A	03314 D	03646 D
02657 C	02863 B	03065 C	03451 B	03647 A
02658 B	02864 A	03066 B	03452 C	03648 B
02659 A	02865 C	03067 B	03453 B	03649 A
02660 C	02866 C	03068 B	03454 C	03650 C
02661 B	02867 B	03069 A	03455 B	03652 D
02662 A	02868 A	03070 B	03456 D	03653 C
02663 D	02869 C	03071 C	03457 C	03751 A
02664 B	02870 B	03072 C	03458 B	03752 A
02665 C	02871 D	03073 C	03459 A	
02666 A	02872 B	03074 B	03460 C	
02667 C	02873 D	03075 A	03461 D	
02668 B	02874 D	03076 B	03462 C	
02669 B	02875 C	03077 A	03463 C	
02670 C	02877 B	03078 D	03464 B	
02671 B	02878 C	03079 C	03465 A	
02672 C	02879 A	03080 D	03466 B	
02673 C	02880 B	03081 D	03467 A	
02674 A	02881 A	03082 D	03468 B	
02675 D	02882 C	03083 A	03469 A	
02676 B	02883 B	03084 A	03470 C	
02677 A	02884 C	03085 A	03471 A	
02678 C	02885 C	03086 B	03605 B	
02679 C	02886 B	03087 A	03606 A	
02680 B	02887 B	03088 D	03607 D	
02681 B	02888 C	03089 B	03608 A	
02682 A	02889 A	03090 C	03609 A	
02683 C	02890 B	03091 A	03610 A	
02684 C	02891 A	03092 B	03611 D	
02685 C	02892 C	03093 D	03612 D	
02686 B	02893 D	03094 C	03613 B	
02687 D	02894 B	03095 A	03614 A	
02688 C	02895 C	03096 D	03615 A	
02689 A	02896 D	03097 B	03616 A	
02690 B	02897 B	03098 C	03617 A	
02691 A	02898 A	03099 A	03618 B	
02692 C	02899 B	03100 D	03619 D	
02693 B	02900 C	03101 C	03620 C	
02694 B	02901 A	03102 A	03621 B	
02695 C	02902 C	03103 D	03622 C	
02696 B	02903 D	03104 D	03623 A	
02697 C	02904 C	03105 A	03624 C	
02698 A	02905 D	03106 B	03625 D	
02699 C	02906 C	03107 C	03626 B	
02700 A	02907 D	03108 D	03627 D	
02701 C	02908 C	03109 D	03628 C	
02702 B	02909 D	03110 C	03629 A	
02703 C	02910 D	03111 C	03630 B	
02704 D	02912 B	03299 C	03631 C	
02705 D	03050 D	03300 C	03632 D	
02706 D	03051 A	03301 B	03633 C	
02707 A	03052 D	03302 D	03634 B	
02851 B	03053 A	03303 C	03635 A	
02852 C	03054 B	03304 A	03636 C	
02853 A	03055 C	03305 B	03637 C	
02854 C	03056 A	03306 C	03638 A	
02855 B	03057 C	03307 B	03639 A	
02856 D	03058 D	03308 C	03640 B	

1801. The wind used to propel a sailing vessel the:

. rational wind
. true wind
. apparent wind
. sensible wind

1802. You are on a broad reach on the port ack with the mainsail and a spinnaker set. Which statement is FALSE?

A. The spinnaker pole should be eased forward as you sail closer to the wind.
B. The mainsail should be sheeted in to keep the leach of the spinnaker open.
C. The spinnaker sheet should be led to a point well aft.
D. As speed increases, heeling force increases and balance is harder to maintain.

01805. A sloop is a sailing vessel with:

A. one mast
B. two masts: with the mizzen stepped abaft the sternpost
C. two masts: with the mizzen stepped forward of the sternpost
D. two masts: a forward and a main

01807. Which of the following is standing rigging?

A. halyards
B. stays
C. sheets
D. downhauls

01808. You are running with a spinnaker set. The luff has started to curl. What should you do?

A. Haul on the spinnaker pole guy to harden the luff.
B. Slack the spinnaker pole guy to increase the angle of the leach to the wind.
C. Give a sharp tug to the sheet.
D. Lower the spinnaker boom to spread the spinnaker.

01812. If the sails are always properly set and trimmed, as a vessel luffs from a beam reach to close hauled the:

A. apparent wind moves forward
B. heeling moment decreases
C. side slip decreases
D. speed increases

01815. If the sails are always properly set and trimmed, as a vessel luffs from a beam reach to close hauled the:

A. speed increases
B. side slip decreases
C. heeling moment decreases
D. apparent wind moves forward

01816. INTERNATIONAL AND INLAND
Unless specifically required by the rules, a sailing vessel is not required to keep out of the way of a:

A. vessel engaged in fishing
B. vessel anchored
C. power-driven pilot vessel on station
D. vessel setting a buoy

01818. When setting the spinnaker:

A. the spinnaker pole is always set on the leeward side
B. the jib must be furled or lowered
C. it is controlled easier when hoisted to leeward
D. it should be hoisted slowly to control the set as it comes up

01824. On a topsail schooner the square sails are controlled by:

A. guys
B. vangs
C. braces
D. brails

01829. A sailing vessel with the wind coming from 220° relative would be:

A. close hauled on the port tack
B. close hauled on the starboard tack
C. running free
D. on a broad reach on a port tack

01832. A sail may be made of several pieces of material, each piece of which is known as a:

A. section
B. panel
C. gore
D. layer

01838. When a sail is reefed, the reef band is pulled taut by hauling on the:

A. reef cringle
B. bolt rope
C. reef points
D. Cunningham

01839. A sailing vessel with the wind coming from 020° relative would be:

A. coming about
B. close hauled on the port tack
C. running free
D. on a broad reach on the starboard tack

01842. Which action will NOT help in preventing an hourglass fouling of a spinnaker when it is being set?

A. Hoist quickly.
B. Haul on the sheet.
C. Haul on the guy.
D. Haul on the boom downhaul.

01843. In heavy weather under sail, which of the following actions will NOT improve the seaworthiness of the vessel?

A. reduce wind resistance
B. slow to bare steerageway
C. improve the sail's driving angle if possible
D. increase righting power

01846. You are under sail. While steady on course, you reef the mainsail and your speed slows. If the wind is steady the apparent wind:

A. is unchanged
B. increases and draws aft
C. increases and draws forward
D. decreases and draws aft

01849. Which of the following lines would NOT be used in handling a jib or staysail?

A. halyard
B. downhaul
C. uphaul
D. sheet

01856. A sailing vessel with the wind coming from 175° relative would be:

A. close hauled on the starboard tack
B. close hauled on the port tack
C. on a broad reach on a port tack
D. running free

01858. A sailing vessel with the wind coming from 183° relative would be:

A. close hauled on the port tack
B. close hauled on the starboard tack
C. running free
D. on a broad reach on a starboard tack

01859. All of the following parts of the sail illustrated are labeled correctly EXCEPT the part labeled: (see illustration D003SL)

A. head
B. leach
C. luff
D. tack

01869. The three corners of the sail illustrated are labeled: (see illustration D002SL)

A. head, fore, and aft
B. luff, leech, and spar
C. headboard, foot, and tail
D. head, tack, and clew

01876. A sailing vessel with the wind coming from 140° relative would be:

A. close hauled on the starboard tack
B. close hauled on the port tack
C. on a broad reach on a starboard tack
D. running free

01882. A sailing vessel with the wind coming from 268° relative would be:

A. on a close reach on a port tack
B. reaching on a port tack
C. on a broad reach on a port tack
D. running free

01889. You are on a sloop rig in heavy weather. If you reef the mainsail, which of the following will tend to relieve the vessel if it then carries excessive lee helm?

A. Shift weight aft.
B. If equipped with a centerboard, partially raise it.
C. Take a double reef in the mainsail.
D. Set a smaller jib.

01896. The side of the sail labeled "A" is known as the: (see illustration D001SL)

A. leech
B. clew
C. luff
D. headboard

01897. What is a part of a vessel's standing rigging?

A. sheet
B. backstay
C. topping lift
D. downhaul

01902. You are on a broad reach on the port tack with the mainsail and a spinnaker set. Which statement is TRUE?

A. The spinnaker pole should be set at almost a right angle to the keel.
B. The mainsail should be sheeted close to the centerline to keep the spinnaker's leach open.
C. The spinnaker should be sheeted in close to the mast (or foremast).
D. As speed increases, heeling force increases and balance is harder to maintain.

01904. A sailing vessel with the wind coming over the port side is said to be on a:

A. port jibe
B. starboard jibe
C. port tack
D. starboard tack

01905. What fitting on the mast works in conjunction with the shrouds to control side bend of the mast?

A. chainplate
B. hound
C. crowfoot
D. spreader

01911. A ketch is a sailing vessel with:

A. one mast
B. two masts: with the mizzen stepped abaft the sternpost
C. two masts: with the mizzen stepped forward of the sternpost
D. two masts: a forward and a main

01915. If the sails are always properly set and trimmed, as a vessel luffs from a beam reach to close hauled the:

A. apparent wind moves aft
B. heeling moment increases
C. side slip decreases
D. mainsheet must be eased

01916. What is part of a vessel's standing rigging?

A. sheet
B. backstay
C. topping lift
D. downhaul

01919. A sailing vessel with the wind coming from 050° relative would be:

A. close hauled on the starboard tack
B. reaching on a starboard tack
C. on a broad reach on a port tack
D. running before the wind

01922. INTERNATIONAL ONLY
A sailing vessel shall not impede the safe passage of a:

A. power-driven vessel following a traffic lane
B. pilot vessel en route to a pilot station
C. law enforcement vessel
D. all of the above

01926. A "reaching" course is one in which the wind:

A. comes directly over the bow
B. comes directly over the stern

C. comes over an area extending from the bow to the quarter
D. has no effect on the vessel

01929. You are underway in your schooner with all sails set when a sudden squall hits with strong winds from abeam. You should:

A. bear off
B. sheet in
C. harden up
D. come up into the wind

01932. Which statement about sailing close-hauled is TRUE?

A. If you ease the sheets, you can sail faster and closer to the wind.
B. If you ease the sheets, you can sail faster on the same course.
C. If you steer closer to the wind, you will slow.
D. If you sheet your sails closer to the centerline, you must bear away from the wind.

01934. Which would NOT reduce the possibility of capsizing in heavy winds?

A. partially raising the centerboard to improve balance
B. increasing tension on the clew outhaul
C. reducing sail area by reefing
D. shifting weight in the vessel to the leeward side

01942. You are on a broad reach on the port tack with the mainsail and spinnaker set. Which statement is TRUE?

A. The spinnaker pole should be set at almost a right angle to the keel.
B. The mainsail sheet should be eased to where the mainsail is ready to quiver.
C. The spinnaker's leach must be kept open by every possible means.
D. The spinnaker's sheet should be led into a point well forward.

01943. You are under sail. While steady on course you shake out a reef and your speed increases. If the wind velocity is steady, the apparent wind:

A. is unchanged
B. increases and draws aft
C. increases and draws forward
D. decreases and draws aft

01947. INTERNATIONAL AND INLAND
Your 18-meter vessel is under sail at night displaying sidelights, sternlight, and a red light over a green light at the masthead. If you start the auxiliary engine and engage the propeller, what change must you make in the vessel's lights?

A. none as long as the sails are set
B. Show two green lights instead of a red and green at the masthead.
C. Display a white light in sufficient time to prevent collision.
D. Replace the all-round red and green lights with a white masthead light.

01953. Which of the following statements is TRUE concerning the gooseneck?

A. It is a sailing maneuver which brings the vessel's head through the wind.
B. It connects the boom to the mast and allows the boom to swing freely.
C. It is a sailing condition where there is a loss of air flow over the sails.
D. none of the above

01964. Which step should be taken to reduce the possibility of capsizing when experiencing heavy winds?

A. Ease the mainsheet when running before the wind.
B. Ease tension on the vang.
C. Increase tension on the clew outhaul.
D. all of the above

01966. A sailing vessel with the wind coming from 090° relative would be:

A. close hauled on the starboard tack
B. reaching on the starboard tack
C. on a broad reach on the starboard tack
D. close hauled on the port tack

01969. A sailing vessel with the wind coming from 290° relative would be:

A. on a close reach on a port tack
B. close hauled on a starboard tack
C. on a broad reach on a port tack
D. on a beam reach on a starboard tack

01972. Which statement about sailing close-hauled is TRUE?

A. If you ease the sheets, you can sail faster but not so close to the wind.
B. If you ease the sheets, you will be in irons.
C. If you sheet your sails closer to the centerline, you can sail closer to the wind and decrease leeway.
D. If you sheet your sails closer to the centerline, you will luff.

01974. When experiencing heavy winds, you should reef sails in order to:

A. bring the sails parallel to wind flow
B. reduce sail area exposed to wind flow

C. allow the sails to catch more wind
D. remove all tension on the main and jib sheets

01976. A capsized vessel is best righted when what part of the vessel is downwind?

A. stern
B. bow
C. centerboard
D. mast

01977. A stay is an example of:

A. standing rigging
B. a downhaul
C. a halliard
D. a jib

01978. Which action is recommended in attempting to right a capsized sailing vessel with the mast downwind?

A. Position all personnel at the stern and rock the vessel upright.
B. Position all personnel around the mast and lift the vessel upright.
C. Lock the centerboard in the down position, stand on the centerboard, and haul on a line attached to the mast.
D. Put the centerboard in the up position and have all personnel haul in on the line attached to the mast.

01982. A spinnaker is properly trimmed when:

A. the luff is almost ready to curl in or break
B. the spinnaker pole is parallel to the deck at a right angle to the centerline
C. it has a deep, V-shaped cross section to catch the wind
D. the clew is higher than the tack, and the leach is curled in

01989. What is the proper method to fix running rigging to a cleat?

A. half-hitches then a round turn
B. one round turn
C. a series of half-hitches
D. a round turn, figure eights, and a half-hitch

01992. The primary advantage of a deep keel on a sailing vessel is that the:

A. resistance to lateral movement is increased
B. length-depth ratio is decreased resulting in a faster hull design
C. height of the center of gravity above the hull is increased resulting in a more stable vessel
D. mast height can be increased to compensate for increased area of lateral resistance

01994. You are close hauled on the starboard tack. There is a rock awash one point on your port bow at a distance of one mile. You will weather the rock:

A. when the rock moves to the left in relation to the background
B. when the rock remains on any bearing on the port side
C. when the rock remains about one point on the port bow as you approach
D. if you ease your sheets and point closer to the wind

01998. INTERNATIONAL AND INLAND
You are under sail making 5 knots. The apparent wind is broad on the starboard beam at 10 knots. Another sailing vessel is sighted dead ahead but you cannot determine if you are meeting or overtaking. What action is correct?

A. You must keep out of the way only if you determine you are overtaking the other vessel.
B. The other vessel must keep clear because you have the wind on the starboard side.
C. You must keep clear because you are to windward of the other vessel.
D. Both vessels are required to maneuver to keep out of the way.

01999. You are on a sloop rigged vessel with the mainsail and jib set. What will happen if you reef the mainsail?

A. The vessel will tend to luff if wind speed increases.
B. The helmsman should expect the vessel to carry lee helm.
C. The center of effort of the sails will tend to move aft.
D. A larger jib should be set to balance the sail plan.

02007. The heel of the mast rests on the:

A. foot plate
B. sole plate
C. hounds
D. step

02012. Twisting of the mainsail can best be controlled by:

A. inserting shorter sail battens in the batten pockets
B. increasing tension on the kicking strap
C. slacking the main outhaul
D. easing the mainsheet

02015. A shroud is an example of:

A. a light sail
B. a topmast stay

C. a sheet
D. standing rigging

02018. The vertical spar extending down from the bowsprit is called the:

A. spritspar
B. dolphin striker
C. jibboom
D. fish stick

02021. If the sails are always properly set and trimmed, as a vessel luffs from a beam reach to close hauled the:

A. true wind increases
B. heeling moment decreases
C. side slip increases
D. jib sheet must be eased

02024. Sail battens are used to:

A. keep the leach extended and prevent sail edge flutter
B. secure the sail corners to the mast, boom and sheet
C. protect the sail edges during heavy weather
D. keep tension on the clew outhaul and downhaul

02025. INTERNATIONAL AND INLAND
You are under sail with the auxiliary engine running and the propeller turning. Which statement is TRUE?

A. This condition is indicated by a conical shape, apex downwards.
B. You should maintain course and speed when approaching a power-driven vessel.
C. You must display two green lights in a vertical line at or near the masthead.
D. You are considered sailing as long as sail propulsion affects the vessel's maneuverability.

02026. Which of the following statements is TRUE concerning the gooseneck?

A. It is a sailing maneuver which brings the vessel's head through the wind.
B. It connects the boom to the mast and allows the boom to swing freely.
C. It is a sailing condition where there is a loss of air flow over the sails.
D. none of the above

02029. A yawl is a sailing vessel with:

A. a single mast
B. two masts: with the mizzen stepped abaft the sternpost
C. two masts: with the mizzen stepped forward of the sternpost
D. two masts: a forward and a main

02035. You are under sail. While steady on course the true wind decreases from 15 to 10 knots. If you maintain the same speed, the apparent wind:

A. increases and draws aft
B. decreases and draws forward
C. is unchanged
D. decreases and draws aft

02036. Which statement is TRUE concerning the spinnaker pole?

A. Its purpose is to hold the head of the sail rigid to the mast.
B. It is attached to the clew of the spinnaker.
C. It is set on the side opposite the main boom.
D. It is set such that the spinnaker is inboard of the forestay.

02042. Which line would be used to hoist a sail?

A. forestay
B. halyard
C. mainsheet
D. foreguy

02044. INTERNATIONAL AND INLAND
You are under sail making 5 knots. The apparent wind is broad on the port beam at 10 knots. Another sailing vessel is sighted dead ahead on a meeting course. What action is correct?

A. Both vessels maneuver to avoid collision.
B. You must keep out of the way of other vessel.
C. Only the other vessel must maneuver to avoid collision.
D. You are only required to maneuver if collision cannot be avoided by maneuver of other vessel.

02049. The bottom of the mast is the:

A. foot
B. heel
C. step
D. sole

02056. Which line would NOT be used to rig a spinnaker?

A. guy
B. downhaul
C. headstay
D. uphaul

02058. The purpose of a vang is to hold down the boom and control slack in the:

A. leech
B. luff
C. foot
D. tack

02059. What standing rigging supports the mast in the fore and aft and athwartships directions?

A. sheets and guys
B. guys and vangs
C. vangs and shrouds
D. shrouds and stays

02062. If you were running before the wind in a fresh breeze, a boom may be prevented from accidently jibing by using a(n):

A. buntline
B. clewline
C. outhaul
D. lazy guy

02064. INTERNATIONAL AND INLAND
You are under sail and overtaking a tug and tow. What action is correct?

A. The power-driven tug must maneuver to avoid collision.
B. You must maneuver to avoid the tug and tow.
C. You must maneuver to avoid collision only if the tug is to leeward and the wind is on your port side.
D. Both vessels are required to maneuver to avoid collision.

02066. Vangs are used to:

A. steady the gaff
B. draw the head of the sail to windward
C. tauten the standing rigging
D. douse the gaff topsail

02069. The metal horseshoe-shaped pieces used to bend a staysail onto a stay are called:

A. hanks
B. shackles
C. warps
D. gudgeons

02072. Which of the following would most likely be wormed, parceled and served?

A. sheet
B. downhaul
C. brail
D. shroud

02076. If you reef the mainsail of a sloop, the center of effort:

A. moves forward and down
B. moves forward and up
C. moves aft and down
D. does not move

02077. INTERNATIONAL AND INLAND
You are proceeding under sail with the auxiliary engine running and the propeller turning. Which statement is TRUE?

A. If most of the propelling power comes from the sails, your vessel is considered a sailing vessel.
B. You must display a red light over a green light at the masthead.
C. In fog you must sound one prolonged blast at two-minute intervals when making way.
D. By day, you must display a black diamond shape forward.

02078. A spinnaker moves a vessel forward primarily by:

A. reducing air flow across the sail to a minimum
B. building up air pressure on the leeward side of the sail
C. catching the wind in the sail
D. balancing the wind pressure on both sides of the sail

02088. A bolt rope is a rope:

A. used to secure a dead eye
B. sewed on the edges of sails
C. used as a center in wire rope
D. used to secure a bolt

02095. Sails may be goosewinged when:

A. close hauled
B. tacking
C. wearing
D. sailing with the wind aft

02102. If the sails are always properly set and trimmed, as a vessel luffs from a beam reach to close hauled the:

A. apparent wind remains steady
B. heeling moment decreases
C. side slip decreases
D. speed decreases

02103. You are under sail. While steady on course the true wind increases from 10 to 15 knots. If you maintain the same speed, the apparent wind:

A. increases and draws aft
B. does not change
C. decreases and draws forward
D. decreases and draws aft

02107. Which of the following is NOT running rigging?

A. downhaul
B. backstay

C. halyard
D. sheet

02111. The universally jointed fitting used to attach the boom to the mast is the:

A. gooseneck
B. step
C. swivel
D. pintle

02112. "Luffing" is a sailing maneuver which:

A. brings main boom from one side of the vessel to the other when running before the wind
B. changes the vessel's tack by bringing the stern through the wind
C. brings the vessel's head more into the wind
D. reduces sail area by rolling the foot of the sail around the boom

02117. INTERNATIONAL AND INLAND
You are under sail and approaching another sailing vessel. Your vessel is to leeward and appears to have a relative bearing of 240° to 250° from the other vessel. What action is correct?

A. The other vessel must maneuver to avoid collision.
B. You must maintain course and speed.
C. You are required to maneuver only if the other vessel is taking insufficient action.
D. You should maneuver as if you are an overtaking vessel.

02154. When shifting to a course where the wind comes more from astern, easing the main outhaul would:

A. allow the boom to swing more easily to leeward
B. decrease the force needed to haul on the main sheet
C. bring the head of the sail down from the top of the mast
D. allow the sail to catch more wind

02155. When sailing with the wind aft, a vessel may carry sails on both sides at the same time. The sails in this condition are:

A. goosewinged
B. luffed
C. reefed
D. cringled

02165. A schooner is a fore-and-aft rigged vessel with:

A. a single mast
B. two masts: with the mizzen stepped abaft the sternpost

C. two masts: with the mizzen stepped forward of the sternpost
D. at least two masts: a forward and a main

02177. If you reef the mainsail of a sloop, the center of effort moves:

A. aft and up
B. forward and up
C. aft and down
D. forward and down

02187. INTERNATIONAL AND INLAND
Your 18-meter vessel is underway propelled by sail and power. What is required when the engine is stopped?

A. Have a white light ready for display in sufficient time to prevent collision.
B. Display red over green all-around lights near the top of the mast.
C. Display the sidelights and sternlight in a combined lantern at the masthead.
D. Turn off the white masthead light.

02189. Changing direction by bringing the stern of the vessel through the eye of the wind is known as:

A. jibing
B. running before the wind
C. tacking
D. reefing

02196. INTERNATIONAL AND INLAND
You are on a sailing vessel with the wind on the starboard side and are approaching another vessel that has the wind on the port side. What action should you take?

A. Reduce sail and hold course.
B. Alter course away from the other vessel.
C. Maintain course and speed.
D. any maneuver to avoid collision

02198. Which statement is TRUE concerning sails sheeted in close to the center line of the vessel?

A. The more the sails are sheeted in, the greater your speed will be when sailing downwind.
B. As the sails are sheeted in, the vessel will heel less when sailing close hauled.
C. As the sails are sheeted in on a close hauled course, speed will increase as the side forces on the vessel decrease.
D. Sheeting in the sails will allow the vessel to sail closer to the wind but with a decrease in speed.

02204. In order to maintain forward speed when changing from a close reach to a broad reach, you should:

A. ease sheets and shift weight inboard
B. ease sheets and shift weight outboard
C. haul in sheets and shift weight inboard
D. haul in sheets and shift weight outboard

02206. Which of the following actions will NOT reduce heeling of a vessel when sailing on a tack?

A. shifting weight to windward
B. easing sheets
C. reefing sails
D. changing to larger sails

02208. When sailing with the wind from dead astern, the main advantage of a centerboard is to:

A. provide weight stability low in the vessel
B. increase drag on the hull
C. decrease the heeling forces on the vessel
D. aid in steering

02212. In order to maintain speed while changing course from a close reach to a broad reach, the sails should be:

A. lowered
B. reefed
C. hauled in
D. eased out

02214. In order to tighten the luff of a sail, you would increase tension on the:

A. backstay
B. headstay
C. downhaul
D. outhaul

02216. Your vessel is about to capsize with both a mainsail and spinnaker. You have eased the mainsheet but the vessel still has excessive heel. What should be your next action?

A. Haul in on the mainsheet and attempt to set a jib to increase sail power.
B. Haul in on the mainsheet and ease the spinnaker sheet.
C. Attempt to bring the vessel more into the wind and haul in on all sheets.
D. Attempt to bear away from the wind and let the spinnaker sheet run.

02222. INTERNATIONAL AND INLAND
Your 18-meter vessel is underway propelled by sail and power. What action is required when the engine is stopped?

A. Turn off the white masthead light.
B. Display a black cone, apex downwards, in the forepart of the vessel.

C. Display the sidelights and sternlight in a combined lantern.
D. Display red over green all-around lights near the top of the mast.

02224. Your vessel is drifting with the wind broad on the port beam. The sail is set and flapping free. As you sheet in, the maximum drive is attained when the sail:

A. is at right angles to the true wind
B. first takes the shape of an airfoil
C. is filled with a slight flap at the leech
D. is 45° from the apparent wind

02225. INTERNATIONAL AND INLAND
You are under sail at 5 knots with the wind from astern. Another sailing vessel is broad on your port beam with a steady bearing and decreasing range. What action is correct?

A. Both vessels must keep out of the way to avoid collision.
B. You must maneuver to avoid the other vessel.
C. You must maneuver to avoid collision only if your mainsail is set to port.
D. You are being overtaken and must maintain course and speed.

02226. A vessel is sailing on a close reach when a strong wind suddenly heels the vessel hard over to one side. In order to reduce the heeling and yet maintain speed, you should:

A. ease the mainsheet and bear more away from the wind
B. haul in on the mainsheet and steer more towards the wind
C. haul in on the mainsheet and ease the jib sheet
D. ease all sheets and bear more into the wind

02228. If your sails are properly trimmed while on a reaching course, changing to a close hauled course will:

A. require you to sheet in to maintain the maximum forward sailing force
B. result in a reduction of speed
C. cause a greater heeling force to leeward
D. all of the above

02229. In order to get the maximum sailing effect when using both a mainsail and jib, the two sails should be trimmed such that:

A. the jib is on one side of the vessel and the mainsail on the other
B. an air slot is formed between the two sails
C. one sail is as close to a right angle as possible to the other
D. as much of a gap as possible exists between the two sails in order to catch the most wind

02232. Your vessel is sailing on a port tack when a sudden gust of wind heels the vessel sharply to starboard. Which action will reduce the heeling of the vessel?

A. Attempt to sail the vessel closer to the wind.
B. Ease the sheets to allow air flow to spill off the sail.
C. Shift weight to the port side of the vessel.
D. all of the above

02234. As a vessel falls off the wind from close-hauled to a beam reach, the tendency for the vessel to move sideways through the water will:

A. increase
B. decrease
C. change only if the vessel comes about on the opposite tack
D. not change

02238. You are sitting on the port side of your vessel and steering by tiller. If you pull the tiller arm towards you, the vessel's head will:

A. turn to port
B. turn to starboard
C. only turn with a corresponding change in sail trim
D. only turn if the centerboard is fully down

02239. A method by which you can temporarily slow or stop a sailing vessel is to:

A. put the wind off the beam and sheet in
B. put the wind off the stern and ease all sheets
C. bring the vessel's head into the wind and let the sails luff
D. raise the centerboard when running before the wind

02275. INTERNATIONAL AND INLAND
Your 18-meter vessel is propelled by sail and power. What action is required when the engine is stopped?

A. Display a black diamond shape forward.
B. Remove the black cone shape from forward.
C. Remove the black balls (one at the masthead and one on each spreader).
D. Display a black cylindrical shape at the masthead.

02277. If you reef the mainsail of a sloop, the center of lateral resistance:

A. moves forward and up
B. moves forward and down
C. moves aft and down
D. does not move

02283. Sails are goosewinged when:

A. tacking
B. on a close reach
C. sailing with the wind aft
D. anchored or drifting

02320. You are attempting to recover an object floating in the water. If your approach to the object is made on a port tack, which action should you take in order to slow the vessel as you draw near?

A. Quickly change to a starboard tack as you reach the object.
B. Shift the rudder from port to starboard several times as you reach the object.
C. Bring the wind so that it comes over the stern and ease all sheets.
D. Bring the wind directly over the bow and allow the sails to flap.

02330. What is the purpose of a centerboard when sailing on a tack?

A. to reduce heeling of the vessel to windward
B. to add weight stability low in the vessel
C. to reduce side slip of the vessel downwind
D. to prevent the vessel backing into the wind

02337. Sideways movement of the mast is resisted by the:

A. weather shroud
B. weather halliard
C. lee sheet
D. forestay

02340. When attempting to pick up a person in the water, your approach should normally be made:

A. with your stern towards the person
B. to windward of the person
C. to leeward of the person
D. with all sails sheeted in

02642. When properly set and drawing, a fore-and-aft sail has a cross section that:

A. is a uniform curve
B. is a curve with more curve at the luff
C. is a curve with more curve at the leach
D. approximates a straight line

SAIL ENDORSEMENT ANSWERS

01801 C	02025 A
01802 D	02026 B
01805 A	02029 B
01807 B	02035 B
01808 C	02036 C
01812 A	02042 B
01815 D	02044 B
01816 C	02049 B
01818 C	02056 C
01824 C	02058 A
01829 D	02059 D
01832 B	02062 D
01838 A	02064 B
01839 A	02066 A
01842 D	02069 A
01843 B	02072 D
01846 D	02076 A
01849 C	02077 C
01856 D	02078 C
01858 C	02088 B
01859 C	02095 D
01869 D	02102 D
01876 C	02103 A
01882 B	02107 B
01889 D	02111 A
01896 C	02112 C
01897 B	02117 D
01902 B	02154 D
01904 C	02155 A
01905 D	02165 D
01911 C	02177 D
01915 B	02187 D
01916 B	02189 A
01919 A	02196 C
01922 A	02198 D
01926 C	02204 A
01929 D	02206 D
01932 C	02208 D
01934 D	02212 D
01942 C	02214 C
01943 C	02216 D
01947 D	02222 A
01953 B	02224 B
01964 C	02225 A
01966 B	02226 A
01969 A	02228 D
01972 A	02229 B
01974 B	02232 D
01976 D	02234 B
01977 A	02238 B
01978 C	02239 C
01982 A	02275 B
01989 D	02277 D
01992 A	02283 C
01994 A	02320 D
01998 C	02330 C
01999 B	02337 A
02007 D	02340 C
02012 B	02642 B
02015 D	
02018 B	
02021 C	
02024 A	

EXAMINATION ILLUSTRATIONS

RULES OF THE ROAD

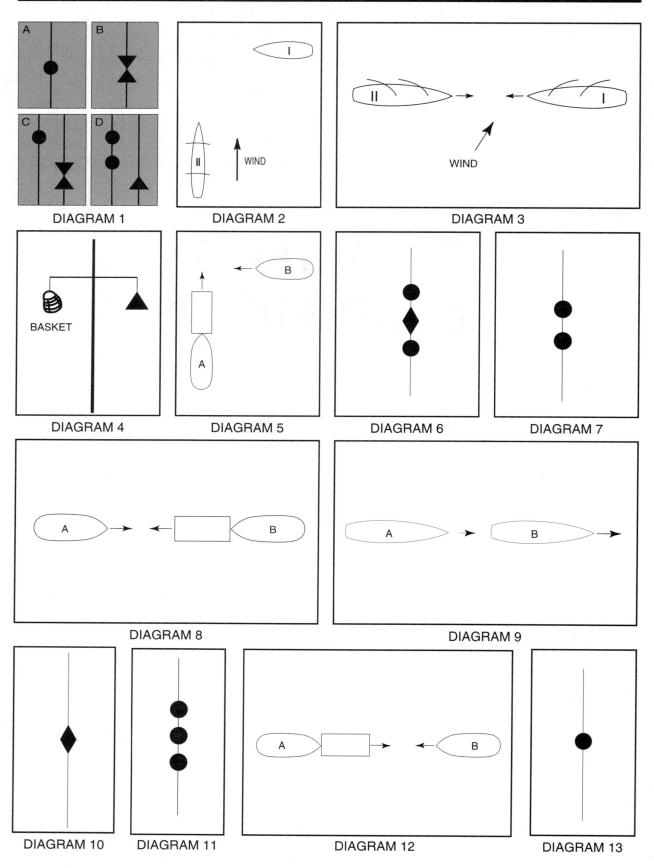

DIAGRAM 1

DIAGRAM 2

DIAGRAM 3

DIAGRAM 4

DIAGRAM 5

DIAGRAM 6

DIAGRAM 7

DIAGRAM 8

DIAGRAM 9

DIAGRAM 10

DIAGRAM 11

DIAGRAM 12

DIAGRAM 13

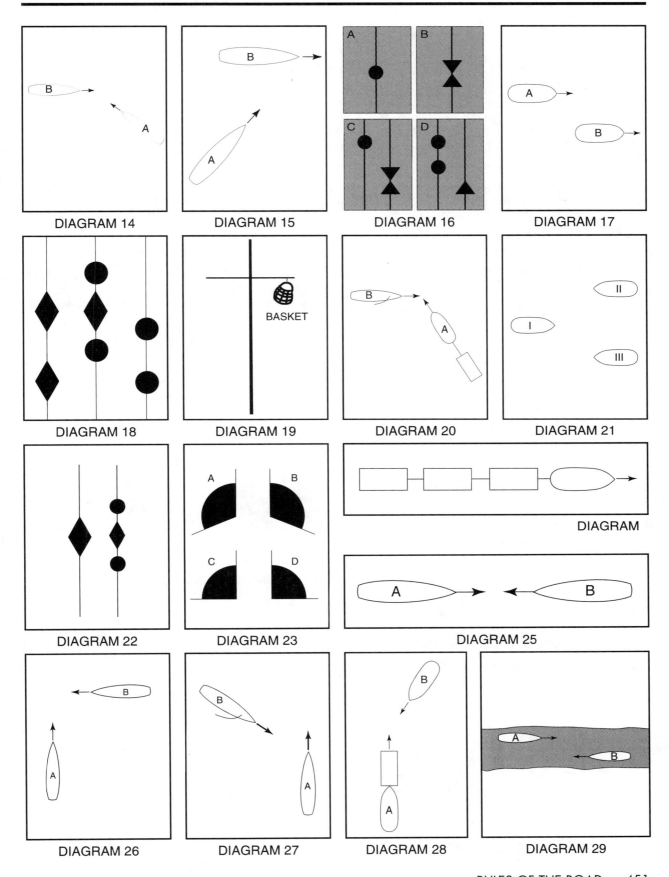

DIAGRAM 14

DIAGRAM 15

DIAGRAM 16

DIAGRAM 17

DIAGRAM 18

DIAGRAM 19

DIAGRAM 20

DIAGRAM 21

DIAGRAM 22

DIAGRAM 23

DIAGRAM

DIAGRAM 25

DIAGRAM 26

DIAGRAM 27

DIAGRAM 28

DIAGRAM 29

BASKET

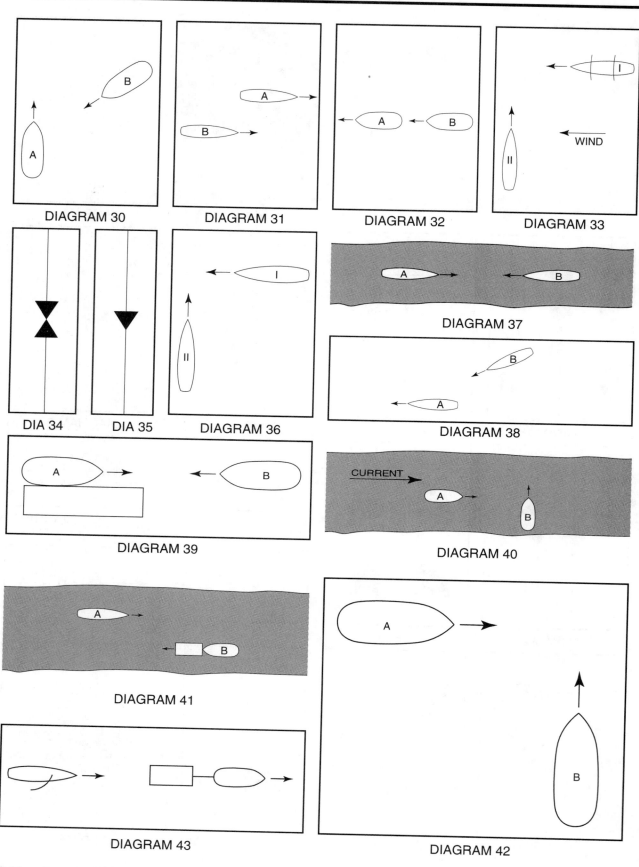

DIAGRAM 30

DIAGRAM 31

DIAGRAM 32

DIAGRAM 33

DIA 34

DIA 35

DIAGRAM 36

DIAGRAM 37

DIAGRAM 38

DIAGRAM 39

DIAGRAM 40

DIAGRAM 41

DIAGRAM 42

DIAGRAM 43

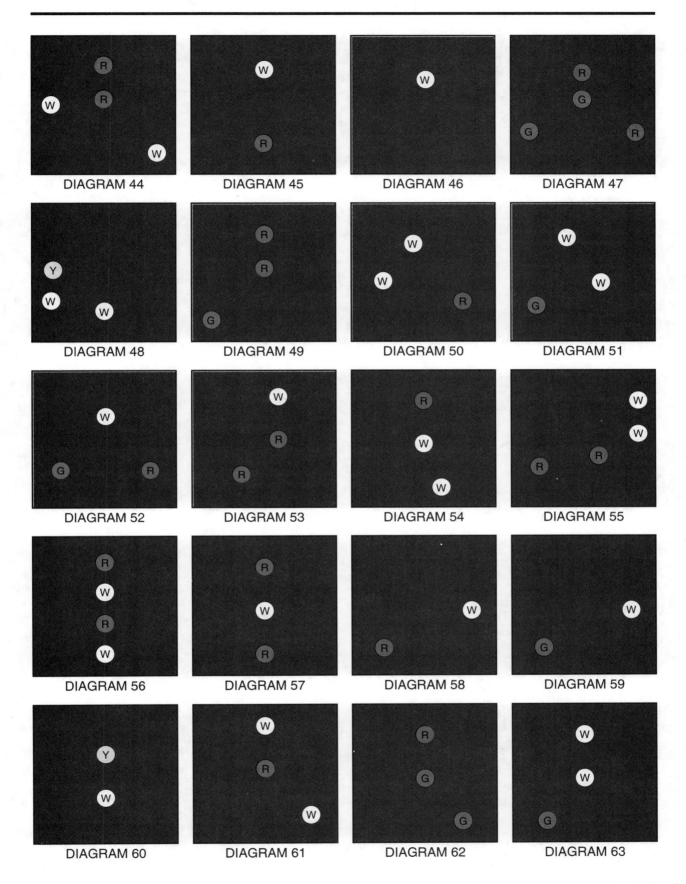

DIAGRAM 44 DIAGRAM 45 DIAGRAM 46 DIAGRAM 47

DIAGRAM 48 DIAGRAM 49 DIAGRAM 50 DIAGRAM 51

DIAGRAM 52 DIAGRAM 53 DIAGRAM 54 DIAGRAM 55

DIAGRAM 56 DIAGRAM 57 DIAGRAM 58 DIAGRAM 59

DIAGRAM 60 DIAGRAM 61 DIAGRAM 62 DIAGRAM 63

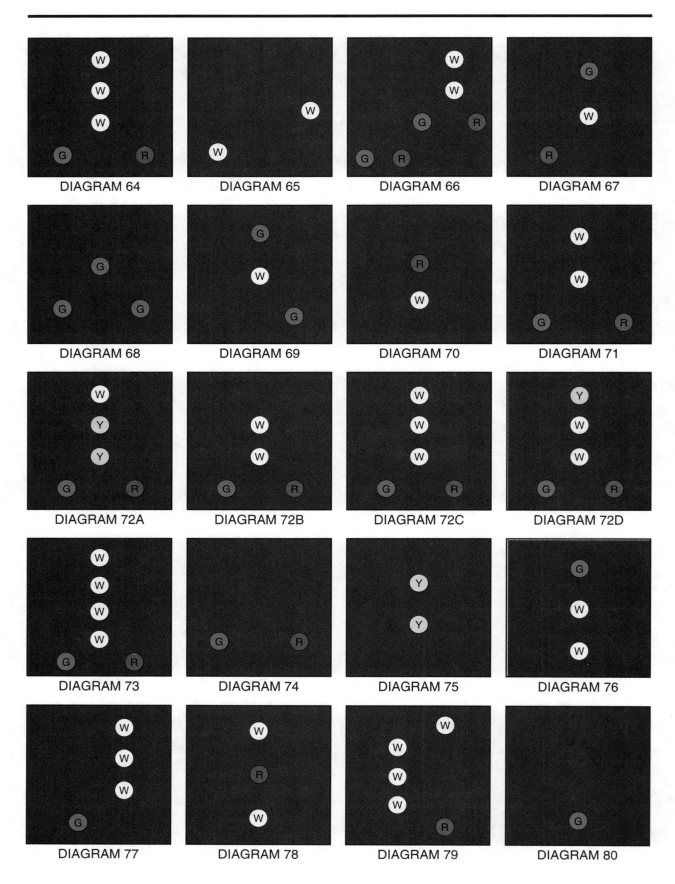

DIAGRAM 64   DIAGRAM 65   DIAGRAM 66   DIAGRAM 67

DIAGRAM 68   DIAGRAM 69   DIAGRAM 70   DIAGRAM 71

DIAGRAM 72A   DIAGRAM 72B   DIAGRAM 72C   DIAGRAM 72D

DIAGRAM 73   DIAGRAM 74   DIAGRAM 75   DIAGRAM 76

DIAGRAM 77   DIAGRAM 78   DIAGRAM 79   DIAGRAM 80

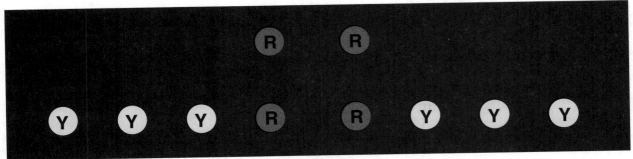

DIAGRAM 81

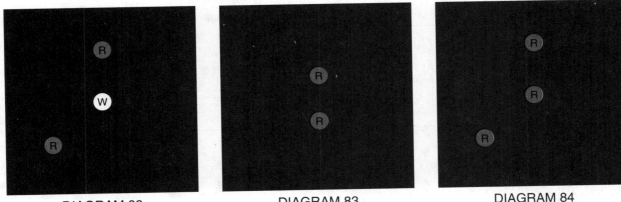

DIAGRAM 82   DIAGRAM 83   DIAGRAM 84

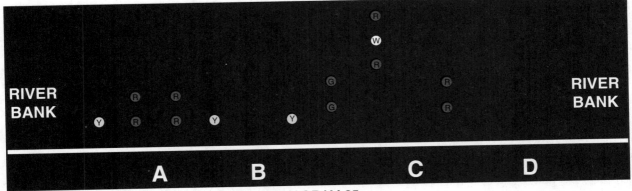

DIAGRAM 85

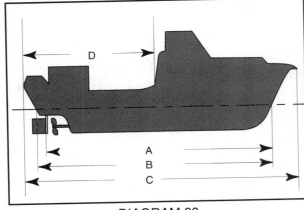

DIAGRAM 86

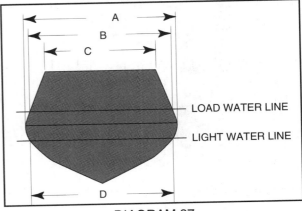

DIAGRAM 87

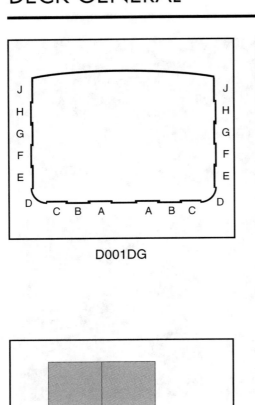

D001DG

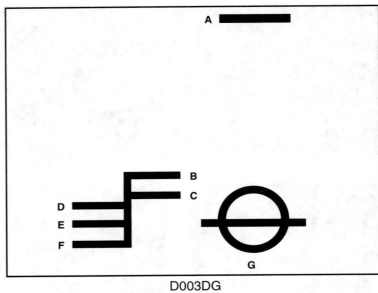

D003DG

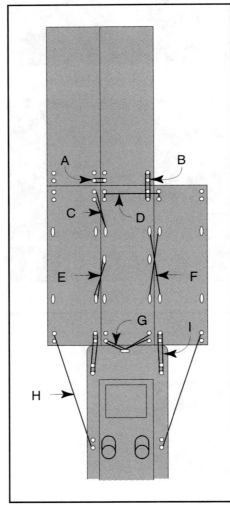

D024DG

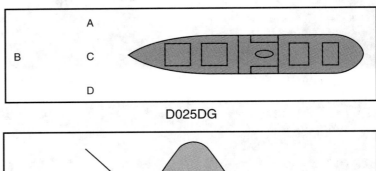

D025DG

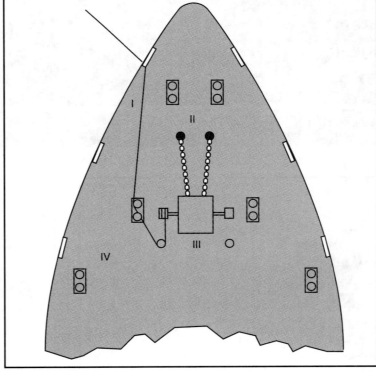

D019DG

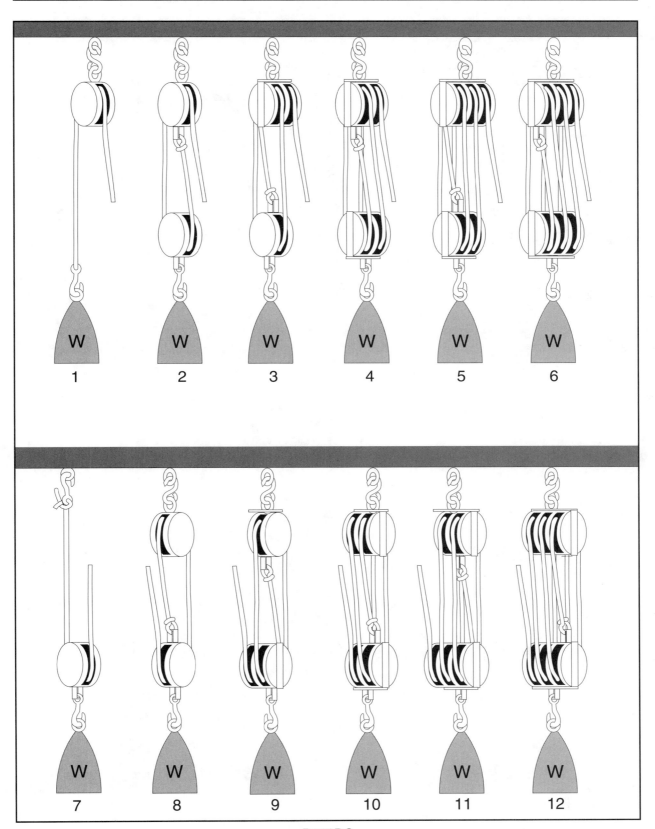

1   2   3   4   5   6

7   8   9   10   11   12

D029DG

D030DG

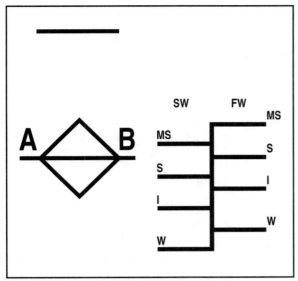

D031DG

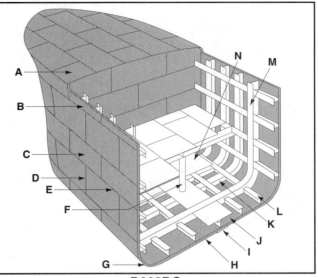

D033DG

HEADING (TRUE)	BEARING (TRUE)	RANGE (YARDS)	REMARKS
228°			Initial heading
228°	232°	2260	on initial course.
228°	234°	1700	Right full rudder
230°	236°	1490	ordered
252°	235°	1275	
275°	231°	1000	
316°	214°	850	
352°	198°	975	
022°	194°	1210	
053°	197°	1430	
087°	202°	1600	
115°	209°	1690	
151°	217°	1700	
183°	225°	1600	
218°	232°	1350	
228°	235°	1125	Rudder amidships Steady on 228° T

D034DG

HEADING (TRUE)	BEARING (TRUE)	RANGE (YARDS)	REMARKS
333°			Initial heading
333°	315°	2125	on initial course.
333°	310°	1650	LEFT full rudder
327°	307°	1475	ordered
310°	303°	1250	
278°	302°	1050	
268°	305°	900	
236°	318°	750	
196°	337°	800	
157°	344°	1100	
113°	340°	1350	
079°	332°	1525	
050°	324°	1575	
022°	318°	1550	
343°	308°	1400	
333°	302°	1175	Rudder amidships Steady on 333° T

D035DG

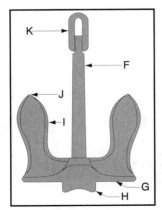

D038DG

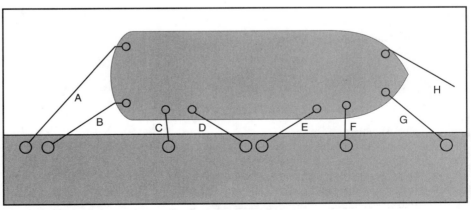

D044DG

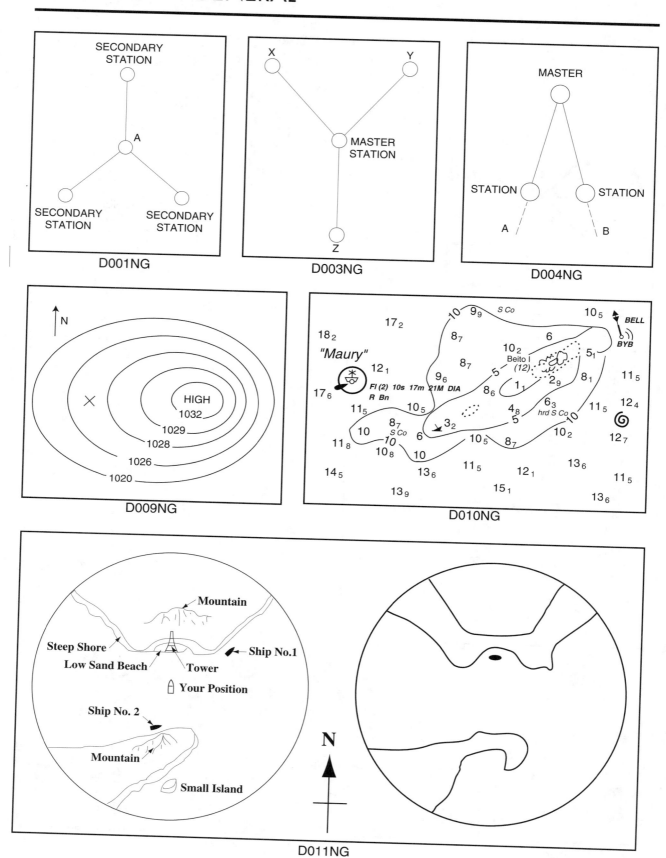

D001NG

D003NG

D004NG

D009NG

D010NG

D011NG

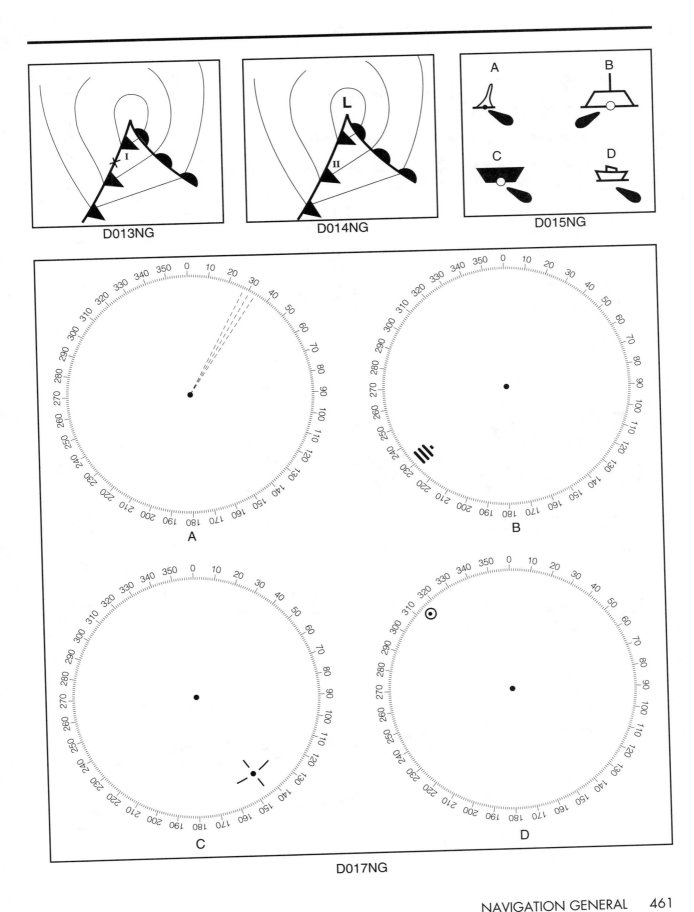

D013NG

D014NG

D015NG

A

B

C

D

D017NG

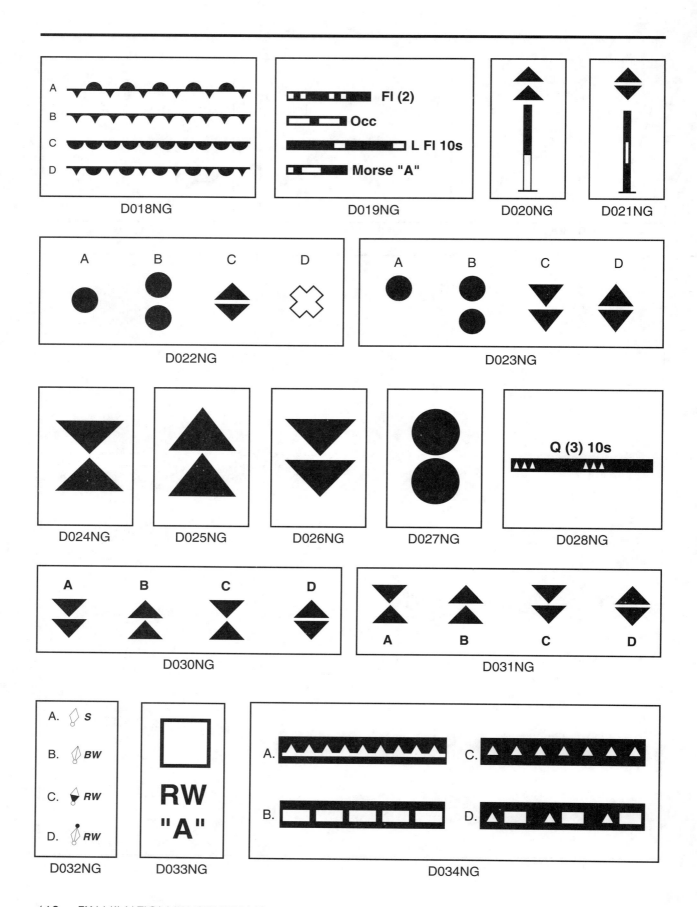

D018NG

D019NG

Fl (2)
Occ
L Fl 10s
Morse "A"

D020NG

D021NG

D022NG

D023NG

D024NG

D025NG

D026NG

D027NG

D028NG

Q (3) 10s

D030NG

D031NG

D032NG

A. S
B. BW
C. RW
D. RW

D033NG

RW "A"

D034NG

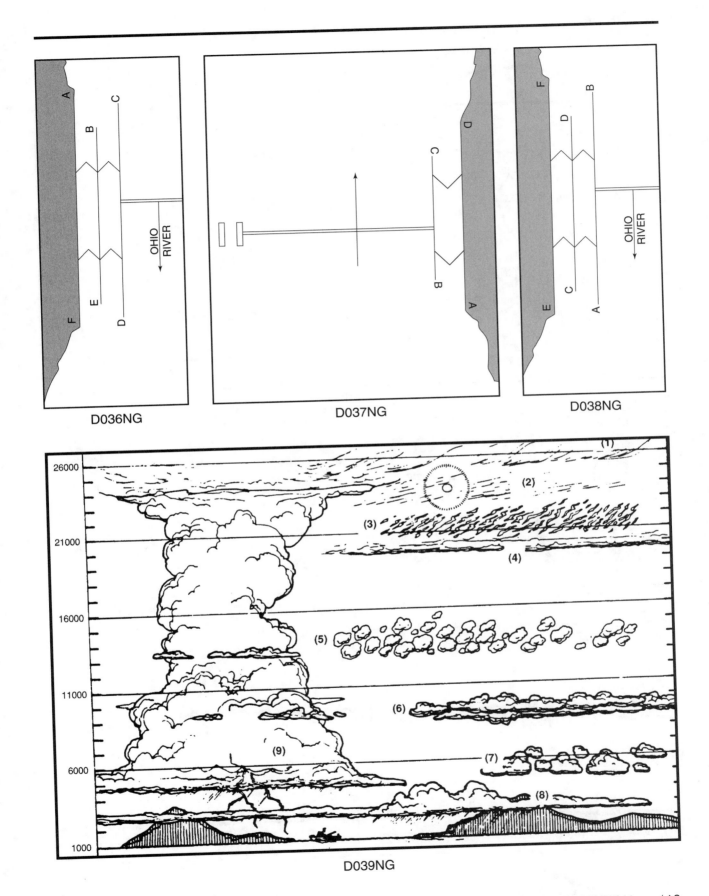

D036NG

D037NG

D038NG

D039NG

F

G

H

I

K

L

M

N

O

P

Q

D042NG

A B C D

D044NG

A B C D

D045NG

RED
A

RED
B

GREEN
C

GREEN
D

D046NG

D047NG

D048NG

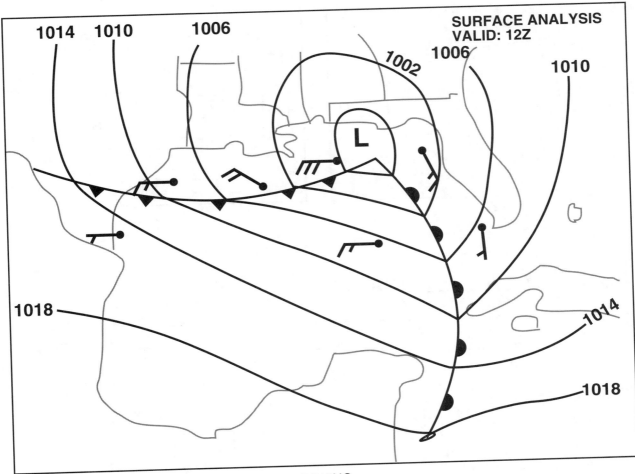

SURFACE ANALYSIS
VALID: 12Z

D049NG

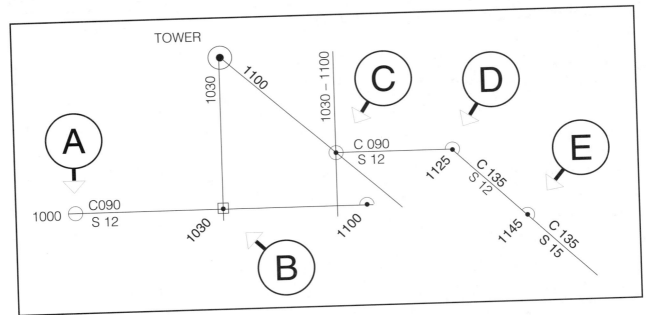

D051NG

SAFETY ILLUSTRATIONS

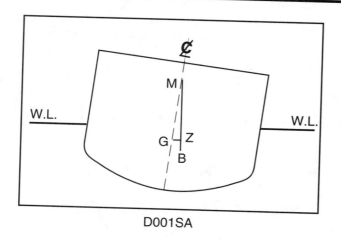

D001SA

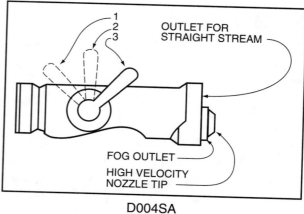

D004SA

AUXILIARY SAIL ILLUSTRATIONS

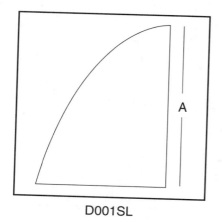

D001SL

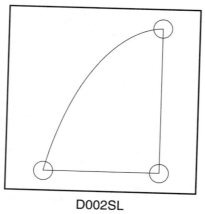

D002SL

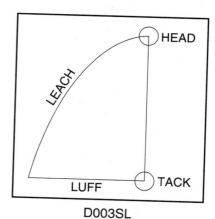

D003SL

APPENDIX:
COLREGS

PART A—GENERAL

RULE 1
Application

(a) These Rules shall apply to all vessels upon the high seas and in all waters connected therewith navigable by seagoing vessels.

These Rules apply to all vessels upon the inland waters of the United States, and to vessels of the United States on the Canadian waters of the Great Lakes to the extent that there is no conflict with Canadian law.

(b) Nothing in these Rules shall interfere with the operation of special rules made by an appropriate authority for roadsteads, harbors, rivers, lakes or inland waterways connected with the high seas and navigable by seagoing vessels. Such special rules shall conform as closely as possible to these Rules.

(c) Nothing in these Rules shall interfere with the operation of any special rules made by the government of any State with respect to additional station or signal lights, shapes or whistle signals for ships of war and vessels proceeding under convoy, or with respect to additional station or signal lights or shapes for fishing vessels engaged in fishing as a fleet. These additional station or signal lights, shapes or whistle signals shall, so far as possible, be such that they cannot be mistaken for any light, shape or signal authorized elsewhere under these Rules.

(d) Traffic separation schemes may be adopted by the Organization for the purpose of these Rules.

(e) Whenever the Government concerned shall have determined that a vessel of special construction or purpose cannot comply fully with the provisions of any of these rules with respect to the number, position, range or arc of visibility of lights or shapes, as well as to the disposition and characteristics of sound-signalling appliances, without interfering with the special function of the vessel, such vessel shall comply with such other provisions in regard to the number, position, range or arc of visibility of lights or shapes, as well as to the disposition and characteristics of sound signalling appliances, as her Government shall have determined to be the closest possible compliance with these Rules in respect to that vessel.

RULE 2
Responsibility

(a) Nothing in these Rules shall exonerate any vessel, or the owner, master or crew thereof, from the consequences of any neglect to comply with these Rules or of the neglect of any precaution which may be required by the ordinary practice of seamen, or by the special circumstances of the case.

(b) In construing and complying with these Rules due regard shall be had to all dangers of navigation and collision and to any special circumstances, including the limitations of the vessels involved, which may make a departure from these Rules necessary to avoid immediate danger.

RULE 3
General Definitions

For the purpose of these Rules, except where the context otherwise requires:

(a) The word "vessel" includes every description of water craft, including nondisplacement craft and seaplanes, used or capable of being used as a means of transportation on water.

(b) The term "power-driven vessel" means any vessel propelled by machinery.

(c) The term "sailing vessel" means any vessel under sail provided that propelling machinery, if fitted, is not being used.

(d) The term "vessel engaged in fishing" means any vessel fishing with nets, lines, trawls or other fishing apparatus which restrict maneuverability, but does not include a vessel fishing with trolling lines or other fishing apparatus which do not restrict maneuverability.

(e) The word "seaplane" includes any aircraft designed to maneuver on the water.

(f) The term "vessel not under command" means a vessel which through some exceptional circumstance is unable to maneuver as required by these Rules and is therefore unable to keep out of the way of another vessel.

(g) The term "vessel restricted in her ability to maneuver" means a vessel which from the nature of her work is restricted in her ability to maneuver as required by these Rules and is therefore unable to keep out of the way of another vessel.

The term "vessels restricted in their ability to maneuver" shall include but not be limited to:

(i) a vessel engaged in laying, servicing or picking up a navigation mark, submarine cable or pipeline;

(ii) a vessel engaged in dredging, surveying or underwater operations;

(iii) a vessel engaged in replenishment or transferring persons, provisions or cargo while underway;

(iv) a vessel engaged in the launching or recovery of aircraft;

(v) a vessel engaged in mineclearance operations;

(vi) a vessel engaged in a towing operation such as severely restricts the towing vessel and her tow in their ability to deviate from their course.

(h) The term "vessel constrained by her draft" means a power driven vessel which because of her draft in relation to the available depth of water is severely restricted in her ability to deviate from the course she is following.

NOTE: There is no mention of a "vessel constrained by her draft" anywhere in the Inland Rules.

(i) The word "underway" means that a vessel is not at anchor, or made fast to the shore, or aground.

(j) The words "length" and "breadth" of a vessel means her length overall and greatest breadth.

(k) Vessels shall be deemed to be in sight of one another only when one can be observed visually from the other.

(l) The term "restricted visibility" means any condition in which visibility is restricted by fog, mist, falling snow, heavy rainstorms, sandstorms or any other similar causes.

PART B—STEERING AND SAILING

Section I—Conduct of Vessels in Any Condition of Visibility

RULE 4
Application

Rules in this Section apply to any condition of visibility.

RULE 5
Look-out

Every vessel shall at all times maintain a proper look-out by sight and hearing as well as by all available means appropriate in the prevailing circumstances and conditions so as to make a full appraisal of the situation and of the risk of collision.

RULE 6
Safe Speed

Every vessel shall at all times proceed at a safe speed so that she can take proper and effective action to avoid collision and be stopped within a distance appropriate to the prevailing circumstances and conditions.

In determining a safe speed the following factors shall be among those taken into account:

(a) By all vessels:

(i) the state of visibility;

(ii) the traffic density including concentrations of fishing vessels or any other vessels;

(iii) the maneuverability of the vessel with special reference to stopping distance and turning ability in the prevailing conditions;

(iv) at night the presence of background light such as from shore lights or from back scatter of her own lights;

(v) the state of wind, sea and current, and the proximity of navigational hazards;

(vi) the draft in relation to the available depth of water.

(b) Additionally, by vessels with operational radar:

(i) the characteristics, efficiency and limitations of the radar equipment;

(ii) any constraints imposed by the radar range scale in use;

(iii) the effect on radar detection of the sea state, weather and other sources of interference;

(iv) the possibility that small vessels, ice and other floating objects may not be detected by radar at an adequate range;

(v) the number, location and movement of vessels detected by radar;

(vi) the more exact assessment of the visibility that may be possible when radar is used to determine the range of vessels or other objects in the vicinity.

RULE 7
Risk of Collision

(a) Every vessel shall use all available means appropriate to the prevailing circumstances and conditions to determine if risk of collision exists. If there is any doubt such risk shall be deemed to exist.

(b) Proper use shall be made of radar equipment if fitted and operational, including long-range scanning to obtain early warning of risk of collision and radar plotting or equivalent systematic observation of detected objects.

(c) Assumptions shall not be made on the basis of scanty information, especially scanty radar information.

(d) In determining if risk of collision exists the following considerations shall be among those taken into account:

(i) such risk shall be deemed to exist if the compass bearing of an approaching vessel does not appreciably change;

(ii) such risk may sometimes exist even when an appreciable bearing change is evident, particularly when approaching a very large vessel or a tow or when approaching a vessel at close range.

RULE 8
Action to Avoid Collision

(a) Any action taken to avoid collision shall, if the circumstances of the case admit, be positive, made in ample time and with due regard to the observance of good seamanship.

(b) Any alteration of course and/or speed to avoid collision shall, if the circumstances of the case admit, be large enough to be readily apparent to another vessel observing visually or by radar; a succession of small alterations of course and/or speed should be avoided.

(c) If there is sufficient sea room, alteration of course alone may be the most effective action to avoid a close-quarters situation provided that it is made in good time, is substantial and does not result in another close-quarters situation.

(d) Action taken to avoid collision with another vessel shall be such as to result in passing at a safe distance. The effectiveness of the action shall be carefully checked until the other vessel is finally past and clear.

(e) If necessary to avoid collision or allow more time to assess the situation, a vessel shall slacken her speed or take all way off by stopping or reversing her means of propulsion.

RULE 9
Narrow Channels

(a) A vessel proceeding along the course of a narrow channel or fairway shall keep as near to the outer limit of the channel or fairway which lies on her starboard side as is safe and practicable.

A vessel proceeding along the course of a narrow channel or fairway shall keep as near to the outer limit of the channel or fairway which lies on her starboard side as is safe and practicable.

Notwithstanding paragraph (a)(i) and Rule 14(a), a power driven vessel operating in narrow channels or fairways on the Great Lakes, Western Rivers, or waters specified by the Secretary, and proceeding downbound with a following current shall have the right-of-way over an upbound vessel, shall propose the manner and place of passage, and shall initiate the maneuvering signals prescribed by Rule 34(a)(i), as appropriate. The vessel proceeding upbound against the current shall hold as necessary to permit safe passing.

(b) A vessel of less than 20 meters in length or a sailing vessel shall not impede the passage of a vessel which can safely navigate only within a narrow channel or fairway.

(c) A vessel engaged in fishing shall not impede the passage of any other vessel navigating within a narrow channel or fairway.

(d) A vessel shall not cross a narrow channel or fairway if such crossing impedes the passage of a vessel which can safely navigate only within such channel or fairway. The latter vessel may use the sound signal prescribed in Rule 34(d) if in doubt as to the intention of the crossing vessel.

(e)(i) In a narrow channel or fairway when overtaking can take place only if the vessel to be overtaken has to take action to permit safe passing, the vessel intending to overtake shall indicate her intention by sounding the appropriate signal prescribed in Rule 34(c)(i). The vessel to be overtaken shall, if in agreement, sound the appropriate signal prescribed in Rule 34(c)(ii) and take steps to permit safe passing. If in doubt she may sound the signals prescribed in Rule 34(d).

In a narrow channel or fairway when overtaking, the vessel intending to overtake shall indicate her intention by sounding the appropriate signal prescribed in Rule 34(c) and take steps to permit safe passing. The overtaken vessel, if in agreement, shall sound the same signal. If in doubt she shall sound the danger signal prescribed in Rule 34(d).

(ii) This Rule does not relieve the overtaking vessel of her obligation under Rule 13.

(f) A vessel nearing a bend or an area of a narrow channel or fairway where other vessels may be obscured by an intervening obstruction shall navigate with particular alertness and caution and shall sound the appropriate signal prescribed in Rule 34(e).

(g) Any vessel shall, if the circumstances of the case admit, avoid anchoring in a narrow channel.

RULE 10
Traffic Separation Schemes

(a) This Rule applies to traffic separation schemes adopted by the Organization.

(b) A vessel using a traffic separation scheme shall:

(i) proceed in the appropriate traffic lane in the general direction of traffic flow for that lane;

(ii) so far as practicable keep clear of a traffic separation line or separation zone;

(iii) normally join or leave a traffic lane at the termination of the lane, but when joining or leaving from either side shall do so at as small an angle to the general direction of traffic flow as practicable.

(c) A vessel shall so far as practicable avoid crossing traffic lanes, but if obliged to do so shall cross as nearly as practicable at right angles to the general direction of traffic flow.

(d) Inshore traffic zones shall not normally be used by through traffic which can safely use the appropriate traffic lane within the adjacent traffic separation scheme. However, vessels of less than 20 meters in length and sailing vessels may under all circumstances use inshore traffic zones.

(e) A vessel other than a crossing vessel or a vessel joining or leaving a lane shall not normally enter a separation zone or cross a separation line except:

(i) in cases of emergency to avoid immediate danger;

(ii) to engage in fishing within a separation zone.

(f) A vessel navigating in areas near the terminations of traffic separation schemes shall do so with particular caution.

(g) A vessel shall so far as practicable avoid anchoring in a traffic separation scheme or in areas near its terminations.

(h) A vessel not using a traffic separation scheme shall avoid it by as wide a margin as is practicable.

(i) A vessel engaged in fishing shall not impede the passage of any vessel following a traffic lane.

(j) A vessel of less than 20 meters in length or a sailing vessel shall not impede the safe passage of a power-driven vessel following a traffic lane.

(k) A vessel restricted in her ability to maneuver when engaged in an operation for the maintenance of safety of navigation in a traffic separation scheme is exempted from complying with this Rule to the extent necessary to carry out the operation.

(l) A vessel restricted in her ability to maneuver when engaged in an operation for the laying, servicing or picking up of a submarine cable, within a traffic separation scheme, is exempted from complying with this Rule to the extent necessary to carry out the operation.

Section II—Conduct of Vessels in Sight of One Another

RULE 11
Application

Rules in this Section apply to vessels in sight of one another.

RULE 12
Sailing Vessels

(a) When two sailing vessels are approaching one another, so as to involve risk of collision, one of them shall keep out of the way of the other as follows:

(i) when each has the wind on a different side, the vessel which has the wind on the port side shall keep out of the way of the other;

(ii) when both have the wind on the same side, the vessel which is to windward shall keep out of the way of the vessel which is to leeward;

(iii) if a vessel with the wind on the port side sees a vessel to windward and cannot determine with certainty whether the other vessel has the wind on the port or on the starboard side, she shall keep out of the way of the other.

(b) For the purposes of this Rule the windward side shall be deemed to be the side opposite to that on which the mainsail is carried or, in the case of a square-rigged vessel, the side opposite to that on which the largest fore-and-aft sail is carried.

RULE 13
Overtaking

(a) Notwithstanding anything contained in the Rules of Part B, Sections I and II any vessel overtaking any other shall keep out of the way of the vessel being overtaken.

(b) A vessel shall be deemed to be overtaking when coming up with another vessel from a direction more than 22.5 degrees abaft her beam, that is, in such a position with reference to the vessel she is overtaking, that at night she would be able to see only the sternlight of that vessel but neither of her sidelights.

(c) When a vessel is in any doubt as to whether she is overtaking another, she shall assume that this is the case and act accordingly.

(d) Any subsequent alteration of the bearing between the two vessels shall not make the overtaking vessel a crossing vessel within the meaning of these Rules or relieve her of the duty of keeping clear of the overtaken vessel until she is finally past and clear.

RULE 14
Head-On Situation

(a) When two power-driven vessels are meeting on reciprocal or nearly reciprocal courses so as to involve risk of collision each shall alter her course to starboard so that each shall pass on the port side of the other.

(b) Such a situation shall be deemed to exist when a vessel sees the other ahead or nearly ahead and by night she could see the masthead lights of the other in a line or nearly in a line and/or both sidelights and by day she observes the corresponding aspect of the other vessel.

(c) When a vessel is in any doubt as to whether such a situation exists she shall assume that it dues exist and act accordingly.

Notwithstanding paragraph (a) of this Rule, a power-driven vessel operating on the Great Lakes, Western Rivers, or waters specified by the Secretary, and proceeding downbound with a following current shall have the right-of-way over an upbound vessel, shall propose the manner of passage, and shall initiate the maneuvering signals prescribed by Rule 34(a)(i), as appropriate.

RULE 15
Crossing Situation

When two power-driven vessels are crossing so as to involve risk of collision, the vessel which has the other on her own starboard side shall keep out of the way and shall, if the circumstances of the case admit, avoid crossing ahead of the other vessel.

Notwithstanding paragraph (a), on the Great Lakes, Western Rivers, or water specified by the Secretary, a vessel crossing a river shall keep out of the way of a power-driven vessel ascending or descending the river.

RULE 16
Action by Give-Way Vessel

Every vessel which is directed to keep out of the way of another vessel shall, so far as possible, take early and substantial action to keep well clear.

RULE 17
Action by Stand-On Vessel

(a)(i) Where one of two vessels is to keep out of the way the other shall keep her course and speed.

(ii) The latter vessel may however take action to avoid collision by her maneuver alone, as soon as it becomes apparent to her that the vessel required to keep out of the way is not taking appropriate action in compliance with these Rules.

(b) When, from any cause, the vessel required to keep her course and speed finds herself so close that collision cannot be avoided by the action of the give-way vessel alone, she shall take such action as will best aid to avoid collision.

(c) A power-driven vessel which takes action in a crossing situation in accordance with subparagraph (a)(ii) of this Rule to avoid collision with another power-driven vessel shall, if the circumstances of the case admit, not alter course to port for a vessel on her own port side.

(d) This Rule does not relieve the give-way vessel of her obligation to keep out of the way.

RULE 18
Responsibilities between Vessels

Except where Rules 9, 10 and 13 otherwise require:

(a) A power-driven vessel underway shall keep out of the way of:

(i) a vessel not under command;

(ii) a vessel restricted in her ability to maneuver;

(iii) a vessel engaged in fishing;

(iv) a sailing vessel.

(b) A sailing vessel underway shall keep out of the way of:

(i) a vessel not under command;

(ii) a vessel restricted in her ability to maneuver;

(iii) a vessel engaged in fishing.

PART C—LIGHTS AND SHAPES

(c) A vessel engaged in fishing when underway shall, so far as possible, keep out of the way of:

(i) a vessel not under command;

(ii) a vessel restricted in her ability to maneuver.

(d) (i) Any vessel other than a vessel not under command or a vessel restricted in her ability to maneuver shall, if the circumstances of the case admit, avoid impeding the safe passage of a vessel constrained by her draft, exhibiting the signals in Rule 28.

(ii) A vessel constrained by her draft shall navigate with particular caution having full regard to her special condition.
NOTE: There is no mention of a "vessel constrained by her draft" anywhere in the Inland Rules.

(e) A seaplane on the water shall, in general, keep well clear of all vessels and avoid impeding their navigation. In circumstances, however, where risk of collision exists, she shall comply with the Rules of this Part.

Section III—Conduct of Vessels in Restricted Visibility

RULE 19
Conduct of Vessels in Restricted Visibility

(a) This Rule applies to vessels not in sight of one another when navigating in or near an area of restricted visibility.

(b) Every vessel shall proceed at a safe speed adapted to the prevailing circumstances and conditions of restricted visibility. A power-driven vessel shall have her engines ready for immediate maneuver.

(c) Every vessel shall have due regard to the prevailing circumstances and conditions of restricted visibility when complying with the Rules of Section I of this Part.

(d) A vessel which detects by radar alone the presence of another vessel shall determine if a close-quarters situation is developing and/or risk of collision exists. If so, she shall take avoiding action in ample time, provided that when such action consists of an alteration of course, so far as possible the following shall be avoided:

(i) an alteration of course to port for a vessel forward of the beam, other than for a vessel being overtaken;

(ii) an alteration of course towards a vessel abeam or abaft the beam.

(e) Except where it has been determined that a risk of collision does not exist, every vessel which hears apparently forward of her beam the fog signal of another vessel, or which cannot avoid a close-quarters situation with another vessel forward of her beam, shall reduce her speed to the minimum at which she can be kept on her course. She shall if necessary take all her way off and in any event navigate with extreme caution until danger of collision is over.

PART C—LIGHTS AND SHAPES
RULE 20
Application

(a) Rules in this Part shall be complied with in all weathers.

(b) The Rules concerning lights shall be complied with from sunset to sunrise, and during such times no other lights shall be exhibited, except such lights as cannot be mistaken for the lights specified in these Rules or do not impair their visibility or distinctive character, or interfere with the keeping of a proper look-out.

(c) The lights prescribed by these Rules shall, if carried, also be exhibited from sunrise to sunset in restricted visibility and may be exhibited in all other circumstances when it is deemed necessary.

(d) The Rules concerning shapes shall be complied with by day.

(e) The lights and shapes specified in these Rules shall comply with the provisions of Annex I to these Regulations.

RULE 21
Definitions

(a) "Masthead light" means a white light placed over the fore and aft centerline of the vessel showing an unbroken light over an arc of the horizon of 225 degrees and so fixed as to show the light from right ahead to 22.5 degrees abaft the beam on either side of the vessel *except that on a vessel of less than 12 meters in length the masthead light shall be placed as nearly as practicable to the fore and aft centerline of the vessel.*

(b) "Sidelights" means a green light on the starboard side and a red light on the port side each showing an unbroken light over an arc of the horizon of 112.5 degrees and so fixed as to show the light from right ahead to 22.5 degrees abaft the beam on its respective side. In a vessel of less than

20 meters in length the sidelights may be combined in one lantern carried on the fore and aft centerline of the vessel *except that on a vessel of less than 12 meters in length the sidelights when combined in one lantern shall be placed as nearly as practicable to the fore and aft centerline of the vessel.*

(c) "Sternlight" means a white light placed as nearly as practicable at the stern showing an unbroken light over an arc of the horizon of 135 degrees and so fixed as to show the light 67.5 degrees from right aft on each side of the vessel.

(d) "Towing light" means a yellow light having the same characteristics as the "sternlight" defined in paragraph (c) of this Rule.

(e) "All-round light" means a light showing an unbroken light over an arc of the horizon of 360 degrees.

(f) "Flashing light" means a light flashing at regular intervals at a frequency of 120 flashes or more per minute.

"Special flashing light" means a yellow light flashing at regular intervals at a frequency of 50 to 70 flashes per minute, placed as far forward and as nearly as practicable on the fore and aft centerline of the tow and showing an unbroken light over an arc of the horizon of not less than 180 degrees nor more than 225 degrees and so fixed as to show the light from right ahead to abeam and no more than 22.5 degrees abaft the beam on either side of the vessel.

RULE 22
Visibility of Lights

The lights prescribed in these Rules shall have an intensity as specified in Section 8 of Annex I to these Regulations so as to be visible at the following minimum ranges:

(a) In vessels of 50 meters or more in length:

—a masthead light, 6 miles;

—a sidelight, 3 miles;

—a sternlight, 3 miles;

—a towing light, 3 miles;

—a white, red, green or yellow all-round light, 3 miles.

—*a special flashing light, 2 miles.*

(b) In vessels of 12 meters or more in length but less than 50 meters in length:

—a masthead light, 5 miles; except that where the length of the vessel is less than 20 meters, 3 miles;

—a sidelight, 2 miles;

—a sternlight, 2 miles;

—a towing light, 2 miles;

—a white, red, green or yellow all-round light, 2 miles.

—*a special flashing light, 2 miles.*

(c) In vessels of less than 12 meters in length:

—a masthead light, 2 miles;

—a sidelight, 1 mile;

—a sternlight, 2 miles;

—a towing light, 2 miles;

—a white, red, green or yellow all-round light, 2 miles.

—*a special flashing light, 2 miles.*

(d) In inconspicuous, partly submerged vessels or objects being towed: —a white all-round light, 3 miles.

RULE 23
Power-Driven Vessels Underway

(a) A power-driven vessel underway shall exhibit:

(i) a masthead light forward *except that a vessel of less than 20 meters in length need not exhibit this light forward of amidships but shall exhibit it as far forward as is practicable;*

(ii) a second masthead light abaft of and higher than the forward one; except that a vessel of less than 50 meters in length shall not be obliged to exhibit such light but may do so;

(iii) sidelights;

(iv) a stern light.

(b) An air-cushion vessel when operating in the non-displacement mode shall, in addition to the lights prescribed in paragraph (a) of this Rule, exhibit an all-round flashing yellow light.

(c)(i) A power-driven vessel of less than 12 meters in length may in lieu of the lights prescribed in paragraph (a) of this Rule exhibit an all-round white light and sidelights;

(ii) a power-driven vessel of less than 7 meters in length whose maximum speed does not exceed 7 knots may in lieu of the lights prescribed in paragraph (a) of this Rule exhibit an all-round white light and shall, if practicable, also exhibit sidelights; *(This exception does exist in Inland Rules.)*

(iii) the masthead light or all-round white light on a power driven vessel of less than 12 meters in length may be displaced from the fore and aft centerline of the vessel if centerline fitting is not practicable, provided that the sidelights are combined in one lantern which shall be carried on the fore and aft centerline of the vessel or located as nearly as practicable in the same fore and aft line as the masthead light or the all-round white light. *(This exception does exist in Inland Rules.)*

A power-driven vessel when operating on the Great Lakes may carry an all-round white light in lieu of the second masthead light and sternlight prescribed in paragraph (a) of this Rule. The light shall be carried in the position of the second masthead light and be visible at the same minimum range.

RULE 24
Towing and Pushing

(a) A power-driven vessel when towing shall exhibit:

(i) instead of the light prescribed in Rule 23(a)(i) or (a)(ii), two masthead lights in a vertical line. When the length of the tow, measuring from the stern of the towing vessel to the after end of the tow exceeds 200 meters, three such lights in a vertical line;

(ii) sidelights;

(iii) a stern light;

(iv) a towing light in a vertical line above the sternlight;

(v) when the length of the tow exceeds 200 meters, a diamond shape where it can best be seen.

(b) When a pushing vessel and a vessel being pushed ahead are rigidly connected in a composite unit they shall be regarded as a power-driven vessel and exhibit the lights prescribed in Rule 23.

(c) A power-driven vessel when pushing ahead or towing alongside, except in the case of a composite unit, shall exhibit:

(i) instead of the light prescribed in Rule 23(a)(i) or (a)(ii), two masthead lights in a vertical line;

(ii) sidelights;

(iii) a sternlight.

(iii) two towing lights in a vertical line.

(d) A power-driven vessel to which paragraph (a) or (c) of this Rule apply shall also comply with Rule 23(a)(ii).

(e) A vessel or object being towed, other than those mentioned in paragraph (g) of this Rule, shall exhibit:

(i) sidelights;

(ii) a stern light; and

(iii) when the length of the tow exceeds 200 meters, a diamond shape where it can best be seen.

(f) Provided that any number of vessels being towed alongside or pushed in a group shall be lighted as one vessel,

(i) a vessel being pushed ahead, not being part of a composite unit, shall exhibit at the forward end, sidelights; *and a special flashing light;*

(ii) a vessel being towed alongside shall exhibit a sternlight and at the forward end, sidelights.

(g) An inconspicuous, partly submerged vessel or object, or combination of such vessels or objects being towed, shall exhibit:

(i) if it is less than 25 meters in breadth, one all-round white light at or near the forward end and one at or near the after end except that dracones need not exhibit a light at or near the forward end;

(ii) if it is 25 meters or more in breadth, two additional all round white lights at or near the extremities of its breadth;

(iii) if it exceeds 100 meters in length, additional all-round white lights between the lights prescribed in subparagraphs (i) and (ii) so that the distance between the lights shall not exceed 100 meters;

(iv) a diamond shape at or near the aftermost extremity of the last vessel or object being towed and if the length of the tow exceeds 200 meters an additional diamond shape where it can best be seen and located as far forward as is practicable.

(iv) a diamond shape at or near the aftermost extremity of the last vessel or object being towed; and

(v) the towing vessel may direct a searchlight in the direction of the tow to indicate its presence to an approaching vessel.

(h) Where from any sufficient cause it is impracticable for a vessel or object being towed to exhibit the lights or shapes prescribed in paragraph (e) or (g) of this Rule, all possible measures shall be taken to light the vessel or object towed or at least to indicate the presence of such vessel or object.

(i) Where from any sufficient cause it is impracticable for a vessel not normally engaged in towing operations to display the lights prescribed in paragraph (a) or (c) of this Rule, such vessel shall not be required to exhibit those lights when engaged in towing another vessel in distress or otherwise in need of assistance. All possible measures shall be taken to indicate the nature of the relationship between the towing vessel and the vessel being towed as authorized by Rule 36, in particular by illuminating the towline.

Notwithstanding paragraph (c), on the Western Rivers (except below the Huey P. Long Bridge on the Mississippi River) and on waters specified by the Secretary, a power-driven vessel when pushing ahead or towing alongside, except as paragraph (b) applies, shall exhibit:

(i) sidelights; and

(ii) two towing lights in a vertical line.

RULE 25
Sailing Vessels Underway and Vessels under Oars

(a) A sailing vessel underway shall exhibit:

(i) sidelights;

(ii) a sternlight.

(b) In a sailing vessel of less than 20 meters in length the lights prescribed in paragraph (a) of this Rule may be combined in one lantern carried at or near the top of the mast where it can best be seen.

(c) A sailing vessel underway may, in addition to the lights prescribed in paragraph (a) of this Rule, exhibit at or near the top of the mast, where they can best be seen, two all-round lights in a vertical line, the upper being red and the lower green, but these lights shall not be exhibited in conjunction with the combined lantern permitted by paragraph (b) of this Rule.

(d)(i) A sailing vessel of less than 7 meters in length shall, if practicable, exhibit the lights prescribed in paragraph (a) or (b) of this Rule, but if she does not, she shall have ready at hand an electric torch or lighted lantern showing a white light which shall be exhibited in sufficient time to prevent collision.

(ii) A vessel under oars may exhibit the lights prescribed in this Rule for sailing vessels, but if she does not, she shall have ready at hand an electric torch or lighted lantern showing a white light which shall be exhibited in sufficient time to prevent collision.

(e) A vessel proceeding under sail when also being propelled by machinery shall exhibit forward where it can best be seen a conical shape, apex downwards. *A vessel of less than 12 meters in length is not required to exhibit this shape, but may do so.*

RULE 26
Fishing Vessels

(a) A vessel engaged in fishing, whether underway or at anchor, shall exhibit only the lights and shapes prescribed in this Rule.

(b) A vessel when engaged in trawling, by which is meant dragging through the water a dredge net or other apparatus used as a fishing appliance, shall exhibit:

(i) two all-round lights in a vertical line, the upper being green and the lower white, or a shape consisting of two cones with their apexes together in a vertical line one above the other; a vessel of less than 20 meters in length may instead of this shape exhibit a basket;

(ii) a masthead light abaft of and higher than the all-round green light; a vessel of less than 50 meters in length shall not be obliged to exhibit such a light but may do so;

(iii) when making way through the water, in addition to the lights prescribed in this paragraph, sidelights and a sternlight.

(c) A vessel engaged in fishing, other than trawling, shall exhibit:

(i) two all-round lights in a vertical line, the upper being red and the lower white, or a shape consisting of two cones with apexes together in a vertical line one above the other; a vessel of less than 20 m in length may instead of this shape exhibit a basket;

(ii) when there is outlying gear extending more than 150 meters horizontally from the vessel, an all-round white light or a cone apex upwards in the direction of the gear;

(iii) when making way through the water, in addition to the lights prescribed in this paragraph, sidelights and a sternlight.

(d) A vessel engaged in fishing in close proximity to other vessels engaged in fishing may exhibit the additional signals described in Annex II to these Regulations.

(e) A vessel when not engaged in fishing shall not exhibit the lights or shapes prescribed in this Rule, but only those prescribed for a vessel of her length.

RULE 27
Vessels Not under Command or Restricted in Their Ability to Maneuver

(a) A vessel not under command shall exhibit:

(i) two all-round red lights in a vertical line

where they can best be seen;

(ii) two balls or similar shapes in a vertical line where they can best be seen;

(iii) when making way through the water, in addition to the lights prescribed in this paragraph, sidelights and a sternlight.

(b) A vessel restricted in her ability to maneuver, except a vessel engaged in mineclearance operations, shall exhibit:

(i) three all-round lights in a vertical line where they can best be seen. The highest and lowest of these lights shall be red and the middle light shall be white;

(ii) three shapes in a vertical line where they can best be seen. The highest and lowest of these shapes shall be balls and the middle one a diamond;

(iii) when making way through the water, a masthead light or lights, sidelights and a sternlight, in addition to the lights prescribed in subparagraph (i);

(iv) when at anchor, in addition to the lights or shapes prescribed in subparagraphs (i) and (ii), the light, lights or shape prescribed in Rule 30.

(c) A power-driven vessel engaged in a towing operation such as severely restricts the towing vessel and her tow in their ability to deviate from their course shall, in addition to the lights or shapes prescribed in Rule 24(a), exhibit the lights or shapes prescribed in subparagraphs (b)(i) and (ii) of this Rule.

(d) A vessel engaged in dredging or underwater operations, when restricted in her ability to maneuver, shall exhibit the lights and shapes prescribed in subparagraphs (b)(i), (ii) and (iii) of this Rule and shall in addition, when an obstruction exists, exhibit:

(i) two all-round red lights or two balls in a vertical line to indicate the side on which the obstruction exists;

(ii) two all-round green lights or two diamonds in a vertical line to indicate the side on which another vessel may pass;

(iii) when at anchor, the lights or shapes prescribed in this paragraph instead of the lights or shape prescribed in Rule 30.

(e) Whenever the size of a vessel engaged in diving operations makes it impracticable to exhibit all lights and shapes prescribed in paragraph (d) of this Rule, the following shall be exhibited:

(i) three all-round lights in a vertical line where they can best be seen. The highest and lowest of these lights shall be red and the middle light shall be white;

(ii) a rigid replica of the International Code flag "A" not less than 1 meter in height. Measures shall be taken to ensure its all round visibility.

(f) A vessel engaged in mineclearance operations shall in addition to the lights prescribed for a power-driven vessel in Rule 23 or to the lights or shape prescribed for a vessel at anchor in Rule 30 as appropriate, exhibit three all-round green lights or three balls. One of these lights or shapes shall be exhibited near the foremast head and one at each end of the fore yard. These lights or shapes indicate that it is dangerous for another vessel to approach within 1000 meters of the mineclearance vessel, *or 500 meters on either side of the minesweeper.*

(g) Vessels of less than 12 meters in length, except those engaged in diving operations, shall not be required to exhibit the lights and shapes prescribed in this Rule.

(h) The signals prescribed in this Rule are not signals of vessels in distress and requiring assistance. Such signals are contained in Annex IV to these Regulations.

RULE 28
Vessels Constrained by Their Draft

A vessel constrained by her draft may, in addition to the lights prescribed for power-driven vessels in Rule 23, exhibit where they can best be seen three all-round red lights in a vertical line, or a cylinder. *NOTE: There is no mention of a "vessel constrained by draft" anywhere in the Inland Rules.*

RULE 29
Pilot Vessels

(a) A vessel engaged on pilotage duty shall exhibit:

(i) at or near the masthead, two all-round lights in a vertical line, the upper being white and the lower red;

(ii) when underway, in addition, sidelights and a sternlight;

(iii) when at anchor, in addition to the lights prescribed in subparagraph (i), the light, lights or shape prescribed in Rule 30 for vessels at anchor.

(b) A pilot vessel when not engaged on pilotage duty shall exhibit the lights or shapes prescribed for a similar vessel of her length.

RULE 30
Anchored Vessels and Vessels Aground

(a) A vessel at anchor shall exhibit where it can best be seen:

    (i) in the fore part, an all-round white light or one ball;

    (ii) at or near the stern and at a lower level than the light prescribed in subparagraph (i), an all-round white light.

(b) A vessel of less than 50 meters in length may exhibit an all round white light where it can best be seen instead of the lights prescribed in paragraph (a) of this Rule.

(c) A vessel at anchor may, and a vessel of 100 meters and more in length shall, also use the available working or equivalent lights to illuminate her decks.

(d) A vessel aground shall exhibit the lights prescribed in paragraph (a) or (b) of this Rule and in addition, where they can best be seen:

    (i) two all-round red lights in a vertical line;

    (ii) three balls in a vertical line.

(e) A vessel of less than 7 meters in length, when at anchor, not in or near a narrow channel, fairway or anchorage, or where other vessels normally navigate, shall not be required to exhibit the lights or shape prescribed in paragraphs (a) and (b) of this Rule.

(f) A vessel of less than 12 meters in length, when aground, shall not be required to exhibit the lights or shapes prescribed in subparagraphs (d)(i) and (ii) of this Rule.

A vessel of less than 20 meters in length, when at anchor in a special anchorage area designated by the Secretary, shall not be required to exhibit the anchor lights and shapes required by this Rule.

RULE 31
Seaplanes

Where it is impracticable for a seaplane to exhibit lights and shapes of the characteristics or in the positions prescribed in the Rules of this Part she shall exhibit lights and shapes as closely similar in characteristics and position as is possible.

PART D—SOUND AND LIGHT SIGNALS
RULE 32
Definitions

(a) The word "whistle" means any sound signalling appliance capable of producing the prescribed blasts and which complies with the specifications in Annex III to these Regulations.

(b) The term "short blast" means a blast of about one second's duration.

(c) The term "prolonged blast" means a blast of from four to six seconds' duration.

RULE 33
Equipment for Sound Signals

(a) A vessel of 12 meters or more in length shall be provided with a whistle and a bell and a vessel of 100 meters or more in length shall, in addition, be provided with a gong, the tone and sound of which cannot be confused with that of the bell. The whistle, bell and gong shall comply with the specifications in Annex III to these Regulations. The bell or gong or both may be replaced by other equipment having the same respective sound characteristics, provided that manual sounding of the prescribed signals shall always be possible.

(b) A vessel of less than 12 meters in length shall not be obliged to carry the sound signalling appliances prescribed in paragraph (a) of this Rule but if she does not, she shall be provided with some other means of making an efficient sound signal.

RULE 34
Maneuvering and Warning Signals

(a) When vessels are in sight of one another, a power-driven vessel underway, when maneuvering as authorized or required by these Rules, shall indicate that maneuver by the following signals on her whistle:

—one short blast to mean "I am altering my course to starboard";

—two short blasts to mean "I am altering my course to port";

—three short blasts to mean "I am operating astern propulsion."

(b) Any vessel may supplement the whistle signals prescribed in paragraph (a) of this Rule by light signals, repeated as appropriate, whilst the maneuver is being carried out:

(i) these light signals shall have the following significance:

—one flash to mean "I am altering my course to starboard";

—two flashes to mean "I am altering my course to port";

—three flashes to mean "I am operating astern propulsion";

(ii) the duration of each flash shall be about one second, the interval between flashes shall be about one second, and the interval between successive signals shall be not less than ten seconds;

(iii) the light used for this signal shall, if fitted, be an all-round white light, visible at a minimum range of 5 miles, and shall comply with the provisions of Annex I to these Regulations.

(c) When in sight of one another in a narrow channel or fairway:

(i) a vessel intending to overtake another shall in compliance with Rule 9(e)(i) indicate her intention by the following signals on her whistle:

—two prolonged blasts followed by one short blast to mean "I intend to overtake you on your starboard side";

—two prolonged blasts followed by two short blasts to mean "I intend to overtake you on your port side."

(ii) the vessel about to be overtaken when acting in accordance with Rule 9(e)(i) shall indicate her agreement by the following signal on her whistle:

—one prolonged, one short, one prolonged and one short blast, in that order.

(d) When vessels in sight of one another are approaching each other and from any cause either vessel fails to understand the intentions or actions of the other, or is in doubt whether sufficient action is being taken by the other to avoid collision, the vessel in doubt shall immediately indicate such doubt by giving at least five short and rapid blasts on the whistle. Such signal may be supplemented by a light signal of at least five short and rapid flashes.

(e) A vessel nearing a bend or an area of a channel or fairway where other vessels may be obscured by an intervening obstruction shall sound one prolonged blast. Such signal shall be answered with a prolonged blast by any approaching vessel that may be within hearing around the bend or behind the intervening obstruction.

(f) If whistles are fitted on a vessel at a distance apart of more than 100 meters, one whistle only shall be used for giving maneuvering and warning signals.

RULE 34
Maneuvering and Warning Signals

(a) When power-driven vessels are in sight of one another and meeting or crossing at a distance within half a mile of each other, each vessel underway, when maneuvering as authorized or required by these Rules:

(i) shall indicate that maneuver by the following signals on her whistle: one short blast to mean "I intend to leave you on my port side"; two short blasts to mean "I intend to leave you on my starboard side"; and three short blasts to mean "I am operating astern propulsion."

(ii) upon hearing the one or two blast signal of the other shall, if in agreement, sound the same whistle signal and take the steps necessary to effect a safe passing. If, however, from any cause, the vessel doubts the safety of the proposed maneuver, she shall sound the danger signal specified in paragraph (d) of this Rule and each vessel shall take appropriate precautionary action until a safe passing agreement is made.

(b) A vessel may supplement the whistle signals prescribed in paragraph (a) of this Rule by light signals:

(i) These signals shall have the following significance: one flash to mean "I intend to leave you on my port side"; two flashes to mean "I intend to leave you on my starboard side"; three flashes to mean "I am operating astern propulsion";

(ii) The duration of each flash shall be about 1 second; and

(iii) The light used for this signal shall, if fitted, be one all-round white or yellow light, visible at a minimum range of 2 miles, synchronized with the whistle, and shall comply with the provisions of Annex I to these Rules.

(c) When in sight of one another:

(i) a power-driven vessel intending to overtake another power-driven vessel shall indicate her intention by the following signals on her whistle: one short blast to mean "I intend to overtake you on your starboard side"; two short blasts to mean "I intend to overtake you on your port side"; and

(ii) the power-driven vessel about to be overtaken shall, if in agreement, sound a similar sound signal. If in doubt she shall sound the danger signal prescribed in paragraph (d).

(d) When vessels in sight of one another are approaching each other and from any cause either *vessel fails to understand the intentions or actions of the other, or is in doubt whether sufficient action is being taken by the other to avoid collision, the vessel in doubt shall immediately indicate such doubt by giving at least five short and rapid blasts on the whistle. This signal may be supplemented by a light signal of at least five short and rapid flashes.*

(e) A vessel nearing a bend or an area of a channel or fairway where other vessels may be obscured by an intervening obstruction shall sound one prolonged blast. This signal shall be answered with a prolonged blast by any approaching vessel that may be within hearing around the bend or behind the intervening obstruction.

(f) If whistles are fitted on a vessel at a distance apart of more than 100 meters, one whistle only shall be used for giving maneuvering and warning signals.

(g) When a power-driven vessel is leaving a dock or berth, she shall sound one prolonged blast.

(h) A vessel that reaches agreement with another vessel in a meeting, crossing, or overtaking situation by using the radiotelephone as prescribed by the Bridge-to-Bridge Radiotelephone Act (85 Stat. 165; 33 U.S.C. 1207), is not obliged to sound the whistle signals prescribed by this Rule, but may do so. If agreement is not reached, then whistle signals shall be exchanged in a timely manner and shall prevail.

RULE 35
Sound Signals in Restricted Visibility

In or near an area of restricted visibility, whether by day or night, the signals prescribed in this Rule shall be used as follows:

(a) A power-driven vessel making way through the water shall sound at intervals of not more than 2 minutes one prolonged blast.

(b) A power-driven vessel underway but stopped and making no way through the water shall sound at intervals of not more than 2 minutes two prolonged blasts in succession with an interval of about 2 seconds between them.

(c) A vessel not under command, a vessel restricted in her ability to maneuver, a vessel constrained by her draft, a sailing vessel, a vessel engaged in fishing and a vessel engaged in towing or pushing another vessel shall, instead of the signals prescribed in paragraphs (a) or (b) of this Rule, sound at intervals of not more than 2 minutes three blasts in succession, namely one prolonged followed by two short blasts.

(d) A vessel engaged in fishing, when at anchor, and a vessel restricted in her ability to maneuver when carrying out her work at anchor, shall instead of the signals prescribed in paragraph (g) of this Rule sound the signal prescribed in paragraph (c) of this Rule.

(e) A vessel towed or if more than one vessel is towed the last vessel of the tow, if manned, shall at intervals of not more than 2 minutes sound four blasts in succession, namely one prolonged followed by three short blasts. When practicable, this signal shall be made immediately after the signal made by the towing vessel.

(f) When a pushing vessel and a vessel being pushed ahead are rigidly connected in a composite unit they shall be regarded as a power-driven vessel and shall give the signals prescribed in paragraphs (a) or (b) of this Rule.

(g) A vessel at anchor shall at intervals of not more than one minute ring the bell rapidly for about 5 seconds. In a vessel of 100 meters or more in length the bell shall be sounded in the forepart of the vessel and immediately after the ringing of the bell the gong shall be sounded rapidly for about 5 seconds in the after part of the vessel. A vessel at anchor may in addition sound three blasts in succession, namely one short, one prolonged and one short blast, to give warning of her position and of the possibility of collision to an approaching vessel.

(h) A vessel aground shall give the bell signal and if required the gong signal prescribed in paragraph (g) of this Rule and shall, in addition, give three separate and distinct strokes on the bell immediately before and after the rapid ringing of the bell. A vessel aground may in addition sound an appropriate whistle signal.

(i) A vessel of less than 12 meters in length shall not be obliged to give the above-mentioned signals but, if she does not, shall make some other efficient sound signal at intervals of not more than 2 minutes.

(j) A pilot vessel when engaged on pilotage duty may in addition to the signals prescribed in paragraphs (a), (b) or (g) of this Rule sound an identity signal consisting of four short blasts.

The following vessels shall not be required to sound signals as prescribed in paragraph (f) of this Rule when anchored in a special anchorage area designated by the Secretary:

(i) a vessel of less than 20 meters in length;

(ii) a barge, canal boat, scow, or other nondescript craft.

PART E—EXEMPTIONS

RULE 36
Signals to Attract Attention

If necessary to attract the attention of another vessel, any vessel may make light or sound signals that cannot be mistaken for any signal authorized elsewhere in these Rules, or may direct the beam of her searchlight in the direction of the danger, in such a way as not to embarrass any vessel. Any light to attract the attention of another vessel shall be such that it cannot be mistaken for any aid to navigation. For the purpose of this Rule the use of high intensity intermittent or revolving lights, such as strobe lights, shall be avoided.

NOTE: There is no restriction on the use of strobe lights in the Inland Rules.

RULE 37
Distress Signals

When a vessel is in distress and requires assistance she shall use or exhibit the signals described in Annex IV to these Regulations.

The distress signals for inland waters are the same as those for international waters with the following additional signal described: A high intensity white light flashing at regular intervals from 50 to 70 times per minute.

PART E—EXEMPTIONS
RULE 38
Exemptions

Any vessel (or class of vessels) provided that she complies with the requirements of the International Regulations for Preventing Collisions at Sea, 1960, the keel of which is laid or which is at a corresponding stage of construction before the entry into force of these Regulations may be exempted from compliance therewith as follows:

Any vessel or class of vessels, the keel of which is laid or which is at a corresponding stage of construction before the date of enactment of this Act, provided that she complies with the requirements of—

(a) The Act of June 7, 1897 (30 Stat. 96), as amended (33 U.S.C. 154–232) for vessels navigating the waters subject to that statute;

(b) Section 4233 of the Revised Statutes (33 U.S.C. 301–356) for vessels navigating the waters subject to that statute;

(c) The Act of February 8, 1895 (28 Stat. 645), as amended (33 U.S.C. 241–295) for vessels navigating the waters subject to that statute; or

(d) Sections 3, 4, and 5 of the Act of April 25, 1940 (54 Stat. 163), as amended (46 U.S.C. 526 b, c, and d) for motorboats navigating the waters subject to that statute; shall be exempted from compliance with the technical Annexes to these Rules as follows:

(a) The installation of lights with ranges prescribed in Rule 22, until four years after the date of entry into force of these Regulations, *except that vessels of less than 20 meters in length are permanently exempt.*

(b) The installation of lights with color specifications as prescribed in Section 7 of Annex I to these Regulations, until four years after the date of entry into force of these Regulations, *except that vessels of less than 20 meters in length are permanently exempt.*

(c) The repositioning of lights as a result of conversion from Imperial to metric units and rounding off measurement figures, permanent exemption.

(d)(i) The repositioning of masthead lights on vessels of less than 150 meters in length, resulting from the prescriptions of Section 3(a) of Annex I to these Regulations, permanent exemption.

(ii) The repositioning of masthead lights on vessels of 150 meters or more in length, resulting from the prescriptions of Section 3(a) of Annex I to these Regulations, until 9 years after the date of entry into force of these Regulations.

(e) The repositioning of masthead lights resulting from the prescriptions of Section 2(b) of Annex I to these Regulations, until 9 years after the date of entry into force of these Regulations.

(f) The repositioning of sidelights resulting from the prescriptions of Sections 2(9) and 3(b) of Annex I to these Regulations, until 9 years after the date of entry into force of these Regulations.

(g) The requirements for sound signal appliances prescribed in Annex III to these Regulations, until 9 years after the date of entry into force of these Regulations.

The requirements for sound signal appliances prescribed in Annex III to these Rules, until 9 years after the effective date of these Rules.

(h) The repositioning of all-round lights resulting from the prescription of Section 9(b) of Annex I to these Regulations, permanent exemption.

(vi) power-driven vessels of 12 meters or more but less than 20 meters in length are permanently exempt from the provisions of Rule 23(a)(i) and 23 (a)(iv) provided that, in place of these lights, the vessel exhibits a white light aft visible all round the horizon; and

(vii) the requirements for sound signal appliances prescribed in Annex III to these Rules, until 9 years after the effective date of these Rules.

ANNEX I— Positioning and Technical Details of Lights and Shapes

1. Definition

The term "height above the hull" means height above the uppermost continuous deck. This height shall be measured from the position vertically beneath the location of the light.

The term "practical cut-off" means, for vessels 20 meters or more in length, 12.5 percent of the minimum luminous intensity (Table 84.15(b)) corresponding to the greatest range of visibility for which the requirements of Annex I are met.

The term "Rule" or "Rules" means the Inland Navigation Rules contained in Sec. 2 of the Inland Navigational Rules Act of 1980 (Pub. L. 96-591, 94 Stat. 3415, 33 U.S.C. 2001, December 24, 1980) as amended.

2. Vertical positioning and spacing of lights

(a) On a power-driven vessel of 20 meters or more the masthead lights shall be placed as follows:

(i) the forward masthead light, or if only one masthead light is carried, then that light, at a height above the hull of not less than 6 meters, and, if the breadth of the vessel exceeds 6 meters, then at a height above the hull not less than such breadth, so however that the light need not be placed at a greater height above the hull than 12 meters;

The forward masthead light, or if only one masthead light is carried, then that light, at a height above the hull of not less than 5 meters, and, if the breadth of the vessel exceeds 5 meters, then at a height above the hull not less than such breadth, so however that the light need not be placed at a greater height above the hull than 8 meters;

(ii) when two masthead lights are carried the after one shall be at least 4.5 meters vertically higher than the forward one.

When two masthead lights are carried the after one shall be at least 2 meters vertically higher than the forward one.

(b) The vertical separation of masthead lights of power-driven vessels shall be such that in all normal conditions of trim the after light will be seen over and separate from the forward light at a distance of 1000 meters from the stem when viewed from sea level.

(c) The masthead light of a power-driven vessel of 12 meters but less than 20 meters in length shall be placed at a height above the gunwale of not less than 2.5 meters.

(d) A power-driven vessel of less than 12 meters in length may carry the uppermost light at a height of less than 2.5 meters above the gunwale. When however a masthead light is carried in addition to sidelights and a sternlight, then such masthead light shall be carried at least 1 meter higher than the sidelights.

The masthead light, or the all-round light described in Rule 23(c), of a power-driven vessel of less than 12 meters in length shall be carried at least one meter higher than the sidelights.

(e) One of the two or three masthead lights prescribed for a power-driven vessel when engaged in towing or pushing another vessel shall be placed in the same position as either the forward masthead light or the after masthead light; provided that, if carried on the aftermast, the lowest after masthead light shall be at least 4.5 meters vertically higher than the forward masthead light.

One of the two or three masthead lights prescribed for a power-driven vessel when engaged in towing or pushing another vessel shall be placed in the same position as either the forward masthead light or the after masthead light, provided that the lowest after masthead light shall be at least 2 meters vertically higher than the highest forward masthead light.

(f)(i) The masthead light or lights prescribed in Rule 23(a) shall be so placed as to be above and clear of all other lights and obstructions except as described in subparagraph (ii).

(ii) When it is impracticable to carry the all-round lights prescribed by Rule 27(b)(i) or Rule 28 below the masthead lights, they may be carried above the after masthead light(s) or vertically in between the forward masthead light(s) and after masthead light(s), provided that in the latter case the requirement of Section 3(c) of this Annex shall be complied with.

(g) The sidelights of a power-driven vessel shall be placed at a height above the hull not greater than three quarters of that of the forward masthead light. They shall not be so low as to be interfered with by deck lights.

The sidelights of a power-driven vessel shall be placed at least one meter lower than the forward masthead light. They shall not be so low as to be interfered with by deck lights.

(h) The sidelights, if in a combined lantern and carried on a power-driven vessel of less than 20 meters in length, shall be placed not less than 1 meter below the masthead light. *[Reserved]*

(h) (i) When the Rules prescribe two or three lights to be carried in a vertical line, they shall be spaced as follows:

(i) on a vessel of 20 meters in length or more such lights shall be spaced not less than 2 meters apart, and the lowest of these lights shall, except where a towing light is required, be placed at a height of not less than 4 meters above the hull;

On a vessel of 20 meters in length or more such lights shall be spaced not less than 1 meter apart, and the lowest of these lights shall, except where a towing light is required, be placed at a height of not less than 4 meters above the hull;

(ii) on a vessel of less than 20 meters in length such lights shall be spaced not less than 1 meter apart and the lowest of these lights shall, except where a towing light is required, be placed at a height of not less than 2 meters above the hull;

(iii) when three lights are carried they shall be equally spaced.

(j) The lower of the two all-round lights prescribed for a vessel when engaged in fishing shall be at a height above the sidelights not less than twice the distance between the two vertical lights.

(k) The forward anchor light prescribed in Rule 30(a)(i), when two are carried, shall not be less than 4.5 meters above the after one. On a vessel of 50 meters or more in length this forward anchor light shall be placed at a height of not less than 6 meters above the hull.

3. Horizontal positioning and spacing of lights

(a) When two masthead lights are prescribed for a power-driven vessel, the horizontal distance between them shall not be less than one half of the length of the vessel but need not be more than 100 meters. The forward light shall be placed not more than one quarter of the length of the vessel from the stem.

Except as specified in paragraph (b) of this section, when two masthead lights are prescribed for a power-driven vessel, the horizontal distance between them shall not be less than one quarter of the length of the vessel but need not be more than 50 meters. The forward light shall be placed not more than one half of the length of the vessel from the Stem.

(b) On a power-driven vessel of 20 meters or more in length the sidelights shall not be placed in front of the forward masthead lights. They shall be placed at or near the side of the vessel.

On power-driven vessels 50 meters but less than 60 meters in length operated on the Western Rivers, the horizontal distance between masthead lights shall not be less than 10 meters.

(c) When the lights prescribed in Rule 27(b)(i) or Rule 28 are placed vertically between the forward masthead light(s) and the after masthead light(s) these all-round lights shall be placed at a horizontal distance of not less than 2 meters from the fore and aft centerline of the vessel in the athwartship direction.

4. Details of location of direction-indicating lights for fishing vessels, dredgers and vessels engaged in underwater operations

(a) The light indicating the direction of the outlying gear from a vessel engaged in fishing as prescribed in Rule 26(c)(ii) shall be placed at a horizontal distance of not less than 2 meters and not more than 6 meters away from the two all-round red and white lights. This light shall be placed not higher than the all-round white light prescribed in Rule 26(c)(i) and not lower than the sidelights.

(b) The lights and shapes on a vessel engaged in dredging or underwater operations to indicate the obstructed side and/or the side on which it is safe to pass, as prescribed in Rule 27(d)(i) and (ii), shall be placed at the maximum practical horizontal distance, but in no case less than 2 meters, from the lights or shapes prescribed in Rule 27(b)(i) and (ii). In no case shall the upper of these lights or shapes be at a greater height than the lower of the three.

5. Screens for sidelights

The sidelights of vessels of 20 meters or more in length shall be fitted with inboard screens painted matt black, and meeting the requirements of Section 9 of this Annex. On vessels of less than 20 meters in length the sidelights, if necessary to meet the requirements of Section 9 of this Annex, shall be fitted with inboard matt black screens. With a combined lantern, using a single vertical filament and a very narrow division between the green and red sections, external screens need not be fitted.

On power-driven vessels less than 12 meters in length constructed after July 31, 1983, the masthead light, or the all round light described in Rule 23(c) shall be screened to prevent direct illumination of the vessel forward of the operator's position.

6. Shapes

(a) Shapes shall be black and of the following sizes:

(i) a ball shall have a diameter of not less than 0.6 meter;

(ii) a cone shall have a base diameter of not less than 0.6 meter and a height equal to its diameter;

(iii) a cylinder shall have a diameter of at least 0.6 meter and a height of twice its diameter; *(There is no cylinder in Inland Rules.)*

(iv) a diamond shape shall consist of two cones as defined in (ii) above having a common base.

(b) The vertical distance between shapes shall be at least 1.5 meters.

(c) In a vessel of less than 20 meters in length shapes of lesser dimensions but commensurate with the size of the vessel may be used and the distance apart may be correspondingly reduced.

7. Color specification of lights

The chromaticity of all navigation lights shall conform to the following standards, which lie within the boundaries of the area of the diagram specified for each color by the International Commission on Illumination (CIE).

The boundaries of the area for each color are given by indicating the corner coordinates, which are as follows:

(i) White:

x	0.525	0.525	0.452	0.310	0.310	0.443
y	0.382	0.440	0.440	0.348	0.283	0.382

(ii) Green:

x	0.028	0.009	0.300	0.203
y	0.385	0.723	0.511	0.356

(iii) Red:

x	0.680	0.660	0.735	0.721
y	0.320	0.320	0.265	0.259

(iv) Yellow:

x	0.612	0.618	0.575	0.575
y	0.382	0.382	0.425	0.406

8. Intensity of lights

(a) The minimum luminous intensity of lights shall be calculated by using the formula:

$$I = 3.43 \times 10^6 \times T \times D^2 \times K^{-D}$$

where I is luminous intensity in candelas under service conditions

T is threshold factor 2×10^{-7} lux,

D is range of visibility (luminous range) of the light in nautical miles,

K is atmospheric transmissivity. For prescribed lights the value of K shall be 0.8, corresponding to a meteorological visibility of approximately 13 nautical miles.

(b) A selection of figures derived from the formula is given in the following table:

Range of visibility (luminous range) of light in nm, D	Luminous intensity of light in candelas for K = 0.8
1	0.9
2	4.3
3	12
4	27
5	52
6	94

Note: The maximum luminous intensity of navigation lights should be limited to avoid undue glare. This shall not be achieved by a variable control of the luminous intensity.

9. Horizontal sectors

(a)(i) In the forward direction, sidelights as fitted on the vessel shall show the minimum required intensities. The intensities shall decrease to reach practical cut-off between 1 degree and 3 degrees outside the prescribed sectors.

(ii) For sternlights and masthead lights and at 22.5 degrees abaft the beam for sidelights, the minimum required intensities shall be maintained over the arc of the horizon up to 5 degrees within the limits of the sectors prescribed in Rule 21. From 5 degrees within the prescribed sectors the intensity may decrease by 50 percent up to the prescribed limits; it shall decrease steadily to reach practical cut-off at not more than 5 degrees outside the prescribed sectors.

(b) All-round lights shall be so located as not to be obscured by masts, topmasts or structures within angular sectors of more than 6 degrees, except anchor lights prescribed in Rule 30, which need not be placed at an impracticable height above the hull, *and the all-round white light described in Rule 23(d), which may not be obscured at all.*

10. Vertical sectors

(a) The vertical sectors of electric lights as fitted, with the exception of lights on sailing vessels, *and on unmanned barges,* shall ensure that:

(i) at least the required minimum intensity is maintained at all angles from 5 degrees above to 5 degrees below the horizontal;

(ii) at least 60 percent of the required minimum intensity is maintained from 7.5 degrees above to 7.5 degrees below the horizontal.

(b) In the case of sailing vessels the vertical sectors of electric lights as fitted shall ensure that:

(i) at least the required minimum intensity is maintained at all angles from 5 degrees above to 5 degrees below the horizontal;

(ii) at least 50 percent of the required minimum intensity is maintained from 25 degrees above to 25 degrees below the horizontal.

In the case of unmanned barges the minimum required intensity of electric lights as fitted shall be maintained on the horizontal.

(c) In the case of lights other than electric these specifications shall be met as closely as possible.

11. Intensity of non-electric lights

Non-electric lights shall so far as practicable comply with the minimum intensities, as specified in the Table given in Section 8 of this Annex.

12. Maneuvering light

Notwithstanding the provisions of paragraph 2(f) of this Annex the maneuvering light described in Rule 34(b) shall be placed in the same fore and aft vertical plane as the masthead light or lights and, where practicable, at a minimum height of 2 meters *(0.5 meter)* vertically above the forward masthead light, provided that it shall be carried not less than 2 meters *(0.5 meter)* vertically above or below the after masthead light. On a vessel where only one masthead light is carried the maneuvering light, if fitted, shall be carried where it can best be seen, not less than 2 meters *(0.5 meter)* vertically apart from the masthead light.

13. Approval

The construction of lights and shapes and the installation of lights on board the vessel shall be to the satisfaction of the appropriate authority of the State whose flag the vessel is entitled to fly.

ANNEX II—Additional Signals for Fishing Vessels Fishing in Close Proximity

1. General

The lights mentioned herein shall, if exhibited in pursuance of Rule 26(d), be placed where they can best be seen. They shall be at least 0.9 meter apart but at a lower level than lights prescribed in Rule 26(b)(i) and (c)(i). The lights shall be visible all around the horizon at a distance of at least 1 mile but at a lesser distance than the lights prescribed by these Rules for fishing vessels.

2. Signals for trawlers

(a) Vessels when engaged in trawling, whether using demersal or pelagic gear, may exhibit:

(i) when shooting their nets: two white lights in a vertical line;

(ii) when hauling their nets: one white light over one red light in a vertical line;

(iii) when the net has come fast upon an obstruction: two red lights in a vertical line.

(b) Each vessel engaged in pair trawling may exhibit:

(i) by night, a searchlight directed forward and in the direction of the other vessel of the pair;

(ii) when shooting or hauling their nets or when their nets have come fast upon an obstruction, the lights prescribed in 2(a) above.

3. Signals for purse seiners

Vessels engaged in fishing with purse seine gear may exhibit two yellow lights in a vertical line. These lights shall flash alternately every second and with equal light and occultation duration. These lights may be exhibited only when the vessel is hampered by its fishing gear.

ANNEX III—Technical Details of Sound Signal Appliances

1. Whistles

(a) Frequencies and range of audibility.

The fundamental frequency of the signal shall lie within the range 70-700 Hz *(70-525 Hz).* The range of audibility of the signal from a whistle shall be determined by those frequencies, which may include the fundamental and/or one or more higher frequencies, which lie within the range 180-700 Hz (±1 percent) and which provide the sound pressure levels specified in paragraph 1(c) below.

(b) Limits of fundamental frequencies.

To ensure a wide variety of whistle characteristics, the fundamental frequency of a whistle shall be between the following limits:

(i) 70-200 Hz, for a vessel 200 meters or more in length;

(ii) 130-350 Hz, for a vessel 75 meters but less than 200 meters in length;

(iii) 250-700 Hz *(250-525 Hz)*, for a vessel less than 75 meters in length.

(c) Sound signal intensity and range of audibility.

A whistle fitted in a vessel shall provide, in the direction of maximum intensity of the whistle and at a distance of 1 meter from it, a sound pressure level in at least one $^1/_3$-octave band within the range of frequencies 180-700 Hz (±1 percent) of not less than the appropriate figure given in the table below.

Length of vessel in meters	$^1/_3$-Octave band level at 1 m in dB referred to $2 \times 10\text{-}5$ Nm^2	Audibility range in nm
200 or more	143	2
75 but less than 200	138	1.5
20 but less than 75	130	1
less than 20	120	0.5

The range of audibility in the table above is for information and is approximately the range at which a whistle may be heard on its forward axis with 90 percent probability in conditions of still air on board a vessel having average background noise level at the listening posts (taken to be 68 dB in the octave band centered on 250 Hz and 63 dB in the octave band centered on 500 Hz).

In practice the range at which a whistle may be heard is extremely variable and depends critically on weather conditions; the values given can be regarded as typical but under conditions of strong wind or high ambient noise level at the listening post the range may be much reduced.

(d) Directional Properties.

The sound pressure level of a directional whistle shall be not more than 4 dB below the prescribed sound pressure level on that axis at any direction in the horizontal plane within ±45 degrees of the axis. The sound pressure level at any other direction in the horizontal plane shall be not more than 10 dB below the prescribed sound pressure level on the axis, so that the range in any direction will be at least half the range on the forward axis. The sound pressure level shall be measured in that one-third octave band which determines the audibility range.

(e) Positioning of whistles.

When a directional whistle is to be used as the only whistle on a vessel, it shall be installed with its maximum intensity directed straight ahead.

A whistle shall be placed as high as practicable on a vessel, in order to reduce interception of the emitted sound by obstructions and also to minimize hearing damage risk to personnel. The sound pressure level of the vessel's own signal at listening posts shall not exceed 110 dB (A) and so far as practicable should not exceed 100 dB (A).

(f) Fitting of more than one whistle.

If whistles are fitted at a distance apart of no more than 100 meters, it shall be so arranged that they are not sounded simultaneously.

(g) Combined whistle systems.

If due to the presence of obstructions the sound field of a single whistle or of one of the whistles referred to in paragraph 1(f) above is likely to have a zone of greatly reduced signal level, it is recommended that a combined whistle system be fitted so as to overcome this reduction. For the purposes of the Rules a combined whistle system is to be regarded as a single whistle. The whistles of a combined system shall be located at a distance apart of not more than 100 meters and arranged to be sounded simultaneously. The frequency of any one whistle shall differ from those of the others by at least 10 Hz.

Towing vessel whistles

A power-driven vessel normally engaged in pushing ahead or towing alongside may, at all times, use a whistle whose characteristic falls within the limits prescribed for the longest customary composite length of the vessel and its tow.

2. Bell or gong

(a) Intensity of signal.

A bell or gong, or other device having similar sound characteristics shall produce a sound pressure level of not less than 110 dB at a distance of 1 meter from it.

(b) Construction.

Bells and gongs shall be made of corrosion-resistant material and be designed to give a clear tone. The diameter of the mouth of the bell shall be no less than 300 mm for vessels of 20 meters or more in length, and shall be no less than 200 mm for vessels of 12 meters or more but of less than 20 meters. Where practicable, a power-driven bell striker is recommended to ensure constant force but manual operation shall be possible. The mass of the striker shall be not less than 3 percent of the mass of the bell.

3. Approval.

The construction of sound signal appliances, their performance and their installation on board the vessel shall be to the satisfaction of the appropriate authority of the State whose flag the vessel is entitled to fly.

ANNEX IV—Distress Signals

1. Need of assistance.

The following signals, used or exhibited together or separately, indicate distress and need of assistance:

(a) a gun or other explosive signal fired at intervals of about a minute;

(b) a continuous sounding with any fog-signalling apparatus;

(c) rockets or shells, throwing red stars fired one at a time at short intervals;

(d) a signal made by radiotelegraphy or by any other signaling method consisting of the group . . .———. . . (SOS) in the Morse Code;

(e) a signal sent by radiotelephony consisting of the spoken word "Mayday";

(f) the International Code Signal of distress indicated by N.C.;

(g) a signal consisting of a square flag having above or below it a ball or anything resembling a ball;

(h) flames on the vessel (as from a burning tar barrel, oil barrel, etc.);

(i) a rocket parachute flare or a hand flare showing a red light;

(j) a smoke signal giving off orange-colored smoke;

(k) slowly and repeatedly raising and lowering arms outstretched to each side;

(l) the radiotelegraph alarm signal;

(m) the radiotelephone alarm signal;

(n) signals transmitted by emergency position-indicating radio beacons.

(o) A high intensity white light flashing at regular intervals from 50 to 70 times per minute.

2. The use or exhibition of any of the foregoing signals except for the purpose of indicating distress and need of assistance and the use of other signals which may be confused with any of the above signals is prohibited.

3. Attention is drawn to the relevant sections of the International Code of Signals, the Merchant Ship Search and Rescue Manual and the following signals: (a) a piece of orange-colored canvas with either a black square and circle or other appropriate symbol (for identification from the air);   (b) a dye marker.

ANNEX V—Pilot Rules

Purpose and applicability.

This part applies to all vessels operating on United States Inland waters and to United States vessels operating on the Canadian waters of the Great Lakes to the extent there is no conflict with Canadian law.

Definitions.

The terms used in this part have the same meaning as defined in the Inland Navigational Rules Act of 1980.

Copy of Rules.

After January 1, 1983, the operator of each self-propelled vessel 12 meters or more in length shall carry on board and maintain for ready reference a copy of the Inland Navigation Rules.

Temporary exemption from light and shape requirements when operating under bridges.

A vessel's navigation lights and shapes may be lowered if necessary to pass under a bridge.

Law enforcement vessels.

(a) Law enforcement vessels may display a flashing blue light when engaged in direct law enforcement activities. This light shall be located so that it does not interfere with the visibility of the vessel's navigation lights.

(b) The blue light described in this section may be displayed by law enforcement vessels of the United States and the States and their political subdivisions.

Lights on barges at bank or dock.

(a) The following barges shall display at night and, if practicable, in periods of restricted visibility the lights described in paragraph (b) of this section—

(1) Every barge projecting into a buoyed or restricted channel.

(2) Every barge so moored that it reduces the available navigable width of any channel to less than 80 meters.

(3) Barges moored in groups more than two barges wide or to a maximum width of over 25 meters.

(4) Every barge not moored parallel to the bank or dock.

(b) Barges described in paragraph (a) shall carry two unobstructed white lights of an intensity to be visible for at least one mile on a clear dark night, and arranged as follows:

(1) On a single moored barge, lights shall be placed on the two corners farthest from the bank or dock.

(2) On barges moored in group formation, a light shall be placed on each of the upstream and downstream ends of the group, on the corners farthest from the bank or dock.

(3) Any barge in a group, projecting from the main body of the group toward the channel, shall be lighted as a single barge.

(c) Barges moored in any slip or slough which is used primarily for mooring purposes are exempt from the lighting requirements of this section.

Lights on dredge pipelines.

Dredge pipelines that are floating or supported on trestles shall display the following lights at night and in periods of restricted visibility.

(a) One row of yellow lights. The lights must be—

(1) Flashing 50 to 70 times per minute,

(2) Visible all around the horizon,

(3) Visible for at least 2 miles on a clear dark night,

(4) Not less than 1 and not more than 3.5 meters above the water,

(5) Approximately equally spaced, and

(6) Not more than 10 meters apart where the pipeline crosses a navigable channel. Where the pipeline does not cross a navigable channel the lights must be sufficient in number to clearly show the pipeline's length and course.

(b) Two red lights at each end of the pipeline, including the ends in a channel where the pipeline is separated to allow vessels to pass (whether open or closed). The lights must be—

(1) Visible all around the horizon, and

(2) Visible for at least 2 miles on a clear dark night, and

(3) One meter apart in a vertical line with the lower light at the same height above the water as the flashing yellow light.